A BRASHEAR(S) FAMILY HISTORY,

Descendants of Robert and Benois Brasseur

VOL. 9
Brashear(s) Family Additions, Corrections, Strays

Assembled and Published by
Charles Brashear

www.charlesbrashear.com

ISBN: 0-933362-19-6

(Version of 21 March 2008)

A Brashear(s) Family History: Descendants of Robert and Benois Brasseur: Vol. 9, Brashear(s) Family Additions, Corrections, Strays, by Charles Brashear

Copyright 2008, by Charles Brashear

ISBN: 0-933362-19-6

I am and have been for 40-something years actively engaged in research on the Brashear(s) Family, in all its branches, in all spellings of the surname. Some years ago, Troy Back and Leon Brashear gave me their blessing and permission to "update" their book, *THE BRASHEAR STORY, A FAMILY HISTORY*, but the more data I collected, the more I realized that this family history will never again fit into one volume, especially if you include the amount and kind of detail that I like to include. I now have produced nine books on the family history; below is the plan for these nine volumes.

Plan for a 9-vol. "A BRASHEAR(S) FAMILY HISTORY"

Vol. 1. **The First 200 Years of Brashear(s) in America** and *Some Descendants in Maryland.*

Vol. 2. **Robert C. Brashear of North Carolina** and *Some Descendants in TN, KY, MO, TX, etc.*

Vol. 3. **Robert Samuel Brashears, the "Rolling Stone,"** and *Some Descendants in TN and KY.*

Vol. 4. **Brashear(s) Families of the Ohio Valley**

Vol. 5. **Two Brashear(s) Families of the Lower Mississippi Valley**, *their Choctaw, and other Descendants*

Vol. 6. **Basil Brashear and his Brashears, Breshears, Beshears, Boshears and Other Descendants**, in MO, ID, TX, etc

Vol. 7. **Basil Brashear and His Brashears, Boshears, Beshears Descendants in TN, IL, MO, KY, etc**

Vol. 8. **Brashear(s) Families West of the Mississippi River**

Vol. 9. **Brashear(s) Family** *Additions, Corrections, and Non-Brashear(s) Families*

Go to my website: www.CharlesBrashear.com and click on **Family Histories**, for further information.

Order published books from me: Charles Brashear, (please add $3 postage and packaging for the first book, $1 each for each additional book sent to the same address).

Contents

Preface Xiii
A Few Words about My Conventions: Xiii

Descendants of Philip Brashear, 1727–1797

1. ABSALOM BRASHEAR AND POLLY PHILLIPS 17
William Abner Beshears and Millie Jane Lamb 18
   Thomas Wesley Beshears and Alice Mae Raines 19
   Bitty Idamae Beshears and Benjamin Franklin Raines . . . 20
   Cleo Abner Beshears and Beulah Hazel Raines 21
Preston Pebble Beshears and His Six Wives 24
   Luther Andrew Beshears and Nellie Edith Moore 26
   Onie Nell Dell Beshears and Art J. Parker 28
   Cyrus Edward Beshears, and Bessie Inez Debusk 29
   Ava Aldreen Beshears and Virgil Ray Haley 30
   Beulah May Beshears and Glover Franklin Bradford 30

2. JESSE BRASHEARS AND BETSY SHELL 31
Valdon A. Brashears and Julia Ann Murphy 33
Mary Ann "Polly" Brashears and John J. Williams 33
   James N. Williams and Elizabeth Butler 35
   John Joseph Williams and Margaret Bodine 35
   Pinkney David Williams and Margaret Angelina Bennett . . 36
   Newton Charles Williams and Mary Jane Newman 37
   Phillip Allen Williams and Sarah Frances Day 53
   Enoch Williams and Sarah Catherine Cooperrider 64
John William Brashears and Mary Jane Daniel Blanks 65
   John William "Willie" Brashears Jr and Lucy Blythe 68
     Henry G. Brashears and Artis Bell Stewart 68
William James Leftwich Brashears and Sarah "Sally" Herrin . 69
   Nellie Brashear and Richard Taylor 69
   Henry A. Brashear and Susie Ann Redmon 69
   Sydney Brashears and John A. Taylor 70
   Kansas (Or Arkansas) Brashear
     and Isaac Perry/ T. J. Cagle 71

3. JAMES ANDERSON BESHEARS
and His Sister, **ELIZABETH C. (BESHEARS) MILLS** 72
   Elizabeth C. Beshears and Caswell Mills 74
   James Anderson Beshears and Millie Francis Roberts 78

4. ROBERT BRASHEARS/BESHEARS
   AND ELIZABETH WHITTEN, of Pike Co,MO 83
   Records in Henry Co, VA 83
   Paulina Beshears and Joseph Keithley Sr 85
   Elijah Beshears and Sarah Long 88
      Nancy Beshears and Bryant Silvey 89
      Robert T. Beshears and Mary Ann Allison 90
         William Elze Beshears and Julia Delia Arendt 90
            Dora Lee Beshears and Joe W. Epperson 92
            Reuben Alfred Beshears and Zoleta Dailey 92
            Nora Perditta Beshears
               and William Melvin Roberts 94
     James W. Beshears and Melinda Wilson/ Clarinda Brown . . . 97
      Joel Marion Beshears and Elizabeth Givens Gray 98
         Clyde Marion Beshears and Emily Klein 102
   Judge William Bazwell Beshears
      and Zephalinda Llewellyn/ Margaret E. Rogers 106
      James Robert Breshears and Anna Elizabeth Dunford . . 109
      William H. Beshears and Mary Eliza Tredway 110
      Basil Lorenzo Beshears and Katherine Clayton 112
   Robert Anderson Beshears and Lucretia A. Unsell 114
   Jackson "John" Beshears and Elizabeth Keithley 118
      Lucinda Jane Beshears and Charles W. Howser 125

5. PARTHENA (BRASHEARS) REA 134
   James Henry Rea and Nancy Eubanks 135
   Adeline Elizabeth Rea and William Henry Mansker 137
      Mansker Family Stories 144

6. ABSALOM BRASHEAR AND NANCY _____ 154
   Census Data: 154
   Anna Crosnon and Ira Brashear 155
   Unaccounted for Data 157
   Braden (Brandon) Brashears and Tabitha Asberry 158
      William Cleveland Beshears and Minnie Hayslip: 160

7. BENJAMIN AND JANE BRASHEARS of Greene Co, MO 162
   Family of Benjamin Brashears and Jane __ 163
      Jesse Brashears and Mary Wilkerson 164
      Jemima Brashears and James Alfred Mitchem 166
      Samuel Brashears and Sarah Pursley 166
         John Brashears and Nannie Sanders 168
      Martin Brashears and Louisa Austin 171
         Charles G. Beshears and Effie J. Fowler 174
      Lewis Brashears and Mary Ann Petty 175
         Robert Lewis Brashears and Claudia Ann Pierson ... 180
      Marina Brashear and Gabriel M. Freeman 181
      Artina Brashears and Wesley Austin 181

8. ALEXANDER MARTIN BRASHEARS 182

Other Brashear(s) Families

9. HARDIN CO, KY, FAMILIES 183
   The Estate of Eliza C. Brashear 183
   James Harrison Brashear and Laura Landis 185
   Micajah Samuel Brashear and Alma Ellen Carman 185
   And Another Hardin Co, KY Family 190
   Descendant of Medora Brashear 192

10. THREE SONS OF ASA D. BRASHEAR 193
   Lemuel Brashear and Asa D. Brashear 193
      Ellis M. Brashear and Mattie Hinton/ Amanda Moore ... 195
      Meade E. Brashear and Mary Sue Eathridge 197
      Alonzo D. Brashear and Martha Sprouse 204

11. SEABORN BRASHER
   AND RACHEL WRIGHT/ LOUISIANA DAVIS 208
   Family of Seaborn Brasher and Rachel Wright 208
      Bert Valentine Brasher Sr and Mary Louise Frey 210

12. PHOEBE BRASHEARS
   AND NATHANIEL MASON/ STEPHEN RICE 213
   Partial Family 215
      Jesse H. Mason and Mary "Polly" Ruth 215
      Margaret Mason and George Hopkins Speer 216
      Elizabeth Mason and John Speers, Jr 218
   Phoebe Brashears and Stephen Rice 220

13. JAMES BASHAM BRASHEAR
    AND SARAH JANE BLADES 222
    Harvey Smith Brashear and Ora Florence Williams 224
    Ella Louise Brashear and George William Logan 227
    Bettie Brashear and Albert Rose 229
    John William "Bill" Brashear
        and Effie Robertson/ Elsie Braden 236

14. VOL. 1 MISCELLANEOUS 238
    Three Daughters of
        Thomas Cook Brashear and Ann Maria Pitts 238
    Biddlecombe Family 244
    Moseley Family 245
    William Jones, ... 247
    Joseph Brashear, b. 1722 248
    Margery (Brashears) Jenkins 248
    William Clayton Brashears, of Texas Navy 249
    Benedict Brashear of Brooke Co, WV, ... 250
    Hood/Brashear Data 251
    Washington Co, MD, Brashears 252
    Van Brashear and Emily Gridley 254
    Robert J. Brashear, of Philadelphia 255
    Henry Cartwright Brashear 256

15. VOL. 2 MISCELLANEOUS 257
    More on Isaac Wright Brashear 257
    Elizabeth Brashear and Michael Straisner 260
    More on Neil S. Brown Boshears and Margaret Tidwell 261

16. VOL. 3 MISCELLANEOUS 262
    Edward Hambleton 262
    Roane Stray Shows up 262
    Roberts Families 264
    Robert Terrel Brashear, of Greene Co, Ar 272
        Doulis W. "Woody" Brashers Sr 276
    Error on Sarah Rhea Hankins Brashear 276
    Hobert Brashear 278

17. VOL. 4 MISCELLANEOUS 279
    Francis "Frank" Brashear,
        Brother of Dr. John Alfred Brashear 279
    Family of Joseph Brashear and Harriet Wolf 279
    Otho R. Brashear and Elizabeth Davidson 280
    Lafayette M. Brashears 283
    Capt Samuel Ray Brashear 285

Jent/Combs Family Additions 286
Katie Lee Brashear 287
Everett R. Brashear 288
Larue Co, KY, Brashears Families 288
Descendants of Ignatius Brashear Jr 291
Philip Boyer Brashear and Queen "Tiny" Adams 292
Lieutenant Absalom J. Brashears, of Hickman Co, Ky 295

18. VOL. 5 MISCELLANEOUS 296
Enoch Brashear and Luclihoma Moore 296
Sarah White Brashears
       and George Jackson/ Ambrose Foster 300
Lindsay/Brashear Families: 303
Brashears on Dawes Final Rolls 305

19. VOL. 6 MISCELLANEOUS 308
John T. Brashear and Sarah J. Rose 308
Descendants of Berry Franklin Brashears 309
Giles Co, Tn 312
Atsy Breshears and Joseph Arter 312
Madison Golman Breshears' Last Child 313
Orvillle and Frank Brashear 313
Corrections on Breshears, Vol. 6 314

20. VOL. 7 MISCELLANEOUS 316
Samuel Brashear and Elizabeth Mason 316
       Phoebe Brashear and Charles Westfall 318

21. VOL. 8 MISCELLANEOUS 320
Samuel Marion Brashear 320
Fragments from Various States: 321
       Stamp Brashears 321
       Brashears/Starns 322
       Beshears/Pendergraft 324
       John Willis Brashears and Cora Shea 327
       Isaac Brasier and Sarah "Sally" Curry 329
       John Brashear and America Thompson 332
       William Henry Brashear and Nora Worster 336
       Ruth Brashears and Henry Tabor 336
       James "Jim" Brashears and Elizabeth Stone 340
       Earna R. Breshears and Etha Pearl Dooly 340

22. BESHEARS FAMILIES OF WILKES COUNTY, NC 342
Family of Martha Brashears/Bishears 342
Catherine "Catie" Bishears 343
   Aaron Beshears and Alia Owens 344
      Clarissa Catherine Beshears and Henry Church 346
      John Beshears and Selena Church 347
      John Sherman Beshears and Lillie Beshears 349
      Aaron Essley Beshears and Cynthia Younce 349
         James Dickson Beshears and Florence Calloway . 350
      Winfield Scott Beshears and Selona Walsh 351
         John Leonard Beshears and Bertha Anderson . . . 352
         Odell Beshears and Lenora Miller 353

JAMES BRAZIER,
OF CUMBERLAND CO, NC

23. POSSIBLE ANCESTRY OF JAMES BRAZIER 356
John Brasseur, of Nansemond Co, VA 356
John Brazer Jr and Ann Grill 359
John Brasier III and Elizabeth Holt 361
John Brazier IV and Elizabeth Simmons 363

24. JAMES AND SARAH BRAZIER OF CUMBERLAND CO, NC 366
James Brazier's Land Records 366
Estate Records and Family of James Brazier 368

25. WILLIAM BRAZIER, s/o James Brazier of Cumberland 372
Rev. Laban Brazier and Deborah Dial 374
Nancy Brazier and Reuben Lloyd 378
Elijah Brazier and Lydia Whitaker 382
John Brazier, of Clermont Co, OH 384

26. JAMES BRAZIER AND MARY "POLLY" SMITH,
  of Lincoln Co, TN 386
Land and Estate Records 386
Family of James Brazier and Polly Smith 387
   Sally M. Brazier and Green Berry Kitchens 389
   Nancy Ellen Brazier and William Barnet Kemp 392
      Thomas Lafayette Kemp and Sarah Florence Lusk . . 394
         Fanny Florence Kemp
           and Rufus Clay Richardson 395

Hattie Louisa Kemp and Curt Henry Noble 403
Sion S. Brazier and Mary L. Baker 405

27. WILLIAM JEAN "BILLY" BRAZIER
AND PERLINA HAZELWOOD 407
Thomas Newton "Newt" Brazier and Lucy C. Kelly 410
   Robert Walter Brazier and Lizzie Marshall 418
Zachary Taylor Brazier and Martha Newman 420
   John William Brazier and Alma Strain 421
   Otho Benjamin C. Brazier and Cordia Anne Townsend . . 423
   Suella Brazier and _____ Minor/ George W. Strain 424
   Laura Oleva Brazier and George W. Strain 426
   James Henry Taylor Brazier and Annis Humphrey 426
Frances Asberry Brazier and Alice Womack 427
Perlina Brazier and William Jacob Evans 430
   Myrtle Joyce Evans and John Wesley Limbaugh 432
   Robert Renegar Evans and Della Allen 436

28. REV. ELIJAH BRAZIER, OF NC & TN 439
Census Data 439
Family of Rev. Elijah Brazier 442
   William "Wiley" J. Brazier and Elizabeth Dowthard 443
   Elijah Brazier Jr and Elizabeth McElroy 446
      Unaccounted For: 446
      Unsolved Question: James E. Brazier 447
      Family of James E. Brazier and Rachel Brandon 449

29. ELIJAH BRAZIER, s/o James Brazier of Cumberland 450
Family of Elijah Brazier and Sarah ____: 452
Sarah Anne Brazier and Charles Blalock: 453
Bathsheba Brazier and John Wesley Mcdougal 454
Rebecca Brazier and Richard Smith 455
Elijah Wesley Brazier and Anna Jordan 457
Elijah Wesley Brazier Jr and Amanda Bush 459

30. ELIJAH BRAZIER, BROTHER?
Of James Brazier, of Cumberland Co, NC 461
Elijah Brazier, b. 1726 462
Elijah Brazier, Jr, b. c1750 462
Elijah Brazier, III, b. 1776 462
Unaccounted for Data: 463

31. ELIJAH BRAZIER SR, OF JACKSON CO, AL 466
Background Records 466
Elijah Brazier Jr and Betsy Stephens 470
    Elizabeth Brazier and Ezekial Faulkner 472
    Sarah Brazier and James Colbert 472
    Nancy Brazier and Solomon S. Stephens 473
    Amanda Jane Brazier and Andrew Worthen 474
    George Washington Brasher and Ida Loveless 476
    Rebecca Brazier and Joseph Henry Fears 478
    Louisa Brazier and Allen J. Messer 479
    Elijah Brashear, III and Rebecca Cornelison 480
    Lewis Weldon Brashear and Daisy Bell 483

32. HARRIS, WILLIAM AND GIDEON BRAZIER,
  of Iredell Co, NC 488
Harris Brazier 488
William Brazier 489
    Strays 490
Gideon Brazier/Bosher 490
    Is this Gideon II? 490

NON-BRASHEARS FAMILIES

THE BRASHER, BRÉSER, BRASIER, BRAZIER FAMILY, OF NEW YORK CITY

33. HENRY BRÉSER/BRASHER, French Huguenot,
AND SUSANNAH SPICER 492
    Henry Bréser's Land Records 494
    Spicer Family 496
    Henry and Susannah's Wills 496
    Henry and Susannah's Family 499
        Susannah Brasier and Lt. William Churchill 501

33A. ANOTHER HENRY/HARRY BRESER/BRASHER? . . . 502
    Garret Brasher and Catherina Hardenbrook 502
    More Strays 504

33B. ISAAC BRAISJER AND HIS SONS 506
  Henricus (Henry) Brasher and Abigail Pearsall 506
    Henry Jr's Estate 507
    Aaltje (Or Ellen) Brasher and John Berrien 509
  Isaac Braisjer or Bradejor Jr and Jannet Devor 509

33C. ABRAHAM BRASIER, the Revolutionist,
  AND LYSBET SHOUTEN 511
  Lucas "Luke" Brasher and Judith Gasherie 512
  John Brasher and Susannah Baker 513
  Abraham Brasher Jr and Elizabeth Daly 514

33D. COL. ABRAHAM BRASHER, THE LIBERTY BOY 516

33E. LT./CAPT. HENRY BRASHER AND LUCY CLARKE . . 522
  John Brasher, s/o Capt. Henry 524
  Robert Clarke Brasher and Hannah Seamon 526
  Jacob Brasher and Sarah Black 527
    Westerfields 528

33F. LT. EPHRAIM BRASHER JR AND HIS DOUBLOON . . 530
  Ephraim Brasher's Estate 534

33G. PHILIP BRASHER, THE ADJUTANT 535
  Philip Brasher, Alderman 536
  Rex Brasher, Painter of Birds 539

Other Non-Brashears Families

34. REV. PLEASANT BRASHIER, OF SC, AND MS 542
Pleasant Brashier and Rebecca Moore 544
Benjamin F. Brashier and Sarah Jane _____ / K.J. Caliway 546
John Washington Brashier and Antoinette S. Arrington 546
  John Calhoun Brashier and Julia Eugenia Parker/
    Martha Jane Evans Boyce/ Belle Hailes 548
    Benjamin Thomas Brashier
      and Margaret Clara Rigby 550
      Clifton Leonard Brashier and Ellen Lesley Lyons . 552
    Benjamin Franklin Brashier
      and Belinda Jane McDonald 554
      Robert Harvey "Harry" Brashier and Estelle Smiley . . 555
William M. Brashier and Sarah Jane Touchstone 556

James T. Brashier and Nancy _____ 560
Christopher Dudley Brashier and Nancy Jane Sykes 561
   Charles Dudley Brashier and Jennie Bell Baker 562
   Nancy Alice Brashier and Benjamin Forest Holland 564
   William Robert Brasher and Sallie Estelle Allen 565
Robert B. Brashier and Louise Isabell Welsen 567
      Salem Cem, Quitman, Clarke Co, MS 567
      Stray Data: 570

35. ZACHARIAH BRAZIER/BRASHER 572
      Francis LeBrasseur, of Charlestown, SC 572
Captain Zachariah Brazier's First Marriage 574
Captain Zachariah Brazier and Elizabeth Fowke 574
   Chandler Fowke and Mary Tassaker 576
   Elizabeth Fowke and Col. William Philips 578
Zachariah and Elizabeth's Pre-nuptial Arrangements 578
   Brazier Family of Kent Co, England 579

36. TWO (OR MORE) WILLIAM BRASIERS, ... 581
Dr. William Brasier, of Edgefield Co, SC 581
Dr. William Brazier, Surgeon, of VA 583
William Braziers of the Eastern Shore of Maryland 584
   William, William, and James Mumford Brazier 584
   Other William Braziers 585
   Another William Brazier, d. c1754: 585
   But We've Still Got William Brazier's Aplenty: 586

37. EDWARD BRASIER, OF CHARLESTOWN, MASS. 588
Thomas Brasier, s/o Edward Brasier 589
Thomas Brasier, Jr, and Hannah Webb 589
   Thomas Brazier, III and Hannah Ivory 590
Edward Brasier and Mary _____/ Esther Frothingham 591
   Benjamin Brasier 592
      Benjamin Brasier, Jr, and Alice Phillips 592
   Thomas Brasier, IV, and Esther Howard 593
Unidentified Brasiers 593

38. GIDEON BRAZIER/BRASHIER 597
Gideon Brashier and Jerusha Thacker 597
A Different Gideon Bosher: s/o John Bosher 597

INDEX 601

Preface

This last volume of *A BRASHEAR(S) FAMILY HISTORY* focuses on additional data that has come in since I produced the original volumes, corrections to what I had written, and several stray families.

I begin with eight chapters on various descendants of Philip Brashear, oldest son of Robert Brashear and Charity Dowell. Philip died in Henry Co, VA, in 1798, or so. His children moved to central KY, then to MO.

After these large chunks, I'm offering twelve chapters on individual families, then the corrections files, and finally non-Brashear(s) families, such as James Brazier of Cumberland Co, NC, and Henry Brasher/Bréser and his family in New York City. Also you'll find data on Pleasant Brashier, of SC and MS; on Zachariah Brazier, of SC and VA; various William Brasiers of The Eastern Shore of Maryland; on Edward Brasier of Charlestown, MA; and on Gideon Brazier.

A FEW WORDS ABOUT MY CONVENTIONS:

Like Troy Back and Leon Brashear, I have marked with an **asterisk** those family lines that are followed up with later, fuller listings or, maybe, a short biographical sketch or some document. Reading genealogies quickly becomes a hopeless, confusing mess; and you just have to flip back and forth between pages, checking birth-dates, wives, etc to trace your line.

Usually, I have put several **generations** in one listing. I've indented and numbered each succeeding generation, thus:

$^{1\text{-}}$1. the parents
　$^{2\text{-}}$1. the children
　　$^{3\text{-}}$4. the grand-children
　　　$^{4\text{-}}$1. the great-grandchildren

▸ The **superscripts** in the outlines represent the number of the generation from Robert Brasseur, the Immigrant Huguenot, who arrived in Virginia about 1635. The ordinal numbers indicate the sequence of that person among his/her siblings. Thus $^{2\text{-}}$1 indicates the second generation, first child in a family; $^{3\text{-}}$4 indicates the third generation, fourth child; etc. Sorry if this makes reading difficult. I hope that it's easier than flipping back and forth over dozens of pages.

▸ Also, I have assigned (or rather let my computer assign) a **serial number** to all members of the Brashear(s) family. In most cases, this serial number is at the beginning of a line on which the member appears. The serial number is preceded by some superscripts. Superscript ^{V1-} refers to the serial number in vol 1; ^{V2-} refers to the serial number in vol 2; etc. Usually, I have also given the serial number assigned by Back and Brashear in parentheses: e.g. Isaac Brashears (Back#168).

- Maybe the serial numbers will help distinguish several people of exactly the same name. The only way you can keep them separate is if they happened to have a known nickname, as did Robert Samuel "Old Bob" Brashear, or you nickname them with their serial number. Much the same is true for the many Othos, Basils, Reginalds, not to mention the Johns, Josephs, Jameses, Williams, Roberts, Elizabeths, Marthas, Margarets, Nancys, etc.

- I've **boldfaced** the people whose birth names were some form of the family name: Brashear, Brashears, Brasher, Brashers, Beshears, Boshears, etc. I have tried to give their surnames as they occur in the documents (even when obviously misspelled), sometimes with and sometimes without the "s." My great grandfather's will spells his name three ways and is indexed under a fourth possibility!)

- Spouses are given in bold italics: e.g. **_Phoebe Nicks_**. Often, a wife's maiden name and/or former name is indicated in parentheses; "née" (feminine) or "ne" (masculine) (French for "born") indicates the surname at birth; thus Dorothy (née Cager/widow Munroe) Jones.

- "Nicknames" are in quotes; e.g. Robert S. "Old Bob" Brashear.

- If a person was <u>called by a name</u> other than his/her first, I've underlined that name, e.g. Howard <u>Charles</u> Brashers, who was called "Charles." Underlining is also used occasionally to call the reader's attention to a name or some data.

- When all I know are the names of a set of children, I've run them on in a paragraph and separated them by punctuation: e.g. (from a Bell family) Ch: Danny Joe; Karen Lynn; Stanley Farris; and Phillip Drew Bell. The exception is that all Brashear(s) family members get a bold line of their own.

- When I don't know a name, either given or surname, I've offered a **blank**, e.g. Robert Brashier, III, m.1. _____; m.2. c1679, Mrs. Alice Jackson, widow of Thomas Jackson. If you know the name(s) you can fill them in with pen and ink. And, of course, I'd like to receive the data also. These blanks are NOT indexed.

- Information I have reason to believe is accurate, but have **no proof** of, is preceded and/or followed by a question mark; thus "Bill Brashear, b. ?1845" means I'm making an informed guess at his birth date. If you take my information elsewhere, please, please, also take my doubt.

I've used some abbreviations:

HSB = *The Brashear-Brashears Family, 1449-1929*, by Henry Sinclair Brashear (1929), the first book-length history of this family

Back = *The Brashear Story, a Family History, 1637-1963*, by Troy Back and Leon Brashear (1963; 1980), the second book-length history of this family.

BFB = "Br(e)ashe(a)r(s) Family Branches," a newsletter published for more than ten years by Arzella Brashear Spear.

FHL = The Family History Library, Salt Lake City. FHL Arc or ARCfile indicates archive files in that library.

"c" in front of a number means "circa" or about: thus "c1742" should be read "about 1742."

"b." mean "born on/at," "d." means "died on/at,"

"m." means "married," and sometimes a number is added to indicate which of multiple marriages I'm talking about, as "m.2." indicates a second marriage.

"bur" means "is/was buried at" some cemetery ("cem")

"s/o" "d/o" "gs/o" and the like mean "s/o "daughter of" etc.

I have sometimes abbreviated county names: e.g. PGCo is Prince George's Co, MD; LawrCo is Lawrence Co, TN

And in places where it struck me as awkward, or lacked clarity, I haven't used these abbreviations.

In many cases, I've followed descending families with other surnames a few generations, especially when someone in that line is an interested and active genealogist, or the lines intermarry later. Many of these people have contributed substantially to what we know about the Brashear(s) Family. As I've said before and will say again, this sort of book cannot be written by one person, because there is simply not enough time in one lifetime to go to all the places, do all the research, and write it up. Any family historian is forced to rely on the research of many a cousin, most of them bearing a different surname. We all owe them heavy thanks for the money and sweat they have expended on our common family history. I'll try to acknowledge them at the end of the chapter to which they contributed, and each at the spot where they contributed most.

This has been a labor of love. There were times when I thought the project would die unfinished; but it's over, completed. I'm going for a long vacation up the Inland Passage!

Descendants of Philip Brashear, 1727–1797

and Ann Wilson

1. ABSALOM BRASHEAR and POLLY PHILLIPS

^{V2-}52. **Absalom Brashears**, (probably s/o Robert Brashears, gs/o Philip Brashears, Jr, and Elizabeth _____, and ggs/o Philip Brashears, Sr, and Ann Wilson), b. 10 March 1817 in Kentucky, d. 9 April 1862 in a civil war battle (probably at Pea Ridge, Elkhorn Tavern, Arkansas.); m. *Martha Ann "Polly" Phillips*, 26 Dec 1838, Casey County, Kentucky. New data from Hazel (Beshears) Palmer, <flahpalmer@yahoo.com>, for which many thanks. Thanks also to Marta Beshears Croom <txcrew@worldnet.att.net>

See vol 2, p.230, for main family of Absalom Brashears and Martha Ann "Polly" Phillips. Their sixth child was John Wesley Bolling Brashears.

^{V2-}1566. ¹⁰⁻6. **John Wesley Bolling Brashears**, (s/o Absalom Brashears and Martha Ann "Polly" Phillips), b. 5 June 1848, Kentucky, d. after 1910; m.1. c1865, *Rebecca McNeeley* b. c1842, MO, (1 ch; div); m.2. 16 Nov 1877, Alton, Oregon Co, MO, *Mary E. Mervin*, b. c1852, KY (6 ch).

Child of John Wesley Bolling Brashears and Rebecca McNeeley:
^{v2-}1691.   ¹¹⁻1. **Thomas Jackson Beshears**, b. 7 Oct 1866, Maries Co, MO, d. 17 July 1900, bur Elvins, St Francis Co, MO; m. *Sarah Ann White*. See Vol 2, p. 229.
Family of John Wesley Bolling Brashears and Mary E. Mervin:
²⁻1695.   ¹¹⁻2. ***William Abner Beshears**, (s/o John Wesley Bolling

Brashears and Mary E. Mervin), b. 28 Jan 1879, Cleburne, AR, d. 26 Dec 1958, Denison, TX; m.1. *Millie Jane Lamb*, (See family below)

V2-1700.   11-3. **Henry Arthur "Art" Beshears**, b. 1 Jan 1881, AR, d. 27 Nov 1963, bur Goodloe Cem, Quitman, AR; m. *Rowena Smith*, d/o George Andrew Jackson Smith (b. 1850, AR) and Emily Ann Bean (b. March 1844, AR), and sister of his brother Preston Beshears's wife. Children of Art & Rowena: (in V.2, I offered ch: Annie; Dell; Clarence; and Cyrus Beshears) (data from Virginia Bradford Rose <jrose10@pacbell.net>)

V9-2.   12-1. **Joe Beshears**, lives in Cabot, AR, married *Ollie*
_____

V9-3.   12-2. **Ollie Mae Beshears**, b. Aug. 28, 1912 Miller, AR. died: Feb. 6, 2001 Beverly Health Care, Heber Springs, AR; m. *Otis Ray Johnson*. He still lives in Quitman, AR. They had 3 sons. D. Johnson, lives in Bryant, Fred Johnson, and Charlie D. Johnson, he lives in Quitman, AR.

V9-4.   12-3. **Thurman Beshears**, lives in Wynne
V9-5.   12-4. **Virgie Beshears**, lives in Winchester, Indiana; married _____ *Kennedy*
V9-6.   12-5. **Zola Beshears**, married *J.W. Ray*
V9-7.   12-6. **Annie C. Beshears** b. c1906 in AR. died very young
V9-8.   12-7. **Cyrus Beshears**, b. 1908
V9-9.   12-8. **Clarence Beshears** b. bef. 1925, died unk.
V2-1705.   11-4. **Missoura Pearlina Beshears**, b. Oct 1883, AR; m. April 1901, *John Neuson*
V2-1706.   11-5. ***Preston Pebble "Presley" Beshears**, b. 25 Feb (or 23 Jan) 1884, Eureka Springs, AR, d. 19 Oct 1976, age 97, Hope, Hempstead Co, AR; m.1. *Ida Andrew Smith*; m.2. *Florence Loven*, who died in childbirth with her first child; m.3. *Ivy New Kimbell*; m.4. his first wife, *Ida Andrew (Smith) Beshears*; m.5. *Ella Mae Biggs*; m.6. c1927, *Mary Magdaline Moore*, (See family below)
V2-1708.   11-6. **Ida Beshears**, b. March 1889, AR
V2-1709.   11-7. **Lizzie or Anna Beshears**, b. Dec 1892, AR

William Abner Beshears and Millie Jane Lamb

V2-1695. 11-2. **William Abner Beshears**, (s/o John Wesley Bolling Brashears and Mary E. Mervin), b. 28 Jan 1879, Cleburne, AR, d. 26 Dec 1958, Denison, TX; m.1. *Millie Jane Lamb*, b. 24 Jan 1880, d. 6 Jan 1941, Denison, TX. Both are buried Fairview Cemetery, Denison, TX; m.2. c1943, *Ella Carlet Baker.*

Family of William Abner Beshears and Millie Jane Lamb:

V9-10. 12-1. ***Thomas Wesley Beshears**, b. 9 Aug 1901, AR, d. 18 Jan 1967, Denison TX; m. Jan 1918, McKinney, Collin Co, TX, *Alice Mae Raines*, b. 9 Oct 1903, d. 5 June 1982, Denison, TX, bur Cedarlawn Cem, Denison, TX.

V9-11. 12-2. **Sarah Beshears**, b. 2 Feb 1905, AR, d. Aug 1986, Denison, TX; m.1. *Bill Wright*; m.2. *Lewis Shields*.

V9-12. 13-1. Mattie Jane Wright

V9-13. 13-2. Edna Mae Wright

V9-14. 13-3. Edgar Lee Wright

V9-15. 12-3. **Lillie Beshears**, b. 5 March 1908, Little Rock, AR, d. 28 June 1988, Arizona; m.1. _____*Steelman*; m.2. *Frank Argo*

V9-16. 13-1. Lonnie Steelman

V9-17. 12-4. **Lola Beshears** b. 5 May 1910, Little Rock, AR, d. 16 Aug 1994, Arizona; m. *Joseph Ellis Steelman*, b. 29 Sept 1907, d. Feb. 1987, Arizona.

V9-18. 13-1. Beulah Steelman b. bef. 1930

V9-19. 13-2. Annie Steelman

V9-20. 13-3. J. E. Steelman

V9-21. 13-4. L. C. Steelman b. bef. 1937

V9-22. 12-5. **Cordelia Beshears** – no info

V9-23. 12-6. ***Bitty Idamae Beshears** (Biddie, Biddis, Betty?) b. 1907? AR, d. the early 1940's; m. *Benjamin Franklin Raines*, b. 20 May 1905, McKinney, Collin Co, TX, d. 17 March 1965, Denison, TX.

V9-24. 12-7. ***Cleo Abner Beshears**, b. 30 Dec 1911, AR, d. 4 Feb 1974, Austin, TX; m. 25 Aug 1935, McKinney, TX, *Beulah Hazel Raines*, b. 17 March 1912, McKinney, TX, d. 24 Nov 1998, Austin, TX. Cleo and Beulah are both buried, Capitol Memorial Park and Gardens, Austin, TX.

V9-25. 12-8. **Alvis Leo Beshears**, b. 29 Dec 1919, d. 23 Dec 1953, Denison, TX; m. *Mary Adams.*

V9-26. 13-1. **Freddie Joe Beshears**, b. 4 Oct 1939, d. Sept1993.

V9-27. 13-2. **Lonnie Joe Beshears**, b.&d. 7 July 1940,

Thomas Wesley Beshears and Alice Mae Raines

12-4. **Thomas Wesley Beshears**, (s/o William Abner Beshears and Milly J. Lamb), b. 9 Aug 1901, AR, d. 18 Jan 1967, Denison TX; m. *Alice Mae Raines*, b. 9 Oct 1903, d. 5 June 1982, Denison, TX; m. Jan 1918, McKinney, Collin Co, TX. Buried, Cedarlawn Cemetery, Denison, TX.

Family of Thomas Wesley Beshears and Alice Mae Raines:

V9-28. 13-1. **Minnie Lorene Beshears**, b. 29 Dec 1921, d. Nov 1984, Denison, TX; m. *Odus B. Shlinder*.

V9-29.   14-1. Minnie Lou Shlinder; m. Gary Mosteller
V9-30.   14-2. Thomas Shlinder
V9-31.   14-3. Glen Ray Shlinder
V9-32.   14-4. Linda Joyce Shlinder
V9-33.   14-5. James Herman Shlinder
V9-34.   14-6. Millie Shlindeer
V9-35.   13-2. **Carl Ray Beshears**; m. ***Peggy Copeland***. No children
V9-36.   13-3. **Herman Dee Beshears**, b. 2 May 1926, d. Feb. 1982, Carterville, Tx; m. ***Martha Lee Parsons***, b. 1932; m. 1 July 1948, Arizona.
V9-37.   14-1. **Thomas Lee Beshears**
V9-38.   14-2. **Herman Donald Beshears**
V9-39.   14-3. **William Ray Beshears**
V9-40.   14-4. **Marta Gayle Beshears**; m. _____ ***Croom***
V9-41.   13-4. **Leonard Lee Beshears**, b. 18 Feb 1930; m. ***Joyce May*** on 16 Sept. 1948, Sherman, TX.
V9-42.   14-1. **David Beshears**,; m. ***Patricia*** _____?__
V9-43.   15-1. **Adam Beshears**,
V9-44.   15-2. **Chandra Beshears**,
V9-45.   13-5. **Cassie Marie Beshears**, b. 1936; m. ***James Bayless***, 4 May 1954.
V9-46.   14-1. Dennis Ray Bayless, b. 5 March 1955. d. a few days after birth.
V9-47.   14-2. James Earl Bayless, b. 28 Jan 1958; m. Durleene Bowels
V9-48.   15-1. Quincy Jameson Bayless, b. 5 Aug 1995, Denison, TX.
V9-49.   14-3. Cynthia Ann Bayless, b. 17 Jan 1961, Denison, TX; m. _____Wineinger.
V9-50.   15-1. Cassandra Loraine Wineinger, b. 20 Dec 1986
V9-51.   15-2. Wesley Wineinger, b. 15 March 1990.

Bitty Idamae Beshears
and Benjamin Franklin Raines

12-4. **Bitty Idamae Beshears** (Biddie, Biddis, Betty?), (d/o William Abner Beshears and Milly J. Lamb), b. 1907?, d. early 1940's; m. ***Benjamin Franklin Raines***, b. 20 May 1905, McKinney, Collin Co, TX, d. 17 March 1965, Denison, TX.

Family of Bitte Idamae Beshears and Benjamin F. Raines:
V9-52.   13-1. Alfred Lee Raines, was killed at age 12 (accident?)
V9-53.   13-2. Henry Edward Raines,; m. Lois _____ No children (raised one of his brother's children)
V9-54.   13-3. Othal Viola Raines

V9-55.   13-4. Jerry William Raines, b. 13 Sept 1925, Maybank, Kaufman, TX; m. on 1 Oct 1945, Betty Jo Murr, b. 10 Sept 1929, Denison, Grayson Co, TX. J.W. Raines and Betty Jo Murr were divorced, and he married 22 Feb 1968, her younger sister, Bonnie Mae Murr, b. 20 Aug 1946.

                  Family of Jerry William Raines and Betty Jo Murr:

V9-56.   14-1. Larry Wayne Raines, b. 23 Feb 19__; m. Rita Carr
V9-57.   14-2. Rose Marie Raines, b. 2 Aug 19__; m. Henry Allen
V9-58.   14-3. Judith Ann Raines, b. 30 May 1947, Denison, Tex.
V9-59.   14-4. Geraldine Raines, b. 5 June1948, Sherman, Tex.
V9-60.   14-5. Wanda Laverne Raines, b. 23 April1953, Denison, Tex.
V9-61.   14-6. Ruby Mae Raines, b. 17 July1954, Denison, TX; m. Steven Perez
V9-62.   14-7. Carolyn Sue Raines, b. 24 July1956; m. Eldon T. Turner
V9-63.   14-8. Oleta Faye Raines, b. 30 April 1963
V9-64.   14-9. Evelyn Kay Raines, b. 10 July1965, Dallas, Tex.

                  Family of Jerry William Raines and Bonnie Mae Murr,

V9-65.   14-10. Dale Willey Raines, b. 21 March1965, Dallas, Tex.
V9-66.   14-11. Melvin Ray Raines, b. 28 July1966, Dallas, Tex.
V9-67.   14-12. Jerry Ben Raines, b. 7 Aug1968, Dallas, Tex.
V9-68.   14-13. Bonnie Elaine Raines, b. 6 Aug1972, Denison, Tex.
V9-69.   13-5. Leamon Oscar Raines, b. 12 July 1932,; m. Norma Ann Renfro.
V9-70.   14-1. Leah Darlene Raines, b. Grayson Co, TX
V9-71.   14-2. Mark Stevan Raines, b. Grayson Co, TX
V9-72.   14-3. Forest Mathew Raines, b. Grayson Co, TX

Cleo Abner Beshears and Beulah Hazel Raines

12-4. **Cleo Abner Beshears**, (s/o William Abner Beshears and Milly J. Lamb), b. 30 Dec 1911, AR, d. 4 Feb 1974, Austin, TX; m. **Beulah Hazel Raines**, 25 Aug 1935, McKinney, TX. Beulah was b. 17 March 1912, McKinney, TX, d. 24 Nov 1998, Austin, TX. Cleo and Beulah are both buried, Capitol Memorial Park and Gardens, Austin, TX.

Notes on Cleo Abner Beshears – (this story was told to Hazel Beshears Palmer by her father, Cleo Abner Beshears, sometime, the late 1940's.)

My father left home at age 15 or 16 because he didn't intend to take another beating from his father, William Abner Beshears. William Abner was a Baptist preacher and a very strict disciplinarian. He used a long "blacksnake" whip to beat his children if he was mad at them.

One day, when my dad got home, he heard Lola (his sister) crying and screaming. William Abner was beating her with his whip. My dad was able to take the whip away from William Abner, and he then helped Lola pack some things and leave home. She was married soon afterwards.

My Dad got rid of the whip while he was riding in the back of a wagon on his way home from church, by cutting the whip into small pieces and dropping them into the dirt road. His father never knew what happened to his whip. Soon after that, my Dad went to live with a family by the name of Reeves, in Platter, Oklahoma. I remember visiting the Reeves family when I was just a young girl. Cleo and his family lived in Denison, Sherman, and McKinney, TX after he and Beulah were married, until June 1952 when the family moved to Austin, TX, in order to be near the Texas State School for the deaf, so their daughters, Lois Ellen and Melba Joyce, could attend school and live at home.

Cleo was on his way to work on the day after Labor Day, 1952, when he was involved in a car-train accident. He was severely injured – fractured skull, concussion, broken left arm, crushed left leg, and internal injuries. His health was never good after the accident. He suffered from heart problems, high blood pressure, diabetes and a stroke, 1972.

He owned and operated a Texaco Service Station, located at the corner of Riverside Drive and Congress Avenue, Austin, TX for many years. His son, Cleo Edward Beshears, worked with him and did mechanical work, as well as other duties.

Cleo died of heart failure at his home at 1402 Drake Avenue, Austin, TX on Feb. 4, 1974.

Family of Cleo Abner Beshears and Beulah Hazel Raines:

V9-73.   13-1. **Hazel Bernice Beshears**, b. 6 Nov 1936, McKinney, TX; m. *Floyd Duane Palmer*, 14 Jan 1956, Austin, TX.

V9-74.   14-1. Floyd Wayne Palmer, b. 9 Jan 1957, Rochester, Fulton Co, Indiana; m.1. Marshall Co, IN, 1 Aug 1976, Kathryn Marie Fouts (1 ch); m.2. Argos, IN, 8 May 1983, Jenise Renee Clark (1 ch), b. 7 Dec 1956,

V9-75.   15-1. Kelly Ann Palmer, b. 28 Nov 1978; m. 24 Oct 2000, K. Curtis Dale Rodgers, b. 5 Nov 1978.

V9-76.   161. Jordan Dale Rodgers, b. 2 Aug1996.

V9-77.   162. Alexandra Megan Rodgers, b. 17 Sept. 2001

V9-78.   15-2. Scott Michael Palmer, b. 11 July 1988.

V9-79.   14-2. Curtis Duane Palmer, b. 20 March 1959, Plymouth, Marshall County, Indiana; m. 14 Aug 1982, Greensburg, IN, Deborah Kathryn Endris, b. 7 Dec 1959, Greensburg, IN

V9-80.   15-1. Victoria May Palmer, b. 7 Nov 1985, South Bend, IN

V9-81.   15-2. Jacob Daniel Palmer, b. 10 June 1988, Plymouth,

V9-82.   15-3. Adrienne "Addie" Christine Palmer, b. 2 Nov 1992, Plymouth, IN

V9-83.   14-3. Alan Lee Palmer, b. 11 March 1965, Plymouth, Marshall County, In; m. Marilyn Sue Geis, b. 11 Sept 1968, Greensburg, Indiana, on 16 June 1990, Greensburg, IN

V9-84.   15-1. Kyle Alan Palmer, b. 22 Jan 1996, Aiken, S.C.

V9-85.   15-2. Grant Joseph Palmer, b. 17 July 1998, Indianapolis, IN.

V9-86.   15-3. Benjamin Cole Palmer, b. 2 July 2001, Indianapolis, IN.

V9-87.   13-2. **Lois Ellen Beshears**, b. 25 Dec 1938, McKinney, TX; m. 11 Dec 1957, Austin, TX, *Richard Duncan*,; m.2. *Bobby Love*.

V9-88.   14-1. Dale Calvin Duncan, b. 15 March 1959, TX; m. Fawn _____?

V9-89.   15-1. Kaitlynn Duncan, b, Austin, TX

V9-90.   15-2. Kristen Duncan, b, Austin, TX

V9-91.   14-2. Kim Ellen Duncan, b. 14 Oct 1963,; m. Terry Lee Hicks on 27 May 1983, Little Rock, AR. Terry Lee Hicks, b. 10 Oct 1956, Whitehall, AR

V9-92.   15-1. Timothy Lee Hicks, b. 11 May1984, Little Rock, AR.

V9-93.   13-3. **Cleo Edward Beshears**, b. 8 Sept 1940, McKinney, TX, d. Sept. 8, 2000, Austin, TX. (yes – he died on his 60th birthday); m. *Monette Lacy Carnline*, 1973?, Austin, TX. Cleo died from a heart attack and complications. Monette died after a two year battle with cancer. Cleo and Monette both buried, Cook-Walden/Memorial Hill Cemetery, Pflugerville, TX.

V9-94.   13-4. **Gene Abner Beshears**, b. 24 Oct 1942, Sherman, TX; m. 19 March 1960, Austin, TX, *Lora Lee Yocum*, b. 14 Dec 1943.

V9-95.   14-1. **Traci Jean Beshears**, b. 13 Nov 1960, Austin, TX; m. *Tommie Thomas*

V9-96.   15-1. Clinton Andrew Thomas, b. 21 April 1980

V9-97.   15-2. Cory David Thomas, b. 1 Dec 1984; m. 27 July 2001, Christopher Rager, b. 25 Dec1960,

V9-98.   14-2. **Sherry Lynn Beshears**, b. 4 Oct 1961, Austin TX; m. *Brian John Thomas*, b. 24 March 1959; m. 19 March 1980

V9-99.   15-1. Jonathan Brian Thomas, b. 1 Aug 1986

V9-100.   14-3. **Brenda Lee Beshears**, b. 14 Dec 1962, Austin, TX; m. 24 Sept 1983, *Tracy Dean Craytor*, b. 20 July1960

V9-101.   151. Amanda Gail Craytor, b. 28 Jan 1986

V9-102.	152. Kyle James Craytor, b. 26 Dec 1989
V9-103.	153. Cody Wayne Craytor, b. 8 April 1992
V9-104.	14-4. **Gene Elliott Beshears**, b. 26 April 1964, Austin, TX; m. to **Connie Fishler** (2 ch); m.2. 25 June 1992, **Cindy Lynell Thornton** (2ch), b. 25 May 1965.
V9-105.	151. **Shane Elliott Beshears**, b. 11 June 1986
V9-106.	152. **Garret Patrick Beshears**, b. 29 July 1988
V9-107.	153. **Joe Brandon Beshears**, b. 8 Dec 1992
V9-108.	154. **Wesley Aaron Beshears**, b. 25 Aug 1997
V9-109.	13-5. **Melba Joyce Beshears**, b. 2 March 1945, Sherman, TX; m. **James David Dailey** on 22 Aug 1963. He was b. August 4, 1942, d. 23 Sept 1966; m.2. Michael Nunn.
V9-110.	14-1. Barry David Dailey, b. 6 Sept 1964
V9-111.	14-2. Vincent Eugene Dailey, b. 6 Oct 1965

Alice, Benjamin, & Bert Edward Raines were siblings, children of Jeremiah Oscar Raines, b. Jan. 9, 1858, d. 16 Feb 1925, bur Mabank, TX; married 1881, Emma Barber.

Jeremiah Oscar Raines was s/o James Alfred Raines & Rosanna Harvey.

James Alfred Raines was s/o George Rains (note spelling) and Jane Sharp.

For more on Raines, contact Hazel (Beshears) Palmer, 19220 Michigan Rd, Argos, IN 46501 <flahpalmer@yahoo.com>.

Preston Pebble Beshears and His Six Wives

V2-1706. 11-5. ***Preston Pebble "Presley" Beshears**, (s/o John Wesley Bolling Brashears and Mary E. Mervin [s/o Absalom Brashears and Martha Ann "Polly" Phillips]), b. 25 Feb 1884, Eureka Springs, AR, d. 19 Oct 1976, age 97, Hope, Hempstead Co, AR; m.1. 24 Dec 1903 (Cleburne Co, AR, Marr Bk 4, p.307), **Ida Andrew Smith**, d/o George Andrew Jackson Smith and Emily Ann Bean, and sister of his brother Art's wife; Art was bondsman to the wedding;

m.2. **Florence Loven**, who died in childbirth with her first child; m.3. **Ivy New Kimbell**;

m.4. his first wife, **Ida Andrew (Smith) Beshears**;

m.5. **Ella Mae Biggs**;

m.6. c1927, **Mary Magdaline Moore**, b. 19 Nov 1892, Mt Vernon, IL, d. of tuberal pregnancy, 16 March 1929, Quitman, AR, sister of his son Luther Beshears' wife, Nellie Moore. (Mary M. Moore had been married previously to Harry H. Bennett (b. 29 Jan 1889, Pearson, AR, d. 25 Feb 1926, Falkner Co, AR) and had 4 ch.

George Andrew Jackson "Jack" Smith, b. 1850, AR, m. Emily Ann Bean, b. March 1844 in AR. Their children were:

a. Rebecca "Becky" Smith, b. Nov. 1873, married _____ Boyce
b. Mary J. Smith, b. 1874
c. John M. Smith, b. 1876
d. Jess Smith, b. Aug. 1883
e. *Rowena Smith, b. Jan. 1885, bur Rose Bud, AR; m. **Henry Arthur "Art" Beshears**.
f. *Ida Andrew Smith, b. 12 March 1885, Heber Springs, AR, d. 3 July 1971 Madera, CA, bur Arbor Vitae Cem.; m. **Preston Pebble Beshears**
g. Isabelle "Lucy" Smith, married Joe Hulse

<u>Family of Preston Pebble Beshears and Ida Andrew Smith</u>. They had 10 children, but only six are listed, the other four having died young.

V9-112.   12-1. ***Luther Andrew Beshears**, b. Aug. 7, 1905, Heber Springs, AR. d. July 2, 1970, Madera, CA, bur Arbor Vitae Cem; m. 7 Oct 1923, in AR, **Nellie Edith Moore**, b. June 19, 1904

V9-113.   12-2. ***Onie Nell Dell Beshears**, b. June 17, 1910 in Cleburne Co, AR, d. April 21, 1999 in Madera, CA, bur Arbor Vitae Cem; m.1. Jan. 4, 1928 Harrison, AR, **Art J. Parker**, m.2. **Lloyd Childers**.

V9-114.   12-3. ***Cyrus Edward Beshears**, b. May 12, 1914, Miller, Heber Springs, AR, d. Oct. 13, 1999 in Sherman, Texas, bur Oct 27 at Wesley Cem in Quitman, AR; m.1. **Bessie Inez DeBusk**, they divorced; m.2. Etta Mae _____ ; m.3. Virginia _____ ,

V9-115.   12-4. ***Ava Aldreen Beshears**, b. Sept. 12, 1916, AR, d. June 1, 1994 in Madera, CA, bur Arbor Vitae Cem; m.1. **Virgil Ray Haley**; m.2 **Al Rice**; m.3. **Jim May**.

V9-116.   12-5. **Preston Brashears**, b. 18 Aug 1918, AR, d. 5 May 1962, Garland Co, AR. Preston died while serving in the U.S. Army Air Force. He appears to have gone back to the "Brashears" surname.

V9-117.   12-6. ***Beulah May Beshears**, b. July 1, 1920, Highden, AR; m.1. 21 Dec 1935, in Cleburne Co, AR, **Glover Franklin Bradford**, they divorced; m.2. **Samuel Seedal Meeks**.

<u>Family of Preston P. Beshears and Florence Loven</u>
V9-118.   12-x. **Wanda Sue Beshears**, who lives in Memphis, TN

<u>Family of Preston P. Beshears and Ivy New Kimbell</u>
V9-119.   12-x. **Edmond Beshears**, who lived in Lancaster, CA

Family of Preston P. Beshears and Ella Mae Biggs
¹²⁻-x. "they had 10 children, a Billy, Luke, Dell, and Mary, and names unknown. Seems he named some of his children with his last wife, the same names of children he had with Ida Smith"

Luther Andrew Beshears and Nellie Edith Moore

V9-120.   ¹²⁻1. **Luther Andrew Beshears**, b. Aug. 7, 1905, Heber Springs, AR. d. July 2, 1970, Madera, CA, bur Arbor Vitae Cem; m. 7 Oct 1923, in AR, *Nellie Edith Moore*, b. June 19, 1904 in Quitman, AR, d. Jan. 9, 1991 in Fresno, CA, bur Arbor Vitae Cem, Madera, CA, d/o Rev. James Shaw Moore and Margarita "Maggie" Bain.

V9-121.   ¹³⁻1. **Evelyn Elizabeth Beshears**, b. April 23, 1925 in Heber Springs, AR; m. Oct. 11, 1941 in Madera, CA, *Macy Ofield Smith*.

V9-122.   ¹⁴⁻1. Linda Fay Smith, b. Oct. 18, 1942, Madera, CA; m.1. Nov. 4, 1959 in Fresno, CA, Russell Crandall; m.2. Robert Lozano.

V9-123.   ¹⁵⁻1. Clifton Wesley Crandall b. Oct. 15, 1960 in Indiana married Nov. 12, 1988 to Natalie Davis in Washington. 3 children: Kyle Crandall, b. Aug. 20, 1985, in Fresno, CA. Russell Crandall, b. April 8, 1986 in Fresno, CA. and C.J. Crandall b. May 1, 1990 in Fresno, CA.

V9-124.   ¹⁵⁻2. Lynnette Crandall b. Jan. 25, 1962 in Fresno, CA. Married Holland, They had 3 children: Amanda Holland, b. Sep. 17, 1983, Luke Holland b. Aug. 20, 1986 and Dusty Holland, b. Aug. 20, 1986. Then she married Ken Keeley 1989 in Washington.

V9-125.   ¹⁵⁻3. Teresa Crandall b. May 29, 1963 in Fresno, CA. Married Peter Shankel Nov. 27, 1985 in Fresno, CA. One child, Elisha Shankel, b. Jan. 30, 1987 in Fresno, CA.

V9-126.   ¹⁴⁻2. Lonnie Charles Smith, b. June 24, 1946, Madera, CA; m. Feb. 24, 1987 in Fresno, CA. to Lynn Koller, had two children: Kathy Smith b. July 17, 1969 in Florida. Chad Andrew Smith b. Jan. 26, 1976. 2nd wife, Patricia Ford she was born Oct. 27, 1954 in Iowa.

V9-127.   ¹³⁻2. **L.G. Beshears**, b. June 2, 1929, Cleburne Co, AR; m. 7 July 1949, in Madera, CA, *Helen Christine Woodley*, they divorced; m.2. *Bonnie* _____ ,

V9-128.   ¹⁴⁻1. **Kathy Beshears**, b. April 1, 1949 in Madera, CA; m. 23 Aug 1969, in Carson City, NV, Jimmie Johnson, they divorced; m.2. on July 22, 1989 in

Juneau, Alaska, Donald O. Perrin, b. Dec. 21, 1952 in Warren, Ohio.

V9-129.   15-1. Jimmie Greg Johnson b. April 4, 1970 in Anaheim, CA. Died April 4, 1970 in Anaheim, CA.

V9-130.   15-2. Tonya Michelle Johnson, b. April 7, 1971 in Oakhurst, CA. Married Aug. 2, 1992 to Vince Gomez Isturis III, in Juneau, Alaska. They have two children:

V9-131.   16-1. Vincent Gomez Istruis, IV b. Feb. 5, 1992 in Seattle, Washington.

V9-132.   16-2. Dereck Micheal Isturic b. March 30, 1994 in Juneau, Alaska.

V9-133.   15-3. Jimmie Brent Johnson, b. Oct. 21, 1974 in Fresno, CA. Married Rachele Michelle Wall Nov. 28, 1993 in Greenbrier, AR. They have 1 child.

V9-134.   16-1. Jimmie Austin Johnson b. Feb. 22, 1995 in Conway, AR.

V9-135.   14-2. **Rhonda Beshears**, b. Dec. 11, 1951 in Madera, CA; m. April 12, 1980 in Madera, CA Bruce L. Johnson. They have two children:

V9-136.   15-1. Liesel Dristin Johnson, b. Dec. 3, 1983 in Fresno, CA.

V9-137.   15-2. Leah Michelle Johnson, b. Aug. 30, 1988 in Fresno, CA.

V9-138.   14-3. **Konnie Beshears**, b. June 14, 1954 in Madera, CA; m.1. Aug. 5, 1972 in Madera, CA, Donnie Goetz, b. Nov. 16, 1955 in Chicago, Illinois, d. Oct. 29, 1993 in Chowchila, CA (3 ch); m.2. 2 April 1992, Emmit Robert Boss,

V9-139.   15-1. Brandel Lee Goetz, b. Jan. 31, 1973 in Chowchilla, CA.

V9-140.   15-2. Jason Lee Goetz, b. Feb. 7, 1981 in Yucca Valley, CA.

V9-141.   15-3. Angelea Christine Goetz, b. July 29, 1983 in Chowchilla, CA.

V9-142.   13-3. **Wanda Lou Beshears**, b. Jan. 5, 1932 Heber Springs, AR; m. June 23, 1951 in Madera, CA, *Bobby Lee Truhitte*.

V9-143.   14-1. Ronnie Lee Truhitte b. March 29, 1952 in Madera, CA. Married June 3, 1972 in Fresno, CA. to Martha Louise Masini. she was born April 17, 1952 in Fresno, CA. they have 3 children.

V9-144.   15-1. Robert Leonard Truhitte b. July 17, 1977 in Oceanside, CA.

V9-145.   15-2. Jeffery Michael Truhitte, b. Aug. 31, 1978 in
                 Oceanside, CA.

V9-146.   15-3. Jacklyn Lavern Truhitte, b. Sept. 8, 1982 in
                 Santa Cruz, CA.

V9-147.   14-2. Carolyn Annette Truhitte, b. May 27, 1955 in
                 Madera, CA. Married Dwayne Lawrance Lucckesi on
                 June 16, 1973 in Madera, CA. He was born Sept. 3,
                 1961 in Madera, They have 2 children:

V9-148.   15-1. Stephanie Marie Lucckesi, b. Sept. 8, 1977 in
                 Fresno, CA.

V9-149.   15-2. Nickolas Giovanni Lucckesi, b. Aug. 3, 1983 in
                 Fresno, CA.

Onie Nell Dell Beshears and Art J. Parker

Children for 12-2. Onie Nell Dell Beshears and Art J. Parker, he was
born Jan. 4, 1910 in Harrison, AR. died Sept. 1952 in Henderson Co,
Reno, Nevada, buried Madera, CA, at Arbor Vitae, Cemetery. They had
two sons. Dell's second husband, Lloyd Childres, died May 10, 1994,
in Madera, CA, and buried at Arbor Vitae Cem.

V9-150.   13-1. Riley Dennis Parker, b. Nov. 1, 1929 in Heber Springs,
                 AR., d. July 21, 1970 in Fresno, CA. buried in Fresno.
                 He first married Anna Maxine Keith on April 9, 1945.
                 She was born March 28, 1928 in Delhi, Oklahoma, Died
                 May 28, 1991 in Reno, Nevada They had a daughter.
                 Riley and Maxine divorced, he then married Hazel
                 Ramona Bradshaw on Feb. 22, 1953, and they had a
                 son

V9-151.   14-1. Patricia Ann Parker, born March 17, 1946 in
                 Madera, CA. Married Jeffrey Wayne Zahourek Feb.
                 14, 1969 in Sacramento, CA. They had two sons,
                 and then divorced.

V9-152.   15-1. Michael Shawn Zahourek b. Feb. 10, 1969 in
                 Reno, Nevada, Married Dec. 31. 1991 to
                 Kimberly Ann Splinter in Reno, Nevada. She was
                 born Feb. 17, 1965 in Bakersfield, CA. They had
                 two children:

V9-153.   16-1. Stak Conard Zahourek, b. July 31, 1989
                 Bakersfield, CA.

V9-154.   16-2. Macy Lynne Zahourek, b. Nov. 22, 1993 in
                 Fresno, CA.

V9-155.   15-2. Bart Mitchel Zahourek b. Dec. 31, 1970 in
                 Sacramento, CA. Married April 12, 1993 in
                 FResno, CA. to Christi Jean Yager, born April 5,
                 1960 in Fresno, CA. They had two children: His
                 second wife was Jenna Johnston, born Jan. 25,

	1973 in Bakersfield, CA. They had 1 child.
V9-156.	16-1. Jeri Ann Zahourek b. May 15, 1991 in Bakersfield, CA.
V9-157.	16-2. Carley June Zahourek, b. Dec. 21, 1994 in Coos Bay, Oregon.
V9-158.	16-3. Christol Joy Zahourek, born Oct. 30, 1984 in Fresno, CA.
V9-159.	14-2. Cecil Raymond Parker, born July 17, 1954 in Fresno, CA. Hazel was born Feb. 12, 1929 in Meeker, Oklahoma. Cecil married Jennifer Wilcox, had 3 children: They divorced, Cecil then married unknown Underwood, they divorce, he married 3rd. wife Sharaon Siler who was born July 3, 1950 in Fresno, CA. They married July 23, 1995 in South Lake Tahoe, Nevada.
V9-160.	15-1. Jennifer Melissa Parker b. Sept. 26, 1976 in Lompoc, CA.
V9-161.	15-2. Emily Lou Parker, b. Sept. 1, 1978 in Lompoc, CA.
V9-162.	15-3. Jacob Raymond Parker, b. Oct. 23, 1989 in Merced, CA.
V9-163.	13-2. Edward Guy Parker, b. March 21, 1931 Heber Springs, AR, Married Jan. 10, 1954 in Madera, CA. to Peggy Kathryn Campbell born Oct. 11, 1933 in Madera, CA. They had two children:
V9-164.	14-1. Edward Arthur "Tuffy" Parker, b. Feb. 1, 1956 in Madera, CA. Married Lisa Fredrica Patterson, in Snelling, CA. they divorced.
V9-165.	14-2. Debra Elaine Parker, b. Aug. 22, 1960 in Madera, CA.

Cyrus Edward Beshears, and Bessie Inez DeBusk

Family of Cyrus Edward Beshears and Bessie Inez DeBusk:

V9-166.	13-1. **Wilburn Lee Beshears**, b. Dec. 19, 1933 in Miller, AR; married *Lillian "Billie" Noleen* in Merced, CA. Two Children:
V9-167.	14-1. **Janet Beshears**, b in Merced, CA. Married in Merced CA to *Steve Schurbutt*.
V9-168.	14-2. **Brian Edward Beshears**, born in Merced, CA, Married in Merced to Cherie.
V9-169.	13-2. **Max Edward Beshears**, b. July 9, 1935 in Miller, AR; married *Nita Kay Morehead*, born July 30, 1939 Her parents were J.R. Morehead and Ileene Francis. 2 ch:
V9-170.	14-1. **Lisa Mechele Beshears**, b. Sept. 26, 1958 married *Steve McMichael*, they had 3 children.

V9-171.	15-1. Cayla McMichael
V9-172.	15-2. Cody McMichael
V9-173.	15-3. Christa McMichael
V9-174.	14-2. **Sheila Kay Beshears**, b. May 4, 1961, married **Dan Carlile**. They had two children:
V9-175.	15-1. David Carlile
V9-176.	15-2. Danielle Carlile

Ava Aldreen Beshears and Virgil Ray Haley

Family of Ava Aldreen Beshears and Virgil Ray Haley:

V9-177.	13-1. Virgil Ray Haley, Jr, b. Feb. 6, 1939 in Madera, CA, died Dec. 23, 1955 in Madera, CA in a terrible truck and car accident, buried at Arbor Vitae cem in Madera
V9-178.	13-2. Robert Lee Haley, b. July 9, 1943 in Madera, CA; married Lois Krum on April 25, 1963 in Madera, CA. Robert & Lois divorced, he then married Betty Haley Sep. 10, 1972, (That was her maiden name) no children, they divorced, he then married #3, Jeannie R. Hogan on Sept. 24, 1994 in Madera, CA.
V9-179.	14-1. Sean Lee Haley, b. Aug. 26, 1966 in Madera, CA; married Kimberly Ann Krezman on June 4, 1994 in Madera, CA. divorced. Kimberly born Oct. 26, 1970 in Madera, CA.
V9-180.	14-2. Ryan Haley, born Sept. 12, 1968 in Madera, CA; married Danica Louise Harmacek March 25, 1995 in Alamo, CA. Danica born Nov. 10, 1963 in Sacramento, CA. They have two children:
V9-181.	15-1. Dallas Lee Ann Haley b. June 29, 1996 in Gig Harbor, Washington,
V9-182.	15-2. Colton David Haley, born Jan. 17, 1999 in Walnut Creek, CA.

Beulah May Beshears
and Glover Franklin Bradford

V9-119. 12-6. **Beulah May Beshears**, b. 1 July 1920, Higden, AR; m.1. in Cleburne Co, AR, 21 Dec 1935, **Glover Franklin Bradford**, b. 19 April 1918, in Higden, Cleburne Co, AR, s/o David Crockett Bradford and Florence Ellen Ramsey; they divorced; m.2. **Samuel Seedal Meeks**. Beulah and Frank had 4 children:

V9-183.	13-1. Virginia May Bradford (who sent data; thanks); m. _____ Rose
V9-184.	13-2. Herbert Franklin Bradford
V9-185.	13-3. Frank Edward Bradford
V9-186.	13-4. David Lee Bradford

2. JESSE BRASHEARS
and BETSY SHELL

[V2-]55. **Jesse Brashears**, (probably s/o Philip Brashears Jr, of Henry Co, VA, and Elizabeth _____; gs/o Philip Brashears, Sr and Ann Wilson, of Henry Co, VA), d. 1811-20, Warren Co, TN; m. 24 Nov 1795, *Elizabeth "Betsy" Shell*, age 21 (b. c1774). See **vol. 2, p. 270**, for the discussion of Jesse and Betsy's moves.

Family of Jesse Brashears and Betsy Shell:

[V9-]187.   [9-]1. **Philip Brashears**, b. bef 1794, VA, maybe d. 1846, Franklin Co, IL

[V9-]188.   [9-]2. **Marvin Melvery Brashears**, b. 1794-1800. Melvery spent his life in Warren Co, TN. See vol 2 for details.

[V9-]189.   [9-]3. ***Valdon A. Brashears**, b. VA, 1797; m.1. _____; m.2. *Julia Ann Murphy*. There is considerable extra, new data on Valdon's descendants, below.

[V9-]190.   [9-]4. dau; m. *Hollis Cooper*

[V9-]191.   [9-]5. **Ann Brashears**, b. 1803, VA; m. c1826, *James Cooper*

[V9-]192.   [9-]6. ***William James Leftwich Brashears**, b. 4 Aug 1803, VA, d. 15 Dec 1897, Warren Co, TN; m.1. _____; m.2. 10 Dec 1842, Cannon Co, TN, *Nancy Nokes*; m.3. 1 Nov 1845, Cannon Co, TN, *Sarah "Sally" Herrin*. There is additional data on them, below.

Thanks to Georgene Humphreys for Xeroxes of Tennessee Land Grant #3300, on next page. This is apparently the land where Betsy lived in 1820, and the base from which their sons settled in several neighboring valleys and hollows.

* *

The State of Tennessee — No. 3300
To all whom these presents shall come—GREETING:

Know Ye, That by virture of part of Certificate No. 611, dated March 10th 1810, issued by the legislature of West Tennessee to Abraham Wright and Jason Thompson and entered on the 11th of December 1810, by No. 5584

there is granted by the said state of Tennessee unto Jesse Brashear, assignee of the said Abraham Wright and Jason Thompson

a certain tract or parcel of land, containing twenty three acres, lying in Warren County, in the first District in a hollow known by name of bare hollow, on the waters of the main East fork of the three forks of Stones River—Beginning at a poplar marked with the letters W.M., being the South East corner of survey or entry in the name of Charles Rudy for eight acres, thence East sixty and one half poles to a ?xtxxxat? standing on the West side of a steep hill, thence North sixty one poles to a Small White oak, thence West sixty and a half poles to a stake in the East boundary line of said Charles Rudy's eight acre survey, thence with his line South Sixty one poles to the Beginning, and including the house and improvements whereon William Middleton Junr lives. Surveyed 23rd March 1811 by Jesse Brashear, D.C.

with the hereditaments and appurtenances—to have and to hold the said tract or parcel of land, with its appurtenances, to the said Jesse Brashear

and his **heirs forever—In witness whereof**   Willie Blount **Governor of the state of Tennessee, hath herunto set his hand and caused the great seal of the state to be affixed, at Knoxville, on the** Seventh **day of** August **in the year of our Lord on thousand eight hundred and** eleven **and of the Independence of the United States the thirty** sixth.

By the Governor,
/s/ R. Houston, **Secretary.**   Willie Blount
* *

VALDON A. BRASHEARS
and JULIA ANN MURPHY

Circumstantial evidence (but no hard documents) strongly suggests that the Mary Ann Brashears, **v-2, p.285**, who married John J. Williams was the oldest daughter of Valdon A. Brashears and his first (unknown) wife. Mary Ann Brashears and John Williams were married in Jefferson Co, IL, where Valdon lived, and they named a child Valdon. I can't imagine Mary Ann naming a child Valdon, unless her father were Valdon A. Brashears. (Thanks to K. Dwaine Williams, of Odin, IL, for the data.)

v2-2323. **Valdon A. Brashears**, (s/o Jesse Brashear and Elizabeth "Betsy" Shell), b. c1797, VA (per 1850 Census, Rutherford Co, TN, HH #1011-437); m.1. ____, b. c1794-1802; m.2. 28 Aug 1842 (*Marriages, Jefferson Co, IL, 1819-1863*) **Julia Ann Murphy**, b. NC, c1821 (29 in 1850). Val received a land grant in TN on 3 Dec 1828: to Valdon Brashear, 34 a., TN Genl Land Grant #413, Warren Co, TN, Book A:279. He and his first wife apparently moved to IL about 1830.

Circumstantial and partially documented family of Valdon A. Brashears,

V9-193.   10-1. ***Mary Ann "Polly" Brashears**, b. 1810-20, indicated by 1820 Census; m. 19 July 1838, in Jefferson Co, IL (Bk 1, p.31; Bk 2, p.84), **John J. Williams**

V9-194.   10-2. fem, b. 1810-20, indicated by 1820 Census

V9-195.   10-3. male, b. 1810-20, indicated by 1820 Census

V9-196.   10-4. ?**James L. Brashears**, b. IL or TN, 1821, (29 in 1850, Rutherford Co, TN); m.1. **Mary A.** ____, m.2. **Eliza ____**,

V9-197.   10-5. **Gilbert Brashears**, b. IL, 1831-32 (19 in 1850, Rutherford Co, TN; and near Val); m. 17 March 1848, **Sarah Crick**, in Rutherford Co, TN

V9-198.   10-6. ***John Brashears**, (15 in 1850, Rutherford Co, TN; child in Val's HH); I believe this to be John William Brashears, b. 1837, Jefferson Co, IL.

V9-199.   10-7. **Nancy C. Brashears**, b. c1849, (1 in 1850, Rutherford Co, TN; child in Val's HH)

Mary Ann "Polly" Brashears
and John J. Williams

10-1. **Mary Ann "Polly" Brashears**, b. 1810-20, TN, indicated by 1820 Census of Valdon A. Brashears, d. 22 Feb 1895, Marion Co, IL, bur Andereck-McClelland Cem; m. 19 July 1838, in Jefferson Co, IL

(Bk 1, p.31; Bk 2, p.84), **John J. Williams**, b. c1812, TN, or NC (34 in 1850; 40 in 1860), d. 5 Oct 1876, bur Andereck-McClelland Cem, Marion Co, IL.

1840 census, Jefferson Co, IL, p.299: Williams, J.J. (20001-0001)

They are hh #667-689, p.48-b, in the 1850 Census of Franklin Co, IL, taken 14 Oct 1850, and the 1860 census of Jefferson Co, IL, McClelland twp, taken 20 July 1860.

Family of John J. Williams and Mary Ann Brashears:

V9-200.   11-1. *James N. Williams, b. 28 March 1839 (11 in 1850; 21 in 1860), died 1918; m. 14 Nov 1862, in Jefferson Co, IL, Elizabeth Butler

V9-201.   11-2. *John Joseph Williams, b. 22 June 1840 (10 in 1850; 19 in 1860), d. 5 Jan 1877, Marion Co, IL, bur Andereck-McClelland Cem; m. 5 Sept 1861, in Jefferson Co, IL, Margaret Bodine

V9-202.   11-3. William Williams, b. 10 Feb 1843 (7 in 1850; 17 in 1860). It is reported that his father drove him away from home.

V9-203.   11-4. Elizabeth Williams, b. 1 Jan 1845 (5 in 1850; 15 in 1860), d. 2 April 1884, bur Andereck-McClelland Cem; m. 24 Sept 1861, in Jefferson Co, IL, Ezekiel Wilson, b. 1841, d. 1 April 1884, bur Andereck/McClelland Cem, s/o Elisha Wilson and Tabitha (ch)

V9-204.   12-1. Mary Wilson, b. 1867,
V9-205.   12-2. William Wilson, b. 1869,
V9-206.   12-3. George Wilson, b. 1879,
V9-207.   12-4. Phillip Wilson, b. 1882, d. 1903; m. 1903, Jefferson Co, IL, Ethel Newell

V9-208.   11-5. *Pinkney David Williams, b. 10 Feb 1876, Buckner, Franklin Co, IL (4 in 1850; David, 13 in 1860), d. 12 Dec 1896, bur Kirk Cem, Jefferson Co, IL; m. 20 Feb 1876, in Marion Co, IL, Margaret Angelina Bennett,

V9-209.   11-6. Dicy (or Lucy) Williams, b. 20 June 1849, Buckner, Franklin Co, IL (Lucy, 2 in 1850; Dicy, 10 in 1860); m. 22 Sept 1870, in Marion Co, IL, Isaac Benjamin Myers, b. 1847, s/o George Myers & Catherine. This family moved to Rend Co, Kansas (ch)

V9-210.   12-1. Hattie Myers,
V9-211.   12-2. Mattie Myers; m. James Willies
V9-212.   12-3. Rosie Myers,
V9-213.   12-4. Effie Myers; m. George Wetzler (ch: John, William, and Georgie Wetzler)
V9-214.   12-5. Willie Myers,
V9-215.   12-6. John Myers,

V9-216.   12-7. George Myers,

V9-217.   11-7. *Newton Charles Williams, b. 7 July 1851, Buckner, Franklin Co, IL (g-gfa of Dwaine Williams), d. 1 Dec 1901, Marion Co, IL, bur Zion Hill Cem; m. Mary Jane Newman, d/o Samuel Newman and Sarah Jane Holt

V9-218.   11-8. *Philip Allen Williams, b. 16 Feb 1853, Buckner, Franklin Co, IL (8 in 1860), d. 24 Jan 1938, Marion Co, IL, bur Andereck-McClelland Cem; m. 28 Oct 1875, in Marion Co, IL, Sarah Frances Day

V9-219.   11-9. *Enoch Williams, b. 5 July 1854, Buckner, Franklin Co, IL (6 in 1860), d. 1933, bur Odin Peaceful Valley Cem; m. 25 Oct 1885, in Marion Co, IL, Sarah Catherine Cooperrider. His mother, Mary Williams, 62, was living in his household in Marion Co, IL, 1880.

V9-220.   11-10. Sarah Margaret Williams, b. 19 Nov 1856, Buckner, Franklin Co, IL (4 in 1860); m. 10 Aug 1876, Thomas W. Fowler

V9-221.   11-11. Mary Williams, b. 9 April 1857, Buckner, Franklin Co, IL

V9-222.   11-12. Valdon Williams, b. c1858 (2 in 1860)

James N. Williams and Elizabeth Butler

V9-223.   11-1. James N. Williams, b. 28 March 1839, d. 1918; m. 14 Nov 1862, Jefferson Co, IL, Elizabeth Butler. (9ch)

V9-224.   12-1. Tom J. Williams, b. 1863, Franklin Co, IL

V9-225.   12-2. James Bunt Williams, 1864, Franklin Co, IL

V9-226.   12-3. Dicy C. Williams, b. 4 April 1866 Jefferson Co, IL, d. 7 Jan 1946 buried South Hickory Hill Cem; m. 9 Aug 1885 Jefferson Co, IL, Ananias Sinclair

V9-227.   12-4. John Williams, b. Franklin Co, IL

V9-228.   12-5. Sarah Williams; m. 13 Nov 1889 Jefferson Co, IL, Richard Richards

V9-229.   12-6. Willard Williams, b. 1880, Sessor; m. Rachel Malrey

V9-230.   12-7. Otto Williams,

V9-231.   12-8. Minnie Amilia Williams, b. 1887; m. Jim Cochrum

V9-232.   12-9. Jim Pete Williams,

John Joseph Williams and Margaret Bodine

V9-233.   11-2. John Joseph Williams, b. 22 June 1840, d. 5 Jan 1877, Marion Co, IL, buried Andereck/McClelland Cem; m. 5 Sept 1861, Jefferson Co, IL, Margaret Bodine, b. 1 April 1844, Jefferson Co, d. 1927 or 1929, bur Andereck/McClelland Cem, Marion Co, IL, (2 ch), d/o James and Ellen Bodine. She m.2. 20 Aug 1879, John Myers

V9-234.   12-1. Allie Alice Eliza Williams, b. 21 June 1870, Marion Co, IL, b. 12 Nov 1954, bur Andereck/McClelland Cem; m.1. 28 Sept 1887, Marion Co, IL, (D-194-162), William Joseph Jackson, b. 5 Aug 1856, d. 6 July 1920, bur Andereck/McClelland Cem. s/o Elisha Jackson & Eliza A. Stanley (ch)

V9-235.   13-1. Clyde Jackson, b. 11 Oct 1891, d. 29 Sept 1898, buried Andereck/McClelland Cem.

V9-236.   13-2. Earnest Todd Jackson, b. 1888, Marion Co, IL, d. 2 Aug 1944, Springfield, IL , bur Griffiths Cem. Brownstown, IL

V9-237.   14-1. Nancy Jackson,

V9-238.   13-3. Marguerita E. Jackson, b. 31 Jan 1896, Marion Co, IL, d. 23 Jan 1973, buried Old Coventry Cem; m. 14 June 1917, Marion Co, IL, John Alva Summerville, b. 22 Aug 1882, d. 12 Aug 1971, buried Old Coventry Cem. s/o Robert Summerville and Margaret Annett Baldridge (ch)

V9-239.   14-1. Jack Summerville,

V9-240.   14-2. Annetta Summerville; m. ? In Ventura, CA, Robert Stover

V9-241.   13-4. Earl J. Jackson, b. 23 Jan 1901, Marion Co, IL, d. 24 Aug 1987, Andereck/McClelland Cemetery; m.1. 10 Aug 1921, Marion Co, IL, (F-78-1849), Grace R. Ross, b. 5 Feb 1903, d. __ June 1978, buried Andereck/McClelland Cem. d/o Isaac John Ross and Emma M. Shanefelt (ch); Earl; m.2. 1979, Velma Aldrich. Alice m.2. 12 April 1925, Marion Co, IL, (bk.F-p.109-4245), Elisha "Lish" Johnson

V9-242.   12-2. Johnnie Williams, b. 15 Feb 1877, d. 29 July 1877, buried Andereck/ McClelland Cem.

Pinkney David Williams
and Margaret Angelina Bennett

V9-243.   11-5. Pinkney David Williams, b. 10 Feb 1847 Buckner, Franklin Co. IL, d. 12 Dec 1896, buried Kirk Cem, Jefferson Co, IL; m. 20 Feb 1876, Marion Co, IL, Margaret Angelina Bennett, b. 5 Jan 1855, d. 27 Jan 1884, buried Antiock Cem, Jefferson Co, IL, (ch)

V9-244.   12-1. Rosa Ellen Williams, b. 11 March 1877, d. 3 Sept 1965, buried Kirk Cem, Jefferson Co, IL; m.1. 21 Nov 1894 Jefferson William Lawson Williams, b. ?, d. 9 Jan 1913, buried Kirk Cem, Jefferson Co, IL, s/o Silas Williams (9ch); Rose Ellen m.2. Ray

Meredith

V9-245. 13-1. Arthur Franklin Williams, b. 23 Aug 1895, d. 29 Aug 1895

V9-246. 13-2. Sadie Pearl Williams, b. 5 Oct 1896, d. 28 Oct 1935

V9-247. 13-3. Silas Earl Williams, b. 24 Dec 1897, d. 5 March 1902

V9-248. 13-4. Walter Enoch Williams, b. 1 Feb 1901, d. 17 Feb 1901

V9-249. 13-5. Bessie May Williams, b. 16 Sept 1902, d. 23 Oct 1920

V9-250. 13-6. Ursula Gertrude Williams, b. 7 Dec 1904, d. 31 Oct 1906

V9-251. 13-7. Minnie Lucille Williams, b. 18 May 1907; m. 2 Sept 1924, Andrew Sinks

V9-252. 13-8. Clarence Edward Williams, b. 7 July 1909, died

V9-253. 13-9. Ernest Clyde Williams, b. 7 Dec 1911; m. Marie Robinson

V9-254. 12-2. James Henry Williams, b. 17 Oct 1878, d. 3 Jan 1879

V9-255. 12-3. Cora Ann Williams, b. 19 Jan 1881, d. 20 April 1952; m. Peter S. Cummings

V9-256. 12-4. Walter Harrington Williams, b. 28 Jan 1883, d. 24 April 1932; m. 1906, Jefferson Co, IL, Pearl Browder

Newton Charles Williams and Mary Jane Newman

V9-257. 11-7. Newton Charles Williams, b. 7 July 1851 Buckner, Franklin Co, d. 1 Dec 1901, Marion Co, IL, bur Zion Hill Cem; m. 16 Jan 1879, Marion Co, IL, Mary Jane Newman, b. 14 March 1860, Jefferson Co, IL, d. 2 Feb 1939, buried Zion Hill Baptist Cem. d/o Samuel Newman and Sarah Jane Holt (ch)

V9-258. 12-1. James Luther Williams, b. 26 Nov 1879, d. 11 Dec 1879, buried Andereck/McClelland Cem.

V9-259. 12-2. Elsie Viola Williams, b. 19 Jan 1881, d. 25 Oct 1888, buried Zion Hill Baptist Cem.

V9-260. The story is told that as Elsie was dying, she said "I see Jesus and Grandma waiting in Heaven for Me." Grandma was Sarah Jane Holt Newman Fox, but Elsie had never seen this grandmother, so the family asked her to describe the woman. Elsie gave a description that the family said was just like Sarah, so they believed her.

V9-261. 12-3. Edgar Allen Williams, b. 15 Aug 1883, d. 21 May 1955, buried Andereck/McClelland Cem; m. 5 June 1913, Marion Co, IL, Eliza Jane "Jennie" Andereck,

b. 9 April 1889, d. 23 Nov 1956, buried
Andereck/McClelland Cem. (ch)

V9-262.   ¹³⁻1. Hazel Dell Williams, b. 17 Aug 1914, d. living
2001; m. 26 Sept 1932, Orville H. Mason, b. 27
Dec 1911, d. 7 Dec 1991 s/o Charles Edgar
Mason and Emma Jane Green (ch)

V9-263.   ¹⁴⁻1. Allen D. Mason, b. 1934; m. Rita Marsell
(ch: Susan Alana; Julie Ann; Sharlene Kay;
and Diana Mason)

V9-264.   ¹⁴⁻2. Linda Jane Mason, b; m. 8 Feb 1959 Flora,
IL, Jim O. Simpson, b. 10 Jan 1939, d. 13
June 2000, buried Andereck/McClelland
Cem. s/o Elmer Simpson and Murle Arers
(ch: Jane; and Jamie Simpson)

V9-265.   ¹⁴⁻3. Raymond Neal Mason; m. Diana Rettig, (ch:
Robert Doyle Mason)

V9-266.   ¹⁴⁻4. James Phillip Mason; m. Paula Campbell,
(ch: Trent James; and Trey William Mason)

V9-267.   ¹⁴⁻5. Donald O. Mason, b. 10 May 1935, d. 2 Jan
1936, buried Andereck/McClelland Cem.

V9-268.   ¹⁴⁻6. Nancy M. Mason, b. 25 July 1936, d. 5 Aug
1936, buried Andereck/McClelland Cem.

V9-269.   ¹³⁻2. Glen Allen Williams, b. 8 July 1917, Prinston,
IN; m. 19 July 19__, Alice Mae Joyce, (ch:
Glenda Joyce; and Michael Williams)

V9-270.   ¹³⁻3. Merle Edgar Williams, b. 6 Jan 1922; m. 21 Oct
_____ Mt. Vernon, IL, Shirley Vaughan,

V9-271.   ¹⁴⁻1. Stephen Edgar Williams, b. 16 Oct 1949,
Champaign-Urbana Champaign, IL; m.
Marcina Gant, b. 21 Aug 1949

V9-272.   ¹⁵⁻1. Keith Byran Williams, b. 6 Oct 1970

V9-273.   ¹⁴⁻2. Ronald "Ronnie" Wayne Williams, b. 22 Dec
1950, Jefferson Co, IL,

V9-274.   ¹⁴⁻3. Keith Douglas Williams, b. 15 March 1953
Evansville, IN; m. Robin Boldwyn, b. 14 May
1954; m.2. Mike Herzing (ch)

V9-275.   ¹⁵⁻1. John Paul Williams (adopted), b. 19 May
1972

V9-276.   ¹⁵⁻2. Kip Lea Williams (adopted), b. 11 June
1973; m. Brett E. Felty, b. (ch)

V9-277.   ¹⁶⁻1. Danielle Felty, b. 18 Nov 1990, d. 3
Jan 1991, buried Oakwood Mt.
Vernon

V9-278.   ¹⁵⁻3. Tobbie Lynn Williams, b. 22 Oct 1975

V9-279.   ¹⁴⁻4. Bradley Paul Williams, b. 7 July 1955,

Jefferson Co, IL,

V9-280.   14-5. Brian Robert Williams, b. 7 July 1955, Jefferson Co, IL,

V9-281.   14-6. Nancy Ellen Williams, b. 29 Sept 1962, Jefferson Co, IL; m. 7 June 1986 Mt. Vernon, IL, Gary Nagel

V9-282.   12-4. John Harvey Williams, b. 28 May 1885, Marion Co, IL, d. 4 May 1977, buried Zion Hill Cem; m. 1 Jan 1910, Marion Co, IL, Mary Skillman, b. 14 April 1886, Marion Co, IL, d. 2 Jan 1978, buried Zion Hill Baptist Church cem. d/o Josiah Skillman & Lucy A. Calhoun. As a child Mary lived with Henry Clay & Elizabeth True and helped with the housework (ch)

V9-283.   13-1. Mary Lucille Williams, b. 31 May 1911; Lived in Odin, IL, d. 21 April 1992, buried Zion Hill Cem; m. 27 June 1931, Donald Burge, b. 27 Dec 1911, d. ? , buried Hillcrest Cem. (ch)

V9-284.   14-1. Paul Dwight Burge, b. 18 June 1932; Lives in Enid, OK 73703; m. 31 Oct 1949, Jeanine Hawley (ch)

V9-285.   15-1. Paul Steven Burge, b. 15 Nov 1952, Marion Co, IL, IL, d. 28 March 1995, Odin Peaceful Valley Cem; m.1. 11 March 1972, Enid, Ok, Karen Sue Goeke (ch)

V9-286.   16-1. Michael Paul Burge, b. 11 July 1972, Germany; m.2. 21 April 1979, Valerie Ann Scaggs. Paul Steven adopted Valerie's son Chad (ch)

V9-287.   16-2. Chad Ernie Burge, b. 5 Oct 1973

V9-288.   16-3. Khristy Dawn Burge, b. 20 Feb 1981; m. 22 July 2000, Stephen Joseph Felgenhauser (ch)

V9-289.   17-1. Steven Michael Felgenhauer, b. 15 Aug 1999

V9-290.   15-2. David Kieth Burge, b. 25 Jan 1955, Marion Co, IL, IL. Lives in Enid, Ok; m. Kathy Jones (ch)

V9-291.   16-1. Tyler Paul Burge, b. 14 July 1988

V9-292.   16-2. Angie Nicole Jones, b. 9 Dec 1982

V9-293.   15-3. Tina Marie Burge, b. 19 Dec 1959 Wayne Co, IL; m.1. 10 Aug 1979, Rick Spencer, b. 8 June 1960; m.2. 3 Jan 1999, David Gerald Quick, b. 9 April 1965

V9-294.   [16-]1. Sara Michelle Spencer, b. 11 March 1981, Marion Co, IL, IL

V9-295.   [16-]2. Ryan Matthew Spencer, b. 1 Dec 1986, Marion Co, IL, IL

V9-296.   [14-]2. Barbara Lua Burge, b. 4 Oct 1934. Lives Marion Co, IL, IL; m. 7 June 1952, Donald Lee Williams, b. 5 Aug ____ (no Relation). Barbara works for Petrolane Corp. Divorced 23 Dec 1989 (ch)

V9-297.   [15-]1. Denny Lee Williams, b. 1 July 1953; m.1. Christine Breder (1ch); m.2. Lori Ubanks (1ch); m.3. Connie Badger (1ch)

V9-298.   [16-]1. Stephanie Marie Williams, b. 18 March 1974; children by Tyron Clasper

V9-299.   [17-]1. MacKenzie Clasper,

V9-300.   [17-]2. Austin Clasper, b. 1996, d. 1997

V9-301.   [16-]2. Kelly Ann Williams, b. 7 May 1980

V9-302.   [16-]3. Doug Williams, adopted,

V9-303.   [15-]2. Anthony Wayne Williams, b. 2 Feb 1959, d. 2 April 1995, buried Zion Hill Cem; m.1. 23 June 1979, Tanna Rae Pontious (no ch); m.2. Cindy Warren (no ch); m.3. Beverly J. Ward (no ch)

V9-304.   [15-]3. Gregory Allen Williams, b. 25 July 1963; Lives Centralia, IL; m. Rebecca "Becky" Burleyson (ch)

V9-305.   [16-]1. James Matthew Williams, b. 13 March 1989

V9-306.   [16-]2. Victor Blake Williams, b. 31 Oct 1991

V9-307.   [16-]3. _____ Curtis Williams, b. 1994

V9-308.   [14-]3. Nonda Fay Burge, b. 10 Aug 1937; Lives in Odin, IL; m. 18 June 1955, Bertram Joseph Rostance, b. 25 Sept 1933 s/o Joseph L. Rostance & _____. (ch)

V9-309.   [15-]1. Rebecca Sue Rostance, b. 13 July 1953; Lives in Odin, IL; m.1. 31 July 1974, Steve Wayne Lee, b. 3 Dec 1953, d. 4 May 1998, buried Odin Peaceful Valley Cem. s/o Harold Lee and Neva Redman (3ch); Rebecca m.2. 16 Dec 2000, Marion Co, IL, Brent Leininger

V9-310.   [16-]1. Shannon Sue Lee, b. 19 March 1975; m.1. Troy Owens; m.2. James

Russell,

V9-311.   [17]-1. Olivia Owens, b. 16 Sept 1993

V9-312.   [17]-2. Nicholas Russell, b. 1 May 1997

V9-313.   [16]-3. Bruce Wayne Lee, b. 30 June 1980

V9-314.   [16]-4. Brandy Lynn Lee, b. 31 Aug 1981 (ch)

V9-315.   [17]-1. Trever Maxwell Hill, b. 14 Feb 2001

V9-316.   [15]-2. Jeffery Allen Ronstance, b. 8 Dec 1960, Lives in, Marion Co, IL; m. 26 April 1979, Vanessa Stewart, b. 25 Dec 1960 (ch)

V9-317.   [16]-1. Aaron Joseph Ronstance, b. 24 Nov 1979

V9-318.   [16]-2. Stacy Jo Ronstance, b. 12 June 1981; m. 16 Oct 1999, Michael Allen Hancock, s/o Donnie Hancock & Debbie Crippen

V9-319.   [15]-3. Scott Joseph Ronstance, b. 19 Nov 1967; m. 24 Aug 1991, Amy Lynn Blumenstock, at New Baden, IL (ch)

V9-320.   [16]-1. Noah Scott Ronstance, b. 5 April 2000

V9-321.   [14]-4. John Scott Burge, b. 6 June 1948; m.1. 13 Aug 1966, Jefferson Co, IL, IL, Jane Alice Latta (ch). John m.2. 20 Dec 1977; Jefferson Co, IL, Sherry Snow, b. 5 April 1959, d/o Robert L. Snow & Wilma Bandy (ch)

V9-322.   [15]-1. John Paul Burge, b. 26 July 1967, Marion Co, IL, IL; m. Leann Andrew (ch: Alyssa; and Aaron Andrew)

V9-323.   [15]-2. Christopher Edwin Burge, b. 10 March 1969, Marion Co, IL, IL; m. 18 Aug 1990, Shiela Colton ch)

V9-324.   [16]-1. Connor Burge, b. 29 March 1992

V9-325.   [15]-3. Jerry Lee Burge, b. 4 Jan 1981

V9-326.   [15] 4. Tiffy Burge, b. 3 Jan 1984

V9-327.   [13]-2. Kenneth Dwight Williams, b. 20 Aug 1912; Lived near Odin, IL, d. 8 Aug 1990, buried Odin Peaceful Valley Cem; m. 9 Sept 1940, St. Louis, Mo, Ruth Amanda Groff, b. 6 April 1921, Marion Co, IL, IL, d. 17 Jan 1999, buried Odin Peaceful Valley Cem. (ch)

V9-328.   [14]-1. Kenneth Dwaine Williams, b. 12 June

	1941. Lives in Marion Co, IL; not married
V9-329.	14-2. Lonnie Ray Williams, b. 30 March 1942. Lives in Marion Co, IL, IL; not m; Served in Vietnam, in Army
V9-330.	14-3. Judy Arlene Williams, b. 11 Aug 1944; Lives in Indianapolis, IN; m. 30 May 1964, Willard Ray Marshall, b. 22 April 1942 (ch)
V9-331.	15-1. Christine Ann Marshall, b. 22 March 1966; Chattanooga TN. lives in Indianapolis, IN; m. 15 May 1993, William Kurt Beanblossom, b. 28 Dec 1968 (ch)
V9-332.	16-1. Grant Marshall Beanblossom, b. 29 Dec 1996 2:04 AM
V9-333.	16-2. William Dane Beanblossom, b. 9 Feb 2000
V9-334.	15-2. Anthony Ray Marshall, b. 18 May 1974; Indianapolis, IN; m. 31 March 2001, Indianapolis, IN, Deena Renee Bingham , d/o Darrell Bingham & Vicki Lee Fisher, b. 31 May 1977
V9-335.	14-4. Randy Kieth Williams, b. 31 Jan 1952. Lives near Centralia, IL; m.1. 18 May 1985, Divorced 1991, Lisa Braddy (ch);Randy; m.2. 26 Dec 1992, Patti Jo Wooters, b. 30 Oct 1961, d/o Guy Wooters & Bobbie Fant
V9-336.	15-1. Neysa Catherine Williams, b. 30 Aug 1977; m. 16 Oct 1999, Joshua Leon Dix s/o James Hobert Dix & Barbara Posey (ch: Sydney Jean Dix)
V9-337.	14-5. Kathy Lynn Williams, b. 4 Aug 1958, Lives in, Marion Co, IL, IL; not married
V9-338.	14-6. Nena Kay Williams, b. 11 Nov 1960; m. 9 Nov 1996, Centralia, IL, Bradley Dean Benjamin, b. 30 Dec 1970, s/o Don Benjamin & Shirley Bierman. Lives in, Marion Co, IL (ch)
V9-339.	15-1. Mikaela Brooke Benjamin, b. 7 April 1997
V9-340.	13-3. Dorothy May Williams, b. 3 April 1915; Lives near Salem, IL; m. 23 March 1932, Raymond Chesley Luttrell, b. 16 Nov 1913, d. 27 Dec 2000, Bethlehem Baptist Church Cem. s/o Charles Fredrick Luttrell & Daisy Bryant (ch)
V9-341.	14-1. Raymond Leroy Luttrell, b. 30 March 1933;

Lives Union, MO, d. 18 Dec 2000, Washington, MO; m. 23 June 1951, Patrica Louise Mulvaney, b. 18 March 1933 (ch)

V9-342.   [15]-1. Arlin Leroy Luttrell, b. 22 Aug 1952, Ca; m.1. 16 Jan 1976; divorced, Kathy _____, b. 21 Jan 1952 (ch); m.2. 5 June 1982; divorced Kathlene Marie Schmitt, b. 13 June 1956 (ch); m.3. in Augusta, MA, Debbie Kasten, lives Augusta, Maine

V9-343.   [16]-1. Aaron Lee Luttrell, b. 29 May 1977

V9-344.   [16]-2. Kelly Marie Luttrell, b. 6 May 1983

V9-345.   [16]-3. Kevin Patrick Luttrell, b. 7 May 1985

V9-346.   [15]-2. Gary Lee Luttrell, b. 17 Sept 1953; Lives Perryville, MO; m. 19 Feb 1988, Ivyline Ann Ernst, b. 3 Feb 1988 (ch)

V9-347.   [16]-1. Garrison Robert Luttrell, b. 30 Nov 1988

V9-348.   [16]-2. Garrett Raymond Luttrell, b. 6 Dec 1989

V9-349.   [16]-3. Carissa Lynn Luttrell, b. 19 July 1991

V9-350.   [16]-4. Crystal Luttrell ?, b. 16 May 1997

V9-351.   [16]-5. Cara Luttrell ?, b. 8 Dec 1999

V9-352.   [16]-6. Eric Kasten, b. 28 Sept 1989

V9-353.   [16]-7. Tiffany Kasten, b. 19 Aug 1981

V9-354.   [17]-1. Alexix Sample, b. 2000

V9-355.   [15]-3. Cheryl Lynn Luttrell, b. 27 Sept 1960; Lives St. Louis, MO; m. Cecil Meadows (ch)

V9-356.   [16]-1. Leslie Meadows,

V9-357.   [14]-2. Ramonda May Luttrell, b. 5 Nov 1945; Lives Salem, IL; m. 3 June 1969, Alan Porter Wilson, b. 5 April 1945 s/o Sam Wilson & Eleanor Porter (ch)

V9-358.   [15]-1. David Alan Wilson, b. 17 Oct 1974 lives Mt. Vernon; m. 10 Aug 1999, Disney World, Arlando, FL, Melissa Ann Copeland, b. 1 Jan 1976, d/o Paul Copeland & Diane _____

V9-359.   [15]-2. James Franklyn Wilson lives Springfield, b. 16 March 1979

V9-360.   [13]-4. John Harry Williams, b. 31 July 1917; Lives Decatur, IL; m. 28 June 1939, Mable Maxine

Hargett (ch)

V9-361.   14-1. Harry Eugene Williams, b. 25 April 1940;
            Lives in Decatur, IL; m.1. 28 July 1961,
            Barbara Ann Maguet, d. 1965 (ch)

V9-362.   15-1. Susan Diane Williams, b. 23 March
                1961; Lives Roundhouse, IL; m.1.
                Tommy Thompson (ch); m.2. Carl May

V9-363.   16-1. Tommy Joseph Thompson, b. Nov,
                    1988

V9-364.   16-2. Tyler John Thompson, b. 11 Aug
                    1992

V9-365.   14-2. Gerald Dean Williams, b. 10 Sept 1942, d.
            18 Jan 1972; m.1. 17 Oct 1959, Karen Irene
            Crosser (3ch); m.2. 21 Oct 1964, Lynn Ann
            Atkins Peterson (1ch)

V9-366.   15-1. Teri Lynn Williams, b. __ Feb 1960

V9-367.   15-2. Victoria Jean Williams, b. __ Feb 1961

V9-368.   15-3. Brian Scott Williams, b. __ Sept 1962, d.
                __ Dec 1978

V9-369.   15-4. Robert Floyd Williams, b. 15 June 1965;
                (ch)

V9-370.   16-1. Brittany Williams

V9-371.   16-2. Amber Williams, not m. to Norma
                    Jean Pocernish (ch)

V9-372.   17-5. Jerri Lynn Pocernich, b. 10 Oct
                        1966

V9-373.   13-5. Russell Dean Williams, b. 25 March 1924; lived
            in Odin, IL, d. 4 Dec 1993, buried Odin Peaceful
            Valley Cem; m. 20 April 1950, Jeanetta Evilsizer,
            b. 4 Aug 1930 (ch)

V9-374.   14-1. Elizabeth Ann Williams, b. 21 June 1953;
            Lives near Worden, IL; m. 18 Dec 1971,
            Gregg Yaw (ch)

V9-375.   15-1. Lauren Christine Yaw, b. 22 June 1981

V9-376.   15-2. Charles Martin "Marty" Yaw, b. 29 June
                1987

V9-377.   14-2. Michael Alan Williams, b. 7 July 1956; Lives
            in Odin, IL; m. 5 Feb 1977, Victoria Cavin
            (ch)

V9-378.   15-1. Jessica Nichole Williams, b. 18 Sept
                1988

V9-379.   15-2. John Michael Williams, b. 16 June 1991

V9-380.   12-5. Mary (May) Williams, b. 11 Feb 1887, Marion Co,
            IL, d. 18 June 1971 Benton Harbor, Mich; m. 23

Nov 1907, Marion Co, IL, Frank Watkins, b. 24 April
1889, d. 12 Jan 1956, buried Benton Harbor, Mich.
s/o Eli Watkins and Ellie Chaffin (ch)

V9-381.   13-1. Frank (Brown) Eli Watkins, b. 26 June 1908, d.
1979; m. 5 May 1938, Maxine Meyers (ch)

V9-382.   14-1. Ellen Faye Watkins, b. 5 May 1937

V9-383.   14-2. Thomas Franklin Watkins, b. 1939

V9-384.   13-2. Ruby Watkins, b. 17 June 1909, d. Feb 1932;
m. 27 June 1928, Carl Wagner (ch)

V9-385.   14-1. Emily May Wagner, b. 8 March 1929

V9-386.   14-2. Frank Earl Wagner, b. Aug 1930

V9-387.   13-3. Newton Edwin "Tony" Watkins, b. 22 Aug 1910;
m. 1932, Barbara Eish (ch)

V9-388.   14-1. Dorthy May Watkins, b. 1933

V9-389.   14-2. Helen Faye Watkins, b. 1934

V9-390.   14-3. Mary Louise Watkins, b. 1938

V9-391.   14-4. Edward Eli March Watkins, b. 1939

V9-392.   14-5. Leroy Joseph Watkins, b. 1941

V9-393.   13-4. Alice May Watkins, b. ?, d. 1991 ?; m. Clarence
O'Keefe

V9-394.   14-1. Norma Jean O'Keefe, b. 1933

V9-395.   14-2. Gerald Edgar O'Keefe, b. 30 May 1935

V9-396.   13-5. Irma L. (Bonnie) Watkins, b, d; m. 29 Aug 1936,
Albert W. Mayhill

V9-397.   13-6. Floyd Raymond "Bill" Watkins, b. 12 July 1917;
m. Cooleen Cody, b. 19 April 1925 ? (ch)

V9-398.   14-1. John Floyd Watkins, b. 26 April 1947; m.
Debra Lyn Dalton (ch)

V9-399.   15-1. Rebecca Lyn Watkins, b. 5 Dec 1976

V9-400.   15-2. Kara Colleen Watkins, b. 17 Feb 1978

V9-401.   15-3. Andrew John Watkins, b. 18 Feb 1981

V9-402.   15-4. Wendy Watkins, b. 12 June 1982

V9-403.   15-5. Glen Raymond Watkins, b. 8 June 1984

V9-404.   14-2. Joyce Colleen Watkins, b. 29 May 1945

V9-405.   14-3. Shirley Ann Watkins, b. 19 Oct 1952; m.
Benjamin Watkins

V9-406.   13-7. Eva Watkins, b. 20 June 1920; m.1. 7 Oct
1936, Alfred Castellari, b. 13 Nov 1915 (ch)

V9-407.   14-1. Alice Marie Castellari, b. 7 June 1937; m.1.
Jan 1954, Robert Allen Whitney Jr. (ch); m.2.
Kenneth Allen Newberry (ch)

V9-408.   15-1. Robert Allen Whitney III, b. 15 June
1956

V9-409.   15-2. Debora Marie Whitney, b. 11 July 1958
(Adopted Out)

V9-410.   ¹⁵-3. Elenor Louise Whitney, b. 23 Nov 1959 (Adopted Out)

V9-411.   ¹⁵-4. Steven Anthony Whitney, b. 11 April 1961 (Adopted Out)

V9-412.   ¹⁵-5. Christine Francetta Whitney, b. 12 June 1962 (Adopted Out)

V9-413.   ¹⁵-6. Julie Gaye Whitney, b. 17 March 1965 (Adopted Out)

V9-414.   ¹⁵-7. John Ira Whitney, b. 17 March 1965 (Adopted Out)

V9-415.   ¹⁴-2. Shirley Ann Castellari, b. 5 June 1938, d. ?; m.2. Ira M. Curtis; m. (3) 27 Oct 1973, Victor D. Warren, b. 28 March 1919, Marion Co, IL, d. 9 Jan 1995 s/o Phillip Warren and Clara Frank

V9-416.   ¹³-8. John D. Watkins, b. 25 Sept 1921; m. Maxine
_____

V9-417.   ¹⁴-1. J.D. Watkins,

V9-418.   ¹⁴-2. Kevin Watkins,

V9-419.   ¹³-9. Leah Watkins; m. Ted George.

V9-420.   ¹⁴-1. John George, b. 1963

V9-421.   ¹³-10 Arlene Fay Watkins, b. 6 March 1924; m.1. 1940, Ralph Shaw (ch); m.2. 10 Feb 1945, Samuel Schaffer, b. 25 Feb 1921 (ch)

V9-422.   ¹⁴-1. Danny Ray Shaw, b. 19 Jan 1943 (ch)

V9-423.   ¹⁵-1. Susan Darlene Shaw, b. 27 Nov 1966

V9-424.   ¹⁴-2. Sandra Sue Schaffer, b. 16 June 1947

V9-425.   ¹⁴-3. Robert Michael Schaffer, b. 19 June 1952 (ch)

V9-426.   ¹⁵-1. Christine Marie Schaffer, b. 2 May 1975

V9-427.   ¹³-11 Silvia May Watkins, b. dead

V9-428.   ¹²-6. Newton Anderson Williams, b. 14 Feb 1889, d. 26 May 1972 Wayne City, IL; m. 14 March 1918, Eliza Maude Haile

V9-429.   ¹³-1. Ester Bernice Williams, b. 9 Jan 1919 (ch)

V9-430.   ¹⁴-1. Mary Alice Williams

V9-431.   ¹⁴-2. Larry Edward Williams, b. 11 Oct 1940; m. _____ Aug 1960, Delorse Ann Lee, b. 27 Oct 1939 (ch)

V9-432.   ¹⁵-1. Richard Anthony Williams, b. 3 June 1961

V9-433.   ¹⁵-2. Renee Arlette Williams, b. 6 June 1962

V9-434.   ¹⁵-3. Edward Lee Williams, b. 5 Oct 1967; m. 11 Oct 1951, Ermil Pierce

V9-435.   ¹³-2. Virgil Newton Williams, b. 28 Oct 1920; m. 12

	Sept 1942, Mary Viola Rouley, b. 22 April 1921
V9-436.	[14]-1. Mary Virginia Williams, b. 8 Dec 1943; m. __ Oct 1973, Kenneth Barriage
V9-437.	[14]-2. Diana Lee Williams, b. 12 Oct 1946 (ch)
V9-438.	[15]-1. Kathy Williams, b. 6 July 1967; m. 1974, Wayne Smith
V9-439.	[13]-3. Eleanor Maude Williams, b. 7 June 1923, d. 9 Dec 1979; m. 12 Aug 1940, Loren Allen McKinney, b. 30 Aug 1921 (ch)
V9-440.	[14]-1. Charles Elbert McKinney, b. 9 May 1941; m. 23 Dec 1961, Jean Carol Sailor, b. 15 Feb 1944 (ch)
V9-441.	[15]-1. Tammy Lee McKinney, b. 13 Dec 1967
V9-442.	[15]-2. Terri Jean McKinney, b. 14 Sept 1968
V9-443.	[14]-2. Loren Allen McKinney Jr, b. 26 Sept 1942; m. __ Feb 1962, Joyce Ann Koester, b. 12 Feb 1944 (ch)
V9-444.	[15]-1. Loren Allen McKinney III, b. 5 Feb 1964
V9-445.	[15]-2. Glen Travis McKinney, b. 2 May 1965
V9-446.	[14]-3. Loretta Jean McKinney, b. 4 Nov 1946; m. 25 Oct 1975, William Ray DeBoer, b. 18 Feb 1939 (ch)
V9-447.	[15]-1. William David McKinney, b. 26 Nov 1964
V9-448.	[15]-2. Edward Allen McKinney, b. 27 Feb 1967
V9-449.	[15]-3. Trina Lynn McKinney, b. 16 Jan 1972
V9-450.	[14]-4. Linda Irene McKinney, b. 15 Jan 1951; m. 6 Sept 1975, John Bain
V9-451.	[14]-5. Eleanor Sue McKinney, b. 4 Dec 1956, d. 4 July 1995, buried Olive Branch Cem. Wayne City,IL; m. 14 Dec 1974, Johnny Ray Marshel, b. 12 Aug 1946 s/o Earl Marshel and Ruby _____ (ch)
V9-452.	[15]-1. Michael Ray Marshel, b. 26 June 1976
V9-453.	[15]-2. Melinda K. Marshel, b. 15 Dec 1981, d. 4 July 1995 (Shot by Father)
V9-454.	[13]-4. Wilburn Haile Williams, b. 18 Nov 1924; m. 14 Aug 1947, Evelyn Martha Easten
V9-455.	[13]-5. Charles Wayne Williams, b. 25 July 1929; m. 24 Jan 1948, Vera van Leesburgh, b. 15 May 1930 (ch)
V9-456.	[14]-1. Mary Margaret Williams, b. 20 May 1949; m. 8 April 1972, James Morgan, b. 15 Aug 1947 (ch)

V9-457.   [15]-1. Michael Morgan, b. 11 July 1975

V9-458.   [14]-2. Charles Wayne Williams Jr, b. 13 Sept 1951; m. 8 March 1975, Mary Kruger, b. 26 Aug 1957 (ch)

V9-459.   [15]-1. Charles Wayne Williams III, b. 26 Aug 1975

V9-460.   [15]-2. Timothy Michael Williams, b. 1 July 1977

V9-461.   [14]-3. Arthur Newton Williams, b.13 May 1958

V9-462.   [12]-7. Charles E. Williams, b. 4 Feb 1891, d. 28 Nov 1972 Johnson City, IL; m. 17 Jan 1916, Jessie M. Jones, b. 11 Dec 1897, d. 8 Dec 1971 (ch)

V9-463.   [13]-1. Helen Glendabell Williams, b. 10 Dec 1915; m. 16 Oct 1938, R.J. Jent, b. 8 Jan 1915 (ch)

V9-464.   [14]-1. James Wendell Jent, b. 6 April 1941; m. 17 Oct 1963, Sandra Kay Hill, b. 22 Oct 1946 (ch)

V9-465.   [15]-1. Lesa Anne Jent, b. 7 Sept 1965

V9-466.   [15]-2. David Wendall Jent, b. 10 Aug 1970

V9-467.   [15]-3. Mark Alan Jent, b. 30 Jan 1972

V9-468.   [14]-2. Glenda Kay Jent, b. 7 Sept 1946

V9-469.   [13]-2. Delbert Melvin Williams, b. 21 Feb 1917; m. Mary Louise Slater, b. 15 July 1920 (ch)

V9-470.   [14]-1. Delbert Melvin Williams, Jr, b. 21 Nov 1947; m. Leah Marie Mornewer, b. 11 Dec 1977 (ch)

V9-471.   [15]-1. Bryce Michael Williams, b. 28 March 1977

V9-472.   [13]-3. Wanda Williams, b. 1919 ?; m. Bernard Eisnmann,

V9-473.   [14]-1. Ronnie Eisnmann

V9-474.   [13]-4. Zola M. Williams, b. 7 Sept 1920, d. 1 Sept 1978; m.1. Ralph Hoffart (ch)

V9-475.   [14]-1. Judith Ann Hoffart, b. 1 May 1942; m. 19 Aug 1960, Richard Hafley, b. 3 Nov 1938 (ch)

V9-476.   [15]-1. Gwen Ann Hafley, b. 18 Oct 1961

V9-477.   [15]-2. Marilyn Kay Hafley, b. 3 Feb 1963

V9-478.   [15]-3. Michael Hafley, b. 22 March 1964

V9-479.   [15]-4. Kyle Hafley, b. 28 May 1969; m.2. 15 Oct 1946, Benjamin Hill (ch)

V9-480.   [14]-2. Mary Kathryn Hill, b. 15 Nov 1950; m. 16 April 1977, Randy Johnson

V9-481.   [13]-5. Robert Williams, b. 28 June 1924; m. Ester Eberhard, b. 28 Sept 1926 (ch)

V9-482.	[14]-1. Ann Williams, b. 5 June 1952
V9-483.	[14]-2. Zola Louise Williams, b. 21 March 1953; m. 14 May 1974, Gus Rappeli (ch)
V9-484.	[15]-1. Joy Lynn Rappeli, b. 25 Sept 197?
V9-485.	[15]-2. Danny Raymai Rappeli, b. 25 Sept 197?
V9-486.	[14]-3. Joy Williams, b. 23 Jan 1957
V9-487.	[14]-4. Gay Williams, b. 23 Jan 1957
V9-488.	[13]-6. Charles Newton Williams, b. 9 Aug 1928; m. 23 Oct 1948, Barbara Jean Carter, b. 17 June 1930 (ch)
V9-489.	[14]-1. Mary Ellen Williams, b. 7 Dec 1950, d. 25 Feb 1957
V9-490.	[14]-2. Julia Lee Williams, b. 21 Aug 1954; m. 20 Sept 1972, Timothy Carter Kennard, b. 25 May 1954 (ch)
V9-491.	[15]-1. Timothy Michael Kennard, b. 17 Jan 1973
V9-492.	[15]-2. Jennifer Jean Kennard, b. 1 Feb 1977
V9-493.	[14]-3. Charles Carter Williams, b. 18 May 1956; m. 16 April 1977, Linda Jean Davis
V9-494.	[14]-4. Lisa Jean Williams, b. 14 April 1959; m. 15 July 1978, Larry Joe Ashley
V9-495.	[13]-7. Earl Dale Williams
V9-496.	[12]-8. Willie W. Williams, b. 18 July 1892, d. 20 Aug 1892, buried Zion Hill Cem.
V9-497.	[12]-9. Jessie M. Williams, b. 23 Aug 1893, d. 12 March 1917, buried Zion Hill Cem.
V9-498.	[12]-10. Dicy Daisey Williams, b. 16 Sept 1894, d. 27 Sept 1894, buried Zion Hill Cem.
V9-499.	[12]-11. Samuel Casey Williams, b. 25 Oct 1896, d. 12 Dec 1988, Atlanta, GA; m. 5 March 1920, Corrine Bellzora Allen, b. 27 Sept 1887, d. 29 Nov 1967, Atlanta, GA (ch)
V9-500.	[13]-1. Dorthy Jane Williams, b. 6 July 1923, Atlanta, Fulton Co, GA; m. 5 Dec 1953, Atlanta GA, Samuel Paul Phillips, b. 29 Sept 1916, Atlanta, Fulton Co, GA. (ch)
V9-501.	[14]-1. Freddy Phillips, b. 12 May 1956, Atlanta, Fulton Co, GA.
V9-502.	[14]-2. Carol Phillips, b. 26 Dec 1958, Atlanta, Fulton Co, GA.
V9-503.	[13]-2. Everett Samuel Williams, b. 3 April 1926, Atlanta, Fulton Co, GA; m. 27 April 1946, Vancouver, Canada, Irene Cormick, b. 20 Oct 1927, Romania, Europe (ch)

V9-504. 14-1. Rick Williams, b. 27 Oct 1947
V9-505. 14-2. Roger Williams, b. 7 Nov 1948
V9-506. 13-3. Evelyn Gertrude Williams, b. 3 April 1926; m. 23 Dec 1945, Atlanta, GA, William Jackson Young, b. 3 June 1920, Chauncy, Dodge Co, GA. s/o Norman J. Young and Katie May Kelly (ch)
V9-507. 14-1. Diane Elizabeth Young, b. 15 Dec 1946, Memphis, Shelby Co, TN; m. 30 Jan 1970, Ronnie Lester Graybeal (ch)
V9-508. 15-1. Samuel Earl Graybeal, b. 13 March 1972
V9-509. 15-2. Rachel Corrine Graybeal, b. 20 Feb 1974
V9-510. 15-3. Sarah Elizabeth Graybeal, b. 29 Dec 1975
V9-511. 15-4. Eve Adel Graybeal, b. 21 Dec 1978
V9-512. 14-2. William Jackson Young Jr, b. 17 March 1948, Atlanta, Fulton Co, GA; m. 26 Jan 1970, Ydona Higgenbotham (ch)
V9-513. 15-1. Tracy Lynn Higgenbotham, b. 1 Dec 1971
V9-514. 14-3. Barry Allen Young, b. 21 May 1954, Atlanta, Fulton Co, GA; m. 1 Sept 1975, Sarah Beth Blichington
V9-515. 14-4. Clifford Lee Young, b. 15 Feb 1963, Atlanta, Fulton Co, GA.
V9-516. 12-12. Oliver David Williams, b. 28 Feb 1897, d. 16 Aug 1897, buried Zion Hill Cem.
V9-517. 12-13. Berthold Williams, b. 27 Aug 1898, d. 30 Aug 1898, buried Zion Hill Cem.
V9-518. 12-14. Nancy Minerva "Minnie" Williams, b. 15 June 1900, d. 21 Dec 1995, Patoka Cem; m. 17 June 1920, Marion Co, Benjamin Franklin Parker, b. 15 June 1900, d. 25 Jan 1979, Patoka Cem. s/o Frank Parker and Caroline Yardley (ch)
V9-519. 13-1. Fern Adeline Parker, b. 8 Sept 1922, Marion Co, IL, d. 12 Jan 1994; m. 3 Aug 1942, Pearl Reed, b. 21 July 1900, Marion Co, IL, (ch)
V9-520. 14-1. Danny Gayle Reed, b. 27 Aug 1943, Marion Co, IL; m. 11 Feb 1965, First Baptist Church, Salem, IL, Delores Faye Carnell, b. 16 Dec 1945, d/o Jesse Warren Carnell Jr. and Valta Lou Campbell (ch)
V9-521. 15-1. Danny Gayle Reed Jr, b. 11 Sept 1965,

	Rockford, IL
V9-522.	[15]-2. Diana Dawn Reed, b. 24 Nov 1966, Marion Co, IL,
V9-523.	[15]-3. David Warren Reed, b. 18 Aug 1968, Marion Co, IL,
V9-524.	[15]-4. Dennis Jason Reed, b. 21 Sept 1973, Marion Co, IL,
V9-525.	[14]-2. Robert Bruce Reed, b. 7 Feb 1950, Marion Co, IL; m. _ July 1970, Carolyn Githers (ch)
V9-526.	[15]-1. Tammy Michele Reed, b. 1 Sept 1970
V9-527.	[14]-3. Joyce Jean Reed, b. 11 Aug 1956, Marion Co, IL; m. _____ Champaign, IL
V9-528.	[13]-2. Clara Mae Parker, b. 25 Feb 1925, Marion Co, IL; m. Lee Farmer, b. 10 Sept 1924, d. _ July 1971 (ch)
V9-529.	[14]-1. Carol Ann Farmer, b. 10 Sept 1946; m.1. Richard Therman (ch); m.2. Charles Pelton (ch)
V9-530.	[15]-1. Jill Therman, b. 15 Aug 1965
V9-531.	[15]-2. John Pelton, b. 1969
V9-532.	[14]-2. Sharon Lee Farmer, b. ? July 1948; m. Larry Moore (ch)
V9-533.	[15]-1. Tina Marie Moore, b. 15 Sept ____
V9-534.	[14]-3. William James Farmer, b. 15 Sept 1956
V9-535.	[14]-4. Mark Douglas Farmer, b. 15 April 1960
V9-536.	[14]-5. Michael Roy Farmer, b. 16 Feb 1963
V9-537.	[14]-6. Kimberly Lynne Farmer, b. 23 Aug 1966
V9-538.	[13]-3. Evelyn Parker, b. 29 Aug 1926; m. 11 Oct 1944, Roy Gonser, b. 24 July 1923 (ch)
V9-539.	[14]-1. Gloria Jean Gonser, b. 10 April 1947; m. 5 Dec 1970, Harold Feldon Markham, b. 1 Aug 1930 (ch)
V9-540.	[15]-1. Larry Wayne Feldon Markham, b. 28 June 1971
V9-541.	[14]-2. Larry Junior Gonser, b. 5 Nov 1948, d. 9 April 1966
V9-542.	[14]-3. Sandy June Gonser, b. 13 Dec 1951; m. 27 Sept 1969, Stephen Wayne Myers, b. 17 Oct 1950 (ch)
V9-543.	[15]-1. Stephenie Diana Myers, b. 13 July 1970
V9-544.	[15]-2. Stephen Wayne Myers Jr, b. 27 Sept 1971
V9-545.	[15]-3. Sandra Jeremy Myers, b. 9 Jan 1976
V9-546.	[14]-4. David Gonser, b. 11 Feb 1955; m. 24 Feb

1973, Brenda Allen, b. 6 June 1953 (ch)

V9-547.   15-1. Cinthia Alien Gonser, b. 21 April 1974

V9-548.   15-2. Brenda Gonser, b. 26 Jan 1975, d. 26 Jan 1975

V9-549.   15-3. Amanda Lynn Gonser, b. 4 Sept 1977

V9-550.   14-5. Frank Arthur Gonser, b. 21 Aug 1956

V9-551.   14-6. Patricia Louise Gonser, b. 7 Jan 1958

V9-552.   13-4. William Dwain Parker, b. 6 May 1929, d. 5 Jan 1995; m. 14 May 1965, Fairman Baptist Church Jaunita Luginia Webb, b. 31 March 1946 (ch)

V9-553.   14-1. Jaunita Luginia Webb, b. 24 March 1966

V9-554.   14-2. Ann Lynn Webb, b. 26 Oct 1968

V9-555.   14-3. Peggy Sue Webb, b. 24 Oct 1972

V9-556.   13-5. Mary Elizabeth Parker, b. 27 Sept 1931; m. Raymond Edward Harley, b. 12 Nov 1930 (ch)

V9-557.   14-1. Linda Diane Harley, b. 15 April 1952; m. Tom McCoy (ch)

V9-558.   15-1. Shannon Lynn McCoy

V9-559.   14-2. Susan Rae Harley, b. 24 Jan 1954; m. Ramiro Tijerina (ch)

V9-560.   15-1. David Ricardo Tijerina, b. 22 Jan 1972

V9-561.   15-2. Maria Susan Tijerina, b. 10 Sept 1974

V9-562.   14-3. Stephen Craig Harley, b. 12 April 1955

V9-563.   14-4. Debora Kay Harley, b. 25 Sept 1956

V9-564.   14-5. Raymond Edward Harley Jr, b. 3 May 1959

V9-565.   14-6. Randal Todd Harley, b. 31 Dec 1965

V9-566.   14-7. Jason Lee Harley, b. 3 Jan 1972

V9-567.   13-6. Lois Faye Parker, b. 27 Aug 1933; m. 21 Jan 1952 Gordon Vaughn Clossen, b. 23 Sept 1928 (ch)

V9-568.   14-1. Michael Vaughn Closson, b. 14 Oct 1952, Benton Harbor, Mich; m. 1 Sept 1973, Rhonda Gale Bell, b. 28 Aug 1957 (ch)

V9-569.   15-1. Michael Vaughn Closson Jr, b. 21 Feb 1975, St. Joseph, MO

V9-570.   14-2. John Adams Closson, b. 18 Dec 1953, Benton Harbor, Mich; m. 10 June 1978, Heidi Lynn Bishop

V9-571.   14-3. Sallie Ann Closson, b. 18 April 1954, Benton Harbor, MI; m. 6 May 1978, Clarence Herbert Norem

V9-572.   14-4. Nancy Jane Closson, b. 19 Aug 1957, Benton Harbor, Mich.

V9-573.   14-5. Lisa Michele Closson, b. 21 July 1970, Herrin Springs, Mich.

V9-574.   13-7. James Allen Parker, b. 21 Aug 1937, d. __
                 _____, buried Patoka Cem; m. Martha Ellen
                 _____, b. 2 June 1942 (ch)
V9-575.   14-1. Debra Ellen Parker, b. 9 July 1959
V9-576.   14-2. James Allen Parker Jr, b. 30 March 1961
V9-577.   14-3. Lori Denise Parker, b. 8 Jan 1964
V9-578.   13-8. Doris Jean Parker, b. 5 June 1939; m. 21 Aug
                 ____, Leroy Allen Rudy, b. 3 Feb 1937 (ch)
V9-579.   14-1. Carol Sue Rudy, b. 24 Feb 1962
V9-580.   14-2. Kenneth Allen Rudy, b. 20 June 1963
V9-581.   14-3. Mellissa Jean Rudy, b. 14 Jan 1965
V9-582.   14-4. Leroy Willford Rudy, b. 12 Jan 1966
V9-583.   13-9. Donald Parker, b. 21 Feb 1944; m. Linda Basil
V9-584.   13-10. Ruth Ann Parker, b. 16 July 1945; m. James
                 Edward Crayens, b. 27 Oct 1949 ? (ch)
V9-585.   14-1. Tammy Lynn Crayens, b. 5 Sept 1969
V9-586.   14-2. James Edward Crayens Jr, b. 23 Sept 1971
V9-587.   14-3. Staci Lynn Crayens, b. 7 Aug 1974
V9-588.   14-4. Traci Lynn Crayens, b. 7 Aug 1974
V9-589.   14-5. Edward Allen Crayens, b. 6 May 1976

Phillip Allen Williams
and Sarah Frances Day

V9-590.   11-8. Phillip Allen Williams, b. 16 Feb 1854, Buckner,
Franklin Co, d. 24 Jan 1938, buried Andereck/McClelland Cem; m. 28
Oct 1875, Marion Co, IL, Sarah Frances Day, b. 22 May 1857, d. 24
March 1929, buried Andereck/McClelland Cem. d/o William T. Day
and Rachel Carder (ch)
V9-591.   12-1. Lillie Belle Williams, b. 11 April 1877, Marion Co,
                 IL, d. 28 Oct 1963, buried Hillcrest Cem, Centralia;
                 m. 17 Dec 1893, Marion Co, IL, Franklin Yates, b. 1
                 Sept 1873, Parkville, Champaign Co, IL, d. 3 Nov
                 1952 Rock Falls, Whiteside Co, IL, s/o Lewis Yates
                 and Tamzine Jane Laughlin (ch). Frank m.2. Minnie
                 (Renske) Kilman
V9-592.   13-1. Orville Roy Yates, b. 3 July 1895, Parkville,
                 Champaign Co, IL, d. 29 June 1914, Drown
                 canoe accident, Alfresco Park, Peoria, bur
                 Fairlawn Cem, Decatur, Macon Co, IL
V9-593.   13-2. Robert Leslie Yates, b. 28 April 1899, Parkville,
                 Champaign Co, IL, d. Feb 1979, Elmwood Cem,
                 Centralia, IL; m. 1928, Hattie Glenn (ch)
V9-594.   14-1. Evelyn Mae Yates; m. Breeze, IL, Sylvester
                 Wempe

^{V9-}595.   ¹³⁻3. Ethel May Yates, b. 20 April 1901, Parkville, Champaign Co, IL, d. 25 Dec 1962, Hillcrest Cem, Centralia, IL; m. 24 Sept 1919, Marion Co, IL, Fredrick H. Overbeck, b. 5 Aug 1897, St. Louis, MO, d. 24 Sept 1919, Marion Co, IL, s/o August Overbeck and Mary C. Koeppe (ch)

^{V9-}596.   ¹⁴⁻1. Mary Kathryn "Bunny" Overbeck, b. 15 Dec 1930, Marion Co, IL; m. 3 June 1950, Marion Co, IL, Charles Monroe "Jim" Lyons, b. 3 Oct 1929, Beckmeyer, Clinton Co, IL s/o Charles Franklin Lyons and Edna Ruth Deadmond (ch)

^{V9-}597.   ¹⁵⁻1. Marie Annette Lyons, b. 21 March 1951, Marion Co, IL; m. 11 Oct 1969, Marion Co, IL, Larry Earl Miller

^{V9-}598.   ¹⁵⁻2. Jerome Christopher Lyons, b. 20 July 1952, Marion Co, IL; m. 20 Aug 1972, Base Chapel San Onofre Camp, Pendleton, San Diego Co, CA, Patricia Marie Fechtler

^{V9-}599.   ¹⁵⁻3. Charles Fredrick Lyons, b. 3 Dec 1953, Marion Co, IL; m. 24 Dec 1971, Marion Co, IL, Charlotte Cathy Howell

^{V9-}600.   ¹⁵⁻4. James Monroe Lyons, b. 12 Aug 1955, Marion Co, IL; m. 12 June 1976, Marion Co, IL, Terri Gayle Livesay

^{V9-}601.   ¹⁵⁻5. Patrick William Lyons, b. 15 April 1957, Taylor Co, Texas; m. 9 Oct 1975, Marion Co, IL, Kimberly Sue Pryor

^{V9-}602.   ¹⁵⁻6. Reginald Ferinand Lyons, b. 17 March 1959, Marion Co, IL,

^{V9-}603.   ¹⁵⁻7. Mitchell Lane Lyons, b. 5 March 1961, Marion Co, IL,

^{V9-}604.   ¹⁵⁻8. Angela Ruth Lyons, b. 11 Dec 1962, Odessa, Texas

^{V9-}605.   ¹⁵⁻9. Dale Rodney Lyons, b. 22 Aug 1964, Marion Co, IL,

^{V9-}606.   ¹⁵⁻10 Melanie Leann Lyons, b. 9 May 1966, Marion Co, IL,

^{V9-}607.   ¹⁵⁻11 Anissa Mickela "Mickie" Lyons, b. 8 Aug 1968, Marion Co, IL,

^{V9-}608.   ¹⁵⁻12 Daren Michael "Darry Mike" Lyons, b. 15 Jan 1971, Marion Co, IL,

^{V9-}609.   ¹⁴⁻2. Lillie May "Lil" Overbeck, b. 26 Oct 1937, Marion Co, IL, d. 25 May 1962, Reno,

---

Washoe Co, Nevada; m.1. 2 March ?, Richard
J. Tibbs Sr; m.2. Robert Gordon Page

V9-610.   14-3. Elizabeth Lucille Overbeck, b. 22 Nov 1940,
Marion Co, IL, d. 22 Nov 1940, Stillborn,
Hillcrest Cem, Centralia,

V9-611.   14-4. Ada Angeline Overbeck, b. 17 Oct 1941,
Marion Co, IL, d. 19 Oct 1941, Hillcrest Cem,
Centralia, IL, Ada and Elizabeth are both,
buried in unmarked graves at the foot of
Mrs. Mary C. (Koeppe) Ovarback's grave

V9-612.   13-4. Eva Francis Yates, b. 27 April 1904, Marion Co,
IL, d. 30 Aug 1951, Hillcrest Cem, Centralia IL;
m. 24 Sept 1919, Marion Co, IL, Chester M.
Chambers, b. ?, d. 5 March 1965 (ch)

V9-613.   14-1. Fredrick Leroy Chambers, not married
V9-614.   14-2. Robert Chester Chambers; m. Betty _____
V9-615.   14-3. William Edward Chambers,

V9-616.   12-2. George Newton Williams, b. 21 Sept 1878, Marion
Co, IL, d. 16 Dec 1957, Andereck/McClelland Cem;
m.1. Lulu Sims; m.2. Della _____ (ch)

V9-617.   13-1. George Williams,

V9-618.   12-3. Robert Douglas Williams, b. 12 Sept 1880, d. 1963,
Deadmond Cem, Sandoval, IL; m. 1 Jan 1899,
Myrtle F. Deadmond, b. 18 July 1881, d. 1958,
buried Deadmond Cem. d/o Jefferson Deadmond
and Ellia Day (ch)

V9-619.   13-1. Leslie Allen Williams, b. 2 Oct 1899, d. 11 June
1962, buried Odin Peaceful Valley Cem; m. 31
March 1920, Marion Co, IL, (F-68-1405), Bessie
Marie Luttrell, b. 24 Feb 1902, d. 2000 ? d/o
Charles Frederick Luttrell & Daisy Bryant (ch)

V9-620.   14-1. Cleo I. Williams, b. 3 Jan 1922, d. 29 March
1995 Odin Peaceful Valley; m. 19 March
1940, St. Louis, MO, Bernard B. Ross, b. 21
Sept 1911, d. 29 Jan 1976, Odin Peaceful
Valley Cem. s/o Isaac Ross & Emma
Shanafelt

V9-621.   14-2. Cary Robert Williams, b. 23 Dec 1923; m.
Madaline Hardy (ch)

V9-622.   15-1. Bobbie Williams; m.1. Mary Ann Hodge
(ch: Roger Williams)

V9-623.   15-2. Kenneth Williams; m. Judy Boatright
(ch)

V9-624.   16-1. Kim Williams,

V9-625.   16-2. Kerry Williams,

V9-626.   16-3. James Leslie Williams; girlfriend, Mindy Finckbone (ch)

V9-627.   17-1. Devin Clay Finckbone, b. 15 July 1997

V9-628.   15-3. Billy Mark Williams, b. 30 Dec 1957

V9-629.   14-3. Nelda Fay Williams, b. 3 Oct 1928; m. Walter Rexall Hensley (ch)

V9-630.   15-1. Michael Hensley, 2 wives, 2 sons

V9-631.   15-2. Peggy Hensley; m. John Tate (ch)

V9-632.   16-1. Gary Tate,

V9-633.   13-2. Everett Lawrence Williams, b. 20 May 1902, d. 1980; m.1. Eva Pigg, b. 19 May 1900 (ch)

V9-634.   14-1. Opal "Azalie" Williams, b. 28 March 1921, Gordon Grove, Ca, d. 8 Feb 2001, buried in California; m.1. Elmer Jackson (ch); m.2. John Wolski (ch); m.3. 18 Dec 1952, Jack Timmerman (ch)

V9-635.   15-1. Baby Boy

V9-636.   15-2. Eleanor Jackson

V9-637.   15-3. Adrian Clark Jackson

V9-638.   15-4. Everet Jackson

V9-639.   15-5. Michael Wolski

V9-640.   15-6. Tim Hugh Timmerman, works at Smithsonian

V9-641.   14-2. Everett Williams Jr, b. 13 Jan 1923, New Jersey; m. _____ Leanord; m.2. Fern Garren (ch)

V9-642.   14-3. James Lawrence Williams, b. 1926; m. Dotty Anderson

V9-643.   14-4. Mildred Lucille Williams, b. 18 March 1929, Marion Co, IL, d. 29 March 1974, buried Hillcrest Cem; m.1. Jack Overturf (ch); m.2. George Shaw (ch)

V9-644.   15-1. Richard Overturf, b. Houston, Texas

V9-645.   15-2. Robin Shaw

V9-646.   14-5. Doug Williams

V9-647.   14-6. Mary Ann Williams

V9-648.   14-7. Barbara Williams, b. 22 July 1938; m. Bob Ross (ch)

V9-649.   15-1. Jack Ross

V9-650.   13-3. Fannie Mae Williams, b. 31 Aug 1904, d. 29 April 1980 Deadmond Cem; m. 1 Nov 1922, Marion Co, IL, (F-88-2316), Charles Earl Carter, b. 16 May 1900, d. 5 Dec 1985 Deadmond Cem.

	s/o Will Carter & Belle Deadmond (ch)
V9-651.	14-1. Earline Carter, b. 3 Nov 1925; m.2. 9 March 1951, Piggot, AR, Dwight Creed (ch)
V9-652.	15-1. Garry Earl Creed, b. ? adopted (ch)
V9-653.	16-1. Garry Earl Creed Jr.
V9-654.	13-4. Bessie Mildred Williams, b. 2 Oct 1906, Marion Co, IL; m. 20 Jan 1924, Linnie R. Deadmond, b. 28 May 1902, d. 10 Nov 1982, buried Deadmond Cem. s/o Samuel Allen Deadmond and Mary Frances McClelland (ch)
V9-655.	14-1. Dalene Deadmond, b. 20 Aug 1924, d. 4 Jan 2000, Odin Peaceful Valley Cem; m. 1 Dec 1945, Marion Co, IL, Jess Morrison Jr, b. 7 May 1921, d. 5 Feb 1981, Odin Peaceful Valley Cem. s/o Jess E. Morrison & Lena Harris (ch)
V9-656.	15-1. Michael Morrison; m. 5 June 1971 1st Christian Church Odin, Susan Evans
V9-657.	15-2. Stanley Morrison; m. Diane Holsapple, d/o Robert Holsapple and _____ _____ (ch)
V9-658.	16-1. Derek Craig Morrison, b. 19 Nov 1971
V9-659.	15-3. Diana Morrison; m. John Schoonover s/o Al Schoonover and _____ _____ (ch)
V9-660.	16-1. Kevin Scott Schoonover, b. 3 Dec 1965, Marion Co, IL, d. 29 July 1974, buried Peaceful Valley Cem.
V9-661.	16-2. Jill Schoonover
V9-662.	16-3. Timmy Schoonover, b. 30 Nov 1972
V9-663.	13-5. Ada Lucille Williams, b. 18 Jan 1912; m. 1 May 1929, Herbert Edward Myers, b. 17 Aug 1905, d. 9 Feb 1978, Salem East Lawn Cem.
V9-664.	14-1. Robert William Myers, b. 23 Dec 1929, d. 28 Dec 1929
V9-665.	14-2. Edward Eugene Myers, b. 25 Nov 1930; m. 23 July 1955, Doris J. West, b. 27 Nov 1936, Fort Worth, Texas (ch)
V9-666.	15-1. Thresia Lynn Myers, b. 23 April 1956
V9-667.	15-2. Tylaine Gayle Myers, b. 14 Oct 1958
V9-668.	15-3. James Edward Myers, b. 17 June 1966
V9-669.	15-4. Mischelle Jean Myers, b. 27 Oct 1969
V9-670.	14-3. Virgil Lee Myers, b. 13 Aug 1932, d. 13 Aug 1932
V9-671.	14-4. Frankie Lee Myers, b. 28 Nov 1947, d. 2

Dec 1947

V9-672.   13-6. Olive Zoelle Williams, b. 23 Feb 1917, d. 6 March 1917, bur Deadmond Cem.

V9-673.   13-7. Velma Dene Williams, b. 8 July 1923; m. 11 June 1941, Glen Albert Scarbrough, b. 28 Sept 1919 s/o Levi Scarbrough and Elizabeth Walker (ch)

V9-674.   14-1. Glen Earl Scarbrough, b. 28 Feb 1943; m. 30 April 1960, Sandra Kay Moore, b.11 Aug 1943, d/o Lawrence Moore and Vivian Gibbs (ch)

V9-675.   15-1. Ronnie Gene Scarbrough, b. 4 Nov 1960; m. 6 Nov 1982, Barr Christian Church, Felicia Jeffords

V9-676.   15-2. Darla Kay Scarbrough, b. 28 Oct 1961; m. Steve Deadmond

V9-677.   15-3. Rocky Lee Scarbrough, b. 8 July 1964

V9-678.   14-2. Kay LaVonne Scarbrough, b. 5 July 1945; m. 10 Feb 1963, Barr Christian Church Odin, LaVerne Bland, b. 18 Ded 1942 s/o Vernon Virgil Bland and Ester Jewel Hanley (ch)

V9-679.   15-1. Patricia Denise Bland, b. 25 July 1964

V9-680.   15-2. Christine Louise Bland, b. 27 May 1965, d. ?, buried Deadmond Cem.

V9-681.   15-3. Laverne Bland, b. 31 Aug 1970

V9-682.   13-8. Lola Idene Williams, b. 10 March 1926, d. 15 June 1995, buried Deadmond Cem; m. 26 Jan 1944, Ivan Eugene McDaniel, b. 25 Dec 1925 (ch)

V9-683.   14-1. Lola Jean McDaniel, b. 7 Aug 1945; m. 7 April 1963, James O. Branch

V9-684.   14-2. Larry Edward McDaniel, b. 10 March 1947; m. 26 June 1966, Phyllis Jean Harper

V9-685.   14-3. Kathy Marlain McDaniel, b. 24 March 1940; m. Sheldon Walker

V9-686.   14-4. Ivan Wayne McDaniel, b. 16 July 1952; m. Christie Frimel (ch: Ivan Anthony; Lynn; and Margina McDaniel)

V9-687.   14-5. Jeffery Keith McDaniel, b. 19 March 1959; m. 1980, Patricia Sue Howell

V9-688.   12-4. Addeline Ada Williams, b. 2 Oct 1882, d. 12 Dec 1964, Andereck/McClelland Cem; m. 12 Feb 1902, Lawrence W. Sproull, b. 24 Nov 1877, Mulberry Grove, IL, d. 11 Sept 1963, buried

Andereck/McClelland Cem. s/o William R. Sproull
and Sarah Conner (ch)

V9-689.   [13-]1. Raymond Franklin Sproull, b. 17 May 1903; m.
14 Aug 1924, Lovell Lynora Deadmond (ch)

V9-690.   [14-]1. Lenora Fern Sproull, b. 1928; m. 30 June
1945, Clayton Vowell

V9-691.   [13-]2. Nellie Louise Sproull, b. 10 Dec 1905; m. 23
April 1924, Clifford Deadmond, b. 23 Jan 1903,
d. 26 Oct 1969, Deadmond Cem. s/o Joseph
Oscar Deadmond and Eva McKnoun (ch)

V9-692.   [14-]1. Hershel Dean Deadmond, b. 16 Dec 1924;
m. 24 Aug ??, Piggott, AR, Glenda Jean
Modlin, d/o Clyde Modlin (ch)

V9-693.   [15-]1. Garry Dean Deadmond, b. 4 Aug 1947,
Centralia, IL; m. 24 April 1967,
Olongappo City, Phillipines, Lug Palino
Lipprado

V9-694.   [15-]2. Gail Dee Deadmond, b. 4 March 1952,
Taylorville, IL; m. 27 June 1970, Odin
Methodist Church, Christopher
Whitehead (ch)

V9-695.   [16-]1. Tammy Lee Whitehead, b. 5 May
1971

V9-696.   [16-]2. Christopher Casey Whitehead, b. 14
July 1977

V9-697.   [15-]3. Ivan Lynn Deadmond, b. 15 Nov 1954;
m. 20 Nov 1976, Patricia Kelly

V9-698.   [14-]2. Delores Fern Deadmond, b. 16 July 1927;
m. 25 Aug 1945, Marion Co, IL, Thomas
Jourdan s/o George Jourdan (ch)

V9-699.   [15-]1. Tomona Fern Jourdan, b. 30 Aug 1946;
m. __ Jan 1967, Tulley Andrew Donoho

V9-700.   [16-]1. Brett Alan Donoho, b. 11 Dec 1967

V9-701.   [16-]2. Brad Andrew Donoho, b. 21 Aug
1969

V9-702.   [16-]3. Janice Leight Donoho, b. 6 Feb 1971

V9-703.   [15-]2. Wilma Jean Jourdan, b. 3 Nov 1947; m.
19 Nov 1965, Jerry Lee Brown

V9-704.   [16-]1. Keith Lee Brown, b. 2 Oct 1967

V9-705.   [16-]2. Vicki Jean Brown, b. 2 July 1971

V9-706.   [15-]3. Ronnie Lee Jourdan, b. 11 Aug 1949; m.
31 Aug 1967, St. Louis, MO, Wilma D.
Wilkes

V9-707.   [16-]1. Ronnie Lee Jourdan, Jr, b. 1 Nov
1967

V9-708.   [16-]2. Willford Wayne Jourdan, b. 12

	March 1970
V9-709.	[16]-3. Adam Leroy Jourdan, b. 10 July 1972
V9-710.	[15]-4. Stanley David Jourdan, b. 22 March 1958; m. Sheryl Lynn Bryant
V9-711.	[16]-1. Patti Jean Jourdan, b. 17 March 1978
V9-712.	[14]-3. Darrell Leroy Deadmond, b. 2 Nov 1930, d. 30 Sept 1999, Deadmond Cem; m.1. 27 Aug 1947, Eloise Sue Tate (ch); Darrell m.2. 11 May 1959, Julia Mae Harmon (ch)
V9-713.	[15]-1. Richard Lee Deadmond, b. 30 April 1949; m.1. 12 March 1971, Kathleen Wilkes (ch)
V9-714.	[16]-1. Tammy Lea Deadmond, b. 8 Jan 1972; m. 19 March 2000, Richard Ray Sadler
V9-715.	[16]-2. Richard Lee Deadmond Jr, b. 21 Feb 1977; m. Jody Lynn _____ (ch); m.2. Sandy Moore Scarbough
V9-716.	[17]-1. Briana Kay Deadmond, b. ?
V9-717.	[17]-2. Brenton Keith Deadmond, b. 23 Oct 1999
V9-718.	[15]-2. Darrus Eugene Deadmond, b. 13 June 1951; m. 16 June 1969, St. Louis, MO, Kathryn Sue Pokojski
V9-719.	[16]-1. Stacy Lynn Deadmond, b. 18 Jan 1970
V9-720.	[16]-2. Michael Lawrence Deadmond, b. 22 Aug 1972
V9-721.	[15]-3. Steven Leroy Deadmond, b. 5 Dec 1959; m. Darla Scarbrough
V9-722.	[16]-1. Steven Deadmond, b. ?
V9-723.	[15]-4. Rebecca Lynn Deadmond, b. 11 March 1961
V9-724.	[15]-5. Kevin Wayne Deadmond, b. 22 Nov 1962
V9-725.	[15]-6. Karen Rae Deadmond, b. 8 April 1972; m. Stacey Shoemaker, b. 13 Oct 1968
V9-726.	[16]-1. son
V9-727.	[14]-4. Phyllis Maxine Deadmond, b. 27 July 1934; m. 3 April 1953, Richview, Washington Co. IL, Paul Ray Davis, b. 12 Feb 1934, s/o Ray Davis and Ethel Donoho (ch)

V9-728.   15-1. Douglas Arthur Davis, b. 28 Sept 1954; m. 8 June 1974, Diana Lynn Sligar
V9-729.   16-1. Christi Lynn Davis, b. 4 June 1975
V9-730.   15-2. Donald Ray Davis, b. 12 Nov 1957, d. 21 April 1978, Deadmond Cem.
V9-731.   15-3. Debra Nell Davis, b. 2 Feb 1962
V9-732.   15-4. Darren Paul Davis, b. 15 Jan 1969
V9-733.   15-5. Darri Clifton Davis, b. 23 Aug 1970
V9-734.   15-6. Donya Dee Davis, b. 5 May 1974
V9-735.   14-5. David Allen Deadmond, b. 3 April 1939; m. _____, Barr Christian Church, May Margaret Green (ch)
V9-736.   15-1. Mitchell Allen Deadmond, b. 5 April 1960, Tampa, Fla
V9-737.   15-2. Roger Keith Deadmond, b. 19 April 1962, Salem, IL
V9-738.   15-3. Brian Wayne Deadmond, b. 3 May 1963
V9-739.   15-4. Matthew Dirk Deadmond, b. 19 Nov 1967
V9-740.   15-5. Marnell Elaine Deadmond, b. 16 July 1970
V9-741.   15-6. Calila Mae Deadmond, b. 8 Feb 1971
V9-742.   14-6. Donna Ellen Deadmond, b. 3 April 1939; m. 3 Nov 1958, Aberdeen, MD, Carmen E. Frimel (ch)
V9-743.   15-1. Danty Eugene Frimel, b. 12 Aug 1961
V9-744.   15-2. Denesise Ellen Frimel, b. 26 May 1964
V9-745.   15-3. Kenton Ellis Frimel, b. 19 May 1965
V9-746.   12-5. Ira Thomas Williams, b. 12 Aug 1884, d. 17 March 1929, Hillcrest Cem, Centralia, IL; m. 6 July 1909 or 1907, Mary Ruth Ballinger, b. 31 Jan 1888, Warrensburg, IL, d. 18 Sept 1971, Hillcrest Cem. d/o Robert Ballinger and Nora Major (ch)
V9-747.   13-1. Nora Frances Williams, b. 15 April 1909, Decatur, d. 18 Sept 2001, Hillcrest Cem; m. 16 Sept 1926, Salem, Roy W. Noller Sr, b. 26 Feb 1906, d. 26 July 1997, Hillcrest Cem. s/o August Noller and Nellie Britton (ch)
V9-748.   14-1. Roy W. Noller Jr; m.1. Phyliss Barr; m.2. _ June 1952, Marion Co, IL, Ada Mae Crane (ch)
V9-749.   15-1. Randy Noller; m. Letsy _____
V9-750.   15-2. Kevin Noller; m. Cheryl _____
V9-751.   15-3. Valeri Noller; m. Terry Shutt (ch: Travis, Dusty, Holly, Bethany, Brad, and

Cassandre Shutt, and Sheri Thomas?)

V9-752.   [13]-2. Emma May Williams; m.1. Clarence Schaubert.
(3ch:) Emma; m.2. _____ White

V9-753.   [14]-1. Hazel Marie Schaubert; m. 28 Feb 1947,
Marion Co, IL, Gerald Bopp, s/o Harry Bopp
and _____

V9-754.   [15]-1. Gary Bopp , (ch: Gary, Jr, and Michelle
Bopp)

V9-755.   [15]-2. Robert Bopp

V9-756.   [14]-2. Maxine Schaubert; m. Wilbur Folt

V9-757.   [14]-3. Robert Clarence Schaubert; m. 1 Aug 1956
Carolyn Eastman

V9-758.   [13]-3. Harry Thomas Williams; m. Christine Laffew

V9-759.   [13]-4. Ella Marie Williams, b. 4 June 1916, Marion Co,
IL, d. 1 May 1975, Oak Hill Cem, Danville, IL; m.
Eugene Schleuter, b. Nashville, Washington Co,
d. 12 Dec 1977, St Lawrence Cem, Sandoval, IL,
s/o William Schleuter and Emma Cruger (ch);
Marie m.2. _____ Turner

V9-760.   [14]-1. William A. Schleuter, b. Oakwood, IL

V9-761.   [14]-2. Barbarba Ruth Schleuter, b. Crawfordville,
IL; m. Milton _____

V9-762.   [12]-6. Nellie May Williams, b. 12 Aug 1886, Marion Co, IL,
d. 22 Jan 1972, Andereck/McClelland Cem; m.1.
1906, Lee Joshua Meador, b. 8 April 1883, Wayne
Co, IL, d. 27 April 1946, Andereck/ McClelland Cem.
(ch); m.2. Oscar Farthing; m.3. _____ van Sycle

V9-763.   [13]-1. Ada Leota Meador, b. 23 Sept 1907, d. 25 Dec
1918, Andereck/McClelland Cem.

V9-764.   [13]-2. Phillip Laurence Meador, b. 8 March 1911; m.
26 Sept 1929, Marion Co, IL, Juanita Harris (ch)

V9-765.   [14]-1. Charles Lee Meador, b. California

V9-766.   [12]-7. Phillip Logan Williams, b. 20 July 1888, Marion Co,
IL, d. 24 April 1959, Sandoval Cem; m.1. 23 Dec
1909, Jessie Moore, b. 7 Dec 1892, d. 26 Dec 1918
(ch); m.2. Edna McMarty; m.3. Reba Doyd

V9-767.   [13]-1. Vivian Fern Williams, b. July 1918, d. 28 Nov
1918, Sandoval Cem.

V9-768.   [12]-8. Maude Louise Williams, b. 13 Nov 1890, Marion Co,
IL, d. ?; m. 10 June 1908, Marion Co, IL, Pleasant
Garfield Carlyle, b. 5 April 1882, Franklin Co, IL, d.
23 March 1932, Hillcrest Cem. s/o James Carlyle
and Mary Phillips (ch)

V9-769.   [13]-1. Zelma Irene Carlyle, b. 15 Feb 1914; m.1.

Alfred Newald; m.2. James Dean

V9-770.   13-2. William Loren Carlyle, b. 30 May 1909, d. 10 Sept 1939, Hillcrest Cem; m. 10 May 1935, Carbondale, IL, Maggy Huckenberry (ch)

V9-771.   14-1. Bob Loren Carlyle

V9-772.   13-3. Myrtle Anna Carlyle, b. 27 Jan 1911; m.1. 20 May 1930, Robert Foltz, b. 1907 (ch); Myrtle; m.2. 1951, Robert Lusch (ch)

V9-773.   14-1. Wanda Faye Foltz, b. __ Dec ___; m.1. 21 July 1961, _____ Dyer; m.2. John Chappell

V9-774.   14-2. Donna Mae Foltz, b. __ Dec ___; m. 11 Oct, Marion Co, IL, Earl Vaughn

V9-775.   14-3. Connie Lusch; m. 28 Dec 1973, Rick Jackson

V9-776.   13-4. Charles Edwin Carlyle, b. 6 April 1916, d. 24 Feb 1950, Hillcrest Cem; m. 14 Sept __, Mt. Auburn Methodist Church, St. Louis, MO, Laverne Ruth Barker

V9-777.   13-5. Flossie Lillian Carlyle, b. 7 June 1917; m.1. Walter Voss (ch); m.2. Albert Burning, b. 1917, d. 19 Dec 1973, Odin Peaceful Valley Cem. (ch)

V9-778.   14-1. Harry Voss; m. Mary Edwards (ch)

V9-779.   15-1. Lisa Voss

V9-780.   15-2. Troy Richard Voss, b. 30 Dec 1961

V9-781.   14-2. Charles Voss; m. Reba Snyder, d/o Harold Snyder and Louise Warren (ch)

V9-782.   15-1. Theresa Voss, b. 9 May 1961

V9-783.   15-2. Christina Voss, b. 22 May 1963

V9-784.   15-3. Cindy Voss, b. 30 Nov 1966

V9-785.   15-4. Charles Voss Jr, b. Nov 1971

V9-786.   14-3. Brenda Burning; m. Elmer Brown

V9-787.   14-4. Sandra Burning; m. Eddie Shopteaw

V9-788.   14-5. Brad Burning; m. Susan Whalen

V9-789.   13-6. Archie Logan Carlyle, b. 20 Nov 1924, d. 7 Feb 1968, Hillcrest Cem; m. 24 June 1946, Barbara Wesley

V9-790.   12-9. Claude Wellington Williams, b. 5 Oct 1892, d. 13 May 1940, Sandoval Cem; m. 29 Aug 1911, Marion Co, IL, Nora "Mae" Moore, b. 1896, Jefferson Co, IL, d. 7 April 1932, Sandoval Cem, d/o Harvey Moore and Lulu Perry, (ch)

V9-791.   13-1. Lulu Monita Williams; m.1. Adriah Sandy, (2ch); m.2, Hershall Myers, (5daus)

V9-792.   13-2. Viola Irene Williams, b. 12 Sept 1914, Marion Co, IL, d. 11 March 1943, Sandoval Cem, m.

	Ralph/Kenneth Carpenter
V9-793.	13-3. Lorene Rose Williams, b. 1925, West Frankfort, IL, d. 8 June 1973, Sunset Hill Cem. Edwardsville, IL, m. Thomas Goodrich
V9-794.	13-4. Willard Williams,
V9-795.	13-5. Pansey Alice Williams, b. 1 Nov ___; m.1. Kenneth Carpenter; m.2. Clarence Suddeth
V9-796.	13-6. Naomi Ruth Williams, m. _____ Van Meter
V9-797.	13-7. Thelma Mae Williams, m. _____ Arnett
V9-798.	13-8. Hazel Fern Williams, b.&d. 1918, Sandoval Cem.
V9-799.	13-9. Virginia Lee Williams, b. 1932, d. 1932, Sandoval Cem.
V9-800.	12-10 Clyde Williams, b. 16 July 1895, d. 17 July 1895, Andereck/McClelland Cem. East side Cedar tree
V9-801.	12-11 Bertha Williams, b. 24 Sept 1897, d. 24 Sept 1897, Andereck/McClelland Cem.
V9-802.	12-12 Myrtie Williams, b. 24 Sept 1897, d. 24 Sept 1897, Andereck/McClelland
V9-803.	12-13 Earnie Lawrence Williams, b. 30 Sept 1899, d. 12 April 1901, Andereck/McClelland Cem.

Enoch Williams
and Sarah Catherine Cooperrider

V9-804.   11-11. Enoch Williams, b. 5 July 1858 Buckner, Franklin Co, IL, d. __ Sept 1933, buried Odin Peaceful Valley Cem; m. 25 Oct 1885, Marion Co, IL, (F-180-165), Sarah Catherine Cooperrider, b. 1 Jan 1969, d. 10 June 1953, Odin Peaceful Valley Cem. d/o William Cooperrider and Catherine Russler (ch)

V9-805.	12-1. William Williams, b. 1 May 1886, Marion Co, IL, d. 25 July 1886, McClelland Cem.
V9-806.	12-2. Clara Alice Williams, b. 18 Nov 1887, Marion Co, IL, d. 28 Feb 1974, Peaceful Valley Cem; m.1. 31 Dec 1908, Marion Co, IL, Joseph E. Deadmond, b. 1872, d. 1933, Odin Peaceful Valley Cem, s/o John Deadmond & Elizabeth Day, (ch); m.2. 27 June 1944, Everett E. Deadmond
V9-807.	13-1. Irma Deadmond, m. _____ Hawkins
V9-808.	13-2. Isabelle Deadmond, m. Ed Ross
V9-809.	13-3. Ira Deadmond, b. 8 Sept 1910, d. 10 April 1988, Odin Peaceful Valley Cem.
V9-810.	13-4. Joseph Deadmond,
V9-811.	13-5. Wilson Deadmond, b. 28 Dec 1916, d. 1 Feb 2000, Odin Peaceful Valley Cem.

V9-812.	13-6. Charles Deadmond,
V9-813.	13-7. Dean Deadmond,
V9-814.	13-8. Irwin Dale Deadmond,
V9-815.	12-3. Gertrude Ellen "Alice" Williams, b. 26 Jan 1890, d. 17 Feb 1947, Hillcrest Cem; m. __ May 1910, John Deadmond, (ch: Floyd; Larkin; and Dwight Deadmond)
V9-816.	12-4. Bertha Williams, b. ?, d. 15 Feb 1894, from old ledger 2 yrs old, Zion Hill Cem.
V9-817.	12-5. Grace Williams, d. 18 July 1896, Zion Hill Cem.
V9-818.	12-6. Dan Williams, b. 17 Dec 1898, Marion Co, IL; m. 10 March 1918, Marion Co, IL, Nellie Uhls, (ch: Reggie; Virginia; Elaine; and Betty Williams)
V9-819.	12-7. Raymond Williams, b. 2 Aug 1901; m.1. 28 Aug 1925, Marion Co, IL, Lillian Dell Deadmond; m.2. 1 Feb 1947, Josephine Forch
V9-820.	12-8. Ruby Diamond Williams, b. 2 Aug 1901, d. 19 March 1968, Antoich Cem; m. 22 Oct 1920, Rollins Sands, (ch: Wayne; Earl Raymond; Eugene Rollin; and Glen Sands)
V9-821.	12-9. Harold Williams, b. 17 July 1904, Marion Co, IL, d. 1970, Rock Falls, IL, m. Velma "Wilma" McNecky, (2ch: Esta May; and Lloyd Enoch Williams)
V9-822.	12-10. Ferrold Williams, b. 9 Aug 1906; m. 27 June 1929, Floyd Nelson Johnston, b. 17 March 1902, d. 8 July 1980, Odin Peaceful Valley Cem, (ch)
V9-823.	13-1. Gerald Johnston, b. 25 Aug 1930, d. 1 Nov 1998, Kentucky; m.1. 15 Dec 1951, Eleanor Anderson, (4ch: Brad; Bruce; Brian; and Brenda Johnston). Gerald m.2. 10 Sept 1978, Erlanger, Ky, Lucille Muldoon
V9-824.	13-2. Gail Gale Johnston, b. 7 Oct 1934; m. 12 June 1955, Marsha Myers
V9-825.	13-3. Roma Johnston, b. 16 Oct 1936; m.1. 30 Nov 1954, Noah Gerald Clark; m.2. _____ Look

John William Brashears
and Mary Jane Daniel Blanks

v-2, p.288: Family of John William Brashears. Vera Brashears, widow of William Marquess Brashears Sr, sent additional data and corrections. Here is the revised section on **John William Brashears**:

v2-2506. **John William Brashears Sr**, (apparently a s/o Valdon A. Brashears and his first wife), b. 22 May 1837, Jefferson Co, IL (says the family Bible), d. 10 April 1922, Trigg Co, KY; m. 3 Sept 1863 (or 1862), **Mary Jane Daniel Blanks**, and had four children. After Mary Jane died, John William Brashears had four children by **Eliza Griffey** (no marriage found).

[The E. Morton Brashears narrative remains the same.]

Children of John William Brashears Sr and Mary Jane Daniel Blanks:

V9-826.   11-1. ***John William "Willie" Brashears Jr**, b. 26 May 1863, Trigg Co, KY, d. 10 Jan 1910, Trigg Co; m. 22 Feb 1889, **Mrs. Lucy Adeline (Blythe) Bridges**, b. 1 Aug 1858,

V9-827.   11-2. **Nancy Ella Brashears**, b. 1 Aug 1866, Trigg Co, KY; m. **John Williams**.

v2-2522a   12-1. Maude Williams,
v2-2522b   12-2. Clay Williams,
v2-2522c   12-3. Myrlle Williams,
v2-2522d   12-4. Tommy Williams,
v2-2522e   12-5. Lavenia Williams,
v2-2522f   12-6. Robert Williams,
v2-2522g   12-7. Maybelle Williams,

V9-828.   11-3. **Walter Scott Brashears**, b. 1870, Trigg Co, KY, d. 9 Jan 1910, Trigg Co, KY; m. **Ella McKinney**, b. 1872, Trigg Co, KY, d. 29 May 1857, Fulton, KY

v2-2523a   12-1. **Walford Brashears**,
v2-2523b   12-2. **Marie Brashears**,
v2-2523c   12-3. **Wilbur Brashears**,
v2-2523c   12-4. **Myrtle Brashears**,
v2-2523d   12-5. **Wardell Brashears**,
v2-2523e   12-6. **Luella Brashears**,

V9-829.   11-4. **James W. "Jim" Brashears**, b. 1872, Trigg Co, KY, d. Franklin Co, IL (?); m. 15 July 1892, **Ora Blythe**, b. 1875, Trigg Co, KY, d. IL. Both ch on 1910, Williamson Co, IL, census.

v2-2524a   12-1. **Beulah Brashears**, b. c1893
v2-2524b   12-2. **Clara Brashears**, b. c1895

Children of John William Brashears Sr and Eliza Griffey:

V9-830.   11-5. **Ernest Napoleon Brashears**, b. 23 Feb 1877, Trigg Co, KY, d. 30 Nov 1952, Trigg Co, KY; m. 28 Sept 1903, **Pearl Elizabeth Cook**, b. 2 June 1883, Caldwell Co, KY, d. 2 April 1939, Trigg Co, KY, d/o Sanford D. Cook and Nancy E. Pickering

V9-831.   12-1. **E. Morton Brashears**, b. 16 June 1904, Trigg Co, KY, d. 16 June 1989, Christian Co, KY; m. 4 June 1931, **Hattie Pearl Fuller**

v2-2526a   12-2. **Lois Cornelia Brashears**, b. 27 July 1905, Trigg Co, KY, d. 1966, Trigg Co, KY; never married v2-2526b   ¹²⁻3. **Bernice Gertrude Brashears**, b. 16 May 1907, Trigg Co, KY, d. 1 Dec 1992, Trigg Co, KY; never married

v2-2526c   ¹²⁻4. **Furmon Brashears**, b. 6 Nov 1909 (twin), Trigg Co, KY, d. 15 Jan 1995; m. 19 March 1932, *Irene Clowe*, b. 6 Dec 1913, d. 2 April 1982, Christian Co, KY

v2-2526d   ¹²⁻5. **Thurmon Brashears**, b. 6 Nov 1909 (twin), d. at birth

v2-2526e   ¹²⁻6. **Thelma Mae Brashears**, b. 8 May 1912, Trigg Co, KY, d. 24 May 1983; m. 16 Jan 1930, *Laymon P'Pool*

v2-2526f   ¹²⁻7. **Lewis Hayden Brashears**, b. 17 Oct 1915, Trigg Co, KY, d. 23 July 1983; m. 6 Nov 1937, *Frances P'Pool*, b. 13 June 1915, Trigg Co, KY, d. 31 March 1978

v2-2526g   ¹²⁻8. **Urey Hubert Brashears**, b. 19 April 1919, Trigg Co, KY, d. 5 Sept 1990, Trigg Co, KY; m. 9 Dec 1951, *Helen Hendricks*, b. 3 July 1928

v2-2526h   ¹²⁻9. **Anna Pearl Brashears**, b. 29 May 1922, Trigg Co, KY; m. 23 Aug 1942, *Charles R. Burgess*

V9-832.   ¹¹⁻6. **Charles W. Brashears**, b. 1 Jan 1879, Trigg Co, KY, d. 18 Oct 1913 (in a mental institute, of TB), Christian Co, KY; single.

V9-833.   ¹¹⁻7. **Oscar E. Brashears**, b. 1 May 1881, Trigg Co, KY, d. 23 Nov 1950 (in a mental institute, of uremia), Christian Co, KY; single.

V9-834.   ¹¹⁻8. **Grover Cleveland Brashears**, b. 18 June 1889, Trigg Co, KY, d. 8 Aug 1966, Trigg Co, KY; m. 29 March 1916, *Fanny Mae Pollard*, b. ?, d. 10 Oct 1983, Trigg Co, KY, d/o Samuel Pollard and Addie "Nancy" Perry

v2-2529a   ¹²⁻1. **Bertrand Brashears**, b. 26 Feb 1917, Trigg Co, KY; m. 18 Nov 1934, *Perry Poindexter*, b. 14 June 1894, Trigg Co, KY, d. 14 Nov 1974, Christian Co, KY

v2-2529b   ¹²⁻2. **Evangeline Brashears**, b. 6 Feb 1919, Trigg Co, KY, d. TN; m. *Garner Burgess*

v2-2529c   ¹²⁻3. **Garland C. Brashears**, b. 16 Jan 1921, Trigg Co, KY; d. 23 Aug 1982, Christian Co, KY; m. 14 Nov 1947, *Naomi Yates*, b. 12 Nov 1928

v2-2529d   ¹²⁻4. **Orland Yates Brashears**, b. 18 Sept 1924, Trigg Co, KY, d. 18 June 1954, Utah; m. *Marie Brown*

v2-2529e   ¹²⁻5. **Elizabeth L. Brashears**, b. 17 May 1928, Trigg Co, KY, d. 14 Nov 1994, FL; m.1. _____ *Belew*; m.2 _____ *Doyle*; m.3. _____ *Wright*

John William "Willie" Brashears Jr and Lucy Blythe

^{v2}-2521. **John William "Willie" Brashears Jr**, (s/o John William Brashears Sr and Mary Jane Daniel Blanks), b. 26 May 1863, Trigg Co, KY, d. 10 Jan 1910, Trigg Co; m. 22 Feb 1889, *Mrs. Lucy Adeline (Blythe) Bridges*, b. 1 Aug 1858, TN, d. 14 Dec 1929, Trigg Co, KY, d/o William Blythe and Margaret Keeler and widow of John W. Bridges, who was accidentally shot and killed while fishing in the Cumberland River in Trigg Co, KY, c1877, leaving a son, John W. Bridges, Jr, b. 3 March 1876, and a pregnant wife: son, Leonard Lisha Bridges, b. 10 Sept 1877. About 11 or 12 years later, John William Brashears and Lucy Bridges married. John William Brashears and Lucy had three children (re: Caldwell Co, History, p.93, biog of John W. Bridges):

^{V9}-835. ^{12}-1. ***Henry G. Brashears**, b. 13 June 1890, d. 4 Aug 1910, Trigg Co, KY (run over by a train); m. 23 Aug 1905, *Artis Bell Stewart*, b. 27 Jan 1890, d. 9 Aug 1982, Trigg Co, KY

^{V9}-836. ^{12}-2. **Maxie L. Brashears**, b. 29 June 1892, Trigg Co, KY, d. 9 Aug 1983, Caldwell Co, KY; m. 1913, *Artis Bell (Stewart) Brashears*, widow of his brother, b. 27 Jan 1890, d. 9 Aug 1982, Trigg Co, KY

^{V9}-837. ^{13}-1. **Dennis Brashears**, b. 24 Nov 1913, Trigg Co, KY
^{V9}-838. ^{13}-2. **Maybelle Brashears**, b. 22 Feb 1916, Trigg Co, KY
^{V9}-839. ^{13}-3. **Arnold Brashears**, b. 5 Feb 1925, Trigg Co, KY
^{V9}-840. ^{12}-3. **Thomas Brashears**, b. 1899, Trigg Co, KY, d. 29 March 1966, Christian Co, KY; m. *Flora Owen*

Henry G. Brashears and Artis Bell Stewart

v2-2532. **Henry G. Brashears**, (s/o John William "Willie" Brashears Jr and Lucy Adaline Blythe), b. 13 June 1890, d. 4 Aug 1910, Trigg Co, KY; m. 23 Aug 1905, Springfield, TN, *Artis Bell Stewart*, b. 27 Jan 1890, d. 9 Aug 1982, Trigg Co, KY, d/o William John Stewart and Georgann McQuery. Henry and Artis had only one child. After Henry was killed by a train, Artis m.2. his brother, Maxie Brashears.

^{V9}-841. ^{13}-1. **William Guy Brashears**, b. 8 Aug 1906, Trigg Co, KY, d. 18 June 1948, Christian Co, KY; m. 15 Sept 1928, *Helen Louise Marquess*, b. 5 Sept 1908, Christian Co, KY, d. 11 Aug 1993, Christian Co, KY. They had only one child.

^{V9}-842. ^{14}-1. **William Marquess Brashears Sr**, b. 26 Sept 1929, Christian Co, KY; m. *Vera James*,

v2-2539a ^{15}-1. **William Marquess Brashears Jr**, b. 25 June 1953

v2-2539b ^{15}-2. **Gregg Thomas Brashears**, b. 4 April 1957

William James Leftwich Brashears
and Sarah "Sally" Herrin

Additions to WARREN/CANNON CO, TN: Douglas R. Besherse, <Dbesherse@webtv.net> and others sent additions to family of William James Leftwich Brashear and Sarah "Sallie" Herrin (or Nerrin):

v2-2326. ***William James Leftwich(?) Brashears**, (s/o Jesse Brashears and Elizabeth "Betsy" Shell), b. 4 Aug 1803, VA, d. 15 Dec 1897, Warren Co, TN, bur Hills Creek Cem, Warren Co, TN; m.1. _____ (4 ch indicated by 1830 census, Warren Co, TN); m.2. 10 Dec 1842, **Nancy Nokes** (no known children, and they apparently divorced); m.3. 1 Nov 1845, Cannon Co, TN, **Sarah "Sally" Herrin**, b. 1831, d. 7 June 1888, bur Hills Creek Cem, Warren Co, TN.

Nellie Brashear and Richard Taylor

V2-2541. [10-1]. **Nellie Brashears**, b. 1820-25 (per 1830 census); m. 1845, in Cannon Co, TN, **Richard Taylor**, who died in the Mexican War, 1847-48.

V2-2541a. [11-1]. Richard Taylor, Jr, b. 1847, White Co, TN. Migrated to Texas.

Robbie Taylor Read <robbie2@wf.net> writes:

My GG Grandparents, **Nelly Brashears** & **Richard Taylor** married in 1845 in Cannon Co, TN. My G Grandfather, also named Richard Taylor was born in 1847 in White Co, TN. My GGGrandfather was said to have died in the War with Mexico in 1847 or 48. Does anyone have any information on Nelly after he died? I don't know if she remarried or if they had any other children in their short marriage. My G Grandfather, Richard ended up in TX, but I don't know at what age he came here. Any information on what happened to Nelly would be greatly appreciated.
Thanks!

Henry A. Brashear and Susie Ann Redmon

v2-2545. [10-5]. **Henry A. "Hank" Brashears**, (s/o William James Leftwich Brashears and Sarah "Sally" Herrin), b. 1848, TN, d. 5 Nov 1932, Atlanta, TX; m.1. 9 June 1867, Dekalb Co, TN, **Susie Ann Redmon**, m.2. **Ann** _____, m.3. **Della Moore**, (partner on death cert. is "Idella"). Contact: Douglas R. Besherse, <Dbesherse@webtv.net>

Obit: HENRY A. "HANK" BESHERSE

Henry A. "Hank" Besherse, age 83, longtime Oak Harbor resident, died at Life Care Center of Skagit Valley in Sedro Woolley [Washington state] on Wed., Oct. 19, 2005.

Mr. Besherse was born on March 12, 1922, in Waurika, OK, to Solomon Besherse and Sarah (King) Besherse. He moved with his family to Whidbey Island from New Mexico in 1937. Hank was married to Helen Vandenburg on July 20, 1941 in Sedro Woolley. He served his country in the Army during World War II, receiving the Silver Star Medal. Following his Honorable Discharge on Feb. 9, 1946, he was employed by Civil Service at NAS Whidbey as a truck driver for thirty-six years, retiring on May 30, 1984. Hank and Helen together were charter members of the Oak Harbor Church of the Nazarene, and served there actively for many years.

Hank is survived by his two sons, **Alvin Lewis Besherse** of Sedro Woolley and **Doug Besherse** and wife Jayne of Okanogan; five grandchildren; 11 great-grandchildren; also, several nieces and nephews. He was preceded in death by his wife Helen on July 26, 1993, and by two brothers and one sister.

A Graveside Service will be Monday, October 24, 2005, 1:00 p.m. at Sunnyside Cemetery, Pastor Ivan Lathrop officiating. Memorials may be made to the Salvation Army, 3001 R Ave. #100, Anacortes, WA 98221. Arrangements under direction of Burley Funeral Chapel.

> Douglas Besherse
> From: DougandJayne509@aol.com
> Date: Thu, 7 Dec 2006 13:30:20 EST
> To: brashear@mail.sdsu.edu

Sydney Brashears and John A. Taylor

v2-2549. [10]-6. **Sydney (or Synda) Brashears**, (d/o William James Leftwich Brashears and Sarah "Sally" Herrin), b. c1861, d. 27 Nov 1938; m. 7 Dec 1881, *John A. (or H.) Taylor*, Warren Co, TN (IGI: M519792), s/o William Arthur Taylor and Nancy Vance. (Data from Deb Jansons <chevygirl40usa@yahoo.com>. Ch:

V9-843. [11]-1. Octavia "Octie" Taylor, b. unknown
V9-844. [11]-2. Nancy Taylor, b. unknown
V9-845. [11]-3. Delie Taylor, b. unknown
V9-846. [11]-4. Sarah Leweller Taylor, b. 18 Sept 1882, d. 31 Oct 1882
V9-847. [11]-5. Lemuel Eugene Taylor (Deb's g-grandfather), b. Sept 23, 1884 in Warren County, TN, d. Jan. 31, 1973 in Pinson, Jefferson County, Alabama and is buried at the

Maple Hill Cemetery in Huntsville, Madison County, Alabama. Lemuel married Ada Mae Campbell (d/o Smith Alexander Campbell and Martha Julia "Pink" Golden) on Sept. 29, 1908, in Madison County, Alabama.

Deb Jansons writes: "Sidney Beshears' husband, John A. Taylor, died on March 4, 1897 in Warren County, TN of possible pneumonia. He is buried at the Hills Creek Cemetery in Warren County.

Some time after John's death, Sidney and her children moved to Alabama and she never remarried. My g-grandfather, Lemuel, was about 13 when his father died and he went to work and supported the family. Sidney later moved to the Fayetteville, Lincoln County, TN, area with her daughter, Octavia. This is where she died and according to her grandchildren (my g-aunts and uncles that are still living), she was buried in the Kelso Community, which is located close to Fayetteville, TN and not the Hills Creek Cem. in Warren County."

Kansas (or Arkansas) Brashear and Isaac Perry/ T. J. Cagle

V2-2552.   [10]-8. **Kansas (or Arkansas) Brashears**, b. c1866; m.1. 19 Dec 1882, *Isaac Perry*, at McMinnville, Warren Co, TN (IGI: M519792); m.2. *John J. Cagle*, or *Thomas Jefferson Cagle*, b. 21 June 1867, Warren Co, TN, d. 30 Dec 1948, Modesto, CA

V9-848.   [11]-1. Isaac Floid Perry, b. & d. 12 March 1884

....

V9-849.   [11]-x. James Alexander Cagle, (s/o Thomas Jefferson Cagle and **Arkansas Brashears**, data from Laurie Wier <Sibling3@aol.com>) b. 26 March 1896, McMinnville, TN, d. 1986, Phoenix, AZ; m.1. Martha Miranda McNeley, b. 24 June 1899, Clarkesville, Pope Co, AR, d. 15 Oct 1938, Tulsa, OK. J.A. Cable was a bootlegger during Prohibition. J.A. Cagle, m.2.

_____.

V9-850.   [12]-x. Aretha Lorraine Cagle, b. 8 Jan 1930, Picher, OK, d. 4 Sept 1977, Montgomery Co, TX.

3. JAMES ANDERSON BESHEARS
and his sister,
ELIZABETH C. (BESHEARS) MILLS

^{V2-}56. **?Wilson? Brashears/Beshears; m.** *Patty* _____ ,

^{V9-}851.   ⁹⁻x. **Elizabeth C. Beshears**, b. June 1830, d. 1905; m. 1845, ***Caswell Mills***,

^{V9-}852.   ⁹⁻y. **James Anderson Beshears**, b. 23 Oct 1835, IN, d. 27 Sept 1883; m.1. ***Mary Francis Green***, (no record of children); m.2. 11 March 1863 in Daviess Co, MO (a notation in the marriage book says he lived in Grundy Co, MO at the time), ***Millie Frances Roberts***, b. 25 April 1843, MO, d. 5 Aug 1899,

We don't really know who the parents of these siblings were. In her Civil War Widow's Pension application, Elizabeth Mills said she is second cousin to William [Bazil] and [Robert] Anderson Beshears of Madisonville, Ralls Co, MO. She calls her mother "Patty," says she has one brother, James Anderson Beshears, whose wife is Milly Frances, but she has no sister and all her [other] brother_s_ are dead.

We have one family that might fit that set of circumstances— Wilson Beshears, who was on the 1830 census of Marion Co, TN.

1830 Census, Marion Co, TN; (0121001-100001)

Wilson Beshears	40-50	b. 1780's
(wife)	30-40	b. 1790's
(son)	15-20	b. 1810-1815
(son)	10-15	b. 1815-1820
(son)	10-15	b. 1815-1820
(son)	5-10	b. 1820-1825
(dau)	0-5	b. 1825-1830

That daughter at the end is a good candidate for being Elizabeth C. (Beshears) Mills. She has no sisters, but a good number of older brothers who would probably be dead by 1902, when Elizabeth was applying for a Civil War Widow's Pension. The brother, James Anderson Beshears, was born five years later than this record—in 1835, in Indiana, say his descendants.

This Wilson Beshears of Marion Co, TN, is believed to be a son of

Philip Brashears, Jr, and his wife, Elizabeth _____, who lived in Henry County, Virginia, in 1810, along with a number of Brashears and Wilson relatives. (See 1810 Henry Co, VA tax lists below.)

There were two other Wilson Beshears in the same time period—one, a son of Robert Brashears and Patsy Wilson, and therefore cousin to this Wilson Beshears; he lived in Perry Co, IL, in 1830. The other Wilson Beshears, was a son of Jeremiah Brashears/Beshears Jr, of Hopkins Co, KY, where he died in 1831, naming a brother, Thomas, his only heir.

The Wilson Beshears who was in Marion Co, TN, in 1830, and several of his brothers and cousins are on a Tax List/ Census of Henry Co, VA, in 1810 (The actual census was lost, this was a re-created census, using tax records):

from *Supplement to 1810 Census of VA*, comp. by. W.S. Yantis:
in Henry Co, VA (males over 21, therefore born bef. 1789):

name	white tithes	slaves	horses
Jesse Brashears,	1	0	0
Philip Brashears,	1	0	1
Wilson Brashears,	1	0	1
Zaza Brashears,	1	0	0
Thomas Wilson Sr (s/o James),	1	2	1
Thomas Wilson Jr,	3	0	7
Gabriel Wilson,	1	0	0
Moses Wilson (s/o James),	1	0	0
Aaron Wilson Sr,	3	0	1
Aaron Wilson Jr,	1	0	1
Thomas Wilson (s/o Aaron),	1	0	1
John Wilson,	1	0	0
Thomas Wilson (s/o Moses),	1	0	3
Daniel Wilson,	1	4	7

Philip Brashears, Jr, was a son of Philip Brashears, Sr, b. 1727, Brashears Meadow, Prince George's Co, MD, d. Henry Co, VA, 1798, oldest son of Robert Cager Brashear and Charity Dowell. Philip Brashears Sr was married to Ann Wilson, daughter of James Wilson, who died in Henry Co, VA, in 1777.

Shortly after 1810, a number of Ann Wilson's brothers moved to south central Kentucky (Wayne, Russell, Pulaski, Montgomery, Bath Counties). Several of the sons of Philip Brashears, Jr, went with this Wilson Clan— Robert, Absalom, Thomas, Zaza, Isaac/ Isaiah. Such close ties would account for different branches of this family using "Wilson" as a given name.

But two other sons of Philip Brashears, Jr— Jesse and Wilson — went down the Tennessee River to Warren Co, TN. Warren County borders Marion County on Marion's northwestern side. Jesse's sons later re-joined his kin folks in Kentucky and Illinois, where some of them had moved about 1830. We do not know where Wilson Beshears' paper track led from Marion Co, TN, but it is likely that he went back to KY to be near his kin folks.

Elizabeth remembered two second cousins, William and Anderson Beshears, of Madisonville, Ralls Co, MO. These were sons of Robert Brashears/Beshears and Elizabeth Whitton, who was a cousin to Wilson Beshears. Philip Brashears Jr (presumed father of Wilson Beshears) was a brother to Robert Brashears, who married (we believe) Patsy Wilson, and was father to Robert Brashears/Beshears (m. Elizabeth Whitton). I have drawn a scheme of this:

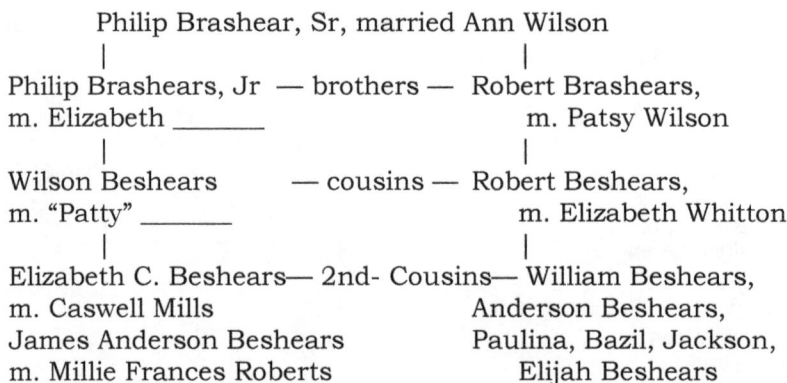

```
              Philip Brashear, Sr, married Ann Wilson
              |                              |
Philip Brashears, Jr  — brothers —   Robert Brashears,
m. Elizabeth _____                        m. Patsy Wilson
              |                              |
Wilson Beshears       — cousins —    Robert Beshears,
m. "Patty" _____                          m. Elizabeth Whitton
              |                              |
Elizabeth C. Beshears— 2nd- Cousins— William Beshears,
m. Caswell Mills                     Anderson Beshears,
James Anderson Beshears              Paulina, Bazil, Jackson,
m. Millie Frances Roberts            Elijah Beshears
```

Let me emphasize, there is no proof of this, only circumstances to suggest it. But it is a scheme, which if proven true, would agree with and validate Elizabeth's affidavit in 1902.

Elizabeth says she and her mother were living in Garrard Co, KY, but visiting cousins in Cumberland County, KY (borders Wayne and Russell Counties) in 1845, when she ran away and married Caswell Mills.

ELIZABETH C. BESHEARS
and CASWELL MILLS

[9]-x. **Elizabeth C. Beshears**, (d/o _____ (Wilson?) Beshears and Patty _____), b. June 1830 (just past 15 at time of marriage), d. Nov-Dec, c1905, possibly Yell Co, AR; m. 10 Oct 1845, probably Clay Co, TN, **Caswell Mills**, b. 1828, d. 3 May 1895, Picton, Hopkins Co, TX. Data from Dolly (Baker) Mills; jmills@3lefties.com

1. Caswell and Elizabeth C. (Beshears) Mills were in Green County, IL, in 1850. (US Census);

2. in 1860, in Harrison County, MO, (US Census);
3. in 1870, in Douglas Co, MO, (US Census and land records);
4. in 1880 in Cedar Co, MO, (US Census);
5. between 1880-1889, in Dade Co, MO, which they left and went into Hopkins Co, TX, where Caswell died 3 May 1895. (Civil War Pension Records).
6. In 1902, Elizabeth was in Yell County, Arkansas. On 27 May 1902, Elizabeth C. Mills applied for a pension on her deceased husband's Civil War service. Elizabeth received a pension and died in Nov or Dec, 1905, probably in Arkansas.

Her deposition contained these facts: her middle initial was "C," which we hadn't known.

7. Elizabeth names one brother, James A. Beshears and his wife Milley Francis. All her [other] brothers are dead, she says, and she has no sisters.
8. She remembers two second cousins, William and Anderson Beshears, of Madisonville [Ralls Co, MO]. (Dolly Mills heard from Linda M. Seevers whose ggggrandfather, Elijah Beshears, was a brother to William and Anderson. In addition there was a sister Pauline and other brothers James W. and Jackson. These were the children of Robert and Elizabeth (Whitton) Beshears.
9.   If these were second cousins of Elizabeth, it seems reasonable to me [Dolly] that Elizabeth and Robert would have been cousins. At that time, I am not certain that they were cousins "once removed" in counting the generations as we do today.)
10. Elizabeth and Caswell ran away and were married somewhere in northern Tennessee (could be Clay County). He was just past 17 and she was 15 as of June, before their marriage on 10 Oct. 1845. She said Caswell Mills lived in Cumberland County, KY, near Albany. (Albany is now in Clinton County, KY), but not far from the line.
11. She mentions that she lived in Garrard County, KY, near what was then known as Old Town.
12. She also said she and her mother, **Patty Beshears**, were visiting cousins in Cumberland County when she met Caswell. The cousins' names (as far as Dolly could make out from the writing— ("you know what trying to read old documents is like") were J--- Asbury, Lindsey Asbury and another name she could not decipher.
13. Elizabeth said "Our home was near Illinois, Sharpsburg, or Madisonville, Garrard Co, KY. I was raised there". She also mentions knowing some folks in Mt. Sterling, [Montgomery Co], KY.
14. Elizabeth mentions "Tom Kennedy my uncle Jim Fletcher near Madisonville or Sharpsburg" (no punctuation, so which one is her

uncle??) She knew these folks.

Elizabeth's sense of geography is very be faulty. Garrard Co, KY, is nowhere near Illinois; it's two counties north of Pulaski Co, which borders both Wayne and Russell Counties, which border Cumberland Co. This is the region where children of Philip Brashears and Ann Wilson lived c1810-1840. Garrard to Cumberland would not be a terrible trip.

The town of Sharpsburg, however is several counties to the northeast from there— in Bath Co, KY. "Second cousin" William Beshears was born in Montgomery Co, KY (borders Bath Co on the southwest) and "second cousin" Anderson Beshears was born in Bourbon Co, KY which borders both Bath and Montgomery Counties on the west. This is the area where Robert Brashear and Elizabeth Whitton lived when their children were born.

Madisonville, KY, is the county seat of Hopkins County, several counties to the west, no where near Garrard County— not likely to be connected to this branch of the family. She may have been thinking of relatives who lived in Sharpsburg, Bath Co, KY, who moved to Madisonville, Ralls Co, MO.

Family of Elizabeth C. Beshears and Caswell Mills: (Thanks to Dolly (Baker) Mills, 949 SR 77, Clovis, NM 88101; 505-762-7807; jmills@3lefties.com for the data)

V9-853. 10-1. Mary Ann Mills, b. 1845, KY; m.1. Napolian Clark, b. 1849, MO; m.2. 2 June 1885, Henry Burleson,

V9-854. 11-1. Elizabeth M. Clark, b. 1866, MO

V9-855. 11-2. John E. Clark, b. 1867, MO

V9-856. 11-3. Rebecca F. Clark, b. 1869, MO

V9-857. 10-2. John Thomas Mills, b. 1848, KY; m. 10 March 1869, Susanna J. Goodnight, b. c1849,

V9-858. 11-1. Millie Frances Mills, b. 6 Jan 1880, Pike Co, MO, d. c1949, at home in Industry, IL; m. 19 Sept 1897, Joseph Henry Alexander, b. 27 April 1875, Scott's Mills, south of Rushville, MO, d. 8 Sept 1958, Jerseyville, IL,

V9-859. 11-2. Terry Mills,

V9-860. 11-3. Charles Mills,

V9-861. 11-4. John Mills,

V9-862. 11-5. Jesse Mills,

V9-863. 10-3. James William Mills, b. 1851, IL; m. Emeline Daniel, b. c1852, MS

V9-864. 11-1. Mary E. Mills, b. c1873, MO

V9-865. 11-2. Ida M. B. Mills, b. c1875, MO

V9-866. 11-3. Hulds L. Mills, b. c1879, MO

V9-867.   10-4. George W. Mills, b. 1853, MO; m. 4 Oct 1890, Sarah _____, b. c1852, MO

V9-868.   11-1. George B. Mills, b. c1873, MO

V9-869.   11-2. Matilda L. Mills, b. c1875, MO

V9-870.   11-3. Nancy C. Mills, b. c1879, MO

V9-871.   10-5. Leonidas L. Mills, b. c1855, MO

V9-872.   10-6. Madison H. Mills, b. c1867/58, MO; m. 9 Dec 1977, Martha E. Marcus, b. c1859

V9-873.   11-1. William R. C. Mills, b. c1879, MO

V9-874.   10-7. Frederic Mills, b. ca. Feb 1860, MO, d. be 1870, MO

V9-875.   10-8. Anderson Prentis Mills, b. 1 March 1862, Douglas, MO, d. 27 Nov 1908, Pindall, Searchy Co, AR; m. 25 July 1878, Cynthia Green, b. 11 July 1858, Webster Co, MO, d. 11 May 1936, Pindall, Searcy Co, AR,

V9-876.   11-1. Benjamin Franklin Mills, b. 30 Jan 1880, Christian Co, MO, d. 8 Sept 1963, Strasburg, Cass Co, MO; m.1. 20 July 1902, Rosa Lea Trammell, b. 15 Aug 1887, Pindall, Searcy Co, AR, d. there, 6 April 1943; m.2. 26 Feb 1947, Essie Philips.

V9-877.   11-2. William Robert Mills, b. 9 Aug 1881, Fordland, Webster Co, MO, d. 13 Feb 1966, Harrison, Boone Co, AR; m. 5 May 1901, Walsie Ellen Battenfield, b. 7 Nov 1886, Pindall, Searcy Co, AR, d. 25 Oct 1964, Harrison, Boone Co, AR

V9-878.   11-3. Vicie E. Mills, b. 17 Feb 1883, Webster Co, MO, d. 22 June 1970, Florida; m. 16 June 1901, William Perry Trammell, b. 4 July 1861, Pindall, Searcy Co, AR, d. 11 Jan 1930, Olathe, Johnson Co, KS,

V9-879.   11-4. Henry Wilson "Dick" Mills, b. Aug 1885, Marshfield, Webster Co, MO, d. 11 March 1957, K.U.Med Center, Johnson Co, KS; m. 1903, Lilly M. Trammell, b. 7 March (?year), Pindall, Searcy Co, AR, d. June 1949, Olathe, Johnson Co, KS

V9-880.   11-5. Johney Jacob "Jake" Mills, b. 16 Sept 1887, Webster Co, MO, d. 27 Oct 1960, Boone Co, AR; m. 1 Jan 1910, Martha Ellen Taylor, b. 14 May 1889, Searcy Co, AR, d. 17 May 1969, Okemah, Okfuskee Co, OK,

V9-881.   11-6. Byrd Francis Mills, b. Sept 1889, Webster Co, MO; m. 15 Nov 1913, Leona Holliday, b. 3 June 1882, d. 2 April 1969, AR

V9-882.   11-7. Bertha Mills, b. Sept 1889, Webster Co, MO

V9-883.   11-8. Harvey Anglish "Harve" Mills, b. 16 Sept 1892, Webster Co, MO, d. 30 Sept1977, Pindall, Searcy Co, AR; m. 13 Feb 1913 (div), Lola Isabell Hoppis, b.

3 Dec 1894,

V9-884.   11-9. Joel Jackson "Jack" Mills, b. 14 Oct 1896, Fordland, Webster Co, MO, d. 27 Oct 1963, Fayetteville, Washington Co, AR; m. 13 Dec 1919, Zora Addie Gary, b. 16 May 1900, Carthage, Jasper Co, MO, d. 25 Aug 1992, AR

V9-885.   10-9. Charles H. Mills, b. 1864, MO

V9-886.   10-10. Albert N. Mills, b. 1867, MO; m. 19 June 1887, M.C. Evans, b. bef 1869

V9-887.   10-11. Lucy Iona Mills, b. Aug 1870, MO; m. Peter E. Hughs, b. c1859

V9-888.   11-1. Charles E. Hughs, b. Aug 1894, TX

V9-889.   11-2. Ina A. Hughs, b. April 1897, TX

V9-890.   11-3. William O. Hughs, b. July 1899, TX

V9-891.   10-12. Caswell Jackson (Magor) Mills, b. Nov 1874, MO

JAMES ANDERSON BESHEARS
and MILLIE FRANCIS ROBERTS

9-y. **James Anderson Beshears**, b. 23 Oct 1835, IN, d. 27 Sept 1883; m.1. *Mary Francis Green*, (no record of children); m.2. 11 March 1863 in Daviess Co, MO (a notation says he lived in Grundy Co, MO at the time), *Millie Frances Roberts*, b. 25 April 1843, MO, d. 5 Aug 1899, per their gravestones in Beshears Cem, west side of Long Creek, Taney Co, MO, which was moved to Bowman's Cem, Stone Co, MO, when Table Rock Dam was constructed. Milly Frances was d/o James E. and Nancy Roberts, according to Paula B. Christiansen <cajunchil@earthlink.net> (Other data from Cynthia (Tinnon) Beshear, wife of Sanford L. Beshear Jr.)

V9-892.   10-1. **Harvey S. Beshear**, b. 1863, bur Catoosa, OK; m. in Boone Co, AR, (Book C, p.109), *Louisa P. Watts*,

V9-893.   10-2. **William "Bill" Riley Beshear**, b. 11 Aug 1864, MO; lived in Henderson Co, TX; d. 31 July 1948, at a Wichita Falls Hospital, Wichita Co, TX, bur Oakwood Cem, Jacksboro, TX, s/o James Anderson Beshear and Millie Frances Robert; m. *Mary Elizabeth Whorton*, b. 6 March 1868, Whorton Creek, Madison Co, AR, d. 5 June 1894, Hollister, MO, d/o Miranda Clinton Whorton and Susan Catherine Bollinger: m.2. *Delilah Purtle*; m.3. *Alice ____*. ...?from his obit: Mr. Beshear was living in Quinton, OK. Survived by two sons, four daughters, 2 sisters, 21 gr-ch and 10 gr-gr-ch:

Family of William Riley Beshear and Mary E. Whorton:

V9-894.   11-1. **George Beshear**,

V9-895.   11-2. **Martha Beshear**, m.1. 9 Oct 1903, *L.P. Logan*, m.2. *William A. Green*, of Spencer, OK

V9-896.   11-3. **Luster Clarence "Buster" Beshear**, b. Oct 1893, Kirbyville, Taney Co, MO, d. May 1960, Winthrop, Little River Co, AR; m. 5 June 1914, N. Miami, OK, *Letha Gladys Felkins*, b. 5 Feb 1897, Joplin, MO, d. 14 April 1974, enroute to a hospital in Dallas, TX.

V9-897.   12-1. **Irvin Cecil Beshear**, b. 4 July 1917, Jopelin, Jasper Co, MO, d. 4 dec 1972, d. 4 Dec 1972. San Francisco, CA; m. 24 Dec 1935, at Winthrop, Little River Co, AR, Alma Copelin, d/o James Larkin Copelin and Alice Audna Alford. They had 4 ch.

V9-898.   12-2. unknown, (next child listed on birth certificate as third in family)

V9-899.   12-3.   **Sanford L. Beshear Sr**, b. 5 July 1921, Blockner, Pittsburg Co, OK (he added the "L" to his name when enlisting in the Army in WWII); m. 25 June 1942, Elco, NV, *Lydia Geraldine Bollinger*, b. 10 April 1922, Carrogordo, Little River Co, AR, d/o Devoe Bollinger and Edna Earle Brasil.

V9-900.   13-x. **Sanford L. Beshear Jr**, b. 23 April 1944, DeQueen, Sevier Co, AR; m. 6 July 1983, Mountain Home, AR, *Cynthia Ann "Cindy" Tinnon*, b. 29 Nov 1942, Vernon, Willbarger Co, TX.

V9-901.   12-4. **Lee Iris Beshear**, b. 10 Feb 1930, Foreman, Little River Co, AR; m. 21 Aug 1948, *James Talley*. 4 ch.

V9-902.   11-4. **Edna Beshear**, m. *Jobe Southard*, of Quinton, OK

V9-903.   11-5. **Esther Beshear**, m. *Charles Southard*, of Chandler, AZ

V9-904.   11-6. **Eva Beshear**, m. _____ *Hicks*,

V9-905.   11-7. **Erma Beshear**, m.1. *Carl Brown*, m.2. *Ted Malone*, of Tulsa, OK

V9-906.   11-8. **Ernest Beshear**, of Jacksboro, OK; m. 12 Nov 1930, *Etta Lou Brown*,

V9-907.   12-1. **Ernest Beshear Jr**,

V9-908.   12-2. **Donald Beshear**,

V9-909.   12-3. **Jerry Beshear**,

V9-910.   12-4. **Sharon Beshear**, m. *Gerald Henry*

V9-911.   11-9. **Elvin Beshear**, d. in his teens.

V9-912.   10-3. **Benjamin "Dick" "Benny Dick" Beshear**, b. 25 Dec 1869, Boone Co, MO, d. 5 June 1934, Pittsburgh, OK, bur Ash Creek Cem, Pittsburgh, OK, as "Dick Beshear," the name the family knew him by. According to Cynthia Tinnon Beshear, listed in one US Census as Bengon D. Beshear, "deformed." Benny Dick m. c1890-92, (according to Ben Chester Beshear and Boone Co, AR, Book D, p.269), *Mary Alice "Allie" Gilbert*, b. 5 July 1873, Taney Co, MO, d. 18 Dec 1961, McAlester, Pittsburgh Co, OK, bur Ash Creek Cem, youngest d/o Moses Gilbert, who was half-indian, and his second wife, Mahala _____ . Moses Gilbert, b. TN, c1820, prob Roane Co, moved to MO c1844, was in Lawrence Co, MO, in 1850 with 1st- wife and several children. First wife d. c1856 and Moses m.2. 1857, Mahala; they had 3 daus. Moses & Mahala in Taney Co, MO, in 1860, until after 1900. Moses bur Omaha, NE. Margaret Jane Gilbert, b. 1862; m. Francis Marion Youngblood, lived in Boone Co, AR (ancestor of Vicki Huffman, who posted this info 25 April 2000 on Beshear GenForum); Martha Gilbert; m. _____ Davis, lived near Pilcher, OK; Mary Alice "Allie" Gilbert, m. Benny Dick Beshear and lived in McAlester, OK. (Data from Gaytha Beshear Wallace <Ajquaid@aol.com> from interview with Ben Chester Beshear, 1978; Arthur Beshear obit; vital stats obtained from headstones at Ashcreek Cemetery, Pittsburgh Co, OK. Note: notice attempt to name children with same beginning letter. Appears to be something of a family tradition!)

V9-913.   11-1. **Aubry Beshear**, b. 1892, d. 1927, Pittsburgh Co, OK, per stone in Ash Creek Cem, Pittsburgh Co, OK

V9-914.   11-2. **Arie Beshear**, b. ?

V9-915.   11-3. **Arney M. Beshear**, b. 31 Aug 1895, d. 21 Feb 1965; m. *Grace* ____, b. 18 Nov 1898, per stone in Ash Creek Cem, Pittsburgh Co, OK

V9-916.   11-4. **Audra Beshear**, b. 1898, d. 1925, per stone in Ash Creek Cem, Pittsburgh Co, OK; m. *Alfred Lee*

V9-917.   12-x. Venie Mae Lee, b. 23 Feb 1919, d. 11 March 1919, d/o Audra Beshear Lee and Alfred Lee

V9-918.   11-5. **Ben Chester Beshear**, b. 12 March 1902 Fairland, OK (born in covered wagon; it is not known if family was moving from AR to OK, or returning to AR from OK, or merely visiting), d. 29 April 1982 McAlester, Pittsburgh Co, OK, bur Oak Hill Cemetery, McAlester, OK; m. *Audie Faye Elizabeth Rodden*.

Ben Chester worked as a coal miner in Pittsburgh Co, OK area.

V9-919. ^{12}-x. **Lillie Faye Beshear**; m. *Homer Leon House*,
V9-920. ^{13}-x. Joyce House; m. _____ Hewitt (Joyceh3036 @aol.com), lives near Sulphur Springs, TX
V9-921. ^{11}-6. **Arthur "Doc" Leon Beshear**, b. 15 March 1905, Rogers, AR, d. 28 May 1974 McAlester, Pittsburgh Co, OK; m. 27 Sept 1924, at Crowder, OK, *Ruby Short*. Arthur worked as a coal miner in Pittsburgh Co, OK area.
V9-922. ^{11}-7. **Elmer Beshear**, b. 9 Aug 1907, Siloam Springs, AR
V9-923. ^{12}-x. **Elmer Beshear, Jr**, b. Krebs, OK
V9-924. ^{13}-x. **Leanne Beshear**, m. _____ *McKnight* (leighannemc@att.net)
V9-925. ^{11}-8. **Alma Beshear**, b. Siloam Springs, AR
V9-926. ^{11}-9. **Roy Beshear**, b. 10 Feb 1910, Siloam Springs, AR, d. Tulare, CA; m. *Ernest* _____. Roy Beshear was the only son to use "s" at the end of Beshear.
V9-927. ^{12}-x. **Troy Cleo Beshear**, b. 3 Oct 1933 (twin), d. 3 Oct 1933, bur Ash Creek Cem
V9-928. ^{12}-y. **Roy Leo Beshear**, b. 3 Oct 1933 (twin), d. 4 Oct 1933, bur Ash Creek Cem
V9-929. ^{11}-10. **Troy Beshear**, b. 8 Jan 1913.
V9-930. ^{11}-11. **Alta Beshear**,
V9-931. ^{10}-4. **Ira B. Beshear**, b. 1870, reported by Gaytha Beshear; no further data
V9-932. ^{10}-5. **Alice Beshear**, b. 25 Aug 1874, d. 12 Sept 1878, "d/o J.A. & M.F." Beshear Cem, Stone Co, MO
V9-933. ^{10}-6. infant **Beshear**, b. 5 Jan 1878, d. 7 Jan 1878, "s/o J.A. & M.F." moved to Bowman's Cem, Stone Co, MO
V9-934. ^{10}-7. **James H. "Jim" Beshear**, b. 1879, living in 1916
V9-935. ^{10}-8. **Richard "Dick" Beshear**,
V9-936. ^{10}-9. **Millie Francis Beshear**, (sister to W.R. Beshear) b. 13 Oct 1881, d. 17 Nov 1969, McAlester, Pittsburg Co, OK; m. *Alexander Wilbur "Dick" Whorton*, of Haywood, OK, brother to wife of William Riley Beshear.
V9-937. ^{11}-x. ch: Oscar, Austin, Alford, Sylvester, Orville, Clifford, Della, Lula, twins Fay and Jay, Beulah, and Ruby Whorton.
V9-938. ^{10}-10. **Thursday (or Tuesday) Beshear**, (fem) b. 1883, Taney Co, MO
V9-939. ^{10}-11. **Etta Beshear**, (sister to W.R. Beshear), b. March 1884; m. _____ *Long*, of Joplin, MO

Other Burials in Ash Creek-Union Baptist Church Cemetery, Ash Creek, Pittsburg Co, OK, recorded by Gaytha Beshear Wallace <Ajquaid@aol.com>, 1978:

Benny Harrison Beshear, b. 25 Oct 1921, d. 21 Jan 1970, OK. PFC Co. C 602 Engr CBT BN WWII

Leon Beshear no dates

Ruby Beshear 12 Sept 1919-31 Oct 1921

Artie Beshear 16 Jan 1939-1 Feb 1939

Geraldene Harris Jan. 1927-1927

Earlene Harris Jan. 1927-1927

George Beshear no dates

Gaytha (Beshear) Wallace <Ajquaid@aol.com>
Date: Thu, 13 Jan 2000 19:29:53 EST

Glancing through the index of your book, I do not find a connection but wonder if you are aware of one. My maiden name was Beshear and my family's known residences go back to Ark., MO, TN, and Kentucky. I was born in Pittsburgh Co., OK, my great uncles were born in ARK while my Great grandfather, Benjamin Beshear, was born in MO. His father, James Anderson Beshear, was born abt 1815 and had lived in an unknown county in TN prior to moving to MO about 1850. James Anderson Beshear married Milly Frances Roberts in 1863 in Daviess Co., Mo but a notation states that he lived in Grundy Co, MO at the time. At the time of James's death, he lived in Taney Co, MO.

Another researcher adds that James Beshear had a brother named Carter, but I do not have supporting documentation to substantiate the family connection. AS a matter of fact, I have no documentation to make any family connections other than the five between me and James Beshear. Do you know of any connections between my Beshear family and the one that you have so extensively researched? Thanks, Gaytha (Beshear) Wallace

Do not confuse this James Anderson Beshears with another James Anderson Beshears, of Hopkins/Christian Co, KY, of the Jeremiah Beshears/Brashears and Elizabeth _____ line of Spartanburg Co, SC.

4. ROBERT BRASHEARS/BESHEARS
and ELIZABETH WHITTEN,
OF PIKE CO, MO

**With Special Thanks to Larry Howser
and Linda Seevers**

$^{v2-}$61. **Robert Brashears/Beshears** (probably s/o $^{v2-}$32, Robert Brashears and? Patsy Wilson), b. 1782, VA, d. 1872, Peno twp, Pike Co, MO; m. c1800, *Elizabeth Whitton*, b. 1781, MD or VA (parents both b. MD), d. 1870, Pike Co, MO.

See 1810 Census of Nelson Co, KY; 1820, 1830 Census of Bath Co, KY; 1840, 1850 Census of Pike Co, MO; 1860, 1870 census of Ralls Co, MO; *History of Audrain Co, MO,* 1884, p.429; *Pioneer Families of Audrain Co, MO,* 1887; *Portrait and Biographical Record of Marion, Ralls, and Pike Co, MO,* 1895.)

While Robert Beshears/Brashears' parents are unknown and unproven, circumstances suggest he is a grandson of Philip Brashears Sr, who died 1798, in Henry Co, VA, and his wife, Ann Wilson. Shortly after Philip's estate was settled in 1807, Ann (Wilson) Brashears moved with her brothers to south-central Kentucky; her sons, Robert and Philip Brashears, and daughter, Nancy, moved there also.

Records in Henry Co, VA

Philip Brashears Sr and his sons, Robert and Philip Jr, are on the Henry Co, Tax Lists 1782-87, as is a William Whitten, possibly Elizabeth's father. Jeremiah, Thomas Sr, and Thomas Jr Whitton are on the Montgomery Co, VA, Tax Lists for the same period, about fifty miles northwest of Henry Co.

These names are harmonious with the last will and testament of a William Whitton, who died two generations earlier in Caroline Co, VA, 1729, naming wife Mary, son George Whitton, dau Anne Davis, and "my six youngest children," Thomas, William, Robert, and Jeremiah Whitton, Mary and Elizabeth Whitton. (*Genealogies of VA Fams*, Copies of Extant Wills from Counties, p.642-3)

The children of Robert Brashears, b. c1759, are undocumented, but circumstances suggest a Philip Brashears, b. c1783, and Absalom

---

Brashears, b. c1786, for they moved with Robert to KY, then to Franklin Co, IL. Robert probably had a son, Robert Jr, b. 1782, who married in Henry Co, VA, before his father and brothers left, but decided to go to Bath Co, KY (which shares a boundary with Montgomery Co, KY, where his son, William Bazwell Brashears, was born), then moved in 1833 to Pike Co, Missouri to seek his fortunes.

This makes it look possible that Robert Beshears/ Brashears, b. 1782, could be a son of v2-32. Robert Brashears, b. c1759, s/o Philip Brashears Sr of Henry Co, VA. Now, all we need is some documentation. That would put Robert Beshears/Brashears in the eighth generation of Brashears in America, and, for want of a better idea, I'm going to start numbering his descendants accordingly.

Robert and Elizabeth are apparently the Robert Brashears family in the 1820 census of Bath Co, KY, p.152, and the Robert Beshears family in the 1830 census, Bath Co, KY, p.198. Later records show that their children were born in this area of KY in this period.

In the 1840 census, Peno twp, Pike Co, MO, p.57, l.24, Robert, J.W., and William B. are listed with the surname, Brashears. Robert and Elizabeth had one male, 20-30 living with them, and one female, [15-]20.

Robert Beshears was age 68 in the 1850 census, Pike Co, MO, and his wife, Elizabeth was 69. Living near them were their married children and their families.

Family of Robert Brashears and Elizabeth Whitton:

V9-940.   9-1. son **Beshears**, b. c1803 ([16-]26 in 1820 census)
V9-941.   9-2. dau **Beshears**, b. 1804
V9-942.   9-3. *Paulina Beshears*, b. 1807, KY (43 in 1850); m. 23 April 1835, in Pike Co, MO, ("by Samuel Lewellyn, JP"; second wife of) *Joseph Keithley Sr*.
V9-943.   9-4. *Elijah Beshears*, b. 1810, KY (40 in 1850); m. *Sarah Long*, b. c1813 (37 in 1850). 8 Children.
V9-944.   9-5. dau **Beshears**, b. 1811
V9-945.   9-6. *James W. Beshears*, b. 1812, KY (35 in 1850), shot on his front porch during the Civil War, 1 Aug 1864, d. 9 Aug 1864, MO; m.1. 18 Oct 1831, Bath Co, KY, *Melinda Wilson*, b. KY, c1812 (38 in 1850) (6 ch); m.2. 13 June 1852, *Clarinda Brown*, b. 13 Feb 1822, d. 2 Feb 1908, bur Barkley Cem, New London, Ralls Co, MO.
V9-946.   9-7. *Judge William Bazwell (Basil) Beshears*, b. 24 Aug 1814, Montgomery Co, KY, d. 17 Sept 1899, MO; m.1. 10 March 1836, Ralls Co, MO (Book A, p.77), *Zephalinda Llewellyn*, b. 18 May 1818, d. 11 Feb 1866, bur Salem Cem, Ralls Co, MO (5 ch in census); m.2. *Mrs. Margaret E. (Rogers) Hutchinson*, a widow.

V9-947. 9-8. **Robert Anderson Beshears**, b. 8 July 1815, Bourbon Co, KY (34 in 1850), d. 10 Dec 1891, Ralls Co, MO (per obit); m. 12 July 1843, Pike Co, MO (Book B, p.94), *Lucretia A. Unsell*, b. c1821, ?Pike Co, MO, d. 1895, both bur Olivet Cem, Center, Ralls Co, MO.

V9-948. 9-9. ***Jackson "John" Beshears**, b. 8 Oct 1818, Bourbon Co, KY, d. 28 June 1882, Ralls Co, MO; m. c1843, *Elizabeth Keithley*, b. 15 Aug 1824, d. 23 May 1903, d/o Joseph Keithly Sr, 2nd husband of Paulina Beshears.

V9-949. 9-10. dau **Beshears**, b. 1820

PAULINA BESHEARS
and JOSEPH KEITHLEY Sr

v2-1883. **Paulina Beshears**, (d/o Robert Brashears and Elizabeth Whitton), b. 1807, KY (43 in 1850); m. 23 April 1835, in Pike Co, MO, ("by Samuel Lewellyn, JP"; second wife of) *Joseph Keithley Sr*, a widower with 11 children, b. 30 April 1786, KY, d. 1852, Pike Co, MO, s/o Jacob Keithly and Barbara Roland. Joseph and Paulina had 6 children.

Note: Joseph Keithley Sr, m.1. Elizabeth Burkett, and had children: 1. Matilda, 2. Eli, 3. Levicy, 4. Delila, 5. Silas, 6. William, 7. *Joseph Jr, 8. *Elizabeth, 9. Sarah "Sally", 10. Pettis, and 11. Irena Keithley.

#7. Joseph Keithley Jr, b. 14 March 1823, d. 9 April 1884; m. 9 Sept 1851, Pike Co, MO, Matilda C. May, b. 22 Sept 1839, d. 12 July 1884, both bur Salem Cem, Ralls Co, MO

x. William E. "Eddie" Keithley, b. c1857; m. 25 Aug 1880, in Spencerburg, Pike Co, MO, **Elizabeth T. "Dixie" Brashear**, b. 8 Aug 1862, d/o James Barton Brashear and Jemima James, gd/o Richard M. Brashear and Emily Leake, ggd/o Barton Brashear of PGCo, MD.

#8. Elizabeth Keithley, b. 15 Aug 1824, d. 23 May 1903; m. **Jackson "John" Beshears**, Paulina's brother. See their family below.

Family of Paulina Brashears and Joseph Keithly Sr: (Ford data from George Teague, 13660 Annandale Dr, Apt 23J, Seal Beach, CA 90740, via Larry Howser)

V9-950. 10-1. Emily Jane Keithley, b. 20 Jan 1836, d. 20 Aug 1864, bur Mount Pleasant Cem, Frankford, Pike Co, MO; m. 27 April 1852, Benjamin Thomas Ford, b. 1838 (or 9 Oct 1833), MO, d. 17 July 1881, s/o Rev. Timothy

Ford of Frankford, MO; gs/o John or Jonathan Ford, b. c1760-65, VA, who moved to KY

V9-951.   11-1. Timothy J. Ford, b. c1852-53, MO

V9-952.   11-2. Renora A. "Nora" Ford, b. 17 April 1855, Pike Co, MO; m. _____ Griffith

V9-953.   11-3. Claudius C. Ford, b. Jan 1857, MO

V9-954.   11-4. Adella B. Ford, b. 1 Dec 1860. MO

V9-955.   11-5. Stephen F. Ford, b. 21 July 1863, MO

V9-956.   11-2. Burt Ford, b. c1865; m. _____,

V9-957.   10-2. Martha A. Keithley, b. 2 March 1838, d. 22 Nov 1879, bur Barkely Cem, New London, Ralls Co, MO; m. 27 March 1855, William Green Hayden, b. 17 Oct 1829, d. 4 Feb 1900. Seven children, all b. Pike Co, MO.

V9-958.   11-1. Woodson Hayden, b. 20 Feb 1856, d. 21 April 1927; m. Louise Virginia Holman, b. 26 Feb 1854

V9-959.   12-1. Claude Hayden, b. 8 Oct 1873, d. 29 Jan 1944

V9-960.   12-2. Mamie Hayden, b. 15 Nov 1875; m. Homer Scott

V9-961.   13-1. Louise Scott,

V9-962.   12-3. Sarah Gertrude Hayden, b. 31 Jan 1877

V9-963.   12-4. Zoron (or Zora) P. Hayden, b. 7 Sept 1879, d. 26 Feb 1926

V9-964.   12-5. Virgil Hayden, b. 2 Oct 1884, d. 24 Jan 1930

V9-965.   12-6. Etta Elizabeth Hayden, b. 24 May 1890, d. 4 Nov 1918

V9-966.   12-7. Joseph Leo Hayden, b. 28 March 1895, d. 27 July 1947; m. Helen _____, b. 1896, MO

V9-967.   12-8. Ruby Davis Hayden, b. 28 April 1895, d. 28 Oct 1976 [???Something is wrong with the dates; Ruby is born 1 month after Joseph.]

V9-968.   11-2. William J. Hayden, b. 31 Jan 1857, d. 4 Sept 1924; m.1. Sarah Ada Hayden, (mother of the children) b. 9 July 1860, d. 30 April 1942; m.2. Alva _____, b. 1860

V9-969.   12-1. Garnet Hayden, b. 12 Nov 1880, d. 10 Dec 1968

V9-970.   12-2. Tuie Hayden, b. Sept 1882

V9-971.   12-3. Mattie Lena Hayden, b. 1887, d. 1967

V9-972.   12-4. Garrett Hayden, b. 22 Oct 1887

V9-973.   12-5. Bryan Hayden, b. 2 Nov 1896, d. March 1983

V9-974.   12-6. George E. Hayden, b. MO

V9-975.   11-3. Emily V. Hayden, b. 1862; m. William R. Matson,

V9-976.   11-4. Ida May Hayden, b. 10 June 1864, d. 10 March 1884; m. Thomas Clark,

V9-977.   11-5. Maggie Belle Hayden, b. 10 Jan 1867, d. 7 April

	1919; m. Andrew Jackson, b. 15 July 1863
V9-978.	12-1. Ada May Jackson, b. 23 Dec 1890
V9-979.	12-2. Lola Belle Jackson, b. 15 Feb 1892
V9-980.	12-3. Horace Green Jackson, b. 6 Jan 1894
V9-981.	12-4. Irl Raymond Jackson, b. 6 Feb 1898

V9-982.   11-6. Marshall Hayden, b. 15 Oct 1868, d. 1936; m. Fannie Ellen Hostetter,

V9-983.   12-1. Gloyd Hayden, b. 28 June 1900, MO, d. 1936

V9-984.   11-7. Mattie Lucy Hayden, b. 1872, d. 1908, Walla Walla, WA

V9-985.   10-3. Lucy W. Keithley, b. 8 Aug 1842, d. 15 May 1868; m. John Steele Ford, b. 1828, d. 1883, both bur Mount Pleasant Cem, Pike Co, MO. John Steele Ford s/o Benjamin Eagleton Ford, I, who was s/o John or Jonathan Ford, b. c1760-65, VA, moved to KY

V9-986.   11-1. Belle Ford,

V9-987.   11-2. Purlina Margaret Ford, b. 1857, d. 1914; m. George Teague, ancestors of George Teague, of Seal Beach, CA, who sent data.

V9-988.   11-3. Emily J. Ford, b. 1858, d. 1933; m. Robert Beasley, b. March 1856, MO

V9-989.   12-1. Minnie B. Beasley, b. Sept 1877

V9-990.   12-2. Owen S. Beasley, b. Feb 1879; m. Opal L. _____, b. 1889, MO,

V9-991.   13-1. Edna J. Beasley, b. 1910

V9-992.   12-3. Jessie L. Beasley, b. May 1881,

V9-993.   12-4. John V. Beasley, b. June 1885; m. Georgia _____, b. 1893, Ind. Terr.

V9-994.   12-5. Thomas Alvie Beasley, b. 13 Oct 1887

V9-995.   11-4. John D. Ford, b. 1860, d. 1936; m. Grace Llewellen, b. _?_, d. 1943

V9-996.   11-5. Mary Ford, b. 1861, d. 1950; m. James G. Hicks,

V9-997.   11-6. Katherine Ford, b. 1864; m. Grand Stidum,

V9-998.   10-4. Mary H. Keithley, b. 1843 (7 in 1850); m. Daniel Boone Ford, b. 1830, MO, s/o Rev. Timothy Ford of Frankford, MO; gs/o John or Jonathan Ford, b. c1760-65, VA, who moved to KY

V9-999.   11-1. William "Willie" A. Ford, b. 1858

V9-1000.   11-2. Laura Ford, m. Edward Torley, lived Frankford, MO

V9-1001.   11-3. Ida May Ford, b. 1865, lived Frankford, MO

V9-1002.   11-4. Nancy Ford, b. 1866 (1880 census, Peno, Pike Co, MO)

V9-1003.   11-5. Roy Ford, lived Burlington, IA

V9-1004.   11-6. Ella R. Ford, b. 1870, lived St. Louis, MO

V9-1005.   11-7. Emma Netta Ford, b. 1872, lived Sacramento, CA

V9-1006.   11-8. Thomas Ray Ford, b. 1880 lived Kansas City
V9-1007.   10-5. Margaret Paulina Keithley, b. 1845, d. 1920, bur. Fairview Cem, Frankford, Pike Co, MO; m.1. Robert T. McIntosh, m.2. William T. Bonham,
V9-1008.   11-1. William B. Bonham, b. 1865, MO
V9-1009.   11-2. M. Bonham, b. 1870, MO
V9-1010.   10-6. John Keithley, b. 1848, d. 1944, bur Fairview Cem, Pike Co, MO; m. Sarah L. Keithley, b. 1855, MO
V9-1011.   11-1. Charles W. Keithley, b. 1876, MO

ELIJAH BESHEARS
and SARAH LONG

v2-1884. 9-4. Elijah Beshears (s/o Robert Brashears and Elizabeth Whitton), b. 8 May 1812 in KY, d. 5 April 1886 in Mt. Vernon, Lawrence County, MO; m. c1830, **Sarah Long**, b. 1 Feb 1813 in KY, d. 30 May 1890 in Mt. Vernon, Lawrence County, MO. Both are buried in the Goss Cemetery. Thanks to Linda Seevers for research and data.

In 1850, they lived in Peno twp, Pike Co, MO
In 1870, they lived in Prairie twp, Montgomery Co, MO
In 1880, they lived in Mt. Vernon, Lawrence Co, MO

Family of Elijah Beshears and Sarah Long:
V9-1012.   10-1. *Nancy Beshears*, b. 1834 in KY; m. 10 Aug 1856 in Pike Co, MO, **Bryant Silvey**,
V9-1013.   10-2. **Elizabeth Beshears**, b. 1832 in KY; m. 17 Sept 1856 in Ralls Co, MO, **William Hostetter**, b. 1835 in MO, d. 1860 in MO. They are in the 1850 and 1860 U.S. Censuses, of Peno, Pikd Co, MO;
V9-1014.   11-1. Harry Hostetter, b. 1853 in MO.
V9-1015.   11-2. William Hostetter, b. 1855 in MO.
V9-1016.   11-3. James E. Hostetter, b. 1860 in MO.
V9-1017.   10-3. **Caroline Beshears**, b. 1836 in KY; m. 9 Sept 1859 in Pike Co, MO, **John Weber**, b. c1829 in Pennsylvania.
V9-1018.   11-1. Susan Weber, b. 1860 in MO.
V9-1019.   10-4. *Robert T. Beshears*, b. 3 Nov 1842 in MO; d. 7 Dec 1914 in MO; m. 5 April 1860 in MO, **Mary Ann Allison**,
V9-1020.   10-5. **Johanna F. Beshears**, b. 1843 in KY; m. **Sterling Laws**.
V9-1021.   11-1. _____ Laws, b. 14 Sept 1884 in Mr. Vernon, Lawrence Co, MO.
V9-1022.   10-6. **James N. Beshears**, b. 1846 in KY.
V9-1023.   10-7. **Susan G. Beshears**, b. 1846 in KY; m. **Dranis A.**

McDannold, 13 Jan 1867 in Pike Co, MO; born c1842 in KY.

V9-1024.   10-8. **Martha C. Beshears**, b. 1848 in KY.

V9-1025.   10-9. **Mary A. Beshears**, b. 1858 in MO; d. 1945 in Aurora, Lawrence Co, MO; m. **James Monroe Allison,** b. 1850 in MO, d. 1914 in Aurora, Lawrence Co, MO, s/o Elsey Allison and Lucinda Poe. 1870 U.S. Census, Prairie, Montgomery Co, MO. Note: Maggie and Lottie are both adopted.

V9-1026.   11-1. Maggie Adams Allison, d. in Aurora, Lawrence Co, MO; m. Champ Phillips, d. in Aurora, Lawrence Co, MO.

V9-1027.   11-2. Lottie Ann Patterson Allison, b. 1886; d. 1976; m. Ernest McClain, b. 1884, d. 1951.

V9-1028.   12-1. Blaine L. McClain, b. 1911 in Aurora, Lawrence Co, MO; d. there 1913

V9-1029.   12-2. Mildred McClain, b.&d. 1914 in Aurora, Lawrence Co, MO

V9-1030.   12-3. Raymond McClain, b.&d. 1920 in Aurora, Lawrence Co, MO

V9-1031.   12-4. Raygene McClain, b.&d. 1926 in Aurora, Lawrence Co, MO

V9-1032.   12-5. Jesse McClain.

V9-1033.   12-6. Helen McClain.

V9-1034.   12-7. Delbert McClain.

V9-1035.   12-8. Chester McClain.

Nancy Beshears and Bryant Silvey

10-1. **Nancy Beshears** (d/o Elijah Beshears and Sarah Long) was born 1834 in KY; m. 10 Aug 1856 in Pike Co, MO, **Bryant Silvey**, b. 1830 in KY, d. bet. 1870 - 1880 in MO. The family is in the 1860, U.S. Census, Salt River, Pike Co, MO; the 1870 and 1880 U.S. Census, Peno, Pike Co, MO

V9-1036.   11-1. Samuel Louis Silvey, b. 30 May 1855 in Frankfort, Franklin Co, Kentucky; d. 17 Feb 1923 in Bowling Green, Pike Co, MO.

V9-1037.   11-2. Sarah E. Silvey, b. 1857 in MO.

V9-1038.   11-3. Margaret A. Silvey, b. 1858 in MO; m. George McCoun. b. 1847 in MO. Living with Jane Pitzer, 58, widow- 1880 U.S. Census, Calumet, Pike Co, MO.

V9-1039.   12-1. Robert McCoun, b. 1879 in MO.

V9-1040.   11-4. James H. Silvey, b. 1862 in MO.

V9-1041.   11-5. Susan E. Silvey, b. 1864 in MO.

V9-1042.   11-6. Loudustie Silvey, b. 1866 in MO.

V9-1043.   11-7. William E. Silvey, b. Feb 1870 in MO.

Robert T. Beshears and Mary Ann Allison

[10]-4. **Robert T. Beshears** (s/o Elijah Beshears and Sarah Long), b. 3 Nov 1842 in MO, d. 7 Dec 1914 in MO, bur Frankford, Pike Co, MO; m. 5 April 1860 in MO, *Mary Ann Allison*, b. 30 Jan 1834 in MO, d. 30 April 1891 in MO, d/o Elsey Allison and Lucinda Poe. They are in the 1880 U.S. Census, Peno, Pike Co, MO;

Children of Robert T. Beshears and Mary Ann Allison:
[V9]-1044.	[11]-1. **Sarah Beshears**, b. 1864.
[V9]-1045.	[11]-2. **Agnes Beshears**, b. 1866.
[V9]-1046.	[11]-3. **Dulcemia Beshears**, b. 1868 in MO.
[V9]-1047.	[11]-4. **Katherine Beshears**, b. 1870 in MO; m. 1900, _____ *Elder*, b. c1870 in Pike Co, MO.
[V9]-1048.	[11]-5. ***William Elze Beshears**, b. 4 Feb 1872 in MO; d. 29 March 1938 in MO.
[V9]-1049.	[11]-6. **James Beshears**, b. 1874 in Pike County, MO.
[V9]-1050.	[11]-7. **Loucinda Beshears**, b. 1879 in MO; m. **George Bradford** 1900. 1880 U.S. Census, Peno, Pike Co, MO
[V9]-1051.	[12]-1. Unk Son Bradford.

William Elze Beshears and Julia Delia Arendt

[11]-5. **William Elze Beshears** (s/o Robert T. Beshears and Mary Ann Allison), b. 4 Feb 1872 in MO, d. 29 March 1938 in MO; m. 11 Nov 1891 in MO (Source: Marriage License; State of MO, County of Pike, License to solomnize marriage between William E. Beshears and Julie Arendt, by Justice of Peace L. A. Donovue on the 11th day of November 1891), **Julia Delia Arendt**, b. 25 April 1872 in MO, d. 4 June 1950 in MO, d/o Peter Arendt and Alcestes McHatton. William and Julia both bur Frankford, Pike Co, MO. 1880 U.S. Census, Peno, Pike Co, MO. 1910 U.S. Census, Spencer Twp, Ralls Co, MO; 1930 U.S. Census, Hannibal, Marion Co, MO.

Children of William Elze Beshears and Julia Delia Arendt:
[V9]-1052.	[12]-1. ***Dora Lee Beshears**, b. 4 March 1892 in Frankford, Pike Co, MO; m. *Joe W. Epperson*,
[V9]-1053.	[12]-2. **Leroy Beshears**, b. Aug 1893 in Frankford, Pike Co, MO; d. in MO.
[V9]-1054.	[12]-3. ***Reuben Alfred Beshears**, b. 21 Aug 1895 in Ashburn, MO; d. 1 May 1934 in Frankford, Pike Co, MO.
[V9]-1055.	[12]-4. **Mollie Beshears**, b. 1896 in Frankford, Pike Co, MO; d. 1918 in St. Louis, MO; m. **Halley M. Gregory**, b. 1896 in MO, d. in MO.
[V9]-1056.	[13]-1. Halley Gregory, b. April 1917 in St. Louis, MO.

V9-1057.   12-5. **Nora Perditta Beshears**, b. 5 Feb 1900 in Frankford, Pike Co, MO; d. 10 Dec 1980 in Edwardsville, Wyandotte Co, KS.

V9-1058.   12-6. **Ruby Beshears**, b. 1901 in Frankford, Pike Co, MO; m. Bert Epperson,

V9-1059.   12-7. **Mattie Beshears**, b. 18 Feb 1902 in Frankford, Pike Co, MO; d. Nov 1986 in MO; m. 24 Dec 1916 in MO, **Roy Epperson**, b. 1 March 1895 near New London, MO (Source: Obituary), d. 19 July 1968 in Frankford, MO, s/o Anthony Epperson and Polly Sinklear. 1920, 1930 U.S. Census, Spencer, Ralls Co, MO,

V9-1060.   13-1. James Epperson, b. 1919
V9-1061.   13-2. Eugene Epperson, b. 1929
V9-1062.   13-3. William Epperson.
V9-1063.   13-4. Richard Lee Epperson.
V9-1064.   13-5. Franklin Epperson.
V9-1065.   13-6. Robert Epperson.

V9-1066.   12-8. **Robert Arendt Beshears**, b. 1904 in MO; d. 15 Sept 1979 in MO, bur Grand View Cemetery, Hannibal, Marion Co, MO; 1930 U.S. Census, Hannibal, Marion Co, MO

V9-1067.   12-9. **Martha Beshears**, b. 1906 in Frankford, Pike Co, MO; m. _____ *Epperson.*

V9-1068.   12-10. **Raymond C. Beshears, Sr**, b. 31 March 1908 in MO; d. 25 Dec 2001 in New London, Ralls, MO, bur Grand View Burial Park, Hannibal, Marion Co, MO; m. 31 Dec 1954 in Kansas City, KS, **Betty Cutburth**.

V9-1069.   13-1. **Raymond C. Beshears, Jr**. b. 15 April 1957.

V9-1070.   12-11. **Rexie Coulter Beshears**, b. 22 Sept 1910 in Frankford, Pike Co, Mo; d. Sept 1976 in Bucklin, Linn Co, MO. 1930 U.S. Census, Hannibal, Marion Co, MO

V9-1071.   12-12. **Maggie D. Beshears**, b. 12 Feb 1915 in Frankford, Pike Co, MO; d. 13 Aug 1981 in MO, bur Fairview Cemetery, Frankford, Pike Co, MO; m.1. *Elmer Ellis, Sr*, b. in MO; m.2. 12 Aug 1954 in Frankford, Pike Co, MO, *Olie Pritchett*, b. 12 Aug 1889, d. 28 Sept 1998 in Hannibal, Marion Co, MO, s/o Claude Pritchett and Daisey Campbell. 1930 U.S. Census, Hannibal, Marion Co, MO. In a 1950 obit, Maggie was listed as Mrs. Maggie Bogue.

V9-1072.   13-1. Elmer S. Ellis, Jr; m. Robin A. _____.
V9-1073.   14-1. Susan Ellis; m. _____ Pickerton.
V9-1074.   14-2. Greg Ellis, b. in MO.

Dora Lee Beshears and Joe W. Epperson

¹²⁻1. **Dora Lee Beshears**, (d/o William Elze Beshears and Julia Delia Arendt), b. 4 March 1892 in Frankford, Pike Co, MO, d. 7 April 1976 in New London, MO; m. 1912 in MO, *Joe W. Epperson*, b. 27 Nov 1884 in MO, d. 17 Dec 1946 in New London, MO, s/o Anthony Epperson and Polly Sinklear. Both bur Barkley Cemetery, New London, MO; 1930, U.S. Census, Spencer, Ralls Co, MO,

Family of Dora Lee Beshears and Joe W. Epperson:

^{V9-}1075. ¹³⁻1. Garnett Lee Epperson, b. 18 May 1910 in Frankford, MO; d. 22 Nov 2000 in New London, MO; m. William Everett Gordon, 30 June 1928 in Hannibal, Marion Co, MO.

^{V9-}1076. ¹⁴⁻1. Everett L. Gordon; m. Margaret _____.

^{V9-}1077. ¹⁵⁻1. Jane Gordon; m. Eddie Glover,

^{V9-}1078. ¹⁵⁻2. Johnny Gordon,

^{V9-}1079. ¹⁴⁻2. JoAnn Gordon; m. Raymond Briscoe; d. Bef. 2000.

^{V9-}1080. ¹⁵⁻1. Jerry Briscoe,

^{V9-}1081. ¹⁵⁻2. David Briscoe,

^{V9-}1082. ¹³⁻2. William Edward "Huck" Epperson, b. 8 June 1912 in MO; d. 16 Dec 1990 in MO, bur Barkley Cemetary, New London, MO. Huck Epperson was blind, according to Cousin Booney Miller (descendant of Rueben Beshears), who used to mow his lawn. He was also an avid Citizen Band operator and talked with family and friends for hours.

Reuben Alfred Beshears and Zoleta Dailey

¹²⁻3. **Reuben Alfred Beshears** (s/o William Elze Beshears and Julia Delia Arendt), b. 21 Aug 1895 in Ashburn, MO, d. 1 May 1934 and bur in Frankford, Pike Co, MO; m. **Zoleta Dailey**. He and his family are listed as BESHERS in the 1930 US Census, Saverton, Ralls Co, MO.

Family of Rueben Alfred Beshears and Zoleta Dailey:

^{V9-}1083. ¹³⁻1. **Lula Dee Beshears**, b. 19 Dec 1919; d. 1987 in Hannibal, Marion Co, MO, bur Grandview Burial Park, Hannibal, MO; m.1. *George Elliott* (no ch). She partnered with (2) *Owen Cravens*, b. 5 June 1898, d. 20 May 1980 in Hannibal, Marion Co, MO, bur Grandview Burial Park, Hannibal, MO. 1930 US Census, Saverton, Ralls Co, MO,

^{V9-}1084. ¹⁴⁻1. **Mildred Beshears**; m. *Gene Wheeler*.

^{V9-}1085. ¹⁵⁻1. Donna Wheeler, m. Mike Deatch,

^{V9-}1086. ¹⁶⁻1. Dawn Deatch,

V9-1087.	[16]-2. Bradley Deatch,
V9-1088.	[15]-2. Vernon Wheeler,
V9-1089.	[15]-3. Ellie May Wheeler,
V9-1090.	[15]-4. Johnny Wheeler,
V9-1091.	[15]-5. Darrell Wheeler,
V9-1092.	[15]-6. Patricia Wheeler,
V9-1093.	[14]-2. **Myrtle Beshears**; m.1. *William D. Miller, Jr*, m.2. *Roman Kamrowski*,
V9-1094.	[15]-1. James Miller; m. Barbara _____
V9-1095.	[16]-1. Jennifer Miller,
V9-1096.	[16]-2. James Miller,
V9-1097.	[15]-2. Owen "Booney" Miller; m. Mary Ellen Dotson,
V9-1098.	[16]-1. Brandon D. Miller; m. Jessica Light,
V9-1099.	[16]-2. Bryan J. Miller,
V9-1100.	[16]-3. Laura L. Miller,
V9-1101.	[16]-4. Paige D. Miller,
V9-1102.	[16]-5. William R. Miller,
V9-1103.	[15]-3. William D. Miller, b. 28 Aug 1964, d. 30 July 1997
V9-1104.	[15]-4. Donold Kamrowski; m.1. Kelly _____ (1 ch); m.2. Phylis Fogal (1 ch)
V9-1105.	[16]-1. Kimberly Kamrowski,
V9-1106.	[16]-2. Tyler Kamrowski,
V9-1107.	[15]-5. Anthony Kamrowski; m. Carrie _____
V9-1108.	[16]-1. Madison Kamrowski,
V9-1109.	[16]-2. Johnathon Kamrowski,
V9-1110.	[15]-6. Robert Kamrowski; m. Vanessa Turnbough
V9-1111.	[16]-1. Jacob Kamrowski,
V9-1112.	[16]-2. Breanna Kamrowski,
V9-1113.	[15]-7. Michael Kamrowski, b. 7 Aug 1978, Hannibal, Marion Co, MO, d. 24 July 2000; m. Patricia Walkley,
V9-1114.	[16]-1. Michael David Kamrowski, II
V9-1115.	[15]-8. Myrtle Kamrowski; m. Jerry Dotson,
V9-1116.	[16]-1. Cody Dotson,
V9-1117.	[16]-2. Shanna Dotson,
V9-1118.	[13]-2. **Bertha L. Beshears**, b. 1922; m. 7 Nov 1934. **George L. Elledge**, b. 7 Feb 1909 in Hannibal, MO, d. 7 Dec 1983 in Columbia. They were in the 1930 U.S. Census, Saverton, Ralls Co, MO
V9-1119.	[14]-1. Sandra Elledge.
V9-1120.	[14]-2. Millie Elledge.
V9-1121.	[14]-3. Betty Elledge.
V9-1122.	[14]-4. Jackie Elledge.
V9-1123.	[14]-5. John Elledge.

V9-1124.   14-6. George Elledge, Jr
V9-1125.   13-3. **Lucille E. Beshears**, b. 19 April 1923 in MO; d. 28 Jan 2000 in St. Joseph Health Center in St. Charles, MO, bur Grandview Burial Park, Hannibal, MO; m.1. _____ *Smith*; m.2. 15 March 1951 in Hannibal, Marion Co, MO, *Noel Shonhart*, d. 22 Sept 1981. 1930 U.S. Census, Saverton, Ralls Co, MO,
V9-1126.   14-1. Harry Smith.
V9-1127.   14-1. Infant Shonhart.
V9-1128.   14-2. Infant Shonhart.
V9-1129.   13-4. **Billy Joe Beshears**, b. 28 April 1927 in Frankford, MO; d. 8 Jan 2004 in Pike County Memorial Hospital in Louisiana, MO; m.1. *Carrie Mae Coleman* (2 ch; divorced 1979); m.2. 5 April 1982 in New London, MO, *Shirley Wagner* (3 ch). 1930 U.S. Census, Saverton, Ralls Co, MO,
V9-1130.   14-1. **Billie Ray Beshears**.
V9-1131.   14-2. **David Beshears**.
V9-1132.   14-1. **Billie Joe Beshears, Jr**, b. 19 Jan 1982; d. 5 Dec 2003 in Pike Co, MO.
V9-1133.   14-2. **Katie D. Beshears**.
V9-1134.   14-3. **Marita M. Beshears**.
V9-1135.   13-5. **Robert Archie Beshears**, b. 24 Nov 1931 in New London, MO; d. 15 June 2003 in ER of Hannibal Regional Hospital, bur Grandview Burial Park, Hannibal, MO; m.1. *Darlene Stull* (no ch); m.2. 16 Aug 1997, *Grace Pursifull.*
V9-1136.   14-1. **Robin Beshears**; m. _____ *Thomas*. Residence: June 2003, Las Vegas, NV from obit of Robert Archie Beshears
V9-1137.   14-2. **Hazil Beshears**; m. _____ *Purvis*. Residence: June 2003, Greensboro, KY from obit for Robert Archie Beshears
V9-1138.   13-6. **George R. Beshears**, b. Jan 1934 in MO; m. *Martha* _____. Residence: June 2003, Bucyrus, MO from obit for Robert Archie Beshears
V9-1139.   14-1. **April Beshears**.

Nora Perditta Beshears and William Melvin Roberts

12-5. **Nora Perditta Beshears** (d/o William Elze Beshears and Julia Delia Arendt), b. 5 Feb 1900 in Frankford, Pike Co, MO, d. 10 Dec 1980 in Edwardsville, Wyandotte, KS; m. c1918 in MO, *William Melvin Roberts*, b. 22 March 1886 in Moberly, Randolph Co, MO, d. 4 July 1950 in Kansas City, Wyandotte, KS, s/o Andrew Roberts and Georgia Slaughter. 1930 U.S. Census, Kansas City, Wyandotte Co,

Kansas

Linda Seevers found this article in her grandmother's Bible. There were no dates on the article, but it has to be prior to 1950.

Worker Injured in Fight

A.A. Burgard Says Another Lineman
Struck Him With Crowbar.

Al A. Burgard, 1508 Tauromee Avenue, Kansas City, Kansas, a lineman for the municipal light department of Kansas City, Kansas, suffered severe head injuries late yesterday when he was struck with a crowbar by a fellow worker at Forty-second Avenue and Metropolitan Boulevard. He was taken to Providence Hospital where his condition was said to be not dangerous. Burgard told the police his assailant was *Melvin Roberts*, 50 North Tenth Street, a lineman's helper.

Children of Nora Perditta Beshears and William Melvin Roberts:

V9-1140. 13-1. Georgia Ruth Roberts, b. 1 Dec 1919 in MO; d. 15 July 1989 in KS; m. William Ernest Sells 27 May 1938. 1930 U.S. Census, Kansas City, Wyandotte Co, Kansas

V9-1141. 14-1. William Ernest Sells, Jr, b. 6 April 1936.

V9-1142. 13-2. William Charles Roberts, b. 22 Feb 1921 in Frankford, Pike Co, MO; d. 1 Sept 1987 in Clinton, MO, bur Englewood Cem, Clinton, Henry Co, MO; m. 1940, Hazel Lorraine Smith, b. 14 March 1926.

V9-1143. 14-1. Caroline Jean Roberts, b. 17 Jan 1943.

V9-1144. 14-2. Nancy Ruth Roberts, b. 29 Sept 1944.

V9-1145. 14-3. Charles Melvin Roberts, b. 8 Feb 1952.

V9-1146. 14-4. Nora Lee Roberts, b. 27 Feb 1956.

V9-1147. 13-3. Frank Aubrey Roberts, b. 5 July 1922 in MO; m. 1940, Vera May Thayer, b. 21 May 1920.

V9-1148. 14-1. Frank Andrew Roberts, b. 4 Dec 1949.

V9-1149. 13-4. Richard Roberts, b. 8 May 1924 in Quincy, Adams Co, IL; d. 12 Aug 1993 in Independence, Jackson, MO , bur Park Lawn Cem, Kansas City, Jackson Co, MO; m.1. 24 Oct 1947 in Jackson Co, MO, Georgia Marie Michaud (2 ch), b. 9 March 1928 in Kansas City, Jackson Co, MO, d/o Philip Michaud and Josephine Paul; m.2. 1952 in Kansas City, Jackson Co, MO, Alma Marie Jones (1 ch), b. 10 April 1922 in Kansas City, Jackson Co, MO, d. 17 Feb 2001 in Independence, Jackson, Jackson Co, MO. 1930 U.S. Census, Kansas City, Wyandotte Co, Kansas.

V9-1150. 14-1. Linda Margaret Roberts, b. 24 Dec 1949 in Kansas City, Jackson Co, MO; m. 26 June 1970 in Kansas City, Jackson Co, MO, Charles Newton Seevers, II, b. 17 Feb 1951 in Independence, Jackson Co, MO.

Linda Margaret Roberts: Graduation: 1997, Messenger College, BA in Biblical Studies. Linda Seevers is a researcher in this branch of the family.

V9-1151.   15-1. Charles Thomas Seevers, b. 29 Dec 1973, Oakland, CA; m. Yvette Marie Lewis, b. 23 Feb 1976

V9-1152.   16-1. Tanner Ryan Seevers, b. 27 Dec 1995
V9-1153.   16-2. Jaden Thomas Seevers, b. 15 Nov 2000
V9-1154.   15-2. Joylynn Rose Seevers, b. 20 Jan 1975, Oakland, CA; m. David Lee Parkman, b. 7 Sept 1973

V9-1155.   16-1. Ian Geoffrey Parkman, b. 9 Nov 2000, Joplin, Jasper Co, MO.

V9-1156.   14-2. Richard Lee Roberts, b. 13 May 1951 in Kansas City, Jackson Co, MO; m.1. 27 March 1971, Dinah Shain, (3 ch) b. 25 Feb 1953; m.2. Alma Marie Jones, b. 10 April 1922, Kansas City, Jackson Co, MO, d. 17 Feb 2001, Independence, MO. Richard L. Roberts: Grad: 1999, DeVry Inst of Technology, BS in Telecommunications.

V9-1157.   15-1. Julie Lynette Roberts, b. 4 April 1973; m. Jeff Eakright, b. 10 Dec 1973

V9-1158.   16-1. Victoria Nicole Eakright, b. 5 July 1994
V9-1159.   16-2. Logan Steven Eakright, b. 30 June 1995
V9-1160.   16-3. Alexander Blake Eakright, b. 24 March 1997

V9-1161.   15-2. Richard Lee Roberts, Jr, b. 1 Oct 1976; m. Carrie Leigh Steppe, b. 10 Dec 1981, St Joseph, Buchanan Co, MO

V9-1162.   16-1. Emilee Cheyenne Roberts, b. 4 Sept 2003
V9-1163.   15-3. Daniel Jerod Roberts, b. 13 Aug 1979; m. Jessica Marie Weimholt, b. 22 Aug 1979

V9-1164.   14-3. Nellie Marie Roberts, b. 1952; m.1. Dale Carlson; m.2. Douglas Edwards.

V9-1165.   15-1. Charity Carlson,
V9-1166.   15-2. Angela Edwards,

JAMES W. BESHEARS
and MELINDA WILSON/ CLARINDA BROWN

[v2-]1886. **James W. Beshears**, (s/o Robert Brashears and Elizabeth Whitton), b. 1812, KY (35 in 1850), shot on his front porch, 1 Aug 1864, d. 9 Aug 1864, bur Spencersburg Cem, Pike Co, MO; m.1. 18 Oct 1831, Bath Co, KY, *Melinda Wilson*, b. KY, c1812 (38 in 1850) (6 ch); m.2. 13 June 1852, *Clarinda Brown*, b. 13 Feb 1822, Spencersburg, MO, d. 2 Feb 1908, bur Barkley Cem, New London, Ralls Co, MO, d/o William Brown.

James W. Beshears and wife, Clarinda, and three children: James C. 18, William H. 13, and Martha E. 7, are #374-368, 1860 census, Spencer twp, Ralls Co, MO.

"On Sunday evening, 1 Aug 1864, Mr. Beshears was sitting on the porch reading his paper. A folded bed comfort was over the bannister in front of him. Others on the porch were William W. Beatty, Hunt Coleman, and one of the Pierces. Negroes were visiting in the back yard. Suddenly, a gun was fired from the opposite hillside, the blue cloud of smoke was seen. Mr. Beshears clapped his hand to his side, rose from his chair and walked inside to say, "Wife, I am shot." When he took off his boot, a large minie ball rolled out. It had passed through the comfort, hit his watch and driven particles of it into Beshears' side, severing the intestines, Doctors Barkley and Bartlett were summoned and rendered all the possible aid until he died nine days later. It was war time and there was much personal bitterness in the community. Detectives were hired, but no clue was found, and no one was arrested." *Ralls County Missouri*, by Goldena Roland Howard, 1980.

Family of James W. Beshears and Melinda Wilson: all b. MO:
[V9-]1167.   [10-]1. **John W. Beshears**, b. MO, c1834 (16 in 1850; 26 in 1860); m. 16 Nov 1854, *Elvira J. Llewellen*, b. c1834 (26 in 1860), d. 6 March 1876, aged 42, bur Old Hostetter Family Graveyard, Ralls Co, MO. They are #376-370 in 1860 census, Spencer twp, Ralls Co, MO, with two children, right next door to his father.

[V9-]1168.   [11-]1. **Alice Beshears**, b. c1856 (4 in 1860)
[V9-]1169.   [11-]2. **Reid W. Beshears**, b. c1860 (1/12 in 1860), d. 5 Sept 1876
[V9-]1170.   [11-](?) ??**Eugene Beshears**, "s/o JJ and Elvira Beshears," d. 5 Sept 1875, age 15 yrs, 5 mos, 15 days, [i.e. b. 16 March 1860] bur Barkely Cem, New London, Ralls Co, MO. [I believe Reid and Eugene are the

same person.]

V9-1171.   ¹¹⁻3. **James J. Beshears**, b. 1865, Frankford, Pike Co, MO, d. 1914; m. *Birdie Beshears*, b. 1872, d. 1960

V9-1172.   ¹²⁻1. **Eura May Beshears**, b. 1907, Pike Co, MO

V9-1173.   ¹⁰⁻2. **Julia A. Beshears**, b. c1836, MO (14 in 1850)

V9-1174.   ¹⁰⁻3. ***Joel Marion Beshears**, (a.k.a. Joseph Marion Beshears) b. c1838, MO (12 in 1850); m. *Elizabeth Givens Gray*, b. 1849.

V9-1175.   ¹⁰⁻4. **Mary E. Beshears**, b. c1841 (9 in 1850); m. *Sidney Pritchett*, b. 1833, MO

V9-1176.   ¹¹⁻1. Emily Pritchett, b. 1859; m. _____ Hostetter

V9-1177.   ¹¹⁻2. Clarinda Pritchett, b. 1862; m. _____ Hostetter

V9-1178.   ¹¹⁻3. William Pritichett, b. 1864

V9-1179.   ¹¹⁻4. Harvey Pritchett, b. 1866

V9-1180.   ¹¹⁻5. Ada Pritchett, b. 1868

V9-1181.   ¹¹⁻6. Mattie Pritchett, b. 1870

V9-1182.   ¹¹⁻7. Edward Pritchett, b. 1873

V9-1183.   ¹¹⁻8. Jessie Pritchett, b. 1874

V9-1184.   ¹⁰⁻5. **James C. Beshears**, b. c1843, Spencer, Ralls Co, MO (7 in 1850; 18 in 1860)

V9-1185.   ¹⁰⁻6. **William H. Beshears**, b. c1847 (3 in 1850; 13 in 1860); m. 29 Dec 1874, *Louisa Raymond*,

Child of James W. Beshears and Clarinda Brown:

V9-1186.   ¹⁰⁻7. **Martha E. "Mattie" Beshears**, b. 29 March 1853, Spencer, Ralls Co, MO, d. 12 Aug 1870, bur Spencersburg Cem, Pike Co, MO; m. *Samuel R. Caldwell*, b. MO.

Joel Marion Beshears and Elizabeth Givens Gray

V2-1928. ¹⁰⁻3. **Joel Marion Beshears**, (aka Joseph Marion Beshears, s/o James W. Brashears and Melinda Wilson), b. 8 June 1837, Pike Co, MO, d. 21 Jan 1890, Vandalia, Audrain Co, MO; m. 13 Dec 1865, in Pike Co, MO (Pike Co Marriages, v.3, p.3), *Elizabeth Givens Gray*, b. 7 June 1840 (2 June says her stone), Cynthiana, Harrison Co, Kentucky, d. May 23, 1898, Vandalia, Audrain Co, MO; d/o Samuel Riley Gray, who was a Kentucky Confederate Volunteer in the Civil War, and Elizabeth Crawford Givens. (Thanks to Maureen Beshears Morisano, of Staten Island, NY, for all of this research.)

Joel/Joseph/"James" seems to have used a number of variations of his name during his lifetime, which makes it a bit difficult to follow him in the records. See his obituary below, in which the writer invites "Christian charity" in assessing his faults, yet credits him with social progress in the town.

In the 1870 Census of Peno twp, Pike Co, MO, Joel M. Beshears is a Grocer, 33 years old. Elizabeth is 29, and their first child, Ella, is 2.

In the 1880 Census of Cuivre twp, Audrain Co, MO, "James"

Brashear is 45; wife, Lizzie, is 33; daughter, Ella, is 12; son, Clide, is 5; and son, Charlie, is 3. A black man named John Minor, age 23, is living with them.

In 1890, the Audrain Co, MO, tax list shows J.M. Beshears living in twp 52, Range 5. He owned real property valued at $130 and personal property worth $100. He also owned 20 neat cattle.

In 1875, Joel M. Brashears and others sued Barbara Cook for division of her late husband's estate. The suit is Joel M. Brashears et al (John Thole, guardian of Mary and Francis Kochling) vs. Barbara Cook et al (William, husband of Barbara) for partition of estate of Joseph Kochling, who died in 1870. Barbara had remarried to William Cook. Kochling children, besides Mary and Francis are Regina and Catherine, these four living in Audrain County, and Enoch, Joseph, and William of Ralls County.

In 1887, Joseph M. Beshears sued the Chicago & Alton Rail Road for damages for injuries received in a collision between two of their trains.

Joel Marion Beshears
Photo: Maureen Morisano

Elizabeth Givens Gray
Photo: Maureen Morisano

Obit: J.M. Beshears, who has been confined to his bed since last August, died Tuesday morning at one o'clock. His remains were laid to rest in the Vandalia cemetery at 3 o'clock, Tuesday evening with Masonic honors, of which order he was a member. Like all men, Joe had his faults, but we, as a christian people, should spread the mantle of charity over his short-comings and remember only the good deeds of his life. To his untiring energy and dauntless courage, Vandalia as a town owes the greater part of her prosperity. He leaves a wife and three children– a married daughter and two small boys– to mourn his loss. The family has the heartfelt sympathy of the entire community in this their sad hour of bereavement. (*Bowling Green Times*, 23 Jan 1890, p.2, col.2)

Obit: Mrs. Joseph M. Beshears: Vandalia, MO, May 23rd-, 1898: Died this a.m. at her son-in-law's residence, two miles west of here, Mrs. Joseph M. Beshears. Three weeks ago, deceased stepped on a rusty nail, which penetrated an inch or more into the flesh, producing this morning what physicians pronounce lockjaw. Deceased formerly owned and lived in the Helm residence in south Mexico. She leaves two sons and one daughter. (DI, 23 May 1898, p.1, col.2)

Both Joel and Elizabeth are buried in Section 1, Row 19, Vandalia City Cemetery, just north of the town.

Family of Joel Marion Beshears and Elizabeth Givens Gray:

[V9-]1187. [11-]1. ***Ella Gray Beshears**, b. 8 June 1868, Frankfort, Pike Co., MO, d. 24 Jan 1949, Idaho Falls, Bonneville Co, Idaho, age 80, bur Rose Hill Cem; m. 27 Nov 1889, in Vandalia, Audrain Co, MO, *James McGee Orr*, b. 2 Nov 1863, Louisiana, MO, d. 3 Sept 1955, Idaho Falls, ID; s/o William Campbell Orr and Eliza Jane Jordan.

Ella Gray (Beshears) Orr
Photo: Maureen Morisano

[V9-]1188. [12-]1. Marion Campbell Orr, b. 13 March 1892, Vandalia, MO; d. 20 March 1954, Idaho Falls, Idaho; never married.

[V9-]1189. [12-]2. Elizabeth Jane Orr, b. 13 Sept 1899, Vandalia, MO; d. 3 July 1993, Idaho Falls, Idaho, age 93; never married.

[V9-]1190. [11-]2. **William Beshears**, b. 26 Nov 1872, Frankfort, Pike Co, MO, d. 24 Jan 1874, age 15 months

[V9-]1191. [11-]3. ***Clyde Marion Beshears**, b. Dec 16, 1874, Pike Co, MO, d. July 11, 1913, Texas. Military service: volunteer in U.S. Army Cavalry Unit during the Spanish American War. He also served in the U.S. Navy and was stationed on a submarine, *USS Prairie*. Married **Emily Klein**, b. New York, c1893, d. March 1953, Brooklyn, Kings Co, New York

[V9-]1192. [11-]4. **Charles Daniel Beshears, Sr**, b. 13 March 1878, Vandalia, Audrain Co, MO; m. in Curryville "by Justice Awis," 15 Aug 1895, reported in Vandalia Leader, **Anna Bell Baker**, d/o Jerry Baker, of Vandalia. Charles worked for Standard Loan and Investment Co, of Vandalia.

Charles Daniel Beshears
Photo: Maureen Morisano

Clyde Marion Beshears
Photo: Maureen Morisano

V9-1193.   12-1. **Charles Daniel Beshears, II**, b. 1918. Was President of Framers Insurance Group, of Los Angeles, CA. He married "a California Girl" and returned from his honeymoon to Vandalia on 7 Dec 1941.

V9-1194.   13-1. a daughter
V9-1195.   13-2. **Charles Daniel Beshears, III,**
V9-1196.   13-3. a son
V9-1197.   13-4. a daughter
V9-1198.   12-2. a daughter??

Clyde Marion Beshears and Emily Klein

11-3. **Clyde Marion Beshears**, (s/o Joel M. Beshears and Elizabeth Givens Gray), b. 16 Dec 1874, Pike Co, MO, d. 11 July 1913, Tomball, Texas; m. in Fort Hamilton, Baybridge, Brooklyn, NY, c1907, *Emily Klein*, b. c1893, New York, d. 31 March 1953, whose parents were both born in Germany. Clyde Marion Beshears and Emily Klein had only one child: Joseph Clyde Beshears (see below). After Clyde died, Emily m.2. also at Fort Hamilton, c1913,

From Left: Charles Daniel Beshears, Sr (holding Charles Daniel Beshears, Jr), Anna Bell (Baker) Beshears, Ella Gray (Beshears) Orr, James McGee Orr. In foreground: Elizabeth Jane Orr and
Marion Campbell Orr. Photo: Maureen Morisano

Olaf John Paulson, and had two children:
      Elberta "Bert" Paulson (m. _____ McNally)
      May Emily Paulson (m. _____ Burns)
the beloved half-sisters of Joseph Clyde Beshears.

    Clyde Marion Beshears served 11 years in the U.S. Army Cavalry, from 4 May 1898 (in Spanish-American War), to May, 1909. He took a discharge and then served two years, from May, 1909, to May, 1911, in the U.S. Navy on the submarine *Prairie*. In the 1910 census, he was a crew-member of the *Prairie*.

Child of Clyde Marion Beshears and Emily Klein:

V9-1199.   12-1. ***Joseph Clyde Beshears**, b. 15 Sept 1908, d. 4 Sept 1994; m.1. 7 Nov 1926, St. Paul's Roman Catholic Church, Brooklyn, Kings Co, NY, ***Frances Teresa McCarthy***, b. 7 May 1909, Brooklyn, d. 24 Feb 1934, d/o Owen McCarthy and Agnes Doyle; m.2. 12 April 1937, ***Margaret Marie Quinlan***, b. 20 Aug 1918, Staten Island, N.Y.

Charles Daniel Beshears
Photo: Maureen Morisano

Elizabeth Jane Orr
Photo: Maureen
Morisano

Marion Campbell Orr
Photo: Maureen
Morisano

Obit: (from *Staten Island Advance*, 5 Sept 1994) Joseph C. Beshears, 85, of Bulls Head, a retired shipyard supervisor, died Sunday at home.

Born in Brooklyn, Mr. Beshears had lived in Valley Stream, L.I. for 20 years and Fort Lauderdale, Fla. for 15 years. He moved to Bulls Head in 1992.

He worked as a supervising shipfitter at the Brooklyn Navy Yard, retiring in 1960. He later worked as a shopkeeper for a sanitation landfill in Hempstead L.I. for more than 10 years.

He was a former parishioner of Our Lady of Good Counsel, R.C. Church, Tompkinsville. Mr. Beshears was a member of the Nassau Aerie Post of the Fraternal Order of the Eagles, Elmont, N.Y. He enjoyed reading and joggiing.

His wife, the former Margaret Quinlan, died in 1992. He is survived by three sons: Joseph F., Eugene, and Richard; three daughters, Agnes Gorton, Nannette Marano, and Elberta Culmore; a sister, Alberta McNally, 26 grandchildren, and 26 great-grandchildren.

The funeral ... Casey Funeral Home, Castleton Corners, with a mass at 10 a.m. in Our Lady of Good Counsel Church. Burial will be in Resurrection Cemetery, Pleasant Plains.

Joseph Clyde Beshears was affectionately known in the family as "Pop."

Family of Joseph Clyde Beshears and Francis Teresa McCarthy:
V9-1200.   13-1. **Joseph Francis Beshears**, b. 2 Nov 1927, Brooklyn, NY, residence Brick, NJ, d. 2 July 2006; m. 8 Sept 1956, Brooklyn, NY, **Helen Theresa McNally**, b. 20

Dec 1933. Four children, all born in Brooklyn, NY:

V9-1201.   14-1. **Maureen Frances Beshears**, b. 25 July 1957; m. 28 May 1983, *Anthony John Morisano, Jr.* Maureen sent data, for which many thanks.

V9-1202.   15-1. Sarah Marie Morisano,

V9-1203.   15-2. Anthony Nicholas Morisano,

V9-1204.   14-2. **Patricia Ann Beshears**, b. 7 Sept. 1958; m. _____ *Earl.*

V9-1205.   14-3. **Theresa M. Beshears**, b. 11 May 1963 (twin); m. _____ *Coranante.*

V9-1206.   14-4. **Francis Joseph Beshears**, b. 11 May 1963 (twin)

V9-1207.   13-2. **Agnes Teresa Beshears**, b. May 15, 1929; married *Ronald Gorton*, currently resides in Brooklyn, NY

V9-1208.   14-1. Frances Gorton, b. 10 March 1953; m. _____

V9-1209.   15-1. Rachel _____ , 1972

V9-1210.   15-2. Alyssa _____ , 1974

V9-1211.   14-2. Kathleen Gorton, b. 26 Dec 1955

V9-1212.   14-3. Michael Gorton, b. 25 June 19__; m. _____

V9-1213.   15-1. Michael Gorton, 1973

V9-1214.   15-2. Timothy Gorton, 1975

V9-1215.   15-3. Matthew Gorton, 1978

V9-1216.   14-4. Roland Gorton, b. 11 Dec 196_

V9-1217.   14-5. Stephan Gorton, b. 22 Jan 1965

V9-1218.   14-6. Brian Gorton, b. 13 Oct 1966

V9-1219.   13-3. **Eugene Beshears**, b. Feb 10, 1934; m. *Patricia Garland*, currently resides in Framingham, MA.

V9-1220.   14-1. **Paul Beshears**, b. 1 April 1958

V9-1221.   14-2. **Laura Beshears**, b. 8 Sept 1959

V9-1222.   14-3. **Ginnie Beshears**, b. 20 May 1961

V9-1223.   14-4. **Elizabeth Ann "Beth" Beshears**, b. 22 March 1963

V9-1224.   14-5. **Clare Beshears**, b. 23 March 1969

Family of Joseph Clyde Beshears and Margaret Marie Quinlan:

V9-1225.   13-4. **Nannette Sarah Beshears**, b. 11 June 1938, Brooklyn, NY; m. *Mike Marano.*

V9-1226.   14-1. Michael Marano, b. 6 Sept 1956

V9-1227.   14-2. Melissa Marano, b. 23 March 1969

V9-1228.   13-5. **Elberta Ann Beshears**, b. 19 Oct 1939, Brooklyn, NY; m. *Albert Culmore.*

V9-1229.   14-1. Lisa Culmore, b. 16 Oct 1963

V9-1230.   14-2. Geralynn Culmore, b. 26 May 1965

V9-1231.   14-3. Albert Culmore, Jr, b. 14 June 1969

V9-1232.   13-6. **Richard Clyde Beshears**, b. 30 Jan 1942; m. *Ellen* _____,

V9-1233.   14-1. **Kevin Beshears**, b. 16 Dec 1966

V9-1234.   14-2. **Ricky Beshears**, b. 8 April 1968
V9-1235.   14-3. **Keith Anthony Beshears**, b. 27 June 1975
V9-1236.   14-4. **Joseph Beshears**, b. July 1908

JUDGE WILLIAM BAZWELL BESHEARS and ZEPHALINDA LLEWELLYN/ MARGARET E. ROGERS

v2-1887. **Judge William Bazwell (?Basil) Beshears**, (s/o Robert Brashears and Elizabeth Whitton), b. 24 Aug 1814, Montgomery Co, KY, d. 17 Sept 1899, MO; m.1. 10 March 1836, (Ralls Co, MO, Bk A, p.77--"groom of Pike Co"; ceremony "by David Biggs, Min"), **Zephalinda Llewellyn**, b. 18 May 1818 (8 Jun, says her stone), d. 11 Feb 1866, bur Salem Cem, Ralls Co, MO (5 ch in census); m.2. **Mrs. Margaret E. (Rogers) Hutchinson**, a widow.

A biography of Judge William B. Beashears appeared in 1884 in the *History of Audrain Co, MO*: "retired farmer and businessman, Vandalia. Judge Beshears, who in a few months will have completed the allotted age of three-score and ten years, is an old gentleman still well preserved in mind and body, and has brought down with him to his old age the confidence and esteem of those who have known him through the long years of his past career. His life has been one of great activity and industry, and has not been left without the substantial rewards of energetic and well directed employment. Though not a wealthy man, he has an ample competency to support him and his family through the twilight of his old age, and until the sun shall sink down below the Western seas on his career forever.

Judge Beshears was born in Montgomery County, Kentucky, on 24th day of August, 1814. He was reared in that county up to the age of nineteen, when his parents, Robert and Elizabeth (Whitton) Beshears, his father a native of Virginia, but his mother formerly of Maryland, came to Missouri and settled in Pike County, where the father died in 1872 and the mother two years before.

Judge Beshears was reared to the occupation of a farmer, and on the 10th of March, 1836, he was married, in Ralls County, to Miss Zethalinda Llewellyn. He followed farming in that county after his marriage until 1847, when he removed to Clark County, where he engaged in merchandising after having farmed there for about ten years. In 1847, Judge Beshears returned to Pike County, but four years afterward removed to Montgomery County where he was engaged in both farming and merchandising, or rather one or the other, for about fourteen years.

In Montgomery county, he was very successful, both as a farmer and in business, and attained to an honorable prominence as an influential citizen of that county. While a resident there, he was three times elected a member of the county court, and held the office continuously from the time of his first election up to 1863, when he was ousted by operation of the test oath prescribed by the Drake constitution, which he refused to take.

In 1865, Judge Beshears returned to Pike County, but in the fall of the same year he located in Ralls County, going, however, to Frankfort where he engaged in merchandising. In about 1867, Judge Beshears settled on a farm in Pike county, where he remained for several years. Following this, in 1870, he removed to Curryville, where he was engaged in selling goods for about a year. Soon afterwards, Judge Beshears went to Ralls county, but shortly settled near Vandalia, where he lived until January, 1880, when he came to this place. Since coming to Vandalia, Judge Beshears has led a retired life, having withdrawn from all business and farming interests.

During the years of his activity, he was an extensive land-holder, and dealt somewhat largely in real estate-trading, buying and selling- and owning different farms at different times; this fact necessitated frequent removal of his place of residence, so that instead of making his home in one county all the time, he has lived wherever his landed and other interests required his personal presence.

Judge Beshears lost his first wife in 1866. She left him six children, of a family of nine born to them. The living are as follows: James H., Thomas J., William H., Bazil L., Pauline E., now Mrs. Shackleford, and John G. Judge Beshears' present wife, before her marriage to him, was a Mrs. Margaret Elizabeth Hutchinson, of Pike County. Her maiden name was Rogers, and she was a widow lady at the time of her marriage to the Judge. But two of the children of a family of five from this union are now living: Verna L. and Pearly L. By her former marriage, Mrs. Behears had two children, one of whom is still living, Charles L. [Hutchinson].

Judge Beshears is a man of fine intelligence, wide and varied information, and a most interesting and entertaining conversationalist. He has had a long experience in business and public affairs, and has been a diligent reader, both of the current events of the times and of historical and general literature, so that he is well prepared to talk on most of the questions of interest to the generality of men. No pleasanter hour can be spent than with him when he his disposed to discuss questions of general concern on which he is posted. He is a man whose acquaintance every one who knows him prizes as of great value." (*History of Audrain County, Missouri*, 1884, p.42[9]-31)

"Judge William Beshears. Robert, his father, and his mother, Elizabeth (Whitton) Beshears are natives of Virginia, but his mother formerly of Maryland." (*Pioneer Families of Audrain County, Missouri,* 1887, by Bryan and Rose).

Family of William Bazwell Beshears and Zephalinda Llewellen:
all b. MO:

V9-1237.   10-1. **Mary Elizabeth Beshears**, b. 21 Dec 1836 (14 in 1850), d. bef 1884; m. Nov 1856, ***John G. Moore,***

V9-1238.   10-2. ***James Robert Breshears**, b. 9 Oct 1839 (11 in 1850), d. 8 April 1911; m. 24 Nov 1868, **Anna Elizabeth Dunford**, b. 24 March 1852*

V9-1239.   10-3. **Paulina A. Beshears** b. 29 Sept 1841 (9 in 1850), d. 1916; m. 29 Sept 1858, Montgomery Co, MO, ***Willis Green Shackleford**, b. 1836, MO*

V9-1240.   11-1. Ione E. Kirtly Shackleford, b. 1861

V9-1241.   11-2. Mollie Shackleford, b. 1865

V9-1242.   11-3. Cora Shackleford, b. 1872

V9-1243.   10-4. ***William H. Beshears**, b. 2 March 1844 (6 in 1850), d. 2 March 1904; m. 25 Sept 1866, **Mary Eliza Tredway**, b. 20 Jan 1848; ancestors of Mrs. Nelda E. McCrory,*

V9-1244.   10-5. **Charlotte A. Beshears**, b. 14 Feb 1846, d. 10 Sept 1846, 7 mos.

V9-1245.   10-6. **Thomas J. Beshears**, b. 15 May 1849 (1 in 1850), d. 17 Jan 1917; m. 25 Dec 1871, ***Annie E. King**, b. 1848, KY*

V9-1246.   11-1. **Jodica Beshears**, b. 1892, MO

V9-1247.   10-7. **Cordelia "Goldie" Keturah Beshears**, b. 15 Nov 1851, d. 12 or 17 Oct 1868, age 16, bur Salem Bapt Cem, Rall Co, MO, "w/o G.T. Howard; d/o Wm. B. and Zephalinda Beshears"; m. 12 April 1865, in Pike Co, MO, ***G.T. Howard,***

V9-1248.   10-8. **John Napoleon Beshears**, b. 26 Aug 1856, d. 14 Nov 1877 in Texas; m. 25 Nov 1876, in Ralls Co, MO, ***Clara G. Clayton**, b. 1860*

V9-1249.   11-1. **Arthur K. Beshears**, b. 1879, MO; m. ***Celia* _____**, b. 1883,

V9-1250.   10-9. ***Basil Lorenzo Beshears**, b. 6 Nov 1857, d. 23 Nov 1897; m. 27 Feb 1879, Audrian Co, MO, **Katherine "Kate" Clayton**, b. 15 June 1863,*

Family of William Bazwell Beshears and Margaret E. Rogers:

V9-1251.   10-10. **Emma P. Beshears**, b. 4 Sept 1867, d. 23 Oct 1867, six weeks old

V9-1252.   10-11. **Vernie Lee Beshears**, b. 4 Oct 1870; m. ***Iola Utterback,***

V9-1253.   10-12.

V9-1254.   10-13. **Mertie May Beashears**, b. 16 Feb 1877, d. 27 Jan

1878, 4 mos

V9-1255.   10-14. **Perlie Logene Beshears**, (male) b. 27 Sept 1877, d. 20
             Jan 1901; m. 25 June 1898, *Georgia Anderson,*

V9-1256.   10-15. **Percie Orah Beshears**, b. 5 Nov 1879, d. 3 Aug 1880,
             near Vandalia, Audrain Co, MO, 8 mos.

James Robert Breshears
and Anna Elizabeth Dunford

10-2. **James Robert Breshears**, (s/o Judge William Bazwell Beshears
and Zephalinda Llewellen), b. 9 Oct 1839, Pike Co, MO, d. 8 April 1911,
?Stillwell, OK; m. 24 Nov 1868, (?in CA) *Anna Elizabeth Dunford*, b.
24 March 1832, Hancock Co, ?OK, d. 1932, d/o Peter and Julia
Harding, natives of Ohio and IL respectively. (data from *Pioneers of the
Prairie* sent to Shirley McCoy in 1986 from James M. Neill, Rt 3, Box
222, Carthage, IL 62321). James Robert Breshears re-inserted an "r"
in his surname.

Family of James Robert Breshears and Anna Elizabeth Dunford:
V9-1257.   11-1. **Florence Breshears**, b. 1870 (?d. young? name re-
             used.)
V9-1258.   11-2. **Zephalinda Breshears**, b. 1872, CA, d. 18 Dec 1945;
             m. 6 March 1893, *William Crear,* b. 9 March 1872,
             Basco, IL, d. 1945, both bur Woodville Cem
V9-1259.   12-1. Mary Louise Crear; m. Maurice Bettisworth
V9-1260.   11-3. **Julia Florence Breshears**, b. 1874 (or 1879), d. 30 May
             1933; m. *Henry Tanner*, b. 1868. Moved 1900 to CA.
V9-1261.   12-1. Raymond Tanner, b. 24 Feb 1896
V9-1262.   11-4. **William Lewis Breshears**, b. 1875 (working for Frank
             Tanner at a sawmill in Stillwell, in 1900)
V9-1263.   11-5. **Gertrude Ellen Breshears**, b. 1878
V9-1264.   11-6. **Daisy Breshears**, b. 1897, d. 1897

Pioneers of the Prairie, p. 248: "Breshears, J. Robert- born October
9, 1839, in Pike County, Missouri, died April 8, 1911. In 1852, Mr.
Breshears went to California, where he engaged in farming until 1867
when he went to Hamilton, Nevada. On November 24, 1868, he
married Anna Elizabeth Dunford, born March 24, 1852, in Hancock Co.
She died in 1932, a daughter of Peter and Julia Harding, natives of
Ohio and Illinois respectively. Mr. and Mrs. Breshears returned to
Stillwell on the newly completed railroad. They bought 120 acres of
land and he went into farming. Children: (as above). Mr. Breshears
was also a retail merchant in Stillwell. They were members of the
Stillwell Methodist Church. They are buried in Woodville Cemetery."

ibid. p.22: Stillwell Methodist Church, June 1873: lots were deeded to church trustees, including James Brashears.

ibid. p.86: J.R. Breshears, a citizen of Stillwell, is very enterprising and industrious. Men like him make the county thrive (9 April 1873).

ibid. p.106 (quoting an old newspaper): In the March 1887 St. Alban Twp election, elected J.R. Breshears constable.

ibid. p.310: William Crear, b. 9 March 1872, Basco, IL, d. 1945; m. 6 March 1893, Zephlinda Breshears, b. 1872, CA, d. 18 Dec 1945, buried (shared stone) Woodville Cemetery. Lived in Oklahoma where he managed a ranch, came back to Stillwell where he farmed and had a grain elevator business. Sold it in 1911. Organized and was cashier of Farmers Bank of Stillwell. He was a member of I.O.O.F., Methodist Church. "They raised Mary Louise Crear, who married Maurice Bettisworth."

ibid. p.402: Ellis Hart, m. 9 Sept 1839, Margaret Breshears.

ibid, p.548: William Breshears in 1900 working for Frank Tanner at a sawmill in Stillwell

ibid. p.752: Henry Tanner, b. 1868; m. Julia Florence Breshears, b. 1874, dau of James Robert Breshears and Elizabeth Dunford. Son Raymond, b. 24 Feb 1896. They moved 1900 to CA.

ibid. p.621: John Owen boarded with the James Brashears family in 1880, St. Albans Twp.

William H. Beshears
and Mary Eliza Tredway

[10]-4. **William H. Beshears**, (s/o Judge William Bazwell Beshears and Zephalinda Llewellen), b. 2 March 1844, Pike Co, MO (6 in 1850), d. 2 March 1904; m. 25 Sept 1866, **Mary Eliza Tredway**, b. 20 Jan 1848, Pike Co, MO, d. 28 July 1922, Ralls Co, MO, d/o William F. Tredway and Paulina Eades, (data from Nelda E. McCrory, 2205 Ridgemont, Columbia, MO 65203, via Larry Howser)

Family of William H. Beshears and Mary Eliza Tredway:
[V9]-1265.	[11]-1.	**Zepha S. Beshears**, b. 5 Oct 1870, d. 21 March 1944, bur Vandalia Cem, Vandalia, MO; m.1. **Fount L. Darnell**, m.2. **Ed. Turley**,
[V9]-1266.	[12]-1.	Ernest Darnell, eldest child, b. 7 Nov 1891, d. 31 March 1980, bur Vandalia, MO
[V9]-1267.	[12]-2.	Edna Florence Darnell, (twin) d. young, bur Vandalia Cem
[V9]-1268.	[12]-3.	Edwin Lawrence Darnell, (twin)
[V9]-1269.	[11]-2.	**Sallie (or Sarah) Ellen Beshears**, b. 21 Sept 1872, Ralls Co, MO, d. 10 Aug 1957, Hannibal MO Hospital; m. 8 March 1894, **William Henry Evans**, b. 13 Feb

1868, d. 3 Dec 1935, Ralls Co, MO, s/o Francis Marion Evans and Elizabeth Ann Johnson,

V9-1270.   12-1. Paul Benn Evans, b. 6 May 1895, d. 16 Oct 1966, bur Monroe Co, MO; m. 1 Oct 1919, Louise Keller,

V9-1271.   12-2. Bessie Edith Evans, (twin) b. 12 May 1898, d. young, 6 Jan 1899, bur Vandalia Cem

V9-1272.   12-3. Beulah Ethel Evans, (twin) b. 12 May 1898, d. 20 June 1971, Pike Co Nursing Home; m. 18 April 1920, Chester Arthur Rohr, b. 23 Aug 1897, Ralls Co, MO, d. 9 Dec 1973, s/o Wyman Mitchell Rohr and Susan Morton Wasson.

V9-1273.   13-1. Eugene Mitchel Rohr, b. 16 June 1921, d. 28 Sept 1993; m. 26 July 1942, Elva Eileen Jackson, 2 ch:

V9-1274.   14-1. Cary Eugene Rohr, b. 20 July 1943,

V9-1275.   14-2. Kerwin Dean Rohr, b. 29 Dec 1948

V9-1276.   13-2. Nelda Evans Rohr, b. 8 Aug 1925, Ralls Co, MO, m. 14 July 1950, John Knox McCrory Sr, b. 16 Nov 1925, Vernon Co, MO. Nelda McCrory contributed data to this article.

V9-1277.   14-1. John Knox McCrory Jr, b. 28 Aug 1951

V9-1278.   14-2. Sally Kay McCrory, b. 3 Oct 1953

V9-1279.   14-3. James Vincent McCrory, b. 18 July 1955

V9-1280.   14-4. Nancy Sue McCrory, b. 19 July 1958

V9-1281.   11-3. **William Bazil Beshears**, b. 29 Jan 1875, d. 3 Sept 1936 in CO; lived in Minnesota, bur Vandalia Cem; m.1. 25 Dec 1899, **Rosa Laird**, of Pike Co, MO; m.2. **Ethel _____**, in MN. All his children b. MN:

V9-1282.   12-1. **Edna Beatrice Beshears**, b. 9 Oct 1900, d. 22 June 1997, Olympia, Thurston Co, WA; m. 15 Jan 1928, **Paul J. Garberg**, b. 1899, MN.

V9-1283.   12-2. **Floyd William Beshears**, b. 1 Jan 1902, Minneapolis, d. there 19 Nov 1985

V9-1284.   12-3. **Mary Blanche Beshears**, b. 24 March 1903, d. 2 March 1988, St Paul, Ramsey Co, MN; m.1. 19 July 1924, **Roland Rentz**, b. 1901, MN; m.2. **Pete Mitras**,

V9-1285.   13-1. Foah O. Rentz, b. 1925, MN

V9-1286.   13-2. Roland Rentz, Jr, b. 1930, MN

V9-1287.   12-4. **Velma Gladys Beshears**, b. 20 June 1904, d. 13 Nov 1985, Phoenix, Maricopa Co, AZ; m.1. Nov 1922, **James Woodhall**, m.2. **Gordon Flynn,**

V9-1288.   12-5. **Roland Freeman Beshears**, b. 3 Au 1905, d. 13 May 1982, Las Vegas, Clark Co, NV; m. 1931, **Marian Slabaugh,**

V9-1289.   12-6. **Addison Clyde Beshears**, b. Jan 1910, d. Dec 1987; m. *Lois* _____,

V9-1290.   11-4. **Homer B. Beshears**, b. 1879, d. 1940, lived Curryville, MO; m. *Zella Wheeler*, b. 15 Oct 1888, IN, d. 15 May 1968, Sonoma Co, CA

V9-1291.   12-1. **Marvin Wheeler Beshears**, b. 16 Feb 1905, MO, d. 15 May 1983, Humboldt, CA

V9-1292.   12-2. **James William Beshears**, b. 26 May 1911, MO, d. 28 Sept 1993, Shasta, CA

V9-1293.   12-3. **Ollie Eugene Beshears**, b. 18 Aug 1913, MO, d. 6 Dec 1992, Shasta, CA

V9-1294.   11-5. **Annie E. Beshears**, b. Feb 1881, d. 15 June 1888, age 7 1/2, drowned when a buggy was swept away in high water.

V9-1295.   11-6. **Leni I. Beshears**, b. Jan 1886, d. 15 June 1888, age 2 1/2, drowned at the same time as Annie, bur Vandalia Cem.

V9-1296.   11-7. unknown,

V9-1297.   11-8. **Rose Ethel Beshears**, b. 15 June 1889, d. 5 Sept 1959, Los Angeles, CA; m. 27 Dec 1906, *Orien Ray Brown*, b. 27 May 1888, Curryville, MO, d. 16 March 1956, Los Angeles, CA

V9-1298.   12-1. Mary Lillian Brown, b. 1907, MO; living San Marino, CA in 1994; m. Alfred B. Post,

V9-1299.   12-2. Charles William Brown, b. 1912, MO

V9-1300.   12-3. Clarence Lloyd Brown, b. 1914, MO

V9-1301.   12-4. Homer Ben Brown, b. 1917, MO

V9-1302.   12-5. Raymond Rose Brown, b. 1923, CA

V9-1303.   12-6. Barbara Louise Brown, b. 1927, CA

Basil Lorenzo Beshears
and Katherine Clayton

10-9. **Basil Lorenzo Beshears**, (s/o Judge William Bazwell Beshears and Zephalinda Llewellen), b. 6 Nov 1857, d. 23 Nov 1897; m. 27 Feb 1879, Audrian Co, MO, *Katherine "Kate" Clayton*, b. 15 June 1863, Ralls Co, MO, d. 26 March 1952, bur Vandalia Cem, Audrain Co, MO, d/o George W. Clayton. They had 8 children. After Basil died, Kate m.2. 1 April 1900, James M. Hill, d. 25 Feb 1949, age 93, and had two sons: Sibert and Clayton Hill.

The Vandalia Leader reported that Basil Beshears and his brother John N. Beshears left for Texas 1 Dec 1881, to engage in stock raising. But they must have come back: 21 Nov 1895, the Leader reported "B.L. Beshears and family left Wednesday for Abeline, TX, to remain permanently." Then on 12 Nov 1896, "The family of B.L. Beshears who left for Texas some time ago has returned."

B.L. Beshears, son of W.B. Beshears, met death, Tuesday morning. Jimmie Beshears, aged 14, was with his father at the time of the accident. The deceased was 40 years and 17 days old. He leaves a wife and seven children. Robert Beshears and family of Stillwell, IL, and V.L. Beshears and P.L. Beshears of IL, arrived yesterday to attend the funeral. (Vandalia Leader, 25 Nov 1897)

Family of Basil Lorenzo Beshears and Katherine Clayton:

V9-1304.   11-1. **Charles McCune Beshears**, b. 18 May 1880, d. 10 March 1924; m. *Daisy Edith Boyd*, b. 19 July 1882, d. 21 Dec 1913, both bur Madisonville Cem, Madisonville, Ralls Co, MO, d/o John Wasson Boyd and Mary Smith.

V9-1305.   12-1. **Averil Wayne Beshears**, b. 4 Dec 1903, m. 18 Feb 1928, *Madge Addie Palmer*, b. 5 May 1911, d. 3 Feb 1999, Center, MO; d/o Thomas G. Palmer,

V9-1306.   13-1. **Averil Wayne Beshears Jr**, b. 15 Jan 1931; m. 20 Aug 1966, *Muriel Ann Martin*, d/o Sam Perry Martin,

V9-1307.   14-1. **Beth Michelle Beashears**, b. 15 Aug 1969

V9-1308.   14-2. **Aaron Wayne Beshears**, b. 29 Jan 1973

V9-1309.   14-3. **Brendon Boyd Beshears**, b. 25 Jan 1976

V9-1310.   13-2. **Reta Louise Beshears**, b. 2 Sept 1941; m. *Lee Gore*,

V9-1311.   14-1. Melaney Lee Gore, b. 13 Aug 1956

V9-1312.   14-2. Lisa Ellen Gore, (Adopted) b. 29 March 1966

V9-1313.   14-3. Eric Wayne Gore, b. 1 May 1974

V9-1314.   12-2. **Oneta Fern Beshears**, b. 1908, m. 16 Nov 1931, *Joseph Errett Palmer*, b. 1905, d. 1948, bur Olivet Cem, Ralls Co, MO

V9-1315.   13-1. Robert Joseph Palmer, b. 16 Dec 1931

V9-1316.   11-2. **James E. Beshears**, b. 1882, drowned in Spencer Creek

V9-1317.   11-3. **Roy E. Beshears**, b. Aug 1884

V9-1318.   11-4. **Jesse Bazel Beshears**, b. 21 Nov 1886, d. 26 June 1975; m. *Nannie Boyd Kraft*,

V9-1319.   12-1. **Ida Catherine Beshears**, m. *Flemon Miller*,

V9-1320.   13-1. Marvin Miller,

V9-1321.   13-2. Richard Miller,

V9-1322.   13-3. Pittman Miller,

V9-1323.   13-4. Nancy Miller,

V9-1324.   13-5. Kathy Miller,

V9-1325.   13-6. _____ Miller,

V9-1326.   12-2. **Thelma Sue Beshears**, m. *Henry Bell*, (div)

V9-1327.	13-1. Doris Bell,
V9-1328.	13-2. Nancy Bell,
V9-1329.	13-3. "Buddy" Bell,
V9-1330.	13-4. Patty Bell,
V9-1331.	13-5. Betty Bell,
V9-1332.	13-6. Johnny Bell,
V9-1333.	13-7. Jimmy Bell,
V9-1334.	12-3. **Bazy (Bazil?) Beshears**, m. *Mary Jo Bland,*
V9-1335.	13-1. **Jay Bazzel Beashears,**
V9-1336.	13-2. **Deanna Beshears,**
V9-1337.	13-3. **Daniel Ray Beshears,**
V9-1338.	11-5. **Ray Thomas Beshears**, b. 18 May 1890, d. 3 Jan 1951; m. *Lola Z. Evans*, b. 31 Aug 1899, d. 14 Dec 1973, both bur Olivet Cem, Ralls Co, MO
V9-1339.	12-1. **Marjorie Ruth Beshears**, m. *Loren Waldmeier,*
V9-1340.	13-1. Thomas Frank Waldmeier,
V9-1341.	12-2. **Raylene Sue Beshears**, m. *Ronnie Scott,*
V9-1342.	13-1. Mitchel Eugene Scott, b. 9 June 1961
V9-1343.	13-2. Michael Ray Scott, b. 11 June 1963
V9-1344.	11-6. **Arthur C. Beshears**, b. Jan 1895
V9-1345.	11-7. **Eva Beshears**, b. June 1896, d. 3 Oct 1972, CA; m. *William Bryan,*
V9-1346.	11-8. **Ruth Cleveland Beshears**, b. June 1896, d. 3 Oct 1972

ROBERT ANDERSON BESHEARS
and LUCRETIA A. UNSELL

v2-1888. **Robert Anderson Beshears**, (s/o Robert Brashears and Elizabeth Whitton), b. 8 July 1815, Bourbon Co, KY (34 in 1850), d. 10 Dec 1891, Ralls Co, MO (per obit; survived by two sons and one dau); m. 12 July 1843, Ralls Co, MO (Book B, p.94), *Lucretia A. Unsell*, b. c1821, ?Pike Co, MO, d. 1895, both bur Olivet Cem, Center, Ralls Co, MO. Robert moved with his parents to Pike Co in 1831; he and wife, Lucretia, moved to Ralls Co, MO, in 1851, where they died. They are #586-573 in 1860 census, Spencer twp, Ralls Co, MO, with three children at home: William, 13; Elizabeth, 9; and Lucy, 3. They were members of the Christian Church and had six children.

Family of Robert Anderson Beshears and Lucretia Unsell: all b. MO:

V9-1347.	10-1. **William B. Beshears**, b. 1845, MO, d. 1915; m. 19 Dec 1867, *Mary Jane Gregory*, b. 1849, d. 1892, both bur Olivet Cem, Ralls Co, MO, d/o James P. Gregory and

Amanda E. Crawford; m.2. 1893, *Fannie* ____, b. c1860.

V9-1348.   ¹¹⁻1. **Ezra M. Beshears**, b. 6 Nov 1870, d. 23 Sept 1925, Fulton, MO; m.1. 26 Dec 1896, *Effie M. Parker*, from his Obit: Died in Fulton, Wednesday morning at 6 A.M. at the age of 55 years. He was reared in Ralls County and moved to his farm east of Vandalia. He has been identified with the banks of this city and has held considerable of their capital stock. He was extremely wealthy and had one of the best improved farms in Pike County.

V9-1349.   ¹²⁻1. **Mary E. Beshears**, b. 1896, d. 1950; m. *Frank Wallace*, b. 1892, WV

V9-1350.   ¹³⁻1. Alpha O. Wallace, b. 1920, Jasper, Ralls Co, MO

V9-1351.   ¹³⁻2. Eugene P. Wallace, b. 1923, Jasper, Ralls Co, MO

V9-1352.   ¹²⁻2. **Lena Beshears**, b. 1898, d. 1940, MO; m. *Otis Williams*,

V9-1353.   ¹²⁻3. **Alva M. Beshears**, b. 16 July 1903, d. 4 March 1922, suicide at age 19; m. 21 Dec ___, *Ruth Griggs*, d/o N.J. Griggs,

V9-1354.   ¹¹⁻2. **Eva Lena Beshears**, b. 1875, d. 1960; m. *William "Will" T. Clark*, b. 1866, d. 1936, both bur Olivet Cem, Ralls Co, MO

V9-1355.   ¹¹⁻3. **Arthur Roy Beshears**, b. 26 Nov 1878, Center, Ralls Co, MO, d. 22 Oct 1956; m. 30 Sept 1900, *Celia Frances Boyd*, b. 27 Aug 1882, Ralls Co, MO, d. 6 July 1954 at Mount Vernon Sanatariam, MO, d/o R.I. Boyd and Fannie Gore; both bur Olivet Cem, Ralls Co, MO

V9-1356.   ¹¹⁻4. **Homer Anderson Beshears**, b. 26 Sept 1882, Center, Ralls Co, MO, d. 4 May 1938, bur Grandview Cem, Ralls Co, MO; m.1. *Crystal* _____, b. 1887(4 ch); m.2. *Fannie Evans*, (?ch); m.3. *Lovanna Mae Paxton*, (1 ch)

V9-1357.   ¹²⁻1. **Kenneth Beshears**, b. 13 June 1913, MO, d. 15 June 1984, Sacramento, CA

V9-1358.   ¹²⁻2. **Devin Roy Beshears**, b. 1914, MO
V9-1359.   ¹²⁻2. **Earl A. Beshears**,
V9-1360.   ¹²⁻3. dau **Beshears**, m. *Kenneth Nearmyer*,
V9-1361.   ¹²⁻4. **Mary Margaret Beshears**, d/o Homer Beshears and Lovanna Paxton, b. 15 Dec 1921, d. 20 Dec 1921, five days old, bur Salem Cem, Center, Ralls Co, MO

V9-1362.   11-5. **William Beshears**, b. 1902, s/o William B. Beshers and Fannie _____ .

V9-1363.   10-2. **Lucretia Elizabeth "Lizzie" Beshears**, (her tombstone says Lucretia "Lizzie") b. 2 Feb 1848, MO (3 in 1850), d. 17 Aug 1934, bur Olivet Cem, Ralls Co, MO, probate completed, Dec 1942; m.1. 2 Feb 1870, *Luther R. Smith*, (2 ch); m.2. 7 Sept 1876, *Jesse McGrew*, (1 ch), b. 10 Jan 1830, d. 13 Jan 1894; m.3. 31 Oct 1895, *Daniel H. Pollard*, b. 19 Feb 1846. (data from Lorrie E. (Peirce) Riemer, P.O.Box 547, Oswego, IL 60543; 630/554-0554 <LRiemer894@aol.com>, for which many thanks.)

V9-1364.   11-1. Ollie Edwin Smith, b. Oct 1871, d. 5 April 1947; m. 1893, Cordelia Cowden, b. Jan 1873, d. 1938

V9-1365.   12-1. Eunice "Lora" Smith, b. June 1897; m.1. Ollie Blanton Robinson; m.2. ____Love,

V9-1366.   13-1. Ollie Blanton Robinson Jr; m. Helen ____

V9-1367.   12-2. Everett F. Smith, b. Dec 1898

V9-1368.   12-3. Ollie Edwin Smith Jr, b. 6 Aug 1903, d. 13 June 1975; m.1. Melvina ____ (1 ch); m.2. Carol ____

V9-1369.   13-1. Rita Kay Smith

V9-1370.   11-2. Samantha May Smith, b. 29 Nov 1872, d. 27 Sept 1952; m. 28 Nov1891, Charlie Larson, b. 24 Sep1868, d. 30 Aug1945

V9-1371.   12-1. Anderson Eugene Larson, b. 4 Aug 1893, d. 7 Oct 1896

V9-1372.   12-2. Grace Elizabeth Larson, b. 18 Dec 1897, d. 15 Aug 1973; m.1. 16 Oct 1916, Edgar Lee Peirce, b. 12 Oct 1892, d. 24 Feb 1970; m.2. 7 Dec 1960, James Frank Baley, b. 3 Nov 1906, d. 9 Jan 1975

V9-1373.   13-1. Charles Lee Peirce, b. 20 Aug 1917, d. 14 Sept 1993; m.1. 4 Dec 1945, Jane Sprague, b. ?, d. 1994; m.2. 18 Dec 1956, Margaret Brockell, d. 27 Dec 1995

V9-1374.   13-2. Raymond Earl Peirce, b. 8 April 1927; m. 6 Dec 1947, Mary Ellen Reinert, b. 31 July 1924, d. 23 May 1988; m.2. 18 Nov 1993, Mary Jane Williams, b. 30 Aug 1931

V9-1375.   14-1. Lynne Marie Peirce, b. 9 Dec 1949; m. 29 Sept 1973, Robert Schmidt, b. 16 Jan 1943

V9-1376.   15-1. John Scott Schmidt, b. 18 July 1983 (adopted)

V9-1377.   15-2. Judianne Marie Schmidt, b. 20Aug 1984 (adopted)

V9-1378.   14-2. Lorrie Ellen Peirce, b. 22 May 1952; m. 24 Nov 1973, Paul Gerhardt Riemer Jr, b. 13 Nov 1947. Lorrie Riemer sent data.

V9-1379.   15-1. Stefanie Lynne Riemer, b. 9 Jan 1978

V9-1380.   15-2. Kimberly Ann Riemer, b. 30 Dec 1979

V9-1381.   15-3. Jonathan Paul Riemer, b. 22 Dec 1983

V9-1382.   14-3. Ronnie Ray Peirce, b. 18 Dec 1954; m.1. 20 Aug 1973, Pamela Sue Ott, b. 16 April 1956 (1 ch); m.2. 1979, Sharon Kay Lammers (no ch); m.3. 22 May 1987, Linda Ann Marklein, b. 14 Feb 1961 (2 ch)

V9-1383.   15-1. Christopher Sean Peirce, b. 19 Sept 1973; m. Jan 1993, Genevieve Elizabeth Hogan, b. 28 July 1975

V9-1384.   16-1. Aaron Scott Peirce, b. 17 Jan 1994

V9-1385.   15-2. Stacy Lynn Peirce, b. 3 Spe 1987

V9-1386.   15-3. Rachel Lee Peirce, b. 3 Aug 1993

V9-1387.   12-3. Glenn Harold Larson, b. 11 June 1901, d. 25 Feb 1902

V9-1388.   12-4. Cloletus A.R. Larson, b. 7 Feb 1903, d. 19 March 1903

V9-1389.   12-5. Charles Alfred Larson, b. 20 Aug 1904, d. 31 Oct 1966

V9-1390.   12-6. Otis Ray Larson, b. 6 Aug 1906, d. 27 June 1992

V9-1391.   11-3. William E. McGrew,

V9-1392.   10-4. **Elias Beshears**, b. 18 May 1851, d. 14 Dec 1855, age 4, bur Madisonville Cem, Madisonville, Ralls Co, MO

V9-1393.   10-5. **Lucy J. Beshears**, b. 8 Nov 1857, d. 22 Aug 1883; m. *Thad A. Briscoe*, b. 2 Jan 1856, d. 31 July 1908, both bur Olivet Cem, Center, Ralls Co, MO, s/o John Briscoe and 2nd wife, Martha Hays. Thad m.2. Rhoda Rice, d/o Andrew Rice.

V9-1394.   10-6. **Orville Anderson Beshears**, b. Jasper, Ralls Co, MO, 21 June 1860, d. 10 Nov 1936, bur Olivet Cem, Ralls Co, MO; unmarried. Very wealthy. He was the largest individual tax-payer in Ralls Co, MO, for several years.

JACKSON "JOHN" BESHEARS
and ELIZABETH KEITHLEY

v2-1889. **Jackson "John" Beshears**, (s/o Robert Brashears and Elizabeth Whitton), b. 8 Oct 1818, Bourbon Co, KY, d. 28 June 1882, Ralls Co, MO; m. c1843, **Elizabeth Keithley**, b. 15 Aug 1824, Randolph or Pike Co, MO, d. 28 May 1903, Ralls Co, MO, d/o Joseph Keithley Sr and his first wife, Elizabeth Burkett. Both John and Elizabeth bur Salem Cem, Ralls Co, MO.

He owned the second farm south of Salem Baptist Church on the same side of the road. Jackson and Elizabeth Beshears are #500-490 in 1860 census, Spencer twp, Ralls Co, MO, with three children: Lucinda, 16; Arminty, 14; and Martha, 12. For some reason, 4 children: Hiram E., 10; William R., 7; Malissa, 5; and Sarilda, 2 were enumerated separately in hh #500-549.

Family of Jackson "John" Beshears and Elizabeth Keithley:

V9-1395. 10-1. ***Lucinda Jane Beshears**, b. 6 March 1844, Peno Twp, Pike Co, MO, d. suddenly (see letter below), 10 Nov 1890, Fairview, Cooke Co, TX, bur Whitesboro Cem, Grayson Co, TX; m. 25 April 1869 in Ralls Co, MO, **Charles W. Howser**, b. 18 Dec 1816, Oldham, KY, d. 31 Aug 1916, Cooke Co, TX (*data from Larry Howser)

V9-1396. 10-2. **Araminta Beshears**, b. 8 Feb 1846, Peno twp, Pike Co, MO, d. 25 Nov 1909, bur Hays Creek Christian Cem, Ralls Co, MO; m. 5 Oct 1865, Ralls Co, MO (Book B, p.1402), **Noah Trammell Hendrix**, b. 5 June 1840, d. 14 Sept 1915, b. Pike Co, MO. Elizabeth Beshears, b. Aug 1824, mo-in-law, is in their household in 1870, Jasper Twp, Ralls Co, MO.

V9-1397. 11-1. Mary Hendrix, b. c1866, d. 7 Feb 1889, age 23; m. _____ Roland; son, _____ Roland, d. 23 Feb 1889 at age 6 mos.

V9-1398. 11-2. Hiram J. "Jack" Hendrix, m. Mirtie Clark, no ch

V9-1399. 11-3. Frank Conn Hendrix, m.1. Alice Ely, m.2. Margaret Tomilson,

V9-1400. 12-1. Lloyd Trammell Hendrix, m. Margaret Hastings,

V9-1401. 12-2. Alice Margaret Hendrix, m. Jack Moseley,

V9-1402. 12-3. Ruth Hendrix, m. Brad (Oland?),

V9-1403. 11-4. Leona Bell Hendrix, b. 13 Sept 1869, d. 1956; m. George Edward Wilson, b. 4 July 1863, d. 1937

V9-1404. 12-1. Coy Wilson, m. Fern Gregory. ch: Gwynn Wilson and Doris Wilson,

V9-1405.	12-2. Lloyd Wilson, m. Ann Denniston. ch: Jane (Denniston), step-dau
V9-1406.	12-3. Ray Wilson, d. age 16
V9-1407.	12-4. Mary Arminta Wilson, b. 25 March 1909; m. 21 Sept 1931, Guy Williams,
V9-1408.	13-1. Peggy Ann Williams, m. William H. McClain. ch: Linda Lee McClain, Teresa Ann McClain, Dennis Harvey McClain
V9-1409.	10-3. **Martha A. Beshears**, b. 4 Feb 1848, Peno twp, Pike Co, MO, d. 17 Nov 1914, Center, MO, bur. Salem Cem; m. 15 Nov 1870, Ralls Co, MO, (2nd wife of) *Moses E. Jewell,*
V9-1410.	11-1. Lem Jewell, b. 23 Oct 1872, d. 19 Jan 1919, bur Salem Cem, Ralls Co, MO
V9-1411.	11-2. Minnie Jewell, b. 1875, d. 1939; m. Joe Brown,
V9-1412.	11-3. Ella Jewell, b. 27 ov 1875, d. 5 May 1960; m. _____ Clark,
V9-1413.	11-4. Felix Jewell, b. 4 Oct 1878, d. 9 Dec 1955, bur Salem Cem.
V9-1414.	11-5. Leta Jewell, m. _____ Owens,
V9-1415.	11-6. Elizabeth Jewell, b. 1882, d. 1931; m. _____ Bigge,
V9-1416.	11-7. Claud V. Jewell, b. 29 March 1885, d. 30 Oct 1928, bur Salem Cem
V9-1417.	10-4. **Hiram E. Beshears**, b. 2 or 22 April 1850, Ralls Co, MO, d. 12 May 1916, Center, MO, bur Mt Olivet Cem; m.1. 5 June 1893, Ralls Co, MO, *Ella N. Floweree*, (1 ch), b. 1 March 1861, d. 17 June 1908; m.2. 1911, *Elizabeth Mariah (Evans) Hutchison*, b. 16 Aug 1856, Howard Co, MO, d. 4 Feb 1934 (no ch); Elizabeth was d/o Francis Marion Evans and Elizabeth Ann Jackson, and a widow with a son, Norman Hutchinson,
V9-1418.	11-1. **Fay Everette Beshears**, b. 19 July 1896, d. 4 Oct 1967, bur Olivet Cem, Ralls Co, MO; unmarried.
V9-1419.	10-5. **William Robert Beshears**, b. 24 Feb 1853, Ralls Co, MO, d. 27 July 1912, bur Vandalia Cem, Vandalia, Audrain Co, MO; m. *Mary Jane Cluster*, b. 6 Nov 1859, d. 28 July 1923, MO.
V9-1420.	11-1. **Walter R. Beshears**, b. 1884, d. 1929, bur Vandalia, MO; m. *Jessie P. Maiden,*, b. 1888, MO
V9-1421.	12-1. **Ruby V. Beshears**, b. 1908, MO
V9-1422.	12-2. **Evaline Ruth Beshears**, b. 1910, MO
V9-1423.	12-3. **Walter Carl Beshears**, b. 1911, MO
V9-1424.	12-4. **Edith E. Beshears**, b. 1914, MO
V9-1425.	12-5. **Paul W. Beshears**, b. 1918, MO

V9-1426. ¹¹-2. **Cordelia Beshears**, b. 1887, d. 1966, bur Vandalia Cem; m. ***Preston Hoagland***, b. 1892, MO

V9-1427. ¹²-1. Lawrence Hoagland, b. 1913, MO

V9-1428. ¹²-2. Marie Hoagland, b. 1914, MO

V9-1429. ¹¹-3. **Bessie Beshears**, b. 1890, d. 1954, bur Quincy, IL; m. ***Allen Woodson***, b. 1887, MO

V9-1430. ¹²-1. Lestie May Woodson, b. 1912, MO

V9-1431. ¹²-2. George Woodson, b. 1914, MO

V9-1432. ¹²-3. Mayo Woodson, b. 1916, MO

V9-1433. ¹²-4. Mabel Woodson, b. 1919, MO

V9-1434. ¹²-5. Lloyd Woodson, b. 1921, MO

V9-1435. ¹²-6. Mary Belle Woodson, b. 1925, MO

V9-1436. ¹²-7. Leonard Woodson, b. 1926, MO

V9-1437. ¹⁰-6. **Melissa "Sis" Beshears**, b. 1855, Ralls Co, MO; m. 8 Sept 1884, Ralls Co, MO, ***Henry A. Johnson***,

V9-1438. ¹⁰-7. **Zerelda Hazeltine Beshears**, b. 30 Nov 1857, Ralls Co, MO, d. 29 Nov 1916, bur Hays Creek Christian Cem, Ralls Co, MO; m. 13 Feb 1883, Ralls Co, MO, ***Leonard Smith McGrew***,

V9-1439. ¹¹-1. Susan Melissa McGrew, b. Jan 1884, d. 1961, bur Vandalia, MO; m. Everett Galloway, b. 11 Nov 1883, d. June 1969, Vandalia, Audrain Co, MO. no ch.

V9-1440. ¹¹-2. Iola McGrew, b. Nov 1887, d. 1969, bur Hays Creek Cem, Ralls Co, MO; m. Thomas F. "Tom" Fike, b. 30 March 1887, MO, d. May 1966, Bloomington, McLean Co, IL.

V9-1441. ¹²-1. Leonard Hamilton Fike, b. 1906, mo, d. 1 Nov 1989, Vandalia, Audrain Co, MO; m. Willie Maud _____, b, 1912, MO

V9-1442. ¹²-2. Esther L. Fike, b. 1909, d. 15 Dec 1999, Vandalia, Audrain Co, MO

V9-1443. ¹¹-3. Vicy McGrew, b. 8 Aug 1889, d. 1990, bur Vandalia Cem; m. Walter Rose, b, 1887, MO

V9-1444. ¹²-1. Alma Rose, b. 1911, MO

V9-1445. ¹¹-4. Elizabeth McGew, b. April 1893; m. Jesse Elzea, b. 1891, MO

V9-1446. 1. Alta M. Elzea, b. 1917, MO

V9-1447. ¹¹-5. Alma McGrew, b. 1899, d. 1900, bur Hays Creek Cem, Ralls Co, MO

V9-1448. ¹¹-6. infant son, still born 1898

V9-1449. ¹⁰-8. **Cordelia Beshears**, b. 26 Nov 1860, Spencerburg, Pike Co, MO, d. 24 Feb 1906, Spencerburg, bur Hayes Creek Cem, Ralls Co, MO; m. 7 Sept 1882, Ralls Co, MO, ***James Samuel Brice***, b. 6 Jan 1853, Spencersburg, Pike Co, MO, d. there.

V9-1450.   11-1. Lena Brice, b. 6 Jan 1884, Spencersburg, Pike Co, MO, d. June 1978, Vandalis, Audrain Co, MO; m. Lewis Outlaw, b. 1884, IL
V9-1451.   12-1. John W. Outlaw, b. 1908, MO
V9-1452.   12-2. Inez L. Outlaw, b. 1910, MO
V9-1453.   12-3. Raymond B. Outlaw, b. 1920, Mo, d. 11 Oct 1996, Vandalia, Audrain Co, MO
V9-1454.   11-2. Bessie Brice, b. 1886, d. 12 Aug 1893, bur Hays Creek Cem, Ralls Co, MO
V9-1455.   11-3. Delcie Brice, b. 8 Oct 1888, MO, d. Dec 1974, Vandalia, Audrain Co, MO; m. Byrd Hayden, b. 22 Aept 1886, IL, d. Sept 1973, Vandalia, Audrain Co, MO
V9-1456.   12-1. James Hayden, b. 1914, MO
V9-1457.   12-2. Gilbert Hayden, b. 1917, MO
V9-1458.   12-3. Elladee Hayden, b. 1922, MO
V9-1459.   12-4. Ruby Hayden, b. 1927, MO
V9-1460.   11-4. Zelma Brice, b. 1891, d. 9 Sept 1893, bur Hays Creek Cem, Ralls Co, MO
V9-1461.   11-5. infant son Brice, b.& d. 10 March 1893, bur Hays Creek Cem, Ralls Co, MO
V9-1462.   11-6. Cutie Inez Brice, b.7 April 1894, d. 28 April 1967; m. Orville L. Bland Sr, b. 1894, MO
V9-1463.   12-1. Elmo Bland, b. 1921, MO
V9-1464.   12-2. Pauline Bland, b. 1924, MO
V9-1465.   12-3. Leland B. Bland, b. 1927, MO
V9-1466.   12-4. Orville L. Bland, Jr, b. MO
V9-1467.   11-7. Elizabeth Brice, b. 1897, MO; m. James Asbury
V9-1468.   11-8. James Roy Brice, b. 21 Jan 1900, d. 17 April 1966; m. Dorothy _____,
V9-1469.   10-9. **John Lee Beshears**, b. 23 Feb 1863, MO, d. 25 Feb 1927; m.1. 10 Sept 1891, Ralls Co, MO, **Matilda Tea Caldwell**, (6 ch); m.2. **Nancy Sunser**, (no ch)
V9-1470.   11-1. **Lester Lee Beshears**, b. 1892, MO, d. 1914
V9-1471.   11-2. **Robert Hurley Beshears**, b. 27 Feb 1894, MO, d. Jan 1974, OkCity, OK; m. Maybelle _____, b. 1895, OK
V9-1472.   12-1. **Don O. Beshears**, b. 9 Sept 1920, Enid, Garfield Co, OK, d. there, Aug 1982.
V9-1473.   12-2. **Robert L. Beshears**, b. 17 Sept 1927, Enid, OK, d. 16 March 1995, OkCity, OK
V9-1474.   11-3. **Katherine Florence Beshears**, b. 1896, d. 7 April 1975; m. **Walter B. Garnett**, b. 1885, MO
V9-1475.   12-1. Victoria M. Garnett, b. 1914, MO
V9-1476.   12-2. Sarah B. Garnett, b. June 1917, MO

^{V9-}1477.   ¹²⁻3. Virginia Lee Garnett, b. Feb 19198, MO

^{V9-}1478.   ¹²⁻4. Butler Edward Garnett, b. Jan 1820, MO

^{V9-}1479.   ¹²⁻5. Gilbert S. Garnett, b. 23 Aug 1921, MO, d. July 1981, MO

^{V9-}1480.   ¹²⁻6. Hurley W. Garnett, b. 11 Sept 1923, MO, d. April 1984, Laddonia, Audrain Co, MO

^{V9-}1481.   ¹²⁻7. Rachel J. Garnett, b. 1926, MO

^{V9-}1482.   ¹²⁻8. Stanley R. Garnett, b. 1928, MO

^{V9-}1483.   ¹²⁻9. Dacheal N. Garnett, b. 1929, MO

^{V9-}1484.   ¹¹⁻4. **Russell Caldwell Beshears**, b. 1898, MO, d. Oct 1979, Youngtown, Maricopa Co, AZ; m. Edna M. _____, b. 9 Aug 1899, TX, d. 18 March 1989, Houston, Harris Co, TX

^{V9-}1485.   ¹²⁻1. **Richard L. Beshears**, b. 1929, OK

^{V9-}1486.   ¹¹⁻5. **infant beshears**, b.&d. 3 July 1901

^{V9-}1487.   ¹¹⁻6. **Glenn Newton Beshears**, b. 1904, Ok, d. Sept 1967, Youngtown, Maricopa Co, AZ; m. *Eva Matthews*, b. 1900, TX

^{V9-}1488.   ¹²⁻1. **Jack R. Beshears**, b. 21 March 1927, OK, d. 15 Sept 1996, Hemet, Riverside Co, CA

^{V9-}1489.   ¹⁰⁻10. **Emma Lucretia Beshears**, b. 31 Oct 1865, Ralls Co, MO, d. 16 Dec 1934, Shelby Co, MO, bur Shelbina Cem, Shelbina, Shelby Co, MO; m. 2 Nov 1890, Ralls Co, MO, *Joseph Newton Griggs*, b. 11 March 1867, IL, d. 26 Jan 1936, s/o Newton Griggs and Caroline M. Roberts.

^{V9-}1490.   ¹¹⁻1. Mollie Pearl Griggs, b. 25 Sept 1891, d. 3 Aug 1952; m. 13 Feb 1910, Jacob Bruce Brengle,

^{V9-}1491.   ¹²⁻1. Mildred Brengle, b. 1913, MO

^{V9-}1492.   ¹²⁻2. Helen Brengle, b. 1918, MO

^{V9-}1493.   ¹²⁻3. Harold G. Brengle, b. 2 June 1922, MO, d. 30 Sept 1988, Springfield, Greene Co, MO

^{V9-}1494.   ¹²⁻4. Doris Brengle, b. 1925, MO

^{V9-}1495.   ¹¹⁻2. Carson "Carsie" Griggs, b. 27 Nov 1893, d. young

^{V9-}1496.   ¹¹⁻3. Roxie May Griggs, b. 13 Jan 1895, d. 29 Dec 1956; m. 20 Feb 1916, Franklin D. Tanner, b. 1886, MO

^{V9-}1497.   ¹²⁻1. Lin Tanner, b. 1919, MO

^{V9-}1498.   ¹¹⁻4. Arthur Bryan Griggs, b. 24 Dec 1896, d. 17 Jan 1969; m. 30 Nov 1962, Martha Virginia Abell,

^{V9-}1499.   ¹¹⁻5. Claude Vincil Griggs, b. 4 Sept 1899, d. 4 June 1970; m.1. Frances Huffman, m.2. Mary (Lankford) Keller,

^{V9-}1500.   ¹¹⁻6. Joseph Hurley Griggs, b. 3 Oct 1901, MO, d. 22 May 1966; m. Dorothy Turner,

^{V9-}1501.   ¹¹⁻7. Charles Vaughn Griggs, b. 19 Nov 1903, MO, d. 16

July 1964; m. 30 June 1926, Alzoma Ridgway, b. 14 Sept 1900, MO, d. Nov 1973, Anabel, Macon Co, MO

V9-1502.   12-1. Charles M. Griggs, b. 12 June 1929, MO, d. Jan 1994, Anabel, Macon Co, MO

V9-1503.   11-8. Lucy Bell Griggs, b. 17 Aug 1906, MO; m. 22 Dec 1937, Joe G. Atterbury,

V9-1504.   11-9. Anna Pauline Griggs, b. 8 July 1910; m. 11 Aug 1928, Stanley Weatherford,

V9-1505.   10-11. **Idona Beshears**, b. May 1868, Ralls Co, MO, d. 1931, Center, MO bur. Mt Olivet Cem, Ralls Co, MO; m. 15 Nov 1893, *Francis Alvin Sayre*, b. 1864, MO

V9-1506.   11-1. John Henry "Hank" Sayre, b. 1895, d. 1950, bur Center, MO; m. Zoleta Iola _____, b. 1899, IL

V9-1507.   12-1. Edith Geneva Sayre, b. 1920, MO

V9-1508.   11-2. Hazel Sayre, b. 11 Nov 1896, MO, d. 1942, bur Milwaukee, WI; m. _____ Griffith,

V9-1509.   11-3. Elizabeth Sayre, b. 1899, MO, d. 1954, bur Salem Cem, Ralls Co, MO; m. Sylvester Turner, b. 1896, Mo, d. 1957

V9-1510.   12-1. Infant Turner, b.&d. 1 July 1917

V9-1511.   12-2. Earl Turner, b. 1913, MO

V9-1512.   12-3. Zella R. Turner, b. 1921, MO

V9-1513.   12-4. Virginia L. Turner, b. 1924, MO

V9-1514.   11-4. Annie Lee Sayre, b. 12 Feb 1904, MO, d. 13 Nov 1998, Osage Beach, Camden Co, MO; m. Ben Isman,

V9-1515.   10-12. **Ambrose B. Beshears**, b. 19 Aug 1871, Ralls Co, MO, d. 4 May 1936, bur Vandalia Cem, Vandalia, Audrain Co, MO; m. 23 Oct 1893, Ralls Co, MO, *Myra V. Butler*, b. 24 July 1871, Ralls Co, MO, d. 3 Jan 1919, bur Vandalia Cem, Vandalia, Audrian Co, MO, d/o Francis M. Butler and Nancy Hazelwood.

V9-1516.   11-1. **Della A. Beshears**, b. 7 Aug 1893, d. 21 Aug 1970; m. *Arch Schumbach*, b. 11 Nov 1894, d. 9 June 1959, no ch

V9-1517.   11-2. **Francis Earl Beshears**, b. 10 March 1895, MO, d. 10 Oct 1953, MO; m. 18 April 1918, *Fern Almeta Evans*, b. 1898, d. c1960, MO

V9-1518.   12-1. **Francis Earl Breshears Jr**, m. *Helen Anderson*,

V9-1519.   13-1. **Judith Ann Beshears**, m. 16 Jan 1960, *Sam Winner*,

V9-1520.   14-1. Lisa Winner, b. 20 Aug 1960

V9-1521.   14-2. Leon Winner, b. 8 Dec 1962

V9-1522.   13-2. **Janice Gay Beshears**, m. 1 June 1961,

		Claudie Burroughs,

V9-1523.   14-1. Sheila Renee Burroughs, b. 21 July 1962

V9-1524.   14-2. Scott Alan Burroughs, b. 4 March 1965

V9-1525.   14-3. Sara Beth Burroughs, b. 18 Feb 1969

V9-1526.   14-4. Shawn Christopher Burroughs, b. 18 Sept 1973

V9-1527.   13-3. **Gerald Wayne Beshears**, m. 12 Jan 1973, Janice Kay McMillen,

V9-1528.   14-1. **Albert Wayne Beshears**, b. 19 Jan 1975

V9-1529.   11-3. **Eula Mercedes Beshears**, b. 31 July 1900, d. 1986; m. 20 June 1920, **Walker Featherstone**, b. 1900, d. 1970, no ch

V9-1530.   11-4. **Wanda Beatrice Beshears**, b. 4 Jan 1903, d. 6 Oct 1944; m. **Warren Stanton,**

V9-1531.   11-5. **Velma May Beshears**, b. 30 May 1905, d. 1985, MO; m. **Rex Griggs**, b. 1900, d. 1940, 2 sons

V9-1532.   11-6. **Elmer Jackson Beshears**, b. 22 March 1907, d. 12 Feb 1979; m. 2 Jan 1932, **Ruby Mae Olebeare**, b. 16 Oct 1914, no ch

V9-1533.   11-7. **Austin Butler Beshears**, b. 30 Jan 1910, d. 14 Jan 1971, bur Vandalia Cem; m. **Edith Waterman,**

V9-1534.   12-1. **Wanda Sue Beshears,**

V9-1535.   12-2. **Austin Butler Beshears Jr**, unm in 1974; lives St. Louis, MO.

V9-1536.   11-8. **Willard Wayne Beshears**, b. 1 March 1913, d. 23 Nov 1926, age 13.

Madisonville, Ralls Co, Missouri
November the 5th, 1887

Dear sister and brother and Nieces and nephews,

I sit down this pleasant morning to answer your letter which came to hand. Some time ago we was glad to hear from you all. And that you all was well. I sure haven't much of importance to write. We all aren't married yet. Serraldo and Sis is married and both of them live in Barton County. Serraldo has been married four years in February. She was out to see us all two years ago this fall. Sis was married while she was out here in September the 8th to Henry Johnson. Serraldo stayed out here six weeks and this fall, her and Lenora came out to see us and stayed a month, while Sis and Henry taken care of things there. They live a quarter of a mile from one another and Sis and Henry came out too and stayed a month, too. They both have a girl. They are awful pretty. Sis's has black eyes just like her mom. She is awful pretty. Dea has a girl too. It looks just like Lenard did.

Her name is Lena Iola. She is awful sweet. She acts just like a little lady. Well you all must make up your mind to come out here to live in this county from Texas. We haven't long to live in this troublesome world. I think we might live so we can see one another. We all think about you all often way out there where we never hear from you all any more. We didn't know what to think. They're isn't hardly a day what Ma says something about you all. Ma says for you all to come out here to live. Ma says for you all to tell Uncle Will she would like to see him and his woman. She was glad to here from them that they was well. Well I will tell my affliction. I have the spinal disease. I haven't seen a well day since I had the nerves affliction. I can't hardly write. I tremble so.

Well I would write more, but I am getting tired and nervious. So will close for this time. Excuse the bad writing and spelling for this time and hoping to here from you all soon.

So good bye to all,
                    Your affectionate sister,
                    E.L. Besheare [Emma Lucretia Beshears]
(text of letter from Larry Howser <txace46@yahoo.com>
see BFB #116, p.10)

Lucinda Jane Beshears
and Charles W. Howser

v2-2079. **Lucinda Jane Beshears**, (d/o Jackson "John" Beshears and Elizabeth Keithley), b. 6 March 1844, Peno Twp, Pike Co, MO, d. 10 Nov 1890, Fairview, Cooke Co, TX, bur Whitesboro Cem, Grayson Co, TX; m. 25 April 1869 in Ralls Co, Missouri, **Charles W. Howser**, b. 18 Dec 1816, Oldham, KY, d. 31 Aug 1916, Cooke Co, TX, s/o Elijah Howser and Nancy Bridgewater. Charles W. Howser served in the 2nd Mo Infantry, Confederate States Army.

Whitesboro, TX,
Nov 19, 1890

Dear Mother,
I take this opportunity to break the bad news of our misfortune on the 10 of Lucinda's death. She was to all appearances as well as she was when you left though it was hard all day Monday. She was helping Armanthia to make Leon a shirt until eleven o'clock when they went in the kitchen to get dinner. Leon and I was sitting in the house a hulling peas. They were talking and laughing about how well we was getting along without Lenora and if the weather was there in proportion to here, how Nora was wishing herself back in Texas until they had dinner near ready on about twelve o'clock when Armanthia called to me to come there quick to ma. She was sitting in a chair by

the stove when I ran in. I said what is the matter ma. She said, "Oh, my feet tingles and I tingle all over." I began to rub her hands and told Leon to run down after Miss Day. After he had started, she screamed three or four times as though in great pain. She was only conscious perhaps about three minites after I got to her. I tingle all over was the only words she spoke. Mrs. Day and Bill came and we carried her in the house, then sent for the doctor. He got there too late to be of any service. She only lived a few minites after he got there. She was taken about twelve and owing to the rain that morning the children could not go to school. The doctor said if he

Charles W. Howser and Lucinda Beshears in back row. Couple directly in front of them is believed to be John Jackson Beshears and Elizabeth Keithley. Older woman at left, believed to be Elizabeth Whitton Beshears (Photo from Larry Howser).

had been there at the time she was taken, he could have done nothing as it was a death stroke. [page missing?]

And died at 1/2 past three and was buried the next evening. I would have wrote to you sooner, but the doctor thought best to call Lenora home before she heard what had happned as it would have been a terrible shock to her there and also on the way home when she got here. This leaves us all well except colds hoping to hear from you soon. I remain as ever yours truely,

C.W. Houser [Charles W. Howser]

Postmarked Nov 19, 1890, Whitesboro, TX:

To Elizabeth Beshears, Madisonville, MO

Family of Charles W. Howser and Lucinda Jane Beshears: (data from Larry Howser <txace46@yahoo.com>)

V9-1537.   11-1. Lenora Ella Howser, (d/o Charles W. Howser and Lucinda Jane Beshears), b. 6 March 1870, Jasper twp,

Ralls Co, MO, d. 18 Jan 1971, Cooke Co, TX, bur Oakwood Cem, Whitesboro, Grayson Co, TX; m. 15 Nov 1894, (in C.W. Howser home, Cooke Co, TX), Robert Brown Sims Jr, b. 6 April 1862, Stony Point, Collin Co, TX, d. 1 Jan 1948, Callisburg, Cooke Co, TX, bur Oakwood Cem, Whitesboro, Grayson Co, TX, s/o Robert Brown Sims Sr.

V9-1538.   12-1. William Horace Sims, b. 20 Oct 1895, Callisburg, Cooke Co, TX; d. 9 Aug 1981, Houston, Harris Co, TX; m. 1953, Mary Knollie; no ch

V9-1539.   12-2. Robert Milton Sims, b. 18 Feb 1897, Collinsville, Grayson Co, TX, d. 27 July 1982, bur Callisburg cem, Callisburg, Cooke Co, TX; m. 19 Aug 1919, Elizabeth Cornelia Clements, b. 12 May 1901, Callisburg, Cooke Co, TX, d. 19 Oct 1981, Sherman, Grayson Co, TX, bur Callisburg Cem, Cooke Co, TX.

V9-1540.   13-1. Milton Carlisle Sims, b. 29 Aug 1922, Whitesboro, Grayson Co, TX, d. 25 Sept 1996, Sherman, Grayson Co, TX; m.1. 12 March 1941, at Marietta, Love Co, OK, Lucille Marie Watson, b. 22 Dec 1923, Cooke Co, TX; m.2. 2 Feb 2002, Guadalajara, Mexico, Sylvia Navarro Rodriguez, b. 1955. Ch (1st- marriage):

V9-1541.   14-1. Billie Don Sims, b. 1 April 1942, Cooke Co, TX, d. 7 Jan 2004, bur Oakwood Cem, Whitesboro, Grayson Co, TX

V9-1542.   13-2. Johnny Maurice Sims, b. 3 May 1926, Whitesboro Grayson Co, TX; m. 18 Oct 1947, in Cooke Co, TX, Sallie M. Ball, b. 1933, Whitesboro, Grayson Co, TX. Ch:

V9-1543.   14-1. Larry Sims, b. 1948, Collinsville, Grayson Co, TX;

V9-1544.   14-2. Robert Sims, b. 1950;

V9-1545.   14-3. James Carlisle Sims, b. 3 Oct 1953, Canadian Hemphill Co, TX, d. 15 July 1968, Gaines Co, TX, bur Denver City Mem'l Park cem, Yoakum Co, TX;

V9-1546.   14-4. Jo Dene Sims (adopted).

V9-1547.   12-3. Johnnie Raymon Sims, b. 10 April 1900, Callisburg, Cook Co, TX, d. 27 Sept 1980, bur Callisburg cem, Cooke Co, TX; m.1. 6 Aug 1922, Leona Laura Tipps, b. 25 July 1903, Cooke Co, TX, d. 26 Aug 1959 (2 ch); m.2. 16 June 1963, Clara Roberson Flowers, b. 3 April 1901, Woodbine, Cooke Co, TX, d. 1 March 1994, Lewisville, Denton

Co, TX, bur Callisburg cem, Cooke Co, TX (no ch).

V9-1548.   13-1. John Robert Sims, b. 15 Oct 1930, Wichita Falls, TX; m.1. 28 June 1952, in Seattle, King Co, WA, Martha V. Knight, b. 17 Oct 1932, Dallas, TX; d. there 7 Sept 1990, bur Callisburg cem, Cooke Co, TX (3 ch). John Robert Sims, m.2. 24 May 1992, in Gainesville, Cooke Co, TX, Georgia Ann Van Ness, b. 1937 (no ch).

V9-1549.   14-1. Michael Sims,

V9-1550.   14-2. Mark Sims, b. 20 Jan 1958, d. 9 Oct 2000, bur Callisburg Cem, Cooke Co, TX, and

V9-1551.   14-3. Lisa Ann Sims, m. 23 Jan 1981, in Callisburg, Cooke Co, TX, Buddy Ray Moore, b. 23 May 1958, Grayson Co, TX.

V9-1552.   13-2. Mildred Pauline Sims, b. 1928; m. 1945, in Wichita Falls, TX, Thomas W. Parker, b. 1927, d. 23 May 1972, Wichita Co, TX. ch:

V9-1553.   14-1. Laura Katherine Parker

V9-1554.   12-4. Abner Austin Sims, b. 25 Feb 1905, Callisburg, Cooke Co, TX, d. there 4 Aug 1969, bur Callisburg Cem, Cooke Co, TX; m. 17 Oct 1936, in Durant, Bryan Co, OK, Essie Jeannetta Williams, b. 30 Sept 1914, Callisburg, Cooke Co, TX; d. 24 May 1995, Gainesville, Cooke Co, TX.

V9-1555.   13-1. Wanda Fae Sims, (twin) b.&d. 10 Nov 1939

V9-1556.   13-2. Fonda Sims, (twin) b.&d. 10 Nov 1939

V9-1557.   13-3. Judith Ann Sims, b. 24 Jan 1943, Cooke Co, TX; m. 24 Feb 1967, in Gainesville, Cooke Co, TX, (1 ch; div 1990), Grady Don Blanton, b. 22 Jan 1947, Cooke Co, TX.

V9-1558.   14-1. Brian Keith Blanton, b. 29 July 1971, Gainseville, Cooke Co, TX; m.1. Nov 1991, Stacy Marie Johnson, b. 26 Aug 1971, Cooke Co, TX (div 1996; 1 dau); m.2. 27 June 1998, in Gainesville, Cooke Co, TX, Laura Jean Blevins, b. 15 Nov 1974, Grayson Co, TX.

V9-1559.   15-1. Mikalya Dawn Blanton, b. 1995

V9-1560.   13-4. Janiece Aline Sims, b. 15 Jan 1946 Cooke Co, TX; m.1. 9 Aug 1968, in Callisburg, Cooke Co, TX, Danny L. White (1 ch; div); m.2. Frank Maynard.

V9-1561.   14-1. Rodney Lee White, b. 18 July 1972, Wise Co, TX; m. 10 Oct 1993, in Gainesville, Cooke Co, TX, Shannon Leigh Baker, b. 3

Sept 1968, Cooke Co, TX (1 ch)

^{V9-}1562.   ¹⁵⁻1. Zachary Lee White, 28 Sept 1993, Gainesville, Cooke Co, TX.

^{V9-}1563.   ¹²⁻5. Arthur Paul Sims, b. 28 Nov 1907, Callisburg, Cooke Co, TX, d. 24 Jan 1928, Cooke Co, TX, bur Oakwood Cem, Whitesboro, Grayson Co, TX; nm.

^{V9-}1564.   ¹²⁻6. Wesley Ralph Sims, b. 5 Feb 1914, Cooke Co, TX, d. 21 Oct 1995, Gainesville, Cooke Co, TX; m. 9 Oct 1937, in Thackerville, Love Co, OK, Jo Ann Dutton, b. 26 April 1920, Whitesboro, Grayson Co, TX, d. 2002, bur Callisburg cem, Cooke Co, TX.

^{V9-}1565.   ¹³⁻1. Margaret Ann Sims, b. 10 Aug 1938, Callisburg, Cooke Co, TX, d. 25 Nov 1999, Gainesville, Cooke Co, TX; m.1. 27 Nov 1960, in Whitesboro, Grayson Co, TX, Thomas Baker Brooksheare; m.2. Jerry Stailfy; no ch.

^{V9-}1566.   ¹³⁻2. Charles Edward Sims, b. 15 March 1941, Cooke Co, TX; m.1. 20 Aug 1966, in Gainesville, Cooke Co, TX, Sandra Sue Bond, b. 1944 (2 ch); m.2 Debra J. _____

^{V9-}1567.   ¹⁴⁻1. Charles Edward Sims Jr, b. 18 Jan 1968, Gainesville, Cooke Co, TX; m. 24 Feb 1991, in Gainesville, Cooke Co, TX, Michelle Jean Woolsey. (3 ch, all b. Gainesville, Cooke Co, TX)

^{V9-}1568.   ¹⁵⁻1. John Anthony Sims, b. 28 June 1991,
^{V9-}1569.   ¹⁵⁻2. Chelsea Renee Sims, b. 26 Sept 1994,
^{V9-}1570.   ¹⁵⁻3. Christopher Ryan Sims, b. 30 Jan 1997.
^{V9-}1571.   ¹⁴⁻2. Steven Ray Sims, b. 7 Jan 1971, Gainesville, Cooke Co, TX; m. 19 Aug 1994, in St. Thomas, Virgin Islands, Kristie Paige West, b. 19 July 1973, Cooke Co, TX.

^{V9-}1572.   ¹³⁻3. Sandra Sue Sims, b. 3 March 1943, Callisburg, Cooke Co, TX; m. 30 July 1966, in Custer City, Cooke Co, TX, William Elmer Cunningham, b. 17 Jan 1943, Gainesville, Cooke Co, TX, d. there 3 July 1989, bur Callisburg cem, Cooke Co, TX.

^{V9-}1573.   ¹⁴⁻1. Cassandra Lynn Cunningham, b. 13 May 1969, Gainesville, Cooke Co, TX; m. 3 Oct 1992, in Gainesville, Cooke Co, TX, Lewis Edward Moreland, b. 3 Sept 1970, (1 ch)

^{V9-}1574.   ¹⁵⁻1. William Riley Moreland, b. 10 May 1997, Gainesville, Cooke Co, TX,

^{V9-}1575.   ¹⁴⁻2. Tawni Leann Cunningham, b. 8 June 1971,

V9-1576.   13-4. Nancy Kaye Sims, b. 14 Dec 1946, Gainesville, Cooke Co, TX; m. 5 June 1969, Gary Don Perryman, b. 2 Nov 1946

V9-1577.   14-1. Tony Shea Perryman, b. 2 Nov 1973, Muenster, Cooke Co, TX

V9-1578.   11-2. Susan Armanthia Howser, (d/o Charles W. Howser and Lucinda Jane Beshears), b. 21 Nov 1873, Cooke Co, TX, d. 29 Nov 1927, bur Spring Creek Cem, Cooke Co, TX; m. 12 April 1911, in Cooke Co, TX, Lee B. Speake, a widower with 8 children. Susan did not have any children of her own. She died of a ruptured appendix.

V9-1579.   11-3. Hattie Jane Howser, (d/o Charles W. Howser and Lucinda Jane Beshears), (twin) b. 30 Oct 1876, Cooke Co, TX, d. 14 May 1878, Cooke Co, TX, bur Whitesboro, Grayson Co, TX

V9-1580.   11-4. Mattie Jane Howser, (d/o Charles W. Howser and Lucinda Jane Beshears), (twin) b. 30 Oct 1876, Cooke Co, TX, d. 17 May 1878, Cooke Co, TX, bur Whitesboro, Grayson Co, TX

V9-1581.   11-5. William Leon Howser, (s/o Charles W. Howser and Lucinda Jane Beshears), b. 19 June 1879, Cooke Co, TX, d. 17 Jan 1947, Cooke Co, TX, bur Oakwood Cem, Whitesboro, Grayson Co, TX; m. 7 Oct 1908, at Vashti, Clay Co, TX, Clara Karstetter, b. 6 Jan 1888, Cooke Co, TX, d. there 8 Jan 1955, bur Oakwood cem, Whitesboro, Grayson Co, TX (Ancestors of Larry Howser).

V9-1582.   12-1. Chauncey Loren Howser, b. 7 Jan 1912, Cooke Co, TX, d. 17 June 1978, San Antonio, Bexar Co, TX; m.1. 1932, in OK, Lorraine Wallace (no ch; div); m.2. 1949, Mrs. Edith Teague Kelly, b. 13 Nov 1907, Floresville, Wilson Co, TX, d. 29 June 2003; no ch.

V9-1583.   12-2. infant son Howser, b. & d. 13 June 1916

V9-1584.   12-3. Otis Roy Howser, b. 8 Sept 1917, Cooke Co, TX; m. 4 Dec 1940, at Gainesville, Cooke Co, TX, Velma Faye Thomas, b. 18 May 1918, Cooke Co, TX, d. there 8 April 2004, bur Callisburg cem, Cooke Co, TX.

V9-1585.   13-1. Larry Dean Howser, (twin) b. 4 Nov 1946, Gainesville, Cooke Co, TX; m. 29 May 1976, at Waco, McLennan Co, TX, Barbara Yvonne Riser, b. 22 March 1952, Longview, Gregg Co, TX, d/o Deryl Calcote Riser and Elisabeth Regina Anna Diehl. Larry Dean Howser is a researcher in this

	branch of the family.
V9-1586.	[14]-1. Michael Christopher Howser, b. 11 April 1979, Denton, TX
V9-1587.	[14]-2. Marcus Joseph Howser, b. 12 Feb 1985, Grand Prairie, Dallas Co, TX
V9-1588.	[13]-2. Ronnie Gene Howser, (twin) b. 4 Nov 1946, Gainesville, Cooke Co, TX; m. 3 June 1970, at Gainesville, Cooke Co, TX, Mary Ruth Wood, b. 22 May 1949, Cooke Co, TX
V9-1589.	[14]-1. Melanie Ruth Howser, b. 24 March 1972; m. 19 July 1997, Matthew Thomas McKnight, b. 16 July 1972
V9-1590.	[14]-2. Heather Marie Howser, b. 13 March 1985
V9-1591.	[12]-4. Otto Lloyd Howser, b. 3 Sept 1919; m. 15 Nov 1941, Winnie Doris Henderson, b. 24 Sept 1920
V9-1592.	[13]-1. Lloyd Gary Howser, b. 24 Dec 1942; m.1. Beverly Ann Hurley (no ch); m.2. Donna Jean Broak (no ch); m.3. Linda Kay Williams (1 ch); m.4. Andrea Ann Phelps (1 ch)
V9-1593.	[14]-1. Julia Dianne Howser, b. 13 Nov 1967; m. Jesse Linton Wilson (2 ch; div); m.2. 22 Sept 1995, in Denton Co, TX, Lowell L. Land (1 ch)
V9-1594.	[15]-1. Jessica Diane Wilson, b. 13 March 1988, Gainesville, Cooke Co, TX
V9-1595.	[15]-2. Jack Clinton Wilson, b. 22 June 1989, Gainesville, Cooke Co, TX
V9-1596.	[15]-3. Taran Elaine Land, b. March 1996, Denton Co, TX
V9-1597.	[14]-2. Shalanna D'Ann Howser, b. 25 Dec 1984
V9-1598.	[13]-2. Jimmie Leon Howser, b. 20 Dec 1950, Gainesville, Cooke Co, TX; m.1. 20 March 1970, in Gainesville, Cooke Co, TX, Sandra Jo Leach, b. 1950 (div 1975; 1 ch); m.2. 13 March 1976, in Dallas Co, TX, Debbie L. Kepley, b. 1954 (div 1977; no ch); m.3. 5 Nov 1977, Denise Mullins, b. 7 Dec 1954 (div 2001; 2 ch); m.4. Michelle
V9-1599.	[14]-1. Kali Jo Howser, b. 24 Feb 1975, TX; m. 15 Nov 2003, in San Francisco, CA, Josh Summer
V9-1600.	[14]-2. Sommer Michelle Howser, b. 10 Nov 1978, Smith Co, TX,
V9-1601.	[14]-3. James Micah Howser, b. 18 Nov 1982, Smith Co, TX

V9-1602.   12-5. Connie Lois Howser, b. 5 Jan 1921, Cooke Co, TX; m. 15 Sept 1941, William Ellis Moore Jr, b. 15 Sept 1919, Cooke Co, TX, d. there 2 June 1979, bur Callisburg cem, Cooke Co, TX (4 ch); m.2. 27 May 1988, in Cooke Co, TX, Joseph Oscar Fox, b. 26 July 1913, Cooke Co, TX, d. there 29 July 1989, bur Fairview Cem, Gainesville, Cooke Co, TX (no ch)

V9-1603.   13-1. Martha Ann Moore, b. 20 June 1943, San Antonio, Bexar Co, TX; m. 24 Feb 1962, in Cooke Co, TX, George Earl Cox, b. 27 July 1942, Tioga, Grayson Co, TX

V9-1604.   14-1. David Earl Cox, b. 16 May 1963, Cooke Co, TX; m. 1991, Crystal Bateman.

V9-1605.   15-1. Whitney Ann Cox, b. 8 May 1992, Sherman, Grayson Co, TX

V9-1606.   14-2. Deborah Lynn Cox, b. 25 April 1967, Cooke Co, TX; m. 31 Aug 1991, in Cooke Co, TX, James Mark Emerson Jr, b. 16 Nov 1968, Knox Co, TX (div 1995; 1 ch); Deborah m.2. 21 June 1997, in Cooke Co, TX, Ronald Mark Wolper, b. 1 July 1971

V9-1607.   15-1. Calvin Ray Emerson, b. 6 March 1994

V9-1608.   14-3. Terrie Ann Cox, b. 28 May 1975, Cooke Co, TX; m. 18 April 1998, in Cooke Co, TX, Terry Joe Thomas Jr, b. 8 Nov 1967, Washington Co, TX

V9-1609.   13-2. William Royce Moore, b. 24 April 1945, Cooke Co, TX; m. 10 Sept 1966, in Cooke Co, TX, Linda Faye Woolsey, b. 3 Nov 1946, Wise Co, TX

V9-1610.   14-1. Anna Michelle Moore, b. 29 June 1968, Cooke Co, TX; m. 1 June 1991, Bryan Keith Rains,

V9-1611.   15-1. Caleb Zachary Rains, b. 10 April 1996, Denton, Denton Co, TX;

V9-1612.   15-2. Colton Daniel Rains, b. 28 Feb 1998, Denton, TX;

V9-1613.   15-3. Cayden Matthew Rains, b. 20 Dec 2001, Denton, TX

V9-1614.   14-2. Carol Denise Moore, b.&d. 21 March 1971, Cooke Co, TX, bur Fairview cem, Gainesville, Cooke Co, TX.

V9-1615.   14-3. Timothy William Moore, b. 13 June 1972, Cooke Co, TX; m. 25 April 1998, in Cooke Co, TX, Trina Jo Ward, b. 6 July 1976;

V9-1616.   15-1. Morgan LeAnn Moore, b. 14 July 2001,

	Cooke Co, TX;
V9-1617.	15-2. Ethan William Moore, b. 15 Sept 2003, Cooke Co, TX
V9-1618.	13-3. Jimmie Ellis Moore, b. 6 Jan 1947, Cooke Co, TX; m. 21 Dec 1956, in Ft Worth, Tarrant Co, TX, Jessa Dene Moore, b. 5 Feb 1949, Tarrant Co, TX, d/o Rev. L.O. Moore. (two adopted ch)
V9-1619.	14-1. John Eric Moore, b. 1 Sept 1972; m.1. May 1995, Karen Sue Green. (div 2000; 1 ch); m.2. 9 Aug 2002, in Wichita Co, TX, Kathy Smith Tucker.
V9-1620.	15-1. Natalie Sue Moore, b. 14 June 1995, Wichita Co, TX
V9-1621.	14-2. Victoria Renee Moore, b. May 1974, South America. (1 ch)
V9-1622.	15-1. Brianna Renee Chester, b. 3 Dec 1997, Cooke Co, TX (father: David Chester)
V9-1623.	13-4. Betty Jean Moore, b. 9 Sept 1956, Cooke Co, TX; m. Aug 1974, Cooke Co, TX, Lewis Wayne Moore, b. 29 Aug 1955
V9-1624.	14-1. Lisa Elaine Moore, b. 17 Dec 1975, Cooke Co, TX; m. 22 Oct 1994, in Cooke Co, TX, Jerry Daniel Jones, b. 23 Aug 1976, Cooke Co, TX (2ch: Tanner Jones; Micah Jones)
V9-1625.	14-2. Amy Karis Moore, b. 4 Nov 1976, Cooke Co, TX; m. 25 May 1998, in Cooke Co, TX, Aaron Mitchell Davis, b. 26 June 1976, Hemphill Co, TX. (ch: Karis Nicole Davis, b. 4 March 2002, Cooke Co, TX)

Contacts who sent data:
- Larry Howser, 2910 Vineyard Drive, Arlington, TX 760[15-2027], (see BFB, #112:p.7); (txace46@yahoo.com)
- Mrs. Linda Seevers, 4050 Azalea Lane, Apt C, Joplin, MO 64801;
- Mrs. Bryan Griggs of Shelbina, MO;
- Mrs. Nelda McCrory, 2205 Ridgemont, Columbia, MO 65203-1539;
- Peggy McClain, Rt 1, Wellsville, MO 63384.
- Maureen Morisano, 52 Winham Ave, Staten Island, NY 10306

5. PARTHENA (BRASHEARS) REA

V2-72. [9-2]. **Parthena "Thena" Brashears,** (d/o 8-2. Phillip Brashears, of Jackson Co, IL in 1850, gs/o Robert Brashears and Patsy Wilson, ggs/o Phillip Brashears, Sr, and Ann Wilson) was born 14 July 1811 in Rutherford County, TN, and died 10 May 1896 in Webster County, MO, Burial: Timber Ridge Cemetery, Webster County, MO. She married (1) 1830 in Benton, Franklin Co, IL, *Thomas Henry Rea*, IL, s/o Abner Rea and Nancy Phillips. He was born 11 June 1811 in Bedford County, TN, and died April 1861 in Franklin County, IL. She married (2) 8 Aug 1853, *Henry Tefertillar*. He was born c1811.

"Thena" and Thomas Henry Rea apparently got a divorce after their daughter, Adeline, was born in 1849 and before the 1850 census enumeration. (Thomas did not die until 1861.) Thena was enumerated in the household of her father in 1850.

1850 Census, Jackson County, IL - Northern District
Phillip Brashears -   67 - b. VA - value is 100
Thena Ray   38 b. cannot read it
Betsey Ray   29 b. TN
William J. P. Ray 10 b. IL
James Henry Ray   5 b. IL
Thomas H. B. Ray   8 b. IL
Adeline E. Ray   1 b. IL
Carthena Ray   3/12 IL

1860 Franklin County, IL Census
Henry Tefertillar   79, married and a farmer
"Sena" Terfertillar49 b. in VA.
William J. Rea,   20, Farm laborer, b. IL
James H. Rea,   15, Farm Laborer b. IL
Adeline H. Rea   10

Children of Parthena Brashears and Thomas Rea:

V2- 76.[10-1]. William J.P. Rea, b. c1840, Franklin Co, IL; m. Mary Woods, 13 July 1863, Franklin Co, IL; b. Bef. 1850.

V2-77.   [10-2]. Thomas H. B. Rea, b. c1842, Franklin Co, IL; m. Mary Ann Overturf, 21 Dec 1863, Franklin Co, IL; b. Franklin Co, IL.

V9-1626.   [10-3]. Daniel Robert Rea, b. c1843, Franklin Co, IL; d. 1895. He married (1) Anna Wilson, daughter of _____ Wilson and Ferby Rea. b. c1843. He married (2) Amanda Lucy Brashears. b. c1843.

V9-1627.   11-1. James Thomas Rea, b. 1874; d. 1954.

V2-78.   10-4. *James Henry Rea, b. 29 June 1845, Franklin Co, IL; d. 14 Nov 1919, Dallas Co, MO; m. Nancy Eubanks, b. 4 Jan 1843

V2-79.   10-5. Carthena Rea, b. 1850, Franklin Co, IL.

V2-80.   10-6. *Adeline Elizabeth Rea, b. 6 - 8 April 1849, Franklin Co, IL; d. 5 Oct 1921, Manes, Wright Co, MO; m. William Henry Mansker.

James Henry Rea and Nancy Eubanks

V2-78. 10-3. James Henry Rea was born 29 June 1845 in Franklin Co, IL, and died 14 Nov 1919 in Dallas Co, MO. He married Nancy Eubanks 7 Jan 1865 in Mulkeytown, Franklin Co, IL, daughter of John D. Eubanks and Nancy Smothers. She was born 14 Jan 1843 in Franklin Co, IL, and died 18 Jan 1931 in Charity, Dallas Co, MO. James was a member of the Church of Christ. Samuel Brashear, M.G., his cousin and son of Absalom Brashear and Nancy _____, performed the wedding ceremony.

Nancy Eubanks was the daughter of John D. Eubanks, MD, born July 1800. He was a chaplain and surgeon in Mexican War and died at Tampico, Mexico in December 1847.

In Feb 1862, James enlisted in Company K, 30th Illinois Infantry. Later in Company A, 136th Illinois Infantry. Mustered out in October 1864. Was at Chickamanga, Moscow, and siege of Vicksburg and Lookout Mountain, Tennessee and "many minor engagements." Was wounded at Chickamanga. At close of Civil War returned to Illinois where he lived until fall of 1877 when he moved to Greene Co, Missouri until 1884. He then moved to Webster Co, MO where he lived until 1898 when he moved to Dallas Co, MO.

-Paraphrased from an article in the "Buffalo Reflex" - Buffalo, MO, November 20, 1919

According to records applying for veterans pension, James was vaccinated for Smallpox upon entry into the Union Army. At this time he, along with many others in his company, were (by testimony of several) infected with syphilis from blood taken from the arm of one infected with the disease.

A detailed account of his health is in the application for pension made by his widow. It would appear she and James went to great lengths to show that he was healthy when going into the army and further to show that he acquired the disease as the result of infected blood taken from another and not from any action of his own.

He was also said to have suffered sunstroke while in the service and to have only been able to do the work of 1/3 of a man after returning home following the war.

Jewel Rayborn Neilson has many papers containing this testimony from both doctors and his commanding officer in the Union Army.

Children of James Henry Rea and Nancy Eubanks:

V9-1628. 11-1. Emma D. Rea, b. 16 Nov 1865, Franklin Co, IL; d. 13 April 1957, Southgate, CA; m. John Valentine Atterberry, 21 March 1885, Webster Co, MO; b. 8 March 1863, Elkland, MO; d. 21 Nov 1950. Both bur Charity Cemetery, Dallas Co, MO

V9-1629. 11-2. J. Harvey Rea, b. 11 Oct 1867, Franklin Co, IL; d. Wichita, KS; m. Ethel B. Stepp, 31 Jan 1891, Dallas Co, MO; bur Kiowa, KS

V9-1630. 11-3. Rosie E. Rea, b. 6 April 1870, Franklin Co, IL; d. c1945, California; m. Charlie Washington Atteberry, 17 Jan 1885, Webster Co, MO; b. 14 April 1866.

V9-1631. 11-4. Benjamin F. Rea, b. 7 Aug 1872, Franklin Co, IL; d. 16 March 1970, Springfield, MO; m. (1) Alice Atterberry, 30 June 1897, Webster Co, MO; m. (2) Carrie Owensby, 8 Aug 1908, MO; b. 6 Feb 1879; d. 22 March 1947, MO. Both bur Oaklawn Cemetery, Buffalo, MO

V9-1632. 11-5. Thomas Edison Rea, b. 19 Sept 1874, Franklin Co, IL; d. Deer Creek, Grant Co, OK; m. Melvina Highfill, 29 Sept 1896, Dallas Co, MO; b. c1877; d. 1961; bur Mount Olive Cemetery, Deer Creek, Oklahoma. (contact: Richard S. Fulton, 4050 Frankford Rd, #302, Dallas, TX 75827)

V9-1633. 12-1. Harry Rea, b. 1897

V9-1634. 12-2. Chloe Dora Rea, b. 1899, d. 1980; m. Francis J. George

V9-1635. 13-1. Billie George, b. 1921; m.1. Charlie Combs, m.2. Bob Holloway. Children: Judy Combs, b. 1943, m. Bob Rea; Nancy Combs, b. 1950, m. Shelly Handleman

V9-1636. 13-2. George Rea George, b. 1924

V9-1637. 13-3. Robert Lee George, b. 1926; m. Olivette Belander. Children: Olivette M. George, b. 1956, m.1. Gary Dean Bartel, m.2. Richard S. Fulton; Mimi George, b. 1961, m. Tommy Bracey

V9-1638. 12-3. Burl Rea, b. 1901, m. Matty George,

V9-1639. 12-4. Dearl Rea, b. 1903

V9-1640. 12-5. James Rea, b. 1905

V9-1641. 12-6. Oleta Rea, b. 1907

V9-1642. 12-7. Wayne Rea, b. 1909

V9-1643. 12-8. Clifford Rea, b. 1914

V9-1644. 12-9. Madeline Rea, b. 1915
V9-1645. 11-6. Harry Rea, b. 10 Aug 1877, Franklin Co, IL; d. 21 Dec
          1955, St. Joseph, MO; m. 27 Feb 1901, Dallas Co, MO,
          Alma Alford, b. 21 Jan 1882, Dallas Co, MO; d. 8 Nov
          1973, Dallas Co, MO.
V9-1646. 12-1. Hazel Rea, b. 1902; late of Buffalo, MO. Hazel sent
          data, for which many thanks.
V9-1647. 12-2. Paul Rea, b. 1904
V9-1648. 12-3. Hallie Rea, b. 1907
V9-1649. 12-4. Ward Rea, b. 1909
V9-1650. 12-5. Irene Rea, b. 1912
V9-1651. 11-7. Maurice Van Rea, b. 29 Feb 1880, Greene Co, MO; d.
          19 Jan 1950, California; m. Lola Jane Fultz, 15 June
          1907, Dallas Co, MO; b. 30 Nov 1889; d. 20 Jan 1969.
          Both bur Charity Cemetery, Dallas Co, MO
V9-1652. 11-8. Abraham S. Rea, b. 24 May 1882, Greene Co, MO; m.
          (1) Gertie Dooley, 8 Aug 1904, MO; m. (2) Sarah Skaggs,
          25 June 1909, Dallas Co, MO; Bur Waverly, MO

Adeline Elizabeth Rea
and William Henry Mansker

Adeline Elizabeth Rea was born 6–8 April 1849 in Franklin Co, IL,
and died 5 Oct 1921 in Manes, Wright Co, MO; bur Coon Creek
Cemetery, Wright Co, MO. She married, at the home of James Rea,
William Henry Mansker on 5 Aug 1866 in Franklin Co, IL, s/o Michael
W. Mansker and Martha Wilson. He was born bet. 14 Feb 1841 in
Franklin Co, IL, and died 11 April 1926 in Blackwell, OK.

William Henry Mansker, Private, Company F, 44th Illinois Infantry.
He enlisted at Chicago on 28 August 1861, and by July 1865 he had re-
enlisted and was stationed at Port Lavaca, Texas, where he contracted
a kidney ailment caused by exposure to the elements and by hard
marching. He was discharged at Camp Irwin, Texas, on 25 September
1865.

William Henry Mansker got several Land Grants:
#1 E⌐SW 34/ 32-N 19-W N 5th Principal Meridian 0   acres Webster
#2 SWSE 34/ 32-N 19-W N 5th Principal Meridian 0   acres Webster
#3 E⌐2NW 3/ 31-N 19-W N 5th Principal Meridian 155.25 acres Webster

William Henry had 2 children in IL and then moved to MO. They
settled on a farm near The Rock Stare, North of Hartville. Around the
turn of the century, they moved to Manes, MO, where they lived until
their deaths. They had 7 children while living in MO.

Children of Adeline Rea and William Mansker

V9-1653.   11-1. Laura Bell Mansker, b. 8 Sept 1869, Duquoin, Perry Co, IL; d. 1 Oct 1957, Springfield, MO. She married James W. Reaves c1888 in MO. He was born c1865 in MO in MO.

V9-1654.   12-1. Elmer Reaves,
V9-1655.   12-2. Rhoda Reaves,
V9-1656.   12-3. Stella Reaves,
V9-1657.   12-4. William Reaves,
V9-1658.   12-5. Ollie Reaves,
V9-1659.   12-6. Gladys Reaves,
V9-1660.   12-7. Nellie Reaves,
V9-1661.   12-8. Ila Reaves,
V9-1662.   12-9. Albert Reaves,

V9-1663.   11-2. Ollie Rayborn Mansker, b. 25 May 1872, Duquoin, Perry Co, IL; d. 8 Aug 1950, Tulsa, OK. She married (1) George Washington Rayborn 14 May 1896 in MO. He was born 15 June 1861 in McMinn Co, TN, and died 9 March 1930 in Tulsa, OK. Both bur Green Mountain Cemetery, Mountain Grove, MO. She married (2) Lens W. Hensley 1936. He died 1939 in Hartville, Wright Co, MO.

V9-1664.   12-1. Jesse Winett Rayborn, b. 15 Feb 1897, Rayborn, Wright Co, MO; d. 19 Sept 1957, Cairo, IL. He married Gertie Lula Alice Dake, 5 May 1917 in Tulsa, OK. She was born 18 July 1898 in Mountain Grove, Wright Co, MO, and died 8 July 1980 in Tulsa, OK.

V9-1665.   13-1. Jewel Juanita Rayborn, b. 23 April 1918, Tulsa, OK; d. 31 Oct 1998, Houston, TX.

V9-1666.   13-2. Marjorie Leone Rayborn, b. 9 June 1920, Tulsa, OK; d. 31 Dec 1992, Joshua Tree, CA.

V9-1667.   13-3. Wilma Ione Rayborn,
V9-1668.   13-4. William Howard Rayborn,

V9-1669.   11-3. Ella Mae Mansker, b. 11 April 1874, Duquoin, Perry Co, IL; d. 9 Jan 1951, Hartville, Wright Co, MO. She met Jesse Wood 1 June 1898 in Hartville, Wright Co, MO. He was born 13 Sept 1864 in Tennessee, and died 5 July 1937 in MO.

V9-1670.   12-1. Nettie Arlie Wood, b. 22 March 1899;
V9-1671.   12-2. Baby Girl Wood, b. 14 Oct 1903, MO; d. 14 Oct 1903, MO.
V9-1672.   12-3. Jewell Gladys Wood, b. 13 Jan 1905.
V9-1673.   12-4. Opal Wood, b. 27 April 1906, MO; d. 13 March 1973; m. Vearl Rowe;

V9-1674.   12-5. Agnes Wood,
V9-1675.   12-6. Nora Velma Wood, She married Loman Ferriel
V9-1676.   13-1. Joyce Dorene Ferriel,
V9-1677.   13-2. Esther Carrol Ferriel,
V9-1678.   13-3. Wilda Ferriel,
V9-1679.   11-4. William Harry Mansker, b. 25 Sept 1876, Franklin Co,
                  IL; d. of heart attack, 6 March 1954, Wright Co, MO. He
                  married (1) Mayme Jane Wilson c1896 in MO, d/o
                  Thomas Davis and Mary McDavies. She was born 13
                  Nov 1876 in Hartville, Wright Co, MO, and died 26 Feb
                  1920 in Hartville, Wright Co, MO. He married (2) Nora
                  Hawk. She was born 4 March 1883 in Columbus, OH,
                  and died 5 April 1976 in Wright Co, MO.
V9-1680.   12-1. Ada Mae Mansker, b. 1 Oct 1897, MO; d. c1900,
                  MO.
V9-1681.   12-2. Clella Mansker, b. Nov 1898, MO; d. c1900, MO.
V9-1682.   12-3. Berchia Ethyl Mansker, b. 23 Jan 1900, MO; d.
                  1983, Tulsa, OK. She married Virgil Marvin Edgar
                  Lee Moore 28 April 1920 in Hartville, Wright Co, MO.
                  He died Unknown in Tulsa, OK.
V9-1683.   13-1. Verna Ruth Moore,
V9-1684.   13-2. Noel Dean Moore,
V9-1685.   13-3. Maxine Moore; m. Asa Albert Hogue
V9-1686.   13-4. Eugene Albert Moore,
V9-1687.   13-5. Theodore Moore,
V9-1688.   12-4. Stella Mae Mansker, b. 13 Oct 1903, MO; d. 1 April
                  1987, Charleroi, PA. She married William Adam Fry
                  in MO. He was born 5 Aug 1892 in MO, and died 21
                  Dec 1951 in Fallowfield Twp, PA.
V9-1689.   13-1. Marjorie Glee Fry,
V9-1690.   13-2. Maymie Glee Fry,
V9-1691.   12-5. Kermit Braden Mansker, b. 11 Oct 1907, MO; d. 29
                  July 1969, Lebanon, MO. He married Nell M. Brook
V9-1692.   13-1. Russell Mansker,
V9-1693.   12-6. Delsa Leather Mansker, b. 18 Feb 1912, MO; d. 7
                  Nov 1979, Planada, CA. She married (1) Leonard
                  England. She married (2) Bill Knudsen. She married
                  (3) Edward Rose
V9-1694.   13-1. Sue England,
V9-1695.   12-7. Thurman "Bill" Hayden Mansker, b. 5 April 1915,
                  Wright Co, MO; d. 29 June 1986, Lebanon, LaClede
                  Co, MO. He married (1) Francis Curtis (2 ch);
                  married (2) Virginia Gail Gibbons (6 ch)
V9-1696.   13-1. Curtis Layne Mansker; m. Carole Fisk,
V9-1697.   13-2. Beverly Ann Mansker,

V9-1698.   13-3. Michael Hayden Mansker,

V9-1699.   13-4. Patrick Alan Mansker,

V9-1700.   13-5. Stephen Dale Mansker,

V9-1701.   13-6. Gail Jeanne Mansker,

V9-1702.   13-7. Lela Jane Mansker,

V9-1703.   13-8. William L. Mansker,

V9-1704.   11-5. Margaret Eva "Maggie" Mansker, b. Bet. 19 Dec 1879 -
              1880, Pinckneyville, Perry Co, IL; d. 7 Aug 1949,
              Mountain Grove, Wright Co, MO. She married (1) Cecil
              Earl Wood. He was born bet. 11 Jan 1880–1888 in
              Hartville, Wright Co, MO, and died 13 Nov 1958 in
              Mountain Grove, Wright Co, MO. She married (2) James
              W. Pettyjohn 30 Aug 1897 in Wright Co, MO. He was
              born 19 Feb 1877 in MO, and died 16 Aug 1909.

V9-1705.   12-1. Jesse Hayden Wood,

V9-1706.   12-2. Ruth Wood,

V9-1707.   12-3. Everett C. Pettyjohn, b. Feb 1898;

V9-1708.   12-4. Ella N. Pettyjohn, b. April 1900;

V9-1709.   12-5. William T. Pettyjohn, b. 1905;

V9-1710.   12-6. Pearl Pettyjohn,

V9-1711.   12-7. Howard Pettyjohn,

V9-1712.   11-6. Icy Ola Mansker, (twin) b. 11 Feb 1883, Illinois; d. 18
              Aug 1905, Wright Co, MO. She died at childbirth or soon
              after her son Orville Carter was born. Although it cannot
              be verified, it was told to Jewel Rayborn that the cause
              of death was "Her husband starved her to death." -Jewel
              Rayborn Neilson. "and as a result her family never spoke
              to her husband again." -Gail Mansker. She married Silas
              Adam Carter 30 Nov 1901 in Wright Co, MO, s/o
              Cornelius Carter and MO Elizabeth. He was born 9 Aug
              1869 in Wright Co., MO, and died 23 Aug 1949 in
              Hartville, Wright Co., MO.

V9-1713.   12-1. Orville Carter, b. 1901, MO; m. (1) Blanche Carder;
              m. (2) Alsie Walker,

V9-1714.   11-7. Nellie Dora Mansker, (twin) b. 11 Feb 1883, MO; d.
              1883, Manes, MO. died at 7 months.

V9-1715.   11-8. Benjamin Franklin Mansker, b. 19 Oct 1888, Webster,
              MO; d. 5 Oct 1978, Lebanon, LaClede Co, MO. He
              married Stella Joan Bresler 23 April 1923 in MO. She
              was born 18 Sept 1895 in MO, and died 1 Nov 1977 in
              Lebanon, LeClede Co, MO.

V9-1716.   12-1. James Mansker, He married Norma _____

V9-1717.   13-1. Kenneth James Mansker, b. 27 Aug 1958; d. 10
                   July 1993.

V9-1718.   12-2. Paul Mansker, b. 16 March 1924, MO; d. MO. He married Edith Tate

V9-1719.   13-1. Frieda Joan Mansker,

V9-1720.   13-2. Dennis Mansker,

V9-1721.   12-3. B.F. Mansker, b. 17 Sept 1932, Wright Co, MO; d. MO. He married Ada Marie Cuthbirth Shields 22 June 1955 in Lebanon, LeClede Co, MO. She was born 1 June 1931 in Long Lane, Dallas Co, MO

V9-1722.   13-1. Sheila Faye Mansker,

V9-1723.   13-2. Larry Dale Mansker, b. 1 Feb 1958, MO; d. March 1958, MO.

V9-1724.   13-3. Ralph Douglas Mansker,

V9-1725.   13-4. Sharon Kay Mansker,

V9-1726.   13-5. Lisa Marie Mansker, b. 7 Sept 1968, MO; d. Sept 1968, MO.

V9-1727.   13-6. Darren Keith Mansker,

V9-1728.   12-4. Virginia Mansker,

V9-1729.   12-5. Laura Mansker,

V9-1730.   12-6. Margaret Mansker,

V9-1731.   12-7. Gertrude Mansker,

V9-1732.   12-8. Agnes Mansker,

V9-1733.   12-9. Geneva Irene Mansker, b. 16 Oct 1928, MO; d. 27 Jan 1940, MO.

V9-1734.   11-9. John Henry Mansker, b. bet. 1 Oct 1865 - 1867, Franklin Co or Macon Co, IL; d. 15 June 1954, Hartville, Wright Co, MO. He married (1) Zelpha Adeline Ray in Springfield, MO, d/o James Ray and Louisa Ray. She was born 1870 in MO, and died Oct 1907 in Hartville, MO (Wright Co). He m. (2) Arminta Elizabeth Sullivant 15 Sept 1909 in MO, d/o John Jr and Rosetta Hammonds. She was born 5 Oct 1879 in MO, and died 20 July 1967 in Wright Co, MO.

Children of John Mansker and Zelpha Ray:

V9-1735.   12-1. Unknown Son,

V9-1736.   12-2. Wiley Mansker, b. 29 Oct 1905, Manes, Wright Co, MO; d. 18 July 1964, Decatur, Macon Co, IL. He married Mary Emily Hopkins 10 Dec 1923 in Iola, KS, d/o Henry "Bunk" Hopkins and Sarah Suey. She was born 1 Sept 1897 in Cherryvale, Montgomery Co, Kansas, and died 18 April 1963 in Peoria, IL.

V9-1737.   13-1. Mary Ellen Mansker, b. 22 Aug 1929, Peoria, IL; d. 15 Oct 1987, Washington, IL buried in Swan Lake Memorial Gardens, Peoria, IL.

V9-1738.   13-2. Beverly Mansker,

V9-1739.   13-3. Wiley Mansker Jr.,

V9-1740.   13-4. Nancy Lee Mansker,
V9-1741.   13-5. Frances Evelyn Mansker, b. 9 Dec 1925,
                  Cherryvale, KS; d. 15 Feb 2003, Bartonville,
                  Peoria Co, IL.
V9-1742.   13-6. Shirley Lavon Mansker,
V9-1743.   13-7. Delores May Mansker,
V9-1744.   13-8. Donna June Mansker,
V9-1745.   13-9. Barbara Jean Mansker,
V9-1746.   12-3. May Mansker, b. 26 Nov 1896, MO; d. Sioux Falls,
                  SD. She married Sherman Ralph Bartholow. He was
                  born 8 Aug 1891 in McCook Co, SD, and died 13
                  July 1970 in Sioux Falls, SD.
V9-1747.   13-1. Donald Bartholow,
V9-1748.   12-4. John Leslie Mansker, b. bet. 21 Jan 1900 - 10 Jan
                  1901, Joplin, MO; d. 30 June 1965, Portland, OR
                  (or Pendleton, OR). He married Georgia Pierce
V9-1749.   13-1. Gary Lee Mansker,
V9-1750.   13-2. Wilma Mansker,
V9-1751.   12-5. Twin to Dudley Mansker, b. 11 Oct 1903; d. 11 Oct
                  1903.
V9-1752.   12-6. Earnest Earl Mansker, b. 18 Oct 1898, Ranger, TX;
                  d. 18 Nov 1959, Springfield, Green Co, MO. He
                  married (1) Laura Mae Alexander (4 ch) He married
                  (2) Lena Marie Inez Bush (2 ch) in Possibly Idaho.
                  She was born 3 Dec 1900 in Bartlesville, OK, and
                  died 19 Aug 1987 in Humble, TX.
V9-1753.   13-1. Rosa Lee Mansker,
V9-1754.   13-2. Earnest Mansker Jr.,
V9-1755.   13-3. Johnny Mansker,
V9-1756.   13-4. Daniel Elijah Mansker,
V9-1757.   13-5. Willard Gene Mansker, b. 22 Jan 1927,
                  Seminole, OK; d. 11 Nov 1997, Spring,
                  Montgomerty Co, TX.
V9-1758.   13-6. Donald Louis Mansker,
V9-1759.   12-7. Minnie Mansker, b. 20 Dec 1894, Wright Co, MO; d.
                  16 Jan 1982, Seattle, WA. She married (1) Walter
                  Garner. She married (2) Hoffman. She married (3)
                  Odell.
V9-1760.   13-1. Zelma Garner,
V9-1761.   13-2. Lyle Garner,
V9-1762.   13-3. Eugene Garner,
V9-1763.   12-8. Rosa Adeline Mansker, b. 24 Oct 1907, Wright Co,
                  MO; d. 17 July 1999, Peoria, IL. She met (1) Willard
                  Cecil McCabe 27 Oct 1924 in Iola, KS. He was born
                  9 Aug 1900, and died 1989. She married (2) Jerry

Pheasant 22 Aug 1959 in Preston, MN, s/o David Pheasant and Blanche Hooper. He was born 6 Nov 1906 in Huntington, PA, and died 6 Sept 1996 in Peoria, IL.

V9-1764. 13-1. Nadine McCabe; m. Michael Vecchio
V9-1765. 13-2. Darrell McCabe; m. Lela Christenson
V9-1766. 13-3. Emmaglee McCabe; m. William Dunn
V9-1767. 13-4. Patsy Lou McCabe; m. Phillip Morgan
V9-1768. 13-5. Robert Pheasant,
V9-1769. 12-9. Laura May Mansker, b. 26 Nov 1896, MO; d. 17 Oct 1993, Sioux Falls, SD. She married Sherman Ralph Bartholow 19 Oct 1919 in Manes, Wright Co, MO. He was born 8 Aug 1891 in McCook Co, SD, and died 13 July 1970 in Sioux Falls, SD.
V9-1770. 13-1. Thelma Lorene Bartholow,
V9-1771. 13-2. Glenda Ola Bartholow,
V9-1772. 13-3. Darlene Etta Bartholow,
V9-1773. 13-4. Donald Eugene Bartholow, b. 11 July 1932, Sioux Falls, SD; d. 21 July 1991, Sioux Falls, SD.
V9-1774. 13-5. Norman Ralph Bartholow,

Children of John Mansker and Arminta Sullivant:

V9-1775. 12-10. Beulah Pearl Mansker, b. 1 Oct 1910, Hartville, Wright Co, MO; d. 21 July 1996, Springfield, MO. She married Calva Perkins bet. 13 Oct 1928 - 1929 in Hartville, Wright Co, MO, s/o Worth Perkins and Minnie Grimes. He was born 1 Jan 1909 in Wright Co, MO, and died 5–6 May 1979 in Springfield, MO.
V9-1776. 13-1. Imogene Perkins; m. Paul Keeling
V9-1777. 13-2. Geraldine Perkins,
V9-1778. 12-11. Fred Mansker, b. 27 June 1912, Wright Co, MO; d. 16 March 1995, Lynchburg, MO. He married Allie Mae Atchley 29 Jan 1933. She was born 25 Sept 1910 in Wright Co, MO, and died 23 July 1996 in Hartville, Wright Co, MO.
V9-1779. 13-1. Dixie Mansker,
V9-1780. 13-2. Marilyn Mansker,
V9-1781. 13-3. Jeanetta Mansker,
V9-1782. 13-4. Karen Mansker,
V9-1783. 13-5. Brenda Mansker; m. Delbert Tate
V9-1784. 12-12. Ollie Mansker, b. 21 July 1915, MO; d. Marshfield, Webster Co, MO. She married Otto Wilson Claxton 15 Sept 1937 in Wright Co, MO, s/o Noah Claxton and Pearly McClanahan. He was born 17 Aug 1914 in Wright Co, MO, and died 19

Aug 1976 in Webster Co, MO.

$^{V9-}$1785. $^{13-}$1. Judith Ann Claxton; m. Cloval Letterman
$^{V9-}$1786. $^{13-}$2. Freda Sue Claxton,

Mansker Family Stories
By Gail Gibbons Mansker

Note: Gail Gibbons Mansker was the wife of Thurman "Bill" Hayden Mansker of Wright Co, MO. Thurman "Bill" was the s/o William Harry Mansker and the great-grandson of Michael W. Mansker.

The following narrative was written in several e-mail installments in 1998 by Gail Gibbons Mansker to her granddaughter, Vicki Finger victoria@attbi.com , who compiled it into one document and shared it with us. Thanks, Vicki!

As far as I know, all the Manskers were farmers and traders. At one time, William Harry Mansker, your Great-Grandfather, ran a store. Most stores in those days sold feed, groceries, bought cream and eggs and ran customers on "bills" a month at a time. They were the meeting place for people who came in to buy or sell and constituted the place where people exchanged news. Most stores would have a "loafing" bench where the men (mostly) could whittle, chew tobacco, and trade stories of their latest trade or coon hunt. Harry was a hunter and fisherman, he raised foxhounds and sent them all over the country. He also at some time hauled gravel with a wagon and team, and kept milk cows.

The job of your Grandpa Bill was to keep the wood box full in winter. He told the story one time of living in a house so cold that the wind blew the linoleum up and down on the floor. They only had a fireplace to heat with, and he and his brother, Kermit, had to turn to, the minute they got home from school chopping wood until dark. That supply would only last until the next evening, when it had to be done all over again.

They had to use an axe and a crosscut saw, only cutting "blackjack" oak as it was considered a trash tree and burned very well. The trouble with the blackjack was that is was rough and crooked, so didn't work up very well.

Your Grandpa (Thurman) Bill was the youngest child, and his Mother, Mayme, died of what they thought was Tuberculosis when he was 5 years old. After that, he was in the care of the big sisters, who took over managing the house, and it was hard for a little boy to stay clean and please them. He was stubborn and spoiled also, but ever after said how mean his oldest sister was to him. He would run to hide from her anger under the house until his Dad came home and rescued him.

When he was just old enough to handle a horse and cultivator, he was given a plot of ground on which to raise corn. One day, he was riding the cultivator when he went to sleep and fell off and the cultivator wheel ran over his leg and broke it. Doctors were few and money was scarce, so Bill said they had the old "horse doctor" set his leg.

When it was nearly well, he and his brother, Kermit, were chasing each other, when Bill ran upstairs and with Kermit hot on his trail. He jumped out the window, breaking the leg again. He never told his Dad and was a long time healing, eventually having one leg an inch shorter than the other.

Bill loved horses and traded for them. They were the main form of transportation then. His Grandfather, William Henry, was a mule trader when they lived at Manes, Mo. and Thurman "Bill" was a little boy. William Henry would let him ride on the back behind him when they took a trip to town. People began to call them "Big Bill" and "Little Bill" so the name of Bill or Billy stuck, and he was called that name all his life.

When he was old enough to raise the corn crop, he had his own hogs, the corn being raised to feed them. When he sold his hogs, he was expected to buy his school clothes out of that money. One of the first things he bought out of his hog money was a prized .22 caliber rifle. Then he hunted squirrels for the table. They also trapped rabbits in a trap called a "gum." They could sell them for 5 cents apiece at the store.

He was 14 when he and his Dad had a difference of opinion over a horse Bill wanted. He left home and rode a freight train out west. This was in the middle of the depression, and he didn't realize there was no work for grown men, let alone a 14 year old. He went hungry and stayed some with some hobos and said it was the worst time of his life. He couldn't go back home as he had no money, and he said it was no use to ask his Dad, as he had none either.

Eventually he and several others were offered a job putting up hay for room and board and some tobacco. The farmer didn't have enough money to pay them. However, it was a godsend, because at least he had food and a place to stay. As he said, when he got the wrinkles out of his belly, he found other work and ended up riding the rails back home. Said when he left home his Dad was the most ignorant man in the world, and by the time he got his feet back under his Dad's table, it was amazing how smart he had become!

Grandpa William Henry Mansker was said to be a contrary character. I think most of the Mansker's were very independent. Once Grandpa Mansker was upset at his wife, Adeline, and threatened to burn down the house. She took her rocking chair into the yard and sat smoking her pipe. When he saw she was not going to do anything, he put the fire out.

Your Grandpa Bill said his Grandpa, William Henry Mansker, called him a "damned little rebel." He could tell stories of his life in the Union side of the Civil War, told him he was a "sharpshooter" which meant he was a good marksman. Often then they climbed trees to have a good view of the Confederates. Bill said as Grandpa Mansker got older and Grandma Mansker had died, he lived a few months with each of his children.

When he lived with them, he would take his money, which he carried in a roll with a rubber band around it, and count it, losing some in the process. Harry, knowing his mind was getting bad, cut money sized newspaper pieces, and Bill said Grandpa would count those newspaper pieces, the same as he had the money, roll it up and put the rubber band back on it. It was Bill's job to kind of follow him around and see he didn't hurt himself.

When Bill was 11, Harry married Nora Hawks. Bill always said she was a "mail order bride." When she came into the household, she had never been married, and the kids resented her mightily. Nora's mother, Grandma Hawks came with her to live with them. Bill said as long as Grandma Hawks was alive, all the house was clean and she was a good cook.

When she died, poor Nora who had never taken responsibility, tried to manage the house and the unruly kids. They made it so miserable for her she gave up and went back to Texas. Bill said that didn't last long, because Harry went and brought her back. Berchia, Bill's sister, taught school when she was 16. You didn't need a degree in those days.

Because of the depression, families moved in with each other and shared expenses. This was true of theirs. It was some years before things improved, so sometimes the ones who had jobs footed the bill for the ones who didn't. Gradually they moved around. Berchia to Tulsa, OK. Jean to Tulsa, and then California, Stella to Pennsylvania. Bill and Frances visited and lived in Tulsa and Pennsylvania.

In Pennsylvania, Bill went to work in the zinc smelters along with Kermit, his brother who was living in Donora. They went to work at 3 or 4 in the morning and worked until 10. This work was exhausting as it was a process of taking a shovelful of zinc ore and having to place it into the very back of the furnace. If it was not placed exactly the hot ore could blow back onto your body, and burns were frequent.

When the "retort" (furnace) was full, it was sealed off to burn the ore into pure zinc. Bill said it sweat all the salt out of your system in the heat, and he and Kermit would go home and drink quarts of salty lemonade. However, he said this was one of the healthiest periods of his life, I guess any germs or impurities couldn't survive that routine.

There is not much knowledge about Frances and Bill's life together. Everything was kept very hush-hush and Bill did not like to talk about it, as it was a very painful memory. I know Frances had several miscarriages, and had two children who died. Jerry Lee, buried in Hartville, and Beverly Ann, buried in Tulsa. Curtis Layne was 3 years old when they divorced and Bill was forced out of their life.

As you know, Bill and Curt did not meet again until Curt was 20 years old. It took many years for the truth of the situation to come out. After Bill and Frances divorced, Bill then went into a series of jobs and experiences.

In California where Jean lived, he tried to join the Army in World War II, they wouldn't take him because of the one shorter leg. He then joined the Merchant Marine in a capacity of electrician, but was told he was really hired in a position of intelligence. If he was to ever be captured or killed, they would not acknowledge him.

He was on board ship in a convoy headed for Europe when his ship was torpedoed. He found himself in the water, the ship on fire, and burning oil all around him. Many died, and he was among those who were rescued in the water. They then put them on a ship, which carried them to Murmansk, Russia.

From there he traveled by train, saying the Russian people were very friendly and handed them food through the windows. It was years before he ever told me this story. One of the reasons he did tell me was that I didn't understand the peculiar nightmares he sometimes had. He would wake suffering and shaking when he had these. He was reliving the torpedoing of the ship and seeing it all in his dream.

When he returned, he drove a bus in Oakland, California, worked on ranches in Wyoming and Montana, worked in Hanford, Washington as a driving tester for licenses in the Government project there.

Bill loved to gamble and was arrested for it while in Washington. When the policeman who arrested him showed up at the Hanford site to take a driver's test, Bill asked to take him. He refused to pass the policeman. When he complained it was because he had arrested him for gambling, none of the other testers would change Bill's test. The story was that the policeman said, "Don't make any trouble for that man, or you will never get your driver's license."

Bill signed up for a year to work on the Alcan Highway in Alaska. This was very good money, but there were no places to go, and the work was grueling, mosquitoes big enough to carry you off, and only a work camp to live in. The biggest mistake he ever made he said was when he decided he had had enough and wanted to quit and go back to the States. Okay, they said, and released him.

When he asked about the next transportation back they said "Sorry, not for several months." He said he had been getting room and board, plus his salary, then when he quit, he had to spend every cent he had made to pay room and board, until he got a way to leave. He said that really taught him a good lesson.

Before I married Bill, he was sick at one time and went to the Doctor, who told him about his circulation problems, and said he should not work for a while. This was devastating to him because of course he had to work at something to support himself. At any rate he was in a beer joint (which is where ranch hands and day workers went to find work in the West).

While he was there a man came in looking for a sheep-herder. Bill told him he was his man. The man said have you ever herded sheep before, (of course he hadn't) but he told him "Yes sir, he sure was a sheep herder." So they go out to the man/Æs ranch and load up the sheep camp which is like a little covered wagon and pulled by horses. They go up the mountain to where the sheep are, Bill had a horse given to him, and a dog (he thinks it is nice to have a dog for company). The boss leaves, and Bill settles in for the night.

About dark he hears the bells on the sheep begin to ring. Looking out, he discovers that the herd is leaving the bedground. He gets on the horse quickly and begins to try to round them up. He has the dog running along side panting and excited. The sheep are getting scattered and though he has ridden as fast as he can to stop them, they are spreading out. He has visions of sheep never found again, and losing this job.

Finally he gets down and sits on a rock, (dog still panting and excited). Bill said he looked at that dog and threw his hat down on the ground and said, "Okay, you know so much, YOU go get them!" The dog took off like a flash and in a few minutes had the sheep all rounded up and back on the bedground. He always laughed at how that dog could do his job, and he was to learn what the dog was for.

He also had a dog one time that stood at the back door of the sheep camp and waited for him to throw scraps out of the door. One morning he baked a pan of biscuits and burned them. Tossed them out the door and thought about the dog too late. The dog caught one of those red-hot biscuits in the air. Bill said no matter what he threw out after that the dog would always wait to see how hot it was before it went into his mouth. He had sheep he herded in the winter on the desert and in the mountains in the summer.

He loved the life, because he could fish and hunt and read, listen to the radio, had his food furnished, and his paycheck would be waiting at the end of the season. Sometimes, he worked on the ranch during lambing time. He said if a ewe didn't accept her lamb, they would put some vanilla on it, which confused the ewe so she wasn't sure if it was hers and most generally took it. If her lamb died, they would skin the lamb and put the hide over another lamb, and she thought it was hers as the smell was still there. Most ewes had two lambs, so it was easy to find the new one.

Coyotes and bears were the biggest problem with the sheep. Bill shot coyotes often, but the bears were more trouble. They would kill the sheep and leave them. One time they found 2 young bears killing the sheep, shot one and wounded it, so it was making a lot of noise, he said they were petrified that mother bear would come after it, and that would have been very dangerous. They did kill both the young ones, and saw nothing of the mother.

Moose was another problem, he said they were bad to come on in mating season. Once he had gotten off his horse and the horse went wild running around a tree, when he looked up there stood a huge moose. He tried to get to the horse and his gun in the scabbard, but the horse wouldn't let him get to him. He said he was very fortunate that the moose finally just left, but he was scared he might have been attacked.

I had never lived in the country where there were no electric lights or running water to say nothing of inside bathrooms. When I first married Bill I lived in Tulsa and we soon decided to move to MO. David was 4 and Billy 3, and thought this was a lot of fun. We moved into a farmhouse with 120 acres.

I had to learn to pump up a white gas lantern, which we hung from the ceiling. We also filled kerosene lamps for light. Drawing water out of the well was done by lowering a "bucket", (a long tube with an opening and closing valve on the bottom). You let the bucket down the well until you heard it hit the water, this created a vacuum, which pushed the water up the bucket and then the valve closed. You pulled the rope hand over hand to the top and held the bucket over your pail, then you had a metal loop you pulled which opened the valve and the water was transferred to the pail. This was a slow task, but the only way of transferring water to the house.

Bill cut trees down with an axe, split up the wood and it was carried to the house, small wood for the cook stove, bigger wood for the heating stove. I soon learned with Aunt Stell's help (she was Bill's Uncle Ben's wife--this for benefit of you kids who were not fortunate enough to have known and loved her) how to find wild greens, how to plant a garden, how to can on a wood stove. She was a wonderful, loving and patient woman, and so good to me.

I can not remember a time when we were not poor in the country, but she taught me so many things to use from nature and how to make do with what we had. Her recipe for chest rubs for colds and croup was equal parts of turpentine, kerosene and lard, melted together, rubbed into the chest and covered with an old piece of outing flannel, you would be cured by morning.

She made the little boys mittens out of old sweaters, putting their hand down, she drew the outline of their hand, sewed on the line, cut them out, and turned them inside out. Old sweaters also made stocking caps. Every old shirt or dress or feedsack went into something. She made my little boys diaper shirts, a button down the front shirt long enough to cover the top of the diaper.

In those days, sugar and flour sacks and printed feed sacks were made into lots of things. Pillow cases, slips, aprons, pot-holders, quilts. Also the flour and feed people gave away coffee cups with their products. Coffee jars were made so that they could be used as canning jars. Oatmeal had small bowls and glasses in every box, and those are the collectibles of today. I still have a cookie recipe book I got free with Gold Medal flour.

No one went and bought new canning jars. Instead you went to "sale" at auctions held mostly on people's farms where they were moving. All farm equipment and animals, cows, horses and mules, pigs, chickens, sometimes canned fruit and vegetables, along with the furniture and anything else they didn't want to take with them was sold at those auctions. It was a wonderful opportunity to visit with your neighbors and outbid them if you could.

Aunt Stell and Uncle Ben had a little daughter named Geneva. She developed strep throat, and because they didn't know what that was, she got rheumatic fever, which damaged her heart. When she was 11 she died, and Bill always told the story of how much he loved her and what a sweet little girl she was. She loved to have him visit her.

On the night she died it was a cold January, they went to take her to the hospital and found the tires on their old car were flat. Aunt Stell said they stuffed the tires with rags and started for the hospital. When a highway patrolman saw them and saw how bad Geneva was he drove ahead of them, so they would get there all right.

Once Uncle Ben got a government loan to help him on his farm, the government lady would come and visit you several times a year and was supposed to teach you how to sew and can and use the farm to make money. Of course this was all Uncle Ben and Aunt Stell had ever done so they had to listen and act like they were taking it in, and then when the lady left they did as they pleased. They milked cows and she saved the cream to sell to make the farm payment. It was a hard life but they always had their own food they raised, and so I learned a lot from her about how to get along with what we had. I really believe that we were healthier and happy even though we had no money to speak of.

Many of the things we did, we did as a family, work and play, having to enjoy some of the simpler pleasures. When farmers butchered, usually hogs, they needed help to take care of the meat. Neighbors would go to help and as their pay they would receive a side of ribs or liver or some part of the meat that was most welcome. Neighbors also helped at haying and other harvest times. It was a way to help and enjoy each other's company at the same time.

Men did a lot of trading. Sometimes they traded farm machinery or cows, mules or horses. Sometimes dogs. It was a favorite pastime to go coon hunting, and usually the family would come to stay all night while the men went coon hunting. It was brag time when each thought they had the best dog. Sometimes they were gone all night and the dogs would come in lanky from running and might even go in to a neighbor's place and be put up until the owner came after them.

Bill said their favorite time when he was young was the 4th of July. All the families would get together and go to the river, where they stayed several days. In the evening and morning, the men would hitch up the wagons and go home and milk and feed and come back to the river.

One of the worst times he could remember was when the camp meetings would be held and they would have revival for several days. He was afraid of the "hellfire and damnation" the preachers preached, and, as a result of his experiences, he never told his children they had to go to church and let them choose to if they wanted or not.

When we lived in Ponca City, Oklahoma, we rented a big two-story house that had a big wheat acreage on it. The part we rented had 40 acres and a stream of water going through it. The wheat pasture part was rented by a farmer who hired David and Billy to work on the tractors.

First the ground had to be plowed, so David worked all night, and Billy worked all day. I think David was 16 that year and Billy 14. It was very long hours, hot and windy in the daytime and cool and full of bugs at night who were attracted to the tractor lights. It was hard for David to sleep in the day, because of course we had no air conditioning.

Billy had to be up and at work at 7 and worked until 7, David would get on the tractor then at 7 that night and work the 12 hours until 7 in the morning. Wheat farming was a no nonsense job and it was important to get it all in and done. In the winter when the wheat was coming up, we had a good advantage, as the farmer who had the pasture had cattle he put on it. The idea being that the more it was eaten the more shoots of wheat would "stool" out and so the more wheat stems there would be, thus more wheat.

Because we had water on our side of the farm, we traded our water for his cattle and we got to pasture our cattle with his, so it was a really good feed saving for us. Then in the summer when the wheat was ready to harvest, Billy and David got the job working at that, and they all drove to the storage and put the wheat in. It was hard work but good pay, and Billy and David bought their school clothes out of their pay and had some left over to spend.

We had lots of garden on that place, and raised cows and hogs and chickens. Something was producing all the time. In the spring we bought baby chickens and raised them to eat and saved some for laying hens. One year, the snow was so deep there was nothing for the wild quail to eat, as they couldn't get to the ground. We had a path dug to the barn and fed our chickens in that path, then found the quail eating with them. Ordinarily, we couldn't have gotten within a mile of them, but they were hungry, so it was a special treat to get to see them up close. The boys also brought rabbit to eat and, of course, had to be the ones to kill and pluck the chickens. It was my job to clean and put them in the freezer, and then to cook them. We butchered our own hogs, so mostly had meat all the time.

One time during the winter, we had a little bull who got shoved into the feed trough. He could not get out and it froze one of his feet. We thought he might die, but survived and lost his hoof. Then Bill made him a leather boot, which he wore until he was big enough to eat. We didn't butcher much beef, as it was worth too much on the market. But this one made a lot of good meat.

Not having an inside bathroom, the creek made a wonderful place to take baths in the summer, also a very peaceful and beautiful place to sit and rest. There was an old rock quarry down on the bottom end of the place and the kids played Cowboys and Indians. Their name for it was Ambush Canyon.

We had horses and one time Bill traded for a goat with a horse. That goat was such a nuisance he decided to trade him back to his friend, but the friend refused to take him, so Bill had to pay him to take him back.

Ponca City, out in the western part of Oklahoma was always subject to thunderstorms and we often took to the storm cellar when it looked bad and we thought there would be a tornado. You could stand in the yard and see the tails develop on the bottom of the clouds, but the only tornado we had was at night when we had gone to bed and that was so fast we would never had time to get to the cellar.

When it went over the house it sounded like a freight train, and when we got up, the down draft in the chimney had spread soot all over the floor and carried it up the stair to the upstairs. Some of the stuff outside was moved down to the barn, and even though we had no bad effects, it was pretty scary to realize what could have happened if it had gotten down to the ground.

We always had lots of company and the kids had to give up their beds to them. Lots of nights they took quilts and went to the yard to sleep. When we moved back to MO and lived in the little house on Paul's place, they also had to sleep up in the attic of the house without many comforts. Later, they said how darn cold that upstairs was when the stove went out below.

Bill would let them take the tractor there to the creek. When I worried they might get themselves hurt, he said not to worry there was a governor on it that wouldn't let them go fast. Years later, they told us how one of them would stand on the governor to keep it open so they could go as fast as they wanted to.

It was not an easy life with all the work to do, and not a lot of money, but we all worked together and played together. We played cards and visited, most people when they came to visit stayed all day, as that was the country custom. Sometimes if there was work to do they came and stayed all day to do that. The kids could always go fishing and we kept a kit of camping stuff for them when they went, as sometimes they stayed all night.

One time they had borrowed a boat to take fishing and were going under a big tree limb when a cottonmouth snake fell into the boat with them. They let the snake have the boat! Also they lost several of my good cooking things, as they were at the bottom of the creek There was always a bunch of hazards to being in the woods, ticks, and snakes and poison ivy, but they didn't seem to mind.

Bill was an excellent horseman, he could ride anything, but was very protective about the kids on horses. He made them go two at a time, the same as when they were hunting, so that if one got hurt the other could go to the house to get help.

He was also very strict about taking them places. If they wanted to go out for track or basketball they had to get a ride or arrange it themselves. One of the best times I ever had was when he let Billy and me go to the horse show being held for the senior trip. We took our big old truck and while Billy worked on the show part, I worked in the concession stand. We got home about midnight, but everyone had fun getting those kids their trip money.

6. ABSALOM BRASHEAR
and NANCY _____

Absalom Brashear, (**Vol.2, p.64–67**; s/o Robert Brashears and Patsy Wilson, gs/o Philip Brashears, Sr, and Ann Wilson), b. 1786, VA; m. **Nancy** _____, b. 1790, VA.

Absalom was on the 1813 tax list of Lee Co, VA, alongside Robert and Philip Brashears. From 1821 to c1824, Absalom lived in Tennessee, where some of his children were born.

On 18 Jan 1825, Absalom received a 50 acre KY land grant on Wolf Creek in Wayne Co, KY, (Wayne Co, KY Deeds, Book U, p.307). On 1826-27 Tax Rolls of Russell Co, KY for property formerly in Wayne Co.

When Absalom sold this patent to William Caughron for $120 on 9 Mar 1829, the land was described as "a certain tract or parcel of land situated, lying, and being in the County of Russell and State of Kentucky on the waters of Cumberland River on the ridge between Cumberland River and Wolf Creek, taken and patented to me, Absalom Brashers, containing fifty acres by survey..."

/s/ Absalom Brashers   /s/ Nancy Brashers
(Russell Co, KY, Deed Bk B, p.30, dated 9 March 1829;
executed and delivered to Mr. Craugham 18 Jan 1830,
recorded by William Patterson, clerk).

Census data:

Robert Beshears, 70-80, Absolim Beshears, 30-40, and Philip Beshears, 40-50, are side by side on the 1830 census, Franklin Co, IL.

1840 Franklin Co, IL Census:
Absolem Bershears, 00020001-01110001
1. girl, 15-20, b. 1820-25
2. boy, 15-20, b. 1820-25
3. boy, 15-20, b. 1820-25
4. girl, 10-15, b. 1825-30
5. girl, 5-10, b. 1830-35

In vol. 2, I searched the census data for a family that would meet those criteria. The only person for whom data is unequivocal was Martha Brashear, b. 1829, who is in Absalom and Nancy's household in 1850; she m. 1 Feb 1852, Thomas Baldwin.

1850 census, Franklin Co, IL, p. 46, #65[9]681
Absalom Bershears,   64, b. VA, c1786
   Nancy Bershears,   60, b. VA, c1790
   Martha Bershears,   21, b. KY, c1829
   Neighbors: Abner Rea, Aley Rea, Robt Rea, more Reas and Wilsons

I grouped with them these people who were living practically next door.

1850 Census, Franklin Co, IL, p. 46, #646-667
Sam'l Besares,   25, b. KY, c1825
   Nancy Besares,   24, b. TN, c1826
   Manerva C. Besares,   4, b. MO, c1846
   William Besares,   3, b. MO, c1847
   Safrona Besares,   5/12, b. IL, c1850
   Neighbors: Henry Teftiller, Joseph Teftiller, Jno Crawford

1850 Census, Franklin Co, IL, p.48, #668-690
Anna Crosnon,   28f, b. TN, c1822
   George T. Crosnon,   6, b. c1844
   Reuben L. Crosnon,   5, b. c1845
   Elizabeth E. Crosnon,   4, b. c1846
   L.C. Crosnon,   2f, b. c1848
   Ira Bershers,   26, b. TN, 1824
   Sarah Bershers,   21

Anna Crosnon and Ira Brashear

Note that Anna Crosnon and Ira Brashears were born in Tennessee.

Family of Absalom Brashears v2-63 and Nancy _____:
[V9]-1787.   [9]-1. **?Anna Brashears**, b. Tennessee, c1822 (28 in 1850); m. _____ ***Crosnon***, d. c1848-50. Anna was apparently a widow in the 1850 census, with four children and her brother, Ira, and his wife, Sarah, in the household.
[V9]-1788.   [10]-1. George T. Crosnon, b. c1844
[V9]-1789.   [10]-2. Reuben L. Crosnon, b. c1845
[V9]-1790.   [10]-3. Elizabeth E. Crosnon, b. c1846
[V9]-1791.   [10]-4. L.C. Crosnon, (fem), b. c1848

[V9]-1792.   [9]-2. **?Ira Brashears**, b. Tennessee, c1824 (26 in 1850), d. c1859; m.1. ***Sarah*** _____, b. c1829 (21 in 1850), apparently d. bef 1852; Ira m.2. 3 Aug 1852, (Franklin Co, IL, Bk 2, p.54), ***Mary Overturf***, b. c1835, IL, ("Farmeress", 25, in 1860, Franklin Co, IL, #558-558, with 2 ch; also in hh, Levi Overturf, 19, b. IL). Mrs. Polly Brashears m. 12 May 1861, (Franklin Co, IL, Bk 3, p.290), John Thomas Davis.

V9-1793.   10-1. **Nancy J. Brashears**, b. c1855, IL (5 in 1860); m. 11 July 1872, (Franklin Co, IL, Bk 3, p.577), *John Scrivner*

V9-1794.   10-2. **John Brashears**, b. c1859, IL (1 in 1860)

V9-1795.   9-3. ?**Samuel Brashears**, b. Kentucky, c1825 (25 in 1850; 35 in 1860; 56 in 1880--parents b. NC); m.1. c1845, *Nancy W. _____*, (mother of the children), b. c1826 (34 in 1860; listed as "weaving" in 1860); m.2. 27 Sept 1868, Franklin Co, IL (Bk 3, p.264), *Mrs. Nancy J. (Norman) Owens*, b. c1831, TN (49 in 1880; parents b. TN). Stepson, Amos Owens, 19, b. IL, fa TN, mo TN, in household in 1880, #133-133.

V9-1796.   10-1. **Manerva C. Brashears**, b. c1846, MO, (4 in 1850; 14 in 1860); m. 5 July 1873, (Franklin Co, IL, Bk 3-B, p.51), *Franklin Booker*,

V9-1797.   10-2. **William J. Brashears**, b. c1847, MO, (3 in 1850; 13 in 1860); m. 16 July 1874, Franklin Co, IL (Bk C, p.6), *Anna F. Brown*

V9-1798.   10-3. **Safrona C. Brashears**, b. c1850, IL, (5/12 in 1850; 10 in 1860)

V9-1799.   10-4. **Lovinia J. Brashears**, b. c1853, IL (7 in 1860); m. 9 April 1872, Franklin Co, IL (Bk 3, p.560), *James Trent*

V9-1800.   10-5. **Samuel R. Brashears**, b. c1855, IL (5 in 1860)

V9-1801.   10-6. **John H.J. Brashears**, b. c1858, IL (2 in 1860)

V9-1802.   9-4. **Martha "Patsy" Brashears**, b. KY, c1829 (21 in 1850; 41 in 1870); m. 1 Feb 1852, Franklin Co, IL (Bk B, p.43) *Thomas Baldwin.* Census: 1860, Butler County, Missouri. Martha Baldwin, 53, is widowed mother in HH of Absalom Baldwin, 27, in 1880, Franklin Co, IL census, #141-141. Also in hh in 1880: Corrinda Brashars, 10, IL IL IL, servant.

V9-1803.   10-1. Absalom Baldwin, b. c1853, IL (listed as Annie, male, 17 in 1870); m. Laura A. Wilson, b. IL, c1858 (22 in 1880; fa b. VA, mo b. TN)

V9-1804.   11-1. Sarah F. Baldwin, b. IL, c1789 (3 in 1880)

V9-1805.   11-2. Hester M. Baldwin, b. IL, c1880 (6/12 in 1880)

V9-1806.   10-2. Samantha Baldwin, b. 1855, IL

V9-1807.   9-5. dau **Brashears**, b. 1830-35 (indicated by 1840 census). Probably **Louisa Brashears**, b. 1832, Franklin Co, IL (5-10 in 1840, hh of Absalom Brashear); m. 29 June 1850, *Sylvester Lilburn Baldwin*, b. 1831.

V-2, p.66: Corliss E. Wright <corvettew68@netzero.net> Sent information on that fifth, unknown child of Absalom Brashears and Nancy ____. Her name was Louisa Brashears. She had married before the 1850 census.

A[bsalom] Besheers, male, widower, is 80, b. c1790, VA, in 1870 census, Franklin Co, IL, Mulkeytown P.O. (#1^{12}-112), with Martha Baldwin, 41, b. KY; Annie Baldwin, 17, b. IL (listed as male); and M.C. Besheers, (fem), 24, b. MA [sic], in his household.
NOTE: Martha "Patsy" Brashears, m. 1 Feb 1852, Franklin Co, IL (Bk B, p.43) Thomas Baldwin.

Unaccounted for Data
Of course, my listing may be in error, but it seems to me to account for the most data. The following is data I can't account for.

1850 Census, Franklin Co, IL, p.48, #66^9-691
Rich I. Buckner,   46, b. TN, c1804
   Bretanna Buckner,   56, b. KY, c1794 [Britannia, 67, in 1860]
   James G. Buckner,   24, b. IN, c1826 [m. Sarah Brashears; see below]
   Moses Buckner,   22, b. IN, c1828
   Rebecca Bersheres, 21, b. TN, c1829
   B.E. Bersheres,   2, b. IL, c1848 [Britannia E. Brashears, 12, in 1860]
   Mary M. Bersheres,   6/12, b. IL, c1850 [Mary M. Brashears, 10, in 1860]

   [?Did Rebecca Buckner m. ____ Brashears? And have two little girls before he passed away?]
Britannia E. Brashears, m. 7 May 1865, Franklin Co, IL (Bk 3, p.543), Franklin Rea.
Mary M. Brashears, m. 4 Nov 1869, Franklin Co, IL (Bk 3, p.357), Jonathan Overturf.

JerryDon <jerrydon1947@netzero.net> sends these families that don't belong here, but belong somewhere near here:

V9-1808.   **Mary "Polly" Brashear**, b. 1826, KY; m. 17 March 1850, ***William Baldwin***, b. 1831, IL
V9-1809.   1. Nancy Baldwin, b. 1851; m. 12 Aug 1869, Newton Ray/Rae, b. 1851 had only one child
V9-1810.   1. James Marlon Ray, b.12 Aug 1870

V9-1811.   **Sarah Brashears**, b. 1829; m. 25 Aug 1850, ***James G. Buckner***, b. 1825, IN. Sarah and James had the following children:
V9-1812.   1. Richard Buckner, b. 1852; m. Martha Baldwin
V9-1813.   1. Emma Buckner,

V9-1814.	2. Ellen Buckner,
V9-1815.	3. Edward Buckner
V9-1816.	2. Francis Buckner, b. 1855,
V9-1817.	3. Brittania Buckner, b. 1858,
V9-1818.	4. Stephen Buckner, b. ?,
V9-1819.	5. William Buckner, b. 1859; m. 10 April 1878, Cordella Baldwin, b. 1859, d/o William Baldwin and Mary "Polly" Brashears. Cordella and her husband, William Buckner, are cousins.
V9-1820.	6. Mary A. Buckner, b. 1861,
V9-1821.	7. Rachel Buckner, b. 1863,
V9-1822.	8. Louisa Buckner, b. 1869,
V9-1823.	9. James Buckner, b. 1870, and
V9-1824.	10. Hettie Buckner, b. 1868 an adopted daughter.

Braden (Brandon) Brashears and Tabitha Asberry

v-2, p. 67. Barbara Snyder Sargent <BSarg99072@aol.com>, 6002 Whipering Lake, San Antonio, TX, 210/648-3053, has found additional data regarding two strays, living with William Haines on the 1870 census of Osage P. O., Jackson Co, IL:

> **W. R. Brashears**, 20, b c1850, IL,
> **Samuel Brashears**, 11, b. c1859, IL.

The boys' father had died c1860-70, and their mother, Tabitha, had married, second, William Haines.

Samuel's third marriage license identifies him as a son of **Braden Beshears** (unidentified; perhaps "Brandon") and Tabitha Asberry. The surname is spelled variously as Brashears, Beshears, Bershertz, etc.

1880 Census, Franklin Co, IL, #7[9]-80
Bershertz, W.R.	30, b. c1850, IL KY IL, farm laborer
Mary A.	20, b. c1860, IL IL IL, wife

1880 Census, Franklin Co, IL, #164-166
Bershertz, R.	25, b. c1855, IL MO MO, farmer
Adaline	25, b. c1855, KY VA TN, wife
John H.	6, b. c1874, KY IL KY, son
Nancy J.	4. b. c1878, KY IL KY, dau

1880 Census, Franklin Co, IL, #228-231
Beshertz, Andrew	30, b. c1850, IL IL IL, farmer
Millie A.	22, b. c1858, IL IL IL, wife
Clara	1, b. c1879, IL IL IL, dau

These are Brashears JerryDon has found but can't put them with any family lines, but knows they are related to the rest of the

---

Brashears.
Andrew Brashear, b. 1851; m. Millie Lefler, daughter of George and
Matilda Eddington,
Clara Brashears, b. 1875; m. William Carpenter, son of N.F. Carpenter
and T.J. Garrison
Samuel T. Brashears, b. 1863; m. Nettie Clark, daughter of S. G. Clark
and _____ Dunnigan

Family of Brandon Beshears and Tabitha Asberry:
V9-1825.   1-x. **Braden (?Brandon) Beshears**, b. KY, d. IL, c1860-70;
            m. *Tabitha Asberry*, b. IL
V9-1826.   2-1. **William R. Beshears or Brashears**, b. c1850, IL; m.
            Mary A. ____, b. c1860, IL (no ch in 1880; and no
            further info)
V9-1827.   2-2. ***Samuel T. Beshears or Brashears**, (s/o Braden
            Beshears and Tabitha Asberry, per Samuel's third
            marriage license), b. 1859, IL, d. 1927, IL, bur
            Miners Cem, Royalton, Franklin Co, IL; m.1. 2 Aug
            1883, in Williamson Co, IL, *Caledonia "Callie"
            Sanders*, b. c1861, IL; m.2. 18 March 1892,
            Franklin Co, IL (Bk 2, p.121), *Nettie Clark*; m.3. 20
            May 1899, Franklin Co, IL (Bk 2, p.83), *Rosa
            Marshall*

Marriages in Franklin Co, IL (source: Illinois Archives: loose leaf binder
of computer generated list in Franklin Co Publ Lib, Benton, IL)
Samuel T. Beshears, m. 18 March 1892, Franklin Co, IL (Bk 2, p.121),
Nattie Clark
Samuel Beshers, m. 20 May 1899, Franklin Co, IL (Bk 2, p.83), *Rosa
Marshall*
Children of Samuel T. Brashears and Caledonia Sanders:
V9-1828.   3-1. **Lillian "Lillie" Beshears**, b. ?
V9-1829.   3-2. **Jesse Beshears**, b. 21 Nov 1886, d. June 1975,
            Laddonia, MO
V9-1830.   3-3. ***William Cleveland Beshears**, b. 18 July 1888 in
            Franklin Co, IL, d. 13 May 1928 in IL.
Children of Samuel Brashears and Rosa Marshall:
V9-1831.   3-4. **Sid Beshears**, b. 24 Feb 1902, IL, d. Aug 1969,
            Desoto, Jackson Co, IL
V9-1832.   3-5. **Ambrose Beshears**, b. 12 Feb 1908, IL, d. June 1987,
            Hurst, Williamson Co, IL
V9-1833.   3-6. **Harley Beshears**,

William Cleveland Beshears and Minnie Hayslip:

3-3. **William Cleveland Beshears**, (s/o Samuel T. Brashears and Caledonia Sanders), b. 18 July 1888, Franklin Co, IL, d. 13 May 1928; m.1. _____. (Barbara Sargent: "I'm not sure if William was married before 1909 or not, but on the 1920 census there is a **Goldie Beshears**, b. c1907, IL, as his daughter"); m.2. 13 Jan 1909, Franklin Co, IL (Bk 3, p.90) *Minnie Rosette Hayzlip*, b. 7 Aug 1891, Franklin Co, IL, d. 16 June 1958, Oak Ridge, Anderson Co, TN, bur Miners Cem, Royalton, Franklin Co, IL.

Family of William Cleveland Beshears by first marriage:

V9-1834.   4-1. **Goldie Beshears**, b. c1907

Family of William Cleveland Beshears and Minnie Hayzlip:

V9-1835.   4-2. ***Bertha Rachel Beshears**, b. 22 April 1911, Zieglar, Franklin Co, IL, d. 24 May 1983, Tucson, Pima Co, AZ; m.1. c1927, IL, *Carl Lee Snyder*, b. 1 Aug 1909, Desoto, Jackson Co, IL, d. 8 Jan 1967, Pittsburgh, Allegheny Co, PA; m.2. c1950, *Julius DuBose*, b?, d. 10 Sept 1980, Tucson, Pima Co, AZ; m.3. c1975, *Fobert Bejar*, b. 7 June 1896, d. Dec 1981, Tucson, Pima Co, AZ.

V9-1836.   4-3. **Edith A. Beshears**, b. 7 Aug 1913, Zieglar, Franklin Co, IL, d. 15 Feb 1990 in Tucson, Pima Co, AZ; m. *Walter "Pat" Alexander*,

V9-1837.   4-4. **Dorotha Beshears**, b. c1915, Franklin Co, IL; m. Wayne Broadway, b. 10 April 1915, d. Feb 1983, Carbondale, Jackson Co, IL

V9-1838.   4-5. **Juanita Beshears**, b. 1925, IL, d. 17 Feb 1997, Knoxville, Knox Co, TN; m. *Jack Minton*, b. 29 Aug 1927, d. 13 March 1996, Powell, Knox Co, TN.

V9-1839.   5-1. Marylin Minton, b. TN
V9-1840.   5-2. Carylin Minton, b. TN

Family of Bertha Rachel Beshears and Carl Lee Snyder:

V9-1841.   5-1. William Snyder, b. 13 Sep1928, Desoto, Jackson Co, IL; m. 5 June 1958, in Nogales, Santa Cruz Co, AZ, Gloria Peckat.

V9-1842.   6-1. Janet Snyder,
V9-1843.   6-2. Mark Snyder,
V9-1844.   5-2. Raymond Lee Snyder, b. 3 Sep1930, Desoto, Jackson Co, IL, d. 19 Feb1993 in Las Vegas, Clark Co, NV and buried in San Antonio, Texas at Ft. Sam Houston Cem; m. 11 June 1951 in Seguin, TX, Helen Ruth Deike, b. 7 Jan 1929 in Hye, Blanco Co, TX. (Barbara's father and mother),

V9-1845.	6-1. Barbara Ann Snyder, b. 16 April 1952, Albuquerque, Valencia Co, NM; m. 9 Feb 1969, in San Antonio, Bexar Co, TX, Robert Duane Sargent, b. 28 Nov 1949, Washington, Washington Co, PA, d. 5 Jan 2000, San Antonio, TX
V9-1846.	7-1. Robert Duane Sargent Jr, b. 28 Sept 1971, San Antonio, TX; m. Rebecca Ann Tipton, b. 26 Oct 1974 Texas City, Galveston Co, TX
V9-1847.	8-1. Robert Duane Sargent III, b. 28 Oct 1991, San Antonio, TX
V9-1848.	8-2. Bradley Jonathan Sargent, b. 29 Dec 1993, San Antonio, TX, d. 8 March 1994, San Antonio, TX
V9-1849.	8-3. Tyler Lee Sargent, b. 14 Oct 1998, San Antonio, TX
V9-1850.	7-2. Steve Raymond Sargent, b. 10 July 1975, San Antonio, TX
V9-1851.	6-2. Diana Lynn Snyder, b. 28 July 1959, San Antonio, Bexar Co, TX; m. 4 March 1978, in San Antonio, TX, Jody Ray Sargent, b. 28 Sept 1957, Washington, Washington Co, PA
V9-1852.	7-1. Crystal Faith Sargent, b. 26 Aug 1983, San Antonio, TX
V9-1853.	7-2. Christopher Ray Sargent, b. 8 Dec 1988, San Antonio, TX
V9-1854.	5-3. James Snyder, b. 29 Sept 1932, Desoto, Jackson Co, IL, d. Nov 1976, Tucson, Pima Co, AZ; m.1. _____ (2 ch); m.2. Joann ____ (2 ch)
V9-1855.	6-1. Evelyn Snyder,
V9-1856.	6-2. LaDonna Snyder,
V9-1857.	6-3. Deborah Snyder,
V9-1858.	6-4. Michael Snyder,

Barbara writes: I am writing to Southern Illinois University-IRAD for info. (birth and death cert.), but you can only ask for 2 people at a time. I am hoping to find Samuel Brashears' father thru his death cert. Also my grandmother told me we had some French and Indian in us. A whole lot of French, but just a little bit of Indian.

I hope this help you and Thanks again for the information.
Barb

7. BENJAMIN and JANE BRASHEARS
OF GREENE CO, MO

v-2, p.264: So much new information has come in on Benjamin Brashears of Greene Co, MO, and his descendants, that I revised the whole chapter. (Thanks to descendant, Ron Fowler, for much of this new information and the documents.)

V2-67. **Benjamin Brashears** (possibly s/o v2-32, Robert Brashears ?and Patsy Wilson), b. c1790-93 in Virginia, probably Henry Co, where Robert lived until after 1810. Benjamin was 60 in 1850; 67 in 1860; he lived in Cumberland Co, KY at least from 1822 to 1835, when his children were born; moved bef 1840 census to Greene Co, MO, d. c1869, Greene Co, MO; m. *Jane* _____, b. c1798, NC.

Considering his birthplace and movements, I think this Benjamin Brashears may be a grandson of Philip Brashears Sr and Ann Wilson, of Henry Co, VA, probably a son of v2-32, Robert Brashears, b. c1759, ?and Patsy Wilson. Lacking documentation, that's the way I'm going to number him and his family.

The first record we have of Benjamin shows he was granted 50 acres of land on Spring Creek in Cumberland Co, KY, in 1824 (Kentucky Land Warrants, Book Q, p.440, surveyed 23 Dec 1824; thanks to Ron Fowler for a copy). Descendants say he was already married by that time and had two children. By 1837, the family had grown to nine and had relocated to Greene Co, MO, just southeast of Springfield.

Benj. Brasheers was on the Tax Assessor's list of Greene Co, MO, 1843: taxed for 2 horses, $90; 5 cattle, $83; 1 timepiece, $25; 1 Jack & mule, $30; total $228.

Benjamin and Jane are in the 1850 census of Greene Co, with six of their nine children. By 1860, Jane was apparently dead, and only one of the children, Lewis, was still at home.

Benjamin and his family were sympathetic to the Southern Cause during the Civil War. Some of his sons served in the war. It is said that Benjamin died during the war, while hiding in a cave from Union forces.

"Springdale Cave"—About six miles from Springfield, on the Springfield and James River bridge road, and on the line of the Springfield and Southern R.R., about three quarters of a mile above

Gallaway station, is a cave of considerable note. From it issues one of the finest streams of water in Greene County and the Southwest, and on account of this spring it became the site of one of the earliest settlements, having been entered in 1840 by Jacob Painter. During the [Civil] war, it was owned by Benj. Brashears, a Confederate soldier and ranger, who is said to have contracted a cold which caused his death while hiding in the cave from his enemies, the Federals. (*History of Greene Co, MO*, p.691; thanks to Dodie Haight for a Xerox copy.)

Letters of administration: Bond was given on 1 Oct 1869 by G.M. [Gabriel M.] Freeman, principal (i.e. an heir: son-in-law) and administrator, with J.W. Leather and L.J. Freeman, securities, in the amount of $1,200, in the estate of Benjamin Brashears, deceased (Will Book A, p.553, Greene Co, MO, Probate Records; thanks to Dodie Haight for a Xerox copy.)

Family of Benjamin Brashears and Jane __

1840 Census, Greene Co, MO:
Benj. Brashears, 40-50, b. 1790-1800   (0032001-0310001)
wife, 40-50, b. 1790-1800 — Jane _____, b. 1798, NC
    boy, 15-20, b. 1820-25 — Thomas
    boy, 15-20, b. 1820-25 — Samuel
    boy, 10-15, b. 1825-30 — Jesse [he was actually 16]
    girl, 10-15, b. 1825-30 — Jemima
    boy,10-15, b. 1825-30 — Martin
    boy, 10-15, b. 1825-30 — Lewis [he was 10]
    girl, 5-10, b. 1830-35 — Marina
    girl, 5-10, b. 1830-35 — Artina
    girl, 5-10, b. 1830-35 — Sinna

1850 Census, Greene Co, MO, Campbell twp: #98
Benj. Brashear,	60, b. VA 1790
Jane Brashear,	52, b. NC 1798
Thomas Brashear,	28, b. KY, c1822
Jemima Brashear,	23, b. KY, c1827
Martin Brashear,	22, b. KY, c1828
Lewis Brashear,	20, b. KY, c1830
Artina Brashear,	17, b. KY, c1833
Sinna Brashear,	15, b. KY c1835

1860 Census, Greene Co, MO, Clay twp: #88-p.91
Benj. Brashears,   67, b. VA, c1793
Lewis Brashears, 30, b. KY, c1830
Family of Benjamin Brashears and Jane _____(from Censuses, descendants):
V2-2231.   9-1. **Thomas Brashears**, b. c1822, KY (28 and still at home in 1850); was referred to as "Tommy the Preacher." No further record.

V9-1859.   9-2. *Jesse Brashears (also Beshears), b. 30 Jan 1824, Cumberland Co, KY, d. 26 Sep 1894, MO; m. 25 Nov 1843, *Mary Wilkerson*. 3 ch.

V2-2233.   9-3. *Jemima Brashears, b. March 1826, KY, d. after 1900, MO; m.25 Nov 1851, *James Alfred Mitchem*. 9 ch.

V2-2232.   9-4. *Samuel Brashears, b. 1827, KY, d. 1898, Springfield, MO; m. *Sarah Pursley*, b. TN, c1832. 8 ch.

V2-2234.   9-5. *Martin Brashears, b. 1828, Cumberland Co, KY, d. 25 Jan 1902, Springfield, MO; m. 18 Feb 1852, *Louisa Austin*, b. NC c1830/31. 9 ch.

V2-2235.   9-6. *Lewis Brashears, b. 17 Jan 1830, Cumberland Co, KY, d. 26 Jan 1900, Pope Co, AR, about 70 years old; m. *Mary Ann Petty*. See below.

V2-2237.   9-7. *Marina Brashear, b. c1832, KY (38 in 1870), d. after 1900; m. 1 Mar 1849, Greene Co, MO, (Marriages, Bk A, p.184), *Gabriel M. Freeman*, b. c1828, NC, (42 in 1870, Greene Co, MO). 10 ch. G.M. Freeman was an heir and administrator of Benjamin Brashear's estate in 1869.

V2-2238.   9-8. *Artina Brashear, b. 1833, KY; m. 8 Aug 1854, *Wesley Austin*. 4 ch. In 1870, they lived in Madison Co, AR.

V2-2239.   9-9. Sirena or Sinna Brashear, b. 1835, KY; m. *John Burrows* or Burruss. In 1870, Greene Co, MO, census, John and "Sina" Burrows were living with her sister, Marina. Not found in MO in 1880 or 1900.

Jesse Brashears and Mary Wilkerson

V9-2. 9-2. Jesse Brashears (Beshears), (s/o Benjamin Brashears and Jane _____), b. 30 Jan 1824, Cumberland Co, KY, d. 26 Sep 1894, near Springfield, Greene Co, MO; m. 25 Nov 1843, *Mary "Polly" Wilkerson*, b. c1824, MO (36 in 1860) or b. c1830, TN (50 in 1880). Are these the same wife, or did Jesse have a second wife in 1880? 3 ch.

Jesse and his son, John B. Beshears, are in the censuses of Greene Co, MO:

1860 Census, Greene Co. MO, Taylor twp: #690-p.734

Jesse Brashears,	36, b. KY c1824
Mary Brashears,	36, b. MO, c1824
James Brashears,	15, b. MO, c1845
John Brashears,	8, b. MO, c1852

1880 Census, Greene Co. MO, Campbell twp: #202-p.216

Jessie Beshers,	55, b. c1825, VA, VA, TN
Polly	50, TN, TN, TN
Betsey (black servant)	43, TN, TN, TN

<u>1880 Census, Greene Co. MO, Campbell twp</u>: #201-p.215
John B. Beshears,   28, b. 1852, MO, VA, TN. s/o Jessie, #202-216,
   Mary S.   27, MO, TN, TN
   Lillie Beshears,   8, MO, MO, MO
   Martha C. Beshears,   6, MO, MO, MO
   Dora Beshears,   5, MO, MO, MO
   Mirtie Beshears,   4, MO, MO, MO
   James Beshears,   1, MO, MO, MO

Obit: Death of a Pioneer.

Jesse Beshears, residing six miles east of Springfield, died yesterday afternoon, aged 70 years. The deceased was afflicted with cancer of the bowel and has been confined to his bed about two months. Mr. Beshears was a native of Virginia and came to Greene County when a small boy. He was a member of the Methodist Protestant Church and was buried this morning near Turner Station.

<u>Family of Jesse Beshears and Mary Wilkerson:</u>

V9-1860.   10-1. **James Brashears**, b. c1845, MO; m. *Emma* ____. One known child:

V9-1861.   11-1. **Columbus Beshears**, b. c1869

V9-1862.   10-2. **John B. Brashears**, b. May 1851, MO, d. 1923; m. 1871, *Mary Susan Webb*, b. c1853, MO (27 in 1880; parent b. TN). Ten ch. In 1880, they were hh#201-215, living next door to Jesse in Campbell twp, Green Co, MO, and had five children. (one dau married a Steward; I don't know which one.)

V9-1863.   11-1. **Lillie Beshears**, b. c1872, MO (8 in 1880); m. 3 Nov 1890, *Martin Ingram,*

V9-1864.   11-2. **Martha C. Beshears**, b. c1874, MO (6 in 1880)

V9-1865.   11-3. **Dora Beshears**, b. c1875, MO (5 in1880)

V9-1866.   11-4. **Mirtie Beshears**, b. c1876, MO (4 in 1880)

V9-1867.   11-5. **James R. Beshears**, b. c1879, MO (1 in 1880), d. 1934; m. *Maude Grantham,*

V9-1868.   11-6. **Clarence Joseph Beshears**, b. Dec 1882, MO

V9-1869.   11-7. **Henry Beshears**, b. c1885, MO

V9-1870.   11-8. **Chester W. Beshears**, b. Sep 1892, MO; m. *Anna* ____

V9-1871.   11-9. **Blanche H. Beshears**, b. Mar 1894, MO

V9-1872.   11-10. **Helen R. Beshears**, b. June 1896

V9-1873.   10-3. **Marion Columbus Brashears**, b. 27 Feb 1863, d. 1 May 1863.

Jemima Brashears and James Alfred Mitchem

V2-2233. 9-3. **Jemima Brashears**, (d/o Benjamin Brashears and Jane _____), b. March 1826, KY, d. after 1900, MO; m.25 Nov 1851, *James Alfred Mitchem*. 9 ch. In 1880, they were living in Vernon Co, MO.

V9-1874.   10-1. Alexander Mitchem, b. c1850, MO

V9-1875.   10-2. Benjamin Lewis Mitchem, b. c1852, MO; m. Amy _____

V9-1876.   10-3. James E. Mitchem, b. c1853, MO

V9-1877.   10-4. Marina Gabriella Mitchem, b. c1856, n.m.

V9-1878.   10-5. Artina Mitchem, b. c1859, MO

V9-1879.   10-6. Charles Mitchem, b. c1862, MO

V9-1880.   10-7. Samuel B. Mitchem, b. c1866, MO; m. Emma _____

V9-1881.   10-8. John/Johnie Mitchem, b. c1869, MO (listed as male, 1 yr in 1870; as fem 10 in 1880)

V9-1882.   10-9. Edwin Mitchem, b. c1874, MO; m. Marie _____

Samuel Brashears and Sarah Pursley

v2-2232. **Samuel Brashears**, (s/o Benjamin Brashears and Jane _____), b. 1825, KY; m. *Sarah "Sallie" Pursley*, b. c1831-32, Roane Co, TN, d. 1896, Springfield, Greene Co, MO, bur Pursley Cem, Greene Co, MO, d/o William Pursley, III, b. 9 Dec 1789, near Knoxville, Knox Co, TN, d. 8 Dec 1842, Greene Co, MO, m. 26 Jan 1823, in Roane Co, TN, Martha Gallion, b. 1806-09, Roane Co, TN, d. after 1880, Greene Co, MO.

1850 Census, Greene Co, MO, Campbell twp: #282

Samuel Brashear,	25, b. KY, c1825
Sarah	18, b. TN, c1832
Martha J. Brashear,	11/12, b. MO, 1849

1860 Census, Greene Co, MO, Jackson twp: #580-p.616

Samuel Brashears,	35, b. KY c1825
Sarah Brashears,	30, b. TN c1830
Martha Brashears,	10, b. MO, c1850
Mary Brashears,	6, b. MO, c1854
John Brashears,	3, b. MO, c1857
Samuel Brashears,	1, b. MO, c1859
Albert Cargile,	32, place of birth & relationship not given

1880 Census, Greene Co, MO, Taylor twp: #202

Samuel Brashears,	54, b. KY c1826, fa b. SC, mo b. TN
Sarah	49, b. TN c1801, fa. b. TN, mo b. TN
Sousan Brashears,	16, b. MO c1854 = Gabriella Susan Brashears
Ellen Brashears,	14, b. MO, c1856
Sarah Brashears,	5, b. MO, c1875
Isac Berrus,	21, MO, TN, TN - relationship not given. Later Gabriella Susan Brashear's husband.

Family of Samuel Brashears and Sarah Pursley:

V2-2241.   10-1. **Martha J. Brashears**, b. MO, 7 May 1850, MO (11/12 in 1850; 10 in 1860), d. 4 Dec 1931, Springfield, MO (Mo death cert 40632); m. 15 Feb 1866, in Greene Co, MO, (bk C, p.10), *James David Kennemer*. Twelve ch.

J.D. Kennemer and Wife, Martha Brashear

V9-1883.   11-1. William Kennemer, b. c1867, MO

V9-1884.   11-2. Samuel Elijah W. Kennemer, b. 20 June 1870, MO, d. 15 March 1915, Greene Co, MO (MO death cert 15886); m. 19 Oct 1893, Greene Co, MO, Dorothy Ann "Dolly Bacon; ggpa/o Judy A. Wilkinson, of Hyde Park, UT, who sent pictures and death certificates .

V9-1885.   11-3. Nancy Kennemer, (twin), b. c1871, MO
V9-1886.   11-4. Sarah Kennemer, (twin), b. c1871, MO
V9-1887.   11-5. Susan Kennemer, b. c1876, MO
V9-1888.   11-6. John Kennemer, b. c1878, MO
V9-1889.   11-7. Mary Kennemer, b. c1879, MO
V9-1890.   11-8. Lee Kennemer, b. May 1883, MO
V9-1891.   11-9. Nora Kennemer, b. 23 Aug 1885, MO, d. 2 March 1920; m. George Collins
V9-1892.   11-10. Thomas Kennemer, b. March 1877, MO
V9-1893.   11-11. Gabriel "Gabe" Martin Kennemer, b. 21 June 1889, MO, d. 31 March 1949, Redwood City, CA; m. 23 April 1925, in MO, Helen Louise Gorton. They had four children, including:
V9-1894.   12-x. Margaret Kennemer, m. _____ Truesdell <atnmt@mlode.com>
V9-1895.   11-12. James Kennemer, b. July 1891, MO
V2-2242.   10-2. **Mary Brashears**, b. MO, c1854 (6 in 1860)
V2-2243.   10-3. ***John Brashears**, b. MO, Feb 1857 (3 in 1860); m. 30 April 1882, *Nannie Sanders*. Four ch.
V2-2244.   10-4. **Samuel Elijah W. Brashears**, b. MO, 28 June 1859 (1 in 1860), d. 12 March 1920, bur Pursley Cem (MO death cert 12264); m. 8 March 1877, *Mary Jane*

Chapman. Three known ch.

V2-2245. 10-5. **Gabriella Susan Brashears**, b. MO c1864 (16 in 1880); ?may have m. 25 July 1880, *Isaac Burrus*?

V2-2246. 10-6. **Margarette Ellen Brashears**, b. MO, c1865 (14 in 1880); m. 29 Sep 1887, *James Connoy*

J.D. Kennemer and Martha Brashear

V9-1896. 10-7. **Ardella Brashears**, b. Jan 1870
V2-2247. 10-8. **Sarah Brashears**, b. MO, c1875 (5 in 1880)

John Brashears and Nannie Sanders

v2-2243. **John Brashears**, (s/o Samuel Brashears and Sarah Pursley), b. 1858, MO; m. 30 Apr 1882, in Webster Co, MO, *Nannie Sanders* , b. 1857, MO, d/o James Sanders and Eliza C. _____. She appeared on the census, 1880, Greene Co, MO. (thanks to Oneida Lee (Swickard) Bynum, <obynum@ren.net>, for data)

V2-2248. 11-1. **Sarah J. Brashears**, b. 1880, MO. She died before 1950.

V2-2249. 11-2. **Alice Brashears**, b. c1883, MO, d. after 1959, CA; m. _____ *Hicks*

V2-2250. 11-3. **Frank Brashears**, b. 1887, d. 1957, Mesa, AZ; m. c1910, *Viola N.* _____, b. 1894, d. 1957, Mesa, AZ.

V2-2251. 12-1. **Floyd E. Brashears**, b. 1915, d. 1975.

V2-2252. 12-2. **Lee Roy Brashears**, b. 1918, d. 1968.

V2-2253. 11-4. **Iona Elizabeth Brashears**, b. 27 Jan 1891, MO, d. 28 Nov 1950, Konawa, OK, bur Konawa Cem, Konawa, OK; m. 30 Jun 1907, at Franks, Indian Terr, OK, *William Columbus Owens*, b. 4 Dec 1879, TX, d. 14 Jul 1970, Barnsdall, OK, bur Konawa Cem, Konawa, OK, s/o William C. Owens and Susan Butler. He appeared on the census, 1910, OK.

V2-2243. 12-1. Hattie Lee Owens, b. 13 May 1908, Stonewall, OK, d. 21 Mar 1991, Pampa, TX. She appeared on the census, 1910, Pontotoc Co, OK; 1920, Vancouver, Canada; 1930, Pampa, Gray Co, TX. In 1931, she was in Maricopa, Mesa Co, AZ. She was baptised, 1933, Pampa, Gray Co, TX. She was buried on 24 Mar 1991, Fairview Cem, Pampa, TX (Pampa *Daily News*). Hattie Lee Owens m. 14 Feb 1923, at Franks, Ind Terr, Isham Richardson Bynum Sr, b.

14 Feb 1902, Hewett or Wilson, Ind Terr, d. 27 Dec 1967, Newhall, CA, bur Fairview Cem, Pampa, TX. He appeared on the census, 1910, Wilson, Carter Co, OK, and on Church Membership rolls there on 29 Aug 1920. He was an Oilfield pumper between 1929 and 1964, Pampa, Gray Co, TX, where he was on Church Membership rolls, 1930.

V2-2255.   [13]-1. Isham Richardson Bynum Jr, b. 6 Jun 1925, Wilson, OK, baptised, 1933, Pampa , Gray Co, TX; m. on 23 Sep 1951, at Pampa , TX, Hetty Jo Tucker, b. 30 May 1924, Pampa , TX, d/o _____ Tucker and Alvia Josephine Huey. He served in the U.S. Army, 1941-46. After 1947, he worked at Trailways Bus Co, Amarillo, Potter Co, TX

V2-2256.   [14]-1. Bonita Bynum.

V2-2257.   [14]-2. Gregg Richardson Bynum, b. 3 Jul 1955. He, b. 3 Jul 1955.

V2-2258.   [13]-2. John W. Bynum, b. 23 Nov 1927, Vernon, TX, d. 17 Jul 1929, Pampa, TX, bur 19 Jul 1929, Fairview Cem, Pampa, TX.

V2-2259.   [13]-3. Rose Ellen Bynum, b. 16 Nov 1929, Pampa, TX, d. 25 Jun 1931, Phoenix, AZ. She was buried on 26 Jun 1931, Double Butte Cem, Maricopa County, AZ.

V2-2260.   [13]-4. Phillip Melvin Bynum, n. 23 Aug 1930, Pampa, Gray Co, TX, d. 4 Jul 1968, Dumas, Moore Co, TX, bur Fairview Cem, Pampa, TX; m. 3 Jul 1950, at Pampa, TX, Frankie Jean Berry, b. 7 Jul 1933, Pampa, TX.

V2-2261.   [14]-1. LaRita Fern Bynum

V2-2262.   [14]-2. Tina Marie Bynum

V2-2263.   [14]-3. Catherine Lee Bynum

V2-2264.   [13]-5. Eugene Warren Bynum, b. 6 Apr 1933, Pampa, TX; m.1. 1954, at Pampa, TX, Beth Allen (1 ch); m.2. 21 Sep 1959, at Pampa, TX, Amy Louise Rutherford (4 ch), b. 16 Aug 1939, Jackson Co, AR

V2-2265.   [14]-1. Toi Lane Bynum, b. 1953, Pampa, Gray Co, TX

V2-2266.   [14]-2. Rocky Carl Bynum

V2-2267.   [14]-3. Mickey Charles Bynum

V2-2268.   [14]-4. Elizabeth Rose Bynum

V2-2269.   [14]-5. Glenna Faye Bynum

V2-2270.   [13]-6. Elmer Graves Bynum, b. 16 Jul 1935, Pampa, TX, d. 13 Aug 1993, Spearman, TX, bur Fairview

Cem, Pampa, TX; m.1. 1956, at Bremerton, WA, Joan Johnson (3 ch), b. 1938, Bremerton,WA; m.2. 1978, at Phoeniz, AZ, Martha Gold (3 ch); m.3. 22 Feb 1980, at Spearman, TX, Nona Faye McClure, b. 10 Mar 1940.

V2-2271.   14-1. Debra Janet Bynum
V2-2272.   14-2. Vickie Jo Bynum
V2-2273.   14-3. Randall J. Bynum
V2-2274.   14-4. Charlotte A. Bynum
V2-2275.   14-5. Janet Marleta Bynum
V2-2276.   14-6. Linda Bynum
V2-2277.   13-7. Joseph Payne Bynum, b. 6 Jun1938, Pampa, Gray Co, TX; m. 15 Mar 1958, at North Hollywood, CA, <u>Oneida Lee Swickard</u>, b. 25 Jun 1941, Glendale, CA

V2-2278.   14-1. Kevin Bynum
V2-2279.   14-2. Kurtis A. Bynum
V2-2280.   14-3. Kellianne Bynum
V2-2281.   14-4. Karl Joseph Bynum
V2-2282.   13-8. Ralph Edward Bynum, b. 19 Nov 1940, Pampa, TX; m. 9 Apr 1960, in Maine, Mona Jean Doucette (2 ch), b. 14 Jul 1943, Van Buren, ME, d. 30 Aug 1947, Amarillo, Potter Co, TX, d/o Reno Doucette and Pauline Jacques; m.2. 7 Dec 1980, at Dumas, Moore Co, TX, Clo Ann Johnson, b. 26 Nov 1940, Pampa, TX

V2-2283.   14-1. Tammy Lee Bynum
V2-2284.   14-2. Terry Lane Bynum
V2-2285.   13-9. Paul J. Bynum, b. 8 Apr 1946, Pampa, TX; m. 1967, Julie Hopkins (2 ch; div, 1988); m.2. 31 Jul 1988, Silsbee, TX, Caroline Carrel, b. 1959, Rusk, TX

V2-2286.   14-1. Jennine Marie Bynum, b. 14 Jul 1969, Japan
V2-2287.   14-2. Daniel Cade Bynum, b. 9 Oct 1970, Newark, NJ
V2-2288.   14-3. Jason Bynum, b. 11 Nov 1983, Galveston, TX
V2-2289.   14-4. Trent Christopher Bynum, b. 16 Jul 1991, Beaumont, TX
V2-2290.   13-10. Elizabeth (no middle name) Bynum, b. 3 Nov 1948, Pampa, TX; m.1. 1967, at Pampa, TX, Gary Smiley (2 ch); m.2. 1973, in TX, Truett Ledbetter (1 ch); m.3. 1977, in TX, Ron Russell; m.4. 1988, at Amarillo, Potter Co, TX, Richard

Royall; m.5. 1992, at Voldesta, GA, Gary Westberry.

V2-2291.   14-1. Jerry Dean Smiley
V2-2292.   14-2. Richard Lee Smiley, b. 17 May 1969, Pampa, TX, d. 30 Jan 1996, Voldesta, GA
V2-2293.   14-3. Rachel Ledbetter
V2-2294.   12-2. John Quincey Owens, b. 8 Mar 1910, Stonewall, OK, d. 1990, Barnsdall, OK; m. 1936, Virginia
V2-2295.   12-3. Frank Owens, b. 1912, Stonewall, OK

Martin Brashears and Louisa Austin

v2-2234. **Martin Brashears**, (s/o Benjamin Brashears and Jane ____), b. 1828, Cumberland Co, KY; m.1. 19 Feb 1853, Greene Co, MO (Book A, p.64), *Louisa Austin*, b. NC, c1830/31 (mother of all the children); m.2. 10 March 1 8 8 1 , *E m i l y Yarbrough*. Martin was a farmer and stock-raiser in Sec 10, T28, R21, near Springfield, MO. A tax record shows his birthplace as Cumberland Co, KY, and says he came to Greene county in 1837.

Obit: "Old Settler Dead"

Martin Brashears who Came to Greene County 65 years ago.

Martin Brashears, aged 73 years, died yesterday morning of consumption, at 10 o'clock, at his home near Galloway. He came to Greene County 65 years ago and has resided near Galloway ever since that time. He leaves a widow and eight children.

Martin Brashear and Louisa Austin.
Photo: Richard Reese

1860 Census, Greene Co, MO, Campbell twp:

#750-p.798

Martin Brashears,	32, b. KY c1828
Louisa Brashears,	29, b. NC c1821
William Brashears,	6, b. MO, c1854
Greene Brashears,	4, b. MO, c1856
Artemie Brashears,	2, b. MO, c1858
Westley Brashears,	2/12, b. MO, 1860

1880 Census, Greene Co, MO, Clay twp:

Martin Beshears,	52, KY, VA, VA
Louisa Beshears,	40, NC, NC, NC
Lewis Greene Beshears,	25, MO, KY, NC
Wesley Beshears,	19, MO, KY, NC
Martin S.J. Beshears,	17, MO, KY, NC
James Beshears,	14, MO, KY, NC
Gabe Beshears,	10, MO, KY, NC
Louisa Beshears,	6, MO, KY, NC

1880 Census, Greene Co, MO, Clay twp:

William Beshears,	26, b. c1854, MO KY NC; s/o Martin
Martha Beshears,	25, MO, VA, VA

In the 1890s, three children of Martin Breshears and Louisa Austin, Martin Benjamin Beshears, Charles Gabriel Beshears, Louisa Beshears, and possibly one other brother migrated to Visalia, Tulare Co, CA, where (at least) Charles and Louisa married and lived. See obituaries below.

Family of Martin Brashears and Louisa Austin:

V2-2296.   10-1. **William Lemuel Brashears**, b. 10 March 1854, MO, d. 15 June 1919; m. 15 Jan 1880, **Martha E. Dike**, b. MO c1855. Four ch.

V9-1897.   11-1. **William E. Beshears**, b. Dec 1874, MO
V9-1898.   11-2. **Charles G. Beshears**, b. 28 Oct 1880, MO, d. 24 Nov 1975
V9-1899.   11-3. **Nancy J. Beshears**, b. April 1884, MO
V9-1900.   11-4. **Minnie F. Beshears**, b. Oct 1895, MO
V2-2297.   10-2. **Lewis Greene Brashears**, b. Oct 1856, MO, d. 1939, Springfield, MO; apparently never married.
V2-2298.   10-3. **Nancy Artemie "Nanny" Brashears**, b. Dec 1858, MO; m. 20 April 1876, **Joel H. Haden**
V2-2299.   10-4. **Job Wesley Brashears**, b. May 1860, MO, d. 1934;
V9-1901.   10-5. **Mary Brashears**, b. c1863, d. before 1902
V2-2300.   10-6. **Martin Benjamin Beshears**, b. c1864, MO; m. _____. Martin voted in Tulare Co, CA, in 1898 and was on the Tulare Co, Census in 1900. (See Tulare Co Gen Web site; thanks to Richard Reese for data.)

Matilda Fowler, Effe & Charles Beshears
Gladys Hardaway & Alice Beshears
Tulare County, California 1907

V2-2301. 10-7. **James Freeman Beshears**, b. 4 May 1866, MO, d. 12 Oct 1918 (suicide); m. 4 Dec 1894, *Rosa Strickland*

V9-1902. 11-1. **Nina A. Beshears**, b. c1896, MO

V9-1903. 11-2. **Joe L. Beshears**, b. 28 Aug 1897, MO, d. 21 July 1950

V9-1904. 11-3. **John E. Beshears**, b. c1902, MO

V9-1905. 11-4. **Catherine L. Beshears**, b. c1904, MO

V9-1906. 11-5. **Pearl J. Beshears**, b. c1907, MO

V9-1907. 11-6. **Fred L. Beshears**, b. c1910, MO

V9-1908. 11-7. **Wesley V. Beshears**, b. c1912, MO

V2-2302. 10-8. ***Charles Gabriel "Gabe" Beshears**, b. Springfield, MO, 1870, d. 5 Sept 1931, Porterville, Tulare Co, CA; m. 24 Nov 1901, Tulare Co, CA, *Effie J. Fowler*,

V2-2302. 10-9. **Louisa Beshears**, b. 9 March 1875, Springfield, MO, d. 11 Dec 1928, Tulare Co, CA; m. 18 Oct 1894, in Tulare Co, CA, *John Hahesy*, b. in Ireland, 1852, d. 20 March 1932, Tulare Co, CA.

Obituary of Louise Beshears Hahesy, Tulare Advance Register, Dec 11, 1928

Stricken with a sudden heart attack about 4 o'clock this morning, Mrs. John Hahesy, 53, residing about 8 miles west of Tulare died in a few minutes. She had been in apparent good health previously. She is survived by her husband, John Hahesy and 7 children, W.M. Hahesy of Tulare, Mrs. Helen Litten of Hollister, John Jr. and Chas J.

---

both of Tulare, Mrs. Michael Deaver of Tulare, Thomas of Laguna Beach and Louise of Tulare. Mrs. Hahesy was Louise Beshears prior to her marriage. She was born in Springfield, MO on March 9th- 1875. She came to Tulare about 34 years ago, where she was united in marriage to John Hahesy.

Some ten years later, they moved to their present home and have resided there ever since.

Charles G. Beshears and Effie J. Fowler

V2-2302. [10]-8. **Charles Gabriel "Gabe" Beshears**, (s/o Martin Beshears and Louisa Austin), b. Springfield, MO, 1870, d. 5 Sept 1931, Porterville, Tulare Co, CA; m. 24 Nov 1901, Tulare Co, CA, **Effie J. Fowler**, b. 10 Dec 1880, Deer Creek, Tulare Co, CA, d. 29 June 1965, Visalia, Tulare Co, CA. Charles farmed wheat and raised cattle in Tulare County his entire adulthood. He bought one of the first grain combines powered by 20 mules, and harvested wheat for many other farmers in the area.

Obit Charles G. Beshears, Porterville Recorder, Sept 9, 1931

LOCAL PIONEER DIES

Funeral services were held yesterday afternoon for Charles G. Beshears, 62, who passed away Saturday afternoon at his home. The

Great grandson, Richard Reese, sent the photo of this operation.

Charles G. Beshears Homestead, Tulare County, California 1915

deceased was a native of Missouri and came to California about 30 years ago. He first settled in Visalia and later came to the Sausalito district, where he engaged in farming and stock raising. He was married about 27 years ago to Miss Effie Fowler, who was born in the Deer Creek section of Tulare Co. Mrs. Beshears and a daughter, Mrs. Alice Reese, survive. He also leaves two brothers, who reside at Springfield, Mo. Mr. Beshears had been in failing health for the past two years and his death was not unexpected. He numbered many friends among the older residents.

Charles and Effie had one child:

V9-1909.   11-1. **Alice Beshears**, b. 18 Oct 1902, Tulare Co, CA, d. 17 Dec 1994, Visalia, Tulare Co, CA; m. 17 Sept 1923, in Visalia, Tulare Co, CA, *Chester Reese*, b. 14 Feb 1897, Tulare Co, CA, d. 10 July 1955, Visalia, Tulare Co, CA. (Grandparents of Richard Reese (Reese@ psnw.com), who sent data and documents, for which many thanks.)

Lewis Brashears and Mary Ann Petty

v2-2235. **Lewis Brashears**, (s/o Benjamin Brashears and Jane ____), b. 17 Jan 1830, Cumberland Co, KY, d. 26 Jan 1900, Dover, Pope Co, AR; enlisted in Confederate Army, 1861, under Capt. Campbell, Greene Co, MO, became 2nd Lt, participated in battles at Pea Ridge, Wilson's Creek and Corinth, where he was wounded in 1862; m. 19 Oct 1869, at Dover, Pope Co, AR, *Mary Ann Petty*, b. 4 Sep 1844, d. 13 Feb 1913, Dover, AR. Joyce McCain, of Russellville, AR, sent data which updates this family, for which many thanks.

Lewis owned land in Green Co, MO: E½ SW¼ Sec 10 and E½ NW¼ Sec 10; W½ NE¼ Sec 9; and E½ NW¼ Sec 9, all in Township 28, Range 21. During the war, Lewis's brother-in-law, Wesley Austin (who married Lewis's sister, Artina), sued Lewis for a debt of $102, which with interest and damages came to $123.10. Since Lewis was away at the war and did not appear, the court ruled in favor of Wesley. Lewis's property was seized on 25 Oct 1862 and sold to pay the debt. (See Greene Co, MO, Circuit Court Cases, Book E, p.433 & 593, and Book F, p.74; thanks to Ron Fowler for copies.)

GREENE COUNTY, MISSOURI
Book E, p.433
CIRCUIT COURT CASES
IN GREENE CIRCUIT COURTJANUARY TERM 1863
Wesley Austin Plaintiff
  Vs
  By Attachment
Lewis Brashears   Defendant
  Comes the Plaintiff and files his petition with the Clerk founded on a demand against the Defendant for money paid by Plaintiff for Defendant as security on a bond executed by Defendant to the County of Greene, State of Missouri, for the use of School Township 30 Range 20 for the sum of $102 bearing 10% interest per annum which sum with the interest and costs of suit commenced by the County Court of Greene County against Plaintiff as security on said bond amounting to $123.19 was paid by Plaintiff for which he claims Judgment against the Defendant.   Also, his affidavit stating that the Defendant has absconded or absented himself from his usual place of abode in this State so that the ordinary process of Law cannot be served on him. It is therefore ordered by the undersigned Clerk of said Court in vacation that publication be made in the Springfield Journal notifying said Defendant that an action has been commenced against him by petition and attachment in said Court as above recited that his property is about to be attached and unless he appears at the next term of the Court which will be held on the first Monday in January 1863 and on or before the third day thereof if the term shall so long continue, if not, then before the end of the term Judgment will be rendered against him and his property sold to satisfy the same.
  M.J. Hubble Clerk
  by E.M. Hendrick DC

GREENE COUNTY, MISSOURI
Book E, p. 593/594.
JANUARY TERM 1863
CIRCUIT COURT CASES
Wesley Austin Plaintiff
    Vs Civil Action
Lewis Brashears Defendant
    Now at this day   comes the Plaintiff by attorney and it appearing
to the satisfaction of the Court that Defendant has been duly notified
by publication in the Springfield Journal, a newspaper published in the
State of Missouri, for four weeks successively, the last insertion at least
four weeks previous to the first day of the present term of this Court
and having failed to plead, answer or demur to Plaintiff's petition the
same is taken as true. And this action being founded on a promissory
note for the direct payment of money and the amount ascertained
whereby the Court doth find on an examination of the same that
Defendant is indebted to Plaintiff in the sum of $123.19 debt and also
$4.15 damage. It is therefore considered by the Court that Plaintiff
have judgment interlocutory and unless cause to the contrary be shown
on or before the sixth day of the next term of this Court this judgment
shall be made final.

GREENE COUNTY, MISSOURI
Book F, p.74.
AUGUST TERM 1863
CIRCUIT COURT CASES
Wesley Austin Plaintiff
    vs Civil Action
Lewis Brashears Defendant
    Now at this day   comes the Plaintiff by attorney and it appearing
to the Court that on the 23 October 1862 an attachment issued in this
cause and on the 25 October 1862 was levied on the following real
estate vis: E 1/2, SW1/4, Section 10 and E1/2 NW1/4 Section 10
W1/2 NE1/4 and E1/2 NW1/4 Section 9 all in Township 28 Range 21.
And that at the January Term 1863 of the Court an interlocutory
judgment was rendered against said Defendant he having been duly
notified as the Law directs and having failed to plead, answer or demur
to Plaintiff's petition and no cause having been shown why the same
should not be made final, the Court sitting as a Jury doth find from the
evidence that the Defendant is indebted to the Plaintiff in the sum of
$123.49 debt and $7.49 damage. It is therefore considered and
adjudged by the Court that the Plaintiff have and recover of and from
Defendants his said debt and damage and that he have execution with
10% interest.

This case probably created some sort of family feud, or at least some ill feeling. No doubt, this encouraged Lewis to look elsewhere for a place to live. Mary Ann Petty's brother, Joseph, had been also a Confederate soldier, wounded at Corinth. The two men may have formed a friendship that led to Joseph introducing Lewis to his sister, Mary Ann.

The case may have soured Wesley and Artina on Greene Co, also, for by 1870, they were in Madison Co, AR.

After marriage in 1869, Lewis and Mary Ann lived at various times in Arkansas and Missouri. After 1880, Lewis owned and operated a lumber mill north of Dover, Pope Co, AR. Both Lewis and Mary Ann died and are buried in Dover.

McFadden Cemetery, Dover, Pope Co, AR (Pope Co. Cems. p.184)
Jemima Brashears, 1875–1954
Lewis Brashears, 17 Jan 1830–26 Jan 1900
Mary A. Brashears, 4 Sep 1844–13 Feb 1913

1900 Census, Pope Co, AR, Martin twp, p.198:
Brashears, Will J.   28, b. May 1872, AR
   Minnie A.   45, b. Sep 1844, AR, mother; Mary Ann (Petty) Brashears
   Jemima   25, b. Feb 1875, AR, sister
   R. L.   22, b. Jan 1878, AR, brother
   Minnie   13, b. Mar 1887, AR, sister

Obit: Louis Brashears —
One of Pope County's oldest and well-known citizens, died at his home at Dover, Friday, January 26, 1900, of floating spleen. Burial occurred at the Dover Cemetery at 11 o'clock the following day, the services being conducted by Alec Bringle. Deceased was about 70 years of age and had spent more than half of his life in Pope County. He was an honest and upright citizen and enjoyed the confidence and respect of a large circle of acquaintances. He leaves a wife and five children to mourn the loss of a kind and indulgent husband and father. (Russellville *Courier-Democrat*)

Lewis and Mary Ann had 5 ch: (thanks to Ron Fowler and Cora Majek for data; additional data from Joyce McCain)

V9-1910.   10-1. **William Joshua Brashears**, b. May 1872, Searcy Co, AR; m. **Emma Bradley**. They were living in Bartlesville, OK in 1920

V9-1911.   11-1. **Pauline Brashears**,

V9-1912.   10-2. **Jemima Martha Brashears**, b. Feb 1875, Searcy Co, AR, d. 1954, Dover, AR; never married.

v2-2304.   10-3. *****Robert Lewis Brashears**, b. 23 Jan 1878, Schell City, Vernon Co, MO, d. 7 Nov 1950, Greenleaf, OR; m. 24

May 1901, in Dover, Pope Co, AR, **Claudia Ann Pierson**.. See below.

V9-1913.   10-4. **Mary Ann Brashears**, b. Oct 1879, Schell City, Vernon Co, MO, d. 17 Jan 1977, Pope Co, AR; m. 27 Dec 1896, in Dover, Pope Co, AR, **William J. Bullock**, (6 ch)

V9-1914.   11-1. Valerie Chloe Bullock, d. at birth

V9-1915.   11-2. Robert Lewis Bullock, b. 1899, AR, d. 1935, AR; m. Verna Cartwright (1 ch)

V9-1916.   11-3. Rebecca Ann Bullock, b. Aug 1901, AR, still living in 2001; m. 26 Sep 1920, Willia Ross (6 ch)

V9-1917.   11-4. Claudia Melissa Bullock, b. 1907, AR, d. 8 May 2000, OK; m. Jess Sanders (2 ch)

V9-1918.   11-5. Lu Willie Bullock, b. 7 Dec 1910, AR, still living in 2001; m. Floyd Turner (2 ch)

V9-1919.   11-6. John Harrison Bullock, b. ?; m. Edith Dorland

V9-1920.   10-5. **Minnie Elizabeth Brashears**, b. 4 Mar 1888, Pope Co, AR, d. 11 June 1951, Dover, Pope Co, AR; m. 6 Nov 1904, in Pope Co, AR, **Thomas Jackson McCain**, b. 16 Oct 1880, Scottsville, AR, d. 26 Oct 1938, Dover, Pope Co, AR

V9-1921.   11-1. infant McCain, b.&d. 5 July 1906

V9-1922.   11-2. Ila Lucile McCain, b. 8 Feb 1908, d. 28 June 1972; m. Ben Lay

V9-1923.   11-3. Thomas Lewis McCain, b. 14 Apr 1910, d. 29 June 1912

V9-1924.   11-4. Winnie Kathleen McCain, b. 3 Sep 1912, d. May 1980, San Bernardino, CA; m. Luther Proctor

V9-1925.   11-5. Minnie Euleta McCain, b. 22 April 1915; m. Scott Turner

V9-1926.   11-6. Thomas Jackson McCain Jr, b. 7 Feb 1918, d. 8 Feb 1918

V9-1927.   11-7. Fred Brashears McCain, b. 27 Apr 1919, Dover, AR; m. 24 Aug 1946, Nina Agnes Eubanks, b. 28 Feb 1917, Dover, AR, d. 15 Nov 1998, Dover, AR

V9-1928.   12-1. Ruby Joyce McCain, b. 29 July 1947, Russellville, AR

V9-1929.   12-2. Freddy Dean McCain, (twin) b. 30 July 1949, Russellville, AR; m. 25 May 1968, May Nioka Miller, b. 7 Dec 1948, Alread, AR

V9-1930.   13-1. Cyndia Jeneane McCain, b. 18 Feb 1970, Russellville, AR; m. 6 June 1992, Lloyd Jerome Callan, b. 8 Aug 1968

V9-1931.	14-1. Savannah Faith Callan, b. 15 Mar 1996, Russellville, AR
V9-1932.	13-2. Bradley Dean McCain, b. 18 July 1976, Russellville, AR
V9-1933.	12-3. Ina Jean McCain, (twin) b. 30 July 1949, Russellville, AR
V9-1934.	11-8. Regina Ruth McCain, b. 16 April 1922, d. 1 Oct 1958, Richmond, CA; m. ____ Sutter
V9-1935.	11-9. Richard Powers McCain, b. 11 Sep 1925, d. 19 Apr 1999, Paducah, KY

Robert Lewis Brashears and Claudia Ann Pierson

10-3. **Robert Lewis Brashears**, (s/o Lewis Brashears and Mary Ann Petty), b. 23 Jan 1878, Schell City, Vernon Co, MO, d. 7 Nov 1950, Greenleaf, OR; m. 24 May 1901, in Dover, Pope Co, AR, *Claudia Ann Pierson*. Six ch.

v2-2305.	11-1. **Nina Lillian Brashears**, b. 20 Jan 1902, Pope Co, AR, d. 17 Oct 1988, Ventura, CA (Ron Fowler's and Cora Majek's grandmother); m.1. 4 Nov 1917, Pope Co, AR, *John Albert Fowler* (3 ch); m.2. 15 May 1930, *Marvin Holder* (no ch)
V9-1936.	12-1. Margaret Evelyn Fowler, b. 1 Aug 1918,Dover, Pope Co, AR, d. 24 March 1983, Ventura, CA; m. 12 Jan 1937, Allen Talcott Worthley (3 ch)
V9-1937.	12-2. Robert Alex Fowler, b. 20 Oct 1920, Cultler, CA, d. 22 Dec 1977, Ventura, CA; m. Mable Sullivan, (1 ch)
V9-1938.	13-1. Ron Fowler, who sent data.
V9-1939.	12-3. Arthur James Fowler, b. 16 June 1926, Visalia, CA, d. 9 Feb 1998, Campbell, CA; m. Patricia McCoy, (4 ch)
v2-2306.	11-2. **Robert Lee Brashears**, b. 8 Apr 1904, Pope Co, AR, d. 4 Feb 1979, Eugene, OR; m. *Gladys Metzken* (no ch)
v2-2307.	11-3. **Mary Claudia Brashears**, b. 6 Mar 1908, Pope Co, AR, d. CA; m. *J.F. Pfieffer* (2 ch)
v2-2308.	11-4. **William Emmett Brashears**, b. 2 Mar 1913, Pope Co, AR, d. 6 Nov 1978, Downey, CA; m. *Doris Holstead* (2 ch)
v2-2309.	11-5. **Edward Pierson Brashears**, b. 12 Jul 1915, Pope Co, AR, d. 19 May 1986, New Haven, CT; m. 4 May 1943, in Guilford, CT, *Esther Smith* (1 ch)

Marina Brashear and Gabriel M. Freeman

v2-2237. **Marina Brashear**, (d/o Benjamin Brashears and Jane ____), b. c1832, KY (38 in 1870); m. 1 Mar 1849, Greene Co, MO, Marriages, Bk A, p.184, *Gabriel M. Freeman*, b. c1828, NC, (42 in 1870, Greene Co, MO). Gabriel M. Freeman was a principal (heir) and administrator in the estate of Benjamin Brashear, in 1869. Gabriel and Marina are #61^9-629 in the 1870 census, Springfield, Campbell Twp, Greene Co, MO, with seven children: (thanks to Dodie Haight for data.)

V2-2310.   [10]-1. Samuel Freeman, b. c1851, MO (19 in 1870; "clerk in store")

V9-1940.   [10]-2. Leonard Freeman, b. c1853, d. before 1870

v2-2311.   [10]-3. Sterling Freeman, b. c1855, MO (15 in 1870)

v2-2312.   [10]-4. Ella "Ellen" Freeman, b. c1858, MO ("Ellen", 12 in 1870)

v2-2313.   [10]-5. Alice Freeman, b. c1860, MO (10 in 1870)

v2-2314.   [10]-6. Benjamin Freeman, b. c1861, MO (9 in 1870)

v2-2315.   [10]-7. Jemima Freeman, b. c1868, MO (2 in 1870)

v2-2316.   [10]-8. Marina "Martha" Freeman, b. Sep 1869, MO (9/12 in 1870)

V9-1941.   [10]-9. Myrtle Freeman, b. Feb 1872

V9-1942.   [10]-10. Gabriel Freeman, b. c1873

Artina Brashears and Wesley Austin

v2-2238. [9]-8. **Artina Brashears**, (d/o Benjamin Brashears and Jane _____), b. 1833, KY; m. 8 Aug 1854, Greene Co, MO (Book B, p.2), *Wesley Austin*. 4 ch. They lived in Madison Co, AR in 1870.

V9-1943.   [10]-1. Benjamin Green Austin, b. c1855, MO

V9-1944.   [10]-2. Robert Lewis Austin, b. c1857, MO

V9-1945.   [10]-3. Laura Austin, b. c1863, MO

V9-1946.   [10]-4. John Austin, b. c1865, MO

---

8. ALEXANDER MARTIN BRASHEARS

v-2, p.183: Doyle Fenn <DoyleFenn@aol.com> reports another child for John Wesley Bolling Brashears and Drucilla R. _____, (s/o James Brashears and Nancy Bolling):

"I found the Civil War record on **Alexander Martin Brashears**, aka Martin A. Brashears. He was a son of John Wesley & Drucilla Brashears. He and his brothers John Wesley Brashears, William Colonel Runnels Brashears, and George Alfred Caldwell Brashears, all served in Co E, Griffin's Battalion, Texas Infantry, Confederate States of America.

"Alexander Martin Brashears died from consumption in Parker Co, TX on 28 Sept 1863. His widow, **Nancy R.** _____, received $164.60 that was due him for clothing and back pay. Alexander was born in Lee Co, VA, was 28 when he died, 5' 8" tall, fair complexion, blue eyes and was a farmer by occupation. He enlisted at Weatherford, TX on 19 July 1862. His record shows he had been absent without leave since June 25, 1863. He must have been sick and returned home, where he died.

Other Brashear(s) Families

9. HARDIN CO, KY, FAMILIES

The Estate of Eliza C. Brashear

V4-864. [9-]5. **William Brashear**, (s/o Thomas Brashear and Lucy Lucas; Thomas Brashear was s/o Nicholas Ray Brashear and Martha Simmons; Nicholas Ray Brashear was s/o William Brashear and Anne Ray), b. c1825, Hardin Co, KY (35 in 1860, Audrain Co, MO); m. 2 Jan 1845, in Ralls Co, MO (by George Waters, Church of Christ Minister) *Elizabeth "Eliza" C. Schulse*, b. c1825 (35 in 1850 Audrain Co, MO), d. 17 Feb 1913, Laclede Co, MO, probably d/o Mark Schulse and Susan Musich, of Nicholas Co, KY. (Additional data from Dorothy Goss, 22169 Gresham Lane, Lebanon, MO 65536)

On 21 Feb 1913, A. W. Roberts applied for Letters of Administration on the effects of Eliza C. Brashear, naming heirs as as Eleanor L. Brashear of Laclede Co, MO; Marcus W. Brashear, of Green Co, MO; Nancy N. Blackman, of Laclede Co, MO; Ailcy Dyer, of Laclede Co, MO; Guy H. Brashear, of Green Co, MO; James Brashear, of Camden Co, MO; Cage Brashear, of Fairland Co, OK; Patsy Finks, of Lincoln Co, OK. A.W. Roberts must have been a son-in-law. (Data from Shirley Graham, <Shirl@pe.net>, and Carroll Jenkins <crjcsj@yahoo.com>.)

Receipt No 5 (of estate proceedings)
State of Misouri County of Laclede
Peynob. PO   MO,   April 25th- 1914
Received of A. W. Roberts, Administrator of Eliza C. Brashear Estate, $45.13 (forty five 13/100 Dollars) binging the ful amount due me of the personel estate of Eliza C. Brashears.
/s/ McCager S. Brashear

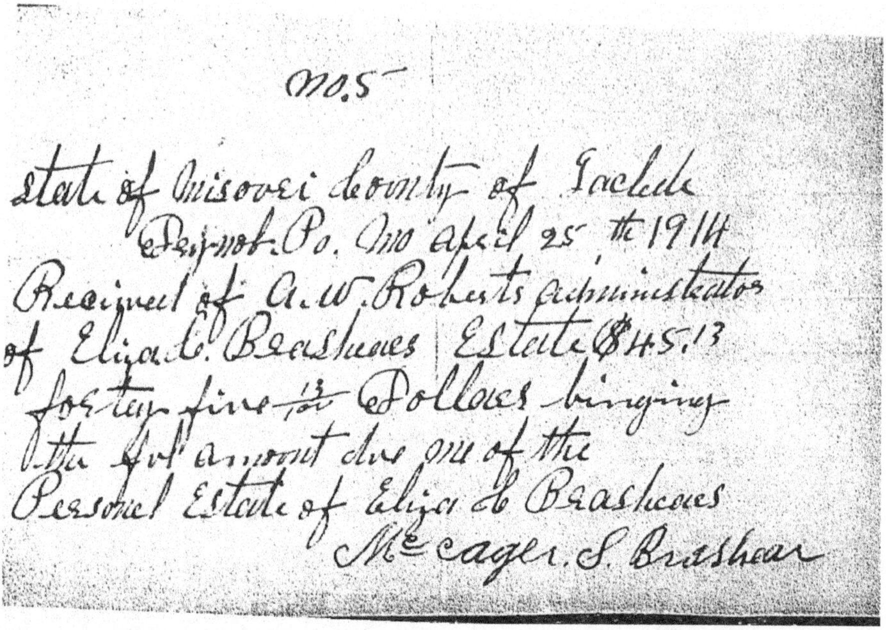

$\mathcal{NO}.5$

[handwritten receipt text, largely illegible]

Which indicates that Samuel's first name was Micajah.

Receipt No 6 is an identical receipt, dated April 11th-, 1914, signed by the mark of Micajah's brother, M. W. Brashears.

Family of William Brashear and Eliza C. Schulse (see 1850, 1860 census of Audrain Co, MO; data and photo from Shirley Graham)

V4-944. 10-1. **Eleanor L. (or C.) Brashear**, b. c1845 (15 in 1860); unmarried; lived Laclede Co, MO in 1913. In 1910 Census of Laclede Co, MO, Eliza is living with Eleanor.

V4-945. 10-2. **Mary A. Brashear**, b. 1846-47 (14 in 1860); d. before 1913

V4-946. 10-3. **John A. Brashear**, b. 1848 (12 in 1860); d. before 1913

V4-947. 10-4. **Marcus William Brashear**, b. 1849 (11 in 1860); lived Greene Co, MO, in 1913

V4-948. 10-5. **Guy Hiram Brashear**, b. 1850 (10 in 1860); lived Greene Co, MO in 1913

V4-949. 10-6. **Sarah Brashear**, b. 1852 (8 in 1860); d. before 1913

V4-950. 10-7. **Nancy Margaret Brashear**, b. 31 Dec 1854 (7 in 1860), d. 5 Jan 1929, Falcon, MO; m. *Lester Blackmon*. lived Laclede Co, MO in 1913. Additional data from ggdau, Kris <kglenn846@aol.com>. Ch: 4 boys, 1 girl, including:

V9-1947. 11-x. Isaac Marshall Blackmon

V9-1948.   10-8. **Ailsey Brashear**, b. 1855 (5 in 1860)lived Laclede Co, MO in 1913; m. April 1879, in Audrain Co, MO, *John William Dyer*, b. VA, d. Laclede Co, MO, c1904. Ancestors of Dorothy Goss, of Lebanon, MO.

V9-1949.   10-9. *****James Harrison Brashear**, b. 1856 (4 in 1860); lived Camden Co, MO in 1913

V4-952.10-10. *****Micajah Samuel Brashear**, b. 1858 (2 in 1860); lived Fairland Co, OK in 1913

V9-1950.   10-11. **Martha "Patsy" Brashear**, b. after 1860, m. _____ *Finks*; lived Lincoln Co, OK in 1913

James Harrison Brashear and Laura Landis

V9-3144.   10-9. **James Harrison Brashear**, b. c1856, MO; m. *Laura Landis*

V9-1951.   11-1. **William Harrison Brashear**, b. 18 July 1892, Mexico, MO (per Gilberte Brashear Parastar <roseozzie@aol.com>

V9-1952.   12-x. **Donald Brashear**
V9-1953.   12-x. **Jimmy Brashear**
V9-1954.   12-x. _____ **Brashear**,
V9-1955.   13-x. **Gilberte Brashear**, m. _____ *Parastar*

Micajah Samuel Brashear and Alma Ellen Carman

V4-952.10-10. **Micajah Samuel "Cage" Brashears**, b. c1858, MO; m. c1876, *Alma Ellen (Carman) Painter*, b. 30 Aug 1860, Monroe Co, MO, d. 5 Sept 1942, Monroe Co, MO, d/o James H. B. Carman (1828–1908) and Mary Ann Shoults (1828–1882). She had been previously married to George H. Painter.(posted by Shirley Graham <Shirl@pe.net>, 11 Sep 1999)

V9-1956.   11-1. **Alva Brashears**, b. 1 May 1886, d. 15 April 1959; m. *Laura Hiatt*

V9-1957.   11-2. **May Brashears**, b. 27 Jan 1888, d. 25 Nov 1959; m. _____ *Postlewait*

V9-1958.   11-3. **Ona Christine Brashears**, b. 27 Jan 1888, d. c1941; m. c.1918, *Morris Bresnehen*

V9-1959.   11-4. **Grace May Brashears**, b. c1891, d. 19 Aug 1963, m. c1910, *Golf Luster*

V9-1960.   11-5. **Leonard Brashears**, b. c1893, d. Oct 1919; m. *Laura Hammer*

V9-1961.   11-6. **Pearl Carman Brashear**, b. c1896, d. 18 Feb 1969; m. *Jessie Lee Kell.* They lived in Bluejacket, Craig

---

Co, OK. Additional data from Caroll (Brashear) Jenkins <crjcsj@yahoo.com>

^{V9-}1962.   ¹²⁻1. **Marie Brashear**, m. Johnny _____

^{V9-}1963.   ¹²⁻2. **Gerald Edwin Brashear**, (married twice; six ch)

^{V9-}1964.   ¹³⁻1. **Carroll Brashear**; m. _____ Jenkins

^{V9-}1965.   ¹³⁻2. _____ Brashear; m. Rosy _____

Alma Ellen (Carman) Painter/Brashears siblings were:
1. Marcus Linus Carman, b. 18 Aug 1850, Ralls Co, MO
2. Isaac Newton Carman, b. 30 April 1853, Ralls Co, MO
3. Elizabeth Eleanor Carman, b. 23 Jan 1854, Ralls Co, MO
4. Mary Jane Carman, b. 16 Feb 1856, Ralls Co, MO
5. Annie Elizabeth Carman, b. 23 Oct 1857, Ralls Co, MO
6. *Alma Ellen Carman*, b. 30 Aug 1860, Monroe Co, MO 7. Margaret Lee Carman, b. 4 May 1862, Monroe Co, MO
8. Emiley Alice Carman, b. 13 Nov 1864, Monroe Co, MO
9. Ella Louise Carman, b. 27 May 1866, Monroe Co, MO
10. James Edward Carman, b. 24 Dec 1876, Monroe Co, MO; m. Agnes

Front row, left to right: Leonard Brashear, Pearl Carman "Babe" Brashear, McCage Brashear and wife, Alma (Carman) Brashear, Mollie (Painter) Link (Alma's daughter by an earlier marriage), Eula (Link) Goodnoa (8 mos old).
Back Row, Left to right: Chris Brashear, James Edward Carman and wife, Agnes Mae (Link) Carman, Alva Brashear, friend Lum Gardner
and "his girl friend," probably Grace Mae Brashear (note the child's dress).

Mae Link. Grandparents of Shirley Graham, who sent data and the photo.

John Richard "J.R." Brashear and GeorgeAnne Upton

David Seay <Seay1964@cox.net> has sent data and a photo of Samuel Eden Brashear, s/o John Richard "J.R." Brashear and Georgianne Upton, d/o Samuel E. Upton and Sarah A. Brashear, in whose household they reside in 1880. The Uptons are both 56 years old, b. c1824; John is 31, b. c1849, George Ann is 30, b. c1850; Samuel Eden Brashear is 3, b. c1777. The census was taken 9th- June, 1880.

Up the page six families, Jos or Jas Brashears is in household of Josiah and Margaret Steth. Jos or Jas is 23, b. c1857, Josiah is 29, b. c1851, Margaret is 20, b. c1860. The couple has a little boy, William L. age 1.

Family of Eden Brashear Jr and Nancy Patterson (sources: 1850 U.S. Census, Kentucky, Hardin Co. & Notes kept by Edith May Brashear):

V4-1885.   10-1. **Andrew P. Brashear**, b. 1843, d. 1917, bur Brashear-Lucas Cem; n.m.

V4-1886.   10-2. **Letitia (or Lutitia) Brashear**, b. 29 May 1845, d. 19 July 1852, bur Geohegan Fam. Cem

V4-1887.   10-3. *****John Richard "J.R." Brashear**, b. c1847 (23 in 1870)

V4-1888.   10-4. **James W. Brashear**, b. 23 March 1851, d. 6 Aug 1852, bur Geohegan Fam. Cem

V4-1889.   10-5. **Margaret P. Brashear**, b. 24 July 1853, d. 2 Oct 1857, bur Geohegan Fam. Cem

V4-1890.   10-6. **Samuel Thomas Brashear**, b. 23 Dec 1855, d. 1 May 1914; m. c1881, **Ada A. (?Anna) Boyd**, b. 6 Oct 1859 (See vol. 4 for family)

V4-1891.   10-7. **Virgil Brashear**, b. 24 June 1858, d. 14 Feb 1863, bur Geohegan Fam. Cem

V4-1892.   10-8. **George Woodford Brashear**, b. 18 Aug 1861 (9 in 1870), d. 23 May 1928, bur Upton City Cem, beside third wife; m.1. **Oma W. Caswell**, m.2. **Minerva Bradley**, m.3. **Cora Belle Jenkins**, d/o James A. Jenkins and Mary "Tom" Brashear, per Jean Smallwood, whose mother was d/o George Woodford Brashear.

V4-1893.   10-9. **inf dau Brashear**, b.& d. 18 Oct 1864, Geohegan Fam. Cem

You'll note that they had trouble keeping their children alive.

John Richard "J.R." Brashears and wife, Georgeanne Epton

V4-1887. [10]-3. **John Richard "J.R." Brashear**, b. 25 Sept 1847, in Cecilia, Hardin Co, KY, d. 20 June 1923, buried Red Mill Cemetery, Elizabethtown, Hardin Co, KY; m. on 21 Nov 1872 (marriage ceremony took place at Samuel E. Upton's home, by Rev. James McGill in Hardin Co, KY) to **Georgeanne Upton**: b. 3 Dec 1849, d. 1932; buried Red Mill Cemetery, Elizabethtown, Hardin Co., KY.

George Anne Upton (V4-1999) was d/o Samuel E. Upton and Sarah A. Brashear, d/o Edward Brashear and Nancy Dyson,

V4-1889. [9]-10. **Sarah A. Brashear**, b. 1823, m. 1 March 1849, **Samuel E. Upton**, ("by S. Lee"; Surety Andrew Brashear [her brother]; Hardin Co Marr Bk C, p.122).

V4-1999. [10]-1. George A. Upton, b. c1850

V4-2000. [10]-2. Millie Upton, b. c1852

V4-2001. [10]-3. Arlosa? Upton, b. c1854

Family of John Richard "J.R." Brashear and Georgeanne Upton:
From V.4, p.349:
V4-2078.   11-1. **Samuel Eden Brashear**, b. 21 Dec 1876, Hardin Co, KY; m. 28 Aug 1895, (Hardin Co, KY, Marriage Register, #2498, p.506). J.R. Brashear, father of the groom consented; father of the lady consulted in Nelson Co, KY. The marriage was entered at Hardin County Court on 27 Aug 1895, with F. L. Woodward signing, in presence of Dudley Woodyard and James Twyman. By G.S. King, Minister), **Minnie Brown Woodward**, b. 1 July 1876, d. 13 April 1929, bur Resthaven Cem, Buechel, Jefferson Co, KY. They had only one child. After Samuel Eden died or left, Minnie m.2. 8 Feb 1910, Nicholas Thomas.

Samuel Eden Brashear
Photo: David Seay

V4-2079.   12-1. **Edith May Brashear**, b. 11 Aug 1898, Cecilia, Hardin Co, KY, d. 1987, Bardstown, Nelson Co, KY, bur Fairview Cem, Fairview, Anderson Co, KY; m. **James Langford Snider**, of Nelson Co, KY.
        Among the children:
V9-1966.   13-X. Doris Ann Snider, m. _____ Seay
V9-1967.   14-y. David Seay, (who sent data)
        From David Seay:
V9-1968.   11-2. **William Irwin Brashear**, b. 1890, Hardin Co, KY, d. 19 Sept 1949, Jefferson Co, KY

Data from Stephanie Clayton:
V4-2079.   12-1. **Edith May Brashear**, b. 11 Aug 1898, who married and raised 10 ch; great-grandmother of Stephanie Clayton, whose e-mail address is no long valid.
    Stephanie: When Edith was about 2 or 3 years old, Samuel disappeared never to be heard from again— whether he fell in the river and drowned accidentally or abandoned his wife and daughter is unknown.

Samuel Eden Brashear, Minnie Brown Woodward,
and their daughter, Edith May Brashear. Photo: David Seay

I know he had an uncle, father, or someone in the family (it was a brother) named Irvin Brashear because my grandmother said that when Edith was an adult, Irvin Brashear cheated her out of much of her inheritance. Apparently, Samuel's living relatives were named in a will of some sort.

And Another Hardin Co, KY Family

7-4. **Thomas C. Brashear**, b. 10 Nov 1764, s/o Ignatius "Nacy" Brashear Sr and Frances Permelia Catryl; m. ***Nancy Brown***, (she d. age 104). [HSB p.87-8 says wife was Francis Berry, but DAR apl #140771 of Mrs. Medora Maynard says Nancy _____. Medora had the wrong Ignatius on her DAR application; so she may well have made another mistake here.]

Their first child was Otho Brashear: (See V.4, p. 375)

Family of **Otho Brashear and Mary Wills**: (birthdates and marriages of 1st four are from *Hancock County KY When it Was Frontier Country*, by Oswald Jett, McDowell Publications, Utica, KY, 1986, p.319)

Thomas Brashear and Lydia Ash

V4-3067.   9-1. **T h o m a s B r a s h e a r**, (Back#345) b. 16 M a r 1 8 1 9, Hardin Co, KY (?or Franklin Co, says HSB p.87), d. 1917; m. 1840 *Lydia Ash*, b. 9 Aug 1819, Hardin Co, KY, d. 1899

V4-3068.   10-1. **Susan Rebecca Brashear**, (Back#543) b. 20 Aug 1841; m. *John James*,

V4-3069.   10-2. **William Henry Brashear**, (Back#544) b. Apr 1844

V4-3070.   10-3. ***Medora Brashear**, (Back#545) b. 30 Oct 1852, Hawesville, Hancock Co, KY; m. *Morton Armand Maynard*, b. 5 March 1840 at Adrian, MI. They lived in Hermosa Beach, CA, in 1929 (sketch in HSB p.87; in 1918, Mrs. Medora Maynard submitted DAR appl #140771, with **incorrect** evidence that her gr-gr-grandfather, Nacy Brashear, was a private in 2nd Regt, Md Troops). That Nacy was s/o Benjamin Brashear, V, of PGCo; see *The First 200 Years of Brashears* for documentation.

V4-3071.   10-4. **Robert A. Brashear**, b. 4 Feb 1857

V4-3074.   9-2. **Ann Marie Brashear**, (Back#342), b. c1820; m. 23 Jul 1836, *Samuel Spotts*,

V4-3075.   9-3. **Eleanor Brashear**, (Back#343), b. c1822; m. 8 Oct 1840, *William W. Nichols*, b. c1819, s/o Shadrack Nichols. [?*Hancock Co ...*, p.324 lists a marriage: Wm. A. Shadrack, m. Elenor Brashear, d/o Otho Brashear.]

V4-3076.   9-4. **Francis Brashear**, (Back#344), b. c1824; m. 23 May 1841, *John S.C. Smart*,

Family of Otho Brashear and Julia Flake:

V4-3077.   9-5. **Mary Jane Brashear**, (Back#346) b. Cloverport, Hancock Co, KY, c1840 (20 in 1860); m. 7 Dec 1860, *Henry M. Mikel*, b. Germany, c1835 (ref: Breckenridge Co Court Records.)

V4-3077a.   10-1. Otho Brashear Mikel,

V4-3078.   10-2. Henry M. Mikel Jr, b. c1876

^{V4}-3079. ^{9}-6. **Emily Brashear**, b. c1845 (15 in 1860); unm. in 1870 & 1880

^{V4}-3080. ^{9}-7. **Jane Brashear**, b. c1847 (13 in 1860)

Descendant of Medora Brashear

(Vol. 4, p.377)
From: "LeeAnn Stevens" <LeeAnn.Stevens@colorado.edu>

Hi Charles,
Thanks a lot for giving me all this info I'm just thrilled to find someone in our current era that shares the same relatives as I do. Janet does this genealogy as her religion, but I don't. It is time consuming and I try to use my lunch or after work to work on it. Hopefully, she gave you all the info on me: sister of Janet (Stevens) Robbins:

^{V9}-1969.   Lee Ann Stevens, m.1. 4 Oct 1969, Daniel Mercado, b. 7 March 1946, (div 1980); m.2. 20 July 1996, William R. Shlegle, b. 15 Aug 1952

^{V9}-1970.   1. Shannon Orr, b. 23 Jan 1969; has three children

^{V9}-1971.   2. John Mercado b. 22 July 1970, m. Juanita Martinez

^{V9}-1972.   3. Christina Mercado b. 22 Feb1975, not married.

I wasn't married when I had my very first child her name is Shannon Orr, b. 1-23-1969 (not the name I chose for her at birth). I named her Genevieve Stevens. She has 3 children (still living with this decision). I divorced No 1 in 1980, went home to mom in Indiana, raised my kids. I left Indiana after the kids were out of school and moved to Fowler, CO where John was living. So again I try marriage, No.2. William R. Shlegle b. 8-15-52, m. 7-20-1996, so put it that way when you get to the volume 8 that I'll be in. I use my maiden name in this marriage.
— LeeAnn Stevens

10. THREE SONS OF ASA D. BRASHEAR

Lemuel Brashear and Asa D. Brashear

re: **V2, p.110**:.

Lemuel Brashear, b. c1787, Guilford Co, NC, d. Nov. 1827, Sumner Co, TN, son of Asa Brashear and Jemima Nelson. On Jan. 6, 1809, in Rockingham Co, NC, Lemuel married **Amelia Mitchell**, b. c1791 in NC. She probably died in Ohio Co, KY, after 1870 (the last census she appears in).

Children of Lemuel Brashear and Amelia Mitchell:

V9-1973.　8-1. ***Asa D. Brashear**, b. 8 April 1810, Guilford Co, NC, d. 11 May 1885, ?Sumner Co, TN, bur Stony Point cem, Scottsville, Allen Co, KY; m. 6 Sep 1852, in Allen Co, KY, **Sarah Jane Ellis**, b. 24 May 1824, Sumner Co, TN, d. 5 July 1913, See below.

V9-1974.　8-2. **Julia Brashear**, b. abt. 1811,

V9-1975.　8-3. **Jeremiah Boshears**, b. c1813, TN. Jeremiah lived in Campbell and Scott counties, TN. He is #v2-439; see Vol 2, p.100 for details.

V9-1976.　8-4. **Jane Brashear**, b. c1815, gg grandmother of (randie66@earth link.net, reported to: BRASHEAR-L@rootsweb.com, 19 May 2004). Jane married **William Miller** on 13 Jan 1831 in Sumner Co, TN. They had seven children:

V9-1977.　9-1. William Henry Miller, b. c1841, TN,

V9-1978.　9-2. George E. Miller, b. Nov. 1843, TN,

V9-1979.　9-3. James Eldon Miller, b. Feb 3, 1848,

V9-1980.　9-4. Charles Floyd Miller, b. c1851,

V9-1981.　9-5. infant female Miller, b.& d. July 23, 1853, Ohio Co, KY,

V9-1982.　9-6. Virgina Miller, b. c1854, Ohio Co, KY,

V9-1983.　9-7. infant female Miller, b. 1856, Ohio Co, KY.

v2-437. p.110, Additional data on Asa D. Brashear, (s/o Lemuel S. Brashear and Amelia Mitchell), and new information on three of his sons: Ellis M. Brashear, Meade E. Brashear, and Alonzo D. Brashear, and their families.

Asa D. Brasher is the grandson named in Capt Asa Brasher's will, 4 Aug 1818, Rockingham Co, NC. (Additions sent by Barbara Lamb, 550 Franklin Road, Scottsville, KY 42164, and Betty Dempsey, who sent pictures <dbdemps@msn.com>).

8-1. **Asa D. Brashear,** (oldest s/o Lemuel S. Brasher and Amelia Mitchell; and grandson of Capt Asa Brasher and Jemima Nelson, of Guilford Co, NC), b. 8 April 1810, Guilford Co, NC, d. 11 May 1885, ?Sumner Co, TN, bur Stony Point cem, Scottsville, Allen Co, KY; m. 6 Sep 1852, in Allen Co, KY, *Sarah Jane Ellis*, b.24 May 1824, Sumner Co, TN, d. 5 July 1913, Simpson Co, KY (Ky Death Cert #20117), d/o Samuel Ellis and Elizabeth Gaines, both b. VA. In 1911, Sarah Jane received a postcard from a son, Rev. Ellis M. Brashear.

Asa D. Brashear and Sarah Jane Ellis had four children:

V9-1984. 9-1. ***Ellis M. Brashear**, b. 19 Nov 1854, in New Roe, Allen Co, KY, d. after 1914; m.1. *Mattie J. Hinton*, b. 1858, d. 2 June 1897 (2 ch); m.2. 27 Oct 1897, *Amanda Jane Moore*, b. c?1858, d. c1904-05. See below.

V9-1985. 9-2. ***Meade E. Brashear**, b. 13 May 1856, d. 8 June 1915; m. *Mary Sue Eathridge*, b. 2 March 1860, d. 30 April 1898 (8 ch; see below)

V9-1986. 9-3. ***Alonzo D. Brashear**, b. 21 May 1859, KY, d. 13 Oct 1902, in Springfield, Robertson Co, TN; m. 3 June 1888, in Robertson Co, TN, *Martha "Mattie" Sprouse*,

V9-1987. 9-4. **Lou Bell Brashear**, b. 19 Dec 1862, Allen Co, KY, d. there, 9 Aug 1922 (Ky Death cert #19168), bur Stony Point Cem, Allen Co, KY; never married, but raised her niece, Ruby Bell Brashear, d/o Ellis M. Brashear.

Ellis M. Brashear
and Mattie Hinton/ Amanda Moore

[9]-1. **Ellis M. Brashear, (s/o Asa D. Brashear** and Sarah Jane Ellis), b. 19 Nov 1854, in New Roe, Allen Co, KY, d. after 1914 (Betty Dempsey has a postcard addressed to Rev. Ellis M. Brashears, dated June 1914, so Ellis was probably living at that time, but [maybe?] died soon after); m.1. *Mattie J. Hinton*, b. 1858, d. 2 June 1897 (2 ch); m.2. 27 Oct 1897, *Amanda Jane Moore*, b. c?1858, d. c1904-05.

Family of Ellis M. Brashear and Mattie J. Hinton:

V9-1988.   [10]-1. **Marvin K. Brashear**, b. 15 July 1882, d. 3 Feb 1967, bur Walker's Chapel, Allen Co, KY; m. *Susie K. Kelsey*, b. 31 Aug 1883, d. 23 Nov 1964

V9-1989.   [11]-1. **Huie Brashear** (fem), b. 16 March 1905; m.1. *Robert Oliver*, b. 1895, d. 1932; m.2. *Isaac Jones*, b. 1907, d. 1979

V9-1990.   [11]-2. **Artie Brashear**, b. 2 Jan 1909, d. at birth, bur Walker's Chapel, Allen Co, KY

Ellis M. Brashear, Marvin K. Brashear, & Mattie J. Hinton

V9-1991.   [10]-2. **James Asa Brashear**, b. 19 Sept 1894, d. 18 Oct 1962; m. 25 July 1918, *Gladys Pardue*, b. 15 Oct 1899, d.1 June 1994, both bur Memorial Gardens, Bowling Green, KY.

V9-1992.   [11]-1. **Jimmye Brashear**, b. 21 Nov 1925; m. 30 Jan 1948, *Lee Sparks* (div)

V9-1993.   [11]-2. **Sammye Brashear**, b. 14 July 1932; m. 8 Sept 1954, *William Graven*, b. 9 July 1931, d. 30 March 2002

V9-1994.   [12]-1. William Robert Graven, II, b. 12 Dec 1955; m. 1 April 1977, Debbie Conner

V9-1995.   [13]-1. Jennifer Elaine Graven, b. 16 April 1974; m. Benton Tower,

---

V9-1996.	[14]-1. Christian Benjamin Tower, b. 9 Feb 1994
V9-1997.	[14]-2. Matthew Ryan Tower, b. 20 Oct 1997
V9-1998.	[13]-2. Christi Lynn Graven, b. 27 Sept 1978; m. Earl Hair
V9-1999.	[14]-1. Ethan Michael Hair, b. 17 Dec 2001
V9-2000.	[12]-2. James Ellis Graven, b. 18 Jan 1968; m. 22 Sept 2000, Jessica Payne

Family of Ellis M. Brashear and Amanda J. Moore:

V9-2001.	[10]-3. **Ruby Bell Brashear**, b. 18 July 1902, d. 27 Jan 1952 (raised by her aunt, Lou Bell Brashear); m. 26 Dec 1924, *John Albridge Dunn*, b. 20 April 1892, d. 3 April 1950
V9-2002.	[11]-1. Harold Wayne Dunn, b. 12 Aug 1926, d. 24 Dec 1988; m. 6 June 1952, Wanda Boyd, b. 7 Feb 1930
V9-2003.	[12]-1. Thomas Jackson Dunn, b. 15 Oct 1954, d. 1956
V9-2004.	[12]-2. Grecia Dunn, b. 22April 1957; m. 10 Oct 1981, Damos Williams, b. 30 Aug 1955
V9-2005.	[13]-1. Lashley Dunn Williams, b. 20 Jan 1985
V9-2006.	[13]-2. Laura Lynn Williams, b. 19 Aug 1988
V9-2007.	[12]-3. Sherri Dunn, b. 23 June 1958; m. 1 July 1995, Chris Skaggs, b. 25 June 19__
V9-2008.	[13]-1. Ali Elizabeth Skaggs, b. 28 May 1996
V9-2009.	[13]-2. Kalee Dunn Skaggs, b. 18 Jan 1999
V9-2010.	[11]-2. Betty Jane Dunn, b. 20 Aug 1932; m. 7 May 1955, Donald Dempsey, b. 27 July 1933
V9-2011.	[12]-1. Timothy Dunn Dempsey, b. 2 July 1957; m.1. 1 July 1978, Anita Laminock, (2 ch); m.2. 21 Sept 1991, Linda Ward (1 ch)

Ruby (Brashear) Dunn

V9-2012.   13-1. Allison Faith Dempsey, b. 14 May 1981
V9-2013.   13-2. Amanda Hope Dempsey, b. 20 June 1986
V9-2014.   13-3. Chloe Marie Dempsey, b. 6 Sep 1996
V9-2015.   12-2. Karen Elizabeth Dempsey, b. 19 May 1959; m.
                12 Dec 1980, Victor Olazabel; m.2. 21 Dec
                1994, Andrew Moutardier,
V9-2016.   13-1. Rachael Olazabel, b. 22 Feb 1982
V9-2017.   13-2. Vic Olazabel, b. 7 Aug 1988

Meade E. Brashear
and Mary Sue Eathridge

9-2. **Meade E. Brashear**, (s/o Asa D. Brashear and Sarah Jane Ellis), b. 13 May 1856, d. 8 June 1915, (his stone at Stony Point Cem, Allen Co, KY says b. 20 April 1858, d. 8 June 1914; it was put up many years after his death by one of his children, who could have had the dates wrong). On 8 Jan 1880, Meade married *Mary Sue Eathridge*, b. 2 March 1860, d. 30 April 1898, both bur Stony Point Church Cem, Allen Co, KY.

Barbara Lamb reports that the family Bible says Meade's wife's name was Mary Sue, but her gravestone at Stony Point says Mary Lou- probably an error in deciphering old handwriting. Data from Barbara Lamb, 550 Franklin Road, Scottsville, KY 42164, for which many thanks.

Meade E. Brashear and Mary Sue Eathridge had 8 children:

Meade E. Brashear

V9-2018.   10-1. **Bertie D. Brashear**, b. 7 March 1881, bur Stony Point Cem, Allen Co, KY; m.1. *Othan Wheat* (div); m.2. _____ *Powell*,
V9-2019.   11-1. Halqua Wheat; m. Mary Woods,
V9-2020.   10-2. **John Leslie Brashear**, b. 15 Feb 1883, d. 29 May 1958, bur Salem Methodist Church Cem, Simpson Co, KY; m. Sept 1919, *Hallie Cuba Mayhew*, b. 5 June 1879, d. 14 Jan 1966,
V9-2021.   11-1. **Myrl C. Brashear**, b. 18 Nov 1921; m. 9 April 1966, *Marcella Clark*, b. 8 July 1927

MARRIAGE CERTIFICATE.

This is to Certify, That on the _21st_ day of _October_ 189_7_

the RITES OF MATRIMONY were legally solemnized by me

between _Ellis M Brashear_

and _Miss Amanda B Moore_

at _the Parsonage in Franklin_ in the County of _Simpson_

in the presence of

J.S. Harris
T.C. Roberton } Signed _G. W. Shugart, G.M._

NOTE.—The Statute requires the names of two witnesses to be inserted in the foregoing Certificate.

V9-2022.   10-3. **Georgia Ann Brashear**, b. 4 Aug 1885, d. ?; m. 17 May 1908, **John Lindsey**, b. c1884, d. 14 March 1910, at age 26, bur unmarked grave, Walker's Chapel, Allen Co, KY; m.2. **Simon Denton, Sr**

V9-2023.   11-1. Lorene Denton; m. Otis Estes,

V9-2024.   12-1. Jo Ann Estes; m. _____ Howell,

V9-2025.   12-2. Leola Estes; m. _____ Salley,

V9-2026.   12-3. Betty Estes; m. _____ Williams,

V9-2027.   11-2. Gene Edward Denton; m. Agnes _____,

V9-2028.   12-1. Barbara Denton,

V9-2029.   12-2. James Denton; m. _____,

V9-2030.   13-1. Dona Denton; m. Steve _____,

V9-2031.   13-2. Dawn Denton; m. Farron Barbour

V9-2032.   14-1. David Denton Barbour,

V9-2033.   14-2. Dana Barbour; m. Joy Settle

V9-2034.   14-3. Sidney Barbour,

V9-2035.   12-3. Steve Denton; m. _____,

V9-2036.   13-1. Summer Denton; m. Eric Vibbert

V9-2037.   11-3. Ruby Denton; m. Victor Vincent,

V9-2038.   11-4. Simon Denton, Jr; m. Celesta Jean Brown,

V9-2039.   12-1. Frieda Denton; m. Bobby _____,

V9-2040.   10-4. **Bevie Glee Brashear**, b. 21 July 1887, bur Walker's Chapel Church, Allen Co, KY; m. 26 Dec 1909, **Levi Perry**, b. 17 Oct 1888, d. 31 March 1961

V9-2041.   11-1. Sadie Mae Perry, b. 7 March 1912, d. 24 May 1989, bur Walker's Chapel; m. 28 Nov 1928,

---

Vernie Clifton Shores, b. 7 Oct 1907, d. 1 April 1973

V9-2042.   12-1. Willis Murl Shores, b. 19 June 1933; m. 5 Aug 1962, Helen Childress, b. 21 Aug 1936,

V9-2043.   13-1. Holly Gayle Shores, b. 29 Dec 1964; m. 22 Nov 1984, Richard Gregory Knowles, b. 18 Aug 1962

V9-2044.   14-1. Andrew Knowles, b. 2 June 1985

V9-2045.   14-2. Rachel Faith Knowles, b. 31 Dec 1989

V9-2046.   13-2. Sue Lynn Shores, b. 11 May 1968; m. 25 Oct 1997; m. David James Hepner, b. 9 March 1967.

V9-2047.   14-1. Aubrey Jane Hepner, b. 27 Auly 2003

V9-2048.   11-2. Anna Belle Perry, b. 11 Nov 1922; m. 26 Dec 1942, Oral Lee Wheat, b. 3 April 1923

V9-2049.   12-1. Joseph Lee Wheat, b. 15 Dec 1943; m.1. Dec 1963, Lillie Taylor (2 ch; div); m.2. 1 Jan 1979, Elizabeth Boatman

V9-2050.   13-1. Joseph Lee Wheat, Jr, b. 19 Aug 1964

V9-2051.   13-2. Keith Taylor Wheat, b. 31 Oct 1966

V9-2052.   12-2. Betty Lou Wheat, b. 10 Jan 1946; m. 9 Aug 1964, Algie Ray Smith, b. 15 April 1941

V9-2053.   13-1. Algie Kipling Smith, b. 3 May 1969

V9-2054.   13-2. Karol Lee Smith, b. 9 April 1973; m. Marcellus Rowe,

V9-2055.   12-3. James Michael Wheat, b. 7 May 1949; m.1. 18 Aug 1967, Sherry Hayes (1 ch, div); m.2. 23 Oct 1981, Vickie Lancaster (1 ch),

V9-2056.   13-1. Leslie Dawn Wheat, b. 23 Dec 1967; m. Larry Pointer (div)

V9-2057.   14-1. Garret Daniel Pointer,

V9-2058.   13-2. Natasha Belle Wheat, b. 20 Dec 1982

V9-2059.   12-4. Virginia Rose Wheat, b. 22 April 1954; m. 7 April 1974, Danny Hayes,

V9-2060.   12-5. Katherine Wheat, b. 30 Oct 1958; m. Johnny Vincent,

V9-2061.   13-1. Megan Vincent, b. 20 Sept 1990

V9-2062.   10-5. **Emma Bell Brashear**, b. 31 Aug 1889; m.1. **Fred Smith**, (they had a son and a daughter, raised by their grandmother Smith); m.2. **A.C. Young**,

V9-2063.   10-6. **Jewell Blake Brashear**, b. 21 May 1892, d. 9 March 1967; m. 1912, **James Harmon Walker**, b. 25 Nov 1884, d. 14 March 1966; both bur Walker's Chapel Church, Allen Co, KY.

V9-2064.   11-1. Thelma Gray Walker, b. 1 March 1913; m. 26 Dec 1929, James Haskell Lamb, b. 20 June 1908, d. 20 Jan 1980

V9-2065.   12-1. Barbara Louise Lamb, b. 17 Sept 1932

V9-2066.   12-2. Stacy Walker Lamb, b. 12 April 1951; m. 14 May 1988, Connie Janine Phillips, b. 6 March 1953

V9-2067.   13-1. Lauren Elizabeth Lamb, b. 18 April 1991

V9-2068.   13-2. Molly Kathryn Lamb, b. 20 Dec 1993

V9-2069.   11-2. Lena Lovell Walker, b. 21 March 1915, d. 24 Nov 1997, bur Crescent Hill Cem, Scottsville, KY; m.1. 26 Sept 1931, Harold Brown, b. 12 July 1911, d. 29 Jan 1947, bur Mt Pleasant Cem, Allen Co, KY; m.2. Mural Garrison; m.3. 12 May 1951 Gobel Young, b. 4 July1914

V9-2070.   12-1. Norma Lee Brown, b. 31 July 1932; m. 31 July 1948, Eugene Garmon, b. 24 Nov 1929, d. 1989

V9-2071.   13-1. Marsha Garmon, b. 17 Aug 1952; m. Gary Jones, b. ?, d. 1998

V9-2072.   14-1. Kerri Lee Jones; m.1. Patrick Epling; m.2. Brian Sitz

V9-2073.   15-1. Amber McKay Epling,

V9-2074.   15-2. Caleb Patrick Epling,

V9-2075.   15-3. Briana Taylor Sitz (twin),

V9-2076.   15-4. Cynthia Lauren Sitz (twin),

V9-2077.   14-2. Chris Jones; m. Kim _____

V9-2078.   15-1. Brittany Jones,

V9-2079.   15-2. Katie Jones,

V9-2080.   13-2. Cheryl Lynn Garmon, b. 5 May 1956; m. 19 July 1975, Jerry Wayne Creek, b. 14 Dec 1955

V9-2081.   14-1. Jeremy Shane Creek, b. 12 May 1978

V9-2082.   14-2. Joshua Cameron Creek, b. 2 Dec 1979

V9-2083.   12-2. Rickie Wilson Young, b. 7 May 1952; m. 20 Aug 1971, Janet Foster, b. 20 Aug 1953

V9-2084.   13-1. Laura Elizabeth Young, b. 25 Oct 1973; m.1. 16 Oct 1991, Randy Shields; m.2. 1 Dec 1997, Brad Wolf, b. 29 Jan 1972

V9-2085.   14-1. Karley Elizabeth Shields, b. 7 June 1992

V9-2086.   14-2. Ada Beth Wolf, b. 13 Nov 1998

V9-2087.   14-3. Dawson Bradley Wolf, b. 2 Aug 2002

V9-2088.   13-2. Leah Jewell Young, b. 12 May 1977; m.
                  Wesley Cunningham, b. 31 March 1975
V9-2089.   14-1. Wesley Cole Cunningham, b. 5 Feb
                        1999
V9-2090.   11-3. Willa Dean Walker, b. 8 Feb 1933; m. 5 June
                  1948, Lucien Shirley Wade, b. 11 March 1926
V9-2091.   12-1. David Meade Wade, b. 4 Jan 1954; m. 7 Aug
                        1976, June Patterson, b. 20 Sept 1954
V9-2092.   13-1. Kyle Dean Wade, b. 25 April 1982
V9-2093.   13-2. Jason Daniel Wade, b. 25 April 1982, d. 9
                        May 1982
V9-2094.   13-3. Alisha Ruth Wade, b. 24 July 1983
V9-2095.   12-2. Deborah Ann Wade, b. 15 May 1956; m. 25
                        Oct 1975, Timothy Daugherty, b. 29 Nov 1955
V9-2096.   13-1. Jordan Michael Daugherty, b. 26 Oct 1983
V9-2097.   13-2. Emily Elizabeth Daugherty, b. 4 Feb 1987
V9-2098.   10-7. **Jenny Clyde Brashear**, b. 14 Oct 1894; m. *Atha*
            Powell, b. 8 Feb 1892, d. 1937
V9-2099.   11-1. Lucylle Powell, b. 27 June 1914, d. 11 June
                  2003; m. 30 Nov 1957, Edwin J. Turner
V9-2100.   11-2. Edward Garnett Powell, b. 13 Nov 1915; m.l.
                  _____ (2 ch); m.2. Nola _____, b. 4 Sept 1925
V9-2101.   12-1. Janice Ann Powell, m. _____
V9-2102.   12-2. Jimmy Powell; m. _____
V9-2103.   11-3. Mayme Lee Powell, b. 23 Oct 1925; m.l. 1944,
                  Homer C. Barton, b. ?, d. 1969; m.2. Gordon
                  Mitchell, b. 6 Dec 1913, d. 10 Aug 1994; m.3. 18
                  Nov 1995, Tom Draper, b. 30 June 1931, d. 2
                  March 2003
V9-2104.   12-1. Robert Keith Barton, b. 12 March 1946
V9-2105.   12-2. Sandra K. Barton, b. 8 Feb 1947; m. 13 Feb
                        1971, Jack L. Harris, b. 19 Nov 1944
V9-2106.   13-1. Tracy Linn Harris, b. 3 Jan 1971; m. 1
                        Dec 1989, Michael Coon
V9-2107.   14-1. Nathan Tyler Coon, b. 31 Dec 1990
V9-2108.   14-2. Zachary Michael Coon, b. 20 Aug 1993
V9-2109.   13-2. Lee Ann Harris, b. 21 Jan 1975; m. 17
                        June 2000, Travis Harrell,
V9-2110.   12-3. Gary Kenneth Barton, b. 22 Oct 1952
V9-2111.   11-4. Sarah E. Powell, m. George S. Stanford,
V9-2112.   12-1. William Clyde Stanford,
V9-2113.   12-2. Larry G. Stanford,
V9-2114.   12-3. Norma Jean Stanford,

V9-2115.   10-8. **Lillie Brashear**, b. 20 Sept 1897; m. *Ervin Stone*
V9-2116.   11-1. Chloe Stone, b. 5 Oct 1925; m.1. 24 Nov 1946,
                   Jack Morlock, b. 27 Feb 1920, d. 23 Oct 1964;
                   m.2. 7 April 1971, Claude Seddelmeyer, b.?, d. 15
                   Sept 1988
V9-2117.   12-1. Terry Morlock, b. 26 April, 1951; m.1. 23 July
                   1969, Carol _____, b. 15 Feb 1952 (2 ch);
                   m.2. 30 July 1977, Judy King, b. 7 Dec 19__ (2
                   ch)
V9-2118.   13-1. Tammy Morlock, b. 15 Feb 1970
V9-2119.   13-2. Timmy Morlock, b. 14 Oct 1972, d. ____
V9-2120.   13-3. Kevin Morlock, b. 9 June 1981
V9-2121.   13-4. Kelly Morlock, b. 18 May 1984
V9-2122.   12-2. Janet Morlock, b. 15 Feb 1949; m. 16 Aug
                   1969, David Whan, b. 5 Aug 1945
V9-2123.   13-1. Jeremy Whan, b. 7 May 1973
V9-2124.   13-2. Kara Whan, b. 14 March 1975
V9-2125.   13-3. Christopher Whan, b. 28 Sept 1979
V9-2126.   11-2. Louie Dale Stone, b. 16 Aug 1928; m. Margaret
                   _____, b. 11 July 1930
V9-2127.   12-1. Michael Stone, b. 14 Feb 1949; m. Karen
                   Leora Bales, b. 1 Nov 1951
V9-2128.   13-1. Nathan Stone,
V9-2129.   13-2. Melissa Stone,
V9-2130.   12-2. John Stone, b. 27 Nov 1951; m. Diana Lynn
                   Cadman, b. 27 July 1956
V9-2131.   13-1. Tracy Stone,
V9-2132.   13-2. Amanda Stone,
V9-2133.   13-3. Robert Stone,
V9-2134.   11-3. Garland Stone, b. 9 May 1921; m. 14 July 1942,
                   Rosemary _____, b. 12 Dec 1923
V9-2135.   12-1. Maureen Stone, b. 6 June 1943, d. 4 April
                   2000; m.1. Larry Marko; m.2. 15 Feb 1969,
                   William Loughrey, b. 7 Nov 1936
V9-2136.   13-1. Lori Marko, b, 8 May 1963; m.1. Daniel
                   Klapp; m.2. Wesley Pender; m.3. 13 Feb
                   1999, David Zimmerman, b. 18 Oct 1955
V9-2137.   14-1. Andrew Klapp, b. 17 July 1980; m. 22
                   Aug 2001, Jamie _____
V9-2138.   14-2. Sean Klapp, b. 8 Jan 1987
V9-2139.   14-3. Molly Pender, b. 21 Feb 1991
V9-2140.   14-4. Corrina Pender, b. 24 Aug 1992
V9-2141.   13-2. David Marko, b. 21 Nov 1964; m. Marla
                   _____
V9-2142.   1. Kayla Marko, b. 19 Dec 1990

V9-2143.   13-3. Daniel Loughrey, b. 4 Aug 1971; m. 17
                  July 1993, Annette Burris, b. 29 June
                  1969
V9-2144.   14-1. William Joseph Loughrey, b. 2 March
                  1996
V9-2145.   14-2. Katherine Loughrey, b. 24 March 1999
V9-2146.   12-2. Gary G. Stone, b. 14 July 1949; m. 14 Sep
                  1970, Melody Rupp, b. 13 July 1930
V9-2147.   13-1. Jeremy Stone, b. 17 Feb 1974; m. 5 Oct
                  2002, Melanie _____, b. 14 Oct 1974
V9-2148.   13-2. Renee Stone, b. 17 Oct 1975
V9-2149.   12-3. Vernon Stone, b. 10 Oct 1950; m. 22 Aug
                  1970, Toni Hendricks, b. 27 Nov 1951
V9-2150.   13-1. Angela Stone, b. 18 May 1974
V9-2151.   13-2. Ryan Stone, b. 22 Aug 1977
V9-2152.   13-3. Lance Stone, b. 8 Jan 1987
V9-2153.   12-4. Rex Stone, b. 17 Oct 1962; m. 17 July 1993,
                  Kathy Zenor, b. 14 May 1961
V9-2154.   13-1. Jill Stone, b. 10 July 1986
V9-2155.   13-2. Traci Stone, b. 20 April 1988
V9-2156.   13-3. Tyler Stone, b. 17 Feb 1994
V9-2157.   12-5. Elaine Stone, b. 21 June 1965; m. Brad
                  Knutti
V9-2158.   13-1. Tara Knutti, b. 15 Feb 1988
V9-2159.   13-2. Timothy Stone Knutti, b. 17 March 1994
V9-2160.   11-4. Donna Stone, b. 20 Feb 1930; m. 29 Aug 1954,
                  Raymond Potts, b. 30 June 1928
V9-2161.   12-1. Lee Potts, b. 6 March 1957; m. 12 Aug 1989,
                  Judy Goddard, b. 9 Aug 1949
V9-2162.   12-2. Craig Potts, b. 26 May 1959; m. _____ (div)
V9-2163.   12-3. Jeff Potts, b. 27 Aug1964; m. _____ (div)
V9-2164.   13-1. Christine Potts, b. 29 July 1995
V9-2165.   13-2. Lindsey Potts, b. 1 July 1997
V9-2166.   11-5. Lottie Stone, b. 3 June 1911, d/o Ervin Stone
                  and his first wife, she was raised by Lillie
                  Brashear, Ervin's second wife, d. 15 Nov 1997; m.
                  Aug 1934, David Krick, b. 15 April 1913, d. 27 Oct
                  1984
V9-2167.   12-1. Marilyn Krick, b. 22 May 1935; m. 26 July
                  1958, Lee Millspaugh, b. 19 Oct 1932, d. June
                  1967
V9-2168.   13-1. David Millspaugh, b. 23 March 1959, d. 4
                  Sept 1996; m. Stacy _____
V9-2169.   13-2. Roger Millspaugh, b. 3 Dec 1964

V9-2170.	13-3. Greg Millspaugh, b. 31 July1961
V9-2171.	12-2. Nila Ardene Krick, b. 13 Nov 1937, d. 11 Jan 1992; m. 11 Nov 1959, Frank Lee Patterson, b. 4 Oct 1932, s/o Lee Crosswhite Patterson, b. 24 July 1907, Yates Center, KS, and Frances Marie Reiff, b. 21 Jan 1909, Gorham, KS.
V9-2172.	13-1. Nicky Lee Patterson, b. 26 Sept 1960; m. 19 June 1981, in OK City, Mary JoAnn Smith, b. 23 Jan 1961. Ch: Jennifer Nicole; Nicholas Lee; and Connor James Patterson.
V9-2173.	13-2. Robby Frank Patterson, b. 29 Aug 1961; m. 22 Feb 1986, in OK City, Pamela Gail Morgan, b. 24 July 1961. Ch: Kyle Anthony "Tony"; and Caroline Frances "Cari" Patterson
V9-2174.	13-3. Michael Frederick Patterson, b. 5 June 1963; m. 12 Jan 1991, in OK City, Toni Reneau Underwood, b. 9 Aug 1967. Ch: Michael Frank; and Jake Aaron Patterson.
V9-2175.	13-4. Penny Lynn Patterson, b. 14 July 1965; not married, no children.
V9-2176.	13-5. Scott Alan Patterson, b. 28 April 1966; m. 7 Feb 1991, in OK City, JoEllen Stephans, b. 13 Nov 1968. Ch: Dillon Scott; and Dean Alan Patterson

Alonzo D. Brashear
and Martha Sprouse

9-3. **Alonzo D. Brashear**, (s/o Asa D. Brashear and Sarah Jane Ellis), b. 21 May 1859, KY, d. 13 Oct 1902, in Springfield, Robertson Co, TN; m. 3 June 1888, in Robertson Co, TN, *Martha "Mattie" Sprouse*, b. 31 Aug 1871, Robertson Co, TN, d. 7 April 1942, d/o John Wesley Sprouse and Tennessee Swift. Data from Sprouse website: Carl M. Sprouse, cs05227@alltel.net:

John Wesley Sprouse, b. 8 Sept 1837, s/o James Sprouse, b. c1795-96, NC, and Mina Moody Owen; m. Tennessee Swift, b. 20 Oct 1842, d/o Richard Moss Swift and Mary Sargent Fulcher. (In the Sprouse Genealogy, A.D. Brashear's name is listed as **Alonzo** D. and he was a "professor." See obit and article below.)

Alonzo and Mattie had only one child:
V9-2177.   10-1. **Lola Beatrice Brashear**, b. April 1889, Robertson Co, TN, d. 26 Dec 1957, Robertson Co, TN; m.1.

William Archie Powell, b. 1852, Robertson Co, TN, d. 25 Aug 1932, Nashville, Robertson Co, TN; m.2. 26 Oct 1910, in Robertson Co, TN, **John Dudley Shannon**, of Springfield, TN, b. 7 Nov 1880, Robertson Co, TN, d. there 22 Sept 1952, s/o William Frances Shannon and Lealan McMurry. Lola and John Shannon are buried in Elmwood Cem, Robertson Co, TN.

A.D. BRASHEAR (from a Robertson Co, TN, history- thanks to Betty Dempsey for a copy)

It was in 1888 that Professor A.D. Brashear, assisted by his wife, Martha Sprouse Brashear, taught school at Ebenezer. The school was supported by Public School Funds. The first building there was erected by the Public School Fund, also.

The little town of Greenbrier was well awakened to the needs now of a good school, and the misses Tichenor and Clark had laid a good foundation upon which to build on. So the Public School Commissioners put forth their best efforts to meet the demands of the people where they were serving in this first growing little town.

Professor Brashear had already proven himself a natural born educator and was most popular among his patrons as a teacher and leader of Robertson County. He married Miss Martha Sprouse, daughter of Mr. and Mrs. J.W. Sprouse of Bethlehem in the previous June, and the two opened the school in the following September, under the most propitious of terms.

Professor Brashear and wife lived in the little town of Greenbrier and drove their beautiful and well-known "Old Ned" to their buggy to and from school each day. Old Ned was a tall, dark brown, two hundred and fifty dollar "High Stepper" of a horse, and if he could speak, he could tell of more of the courting young man who had owned him and he no doubt was the means of helping his master's dreams come true.

Mr. Brashear was born in Allen County, Kentucky, July 24, 1859. He was educated in the schools near his home, and at Lick Fort College, Kentucky. In 1880, he came to Robertson County and taught his first school in the First Civil District, near Cross Plains. After a couple of years, he came to Bethlehem, where he taught until he married in 1888. He and his wife taught at Ebenezer for a couple of years and, after the birth of their daughter, Lois Beatrice, who in 1919 became Mrs. Dudley Shannon, he purchased a farm near Bethlehem and moved his family there.

Again, he was elected principal of the Bethlehem School, a new room was added to the building, an assistant was employed and the

---

Other Brashear(s) Families

school increased and flourished under the leadership of these two popular teachers, Professor Brashear and Elic Robertson.

After a few years of teaching and farming in that vicinity, he sold his farm and moved to Lamont, where he accepted the principalship of the school there. From Lamont, he next accepted the principalship of the school at Adams Station. This wound up his years of teaching. For, after twenty-three years of teaching, he was sought to fill the vacancy in the county as Superintendent of Public Schools. The way he succeeded as Superintendent is shown in the fact that he held this position for several consecutive years, until his death October 13, 1902.

Other teachers who came from Allen County, Kentucky, to teach in the schools of Robertson County, were Asbury Hill, John Hill, A.C. McGuire, S.J. Lovelace, who taught at Bethlehem, Professor Lovelace went back to Scottsville, Kentucky, married and served as City Judge until his death many years later.

On Monday, January 5th-, 1903, the Robertson County Court adopted the following resolution:

- Whereas the death of A.D. Brashear occurred on the 14th- day of October, 1902, and
- Whereas the many substantial and excellent qualities possessed by Mr. Brashear placed him in the front ranks as an educator and supervisor of our public schools and
- Whereas it is entirely proper that we as the representatives of our county express our appreciation and recognition of the valuable services rendered by him in discharging so efficiently the duties of his office.

Therefore, be it resolved by the County Court of Robertson County that in the death of Mr. Brashear the County has lost one of its most worthy and useful citizen, a man of sterling worth and ability, a man who held the confidence and esteem of the public generally.

Be it further resolved that the sincere sympathy of the court be and is hereby extended to his family in this sad bereavement.

/s/ Ed. S. Eckles; Verner Bradley

Last Will and Testament of A.D. Brashear (Robertson Co, TN, Minute Book 31, p.28; Wills and Estates, Bk 27, p.248)

Know all men by these presents that I, being in bad health but of sound mind and memory do make and publish this my last will and testament. First, I desire that my just debts and funeral expenses be first fully paid.

Secondly, I devise to my beloved wife, Mattie Brashear, the house and lot situated in the town of Springfield, Robertson Co, Tennessee, that I now live in, on East May Street. Also my entire household and kitchen furniture (except that part hereafter ?mentioned?), one milch cow, one buggy.

Thirdly, I will to my daughter Lola Brashear my life policy in the K.P. of One thousand dollars, and my desk and piano and books and one thousand dollars in money.

The rest of my estate I will to my wife Mattie Brashear.

If my daughter, Lola, should die before my mother, Sarah J. Brashear, and my sister, Loubelle be still living, then I devise that one thousand dollars of the part I herein will to my daughter be paid to them.

If I should be sick for a time and the necessary expenses of such sickness be such as to not leave to my wife, Mattie Brashear, an equal amount to that above given to my daughter, then and in that case, I desire that they each receive an equal share.

I nominate and appoint my wife, Mattie Brashear, to be the executor of this my last will and testament without bond,
Thus 28th- day of July 1902.
/s/ A.D. Brashear
Witnessed by
T.A. Cook
Wm McNeeley

Written in the margin of the above will: "I desire that my daughter, Lola, be educated under the tutorship of Prof McNeely if it can be done without too much expense to her or inconvenience to Prof McNeely."
(The will entered probate Nov 1st-, 1902)

11. SEABORN BRASHER
and RACHEL WRIGHT/
LOUISIANA DAVIS

v-2, p.142: Pat Cottrell <PatCottrell@prodigy.net> sent additional data on

v2-551. **Seaborn Brasher**, (son of Zaza Brasher Sr, and his second wife, Elizabeth Lomax), was b. c1802, d. bef Oct 1833, Washington Co, MS; m.1. c1821, *Rachel Wright*, d. bef 1832; m.2. 1832, *Louisiana Davis*, d/o Dr. and Mrs. Davis who lived later near Carmel (now Eudora) on Macan Hills, Chicot Co, Arkansas.

Family of Seaborn Brasher and Rachel Wright
(Ref: 1830 Census, Washington Co, MS; Probate records, Washington Co, MS; *Arkansas Census of Confederate Veterans*, transcribed and edited by Bobbie McLane and Capitola Glazner. publ 1911, Vol. I (A thru D), p.57; additional data from descendant Pat Cottrell <PatCottrell@prodigy.net>.)

V9-2178. 8-1. **Charles H. Brasher**, b. 17 Feb 1824, d. 12 Mar 1855

V9-2179. 8-2. **Lomax Brasher**, b. 15 Mar 1828, d. 31 May 1908; m. 7 Jun 1853, *Talitha C. Casey*, b. 14 Aug 1836, d. 13 Apr 1906. (re: Lomax's descendants: Contact Adrian M. Williams, 919 East 13th St. Weslaco, TX 78596; or Pat Cotrell <PatCottrell@prodigy.net>.)

V9-2180. 9-1. **Rachel A. Brasher**, b. 31 May 1854, d. 4 Dec 1880; m. 7 Dec 1871, *Richard Miles Pearce*

V9-2181. 9-2. **Sarah Jane Brasher**, b. 29 Aug 1856, d. 26 Jan 1858

V9-2182. 9-3. **Asis S. (?Asa) Brasher**, b. 20 Feb 1859, d. 22 Oct 1866

V9-2183. 9-4. **William Henry Brasher**, b. 4 Jun 1861, d. 22 Mar 1940; m. 29 Dec 1885, Lamar Co, TX, *Francis Jane Young*, b. 29 Apr 1864, d. 14 Dec 1954, d/o William Rufus Young, b. 1 May 1826, d. 30 Jan 1901, and S_____ Ratliff, b. 2 Apr 1842, d. 1 Nov 1918

V9-2184. 10-1. ***Bert Valentine Brasher Sr**, (called "Sylvester," "Vessie," "BV"), b. 27 Feb 1887,

Lamar Co, TX, d. 17 Nov 1971, Whittier, CA;
m.1. 4 Apr 1907, Dallas, TX, **Mary Louise
Frey**, b. 2 Jun 1887, Wichita Falls, TX, d. 4
Dec 1964, Pico Rivera, CA, d/o Frederick Frey,
b. 25 Feb 1849, d. 25 Feb 1926, and
Madgalena Frank, b. 19 Feb 1854, d. 15 Mar
1920; m.2. 29 Jun 1965, **Edith Hadley
Newson**, b. 21 Aug 1895, d. Sep 1996,
Modesto, CA

V9-2185.   10-2. **Avon E. Brasher**, b. 21 Apr 1895, Roscoe, TX,
d. 15 Jan 1972, Pico Rivera, CA; m.1. 1920,
Winifred Kelley (1 ch; div); m.2. 29 Nov 1930,
Glendale, CA, **Helen Keating Brasher**, b. St
Louis, MO, d. Pico Rivera, CA (Helen was an
aunt to Dorothy Ester Keating, who m. Bert V.
Brasher Jr.)

V9-2186.   11-1. **Marifrancis Brasher**, b. 27 Jan 1921, New
Orleans, LA; m. 1943, New Orleans, LA,
Franklin Hickman. Ch: Franklin,
Charlotte, and Helen Hickman

V9-2187.   9-5. **Tabitha L. Brasher**, (twin), b. 10 May 1872, d. 29
Jun 1890

V9-2188.   9-6. **Talitha C. Brasher**, (twin), b. 10 May 1872, d. 2
Apr 1906; m. 28 Nov 1889, **John L. West**.

V9-2189.   10-1. F.A. West, b. 6 Sep 1890

V9-2190.   10-2. David C. West, b. 10 Nov 1891

V9-2191.   10-3. Frank D. West, b. 14 Feb 1894

V9-2192.   10-4. Camden G. West, b. 7 Apr 1896

V9-2193.   10-5. Samuel L. West, b. 9 Mar 1898

V9-2194.   8-3. **?? son**, b. 1825-1830. Census indicates this child.
Not named in probate, so died young? It is possible
that a first wife died in childbirth. A first marriage
would probably be before they moved to Washington
Co, MS, since first child b. 1824. Second marriage,
1832, to Louisiana Davis would be Washington Co,
MS.

Child of Seaborn Brasher and Louisiana Davis:
V9-2195.   8-4. **Dr. Asa Davis Brasher**, b. 5 Jun 1833, Washington
Co, MS, d. 3 Dec 1863 at Carmel, Chicot Co, AR; m.
18 Aug 1858, at Lake Village, Chicot Co, AR, **Leona
Sumner**. See article on him in Vol 2. p.143.

Bert Valentine Brasher Sr and Mary Louise Frey

[10]-1. **Bert Valentine Brasher Sr**, (s/o William Henry Brasher and Francis Jane Young; called "Sylvester," "Vessie," "BV"), b. 27 Feb 1887, Lamar Co, TX, d. 17 Nov 1971, Whittier, CA; m.1. 4 Apr 1907, Dallas, TX, *Mary Louise Frey*, b. 2 Jun 1887, Wichita Falls, TX, d. 4 Dec 1964, Pico Rivera, CA, d/o Frederick Frey, b. 25 Feb 1849, d. 25 Feb 1926, and Madgalena Frank, b. 19 Feb 1854, d. 15 Mar 1920; m.2. 29 Jun 1965, *Edith Hadley Newson*, b. 21 Aug 1895, d. Sep 1996, Modesto, CA

V9-2196.   [11]-1. **Bert Valentine Brasher Jr**, b. 8 Feb 1908, Roscoe, TX, d. 12 Jan 1983, Ringwood, NJ; m.1. 21 Sep 1934, Huntington Park, CA, *Dorothy Ester Keating*, b. 29 Jun 1914, St Louis, MO, d. 28 Apr 1956, Ringwood, NJ; m.2. 28 Apr 1956, Glen Rock, NJ, *Gertrude Maresca Hartley*, b. 29 Jul 1915 (no ch).

V9-2197.   [12]-1. **Bert Valentine Brasher III**, b. 24 Nov 1935, Maywood, CA; m. 12 May 1962, in NJ, *Janice Klepac*

V9-2198.   [13]-2. **Robert Christopher Brasher**, b. 1 Aug 1963, NJ

V9-2199.   [13]-3. **Catherine Marie Brasher**, b. 5 Jun 1965, NJ; m. 27Aug 1994, in Houston, TX, *Dan V. McGaughey*, b. 10 Oct 1957 (he had two children from a previous marriage: Brandon McGaughey, b. 14 May 1983, and Cameron McGaughey, b. 25 Oct 1985)

V9-2200.   [14]-1. Jordan Thaddeus McGaughey, b. 8 Feb 1997, Houston, TX

V9-2201.   [13]-4. **William Thaddeus Brasher**, b. 12 May 1969, NJ; m. 6 Jan 1996, Kingwood, TX, *Stephanie Denise Cain*, b. 4 Oct 1970

V9-2202.   [12]-2. **Thomas Frederick Brasher**, b. 24 May 1937, Maywood, CA; m. 26 Jan 1957, Ho-Ho-Kus, NJ, *Margaret Mary Farley*

V9-2203.   [13]-1. **Dorothy Brasher**, b. 13 Nov 1957, Waldwick, NJ; m. 24 Oct 1982, Mission Viejo, CA, *Robert Bohrer*, b. 23 Sep 1955.

V9-2204.   [14]-1. Rachel Bohrer, b. 27 Jul 1986
V9-2205.   [14]-2. David Bohrer, b. 23 Jun 1988
V9-2206.   [13]-2. **Thomas Frederick Brasher**, b. 8 Sep 1961
V9-2207.   [13]-3. **Mary Eleanor Brasher**, b. 6 Dec 1964, Diamond Bar, CA; m. 14 Apr 1995, at Silverdao, CA, *Eric Philip Huber*, b. 1965, PA

V9-2208.   14-1. Sarah Noel Huber, b. 31 Dec 1996,
                Redwood City, CA
V9-2209.   14-2. Victoria Marie Huber, b. 19 Nov 1998,
                Redwood City, CA
V9-2210.   12-3. **Patricia Ann Brasher**, b. 28 Jul 1941, Oakland,
                CA; m. 16 May 1965, Ridgewood, NJ, *Arthur
                Albert Cottrell*, b. 4 Apr 1940, Summit, NJ
V9-2211.   13-1. Gail Louise Cottrell, b. 28 May 1965,
                Elizabeth, NJ; m. 28 Jan 1991, at Torrance,
                CA, Richard Lawrence Rodono, b. 6 Jan 1961,
                Seattle, WA
V9-2212.   14-1. Dominic Joseph Rodono, b. 12 Jan 1992,
                Torrance, CA
V9-2213.   14-2. Anthony James Rodono, b. 6 Jun 1993,
                Torrance, CA
V9-2214.   14-3. Paul Arthur Rodono, b. 25 May 1995,
                Torrance, CA
V9-2215.   14-4. Angela Marie Rodono, b. 10 Dec 1997,
                Torrance, CA
V9-2216.   13-2. Timothy Scott Cottrell, b. 19 May 1966,
                Elizabeth, NJ
V9-2217.   13-3. Dawn Marie Cottrell, (twin), b. 8 Dec 1967,
                Lakewood, NJ, d. 18 Apr 1968, Jackson, NJ
                (Sudden Infant Death Syndrome)
V9-2218.   13-4. Denise Mary Cottrell, (twin), b. 8 Dec 1967,
                Lakewood, NJ; m. 8 Aug 1987, at San Pedro,
                CA, Timothy Edward Metcalf
V9-2219.   14-1. Brenda Marie Metcalf, b. 12 May 1988,
                Torrance, CA
V9-2220.   14-2. Jessica Brooke Metcalf, b. 30 Jul 1989,
                Torrance, CA
V9-2221.   14-3. Nicholas Edward Metcalf, b. 1 Jan 1991,
                Torrance, CA
V9-2222.   14-4. Daniel Grady Metcalf, b. 7 Sep 1992,
                Torrance, CA
V9-2223.   14-5. Monica Rose Metcalf, b. 12 Jul 1994,
                Torrance, CA
V9-2224.   14-6. Rebecca Francis Metcalf, b. 25 Sep 1995,
                Couer d'Alene, ID
V9-2225.   14-7. Zachary Joseph Metcalf, b. 21 Apr 1998,
                Coeur d'Alene, ID
V9-2226.   14-8. Alexandra Elizabeth Metcalf, b. 9 Mar
                1999, Coeur d'Alene, ID
V9-2227.   13-5. Eric Martin Cottrell, b. 27 Nov 1969,
                Lakewood, NJ

V9-2228.   12-4. **Helen Marie Brasher**, b. 8 May 1944, Oakland, CA; m.1. *Mel Dow* (div); m.2. *Ward Bolinger* (div)

V9-2229.   13-1. Matthew Daryl Dow, b. 25 Nov 1970, Dodge, WI; m. 23 Jan 1993, at Belflower, CA, Amy C. Hart, b. 12 Apr 1973

V9-2230.   14-1. Heather Michelle Dow, b. 27 Aug 1993, San Pedro, CA

V9-2231.   14-2. Ian Matthew Dow, b. 2 Jun 1997, San Pedro, CA

V9-2232.   13-2. Christian Dawson Bolinger, b. 27 Apr 1980, Harbor City, CA

V9-2233.   13-3. Ryan Dawson Bolinger, b. 1 Oct 1981, Harbor City, CA

V9-2234.   13-4. Jason Dawson Bolinger, b. 16 Jan 1983, Harbor City, CA

V9-2235.   12-5. **Michael Lawrence Brasher**, b. 27 Jan 1953, Ridgewood, NJ; m.1. *Deana Ginger* (2 ch, div); m.2. 12 Feb 1997, *Robin Johnson* (no ch, div)

V9-2236.   13-1. **Derrick Brasher**, b. 10 Feb 1979, Harbor City, CA

V9-2237.   13-2. **Alyssa Brasher**, b. 5 Jan 1982, Harbor City, CA

12. PHOEBE BRASHEARS
and NATHANIEL MASON/
STEPHEN RICE

v2-256; 7-6. **Phoebe Brashears**, (Back#171; d/o Robert Samuel Brashears and Phoebe Nicks), b. 8 July 1768, probably in Guilford Co, NC, where RSB lived at the time, (she is listed in RSB's Bible), d. 1834; m.1. in Knox Co, TN, 9 July 1801 (by Darmand (J.P. or Minister?), *Knox Co Marriages*) **Nathaniel Mason**, b. c1769, VA; m.2. after 1805 and before 1814, **Stephen Rice**, (Stephen and Phoebe (Brashears) Rice were heirs in the estate of Quinton Nicks, her mother's brother, in 1814. Phoebe is referred to as Phoebe Rice in RSB's will, 1815).

Nathaniel Mason was a soldier at South West Point, the garrison at Kingston; he was probably a brother of Daniel Mason, who married Phoebe's sister, Mary Brashears.

1801— Nathaniel Mason, Stephen Rice, Steve Rice, and others are on the petition to create Roane Co, TN, from a portion of Knox Co. Are Stephen Rice and Steve Rice different persons?

1802— Nathaniel and Daniel Mason are in Capt. John Walker's Company (the early county was organized into "companies," which were combination Militia and tax collecting agencies).

1805— "Nathal" Mason, Stephen Rice, and others are on the Tax List of Roane Co, TN.

Soon thereafter, the Roane County Sheriff reported that Nathaniel Mason was "not to be found within the bounds of this county" when he attempted to serve papers on him. We may assume that he skipped the country. It is possible that Nathaniel Mason simply abandoned Phoebe, or that they got a divorce.

A Nathaniel Mason appears in the 1818 Tax List of Lawrence Co, TN, taken by Duncan McIntyre, Esq, along with a Robert Mason and Warren Mason. Nathaniel appears in an 1819 Lawrence Co court record. Robert and Warren Mason are in the 1820 U.S. Census of Lawrence Co, TN, and Warren Mason is in the 1830 census, there. Whether or not these are the same men is undocumented, but they sure look like it.

1830 U.S.Census of Shelby Co, TN (Roll M1^{9}-181, Page 15): (thanks to Clarice Marker <asearcher4@aol.com> for the data) N. Mason males 0 0 2 0 1 00 1 (50-60) females 0 3 0 2 0 0 1 (40-50)

Probably Nathaniel Mason. He is 50-60 years old (should be about 61), and his wife is 40-50 (if that were Phoebe Brashears, she should be 61 or 62). Also, there are three girls 5-10, two boys 10-15, two girls 15-20, and one boy 20-30. Who these are is unknown.

P. Mason males 2 0 0 0 0 1 (30-40) females 2 1 0 0 1 (20-30)
Could be Phillip J. Mason, s/o Daniel Mason and Mary Brashears.

A. Mason (Alexander?) males 1 0 0 0 1 (30-40) female 0 0 0 0 1 (20-30)
Probably Alexander Mason, husband of Mary Mason, d/o Daniel Mason.

A. Brashears male 1 1 0 0 0 1 (30-40) female 2 1 0 0 1 (20-30)

(S?) (J?)Brashers males 2 0 1 1 0 1 (30-40) female 0 0 0 1 1 0 0 0 1 (one female [15-]20, one female 20-30, and one female 60-70 {mother?}

From *Roots of Roane County, TN*, by Snyder E. Roberts, page 49-51: The Mason name in VA was synonymous with wealth and leadership. Col. George Mason (1725-1792) was the best known of the Masons in VA. George Washington was his closest friend and neighbor. His famous home, "Gunston Hall," overlooks the Potomac River only a few miles from Mount Vernon. Col. George Mason is best known as the author of the Bill of Rights, the first ten Amendments to the US Constitution. He married Ann Eilbeck by whom he had nine children. (Names unknown to me.)

Daniel and Nathaniel Mason who were probably brothers, were the first of that name in Roane County. Their relationship to Col. George Mason has not been proven, but, according to Goodspeed's *History of East Tennessee*, "Daniel (b. 1770-80-- d. 1839) came to Fort South West Point as a young man from the Potomac River in either VA or MD. Nathaniel Mason married (7-9-1801) Phoebe Brashears, daughter of Robert Samuel Brashears. Daniel Mason married (3-6-1797) Phoebe's sister, Mary "Polly" Brashears, who was the well-to-do young widow of Robert Gilliland, who had bought 640 acres on the north side of Clinch River from Reed and Swaggerty in 1794 (Knox Co Deeds, Book C, p.22). Roane Co was created from a part of Knox Co in 1801; so the people may not have actually moved, just their boundaries and place names changed.

Partial Family

Data from Clarice Marker suggests that Nathaniel Mason and Phoebe Brashears had (at least) the following children:

V9-2238.   8-1. *Jesse H. Mason, b. 1802, TN
V9-2239.   8-2. *Margaret Mason, b. c1805-10, TN; m. 8 Nov 1829, Shelby Co, TN, George Hopkins Speer, s/o John Speer, Sr; Alexander Mason was bondsman in this marriage.
V9-2240.   8-3. *Elizabeth Mason, b. 1812, TN (birth estimated from 1830 U.S.Census, Fayette Co, TN, roll M-1⁹⁻176, p. 41), d. bef 1860, AR; m. 4 July 1835 Shelby Co, TN, John Speer, Jr. Elizabeth Mason and John Speer Jr named one daughter Phoebe Brashears Speer and a son Nathaniel Mason Speer.

Jesse H. Mason and Mary "Polly" Ruth

8-1. Jesse H. Mason, (s/o Nathaniel Mason and Phoebe Brashears), b. 1802, TN; m.1. Mary "Polly" Ruth, b. 1800, TN, d. before 1838 (1 ch); m.2. Eltin Landrum, b. 1818, Wilson Co, TN, d. 1856, Farmington, St Francis Co, MO (6 ch)

V9-2241.   9-1.Corporal Jesse Green Mason, Sr, b. 12 Feb 1823, Knoxville, Knox Co, TN, d. 4 Aug 1863, St Louis, MO, bur. Vicksburg, MS; m. Mary Louisa Martin, b. 8 Jun 1835, TN
V9-2242.   10-1. William L. Mason, b. 25 Sep 1847, TN
V9-2243.   10-2. James Mason, b. 1851, Crawford Co, MO
V9-2244.   10-3. Nancy Jane Mason, b. 25 Aug 1853, Davisville, Crawford Co, MO, d. before 1863
V9-2245.   10-4. Henry P. Mason, b. 25 Oct 1855, Davisville, Crawford, MO, d. before 1863
V9-2246.   10-5. John Calloway Mason, b. 8 Jul 1858, Berryman, MO
V9-2247.   10-6. Jesse H. Mason, Jr, b. 11 Sep 1860, Davisville, Crawford Co, MO
V9-2248.   9-2. Mary Jane Mason, b. 9 Jan 1840, TN
V9-2249.   9-3. Margaret Lucinda Mason, b. 1 Feb 1842, St Francis Co, MO
V9-2250.   9-4. John W. Mason, b. 1846, St Francis Co, MO
V9-2251.   9-5. Phebe Haney Mason (twin), b. 28 Jun 1848, Farmington, St Francis Co, MO
V9-2252.   9-6. Martha E. Mason (twin), b. 28 Jun 1848, Farmington, St Francis Co, MO
V9-2253.   9-7. Nancy Adeline Mason, b. 1851, St Francis Co, MO

Margaret Mason and George Hopkins Speer

8-2. Margaret Mason, (d/o Nathaniel Mason and Phoebe Brashears), b. c1805-10 (age 20-30, on 1830 U.S.Census, Fayette Co, TN, roll M-1⁹⁻176, p. 41; she is reported to have had a child out of wedlock about 1825; if she were 15 at the time, her birthdate would be approximately 1810); m. 8 Nov 1829, Shelby Co, TN, George Hopkins Speer, s/o John Speer, Sr; Alexander Mason was bondsman in this marriage. (Alexander was husband of Mary Mason, daughter of Daniel Mason & Mary Brashears)

V9-2254. 9-1. Samantha (Mason) Speer, b. 1825-1827, TN, d. AR; family legend says she was a daughter of a Swaringen (Swearingen), who was living in Shelby Co, TN, in 1830. Samantha m. James Wesley Blocker, b. 25 Oct 1819, Illinois, d. 10 Jan 1915, Garland Co, AR, bur. Rock Springs Cem, Garland Co, AR

V9-2255. 10-1. Elijah C. Blocker, b. 22 Aug 1849, Montgomery Co, AR, d. 12 Dec 1919, bur. Rock Springs Cem, Garland Co, AR

V9-2256. 10-2. William Jasper Blocker, b. 1853, Montgomery Co, AR

V9-2257. 10-3. George W. Blocker, b. c1854, AR

V9-2258. 10-4. Michael M. Blocker, b. 9 Nov 1855, Montgomery Co, AR, d. 9 Apr 1930, Garland Co, AR, bur. Rock Springs Cem, Garland Co, AR

V9-2259. 10-5. Elizabeth E. Blocker, b. 22 Mar 1856, Montgomery Co, AR, d. 25 Dec 1941, Garland Co, AR, bur. Rock Springs Cem, Garland Co, AR

V9-2260. 10-6. Susan F. Blocker, b. 1857, AR

V9-2261. 10-7. Amanda Lucindy Blocker, b. 18 Oct 1859, Montgomery Co, AR; m. George Hopkins Speer, b. c1785, North Carolina

V9-2262. 9-1. Sheriff George H. Speer, II, b. 1830, TN, d. 16 Aug 1913, bur. Greenwood Cem, Garland Co, AR; m. Mary Blakely, b. 2 Jun 1839, d. before 1879

V9-2263. 10-1. Cornelius C. Speer, b. 21 Oct 1855, d. 23 Dec 1933, Garland Co, AR, bur. Buckville Cem, Garland Co, AR

V9-2264. 10-2. Thomas Jefferson Speer, b. 15 Mar 1858, AR, d. 27 Nov 1922, Buckville, Montgomery Co, AR

V9-2265. 10-3. William Speer, b. Dec 1859

V9-2266. 10-4. Mary Elmina Speer, b. c1867

V9-2267.   10-5. George Hopkins Speer Jr, b. 4 Dec 1871, AR, d. 24 Jul 1925, bur. Greenwood Cem, Garland, AR; m. Mary Jane Jackson, b. 2 Jun 1839, South Carolina, d. 3 Jun 1915, bur. Greenwood Cem, Garland Co, AR

V9-2268.   9-2. Emley Elizabeth Speer, b. 1833, TN, d. 7 Jun 1904, bur. Rock Springs Cem, Garland Co, AR; m. Michael Mitchell Blocker, b. Apr 1824, Illinois, d. 21 Oct 1905, Garland Co, AR, bur. Rock Springs Cem, Garland Co, AR

V9-2269.   10-1. Emilie Arminda Blocker, b. 9 Jul 1869, AR, d. 7 Dec 1950, Garland Co, AR, bur. Rock Springs Cem, Garland Co, AR

V9-2270.   10-2. Hiram Abraham Blocker, b. 19 Feb 1852, Montgomery Co, AR, d. 1926, Garland Co, AR, bur. Rock Springs Cem, Garland Co, AR

V9-2271.   10-3. George R. Blocker, b. 1853, Montgomery Co, AR, d. 1860, Montgomery Co, AR

V9-2272.   10-4. Catherine Blocker, b. c1854, AR, d. c1864

V9-2273.   10-5. Lyle Blocker, b. 1855, AR

V9-2274.   10-6. John Blocker, b. 1856, Montgomery Co, AR, d. 15 Mar 1899, Garland Co, AR, bur. Blocker-Ellis Cem, Garland Co, AR

V9-2275.   10-7. Joseph Blocker, b. 1857, Montgomery Co, AR

V9-2276.   10-8. Mary Blocker, b. c1858, d. c1864, bur. Mount Pleasant Cem, Garland Co, AR

V9-2277.   10-9. Sarah Blocker, b. 1859, Montgomery Co, AR, d. 1860, Montgomery Co, AR

V9-2278.   10-10. J. Calvin Blocker, b. 30 Mar 1861, Montgomery Co, AR, d. 1 Apr 1898, Garland Co, AR, bur. Rock Springs Cem, Garland Co, AR

V9-2279.   10-11. Samantha Elizabeth Blocker, b. 20 Jan 1867, Garland Co, AR, d. 13 Mar 1924, bur. Rock Springs Cem, Garland Co, AR

V9-2280.   10-12. Drinda Malinda Blocker, b. 25 Jan 1871, Cedar Glades, Montgomery, AR

V9-2281.   10-13. Delitha Ellen Blocker, b. 7 Jul 1873, Garland Co, AR

V9-2282.   9-3. Mary Jane Speer, b. 1835, TN, d. after 1902, Garland Co, AR, bur. Mountain Valley Cem, Mountain Valley, Garland, AR; m. James M. Phillips, b. 7 Jul 1832, TN, d. 22 Jun 1904, Black Fork, Scott Co, AR, bur. Haw Creek Cem, Black Fork, Scott Co, AR

V9-2283.   10-1. Zacharia Phillips, b. 2 Nov 1855, Hot Springs Co, AR, d. 3 Sep 1905, Garland Co, AR, bur. Mountain Valley Cem, Mountain Valley, Garland Co, AR

V9-2284.   10-2. John Phillips, b. c1859, AR, d. before 1870, Montgomery Co, AR

V9-2285.   10-3. James Henry Phillips, b. Aug 1864, Montgomery Co, AR, d. Mo. of Sep aft 1900, bur. Mountain Valley Cem, Mountain Valley, Garland Co, AR

V9-2286.   10-4. William Thomas Phillips, b. c1867, Montgomery Co, AR, d. after 1930, bur. Mountain Valley Cem, Mountain Valley, Garland Co, AR

V9-2287.   10-5. Dr. Joseph A. Phillips, b. 27 Jan 1870, Mountain Valley, Garland Co, AR, d. 3 Apr 1946, Grand Junction, Mesa Co, CO, bur. Memorial Gardens, Pleasant Hill, Garland Co, AR

V9-2288.   10-6. Nancy Jane Phillips, b. May 1872, Montgomery Co, AR

V9-2289.   10-7. Calvin F. Phillips, b. 1875, AR

V9-2290.   10-8. Mary Etta Phillips, b. 7 Jan 1879, Mountain Valley, Garland Co, AR, d. 1936, Muse, Le Flore Co, OK, bur. Muse, LeFlore Co, OK

Elizabeth Mason and John Speers, Jr

8-3. Elizabeth Mason, (d/o Nathaniel Mason and Phoebe Brashears), b. 1812, TN, d. before 1860, AR; m. 4 July 1835 Shelby Co, TN, John Speers, Jr, b. 1811, Kentucky, d. after 1871, AR, s/o John Speers, Sr.

V9-2291.   9-1. Phoebe Brashears Speers, b. c1835, AR; m. Zachariah Phillips, b. c1833, Wilson Co, TN, d. 8 Apr 1864, Little Rock, Pulaski Co, AR, bur. National Cem, Pulaski Co, AR

V9-2292.   10-1. Isabella Ellen Phillips, b. 1859, Montgomery Co, AR; m. John Smith

V9-2293.   9-2. Franklin Monroe Speers, b. Feb 1837, Fayette Co, TN, d. 14 Aug 1906, Garland Co, AR; m. Sarah Frances Phillips, b. May 1845, Dyer Co, TN, d. 1926

V9-2294.   10-1. William Thomas D. Speers, b. Oct 1872, AR

V9-2295.   10-2. Amanda C. Speers, b. 13 Feb 1877, Garland Co, AR, d. 1922, Garland Co, AR

V9-2296.   10-3. Marion Monroe Speers, b. 1 Jan 1879,
               Garland Co, AR, d. 29 Aug 1963, San
               Francisco, San Francisco Co, CA, bur. Novato,
               Marin Co, CA
V9-2297.   10-4. George Speers
V9-2298.   9-3. George Speers, b. 1841, AR
V9-2299.   9-4. Nathaniel Mason Speers, b. c1843, Montgomery
               Co, AR, d. 28 Feb 1887, Garland Co, AR; m.
               Margaret Ann Phillips, b. May 1843, Wilson Co,
               TN, d. 1916, Lenox, Le Flore, OK, bur. Muse Cem,
               Muse, Le Flore, OK
V9-2300.   10-1. James William Speers, b. 1861, Montgomery
               Co, AR
V9-2301.   10-2. Nathaniel H. Speers, b. Jul 1872, AR, d. 3 Dec
               1935
V9-2302.   10-3. John T. Speers, b. c1873, Montgomery Co, AR
V9-2303.   10-4. Elizabeth Speers, b. 1875, Montgomery Co,
               AR, d. after 1880, AR
V9-2304.   10-5. Mary Speers, b. 1879, Montgomery Co, AR, d.
               after 1880, AR
V9-2305.   10-6. Martha Jane Speers, b. 3 Mar 1885, Garland
               Co, AR
V9-2306.   10-7. Anna Louise Tennessee Speers, b. 9 Aug
               1888, Garland Co, AR, d. 17 Jan 1933
V9-2307.   9-5. James William Speers, b. c1845; m. Mary Ann
               Susan Hamilton
V9-2308.   10-1. George Newton Speers, b. 17 Jan 1872,
               Garland Co, AR
V9-2309.   9-6. Samuel Jefferson Speers, b. 10 Nov 1848, AR, d.
               22 Mar 1933, Garland Co, AR, bur. Mountain
               Valley Cem, Mountain Valley, Garland Co, AR; m.
               Johnnie Evelyn Johns, b. 24 Mar 1858, AR, d. 7
               May 1957, Garland Co, AR, bur. Mountain Valley
               Cem, Mountain Valley, Garland Co, AR
V9-2310.   10-1. Virgil Speers, b. 28 Feb 1877, Garland Co,
               AR, d. 25 Jul 1958, Garland Co, AR, bur.
               Mountain Valley Cem, Mountain Valley,
               Garland Co, AR
V9-2311.   9-7. John Lindsey Speers, b. Aug 1854, AR; m. Dosie
               Liza Reynolds
V9-2312.   10-1. Lizzie Speers
V9-2313.   10-2. Maggie Speers
V9-2314.   10-3. Rosetta Speers, b. c1879, d. 1916
V9-2315.   10-4. Minnie Speers, b. c1892

^{V9-}2316.   ¹⁰⁻5. Elmer Speers, b. c1895
^{V9-}2317.   ¹⁰⁻6. Steve Speers, b. c1868, d. 2 Feb 1941

Phoebe Brashears and Stephen Rice

Phoebe Brashears m.2. *Stephen Rice*, who had been in Roane County from its earliest beginnings. Stephen Rice had apparently been married previously:

Stephen Rice, dob, dod, wife, unknown (WFT #3868-Vol 1)
  Rebecca Rice, b. 1796, TN, d. 1860, d/o Stephen Rice; m. 17 Oct 1814, Roane Co, TN, James Flatt, b. 1784, VA, d. 1854, Hardin Co, TN. John [B.?] Rice was bondsman for this marriage.

Stephen Rice *may* have been in Pendleton Dist, SC, at the same time as Robert Samuel Brashears and his daughters, for Stephen Rice got a SC land grant of 167 acres on Brush Creek, a branch of Saluda River, in 1791. (RSB's SC homestead was on George's Creek, a branch of the Saluda River.) Stephen Rice sold this grant to James and Elizabeth Satterfield at some unknown time. James Satterfield then sold the land in 1799:
  On 12 Nov 1799, <u>James</u> Satterfield sold, for $100.00, 167 acres originally granted 6 June 1791 to Stephen Rice, being on Brush Creek of Saluda River, and adjoining George Head, to Jonathan Synard, both of Pendleton Co, SC.
  /s/ James Satterfield, Elizabeth Satterfield
  wit: James Hill, James Cooper, John Fenell, who swore by oath 15 Nov 1798 before Robert Brown JP, recd, 10 March 1801. (Pendleton Co, SC, Deeds, Bk F, p.145)

On 29 Jan 1799, Robert Samuel Brashears sold 41 acres to Stephen Rice, (Knox Co, TN, Deeds, Bk F (VI), p.302)
  It is not known for sure if this is the same Stephen Rice as appears in early Roane Co, TN, records, but it sure looks circumstantial to me.
  In 1801, Stephen Rice appears twice on a petition to create Roane Co, from a portion of Knox Co, TN, along with RSB, some of his sons, and several of his sons-in-law. This may indicate that there were two Stephen Rices in Roane Co in 1801.
  Stephen Rice is the only Rice on the 1805 Tax List of Roane Co (article by Mable Thornton in *Ansearchin' News*, 1963): John McNutt, Moore Matlock, Bazzle Breshears, James Mcintire, Nathal Mason, Thomas Masterson, Stephen Rice, Gray Sims, Nichodemus

Burns. Since Nathaniel Mason was still in the county in 1805, we can presume that he and Phoebe Brashears were still married.

Stephen Rice was closely associated with John B. Rice (who m. Sarah "Sally" Brashears, d/o Isaac Brashears, Phoebe's brother), but what the relationship was is undocumented. Both served in the War of 1812. On 11 June 1814, Stephen and Phoebe (Brashears) Rice gave their power of attorney to John B. Rice to collect Phoebe's share of the estate of Quinton Nicks; this was before John B. Rice m. Sarah "Sally" Brashears, so it indicates some relationship between the Rice men.

Phoebe was called "Phebe Rice" in RSB's will in 1815.

In 1817, Stephen Rice sold his interest in 41 acres to Bazzel Brashears (his brother-in-law) (Roane Co, TN, Deeds, Book E, p.196).

13. JAMES BASHAM BRASHEAR
and SARAH JANE BLADES

[10-]12. **James Basham "Jim" Brashear**, (s/o Walter "Watt" Brashears and Elizabeth Basham), b. 20 Aug 1846, LawrCo, MO; d. 7 Sept 1935, Springfield, Greene Co, MO; m. 3 Jan 1867, Billings, Christian Co, MO (per Mona Rosa Maybee), or 3 Jan 1867, in LawrCo, MO, **Sarah Jane Blades**, b. 2 June 1849, Greene Co, MO, d. 29 May 1940, Hurley, Stone Co, MO, d/o Ransom Blades and Frances Garoutte. (LawrCo, MO Marr. Rec'ds, 1845-1870, p.361: James B. Beshears to Sarah J. Blades of Greene Co, 3 Jan 1867, James M. Jones, M.G.). Both are buried in Blades Cem, Greene Co, MO. New data and photos from Mona Rose Maybee, of Chico, CA.

James's military service: 14 Aug 1862, Pvt. Co. F, 8 Regt, Mo Cav. discharged

```
1880 census Dallas Co, Dallas, Texas, Precinct 7
Brashears, James B   33   MO TN TN    farmer
        Sarah Jane 31   MO TN TN
        Reuben D.       11 son   MO MO MO   at home
        Henry S.        9 son    TX MO MO   at home
        Ella            6 dau    MO MO MO   at home
```

James Basham Brashear and Sarah Jane Blades

Mary D.	3	dau	TX MO MO	at home
Lewis S.	2	son	TX MO MO	at home
Clurdy, Adolphus	29	serv	GA TN TN	farm laborer

1890 Special census Greene Co, MO; Republic
Brashares, James B., 8th MO Cav.

1900 census Greene Co, MO, Pond Creek twp.

14-14 Brashear, James	aug 1846	54	35yrs		MOTN TN	farmer
Sarah J.	June 1849	51	8-6		MO TN MOi	
Lewis	nov 1875	22	son	TX MO MO		farmer
William	oct 1884	15	son	TX MO MO		
Brackins, Deller	July 1876	24	dau	TX MO MO		
Evart	aug1897	2	gson	MO MO TX		

NOTE: the children are numbered in vol 8 as $^{V8\text{-}}4006$–$^{V8\text{-}}4025$.

$^{V9\text{-}}$2318. $^{11\text{-}}$1. **Reuben D. Brashear**, b. 12 Feb 1869, MO, d. 29 March 1889, bur Blades Cem, Greene Co, MO; m. 4 Sept 1887, Greene Co, MO, (Bk H, p.295) *Martha Addie Watson*, b. c1867, MO; d/o Benjamin Watson and Mary _____

$^{V9\text{-}}$2319. $^{12\text{-}}$1. **Myrtle Brashear**,

$^{V9\text{-}}$2320. $^{11\text{-}}$2. ***Harvey Smith Brashear**, b. 19 Jan 1871, Paris, LaMar Co, TX, d. 17 Jan 1962, Chelsea, Rogers Co, OK; m. 31 May 1891, in Greene Co, MO, (Bk J, p.40), *Ora Florence Williams*, b. 2 May 1874

$^{V9\text{-}}$2321. $^{11\text{-}}$3. ***Ella Louise Brashear**, b. 20 Nov 1873, MO, d. 29 Jan 1959, San Gabriel, Los Angeles Co, CA; m. 30 Dec 1888, Greene Co, MO, *George William Logan*, b. 27 Oct 1866

$^{V9\text{-}}$2322. $^{11\text{-}}$4. **Mary Ardella Brashear**, b. 7 July 1876, Texas, d. 26 Dec 1943, Tacoma, Pierce Co, WA; m.1. 19 Jan 1896, in Greene Co, MO, (Bk L, p.87), *James Brackin*, b. 28 Jan 1872, Chesapeake, Lawrence Co, MO, d. 12 Nov 1932, Redlands, San Bernardino Co, CA; s/o James Brackin and Sarah Hood, div. 19 Sept 1898, Greene Co, MO; m.2. 24 Dec 1919, *Walter Cash*, b. 21 June 1873, Bolivar, TX, d. 3 Jan 1942, Wichita, Sedgwich Co, KS

Mary Ardella Brashear

V9-2323.   12-1. Vernon Everett Brackin, b. Aug 1897, MO; m. 26 Sept 1932, in Kansas City, Jackson Co, MO, Jean _____, b. 1914

V9-2324.   13-1. Jerry Anne Brackins,

V9-2325.   11-5. **Mark Lewis "Bud" Brashear**, b.17 Dec 1877, TX, d. 26 May 1941, Hurley, Stone Co, MO, bur Blades Cem, Greene Co, MO; m. 2 March 1924, Stone Co, MO, *Tilda "Tillie" Morris*,

V9-2326.   11-6. **Gilly Ann Brashear**, b. 30 June 1881, d. 29 Nov 1888, age 7, bur Blades Cem, Greene Co, MO.

E. O. DAGGETT, Washington Ave., BILLINGS, MO.

Bill, Bud, Bettie, and Della Brashears

V9-2327.   11-7. ***Bettie Brashear**, b. 3 Oct 1882, Paris, LaMarch Co, TX, d. 3 March 1948, Sutter Creek, Amador Co, CA; m. 1 April 1900, Billings, Christian Co, MO, **Albert Rose**, b. 1 Jan 1878

V9-2328.   11-8. ***John William "Bill" Brashear**, b. 31 Oct 1884, Texas, d. 20 April 1951; m.1. 1 Oct 1905, in McKinley, Lawrence Co, MO, **Effie M. Robertson**, b. 23 Aug 1888, MO; m.2. 1 Sept 1931, **Elsie M. Braden**

Harvey Smith Brashear
and Ora Florence Williams

11-2. **Harvey Smith Brashear**, b. 19 Jan 1871, Paris, LaMar Co, TX, d. 17 Jan 1962, Chelsea, Rogers Co, OK; m. 31 May 1891, in Greene Co, MO, (Bk J, p.40), *Ora Florence Williams*, b. 2 May 1874, Decatur Co, Iowa, d. Sept 1954, Chelsea, Rogers Co, OK, d/o _____ Williams and Jane Craft. They are in the 1900 census of Christian Co, MO.

V9-2329.   ¹²⁻1. **Nola Jane Brashear**, b. 14 Feb 1892, Indian Terr, (OK), d. 25 Feb 1899, bur Blades Cem, Greene Co, MO.

V9-2330.   12-2. **James R. Brashear**, b. 7 Feb 1894, d. 14 Feb 1894, bur Blades Cem, Greene Co, MO.

V9-2331.   ¹²⁻3. **Ella Mae Lorena Brashear**, b. 2 Oct 1895, Republic, Greene Co, MO, d. 21 May 1983, Tulsa, Tulsa Co, OK; m. 22 Dec 1913, in Claremore, Rogers Co, OK, *Hulett Dishman*, b. 4 April 1891, in Strattford, Greene Co, MO, d. 23 May 1943, Chelsea, Rogers Co, OK, s/o Leroy Dishman and Martha _____. Both Ella and Hulett bur Chelsea City Cem, Chelsea, Rogers Co, OK.

Harvey Smith Brashear and family

V9-2332.   13-1. Harvey Lee Dishman, b. 14 March 1915,
           Chelsea, Rogers Co, OK; m. 2 Oct 1938,
           Nowata, OK, Maude C. "Maudie" Russell, ch:
           Russell L.; Jimmy Ray; Linda Ann; Dale
           Hullett; and Harvey Neil Dishman.

V9-2333.   13-2. Ruth Dishman, b. 1 July 1916, Chelsea,
           Rogers Co, OK; m. 29 April 1947,
           Independence, Kansas, Homer Lee Stanert,

V9-2334.   13-3. Hulett Dishman, Jr, b. 3 May 1918, Chelsea,
           Rogers Co, OK; d. March 1987, Tulsa, Tulsa
           Co, OK; m. 26 Sept 1969, Tulsa, Tulsa Co, OK,
           Evelyn Griffin,

V9-2335.   13-4. Hubert Dishman, b. 7 April 1920, Chelsea,
           Rogers Co, OK; m. 28 Dec 1945, Tulsa, Tulsa
           Co, OK, Esther England, ch: Huronica
           Katherine; Patsy; and Hubert Mack Dishman.

V9-2336.   13-5. Ella Mae Dishman, b. 6 Nov 1921, Chelsea,
           Rogers Co, OK; m. 29 June 1947, Chelsea,
           Rogers Co, OK, Francis E. Hood,

V9-2337.   13-6. Mary Alice Dishman, b. 25 June 1926,
           Chelsea, Rogers Co, OK; m. 6 May 1956, Tulsa,
           Tulsa Co, OK, Donald L. Kent, ch: Jay Leroy
           Kent.

V9-2338.   13-7. Florence Earlene Dishman, b. 2 July 1933,
           Chelsea, Rogers Co, OK; m. 25 April 1952,
           Tulsa, Tulsa Co, OK, Franklin D. Cantrell, ch:
           Gary D.; T. Douglas; and Lisa D. Cantrell.

V9-2339.   12-3. **Loren G. Brashear**, b. Jan 1898, MO, d. 3 March
           1901, bur Blades Cem, Greene Co, MO

V9-2340.   12-4. **Clega Lois Brashear**, b. 16 June 1905, Stone Co,
           MO; m. 14 Oct 1922, *Edward Lee Garrison*, s/o
           Joshua Garrison and Terra Grubbs.

V9-2341.   13-1. Aliene Marjory Garrison, b. 29 May 1924,
           Salina, OK; m.1. 1944, Texas, Lowell Wallace
           Dennis; m.2. 1951, William Wynn, ch: Lowell
           Wallace Jr; and Sandra Denise Dennis; and
           Michael Wynn.

V9-2342.   13-2. Della Maxine Garrison, b. 15 Sept 1927,
           Chelsea, Rogers Co, OK; m.1. 1944, Paul
           Elmore; m.2. May 1950, Edwin G. Smith, ch:
           Janice Paulette Elmore; and Roberta Gail; and
           Linda Kay Smith.

V9-2343.   13-3. Bobby Lee Garrison, b. 7 Aug 1930, Pryor,
           OK; m. 1960, Anise Smith, ch: Terry Lorane;
           and Kelly Garrison.

V9-2344.   13-4. Norma Jean Garrison, b. 30 Oct 1932, Pryor, OK; m. 1954, Edward Malla, ch: Michele Denise Malla.

V9-2345.   13-5. Ruth Ann Garrison, b. 10 Feb 1935, Pryor, OK; m. 30 May 1953, William Blain Wampler, ch: Debra Lynn; Bryon Lee; Derrill Jean; Ronda Elaine Wampler.

V9-2346.   13-6. David Hough Garrison, b. 4 April 1938, Pryor, OK; m. Betty Joann Mickoelson, ch: Pamela Sue Garrison.

V9-2347.   13-7. Carolyn Sue Garrison, b. 15 Sept 1943, Salina, OK; m. Carlton Hall, ch: Jeffrey David Hall.

V9-2348.   13-8. Larry Neil Garrison, b. 11 Sept 1945, Salina, OK; m. 22 Nov 1965, Covina, Los Angeles Co, CA, Glenda Sue Scribneron, ch: Torri Jean Garrison.

Ella Louise Brashear and George William Logan

11-3. **Ella Louise Brashear**, b. 20 Nov 1873, MO, d. 29 Jan 1959, San Gabriel, Los Angeles Co, CA, bur Bellevue Mausoleum, Ontario San Bernardino Co, CA; m. 30 Dec 1888, Greene Co, MO, *George William Logan*, b. 27 Oct 1866, Greene Co, MO, d. 16 Feb1920, Republic, Greene Co, MO, bur Wade Cem, Greene Co, MO; s/o James Logan and Mary Lile. In 1900 census, Greene Co, MO, Pond Creek Twp.

V9-2349.   12-1. Gilla Adaline "Addie" Logan, b. 15 Oct 1889, Greene Co, MO; d. 4 Jan 1976, San Gabriel, Los Angeles Co, CA; m.1. 19 March 1910, Springfield, Greene Co, MO, Carl Washam, b. 14 Aug 1889, in Billings, Christian Co, MO, d. 13 April 1952, San Gabriel, Los Angeles Co, CA, s/o John Washam and Mary Laney; m.2. 11 Oct 1960, Las Vegas, Clark Co, Nevada, Roy C. Smith

V9-2350.   13-1. Florine Elizabeth Washam, b. 3 Jan

Ella (Brashears) Logan

1911, Republic, Greene Co, MO; d. 29 July 2001, CA; m. 20 Nov 1937, Las Vegas, Clark Co, Nevada, Robert Hanley Thompson; b. 25 Nov 1909, Salt Lake City, Utah; d. 11 Sept 1974, CA, bur Rose Hill Cem, Whittier, Los Angeles Co, CA, ch:

V9-2351.   14-1. Annette Elizabeth Thompson, m. William Lester Sadler, ch: Erick Thompson

V9-2352.   13-2. Ella Geraldine Washam, b. 13 Jan 1912, MO; d. 19 June 1914, bur Wade Cem, Greene Co, MO

V9-2353.   13-3. Carl Delmer Washam, b. 22 May 1916, Aurora, LawrCo, MO; d. 21 Sept 1918, Tulsa, Tulsa Co, OK, bur Wade Cem, Greene Co, MO

V9-2354.   12-2. Lillie Smith Logan, b. 18 Oct 1890, Greene Co, MO; d. 20 Oct 1941, Booneville, MO, bur Cassville, Barry Co, MO; m. 22 April 1914, in Republic, Greene Co, MO, Tolbert Fanning Plumlee, b. 28 Aug 1887, Jasper, AR, d. July 1978; s/o Dee Plumlee and Ada Massey

V9-2355.   13-1. Lyndall Ada Plumlee, b. 21 Jan 1915, Republic, Greene Co, MO; m.1. 9 April 1934, Berryville, Carroll Co, AR, Ernest Harold Newman; b. 15 May 1913, Cassville, Barry Co, MO; d. 27 Nov 1941, Washington, MO; m.2. 2 Sept 1951, Claremore, Rogers Co, OK, Benjamin Arthur Wohlgeman, ch:

V9-2356.   14-1. Larry Dee Newman, m. Betty Garber, ch: Tone Dee; and Tammy Jo Newman.

V9-2357.   14-2. James Ernest Newman, m. Mary Gresham, ch: Cynthia Ann Newman.

V9-2358.   13-2. Beulah Mae Plumlee, b. 5 Feb 1917, Republic, Greene Co, MO; m. 2 June 1935, Cassville, Barry Co, MO, Pharis C. Clark; b. 20 Sept 1914, Golden, Barry Co, MO; d. Jan 1981, Bartlesville, OK, ch:

V9-2359.   14-1. Peggy Sue Clark, m. Donald H. Allgood, ch: Donna K.; Donnie H.; and Douglas S. Allgood.

V9-2360.   14-2. Dorothy Lea Clark, m. Oscar Ostickenberg, ch: Sandra K.; and Randy H. Ostickenberg.

V9-2361.   13-3. George Dee Plumlee, b. 9 March 1919, Republic, Greene Co, MO; d. May 1982, CA; m.1. bef. 1946 G. Louise Newman; b. 29 July 1921, Cassville, Barry Co, MO; m.2. 9 Jan 1949, OK, Winnona Marguerita Revara; b. 21

Feb 1918; d. Aug 1981, Ahwahnee, CA, ch: Vickie Kay; and Larry Dee Plumlee.

V9-2362.   12-3. Reuben Monroe Logan, b. 17 Dec 1893, Pratt, Pratt Co, Kansas; d. 5 Nov 1983, Greensburg, Kansas; m. 5 April 1956, Lenna _____, b. 9 Nov 1892; d. April 1972, Greensburg, Kansas.

V9-2363.   12-4. Virgil Edward Logan, b. 18 Sept 1895, Pratt, Pratt Co, Kansas; d. 21 Nov 1970, Springfield, Greene Co, MO; m. 16 May 1917, in Springfield, Greene Co, MO, Clara C. Collier, b. 15 Nov 1896, Greene Co, MO, d. 28 Oct 1974, Springfield, Greene Co, MO; s/o Joseph Collier and Lillie McDaniel. Virgil and Clara both bur Wade Cem, Greene Co, MO.

V9-2364.   13-1. Wilma Vineyard, Foster child; m. _____ Keiper

V9-2365.   13-2. David Vineyard, Foster child.

V9-2366.   12-5. Emmett Logan, b. 22 Jan 1898, Greene Co, MO; d. 22 Jan 1898, Greene Co, MO.

V9-2367.   12-6. Infant Logan, b. 27 April 1901, Greene Co, MO; d. 27 April 1901, Greene Co, MO.

V9-2368.   12-7. James Orville Logan, b. 12 Dec 1903, Greene Co, MO; d. 25 Sept 1979, Springfield, Greene Co, MO, bur Wade Cem, Greene Co, MO; m.1. c1935, Mary _____; m.2. 14 Sept 1946, in Harrison, Boone Co, AR, G. Louise Newman, b. 29 July 1921, Cassville, Barry Co, MO; d/o Ray Newman and Faye Garner

V9-2369.   13-1. Bobbie Orville Logan, b. 6 Aug 1947, Springfield, Greene Co, MO.

V9-2370.   13-2. Carolyn Louise Logan, b. 2 May 1952, Springfield, Greene Co, MO.

V9-2371.   12-8. Henry Eldon Logan, b. 15 Jan 1914, Greene Co, MO; d. 12 July 1935, Lockport, Niagara Co, New York.

Bettie Brashear and Albert Rose

11-7. **Bettie Brashear**, b. 3 Oct 1882, Paris, LaMar Co, TX, d. 3 March 1948, Sutter Creek, Amador Co, CA; m. 1 April 1900, Billings, Christian Co, MO, *Albert Rose*, b. 1 Jan 1878, Greene Co, MO, d. 15 Oct 1958, Springfield, Greene Co, MO, s/o Townley Rose and Eglantine Smith. Both bur Maple Park Cem, Springfield, Greene Co, MO

V9-2372.   12-1. Eula Odessa Rose, b. 08 Aug 1901, Greene Co, MO; d. 20 April 1995, Upland, San Bernardino Co, CA; m. 1 Sept 1923, in Republic, Greene Co, MO,

William Ernest Riddle, b. 18 May 1898, Strawberry Plains, Jefferson Co, TN, d. 17 April 1982, Ontario, San Bernardino Co, CA; s/o James Riddle and Cora Bailey. Both Eula and William bur Sunny Slope Cem, Corona, Riverside Co, CA.

V9-2373.   [13]-1. Robert Ellis Riddle, b. 28 June 1924, Republic, Greene Co, MO; d. 12 Oct 2004, Winfield, Kansas; m. 22 Feb 1947, Ft. Scott, Kansas, Mary Christine Walters; b. 13 March 1912, Pawnee, Bourbon Co, Kansas; d. 11 June 1996, Winfield, Kansas, bur Highland Cem, Winfield, KS, ch: Marilyn Roseanne; and Marsh Lea Riddle.

V9-2374.   [13]-2. Elizabeth Arlene Riddle, b. 23 June 1926, Republic, Greene Co, MO; m. 14 Sept 1947, Ontario, San Bernardino, CA, Winthrop Charles "Win" Walker; b. 3 June 1927, Pittsfield, Mass, ch:

V9-2375.   [14]-1. Linda Arlene Walker, m. John Cronquist ch: Catherine Elizabeth Cronquist.

V9-2376.   [14]-2. Ruth Ellen Walker, m. John Irwin Finnie, ch: Scott Charles; Andrew John; and Sean McIlwain Finnie

V9-2377.   [14]-3. James Winthrop Walker,

V9-2378.   [13]-3. Infant Riddle, b. 24 June 1928, Republic, Greene Co, MO; d. 24 June 1928, Republic, Greene Co, MO, bur Wade Cem, Greene Co, MO

V9-2379.   [13]-4. Eula Maxine Riddle, b. 19 June 1930, Ontario, San Bernardino, CA; m.1. 6 Sept 1950, Ontario, San Bernardino, CA, Paul Elmer Fugason; b. 08 Nov 1921, Pomona, Los Angeles, CA; d. in auto accident, 20 Jan 1969, Upland, San Bernardino, CA; m.2. 30 Sept 1972, Peter "Pete" Sewald, ch:

V9-2380.   [14]-1. Susan Joann Fugason, m.1. Ronald Gene Copenhagen; m.2. Donald Edward Olson; m.3. Henry Pillegrini, ch: Traci Diane Olson/Pelegrini; and Timothy Paul Pellegrini.

V9-2381.   [14]-2. Carol Marie Fugason, m. Lester Condrad Hite, Jr, ch: Melissa Mare; and Stefanie Nicole Hite.

Albert Rose, Bettie Brashear, and young family

V9-2382.   13-5. Betty Louise Riddle, b. 9 Oct 1934, Ontario, San Bernardino, CA; m. 11 Oct 1952, Ontario, San Bernardino, CA, Fred Austin Graves; b. 22 Sept 1925, Tellico Plains, Tennessee; d. 12 April 2000, ch:

V9-2383.   14-3. Karen Elaine Graves, m. Peter Howard Kikis, ch: Kelley Renee; Corey Austin; Robin Elaine; and Kristen Nicole Kikis.

V9-2384.   14-2. William Dean Graves,

V9-2385.   14-3. Randall Keith Graves, m. Deanne Marie Winslow, ch: Sarah Odessa; Anne Marie; and Danielle Nicole Graves.

V9-2386.   14-4. Sandra Kay Graves, m. Gary Brian Nelson, ch: Jennifer Anne; and Amy Elizabeth Nelson.

V9-2387.   12-2. Burl Efton Rose, b. 1 Oct 1903, Greene Co, MO; d. 23 Feb 1976, Red Bluff, Tehema Co, CA; m. 1 Oct 1929, in Berkeley, Alameda Co, CA, Dorothy Theresa Hadlen, b. 20 Aug 1909, Berkeley, Alameda Co, CA, d. 17 April 2001, Chico, Butte Co, CA; s/o Charles Hadlen and Dena Hoffman. Both burl and Dorothy bur Sunset View Cem, Contra Costa Co, CA.

V9-2388.   13-1. Joan Darlene Rose, b. 8 Nov 1934, Berkerley, Alameda, CA; d. 18 Nov 1990, Sacramento, Sacramento, CA; m. 19 June 1955, Berkeley, Alameda, CA, Charles Emerson Lundgren; b. 1 March 1934, San Francisco, San Francisco, CA, ch:

V9-2389.   14-1. Nancy Lynn Lundgren, m. Bruce Howard Kolstad, ch: Markus Joel; and Michael Bruce Kolstad.

V9-2390.   14-2. Lisa Joan Lundgren, m. Arthur Olaf Fonden, Jr, ch: Maxwell Arthur Fonden.

V9-2391.   13-2. Nancy Jean Rose, b. 11 Nov 1939, Berkerley, Alameda, CA; d. 16 Dec 1986; m. 7 Feb 1957, Berkeley, Alameda, CA, Frank Marshall Ferry; b. 14 May 1937, ch:

V9-2392.   14-1. Kristopher M. Ferry,

V9-2393.   14-2. Kimberley Ann Ferry, m.1. Jeffrey Alan Damiano; m.2. David Roberts, ch: Ryan; and Robin Marie Damiano.

V9-2394.   12-3. Beulah Helen Rose, b. 21 Feb 1915, Greene Co, MO; d. 6 Dec 2001, Springfield, Greene Co, MO; m.1. 1 March 1934, in Springfield, Greene Co,

MO, Henry Lee Daniel Waddle, b. 2 July 1913, Springfield, Greene Co, MO, d. 1 Nov 1974, Springfield, Greene Co, MO; s/o Henry Waddle and Ada McNatt; m.2. 11 June 1977, in Springfield, Greene Co, MO, Benjamin Barnett "Barney" Johnson, b. 21 Aug 1907, Beaver Dam, KY, d. 8 Aug 1999, Springfield, Greene, Co, MO; s/o Benjamin Johnson and Nora Blockson. Both Beulah and Henry bur Greenlawn Cem, Springfield, Greene Co, MO; Barney bur Wade Cem, Greene Co, MO.

V9-2395. 13-1. Ada Lee Waddle, b. 20 Aug 1935, Springfield, Greene Co, MO; m. 1 March 1953, Springfield, Greene Co, MO, Wayne Carroll Copeland; b. 29 Dec 1929, Ash Grove, Greene Co, MO, ch:

V9-2396. 14-1. Richard Allen Copeland, m. Vicki Sue Wolford, ch: Matthew Allen; and Rubecca Sue Copeland.

V9-2397. 14-2. Gary Wayne Copeland, m.1. Candy Sue VanHooser (2 ch); m.2. Janice Lynn Kepac (1ch):

V9-2398. 15-1. Deborah Renee Copeland, m.1. Todd G. Rickbohm (2 ch); m.2. Scott C. Dickinson, ch: Alexander Save Fickbohm; and Ethan Nicholas Grant

V9-2399. 15-2. Suzanna Michelle Copeland, m. Arron Patrick Seely, ch: Cooper Seely

V9-2400. 15-3. Aaron Thomas Copeland.

V9-2401. 14-3. Peter Lee Copeland,

V9-2402. 13-2. Rose Carol Waddle, b. 24 Aug 1937, Springfield, Greene Co, MO; m. 12 June 1955, Springfield, Greene Co, MO, William Norman Mann; b. 19 Dec 1936, Eldorado Springs, MO, ch: (all three adopted).

V9-2403. 14-1. Carolyn June Mann, m. Richard Lynn Greene, ch: Andrew William Greene.

V9-2404. 14-2. Terressa Lynn Mann, m.1. Douglas James Stewart (1ch); m.2. Randall Jan Steen, (2ch): Ryan Scott Mann; Chad Steen Mann; and Tiffany Renee Steen.

V9-2405. 14-3. Jeffrey Dean Mann,

V9-2406. 13-3. Agaytha Ann Waddle, b. 2 Nov 1939, Springfield, Greene Co, MO; m. 22 July 1961, Springfield, Greene Co, MO, Roger Lee Pryer;

b. 15 Nov 1939, Spokane, Christian Co, MO, ch:

V9-2407.   14-1. Carrie Lynn Pryer, m. James Douglas Nutter, ch: Heather Lynn; and Joshua Nutter.

V9-2408.   14-2. Kevin Lee Pryer, m. Kristine Louise Clemens, ch: Korey Lee Pryer.

V9-2409.   13-4. Donna Jean Waddle, b. 6 Dec 1951, Springfield, Greene Co, MO; m.1. 10 July 1970, Springfield, Greene Co, MO, Richard Alan "Rich" Brown; m.2. 3 April 1982, Robert Perez; b. 7 July 1948; m.3. 15 April 2005, Arizona, Peter Williams; d. 2006.

V9-2410.   12-4. Mona Marie Rose, b. 22 July 1923, Republic, Greene Co, MO; m.1. 13 Aug 1940, Bolivar, Polk Co, MO, Stanley William Cox, b. 21 Jan 1923, MO, d. 27 Aug 1960, Springfield, Greene Co, MO, bur Hazelwood Cem, Springfield, Greene Co, MO; s/o W. Cox and Sybil Lowe; m.2. 19 June 1943, in Santa Barbara, Santa Barbara Co, CA, Orrin Smith Maybee, b. 2 Feb 1917, Trenton, Hastings, Ontario Province, Canada, d. 14 May 2003, Chico, Butte Co, CA, bur Oak Glen cem, Chico, Butte, CA; s/o Harold Maybee and Addie Smith.

V9-2411.   Child of Mona Rose and Stanley Cox:

V9-2412.   13-1. Mary Beth Cox/Maybee, b. 22 March 1941, Springfield, Greene Co, MO; d. 14 April 2003, El Paso, El Paso, Texas; m. 27 May 1960, San Francisco, San Francisco, CA, Gerald Lawrence Rowe; b. 12 July 1939, Sequim, Callam Co, Washington, ch:

V9-2413.   14-1. Gerald Lawrence Rowe, Jr; m.1. Sherrie Perkins (2 ch); m.2. Tina Newell (1 ch): Gerald Lawrence Rowe, III; J.T. Lewis Rowe; and Jeffrey Allen Rowe.

V9-2414.   14-2. David Allen Rowe, m. Teresa Katzmark, ch: Jared Scott; and Julian David Katzmark.

V9-2415.   14-3. John Edward Rowe, m. Kelly Lynn Bradshaw, ch: Karley Alys Rowe

V9-2416.   Children of Mona Rose and Orrin Maybee:

V9-2417.   13-2. Monica Jean "Mickey" Maybee, b. 15 Dec 1943, Springfield, Greene Co, MO; m. 31 May 1963, Mill Valley, Marin, CA, Billy Michael Hayes; b. 10 Dec 1940, Ripley, Tippah Co,

Mississippi, ch: Billy Michael, Jr; Bonnie Adele; and Benjamin David Hayes.

V9-2418.   13-3. Mikelyn Gay "Miki" Maybee, b. 4 April 1947, Ft. Baker, Marin, CA; m.1. 21 May 1966, Cyrpess, Orange Co, CA, Michael James "Mike" Hull; m.2. 5 Dec 1969, Las Vegas, Clark, Nevada, div 1968, Santa Ana, Orange Co, CA, John Dennis Monroe; b. 3 March 1941, OK; m.3. 23 Jan 1976, El Segundo, Los Angeles, CA, Ralph Potter; m.4. 24 Jan 1981, Santa Barbara, Santa Barbara, CA, div 1989, Michael Neal Gray; m.5. 1 Oct 2001, San Francisco, San Francisco, CA, Danny Ross Martin; b. 7 Nov 1949, Terre Haute, Indiana, ch:

V9-2419.   14-1. Jon Christopher Monroe, m. Rejanne SantAna Perriera, ch: Bruno Perriera Monroe.

V9-2420.   13-4. Melody Ann "Dee Dee" Maybee, b. 19 Feb 1949, San Francisco, San Francisco, CA; m.1. 22 Dec 1973, Samoa, Humboldt, CA, Michael Hoy; b. 18 Aug; m.2. 1 March 1986, Paradise, Butte, CA, Fred Carter Bryant; b. 26 Dec 1932, Eminence, Henry Co, Kentucky, ch:

V9-2421.   14-1. Erik Nilson Maybee/Bryant, m. Debbie Ann Turbaugh, ch: Jan Jacob Bryant.

V9-2422.   14-2. Graem Kiernan Bryant.
V9-2423.   14-3. Kaela Leanne Bryant.
V9-2424.   13-5. Mark Orrin Maybee, b. 20 July 1950, Tokyo, Japan; m.1. 27 April 1974, Cypress, Orange Co, CA, div. c1978, Butte Co, CA, Karen Marie Johnson (1 ch); b. 1 March 1953, AR; m.2. 15 Oct 1983, Zephyr Cove, Nevada, div 15 Oct 1983, Zephyr Cove, Nevada, Dean Anita Marsh (1ch); b. 2 June 1951, San Mateo, CA, ch:

V9-2425.   14-1. Jessica Lynn Maybee, m.1. Jeff May; m.2. Lance Travis Hill, ch: Morgan Sheamarie Maybee.

V9-2426.   14-2. Emily Rose Maybee.

John William "Bill" Brashear and Effie Robertson/ Elsie Braden

[11]-8. **John William "Bill" Brashear**, b. 31 Oct 1884, Texas, d. 20 April 1951, Kissee Mills, Taney Co, MO, bur Blades Cem, Greene Co, MO; m.1. 1 Oct 1905, in McKinley, Lawrence Co, MO, *Effie M. Robertson*, b. 23 Aug 1888, MO, d. 18 May 1976, bur Maple Park Cem, Aurora, Lawrence Co, MO; divorced before 1931; d/o James Robertson and Mary Pate; m.2. 1 Sept 1931, *Elsie M. Braden*. Bill and Effie are in the 1910 Census, Lawrence Co, MO, Turnback twp.

Family of John William Brashear and Effie Robinson:

[V9]-2427.   [12]-1. **Fred Loren Brashear**, b. 4 May 1906, Marionville, LawrCo, MO, d. 28 March 1956; m. 11 July 1931, *Carie Irene Harris*, b. 8 June 1909, d. July 1970, Aurora, Lawrence Co, MO; d/o Walter Harris and Mary _____. Both bur Maple Park Cem, Aurora, LawrCo, MO

[V9]-2428.   [13]-1. **Gail Delores Brashers**, b. 12 Nov 1937, Aurora, LawrCo, MO; m. 25 July 1956, *Frank Albert Jirik*, ch: Ann Marie; Anthony Albert; and Dale Robert Jirik.

[V9]-2429.   [13]-2. **Janis Brashers**, b. 12 Aug 1948, Aurora, Lawrence Co, MO; m. 12 Aug 1966, *Dallas Smith*, ch: Lisa Fay Smith.

[V9]-2430.   [13]-3. **Freddie Brashers**, b. after 1948.

[V9]-2431.   [12]-2. **Amy Brashear**, b. 12 July 1908, Marionville, LawrCo, MO, d. 3 July 1998, Aurora, Lawrence Co, MO, bur Maple Park Cem, Aurora, LawrCo, MO; m.1. 26 Nov 1927, *Hugh Keller*, s/o Martin Keller and Lena _____; m.2. 19 Dec 1949, *Jessie Chapman*,

[V9]-2432.   [13]-1. Doyle Keller, b. 1 Jan 1930, Midway, Utah; m. 23 June 1947, Geraldine Sumners, ch: Ronald S.; and Renee Keller.

[V9]-2433.   [13]-2. Infant Keller, b. 12 April 1931; d. 12 April 1931.

[V9]-2434.   [12]-3. **Mary Wilmuth Brashear**, b. 16 Nov 1910, Marionville, LawrCo, MO, d. 28 Nov 2004, Crane, Stone Co, MO; m. 30 June 1928, *Verl N. Talley*, b. 31 Jan 1908, d. 31 Jan 1988, Springfield, Greene Co, MO, s/o W. Talley and Pearl Clines. Both Mary and Verl bur Mt. Olive Cem, McKinley, LawrCo, MO

[V9]-2435.   [13]-1. Edna Mae Talley, b. 18 Jan 1930, Billings, Christian, MO; m. 19 May 1949, Howard Eugene Stewart; b. 16 Oct 1927; d. 8 March 1994,

Springfield, Greene Co, MO, ch: Howard; and
Randy Stewart.

V9-2436.   13-2. Norman Talley, b. 7 March 1931, Billings,
Christian, MO; m. Kathryn Carl, ch: Aletta Key;
and Dennis Talley.

V9-2437.   12-4. **Mildred Leona Brashear**, b. 17 May 1921,
Marionville, LawrCo, MO; m. 12 March 1937,
Marshall Brown, s/o Fred Brown and Etta _____.

V9-2438.   13-1. Larry Duane Brown, b. 1 March 1945.

V9-2439.   13-2. Tamara Lynn Brown, b. 3 Sept 1951.

V9-2440.   12-5. **Guy Winford Brashear**, b. 7 Feb 1924, Marionville,
LawrCo, MO, d. 15 Jan 1965, Springfield, Greene Co,
MO; m. 26 April 1946, ***Betty Jo Clinkenbeard***, d/o
George Clinkenbeard and Lennie _____. Both bur
Maple Park Cem, Aurora, Lawrence Co, MO.

V9-2441.   13-1. **Guyann Brashears**; b. 22 Jan 1953; m. _____
Perryman.

Family of John William Brashear and Elsie Braden:

V9-2442.   12-6. **Winford Richard Brashear**, b. 20 Sept 1932, Salina,
OK; m. 21 Aug 1955, ***Lavonna M. Tidwell***, d/o
Everett Tidwell and Minnie _____.

V9-2443.   13-1. **Vickey Denice Brashears**; b. 15 Feb 1959.

V9-2444.   13-2. **Keith Richard Brashears**; b. 15 Jan 1961.

V9-2445.   12-7. **Jim Gordon Brashear**, b. 7 Aug 1935, Pryor, OK; m.
25 Dec 1955, ***Margie Meredith***, d/o Leonard
Meredith and Audrey _____.

V9-2446.   13-1. **Diane Lenel Brashears**; b. 13 Aug 1958.

V9-2447.   13-2. **Steven Leonard Brashears**; b. 28 Nov 1961.

V9-2448.   13-3. **Linda Kay Brashears**; b. 29 June 1963.

14. VOL. 1 MISCELLANEOUS

Three daughters of
THOMAS COOK BRASHEAR
and ANN MARIA PITTS

#[V1]-**744.** [8]-3. **"Col." Thomas Cook Brashear** ([Back#]186; s/o Dr. Belt Brashear and Ann Cook), b. 15 Jan 1805, New Market, MD, d. there, 15 Jan 1851, bur Hall-Wood Cem, New Market, FredCo, MD; m.1. 30 March 1830, in Frederick Co, MD, *Ann Maria Pitts*, b. 31 Jan 1810, New Market, MD, d. 31 Jan 1843, New Market, Frederick Co, MD; m.2. _____ ?Hall?, mother of the last child, Charles Hall Pitts. The title, "Col," was apparently honorary; there is no evidence that he was ever in the military.

1850 Census, New Market, Frederick Co, MD -- 31 July - #151-157

Thomas C. Brashear,	45 (1805) Farmer $6,000
Ann E. "	19 (1831)
Sarah L. "	17 (1833)
Mary C. "	15 (1835)
Fanny M. "	14 (1836)
Laura J. "	9 (1841)
Thomas P. "	9 (1841)
Charles H. Pitts "	1 (1849)

slaves owned by Thomas Cook Brashear
from 1850 Census, New
Market, Frederick Co, MD
80 yr. black female
55 yr. black female
50 yr. mulatto female
16 yr. mulatto female
7 yr. mulatto female
18 yr. black female
11 yr. mulatto female
55 yr. mulatto male
35 yr. black male
16 yr. mulatto male
17 yr. mulatto male
3 yr. black male
1 tr. mulatto male

Anne Elizabeth "Betty" (Brashear) Dorsey,

The first daughter:

V1747. 9-1. **Anne Elizabeth "Betty" Brashear**, b. 19 Feb 1831, d. 15 Dec 1924; m. 22 Nov 1853, *William Roderick Dorsey*, b. 23 June 1830, d. 20 Sept 1891

V1748. 10-1. Dr. Frank Dorsey, b. 8 Oct 1853, d. 22 Feb 1911; m. Lulu Leaf, 3 ch who d. young

750a. 10-2. Henrietta Dorsey, m. Frank Keen

750b. 11-1. Mary Keen; m. Dr. ____ Bowers; no ch

V1749. 10-3. Lucy Sprigg Dorsey, b. 5 March 1864, d. 13 Feb 1935; unm.

V1750. 10-4. Kate Winder Dorsey, b. 14 Sept 1867, d. 9 Feb 1943; unm.

V1751. 10-5. William Roderick Dorsey Jr, b. 8 Oct 1868, d. 24 Oct 1946; m. Isabelle Kirch, b. 6 June 1868, d. 17 Feb 1964; ch: Lucy Sprigg Dorsey and William Roderick Dorsey, III

Reminiscenses of Mrs. William Roderick Dorsey, (Elizabeth "Aunt Betty" Brashear), pertaining to the South.

Stonewall Jackson paroled prisoners after Harper's Ferry (7,000 men) who camped on Mr. Roderick Dorsey's farm.

When Confederates first came into Maryland, Mrs. Dorsey, knowing two pickets were at her gate and seeing two "Dutch ..." coming down the Pike, ran to her third-story window and waved her bonnet, as a warning to the pickets.

Thomas Pitts Brashear was captured from Capt. Emack's Company at Monterey, July 4th, at midnight.

State Legislature met in what is now Kemp Hall to vote to secede. The ones Aunt Betty remembered were Charles H. Pitts, Teackle Wallis, Henry McTier Warfield, Lawrence Sangster, all arrested and taken to Fort Warren on Massachusetts Bay and kept there. Firey, of Hagerstown, in a speech at the session of the Legislature, said "If Maryland secedes, she will be the ballroom for the "Dance of Death.""

The second daughter:

V1754. 9-4. **Mary Cook Brashear**, b. 21 Feb 1834 (15 in 1850), New Market, MD, d. 29 Jan 1862; m. 4 Oct 1855, Zion Episcopal Ch, Urbana, FredCo, MD, *Thomas Roger Johnson*, b. 17 Nov 1829, in Rock Hall, FredCo, MD, d. 21 Feb 1907, Frederick City Hosp, Frederick, MD, s/o Joseph Johnson and Eleanor Hilleary. He was a brother of William Hilleary Johnson. Thomas Roger Johnson m.2. Elizabeth Davis. His obit names two children.

Family tradition (not confirmed) says Thomas Roger Johnson could not enter service due to stuttering and served on underground railroad to free slaves; he lost all his money going surety for friends. However, according to census, family money was already gone before Thomas Roger. He lived on a plantation belonging to Hilleary sisters, and moved to Georgia with Cunninghams.

From Joseph Alexander's memoirs - he helped found Ku Klux Klan

After his father Joseph's death, the family moved to his aunt's farm 'Selma' outside of Petersville, MD. Thomas

Thomas Roger Johnson

continued to live at and manage his aunt's farm in Petersville. In 1860 at the age of 29, Thomas had real property valued at $3,600 and $3,000 in personal property. He lived with his aunt, sister, his first wife and her brother and sister, and his daughter.

From 1860 Census, FredCo, MD:

Thomas Johnson	29, $3000, $3000
Rebecca (Hilleary?)	70, $2000 (aunt)
Mary Johnson	26 (née Brashear; wife)
Ella Johnson	1 (dau: Mary Eleanor Johnson, b. 27 July 1858,)
Nettie	25 (sister)
Thomas	20 (brother?)
H.	25, $2645 (?sister; Henrietta Johnson?)

The death of his father and the depression of 1837 which had affected the planter class had reduced the Johnson land-holdings, but still left Thomas a member of the planter class. There is no record of Thomas serving in either army, possibly this was because of a severe stammer. Thomas taught his son Joseph that he took the oath of allegiance several times with reservation. He sheltered Southern soldiers returning to Virginia, and helped organize the Ku Klux Klan. Joseph, however, taught his children that Thomas had worked as a part of the Underground Railroad.

Whichever portions of tradition are true, Thomas and his second wife Elizabeth Davis Johnson lost what they had by the end of the war. The 1870 Census shows that they moved to Bostwick, Georgia with Elizabeth's sister's family and claimed no real or personal property of their own. Continuing to move to various places in Georgia, they never settled and in 1880 still reported nothing of value. Thomas apparently returned to Frederick Co, MD, at some time.

21 Feb 1907: Mr. Thomas Roger Johnson, well known resident of this county died suddenly at the Frederick City Hospital at 7:50 this morning while sitting in bed eating his breakfast, death being due to heart failure. The waiter containing his meal was setting on his lap, and he requested that it be taken off, and expired shortly afterwards. He was 77 years old and is survived by one daughter and one son. Mrs. E. R. Plummer of Adamstown, and Mr. Alex Johnson of Baltimore. One sister, Miss Nettie Johnson, of this city, also survives him. He was a brother of the late Dr. William Hilleary Johnson, of Adamstown.

The funeral took place on Saturday at 12 o'clock, from the home of his nephew, Dr. Thomas B[rashear] Johnson, East Patrick street. Services were held at the house, conducted by Rev. Dr. Osborne Ingle, assisted by Rev. Geo. Thomas, of Adamstown. The pallbearers were: John O. Whitter, Arthur Potts, F. Columbus Knott, D. Z. Padgett, G. A. T. Snouffer, and George Snouffer. Interment was made in Mt Olivet cemetery. W. H. B. Edison was the funeral director [on 23 Feb 1907].

Children to Thomas Roger Johnson:

V9-2449. 10-1. stillborn Johnson, per Grammy's handwriting in greatgranddad's memoirs.

V9-2450. 10-2. Henrietta Johnson, b. 8 June 1857, d. 23 Feb 1858. bur Mr. Olivet Cem.

V9-2451. 10-3. Mary Eleanor Johnson, b. 27 July 1858, d. 21 Oct 1886, bur Mr. Olivet Cem (tombstone also reads: "Niece of Henrietta Johnson.")

V9-2452. 10-4. E.R. Johnson (fem); m. _____ Plummer, of Adamstown. Survivor according to obit.

V9-2453. 10-5. Joseph Alexander Johnson, of Baltimore. survivor according to obit.

The third sister:

V1756. 9-6. **Laura Jane Brashear**, b. 17 Feb 1837, Fredco, MD, d. 1 Dec 1895, Adamstown, FredCo, MD; m. **Dr. William Hilleary Johnson**, b. 1 July 1827, Rock Hall, FredCo MD, d. 13 Dec 1901, Adamstown, FredCo, MD, s/o Joseph Johnson and Eleanor Hilleary; both bur Mt. Olivet Cem, Frederick, MD, alongside two of their daus.

William H. Johnson was born in "Rock Hall", a house built by his grandfather Major Roger Johnson in 1812. William attended the University of Maryland and became a Medical Doctor.

During the Civil War, William moved to Missouri and joined the Missouri Home Guards. He served as a surgeon under Gen. Sterling Price in the Trans-Mississippi campaign. Confederate Records vol 2 page 107, register, show that he was 1st Sergt, Capt Parrott's Co (E),

Gentry County Regiment, Missouri, from August 5, 1861 to September 24, 1861. He was last paid July 11, 1864.

He returned to Frederick County after the war and continued his profession as a doctor. From 1865 till 1900, he practiced in Adamstown. He was a member of the Protestant Episcopal Church, FredCo, MD. The 1870 census shows only that he had personal property of $600.

From 1870 Census:

William H. Johnson,	42 physician, $600
Laura	32
Elizabeth	7
William C.	4
Thomas	2
Jacent Gury	25 black male domestic servant
Caroline Gury	5 mo

Five children named in Sketch of Dr. Thomas Brashear Johnson, in Williams, *History of Frederick Co*, p.1208.

V1757.   10-1. Annie Elizabeth Johnson, b. 25 July 1863, d. 27 June 1917; m. 27Aug 1884, Robert Moffett, of Wash, D.C.

V9-2454.   11-1. Eleanor J. Moffett, b. 25 Sept 1885; m. Ray E. Carlson

V9-2455.   12-1. Ray E. Carlson, II

V9-2456.   11-2. Benjamin Moffett, b. 12 March 1887; m. Helen Ramsburg

V9-2457.   12-1. Carrie Moffett,

V9-2458.   11-3. Laura Pritchard Moffett, b. 24 July 1889; m. Wayne Hart

V9-2459.   12-1. Elizabeth Hart,

V9-2460.   11-4. Robert Moffett, II, b. 7 Nov 1892; m. Liaze Sasser

V1758.   10-2. William Channing Johnson, b. 7 March 1866 (or 1865), d. 10 Dec 1933, Frederick Co, MD, lived Washington, D.C.; m. Sally Conrad Fauntleroy

V1759.   10-3. Thomas Brashear Johnson, b. 29 June 1868, Adamstown, MD, d. 1925. Grad U. Maryland, 1889 with M.D.; post-graduate work at Johns Hopkins University, Baltimore, and New York Polyclinic, and became a member of the Medical and Chirurgical Faculty of Maryland. He was a Director of Central National Bank of Frederick, on staff of Frederick City Hospital, manager of W.F. & G.R.R. Co, and other companies; active in Columbia Lodge, Elks, Knights of Pythias; a Democrat and member of Protestant Episcopal Church. "Dr. Johnson is unmarried."

Laura J. Johnson and Mary Louisa
Johnson, about 1903, when Laura died

Thomas Brashear Johnson

V1760.   10-4. Mary Louisa Johnson, b. 23 Jan 1872, d. 2 Sept 1955,
          FredCo, MD
V1762.   10-5. Laura J. Johnson, b. 24 Oct 1875, d. 20 April 1903,
          FredCo, MD

p.15: Sally Gray, acquisitions, National DAR Library,
<openc2@aol.com> sends the following:

I would like to offer one correction to you that will be an addition to
your lineage. Joseph Jordan did not marry Holia Christian. This is a
spelling error. Her name was Filia Christi Akehurst. The name is
Latin for "Daughter of Christ." Her father was Daniel Akehurst, who
was a rather prominent Quaker in early North Carolina. You will find
many references to him in the "Colonial Records of North Carolina" a
multi-volume set recently reprinted by Tom Broadfoot. This will
include a reference to the marriage of Joseph Jordan and Filia Christi
Akehurst, daughter of Daniel Akehurst.

Georgene Humphries <humphri@northrim.net> found some references
in the patent books for North Carolina 1-13: (1663-1729)

Abstracts of Land Patents: Bk.1, p.52, Entry 132: Albermarle Co, VA/NC, William Earle of Craven Co, NC and Ye Reste etc., to Robert West; Thomas West; & John West in common. Feb 1696. 250 acres on flatty Creek in Pascotank (sic) Precinct joining Richard Stamp;

/s/ Jn Archdale

[wits] Danl Akehurst; Francis Toms; Saml Swann; Henderson Walker.

Bk.3, p.236, entry #2596. (original record p.260) John Braizier, 9 Nov 1730; 540 acres in Perquimons precinct on NE side of river, joining former land of Brasuer, Sandersons Dock Landing, and the sd river. Wtn: R'cd Everard; John Lovick; C. Gale; Thom Pollack; Robert West; John Palinn & John Worley

*****

Biddlecombe Family

p.21: Posted by: Elaine Blackman
Date: September 01, 1999 at 06:11:13
In Reply to: Re: Mary Brashears b.1649 by Charles Brashear

Mary Brassieur/ Brashear and James Biddlecombe were my 9th- great-grandparents. My line then descends through
Mary Biddlecombe and James Tarpley;
James Tarpley, Jr. and Mary Camp;
Mary Tarpley and John Camp, b. 1743, d. 1818;
Annie Naomi Camp and John Hill;
Elizabeth Hill and John Awtrey;
Sarah Awtrey and Drewry Alvin Eubanks, m. c1848/9 in Murray Co, GA, Went to Greene Co, AR bef. 1860;
Chaste C. Eubanks and Rachel _____, went to Comanche Co, TX for a short while c1900, back to Polk Co, AR;
Drewry Lyman Eubanks and Mary Elizabeth "Lizzie" Barnes, b. 1873, Hamilton Co, TX;
Chester Lafayette Eubanks, b. 1899, Hamilton Co, TX, and Ila Monehta Martin, b. 1908, Caddo Mills, TX (Elaine Blackman's grandparents).

Terry Joy Jeffers ... "Joy Jeffers" <joydell@the-cia.net sent the following data:
Mary Brassieur married James Biddlecombe and had:
Mary Biddlecombe married James Tarpley and had:
James Tarpley, Jr, married Mary Camp
Winifred Tarpley married Nathaniel Camp
Hosea Camp married Elizabeth Jordan and had:
Margaret "Peggy" Camp married Genubuth Winn and had:

Permelia Foster Winn married James E. Williams and had:
Mattie Attala Williams married James Sydney Slaughter and had:
James Allen Slaughter married Eva Della Fuller and had:
Mattie Lou Slaughter married Terry Lee Jeffers and had:
Terry Joy Jeffers ... "Joy Jeffers" <joydell@the-cia.net

*****

Moseley Family

Henry Moseley, b. 1614, d. 1656; m. Anne Nott, b. 1615, d. 1720
V1-9.   2-1. **William Moseley**, b. 1635, d. 1681; m. **Martha Brasseur**,
            b. 1636, d. 1725 (d/o Robert Brasseur)
        2-2. Henry Moseley, b. 1640
        2-3. Anne Moseley, b. 1642; m. Thomas Harding
        2-4. John Moseley, b. 1645, d. 1668

Family of William Moseley and Martha Brasseur:
V1-24. 3-1. *William Moseley, Jr, b. c1660, d. before 10 April 1700; m.
            Hannah Hawkins, b. c1663, d/o Major Tomas Hawkins, of
            old Rappahannock Co, VA.
V1-21. 3-2.   Edward Moseley, b. c1663, d. 1714
V1-xx. 3-3.   John Moseley, b. before Nov 1669
V1-22. 3-4.   Robert Moseley, b. 1668, d. 1714; m. Martha Reeves, b.
            after 1670, d. after June 1707
            4-x. Benjamin Moseley, b. 1703, d. 1737; m. Crittenden
V1-20. 3-5.   Elizabeth Moseley, b. 1673, d. 1725; m. John Hawkins, b.
            1666, d. 1726
V1-23. 3-6.   Benjamin Moseley, b. c1674
            4-x. John Moseley, b. c1695, d. May 1717
V1-28. 3-7.   Martha Moseley, b. c1690, d. 1717; m. William Thompson,
            b. 1679, d. 1732

Family of William Moseley, Jr, and Hannah Hawkins:
V1-25. 4-1.   William Moseley, III, b. c1692, d. cMar 1770; m. Elizabeth
            Thompson, b. c1700
V9-2461.   5-1. Elizabeth Moseley, b. c1725, d. after 1773; m.
                William Sessions, b. 1730
V9-2462.   5-2. William Moseley, IV, b. 1724, d. after 1790; m.
                Sarah Mason?, b. c1730
V9-2463.   6-1. Robert D. Moseley, b. 1755, d. 1831; m. Margaret
                Vann, b. 1767, d. 10 Oct 1849
V9-2464.   6-2. Benjamin Moseley, b. c1760
V9-2465.   6-3. Sarah\Selah Moseley, b. 1763
V9-2466.   5-3. John Moseley, b. c1730, d. after 1785; m. Margaret, b.
                1730

---

^{V9}-2467.   5-4. Benjamin Moseley, b. c1731, d. 14 Dec 1793; m. Winney Lethure, b. 1740, d. 1800
^{V9}-2468.   5-5. Thomas T. Moseley, b. 1728, d. after 1793; m. Mary Brantley, b. c1735
^{V9}-2469.   6-1. Ann Moseley, b. c1751, d. after 1786
^{V9}-2470.   6-2. Clement P. Moseley
^{V9}-2471.   6-3. Thomas Moseley, b. c1753
^{V9}-2472.   6-4. William Brantley Moseley, b. 1755, d. 1851; m. Sarey Phillips, b. c1760, d. c1845
^{V9}-2473.   5-6. Robert Moseley, b. c1735, d. 12 March 1796; m. Sarah Turpin; m. Mary Bransford, b. 1743
^{V9}-2474.   6-1. Mary Moseley, b. c1760, d. 20 Jan 1857; m. Derrick Holsonbake;
^{V9}-2475.   6-2. Martha Moseley, b. c1762, d. before 1860; m. Malachi Stallings
^{V9}-2476.   6-3. John Moseley, b. c1763, d. 1796
^{V9}-2477.   6-4. Sarah Moseley, b. c1767; m. William Hagwood
^{V9}-2478.   6-5. Susanna Moseley, b. c1769, d. before 1870; m. Adams
^{V9}-2479.   6-6. Elizabeth Moseley, b. c1770, d. 12 Dec 1863; m. Edmond Edward Vann
^{V9}-2480.   6-7. Edward Moseley, b. 5 April 1771, d. 20 May 1834; m. Martha Butler
^{V9}-2481.   6-8. Rachel Moseley, b. c1774, d. c1883; m. Thomas Davis
^{V9}-2482.   6-9. Anna Moseley, b. 22 July 1778, d. 26 Oct 1847; m. Elizer Jeter
^{V9}-2483.   6-10. Lydia Moseley, b. 22 Jan 1780, d. 23 Dec 1843; m. Luke Williams; m. Elisha Moseley, b. 1784, d. 1843
^{V9}-2484.   6-12. Robert T. (S.) Moseley, b. 22 March 1782, d. 20 Sept 1829; m. Rebecca Smith Adams
^{V9}-2485.   6-13. Jesse Moseley, b. 21 March 1784, d. Sept 1827; m. Mildred Copeland, b. 1788, d. 1816
^{V9}-2486.   6-14. Daniel Moseley, b. 16 March 1787, d. 12 May 1856; m. Sarah Mary Copeland, b. 14 Sept 1790, d. 3 Dec 1847
^{V9}-2487.   6-15. Penelope Moseley, b. 21 Feb 1788, d. 4 Sept 1844; m. John Thomas Copeland, b. 15 June 1784, d. 20 Sept 1845
^{V9}-2488.   6-16. Gracey Moseley, b. 26 March 1790
^{V9}-2489.   6-17. Thomas Moseley, b. 1792, d. c1824; m. Nancy Smedley

For more on Moseley, contact "Tammie Wood Deming" <Hurricane4Uonly@aol.com> ; who has more than 500 additional descendants.

*****

William Jones,

p.93: Barbara Watson <emmapeel@fix.net> writes: "I am a direct descendant of Robert Brashear, the Improvident. I have a story about William Jones, the father of Ann and Mary who married the Brashear brothers. This comes from 'The Goe Family' book published in 1996.

"William Jones, collarmaker, is found in the court records several times in Prince George's Co, Md, between 1696 and 1699 as a defendant for failure to pay his debts. In several cases his sons-in-law, Benjamin and Samuel Brashear Sr, provided tobacco to pay his debts and keep him out of jail."

Barbara Watson's line of descent:
Samuel Brashear Sr; m. Ann Jones
Elizabeth Brashear; m. John Turner
Dorcas Turner; m. William Goe II
Mary Goe; m. James Hopkins
Thomas Hopkins; m. Elizabeth Perry
James Perry; m. Isabel Nelson
John Henry Perry; m. Edna Blackburn
Kathryn Perry; m. Gulbran Vinger (first non-Britisher in my family since Brashear)
Barbara Perry (me); m. Robert Watson

Mary Goe's brother, Phillip Goe, m. Daniel Boone's daughter, Rebecca

*****

p.139: JoAnn Hamblin, 913 W. 11 St, Mesa, AZ 85201, sent data regarding:
V1-403.   6-3. **Mary Brasher**, (Back #57), b. 5 Nov 1729, Queen Anne's Parish, Prince George's Co, MD, d/o John Brashear "Jr" and Mary Dowell, m. c1763, in PGCo, MD, *Thomas Ray*.
*****

Joseph Brashear, b. 1722

p.177: "Rich Kurlich" <richkurlich@hotmail.com> sends documents that change data on two of Samuel Brashear Jr and Elizabeth Brashear's children. It's an 1815 court case in Yohogania Co, VA (now West Virginia).

V1-533. 6-3. **Joseph Brashear**, (Back #-73) b. 15 Jan 1722, d. after 1783; m. *Patsy Beaden*. A deposition in an 1815 Yohogania Co, VA, court case says that Joseph Brashier, brother of Jeremiah Brashear, "intermarried with Patsey Beaden by whom he had an only child called Elizabeth." Joseph's inventory of estate filed in Prince George's Co, MD, 7 May 1785, by admrx, Mary Brashear (Book ST#2, p.219. ?His sister who was unmarried? Or a late-in-life second wife?) Joseph Brashear, m. 10 Dec 1780, PGCo, *Mary Cross*, who may have been a widow. In any case, Mary apparently died soon after, for accounts in estate filed by Alexander Duvall, admr, 25 May 1789 (Book ST#2, p.25); further accounts filed by Alex Duvall, 13 March 1795 (Book ST#3, p.90).

V1-533a. 7-1. **Elizabeth Brashear,** only child of Joseph Brashear.

That should shoot down forever the claim that Joseph Brashear, b. 1722, was the father of William Brashear, who had land on Floyd's Fork, Jefferson (later Bullitt) Co, KY, and married Anne Ray.

Margery (Brashears) Jenkins

p.189, Margarey Brashear, (d/o Jeremiah Brashear Sr and Esther Belt):

V1-622. 7-2. **Margery Brashear**, (Back #-132), b. c1758, PGCo, MD; ?m.1. _____ *Wilson*; m.2. 28 Jun 1780, in PGCo, *Joseph Jenkins*, b. 22 May 1755, Prince George's Co, MD, d. Monongalia Co, VA, s/o John Jenkins of PGCo. Joseph and Margery Jenkins lived in Monongalia Co, VA (now West Virginia) in the late 1700's, early 1800's. Margery's surname was Wilson on her marriage to Joseph Jenkins, so we assume she had been married earlier. Depositions in the 1815 court case in Yohogania Co, VA (now West Virginia) prove Margery (Brashear) Jenkins to be d/o Jeremiah Brashear.

Children of Joseph Jenkins and Margery Brashears: (Thanks to Lee Mattei for data.)

^{V9}-2490. ^{8}-1. Joseph Nelson Jenkins, b. 10 Aug 1787; d. 9 Dec 1876, Harrison Co, WVa.

^{V9}-2491. ^{8}-2. Mary Jenkins, b. 1789, PGCo, MD; d. 6 Nov 1880, Monongalia Co, VA; m. 17 May 1812, Monongalia Co, VA, Paul Vandevort, d. Monongalia Co, VA.

^{V9}-2492. ^{8}-3. Levi Jenkins, b. 1790; m. Mary Abercrombie, 9 Dec 1812, Monongalia Co, VA.

^{V9}-2493. ^{8}-4. Osborn Jenkins, b. 1792; m. Gartright Breakiron.

^{V9}-2494. ^{8}-5. James Jenkins, b. 1794, PGCo, MD; d. 1871, Marion Co. WVa.

^{V9}-2495. ^{8}-6. John Jenkins, b. 1795; m. Rebecca Severn.

^{V9}-2496. ^{8}-7. Margaret Jenkins, b. 1796; m. William Vandevort.

^{V9}-2497. ^{8}-8. Hannah Jenkins, b. 1797; m. Henry Rumble.

^{V9}-2498. ^{8}-9. Ann Jenkins, b. 1799, Monongalia Co, VA; d. 1873, Monongalia Co, VA.

For more on Jenkins, contact: "Lee Mattei" <ematt@kellnet.com>

******

William Clayton Brashears, of Texas Navy

p.182: Marion Farrow Noldt, gggd/o Benedict Brashear and Sarah Godman, identifies the stray William C. Brashears of the Texas Navy; she lists Benedict and Sarah's children as:

^{V1}-948. ^{9}-1. **William Clayton Brashears**, b. 1812, d. 31 Oct 184^{9}-This is #948. William C. Brashears of the Texas Navy, p.237.

^{V1}-562a. ^{9}-2. **John Clayton Brashears**, b. c1815; m. *Laura Watson*, and lived in Bedford Springs, PA

^{V1}-564. ^{9}-3. **Dorcas G. Brashears**, b. 1818, d. 1893; m. (second wife of) *Thomas Harvey*. Thomas m.1. Martha Beal and had two daughters, Mary and Catherine. Mary was called "Aimee" and helped raise the two daughters by Dorcas.

^{V1}-564a. ^{10}-1. Clara Catherine Harvey, b. 1855, d. 1914; m. William Watson Farrar, of Washington Co, PA, s/o John Farrar. Clara and William are grandparents of Marion.

^{V1}-564b. ^{11}-1. Mary Watson Farrar, b. 1889, d. c1957; m. Emil L. Koenig and had two sons, Robert Farrar Koenig and Edward L. Koenig.

^{V1}-564c. ^{11}-2. Katherine Watson Farrar, b. 1893, d. 1984; m. Oct 1921, Alvah Howard Farrow.

v1-564d.   12-1. Howard Watson Farrow, b. 1922, d. 1969, m. in 1956, Natalie Farrow Gehl
v1-564e.   12-2. Marion Stratton Farrow, b. 1925; m. _____ Noldt.
v1-564f.   11-3. son Farrar, stillborn, or d. very young.
v1-564g.   10-2. Elizabeth Harvey.
v1-563. 9-4. **Sarah Ann Brashears**, b. 1823
v1-563a.   9-5. **Lucy Elizabeth Cross Brashears**, b. 1820, d. 1842
v1-565. 9-6. **Humphrey Godman Brashears**, b. 1826, d. 1842

******

Benedict Brashear of Brooke Co, WV,

Benedict Brashear, b. c1808, Maryland, d. after 1857, Carpenter and Merchant; m. c1850, ***Anne Elizabeth*** _____, b. c1822, Ohio, d. 30 Dec 1884, Hancock Co, WV.

This is not the Benedict Brashear, (v1-550), s/o Samuel Brashear III and Rachel Brashear, of Prince George's Co, MD, b. ?, d. 1783, PGCo; m. Martha _____. His estate proceedings names son, Samuel. No further information.

Nor is this the Benedict Brashear, (v1-562), s/o John Brashear and Sarah Tilghman, of Prince George's Co, MD, b. c1785-88, d. c14 July 1853, PGCo; m. Sarah Godman. Census and newspaper records show that this Benedict and Sarah had children, William Clayton, John Clayton, Dorcas G., Sarah Ann, Lucy Elizabeth, and Humphrey Godman Brashear.

Both of these Benedicts are from the Samuel Brashear III line (the first is uncle to the second). There are plenty of gaps in that family where this Benedict "could" fit, but there is no evidence at the moment.

- 1846, June 6 — Benedict witnessed the will of Henry Jamison in Brooke Co, WV. Henry Jamison left everything to Lloyd Wilcoxen. (ref: Ruth Brodine Library)
- 1849, July 28 — Benedict bought lot 39 in Bethany, from Thom, Lucy, Ann, John, and Mary Wilson (Brooke Co, WV, Deeds, Bk 16, p.419)
- 1850 — Census, Brooke Co, WV, Third Dist. Benedict and Ann are listed; the column "marr. this year" is checked for everyone, even the children.
- 1851, April 17 — Benedict purchased land in Bethany from Alexander Campbell, UX (Brooke Co, WV, Deeds, Bk 17, p.17)
- 1854, May 27 — Benedict sold land to John Shrimplin for $1100 (Brooke Co, WV, Deeds, Bk 18, p.15)

- 1848-1878 — Benedict is listed as the second treasurer of Hancock Co, (*The History of the Panhandle of West Virginia*, p.428)
- 1857, June 15 — Benedict and Anne Elizabeth sold Lot 38 in New Cumberland to Daniel F. Connell (Hancock Co, WV, Deeds, Bk 3, p.62)
- 1860 — Census, Hancock Co, WV, New Cumberland Post Office. Benedict is listed as merchant. No children in household; Mary Tailor, 52, was living in the household as a domestic.
- 1873, Jan 3 — Anne Elizabeth sold to Richard E. Brandon, Lot 38, Campbell's Addition (located at E. Chester Sr and Vine Alley) (Hancock Co, WV, Deeds, Bk C, p.157). Either this was Anne Elizabeth's separate property, or Benedict had died. However, he is listed as Treasurer until 1878.
- 1884, Dec 30 — Anne dies. Anne Elizabeth [and?] heirs sold to Thomas Bonsall Lot 74 in Campbell's Addition (Hancock Co, WV, Deeds, Bk F, p.151)
- 1885, Jan 12 — Heirs of Anne Elizabeth sold ? to Mary M. Brandon (Hancock Co, WV, Deeds, Bk E, p.589)

*****

Hood/Brashear data

From: RonUlrich <ulrich@erols.com>

I recently bought the LDS 1880 Census CDs ($50 or so) and also the 1900 Census Online from Genealogy.com and have had the capability to search for names with relative ease. I found the following:

1880 US Census, Woodville, Frederick Co, Maryland; FHL Film 1254510;
National Archives Film T9-0510; Page 520A:

William H. HOOD,	32 MD MD MD, farmer (b. Abt 1848)
Francis HOOD,	27 MD MD MD, wife (b. Abt 1853)
Annis A. HOOD,	7, MD MD MD (Dau b. Abt 1873)
Addie M. HOOD,	5, MD MD MD (Dau b. Abt 1875)
Stella HOOD,	3, MD MD MD (Dau b. Abt 1877)
Emma HOOD,	10/12, MD MD MD (Dau b. Abt Aug 1879).

Also listed are:

Julia HOOD,	57, MD MD MD (Mother b. Abt 1823)
Thomas HOOD,	42, MD MD MD (Cousin b. Abt 1838); farm hand
Wm. H. BRASHEARS,	31, MD MD MD (Cousin b. Abt 1849); farm hand
William G. BRASHEARS,	23, MD MD MD (Brother-in-law b. Abt 1857); farm hand
Mary BOWERS,	11, MD MD MD (Other b. Abt 1869); Servant

US Census 1900 (2 June) Maryland, Carroll County, Page 351a, lines 64-69:

William Hood,	52, MD MD MD (b. April 1848) Occ: Merchant
Laura E. _____,	43, MD MD MD (b. April 1857) wife m.1yr, 0 ch

---

Ordean Hood,	27, MD MD MD (dau b. Jun 1872 - 27);
Addie M.	25, MD MD MD (dau b. Oct 1874 - 25);
Harry G. Hood,	18, MD MD MD (son b. Oct 1881 - 18); and
Chester R. Hood,	10, MD MD MD (son b. Dec 1889 - 10)

Which leads me to believe that Francis (Frances) was Frances Brashears, daughter of Richard Gassaway Brashears, and that William Hood was the son of Henry Hood and Julia Ann Brashears (as you already knew). Anyway seems to me to fill a gap.

****

Washington Co, MD, Brashears

From: Anita Louise Magner <SKCM23@aol.com>
Mr. Brashears, I have been working on my Brashears family genealogy for some time and I sent for your book, Vol. 1, "A Brashear(s) Family History" a few years ago. In Chapter 18 of your book, I found several errors. I hope I can correct them for you.

[V1]-493. [8]-1. My 4th great grandfather was **Joshua Brashears, Jr.**, born Aug. 4, 1795 most probably in Anne Arundel County, MD and died Feb. 4, 1842 in Sharpsburg, Wash Co, MD. He was married to **Mary Stiffler**, born abt. 1795 and died Jan 3, 1827 in Sharpsburg, Washington County, MD. She and Joshua are both buried in the Lutheran Graveyard in Sharpsburg. Mary was the daughter of John Stiffler, Jr. and Sarah Gray. I have some information on both of these people also.

[V1]-1128. [9]-1. My 3rd great grandfather was **William Brashears** born March 27, 1822 in Sharpsburg, Wash. Co., MD, and died August 3, 1910 in Sharpsburg, MD. He was married to **Elizabeth A. Benner**, born 1824 and died November 4, 1887 in Sharpsburg, MD. They are buried in Mountain View Cemetery, Sharpsburg, MD. I don't have postive proof yet, but I believe she was the daughter of Daniel Benner and Catherine Renner. William was a stone mason. I have census records, his obituary and death certificate. They had 10 children,

[V1]-1129.	[10]1. **Mary C. Brashears**,
[V1]-1143.	[10]-2. **Thomas Hammond Brashears**, my ggreatgrand father,
[V1]-1149.	[10]-3. **Amelia Frances Brashears**,
[V1]-1150.	[10]-4. **Julia M. Brashears**,
[V1]-1151.	[10]-5. **Clara E. Brashears**,
[V1]-1130.	[10]-6. **George Ridgely Brashears**,
[V1]-1152.	[10]- 7. **William F. Brashears**,
[V1]-1153.	[10]-8. **Cora E. Brashears**,

V1-xxx.   10-9. **Charles V. Brashears**, and
V1-xxx.   10-10. **Ada J. Brashears**,

Thomas Hammond Brashears was born August 4, 1848 in Sharpsburg and died January 11, 1912 in Sharpsburg. He was a carpenter. He married **Sarah Louise Peterman** born January 5, 1851 in Sharpsburg and died February 13, 1943 in Sharpsburg. She was the daughter of George L. and Mary Ann McGraw Peterman. They are buried in Mt. View Cemetery in Sharpsburg. They had 9 children,

V1-1144.   11-1. **George William Brashears**, my greatgrand father,
V1-114?.   11-2. **Thomas Walter Brashears**,
V1-114?.   11-3. **Grafton Finley Brashears**,
V1-1145.   11-4. **James F. Brashears**,
V1-1146.   11-5. twins- **Nan L. Brashears** and
V1-1147.   11-6. **Nina L. Brashears**,
V1-1148.   11-7. **Luva E. Brashears**,
V1-114?.   11-8. **Mary Prudence Brashears**, and
V1-114?.   11-9. **Iva Brashears**.

    I have information about these people. The information you have about Thomas H. Brashears married to Mary Keedy is not my Thomas Hammond. George Ridgely Brashears and his wife Elizabeth "Maggie" Benner had a son named Thomas H. and he married Mary Keedy. My greatgrandfather only had the one wife.

My greatgrandfather was **George William Brashears**, born Nov. 28, 1872 in Sharpsburg and died Dec. 19, 1924 in Hagerstown, MD. He married **Daisy Ellen Domer**, born 1880 in Shepherdstown, WV, and died March 3, 1909 in Sharpsburg. She was the daughter of John and Ida Show Domer. They are buried in Mt. View Cemetery in Sharpsburg. They had 4 children,

V9-2499.   12-1. **Mary Samantha Brashears**,
V9-2500.   12-2. **Katherine Brashears**,
V9-2501.   12-3. **Kenneth Leo Brashears**, my grandfather, and
V9-2502.   12-4. **George William Brashears, Jr.**

    George William was a factory worker and Laborer. I have information about these people also.

I also have done some research on Van Stiffler Brashears, Joshua and Thomas, brothers to my ancestor William.

I would be glad to send you what I have found if you are interested.

Sincerely,

Anita Louise Magner

****

V.1, page 281:

V1-1401. **Henry Alonzo Brashear**, s/o Richard Gassaway Brashear and Catherine A. _____ [of the Dowell Brashears line]

V9-2503.   **Robert Eugene Brashear**, (s/o Henry Alonzo Brashear and _____); m. *Della Irene Jordan*. Among their children:

V9-2504.   **Sarah Alice Brashear**, (mother of Patricia Oldfield, <PatCPC@msn.com>)

*****

Van Brashear and Emily Gridley

From Amanda Brashear:

I am a member of the Brashear family still living in Gallatin County KY. I just came across your info while doing a family history search and seen that it stops at Van Brashear and Emily Gridley, my great, great grandparents. Saw that you asked for info on their descendants. Wanted to share more with you.

v4-3224. [9]10. **Van Swangdon Brashear**, b. 18 Aug 1859, d. 14 Feb 1917; m. 1887, *Dora Harris*. They had 6 boys and two girls.

V9-2505.   [11]1. **Goebel Brashear**, m.1. *Helen Speigel* (no kids); m.2. *Louise Webster* (2 kids)

V9-2506.   [12]1. **Lonnie Van Brashear**,

V9-2507.   [12]2. **Nancy Brashear**; m. _____ Plunkett

V9-2508.   [11]2. **Erve "Seven" Brashear**, (died young, unmarried)

V9-2509.   [11]3. **Robert "Sug" Brashear**, m. *Hazel Morgan*

V9-2510.   [12]1. **Ruthie Brashear**,

V9-2511.   [12]2. **Bobby Brashear**,

V9-2512.   [12]3. **Eva Brashear**,

V9-2513.   [12]4. **Dave Brashear**,

V9-2514.   [11]4. **Roy "Monk" Brashear** (twin), m. *Blanche Morgan*

V9-2515.   [12]1. **Juanita Brashear**, died in infancy

V9-2516.   [12]2. **Joanne Brashear**,

V9-2517.   [12]3. **Donnie Brashear**,

V9-2518.   [13]x. _____ **Brashear**,

V9-2519.   [14]Y. **Amanda Brashear**, (who sent this data)

V9-2520.   [11]5. **Raymond Brashear**, (twin), died young, no children.

V9-2521.   [11]6. **Henry "Six" Brashear**, m. *Luanne Lillard*,

V9-2522.   [11]7. **Mary Brashear** (unmarried, no children)

V9-2523.   [11]8. **Sue Brashear**, m. *Wallace Hon*,

Hope this helps, or at least is not info that you already have.

Thanks, Amanda

*****

Robert J. Brashear, of Philadelphia

V9-2524.   a-x. **Robert J. Brashear** (the elder), b. Maryland (per son's 1900 census), lived and was a painter in Philadelphia until about 1918; m. _____, b. Ireland (per 1900). (Data from Robert H. Brashear, 1117 Gloria Lane, Yardley, PA 19067; 215/736-0659; <Rbrashear@directweb.com>.)

V9-2525.   b-x. **Robert J. Brashear** (the younger), b. June 1866, in Maryland (per 1900 census, Philadelphia, PA), d. ?; m.1. *Ella Dora DeLarue*, b. ?, d. 1895, Philadelphia in a Trolley accident , bur Fernwood Cem, just outside southwest Phila; m.2. *Catherine "Katie"* _____, b. c1870 (30 in 1900), Philadelphia, PA, d. 28 May 1901, Philadelphia (pneumonia), bur Fernwood Cem, just outside southwest Phila, alongside first wife.

1888: Philadelphia City Directory lists an <u>Alvan V. Brashear</u> on 22nd St and a Robert J. Brashear, "painter," on 15th St. Later directories do not list Alvan, but Robert J. continues to be listed, until in 1893 there are two Robert J. Brashears

1893 City Directory lists <u>two</u> Robert J. Brashears, listed as living just blocks from each other, both "painters." Later directories list only one Robert J. Brashear.

1895 City Directory lists Robert J. Brashear (the younger) as living on 48th St. The death notice of his first wife, Ella Dora, gives her address as 48th St.

1897: City Directory lists Robert J. Brashear as living with "<u>Elizabeth Brashear</u>, wid. Eli". We assume that, after the death of Ella in a trolly accident, Robert brought in a relative to help raise the three children. He apparently married again soon, for the 1900 census lists his wife as "Katie," age 30, along with the three children by his first marriage.

1901: second wife, Katie, dies of pneumonia.

1903, and 1907: City Directory lists Robert J. Brashear, "painter," after which he disappears; moved "upstate" according to his granddaughter, who never met him, says Robert H. Brashear.

<u>Family of Robert J. Brashear and Ella Dora DeLarue:</u> (per 1900 census, Philadelphia, PA)

V9-2526.   c-1. **Robert Edward Brashear "Jr,"** b. 1890, (was a printer in Philadelphia and helped develop the embossing process); m. *Mary Pearce Hutton*

V9-2527.   d-1. **Milton C. Brashear**, b. 1910, d. 1972; never married; no ch

V9-2528.   d-2. **Robert E. Brashear**, b. 1912, d. 1923; died young

---

V9-2529.	d-3. **Marion Eleanor Brashear**, b. 1914, d. 1999; m. *Horace March*, no ch

V9-2529.   d-3. **Marion Eleanor Brashear**, b. 1914, d. 1999; m. *Horace March*, no ch

V9-2530.   d-4. **Harold Earl Brashear**, b. 1916, d. 1976 (he was a conductor for Reading Railroad); m. *Evelyn Marie Greenway*

V9-2531.   e-1. **Carol Evelyn Brashear**, b. 1945; m. *Albert Humbert*, no ch

V9-2532.   e-2. **Robert Horace Brashear**, b. 1951; m. *Cheryle A. Hinkle*

V9-2533.   f-1. **Robert Horace Brashear Jr**, b. 1993

V9-2534.   f-2. **Caitlyn Marian Brashear**, b. 1997

V9-2535.   c-2. **Ada A. Brashear**, b. 1893. Allegedly "married an Indian and moved to a reservation in New York state"; possibly died soon after giving birth, but we know nothing more than this.

V9-2536.   d-1. a daughter. ??the "granddaughter" who told of Robert J. Brashear's move to upstate.

V9-2537.   c-3. **Mary Brashears**, b. 1894, no info

******

Henry Cartwright Brashear

Farmer & Stock Feeder; b. Franklin, Penn, Aug 3, 1859; s/o **R. A. Brashear** & Sarah Ann Seaton; educ Franklin, Penn HS; m. *Lenore Golden*, Aug 18, 1884, Franklin, Penn (dec May 4, 1939); sons: **Robert Ayres Brashear** (dec), **John William Brashear**;

1876-86 mfr, dlr in tin & glassware, Franklin, Penn, by means of itinerant traders covered western Penn & eastern OH;

1886 homesteaded Scotts Bluff Co, NE; cattle raiser, captured & sold wild horses, sheep feeder past 20 years, recently began cattle feeding; owner & mgr 3 farms; instrumental in bldg of Mitchell Ditch; Rep; hobbies, baseball, softball; res Scottsbluff.

Who's Who in Nebraska, 1940, SCOTTS BLUFF COUNTY, (NEGenWeb Project - Scotts Bluff County), A. B. Woods, ref: http://www.rootsweb .com/~neresour/OLLibrary/who1940/co/scotbluf1.htm

15. VOL. 2 MISCELLANEOUS

v-2, p.73: Pauline Utterback Dvorak <"ed33913"@navix.net> writes: "The good news is that I received your book-The bad news is that you left out my ancestor-- Bennett Ball, son of Moses Ball Jr and Mary Ann "Molly" Hardin. You have Wesley Ball (#v2-188) married to Nancy Bailey. Wesley married Sarah Bailey, who was a sister to Bennett's wife Nancy. Wesley and Bennett are brothers. Bennett and Nancy Bailey Ball moved to Madison Co. Arkansas and are buried in Wesley cemetery. Their daughter Nancy Ball married William Creech. This is my line."

CB's response: I'm sorry. I can only go by what people send me. I regret the error and omission of Bennett.
******

v-2, p.81: Rebecca Brashear and Elias Roberts had only 10 children, not 11 as mentioned. Sorry about the typo. Thanks to Pat McDonald <patiemac@ infohwy.com> for calling my attention to the error.
*****

v-2, pp.90-101: Pat Kennedy <pakennedy@uswest.net> contributed significantly to unravelling the Ray Co, MO, Brashear clan. Through an oversight, her contribution was not acknowledged. Sorry, Pat, and Thanks a million for the data.
****

More on Isaac Wright Brashear

v-2, p.102: Jim Wheat, of Garland, Texas, sent this newspaper clipping on another descendant of Jesse Brashears of Rutherford Co, TN, s/o Capt Asa Brasher. (From: Dallas [Tex.] *Daily Times Herald*, August 3, 1892, p.2.) Note that it corroborates some of the tentative data in the family of Isaac Wright Brashears.

HE FOUGHT WITH FORREST.

————

SOMETHING OF JOHN BRASHEAR,
WHO DIED RECENTLY.

————

He Was a Gallant Soldier, of
Gentle Birth and Highly Connected.

————

Two weeks ago, John Brashear was found dead on the farm of W. P. Martin. He was an employee of Mr. Martin, who kindly gave him work when the unfortunate man and his family were on the verge of starvation. John Brashear left a widow and two little children in destitute circumstances. The TIMES-HERALD made an appeal to the old Confederates, and not in vain.

The following letter is not only interesting, but pathetic, as well as self-explanatory:

Murfreesboro, Tenn., July 25, 1892.
W. P. Martin, Esq., Dallas, Tex.
Dear Sir:-
   In behalf of Col. Brashear, one of our oldest and best citizens, I want to return you his thanks and the thanks of us all for the interest you took in his son, John Brashear, who it seems died on your place. We all do thank you a thousand times for the kindness you showed him while living and especially the interest you took in him and his wife after his death, and especially do we thank the old confederate soldiers for the interest they manifested in John Brashear and his poor wife and children, and I want you to say to the old Rebs that they never took charge of, or interest in, a more gallant or brave soldier than John Brashear.
   He was one of, and belonged to, Gen. Forrest's escort and you know it took men or boys who never flinched or flickered to ride with the gallant Forrest. John Brashear was one of them, and was complimented more than a half-dozen times in public orders from his officers for gallantry on the field. He was the youngest soldier in Forrest's escort, being only 16 years old then; so that you can say to the old Confederate veterans that what they did was done for as gallant a soldier as ever rode with Forrest.
   Col. Jesse Brasher is one of our most prominent and worthy citizens, and one of the wealthiest men in this part of the state. John, his son, like many other young men that went through the war,

————————————————————————————

contracted bad habits that tended to degrade rather than uplift them. He gave his father much trouble, but the old gentleman stood it all and begged John not to go away, and offered him a splendid farm, well stocked, and all that, but John felt that he wanted to get away from his old associates, thinking he could get rid of his bad habits sooner, and this is the result.

You can say to all those who interested themselves in behalf of the widow and her little ones, that they are now in good hands and will be well taken care of. John was buried yesterday. There was an immense concourse of people there. Old Col. Jesse Brashear don't believe much in preachers. He says they do more mischief than good, and he would not have any services, only asking me to make a short talk to the people, reading your telegrams and such other information as we had received from Dallas. But, when I got on his confederate record, I saw so many old soldiers standing around me shedding tears, I broke completely down and had to give it up.

So, say to your folks and people that they entertained and took care of no common tramp, but a brave and gallant confederate soldier, one that followed the great Forrest and one of gentle birth, but by misfortune, a seeming outcast. My wife is a cousin of John Brashear; his father, Col. Jesse Brashear, is the only uncle she has living.

[Isaac] Wright Brashear, who moved to Houston, Tex., in 1838, and died there many years ago, leaving a large family. John Brashear, a son, who has been since the war, county judge of Harris county, was a cousin of our John, who died in Dallas. He has another cousin who is clerk of the district court at Houston, Texas, Henry Brashear. Col. James W. Jones, of Houston, a prominent lawyer there, married his cousin, Sallie Brashear; and Charley Miller, a prominent real estate man at Houston, married a cousin of his, Annexa Brashear. She was born when Texas was annexed to the United States, hence her name. I give you these facts only to show you that John Brashear belonged to one of the best families in Tennessee and Texas. I was, myself, born at Nacogdoches, Texas, in 1837, and I mustered into the Confederate service nearly all the Texas soldiers in 1861 and 1862.

Perhaps some of you old soldiers will remember me; I mustered in soldiers at San Antonio, Harrisburg, Houston, Galveston, Hempstead and many other places, and finally, was made the first adjutant of the Texas Rangers and fought all through this part of the country, and John Brashear's company was with [me] right most of the time. Respectfully,

J. W. SPARKS.

Kathy McAdams (mcadams@jps.net) sends the following on Col. James W. Jones, the Houston Lawyer, who married a daughter of Isaac Wright Brashear and Sarah Trott. He was the son of James Jones and

Eliza Murray of Jackson Co, Tennessee. James W. left Jackson Co after the Civil War and settled in Houston, Texas. He is the grandson of Thomas Murray and Margaret Mercer. This is the Murray line of Governor William H. (Alfalfa Bill) Murray, of Oklahoma.

****

Elizabeth Brashear
and Michael Straisner

v-2, p. 135: Elizabeth Brashear (v2-546) and Michael Straisner.
From: "Royce Lee Pate" <rlpate@alltel.net>
Subject: Brashear Book

Regarding Zaza Brashear's daughter, Elizabeth, who married Michael Stracener. I have information on them, for they are my great great grandparents. I have a picture of their son Jefferson and most of his 14 kids.

01 Jefferson F. Strasner   (photo)
02 Mary Margaret Strasner (photo)
03 Nancy C. Strasner   (photo)
04 Sarah P. Strasner   (photo)
05 Elizabeth LeAndrea Strasner   (photo)
06 Rose Zinna Rebecca Jane Strasner (photo)
07 Healeder Elizabeth Drucilla Strasner (photo)
08 James Strasner
09 William Jasper Strasner
10 Julia Frances Strasner (photo)
11 Lula Missouri Strasner (photo)
12 Henrietta W. Strasner (photo)
13 Rhoda Charlotty Strasner (photo)
14 Dallas Belzora Strasner (photo)

I also have information on most of these and their families. Elizabeth LeAndrea and Rose Zinna Rebecca Jane are my great grandma's. Elizabeth is on my mother's side and Rose is on my father's side. I have some of these children's pictures. If you would like please let me know. If I scan the pictures on my scanner, can you print them? Also do you put pictures in your book.
Royce L. Pate

****

More on Neil S. Brown Boshears
and Margaret Tidwell

v2-463. **Cornelius "Neil S." Brown Boshears,** (s/o Jeremiah Nathan Boshears and Sarah "Sally" Malicote), b. 19 Oct 1849, Cedar Creek, TN, d. 26 Dec 1930, Knoxville, TN, bur Pond Cem, Grantsboro, Campbell Co, TN; m. c.1867-68, (div 1887, Campbell Co, TN) *Margaret Tidwell,* b. 5 Sep 1834, d. 7 Mar 1906, bur Bakers Forge Cem. Neil S. Brown Boshears was probably named after ?Cornelius "Neil" S. Brown, Governor of Tennessee, 1848-1850, and member of the Whig Party, forerunner of the Republican Party.

Angie Adcock <longtongue1@msn.com> writes. Cornelius Boshears also known as Neals or Neil S. Brown Boshears or Grand Pap Neil. Born 10-19-1849 in LaFollette, Campbell County, TN; d. 12-27-1930 in Knoxville, Knox County, TN, buried in Pond Cemetery in LaFollette, Campbell Co, TN. 1st Marriage Margaret Tidwell in about 1867 or 1868 divorced in 10-21-1887. 2nd marriage 7-23-1889 to Bettie Leach. 3rd marriage 8-21-1898 to Bettie Wright. We think that Bettie Wright was Cherokee. I have all the information on Neil but I didn't know if we were some kin or not? Do you have an e-mail address for Rebecca J. Ellis? I might find it on the internet. If you ever run across a Earnest - Ernest Boshears or a Bettie Malicote Green, please let me know. My grandfather is Earnest Boshears and his mother is Bettie Malicote. Malicote was her maiden name and she never married my grandfather's dad. But she later on married a Howard Green. Earnest b. 1-25-1892 LaFollette, Campbell County, TN; d. 12-28-1957 in LaFollette, Campbell County, TN. It was so good to get your letter. I hope to hear from you soon. Thanks!

16. VOL. 3 MISCELLANEOUS

p.15: Typographical error in the marriage date of Samuel Brashear and Ann Jones. It should be c1693.

Edward Hambleton

p.19; Family of Edward Hambleton: Maryland Calendar of Wills, Volume 4: Will of Edward Hambleton, (innholder), Queen Anne's Co, Maryland, dated 2 Mar 1713; probate: 10 Dec 1716. To 5 child., viz.: William, Edward, Elizabeth, Margaret and Sarah, entire estate. Son Edward and daus. Margaret and Sarah to be in care of their uncle, Walter Quinton, ex.
Exs.: Wife Rachell [Quinton] and friend Walter Quinton, jointly.

That will generates this fragment of family:
Edward Hambleton, m. Rachel Quinton (sister of Walter Quinton)
1. William Hambleton,
2. Edward Hambleton, ward of Walter Quinton after Edward Hambleton's death
3. Elizabeth Hambleton,
4. Margaret Hambleton, ward of Walter Quinton after Edward Hambleton's death; later married William White.
5. Sarah Hambleton, ward of Walter Quinton after Edward Hambleton's death
******

Roane Stray shows up

from: John James Lafayette Brashear

p.108. #574, [10-]5. **Joseph Henry Brashears**, b. 22 Feb 1896, Roane Co, TN (s/o William D. Brashears and second wife, Margaret Fanny Cox). Also Joseph H. Brashears, Ky Pvt, 21 Inf, 1st Div, WW I, on p.113. He was wounded in the war: his hands were crippled by machine-gun fire.

Some time in the early 30s, he moved his family to Harlan Co, KY, "to make big money in the coal mines," as John J.L. Brashear puts it. "The story is that grandpaw Joe sold the farm in Tenn., bought an Auburn, and moved to KY. ... All he could remember of [Great]Grandpaw William was that he was always dressed in black and walked around town (Oliver Springs, TN) with a cane. Sounds like a man of leisure."

Joseph Henry Brashears married twice: first, Pearl Ledford, b. c1902 (17 in 1920, Roane Co, TN), and had 7 children:

[11]1. ***Arnold Lee Brashears**, b. 2 Oct 1920, d. 7 Jan 1986
[11]2. **Earl Brashears**,
[11]3. **Cecil Brashears**,
[11]4. **Floyd Brashears**,
[11]5. **Marvin Brashears**,
[11]6. **Marion Brashears**,
[11]7. **Gladys Brashears**. "I'm not sure how to spell my Aunt's name, so I spelled it the way it sounds."

[11-x]. Joseph Henry Brashears married a second time and had 3 or 4 children, "but I don't know their names or how many. We moved north and lost touch with everybody. I think it must have been the same with my [great]grandfather when they moved from Roane Co, Tenn. to Harlan Co, KY. The families going where the jobs were."

Grandmaw Pearl died of TB soon after the move. She and Joe had eloped around 1936, when they were teen-agers, but her family didn't approve of the marriage ("Dad was from the wrong side of the tracks") and kept the young ones apart until Pearl was 18.

Joseph Henry Brashears died in 1949. "My Uncle Floyd was to transport Joe's body to Tenn. for burial in Dyllis Cemetery (in Roane Co, TN), and have a marker installed, which he didn't. I remember Dad being pretty peeved at Uncle Floyd for a long time after that." The dates on his stone say 22 Feb 1847–20 Oct 1949. (The first seems to be in error; he was born in 1896.)

"Dad," (Arnold Lee Brashears) "had to quit school when he was in the 4th grade to take care of his brothers and sister. When his brother, Earl, was 12 or so, Dad went to work in the mines with Grandpaw (at age 14). ... the war got Dad out of the coal mines (thank goodness) when he got back in 1945. We started moving north out of the mountains around 1953."

Arnold Lee Brashears, Sr, b. 2 Oct 1920, d. 7 Jan 1986; m.1. **Sarita Smith**, b. 29 Jan 1921, d. 1963 (4 ch); m.2. **Joyce Wilma Neely**, b. 21 May 1941, d. 19 Oct 2006 (2 ch).
[12]1. **John James Lafayette Brashears**, b. 22 Feb 1940, living in 2007 in Ohio; "when I was born, it was understood that I, being the first grandson, would be named after Grandpaw Joe (also being born on his birthday as well). At the last minute, Mom changed her mind and named me after her Dad, which hurt Grandpaw Joe and he

wouldn't have much to do with Mom after that (family squabbles are silly).

[12]2. **Pearl Vestina Brashears**, b. 22 Dept 1942
[12]3. **Arnold Lee Brashears, II**, b. 30 Jan 1947
[12]4. **Machell Brashears**, b. 21 Sept 1955
[12]5. **Mark David Brashears**, b. 16 April 1961
[12]6. **Monicha Brashears**, b. 25 Oct 1963

*****

Roberts Families

From: "Chris H. Bailey" <chrisb@esslink.com>
To: "Charles Brashear" <brashear@mail.sdsu.edu>
Subject: Errata and additions to vol 3.

p. 73. #204. Asa Ellis Roberts died Oct. 8, 1887 (not 1877). His son and my ancestor was born in 1884.

p. 101, #536. William Louis Roberts died Aug. 10, 1939 (not 1839).

pp.71-73: I thought I had sent you Roberts info which included the children of Asa and his siblings. Had I known, I could have sent you more complete data on the families of most of Asa's brothers and sisters. Although it is after the fact, I will attach an MS Word file with this data.

[v3]175. Elias R. "Robbie" ROBERTS, son of John Calvin Roberts and Elizabeth Blackwell, was born Oct. 27, 1818 in Roane County, TN. He was married Jan. 9, 1840 in Roane County, TN to *Mary McCormack* who was born about 1824 in TN.

They had the following children born in Roane County, TN:

[v9]2538.   1. Elizabeth Roberts, b. abt. 1840. She married a Mr. Ball.
[v9]2539.   2. John C. Roberts, b. Nov. 10, 1842. He married Mrs. Mary Susan (Toney) Smith, widow of John Smith. They had three children born in Smith County, TN. He died Oct. 27, 1927 at Gallatin, TN and was buried in Russell Family Cemetery.
[v9]2540.   3. Mary A. Roberts, b. abt. 1844. She was married Jan. 5, 1864 in Roane County, TN to William Wright.
[v9]2541.   4. Rebecca J. Roberts, b. abt. 1846. She was married Mar. 9, 1865 in Roane County, TN to James McCravey.

^{V9}-2542.   5. Margaret A. Roberts, b. 1848. She was married Nov. 7, 1872 in Roane County, TN to Samuel Houston Crow (1827-1915). She died in 1927.

^{V9}-2543.   6. George Washington Roberts, b. July 22, 1850. He was married Sep. 22, 1870 in Roane County, TN to Mary Elizabeth Hacker who was born Mar. 6, 1845. They had six children. George W. Roberts died Aug. 15, 1923 and his widow died Sep. 16, 1925. They are buried in New Providence Cemetery, Loudon County, TN.

^{V9}-2544.   7. Amanda Roberts, b. abt. 1852. She married William Hart. They had six children.

^{V9}-2545.   8. William H. Roberts, b. 1854. He was married July 29, 1879 in Roane County, TN to Elizabeth Martin who was born in 1854 in Roane County, TN. They moved to Washington State and had nine children. Elizabeth Roberts died in 1909 and William H. Roberts died in 1935. They are buried at Steptoe, WA.

This family was living in Roane County, TN in 1850 and 1860. "Robbie" was supposedly a veteran of the Civil War and a pensioner. He died in 1902 and is buried in the Tennessee Church Cemetery near Kingston, TN. His grave is marked by a fieldstone.

^{v3}-184; David Roberts, son of John Calvin Roberts and Elizabeth Blackwell, was born April 24, 1820 in Roane County, TN. He was married Oct. 10, 1840 in Roane County, TN to Anna Hester, daughter of William Hester. Ann was born about 1824 in TN. They had only one daughter born in Roane County, TN:

^{V9}-2546.   1. Elizabeth Roberts, b. July 22, 1841. She never married.

David Roberts died before 1848 "with fever" according to his father's bible record. In 1850 David's widow and ten year old daughter were living in her father's home in Roane County, TN. Widow Anna Roberts was married May 29, 1853 in Roane County, TN to Nimrod Underwood. Nimrod was appointed guardian of Anna's daughter, Elizabeth Roberts.

^{v3}-184; **Elijah Roberts**, son of John Calvin Roberts and Elizabeth Blackwell, was born Feb. 10, 1822 in Roane County, TN. He married Sarah J. _____, who was born about 1826. They had four children by 1850:

^{V9}-2547.   1. Sarah E. Roberts, b. abt. 1844.

^{V9}-2548.   2. Hugh F. Roberts, b. abt. 1846.

^{V9}-2549.   3. Mary L. Roberts, b. abt. 1848.

V9-2550.   4. Amanda J. Roberts, b. abt. 1849.

Elijah Roberts was living in Texas by 1848. He was enumerated as "E. Roberts" in the 1850 census of Cherokee County, TX. He was living in Texas in 1852, but died before 1873 "with the black ganders," according to his father's bible.

V3-199; **Francis Marion "Jack" Roberts**, son of John Calvin Roberts and Elizabeth Blackwell, was born Dec. 3, 1825 in Roane County, TN. He was married May 31, 1849 in Roane County, TN to Margaret Ann Lyle who was born Mar. 22, 1824 in TN. They had five childen:

V9-2551.   1. William Lyle Roberts, b. Oct. 15, 1851. He married Sophronia Byrd.
V9-2552.   2. John Francis Roberts, b. May 10, 1856.
V9-2553.   3. Samuel Henry Roberts, b. Apr. 4, 1858. He married Lucinda Ann Hayden.
V9-2554.   4. Elizabeth Jane Roberts, b. Nov. 28, 1860.
V9-2555.   5. Alfred Marion Roberts, b. June 13, 1863. He died Mar. 12, 1897.

In 1850, Francis and his wife were newly married and living next door to his parents in Roane County, TN. They went to Dent County, MO by 1852 but were not located there in the 1860 census. Francis was "lost in the War", according to his father's bible record.

Francis M. Roberts was mentioned in his father's probate settlement of 1877 as being deceased, but had heirs whose names were unknown, but were "thought to be in the State of Missouri." Margaret Roberts died May 26, 1876.

None of Francis' heirs could be found in the 1870 census of Dent County, MO, but the three younger children were enumerated in the home of the oldest son in Lynn Township, Dent County, MO in 1880.

V3-202; **Amanda Roberts**, daughter of John Calvin Roberts and Elizabeth Blackwell, was born Apr. 27, 1831 in Roane County, TN. She first married August 23, 1849 in Roane County, TN to Jonathan Tallent. They had five children, the first two born in Roane County, TN and the remainder in Dent County, MO:

V9-2556.   1. William A. Tallent, b. abt. 1850. He married Vandalia ----.
V9-2557.   2. Lucy A. Tallent, b. abt. 1852 in TN. She married Peter Chandler.
V9-2558.   3. John Tallent. He married Myrtle Sherrell and moved to Oregon.
V9-2559.   4. Margaret Tallent, b. abt. 1857 in MO. She married William Daugherty.

V9-2560.   5. Jane Tallent. She married Peter Malady.

Jonathan Tallent was killed as a soldier in the Civil War in Arkansas. In 1870 Amanda's oldest son was living in Spring Garden Township, Dent County, MO and working as a farm laborer for Abner Harrison. In 1870 two youngest daughters were living in the home of Bazel Roberts, Amanda's younger brother.

Amanda was remarried Sep. 22, 1869 in Roane County, TN to George Washington Byrd as his third wife. George was born July 29, 1819 in TN. (He had first been married to Sarah A. Everett and had 12 children; she died in TN. His second wife was Mary May Silvey who had one son and died in TN.) George and Amanda had two sons:

V9-2561.   1. Joseph Byrd, b. July 9, 1870. He was married to Amanda Stephens who was born in 1866. He died Sep. 25, 1922 and she died in 1933. They are buried in Stone Hill Cemetery, Dent County, MO.

V9-2562.   2. Hugh Roberts Byrd, b. Oct. 14, 1872. He married Eugenia Wood. He died July 2, 1953. They are buried in Stone Hill Cemetery, Dent County, MO.

George W. Byrd died in May, 1878. Amanda Byrd died Oct. 1, 1917 in Dent County, MO. They are buried in Stone Hill Cemetery, Dent County, MO.

v3-203; **Hugh Roberts**, son of John Calvin Roberts and Elizabeth Blackwell, was born Aug. 24, 1833 in Roane County, TN. He was first married Nov. 20, 1856 in Dent County, MO to Sarah J. Hickson (or Hickerson) who was born Aug. 17, 1831 in Dent County, MO. They had at least four children born in Dent County, MO:

V9-2563.   1. Susan Elizabeth Roberts, b. Dec. 29, 1857. She was married Mar. 3, 1880 in Dent County, MO to Timothy Hickman, son of James Hickman and Elizabeth Kinney. Timothy was born in 1852 in Monroe County, OH. She died Mar. 7, 1913 in Texas County, MO. She and her husband are buried in New Hope Cemetery, Dent County, MO.

V9-2564.   2. India A. Roberts, b. abt. 1859.

V9-2565.   3. Julia Ann Roberts, b. abt. 1861. She was married Apr. 25, 1883 in Dent County, MO to Andrew Love. They moved to Newton County, MO.

V9-2566.   4. Mary Lee Roberts, b. July 17, 1862. She was married Jan. 2, 1884 in Dent County, MO to Isaac McAlpin Randolph. She died May 30, 1938 in Dent County, MO.

She and her husband are buried in Cedar Grove Cemetery, Salem, MO.

Sarah J. Roberts died May 12, 1863 in Dent County, MO. Hugh was married a second time on Feb. 1, 1866 in Dent County, MO to Mrs. Sarilda Jane (Garret) Warden, widow of William Warden. Sarilda was born about 1843 in MO. They had three children born in Dent County, MO:

V9-2567. 1. Martha Mandring Roberts, b. Feb. 20, 1867. She was married Jan. 13, 1892 to Ulyssus Grant Yeater. She died Nov. 8, 1954 at Moberly, Randolph County, MO. She and her husband are buried in Cedar Grove Cemetery, Salem, MO.

V9-2568. 2. Sarah Jane Roberts, b. June 20, 1869. She was married to William H. Frank. They lived in a western state where she died Feb. 27, 1898. Her body was returned to Dent County, MO and buried in Cedar Grove Cemetery at Salem, MO. He was buried in the west.

V9-2569. 3. Lucinda Francis Roberts, b. Apr. 24, 1871. She was married Apr. 9, 1902 to Fines Ewing McGee. She died Feb. 15, 1951. She and her husband are buried in New Hope Cemetery, Dent County, MO.

This family was living in Spring Creek Township, Dent County, MO in 1860 and 1870. In the latter Census Sarilda's eight year old daughter, Mary Catherine Warden, was living in their home. (Mary C. Warden was married Dec. 24, 1879 in Dent County, MO to Robert William Jones.)

Hugh Roberts was a veteran of the Civil War, serving in Company "D", 48th Missouri Infantry. He died Apr. 23, 1916 at Salem, Dent County, MO. He was buried with his first wife in Cedar Grove Cemetery, Salem, MO. His widow Sarilda was buried with her first husband in Warden Cemetery, Dent County, MO.

v3-204; **Asa Ellis Roberts**, son of John Calvin Roberts and Elizabeth Blackwell, was born Feb. 18, 1835 (listed as Feb. 28, 1835 in his father's bible), in Roane County, TN. He was married May 19, 1852 in Roane County, TN to Cynthia Minerva Toney. (Name mistakenly listed as "Elizabeth" M. in marriage record). Cynthia was born Mar. 1, 1834.

This family has not been located in the 1860 census, but in 1870 they were living in Jefferson County, IL, near Spring Garden. Asa was listed as a farmer, 36 years old and born in TN. His wife "Minerva" was listed as the same age and also born in TN. They at least six children living in 1870, born in IL:

V9-2570. 1. William Roberts, b. abt. 1853.
V9-2571. 2. George W. Roberts, b. abt. 1856. He first married Henrietta Sherroll and secondly, Mrs. Marriett Cleghorn.
V9-2572. 3. Margaret Roberts, b. abt. 1859. She married a Mr. Porter and had children.
V9-2573. 4. (Dr.) Calvin Roberts, b. abt. 1861. He is buried at Henderson, KY.
V9-2574. 5. Sarah Angeline Roberts, b. 1863. She was married Nov. 25, 1879 in Jefferson County, IL (Bk. 6, p. 7 lic. #215) to Daniel Rufus Baltzell. They had 1 son and 7 daughters. She died in 1929 in Jefferson County, IL. They are buried in the Arnold Cemetery, Jefferson County, IL.
V9-2575. 6. Monroe Roberts, b. abt. 1866. He was buried at Willow Springs, MO.

Asa Roberts' first wife, Cynthia Minerva Roberts died May 26, 1872 age 35 years, 25 days and was buried in New Hope Cemetery near Ina, IL. Buried beside her are four small stones which each say "Infant of A. & C. M. Roberts." No names or dates are given on any of them. A fifth stone remains which has the top part broken and lost. Only the age 3 (or 13) years, 4 months and 7 days remains.

Asa Roberts was married a second time on Aug. 25, 1872 at Spring Garden, Jefferson County, IL to Mrs. Patience Anna (Marshall) Dean, daughter of Jane Marshall. Patience had first been married in 1859 in Jefferson County, IL to Thomas B. Dean who had died Feb. 3, 1863 at Ewing, IL. Patience was born Dec. 30, 1845 in Jefferson County, IL. They had four children born near Spring Garden, Jefferson Co., IL:

V9-2576. 1. Charles Wilson Roberts, b. July 5, 1873. He married Clara Farmer.
V9-2577. 2. Rosa Della Roberts, b. May 26, 1875. She was married Jan. 29, 1891 in Jefferson County, IL to James Lawrence Darrington (1873-1955). They had five children. They died at Tulsa, OK.
V9-2578. 3. Florence Elizabeth Roberts, b. Jan. 21, 1880. She married Francis Perry Scott.
V9-2579. 4. Hugh Ellis Roberts, b. July 2, 1884. He married Clora Dell Scott.

Asa Roberts enlisted as a private in Captain Almon's Company "I", 31st Regiment Illinois Volunteers on Aug. 15, 1861 for three years. He was discharged July 26, 1862 at Cairo, IL for "Chronic Pericarditis and he is Perfectly unfit for Service." His discharge noted "This man has been on furlough in Hospital ever since the battle of Fort Donelson."

At the time of his discharge he was noted as age 26, born in Roane County, TN and was 5 feet 8 inches tall with fair complexion, grey eyes and dark hair and a farmer at the time of his enlistment. Asa applied for a disability pension on Aug. 25, 1867. He was granted a pension until his death.

Neither Asa Roberts or his wife Patience could write. In their pension papers is a deposition by a friend, Thomas J. Ward of Benton, IL, who noted that he made the entries for the births of the oldest three of their four children in the Roberts' family bible.

This family was living in Winifred Town, Elk Prairie Township, Jefferson County, IL in 1880. Asa's step daughter, Elnora Dean, age 17, was living in their home at that time. "Nora" Dean later married Michael Pitchford.

Asa E. Roberts died of heart and lung disease on Oct. 8, 1887 in Jefferson County, IL after having to have a constant attendant for 30 months previous. His widow immediately applied after his death for a widow's pension and was granted it and drew it until her death. She lived at Sesser, IL on July 12, 1917. She died July 26, 1919. They are buried in New Hope Cemetery near Ina, IL.

v3-205; **Robert Samuel Roberts**, son of John Calvin Roberts and Elizabeth Blackwell, was born June 5, 1837 in Roane County, TN. He was first married Nov. 23, 1856 in Roane County, TN to Louisa Hester, daughter of Churchwell Hester. Louisa was born Nov. 18, 1836 in Roane County, TN. They had eight children born in Roane County, TN:

V9-2580.   1. Elizabeth Canses Roberts, b. Sep. 19, 1857. She was married July 22, 1876 to R. C. Martin. She died Mar. 11, 1889. They supposedly settled in Kansas and had three children.

V9-2581.   2. Mary Savannah Roberts, b. Oct. 2, 1859. She was married Jan. 24, 1884 to John Tandy Rice who was born Nov. 10, 1861. They had seven children.

V9-2582.   3. Vina Tennessee Roberts, b. Nov. 6, 1862. She was married Dec. 18, 1879 to William H. Harwell.

V9-2583.   4. Joseph A. Roberts, b. Aug. 19, 1865. He was married July 31, 1884 to Hester Ladd. They resided at Birmingham, AL and had five children.

V9-2584.   5. Manda Isibel Roberts, b. Oct. 18, 1867. She married John Jones and they resided in Morgan County, TN.

V9-2585.   6. Samuel H. Roberts, b. Mar. 8, 1871. He died June 21, 1873.

V9-2586.   7. William Louis Roberts, b. Feb. 16, 1874. He apparently never married and lived at Robertsville, Anderson

County, TN. He died Aug. 10, 1939 and is buried in Robertsville Cemetery.

V9-2587.   8. Scotland L. C. Roberts, b. Aug. 28, 1876. She was married in 1901 to Alfred H. Diggs who was born Mar. 15, 1877. They had three children. Alfred Diggs was in the sawmill and lumber business at Oliver Spring, TN. He died Jan. 29, 1959. Scotland Diggs lived to be 90 years of age and died May 4, 1967 at Oak Ridge, TN. They are buried in the Oliver Springs Cemetery, Oliver Springs, TN.

V9-2588.   9. Walter Roberts, b. May 18, 1880. He was married in 1909 to Bertha Irene Courtney who was born July 26, 1888. They had two children. Walter Roberts died Oct. 14, 1941 and was buried in Robertsville Cemetery, Robertsville, TN.

Robert S. Roberts was a veteran of the Civil War having served in the Union Army in Company "E", 1st Tennesse Infantry. He was a pensioner in later years. In 1880, this family was living in 15th District, Roane County, TN. He lived on a farm in Roane County near the confluence of the Clinch and Emory Rivers until 1890 when he moved to a farm at Robertsville, Anderson County, TN. Louisa Roberts died Jan. 8, 1895. "Samuel" Roberts was married a second time in 1901 to Artelia Sampsell. They had a son born in Anderson County, TN:

V9-2589.   1. James Mitchell Roberts, b. June 21, 1907. He married Nell Pierce. They resided in North Carolina and had two children.

Robert Samuel Roberts died June 9, 1910. He and his first wife are buried in the Kries Cemetery, Sugar Grove Valley, Roane County, TN.

v3-206; **Bazzel Roberts**, son of John Calvin Roberts and Elizabeth Blackwell, was born May 20, 1839 in Roane County, TN. He was married April 3, 1858 in Roane County, TN to Margaret Wester (or Hester) who was born in 1839. They had at least three children born in Roane County, TN:

V9-2590.   1. John Roberts, b. abt. Feb. 1860. He was four months old when the 1860 census was taken. He reportedly married, but his wife deserted him shortly thereafter.

V9-2591.   2. Rebecca Roberts, b. April 12, 1866. "Nellie" was married to Gilbert Bruce Worsham. She died Sept 30, 1912 at San Diego, CA. She and her husband are buried in Stone Hill Cemetery, Dent County, MO.

^{V9}-2592.   3. William L. Roberts, b. abt. 1868. He was living with his cousin, William A. Tallent, in Dent County, MO in 1880.

Bazel Roberts died Feb. 17, 1877 in Dent County, MO. His tombstone in Stone Hill Cemetery, Dent County, lists his age as 38 years, 8 months, 7 days. In May of 1878 his nephew, William C. Tallent noted as administrator of Bazel's estate and had an attorney appointed in Roane County, TN to be agent for an inheritance Bazel was due from his deceased father, John C. Roberts.

^{v3}-207; **Rebecca Elizabeth Roberts**, daughter of John Calvin Roberts and Elizabeth Blackwell, was born Jan. 21, 1841 in Roane County, TN. She was married Oct. 11, 1868 in Roane County, TN to Joseph Brown, an emigrant, and born about 1844 in Saxony. They had one daughter born in Roane County, TN:
^{V9}-2593.   1. Elizabeth Brown, b. abt. 1873.

Curiously, in the 1870 census Rebecca was still listed as Rebecca Roberts and was enumerated in her widowed father's home. Joseph Brown was also living in the home but as a farm laborer and not indicated as Rebecca's husband. Both were living when John C. Roberts' estate was distributed in 1877.
In 1880 Rebecca Brown and her seven year old daughter were living with her aunt, Margaret Roberts, in Roane County, TN.

*****

Robert Terrel Brashear, of Greene Co, AR

^{v3}-**737, V.3, p.127**:
¹⁰-3. **Robert Terrel Brasher**, (s/o Charles Riddle Brasher and Margaret Catherine Wyatt) was born July 3, 1875 in Tennessee, and died October 1920 in Greene Co, AR. He married c1903 in TN, **Annie Elizabeth Chunn**, daughter of John Chunn and Mattie Guinn. She was born September 28, 1886 in Jackson, Madison Co, TN, and died January 2, 1957 in Paragould, Greene Co, AR. Robert Terrel's birth and death dates are from Linwood Cemetery records for Greene Co, on Rootsweb.com. He is said to have died of "stomach troubles," which is now assumed to have been stomach cancer.
In 1910, Annie and husband Robert Brasher are living in St. Francis Township, Greene Co, AR. His age is listed as 32, hers is 24 and their children: Allen is 5, Eva is 2 1/12. Albert Chunn, her brother, age 23, is also living with them.
After Robert Terrel's death, Annie Chunn m.2. Louis Schwamb, and had more children. Her death certificate lists her birth date, September 28, 1886, and she died at age 70. Cause of death is

Coronary Occlusion with Arteriosclerosis. She is buried in Linwood Cem, Paragould, AR. Her husband, Louis Schwamb, is the informant. Data from Bill Boxx, a descendant of Annie Chunn and Louis Schwamb <Twmboxx@aol.com>.

Children of Robert Terrell Brasher and Annie Elizabeth Chunn:

V9-2594. 11-1. ***Robert Allen Brasher, Sr**, b. January 21, 1905, TN; d. September 19, 1987, St. Bernard's Medical Center, Jonesboro, Craighead Co, AR.

V9-2595. 11-2. **Eva Louise Brasher** (d/o Robert Terrel Brasher) was born March 10, 1908 in Jackson, Madison Co, TN, and died December 14, 1994 in Greene Co, AR. She married 1929, Greene Co, AR. *A. Harvey Mclerkin*. He was born August 13, 1894, and died April 30, 1976 in Greene Co, AR. Both buried in Linwood Cemetery, Paragould, AR. Their marriage appears in the marriage records of Greene Co, AR on Rootsweb.com.

V9-2596. 12-1. Carolyn Louise Mclerkin, b. November 10, 1931, Paragould, Greene Co, AR; d. February 18, 2003, Greene Co, AR, bur Linwood Cemetery, Paragould, AR. She married Horace Carmack.

V9-2597. 11-3. **Marguerite Marie Brasher** (d/o Robert Terrel Brasher) was born April 11, 1913 in Greene Co, AR, and died December 11, 1991 in Vicksburg, Mississippi, bur Linwood Cem, Paragould, AR. She married (1) 1934 in Greene Co, AR, *Joe T. Faulkner*. He was born April 15, 1912 in Greene Co, AR. She married (2) 1948, *Walter Cole*. Marguerite owned the Cinderella Cafe in West Plains, MO.

Children of Marguerite Brasher and Joe Faulkner:

V9-2598. 12-1. Kaye Don Faulkner, b. February 08, 1935. Living in Dickson, TN in 1991, per his mother's obituary.

V9-2599. 12-2. Joe E. Faulkner, b. September 28, 1937.

V9-2600. 12-3. Judith Ann Faulkner, b. August 19, 1941. She married James R. Bentley, son of Robert Bentley and Edith Unknown. He was born January 04, 1941.

11-1. **Robert Allen Brasher, Sr,** (s/o Robert Terrel Brasher and Annie Elizabeth Chunn) was born January 21, 1905 in TN, and died September 19, 1987 in St. Bernard's Medical Center, Jonesboro, Craighead Co, AR, bur St. John's Cemetery, Lafe, Greene Co, AR. He married, in 1931, *Ida Hilda Ada Lauchsteadt*, d/o Gustave Lauchsteadt and Mathilda Hundt. She was born August 26, 1902, and died August 24, 1981 in Lafe, Greene Co, AR.

Bill Boxx has a copy of his obituary from 1987 in the Paragould Daily Press. Ida's parents are known from the baptismal records of St. Peter's and St. John's Lutheran Churches on the Greene Co, AR page of Rootsweb.com

Children of Robert Allen Brasher, Sr and Ida Lauchsteadt are: (Sources: Baptismal records of St. Peter's and St. John's Lutheran Churches on the Greene Co, AR page of Rootsweb.com. Marriage records of Greene Co, AR on Rootsweb.com. Thanks to Bill Boxx for the data.)

V9-2601.   12-1. **Robert Allen Brasher, Jr**, b. April 28, 1932, Greene Co, AR; d. November 18, 2000, Paragould, Greene Co, AR, of a heart attack. He married 1951 in Greene Co, AR, *Lucille Tritch*. Death and other information are from his obituary.

V9-2602.   12-2. **Martha Brasher**, b. Abt. 1933. She married 1952 in Greene Co, AR, *William Willis*.

V9-2603.   12-3. **Mary Ida Brasher**, b. December 25, 1935; m. 1955, Greene Co, AR, *Harold G. Dowler*.

V9-2604.   12-4. **Harriette Ellen Brasher**, b. September 02, 1937. She married, 1959, in Greene Co, AR, *Donald R. Lacy*. Donald's name and marriage date is from the marriage records of Greene Co, AR on Rootsweb.com.

V9-2605.   12-5. **Ralph Gustave Brasher**, b. February 26, 1939; m. 1967, Greene Co, AR, *Emma R. Breckenridge*. Emma's name and marriage date are from marriage records of Greene Co, AR on Rootsweb.com.

V9-2606.   12-6. **Mithilda Ann "Tillie" Brasher**, b. January 17, 1941; m. 1956, Greene Co, AR, *John H. Henderson*, 1956, Greene Co, AR.

May be related to John Brashear and Charity Bradley, of Decatur Co, TN:

Elizabeth H. Brashears, m. 2 Nov 1841, in Greene Co, AR (Co seat: Paragould), *John Harmon Wyatt*, Ten children, first 9 b. Green Co, AR.

1. Sarah E. Wyatt, b. 15 Apr 1842
2. Martha A. Wyatt, b. 4 Sep 1844
3. John Wyatt, b. 2 Nov 1847
4. William Wyatt, b. 11 Feb 1849
5. Nancy M. Wyatt, b. 29 Jan 1851
6. Mary Jane Wyatt, b. 9 Apr 1853
7. Tennessee C. Wyatt, b. 8 Aug 1855
8. Sarah M. Wyatt, b. 6 Jan 1857
9. Virginia C. Wyatt, b. 13 May 1861

10. Caroline Wyatt, b. 21 Jan 1872, Washington Co, AR

<u>1850 Census, Greene Co, AR</u>:
Samuel Brashears, b. c1820, AL (30 in 1850), School teacher,
   Susan _____, b. c1825, TN (25 in 1850), cannot read or write
   Mary Brashears, b. c1849, AR (1 in 1850)
Next door: John G. Ishmael,

John R. Brashers, m. *Lucy Elizabeth Kennamore*, possibly from TN; moved to Paragould, AR. Lucy E. Brashers received Confederate Widow's pension #18282, in Greene Co, AR. Her husband, John R. Brashers, had served in Co. D, 3rd Arkansas Cavalry.
   Their children included:
   b-x. **Eveline Brashers**,
   b-x. **Margaret Brashers**,
   b-x. **Obadiah Memery Brashers**, (twin), bur Beech Grove Cem, Paragould, AR
   b-x. **Robert Henry Brashers**, (twin)
      c-y. **Eveline Brashers**,
      c-y. **Margaret Brashers**,
      c-y. **Nathan Brashers**, m. *Bonnie Shipman*
         d-z. **Carolyn Brashers**, m. _____ *Etchison*
         d-z. And 8 others.
Contacts: <Kessins@vfc.com>
<Dolphin19@earthlink.net>
<CBWeinstin@webtv.net>
Carolyn Etchison <EtchisonE@aol.com>
<SHKOALA10@aol.com>

from Carla (Brashers) Weinstein (Walter Brashear and Elizabeth Basham line) The Brashers at Paragould, Nancy Utsinger has been in contact with them. Nancy and Sheila are related to me through Dio Cleshion, a brother Robert W. father of John W. father of John Robert father of Charles Loren which is Nancy and Sheila's father.

b-x. Walter "Watt" Brashears,
   c-x. Robert W. Brashears, brother of Dio Cleshion Brashear
      d-x. John W. Brashears,
         e-x. John Robert Brashears,
            f-x. Charles Loren Brashears,
               g-x. Nancy Brashears, m. _____ Utsinger,
               g-x. Sheila Brashears,

I also just found an e-mail I received from Nancy a while back. It is an obituary:

Doulis W. "Woody" Brashers Sr

Doulis W. " Woody" Brashers, Sr, of Paragould, AR; m. Nellie ____, b. bef 1998; Woody living Paragould, AR, in 1998

   x. **Robert Eugene Brashers**, b. 13 Marcy 1958, "of Paragould", d. 13 Jan 1998, in Dunklin, MO; m. Rose ____, of Paragould

      y. **Deborah Brashers**, of Paragould

      y. **Angela Brashers**; m. ____ Stolz, of Paragould

      y. **April Brashers**; m. ____ Stolz of Paragould

      y. **Tiffany Brashers**; m. ____ Scholesseur, of Huntsville, AL

   x. **Doulis W. Brashers, Jr**, d. bef 1998

   x. **Deborah K. Brashers**, d. bef 1998

   x. **Gary Brashers**, living 1998 in Huntsville, AL

Obituary: Robert Eugene Brashers, 40, of Paragould, AR, died Wednesday Jan 13 1998 in Dunklin Co, MO. He was born March 13, 1958 in Newport News, Va. He was a carpenter. He was preceded in death by his mother, Nellie Brashers, a brother Doulis W. Brashers Jr., and a sister Deborah K. Brashers. Survivors include his wife Rose Brashers of Paragould, 4 daughters Deborah Brashers, Angela Stolz, and April Stolz all of Paragould and Tiffany Scholesseur of Huntsville AL, his father Woody Brashers of Paragould and a brother Gary Brashers of Huntsville AL. A graveside service will be at 10am Saturday at Shiloh Cemetery with Robert Jack officiating. Visitation will be from 6-9 p.m. this evening at the Heath Funeral Home in Paragould.

*****

Error on Sarah Rhea Hankins Brashear

   ERROR regarding Sarah Rhea Hankins Brashear, wife of **v3-15, 8-2.** Robert B. Brashears:

   There is an error in the Robert Brashear/Sarah Rhea Hankins write-up. The data on John Rhea of Giles Co, TN, connected with the Hopkins Lacy estate is ascribed to the wrong Robert Brashear and Sarah Rhea.

   I believe (on scant evidence) that Robert H. Brasher was a brother of Berry Boshears/Brashears, who lived in Lawrence Co, TN, in 1820-26, McNairy Co, TN, in 1830, Tishomingo Co, MS, in 1840, White Co, AR, in 1846-49, Montgomery Co, AR, in 1850, and died after 1860 in Pulaski Co, AR. Both – all? – these families were connected with Giles/Lawrence Co, TN, so when I got a Robert and Sally mentioned in John Rhea's records, I assumed that was proof enough. But (egg on face) there were TWO Robert Brashears and TWO Sallys, who seem to have been associated with TWO John Rheas. Anyway, this John Rhea is NOT "ours." I suggest you strike it out, and if you find any more data, send it to me.

Robert H. Brasher, m. 16 April 1819, (Lawrence Co, AL), *Sally L. Rhea*. Sally Rhea was d/o John Rhea Sr: Loose Records of Madison Co, AL, by Ganrud, vol 4, p.84: estate of John Rhea paid sums to Phillip B. Mason, in right of wife, Nancy; Joseph Nail, in right of wife, Esther; Robert Brashears [in right of wife Sally]; William Rhea's heirs; Margaret Wright's heirs; and John Rhea Jr, all heirs of John Rhea Sr.

On 13 Dec 1834, John Rhea [Jr] made bond in Giles County, TN, regarding the estate settlement of Hopkins Lacy in Madison Co, AL (Loose Bonds, by Ganrud, p.84, no.22). Theophilus Lacy, adm of Hopkins Lacy, dec'd, paid John Rhea, certain sums for Phillip Mason, in right of wife Nancy (Rhea); Joseph Nail, in right of wife Esther (Rhea); Robert Brashears, in right of his wife Sallie Rhea; William Rhea's heirs; Margaret Wright's heirs; and for self (John Rhea); all heirs of John Rhea Sr. (John Rhea Sr probably married a d/o Hopkins Lacy; how else would his children be heirs?)

p.156. Rani Deanne (Clayton) Everett <reverett@centurytel.net> sends these additions and corrections:

Rani; "There was also an old story about William Riley Brashears, Page 154, #983. My grandmother told me that her grandmother told her this story about him. One day he walked out of the house, walked into the woods, and was never seen or heard from him again. They looked for him for years. I just thought that was interesting. Wish we could find out what happened to him."

*****

A different William Riley Brashers:
p.251: The wife of William Riley Brashers (v3-1821) should be Sarah Elizabeth **Jones**, not James. Thanks to grandson Thomas C. Brasher of Saltillo, TN, for the correction.

******

Hobert Brashear

p.285,ff. Vol 3, Update from Donald J. Brashear
<Hanger4B@aol.com>
V9-2607. **Hobert Brashear**, (s/o Carl Brashear and Lucy King);
V9-2608.   x. **Donald J. Brashear**, m. *Donna Rae Pelfrey*
V9-2609.   y. **Joseph Erick Brashear**,
V9-2610.   y. **Joshua Derrick Brashear**,
V9-2611.   y. Johnathan Scott Campbell (stepson)
V9-2612.   z. Dylan Alexander Campbell,
Donald: "I also have a granddaughter, **Amber Mercedes Brashears**."

17. VOL. 4 MISCELLANEOUS

Francis "Frank" Brashear, brother of Dr. John Alfred Brashear

p. 69, #v4-162: A bit of extra data on wives and children of Frank Brashear, brother of Dr. John Alfred Brashear, the Pittsburgh Astronomer:

v4-162:   [9]-5. **Francis "Frank" Brashear**, b. 11 April 1851, d. 9 Oct 1939; m.1. ***"Dolly" Leonard***, d/o _____ Leonard and Elizabeth Wilkison, of Lawrence Co, PA (mother of the children); m.2. c1896 (had been married 4 years in 1900 census), ***Rima*** _____.

v4-163:   [10]-1. **Frank Brashear Jr**, living "northside" Pittsburgh in 1920

            [11]-1. **Eleanor Brashear**, b. c1904 (aged 4 at 89th birthday of Julia (Smith) Brashear) in 1908.

v4-165:   [10]-2. **Irma Brashear**, b. 1883 (per 1900 census), d. in CA

v4-166:   [10]-3. **Elsie Brashear**, b. 1887 (per 1900 census)

******

Family of Joseph Brashear and Harriet Wolf

p. 102, #v4-453: **Ruth M. Brashear**, (d/o Joseph Brashear and Harriet Wolf):

Jane Yohe Lahey, Kenilworth, IL, <Jlahey1134@aol.com> sent information on Ruth M. Brashear, b. 1837 (13 in 1850 and daughter in household of Joseph Brashear and Harriet Wolf, Brownsville, Fayette Co, PA, p. 293, line 18ff, family/dwelling 308; 23 in 1860 and wife of John S. Yohe, of Monongahela, PA).

John S. Yohe served in the Civil War as a blacksmith, and when he was in the hospital, stated that he was a widower, and that his home was Brownsville, PA. I suspect his two children by "Ruth" might have been living with their grandparents or Brashear relatives. The son was named Joseph B. Yohe, possibly after his Brashear grandfather.

Ruth Yohe died 1862/1864. John Yohe was home on furlough 10 August 1862. This could coincide with the birth of Joseph B. Yohe and/or the death of Ruth.

V4-460; [10]-2. **Robert D.L. Brashear**, (s/o Napoleon Reginald Brashear [s/o Joseph Brashear and Harriet Wolf] and Mary Ann Gibson [her surname has been added]) b. 26 Aug 1868, Allegheny Co, PA, d. c190[9]-10; m. 19 July 1894 in Armstrong Co, PA, **Sarah Jane "Sadie" Hill**, b. 1868, Armstrong Co, PA, d. 1932, Allegheny Co, PA, bur Kittanning Cem, Kittanning, PA [her surname is also added: They had children (data from Richard McFerrons : <mcferronsr@wideopenwest.com>). After Robert died, "Sadie" moved the family to Kittanning, PA.

V9-2613.   [11]-1. **Margaret R. Brashear**, b.1896, Tarentum, PA; m. **Howard Rupp,**

V9-2614.   [11]-2. **Joseph E. Brashear**, b.1897, Tarentum, PA; m. **Ethel** _____

V9-2615.   [11]-3. **Laura I. Brashear**, b. 11 July1900, Tarentum, PA; m. **George E. McFerron,**

V9-2616.   [11]-4. **Fay A. Brashear**, b.1906, Tarentum, PA; m. **Albert Claus,**

V9-2617.   [11]-5. **James E. Brashear**, b.1909. Tarentum, PA; m. **Ida** _____ ,

V9-2618.   [12]-x. **James E. Brashear, Jr,**

V9-2619.   [13]-y. **Terence Brashear**, (for data, thanks to <birdnird@yahoo.com>)

****

Otho R. Brashear and Elizabeth Davidson

From V.4, p.117:

v4-549; [9]-8. **Otho R. Brashear**, (s/o Washington Brashear and Rachel Ann Pearth; Washington Brashear was s/o Reginald Brashear and Elizabeth Brown; Reginald Brashear was s/o Otho Brashear and Ruth Brown, of PGCo, MD, and Fayette Co, PA), b. 1837, Redstone, PA (22 in 1860; 44 in 1880), d. 1916; m. 12 March 1862 (per Brodine, *History of Fayette Co*, p.721), **Elizabeth Davidson**, b. 1841 (39 in 1880), Fayette Co, PA (See HSB, p.98), d/o Jacob and Mary Davidson, who were married 2 June 1835. Elizabeth was one of ten children.

In 1869, Otho was assessor of Redstone twp (Brodine, *History of Fayette Co*, p.733). They are dwelling #184 in the 1880 census, Redstone Twp, Fayette Co, PA, with five children. On 25 April 1910, Otho was a widower and lived at 12 Collins Ave, Uniontown, PA, with three of his unmarried daughters.

1880 census, Redstone twp, Fayette Co, PA, taken 19 June 1880, #184

Brashear, Otho	44, head, farmer
Elizabeth	39, wife
William	17, son, farm hand
Jennie	15, dau
Minnie	12, dau

Edgar	10, son
Cassy	2, dau

1910 census, Uniontown, Fayette Co, PA, taken 25 April 1910, #6[12]-214"

Brashear, Otho R.	74, widower
Jennie A.	44, dau, single
Minnie	42, dau, single
Cherrie P.	29, dau, single

Family of Otho R. Brashear and Elizabeth Davidson:

V9-2620. [10-]1. **William Brashear**, b. c1863 (17 in 1880)

V9-2621. [10-]2. **Arnetta Virginia Brashear**, b. c1865 ("Jennie" age 15 in 1880; 44 in 1910), lived Uniontown, PA

V9-2622. [10-]3. **Estella Minnie Brashear**, b. c1868 (12 in 1880; 42 in 1910); lived Uniontown, PA

V9-2623. [10-]4. **Edgar Thorne Brashear**, b. 6 Jan 1870, Redstone twp, Fayette Co, PA; m. 24 Jan 1885, *Margaret Burd*, b. 31 Dec 1871. Edgar was a real estate superintendent for West Pennsylvania Railway Co; he lived in Pittsburgh in 1929 and submitted his family history to Henry Sinclair Brashear; see HSB, p.98-99.

V9-2624. [11-]1. **Donald Everett Brashear**, m. *Katherine Patterson*,

V9-2625. [12-]1. **Patricia Anne Brashear**,

V9-2626. [11-]2. **Edgar Maurice Brashear**, m. *Mary Miller*,

V9-2627. [12-]1. **Mary Jean Brashear**,

V9-2628. [10-]5. **Cherrie Peart Brashear**, b. July 1878 ("Cassy", age 2 in 1880; 29 in 1910); lived Uniontown, PA

Elizabeth Davidson, m. 12 March 1862, Otho R. Brashear; her brother was John H. Davidson, M.D.
(See also vol. 4, Brownsville Colony, family of Reginald Brashear)

JOHN H. DAVIDSON, M.D. Although a young man, Dr. John H. Davidson, of Perryopolis, is one of the prominent physicians of Fayette County. He was born Nov. 15, 1845, in Redstone township, Fayette Co., at the old Brownfield tavern stand, two miles east of Brownsville, on the National pike. His early life was passed upon his father's farm in much the same manner that farmers' boys usually spend their time.

He was educated in the common schools and Dunlap's Creek Academy, and read medicine in the office of Dr. Samuel B. Chalfant, of Upper Middletown, Fayette Co., and attended lectures at and graduated from the Medical Department of the Western Reserve University, of Cleveland, Ohio. He began his course in this college in 1868, and graduated in 1870.

He was married Dec. 26, 1871, to Chilnissae J. Chalfant, daughter of Dr. S. B. and Elizabeth Chalfant. Mrs. Davidson died June 27, 1877. They had one child, Clayton Torrance Davidson, now a bright boy of eight years. The doctor was married again Jan. 10, 1881, to Mary E., the sister of his former wife.

After graduating Dr. Davidson first practiced his profession in company with his preceptor and father-in-law, Dr. Chalfant. He located in Perryopolis in December, 1872. From the beginning his practice there has been large and lucrative. He is recognized as a skillful physician. His judgment is excellent; his knowledge of men and general business acute.

He has held the office of school director in Perry township, and, according to a late county superintendent of schools, was one of the very best directors in Fayette County. His possessions are houses, lands, bank stock, brick-works, book accounts, energy, good health, good sense or brains.

Dr. Davidson is of English stock. His father, Jacob Davidson, was born in Westmoreland County, Pa., and married Hannah Kelley, of the same county. Soon after his marriage he located upon the farm where the doctor was born. He died in 1858. Mr. Davidson's occupation was farming. He was a prominent member of the United Brethren Church, and was noted for his piety, and was a local preacher.

The doctor's grandfather, Jacob Davidson, was born in England. When quite young his father, who was a minister of the gospel, emigrated to America, and located in Philadelphia. Jacob, the doctor's grandfather, married Mary Young, of Franklin County, Pa. They came to Fayette County in 1837, and settled on the Basil Brown tract of land, near Brownsville.

He died April 15, 1856, aged seventy-four years. He was a miller by trade, owned a large amount of land, and was long a director in the Monongahela Bank, of Brownsville.

The doctor's maternal grandfather, Jacob Kelley, was born in England, came to America when young, and settled in Westmoreland County, Pa.

Dr. Davidson's parents, <u>Jacob and Mary Davidson</u>, were married June 2, 1835, and had ten children, nine of whom are living,——
1. Mary Davidson, married to John Rice, Nov. 2, 1855;
2. **Elizabeth Davidson**, m. March 12, 1862, **Otho Brashear**;
3. Kate Davidson, married Jan. 23, 1867, to Benton Bennett;
4. Lou Davidson, married Jan. 3, 1871, to James F. Grable;
5. <u>John H. Davidson</u>, M.D. b. 15 Nov 1845, married Dec. 26, 1871, to Chilnissae J. Chalfant
6. Haddie Davidson, married July 24, 1873, to Jesse Coldren;
7. Anna Davidson, married Nov. 12, 1874, to Luther Noble;

8. Amos W. Davidson, married May 29, 1878, to Maggie Vernon;
9. Ada Davidson, who is single.

History of Fayette County, Pennsylvania : with biographical sketches of many of its pioneers and prominent men. Philadelphia: L.H. Everts & Co., 1882, page 721

****

Lafayette M. Brashears

v.3, p.299. The following is s/o **v3-3237** [10-]1. **Lafayette M. Brashears**, (s/o Ezekiel Brashear: brother to the four who moved to Madison Co, AR) and his first wife, *Joanna Baker*. (See p.299, of Vol 3). Lafayette was briefly in St. Paul, AR, and married as his second wife, *Emily Tennessee Bivens Gentry*, who is buried in the Brashear Cem, St. Paul, AR. Lafayette's obituary identifies a son, William H. Brashears, as living in Danbury, Iowa, in 1938, but he also lived for a time in St. Paul, AR, where he married his wife, Margaret Crawford, in 1902. William H. and Margaret moved to Danbury, Iowa, in 1912, according to her obit.

v3-3245. [11-]3. **William Henry Brashears**, b. 7 Sep 1878, Perry Co, KY, (s/o Lafayette M. Brashears and Joanna Baker), living Danbury, Iowa, in 1934 and 1938; m. 15 Apr 1902, at St. Paul, AR, *Margaret Crawford*, b. 17 Mar 1884, St Paul, AR, d. 4 Nov 1934, Danbury, IA, d/o George Crawford and Nancy Green. Family based on obituary of Mrs. William Brashears, below.

[V9-]2629. [12-]1. **Acie Brashears** (dau), living 1934, Danbury, IA
[V9-]2630.   [13-]x. Dorothy F. Mott, d. 1995; m. _____ Dean
[V9-]2631.   [14-]x. Dana Dean
[V9-]2632.   [14-]y. Michelle Dean
[V9-]2633. [12-]2. dau **Brashears**, m. *Fred Rickert* , living 1934, Danbury, IA
[V9-]2634.   [13-]1. Freddie Rickert , living 1934, Danbury, IA
[V9-]2635.   [13-]2. Nancy Ann Rickert , living 1934, Danbury, IA
[V9-]2636. [12-]3. dau **Brashears**, m. *Bernie Wessling*, of Danbury, IA
[V9-]2637.   [13-]1. Bernajean Wessling , living 1934, Danbury, IA
[V9-]2638. [12-]4. dau **Brashears**, m. *Al Wolterman*, of Sioux City, IA
[V9-]2639.   [13-]1. Billy Wolterman
[V9-]2640. [12-]5. **Percy Brashears**, living 1934, Danbury, IA
[V9-]2641. [12-]6. **Kirby Brashears**, living 1934, Danbury, IA, apparently named for Kirby W. Brashears (v3-3259), a brother of William H. Brashears,

OBIT: November 4, 1934 - Danbury, Iowa

Mrs. William Brashears is Taken by Death   (Former St. Paul resident)

The community deeply regrets the death of Mrs. Wm. Brashears, 50 who passed away in her home here Sunday evening about six o'clock just at the close of a beautiful day. The end came following an illness of four years during which she had suffered much at home and at the hospital.

Funeral services for Mrs. Brashears were held Wednesday afternoon at 2:30 o'clock at the Danbury Methodist church with the pastor, Rev. W.C. Bergman officiating. Special singing was furnished by a quartet composed of Arthur Tatman, Mrs. Fred Schrunk, Dr. W.H. Richards and Miss Reba Richards. Miss Dorothy Durst was the accompanist. Burial was made in the Danbury cemetery under the direction of the Fitzpatrick Service. Both the church and graveside services were well attended by relatives and friends of the family. The pallbearers were Joe Granter, L.D. Smith, Robert F. Driscoll, M.G. Keitges, Henry Osterholtz and Frank Palmer.

Margaret Crawford Brashear, daughter of Mr. and Mrs. George Crawford, was born March 17, 1884 at St. Paul, Arkansas, and died at her home in Danbury, Iowa, at 6pm November 4, 1934. She had attained the age of 50 years, 8 months and 17 days. She was reared to young womanhood at St. Paul and received her education in the public schools of that city. She was united in marriage to William H. Brashears, April 15, 1902 at St. Paul, Arkansas, and the happy couple lived there until 1912 when they came to Danbury where Mrs. Brashears resided up to the time of her death.

The marriage of Mr. and Mrs. Brashears was blessed with six children all of whom with the husband survive her. They are, four daughters, Miss Acie Brashears, Mrs. Fred Rickert, and Mrs Bernie Wessling of Danbury, and Mrs. Al Wolterman of Sioux City, and two sons, Percy Brashears and Kirby Brashears at home. Surviving are also five sisters, three brothers and four grandchildren, who are Freddie and Nancy Ann Rickert, Bernajean Wessling and Billy Wolterman.

Mrs. Brashears had been in poor health for the past four years and through all of this time spent at home and at the hospital, she displayed much patience and fortitude and death alone had the power to relieve her suffering, despite the fact loving hands and medical skill did everything possible to bring her back to her loved ones and friends. Mrs. Brashears was a member of the Methodist church and in health had been a worker for the church. She was a good wife and mother, and many were the friends she made during her life's journey. She is sadly missed in the home and in the community.

William Henry Brashears passed away in Ida Grove, Iowa, in 1957.

Capt Samuel Ray Brashear
p.319:

v3-3600. [9]-9. **(Captain) Samuel Ray Brashear**, (Back #483; s/o Robert S. "Old Bob" Brashear (v3-25) and Mary Everidge, gs/o Capt Samuel Brashear), b. 1841; served as Lieutenant and Captain in 13th-Regiment, Kentucky Cavalry (Confederate) during the Civil War; m. *Mary Ann Hogg*. He had at least two sons who moved to Arkansas and then to Texas; ref: Kay Boyd <Mkdb1405@aol.com>

[V9]-2642.   [10]-1. **Thomas Benton Brashear**, b. c1865, d. 7 May 1935, Sierra Blanca, Hudspeth Co, TX; m. 1 Jan 1885, *Emma Dawson*, b. 31 Jan 1867, d. 17 March 1942, Sierra Blanca, Hudspeth Co, TX

[V9]-2643.   [11]-x. **William C. "Bill" Brashears**, b. 1888, TX, lived Sierra Blanca, TX; m.1. _____ (3 ch); m.2. *Jenny*

[V9]-2644.   [12]-1. **Ruth Brashears**, b. 1909, AZ; m. *Joe H. Thomas*, b. 1904, TX

[V9]-2645.   [13]-1. Bill Thomas,

[V9]-2646.   [12]-2. **Stella Brashears**, b. 1917

[V9]-2647.   [12]-3. **Christina Brashears**, b. 1920; m. _____ *Prine*

[V9]-2648.   [11]-x. **Cosma Brashears**, b. aft 1900

[V9]-2649.   [11]-x. son

[V9]-2650.   [10]-2. **William Silas (W.S.) "Red Will" Brashear**, b. 31 Dec 1867, KY, d. 1 Dec 1933, Golden, CO; m. c1900, in St. Paul, AR, *Ella Katherine Crawford*, b. 27 March 1882, St. Paul, AR, d. 15 Nov 1954, San Antonio, TX, d/o George Crawford and Nancy Green. W.S. Brashears lived in St. Paul, AR, from about 1900 til at least 1917.

[V9]-2651.   [11]-1. **Fannie Ray Brashears**, b. c1901. No one seems to know whatever happened to Fannie. She was the "wild" one and moved to Alaska and married several times. Didn't keep up with her mother or brother.

[V9]-2652.   [11]-2. **Benton Brashears**, b. 14 Mar 1910, St. Paul, AR, d. Fayetteville, AR, 2 May 1929, age 19, bur Brashears Cem, St. Paul. obit: Benton Brashears died in hospital after skull injury from cranking car; bur Combs Cem, near Combs, AR, unmarked grave. Father identified as W.S. Brashear. The Combs Cemetery is also known as the Brashear Cemetery. It is about 300 yards west of Brashear Junction.

[V9]-2653.   [11]-3. **William Silas "Bill" Brashears, Jr**, b. 4 Mar 1917, St. Paul, AR; m. 26 March 1938, in Truth or Consequences, NM, *Rowena Deborah Elizabeth*

	Stromberg, d. 11 Oct 2002, d/o Hjalmar Stromberg and Ester Sponberg.
V9-2654.	¹²⁻1. **William Hjalmar Brashears**, b. 13 Oct 1940, El Paso, TX; m. 8 Jan 1963, in Dallas, TX, *Nancy Annette Cawthon*
V9-2655.	¹³⁻1. **William Brent Brashears**, b. 2 April 1965, Ft Polk, LA; m. 12 June 1993, in Midlothian, TX, *Julie Ann Ball Melton* (div 2002)
V9-2656.	¹⁴⁻1. **Bostyn Logan Brashears**, b. 20 June 1994
V9-2657.	¹⁴⁻2. **Britysh Brashears**, b. 17 June 1996
V9-2658.	¹³⁻2. **William Brannon Brashears**, b. 29 Oct 1969, Arlington, TX; m. 28 March 1996, in Brazos, TX, *Carrie Ann Turner*
V9-2659.	¹⁴⁻1. **William Joey Brashears**, b. 7 Dec 1900
V9-2660.	¹⁴⁻2. **Joshua Brashears**, b. 25 Feb 1998
V9-2661.	¹⁴⁻3. **Jeremey Brashears,** b. 25 Feb 1998
V9-2662.	¹²⁻2. **Gerald Benton Brashears**, b. 14 Jan 1943, San Antonio, TX; m.1. 25 April 1964, in Tivoli, TX, *Mary Ann Payne* (3 ch); m.2. 4 Jan 1989, in Houston, TX, *Robyn Ann Rhodes* (1 adopted ch)
V9-2663.	¹³⁻1. **Jeremy Benton Brashears**, b. 5 Dec 1969, Corpus Christi, TX, d. 5 Deb 1969, bur Roselawn Cem
V9-2664.	¹³⁻2. **Gerald Craig Brashears**, b. 1 March 1971, San Antonio, TX; m. June 1997, in Georgia, *Laurel Otsberg*
V9-2665.	¹⁴⁻1. **Linnea Marie Brashears**, b. 20 June 2002
V9-2666.	¹³⁻3. **Anissa Nicole Brashears**, b. 4 May 1973, San Antonio, TX; m. 6 June 1998, in San Antonio, TX, *Roger Maris Barton* (div 2002)
V9-2667.	¹³⁻4. **Heather Renee Brashears**, b. 2 April 1983 (adopted child)

******

Jent/Combs Family Additions

p.370-71: V3-4755. ¹¹⁻8. Callie Jent, (Back#1123), b. 2 Dec 1900 (or 1901), d. 11 (or 20) Aug 1945, of TB and cervical cancer; m.1. 2 Oct 1917, in Sassafras, Knotts Co, KY, Lindsey Combs, b. Aug 1898, Knotts Co, KY, s/o Billy Combs and Martha Young; m.2. Robert Alvin Feltner Sr, b. 2 May 1895, Perry Co, KY, d. 24 May 1982, Pontiac, MI. Robert Alvin Feltner Sr. had 5 wives and we are still researching the children born—m.1. 22 May 1916, Mayoma Fugate (she was 18); m.2.

11 Jan 1917, Malinda Combs, (ch: Jelias R. B. 11 April 1922); m.3. 18 July 1923, Nannie Minton; m.4. Callie Jent (see below for children); m.5. c1945 (soon after Callie died), Margaret Bach. Robert also had 2 more boys by one of his wives: Wallace and Roy. Roy, m. Glenda _____; he died at age 20 of lung cancer from working in the coal mines. (Contact Rita Feltner <Rfel34@aol.com>) 119 Del Rio Road, Carpentersville, Il. 60110)

Family of Callie Jent and Lindsey Combs:
V9-2668.　　12-1. Watson W. Combs, b. 10 Oct 1919
V9-2669.　　12-2. James Alvery Combs, b. 26 May 1921 (or 1922), Perry Co, Ky.
V9-2670.　　12-3. Flora Combs, b. 25 Sep 1925, Perry Co, Ky.
Family of Callie Jent and Robert Alvin Feltner Sr:
V9-2671.　　12-4. Marcus W. Feltner, b. December 27, 1928, Perry Co, KY
V9-2672.　　12-5. Royal Francis Feltner, b. January 14, 1932, Perry Co, KY
V9-2673.　　12-6. Fred Lonadean Feltner, b. August 21, 1933, Perry Co, KY
V9-2674.　　12-7. Baxter J. Feltner, b. August 25, 1935, Perry Co, KY.
V9-2675.　　12-8. Robert Alvin Feltner Jr, b. November 17, 1937, Perry Co, KY ("the youngest"); m.1. _____; m.2. _____; m.3. 28 Sep 1963, Rita A. _____, who had been married twice previously and has daughters, Barbara Ann _____, b. c1954; Donna Louise _____, b. c 1957; and Verna Marie, b. c1060. Robert Feltner Jr and Rita have one son:
V9-2676.　　13-1. Roy Allen Feltner, b. 1964, (says Rita: "I did not have the heart to name him Alvin. It sounded too much like a Chipmunk that use to be popular way back when"); m.1. c1988, Glenda Thingvold; m.2. 4 Sep 1998, Virgene "Kay" Wright, no ch
V9-2677.　　12-9. Cleda Mae Feltner, b. September 12, 1939, Perry Co, KY
V9-2678.　　12-10-11. Twins Allie & Malley were stillborn

*****

Katie Lee Brashear

My grandmother was **Katie Lee Brashear**, born 1885 in Kentucky. She married Roy Everett Tabb in Hardin County Kentucky, she had 7 children. My father Roy Eldred Tabb was her first born. Katie was the daughter of James Clark Brashear and Leona Upton. Leona died two weeks after Katie was born and her father remarried his housekeeper to have help with his baby Katie. James Clark Brashear died in Elizabethtown Ky. If you need more, dates and etc email me.

sincerely
Jean Tabb Akers <jtakers@earthlink.net>

V9-2679. James Clark Brashear, b. _____, d. _____, Elizabethtown, KY; m. *Leona Upton*, b. _____, d. c1885. Leona died two weeks after Katie was born and James Clark Brashear married his housekeeper to have help with his baby.

V9-2680.   **Katie Lee Brashear**, b. 1885, KY; m. *Roy Everett Tabb*
V9-2681.   1. Roy Eldred Tabb, oldest of seven children
V9-2682.   Jean Tabb; m. _____ Akers

*****

Everett R. Brashear

Vol. 3, p.429
Hello Cousin Charles,

I am Verna Taulbee Smith. Grace Brashear was my Mother. She was the only child of **Everett R. Brashear** and Corzillia York. Everett was killed when my Mother was 3yrs old.

You mentioned that you have my family through 4 children of Grace and Archie Taulbee. You may want to update that info with a fifth child, born Nov 29, 1962, named Dwight David Taulbee.

Grace (Brashear) Taulbee, Verna's Mother, had a massive coronary on Nov. 14 1987 and passed away that day in Cincinnati at Christ Hospital. She was 66yrs. old. Verna's Father passed away on Nov. 13, 1993 from prostate cancer at the age of 83.

Brother, Granvel P. Taulbee was killed in a trucking accident on Sept. 18, 1994 at the age of 42.

Corzillia York Brashear Stacy passed away on June 18, 2000 at the age of 97yrs from natural causes at Windsor Care Nursing Home, Mt. Sterling, Ky.

*****

LaRue Co, KY, Brashears Families

p.179: Martha Lynn Brashear Julian, 952 Frontier Drive, Henderson, KY 42420, sent the following update on:

V9-2683.   ax. **Filip N. Brashears** ("F.N." on gravestone), b. 1840, Larue Co, KY, d. 22 Feb 1914, Larue Co, KY; m. 16 June 1867, in Larue C, KY, *Paralee Brite Upton*, b. 1847, Hardin Co, KY, d. 24 Nov 1928, Larue Co, KY, d/o

George Washington Upton (1820–1891) and Elizabeth Flanders (18174–1899).

Many of the family are buried at Big Spring Cem (also called Upton Fam. Cem.) on Upton-Sonora Road:

F. N. Brashear, b. 1840, d. 1914

Paralee Brashear, wife of F. N., b. 1847, d. 1928 (née Upton)
Clarence Brashear, s/o F. N. and Paralee, b. 26 April 1870, d. 2 March 1875
Adda Brashear, d/o F.N. & P., b. 25 Jan 1872, d. 23 Dec 1878
Clara Brashear, d/o F.N. & P. b. 11 Aug 1873, d. 31 Dec 1873
Ruby Brashear, d/o F.N. & Paralee, b. 3 June 1885, d. 28 Sep 1886
Lawrence Brashear, b. 28 Dec 1874, d. 18 March 1951
Sarah E. Brashear, wife of Lawrence, b. 13 Oct 1896, d. 17 Aug 1966
R.U. Brashear, 1883- 1906
Earl "Shack" Brashear, b. 18 March 1919, d. 12 Oct 1976

Family of Filip N. Brashear and Paralee Brite Upton:

V9-2684.   b-1. **Clarence Brashear**, b. 26 April 1870, d. as child, 2 March 1875

V9-2685.   b-2. **Adda Brashear**, b. 25 Jan 1872, d. as child, 23 Dec 1878

V9-2686.   b-3. **Clara Brashear**, b. 11 Aug 1873, d. as child, 31 Dec 1873

V9-2687.   b-4. **Lawrence "Jake" Brashear**, b. 28 Dec 1874, Hardin or Larue Co, KY, d. 18 March 1951, Larue Co, KY; m.1. *Ethel Newman*; m.2. 15 Feb 1918, *Sarah "Sally" Ellen Payton*, b. 13 Oct 1896, d. 17 Aug 1966, d/o William R. Payton (1857–   ) and Josephine Skaggs (1862–   ).

V9-2688.   c-1. **Russell Clifford Brashear**, b. 20 Dec 1917, Glendale, Hardin Co, KY, d. 21 Dec 1994, Henderson Co, KY; m. 13 July 1939, *Elizabeth Raymer*

V9-2689.   d-x. **Otto Brashear**, son by first wife

V9-2690.   d-x. **Martha Lynn Brashear**; m. _____ Julian

V9-2691.   c-2. **Earl Shacklette "Shack" Brashear**, b. 18 March 1919, Glendale, Harding Co, KY, d. 12 Oct 1976, Warren Co, KY

V9-2692.   c-3. ?**Elizabeth Betty Jane Brashear,** b. ?1932

V9-2693.   b-5. **Ruby Brashear**, b. 12 July 1885, d. as child, 23 Sept 1886

V9-2694.   b-6. **Jesse Brashear**,

V9-2695.   b-7. **Daisy Brashear**, m. Leslie Fletcher

V9-2696. b-8. **Grover Elroy Brashear**; m. Maude Shoat, b. Bonnievill, 6 mi from Upton in Hart Co. They lived in Bloomington, IN. Four daughters and]

V9-2697. c-x. **Grover Elroy Brashear Jr**,

V9-2698. b-9. **Robert Brashear**, killed a young man, Grover Weldon, in argument over a girl.

V9-2699. b-10. **Emma Brashear**, m. William Larkin

V9-2700. b-11. **Agnes Brashear**, m. Harry Fletcher (had three daughters)

V9-2701. b-12. **Minnie Brashear**, m. John Van Nart

V9-2702. b-13. **Ora Brashear**, m. James "Jim" Bradley (1 dau)

****

Some of the West Point, KY, connection: (see **Vol 4, p.332**)
The Davis News, Davis, Murray County, Oklahoma

Thursday, February 7, 1924, Vol. XXX, Number 19
Death of W. J. BRASHEARS

W. J. BRASHEARS passed away at his home six miles northwest of Davis last Saturday, Feb. 2, 1924 at 9:30 a.m. after a long lingering illness. He had the flu in 1918, the disease settled in his lungs, and he was never able to overcome it.

Mr. Brashears was one of our best and most successful farmers. He was born at West Point, Tennessee April 25, 1873, and would have been 51 years of age next April.

At the age of 15, he moved to this country and spent the remainder of his life here. He lived on his home place past 18 years.

He was twice married-first to Miss **Katherine Williams**, and of their five children, two sons and two daughters survive: Douglas V. Brashears of this community and Earl Brashears of Shawnee, Mrs. Banner Broom and Miss May Brashears.

His second marriage was to Miss **Victoria Broom**, and of their two children, one survives, Miss Ora Brashears. A sister, Mrs. Banner Baxter, lives at Lexington and a brother, Lonzo Brashears, lives at Old McGee.

A striking co-incidence is that his brother's 15 year old son died last Saturday morning.

The deceased was a good citizen, well liked, and had a large circle of friends. He had been a member of the Woodmen of the World about 10 years.

Burial was in Green Hill Cemetery at Davis last Sunday at 3:00. Funeral services were conducted by Rev. A. E. Watford, Methodist pastor.

W.J. Brashears was possibly an unknown son of Lenzy Brashear and Martha "Patsy" Stovall, of West Point, KY. See Vol 4, page 332.

V9-2703.　　**W.J. Brashears**, b. 25 April 1873, West Point, KY, d. 2 Feb 1924, Davis, Murray Co, OK; moved c1888 at age 15 to Davis, Murray Co, OK; m.1. in OK, *Katherine Williams* (5 ch); m.2. *Victoria Broom* (2 ch).

V9-2704.　　1. **Douglas V. Brashears**, lived 1924 in Davis, Murray Co, OK

V9-2705.　　2. **Earl Brashears**, of Shawnee, OK (1924)

V9-2706.　　3. **Victoria Brashears**, m. _____ Broom; living in 1924

V9-2707.　　4. **May Brashears**, living in 1924

V9-2708.　　5. unk Brashears, deceased before 1924

Children of the second marriage:

V9-2709.　　6. **Ora Brashears**, living in 1924

V9-2710.　　7. unk Brashears, deceased before 1924.

W.J. Brashears was apparently married a couple more times, if we can believe the tombstones in

Green Hill Cemetery, Murray Co., OK

Brashears, W.J., b. April 26, 1874, d. Feb 2, 1924
Brashears, Melinda C., b. Dec 29, 1874, d. Dec 21, 1910, w/o W.J.
Brashears, Lula V., b. Dec 17, 1882, d. Dec 7, 1918, w/o W.J.

Others in the same cemetery may be descendants or relatives:

Brashears, Roy, b. Feb 2, 1902, d. Mar 17, 1989, m. Nov 9, 1929
Brashears, Iva, b. Feb 1, 1909, d. ????, w/o Roy

Brashears, Ollie Gertrude, b. Dec 1, 1897, d. Nov 2, 1938
Brashears, Lillie C., b. Feb 10, 1900, d. Oct 9, 1900, "d/o Lonzo & Nancy"
Brashears, Iva, b. Feb 1, 1909, d. Apr 30, 1988
Brashears, Gayland B., b. Nov 17, 1934, d. Apr 15, 1994, USA, Korea

*****

Descendants of Ignatius Brashear Jr

Vol 4, pp. 381; Ed Mielock has sent data on descendants for Ignatius Brashear Jr:

Robert H. Brashear. 1836-bef1900; m. *Mary E. Unseld*, 1839-aft 1900
Benjamin H. Brashear, 1863-1914; m. *Mary E. Guthrie*, 1872-1966
Julius Guthrie Brashear, Sr, m. *Beulah Waller*,
Julius Guthrie Brashear, Jr, b. 6 June 1900, West Point, KY, d. 26 Feb 1963, Phoenix, AZ; m. 7 May 1929, in Hartford, KY, *Alma*

Florence Marshall, b. 4 Sept 1900, Fordsville, KY, d. 24 Dec 1985, Phoenix, AZ

Jay Brashear, b. 22 May 1932, Evansville, IN, d. 15 Sept 2007, Gunnison, CO; m. 2 May 1959, in Phoenix, AZ, *Anne Marie Meilock*, b. 1 Sept 1929, Detroit, MI, d. 19 May 2005, Scottsdale, AZ. They have two children:

1. **Jay Michael Brashear**, b. 14 Aug 1960, Scottsdale, AZ; m. 22 April 1994, in Scottsdale, AZ, *Anne Marie Arthur*, b. 6 Feb 1968. They have two sons: **Jonathan Marshall Brashear**, b. 19 Feb 2002, Scottsdale, AZ, and **Joel Brashear**, b. 31 Dec 2003, Scottsdale, AZ

2. **Jolie Ann Brashear**, b. 9 May 1963, Scottsdale, AZ; m. 12 Oct 1996, in Denver, CO, *Thomas Edward Judkins Hazard*. They have a daughter: Olivia Kensington Hazard, b. 20 Feb 1999, Denver, CO

****

Philip Boyer Brashear
and Queen "Tiny" Adams

v.4 p.530: additions to [V4]-4433. Phillip Boyer Brashears:

Philip Boyer Brashears, (s/o Marsham Brashear of Warwick Co, IN, and his wife, Mary Elizabeth Jones) b. May, 1846, IN, says 1900 census of Calhoun Co, AR, parents b. TN; m. 19 Oct 1865, in Hopkins Co, KY, *Queen T. "Tiny" Adams* (per *Marriage Index: Kentucky, 1851-1900*, sent by Terry _____ <gentek@webtv.net>). P.B. Brashears bur Bethel Cem, near Bearden, Ouachita Co, AR; no dates: only inscription: "Co. E, 55 Inf. Indiana". We can reconstruct three children from censuses 1900 to 1920; a look at the 1880 census might fill in some of the others.

[V4]-4434.   [9]-1. **Ida Virginia Brashear**, b. c1868, IN

[V4]-4435.   [9]-2. **John C. Brashears**, b. Jan 1870, IN; m. *Mary Lucinda "Synda" Cathey*, b. May 1876 (per 1900, Calhoun Co, AR), d/o Samuel Newton Cathey and Susan Ann Gibson. Before 1910 census, John and Mary Lucinda moved to Grant Co, AR, where John died July 1915 and is buried in Leola Cemetery. Mary Lucinda d. 8 Jan 1938; also bur Leola Cem.

[V9]-2711.   [10]-1. **Bertha Brashears**, b. Oct 1894, (per 1900, Calhoun Co, AR); m. Clarence Edwards

[V9]-2712.   [10]-2. **Queen A. Brashears**, b. Jan 1897, (per 1900, Calhoun Co, AR)

[V9]-2713.   [10]-3. **Orenia Brashears**, b. Jun 1898 (per 1900, Calhoun Co, AR; 19 in 1920); m. *Bill Simpson*, s/o Robert Simpson & Mary Ann Martin Cathey

V9-2714.   10-4. **Dollie Brashears**, b. c1905 (15 in 1920, dau)
V9-2715.   10-5. **Herbert Brashears**, c1910 (10 in 1920)
V9-2716.   10-6. **Susie Brashears**, b. c19$^{12\text{-}}$14, not in 1920 census, d. 1918, influenza
V9-2717.   10-7. **Alphons Brashears**, b. c1914 (6 in 1920); never married
V9-2718.   9-3. **Annie Elizabeth Brashears**, b. July 1881, AR, (per 1900, Calhoun Co, AR), d. 19 April 1938; m. 28 Feb 1897, Calhoun Co, AR, *William Penn Clemons*, b. Aug 1872 (per 1900, Calhoun Co, AR)
V9-2719.   10-1. Katie Clemons, b. Mar 1898 (per 1900, Calhoun Co, AR; 12 in 1910; 22 in 1920); m. Louis Brown
V9-2720.   10-2. Nellie R. Clemons, b. Sep 1899 (per 1900 Calhoun Co, AR; 10 in 1910); m. Claud Steelman
V9-2721.   10-3. Bessie Clemons, b. c1902 (8 in 1910; 19 in 1920); m. Edgar Lee
V9-2722.   10-4. Mary Clemons, b. c1904 (6 in 1910; 16 in 1920); m. Marvin Gregory
V9-2723.   10-5. David Clemons, b. c1906 (4 in 1910; 14 in 1920); m. Velor Mosley, sister of Bessie Mae Mosley
V9-2724.   10-6. James "Jimmie" Clemons, b. c1908 (2 in 1910; 11 in 1920); m. Bessie Mae Mosley, sister of Velor Mosley
V9-2725.   10-7. Rachel "Dollie" Clemons, b. c1910 (4/12 in 1910; 10 in 1920); m. Bruce Quarles (Qualls)
V9-2726.   10-8. Harvey Clemons, b. c1912 (8 in 1920); m. Floy McGuire
V9-2727.   10-9. Florence Clemons, b. c1915 (5 in 1920); m. _____ Pennington
V9-2728.   10-10. Clary Clemons, b. c1919 (1 7/12 in 1920), son
V9-2729.   10-11. Samuel Clemons,   c1920 (3/12 in 1920, son); m. Clyde McGuire, sister of above
V9-2730.   10-12. Margie Clemons, b. after 1920; m. _____ Davis, Assoc of God Min.
V9-2731.   9-4. **Effie B. Brashears**, b. May 1883, AR (per 1900, Calhoun Co, AR)

From Dorothy H. Cathey, Calion AR 71724 (Anna Locke's sister):

1900 census, Calhoun Co, AR, Caswell twp, June 1:

25-249 P.B. Breshears	b. May 1856, widower, IN TN TN
Effie B.	b. May 1883, dau,AR IN TN
245-250 John Brashears	b. Jan 1874, headAR AR KY
Synda (Cathey)	b. May 1876, wife AR AR AR
Bertha	b. Oct 1894, dau AR AR AR;
	m. Clarence Edwards

```
        Queen A.            b. Jan 1897, dau      AR AR AR
        Orena              b. Jun 1898, dau      AR AR AR
1900 Census, Calhoun Co, AR, Locust Bayou twp
58-68   William P. Clemens  b. Aug 1872, head     AR AR MS
        Annie F. (Brashears) b. Jul 1881, wife     AR IN KY
        Katie B.            b. Mar 1898, dau      AR AR AR
        Nella R.            b. Sep 1899, dau      AR AR AR


1910 census, Calhoun Co, AR, Caswell twp:
145-157 William P. Clemens  36, m. 14 yrs         AR AR AR
        Annie              28, m. 14 yrs ch 7/7   AR KY IN
        Katie              12, dau
        Nellie             10, dau
        Bessie             8, dau
        Mary               6, dau
        David              4, son
        James              2, son
        Rachel             4/12, dau


1920 census, Calhoun Co, AR, Caswell twp, Jan 12
#185-194 William P. Clemens  47, head
        Annie              41, wife
        Katie              22, dau
        Bessie             19, dau
        Mary               16, dau
        Dave               14, son
        Jimmie             11, son
        Dollie             10, dau
        Harvey             8, son
        Florence           5, dau
        Clary              1 7/12, son
        Samuel             3/12, son
#186-195 Sindie Brashears  43, widow            AR TN KY
        Orenia             19, dau;
        Dollie             15, dau
        Herbert            10, son
        Susie              not in 1920 census, d. 1918, influenza
        Alphons            6, son    never married
```

Synda/Sindie is Mary Lucinda Cathey, d/o Samuel Newton Cathey and Susan Ann Gibson. Before 1910 census, John Brashears and Mary Lucinda moved to Grant Co, AR, where John died July 1915 and is buried in Leola Cemetery. Mary Lucinda d. 8 Jan 1938; also bur Leola Cem.

****

Lieutenant Absalom J. Brashears, of Hickman Co, KY

An SBC-Yahoo map shows Hickman is a Mississippi River Town, in Hickman Co, at the extreme western end of Kentucky. It is a short distance north of the TN/KY border and only a few miles upstream from Madrid Bend.

Absalom J. Brashears, b. c1833 (listed in a military record as age 30 in 1863), enlisted 4 Dec 1861, in Co. H, 31st Reg't, Tennessee Infantry, Confederate States Army, commanded by Col. A. H. Bradford, for a period of 1 year, at Columbus, [Hickman County] Kentucky.

His service records indicate that he repeatedly got wounded or lost in battles, but kept doggedly coming back for more, even after he was counted as a deserter several times.

On the back of slip #50019042 of his service records in the National Archives, covering the period 26 Sep 1861 to Jan 1, 1862, is the note "to the hospital but drop as a deserter according to Genl orders."

Promoted from Private to 3rd Lieutenant, 8 May 1862, and his name appears on the muster rolls through Dec 31, 1862.

An undated muster lists 2nd Lt. A.J. Brasher as a deserter as of Jan 1, 1863, and no successor appointed.

A muster dated 12 May 1863, "near Shelbyville, Tenn", lists 2nd Lt. A. J. Brashers, age 30. Under remarks: "deserted from Shelbyville."

On 26 Sep 1864, J. L. Brashers signed the receipt roll, for having been issued clothing.

An undated return lists Lt. A.J. Brasher, Co. H., 31 Regt Tenn Vols, as one of the men in 2d Brigade, 1st Division, 1st Corps, "who have been absent for seven days or more without leave or explanation."

The 31st Regiment, Tennessee Infantry, was organized Oct 12, 1862, and re-organized May 8, 1862(63?). It was temporarily consolidated with the 33rd Regt until May 6, 1863. On 9 Mar 1864, its companies were attached to various regiments, Army of Tennessee, but each company kept its own muster and original designation. About 9 Apr 1865, the 4th, 5th, 19th, 24th, 31st, 33rd, 35th, 38th, and 41st Regiments were assigned to the 3rd Consolidated Regiment, Tennessee Infantry, which was paroled at Greensboro, NC, May 1, 1865.

These may be relatives:
Children of James Brashears and Eliza Hinsley (or Stone) (from births recorded in Hickman Co, KY; thanks to Bill Utterback <billco@ARN.NET> for the data)

---

1. **Eliza Brashears**, b. 18 Nov 1856 at Cane Creek, Hickman Co, KY, dau of James Brashers[sic] & Eliza Hinsley
2. **Amanda M. Brashears**, b. 21 Dec 1857 at Cane Creek, Hickman Co, KY, dau of James Brashears & Eliza Hencely [sic]
3. **Sarah Burton Brashears**, b. -- May 1860 in Hickman Co, KY, dau of James Brashears & Eliza Stone
4. **Adaline Brahear** [Brashears], b. 31 Oct 1861 in Hickman Co, KY, dau of James Brasher & Eliza Stone

18. VOL. 5 MISCELLANEOUS

Enoch Brashear and Luclihoma Moore

Re: **Vol 5, pp. 556-560:**

Choctaw enrollment cards containing additional information have been sent by Charles A. Greene, P.O.Box 3170, Bakersfield, CA 93305, for which many thanks.

These data modify the
Family of Enoch Brashear and Luclihoma (a.k.a. Louisa Moore):

V9-2732. 10-1. **Alfred (or Albert) Brashears**, ½ Choctaw, b. 1852, Skullyville, Leflore Co, I.T., d. c1891; m. 5 March 1885, at Savanna, I.T., **Martha Helen Grissom**, b. 1861, d. 10 Dec 1929, Coalgate, OK, d/o William Grissom and Mary Grissom, both non-citizens. (See vol. 5 for further data). Albert and Martha had one child:

V9-2733. 11-1. **Ira Brashears**, b. 27 Jan 1896, Sandridge, OK, d. 25 June 1953, Los Angeles, CA; m.1. 17 July 1916, in Coalgate, OK, **Viola "Belle" Maybelle Purdy**, b. 6 April 1881, Dallas Co, AR, d. 5 March 1939, Coalgate, OK (mother of the child); m.2. 1939, in Atoka, OK, **Nan (Carlisle) Faulconer**; m.3. 7 Aug 1941, Yuma, AZ, **Pearl Kelso**

V9-2734. 12-1. **Dorothy Marie Brashears**, b. 28 Nov 1921, McAlester, OK, d. 16 March 1991, Salinas, CA; m.1. 12 Nov 1940, in Reno, NV, **Virgil Kenneth Harmon**, b. 1 Aug 1918, Sallisaw, OK, d. 27 Jan 1967, Fresno, CA; m.2. 28 April 1967, in Reno, NV, **Raymond Earl Hicks**, b. 1 May 1928, Sayre, OK,

V9-2735.   13-1. Larry Ronald Harmon, b. 1942, CA; m. in California, Cora Elizabeth "Corky" Myers

V9-2736.   13-2. Deanna Carole Harmon, b. 1950, CA; m.1. in Nevada, Keith O'Mara; m.2. in California, Gordon Arthur Spence; m.3. in Hawaii, Richard Belding

V9-2737.   10-3. **George W. Brashears**, ½ Choctaw, b. 1865 (40 at time of marriage in Sept 1904); m. 4 Sep 1904, in Ada, Chickasaw Nation, Bk H, p.321), **Blanche Wilburn**, b. c1884 (20 at time of marriage), Census Card #2319, Choctaw Roll #6704, [do not confuse him with the George William Brashears on Choctaw Census Card #3172, Choctaw Roll #9171]. (See vol 5 for further details). George and Blanche had a son before the rolls were closed (they may have had more later),

V9-2738.   11-1. **Lovel Sumner Brashears**, 7/16 Choctaw, b. 29 Aug 1905, and enrolled as a minor Choctaw on Card #518, d. Dec 6, 1908, "s/o G.W. & Blanche", bur Hickory Cem, Murray Co, OK.

V9-2739.   10-4. **Mary Brashears**, ½ Choctaw, b. c1870 (age 32 in 1902,) listed on Choctaw Census field card #1567 as daughter of Enoch and Louisa (i.e. Luclihoma) Brashears, and wife of **Gabriel Nelson**, s/o Cole Nelson, dec'd, and his wife, Rhoda Nelson, dec'd, both from Jack Fork County (2 ch). Mary m.2. **James Homer (Homma)** and had one child by him.

V9-2740.   11-1. Laura (or Louisa) Homer, b. c1886 (age 16 in 1902; Roll #5779), d/o James Homer, dec'd, of Kiamitia Co and Mary Nelson, of Kiamitia Co. A notation says that Laura was on the 1893 Pay Roll, page 95, No. 790, Kiamitia Co. She was also on the 1896 Choctaw Rolls as Louisa Homma, page 141, #5779. Another notation says that Laura/Louisa had gone to the Chickasaw Nation.

V9-2741.   10-5. **Isabelle Brashears**, ½ Choctaw, b. c1870 (35 in 1905, enrollment #5776), d/o Enoch Brashears and Louise Moore (Choctaw field card #1510), m.1. **Mack Hulland** (Holland), a non-citizen; m.2. Ambrose L. Rice, b. c1875 (27 in 1902), intermarried white (Choctaw Card #1490), s/o G.W. Rice and Itlema Rice. Isabelle had two children by her first marriage:

V9-2742.   11-1. Amanda Huland, b. c1895 (10 in 1905; Card #1510, Roll #5777)

V9-2743.   11-2. Mattie Huland, b. c1902 (2 in 1905, Card #1510, Roll #5778)

V9-2744. 10-6. **Jane Brashears,** ½ Choctaw, b. c1873 (if about 17 when marrying) (d/o Enoch and Louisa Brashears), d. May 1893; m. 14 Nov 1890, in Paris, Lamar Co, TX (TX Marr Recs online) (first wife of) *John William Wood*, b. 1866, son of William Wood and Nannie _____. They had one child:

V9-2745. 11-1. William Edgar Wood, b. 29 Aug 1891. (11 in 1902; Choctaw Roll #4458)

V9-2746. 10-7. **Amanda A. (or R.) Brashears** (½ Choctaw, Roll #4457; d/o Enoch and Louisa Brashears), b. c1875 (10 on 1885 census); m. 6 July 1894 in Paris, Lamar Co, TX (per data in Choctaw application) (2nd wife of) *John William Wood*, (widower of her sister), b. 1866 (per data in Choctaw application), son of William Wood and Nannie _____. Libby Nations <vnations@gte. net>, writes: "Amanda Brashears was already on the Choctaw roll when she married John W. Wood. And he applied and was listed on the roll because his wife Amanda was. So I would think that Amanda's parents would be on the roll also. Maybe what I need to do is find Enoch on the roll and see if he has an application." [Enoch is NOT on the rolls; he was apparently dead before 1885.] Amanda, age 10, is alone on the 1885 Census, Kiamitia Co, I.T. Four children were enrolled on Choctaw Census Card #1578. The oldest, Edgar, is s/o Jane Brashears (Amanda's sister) and John William Wood.

V9-2747. 11-1. George Henry Wood, b. c1895 (7 in 1902; Choctaw Roll #4459)

V9-2748. 11-2. Thomas L. "Tommy" Wood, b. 6 Jan 1897 (6 in 1902; Choctaw Roll #4460), (Dept Interior affidavit says 3 Jan 1897); d. August 1984, Dallas, TX (SS death records)

V9-2749. 11-3. Robert Dewey Wood, b. 5 Dec 1899, Hugo, OK (SS death records) (3 in 1902; Choctaw Roll #4461); d. Oct 1971, Dallas, TX (SS death records); m. Eunice Rozanna Harris; b. 2 July 1899, Paris, TX (SS death records); d. August 1994, Dallas , TX (SS death records).

V9-2750. Amanda Brashears and John W. Wood *may* have had several other children, after the Choctaw Rolls were closed. Some researchers accredit them with children named: Arthur; Florence; Ina; Ivey; Naomi; Rosie; and Ruth Wood. (No documents.)

Mary Brashear, age 32 in 1902 (b. c1870), is listed on Choctaw Census field card #1567 as wife of Gabriel Nelson, s/o Cole Nelson, dec'd, and his wife, Rhoda Nelson, dec'd, both from Jack Fork County. Enrollment was dated 12 Dec 1902. Mary's father is listed as Enoch Brashears, dec'd, of Kiamitia Co, and Louisa (i.e. Luclihoma) Brashears, also dec'd, of Kiamitia Co. Gabriel Nelson was living at the time at Grant, Kiamitia Co, Indian Territory.

A line is drawn through Mary's entry and the notation is added that she died 1 May 1901. Proof of death was submitted 27 Oct 1902, and the enrollment was canceled 16 Sept 1904. A later notation says that Gabriel Nelson later married Susan Gibson.

Two Nelson children by Gabriel's first(?) marriage were enrolled:

V9-2751.   1. Will Nelson, age 18(i.e. b. c1884), s/o Gabriel Nelson and Nancy Nelson, both of Jacks Fork Co, and

V9-2752.   2. Wilson Nelson, age 14 (i.e. b. c1888) of the same parents.

A step-daughter to Gabriel Nelson was also listed:

V9-2753.   3. Laura Homer, age 16 (b. c1886), d/o James Homer, dec'd, of Kiamitia Co and Mary Nelson, of Kiamitia Co. Notation says that Laura was on the 1893 Pay Roll, page 95, No. 790, Kiamitia Co. She was also on the 1896 Choctaw Rolls as Louisa Homma, page 141, #5779. Another notation says that Laura/Louisa had gone to the Chickasaw Nation.

Isabelle Brashear, another daughter of Enoch Brashears and Luclihoma (Luclihoma is listed this time as Louisa Moore), is listed on field card #1510, dated 12 June 1905, as a widow, Isabelle Huland, with two children. She was age 35 (b. c1870), ½ blood, enrollment #5776, Kiamitia District, 1896, as Isabelle Holland. Her children by Mack Huland, a non-citizen, were Amanda Huland, age 10 in 1905 (b. c1895), 1/4 blood, enrollment #5777, and Mattie Huland, age 3 (b. c1902), 1/4 blood, enrollment #5778. A notation says that Isabelle, Manda, and Mattie were also on the 1896 roll (but Mattie wasn't yet born??). Isabelle is also listed as the present wife of Ambrose L. Rice, Choctaw Card #1490.

Ambrose Rice is listed on card 1490 as an intermarried white, age 27 (b. c1875), s/o G.W. Rice and Itlema Rice, both non-citizens. Ambrose is listed as an intermarried white on enrollment #14974. A notation says he was formerly the husband of Annie L. Rice, #710, on 1893 Roll. Annie died in 1896. Ambrose was listed on the 1896 roll as Embro L. Rice. The Davis Commission dis-enrolled him in 1896 (Choctaw Case #662); no appeal was filed.

Another notation says that Ambrose Rice is now (12 June 1905) the husband of Isabelle Huland, Choctaw Card #1510. Evidence of their marriage was filed on 12 Dec 1902.

Martha H. (Grissom) Brashears, widow of **Albert Brashears** (s/o Enoch Brashears and Luclihoma) is listed on Card #5862. She was age 42 (enrollment 13 Dec 1904, i.e. b. c1862), d/o William Grissom and Mary Grissom, both non-citizens. Card #5862 notes that Albert was on the 1885 Choctaw Census Roll, Atoka County, #824, but is now (1904) deceased. Martha was originally listed for enrollment on Choctaw Card #B-453, dated 8 Dec 1899, and transferred to card #5862 on 21 Nov 1904. (See decision of 9 Nov 1904.)

Card #B-453 listed Martha H. Brashears. Her certificate of marriage to Albert Brashears on 4 March 1885 was exhibited in due form on 26 March 1903, but it was not in a condition to be filed. "As to the marriage and separation, see her testimony." Transferred to Choctaw Card #5862.

*****

SARAH WHITE BRASHEARS
and GEORGE JACKSON / AMBROSE FOSTER

8-4. **Sarah White Brashears**, (d/o of Phillip Brashears and Mary White), b. 1 May 1797, in The Parish of Feliciana, LA; d. 12 April 1843, in The Parish of Concordia, LA; m.1. *George Jackson*, b. _?_, d. 1821, s/o James Jackson, Sr, a neighbor to Sarah's brother, Samuel Brashears. The probate of George Jackson in 1821 names his widow, Sarah Brashiers and gives two children and their ages. (Data from Noel Geissmann <noelueli@bellsouth.net>, for which, many thanks.)

Sarah White Brashears m.2. *Ambrose Foster*, who died in 1835. They had one son. Sarah is listed in Philip's Probate in 1825 as Sarah Foster.

In the 1830 Census of West Feliciana Parish, LA, Sarah Brashears and her three children are listed (next door to an Elizabeth Hadden/Madden, possibly her sister, though Elizabeth is listed in Philip's probate in 1825 as Elizabeth Marbury. Her brother Zadock Brashears also lived in West Feliciana).

Sarah Brashears, 30-40
female, 15-20 (fits for age of Elizabeth, b. 1815)
female, 10-15 (fits for Mary, b. 1817)
son, 5-10 (fits of Marcus, b. 1825)

Ambrose Foster is on the 1830 census in Concordia Parish, living alone. Sarah could have been visiting elsewhere, or they were living apart for some reason. She used her maiden name of Brashears. Remember that West Feliciana Parish and Concordia are next to each other. They could have been just a few miles apart. Ambrose may have gone ahead to locate a new home for his family.

Burials in Morgantown Cemetery, Adams Co, MS.
Sacred To The Memory Of
Ambrose Foster
Who Departed This Life
_____ 22. 1835
An Honest Man Is The Noblest Work Of God

In Memory of Sarah White Foster
Born May 1, 1797
In The Parish Of Feliciana, La.
Died Apr. 12, 1843
In The Parish of Concordia. A Good
Wife, A Fine Mother And A
Christian. God Has Called Her.

Marcus D. LaFayette Foster
Son Of Ambrose & Sarah Foster
Born Nov. 3, 1825
Died June 10, 1844

Family of Sarah White Brashears and George Jackson:
V9-2754.   9-1. Elizabeth A. Jackson, b. 1815; m. c1836, James T. Cain.
V9-2755.   10-x. Martha Francis Cain, m. Frederick Shaffer Jr
V9-2756.   9-2. Mary Jackson, b. 1817
Family of Sarah White Brashears and Ambrose Foster:
V9-2757.   9-3. Marcus D. LaFayette Foster, b. 3 Nov 1825, d. 10 June
                1844, age 18½, bur Morgantown Cemetery, Adams Co,
                MS. This is just across the bridge from Concordia
                Parish, LA.

In Livingston Parish, LA, in December, 1903, James T. Cain and
Elizabeth A. Jackson transferred her inheritance from George Jackson
and Sarah White Brashears to her own daughter, Martha Francis Cain,
and her husband, Frederick Shaffer, Jr:

And now personally came and intervened in these presents Mistress
Elizabeth A. Jackson but now the wife of vendor who declared unto me
Notary that it is her wish and intention to release in favor of the said
purchaser the property herein described from the matrimonial total
paraphernal and other rights and from any claims mortgage or other
privileges to which she is or may be entitled whether by virtue of her
marriage with her said husband or otherwise.
Wherein I the said Notary did inform the said appearers , apart and
out of the presence and hearing of her said husband and before
receiving her signature that she had by law a legal mortgage on the

property of her said husband. Firstly, for the restitution of her dowry and for the reinvestment of her total property sold by her husband and which she brought in marriage reckoning from the celebration of the marriage; Secondly for the restitution and reinvestment of the total property by her since marriage whether by succession or donation from the day the succession was opened or the donation perfected; Thirdly for nuptial presents; Fourthly for debts by her contracted with her said husband; Fifthly, for the amount of her paraphernal property alienated by her and received by her said husband or otherwise disposed of for the individual interest of her said husband and the said appearers did thereupon declare unto me Notary that she was fully aware of and acquainted with the nature and extent of the matrimonial dotal parapernal and other rights and privileges thus secured to her by law on the property of her said husband and that availing herself of the rights secured to her by the second section of an act passed by the Legislature of this State authorizing wives to make valid remunerations etc. approved on the twenty seventh day of March eighteen hundred and thirty five she nevertheless did persist in her intention of renouncing not only all the rights, claims and privileges therein before enumerated and described but all other or any kind or nature whatever to which she is or may be entitled by any laws now or heretofore in force in the State of Louisiana. And the said husband being now present aiding and authorizing his said wife in the execution of these presents she the said wife did again declare that she did and doth hereby make a formal renunciation and relinquishment of all her said matrimonial dotal paraphernal and other rights claims and privileges in favor of the said purchaser binding herself and her heirs at all times to sustain and acknowledge the validity of this renunciation.

Thus done and passed in my office in the said Parish in the presence of George W. Cain and John Buller witnesses of lawful age who hereunto sign their names together with said Parties and me the said Notary on the day and date first afore written.

Attest: Jas. T. Cain
G. W. Cain   Elizabeth A. Cain
John Buller   Martha F. Shaffer
                                 F. Shaffer

G. Albritton, Notary Public
Filed Dec. 30th 1903, Recorded Dec. 31st 1903
M. Cooper, Clerk of Records
(Thanks to Noel Geissmann <noelueli@bellsouth.net> for the copy.)

Lindsay/Brashear Families:

I'm going to start from Robert Brashear, born 1646

Gen 1. Robert Brashear, b. 1646, d. 1712

Gen 2. Samuel Brashear, Sr.   Benjamin Brashear, Sr
     m. Ann Jones   m. Mary Jones

Gen 3. Samuel Brashear, Jr; m.   Elizabeth Brashear

Gen 4. Ignatius Brashear, Sr, b. April 17, 1734; m. Frances Permelia Catryl. b. April 14, 1736

Gen 5. Ignatius Brashear, Jr, b. March 28, 1767; m. Mary Orme, b. 1780

Gen 6. Ruth Caroline Brashear, b. January 22, 1807, d. October 22, 1890, New Orleans, Louisiana; m. William Brashear Lindsay, b. May 13, 1806 in Mississippi, d. August 7, 1866, New Orleans, Louisiana

Gen 7. William Brashear Lindsay, Jr, (from Louisiana); m. Marie Martha Mouton, b. March 1, 1852, Lafayette, Louisiana, d. May 13, 1930, Lafayette, Louisiana

Gen 8. William Brashear Lindsay, III, b. September 27, 1876, Lafayette, Louisiana, d. March 4, 1943, Lafayette, Louisiana; m. Lena Clotile Toups, b. July 2, 1893, Thibodeaux, Louisiana, d. December 18, 1980, Lafayette, Louisiana

    Gen 9.1. William Brashear Lindsay, IV, b. March 2, 1912, Lafayette, Louisiana, d. August 13, 1996, Philadelphia, PA
    Gen 9.2. Bonita Lindsay, b. November 3, 1913, Lafayette, Louisiana
    Gen 9.3. Felix Hubert Lindsay, b. February 23, 1915, Lafayette, Louisiana, d. 1997, Virginia
    Gen 9.4. Peggy Irene Lindsay, b. October 14, 1927, Lafayette, Louisiana; m. Frank Emmett Wilson, Jr, b. January 31, 1922, Church Point, Louisiana, d. March 29, 1986, Lafayette, Louisiana
        Gen. 10.1 Rhonda Anita Wilson, b. October 17, 1950, born Church Point, Louisiana; m. Ross Elliot Whitfield, b. June 22, 1948, Cincinnati, Ohio
            Gen. 11.1 Ross Stuart Whitfield, b. June 15, 1980, Baton Rouge, Louisiana

Gen. 11.2 Lindsay Elizabeth Whitfield, b. November 10, 1982, Baton Rouge, Louisiana

Gen. 10.2 Frank Emmett Wilson, III, b. May 7, 1952, Church Point, Louisiana; m. Janet Faulk, b. March 18, 1953, Rayne, Louisiana

Gen. 11.1 Ashley Rae Wilson, b. December 25, 1979, Crowley, Louisiana

Gen. 11.2 Mark Joseph Wilson, b. September 15, 1983, Lafayette, Louisiana

Gen. 10.3 William Brian Wilson, b. December 14, 1960, Crowley, Louisiana; m. Elizabeth Leicher, b. September 13, 1962, Folsom, Louisiana

Gen. 11.1 Samuel William Wilson, b. September 10, 1991, Slidell, Louisiana

Gen. 11.2 John Emmett Wilson, b. May 31, 1994, Slidell, Louisiana

Gen. 11.3 Maxwell Brian Wilson, b. October 16, 1998, Rockledge, Florida

Also, going back to Robert Brashear, b. 1646

Gen. 1 Robert Brashear, 1646–1712

Gen. 2 Samuel Brashear, Sr.; m. Ann Jones

Gen. 3 Samuel Brashear, Jr.; m. Elizabeth Brashear

Gen. 4 Benjamin Brashear, b. 1666; m. Catherine Belt, b. March 18, 1729/30, Prince Georges Co, Maryland, d. 1773, Brownsville, PA

Gen. 5 Tobias Brashear b. 1756 in Prince Georges Co, Maryland, d. 1807, Port Gibson, Mississippi; m. Martha Brocus, b. 1756 d 1813, Port Gibson, Mississippi

Gen. 6 Martha Brashear, b. 1789, d. July 17, 1821; m. William Lindsay, b. 1769, Henry County, VA, d. 1817, Mississippi

Gen. 7 William Brashear Lindsay, b. May 13, 1806, Mississippi, d. 1866 in New Orleans, Louisiana; m. Ruth Carolina Brashear, b. 1807, d. 1890, New Orleans, Louisiana

The rest is the same.
Thank you
Rhonda Whitfield, 1281 Kings Road, Morgantown, WV 26508

Brashears on Dawes Final Rolls

The Native American Collection, GenRef, Inc. and the Oklahoma Historical Society

Surname	Given Name(s)	Age	Sex	Bld %	Census Cd #	Page Number	Enroll. Number	Tribe

Brashears, Albert, 22, Male, , CC# 437 Page 155, Enr# 5250 Choctaws - Freedmen

Brashears, Amelia, 31, Female, , CC# 554 Page 142, Enr# 3144 Choctaws - Freedmen

Brashears, Bat, 36, Female, , CC# 97 Page 139, Enr# 2577 Choctaws - Freedmen

Brashears, Battieste, 61, Male, , CC# 418 Page 129, Enr# 892 Choctaws - Freedmen

Brashears, Bill, 24, Male, , CC# 255 Page 126, Enr# 322 Choctaws - Freedmen

Brashears, Buster, 2, Male, 5-16, CC# 704 Page 102, Enr# 677 Choctaws - by Blood (New Borns)

Brashears, George, 44, Male, 1-2, CC# 1491 Page 25, Enr# 4170 Choctaws - by Blood
Brashears, Edward, 6, Male, 3-4, CC# 1491 Page 25, Enr# 4172 Choctaws - by Blood

Brashears, George W., 38, Male, 1-2, CC# 3172 Page 55, Enr# 9171 Choctaws - by Blood
Brashears, Ivey, 2, Female, 1-4, CC# 3172 Page 55, Enr# 9173 Choctaws - by Blood

Brashears, Polly, 68, Female, , CC# 882 Page 135, Enr# 1915 Choctaws - Freedmen
Brashears, Willie, 21, Male, , CC# 882 Page 135, Enr# 1917 Choctaws - Freedmen
Brashears, Richard, 20, Male, , CC# 882 Page 135, Enr# 1916 Choctaws - Freedmen

Brashears, Charley, 32, Male, , CC# 883 Page 135, Enr# 1918 Choctaws - Freedmen

---

Brashears, Henrietta, 27, Female, , CC# 883 Page 135, Enr# 1919 Choctaws - Freedmen

Brashears, Henry C., 9, Male, , CC# 883 Page 135, Enr# 1920 Choctaws - Freedmen

Brashears, Augustus, 7, Male, , CC# 883 Page 135, Enr# 1921 Choctaws - Freedmen

Brashears, Flossie, 4, Female, , CC# 883 Page 135, Enr# 1922 Choctaws - Freedmen

Brashears, Eugene, 2, Male, , CC# 883 Page 135, Enr# 1923 Choctaws - Freedmen

Brashears, Carrie, 1, Female, , CC# 144 Page 157, Enr# 47 Choctaws - Freedmen (Minors)

Brashears, Carrie, 19, Female, , CC# 1206 Page 149, Enr# 4319 Choctaws - Freedmen

Brashears, Charley, 20, Male, , CC# 1522 Page 155, Enr# 5239 Choctaws - Freedmen

Brashears, Ed, 52, Male, , CC# 730 Page 149, Enr# 4267 Choctaws - Freedmen

Brashears, Ida, 1, Female, , CC# 437 Page 141, Enr# 2929 Choctaws - Freedmen

Brashears, Isa May, 1, Female, 1-8, CC# 744 Page 102, Enr# 711 Choctaws - by Blood (New Borns)

Brashears, John, 35, Male, 1-4, CC# 3021 Page 53, Enr# 8856 Choctaws - by Blood

Brashears, Benjamin, 26, Male, 1-4, CC# 2564 Page 45, Enr# 7450 Choctaws - by Blood

Brashears, Mary Estella, 3, Female, 1-8, CC# 2564 Page 45, Enr# 7451 Choctaws - by Blood

Brashears, Johnie Tobias, 1, Male, 1-8, CC# 2564 Page 45, Enr# 7452 Choctaws - by Blood

Brashears, Tola, 1, Female, 1-8, CC# 2564 Page 45, Enr# 7453 Choctaws - by Blood

Brashears, Julia F., 20, Female, 1-4, CC# 3172 Page 55, Enr# 9172 Choctaws - by Blood

Brashears, Lida B., 31, Female, I W, CC# 3172 Page 116, Enr# 295 Choctaws - by Intermarriage

Brashears, Lovel Sumner, 1, Male, 7-16, CC# 518 Page 110, Enr# 425
Choctaws - by Blood (Minors)

Brashears, Martha H., 42, Female, I W, CC# 5862 Page 121, Enr# 1234
Choctaws - by Intermarriage

Brashears, Mary J., 61, Female, 3-4, CC# 2536 Page 44, Enr# 7357
Choctaws - by Blood
Brashears, Tobias, 41, Male, 5-8, CC# 2536 Page 44, Enr# 7358
Choctaws - by Blood
Brashears, Bessie, 21, Female, I W, CC# 2536 Page 123, Enr# 1528
Choctaws - by Intermarriage
Brashears, William J., 2, Male, 5-16, CC# 2536 Page 44, Enr# 7361
Choctaws - by Blood

Brashears, Mary Prince, 19, Female, , CC# 437 Page 141, Enr# 2928
Choctaws - Freedmen

Brashears, Minnie, 39, Female, I W, CC# 3021 Page 115, Enr# 281
Choctaws - by Intermarriage

Brashears, Nancy, 47, Female, , CC# 418 Page 129, Enr# 893 Choctaws
- Freedmen

Brashears, Richard, 81, Male, , CC# 1179 Page 146, Enr# 3821
Choctaws - Freedmen

Brashears, Rube, 1, Male, , CC# 179 Page 158, Enr# 302 Choctaws -
Freedmen (Minors)

Brashears, Susie, 14, Female, , CC# 695 Page 155, Enr# 5351 Choctaws
- Freedmen

Brashears, Turner, 24, Male, 1-4, CC# 3066 Page 54, Enr# 8961
Choctaws - by Blood

Brashears, Viola, 1, Female, 5-16, CC# 704 Page 102, Enr# 678
Choctaws - by Blood Newborns)

Brashers, Mary W., 8, Female, , CC# 525 Page 224, Enr# 2183
Chickasaws - Freedmen
Brashers, Bessie, 6, Female, , CC# 525 Page 224, Enr# 2184 Chickasaws
- Freedmen

Dawes Final Rolls - Rejected
**The Native American Collection, Gen Ref, Inc.
and the Oklahoma Historical Society**

Bld Census   Enroll.

Surname   Given Name(s)   Age Sex %   Cd # Page Number Tribe

Brashears, Mary, 27, Female, Full, CC# 1491 Page 77, Enr# 4171
Chickasaws - Freedmen
Brashears,, 4, Female, 3-4, CC# 1491 Page 77, Enr# 4173 Chickasaws -
Freedmen

**Index to Applications for Enrollment, 1896 - 1897
The Native American Collection,
GenRef, Inc. and the Oklahoma Historical Society**

Surname, Given Name(s),   Tribe, Case Number

Brashares	, Napolean P	Choctaw	877
Brashears	, J R	Cherokee	3730
Brashears	, Minnie	Choctaw	883
Brashears	, William	Cherokee	3981
Brashear	, Aggie	Cherokee	2850
Brashear	, Mary L	Cherokee	5063
Brashear	, Sarah M	Cherokee	2850
Brasher	, Susan M	a Cherokee	4310

19. VOL. 6 MISCELLANEOUS

John T. Brashear and Sarah J. Rose

Wayne Brashear <cityjazz@aol.com> of Corona, CA, sent data on:
^{V6}-854. ^{9}-2. **John T. Brashears** (son of Berry Brashears and Francis
Pryor), b. abt 1840, Lawrence Co, TN; m. **Sarah J. Rose**, b. abt 1844,
TN. They were the parents of six children: (re: 1880 census, Giles Co, TN)
^{v6}-855. ^{10}-1. **John W. Brashears**, b. c1872
^{v6}-856. ^{10}-2. **Julia H. Brashears**, b. c1873
^{v6}-857. ^{10}-3. **Cora A. Brashears,** b. c1874
^{v6}-858. ^{10}-4. **Ida L. Brashears**, b. c1875
^{v6}-859. ^{10}-5. ***Robert Leroy Brashears**, b. c1876 (35 in 1910, Giles
Co, TN)
^{v6}-860. ^{10}-6. **Walter Brashears**, b. c1879 (31 in 1910, Giles Co, TN)

^{v6}-859. ^{10}-5. **Robert Leroy Brashears**, b. c1876, (s/o John T. Brashears and Sarah J. Rose), was living in Giles Co, TN, at the time of the 1910, 1920, and 1930 U.S. Censuses. Robert married c1905 (had been married 25 years in 1930) *Sallie J.* _____, b. c1872 (38 in 1910; 48 in 1920; 58 in 1930). In 1910, he was called Leroy Barsheare; in 1920, he was called Robert L. Brasheare; in 1930, he was called Roy L. Barsheare. Robert's younger brother, Walter, is living with them in 1910.

Family of Robert Leroy Brashears and Sallie J. _____:
^{v9}-2758. ^{11}-1. **Mary L. Brashears,** b. c1904 (6 in 1910; 16 in 1920)
^{v9}-2759. ^{11}-2. **Roy English Brashears**, b. c1906 (4 in 1910; 14 in 1920; 25 in 1930)
^{v9}-2760. ^{11}-3. **Sadie L. Brashears**, b. c1908 (2 in 1910; 12 in 1920; 23 in 1930)
^{v9}-2761. ^{11}-4. **Louise M. Brashears**, b. c1912 (8 in 1920; 18 in 1930)

1910 US census, Giles Co, TN District 35, Civil District 19, p.81A, 22 Apr 1910 (Hams Creek Road):
Leroy Barsheare, head, 35, m. 7 yrs, b. TN, TN, TN, farmer, can read and write.
Sallie J., wife, 38, m. 7 yrs, b. TN, TN, TN.
Mary L., dau, 6, b. TN, TN, TN.
English, son, 4, b. TN, TN, TN.
Sadie, daughter, 2, b. TN, TN, TN.
Walter, brother, 31, single, b. TN, TN, TN, farm laborer, can read and write.

1920 US census, Glles Co, TN, District 44, Civil District 19, p. 280B, 2/3 Jan 1920 (Tucker Road):
Robert L. Brasheare, head, 44, b. TN, TN, TN, farmer, general farm.
Sallie B., wife, 48, b. TN, TN, TN.
Mary E., daughter, 16, b. TN, TN, TN.
Ray E., son, 14, b. TN, TN, TN.
Sadie L., daughter, 12, b. TN, TN, TN.
Louise, daughter, 8, b. TN, TN, TN.

1930 US census, Giles Co, TN, District 28, Civil District 19, p.254B, 3 Apr 1930 (Hams Creek Road):
Roy L. Barshears, head, 55, 25 when married, b. TN, TN, TN, farmer, own farm.
Sallie J., wife, 58, 28 when married, b. TN, TN, TN.
Roy E., son, 25, single, b. TN, TN, TN, farmer, own farm.
Sadie L., dau, 23, single, b. TN, TN, TN.
Louise M., dau, 18, single, b. TN, TN, TN.
*****

Descendants of Berry Franklin Brashears

Carl Boshers, of Columbia, TN, sent these additions and correction, even before the ink on vol 6 was dry.

He writes: Thanks very much for the data on Berry Franklin Brashears. Please allow me to make a couple of minor corrections, fill in some blanks and make a few additions.

V6-#890.   12-1. **Charles Henry Brashears,** m. *Edna Earle Arthur*, b. 20 June 1931.

Their children:

V6-891.   13-1. **Donna Carol Brashers**; b. 27 March 1961, m. *William Jeffrey Williams*; b. 30 March 1960. They had two children:

V9-2762.   14-1. Bryan Jeffrey Williams, b. 24 Feb 1987.
V9-2763.   14-2. Rebecca Katelyn Williams; b. 08 April 1991.

V6-892. 13-2. **Charles "Chuck" Henry Brashears, Jr**, b. 24 Nov 1963, m.1. *Cynathia "Cindy" Darlene Perryman*. 1 child, m.2. *Dawn Barbee*; they had 1 child;

V9-2764.   14-1. **William Bradley Brashears**; b. 23 April 1982.
V9-2765.   14-2. **Tyler Wayne Brashears**; b. 22 Jan 2000.

V6-893. 13-3. **Helen Kathleen "Kathie" Brashears**; b. 20 Dec 1955, m.1. *Steve Spivey*; m.2. *Ronald Sanford*, they had 2 children; m.3. *Philip Forrester*, b. 01 May 1947.

V9-2766.   14-1. Samanatha "Sammie" Karon Sanford, b. 10 Oct 1988.
V9-2767.   14-2. Charles Thomas Sanford, b. 15 Feb 1990.

V6-894 13-4. **Cheryl Ann Brashears**; b. 25 Sep 1951, m.1. *Clifton Eugene Tatum*; b. 04 March 1947, they had 2 children

V9-2768.   14-1. Clifton Eugene Tatum Jr, b. 20 March 1970, m. 03 April 1992 to Clara Ann Dugger, b. 06 Sep 1976, they had 3 children; Clifton Eugene Tatum III, b, 26 June 1992; Xanthia Nicole Tatum, b. 11 Sep 1994; and Tiffany Tatum, b. 27 Feb 1997.

V9-2769.   14-2. Philip Scott Tatum; b. 01 April 1974, m.1. Bama Whitney Green, they had 2 children; Bailey Suzanne Tatum, b. 07 Nov 1997. Preston Scott Tatum; b. 07 Sept 1998.

Add:

V6-899,   11-5 **Luna Jewel Brashears**; m. *Vance Tankersley*.
V6-900.   11-6. **William Edwin Brashears** was the full name of Billy Brashears; he was married to *Mary Frances Williams*. He and Mary had one son **Jimmy Brashears**. See the obituaries, below, which Carl sent.

V6-901,   11-7. **Doris Brashears**; m. *Ima Jean Compton*.
V6-902,   11-8. **Lightfoot Veol Brashears**, full name of L.V. "Pete" Brashears (per his son **Ronnie Brashears**)
V6-903.   11-9. **Geraldine Brashears**; m. *Ed Hill Estes*

The Obit for Charles Henry Brashears is not quite correct. It gives Peggy Rogers and Shirley Brashears as Charles's sisters. They were really his step-sisters. Several years after Will Tom Brashears's first wife, Kathleen Young, died, Will Tom married Tavie Newton, who was the widow of Tom Newton. Tavie and Tom Newton had the two daughters, Peggy and Shirley Newton. Will Tom adopted Shirley (she was handicapped). Peggy m. Leonard Rogers. V6-895, [12-]2., and V6-896, [12-]3 are not of the Brashears blood line.

I am posting the **obituaries** of the son and wife of "Billy" Brashears. Note the discrepancies in the two obit's of the middle name of Billy. I do not know which one is correct. It may be that Jimmy's (James) middle name is wrong. Also notice how close their deaths were. — Carl

obit: Mary Frances Brashears. Posted on April 12, 2004
(WKSR Radio) (http://www.wksr.com/)
Mary Frances Brashears died yesterday at Hillside Hospital. She was a native of the Diana community and was a retired employee of Maremont Corporation. She was 85 years old. Visitation will be held today from 4-8pm at Carr & Erwin Funeral Home. Services will be held tomorrow at 2pm in the chapel of Carr & Erwin Funeral Home. Burial will follow in the Diana community.

Survivors include a son, Jimmy Brashears of Manchester, Tennessee, and a twin sister, Sarah Whitworth of Pulaski. Four grandchildren, and three great, grandchildren also survive. She was preceded in death by her husband, William Edwin Brashears.

Carr & Erwin Funeral Home is in charge of arrangements for Mary Frances Brashears.

Obit: James Edom Brashears. Posted on April 16, 2004
(WKSR Radio) (http://www.wksr.com/)
James Edom Brashears died today at his Manchester, Tennessee residence. He was 63 years old and a native of Pulaski. Visitation will be held tomorrow from 5-9pm at Coffee County Funeral Home in Manchester. Services will be held Sunday at 2pm in the chapel of Coffee County Funeral Home with Reverend Wendell Trussell officiating. Burial will follow in the Rose Hill Memorial Gardens in Coffee County.

He was preceded in death by his parents, William Edom & Mary Frances Williams Brashears. There are no local survivors. Coffee County Funeral Home of Manchester is in charge of arrangements for James Edom Brashears.

Giles Co, TN

From Carl Boshers, Date: April 6, 2006

PULASKI- Maxie Pearl Brashears Bobo, 95, died Tuesday, April 4, 2006, at National Health Care.

Services will be 2 p.m. Thursday at the Carr & Erwin Funeral Home. Burial will be in Maplewood Cemetery.

She was the daughter of the late William Henry and Albert Burl Fry Brashears, and was a native of Giles County. She was a homemaker. Survivors include her sister, Margaret Simpkins; several nieces and nephews

[V9]-2770. William Henry Brashears, m. Albert Burl Fry
[V9]-2771.   x. **Maxie Pearl Brashears**, b. c1911, d. 4 April 2006, Pulaski, Giles Co, TN, bur Maplewood Cem; m. _____ Bobo
[V9]-2772.   x. **Margaret Brashears**; m. _____ Simpkins

*****

Atsy Breshears and Joseph Arter

d/o William Arthur Breshears and Anna Ethridge

Norman Combs <bilgerat@sbcglobal.net> sends this information about William Arthur & Anna Ethridge Breshears' daughter, Atsy b. (1834). [V]-[6]1654 [9]7, p. 175.

This Atsy Breshears was my ggmother, m. Joseph Arter 1850's (Pope or Searcy Co AR). They are listed in the 1860 Mtn Twp Searcy Co Ar census just below her parents Wm & Anna Brashears & above bro Hardin & family & sis Sarah Humphreys(sp) & fam.

My ggfather, Joseph Arter probably perished during the Siege of Vicksburg; don't know what happened to Atsy.

My gmother, Sarah & bro Joseph were in Richland twsp, Searcy Co AR in 1880 living with a "Franklin" family; big sis Anna Elizabeth, md to Xerxes Robertson was nearby. Don't know where they were in 1870.

During the early 1880's my gmother, Sarah, md a "Williams." Their two children were Joseph & Atsy Geneva Williams. Mr. Williams was out of the picture by 1888; don't know what happened to Joseph and Atsy G. Williams.

By 1888 Sarah took up with Edward D. Combs. Andrew Jackson Combs was b. Aug. 1889 and Alfred Washington Combs Apr. 1891; both near Plato, MO. After Edward d. Texanna, OK (1895) Sarah dropped the two younger boys off at their older half-sister's and left Plato. These boys never knew their mother like she never knew her father.

There is not much to tell about this boring branch of the family except that Atsy Breshears would probably have been worried about her grandson, Alfred lugging a machine gun around France in 1918, getting both sides of his helmet shot off and spending the last month of the war hospitalized because of mustard gas; concerned about a ggson captured by the Japanese in the Philippines, lucky enough to survive the "Bataan Death March" only to be encamped at Hiroshima, but lucky to be out on a work detail when the bomb hit; she would have been grief stricken when another ggson shot & killed two of his stepsons over a disagreement; devastated when a gggson died from a booby trap in Vietnam; proud that another gggson authored "Wireshark" or "Ethereal" a network protocol analyzer.

*****

Madison Golman Breshears' last child

Posted by: Gerald Hodges, Date: May 24, 2005 at 18:11:59
In Reply to: v.6 Brashears-Breshears Families-TN,MO,etc by Charles Brashear

I was going over your Breshears in Benton and Hickory Co., MO. Under #33- **Madison Golman Breshears**, this last child John Francis "Little Frank" Breshears and Sarah H. Hodges 372? That is an error, Sarah H. is Sarah M. Hodges. Sarah was a Great Aunt of mine, sister to my Great Grandfather, Lewis C. Hodges, who came to TX from Hickory Co, MO. I also have a copy of John and Sarah's marriage papers. I don't really know if that will help you if the book is already printed.
- Gerald Hodges

****

Orvillle and Frank Brashear

From: lodyrose@hotmail.com
To: BRASHEAR-L@rootsweb.com

My grandmother **Lena Carroll** was married to **Orville (AKA Dick) Brashear**.
I would like to have any information on a Frank Brashear. I have some old photos of Linda Jean and Frank, and Karen Leah, dated 1948. Linda age 4 in 1948, on a pony. They lived around Bolivar, Polk Co., MO.

From: j3conner@4edisp.net
To: BRASHEAR-L@rootsweb.com

Following is the only information I have about Frank Brashear. I hope it will be helpful to you:

Frank Wesley Brashear, b. 27 Mar 1911, Bolivar, Polk Co., MO, d. 1 Aug 1988, Bolivar, Polk Co., MO; Burial: Greenwood Cemetery, Bolivar, Polk Co., MO; Occupation: Owner/Operator Bolivar Quarry; Religion: Baptist
Father: John Wesley Brashear (1872-1960)
Mother: Van Rachel Stafford (1874-1961)
Spouses: 1: *Cora Lee Morgan*, m. 21 Jun 1932 Springfield, Greene Co., MO;
Spouse : 2: *Thelma Lovina Teters*, b. 21 Aug 1915 Bolivar, Polk Co., MO, d. 30 Nov 1977 Springfield, Greene Co., MO; Burial: Greenwood Cemetery, Bolivar, Polk Co., MO; Marriage: 25 Aug 1963
- Judy S. Conner, 7408 Greentree Court, Amarillo, TX 79119

****

Corrections on Breshears, vol. 6

"Noble King" <nobleshobby@tri-lakes.net>
To: "Charles Brashear" <brashear@mail.sdsu.edu>
Subject: Breshears Book # 6 Corrections & Additions

Here are some additions and corrections on the MO line that I have put together.
#3360 pages 320 & 353, Marion Lloyd Breshears was the son of Lloyd Thomas Breshears & Fairy Ellen Weaver, not Ruth Morton.
#3862 page 351 John William Breshears married Lydia Jewell Jeffries. They also had a daughter, Barbara Lynn, in addition to the 2 boys. John's second wife was Hettie Mae Shaw. Their children were John Wayne & Juanita Mae Breshears
#3865 Ivan Breshears married Lucy Marie Pitts.
#3128 pages 299 & 300: Walter Joseph Button was not known as Toad. That was another Button relative in the same area.
#3149 page 300 Leta May Button Bybee died Feb 2, 2005.
#3157 page 301 William Ralph Button died Feb 17, 2005.
#3967 page 362 Minnie Elizabeth Breshears died April 24, 1996 Vessie Buel Wright born November 14, 1905 .
#3970 page 363 Hettie Noble Wright married November 24, 1996.
#3971 page 363 Son born to Douglas Shawn Newman : Gabriel Douglas Newman born June 8 2005.
#4215 page 383 Perry Westerfield Breshears His wife was younger than he: Florence was born March 3, 1889
#4216 Helen Breshears born July 16, 1916 married Bill Hentzi -Looks like his birth date might be wrong but I don't have the correction.
#4217 page 383 Leonard Thomas Breshears born April 25, 1920, Avery, MO, died July 9, 1978 Greene Co., MO.
#4584 page 410 Zella Lou Murray was NOT a twin

#4585 Donnie Dale Murray was NOT a twin born October 1949.

#4272 page 388 Donald Dean Brooks died October 12, 2006.

#4263 page 387 Wilma Nadine McKenzie died August 24, 2006.

#3953 page 357 Ralph Breshears died January 20, 2007.

#5528 page 482 James Eddie Prine died December 31, 2006.

#5553 page 487 Christine Lori Breshears married 3rd time October 15, 2005, Gregory Taylor.

#5567 page 488 Homer Durl Henderson born July 20, 1926, died November 29, 2006. Homer was handicapped & stayed with his family as long as they could care for him. He entered a care center in the mid 1990's.

#5580 page 489 Doyle Neil Breshears born about 1941 married to Barbara Howard. Barbara was killed in an auto accident December 20, 2002. Neil married second time to Frances Hammons Yancey.

#5579 page 489 Lowell Breshears born Sept 15, 1909 died Dec. 25, 2002 I didn't have this one written on my list as I was trying to find out for sure that I was right and last night called a son of Roy Horace Button. #3145 page 300, Roy Horace Button was only married once-to Fyrn Dawson. No one in the family knows any Tyru Dawson. They had already seen that and knew what I was asking about right away.

20. VOL. 7 MISCELLANEOUS

Samuel Brashear and Elizabeth Mason

[8]9. **Samuel Brashear**, (s/o Ithra Brashears, Sr, and Hannah Elizabeth Middleton), b. 1816, Crawford Co, IL, d. 1860s; m. 26 Sept 1837, (Crawford Co, IL Marr. Bk A, p.65), **Elizabeth Mason** b. c1816, IL, d. after 1870, IN

Samuel, Elizabeth, and their children apparently moved about the mid-1840s to the vicinity of Vincennes, Knox Co, IN: (Data from "Colleen A. Kelly" <darkeyes222@sbcglobal.net>).

1850 Knox Co., IN, Subdivision 61 enum. 15 Oct by J. W. Wisener

Sam'l Beshears	33	IL	Farmer
Elizabeth	33	IL	
Mary	11	IL	
Elizabeth	9	IL	
Eliza	7	IL	
Albert	5	IL	
James	4	IL	
Phebe	3	IL	
Martha	2	IL	

1860 Knox Co., IN, Vigo Twp., Edwardsport P. O., Enum. 31 Aug

Samuel Brashears	41	IL	Farmer
Elizabeth	41	IL	
Eliza	18	IL	
Albert	17	IL	
James	16	IL	
Phebe	14	IN	
Martha	12	IN	
Edward	10	IN	
Samuel	7	IN	
Elias	5	IN	
Sarah	2	IN	

By 1870, Samuel is no longer listed in Knox Co., IN.
However, in Steen Twp., Wheatland P.O., Knox Co, IN are:

his wife, Elizabeth Brashears	45	IL
James Brashears	24	IL
Phoebe Brashears	21	IN
Edward Brashears	20	IN
Samuel Brashears	16	IN

```
Sarah Brashears      12  IN
John Gilmore             12  IN
```

and
```
Albert Brashears       27  IN
Martha E. (Westfall)   20  IN
Charles E. Brashears    1  IN
Martha A. Brashears    21  IN
```

Family of Samuel Brashear and Elizabeth Mason:

[9]1. **Mary Brashear**, b. c1839, IL (11 in 1850)

[9]2. **Elizabeth Brashear**, b. c1841, IL (9 in 1850)

[9]3. **Eliza Brashears**, b. c1843, IL (7 in 1850; 18 in 1860)

[9]4. **Albert Brashears,** b. c1845, IL (5 in 1850, 17 in 1860); m. 30 April 1868, in Knox Co, IN, *Martha E. Westfall,*

    [10]1. **Charles E. Brashears**, b. c 1869, IN (per census)

[9]5. **James Brashears**, b. c1846, IL or IN (4 in 1850, 16 in 1860)

[9]6. ***Phebe Brashears**, b. Jan 1846, IL or IN (3 in 1850, 14 in 1860), d. 4 June 1916; m.1. 8 May 1871, in Knox Co, IN, *Charles Westfall*, d. bef Feb 1877; m.2. 27 June 1879, in Knox Co, IN, *William "Sanford" Eoff*, b. c1830, d. 3 July 1883.

[9]7. **Martha A. Brashears**, b. c1848, IL or IN (2 in 1850, 12 in 1860); m. 20 Oct 1870, In Knox Co, IN, *George Westfall,*

[9]8. **Edward Brashears**, b. c1850, IN (10 in 1860); m. 26 Feb 1871, in Knox Co, IN, *Lydia Pickle,*

[9]9. **Samuel Brashears**, b. c1853, IN (7 in 1860); m. 23 Aug 1885, in Knox Co, IN, *Martha A. Hooper,*

[9]10. **Elias Brashears**, b. c1855, IN (5 in 1860)

[9]11. **Sarah Brashears**, b. c1858, IN (2 in 1860); m. 28 Dec 1879, in Knox Co, IN, *George Johnson,*

An interesting note: while checking Indiana marriages for Knox County and Brashear, Colleen found:

Albert Brasher (note spelling) and Martha Westfall 4-30-1868

Phebe Brashear and Charles Westfall 5-8-1871

Martha Brashear and George Westfall 10-20-1870

Edward Brashear and Lydia Pickle 2-26-1871

Samuel Brashear and Martha A. Hooper 7-23-1885

Sarah Brashear and George Johnson 12-28-1879

(Colleen's comment: Will let you know if I find the relationships between these Westfalls) Since these Brashears all married within a few years of each other, I am assuming they are the children of Samuel and Elizabeth; but, am checking further and will let you know what I find.

I also found for this time frame:

I. Brashear and Emaline Pickle 9-29-1876

and these Brashears (note the "s")

Other Brashear(s) Families   317

Alice Brashears and Jos. Shaw 5-28-1874
Louisa Brashears and Mahlon (or Mathen) House 9-5-1882
Martha E. Brashears and Martin V. Snyder 10-14-1883

I don't yet know which Brashear(s) these belong to. I will check family tree and see if I can get clues (?) and try to find some sort of documentation as relative proof on info. I've included here. I've learned they are not always factual.

I have not at this point been able to find any further information about these children of Samuel and Elizabeth: Mary, Elizabeth, Eliza, James, or Elias.

Phoebe Brashear and Charles Westfall

[9]6. **Phoebe Brashear**, (d/o Samuel Brashear and Elizabeth Mason), b. Jan 1846, in either Knox or Gibson Co, IN, d. 4 June 1916, Evansville, IN; m.1. 8 May 1871, in Knox Co, IN, **Charles Westfall**, d. before Feb 1877; m.2. 27 June 1879, in Knox Co, IN, **William "Sandford" Eoff**, b. c1830, d. 3 July 1883, in Vincennes, Knox Co, IN, by hanging. (Death Certificate H-26, p. 56: little information except that he was married, a farmer, and cause of death is "Hanging (self to a tree)." No informant it listed. The family swears that he was murdered, that he was a doctor and was killed for the medicine he was carrying. Nothing has been found to substantiate this claim.

Charles Westfall died before Feb 1877, when an appraisal of his estate was ordered. In inventory of the estate of Phebe Westfall, widow of Charles, is valued at $349.75, and includes farm equipment, a couple of horses, cow and calf, bedding, etc.

Then 3 July 1883, her second husband, William Eoff, was found hanging from a tree.

Phoebe never remarried. She had only two sons: Robert Westfall and William Sanford "Jake" Eoff. Indiana death records list her death as 4 June 1916, in Evansville, IN. She was last listed in census in 1900 Vigo, Knox Co., IN, living with her son, Robert Westfall.

Robert Westfall	29 (March 1871)
Sarah J.	26 (Oct. 1873)
Bertha	6 (Oct. 1893)
Hallie	4 (May 1896)
Phoeba Eoff, mother	54 (Jan 1846) widow, has borne 2 ch, 2 are living.

Listed directly above them is Sanford Eoff, servant, farm laborer, 20 (May 1880) IN IN IN, living with Theodore Wampler 48 IN VA Va, and his wife, Martha E. 36 and family.

Children of Phoebe Brashear:

[10]1. Robert Westfall, b. March 1871 (per 1900 census); m. Sarah J. _____, b. Oct 1873 (per 1900 census)

[11]1. Bertha Westfall, b. Oct 1893 (per 1900 census)

[11]2. Hallie Westfall, b. May 1896 (per 1900 census)

[10]2. William "Sanford" Eoff, b. May 1880 (per 1900 census); m. 2 Sept 1903 (or 7 Sept) in Knox Co, IN, Ida Belle Johnson, d/o George W. Johnson and Elizabeth Harbin. They had 3 children:

William Sanford Eoff, (s/o Phoebe Brashear and William Eoff); An out-of-wedlock relationship of William Sanford Eoff with Lena Ann Landreth produced a dau:

[11]x. Ada Mae Eoff/Landreth, b. 18 Nov 1898,

[11]1. William Sanford "Jake" Eoff, b. 3 Dec 1903 in Knox Co, IN, d. c1958 in either Rush or Henry Co., IN; m. Ethel Mae Phillips, (d/o William "Henry" Phillips and Anna Chandler) b. 2 Dec 1895, Petersburg, IN, d. July 1966 Muncie, Delaware Co, IN. Ethel had been married previously to a William Cox, Colleen thinks. They had 2 sons: Kenneth and Byron Cox.

William Sanford "Jake" Eoff and Ethel Mae Phillips had 4 children all born in Vincennes/Bicknell area and all now deceased:

[12]1. Delores June Eoff.

[12]2. Donna Jean Eoff (mother of Colleen A. Kelly" <darkeyes222@sbcglobal.net>)

[12]3. Dorothy Lois Eoff,

[12]4. William Ellsworth Eoff,

[11]2. Ida E. J. "Myrtle" Eoff, b. 4 Sept 1908 ; m. Ted Howard, Lowell Brooks, Mr. McClure

[11]3. Robert Nelson Eoff, b. 27 Aug 1914 Bicknell, IN, d. 5 Nov 1975, Knightstown, Henry Co., IN; m. Ruby Lucille Webb,

Concerning the Westfalls:

1860 Palmyra, Knox Co., Vincennes P.O., IN

Abel Westfall	57	IN	Farmer 2000/550
Indiana	48	IN	
Cassandra A.	27 (24?)		
Charles	21	IN	Farmer
George	16	IN	
Elizabeth	10	IN	
Sarah C.	7	IN	
John Johnson	4	IN	
Ann E. Starr	1	IN	

There is a Martha E. Westfall who would be about the right age to have married Albert Brashear. She is enumerated in neighboring Gibson Co., Montgomery Twp. with the following family:

James Westfall	48	IN	Farmer 2600/1000
Mary J.	29	IN	
Perry A.	9	IN	
Ann M.	7	IN	
Charles R.	4	IN	
James P.	1	IN	

Although there is also a Charles Westfall listed with the above family, he would have been too young to have married Phoebe in 1871. There are 2 men in 1860 named Albert Brashear/Brashears living in or around the Knox County area who would be old enough to marry Martha Westfall in 1868. One, of course, is Albert, 17, the son of Samuel and Elizabeth living in Knox Co., with his parents. Another is Albert, 12, living across the river in Crawford Co., IL. He is the son of Haney, 39, and Eliza, 37. He'd have been about 18 in 1868.

21. VOL. 8 MISCELLANEOUS

Samuel Marion Brashear

Samuel Marion Brashear, (s/o Snoden Trullinger Brashear and Malinda Ellen Breeden), b. 14 June 1884, Attica, Harper Co, KS, d. 13 Jan 1960, Aurora, CO; m.1. **Nell Kincheloe**, m.2. **Hazel Downey**, m.3. **Verna Evans**. Snoden died in Sam's home in Denver. (info from Heidi Baur, posted on GenForum Brashear)

Family of Samuel Marion Brashear and Nell Kincheloe:

V9-2773.	1. **Neil Brashear**, m. _____
V9-2774.	1. **Larry Brashear**,
V9-2775.	2. **Geniene Brashear**,
V9-2776.	3. **Patricia Brashear**,
V9-2777.	4. **girl Brashear**,
V9-2778.	2. **Hazel Brashear**, m. _____
V9-2779.	1. Paula _____

Family of Samuel Marion Brashear and Verna Evans:

V9-2780.	3. **Lois Brashear**, m. _____
V9-2781.	1. Doug _____,
V9-2782.	2. Bonnie _____,

^{V9}-2783.   3. Kristy _____,
^{V9}-2784.   4. Randy _____,
^{V9}-2785.   5. Ricky _____,
^{V9}-2786.   4. **Marion Brashear**, m. _____
^{V9}-2787.   1. **Leslie Brashear**,
^{V9}-2788.   2. **Barbara Brashear**,
^{V9}-2789.   5. **Robert Brashear**, m. _____
^{V9}-2790.   1. **Valerie Brashear**,
^{V9}-2791.   2. **Vicki Brashear**,
^{V9}-2792.   3. **Terry Brashear**,
^{V9}-2793.   6. **Catherine Brashear**, m. _____
^{V9}-2794.   1. Mike _____,
^{V9}-2795.   2. Mark _____,
^{V9}-2796.   3. Gretchen _____,
^{V9}-2797.   4. Heidi _____, m. _____ Baur.

Fragments from various states:

Stamp Brashears

a-x. **Stamp Brashears**, m. *Ethel* _____. Judy (Brooker) Berchak, searching for ancestry, Ozark, Franklin Co, AR:

b-x. **Ethel Brashears**, b. 1886, Ozark, Franklin Co, AR, d. 1981, Fayetteville, AR; m. 30 Nov 1902, in Franklin Co, AR, *W. (William?) Allan Johnson*, b. 1883, Ozark, Franklin Co, AR, s/o "Bud" and Lizzie Johnson.

c-1. Anna Johnson,

c-2. Selma Johnson, b. 2 Nov 1906, Ozark, Franklin Co, AR; m. Harrison Benjamin Belt

d-1. Mildred Geraldine Belt, b. 1921; m. Bennett Brooker (from Florida)

e-1. Judy Lenora Brooker, b. 1943; m. 1963, Henry Lee Berchak

f-1. Judith Katherine "Katie" Berchak, b. 1983

d-2. Florence "Flossie" Belt,

d-3. Willa Bea Belt,

d-4. Harrison Benjamin "Red" Belt, Jr,

c-3. Oma Johnson,

c-4. Hebert Johnson,

c-5. Gordon Johnson,

c-6. Delmer Johnson,

c-7. Helen Johnson,

c-8. Ozea Johnson,

c-9. Lilly Johnson,

*****

Brashears/Starns

a-x. **William Brashears**, b. c1799, SC (50 in 1850, Marion Co, AR), d. 5 Aug 1876, Madison Co, AR; m. c1820, *Mary L._____*, b. 1804, TN (45 in 1850; 76 in 1880, Madison Co, AR, mo-in-law to George W. Starns, b. NC, says F.F. Starns), d. 22 Feb 1888, Madison Co, AR. William and Mary, age 50 and 45, are #76, p.619, 1850 Census, Marion Co, AR, taken 19 Oct, with dau Eliza still at home.

b-1. **Alfred Thomas Brashears/Beshears**, b. 14 Jan 1819, TN (30 in 1850, Union twp, Marion Co, AR, #64, p.618, taken 19 Oct, with wife and four children); m.1. _____ _____ and had two children; m.2. in Taney Co, MO, *Rebecca Adeline King*, b. 27 Feb 1825 (20 in 1850). Alfred Thomas Beshears lived next door to William and Mary Brashears/Beshears in Marion Co, AR in 1850 and in Madison Co, AR in 1860 & 1870. Alfred T. Beshears moved to Texas before 1878, first stopping in Bell Co, then moving to Brown Co by the 1880 Census. Alfred is buried in Brown County and his wife Rebecca is buried in Erath County with her daughter, Emily Bristow. Data from Debbie <Debshasha@aol.com>

Family of Alfred Thomas Beshears and first wife:

c-1. **Amanda Beshears**, b. 1841, TN (9 in 1850, Marion Co, AR)

c-2. **Miranda Beshears**, b. 1843, TN (7 in 1850)

Family of Alfred Thomas Beshears and Rebecca Adeline King:

c-3. **William C. Beshears**, b. 1848 (2 in 1850, Marion Co, AR)

c-4. **Mary Ann Beshears**, b. 8 Aug 1850 (1 in 1850)

c-5. **Margaret Jane Beshears**, b. 1854; m. *William Roles*

c-6. **James Monroe Beshears**, b. 20 Nov. 1855; m. *Mary Arizona Reed*

c-7. **Emily Dulcinia Beshears**, b. 9 June 1858; m. *Samuel Houston Bristow*

c-8. **Alfred Thomas Beshears Jr**, b. 1862; m. *Angie James*

c-9. **Eliza Beshears**, b. 1864

c-10. **Isaac L. Beshears**, b. 22 Aug 1866; m. *Julia Roene Alexander*

c-11. **John R. Beshears**, b. 1869; m. *Alice Cryer*

b-2. **Martha A. Brashears** b. 14 Aug 1822, TN, d. 19 Dec 1882, Madison Co, AR; m. c1842, (second wife of) *George W. Starns*, b. 5 Oct 1819

(1821 says stone), Rhea Co, TN, d. 30 Jan 1885, Madison Co, AR, s/o Nicholas Starns and Barbara Ann Winters; gravestones in Farmers Cem, Madison Co, AR. Martha & George lived in Marion Co, AR until about 1851, when they moved to Madison Co, AR. They are in the 1850 Census, Marion Co, AR; in the 1860, Madison Co, Bowen twp; in the 1870 and 1880, Madison Co, Prairie twp. George W. Starns homesteaded 120 acres in Madison Co, described as E 1/2, NE 1/4, & NE 1/4, SE 1/4, Sec 13, T17N, R27W; appl #1828, Homestead cert #1, U.S. Patent dated 30 Jun 1876, recorded 25 Feb 1890, Madison Co, Deed Book P, p.406.

c-1. William Nicholas Starns, b. 1843, Marion Co, AR, d. c1879, Hindsville, Madison Co, AR; m. c1868, in Madison Co, AR, Elizabeth A. "Bettie" Rucker, b. 1851, MO. Ch: Elliott Franklin, Samantha R., Nancy, Martha, Walter, Jason, and Maude Starns.

c-2. Nancy C. Starns, b. c1846, Marion Co, AR; m. _____ McAdoo.

c-3. Elizabeth Ann Starns, b. c1848, Marion Co, AR; m. George A. Turner.

c-4. Mary E. "Mollie" Starns, b. c1851, Madison Co, AR (29 in 1880); m. G.P. Guthrey.

c-5. Alfred Carter "Alf" Starns, b. c1853, Madison Co, AR, d. after 1900, Pontotoc Co, OK; m. Darcus Belle Phillips, b. 1857, AR (23 in 1880). Ch in 1880: Edgar H. Starns.

c-6. Susan C. Starns, b. c1855, Madison Co, AR (25 in 1880)

c-7. James L. "Jim" Starns, b. c1857, Madison Co, AR

c-8. Lewis N. Starns, b. c1858, Madison Co, AR; m. Mary C. _____, b. c1859, GA (21 in 1880)

c-9. Harry C. "Dock" Starns, b. c1861, Madison Co, AR (19 in 1880); m. L.J. _____.

c-10. George W. "Gus" Starns, b. 1863, Madison Co, AR; m. Emma Frazier, at Hillsboro, Hill Co, TX

c-11. Sallie I. Starns, b. c1865, Madison Co, AR (15 in 1880); m. W.A. Fullerton.

b-3. **Elizabeth "Eliza" Brashears**, b. c1831, TN (19 in 1850, Marion Co, AR)

b-4. **John Brashears**, *May* be the John Brashear who married in 1855, Madison Co, AR, Milly Smith. See below.

Nicholas Starns, or Starnes, father of George W. Starns, was b. 6 Nov 1756, Cecil Co, MD, moved with his family in 1757 to Fairfax Co, VA, moved in 1772 to Craven District, SC. In 1775, he moved to Washington Co, VA (the Watauga Settlement, which would one day be Tennessee). On 13 Sep 1775, he volunteered in Captain Crabtree's Co and served 10 days. In the autumn of 1775, he served three weeks as a sergeant in the same company under Col. William Campbell. From Sep 1780, he served three months as a sergeant, again under Captain Crabtree and Col. William Campbell, and participated in the battle of King's Mountain, as one of "The Overmountain Men." In the autumn of 1780 and winter of 1780-81, he served 5 weeks as sergeant in Captain Truit's Co, and was engaged in the expedition against the Cherokees, when Col. John Sevier burned 16 Indian towns. He receive a Rev. War Pension for these services.

For more on the Starnes Family, see *Of Them That Left a Name Behind*, a History of the Starnes Family's First 125 Years and Beyond in America, by H. Gerard Starnes and Herman Starnes, Gateway Press, Baltimore, 1983; or contact descendant: Frank F. Starns, 206 Sherry Trail, Weatherford, TX 76086-4718; 817/613-9001.
*****

Beshears/Pendergraft

The following info was gathered by Jeannie Thompson, who is researching the Beshears family.
who sent it to Larry Pendergraft <lpenderg@sun1282.spd.dsccc. com>
>forwarded by Carline Doyle, cdoyle@mail.snider.net
>who forwarded it to Joe George: jgeorge@northcoast.com
>who forwarded it to me: Charles Brashear: brashear@mail.sdsu.edu

William David "Bill" Beshears, b. 1851, d. 1889, Franklin Co, AR, (s/o John Beshears and Milly Smith; she was thought to have been born in Ireland); m. 10 Feb 1876, in Franklin Co, AR, **Amanda Joyce Williams**, b. 8 Jul 1852, NC or MO, d. 14 Feb 1925, Scott Co, AR.

William had two sisters, **Dora** and **Amy Beshears**. There possibly were other siblings, but this is uncertain, and nothing further is known about William's siblings, parents, or any previous relatives. Amanda m.2. 22 May 1905, Waldron, Scott Co, AR, John M. Winters— no children by this marriage.

Family of William David "Bill" Beshears and Amanda Joyce Williams:
b-1. **Julia Ubania (or Ann?) Beshears**, b. Nov 1876, AR, d. 3 Dec 1929, Miami, Ottawa Co, OK; m.1. 27 Jan 1894, in Franklin Co, AR, **James A. "Jim" "Doc" Pendergraft**, b. Feb 1877, Logan Co, AR, d. c1910, Scott Co, AR. Julia and Jim had 3 children, then divorced c1899. Julia m.2. c1903 to **Floyd Montgomery Peterson**,

1864-1929 - 5 children. After the divorce, Jim Pendergraft married a widow named Nancy, and had another child, Josey. According to family tradition, Jim Pendergraft was shot & killed in an ambush after an argument with a Mr. Scott.

Children of Julia Ubania Beshears and James A. Pendergraft:

c-1. William David Pendergraft, b. 1894 (Larry Pendergraft's grandfather.)

c-2. Herman Charles Pendergraft, b. 1898

c-3. Rosie Pendergraft, b. c1900-1903

Children of Julia Ubania Beshears and Floyd M. Peterson: (all b. Ind Terr/OK)

c-4. Lee Roy Peterson,

c-5. Matilda Elizabeth "Tilly" Peterson,

c-6. Floyd Douglas Peterson,

c-7. Oscar Tait "Pete" Peterson,

c-8. Mark Peterson,

b-2. **George Washington Beshears**, b. 22 Nov 1879, d. 13 Mar 1967, bur Bloodworth Cem, Scott Co, AR, "s/o Wm. D. & Amanda"; m. 7 Nov 1903, **Fannie Powell**, b. 16 Jun 1883, d. 8 Apr 1935, bur Bloodworth Cem, Scott Co, AR, "Wife of George W. Beshears". - 8 children:

c-1. **Gilbert Guy Beshears**, b. 30 Sep 1907, d. 17 May 1992; m. **Delsie L. ____**, b. 29 Nov 1909, bur together (double stone) in Bloodworth Cem

c-2. **Bernice Beshears**, b. 18 Feb 1911 (error? compare birth to next birth), d. 15 Jul 1933, bur Bloodworth Cem, Scott Co, AR "d/o George and Fannie"

c-3. **Paul Garland "Bruce" Beshears**, b. 23 Feb 1911 (still living in Scott Co, 1995); m. **Gladys Edwards**, b. 15 Mar 1910, d. 22 Sep 1984, (double stone) in Bloodworth Cem

c-4. **Obie Beshears**, b. & d. 14 Nov 1915, bur Bloodworth Cem, "s/o George & Fannie"

c-5. **James Garland Beshears**, b. 22 Jul 1917, d. 24 Nov 1989; m. **Lavern ____**, b. 2 Jan 1922, bur together (double stone) in Bloodworth Cem, Scott Co, AR

c-6. **Elva Beshears**, b. & d. 23 Jul 1917 "d/o George and Fannie" (?a twin, born after midnight? cf. last birth date.)

c-7. **Beatrice Beshears**, (living in Ft. Smith as of 1995),

c-8. **Eva Beshears**,

b-3. **Elmer (Robert/Randall?) Beshears**, b. 1884, d. 28 Dec 1928; m. 11 May 1906, **Parney Metcalf** - 10 children;

c-1. **James Arvell Beshears**, (3 ch),

c-2. **Allen Beshears**, (1 ch),

c-3. **Jack "Archie" Beshears**, (2 ch),

c-4. **Noah Beshears**,

c-5. **Elmer Beshears**, (5 ch),

c-6. **Odis Beshears**, (2 ch),

c-7. **Edith Beshears**, (4 ch),

c-8. **Margaret Beshears**, (6 ch),

c-9. **Marceille Beshears**, (4 ch),

c-10. **Calvin Beshears**, (4 ch),

c-11. **Billy Beshears**, (4 ch).

b-4. **James Franklin Beshears**, b. 18 May 1882, d. Nov 1963; m.1. 2 Nov 1902, *Rosette Pendergraft* (sister of Jim "Doc" Pendergraft) - 2 children; m.2. *Mattie (Hamilton) Edwards* - no children; m.3. *Cordelia (Ashford) Gibson* - no children

c-1. **Elva Beshears**, (at least 1 ch),

c-2. **Lola Beshears**, (2 or more ch)

b-5. **Hubert Oscar Beshears**, b. 9 May 1883, d. 25 Feb 1958, bur Bloodworth Cem, Scott Co, AR, "s/o William D. Beshears"; m.1. 27 Dec 1906, *Effie Reed* - 11 children; m.2. 26 Jun 1928, *Rilla Hines*, b. 9 May 1886, d. 25 Feb 1958 - 10 children;

Children of Hubert Oscar Beshears and Effie Reed:

c-1. **Addie Beshears**, (5 ch),

c-2. **Delphia Beshears**, (6 ch),

c-3. **Loy Oscar Beshears**, (killed by lightning at age 14),

c-4. **Ollie Beshears**, (female, had 4 ch),

c-5. **Louise Beshears**, (lived 5 mos.),

c-6. **Ida Mae Beshears**, (lived about 6 wks),

c-7. **Ona Beshears**, (2 ch),

c-8. **Ola Beshears**, (1 ch),

c-9. **Elva Lucille Beshears**, (3 ch),

c-10. **Willie Mae Beshears**, (3 ch),

c-11. **Jessie Beshears**, (3 ch).

Children of Hubert Oscar Beshears and Rilla Hines:

c-12. **L.T. Beshears**, b. 2 Apr 1929, d. 17 Apr 1929, bur Bloodworth Cem, "s/o Hubert and Rilla"

c-13. **Amanda Jane "MJ" Beshears**,

c-14. **MaeFern Beshears**,

c-15. **Glen Bert Beshears**,

c-16. **Obie Beshears**,

c-17. **A.C. "Pete" Beshears**,

c-18. **Thelma Jo Beshears**,

c-19. **Retha Lou Beshears**,

c-20. **Infant Beshears**, grave in Bloodworth cem, marked with rock

c-21. **Infant Beshears**, grave in Bloodworth cem, marked with rock

b-6. **Susie Beshears**, b. 17 Dec 1888, d. 14 Dec 1958; m. 27 Dec 1903, *Michael C. Solley* - 8 children;

   c-1. William Solley,

   c-2. Alonzo Edwin Solley,

   c-3. Cecil James Solley,

   c-4. Pauline Solley,

   c-5. Marvest Preston Solley,

   c-6. Michael Dale Solley,

   c-7. Wilma Doyce Solley,

   c-8. Ruth Lois Solley,

****

John Willis Brashears and Cora Shea

[10]x. **John Willis Brashears**, b. 31 Aug 1878, Chicago, IL, d. 1954, Evanston, IL; m. 25 Oct 1905, Chicago, IL, *Cora Dorothy Shea*, b. 25 Feb 1886, d. 1953, Mobile, AL

   [11]1. **Lois Cora Brashears**, b. 26 Apr 1907, d. 1984, Eureka, CA; m. *Gardner B. Abbott*, b. 27 Aug 1907

   [12]1. John William Abbott, b. 12 Jun 1934, Evanston, IL; m. 20 Jul 1962, in Mobile, AL, Betty Carney, b. c18 Apr 1938

   [13]1. Lisa Abbott, b. 13 Jul 1960; m. 9 Jul Klammath Falls, OR, Douglas Young, b. 13 Jul 1960

   [14]1. Kirstyn Young, b. 16 Oct 1990

   [14]2. Klyil Mara Young, b. 13 Sep 1994

   [13]2. John W. Abbott, b. 12 Nov 1961; m. 16 Sep 1984, Klammath Falls, OR, Gina Sampo, b. 1960-64

   [14]1. Nathan Lee Abbott, b. 9 Jun 1985

   [14]2. Ashley Renee Abbott, b. 20 Mar 1989

   [13]3. Daniel Sterling Abbott, b. 24 May 1966; m. 16 Aug 1985, Klammath Falls, OR, Jeri Feeback, b. 30 Jul 1966

   [14]1. Jessica Lynn Abbott, b. 20 Mar 1989

   [14]2. Jamie Lee Abbott, b. 7 May 1993

   [12]2. James Gardner Abbott, b. 7 June 1938, Evanston, IL; m. 30 Aug 1960, in Mobile, AL, Elizabeth Foutz, b. 2 Sep 1938

   [13]1. David Michael Abbott, b. 28 Aug 1961, Mobile, AL; m. 30 Nov 1991, in Anderson, SC, Barbara Shaw,

   [13]2. Jennifer Lynn Abbott, b. 10 Oct 1965; m. 28 Nov 1965, Brian Allen Spearman

¹³3. Susanne Noelle Abbott, b. 8 Nov 1968
¹²3. Paul Allen Abbott, b. 28 Nov 1940, Evanston, IL; m. 9 Jun 1963, in Berkeley, CA, Susan Lorraine Walraven, b. 10 Oct 1941, San Francisco, CA
>
> ¹³1. Clifford Allen Abbott, b. 16 Jul 1966, Opelkka, AL; m.1. in Seoul, Korea, In Hwo No, (1 ch) b. South Korea; m.2. 1 Oct 1990, in Junction City, KS, Chong Um Pak, (1 ch) b. 30 Oct 1960, South Korea
>
> > ¹⁴1. Dwayne Allen Abbott, b. 19 Jul 1988, Seoul, Korea
> > ¹⁴2. Brian Willis Abbott, b. 21 Jul 1992, Ft. Riley, KS
>
> ¹³2. Sarah Lorraine Abbott, b. 27 Jun 1969, Hoopa, CA; m. 14 Jun 1992, in Sedona, AZ, Gerald Thoman Heinig, b. 2 Mar 1967
>
> > ¹⁴1. Ciera Elizabeth Abbot Heinig, b. 5 Feb 1994, Bringham City, UT
>
> ¹³3. Elizabeth Anne Abbott, b. 27 Feb 1971, Hoopa, CA; m. 11 Jun 1994, Willow Creek, CA, Clarence Norvin Hostler Jr, b. 17 Jun 1971, Eureka, CA
>
> > ¹⁴1. Joshua Paul Hostler, b. 22 Dec 1994, Eureka, CA

¹¹2. **Robert William Brashears**, b. 26 Feb 1913, d. in St. Peterburg, FL; m.1. 13 Jul 1935, *Dorothy Goetz*, (no ch?); m.2. 1937, in St. Petersburg, FL, *Virginia* _____, b. 30 May 1908, d. 1978, St. Petersburg, FL

¹²1. **Coralee Helen Brashears**, b. 15 Oct 1938, Evanston, IL; m. 15 May 1961, in St. Petersburg, FL, *James Woodsen Hays*, b. 23 Apr 1937, St. Petersburg, FL, (div? 15 May 1972, St. Petersburg, FL)

> ¹³1. Tracey Helen Hays, b. 9 Oct 1961, St. Petersburg, FL; m. 14 Jun 1986, St. Petersburg, FL, Robert Sullivan, b. 1 Dec 1959
>
> > ¹⁴1. Scott Alexander Sullivan, b. 26 Nov 1992
> > ¹⁴2. Jessica Layne Sullivan, b. 17 Mar 1995
>
> ¹³2. Terry Gay Hays, b. 19 Dec 1962, St. Petersburg, FL
> ¹³3. Steven James Hays, b. 11 Sep 1966,
> ¹³4. Julie Ann Hays, b. 6 Dec 1968,

¹²2. **Carol Lynn Brashears**, b. 7 Mar 1942, Evanston, IL; m. 5 Dec 1970, *Frank Edwain Cerio*, b. 23 Dec 1942

> ¹³1. Krista Lauren Cerio, b. 28 Nov 1976

¹²3. **Beverly Ann Brashears**, b. 20 Oct 1946, Evanston, IL; m. 2 Sep 1967, St. Petersburg, FL, *Thomas Harrell*, b. 10 Oct 1946, St. Petersburg, FL (?div 13 Jul 1989, Columbia, SC)

> ¹³1. Richard Todd Harrell, b. 5 Jan 1972

[13]2. Ashlie Layne Harrell, b. 21 Jun 1974
[11]3. **Jeanne Bradley Brashears**, b. 16 May 1914, Chicago, IL; m. 1 Aug 1936, Wilmette, IL, **Robert Alfred Wolff**, b. 4 Jul 1910, Evanston, IL, d. Jan 1983, Minneapolis, MN
   [12]1. Robert Alfred Wolff Jr, b. 24Dec 1940, Evanston, IL; m.1. 8 Apr 1967, Blenheim, New Zealand, Helen Wilks, b. in Blenheim, New Zealand (2 ch; ?div in Shakopee, MN); m.2. 1981, Atlanta, GA, Patricia Woodcock, b. Blenheim, New Zealand (?div Atlanta, GA); m.3. 16 Sep 1983, Atlanta, GA, Sheryle Ann Francis, b. Anderson, IN (?div 1993, Perry, FL)
      [13]1. Kristopher Francis Wolff, b. 25 Jan 1978
      [13]2. Melissa Francis Wolff, b. 23 Oct 1980
   [12]2. Elizabeth Cora Wolff, b. 5 Aug 1946, Evanston, IL; m. 27 Aug 1972, Holy Trinity United Methodist Church, Prior Lake, MN, James Charles Weninger, b. 13 Aug 1946, St. Paul, MN
      [13]1. Virginia Lois Weninger, b. 27 Jun 1978

******

Isaac Brasier and Sarah "Sally" Curry

Isaac Brasier, b. c1771, NC; m. 1803, in Jefferson Co, KY, **Sarah "Sally" Curry**. Isaac and Sally moved their family to Owen Co, IN, before 1820; they are shown in the 1820, 30 & 40 Owen Co, IN census, living in their own household with children. The 1850 census shows them living with son, Hiram, and his second wife, Amanda.
?Is this him?
1820 Census, Indiana: Isaac Brashear, (320010-00100), Wabash Co, page 19 (<MRVE)

Family of Isaac Brasier and Sarah "Sally" Curry: (data from Donna Jo Brasier Sielert <sielertd@esuvm.emporia.edu>; research done by Blanche and Raymond Brasier (now deceased), Helen Bozarth Sinor, and Donna, pieced together from marriage records, tax records, census, county histories and land transactions. To date, Donna has not been able to locate a Bible, Will, or much of anything that will help verify the information.)
b-1. **Hiram Brasier**, b. c1806, KY, m.1. 16 May 1831, **Polly Walters** (Owen County Marriages, 1819-1844, p.3); m.2. 1 Mar 1846, Gosport, Owen Co, IN, **Amanda Hughes**, (Owen County Marriages, Volume II, 1845-1853, p.3). Listed on p.1 of 1843 Tax list, Wayne twp, Owen Co, IN

---

b-2. **Susanna Brasier**, b. c1807, KY, d. 1830 (Blanchard's "History of Morgan, Monroe & Brown Counties, IN," 1884, p.324); m. 18 Sep 1827, Owen Co, IN, *Richard C. Walters* (Owen County Marriages 1819-1844, p.22).

b-3. **Jonathan Brasier**, b. c1808, KY, m. 9 Feb 1832, Gosport, Owen Co, IN, *Ellen Jane Howard*, (Owen County Marriages 1819-1844, p.3). Listed on p.8, 1843 Tax list, Wayne twp, Owen Co, IN

b-4. **Lucinda Brasier**, b. c1810, KY, m. 14 Oct 1830, Owen Co, IN, *William Sandy*, (Owen County Marriages 1819-1844, p.3). William Sand(e)y listed on p.6, 1843 Tax list, Wayne twp, Owen Co, IN

b-5. ***George Washington Brasier**, (Donna Jo Brasier Sielert's grandfather) b. 18 Sep 1812, KY, d. 20 May 1884 in Emporia, Lyon Co, KS. (Dates of birth and death taken from tombstone and obituaries); m. 14 Aug 1836, Owen Co, IN, *Mary H. McGinnis*, (Owen County Marriages 1819-1844, p.3). Listed on p.2, 1843 Tax list, Wayne twp, Owen Co, IN

b-6. **Gideon Brasier**, b. 24 Aug 1814, KY, d. 31 Jan 1888, probably in Hendricks County, IN (dates of birth and death taken from tombstone, Walters Cemetery, p.103); m. 4 Feb 1841, Gosport, Owen Co, IN, *Sarah Jones*, (Owen County Marriages 1819-1844, p.3). Blanchard's 1884 history says that Gideon and Sarah moved from Morgan County, IN, to New Winchester, Hendricks Co, IN. Listed on p.2, 1843 Tax list, Wayne Twp, Owen Co, IN

b-7. **Westley Brasier**, b. c1817, KY,; m. 23 Dec 1849, *Adaline Hughes*, (Owen County Marriages 1845-1853, Vol II, p.3). Listed on p.2, 1843 Tax list, Wayne twp, Owen Co, IN

b-8. Girl **Brasier** - b. c1818 or 1822, KY - Helen Bozarth Sinor

b-9. **Paulina Brasier**, b. 24 Mar 1819, KY, d. 15 Jan 1881 (Dates of birth and death taken from tombstone, Walters Cemetery, p.86); m. 3 Jan 1836, *Harrison P. McGinnis*, (Owen County Marriages 1819-1844, p.15). Harrison McGinnis listed on p.5, 1843 Tax list, Wayne twp, Owen Co, IN

b-10. **John F. Brasier**, b. 20 May 1821, IN, d. 7 Feb 1876 (dates of birth and death taken from Owen County IN Cemetery Listings, Gosport Cemetery, Wayne Township, Owen County, IN, p.627); m. 19 Aug 1848, Gosport, Owen Co, IN, *Emily Caroline Guy* (Owen County Indiana Marriages 1845-1853, Volume II, p.3). Listed on p.2, 1843 Tax list, Wayne twp, Owen Co, IN.

b-5. **George Washington Brasier**, (Donna Jo Brasier Sielert's grandfather) b. 18 Sep 1812, KY, d. 20 May 1884 in Emporia, Lyon Co, KS. (Dates of birth and death taken from tombstone and obituaries); m. 14 Aug 1836, Owen Co, IN, **Mary H. McGinnis**, (Owen County Marriages 1819-1844, p.3). Listed on p.2, 1843 Tax list, Wayne twp, Owen Co, IN

c-x. ***James Dallas Brasier**, b. 7 May 1849, Gosport, Owen Co, IN, s/o George Washington Brasier and Mary McGinnis, d. 12 Jan 1925, Americus, Lyon Co, KS; m. 9 Aug 1870, IN, **Sarah Emeline (Browder) Jones**, b. 28 Jul 1852, Morgan, IN, d. 16 May 1921, Americus, Lyon Co, KS (she had been m. previously to ____ Jones). (Ancestors of Donna Jo Brasier Sielert, 1119 State St, Emporia, KS 66801 (1986) <sielertd@esuvm. emporia.edu>. Seven children:

d-1. **Hattie Effie Brasier**, b. 18 May 1871, Gosport, Owen Co, IN, d. 3 Oct 1956, Americus, Lyon Co, KS; m. **John Floyd**,

d-2. **Samuel Alonzo Brasier**, b. 9 Oct 1873, Gosport, Owen Co, IN, d. 31 Dec 1956, Emporia, Lyon Co, KS; m. **Nettie J. Conway**,

d-3. **Maude Ora Brasier**, b. 14 Feb 1876, Mottoon, Cole Co, IL, d. 23 Aug 1964, Americus, Lyon Co, KS; m. **Harry E. Weaver**,

d-4. **Alice Dora Brasier**, b. 14 May 1878, Mottoon, Cole Co, IL, d. 23 Feb 1968, Colorado Springs, CO; m.1. **Charlie David Brukett**, m.2. **Pete Engessler**,

d-5. **Julie Ann Brasier**, b. 15 Mar 1880, Americus, Lyon Co, KS, d. 23 Jul 1971, Colorado Springs, CO; m. **Benjamin F. Inman**,

d-6. **William Elmer Brasier**, b. 15 Aug 1882, Americus, Lyon Co, KS, d. 30 May 1960 Emporia, Lyon Co, KS; m.1. 23 Jan 1907, Armericus, Lyon Co, KS, **Lois Effa McCosh**, b. 24 Apr 1884, Mount Union, IA, d. 13 Apr 1910, Americus, Lyon Co, KS, d/o Alva Lindly McCosh, b. 4 Dec 1861, d. 12 Jun 1921; m.2. **Iva Ace**, m.3. **Lois Moore**; m.?4. 12 Apr 1883, **Elizabeth Crawford**, b. 28 Nov 1864, d. 1937

e-x. **Donald McCosh Brasier**, b. 11 Sep 1909, Americus, Lyon Co, KS; m. 20 Jul 1930 (Emporia, KS), **Josephine Maude Crook**, b. 10 Oct 1907, Saffordville, Chase Co, KS, d/o John Seldon Crook, b. 13 May 1874, Saffordville, d. 2 Sep 1956, Emporia, KS; m. 3 Aug 1905, Rebecca Elizabeth Bailey, b. 14 Jul 1874, Harveyville, KS, d. 5 Feb 1960, Emporia

F-x. **Donna Jo Brasier**, b. 6 Jan 1933, Emporia, Lyon Co, KS; m. 26 Feb 1952 (Oklahoma City, OK), **David Sielert**, b. 24 Jun 1926, Plymouth, KS

d-7. **Ida Melissa Brasier**, b. 31 Jul 1890, Americus, Lyon Co, KS, d. 3 Jun 1973, Colorado Springs, CO; m. ***Edgar P. Orrill,***
*****

John Brashear and America Thompson

In Loving Remembrance of Mother (Obit) *Corydon Democrat,* Corydon, Harrison Co, IN (south cent part of state; on Ohio River) (thanks to Lois Barger for the clipping):

Just as the clock was on the stroke of 5 Saturday evening, March 20, 1920, the death angel silently visited our home again, and took from it our darling mother.

America Thompson was born August 28, 1851, her age being 69 years, 7 months and 8 days. She was the daughter of <u>Nathaniel and Elizabeth Thompson</u>, now deceased. She united with the M.E. Church at Evans Landing Indiana, at the early age of 13. She was a devoted Christian, believing with all her heart and soul the teachings of Christ.

She was united in marriage to **John Brashear**, April 30, 1873. To this union, 11 children were born, 4 having preceded her to the Great Beyond. She leaves to mourn her sad departure a husband, John Brashear, of Laconia, two sisters, Mrs. Henry Smith, of Laconia, and Mrs. W.B. Summers, of Beulah, Wyoming, and seven children, namely: David Brashear, of Latham, IL; Mrs. D.M. Maynard, of Tipton, IN; W.L. Brashear, of New Albany; Miss Laura Brashear, Mrs. Forest Cotner, and Mrs. J.E. Byrum, of Davidson, IN.

During her illness, she suffered intensely, having not lain down for 14 weeks. Death was due to dropsy. Funeral services were conducted by Rev. Hewitt, of Mauckport, IN, and the remains were laid to rest in the Otterbein cemetery.

> Our sad hearts have learned to feel
> Our Father's will was best,
> That called the earthly to the land
> Of happiness and rest.
> And now while o'er our shortening way,
> The shadows come and go,
> We love to think that thou art free
> From every earthly woe.
> Sleep on, dear mother, thy work is done,
> Thy mortal pang is past,
> Jesus has come and borne you home

Beyond the stormy blast.
The flowers we place upon thy grave
Will wither and decay,
But the love we bear for thee
Will never pass away.
Daughter Mabel

1) The 1851 birth year for America is problematic since she is listed in the 1850 Census under her father, and appears even older in the 1860 census:

1850 Census -- Indiana, Harrison County, District 45, Roll 149, page 366 (taken 1
    November 1850), Dwelling 1209, Family 1209
Line 33. Thompson, Nathaniel W., 33, M, White, Carpenter, born Kentucky
34 ____, Elizabeth, 34 [?], F, White, born Indiana
35 ____, George, 9, M, White, born Indiana
36 ____, Mary, 5, F, White, born Indiana
37 ____, Catharine, 3, F, White, born Indiana
38 ____, Columbia, 1, F, White, born Indiana
39 ____, America, 3 months, White, born Indiana

1860 Census -- Indiana, Harrison County, Taylor Township, Rosewood post office
    (page 0403). National Archive Series Number: M653 National Archive Microfilm
    Number: 264. Family Number: 0457 Dwelling Number: 0466
19A Thompson, Nathaniel M, Head, 45, White, born Indiana, Farmer, Real Property
    $0, Personal $500, literate
20A ____, Elizabeth, F, 42, born Virginia, Housekeeper, literate
21A ____, George, M, 18, born Indiana, Farm laborer, literate
22A ____, Mary, F, 16, born Indiana, Domestic, literate, attended school in past year
23A ____, Catharine, F, 15, White, born Indiana, Domestic, literate, attended school in
    last year
24A ____, Columbus, M, 14, White, born Indiana, literate, attended school [this is
    Columbia, a girl]
25A ____, America, F, 12, White, born Indiana, literate, attended school [born 1848?]
26A ____, William, M, 10, White, born Indiana, literate, attended school
27A ____, Wesley, M, 9, White, born Indiana, literate, attended school
28A ____, Sarah, F, 7, White, born Indiana, literate, no notation about school
29A ____, Abigail, F, 6, White, born Indiana, literate [sic], no notation about school
30A ____, Rebecca, F, 5 months, White, born Indiana, literate [sic]

[These ages seem too old based on the 1850 census -- was it actually taken in 1861?]

Brashear, John, b. Nov 1851, age 48, married 26 years, Blacksmith, illiterate, rents home, born in Indiana, as were parents.

_____, America, b. Aug 1851, age 48, m. 26 yrs, mother of 11 (7 living), literate, born in Indiana, as were parents

_____, William, son, Widower, b. Mar 1875, age 25, Day Laborer, literate

_____, George, son, single, b. July 1877, age 23, Day Laborer, unemployed 8 mos this year, literate

_____, David, son, single, b. Jan 1878, age 22, Day Laborer, unemployed 4 mos, literate, born Kentucky

_____, Mabel, dau, single, b. July 1881, age 18, born Kentucky, literate

_____, Mary, dau, single, b. Aug 1885, age 14, born Kentucky, literate (school)

_____, Annie, dau, single, b. Dec 1888, age 11, born Indiana, literate (school)

_____, Clara, dau, single, b. Jan 1890, age 10, born Indiana, literate (school)

_____, Charles, grandson [son of William], b. Jan 1900, age 4 mos, born Indiana

As near as I can figure out, this is the way John and America's family shaped up. Not sure I've accounted for the eleven children, and I only know for sure a couple of the four who were dead by 1920.

John Brashear, b. Nov 1851, IN, living in Laconia, Harrison Co, IN, in 1920; m. 30 Apr 1873, Harrison Co, IN, **America Thompson**, b. 28 Aug 1850?, d. 20 Mar 1920, Harrison Co, IN, d/o Nathaniel and Elizabeth Thompson (re: obit of America (Thompson) Brashear; additional data from John Thompson).

d-1. **William Brashear,** b. March 1875, IN (widower, 25, in 1900 census), d. Jan 1999, IN

e-1. **Charles Brashear**, b. Jan 1900 (4/12 in 1900 census)

d-2. **George Brashear**, b. July 1876, KY

d-3. **David Brashear**, b. 10 Jan 1878, KY; m. 31 Jan 1907, Harrison Co, IN, *Carrie E. Thompson*, b. 29 June 1881, lived Latham, IL, in 1920

d-4. **Mabel Brashear**, b. July 1881, KY (18 in 1900), living in 1920, author of her mother's obit; m. 2 May 1901, Harrison Co, IN, *John E. Byrum*

d-5. **Bertha Brashear**, d. 16 Oct 1884

d-6. **Mary Brashear**, b. Aug 1885, KY (14 in 1900 census)

d-7. **W.L. Brashear**, lived New Albany, IN, in 1920

d-8. **Laura Brashear**, b. 1888, lived Davidson, IN, in 1920; m. 22 Aug 1908, Harrison Co, IN, *W.P. McIntire*

d-9. **Annie Brashear**, b. Dec 1888, IN (11 in 1900 census) d-10. **Clara Brashear**, b. 21 Jan 1890 (per 1900 census and Marr. Lic), IN; m. 11 April 1908, in Harrison Co, IN (Bk R, p.462), *Forest Cotner*, lived Davidson, IN, in 1920

d-11. **Maggie Brashear**, d. 2 Jul 1893

Either Mary or Annie Brashear, married D.M. Maynard, and lived Tipton, IN, in 1920

John could very well be a son of the William Brashear who was living in Harrison Co, IN. Note that the data I have on William's family ends with the 1850 census and your John was born Nov 1851. John could be #c-6. Note also that John named his first son, William. Data from: "Geraldine Crouch" <gbc34@hotmail.com>

b-x. **William Brashear**, b. c1812, NC (38 in 1850 census, Harrison Co, IN); m. 20 Nov 1836, (Harrison Co, IN, Marriages), *Merinda McEntire*, b. c1813, Harrison Co, IL (37 in 1850), d. 9 Jul 1876, Metropolis, Massac Co, IL. William **MAY** (no proof) be s/o (a-x.) Thomas Brashear, who is in the 1830 Census, Harrison Co, IN. In 1840, next door to William is a Mary Brashear, 60-70, b. c1770-80, possibly his mother; she is not in the 1850 census.

c-1. **Thomas Brashear**, b. c1837, Harrison Co, IN (13 in 1850)

c-2. **William S. Brashear**, b. c1839, Harrison Co, IN (11 in 1850), d. Mound City, IL, 23 Feb 1910; m. 30 Jun 1867, in Massac Co, IL, *Liza Jane Geneau*. William S. Brashear lived in Metropolis, Massac Co, IL in 1876; Gerri Crouch has pages from the Bible of William S. and his funeral card of February 23, 1910

d-1. **William Thomas Brashear**, b. ?, d. shortly after birth

d-2. **Franklin Brashear**, b. ?, d. shortly after birth

d-3. **Anna Holland Brashear**, b. ?, d. ?; m. _____?

d-4. **? _____ Brashear**, b. ?, d. ?; m. _____?

c-3. **Robert N. Brashear**, b. c1845, Harrison Co, IN (5 in 1850). Robert N. Brashear lived in Metropolis, Massac Co, IL in 1876

c-4. **George W. Brashear**, b. c1847, Harrison Co, IN (3 in 1850)

c-5. **Francis Brashear**, b. c1849, Harrison Co, IN (10/12 in 1850)

Family found in 1860 in Smithland, Livingston Co, KY (trade: Cooper), with two more children:

c-6. **Catherine Brashear**, b. c1854 (6 in 1860)

c-7. **John F. Brashear**, b. c1857 (3 in 1860)

******

William Henry Brashear and Nora Worster

William Henry Brashear, b. 22 July 1864, MO; m. 20 April 1893, at Lee, IA, **Nora Ellamus Worster**, b. 30 Oct 1866-68, Keokuk, IA, d. 19 June 1954, Keokuk, IA, bur Greenwood Cem, Hamilton, IL, d/o Thomas M. Worster, b. MO, and Martha A. _____, b. WVa. In the 1900 census, William and Nora were living at 1476 Paleau, Keokuk, in a rented house, next door to Thomas M. and Martha A. Worster. William Henry Brashear deserted his family about 1901, and the children were raised by their Worster grandparents. Nora m.2. 3 June 1916, Hamilton Bell; they lived some of the time in Quincy, Adams Co, MA.

1. **Anna Mae Brashear**, b. 11 Feb 1894, Ft Madison, Lee Co, IA, d. 29 Oct 1970, Lemon Grove, San Diego Co, CA, bur Ft Rosecrans Cem, Point Loma, San Diego, CA; m. 6 Aug 1919, at Hamilton, IL, **Frank Othello Barber**. (data from Anita Barber. as of 1992: 1542, Angelus Ave, Lemon Grove, CA 91945; 619;697-6952)
2. **William Henry Brashear, Jr**, b. 20 June 1896, Keokuk, IA

****

Ruth Brashears and Henry Tabor

from Willie Reeves Hardin Bivins, Oklahoma City <wvbivins@webzone.net>,
Ken Risley <teardrp9@aol.com>,
Don Jennings, Sacramento <dmandthee@aol.com)>,
Bob Wilson, Corvallis, OR, <bob_w_97446@yahoo.com>,
Gloria Taber, Chandler, OK, <gtaber@brightok.net>

1st gen: William Taber and Hagar Stovall
2nd gen: John Taber and Mary Fowler
3rd gen: James Taber; m. Edy ?Russell. William Yates has posted a family tree on rootsweb.com all the way back into England to nobility. They had children:

1. Henry Tabor, who m. **Rutha Brashears**
2. William Tabor,
3. Edy Tabor,
4. James Tabor,
5. Isaac Tabor,
6. Russell Tabor,

Ruth (Rutha, Ruthie, Ruthey) Brashear(s), b. c1805-6, TN (age 59 in 1865 pension application), d. Oct 1870, Ozark Co, MO; m. 8 Feb 1821 in Perry County, TN ("by Rev. William Hodge," according to her affidavit in her pension application in Douglas Co, MO) **Henry Tabor**, b. 1802 in Warren Co, Kentucky, d. 31 Dec 1861 (or 4 Jan 1862) in Rolla, Phelps Co, MO.

Henry and Ruthie showed up in the Ozarks about 1833. Henry lied about his age and went into the Civil War when he was about 60. He died of a combination of illnesses, including measles, while still in camp in MO, not long after he enlisted. Several years after his death, Ruth applied for a pension. Her file is full of documents, and from them we learned that her maiden name was Brashears, according to one document. Others spelled it Butchers, Brasher, Beshers and maybe some other ways.

Silas Turnbo (http//thelibrary.springfield.missouri.org/ lochist/turnbo/), wrote, "Henry Tabur married Ruthy Pershears. Their children were John the preacher (my wife's gg grandfather) who died several years ago. Henry who was killed on Pond Fork in war times and Bob and Jim. The names of their daughters were Nancy who married Hiram Bias, Susan who married Simon Herrean. Phoebe who married Paton Keesee son of the old time settler Paton Keesee, Ede who married Mort Herrean, Manerva who married Cage Duggins and Eliza who married Pinkney Herrean. These early pioneers are all dead and the most of their children that we mention are passed over the great beyond too. Those of them who are living are growing very old and stand on the brink of the grave."

A number of researchers have outlined the Tabor/Taber lineage, but I have found nowhere that anyone has identified Rutha's parents. Her surname is often spelled in various ways (as hhttp//genforum. com/taber/messages/399.html), but I don't think there is much doubt that she comes from the Brashears line. From looking at your notes on volumes 1-6, it's hard to tell which (if any) might cover her birth family. If you have covered her family, we would be interested in that particular volume, but the whole series is far beyond our means.

Bob Wilson: Concerning John M. Tabor's wife, Susan Jane, all the other researchers I have seen have her maiden name as "Riswell", or possibly "Risley", as in the second of your named sources. I lean toward the latter, since there seem to have been quite a number of Risley's in the area, but I have never had names for her parents. I'll have to investigate Noah Risley and Harriett Scott to see what I can stir up. I did obtain a photo of the tombstone for John & Susan at the new

Friend Cemetery; the original Friend Cemetery, together with several others, was relocated to accommodate the building of Bull Shoals Reservoir.

Family of Henry Tabor and Rutha Brashears:
b-1. John M. Tabor, b. 23 Apr 1824, Madison Co, IL, d. 11 Mar 1905, Ozark Co, MO, bur Friend Cem, Ozark Co, MO; m. c1843, in Ozark Co, MO, Susan Jane Risley, b. Sep 1830, IL, d/o Noah Risley and Harriett W. Scott. John and Susan are buried at the New Friend Cem (the Old Friend Cem was relocated to accommodate the building of Bull Shoals Reservoir.)
   c-1. Tabitha Tabor, b. c1844, MO
   c-2. Bennett Tabor, b. c1845, MO (or Hill Co, TX), d. Mar 1897, Ozark Co, MO, bur Friend Cem, Ozark Co, MO; m.1. Cindy Ledbetter, b. ?, bur Chandler, OK (they had 10 ch, including sons, Hiram and Isaac); m.2. c1870, Elizabeth Friend. (data from Gloria Taber <gtaber@brightok.net>
      d-1. John William Taber, (s/o Bennett Tabor and Elizabeth Friend), b. 8 Feb 1882, Lutie, MO, d. Jan 1929, Chandler, OK; m. Elsie Gray
         e-1. George McKinley Taber, bur Chandler, OK
            f-x. John William Taber, bur Chandler, OK; m. Gloria

         e-2. Ray Taber, bur Chandler, OK
         e-3. Averil Taber, bur Chandler, OK
   c-3. William J. Tabor, b. 1851, IL; m. 15 Mar 1870, in Ozark Co, MO, Louisa M. Murphy
   c-4. Manerva Tabor, b. 9 Feb 1854, Gainesville, Ozark Co, MO, d. Aug 1913, Gore, Sequoyah Co, OK, bur Round Mountain Cem, between Gore and Vian, Sequoyah Co, OK; m.1.10 Jun 1870, in Ozark Co, MO, Artus J. Cleveland; m.2. 13 Aug 1878, in Ozark Co, MO, Alexander McNight; m.3. abt 1881 --?-- "Kersey" {Bob Wilson: her name was "Mrs. Manerva Kersey" when she married J. H. Sills. My wife's first cousin Carolyn (Sills) Van Dyck somehow determined that his first name was Paton/Peyton, so I strongly suspect he was one of the several Payton Keesee's in that region at the time); m.4. 1883, Cursey Sills; m.4. 26 Sep 1883, at Isabella, Ozark Co, Missouri, Joshua Henry Sills; m.5. 29 Nov 1891, Crawford Co., Arkansas, Enoch Potts (a son, Fred Potts, b. Oct 1893)

c-5. Rutha Eda (Edy?) Tabor, b. 28 Sep 1856, Ozark Co, MO, d. 12 Jun 1925, Corsicana, Navarro Co, TX, bur Eastern Star plot, Corsicana, TX; m. 23 May 1874, in Ozark Co, MO, Elias Bivins

c-6. Sarah Tabor, b. 1859, MO; m. 26 Aug 1875, in Ozark Co, MO, Levi W. Ledbetter

c-7. Hiram Tabor, b. 25 Dec 1861, MO; m. 8 Feb 1887, Maggie ____

c-8. Phoebe Tabor, b. c1864, MO; m. ____ Wells

c-9. John Franklin Tabor, b. 12 May 1867, MO, d. 12 Jan 1913, Ozark Co, MO, bur Isabella Cem, Ozark Co, MO; m. Mary L. Cooledge

c-10. Robert Tabor, b. 4 Jun 1871, Taney Co, MO; m. Nancy E. ____

c-11. Sally Tabor, b. ?; m. Will Malick/Mallett

b-2. Nancy Jane Tabor, b. 12 Nov 1826, Madison Co, IL, d. 9 Jul 1898, Dugginsville, Ozark Co, MO. bur Hart Cem, Ozark Co, MO; m. 19 Aug 1844, Taney Co, MO, Hiram Bias

b-3. Susan Tabor, b. 1830, Macoupin Co, IL; m. c1846, Simon Herrean

b-4. Phoebe Tabor, b. 1832, Macoupin Co, IL, d. 1898, Itasca, Hill Co, TX, bur Itasca Cem, Itasca, TX; m.1. c1850, ____ Brown; m.2. 1 Oct 1857, Ozark Co, MO, Paton Keesee, s/o Paton Keesee, an old-time settler in MO.

b-5. Ede (Edy?) Tabor, b. 1835, Taney Co, MO; m. c1854, Taney Co, MO, Mort Herrean

b-6. Minerva Tabor, b. c1837; m. c1858, Micajah "Cage" Duggins

b-7. Henry William Tabor, b. 1839, MO (or AR), d. during Civil War, at Pond Fork, AR; m. Katie Ledbetter.

c-1. Fanny Tabor, b. 1870, AR, d. 1947, OK

c-2. Henry William Tabor, b. c1867-78, AR, d. CA, 1952

c-3. Isaac Taber, b. 1872, AR, d. 1952, Antioch, CA; m. Felitha Cumile (Tine) Yocum, b. 1872, AR, d. 1915, OK (grandparents of Don Jennings)

c-4. Jacob Tabor, b. 1874, AR, d. _?_, OK

b-8. Robert Tabor, b. Mar 1841, MO, d. 8 Jul 1907, Leavenworth, Leavenworth Co, KS (or d. 11 Feb 1963 buried long cemetery in OK); m. 8 Jun 1863, in Ozark Co, MO, Tabitha "Betha" Graham, b. 1846, d. 1918

b-9. James Tabor, b. Aug 1843, MO, d. Dec 1914, Ozark Co, MO; m. 12 Jul 1862, in Ozark Co, MO, Mary Tabor

b-10. Eliza Tabor, b. 1847, MO; m. 1870, in Ozark Co, MO, Pinky Herrean

****

James "Jim" Brashears and Elizabeth Stone

Carolyn Higdon's Line:

James "Jim" Brashears, b. c1823, TN; m. *Elizabeth "Lizzie" Stone*, b. c1834, IL (great grandparents of Carolyn A (Brashears) Higdon)

a-x. **Henry William Brashears**, b. 22 Mar 1870, KY, d. 10 Apr 1931, Bertrand, MO; m. 22 Jan 1896, *Rosa Ann Lang*, b. 29 Jul 1882, Carlisle Co, KY, d. 12 Jun 1927, Armor, MO, d/o Charles and Sallie (Grubbs) Lang.

b-x. **Henry Brashears Jr**, b. 17 Oct 1920, Bertrand, MO, d. 26 Sep 1951, Bertrand, MO; m. 31 Jan 1942, _____

c-x. **Carolyn A. Brashears**, b. 11 Nov 1942, Sikeston, MO; m. 13 Apr 1963, *Malcolm Higdon*

*****

Earna R. Breshears and Etha Pearl Dooly

Obit from Independence, MO, *Examiner*

Clora Elizabeth "Liz" Meyers, 58, Odessa, died Wednesday, March 6, 2002, at the Medical Center of Independence.

Mrs. Meyers was born March 17, 1943, in Slater, MO., the daughter of Earna R. and Etha Pearl(Dooly) Breshears. On March 26, 1970, she married Donald W. "Hamburger" Meyers in Marshall, MO., who preceded her in death on Feb. 17, 1997. She had worked for Morgan's Restaurant and Taco John's in Odessa, and Wendy's and Dairy Queen in Oak Grove.

She attended rural school and Marshall High School. She was a member of New Life Assembly of God in Oak Grove, where she had worked in the nursery.

Her survivors include three children, Dwayne Meyers, and Ernie Meyers and wife, Kari Meyers, all of Odessa, and Karen Dieckhoff and husband, Tim, Blue Springs; her mother Etha Pearl Breshears, Holden, Mo.; two brothers, Ralph Lee Breshears, Arrow Rock, Mo., and John Breshears, BeBee, Ark.; a sister, Aline Kirchoff, Holden; five grandchildren, Rayna and Kyle Meyers, and Jordan, Shanna and Colby Dieckhoff; and her mother-in-law, Paula Meyers, Concordia, Mo.

Services will be 1 p.m. Saturday at the church. Burial will be in Mount Tabor Cemetery, Odessa. Friends may call from 6 to 8 tonight at the Ralph O. Jones Chapel, Odessa. The family suggests contributions to your favorite charity. (Posted on GenForum by: Linda M. Seevers, 13 March 2002; thanks Linda.)

from this obit, the following family fragment:

Earna R. Breshears; m. *Etha Pearl Dooly*, Etha living Holden, MO, in 2002

Children included:

x. **Ralph Lee Breshears**, living Arrowrock, MO, in 2002

x. **John Breshears**, living BeBee, AR, in 2002

x. **Aline Breshears**, m. _____ *Kirchoff*, living Holden, MO, in 2002

x. **Clora Elizabeth "Liz" Breshears**, b. 17 March 1943, Slater, MO, d. 6 March 2002, at the Medical Center of Independence, MO; m. 26 March 1970, in Marshall, MO, *Donald W. "Hamburger" Meyers*, d. 17 Feb 1997, s/o _____ Meyers and Paula _____.

    y. Dwayne Meyers, of Odessa, MO, in 2002

    y. Ernie Meyers, m. Kari _____, of Odessa, MO, in 2002

        z. Rayne Meyers,

        z. Kyle Meyers,

    y. Karen Myers, m. Tim Dieckhoff, of Blue Springs, MO, in 2002

        z. Jordan Dieckhoff,

        z. Shanna Dieckhoff,

        z. Colby Dieckhoff,

22. BESHEARS FAMILIES OF WILKES COUNTY, NC

The name Brashears first appears in Wilkes Co, North Carolina, records when **Martha Brashears/Bishears** was listed as head of household in the Census of 1810. Bishears was apparently another misspelling of the surname. She was 16-45 (b. 1765-1794) and had three daughters, two 10-16, and one under 10:

> Catharine "Catie" Bishears;
> Martha Bishears;
> Sarah "Sallie" Bishears.

There was also a listing for Mary Bishears with three people: a male 0-10, a female 0-10 and herself, 10-16. Mary's name never showed up again in the Census, so it is unknown if she was a young mother 16 years of age with 2 small children, nor where she might have gone from Wilkes County. She was apparently in the household of Gabriel Church.

The first Martha, apparently a widow, was said to have come to Wilkes County from the banks of the Potomac River in Virginia. This may have been the Great Southern Branch of the Potomac, called Wappacomo by the Indians, now in West Virginia.

A Beshears descendant and researcher, V. (Church) Taylor of North Carolina (now deceased), thought that Martha may have come to NC from Kentucky.

The following data comes mainly from the *Wilkes County Heritage Book*, published in the 1980's, augmented by research by Lois Beshears, Bernice Beshears, and Brenda Lowe.

V9-2798.   A-x. **Martha Brashears/Bishears,** b. 1765-94 (16-45 in 1810 Wilkes Co, NC). Since she had two daughters in the 1794-1800 period, she was probably b. c1775-80.

Family of Martha Brashears/Bishears

V9-2799.   B-1. **Mary Bishears,** b. c1794 (10-16 in 1810); m. *Gabriel Church.* Family story has it that she and Gabriel were out in the woods hunting squirrels, when his gun accidentally discharged and killed her.

V9-2800.   B-2. ***Catharine "Catie" Bishears,** b. 1797/8, on the banks of the Potomac River in Virginia, d. 1900/01 in Wilkes Co (103 years old!). She was a charter member of the Yellow Hill Baptist Church in Wilkes Co, which was formed in 1853. Catie had three children out of wedlock: the first was the child of **Naamon Woodie**; the other two are believed to be (no proof) children of Gabriel Church, her sisters' husband.

V9-2801.   B-3. **Martha Bishears**, b. c1800, VA (0-10 in 1810), d. c1900, Webster Co, MO; m. 1816, in Wilkes Co, NC, **Kelly Sartin/Sartain**. Possible daughter, reported by Leah (Leah_1963@msn.com). Anyone have any data?

V9-2802.   B-4. **Sarah "Sallie" Bishears,** b. c1805; m. **Gabriel Church**, after her sister Mary's death. Sarah was living with Gabriel and Mary prior to Mary's death (and it looks like Catie lived with them too). Gabriel and Sallie both died after 1880. Since we do not know when Mary was killed and when Gabriel and Sallie married, we do not know which of the sisters was the mother of Gabriel's children:

V9-2803.   C-1. David Church, b. c1815, probably s/o Mary (since Sally was only about 10 years old in 1815). David Church m.1. Elizabeth Crane, m.2. Elizabeth Stuart.

V9-2804.   C-2. Amelia Church, b. c1820; m. 15 Feb 1843, Henry Bumgarner

V9-2805.   C-3. Gabriel Church, III

V9-2806.   C-4. Joel M. Church, b. 8 Oct 1824, d. 18 Feb 1917; m. 29 Sep 1844, Rhoda Catherine Payne

V9-2807.   C-5. Caroline Church, b. 1832; m. Alexander Church, IV

V9-2808.   C-6. Winston Church, b. c1836; m. 13 Dec 1854, Sarah "Sally" Kees

V9-2809.   C-7. Jordon Church, b. 1838; m.1. 24 Jan 1852, Melinda Payne, m.2. Elizabeth Bentley

V9-2810.   C-8. Catherine Church, b. 1838

Catherine "Catie" Bishears

B-2. **Catharine "Catie" Bishears** was said to be born on the banks of the Potomac in Virginia, in 1797/98 and died in Wilkes Co, North Carolina, in 1900/01. The surname was corrupted to "Beshears" in her children, all three of whom seem to have been illegitimate. The Wilkes Co North Carolina Court Minutes of 4 Feb 1818 identify the father of the oldest, Aaron: "Naamon Woodie, Bastardy Bond— in body of

Catherine Beshears. Jonathan Woodie, security." Naamon Woodie was married to Ruth Carter.

V9-2811. C-1. *Aaron Beshears, b. 27 Dec 1817, Wilkes Co, NC, d. 10 Feb 1892; m. *Alia "Alley" Owens*

V9-2812. C-2. Martha "Patsie" Beshears, b. April 1825, possibly (no proof) daughter of Gabriel Church; m. *Jonathan P. Woodie*, b. c1824 in Wilkes Co, s/o Naamon Woodie and Ruth Carter. Jonathan died during the Civil War, 13 March 1863, of Yellow Fever which he contracted while a prisoner in Orange County, Virginia. Patsie died in 1901, in Wilkes Co, NC.

V9-2813. C-3. Mary "Polly" Beshears, possibly (no proof) daughter of Gabriel Church; m. *Rev. William Walker* and they lived in the Lewis Fork community near Fletcher Creek.

Aaron Beshears and Alia Owens

C-1. Aaron Beshears, (s/o Catherine "Catie" Bishears and Naamon Woodie), b. 27 Dec 1817, Wilkes Co, NC, d. 10 Feb 1892 (dates from death certificate); m. c1842, *Alia "Alley" Owens*, b. 3 Feb 1827, d. 29 May 1916, Wilkes Co, NC, d/o Larkin Owens and Elizabeth Greer (data from death certificate). Alley was a granddaughter of Barnard Owens and Benjamin Greer, both Revolutionary War Soldiers.

Aaron was commander of the home-guard in the Summit Area of Wilkes County, a unit formed during the Civil War to hunt slackers and deserters. He and Alley are buried in the Beshears Cemetery in the Summit area.

Children of Aaron Beshears and Alia Owens:

V9-2814. D-1. Malinda "Lin" Beshears, b. c1842; m.1. *Joseph "Pete" Waters*, m.2. *Larkin Griffin*

V9-2815. D-2. Martha Beshears, b. 12 April 1844-5, d. 17 March 1915; m. *Jerry Walker*

V9-2816. D-3. *Clarissa Catherine Beshears, b. 28 July 1846, d. 28 Sep 1943, Wilkes Co, NC; m. 9 March 1865, *Henry Harrison Church*, b. 1844, d. 1917.

V9-2817. D-4. *John Beshears, b. 12 Jan 1850, d. 29 Sep 1936, Wilkes Co, NC; m.1. 27 Oct 1867. *Selena V. Church*, b. 14 Feb 1849, d. 10 Dec 1900; m.2. 9 Oct 1904, *Nelia Shepherd*, b. 24 July 1881, d. 2 July 1953,

V9-2818. D-5. William Franklin Beshears, b. 29 May 1852, d. 31 Jan 1945; m. *Sarah Camilla Blackburn*, b. 9 Feb 1854, d. 21 Nov 1939. William and Sarah were the parents of 12 children and at one time were written up in "The State, A Weekly Survey of NC" as having 600 descendants and unsurpassed by anyone in N.C. (see family of Edmund Blackburn in Heritage Book)

V9-2819.   E-1. **Albert Gaither Beshears**, b. 1873, d. 1961

V9-2820.   E-2. **Zora Adina Beshears**, b. 1876, d. 1968

V9-2821.   E-3. **Cora Ella Beshears**, b. 27 June 1877, d. 21 April 1940, Carborrus Co, NC; m.1. *Martin Philo Phillips*; m.2. *Finley A. Eller*

V9-2822.   E-5. **Rettie Victoria Beshears**, b. 1878, d. 1951

V9-2823.   E-6. **Heg Hamilton Beshears**, b. 1880, d. 1957

V9-2824.   E-7. **Ida Mary Beshears**, b. 1882, d. 1963

V9-2825.   E-8. **Sarah Evelyn Beshears**, b. 1883, d. 1970

V9-2826.   E-9. **Willie Thomas Beshears**, b. 1886, d. 1969

V9-2827.   E-10. **Daniel Fowle Beshears, Sr**, b. 1888, d. 1969

V9-2828.   E-11. **Ray Vaughan "Dock" Beshears**, b. 1890, d. 1980

V9-2829.   E-12. **Lillie Alberta Beshears**, b. 23 Oct 1891, Wilkes Co, NC, d. 21 Marcy 1965, Wilkes Co, NC; m. 4 July 1906, a first cousin, *****John Sherman Beshears**, b. 3 Aug 1887, Wilkes Co, NC, d. there 13 May 1940, s/o John Beshears and Selena V. Church.

V9-2830.   E-13. **Nettie M. Beshears**, b. 1893, d. 1984

V9-2831.   D-6. *****Aaron Essley Beshears,** b. 6 Oct 1855, d. 25 Jan 1948; m.1. *Cynthia Ellen Younce* (or Yountz), m.2. *Nancy Elizabeth Lee*

V9-2832.   D-7. **Elizabeth Beshears**, b. 4 March 1859, d. 27 Nov 1947; m. *Rev. James M. Pilkenton*

Mary Owens, sister of Alley, lived with Aaron and Alley and was the mother of three children by Aaron Beshears. Family members remember Alley raising these children as her own.

Children of Aaron Beshears and Mary Owens:

V9-2833.   D-1. *****Winfield Scott Beshears,** b. 1854, d. 1940-41; m. *Selona "Lon" Josephine Walsh*

V9-2834.   D-2. **Adlaide Beshears**, b. 8 March 1857, d. 18 May 1930; m.1. *John Madison Powell*, m.2. *Thomas South*

V9-2835.   D-3. **Cornelius Clingman Beshears**, b. 25 March 1860, d. 21 Dec 1951; m. *Sarah Jane Owens*, b. July 1886. Sarah Jane was the daughter of Andrew and Mary Phillips Owens. Andrew was the brother of Alia and Mary Owens, making Cornelius and Sarah Jane first cousins.

V9-2836.   E-1. **Marshall Clinton Beshears**, b. 1887, d. 1978, m.1. Martisha Cordelia Roten, b.1883,d. 1938; m.2. Annie Flavil Yates b. 1920, d. 1992.

V9-2837.   E-2. **William Cowles Beshears**, b. 1890 d. 1983; m. 1. Annie Mae Parsons b. 1890, d.1969, m. 1907, divorced 1916. m.2. Clementine Brown Severt b. 1878, d.1964; m.3. Lelia Sheets Wyatt, b. 1890, d. 1960.

V9-2838.   E-3. **Charles H. Beshears**, b. 1893, d. 1899

V9-2839.   E-4. **Aaron Lee Beshears**, b. 1896, d. 1969, m.1. 1915 Margaret Roten, b. 1892, d.1928; m.2. 1929, Mattie Roten (sister of Margaret) b. 1887, d. 1969

Clarissa Catherine Beshears and Henry Church

D-3. **Clarissa Catherine Beshears,** (d/o Aaron Beshears and Alia "Alley" Owens), b. 28 July 1846, Wilkes Co, NC (ref. NC Births), d. 28 Sep 1943, Ashe Co, NC; m. 9 March 1865, *Henry Harrison Church*, b. 22 July 1844, d. 5 March 1917, Burke Co, NC.

Family of Clarissa Catherine Beshears and Henry Harrison Church:

V9-2840.   E-1. Thomas Aaron Church, b. 1866, d. 1943; m.1. Martha Ellen Blackburn (14 ch), b. 1863, d. 1911; m.2. Hattie Rice. Ch:

V9-2841.   F-1. Levi Harrison Church, b. 1884,

V9-2842.   F-2. Grover Cleveland Church, b. 1885,

V9-2843.   F-3. Bynum Lufate Church, b. 1886,

V9-2844.   F-4. Thomas Mack Church, b. 1888,

V9-2845.   F-5. Annie Dora Church, b. 1890,

V9-2846.   F-6. Florence Deona Church, b. 1891-1939; m. Noah Columbus Johnson, 1886-1971,

V9-2847.   F-7. Walter Grady Church, b. 1893,

V9-2848.   F-8. Edmund Call Church, b. 1895,

V9-2849.   F-9. Mary Idella Church, b. 1896,

V9-2850.   F-10. Willard Vann Church, b. 1898,

V9-2851.   F-11. Nettie Church, b. 1900,

V9-2852.   F-12. Willie Church, b. 1901,

V9-2853.   F-13. Coila Mae Church, b. 1905,

V9-2854.   F-14. Richard Hackette Church, 1906.

V9-2855.   E-2. William John Wesley Church, b. 1867, d. 1961; m. Fannie Ellen Church

V9-2856.   E-3. Harrison Loranso Dow Church, b. 1870, d. 1956; m.1.
            Mary Bauguss, m.2. Martha Green
V9-2857.   E-4. Calvin Horace Greely Church, b. 1872, d. 1890
V9-2858.   E-5. Aly Queen Esther Church, b. 1874, d. 1960; m.1. James
            Chappell; m.2. Charles Hackett
V9-2859.   E-6. Daniel Welborn Jones Church, b. 1876, d. 1964; m.
            Alice Lorine Fairchilds, b. 1880, d. 1973. Ch: Clyde
            Mathus; Esther Maybelle; Lena Mary; and Harrison Henry
            Church
V9-2860.   E-7. Zora Camilla Church, b. 1877, d. 1973; m. David S. Lee,
            b. 1874, d. 1953. Ch: Maude; Mamie; Robert; Broadus;
            Pansy; and Wade Lee
V9-2861.   E-8. Winfield Scott Church Sr, b. 1879, d. 1960; m. Selah
            Jane Baker, b. 1883, d. 1961. Ch: V., 1901; Zeb, 1903;
            Mae, 1906; Ina, 1908; Winfield Scott Jr, 1910; Robert
            Page, 1913; and Lillian Church, 1919.
V9-2862.   E-9. Sallie Clarissa Virginia Church, b. 1881, d. 1969; m.
            Cicero Calvin Kees, b. 1878, d. 1943. Ch: Isaac A., 1899;
            Lonnie Levi Sr, 1904; and Turner Harrison Kees, 1909.
V9-2863.   E-10. Rebecca Lou Ellen Church, b. 1883, d. 1971; m.
            Millard Monroe Phillips, b. 1881, d. 1966. Ch: Clara
            Estora, 1904; Greely Curtis, 1906; Lou Eva Mae, 1908;
            Horace Harrison, 1911; William Joseph Sr, 1916; Sarah
            Pauline "Polly", 1923; Wade Harold Phillips, 1927.
V9-2864.   E-11. Nancy Elizabeth Church, b. 1885, d. 1907; m. How
            Columbus Phillips, b. 1882, d. 1949. Ch: Ennis, 1902;
            and James Blaine Phillips, 1906.
V9-2865.   E-12. Laura Church, b. 1888, d. 1888
V9-2866.   E-13. Winnie Mae Church, b. 1890, d. 1962; m. Enoch
            Reeves Mikeal Sr, b. 1883, d. 1956. Ch: Loy Martha
            Catherine, 1907; Lee Edward, 1908; Scott Tillman, 1909;
            Belle Boyd, 1911; Fanny Pearl, 1916; Ruth Marie, 1918;
            Asa Burton, 1920; Enoch Reeves Jr, 1922; John Wilburn,
            1924; Coy M., 1925; Betty Nell, 1930; and Max H. Mikeal,
            1933.

John Beshears and Selena Church

D-4. **John Beshears,** (s/o Aaron Beshears and Alia "Alley" Owens), b.
12 Jan 1850, d. 29 Sep 1936, Wilkes Co, NC; m.1. 27 Oct 1867. **Selena
V. Church**, b. 14 Feb 1849, d. 10 Dec 1900; m.2. 9 Oct 1904, **Nelia
Shepherd**, b. 24 July 1881 (she was younger than some of

John's children!), d. 2 July 1953, d/o Thomas Shepherd and Hannah Caroline Parsons. Eleven ch by 1st marr and six by second: (Thanks to Lois Beshears for data, which looks like Bible notes.)

Family of John Beshears and Selena V. Church:

[V9]-2867.　E-1. **Henry Lee Beshears**, b. 17 Aug 1868, d. 2 Feb 1945; m. 24 Dec 1890, *Laura Ann Green*. 13 ch.

[V9]-2868.　E-2. **Mary Elizabeth Beshears**, b. 22 May 1870, d. 30 May 1958; m. before 1886, *Zackery Greer*

[V9]-2869.　E-3. **Sarah C. Beshears**, b. & d. 1 July 1872

[V9]-2870.　E-4. **William M.R. Beshears**, b. c1875

[V9]-2871.　E-5. **Thomas Aaron Beshears**, b. Oct 1877; m. *Ninnie Church*

[V9]-2872.　E-6. **Aly Adina Beshears**, b. 20 March 1880, d. 24 Dec 1952; m. *J. Osco Cardwell*,

[V9]-2873.　E-7. **Dora B. Beshears**, b. c1883, d. 2 Feb 1883

[V9]-2874.　E-8. **Gertie Beshears**, b. 1 May 1885, d. 30 Aug 1970, Jonesboro, TN; m. _____ *Hodges*,

[V9]-2875.　E-9. ***John Sherman Beshears**, b. 3 Aug 1887, d. 13 May 1940; m.1. 4 July 1906, a cousin, *Lillie Alberta Beshears*, d/o William Franklin Beshears and Sarah Camilla Blackburn. John had four children by Chanie Phillips, b. 1 Jan 1900, at Jobs Cabin twp, Wilkes Co, NC, d. 10 June 1966, Forsyth Co, NC, d/o Nathan Phillips and his 2nd wife, Ellen Canter.

[V9]-2876.　E-10. **Belva Alice Beshears**, b. 11 Nov 1889, d. 11 Sep 1983; m. *James Monroe Church*,

[V9]-2877.　E-11. **Ida Virginia Beshears**, b. Feb 1892; m. *John T. Davis*,

Family of John Beshears and Nelia Shepherd:

[V9]-2878.　E-12. **Robert Glenn Beshears**, b. 28 July 1905

[V9]-2879.　E-13. **Elizabeth Lee Beshears**, (twin) b. 20 June 1907; m.

[V9]-2880.　F-x. Susan _____ ; m. _____ Graybal. In 2004, the only living daughter of Elizabeth Lee Beshears. (Sbavalon2003@yahoo.com)

[V9]-2881.　E-14. **Zebulon Vance "Zeb" Beshears**, (twin) b. 20 June 1907, d. 22 April 1975; m. 19 March 1938, *Bertie Leota Cornett*

[V9]-2882.　E-15. **Parker Beshears**, (twin) b. 30 Jan 1916, d. 23 Dec 1916

[V9]-2883.　E-16. **Paul Beshears**, (twin) b. 30 Jan 1916

[V9]-2884.　E-17. Un-named infant, b.& d. 29 Nov 1919

John Sherman Beshears and Lillie Beshears

[E]-9. **John Sherman Beshears**, (s/o John Beshears and Selena V. Church), b. 3 Aug 1887, d. 13 May 1940; m.1. 4 July 1906, a cousin, **Lillie Alberta Beshears**, d/o William Franklin Beshears and Sarah Camilla Blackburn. John had four children by <u>Chanie Phillips</u>.

The book, "The Phillips Family, Our History, Our Heritage" by Shirley Phillips Friel, says that Chanie Phillips, b. 1 Jan 1900, at Jobs Cabin twp, Wilkes Co, NC, never married, d. 10 June 1966, Forsyth Co, NC, d/o Nathan Phillips and his 2nd wife, Ellen Canter. She had six children:

      1. Vertie Reeves Phillips, b. 5 April 1919, (d/o Chanie Phillips and Cicero Mikeal), m. 13 Jan 1937, Wade Atkins,

      2. Mildred Leota Phillips, b. 27 Jan 1921, (d/o Chanie Philips and Rufus Hamby),

Chanie Phillips also had four children by John Sherman Beshears:

[V9]-2885.   F-1. Johnson Alonzo Phillips, b. 3 Aug 1927

[V9]-2886.   F-2. Delmar Phillips, b. 17 May 1930; m. 7 Nov 1955, Evelyn Darnell

[V9]-2887.   F-3. Anna Snowbell Phillips, b. 27 Feb 1935

[V9]-2888.   F-4. Clyde Iredell "Pat" Phillips, b. 30 Dec 1937

Aaron Essley Beshears and Cynthia Younce

[D]-6. **Aaron Essley Beshears**, (s/o Aaron Beshears and Alia "Alley" Owens), b. 6 Oct 1855, in Wilkes Co, NC (from his death certificate); he d. 25 May 1948, in Wilkes Co, NC and is buried at the Yellow Hill Baptist Cem, at Summit. Essley m.1. **Cynthia Ellen Younce**, b. c1863, d. after 1910. Essley and Cynthia were divorced. Essley m.2. 18 Feb 1892, in Wilkes Co, NC, **Nancy Elizabeth Lee**, b. 28 Sep 1869, d. 15 July 1953 (tombstone in Yellow Hill Baptist Cem), first child of William and Eliza (Mikeal) Lee.

<u>Children of Aaron Essley Beshears and his 1st wife, Cynthia Younce:</u>

[V9]-2889.   E-1. **Joseph Franklin Beshears**, b. 11 July 1881, d. 21 Aug 1939, bur. Yellow Hill Bapt. Cem.; m.1. 25 Dec 1904, **Maggie Tomlinson**, d/o Levi and Mary Alice (Blackburn) Tomlinson; m.2. **Ella T. Tomlinson**, Maggie's sister. Had family, but I don't have data.

[V9]-2890.   E-2. **Julia A. Beshears**, b. 13 March 1883, d. 19 July 1955, bur. Yellow Hill; m. **Robert Franklin Phillips**, s/o Eli Phillips.

V9-2891.   E-3. *James Dickson Beshears, b. July 1884, d. c 1928, bur. Winston-Salem, NC; m. 18 June 1906, *Florence Calloway*, b. 1888, d/o Jim Calloway

Children of Aaron Essley Beshears, and his 2nd wife, Nancy Elizabeth Lee:

V9-2892.   E-4. Julius Martin Beshears, b. 16 April 1894, d. 14 June 1982, Wilkes Co, bur. Arbor Grove Bapt. Cem, at Purlear, Wilkes Co; m. 28 Feb 1914, *Kiter Virginia Beshears*, b. 21 July 1896, d. 1 Aug 1976, d/o Henry Lee and Laura (Green) Beshears. Julius was a Postman for 60 years.

V9-2893.   E-5. Aley Lidy Elizabeth Beshears, b. 28 June 1896; m. *Amos James*

V9-2894.   E-6. William Moody Beshears, b. 23 July 1899, d. 12 Dec 1909, Wilkes Co, NC.

V9-2895.   E-7. Selay Lebeth Beshears, b. 1902; m. *Hubert Notsinger*; they were living in Winston-Salem in 1986

V9-2896.   E-8. Mary Rebecca Beshears, b. 26 Aug 1904; m. *Reece Spencer*; they also live in Winston-Salem, NC.

V9-2897.   E-9. Aaron Hegman Beshears, b. 23 Feb 1907; m. 24 Feb 1924, *Eugenia Diana Teague*

V9-2898.   E-10. Noah Call Beshears, b. 13 Dec 1909; m.1. *Florence Ashley*, d/o Job and James Ashley; m.2. 15 Aug 1959, in Wilkes Co, NC *Winnie Alice Spears*, b. 4 May 1924, d/o Lewis Anderson and Bertha Rosalie (Cornett) Spears.

James Dickson Beshears and Florence Calloway

E-3. James Dickson Beshears, b. July 1884, (s/o Aaron Essley Beshears and his 1st wife, Cynthia Younce), d. c 1928, bur. Winston-Salem, NC; m. 18 June 1906, *Florence Calloway*, b. 1888, d/o Jim Calloway. They had 9 children; (thanks to great-granddaughter, Mary (Jordan) Kriglein (maryj1968@yahoo.com) for data).

V9-2899.   F-1. James Walter Beshears,
V9-2900.   F-2. Webb Beshears,
V9-2901.   F-3. Josephine Beshears,
V9-2902.   F-4. James Dickson Beshears,
V9-2903.   F-5. Howard Beshears,
V9-2904.   F-6. Lacy Beshears,
V9-2905.   F-7. Beatrice Beshears,
V9-2906.   F-8. Elzie Densmore Beshears, b. 8 Aug 1909, Meadow View, VA, d. 15 Nov 1983, Winston Salem, NC; m. John Murphy Styles. They had 9 children.

V9-2907.	G-1. **Carrie Virginia "Sister" Beshears**, (not John Murphy Styles' daughter; she was born before Elzie and he met.)
V9-2908.	G-2. John Murphy Styles, Jr,
V9-2909.	G-3. James "Big Jim" Styles,
V9-2910.	G-4. Shirley Jean Styles, m. Lloyd James Jordan, SR and had 7 ch: Lloyd James, Jr; Caroly Winona (m. Saunders); Sharon Joann (m. Conrad); Sheila Faye (m. Carter); Tina Maire (m. Nail); David Anthony (d. when a few months old); Mary Melissa Jordan (m. Kriglein). Writes Mary Kriglein: "We were raised mainly in Sanford, NC, but lived some in Winston Salem."
V9-2911.	G-5. Flora Direne Styles,
V9-2912.	G-6. Johnsie Styles,
V9-2913.	G-7. Bessie Styles,
V9-2914.	G-8. Margaret Styles,
V9-2915.	G-9. Robert Styles,

Winfield Scott Beshears and Selona Walsh

D-1. **Winfield Scott Beshears**, (s/o Aaron Beshears and Mary Owens), 1854-1940/41; m. **Selona "Lon" Josephine Walsh**, and had 8 children, 5 boys and three girls (order of birth not certain; data from Bernice J. Beshears, 2396 Old Salisbury Rd, Winston-Salem, NC 27127, widow of Alfred Beshears, a grandson):

V9-2916.	E-1. **Grover Cleveland "Cleve" Beshears**, b. Summit, Wilkes Co, NC, 17 Dec 1895 (NC Births), d. 28 Feb 1972; m.1. **Emma Nelson** and lived in Portland, OR. Emma died as a result of burns from an electric heater; then Cleve moved back to North Wilkesboro and m.2. **Manie Beshears**; lived North Wilkesboro, NC.
V9-2917.	F-1. **Alice Beshears**, d/o Emma by a first marriage; went by name of Beshears (may have been adopted)
V9-2918.	F-2. stillborn child, born to Cleve and Emma
V9-2919.	E-2. **Manfield "Max" Beshears**, b. _____, d. _____; m. **Clara** _____ and they lived for a time in Edmonton, Canada, lived in Chicago;
V9-2920.	F-1. **Robert "Bob" Beshears**,
V9-2921.	E-3. ***John Leonard Beshears***, b. 11 May 1891, d. 29 July 1953, left home at an early age, lived in Alberta, Canada and Portland, OR. See below.

V9-2922.   E-4. **Odell Beshears**, b. 16 July 1893, d. 11 July 1971, m. **Nora Miller**. Lived at the old home place in Walsh, Wilkes Co, NC and had 8 children (see below).

V9-2923.   E-5. **Asa Beshears**, b. ____, d. ____, unmarried. He was blinded by gas in World War I; he fathered two daughters, one of whom is or was married to Jerry Lewis, world-known Hollywood comedian.

V9-2924.   E-6. **Laura Beshears**, b. ____, d. ____, m. ____ **Church**; lived in Tennessee; has two dau & 1 son

V9-2925.   E-7. **Ella Beshears**, b. ____, d. ____, m. **Miles Redding**; lived Yadkinville, NC.

V9-2926.   F-1. Essie Redding, b. Feb 1915,

V9-2927.   F-2. Eugene Redding, b. 9 June 1919,

V9-2928.   F-3. Charles Redding, b. 11 March 1921,

V9-2929.   F-4. John L. Redding, b. April 1926,

V9-2930.   F-5. Patsy Redding, b. Nov 1933

V9-2931.   F-6. Betty Redding, b. 11 March 1936

V9-2932.   E-8. **Josephine "Josie" Beshears**, b. ____, d. young ____

John Leonard Beshears and Bertha Anderson

E-3. **John Leonard Beshears**, Sr, b. 11 May 1891, Summit, Wilkes Co, NC; d. 29 July 1953, s/o Winfield Scott and Selona (Walsh) Beshears; lived North Wilkesboro, North Carolina; moved as a young man to Portland, Oregon (his brother "Cleve" either went with him or joined him soon after, for they both lived in Portland). J.L. m. in Washington state, **Bertha Anderson**, b. in Sweden, 3 Nov 1883, d. 9 Aug 1964. They moved to Edmonton, Alberta, Canada, where he married and three children were born; he then moved 1920 back to Portland. J. L. and Bertha divorced early, so the children lost contact with their father. (data from Ruth Beshears Cobb, 55 Langdon Terrace, Bronxville, NY 10708, and Gwen Beshears Reinke):
Children of John Leonard and Bertha (Anderson) Beshears:

V9-2933.   F-1. **Gwendolyn Lenore Beshears**, b. 28 June 1913, living in 1991 in Oregon; m. **Fred Reinke**.

V9-2934.   F-2. **John Leonard "Jack" Beshears, Jr,** b. 1 April 1915, Edmonton, Alberta, Canada, d. 17 May 1978; m. **Ruth Nehring**. After Jack's death, Ruth m.2. Jess Cobb. Jack and Ruth had two children.

V9-2935.   G-1. **John Leonard Beshears, III**, b. 8 Dec 1948; m. 10 June 1979, **Eleanor Mar**; lives (1991) in San Francisco

V9-2936.   H-1. **John Leonard Beshears IV**, b. 10 June 1982
V9-2937.   H-2. **Laura Beshears**, b. 1 July 1985
V9-2938.   G-2. **David Andrew Beshears**, b. 15 Dec 1951; m. 9 Jan
            1982, *Barbara Feihel*; lives (1991) in Brewster, NY
V9-2939.   H-1. **David Andrew Beshears, Jr**, b. 16 May 1984
V9-2940.   H-2. **Danielle Allyssa Beshears**, b. 6 July 1991
V9-2941. F-3. **Irwin Scott Beshears**, b. 12 Nov 1917, d. 28 Dec 1975;
            m. *Norma Thomas*, b. 2 March 1922, still living (1991) in
            Oregon.
V9-2942.   G-1. **Thomas Scott Beshears**, b. 19 Feb 1947, m.1.
            Cheryl ____; m.2. *Nancy (née Allison)*, b. 16 Nov
            1956; Thomas and Nancy have one daughter and live
            in Tigard, OR
V9-2943.   H-1. **Samantha Beshears**, b. 31 July 1984
V9-2944. F-4. **Doris Virginia Beshears**, b. 27 Aug 1923, Portland, OR;
            d. 7 Aug 1926, 20 days before her third birthday.

Odell Beshears and Lenora Miller

E-4. **Odell Beshears**, b. 16 July 1893, d. 11 July 1971, s/o Winfield
Scott and Selona (Walsh) Beshears, m. 28 Nov 1915, in Wilkes Co, NC,
Lenora "Nora" Ethel Miller, b. 24 March 1895 at Obids, Ashe Co, NC,
d. 10 Dec 1979, in Wilkes Co, NC. Both are buried at the Big Ivy Baptist
Cemetery at Purlear, Wilkes Co, NC. Odell seems to have been the one
who stayed in Wilkes Co and farmed the land.
V9-2945. F-1. **Dorothy Faye Beshears**, b. 24 Oct 1916, d. 4 Feb 1982,
            bur. Mountlawn Mem. Park, Wilkes Co; m. 15 Sep 1944,
            Thomas Linderman
V9-2946.   G-1. Judith Ann Linderman, b. 24 April 1947; m. 21 Dec
            1968, Edward Snyder Sr.
V9-2947.   H-1. Edward Snyder, Jr. b. 16 Feb 1970
V9-2948.   H-2. Laura Snyder, b. 3 Jan 1975
V9-2949.   G-2. Sarah Linderman, b. 29 Jan 1949, m. 15 July 1972,
            Danny Pell
V9-2950.   H-1. David Pell, b. 23 April 1974
V9-2951.   H-2. Melissa Pell, b. 24 April 1976
V9-2952. F-2. boy **Beshears**, b. 1 Aug 1918
V9-2953. F-3. **Orpha Beshears**, b. 10 July 1919, m. 1947, *William F.
            Mitchell Sr*
V9-2954.   G-1. William F. "Billy" Mitchell, Jr, b. 12 Dec 1947
V9-2955.   G-2. Robert "Bobby" Mitchell, b. 20 Nov 1948; m. Brigette
            Rogers

V9-2956.   H-1. Shelley Ann Mitchell, b. 31 May 1971
V9-2957.   F-4. **Ray Alfred Beshears**, b. 10 April 1921, d. 16 March 1990, m. 29 Sep 1944, *Bernice Johnston*, d/o Edwin Clive and Fannie Pearl (Hartzog) Johnston
V9-2958.   G-1. **David R. Beshears**, b. 11 July 1946, at Jefferson, Ashe Co, NC; m. *Carol Blackwell*
V9-2959.   F-5. **Vada Blanche Beshears**, b. 3 Aug 1923, m. 23 Dec 1942, *Robert Church*, d. 1971, s/o Alma and Mary (Church) Church
V9-2960.   G-1. Ronald Lee Church, b. 13 May 1945, m. Wanda Porter
V9-2961.   H-1. Christopher Church
V9-2962.   H-2. Michael Church
V9-2963.   G-2. Scott Church, b. 12 Feb 1959, m. 8 Aug 1981, Cheryl Hamby
V9-2964.   F-6. **Doris Mozelle Beshears**, b. 20 Jan 1927, m. 27 Nov 1927, *Harley Moser*. d. 1979
V9-2965.   G-1. Shirley Ann Moser, b. 14 Aug 1959, m. 10 July 1971, Ray Lowe
V9-2966.   H-1. Sharon Lowe, b. 22 Sep 1973
V9-2967.   H-2. Valerie Lowe, b. 14 June 1976
V9-2968.   F-7. **Lela Beshears**, b. 1 Feb 1928, m. 1947, *James Mitchell*
V9-2969.   G-1. Louise Mitchell, b. 12 Aug 1948; m. 1978, Donald Black
V9-2970.   G-2. Lorraine Mitchell, b. 25 Aug 1950; m. Steve Birkette
V9-2971.   H-1. Melissa Birkette, b. 21 May 1978
V9-2972.   H-2. Nathan Birkette, b. 1 Aug 1980
V9-2973.   G-3. James "Jimmy" Mitchell, Jr., b. 30 May 1953
V9-2974.   G-4. David Mitchell, b. 23 Oct 1970
V9-2975.   F-8. **Kathleen Beshears**, b. 27 June 1930, m. 20 Jan 1951, *James Blaine "J.B." Calloway*
V9-2976.   G-1. Benny Calloway, b. 17 Dec 1953; m. Gladys Benton
V9-2977.   G-2. Elaine Calloway, b. 27 Jan 1956, m. Terry West
V9-2978.   H-1. Stephanie West, b. 28 Oct 1973
V9-2979.   H-2. Kristi West, b. 6 June 1979
V9-2980.   H-3. Jason West, b. 13 Oct 1980
V9-2981.   G-2. Michael Calloway, b. 24 Aug 1957
V9-2982.   G-4. Karen Calloway, b. 12 Feb 1961,
V9-2983.   F-9. **Brenda Joyce Beshears**, b. 11 Aug 1941, m.1. 27 March 1959, *Edwin Lowe*, b. 21 Oct 1940, at Moravian Falls, Wilkes Co, NC, d. 20 Dec 1979, Yadkin Co, NC; m.2. *Joe Richardson*

2984.   G-1. Gregory Lowe, b. 5 May 1964, at North Wilkesboro, Wilkes Co, NC.

Contacts:

Lois Beshears, <sassy285@aol.com>	All lines
Rita Woodward <woodward@texas.net>	Sarah Beshears, 1805
Barry <ez@dialpoint.net>	Cora Beshears
Amy <white-tiger81@webtv.net>	Sherman Beshears

Bernice J. Beshears, 2396 Old Salisbury Rd, Winston-Salem, NC 27127, widow of Alfred Beshears
Mary (Jordan) Kriglein (maryj1968@yahoo.com)
Leah (Leah_1963@msn.com)
Susan Graybal (sbavalon2003@yahoo.com)

Descendants of
JAMES BRAZIER,
of Cumberland Co, NC

23. POSSIBLE ANCESTRY OF JAMES BRAZIER

The ancestry of James Brazier is still uncertain. He was a carpenter and farmer of Cumberland County, North Carolina. Circumstances (documentation is missing) tend to link him with John Brasseur of Nansemond County, Virginia, whose descendants lived in Essex Co, VA and Perquimans Co, NC in the early 1700's.

However, the sketch of James's grandson, Elijah Wesley Brazier, in *The History of Stewart County, Georgia*, says that the family came from Ireland at an unknown date. We need evidence.

Here is the paper trail that leads me to believe that James Brazier of Cumberland Co, NC, came from the line of John Brasseur of Nansemond Co, VA. (NOTE: Serial numbers in this chapter are those assigned in *The First 200 Years of Brashears in America*, Vol. 1 of A BRASHEAR(S) FAMILY HISTORY.)

John Brasseur, of Nansemond Co, VA

v1-4. John Brasseur, second son of Robert Brasseur, the Huguenot Immigrant, was born in 1624 in France and his birthdate registered on the Isle of Thanet, Kent County, England, according to the suspect record by Danny Brashear (IGI #8104402:4). Considering that John Brasseur Jr was born about 1650, this date can't be far wrong. He is named "sonn and heir" of Robert Brasseur in a 1667 land record (see below).

When John came to Virginia is uncertain, but Christopher Reyault was granted 600 acres "across Gloucester County," 6 March 1654, for transporting 12 persons, including "John Brashers" (Nugent, *Cavaliers and Pioneers*, I:302).

Virginia Land Patents Book 1, p.318 is a bit more specific: Christopher Regault, 600 acs. Glouster Co, 6 March 1654, "Upon eastward side of the main swamp of Crany Creek, upon the head of Breemans Neck and adj devdt to Mr. Breeman... Transportation of 12 persons: Christopher Regault, William Frost, Symon Parrett (maybe Garrett?), Joan Bugg, Wm Woodars, John Brashere, Thomas Studdel, his wife & child, William Risbixt & his wife, Wm Todd."

Since this is about a year after John's father, Robert Brasseur, got a similar patent in Nansemond County, we have to assume that Robert had sold his "headright" for transporting John.

On 17 April 1667, John Brasseur received a patent in "Nancimond" Co, VA, for "400 acres, adjoining Mr. Francis Spight, 300 acres part thereof was formerly granted to Robert Brasseur and Peter Rey, 24 Feb 1638, and 100 acres for transportation of two persons: Richard Kingsbury and Alice Whitaker. The moiety [i.e. half of an estate] is due the said John Brasseur, sonn and heir of the said Robert Brasseur." (*Va Land Patents*, Book 6, p.72)

This patent would indicate that John was the oldest surviving son (Benois/Benjamin was, of course, dead by this time). The 300-acre portion is half of the 600 acre tract purchased in 1638 by Robert Brassure and Peter Rey. John seems to have gotten the other half of the original 600 acres a few years later, but lost both parcels to the laws of escheatment.

In 1688, in Perquimans Co, NC: John Brasseur, Edw. Streater, Robt. Tooles signed as commissioners of precinct court. (*N.C. Gen. Register*, v.3 p.432.) This could hardly be John III, b. after his father married in 1675; nor John II, who was ensconsed in Essex Co, VA; it has to be the old man, John I, who was literate enough to be a burgess several times and who seems to have enjoyed stoking fires in many distant climes.

John Brasseur, the first, apparently died in the early 1690's. On 17 May 1692, John Brasseur [the son], "of Nansemond Co, now of Surry," [and] Mary Brasseur and Thomas Cocke, of Henrico, convey to William Cocke (brother of Thomas Cocke) a grist mill located in Surry Co. (Boddie, *Southside Virginia Families*, v.1, p.146-7). This is John Jr and his sister selling property they got from John Sr.

Earlier Surry Co records show John Brasseur, owner of this mill, leasing it out. John Brasseur had been active in Surry County, north and west of Isle of Wight County, from the 1660's. The 235 acre patent that came to him in 1674 through his wife, Mary Pitt, adjoined land of "the said Brasseur," in Surry Co. Several years earlier, on 7th 8ber

1668, John Brasseare, of Nansemond Co, leased to John Rawlings of Surry Co, a

> "water mill, land, and housing belonging to said Brasseaur on ye Burson Branch in upper Spipoaks Creek lately in occupation of Hen[ry] Francis. Lease for seven years, paying on 10 Oct. annually 3000 pounds of tobacco, said Rawlings agreeing to keep mill & housing in good repair and to build a dwelling house & to plant that parcell of ground with apple trees part of which is already fenced in to such purpose & to secure ye same & att ye expiration of ye time before said to deliver ye said mill up unto ye said Brasseur his heirs or assigns in good substantial working condition with flood gate & all other things in good order alsoe what housing is now or hereafter ye said Rawlings shall build upon ye said plantation hee is to leave in a tenantable condition." (Recorded, 21 Dec 1668, Surry Co, Deed Book I, p.319.)

The above deed of this mill to William Cocke sounds like John I's children disposing of their inheritance. This, however, does not jibe with John's having been a Burgess in 1695/6, 1696/7. (A different John? Apparently, a grandson.)

John Brasseur Sr may have had many children, but, at this moment, I know of only two, John Jr and Mary; however, I am ascribing to him a stray Richard Brashear, whom circumstances suggest was a son:

Children of John Brasseur and Mary Cocke:

v1-201. 3-1. *John Brasseur Jr, b. c1650, +/-5yrs [John Brasseur Sr would have been 21 in 1645 and John Jr was old enough to be a witness in Surry Co in 1675]; d. 1712/13, Essex Co, VA, and left a will; m. 20 May 1675, Nansemond Co, VA, _____ (unknown, but from Rappahannock Deeds and Estates, we think her name was **Ann Grill**). "John Brasseur of Nansemond witnessed at the marriage of John Brasseur Jr, 20 May 1675." (*Friends of Lower Virginia*).

v1-202. 3-2. **Richard Brasseur**, b. bef 1654. This one is somewhat speculative. In Surry Co, VA, 26 Jan 1675/76, Ann Kersey binds her son, John Kersey, to Richard Brassier as apprentice until age 21. (*Surry County Records*, by Eliz. T. Davis, p.138) This Richard would have to be 21, right? i.e., b. bef 1654. No further record; Richard may have died young, before John Brasseur [Jr] and Mary Brasseur and her husband, Thos Cocke, sold John Brasseur Sr's property. This brother would explain John Jr's naming a son Richard.

Child of John Brasseur and Mary Pitt:

v1-203.   3-3. **Mary Brasseur**, b. c1672-3, d/o John Brasseur and Mary Pitt; m. c1687, **Capt. Thomas Cocke**, b. at Malvern Hills, Henrico Co, VA, 1662-4; d. 1707. Thomas Cocke is reported in "Genealogy of the Cocke Family," (*VA Mag. Hist*, v.II, p.486) to m.2. Frances _____, which would mean that Mary probably died, c1698-1700. Thomas's will, dated 16 Jan 1706, Henrico Co, proved 1 April 1707, named their six children: 1. Thomas Cocke, Jr, 2. James Powell Cocke, 3. Henry Cocke, 4. Brazure Cocke, 5. Mary Cocke, 6. Elizabeth Cocke, (See *The First 200 Years of Brashears in America* for more.)

John Brazer Jr and Ann Grill

#v1-201. 3-1. **John Brasseur/Brazer Jr**, in the third generation of the family in America, was apparently born in Nansemond Co, VA, c1650 +/- 5 yrs, moved c1675 to Surry Co, VA, then later, c1684, to Essex Co, VA, on the Rappahannock estuary, some 40-50 miles north east of present-day Richmond, VA, where he left a will in 1712. He lived in South Farnham Parish; present-day Farnham is in Richmond Co, VA, about ten miles from the Rappahannock River.

John's wife was probably **Ann Grill**. On 9 Nov 1699, Jno Brasier and wife, Ann, were named executors of Jonathan Grill's estate. (Rappahannock Deeds and Wills 10, p.22) Usually, in early Virginia, naming a woman as co-executor of an estate means that she is either the widow or daughter of the deceased man. Since John and Ann had apparently been married since 1675, I'm assuming that Jonathan Grill was her father, and that they had moved to Rappahannock with him, or at the same time.

John's wife, Ann, must have died in the 1700-1710 period and John married a younger woman named **Elizabeth**, which would explain why John stated in his will that he wanted his son, Richard, to stay with his mother-in-law—that is, his step-mother—"until next Christmas."

Will of John Brazer (John Brasseur Jr) of So. Farnham Parish, Essex Co, VA, dated 23 Oct 1712, recorded for probate 14 March 1712/13 (i.e. 1713 by the way we count years).

To son Richard Brazer, all lands;

to wife Elizabeth, a negro man servant,

to son John, a cow and calf.

To son-in-law Robert Davis, a heifer.

Balance of Estate to be divided between wife Elizabeth and son, Richard, they to be Exors.

"I also will and desire that my son, Richard Brazer, stay with his Mother-in-law till next Christmas come twelve months."

signed John [X] Brazer.

Wit: Thomas [X] Russell, Ann [X] Gibbons, and James Edmondson.

(Ref: Essex County, VA, Wills and Deeds, 1711-1714, Book D&W-14, p.112; see also *Virginia Colonial Abstracts*, by Beverly Fleet, original in 34 volumes, reprinted in 3 by Gen. Publ. Co., Inc, 1988. v.II, p.112. Thanks to Jerri Beshears Kennedy for finding the data.)

The will of Richard Brazer, So. Farnham Parish, Essex Co, dated 19 April 1717, proved 21 May 1717 (Deeds and Wills 15, p.46-7), "being sick and weak,"

Unto my brother John Brasier 50 ac of land of the point joining to the Gleabe Swamp near to Covington's Mill Dam. All the rest of my land and plantation to William Hudson's 3 sons, vist: his own two sons, William & John & his son in law Robert Davis. William Hudson, my sole executor, the 50 ac given unto my brother John be under the care of my ex Wm. Hudson until the return of my brother John from where he is gone to and if he never returns the 50 acs to be divided equally to Wm. Hudson's 3 sons.

/s/ Richard [R] Brazier

Wit: Joseph Anderson, Elliner Moody, Frances Moore (Deeds and Wills 15, p.47; *Essex Co VA Records, 1706-1707, 1717-1719*, abs & comp by Dorman, p.46; see also Essex Co Probate Index, 4/19/1717, which names the devisees in the will.)

From the records, I piece together this family group:

Children of John Brasseur Jr and Ann ?Grill:

v1-210.   4-1. ***John M. Brazier/Brassier III**, b. c?1676, just after his parents married; m. bef March 1693, **Elizabeth Holt**, (1595 says *Marriages of Old Rappahannock & Essex Co, VA*, which seems to be following Court Orders, Book I, p.256). *VA Wills and Administrations 1632-1800*, by Torrence, gives John M. Brassier m. Elizabeth Holt, d/o

Richard Holt, "as proven by Holt's will, dated 9 March 1693/4, Essex Co, VA." This would suggest that John and Elizabeth married before March 1693, and the court record is only acknowledging that they are presently, in 1695, married.

v1-211.   4-2. **Richard Brashear/Brassers**, b. 7 July 1678, d. April-May 1717; m. **Elizabeth Howard**, (*Old Rappahannoock Virginia*, marriages of Farnham & Westmoreland Parishes, says 7 July 1678. *The date doesn't work for marriage; it's more likely the date of birth.* American Marriage Records *before 1699*, North Farnham Parish, Richmond Co, VA, by Clemens, give this date of marriage for Richard Brasser and gives the bride's name as Elizabeth How. *That could be just a copyist's abbreviation for Howard, or the page could have been torn.*) They apparently had no children.

v1-212.   4-3. **Elizabeth Brassure**, m. *Robert Davis*,

John Brasier III and Elizabeth Holt

#v1-210. 4-1. **John M. Brasier III** would have been born, probably in Nansemond Co, VA, c1676, shortly after his parents married in 1675; he married **Elizabeth Holt** in Essex Co, VA, apparently before 9 March 1693; and seems to have moved back to Nansemond soon after, then to Perquimans Co, NC (just across the state line), which may be why his father did not give him land in his will. And his brother, Richard, hardly knew "where he had gone to." The following records suggest that he took over his grandfather's holdings in Nansemond Co, VA.

In 1700: "John Brasseur, Patent, 37 Acres in Nansemond Co. In Chuckatuck Parish, adjoining Edward Major, Rogers' Mill and Toby Smith, for transportation of one person. April 24, 1700." (*Va Land Patents*, Book 9, p.259; *Edward Pleasant Valentine Papers*, p.214.)

While one was entitled to 50 acres of free land for tranporting a person, one could settle for less if all the neighboring land was taken. This grant looks like a "wedge" or left-over piece between other grants. Note that, on 5 June 1639, Georg Giles, was granted 100 acres in Upper County of New Norfolk (later absorbed into Nansemond Co), "upon N. side of Nansamund Riv., adj. Edward Major & S.W. upon Robert Brassure. Due for transportation of 2 persons, Georg Giles and John Giles." (*Va Land Patents*, Book 1, p.659.)

John M. Brasier, III, was apparently living where his great-grandfather, Robert Brasseur, had lived.

In 1704, a Mr. Jno. Brasseur was listed on the Quit Rent Rolls of Nansemond County as owning 400 acres (*Virginia Magazine of History*, v.29; and *Rent Rolls of Nansemond Co, VA*, p.204). John Brazur (John Jr) was listed with 300 acres in Essex County, that year, in *A True and Perfect Rent Roll for Essex Co, VA*, p.134. John Brassieur [John III] is also listed as an officer of Nansemond in 1704.

Some time in the 1710s, John Brasseur III moved to the border land between Perquimans and Pasquotank Counties, NC.

10 Sep 1715. John Brasier witnessed a deed from Lewis Davis of Albemarle Co, NC, to John Hardy of Same.... *Chowan Co, NC Abstracts*, Deed Bk 1, p.? Chowan County borders Perquimans on the southwest. Pasquotank Co borders Perquimans Co on the other side, the northeast. Albemarle was the parent county of all three; it no longer exists.

History, v.29; and *Rent Rolls of Nansemond Co, VA*, p.204). John Brazur (John Jr) was listed with 300 acres in Essex County, that year, in *A True and Perfect Rent Roll for Essex Co, VA*, p.134. John Brassieur [John III] is also listed as an officer of Nansemond in 1704.

Some time in the 1710s, John Brasseur III moved to the border land between Perquimans and Pasquotank Counties, NC.

10 Sep 1715. John Brasier witnessed a deed from Lewis Davis of Albemarle Co, NC, to John Hardy of Same.... *Chowan Co, NC Abstracts*, Deed Bk 1, p.? Chowan County borders Perquimans on the southwest. Pasquotank Co borders Perquimans Co on the other side, the northeast. Albemarle was the parent county of all three; it no longer exists.

4 Nov 1718. Richard Brassiers witness to will of William Haig. Pasquotank Co, NC.

4 Nov 1718. James Braezar witness to will of George Anderson, Pasquotank Co, NC. [Looks like John III named sons Richard and James. A generation later, in 1757, James Brazier, later of Cumberland Co, NC, witnessed a will of another George Anderson, in Granville Co, NC.]

9 Nov 1730, John Braizier patented 540 acres in Perquimans precinct on N.E. side of the river, joining former land of said Brazier, Sanderson's dock landing, and the said river. Wit: Richard Eberhard, John Lovick, C. Gale, Tho Pollock, Robt West, John Palin. (*Abstracts of Land Patents, Province of North Carolina, 1663-1729*, p.260; NC Archives file #2596.) This land later went to his son, John Brasseur/Brazier IV, whose widow, Elizabeth, sold portions of it.

Family of John M. Brazier III, and Elizabeth Holt, in Essex Co, VA

v1-213.   5-1. *John Brazier IV, b. c1696, shortly after parents marry,
           d. bef 1743, when widow sold land; m. *Elizabeth
           Simmons*
v1-214.   5-2. Richard Brassier, (speculative) witnessing a will in 1718
v1-215.   5-3. James Braezar, (speculative) witnessing a will in 1718
           for George Anderson, Pasquotank Co, NC)

Richard or James may be the ancestor of James Brazier of Cumberland
Co, NC, who was born 1710-15.

John Brazier IV and Elizabeth Simmons

#v1-213. 5-1. John Brazier IV, b. c1696. d. bef 1743, when widow
sold land; m. *Elizabeth Simmons*, d/o George Simmons, Perquimans
Co, NC (Elizabeth Simmons Brazier m.2. _____ Ranier, and d. c1784.
Dying that late, she couldn't have been born much before 1710, right?
Elizabeth's brother, William Simmons, s/o George and Susan Simmons,
was b. 5 Jan 1715.)

17 Oct 1743.   Elizabeth Brasier, et. al. grant 40 a. to John Griffin.
Perquimans Co, Deeds, Book D, p.122:
    Elizabeth Brazier, relict of John Brazier dec'd of Perquimans Co,
    [&] Susannah Smith relict of Jas. Smith dec'd, [for] 45 pounds ...
    with consent of my mother, sd. Susannah Smith [i.e. said
    Susannah Smith is mother to Elizabeth Brazier—she was widow
    of George Simmons] to John Griffin, 40 a. N.E. side of Pugh River,
    near bridge, part of tract of 90 a. acc. to Wm. Moore, 1st patented
    2/4/1723, assigned to Ric'd Gray to Wm. Carmon, deed of gift
    Geo. Simmons after sa. Simmons death given to his dtr. Eliz.
    Brazier, foot of lower bridge down road to back of said land
    whereon I now dwell to river mouth of bridge.
            /s/ Eliz (I) Brazier
                (i.e., her mark is a capital I)
            Susannah (X) Smith.
                (her mark: a backward S with a tail)
    Dated: 17 Oct 1743.
    Wit: Josiah Bogue, Luke Bond.
    [This practice of individualizing one's mark is characteristic of James
Brazier, d. Cumberland Co, NC, c1789 and also of the Thomas Brazier

---

clan of Orange Co, NC.] Some time after this deed, Elizabeth m. _____ Ranier.

1774. Elizabeth Ranier grants [intervivos] 50 a. to John Brazier. Grantee-Grantor Index #305; Perquimans Co, Deed Book H, p. 305:
Eliz. Ranier for love and consideration I bear my son John Brasher after my decease 50a. plantation formerly known by man [?name] of New Neck Man meek lying in neck, county aforesaid, 23 May 1774. Wit: John Robinson, Luke Bogus.

1774. Ruben Brazier grants 150a. To James Jordan. Perquimans Co, Deeds, Book d, p.358; index #247:
Ruben Brazier of Craven District of Province of South Carolina [should be NC] being son of John Brazier dec'd which did [died] formerly in Perquimans Co, in N.C. £ Soot money [800 pounds VA money?] pd by Jas. Jordan of Chowan Co, NC, land and plantation in Perquimans Co, whereon Eliz. Ranier and John Brazier now live; E. side of Perquimans river, near Tho. Newly, beding on Eliah Griffin & joining of Wm. Whites land and on River Swamp, est. 150 a. 12/16/1773.
signed: Ruben [X] Brazier.
Wit: Zachariah Jordan, Jas. Michal.
Noted: Newbern Dec 20, 1773, Rec. 23 April 1774.
[New Bern, one-time colony capital, is in Craven Co, North Carolina; looks to me like a mistake in the records, though the borders were very uncertain and shifted often.]

Some of the Children of John Brazier IV and Elizabeth Simmons, likely to be born 1720's:
v1-216.   6-1. **John Brazier/ Brasser, V**, living on dad's plantation, Perquimans, 1774, with mother, Elizabeth Ranier; both d. before 1 June 1784, when their property was inherited by a younger George Simmons.
v1-217.   6-2. **Reuben Brazier**, living in Craven Co, NC, in 1774.

Possible brother of Reuben Brasier (no documents):
11 March 1749, Thomas T. Brazzer, witness to will of William Price, of Parish of Prince George, Craven Co, SC (?NC; there was, then, no Craven Co in SC, but there were constant irregularities at that time as to where the border was), probated 9 April 1750 (Vol 6, p.329)

Possible s/o Reuben Brasier (no documents):
16 Oct 1787, John Brashers m. Bridget Conner; bondsman, James McMorris—Craven Co, NC, Marriages.)

If my guesses based on these moves are correct, James Brazier of Cumberland Co, NC, merely continued the migrations that the John Brasseurs, III & IV, had started before him. Others of the family, Reuben and the Jordan cousins, moved in similar paths; why not James Brazier, who showed up first in Granville Co, NC (area later Bute and Wake Co), then moved to Cumberland Co, NC, where he lived out his life.

24. JAMES and SARAH BRAZIER
of Cumberland Co, NC

James Brazier, b. c?1710-15, probably Pasquotank Co, NC, d. 1789-90, Cumberland Co, NC, and left a will; m. **Sarah** ____.

On 16 March 1754, James Brazier of Granville Co, NC, entered a Granville Land Grant of 329 acres on the south side of the Tar River Bridge, "near Simes line." The land was later in Bute Co, a county that has been reallined out of existence; the land seems to have been in present-day Franklin County, but the records are in present-day Warren Co, NC. James Brazier and his wife, Sarah, of Cumberland Co, NC, later sold this land.

James Brazier's Land Records

6 July 1757. James Braizar witness to will of George Anderson. Granville Co, NC. (Grimes, *NC Wills, 1690-1760.*) This has to be our James Brazier; there are no others in the county at that time. The relationship between this James Braizar and the James Braezar who witnessed the will of another George Anderson, 1718, Pasquotank Co, NC, is unknown; we can speculate that the two records indicate some kind of familial relationship. Considerably later, on 1 Feb 1779, John Anderson entered 100 acres (Entry #0261) in Cumberland Co, NC, between William Anderson Sr and surplus land within James Brazier's.

On 22 May 1760, James Brazier's Granville Land Grant #21 of 329 Acres was surveyed. (Thanks to Wes Taukchiray for a copy of Granville Grants, Reel 6, part 34-A, NC State Archives.) "Surveyed for James Brazier, 329 Acres of Land According to the above plan, lying in Granville County on So side Tar River, Begins at a water oak at the letter "a," Runs by Simses line S. 20° W, 216 poles to a Hickory at "b," then west 164 p. to a Hickory at "c," then N. 262 poles to a Maple at "d," then down the various courses of the Creek to the River, then the river to the first station. Sworn Chain carriers: John Burt, John Gun; surveyed by Thos Person."

The grant was made official on the 16th of March 1761. He signed the Indenture with his mark, a cursive "J".

The 1761 tax list, Granville Co, NC, taken by John Pope, lists four taxables in James's household:

James Brazier's Granville Grant

> James Braisher
> William Braisher
> John Braisher
> Indian girl Poll

William and John were named as sons in the will of James Brazier; since they would have to be 21 to be listed as taxable adults, they were both born before 1740, which would set James's birthdate back to the 1710-15 period or before.

Who the Indian girl was has not been determined. A band a Saponi Indians lived between Kitrell and Henderson in present day Vance Co, NC. They numbered 24 to 28 in 1754, half of them men. In 1761, there were 20 men, plus women and children. The "Indian girl Poll" could well have been from this group (thanks to Wes Taukchiray for a copy of the tax list and the information on the Saponi Indians).

On 26 Oct 1762, William and Mary Blake of Johnson Co, NC sold to James Brazier of Granville Co, 460 acres on south side of Tar River on both sides of Mill Creek. Signed: Wm. (X) Blake, Mary N. Blake. Wit: John Burt, Tho. Jones. Rec. 1763. For some years, James traded this and another parcel of land (his Granville Grant) back and forth with neighbors.

Bute Co, Deeds, Book A, p.206: Jas. Brazier and wife Sarah to John Townsend of Caroline Co, VA, for ____ lbs Va. money, 789 acres in two tracts, one by patent, 329 acres on so. side of Tar River, Bellies Creek, adjoining Sims; 460 acres adjoining first tract. Wit: Wm. Brack, Jas. Murry, Wm. Brazar, John Townsend, April 1765, rec. July 1765. [William Brazar is believed to be James's son, who is named in James's will and who moved from the Cumberland/Wake line to Surry Co, NC, c1800.]

Bute Co, Deeds, Book 1, p. 78: John Townsend to Jas. Brazor, carpenter, of Cumberland Co, for 90 lbs Va. money, 789 acres in Bute Co, on so. side of Tar River on Mill Creek, where Townsend now lives. He bought 329 acres of this land 20 Feb 1765 from Jas. Brazor, it being a Granville Grant ... remaining 460 acres was bought from Jas. Brazor 20 July 1765, he having bought it 16 Oct 1762 from Wm. Blake, it being an Earl Granville Grant. wit: Osborn Jeffries, Simon West, Tho. Smith.

Bute Co, Deeds, Book 3, p. 120: Jas. Brazier and Sarah his wife of Cumberland Co, 17 Aug 1768 to Stephen Lowe of Bute Co for 80 lbs Va. money, two tracts, one 329 acres on so side Tar River, adj Sims; two, 460 acres above Jas Murry. Wit: Giles Bowers, Proved by Wm. Russell. Reg. 2/12/1771.

The Tar River headwaters in present-day Person Co near the Virginia line, then runs through Granville, Vance, Franklin (adjoins Warren), Nash, Edgecombe, and Pitt Counties, before emptying into the Pamlico River and Pamlico Sound on the central coast of North Carolina. This is about 90 miles northeast and two major water-ways away from where James ended up in Cumberland County, though a major roadway ran from present-day Fayetteville in Cumberland Co, through Raleigh and Bute Co, and into Virginia.

When James and Sarah Brazier moved to Cumberland County, William Brazier/ Brasser apparently went with them. He bought land there in 1769 and sold it in 1774. The he returned to Wake County. NC Entry permit #136 was issued 4 March 1778 to William Brazier, to enter 100 acres of "vacant land in Wake County, lying on both sides of Reedy Creek, on the upper side of his plantation, joining his own line."

NC entry permit #362, 3 June 1778, to Joseph Blake, allows him to enter 550 acres of "vacant land in Wake County, lying on both sides of Reedy Creek, joining Robertson Hendon's line, and the lines of William Morgan and William Brasser, including his mill and improvements."

Estate Records
and Family of James Brazier

Cumberland County, NC, is directly downstream from Orange/ Chatham. The Haw River is joined by the Deep River near the old Chatham/Cumberland Co line (now in Lee Co), becomes the Cape Fear River, then flows toward the south coast of North Carolina. James Brazier's land in Cumberland County was on Parker Creek, very near the present-day boundary of Wake and Harnett Counties. About a century later, in 1845, C. M. Brazier [who?] sold 40 acres on Long Creek, apparently a branch of Parker Creek, to Joseph Johnson. (Cumberland Co, Deeds, Book 46, p.269)

James Brazier and his descendants favored a number of standard Brazier names: James, John, William, Elijah, Laban, Leah.

Will of James Brazier, Cumberland Co, NC, signed 7 June 1789. Proved 1790. Original in NC Archives, Raleigh (not in county records; it is indexed under "Breazier," but the spelling of the surname in the will is clearly Brazier). "being in a low state of health of body but being in perfect mind and memory — such worldly estate wherewith it has pleased almighty God to bless me in this life. I give devise and dispose of the same in the following manner: first I give and bequeath to my grandson James Brazier, son of Elijah Brazier, two hundred and fifty acres of land where on my mill stands and likewise the mill with it. I give and bequeath to Labon Brazier one negro woman named Trener. I likewise give and bequeath my riding horse bridle and saddle to James Brazier, son of William Brazier. I give and bequeath to William Brazier, son of William Brazier one feather bed and furniture. I likewise give and bequeath one feather bed to Leah Brazier, daughter of John Brazier— and the remaining part of my household furniture with all my stock I give and bequeath to my two sons, William Brazier and Elijah Brazier, to be equally divided between them—I likewise constitute my son Elijah Brazier the soul executor..."

James ("*𝒥*") Brazier

[his mark is a hump with a loop at the bottom, like a cursive "J"]
wits: John Knight, James B. Booker, Zachariah Miller
Proved 27 Oct 1790, by John Knight and James Booker.

Family of James and Sarah Brazier: from wills, estate papers, Bibles:

V9-2985.   b-1. ***William Brazier**, b. before 1740 (21+ on Granville Co, Taxlist in 1761); d. 1814, Surry Co, NC, leaving a will; m.1. _____ ; m.2. 1 May 1803, **Sarah Horne**,

V9-2986.   b-2. **John Brazier**, b. before 1740 (21+ on Granville Co, Taxlist in 1761), deceased bef 1789; probably m. **Christiana** ____,

V9-2987.   c-1. **Leah Brazier**,

V9-2988.   b-3. ***Elijah Brazier**, b. 15 July 1756, d. before March 1818; first on Tax lists in 1777 (he'd just turned 21) in Capt Robt Cobb's District; transferred land intervivos to sons, William and Elijah, 1815; m.1. **Sarah** _____, m.2. **Rebekah** _____

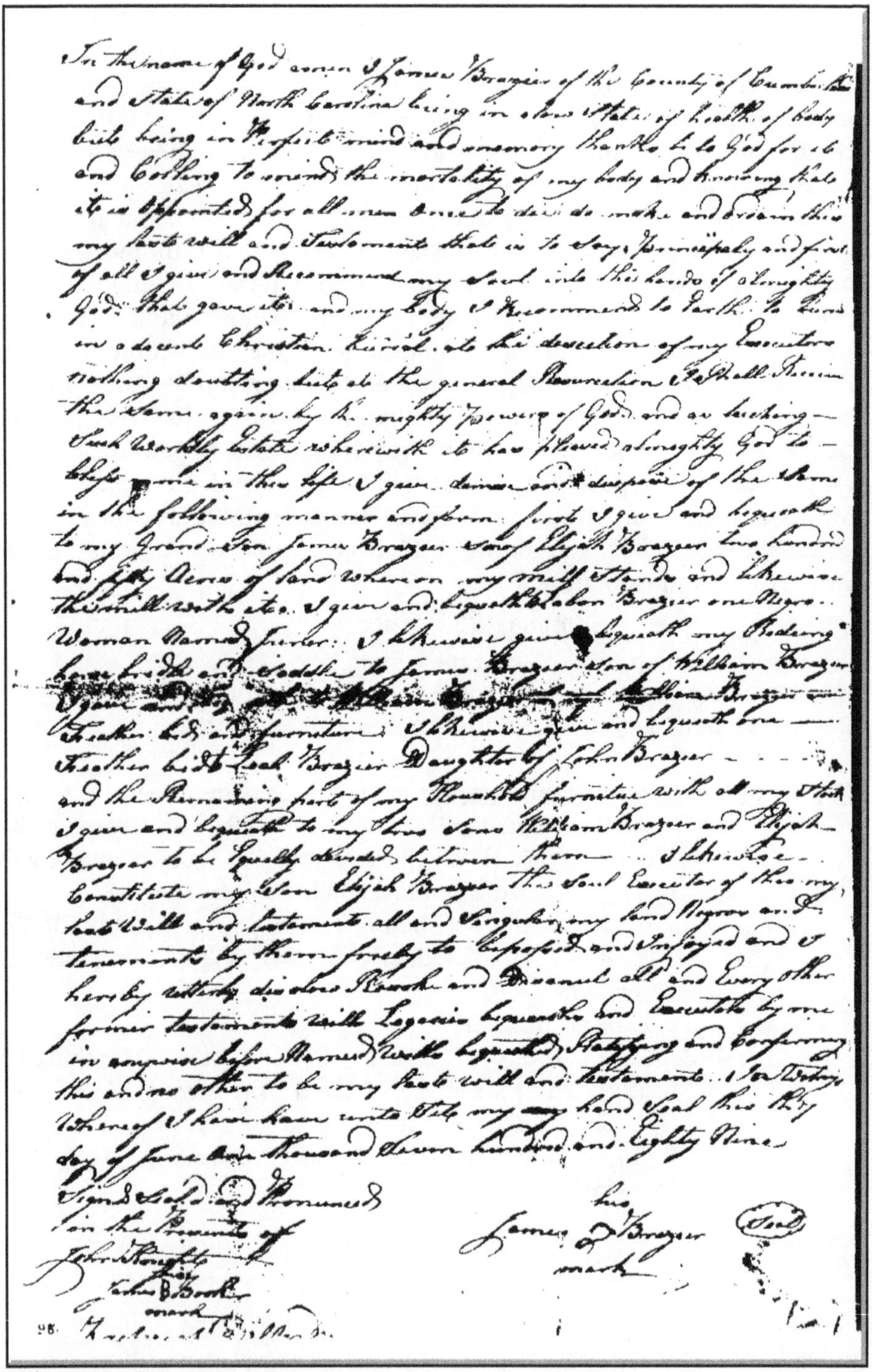

Figure 38: Will of James Brazier, of Cumberland Co, NC.

<u>Christiana</u> <u>Brazier</u>. (Probably widow of John, s/o James; they live in the same tax district.)

1777 Tax list of Cumberland Co, NC, Capt Robt. Cobb's District, Christiania Brazier, 100 acres.

1778, Cumberland Co, NC, entry permit #195 for 200 acres issued to Christine Brazer, including her improvements, adjoining John Copeland's entry #194, on Cape Fear River.

1779 Tax list of Cumberland Co, NC, Capt Robt. Cobb's District, Christiania Brazier, 322 acres.

On 4 Nov 1782, James Brazier of Cumberland Co, NC, deeded to Elijah Brazier of Cumberland Co, NC, "the said James Brazier for and in consideration of the love and affection for my son Elijah Brazier," 100a acres in Cumberland Co, on northeast side of northwest branch of Cape Fear River, being the plantation where I now live, near where the Earl of Granville's line crosses the river.

/s/ James Brazier

wits: John Pope, Thomas Bogs, Wm. Scoggins

(Cumberland Co, NC, Deed Bk 7, p.100)

From Deeds Index, Real Estate Conveyances, Cumberland Co, NC

William Brazier to Samuel Hart	Deed, 200a McNeill Cr.	1774	Bk 6, p.198
James Brazier to Elijah Brazier	Deed, 100a Cape Fear riv.	1783	Bk 7, p.100
al B Brasar to Elijah Brazer	Deed, int Braser Estate	1806	Bk 22, p.272
Rebecca Brasier to Elijah Brazier	Deed, indefinite	1811	Bk 26, p.191
Elijah Brazier to William Brasier al	Deed, 30a & para prep	1815	Bk 28, p.33
Barshabe Brasier to Elijah Brazier	Deed, int J. Brasier est	1815	Bk 29, p.169
Elijah Brazier to William Brazier	Deed, 250a Parkers Cr	1815	Bk 28, p.170
Elijah Brazier to Elijah W. Brazier	Deed, 200a Cape Fear riv.	1817	Bk 25, p.936
Elijah W. Brazier to James Battle	Deed, 200a near Parker cr	1818	Bk 30, p.148
G.M. Brazier to Joseph Johnson	Deed, 40a Long Branch	1845	Bk 46, p.269

25. WILLIAM BRAZIER,
s/o James Brazier of Cumberland

b-1. **William Brazier**, s/o James and Sarah Brazier of Cumberland Co, NC, was listed as a taxable (21 or over) on the 1761 tax list of Granville Co, NC; so he had to be born before 1740.

He was old enough to witness a land transaction in Bute Co, NC in 1765.

About 1768, his father, James, moved to Cumberland Co, NC, and William apparently went with him. He bought 200 acres in Cumberland Co, NC, on McNeill Creek from Neil McNeill in 1769 (Cumberland Co, NC Deeds, Bk 3, p.455); sold same to Samuel Hart in 1774 (Cumberland Co, NC Deeds, Bk 6, p.198; no wife signed). He apparently sold this land to his father, James, who gave part of it in his will to James Brazier "Jr," s/o Elijah Brazier. William apparently moved back to Wake Co.

In June 1777, William bought land in Wake Co, from John Motley (Wake Co, Deeds). He m.1. _____ (mother of the children); m.2. 21 May 1803, **Sarah Horne**, in Wake Co, NC (also listed Surry Co) NC, which is rather too late for her to have been the mother of his children. His youngest daughter was married on the same day.

William Brazier lived in Granville, Bute, and Wake Counties, then moved c1795 to western North Carolina, to the boundary area of Surry/Rowan counties; Rowan Co, Deed Book 14, p.187, 30 May 1795, William Brazier bought 200 acres in the Forks of the Yadkin River, on "Grate" branch.

William Brazier died in Surry Co, NC in 1814, willing the 200 acres of land in Surry Co to sons, James and Elijah; witness: Laban Brazier. William's will, Surry Co, NC, dated 20 Sep 1813, names wife Sarah (Horne), sons Laban, James, Elijah, John, daughters Cretia Brazier and Polly Kerr, and grandson, Wiley, to whom he gave a rifle "or the worth of it." Executors are sons Elijah and James.

Will of William Brazier

In the name of God Amen, I William Brazier of Surry County and State of North Carolina being of sound disposition of mind memory and understanding, considering the certainty of death, and the uncertainty of the time thereof, being desirous to settle my worldly affairs, I do therefore make and publish this my last will and testament in manner and form following that is today.

First and principally I commit my soul into the hands of Almighty God, and my body to the earth, to be decently buried at discretion of my executors have in after named and after my debts and funeral expenses are paid I bequeath as follows:

I give and bequeath to my wife Sarah Brazier all my stock of hogs and all the crop that is on the farm where I now live to dispose of as she pleases, also my good horse I give to her, and if the horse should live longer than she then . . . he shall then belong to my children.

Item, I give and bequeath to my son Laban Brazier fifteen dollars.

Item, I give and bequeath t my son James Brazier all my land on the north side of the branch as follows beginning where my line crosses said branch and runs up said branch near to the upper end of the meadow to a stake thence running near west come by a walnut tree to a large pine on my upper line. Only my son Elijah Brazier shall have half the fruit that the orchard grows on said land while the said Elijah continues where he now lives.

Item, I give and bequeath to my son Elijah Brazier all my land on the south side of the branch including the whole of my land to the line above mentioned.

Item, I give to my grandson Wiley Brazier my gun or the worth of it.

Item, I give to my daughter, Cretia Brazier five shilling.

Item, I give to my daughter Polly Kerr five shillings.

Item, I give and bequeath to my son John Brazier one feather bed and furniture also fifteen dollars.

Item, I give and bequeath to my sons James Brazier and Elijah Brazier all my moveable property that has not been mentioned before, after raising the above fifteen dollars for my son Laban Brazier and the above fifteen dollars for my son John Brazier. They shall equal divide it between them.

And lastly I do appoint and constitute my son James and Elijah Braziers to be the sale executor of this my last will and testament revoking and annulling all former wills by me heretofore made ratifying and confirming this to be my last will and testament.

In testimony whereof I have hereunto set my hand and affixed my seal this Twentieth Day of September in the year of our Lord One Thousand Eight Hundred and Thirteen.

/s/ William Brazier

Witnessed by: John Turner Judge
and J.L. Bird [?probate date 20 Sep 1817]

On 11 March 1816, Elijah and wife, Nancy, sold his part of the land (Rowan Co, Deed Book 23, p.772; he moved to Franklin Co, TN in 1818).

Family of William Brazier: (Order of birth not certain, except that a few have dates.)

V9-2989.　c-1. ***Rev. Laban Brazier**, b. 24 July 1769, NC, d. 16 Dec 1841, Clermont Co, OH; m.1. 4 Sep 1804 in Rowan Co, NC, **Deborah Dial**, b. 23 or 28 Feb 1785, Delaware, d. 12 March 1822, Clermont Co, OH; m.2. **Olive "Olley" (née Warren; widow Ayers)**, b. 14 Dec 1792, Maine, d. 2 Oct 1854, Decatur Co, IN, bur Ridlen Cem, St. Paul, IN.

V9-2990.　c-2. ***John Brazier** moved to Clermont Co, OH, where he d. 1838; see below.

V9-2991.　c-3. **William Brazier**, d. bef. 1813

V9-2992.　　d-1. **Wiley Brazier**,

V9-2993.　c-4. ***James Brazier**, b. 17 Jan 1772, according to his own Bible; moved to Lincoln Co, TN; m. **Mary "Polly" Smith**, in Wake Co, NC, 1801.

V9-2994.　c-5. ***Rev. Elijah Brazier,** b. c1774; m. **Nancy _____**, moved 1818 to Franklin Co, TN

V9-2995.　c-6. **Cretia Brazier**

V9-2996.　c-7. **Mary "Polly" Brazier**, b. c1787 (if 16 when marrying); m. 21 May 1803, Surry Co, NC, **Samson Keen**. They were married the same day as her father married Sarah Horne. William Brazier was bondsman for John Gentle and Eliza (Elizabeth?) Keen, who married 14 Jan 1800.

Of these children, Laban and John moved to Clermont Co, Ohio, about 1810; James and Elijah moved about 1818 to Franklin Co, TN. Wiley, s/o William, joined his uncles in TN about 1830.

Rev. Laban Brazier and Deborah Dial

c-1. **Laban Brazier**, b. 24 July 1769, NC, d. 16 Dec 1841, Clermont Co, OH; m.1. 4 Sep 1804 in Rowan Co, NC, (*Rowan Marriages*, by Brent H. Holcomb), **Deborah Dial**, b. 23 or 28 Feb 1785, Delaware, d. 12 March 1822, Clermont Co, OH, d/o Shadrach Dial and Nancy Horney; m.2. 9 Dec 1824, in Clermont Co, OH "by James Ward, JP," **Olive "Olley" (née Warren; widow Ayers)**, b. 14 Dec 1792, Maine, d. 2 Oct 1854, Decatur Co, IN, bur Ridlen Cem, St. Paul, IN, d/o John Warren Sr, b. 25 April 1772, Berwick, ME, d. 2 Oct 1851, Decatur Co, IN, and

Hannah Witham, b. c1770-75, d. 1841-43 [contact: Jon Stedman, 1919 Eagle Drive, Denton, TX 76201].

1796 (Iredell Co, NC, Deed Book 15, p.490) Laban Brazier. Record pertains to survey of 100 acres in Rowan Co (Iredell split off from Rowan in 1788).

About 1807 or before, Laban Brazier, his wife, her father Shadrach Dial (s/o Robert Dial), and Shadrach's second wife moved from Rowan Co, NC, to Clermont Co, OH, where they are on the County Tax lists for 1810 (*Early Ohio Tax Records*, by Esther W. Powell).

In 1813, Laban is on the Tax list of Union twp, Clermont Co, and received $11 for services to Batavia twp in 1822, where he was property holder No 4455 in 1826. He was minister of Batavia Methodist Episcopal Church in 1817, and is listed (with Elijah Brazier) as an early member of Olive Branch, Methodist Episcopal Church, before 1831.

Rev. Laban Brazier was apparently a circuit riding Methodist minister. A member of the Brazier family gave to Bethesda Hospital, which had a small museum, several letters of Laban and his father-in-law, Shadrach Dial, concerning land titles, and a set of saddlebags said to have belonged to Rev. Laban Brazier. These items are now in the Ohio State Historical Society Library in Cincinnati.

Laban left his family Bible to his second wife, Olive. Someone apparently tried to destroy it, but charred remains of it are now in the Cincinnati Public Library. It has been transcribed in *Bible Records of Thirty Ohio Families*,

Family of Laban Brazier and Deborah Dial:

V9-2997.   d-1. **Mary D. Brazier**, b. 30 Aug 1805, Rowan Co, NC, d. 29 Sep 1867, Marion Co, IN; m. 4 Jan 1824, in Clermont Co, OH (by David Dial, JP), ***Reuben Hunter***, b. c1801, Rowan Co, NC, d. 13 Sep 1846, s/o John Hunter and Mary

V9-2998.   d-2. ***Nancy Brazier**, b. 10 Nov 1807, Clermont Co, OH, d. 16 Jan 1875, Midway, Grass twp, Spencer Co, IN; m. 22 Jan 1827, in Clermont Co, OH, **Reuben Lloyd**, b. 24 Dec 1794, PA, d. 17 July 1863, Spencer Co, IN

V9-2999.   d-3. ***Elijah Brazier**, b. 10 Jan 1810, Clermont Co, OH, d. 26 April 1883, Clermont Co, OH; m. 14 Nov 1834, Clermont Co, OH, ***Lydia Whitaker***, b. 10 April 1810, d. 4 May 1897, both bur Olive Branch Cem, Clermont Co, OH.

V9-3000.   d-4. **John Brazier**, b. 18 April 1811, Clermont Co, OH, d. there 29 Nov 1833

V9-3001.   d-5. **Elizabeth Brazier**, b. 7 July 1813, Clermont Co, OH, d. 4 Dec 1833; m. 1 Sep 1831, _____ **Shearer**,

V9-3002.   d-6. **Lydia Ann Brazier**, b. 11 May 1819, Clermont Co, OH, d. 30 Sep 1849; m. 6 June 1839, _____ **Woodruff**,

V9-3003.   d-7. **Shadrach Brazier**, b. & d. 9 March 1822, three days before his mother.

Family of Laban Brazier and Olive Warren:

V9-3004.   d-8. **Hannah Brazier**, b. 25 Nov 1825, Clermont Co, OH, d. there 1846; will dated 15 July 1846, probate Sep 1846 (Clermont Co, OH, Book F, p.111).

V9-3005.   d-9. **James Brazier**, b. Sep 1827, Clermont Co, OH, d. there 20 Oct 1845.

Tragedy stuck this family more than once. Within one week in 1833, Laban lost a son, John, and a daughter, Elizabeth (Brazier) Shearer. Within the year 1845-6, the two youngest children, Hannah and James, died. Olive then apparently moved to Indiana with some of her relatives.

The Will of Laban Brazier, 15 June 1839, Clermont Co, OH, (Book E, p.296), probate 15 Jan 1842:

At a special Court held before the Honorable Owen T. Fishback, President Judge, and Samuel Hill and George McMahan, Esquires, Associate Judges of the Court of Common Pleas of Clermont County at the Court house in the town of Batavia on the 15th day of January A.D. 1842 for the purpose of attending to Probate and testamentary business:

The last will and testament of Laban Brazier, late of Clermont County dec[d] was this day brought before the Court and was proved by the oaths of David White Jr, and William Thomas, the witnesses thereto, whose examination were reduced to writing and, it appearing to the satisfaction of the Court that the said Laban Brazier at the time of Executing said will was of full age and of sound mind and memory and not under any restraint, it is ordered that said will and the proof so reduced to writing be recorded.

Will, to wit:

In the name of God, Amen. I, Laban Brazier, of Clermont County and State of Ohio, being well in body and sound in memory do by the Grace of God this 15th day of June in the year of our Lord Eighteen hundred and thirty nine, make this my last will and testament. My body I resign to the earth, my soul to God who gave me. As to what little of this world's goods where with it hath pleased God to bless me with, after my just debts and funeral expenses is paid, I will to be disposed of in the following manner. To my wife, Olley Brazier, I give and bequest the plantation which I now live, to receive one third of grain and grass, fruits and vegitables of the land I cleared and fenced, so long as she remains the widow of Laban Brazier, also one horse creture two cows ten sheep ten hogs, fowls of all descriptions, Dwelling house and Kitchen furniture of all kinds and fifty dollars in money over and above what little she hath gathered herself (that I have nothing to do with). When the said Olley ceases to be the widow of the said Laban Brazier, the land to be divided as follows: beginning at a live beech and poplar at the corner where L. Brazier, J.Troy and D.Dial intersects, runs S.East direction Eleven and half poles to a stone near a small run in sd Laban's orchard Plot: thence S.West direction along a lane fence to intersect J.Grays's E. and West line, thirty seven poles E. of J.Grays corner to a Elm and white oak-- Elijah Brazier, to have the N.West side of sd Line as it bound by others' lines, for him and his heirs forever, and James Brazier to have S.East side of sd line as it bound by other lines, for him and his heirs forever.

I will and bequest to my daughter Mary D. Hunter fifty dollars, to Nancy Loyd, fifty dollars, to Elijah Brazier, fifty dollars, to Lydia Ann Woodruff, fifty dollars, to Hannah Brazier, one bed and bedding one cow four sheep and as much household property as to make her equal with the other girls and fifty dollars in money, and James Brazier one horse creture, saddle and bridle, bed and bedding one gun and fifty dollars in money my farming and mechanical tools fan and wagon— icluded [sic] to remain on the farm for the use thereof to be taken care of till the year of forty Eight [when James would turn 21], then whats left for James to have and to receive all thats coming to him and at the death of sd Olley Brazier all the stock and cretures with all the household and kitchen property to belong to Hannah and James Brazier. my bible I give to Olley. Hannah and James School books is there own, all the rest of my books equaly divided among all my heirs. If more money than is mentioned divide in proporation, if less divide in proportion. I wish James to have good English learning and to be bred to work. I do by these presence appoint Elijah Brazier and John Warren Jr, Executors to this my last will and testament. Given under my hand and seal and acknowledged on the day and year above written,

Laban Brazier (seal)

in presence of David White Jr; Wm Thomas

Of the executors, Elijah Brazier is s/o Laban; John Warren Jr is a brother of Olive, Laban's second wife.

Nancy Brazier and Reuben Lloyd

d-2. **Nancy Brazier**, (d/o Rev. Laban Brazier and Deborah Dial), b. 10 Nov 1807, Clermont Co, OH, d. 16 Jan 1875, Midway, Grass twp, Spencer Co, IN; m. 22 Jan 1827, in Clermont Co, OH, **Reuben Lloyd**, b. 24 Dec 1794, PA, d. 17 July 1863, Spencer Co, IN

V9-3006. e-1. John Lloyd,

V9-3007. e-2. Hulder Lloyd,

V9-3008. e-3. Catherine Lloyd, b. 25 June 1828, Clermont Co, OH, d. 1 Aug 1896, Spencer Co, IN; m. 31 Jan 1850, Joseph Beeler, b. 26 Sep 1823, OH, d. 28 Feb 1919

V9-3009. f-1. Ann E. Beeler, b. 1851, Spencer Co, IN; m. 16 Feb 1879, Thomas J. Wilson

V9-3010. f-2. Nancy W. Beeler, b. 1853, Spencer Co, IN

V9-3011. f-3. Mary Alice Beeler, b. 21 Dec 1853, Spencer Co, IN, d. there, 13 Dec 1922; m. 28 Aug 1894, Phillip Atkinson,

V9-3012. f-4. William H. Beeler, b. 1857, Spencer Co, IN, d. 1896, Beatrice, Nebraska

V9-3013. f-5. Lydia A. Beeler, b. 1858, Spencer Co, IN

V9-3014. f-6. Lilly Fremont Beeler, b. June 1861, Spencer Co, IN; m. 23 Dec 1880, Delbert Partridge

V9-3015. f-7. Harriet Beeler, b. 29 March 1862, Spencer Co, IN, d. 6 Sept 1896

V9-3016. f-8. Nettie F. Beeler, b. 29 March 1864, Spencer Co, IN, d. 1937

V9-3017. f-9. Jennie V. Beeler, b. Oct 1868, Spencer Co, IN, d. 1936

V9-3018. e-4. Deborah Lloyd, b. 14 Jan 1830, Clermont Co, OH, d. 4 Sep 1872, Spencer Co, IN; m. 3 March 1853, Andrew Jackson Parr, b. 1832, OH, d. 8 July 1906, Spencer Co, IN

V9-3019. f-1. Mattie Nancy Parr

V9-3020. f-2. Andrew Parr

V9-3021. f-3. Alice J. Parr, b. 5 May 1854, Spencer Co, IN, d. there, 1 Sept 1872

V9-3022. e-4. Labon Brazier Lloyd, b. 23 March 1831, Clermont Co, OH, d. 18 March 1897, Spencer Co, IN; m. 29 Sep 1854, Harriet Durham Gwaltney, b. 19 Feb 1834, Hamilton Co, OH, d. 18 March 1897, Spencer Co, IN

V9-3023. f-1. _____ Lloyd,

V9-3024.   f-2. Charles R. Lloyd, b. 26 Sept 1856, Spencer Co, IN, d. 24 Feb 1922; m. Olive Beeler

V9-3025.   f-3. Aquilla Durham Lloyd, b. 13 March 1858, Spencer Co, IN, d. there, 1 Nov 1930; m. 25 March 1885, Elizabeth Clare Hancock

V9-3026.   f-4. Sarah Alice Lloyd, b. 29 June 1861, Spencer Co, IN, d. there, 31 Dec 1902; m. Julius King Wilkinson

V9-3027.   f-5. Lucie B. Lloyd, b. 23 Aug 1863, d. 17 Sept 1864

V9-3028.   f-6. Reuben L. Lloyd, b. 26 Aug 1864, Spencer Co, IN, d. there, 29 Jan 1901; m. 11 April 1889, Josephine Nunn

V9-3029.   f-7. Nancy Catherine Lloyd, b. 17 Aug 1867, Spencer Co, IN, d. there, 6 Aug 1944; m. 25 Dec 1888, Melville Cox Wilkinson

V9-3030.   f-8. John Meyer Lloyd, b. 13 Aug 1870, Spencer Co, IN; m. 21 Sept 1891, Gertrude Wilson

V9-3031.   f-9. Jackson T. Lloyd, b. 31 Jan 1873, Spencer Co, IN, d. there, 17 April 1893

V9-3032.   e-5. Elijah Lloyd, b. 26 July 1832, Clermont Co, OH, d. 22 Aug 1912, Spencer Co, IN; m.1. 12 Oct 1854, Rebecca A. Gwaltney, b. 20 Oct 1832, d. 4 April 1865; m.2. 22 May 1867, Amanda R. Sheets, b. ?, d. 14 July 1925

V9-3033.   f-1. Mary "Mollie" Lloyd, b. -?-, d. 29 Feb 1936; m. 6 March 1884, Samuel McVey

V9-3034.   f-2. Jackson Lloyd, b. Nov 1855, Spencer Co, IN; m. 25 Feb 1880, Catherine Jenny "Katie" Magee

V9-3035.   f-3. Nancy Lloyd, b. 1863, m. 30 April 1885, Alva G. Giles

V9-3036.   f-4. Clara R. Lloyd, b. Dec 1865; m. 20 Dec 1886, Park R. White

V9-3037.   f-5. Jackson Lloyd, b. 1867

V9-3038.   f-6. Herbert "Bert" Lloyd, b. 6 July Spenser Co, IN; m. Ida Krueger

V9-3039.   e-6. Henry I. Lloyd, b. 23 Oct 1834, Clermont Co, OH, d. 18 Feb 1879, Spencer Co, IN; m. 29 Nov 1859, Eliza Jane Ranger, b. 1832, OH, d. 21 Dec 1902.

V9-3040.   f-1. Timothy Lloyd, b. 1860, d. 1943; m. 11 Jan 1881, Elize A. Richards

V9-3041.   f-2. Ella Lloyd, (twin) b. 12 Oct 1862, d. 15 Jan 1865

V9-3042.   f-3. Eben Lloyd (twin) b. 12 Oct 1862, d. 18 Feb 1863

V9-3043.   f-4. Azula Lloyd, b. Sept 1864, d. Sept 1864

V9-3044.   f-5. Emmet Lloyd, b. 1868, d. 1960; m. 20 Dec 1888, Carrie Myers.

V9-3045.   e-8. Julia Ann Lloyd, b. 23 May 1836, Clermont Co, OH, d. 27 July 1914, Parsons, Labette Co, KS; m. 8 Oct 1857, Thomas Otis Barker, b. 17 June 1835, Midway, Spencer Co, IN, d. 8 April 1918, Parsons, Labette Co, KS (ref: Ruth Barker Morgan. [NB: I wrote 1992; ltr returned: 239 E. Fifth St. San Dimas, CA 91773)

V9-3046.   f-1. Nancy Jane Barker, b. 22 Aug 1858, d. 12 March 1952; m. Dec 1884, William C. Weaver, b. -?-, d. 7July 1902, Parson, Labette Co, KS

V9-3047.   g-1. Nell Elizabeth Weaver, b. 5 Oct 1887, Kingman, KS; m. 26 June 1910, Edward C. Fisher, b. 12 Sept 1886, Humboldt, KS; d. 19 Feb 1972, Parsons, Labette Co, KS. 2 ch: Richard Wayne, and Dana Louise Fisher.

V9-3048.   f-2. Martha Ann Barker, b. 9 Sept 1860, Midway, Spencer Co, IN; d. 14 March 1930; m. 6 Nov 1881, Perry Samuel White, b. 12 Nov 1859, Skelton Twp, IN; d. 9 Aug 1943, Kansas City, MO

V9-3049.   g-1. Herbert O. White, b. 24 Aug 1883, Parson, Labette Co, KS, d. there, 29 June 1885

V9-3050.   g-2. Walter George White, b. 5 Feb 1885, Parson, Labetter Co, KS, d. 6 Nov 1938, Alexandria, LA; m. Clara Cover

V9-3051.   g-3. Faye White, b. 2 Nov 1888, Parson, Labette Co, KS, d. 2 Feb 1962, Kersey, Well Co, CO; m. David C. Durrell

V9-3052.   g-4. Helen Julia White, b. 24 April 1893, Parsons, Labette Co, KS, .d 25 Dec 1958; m. Howard Dudley Clark

V9-3053.   g-5. Laura White, b. 13 Oct 1895, Parsons, Lebatter Co, KS, d. there, 22 May 1899

V9-3054.   f-3. Reuben Lloyd Barker, b. 13 Aug 1862, Midway, Spencer Co, IN, d. 9 Dec 1937, Tulare, Tulare Co, CA; m.1. 29 March 1888; Mattie May Cary, b. 4 July 1865, KS, d. 30 Nov 1915, Burden, Cowley Co, KS; m.2. 1 Dec 1915, Nora Zilpha West, b. 23 May 1881, Pilot Knob, IN, d. 11 May 1959, Los Angeles, CA

V9-3055.   g-1. Eva Estella Barker, b. 21 Feb 1889, Parsons, Labette Co, KS, d. 23 Oct 1916, KS

V9-3056.   g-2. Elmer Lloyd Barker, b. 23 June 1890, Parsons, Labette Co, KS, d. 13 Sept 1910, KS

Brashear(s) Families— Additions, Corrections, Strays

V9-3057.   g-3. Horace Harrison Barker, b. 3 May 1892, Parsons,
              Labette Co, KS, d. 3 Dec 1913, KS
V9-3058.   g-4. Guy Cary Barker, b. 29 Jan 1894, Parsons,
              Labette Co, KS; d. 20 Dec 1977, KS; m. Rosalie
              _____. 2 ch: Wanda, and Virginia Barker
V9-3059.   g-5. Dorothy May Barker, b. 14 Sept 1896, Alabama,
              d. 10 Nov 1897
V9-3060.   g-6. James Dewey Barker, b. 11 Sept 1898, Pulaska,
              Missouri, d. 30 Nov 1976; m. Mariann Bergant.
              2ch: Dorothy, and Georgia Barker
V9-3061.   g-7. Thomas Frank Barker, b. 6 Jan 1901, Garnett,
              Anderson Co, KS; d. Burden, Cowley Co, KS; m.
              26 June 1932, Madeline Jane Hukle, b. 26 June
              1905, Peck, Sumner Co, KS, d. 23 Nov 1984. 3 ch:
              Lyle Frank; Donald Lee; and Ronald Lee Barker
V9-3062.   g-8 Ruth Juliette Barker, b. 18 Sept 1916, Glendive,
              Dawson Co, Montana. d. 9 Sept 1994, La Verne,
              Los Angeles Co, CA; m. 20 Dec 1957, Ira Dawson
              Morgan, b. 19 May 1896, Hilham, Overton Co, TN,
              d. 28 Feb 1982
V9-3063.   f-4. Sarah Anise Barker, b. 21 March 1865, Midway,
              Spencer Co, IN, d.12 Dec 1907; m. 7 Dec 1884,
              Horace M. Merreill
V9-3064.   g-1. Ernest Ray Merreill, b. 9 May 1906, Glendale, Los
              Angeles Co, CA
V9-3065.   f-5. William Ellis Barker, b. 15 July 1867, Midway,
              Spencer Co, IN, d. 9 Oct 1950; m. 28 Feb 1889,
              Maggie Belle Slane, b. 12 Aug 1867, IN, d. 11 Sept
              1956, Winfield, KS
V9-3066.   g-1. Ellis Thomas Barker; m. Daisy Wooley
V9-3067.   g-2. Mabel Barker; m. Earl Walker
V9-3068.   g-3. Fannie Anise Barker; m. Clifford Hite
V9-3069.   g-4. Mildred Barker;
V9-3070.   g-5. Edith Marcelina Barker;
V9-3071.   g-6. Wilbur Eugene Barker; m. Julia Mauney
V9-3072.   g-7. Howard Taft Barker; m. Esther Schaefer
V9-3073.   g-8. Ruth Pauline Barker; m. John Thompson
V9-3074.   g-9. Irma Barker, b. 12 Aug 1891, Labette Co, KS, d.
              6 June 1959; m. Nellie Moore
V9-3075.   g-10. Delbert Barker, b. 20 Nov 1892, Parsons,
              Labette Co, KS, d. 16 May1964, Winfield, Cowley
              Co, KS; m. Grace Thursk

V9-3076.	g-11. Carl Barker, b. 1 Aug 1894, Labette Co, KS; d. 25 July 1966; m. Norma McKnab
V9-3077.	g-12. Edna Barker, b. 19 Feb 1897, Labette Co, KS, d. July 1988, KS; m. Sidney Shields
V9-3078.	g-13. Gladys Blanche Barker, b. 16 March 1909, Winfield, Cowley Co, KS, d. 9 Dec 1988, Willington, Sumner Co, KS; m. Charles Brooks
V9-3079.	f-6. Henry Dean Barker, b. 25 May 1869, Midway, Spencer Co, IN; d. there, 2 Nov 1869
V9-3080.	f-7. Elijah Claude Barker, b. 17 Sept 1870, Midway, Spencer Co, IN, d. there, 31 Aug 1875
V9-3081.	f-8. Julia Flora Barker, b. 5 Sept 1873, Midway, Spencer Co, IN; d. there, 3 Nov 1875
V9-3082.	f-9. Grace Barker, b. 28 March 1875, Midway, Spencer Co, IN, d. 3 Jan 1969, CA
V9-3083.	f-10. Clyde J. Barker, b. 28 March 1879, Midway, Spencer Co, IN

Elijah Brazier and Lydia Whitaker

d-3. **Elijah Brazier**, (s/o Rev. Laban Brazier and Deborah Dial), b. 10 Jan 1810, Clermont Co, OH, d. 26 April 1883; m. 14 Nov 1834, Clermont Co, OH, *Lydia Whitaker*, b. 10 April 1810, d. 4 May 1897, both bur Olive Branch Cem, Clermont Co, OH.

Elijah Brazier, trustee of Batavia twp, 1851 (*Clermont Co Hist*, p.252)

Elijah Brazier, on awarding Committee for Clermont County Agriculture Society, near Batavia, 1857. (p.97)

Melvin C. Brazier, enlisted 13 July 1861, Co E, 39th Ohio Vol Inf.

James Brazier, Noble Grand of Mount Carmel Lodge, No. 190, I.O.O.F., 1879

Family of Elijah Brazier and Lydia Whitaker:

V9-3084.	e-1. **Elmira Brazier**,
V9-3085.	e-2. **William Brazier**,
V9-3086.	e-3. **Mary Brazier**,
V9-3087.	e-4. **Melville Brazier**,
V9-3088.	e-5. **Lucrecia Brazier**,
V9-3089.	e-6. **John Brazier**,
V9-3090.	e-7. **Wilber Brazier**,
V9-3091.	e-8. **Carrie Brazier**,
V9-3092.	e-9. **Hamer Brazier**,

^{V9}-3093.   e-10. **James Madison Brazier**, b. 10 Oct 1848, d. 1934; m. **Edith Jane Phillips**, b. 30 May 1857, OH, d. 1934, d/o Elijah Day Phillips (1826-1898) and Laurena Rose (1828-1909). Laurena Rose was d/o John Rose, a Rev War soldier from NJ, and Jane Douglas.

^{V9}-3094.   f-1. **Fred Brazier**; m. **Maude Emily Price**. She was from England.

^{V9}-3095.   f-2. **Harry Brazier**, m. **Lola** _____

^{V9}-3096.   f-3. **Mabel Brazier**, m. **Bill Nagel**

^{V9}-3097.   f-4. **Edna Brazier**, m. **John Barkl(e)y**

^{V9}-3098.   f-5. **Melville Christy Brazier**, b. 14 Jan 1891, Mt Carmel, Clermont Co, OH, d. 1963-4 in Tampa, Hillsborough Co, FL; b. 1864, Flag Springs Cem, Hamilton Co, OH; m. c1934, in Cincinnati, Hamilton Co, OH, **Grace Etta (Fair) Vogel**, b. 30 April 1903, d. 16 Jan 1965. No ch, but Grace had a daughter by a previous marriage. Data from Judith A. Shamp, step-granddaughter <BLKYGYRL@aol.com> who writes: Grandpa Mel was cremated and his remains were transported to OH, and I was told by his nephew, Lewis Brazier, that he is interred in Flag Springs Cem, Hamilton Co, OH. Grandpa Mel married Grace Etta Fair Vogel (she may have had one more marriage (maiden name Fair). Her daughter, Marjorie Vogel, was my mother; she passed away, 29 Dec 1997, Tampa, FL. There was no issue from this marriage. Mr. Brazier raised my sister, brother, and me, until I was about 11 years of age. I wanted to make certain that I had some information to be entered into the database, as he was with me during my formative years. He was a very practical man. Quiet, soft spoken, and could build anything. He didn't marry until his mother, Edith, passed away. She d. in 1934. I am not certain as to when he and my grandmother married, but I was a very small child. I can still remember things about him from those times even now. He worked at R.K. LaBlonds in Cincinnati, St Brenard, I think, not sure about the area. Once a week, he used to come down the street with a small white pail of oyster stew. That was his supper for the evening. He loved the stuff. (We lived in Cox's Lane at that time.) He drove an old Model A four-door Ford until I was about nine or so. He'd had a heart attack and voluntarily turned in his driver's license. Said "he was afraid that he would have another attack and kill someone." The house in Tampa was at 7210 Highland Ave. It is long gone, now replaced by a concrete block one. The old neighborhood has gone downhill. It isn't the same quiet place that as I child I played around in. I was in Amelia, OH, with an aunt when we got the call that he had passed away. He had gone to dinner with an acquaintance and turned, they said, at the door to wave and his heart gave out. It was sudden, and they do not believe that he suffered any pain. The farmhouse, I am told, still stands on Rose Hill in Mt Carmel, near Newtown, OH.

V9-3099.   g-1. Marjorie Vogel, b. ?, d. 29 Dec 1997, Tampa, FL; 3 ch: 2 girls, 1 boy

John Brazier, of Clermont Co, OH

c-2. **John Brazier**, (brother of Laban and s/o William Brazier (d. 1814, Surry Co, NC), apparently migrated to Clermont Co, OH, soon after Laban. John Brazier's land (corner) was used to establish the boundary of Batavia Township in 1815. He was listed as a viewer of roads in 1814. He was a Justice of the Peace for Union twp in 1814 and 1815, for Batavia twp in 1816. He was a property holder (No. 1671) in Batavia twp in 1826. (*History of Clermont Co, OH*, 1880 p.63, 83, 118-9, 249). These references are obviously not to Laban's son, John, b. 1811, far too late, d. 1833.

"In the southwestern part of the Township (Batavia) John Brazier, of North Carolina, was among the pioneers, and died near what is now known as Centreville Station, in 1838. He had sons named William, Lewis, Oliver, and Henry, the latter yet living (1880) as the sole member of the family not deceased. On an adjoining farm lived Laban Brazier, a local Methodist preacher, who died in 1843. It is said of him that he preached nearly all the early funeral sermons. His sons were James, John, and Elijah, the latter being a resident of Amelia at this time." (*History of Clermont County, Ohio*, 1880, p.248)

Sons of John Brazier:
V9-3100.   d-1. **William Brazier**, d. bef 1880
V9-3101.   d-2. **Lewis Brazier**, d. bef 1880
V9-3102.   d-3. **Henry Brazier**, living in 1880

V9-3103.   d-4. **Oliver Brazier**, b. 1 Feb 1837, d. 20 Sep 1870, ae 43 yr, 7 mo, 20 days, Amelia Cem (*Clermont Co, OH, Cem Rec. v.I, p.6*)

Others in Amelia Cem on State Rd #125: (*Clermont Co, OH, Cem Rec.* v.I, p.6)
Sarah Brazier, d. 13 Sep 1859, age 10 yrs, 9 mo, 2 days,
William Brazier, d. 13 Sep 1870, age 19 yrs, 10 mo, 21 days
Thomas Brazier, no dates

26. JAMES BRAZIER
and MARY "POLLY" SMITH,
of Lincoln Co, TN

c-4. **James Brazier** and his brother, Elijah, (sons of William Brazier, of Surry Co, NC), moved together and lived near each other most of their lives. Elijah is in the 1800 Census of Greenville, SC, with the Thomas Brazier clan. Elijah and James are in the 1810 Rowan, NC Census and the 1820 Franklin Co, TN. Apparently, they moved there about 1818. About 1830, James and Mary "Polly" Brazier moved to Lincoln Co, TN (borders Franklin Co, where many of his children's marriages were recorded). He is not in the 1830 Census of Franklin Co, though Elijah is.

Land and Estate Records

In March, 1830, James Brazier bought 50 acres in Lincoln Co, TN, from Joseph Frost (Deed recorded 31 March 1851). In April, 1831, he bought another 160 acres from Joseph Frost, a parcel adjoining the first one. In 1833, he bought an additional 30 acres from George Waggoner. James Brazier died (19 March 1833) before the paper work was completed on this last purchase, but his heirs completed the deal and recorded the deed on 21 Jan 1834. In 1848, William Jean "Billy" Brazier bought the 240 acres from the other heirs.

William Cobble & Wife, et.al. to William J. Brazier: Joseph Frost by deed dated 22nd of March 1830 conveyed to James Brazier a tract of land containing fifty acres situated in Lincoln County, Tennessee, on the waters of East Mulberry Creek. Said Frost in like manner sold and by deed bearing date of 16th of April 1831, conveyed to said James Brazier a tract of land adjoining the tract first above mentioned, containing one hundred & sixty one acres & 148 poles. Said James Brazier purchased of George Waggoner a tract of land adjoining the tracts of land above mentioned, containing about thirty acres; this tract of land after the death of said Brazier did convey to his heirs by said Waggoner by deed dated 21st January 1834. Said several deeds are of record in the Register office of said County of Lincoln. Said James Brazier died intestate whereby his interest in said land descended to his children: William J. Brazier, Sion S. Brazier, Sarah who has intermarried with Green B. Kitchen, Elizabeth who has intermarried with Morgan Garner, Nancy who has intermarried with William B. Kemp, & Mary H. who has intermarried with William Cobble. The said William J. Brazier has purchased from said other heirs of James Brazier the interest they acquired to said land as before stated & they desire to make conveyance thereof to him and to effect this object this indenture is made between said [heirs enumerated again] and William J. Brazier ... in consideration of $450. ... witness my hand at Office this 18th day of April 1848

Wm. E. Sayles, Clerk

Family of James Brazier and Polly Smith

Family Bible record of James Brazier, son of William Brazier of Surry Co, NC, grandson of James Brazier of Cumberland Co, NC. The Bible was printed in 1828 by Mcarty and Davis of Philadelphia; so most of the entries in it are from hindsight and were probably made all at once. The Bible was lost for many years, then found in a trunk in Florida in recent years by a lady who was not related. She later took the Bible to Tennessee and presented it to Ruthie Brazier Limbaugh, of Belvidere, TN, who d. May 1990. I have rearranged the entries to make a family group sheet:

James Brazier, son of William Brazier Dest (dec'd) was bornd January 17 1772.
Mary Brazier his wife was bornd July 19 1775.
James Brazier married Mary Smith, 3 Sep 1801. [Wake Co, NC Marriage license: James Brazier & Polly Smith, 2 Sep 1801]

Family of James Brazier and Mary "Polly" Smith, all b. North Carolina:

V9-3104.   d-1. ***Sally M. Brazier,** b. 5 April 1803, Wake Co, NC, d. 10 May 1850; m. 28 Feb 1827, **_Green Berry Kitchens_**, b. 26 March 1805, d. 11 July 1868

V9-3105.   d-2. ***Elizabeth Brazier,** b. 18 Aug 1805, d. 13 Sep 1875; m.1. 15 Jan 1824, **_Joseph Graves_**, d. 27 July 1832, age 29 yrs, 3 mos, 3 days; Elizabeth m.2. **_Morgan Garner_**; In Bible: Elizabeth Garner departed this life 13 Sep 1875,

	age 70 yrs, 1 mo, 5 days. Children from James Brazier Bible.
V9-3106.	e-1. Martha Jane Graves, b. 30 Dec 1825; d. 3 Sep 1846, age 20 yrs, 8 mos, 3 days
V9-3107.	e-2. Thompson Wesley Graves, b. 1 June 1829; m. 16 Nov 1852, Luisa Jane Shasteen, b, 14 Nov 1839, d. 23 July 1878. Ch: Martha C., 1859; George W., 1867; and Banner Graves, 1874
V9-3108.	e-3. Joseph F. Graves, b. 13 June 1832, just five weeks before his father died.
V9-3109.	d-3. **Nancy Ellen Brazier,** b. 15 Nov 1807, d. 17 Sep 1892, Merrilltown, Travis Co, TX; m. 4 July 1832, **William Barnett Kemp**, b. 4 Nov 1814, Caswell Co, NC, d. 7 Nov 1885, Merrilltown, TX
V9-3110.	d-4. **Sion S. Brazier,** b. 7 Feb 1810; m. 23 Nov 1841, **Mary J. Baker**, b. c1820 (age 40 in 1860 Lincoln, TN)
V9-3111.	d-5. **William Jean "Billy" Brazier,** b. 5 Nov 1812; m. 28 May 1836, **Perlina A. E. Hazlewood** and had thirteen children. After Perlina Brazier died on 1 Jan 1857, "Billy" m.2. **Martha Hazelwood**, thought to have been a cousin of his first wife, and they had three children. Billy Brazier died 25 Aug 1890 and was buried in the Brazier Cemetery, on his property in Moore Co, TN, a short distance behind his home. Martha Brazier died 23 Dec 1869. See below.
V9-3112.	d-6. **Mary H. "Polly" Brazier,** b. 19 March 1815; m. **William Cobble**
V9-3113.	e-1. Jane Coble
V9-3114.	e-2. Terresa Coble

From the Bible:
James Brazier departed this life on the night of the 19th of March in the year of our LORD 1833, aged 61 yrs, 2 mos, 2 days
Mary Brazier departed this life on the night of the 21st of March in the year of our lord 1855, aged 79 yrs, 8 mos, 2 days

In her book, Mertie Brazier (Rt 2, Box 301, Chico, TX 76030), says that "the youngest son, James Brazier Jr, was not included as an heir, as he was given the home place, since he was living with his parents at the time of his father's death." Since James Sr died intestate, the law would have included James Jr regardless of what arrangements the siblings had made. He is not among the heirs, nor among the sellers when Billy Brazier bought the others' shares. An 1832 Franklin Co Court record establishes that this James Brazier in question was a son and orphan of William Brazier, probably a son of Elijah Brazier and grandson of James Brazier of Cumberland Co, See Unsolved Puzzles below.

Sally M. Brazier and Green Berry Kitchens

d-1. ***Sally M. Brazier,** b. 5 April 1803, Wake Co, NC, d. 10 May 1850; m. 28 Feb 1827, **_Green Berry Kitchens_**, b. 26 March 1805, d. 11 July 1868, s/o Samuel Kitchens and Martha "Patsy" Brooks.

Family of Sally M. Brazier and Green Berry Kitchens: (source: Mertie Brazier)

V9-3115.   e-1. Mary L. Kitchens, b. 1831
V9-3116.   e-2. Nancy Kitchens, b. 1833
V9-3117.   e-3. Elizabeth Kitchens, b. 1835
V9-3118.   e-4. William L. Kitchens, b. c1839, d. young? (name re-used)
V9-3119.   e-5. Samuel Asberry Kitchens, b. 20 Dec 1840, Winchester, Franklin Co, TN, d. 22 Nov 1916, OK (data from a letter from him to the _Dallas Morning News_), m.1. Mary Elizabeth Runnels, b. 14 Nov 1840, d. 30 Aug 1888; m.2. Mary Jane Evans Allen, b. 10 March 1867, d. 12 Jan 1944.
V9-3120.   f-1. Martha L. Kitchens, 1868-1869;
V9-3121.   f-2. James Melton Kitchens, 1860-1870;
V9-3122.   f-3. Sedonia Lora Kitchens, b. 13 Oct 1871, m. Frances Marion Whitford (ch: Lewis; Isaac; Winnie; and Clayborn Whitford);
V9-3123.   f-4. Louis Thomas Kitchens, 1873- 1895;
V9-3124.   f-5. Samuel Westley Kitchens, 1874-1900;
V9-3125.   f-6. Lora Kitchens, 1879, m. James Moss;
V9-3126.   f-7. Winnie Kitchens, 1880, m. Henderson Runnels (ch: Willie; Leonard; Lula; and Ben Runnels);
V9-3127.   f-8. William Newton Kitchens, 1881- 1916, m.1. Mary Jane Evans Allen, b. 1867, d. 1944 (2ch: by 1st m.); m.2. Mary Charlotte "Lottie" Evans, b. 1882, McMinnville, TN, d. 13 Jan 1967, Lubbock, TX (14 ch by 2nd m.):
V9-3128.   g-1. Ina Elizabeth Kitchens; m. _____ Hoskinson
V9-3129.   h-1. Barbara J. Hoskinson, m. Dennis Lange. ch: Samuel Zachary Lange

V9-3130.	g-2. George Washington Kitchens;
V9-3131.	h-1. Paul Stewart Kitchens; m. Velma Oleta Rudloff. Ch: Joel Wayne, Paul Ray, Linda Mae, and Robert Dale Kitchens,
V9-3132.	h-2. Shirley Maxine Kitchens, m. W. A. Bittle. Ch: James Westley; John David; Rebecca Ann; Naomi Ruth; Mary Priscilla; Nathan Aaron; and Paul David Bittle
V9-3133.	h-3. Nettie Janita Kitchens; m.1. Joseph Kennedy; m.2. William Thomas Smith. Ch: David; Rosetta; Jennifer Suellen; Weneton; Mary Lois; Sandra K.; and Andy Smith
V9-3134.	h-4. Naomi Gertrude Kitchens; m. Willie Thomas. ch: James Harlan; and Sylvia Mae Thomas
V9-3135.	h-5. J.T. Asberry Kitchens; m. Goldie K. Markham. ch: George David; and John Timothy Kitchens
V9-3136.	h-6. Otis Roy Kitchens; m. Evelyn Kimmous. Ch: Beverly May; John Joseph; and Donald Kitchens
V9-3137.	h-7. Marvin Lee Kitchens; m. Frances Jeanette Crump. ch: George Steven; and Marvin Keith Kitchens
V9-3138.	h-8. Iva Mae Kitchens; m. D.L. Gee. ch: Leva Maxene; Darmond Legue; Mark Anthony; and Terron Douglass Gee
V9-3139.	h-9. Laguatta Joy Kitchens; m. Shelby Leon Gee. ch: Shelby Larry; Marvin Leon; Lloyd Wade; and Creda Joy Gee
V9-3140.	g-3. (by 2nd m.): Bill Kitchens;
V9-3141.	g-4. Floyd Norman Kitchens;
V9-3142.	g-5. Iliot Duard Kitchens, (m. Roxie Mae Hooper);
V9-3143.	g-6. Milburn Lafayette Kitchens;
V9-3144.	g-7. Ethel Viola Kitchens, (m. Authur Johns);
V9-3145.	g-8. Velma Sedonia Kitchens, 1901-1970 (m. Elmer Patterson);
V9-3146.	g-9. Mary Adeline Kitchens, 1902-1973 (m. Lenny Hodges);
V9-3147.	g-10. Alvin James Kitchens;
V9-3148.	g-11. Pearl Elizabeth Kitchens;
V9-3149.	g-12. Arthur Lee Kitchens;

V9-3150.	g-13. Clifford Dee Kitchens, 1910-1966 (m. Beulah Townsend);
V9-3151.	g-14. Paul Curtis Kitchens, 1913, 1999 (m. Myrtle Townsend);
V9-3152.	g-15. Norma Lee Kitchens, 1918-1996, (m. Roy _____);
V9-3153.	g-16. Grady Otho Kitchens, (m. Nell Hackworth)
V9-3154.	e-6. William Green "Billy" Kitchens, (twin) b. 1 Oct 1841, d. 24 Nov 1918; m.1. in 1864, Martha Ann Webb, b. 23 Nov 1841, TN, d. 1 May 1876; m.2. 25 Oct 1876, in Franklin Co, TN, Mary Lydia Lupkins.
V9-3155.	f-1. Sarah S. Kitchens, 1865;
V9-3156.	f-2. Nancy J. Kitchens, 1869;
V9-3157.	f-3. William Zachariah Kitchens, 1872- 1938, m. Emma Parlee Fairchilds (ch:
V9-3158.	g-1. Minnie May Kitchens; m. _____ Parsely
V9-3159.	h-1. Ruby Parsley; m. E.G. McMasters. Ch: Jennifer; Donna; and Tommy Grant McMasters
V9-3160.	g-2. John Kitchens; m. _____.
V9-3161.	h-1. Corda Mae Kitchens; m. Donald Gelvin. Ch: Diane; and Mike Gelvin
V9-3162.	h-2. Lovell Gene Kitchens; m. Shirley _____. ch: Allen; and Charles Kitchens
V9-3163.	g-3. William Floyd Kitchens; m. _____
V9-3164.	h-1. Emmaline Kitchens; m. Buster Riddle. ch: Debra Kay Riddle (m. _____ Hinkle)
V9-3165.	g-4. Jess Robert Kitchens; m. _____
V9-3166.	h-1. Roberta Evelyn Kitchens; m.1. Edwin Reach; m.2. J.L. Byas;
V9-3167.	i-1. Jack Lynn Byas; m. Peggy Williams. ch: Shelly Nan; and Jana Lynn Byas
V9-3168.	i-2. Steven Dale Byas; m. Donna Marie Moore. ch: Jason Lee Byas
V9-3169.	h-2. Curtis Edward Kitchens; m. Helen Ann Artre.
V9-3170.	i-1. Randall Kitchens; m.1. Lisa Poor (3 ch); m.2. Kelly _____ (1 ch). Ch: Taylor Leigh; Zachary; Madison Danielle; Ashley Kitchens
V9-3171.	i-2. Richard Edward Kitchens; m. _____. ch: Dane Kitchens
V9-3172.	g-5. Jewell Kitchens

V9-3173.　　　g-6. Cecil C. Kitchens; m. _____

V9-3174.　　　　h-1. Larry Dean Kitchens; m. Judy Gore. ch: Charles; and _____ Kitchens

V9-3175.　　　g-7. Hazel Kitchens; m. _____ Richardson

V9-3176.　　　　h-1. Norma Richardson; m. 1. Raymond Farmer; m.2. _____ King; m.3. _____Galliger. Ch: Nathan Douglas; Diane; Dana; and Melissia Farmer

V9-3177.　　　g-8. Fred Kitchens;

V9-3178.　　f-4. Mary L. Kitchens, 1874-1884;

V9-3179.　　f-5. Josie F. Kitchens, 1876, m. William H. Petty (ch: Pearl B. and Ida E. Petty);

V9-3180.　　f-6. James Morrison Kitchens, 1866-1919, m.1. Mary Alice Couch. 1874-1903 (3 ch: Onie Lee; James Henry; and Anna May Kitchens); m.2. Ida Allen (1 ch: William Andrew Kitchens)

V9-3181.　　e-7. William Seth Kitchens, (twin) b. 1 Oct 1841,

V9-3182.　　e-8. Martha A. Kitchens, b. 1843 (twin)

V9-3183.　　e-9. Margaret E. Kitchens, b. 1843 (twin)

V9-3184.　　e-10. Wade M. Kitchens, b. 1847

Nancy Ellen Brazier and William Barnet Kemp

Nancy Ellen Brazier, b. 15 Nov 1807, NC, d. 17 Sep 1892, Merrilltown, Travis Co, TX; m. 4 July 1832, in Normandy, Bedford Co, TN, **William Barnett Kemp**, b. 4 Nov 1814, Caswell Co, NC, d. 7 Nov 1885, Merrilltown, TX, s/o Barnett Kemp and Mary McKee.

Family of Nancy Ellen Brazier and William Barnet Kemp: (Sources: 1850 Franklin Co, TN Census and family group sheet by Wanda Bentley/Irby)

V9-3185.　　e-1. James Barnett Kemp, b. 18 April 1833, Winchester, Franklin Co, TN; d. 27 Dec 1881, Merrilltown, Travis Co, TX; m. 15 June 1854, Coffee Co, TN, (by Rev. Williams), Eliza Sophronia [Ann?] Woodward, b. 14 Jan 1833, TN, d. 15 Dec 1918, Merrilltown, Travis Co, TX, d/o Josiah Grandon Woodward and Nancy Jane Kitchens. James was Capt. Co. D, Waul's Texas Legion; was captured and paroled, but could not work as a blacksmith for the remainder of the Civil War. His Bible records in possession Jessie Newton Yarbrough, Robert Lee, TX; Wanda Irby has Xerox copies.

V9-3186.　　f-1. Viola Tennessee Kemp, b. 27 April 1855, Onion Creek, Travis Co, TX, d. 31 Oct 1929, TX; m. 5 March

1870, Alexander Hoyt Ash, who d. 1892, Williamson Co, TX. Ch: Will, Alvin, Omar, Terrell, Lee, Minnie, Onie, and Viola Ash. Family legend says Alexander Ash was visiting the slave quarters (?slaves ?in 1892) and ignoring his family. As he was returning from Round Rock one night, he was killed by a shot-gun blast near his home. His son, Will Ash, was arrested and tried for the murder of his father, but was acquitted. Family legend says that Viola and Will planned the killing. Viola and Grandma Kemp raised the money for Will's defense. Will Ash made his living as a professional on the rodeo circuit. He married and had a number of children, but became a bootlegger and took up with another woman. He is said to have found his wife taking a nap in the daytime, poured alcohol over her, and set her afire. He then would not let the kids take to her the doctor and she died, 31 Oct 1929. The kids got together and passed a death sentence on him. His son, Samuel Barnett Ash, killed him in 1938, Comanche, TX; since Will was also armed, it was considered self defense. Later, it came out that the law officers were considering arresting him for the murder of his wife, but were afraid of him.

V9-3187.   f-2. Coryell Clementine "Cora-Lee" Kemp, b. 28 Nov 1857, Fayette Co, TX, d. 20 March 1858, TX

V9-3188.   f-3. Lewis Cass Kemp, b. 12 Feb 1859, Winchester, Fayette Co, TX, d. 18 Sep 1949; m.1. 20 Oct 1881, Anna Agnes Ross, m.2. 22 Feb 1905, Laura R.C. Stamp

V9-3189.   f-4. Dora Alice "Allie" Kemp, b. 27 June 1860, Fayette Co, TX, d. 27 Jan 1906; m. Dec 1877, Theodore Printis Smith

V9-3190.   f-5. Nancy Edna Kemp, b. 21 July 1864, Fayette Co, TX, d. 24 Jan 1905; m. 20 Oct 1881, William Joe Graves

V9-3191.   f-6. Sophronia Ann Kemp, b. 5 March 1867, d. 31 May 1951

V9-3192.   f-7. Minnie Rose Kemp, b. 12 April 1870, Merrilltown, Travis Co, TX, d. 18 March 1888

V9-3193.   f-8. Samuel Barnett Kemp, b. 26 Dec 1871, Merrilltown, Travis Co, TX, d. Aug 1962; m. 30 Dec 1903, May Hope

V9-3194.	f-9. Daisy Mae Kemp, b. 18 April 1875, Merrilltown, Travis Co, TX, d. 2 Aug 1917; m. 7 Sep 1892, Edward R. Dickson/Dixon
V9-3195.	f-10. Nancy Lilly Kemp, b. 6 Dec 1877, Merrilltown, Travis Co, TX; m. 24 Jan 1897, George M. Gardner
V9-3196.	e-2. Robert Kemp, b. c1835, TN; not in 1850 census
V9-3197.	e-3. ?Minnie Kemp, b. c1836??
V9-3198.	e-4. Wilson Rudolph "Willie" Kemp, b. 1837; d. 16 Feb 1862, of measles during Civil War at Willard, Torrance Co, NM.
V9-3199.	e-5. Mary Louisa "Lou" Kemp, b. 20 Dec 1839, TN; d. 29 July 1926, TX; m. John M. Smith, of Cunningham Prairie, Fayette Co, TX
V9-3200.	e-6. Sarah Ann Kemp, b. 1843, TN; m. Andrew Jackson "Jack" Ford
V9-3201.	e-7. Nancy Caroline "Callie" Kemp, b. 21 Aug 1846, TN; d. 1904, TX; m. August F. Weber
V9-3202.	e-8. *Thomas Lafayette "Tom" Kemp, b. 14 Sep 1848, TN; d. 9 Oct 1921, Eastland, TX; m. 20 Jan 1876 in Brown Co, TX, Sarah Florence Lusk, b. 29 Jan 1858, d. 17 Dec 1900 (see below for their descendants)
V9-3203.	e-9. Abijah Gotlieb "Bija" Kemp, b. 14 March 1851, TN; d. 2 June 1897, Merrilltown, TX; not married, was handicapped.

Thomas Lafayette Kemp and Sarah Florence Lusk

(Data from descendant Wanda Fay Irby, Seymour, TX)
Descent of Wanda Fay Irby,] from James Brazier of Cumberland Co, NC:
James Brazier of Cumberland Co; d. 1789; m. Sarah _____
William Brazier, d. 1813; m. Sarah Horne
James Brazier, b. 17 Jan 1772; m. Mary "Polly" Smith
Nancy Ellen Brazier, b. 15 Sep 1807; m. William Barnett Kemp
Thomas Lafayette Kemp, b. 14 Sep 1848; m. Sarah Florence Lusk
Fanny Florence Kemp, b. 21 July 1879; m. Rufus Clay Richardson
Walter Calvin Richardson, b. 8 May 1907; m. Ellen Lee Kirkpatrick
Wanda Fay Richardson, b. 1 Oct 1934; m.1. James Alvin Bentley; m.2. Harley Preston Roam; m.3. James Thomas Irby

e-8. Thomas Lafayette "Tom" Kemp, b. 14 Sep 1848, TN; d. 9 Oct 1921, Eastland, TX; m. 20 Jan 1876 in Brown Co, TX, Sarah Florence

Lusk, b. 29 Jan 1858, d. 17 Dec 1900, Thalia, Foard Co, TX, d/o Marion James "Bunk" Lusk and Nancy Amanda Woodward.

V9-3204. f-1. William Josiah Kemp, b. 1 March 1877, TX, d. 17 Aug 1907; m. 23 Dec 1900, Duncan, OK, Emma Jones

V9-3205. f-2. Marion Abijah Kemp, b. 18 June 1878, TX, d. 3 Jan 1946; m. 28 July 1918, Eastland, TX, Myrtle House

V9-3206. f-3. *Fanny Florence Kemp, b. 21 July 1879, Brown, TX, d. 26 Sep 1954, Elbert, Throckmorton Co, TX; m. 26 Nov 1899, DeKalb, Bowie Co, TX, Rufus Clay Richardson, b. 24 Nov 1877,

V9-3207. f-4. Samuel Barnett Kemp, b. 12 June 1881, d. 1 May 1892, Arcadia, LA

V9-3208. f-5. Minnie Maud Kemp, b. 26 Jan 1883, d. Jan 1977

V9-3209. f-6. Nancy Ellen Kemp, b. 28 May 1885, d. Oct 1933

V9-3210. f-7. Thomas Jesse Kemp, b. 5 June 1887, d. Jan 1964, Sweetwater, TX

V9-3211. f-8. Benjamin Franklin Kemp, b. 28 Sep 1895; m. 24 Aug 1919, Albuquerque, NM, Pauline Dotson (div)

V9-3212. f-9. *Hattie Louisa Kemp, b. 3 July 1898, DeKalb, Bowie Co, TX, d. 10 Oct 1985, Albuquerque, NM; m. 17 Aug, Cisco, Eastland Co, TX, Curt Henry Noble.

Fanny Florence Kemp and Rufus Clay Richardson

f-3. Fanny Florence Kemp, b. 21 July 1879, Brown, TX, d. 26 Sep 1954, Elbert, Throckmorton Co, TX; m. 26 Nov 1899, DeKalb, Bowie Co, TX, Rufus Clay Richardson, b. 24 Nov 1877, Hon, Scott Co, AR, d. 21 June 1958, Throckmorton, Throckmorton Co, TX; both are buried at Elbert, Throckmorton Co, TX. Bible records and a journal of Rufus, in possession of Jean Hinson, 1501 Ave C. Graham, TX 76046.

Says Wanda Irby: "Grandad gave everyone a nickname. He called Daddy, "Cal;" Aunt Virgie was "Pete;" Loyd Ray was "High pockets;" Hoyt was "Mutt;" Delma was "Doodle"; many others I don't remember. R.C. was "C Boy." Grandad was a farmer and a carpenter. He built a number of houses in the area. He was an old time gentleman and took care of everything.

Grandma never knew or asked about business. She would tell Grandad she needed shoes or dresses. He brought them from town for her. He ruled the entire family. When Grandad decided something—that is what they did. No one went against Grandad's decisions. He was full of fun and loved to dance...I can remember getting him to do the Double Shuffel and the Buck and Wing. We thought it was so funny.   Grandma was his Queen and was not to be worried about anything."

^{V9-}3213.   g-1. Minnie Leora Richardson, b. 28 Sep 1900, DeKalb, Bowie Co, TX, d. 22 July 1958, Wichita Falls, Wichita Co, TX, bur Elbert, Throckmorton Co, TX; m. 14 Sep 1933, Dwight Davidson Bellah, b. 7 Oct 1879, d. 12 Aug 1943, Elbert, Throckmorton Co, TX, bur there, s/o Samuel Walter Bellah and Emily Henry Josephine Briant.

^{V9-}3214.   h-1. Florence Josephine Bellah, b. 24 Jan 1935, Elbert, Throckmorton Co, TX; m. 18 June 1951, Wichita Falls, Wichita Co, TX, Bobby Lee Blair, b. 10 Oct 1932

^{V9-}3215.   i-1. Dwight Lee Blair, b. 10 Feb 1954, Throckmorton, Throckmorton Co, TX; m. 7 Aug 1977, Judy Elizabeth Flynn, b. 20 Sep 1960, Midland, TX

^{V9-}3216.   j-1. Amber Renee Blair, b. 2 Dec 1980, Lubbock, TX

^{V9-}3217.   j-2. Kristi Dawn Blair, b. 28 Sep 1982, Wichita Falls, TX

^{V9-}3218.   i-2. Bobby Don "Donnie" Blair, b. 24 Dec 1954, Thorckmorton, Throckmorton Co, TX; m.1. 1 June 1972, Sharon Louise Moody, (2 ch; div); m.2. Vicky _____ (2 ch)

^{V9-}3219.   j-1. Justin Don Blair, b. 15 Dec 1972, Olney, Young Co, TX

^{V9-}3220.   j-2. Brandon Lee Blair, b. 26 Oct 1974, Olney, Young Co, TX

^{V9-}3221.   f-2. Vicki Blair,

^{V9-}3222.   j-4. Shawn Blair,

^{V9-}3223.   j-5. Breon Blair, b. 20 Jan 1997

^{V9-}3224.   h-2. Mary Sue Bellah, b. 9 July 1939, Olney, Young Co, TX; m. 9 Dec 1960, Donald Eugene Hale,

^{V9-}3225.   i-1. Tracey LaDon Hale, b. 16 Oct 1962, Wichita Falls, TX

^{V9-}3226.   g-2. Nettie May Richardson, b. 8 March 1902, DeKalb, Bowie Co, TX, d. 9 Sep 1990, Graham, Young Co, TX, bur Elbert, Throckmorton Co, TX; m. 3 Oct1920, Elbert, Thorckmorton Co, TX, John Henry Huffman, b. 27 Oct 1900, Woodland, Red River Co, TX, bur Elbert, Throckmorton Co, TX, s/o Robert E. Huffman and Emma Levitt.

^{V9-}3227.   h-1. Hoyt Leon Huffman, b. 17 July 1921, Elbert, Throckmorton Co, TX; m. 14 Oct 1944, Durham, NC,

	Margie Raye Tenney, b. 18 April 1926, Throckmorton, TX
V9-3228.	i-1. Kenneth Joe Huffman, b. 17 Aug 1943, Ft Worth, Tarrant Co, TX
V9-3229.	i-2. Glenda Kaye Huffman, b. 28 Aug 1945, Ft Worth, Tarrant Co, TX; m. 16 March 1963, Megargel, Archer Co, TX, George Philip Rife, b. 29 May 1943, Graham, Young Co, TX (4 ch; div)
V9-3230.	j-1. Lynda Denise Rife, b. 27 Oct 1963, Fort Worth, TX
V9-3231.	j-2. Philip Ben Rife, b. 3 June 1967, Mineral Wells, Palo Pinto Co, TX
V9-3232.	j-3. Tammy Kaye Rife, b. 19 June 1969, Graham, Young Co, TX
V9-3233.	j-4. Daniel Bryand Rife, b. 26 Oct 1971, Graham, TX
V9-3234.	i-3. Johnnie Ray Huffman, b. 3 June 1947, Olney, Young Co, TX; m. 8 July 1968, Megargel, Archer Co, TX, Danza Raye Guffey, b. 1 Oct 1948, Knox City, Knox Co, TX
V9-3235.	j-1. Christi Dawn Huffman, b. 12 April 1969, Graham, Young Co, TX
V9-3236.	j-2. Jeffery Paul Huffman, b. 23 Jul1971, Stephenville, Erath Co, TX
V9-3237.	h-2. Emma Jean Huffman, b. 5 April 1924, Breckenridge, Stephens Co, TX; m. 3 May 1945, in Jean, Young Co, TX, Roland Wade Sparks, b. 9 Sep 1925, Jean, Young Co, TX, d. 4 May 1959, killed in an oil-field accident, Canadian, Hemphill Co, TX
V9-3238.	i-1. Brenda Ann Sparks, b. 26 April 1947, Olney, Young Co, TX; m. 10 Jan 1964, Graham, Young Co, TX, Louis Dale Marsh, b. 28 Dec 1943, Olney, Young Co, TX
V9-3239.	j-1. Sherman Wade Marsh, b. 21 Oct 1965, Graham, Young Co, TX; m.1. Mary ___ (div); m.2. Beth ___.
V9-3240.	j-2. Kimberly Dell Marsh, b. 27 April 1969, Graham, Young Co, TX; m. 29 July 1991, Graham, Young Co, TX, Brian Lynn Reeves, b. 26 July 1962, Henrietta, Clay Co, TX (2 ch; div); m.2. 10 May 1997, Graham, Young Co, TX, Chad Kynor Dodson, b. 25 March 1968.

V9-3241.   k-1. Jared Brian Reeves, b. 28 May 1991, Wichita Falls, TX
V9-3242.   k-2. Austin John Reeves, b. 23 April 1993
V9-3243.   i-2. Terry Wade Sparks, b. 10 Jan 1953, Graham, Young Co, TX; m. 8 Sep 1973, Loving, Young Co, TX, Sandri Kay Cutburth, b. 4 July 1954, Graham, Young Co, TX
V9-3244.   j-1. Misty Marie Sparks, b. 15 Feb 1976, Fortuna, CA
V9-3245.   j-2. Bryan Wade Sparks, b. 23 Aug 1979, Wichita Falls, TX
V9-3246.   g-3. Virginia Pearl Richardson, b. 31 Dec 1903, DeKalb, Bowie Co, TX, d. 24 Aug 1975, Seymour, Baylor Co, TX, bur Elbert, Throckmorton Co, TX; m. 20 May 1923, Elbert, Thorckmorton Co, TX, Kenneth Raymond Mitchell, b. 12 Sep 1901, Elbert, Throckmorton Co, TX, d. 29 May 1993, Throckmorton, Throckmorton Co, TX, bur Elbert, TX, s/o Beverlie Custer Mitchell and Mary Olevia Bacon.
V9-3247.   h-1. Terrell Wade "T.W." Mitchell, b. 7 Dec 1925, Elbert, TX
V9-3248.   h-2. Doris Ray Mitchell, b. 2 June 1928, Elbert, TX, d. 24 Dec 1974, San Antonio, Bexar Co, TX
V9-3249.   h-3. Richard Franklin Mitchell, b. 10 April 1931, Elbert, Throckmorton Co, TX, d. 2 Sep 1994, of lung cancer, bur Throckmorton, TX; m. Jolene Ingram
V9-3250.   i-1. Kenneth Joe Mitchell,
V9-3251.   i-2. Annette Mitchell,
V9-3252.   i-3. Brenda Mitchell,
V9-3253.   h-4. Harlis Leo Mitchell, b. 12 March 1933, Elbert, TX
V9-3254.   h-5. Delma Lou "Doodle" Mitchell, b. 12 April 1935, Elbert, TX
V9-3255.   g-4. Walter Calvin Richardson, b. 8 May 1907, Thalia, Foard Co, TX, d. 14 June 1946, Elbert, Throckmorton Co, TX, bur there; m. 25 Dec 1930, Throckmorton, Throckmorton Co, TX, Ellen Lee Kirkpatrick, b. 9 Jan 1912, Elbert, TX, d. 23 Jan 1946, Goree, Knox Co, TX, but Elbert, Throckmorton Co, TX, d/o John Kirkpatrick and Annis Cooley. Writes daughter Wanda: "He was tall with dark hair and blue eyes. He was often called Slim so was slender. He was slow moving and soft spoken and full of fun—loved practical jokes even when they were on him. He smoked cigarettes he rolled himself out of Prince

Albert tobacco. He liked hunting and the outdoors." Ellen "was tall, her eyes were blue—so dark that when she was angry they were almost purple. She was artistic and could do almost anything she set her mind to do. She loved animals and the outdoors. She knew all the plants that were good to eat and could make a meal out of the pasture. She said her hair was mouse brown, and it had to be washed really often or was oily. It had a natural wave to it and she was a very pretty woman. She was loving but quick tempered and more so because she was sick most of my life. She loved music, games and people. She was a very social person. Mother would not let us call her Mama—it was always Mother. She always smelled of lavender. She grew flowers in pots when we had to haul all our water. She kept our yard bare and swept clean. When she did the laundry, she also scrubbed all the floors the same day to save water. She played the piano or organ and Grandpa Kirk gave her an old pump organ. She played "by ear" and had never had lessons but she could hear a song and play it. They often had "singings" and "play parties" at our house. All the kids played outside till they were worn out, then put to bed wherever there was space for them. They played games like "42" and Chinese checkers and others I don't remember. When we went to Grandad Richardson's, they played croquet by the hour. They were close knit families—both the Kirkpatricks and Richardsons and had been friends and neighbors for years. The families visited each other and got together every time they possibly could. Those close enough were at Grandma and Grandad Richardson's every Sunday. Mother made all my Valentines to exchange at school. Often they were cookies with painted faces and red hearts. She also made most of our clothes. She liked to read and exchanged magazines and books with all the neighbors. A neighbor saved all the newspapers for her and Daddy. His name was Gifford B. Eggleston. We called him Eggie. He sometimes took us to Seymour on Monday and took us to see our first movie. In between reels, Charlie McCarthy and Edgar Bergan were on stage to keep the people entertained while they changed the film!! I think this was in Seymour."

V9-3256.   h-1. Elinore Nadine Richardson, b. 9 May 1932, Elbert, Throckmorton Co, TX, d. 28 Sep 1933, Throckmorton, TX

V9-3257.   h-2. Wanda Fay Richardson, b. 1 Oct 1934, Goree, Knox Co, TX; m.1. 10 Dec 1957, Wichita Falls, Wichita Co, TX, James Alvin Bentley (3 ch; div), s/o Clyde Samuel Bentley and Ida Miranda Williams; m.2. 3 June 1955, Mineral Wells, Palo Pinto Co, TX, Harley Preston Roam (1 ch; div), b. 22 Dec 1930, AR, s/o Harley Preston Roam and _____ Hargrave; m.3. 19 Oct 1991, Perrin, Jack Co, TX, James Thomas Irby, b. 12 Nov 1928, Ft Worth, Tarrant Co, TX

V9-3258.   i-1. James Ray Bentley, b. 25 Oct 1959, Olney, Young Co, TX; m. 13 March 1983, White Settlement, Tarrant Co, TX, Sherry Elaine Howard, b. 8 June 1964, Ada, Pontotoc Co, OK

V9-3259.   j-1. Phillip James Bentley, b. 22 June 1983, Ada, Pontotoc Co, OK

V9-3260.   j-2. Bryan Adam Bentley, b. 10 July 1985, Ada, OK

V9-3261.   j-3. Dakota Keith Bentley, b. 28 Feb 1988, Ada, OK

V9-3262.   i-2. Miranda Ellen Bentley, b. 15 Feb 1964, Olney, Young Co, TX ; m. 9 May 1985, White Settlement, Tarrant Co, TX, William Estell Harris, b. 23 Dec 1965, Buel, Tuscaloosa Co, AL (div)

V9-3263.   j-1. Summer D'Anne Bentley, b. 7 Feb 1980, Ft Worth, Tarrant Co, TX, (born when Miranda was 15 and unmarried; father: Dickey Ray Garrison)

V9-3264.   j-2. William Taylor "Tye" Harris, b. 23 Dec 1985, Azle, Tarrant Co, TX

V9-3265.   j-3. Clyde Colman "Cole" Harris, b. 28 Jan 1987, Azle, TX

V9-3266.   j-4. Tiffany Ann Bentley, b. 18 April 1995, Ft Worth, Tarrant Co, TX (d/o Miranda's cousin, Theresa Joe Bentley Bennett and taken by Welfare because she showed drugs in her system; placed with Miranda and adopted by her, Aug 1996)

V9-3267.   i-3. Shawn Lee Bentley, b. 18 June 1967, Olney, Young Co, TX; m. 14 Dec 1984, White Settlement,

Tarrant Co, TX, Melissa Louise Willis, b. 21 Aug 1966, Marietta, Cobb Co, GA, d/o Jack Thurmond Willis and Mary Louise Daniel. On 8 Dec 1995, Melissa ran off with her boss, Jeff Walker, leaving Shawn and three children; Shawn filed for divorce, charging adultry and abandonment; granted 19 Feb 1996)

V9-3268.   j-1. Heather Louise Bentley, b. 21 Sep 1985, Ft Worth, Tarrant Co, TX, d. 22 Sep 1985, Ft Worth, TX

V9-3269.   j-2. Bradley Jack Bentley, b. 11 Dec 1986, Ft Worth, TX

V9-3270.   j-3. Patrick Shawn Bentley, b. 17 March 1988, Ft Worth, TX

V9-3271.   j-4. Amber Michelle Bentley, b. 26 Oct 1989, Ft Worth, TX

V9-3272.   i-4. Harley Robin Roam, b. 30 March 1956, Olney, Young Co, TX; m. 25 Dec 1977, White Settlement, Tarrant Co, TX, BokHui Lee, b. 1 March 1948, Taegu, Korea, d/o Jang Uk Lee and Jim Su Kim.

V9-3273.   j-1. Roy Robin Roam, b. 28 March 1979, El Paso, El Paso Co, TX

V9-3274.   j-2. Jennifer Lee Roam, b. 8 Sep 1983, Junction City, Geary Co, KS

V9-3275.   i-5. Wanda Fay Irby.

V9-3276.   h-3. Loyd Ray Richardson, b. 19 Oct 1936, Goree, Knox Co, TX; m. 23 Sep 1958, Amarillo, Potter Co, TX, Lois Ellen McKay, b. 15 Dec 1938, Dustin, OK, d/o Dewey Lee McKay and Gladys Opel White.

V9-3277.   i-1. Anita Gwenn Richardson, b. 14 July 1959, Duman, Moore Co, TX; m. 18 May 1985, Englewood, Arapaho Co, CO, Gary Dean Edwards, b. Denver, CO

V9-3278.   j-1. Cynthia Dian Edwards, b. 23 Aug 1986, Denver, CO

V9-3279.   j-2. Steven Andrew Edward, b. 6 June 1990, Denver, CO

V9-3280.   i-2. Walter Dale Richardson, b. 26 Oct 1961, Dumas, Moore Co, TX; m.1. 15 Oct 1981, Amarillo, Potter Co, TX, Jody Lynn Cisneros, b. 24 July 1964, Houston, Harris Co, TX (div); m.2. 13 June 1986,

Dumas, TX, Deborah Lynn Roark, b. 2 Nov 1964, Guymon, Texas Co, OK

V9-3281.   j-1. Gary Ray Richardson, b. 11 Sep 1981, Borger, Hutchinson Co, TX

V9-3282.   j-2. Rebecca Lynn Richardson, b. 9 Feb 1988, Dumas, Moore Co, TX

V9-3283.   i-3. Karl Ray Richardson, b. 9 Nov 1964, Dumas, Moore Co, TX; m. 5 Dec 1986, Dumas, TX, Pamela Sue Singleton

V9-3284.   j-1. Justin Ray Richardson, b. 17 Feb 1988, Dumas, Moore Co, TX

V9-3285.   j-2. Kristopher James Richardson, b. in March 1989, Dumas, TX

V9-3286.   i-4. Darla Kay Richardson, b. 9 Nov 1964, Dumas, Moore Co, TX; m. 14 Sep 1984, Dumas, TX, Clinton Alan Simmons,

V9-3287.   j-1. Kayla Lynnette Simmons, b. 24 July 1989
V9-3288.   j-2. Jermey Scott Richardson, b. 27 April 1990
V9-3289.   i-5. Randi Michelle Richardson, b. 7 Jan 1980, Dumas, Moore Co, TX

V9-3290.   g-5. Ina Gertrude Richardson, b. 26 Sep 1909, Elbert, Throckmorton Co, TX; m. 16 Feb 1951, Colorado City, TX, Marvin Clifford Pettitt, b. 23 Jan 1914, Taylor Co, TX

V9-3291.   g-6. Clarence Ray Richardson, b. 1 June 1913, Elbert, Throckmorton Co, TX, d. 28 Nov 1983, Olney, Young Co, TX, bur Elbert, Throckmorton Co, TX; m. 6 Nov 1942, Walters, Cotton Co, OK, Jessie Wilkinson, b. 16 Feb 1919, Throckmorton, TX

V9-3292.   h-1. Gordon Clarence Richardson, b. 28 Nov 1943, Haskell, Haskell Co, TX, d. 9 April 1998, Wichita Falls, Wichita Co, TX; m. 15 Aug 1992, Thorberry, Clay Co, TX, Judith Timson.

V9-3293.   h-2. Larry Wayne Richardson, b. 12 April 1948, Olney, Young Co, TX; m. 9 March 1974, Clyde, TX, Marsha Rexroat, b. 25 April 1948, Ranger, TX

V9-3294.   i-1. Necia Leigh Richardson, b. 4 Jan 1976, Abilene, Taylor Co, TX

V9-3295.   h-3. Billy Jack Richardson, b. 25 Aug 1953, Olney, Young Co, TX; m. 21 Jan 1976, Abilene, Taylor Co, TX, Catherine Annette Dodson

V9-3296.   h-4. Jerry Lee Richardson, b. 18 March 1957, Throckmorton, Throckmorton Co, TX; m. 21 Sep

	1985, Vernon, TX, Jeanne Lucille Goins, b. 1 Sep 1959, Bruch, Morgan Co, CO.
V9-3297.	g-7. Ray Cecil Richardson, b. 29 Aug 1917, Elbert, Throckmorton Co, TX, d. 1 Oct 1956, Elbert, Throckmorton Co, TX
V9-3298.	g-8. Lena Lucille Richardson, b. 5 July 1921, Elbert, Throckmorton Co, TX, d. 12 Oct 1989, Wichita Falls, Wichita Co, TX, bur Elbert, Throckmorton Co, TX; m. 28 Feb 1946, Elbert, Throckmorton Co, TX, Samuel Irvin Bellah, b. 3 April 1914, Profitt, Young Co, TX, d. 31 Oct 1977, Elbert, Throckmorton Co, TX, s/o Dwight Davidson Bellah and Eura Dell Cooper.
V9-3299.	h-1. Ronnie Bruce Bellah, b. 9 Dec 1951, Olney, Young Co, TX; m. 13 June 1976, Megargle, Archer Co, TX, Kellie Adelle Smith,
V9-3300.	i-1. Scott Bellah

Hattie Louisa Kemp and Curt Henry Noble

f-9. Hattie Louisa Kemp, b. 3 July 1898, DeKalb, Bowie Co, TX, d. 10 Oct 1985, Albuquerque, NM; m. 17 Aug (or 3 July) 19__, Cisco, Eastland Co, TX, Curt Henry Noble.

V9-3301.	g-1. Curt Henry Noble Jr, b. c1920
V9-3302.	g-2. Clay Noble, b. Feb 1923, Eastland Co, TX
V9-3303.	g-3. Florence Noble, b. 10 May 1925, Gallup, NM, d. 29 Aug 1943, Albuquerque, NM
V9-3304.	g-4. Clint Noble,
V9-3305.	g-5. Cleve Noble,
V9-3306.	g-6. Ned Noble,
V9-3307.	g-7. Ruby Violet Noble, b. 26 Sep 1927, Gallup, McKinley Co, NM, d. 16 June 1996, Farmington, San Juan Co, NM, bur Bloomfield, San Juan Co, NM; m. 9 Feb 1947, James Leroy Ford, b. 20 June 1927, Minerva, Columbiana Co, OH, d. 12 Sep 1959, Albuquerque, Bernalillo Co, NM, bur Gallup, NM, s/o Levi Ford and Berdette Wright.
V9-3308.	h-1. Curtis James Ford, b. 16 June 1949, Canton, Stark Co, OH; m. 5 Aug 1975, Grants, Cibola Co, NM, Civilla Lois Holder, b. 12 Sep 1954, Albuquerque, Bernalillo Co, NM, d/o Floyd L. Holder and Mary Lou Willman; Curtis also had a child by Leona Hargis, not married.

^{V9-}3309.	i-1. Kimberly Lynn Ford, b. 20 Oct 1972, Killeen, Bell Co, TX; m. 8 Sep 1990, Ernie J. Casaus Jr, b. 3 July 1970, Farmington, San Juan Co, NM, s/o Ernest J. Casaus Sr and Paulie Gomez
^{V9-}3310.	j-1. Casey Tye Casaus, b. 18 March 1990, Farmington, NM
^{V9-}3311.	j-2. Montana Rose Casaus, b. 5 Nov 1992, Farmington, NM
^{V9-}3312.	i-2. Tresa Marie Hargis, b. 16 Jan 1975, Durango, La Plata Co, CO; n.m. Tone Dane Beevers
^{V9-}3313.	j-1. Jechariah Dean Beevers, b. 2 May 1994, Farmington, NM
^{V9-}3314.	h-2. Dean Allen Ford, b. 4 Feb 1952, Gallup, McKinley Co, NM; m. 26 May 1971, Bloomfield, San Juan Co, NM, Pricilla Lynn Clark, b. 22 June 1951, Ada, Pontotoc Co, OK, s/o J.D. Clark and Mary Ann Goodrich.
^{V9-}3315.	i-1. Brian Lee Ford, b. 24 Aug 1972, Farmington, San Juan Co, NM
^{V9-}3316.	i-2. Dustin Lee Ford, b. 2 Sep 1980, San Antonio, Bexar Co, TX
^{V9-}3317.	h-3. Dalton Clay Ford, b. 2 Jan 1954, Albuquerque, Bernalillo Co, NM; m. 26 Sep 1983, San Antonio, TX, Linda Kay Rich, b. 20 March 1959, Cortez, Montezuma Co, CO, d/o Lawrence Rich and Pearl Lorrain Remer.
^{V9-}3318.	i-1. Travis Shane Ford, b. 4 April 1984, San Antonio, Bexar Co, TX
^{V9-}3319.	h-4. Carol Ann Ford, b. 8 Feb 1955, Gallup, McKinley Co, NM; m.1. 8 Sep 1975, (div 7 Feb 1990), Alan Lynn Doyle, b. 22 May 1958, s/o Ronald Melvin Doyle and Ida Joan Smith; m.2. 7 June 1991, Durango, La Plata Co, CO, Mike Alan Harris, b. 14 May 1952, Farmington, San Juan Co, NM.
^{V9-}3320.	i-1. Stacy Leann Doyle, b. 11 Nov 1973; m. 31 Aug 1991, Bloomfield, San Juan Co, NM, Dwayne Cruz Archibeque, b. 4 Aug 1971, Farmington, NM, s/o Paul Archibeque and Rosie Sanchez
^{V9-}3321.	j-1. Tiara Cruz Archibeque, b. 28 Jan 1992, Farminton, NM
^{V9-}3322.	j-2. Ashlee Mechelle Archibeque, b. 18 May 1994, Farmington, NM

V9-3323.	i-2. Shawna Renee Doyle, b. 3 June 1978, Big Lake, Reagan Co, TX
V9-3324.	i-3. Jennifer JaNeal Doyle, b. 23 Feb 1986, Farmington, San Juan Co, NM
V9-3325.	h-5. Karen Beth Ford, b. 26 Nov 1958, Gallup, McKinley Co, NM
V9-3326.	h-6. Jimmy Noble Ford, b. 21 Nov 1959, Farmington, San Juan Co, NM; m. 30 Jan 1986, San Antonio, Bexar Co, TX, Doris Williams Nixon, b. 18 April 1959, San Antonio, TX, s/o Bob Claude Williams and Georgia Lucretia Hopson.
V9-3327.	i-1. Matthew Ryan Ford, b. 19 Sep 1988, Marietta, Cobb Co, GA
V9-3328.	g-8. Wilsie Louise "Midge" Noble,

Sion S. Brazier and Mary L. Baker

Sion S. Brazier, b. 7 Feb 1810, NC, d. 28 Oct 1890, TN; m. 23 Nov 1841, **Mary L. Baker**, b. c1820 (age 40 in 1860 Lincoln, TN) (Franklin Co, Tn Marriages: Sion S. Brazier to Mary L. Baker, married by Reuben Stambler, 22 Nov 1841.) She was born 22 May 1820, AL, d. 25 Dec 1890, TN.

Family of Sion S. Brazier and Mary L. Baker: (Source: Mertie Brazier and 1860 Census, Lincoln Co, TN, H/H #81-18))

V9-3329.	e-1. **Rachel Brazier,** b. 25 June 1843
V9-3330.	e-2. **Lydia Brazier,** b. 15 April 1845
V9-3331.	e-3. **Mary Caroline "Callie" Brazier,** b. 22 March 1847, TN, d. 9 Oct 1920, Moore Co, TN; m. **Lewis Massey**
V9-3332.	e-4. **Sarah Brazier,** b. 9 Sep 1848, TN; m. Sterling Washington Allen, b. c1850, TN
V9-3333.	e-5. **Lemuel Brazier,** b. 8 Dec 1850; not in 1860 Census
V9-3334.	e-6. **James A. Brazier,** b. 29 Dec 1851
V9-3335.	e-7. **George W. Brazier,** b. 15 Dec 1853
V9-3336.	e-8. **Cynthia P. Brazier,** b. 23 Dec 1855
V9-3337.	e-9. **Nancy R. Brazier,** b. Dec 1858; m. 23 Oct 1881, **John Woodward**
V9-3338.	e-10. **William E. Brazier,** b. 17 Feb 1861
V9-3339.	e-11. **Martha Elizabeth Brazier,** b. 7 Nov 1864, Franklin Co, TN, d.14 Sept 1943, Ada, Pontotoc Co, OK; m. 31 Oct 1881, McMinnville, TN, James Carroll Evans, b. 31 Oct 1858, TN, d. 7 June 1936, Ada, Ponototoc Co, OK. s/o Isaac C. Evans.

V9-3340.	f-1. Alma Louise Evans; m. Lauron Lemens Sears
V9-3341.	f-2. Mary Charlotte "Lottie" Evans, b. 17 Sept 1882, McMinnville, Tn, d. 13 Jan 1967, Lubbock, TX
V9-3342.	f-3. Donna Almeda Evans, b. 20 Feb 1883, McMinnville, TN, d. 1 Oct 1936, Bakersfield, Kern Co, CA; m. 4 Nov 1900, Jesse Aaron Cook
V9-3343.	f-4. William Arthur Evans, b. 30 Sept 1886, McMinnville, TN, d. 14 Sept 1957, Norman, Cleveland Co, OK; m. 24 Oct 1909, Lena R. Kirk
V9-3344.	f-5. Bertha C. Evans, b. July 1888, McMinnville, TN, d. 7 Oct 1967, Muskogee, Muskogee Co, OK; m. 12 Oct 1902, J. W. Weaver
V9-3345.	f-6. Lucy Josephine Evans, b. 26 May 1892, McMinnville, TN, d. 6 Nov 1962, Ada, Pontotoc Co, OK; m. Owen Norvell
V9-3346.	f-7. Cora I. Evans, b. 20 Aug 1895, Indian Territory, Caddo, OK, d. 1 Feb 1963, Graham, Young Co, TX; m. Perry Johns
V9-3347.	f-8. Clarence I. Evans, b. 28 Oct 1899, Indian Territory, Caddo, OK, d. there, 14 Sept 1900,

27. WILLIAM JEAN "BILLY" BRAZIER
and PERLINA HAZELWOOD

William Jean "Billy" Brazier, b. 5 Nov 1812, d. 25 Aug 1887; m.1. 27 May 1836, ("at John C. Haslewood", i.e. her father's house) *Perlina A.E. (?Elizabeth) Hazelwood*, b. 1 May 1817, d. 1 Jan 1857; m.2. 1 Sept 1864, (Lincoln Co, TN, Marr p.85) *Martha L. Spencer*, b. 10 Jan 1827, d. 23 Dec 1869, age 42y, 11m, 13da. Billy and Perlina had 13 children; Billy and Martha had three.

Will of William Jean Brazier, (Moore Co, TN, Will Bk A, p.36) Typewritten text found among loose papers in the Moore County Courthouse, Lynchburg, Tennessee, 12 Oct 1983: (in the original spelling; passages in parentheses were added above the line, with a typewriter, except the "Sue" of Willia Sue in two places, which were handwritten and the turns marked by (x), which were a hand-made mark—a loop that crossed back upon itself, apparently dividing sentences or items in the will.)

STATE OF TENNESSEE
COUNTY OF MOORE
    I William J. Braizer do make and publish this as my last will and testament hereby revoking and making void all others by me anytime mad.
    First I will that my funerals Expences and all of my Detts be paid as soon after my Death as posbly out of my money that I may Diepossessed of an may com to the hands of my Excutors   I all so will that my personly property property to be sold on twelve months credit as son as posable after my Death I alls will that my land be sold on a credit of one & two and three years credit in two seppert Tract the Devision line to begin at a chestnut the Southwest corner of William Waggoner thence Runing South to my south bounder Line between me and Easlick I will and give my Excutor all the power that I have to sell my lands without a decree from the Cort and make Such title as I have my self and I want the proseed of my land and personey property devided Equal between my children after them Equal (with Thomas N.) with the exception of one

---

James Brazier, of Cumberland Co, NC   **407** that is my daughter Willia A. E. ("Sue") I will her one hundred and fifty Dollars over and abov the balance of my lawful heirs, wich is heare named Mary A. (who married Will Darnell) Elizabeth wich I have gave her one hundred dollars Marrida C. who mared I Gray (I gave he noth) gave and Thomas N. wich I have gave him one hundred and fifty dolar hors(x) Luca J. who mared Thomas McGhee (gave nothing) and Zachary T. I have him one hundred and twentifive Dollars in a hors(x) and Frances A. Braizer I have gave him Eighty Dollars in a hors(x) Nancy C. who mared Henry Armstrong I have gave her nothin her to for Perlinah S. C. who mared Jake Evans (I gave) nothin Gaston W. (nothin) Willia A N ("Sue") I want her to have one hundred and fifty Dollars moore than the rest of the a bove named heirs on the account of her not hearing and talking good wich I have giv her nothing her to fore if any of the above heirs should die before my estate is wound up I want theses heirs to have their fare shars I want it destinkley understood that I want the above named children wich is my lawful heirs made equal with Thomas Nuton Braizer my Excutor in witness wher of I do to this my will set my hand this the 18th day of July 1887 Signed and published in ower presents and we Subscribed ower names her to in the presents of the Testator this the 18th day of July 1887

William Jean Brazier

Tested John L. Ashby & Wm. S. Evans
Probate 12 Sep 1887

Family of William Jean "Billy" Brazier and Perlina Hazlewood all born Lincoln Co, TN. (first seven listed in James Brazier Bible; see also 1850 Census, Lincoln Co, TN, #1054-120, and 1860 Census, Lincoln Co, TN, #82-18):

V9-3348. e-1. **John W. Brazier,** b. 9 Aug 1836; d. 27 May 1840, 4 yrs, 9 mos, 18 days; bur. Brazier Cem on "Billy" Brazier land, Moore Co, TN

V9-3349. e-2. **Mary A. Elizabeth "Polly" Brazier,** b. 14 Dec 1838, lincoln Co, TN; m. 26 Jan 1858, **W.L. "Will" "Billy" Darnell**, b. c1837

V9-3350. f-1. James W. Darnell, b. c1863

V9-3351. f-2. Susan P. Darnell, b. c1865

V9-3352. f-3. W. L. "Billy" Darnell Jr, b. c1867; m. Sissy McGee

V9-3353. g-1. Gracie Darnell, m. Luther Spencer

V9-3354. g-2. James "Jim" Darnell, m. Annie Lee Grammer

V9-3355. g-3. Samuel "Sam" Darnell, m. Gracie Grammer

V9-3356. g-4. John Darnell, m. Louisa Shelton

V9-3357. f-4. Laura L. Darnell, b. c1870

V9-3358.	f-5. Martha Darnell, b. c1874
V9-3359.	f-6. Sarah A. Darnell, b. c1876
V9-3360.	f-7. Mary Darnell, b. c1878
V9-3361.	e-3. **James M. Brazier,** b. 21 April 1840; d. 17 May 1840, aged 26 days; bur Brazier Cem.
V9-3362.	e-4. **Marilda C. "Rilda" Brazier,** b. 21 Sep 1841, Lincoln Co, TN; m. 9 March 1864, (or 18 July 1867) *J.N. "Ike" Gray*, b. 1839. (Her given name is Marianda and Marand in other documents; Marilda in her father's will. Since her nickname was "Rilda," I'm going with Marilda.)
V9-3363.	f-1. James Cullen "Jim" Gray, m. Alice _____
V9-3364.	f-2. Lucy Gray, m. Jim Manning
V9-3365.	f-3. Mattie Gray, n.m.
V9-3366.	f-4. Virginia "Jennie" Gray, m. *Thomas Riley Brazier*, b. 8 March 1870, Lincoln Co, TN, d. 2 Nov 1949, TN, s/o Thomas Newton "Newt" Brazier and Lucy Caroline Kelley
V9-3367.	f-5. Mary Frances Gray, b. 5 Nov 1874; m. Charlie Bryant
V9-3368.	f-6. Catherine Elizabeth Gray, b. c1878
V9-3369.	f-7. John Shelby Gray, b. 12 Sept 1884; m. Maude Miller
V9-3370.	e-5. ***Thomas Newton "Newt" Brazier,** b. 17 Jan 1843; d. 13 July 1910; bur. Brazier Cem; m. 12 Sep 1867, *Lucy Caroline Kelly*, b. 15 May 1847, d. 3 July 1910; eight children; see below.
V9-3371.	e-6. **Lucy J. "Lou" Brazier,** b. 20 Oct 1844; m.1. 30 July 1865, *John J. Daniel*; m.2. *Tom McGeHee*, widower of her sister, Martha, after Martha's death on 5 Dec 1874; m.3. *John C. Evans*
V9-3372.	f-1. Lottie McGeHee
V9-3373.	f-2. Febe Daniel
V9-3374.	f-3. Tom Daniel; living in Nashville, TN in 1915, when he corresponded with his cousin, J.W. Brazier of Chico, TX.
V9-3375.	e-7. **Phoebe (Febe) Ann Brazier,** b. 22 Nov 1845; d. 27 June 1846, aged 8 mos, 7 days
V9-3376.	e-8. **William J. Brazier,** b. 27 Feb 1847; d. as infant, bur. Brazier Cem.
V9-3377.	e-9. ***Zachary Taylor Brazier,** b. 11 May 1848; d. 8 June 1899 at Chico, TX; m. 1 June 1871, *Martha E. Newman*; five children, see below

V9-3378.   e-10. **Francis Asberry "Berry" Brazier,** b. 11 March 1850; m. 19 Dec 1878, *Alice Womack*

V9-3379.   e-11. **Martha M. Brazier,** b. 29 Nov 1852, d. 5 Dec 1874; m. 29 Nov 1873, *Tom McGeeHee*

V9-3380.   e-12. **Nancy C. "Nan" Brazier,** b. 23 July 1854, d. 13 Oct 1929, TN; m. 3 Oct 1886, *Henry B. Armstrong.*

V9-3381.   f-1. Maude Armstrong; m. _____ Fields

V9-3382.   f-2. Ben Armstrong, d. 1936

V9-3383.   f-3. George Armstrong, b. 19 Aug 1889, d. 6 Jan 1946; m. Lora Smith

V9-3384.   g-1. J. B. Armstrong, b. 10 Aug 1914

V9-3385.   g-2. Frank Armstrong, b. 11 April 1917

V9-3386.   g-3. Gladys Armstrong, b. 3 June 1919

V9-3387.   g-4. Maude Armstrong, b. 19 Sep 1920

V9-3388.   f-4. Mary Armstrong; m. Arthur Church

V9-3389.   f-5. Annie Armstong; m. Tom Adcock

V9-3390.   e-13. ***Perlina Susan Cordelia "Deed" Brazier,** b. 5 Oct 1856; m. 20 Aug 1879, *William Jacob "Jake" Evans*

Family of William J. Brazier and Martha Spencer

V9-3391.   e-14. **Gaston W. "Dock" Brazier,** b. 17 Oct 1866, Ashby, Moore Co, TN; m. 9 April 1885, in Moore Co, TN, *Mary Julia Lackey*, b. Oct 1867, TN

V9-3392.   f-1. **Anne Brazier,** b. 8 Feb 1890, TN, d. 19 Aug 1962, Franklin Co, TN; m. *Wiley Hunt,* b. 6 Aug 1888, d. 29 Mary 1974, both bur Memorial Park, Winchester, TN.

V9-3393.   f-2. **Clifford Brazier,** b. Dec 1892

V9-3394.   f-3. **Ethel Emma Brazier,** b. 19 Jan 1898, d. 14 Jan 1969, Franklin Co, TN; m. *Marc Glaspy Conn,* b. 23 July 1889, TN, d. 5 Oct 1959, Franklin Co, TN, both bur Mt. Garner Cem, Decherd, Franklin Co, TN.

V9-3395.   e-15. **Willie (or Wiley) A.E. "Sue" Brazier,** (fem) b. 20 June 1868; partially deaf and mute

V9-3396.   e-16. **Ellen Brazier,** b. 1870; m. *Lee Waggoner*

Thomas Newton "Newt" Brazier and Lucy C. Kelly

e-5. **Thomas Newton "Newt" Brazier,** fifth child of William Jean "Billy" Brazier and his wife, Perlina Hazlewood, b. 17 Jan 1843, TN, d. 13 July 1910, bur. Brazier Cem, Moore Co, TN; m. *Lucy Caroline Kelly,* b. 15 May 1847, Newport, Cocke Co, TN, d. 3 July 1910, Lynchburg, TN, d/o Charles Kelly and Lucy Hudson, who was said to be Cherokee. They lived their lives in Franklin and Moore Counties, TN, as did a younger brother, Frances Asberry Brazier. A third brother, Zachary Taylor Brazier, moved to Wise County, Texas, in 1882. Their children kept up with their Tennessee and Texas cousins, respectively.

A number of their descendants claimed Cherokee rights about 1900, on the basis of Lucy Kelly's supposed Cherokee ancestry. The claims were rejected, apparently for insufficient evidence. However, to be eligible for rights, one had to live in an Indian community and be recognized by members of that community as an Indian. If you had moved out and integrated with white society, you were ineligible.

In the rejected claims for membership in the Eastern Band of Cherokees there are a series of claims of Cherokee blood for descendants of Lucy Caroline (Kelly) Brazier (apparently arranged by her sons Charles William and Thomas Riley Brazier), who was said to have been born in Newport, Cocke County, Tennessee in 1851 and to have died near Lynchburg 7 April 1892, daughter of Charles Kelly (born North Carolina) and Lucy (Hudson) Kelly. Both of her parents were said to have been of Indian blood; her mother, Lucy Hudson, was said to have been born near Newport. Charles William says that Lucy Kelly was 1/8 Cherokee (Nathan Elonzo, who says he was born 8 December 1884, and was not married, says she was 1/4) and that in 1835 his grandmother was 18 and his Hudson great-grandmother was 58.... The claims were based on four cousins, Charles, _____, Nannie, and Belle Hall, children of Jane Kelly Hall, great-aunt of Charles William Brazier, who had gone to the Indian Territory between 1880 and 1890, and receirved lands and annuities as Cherokees by their Kelly descent. (from Robert Dale Sweeney)

Family of Thomas Newton Brazier and Lucy Caroline Kelly:

V9-3397.   f-1. **Charles William "Bill" Brazier,** b. Lincoln Co, TN, 8 Aug 1865, d. 22 Dec 1915, bur Fayetteville, Lincoln Co, TN; m. 9 Feb 1894, in Moore Co, TN, *Minnie Lee Burrow*, b. 5 Jan 1879, TN, d. 6 May 1946, Sylacauga, Talladega Co, AL, d/o John Burrow and Mary Black; 8 children, all born Moore Co, TN.

V9-3398.   g-1. **Dovie Mae Della Brazier,** b. 22 Sept 1894, Lois, Moore Co, TN, d. 6 July 1936, Tullhoma, Coffee Co, TN; m. *Mike Brewer*, b. 8 March 1888, d. May 1955.

V9-3399.   h-1. M.C. Brewer;

V9-3400.   h-2. Clara Mae Brewer;

V9-3401.   h-3. Charles Brewer; m. Jewel Bean. ch: Irene; and Rita Brewer

V9-3402.   g-2. **Thomas William Brazier,** b. 8 Jan 1896, d. 1 May 1981, Sylacauga, Talladega Co, AL; m. *Mattie Lee Wright*

V9-3403.   h-1. **Roland Dawson Brazier,** b. 13 July 1925; m. *Ethel Maudine Coleman.* (Contact: Maudine Brazier, 204 Oakdale Road, Alpine, AL 35014)

V9-3404.   i-1. **Bruce Wayne Brazier,** b. 1 Oct 1951; m.1. *Sebrina Kay Denty,* m.2. *Wanda Annette Easterwood.*

V9-3405.   h-2. **Roy Clayborn Brazier,** b. 1928, Huntsville, Madison Co, AL, d, 27 Oct 2005, Sycamore, Talladega Co, AL; m. *Mildred Joyce Hodge,* d/o Charles Hodge and Mildred Willingham

V9-3406.   i-1. **Roy David Brazier,** m.1. *Gwynn Smith* (1 ch); m.2. *Sharon Alice Holman* (1ch)

V9-3407.   j-1. **David Lee Brazier,**

V9-3408.   j-2. **Michael Roy Brazier,**

V9-3409.   i-2. **Randall Warren Brazier;** m. *Linda Tucker*

V9-3410.   j-1. **Christopher Randall Brazier,**

V9-3411.   j-2. **Corey Thomas Brazier,**

V9-3412.   i-3. **Andrea Lynn Brazier;** m. *Gregory S. Payne,*

V9-3413.   j-1. Geni Lynn Payne,

V9-3414.   i-4. **Mitchell Keith Brazier;** m. *Kelly Mosley*

V9-3415.   j-1. **Adam Keith Brazier,**

V9-3416.   i-5. **Myra Dale Brazier,** b. 19 July 1948, Sylacauga, Talladega Co, AL, d. 25 July 1948

V9-3417.   h-3. **Cleon Freeman Brazier,** b. 21 April 1920, Hunstville, Madison Co, AL, d. there, 28 April 1920, age 1 week.

V9-3418.   g-3. **Lula Caroline Brazier,** b. 15 Aug 1899, Huntsville, Madison Co, AL, d. there, 18 Oct 1994; m. 19 March 1919, in Huntsville, AL, *Charles Thomas Upton,* b. 6 April 1899, Huntsville, AL, d. there, 4 Sept 1977

V9-3419.   h-1. Mary Helen Upton, m.1. William C. Coggins, Sr, b. 19 May 1916, d. 1 May 1983; m.2. Joe Weaver Perkins, b. 24 July 1918, d. Oct 1974

V9-3420.   h-2. Charles Thomas Upton, Jr; m. Norene Mays

V9-3421.   h-3. Wilma May Upton; m. B.W. Williams

V9-3422.   h-4. William Eli Upton; m. Mildred Etheridge

V9-3423.   h-5. Ernest Leonard Upton; m. Virginia Henson

V9-3424.   h-6. Virginia Upton; m.1. Meredith Huckabye; m.2. Noland Smith

V9-3425.   h-7. James Donald Upton; m. Carol Simone Frazier

V9-3426.   h-8. Herbert Clifton Upton; m.1. Ann Daugette; m.2. Sandra J. Dotson

V9-3427.   h-9. Sarah Catherine Upton, b. 9 Sept 1919, Huntsville, Madison Co, AL, d. there 10 Aug 1968; m. 14 June 1942, in Huntsville, AL, Warren Tate, b. 28 Feb 1892, d. 21 Sept 1963, Huntsville, Madison Co, AL

V9-3428.   h-10. Nadean Upton, b. 8 Dec 1924, Hazelgreen Madison Co, AL, d. there, 10 Feb 1925, age 2 mos.

V9-3429.   g-4. **Arthur James Brazier,** b. 7 March 1900, d. 10 Dec 1985, Huntsville, Madison Co, AL; m. ***Bessie Upton***, 20 June 1905, AL, d. 2 March 1980, Huntsville, Madison Co, AL

V9-3430.   h-1. **Thomas Brazier**, b.1922, Huntsville, Madison Co, AL; m. Lillian _____

V9-3431.   h-2. **Thelma Louise Brazier**, b. 1924, Huntsville, Madison Co, AL, d. there, 1924

V9-3432.   h-3. **Margaret Edith Brazier**, b. 3 Nov 1925, Huntsville, Madison Co, AL; m. ***Waymon Garfield***

V9-3433.   h-4. **James Brazier,** b. May 1928, Huntsville, AL; m. ***Virginia Baltimore***

V9-3434.   h-5. **Juanida Brazier**, b. March 1930, Huntsville, Madison Co, AL;

V9-3435.   h-6. **Barbara Ann Brazier**, b. Feb 1931, d. 1947, m. ***Floyd Pogue***

V9-3436.   h-7. **Bobby Gene Brazier**, b. bet. 1931-1947, Huntsville, Madison Co, AL; m. ***Rachel Ann Littlejohn***

V9-3437.   h-8. **Darrell Brazier**, b. bet. 1931-1947, Huntsville, Madison Co, AL; m. ***Carol Hayden***

V9-3438.   h-9. **Diane Brazier**, b. bet. 1931-1947, Huntsville, Madison Co, AL; m. ***Daniel Moore***

V9-3439.   h-10. **Geneva Brazier**, b. bet. 1931-1947 Huntsville, Madsion Co, AL;

V9-3440.   h-11. **Henry Carey Brazier**, b. bet. 1931-1947, Huntsville, Madison Co, AL; m. ***William Jean Billions***

V9-3441.	h-12. **Herbert Moody Brazier**, b. bet. 1931-1947, Huntsville, Madison Co, AL; m. *Linda Stanley*
V9-3442.	h-13. **Arthur James Brazier, Jr**, b. Huntsville, Madison Co, AL; m. *Sylvia Christian*
V9-3443.	i-1. **Debbie Brazier**,
V9-3444.	i-2. **Donald Brazier**,
V9-3445.	i-3. **Dona Brazier**,
V9-3446.	i-4. **Delores Brazier**,
V9-3447.	i-5. **Denise Brazier**,
V9-3448.	h-14. **Joyce Brazier**, b. Huntsville, Madison Co, AL; m. *Monroe Bolden*
V9-3449.	h-15. **Nancy Brazier**, b. Huntsville, Madison Co, AL; m. *Jack W. Ray*
V9-3450.	h-16. **Jimmy Dole Brazier**, b. 1948, Huntsville, Madison Co, AL, d. there, 1948
V9-3451.	g-5. **Charlie Osborn Brazier,** b. 22 Feb 1902, Lois, Moore Co, TN; d. 1 Sept 1958, Guntersville, Marshall Co, AL; m. 11 Dec 1922, in Huntsville, Madison Co, AL, *Lela Lucille Kennemer*, b. 18 Feb 1906, AL, d. 26 May 1987, Gadsen, Etawoh Co, AL, d/o David Kennemer and Melissa Franklin
V9-3452.	h-1. **Larry Joe Brazier**; m. *Rosemary Taylor*, d/o John Taylor and Essie Pearce
V9-3453.	i-1. **Melissa Jo Brazier**,
V9-3454.	i-2. **Charles Alan Brazier**,
V9-3455.	i-3. **Joanna Leigh Brazier**,
V9-3456.	h-2. **Wanda Pauline Brazier**, b. 22 Aug 1923, Huntsville, Madison Co, AL, d. 11 April 1989, Gadsen, Etawoh Co, AL; m. 22 March 1941, in Guntersville, Marshall Co, AL, *G.W. Jackson*, b. 3 Sept 1920, AL, d. 5 Jan 1991, Gadsden, Etowah Co, AL
V9-3457.	i-1. Gerald Wayne Jackson,
V9-3458.	i-2. Janice Paulette Jackson,
V9-3459.	i-3. Leonard Charles Jackson,
V9-3460.	i-4. Terry Martin Jackson,
V9-3461.	h-3. **William Loyd Brazier**, b. 28 April 1929, Huntsville, Madison Co, AL, d. 1 Dec 1998, Birmingham, Jefferson Co, AL; m.1. Dolly Ruth Vest Station; m.2. in Gentersville, Madison Com AL, 14 Dec 1946, *Frances Pauline Cornelius*, b. 11 March 1930, AL, d. 21 Nov 1967, Guntersville,

Madison Co, AL, d/o William Cornelius and Nora Thompson,

V9-3462.   i-1. **Ronald Loyd Brazier,**

V9-3463.   i-2. **Janice Ann Brazier,**

V9-3464.   g-6. **Mattie Jane Brazier,** b. 28 July 1903, d. 5 Oct 1927, Huntsville, Madison Co, AL; m. *Albert McPeters*, b. 22 Jan 1896, d. Aug 1965, Columbus, GA

V9-3465.   g-7. **Lee "R.B." Brazier,** b. 1 May 1906, Lois, Moore Co, TN, d. 29 July 1979, Huntsville, Madison Co, AL; m. in Huntsville, Madison Co, AL, *Rena Odell Young*, b. 2 Nov 1907, d. 1 July 1967, Huntsville, Madison Co, AL

V9-3466.   h-1. **Mildred Brazier,**

V9-3467.   h-2. **Bernice Brazier,**

V9-3468.   h-3. **Lee R. B. "Bud" Brazier**; m. *Jimmie Ruth Pitts*

V9-3469.   h-4. **James Edward Brazier**; m. *Linda Jean Stinnett*

V9-3470.   h-5. **Betty Jean Brazier**; m. *Jerry Edward Stolz*

V9-3471.   h-6. **Donald Brazier,**

V9-3472.   h-7. **Bobby Brazier,**

V9-3473.   h-8. **David Edward "Duck" Brazier,**

V9-3474.   h-9. **J.B. Brazier**, b. & d. 1937, Huntsville, Madison Co, AL

V9-3475.   h-10. **Janie Lavone Brazier**, b. 1 March 1944, Huntsville, Madison Co, AL, d. there, 8 Aug 1983

V9-3476.   g-8. **Earnest Price Brazier,** b. 22 March 1908, Brownton, Moore Co, TN, d. 16 Aug 1988, Huntsville, Madison Co, AL; m. in Huntsville, Madison Co, AL, on 17 Jan 1930, *Nancy Jane Waller*, b, 8 Jan 1910, Scottsboro, Jackson Co, AL, d. 1996, Hunstville, Madison Co, AL.

V9-3477.   h-1. **Betty Lucille Brazier**; m.1. *Vernie L. Brown*, Jr, s/o Vernie Brown and Bertha Cheeves; m.2. Carlos Eugene Pressnell, s/o Joseph Pressnell and Myrtle Morehead.

V9-3478.   i-1. Cheryl Lucille Brown; m. Fred Allen Wilson. ch: Tracy Dawn Wilson

V9-3479.   i-2. Durand Levoyd Brown; m. Cathy Elaine Henson. ch: Chadley; Corey; and Amanda Brown

V9-3480.   i-3. Gary Dale Brown; m. Pamela Hubble. ch: Matthew Brown

^{V9}-3481.	i-4. Kenneth Harold Brown; m. Cynthia Napper. Ch: Bridgett Gail Brown
^{V9}-3482.	i-5. Jeffery Glenn Brown; m. Virginia Hopkins
^{V9}-3483.	i-6. Debra Jo Brown; m. Sam Martin. ch: Angel Michell; and Holy Gail Martin
^{V9}-3484.	i-7. Cathy Lanett Brown; m. Charles Colbert. ch: Bradley Dewite Colbert
^{V9}-3485.	i-8. Rhonda Denise Brown; m.1. James Timothy Thompson, s/o Herman Thompson and Bertha West; m.2. John Edward Ricketts, s/o Luther Ricketts and Edna _____. ch: Steven James Ricketts.
^{V9}-3486.	h-2. **Lavone Brazier**; m.1. *Lee Curmon Hall*, s/o Thomas Hall and Fannie Grimes; m.2. Lloyd William Biggs.
^{V9}-3487.	i-1. Stephanie Lynn Hall; m. Thomas Beshears. ch: Sean Michael Beshears
^{V9}-3488.	i-2. William Jamie Biggs; m. Margo _____. ch: Taylor Aaron Biggs
^{V9}-3489.	h-3. **Earnest Rayman Brazier**; m. *Eloise Williamson*
^{V9}-3490.	i-1. **Angela Robin Brazier**, m. James Steven Ricketts. Ch: Dwayne Steven; and Justin Daniel Ricketts
^{V9}-3491.	i-2. **Cynthia Rae Brazier**,
^{V9}-3492.	h-4. **Billy Glenn Brazier**; m. *Patricia McClusky*
^{V9}-3493.	i-1. **Glenn Brazier**,
^{V9}-3494.	i-2. **Annette Brazier**,
^{V9}-3495.	h-5. **Lilly Faye Brazier**, b. 17 Aug 1938, Huntsville, Madison Co, AL, d. there, 19 June 1978; m. *Bradley Morgan Pigg*, ch: Keith, and Donna Faye Pigg (1956-1958).
^{V9}-3496.	f-2. **Thomas Riley Brazier,** b. Lincoln Co, TN, 21 March 1868; m.1. *Virginia "Jennie" Gray*, d/o Isaac Gray and Maranda Brazier, and had one son; m.2. *Maude Barns* and had two daughters.
^{V9}-3497.	g-1. **George Andrew Brazier,** b. 13 June 1906; m. *Louise Elkins*
^{V9}-3498.	g-2. **Ruby Brazier,** b. 1912 (or 1919); m. *Jesse Ledford*
^{V9}-3499.	g-3. **Lena Mae Brazier,** b. 1914 (or 1913), d. 26 Dec 1980; m. *Holt Robertson*

V9-3500. f-3. **John Asberry Brazier,** b. Lincoln Co, TN, 3 April 1872, d. 21 Oct 1902, bur. Bean Cem. Franklin Co, TN; m. 11 Dec 1882, in Moore Co, TN, *Annie Marshall*, d/o Hayden and Chick(?) Marshall.

V9-3501. g-1. **Edward Brazier,** b. 1 Jan 1894, Moore Co, TN; m. *Lemmie Smith*, b. 15 May 1898, d. Oct 1983, Franklin Co, TN.

V9-3502. g-2. **Alton Brazier,** b. 1897, Moore Co, TN; m. Elsie Mitchell

V9-3503. g-3. **Holland Brazier**; m. *Eula Copley*

V9-3504. g-4. **Lee Roy Brazier,** b. 1902, d. young

V9-3505. f-4. **Lou Anna Brazier,** b. Lincoln Co, TN, 18 Feb 1875, d. 8 Aug 1961, bur. Frame Cem. Moore Co, TN; m. 4 May 1903 (or 29 May 1904), *George Lewis*, b. 5 Jan 1872, d. 10 May 1936, and had three children

V9-3506. g-1. Lem A. Lewis, b. 6 May 1905, TN, d. 20 April 1986

V9-3507. g-2. Leonard Lewis, died early

V9-3508. g-3. James Lewis, b. 1910, disappeared in 1934 and has not been heard from since; m. Mattie Soloman

V9-3509. f-5. ***Robert <u>Walter</u> Brazier,** b. Lincoln Co, TN, 15 Oct 1877, d. 1 Aug 1939, Franklin Co, TN, bur. Beach Hill Cem. Franklin Co, TN; m. 15 Aug 1898, *Mary Elizabeth "Lizzie" Marshall*, b. 4 Jan 1879, Tn, d. 9 Nov 1960, Franklin Co, TN.

V9-3510. f-6. **Obediah "Obe" Brazier,** b. Lincoln Co, TN, 15 March 1879, d. 1910, bur. Brazier Fam Cem; m. 19 Feb1905 (had been married 6 yrs in 1910), *Tennie Johnson Bishop*, b. c1881 (29 in 1910). The 1910 Census of Moore Co, TN, 6th Civil Dist says they had had 6 children, three were living.

V9-3511. g-1. **Edna L. Brazier**, b. c1903 (7 in 1910)

V9-3512. g-2. **Nellie P. Brazier**, b. 3 July 1906 (6? in 1910; hard to read); m. *M. Roy Evans*, (ch: Josie Lou; and Pauline Evans)

V9-3513. g-3. **James M. Brazier**, b. 21 Nov 1908; m. *Bessie Hunt*.

V9-3514. f-7. **James Oscar Brazier,** b. 8 March 1881, d. early, bur. Brazier Fam Cem.

V9-3515. f-8. **Nathan Elonzo "Lon" Brazier,** b. Moore Co, TN, 8 Dec 1884, d. 29 July 1969, Aurora, IL; m. *Daisy Limbaugh*; no children.

V9-3516. f-9. **Willie Suella Brazier,** b. 10 July 1886, d. 1889, Moore Co, TN

Other Franklin Co, TN Marriages:

24 Aug 1859: J.M. Parks to E.Z. Brazier, by D.D. Smith, JP, 24 Aug 1859

5 Feb 1868: Sam'l McKelvey to R.L. Brazier

3 Nov 1868: James W. Brazier to M.J. Brown, by J. Hudgins, MG, 3 Nov 1868

(see 35,000 Tennessee Marriage Records and Bonds, 1783-1870, by Rev. Silas Emmett Lucas, Jr. and Mrs Ella Lee Sheffield, 3 vols.)

Robert Walter Brazier and Lizzie Marshall

f-5. **Robert Walter Brazier,** (s/o Thomas Newton Brazier and Lucy Caroline Kelly), b. Lincoln Co, TN, 15 Oct 1877, d. 1 Aug 1939, bur. Beach Hill Cem. Franklin Co, TN; m. 15 Aug 1898, *Mary Elizabeth "Lizzie" Marshall*, b. 4 Jan 1879, TN, d. 9 Nov 1960, Franklin Co, TN. They had eight children

V9-3517.   g-1. **Nellie Ann Brazier,** b. 23 July 1899, Franklin Co, TN, d. 1985; m. on 3 Dec 1916, in Franklin Co, TN, *Joel H. Limbaugh*, b. 25 Nov 1886, d. 28 July 1958

V9-3518.   h-1. R.J. (or R.T.) Limbaugh, b. 22 June 1918, Franklin Co, TN, d. 27 Sep 1919

V9-3519.   h-2. Letha Zone Limbaugh, b. 5 June 1920; m. Bill Gribble

V9-3520.   h-3. William Benjamin Limbaugh, b. 12 June 1923; m. Joyce Wiley

V9-3521.   g-2. **Ruthie Lee Brazier,** b. 18 July 1902, Moore Co, TN, d. there, 21 May 1990; m. 2 Oct 1921, *Clyde Walter Limbaugh*, b. 12 Nov 1894, d. 13 March 1958

V9-3522.   h-1. Hazel Leola Limbaugh, b. 25 Sep 1923, Franklin Co, TN; m.1. James M. Clark; m.2. Robert Zeleneck

V9-3523.   h-2. Walter Clyde Limbaugh Jr, b. 16 Jan 1925, Franklin Co, TN; m. 1946, Ovena Cowser

V9-3524.   h-3. William Marshall Limbaugh, b. 18 Jan 1927, Franklin Co, TN, d. 13 March 1982, bur. Beech Hill Cem.; m.1. Johnie Lee Ray (3 ch); m.2. Jean Huffer (2 ch)

V9-3525.   g-3. **Harmon D. Brazier,** b. 4 Jan 1904, Franklin Co, TN, d. 12 Sept 1991, Moore Co, TN; m.1. on 30 Jan 1927, TN, *May Turner*, (5 ch) d. 4 Dec 1956; m.2. *Thelma Gunn*

V9-3526.   h-1. **Earlene Brazier,** b. 10 July 1930, Franklin Co, TN; m.1. *Richard Thomas*; m.2. *John Campbell*

^{V9}-3527.	h-2. **Alverene Brazier,** b. 13 Feb 1934, Moore Co, TN, d. 8 Aug 1977; m. *Jimmie Holloway*
^{V9}-3528.	h-3. **Landon Brazier,** b. 14 July 1937, Franklin Co, TN; m. *Barbara Jo Blasbo*
^{V9}-3529.	h-4. **Ovena Brazier,** b. 9 Dec 1941, Franklin Co, TN; m. 1959, *Albert Baker,*
^{V9}-3530.	h-5. **Mable Brazier,** b. 2 Jan 1945, Franklin Co, TN; m. 1963, *Donald Holloway*
^{V9}-3531.	g-4. **Lamar Brazier,** b. 13 April 1907, Moore Co, TN; m.1. *Lillie Turner* (3 ch); m.2. *Johnnie Cantrell* (1
^{V9}-3532.	h-1. **Marvin Brazier,** b. 14 Jan 1932, Franklin Co, TN
^{V9}-3533.	h-2. **Evon Brazier,** b. 7 March 1938; m. *Bob Tucker*
^{V9}-3534.	h-3. **Larry Brazier,** b. 20 Sep (or Oct) 1941; m. *Betsy McGee*
^{V9}-3535.	h-4. **Jackie Brazier,** b. 24 May 1947; m.1. *Kennie Trice*; m.2. *Ricky Cruteson*; m.3. 1970, *Jim Bowman*
^{V9}-3536.	g-5. **Maymie Catherine Brazier,** b. 3 July 1909, Moore Co, TN, d. 3 Aug 1980; m. *Jim Wiley Thornberry*, d. 1974 (both bur. Beech Hill Cem.)
^{V9}-3537.	h-1. Lamar Thornberry, b. 9 Oct 1931; m. 1955, Bobby Sue Smith
^{V9}-3538.	h-2. Jo Ann Thornberry, b. 2 March 1937; m. 5 July 1958, Jessie Shaver, Jr
^{V9}-3539.	h-3. Hazel Ruth Thornberry, b. 12 Oct 1944; m. 28 Dec 1961, John Thomas Taylor
^{V9}-3540.	g-6. **James Walter "Jim" Brazier,** b. 27 Aug 1913, Moore Co, TN, d. there, 6 April 1998; m. 1935, *Edith Rogers*, b. 4 Sept 1914, d. 4 July 2000, Lynchburg, Moore Co, TN.
^{V9}-3541.	h-1. **David Leroy Brazier,** b. 14 June 1936; m. *Martha Strandridge*
^{V9}-3542.	h-2. **Joyce Ann Brazier;** m. *E.W. George*
^{V9}-3543.	g-7. **Rosa M. Brazier,** b. 29 April 1915, Franklin Co, TN; m. 17 April 1932, *Buford Baker*, b. 3 Aug 1906, Lynchburg, Moore Co, TN, d. there, 18 April 1990.
^{V9}-3544.	h-1. Elizabeth Baker; m. Clyde Maples
^{V9}-3545.	h-2. Jimmie Baker, b. Dec 1934 (or 35); m. Lequetta Smith
^{V9}-3546.	h-3. Bobby Baker; m. Patsy _____
^{V9}-3547.	h-4. Wallace Baker; m.1. Carolyn Hayes; m.2. Sarah Cantrell
^{V9}-3548.	h-5. Debbie Baker, b. Sep 1957

V9-3549.　　g-8. **Mattie Pearl Brazier,** b. 2 May 1917, Franklin Co, TN, d. July 1985; m. 23 Sep 1933, **Wallace Clark**, b, 25 Aug 1916, d. 29 June 1995, Memphis, Shelby Co, TN.

V9-3550.　　h-1. Lynda Joy Clark, died in infancy

V9-3551.　　h-2. Barbara Clark,

Zachary Taylor Brazier and Martha Newman

e-7. **Zachary Taylor Brazier** was born 11 May 1848 in Lincoln County, TN, the seventh child of William Jean "Billy" and Perlina (Hazlewood) Brazier, died Wise Co, TX, 8 June 1899. On 1 June 1871, he married **Martha E. Newman** in Lincoln Co, TN, where they lived until all five of their children were born. Martha was b. c1842 in Lincoln Co, TN, d. 11 Dec 1911, in Chico, Wise Co, TX. In 1882, they moved to Texas. Several of the Newman family moved at the same time and settled in Fannin County, Texas.

As family legend has it, Zachary and his family were transported from Moore County to Murfreesboro by his father, where they boarded a train for Fort Worth, Texas. Fort Worth was a progressive town with the Chicago Union Stockyard already open, and public school classes opening just that year. The Braziers and Newmans bought wagons and teams, and moved up the Trinity River into Wise County. They settled near where Lake Bridgeport Dam is located.

Zachary Taylor Brazier died in 1898 from TB and was buried in the Chico, Texas cemetery.

Family of Zachary Taylor and Martha (Newman) Brazier, all born in Moore Co, TN:

V9-3552.　　f-1. *****John William "J.W." Brazier,** b. 16 March 1872; m. **Alma Esther Strain**

V9-3553.　　f-2. *****Otho Benjamin C. Brazier,** b. c1874; m. **Cordia Anne Townsend**

V9-3554.　　f-3. *****Suella Brazier,** b. 9 Sep 1877; m.1. _____ **Minor**, m.2. **George W. Strain**, widower of her younger sister.

V9-3555.　　f-4. *****Laura Oleva Brazier,** b. 5 Nov 1879; m. **George W. Strain**

V9-3556.　　f-5. *****James Henry Taylor Brazier,** b. 1881; m. **Annie Humphrey**

John William Brazier and Alma Strain

f-1. **John William "J.W." Brazier**, s/o Zachary Taylor Brazier and Martha Newman, b. 16 March 1872, Moore Co, TN, d. 18 June 1955, Chico, Wise Co, TX. He was eleven years old when the family moved from Tennessee to Texas, where he married *Alma Esther Strain* in 1897. She was born 28 Jan 1879, TN, d. 2 May 1972, in Chico, Wise Co, TN. For several years, they lived in the Sand Flat community, with Alma's mother, who was a widow. Seven of their nine children were born there.

They took an active part in the affairs of the community. They attended church in a wagon and took their turn at having the traveling preacher to Sunday dinner and supper. And they boarded the teacher of the one-room school when it was their turn. The men maintained the roads and hauled rock with wagon and team to build the last school built in the community.

The family was nearly self-sufficient, as was the style in those days. The Brazier family had a windmill to lift water from their well, and a room under the water-tower cooled by dripping water was storage place for the milk, butter, fruits, etc. The pork was cured and hung in the smokehouse. Beef was available only when some farmer in the neighborhood butchered a calf and passed cuts out to all the neighbors, because there was no ice box nor any way to keep the meat. In due time, another neighbor would do the same. A garden provided fresh vegetables, and an orchard provided fruit. Cotton was the principal money crop, which was picked by hand and hauled by wagon the seven miles to the gin in Chico. Corn was grown for feed and corn-meal.

In 1913, J.W. Brazier sold the farm and moved into Chico so the children could attend high school. There they had twelve acres, plus some rented land, on which they grew peanuts, truck crops of watermelons and cantaloupes.

John W. Brazier died in 1955 and Alma in 1972. They are both buried in the Chico Cemetery.

Family of John W. and Alma (Strain) Brazier:

V9-3557. g-1. **George William Brazier,** b. 4 Sep 1898, d. 11 March 1977. Attended grammar school in Sand Flat and high school in Chico; was a farmer; never married.

V9-3558. g-2. **Mary Esther Brazier,** b. 5 May 1901; attended Chico High and Denton College, after which she taught school in Chico; married *John Crawford*; no children.

---

^{V9-}3559.   g-3. **Wesley Johnson Brazier,** b. 29 Aug 1903, d. 17 May 1981; m.1. in 1933, *Deomae Walthall*; m.2. in 1949, *Jewel Johnson*. Wesley attended Weatherford College, then worked in a dairy, and with a sand and gravel company; he later had his own business in San Angelo, Texas. He had no children, but adopted his first wife's son, John Ross.

^{V9-}3560.   g-4. **Gladys Brazier,** b. 6 May 1905, d. of diphtheria 20 Nov 1906

^{V9-}3561.   g-5. **Mertie Brazier,** b. 6 May 1907; finished high school in Chico, but there were no funds to attend college. Mertie worked at various jobs in Wichita Falls. In 1935, she began working at the Wichita Falls State Hospital, and attended Hardin Junior College and Midwestern University, eventually advancing to social worker, which she continued until retirement in 1970. Mertie wrote a book on the family, which has offered much information.

^{V9-}3562.   g-6. **James Byington Brazier,** b. 2 May 1910; m. *Lucille McDonald*. They moved to California and worked for Consolidated Aircraft, then transferred to the same firm's plant in Fort Worth.

^{V9-}3563.   h-1. **Beverly Ann Brazier,** b. 1 July 1942, m. *William Robert Crosby*

^{V9-}3564.   i-1. Sue Ann Crosby, b. 19 Jan 1963; m. Bruce Rohne

^{V9-}3565.   i-2. Jo Lynn Crosby, b. 16 Sep 1966

^{V9-}3566.   h-2. **Marilyn Sue Brazier,** b. 19 June 1944; m. *Lesley Hadley*

^{V9-}3567.   i-1. Robin Gayle Hadley, b. 25 April 1967

^{V9-}3568.   i-2. Kristen Leigh Hadley, b. 6 July 1969

^{V9-}3569.   i-3. Jon Scott Hadley, b. 6 July 1970

^{V9-}3570.   g-7. **Julia Louise Brazier,** b. 10 Dec 1912; after high school at Chico, Julia moved to Austin, attended the State University, and became a teacher. She m. *Phil Strandtmann*, a draftsman.

^{V9-}3571.   h-1. Donna Theresa Strandtmann, b. 14 Feb 1947; m. Harry Barkley

^{V9-}3572.   i-1. Adam Jay Barkley, b. 6 Sep 1967

^{V9-}3573.   h-2. Mary Jane Strandtman, b. 10 Jan 1949; m. David Sward

^{V9-}3574.   g-8. **Mattie Margaret Brazier,** b. 31 Aug 1915; after high school in Chico, Mattie worked in various homes in Chico

and Denton; then in 1941, she began working for the Wichita Falls State Hospital and attended night classes at college there. She retired in 1976 after 35 years of work.

V9-3575. g-9. **Nora Eloise Brazier,** b. 15 April 1919; after high school in Chico, she worked some at the library, then started, also in 1941, at the Wichita Falls State Hospital. She joined the Navy and served a term, then attended the State University at Austin. Until her retirement in 1978, she worked mostly as a social worker for the Department of Human Resources.

Otho Benjamin C. Brazier
and Cordia Anne Townsend

f-2. **Otho Benjamin C. Brazier**, s/o Zachary Taylor Brazier and Martha Newman, was born in Moore County, TN, c1874, and died in Greer Co, OK, c1905. He moved with the family to Texas, while still a young boy. He married *Cordia Anne Townsend* and lived probably in Wise County, Texas, until after his first child was born, then moved to Greer County, Oklahoma, where he homesteaded some land near Willow and lived in a dug-out while trying to get a start. After about five or six years, Otho Benjamin C. Brazier became ill with tuberculosis and died c1905. Cordia Anne died c1907. The children were reared by some of the Townsend family.

Family of Benjamin C. and Cordia Anne (Townsend) Brazier:
V9-3576. g-1. **Walter Brazier,** b. c1897, either Wise Co, TX or Greer Co, OK; d. of tuberculosis in 1914; bur. Greer Co, OK
V9-3577. g-2. **Beulah Brazier,** b. c1900, either Wise Co, TX or Greer Co, OK; d. 1944, Venice, California; m. 30 Oct 1920, *Oba R. Tolman*; they had four sons:
V9-3578. h-1. Oba Rho Tolman
V9-3579. h-2. Otha Ernest Tolman, m. Irene _____
V9-3580. h-3. Vaughn Tolman
V9-3581. h-4. Tom Tolman
V9-3582. g-3. **Otho Benjamin Brazier, Jr,** b. 31 Oct 1905, Greer Co, OK, six months after his father's death, eighteen months before his mother died. He was raised by his mother's parents, who later sent him to a boarding school in Kansas. He left school at age 14 and went out on his own. Otho Benjamin m. *Daisey Sarilly Leckie* on 4 Jan

1934 in Sayre, OK, and had two children. About 1940, the couple and their young children moved to Montana. Otho Benjamin d. 4 Jan 1984, Laurel, MT; Daisy d. 15 Nov 1961, Hardin, MT.

V9-3583.   h-1. **Patricia Ann Brazier,** b. 10 Nov 1934, Greer Co, OK; m. on 29 Aug 1954 in Hardin, Montana, **Charles Lowell Bullis**, b. 16 Sep 1924, Hardin, MT.

V9-3584.   i-1. Charles Alvin Bullis, b. 12 Jan 1956, Billings, MT

V9-3585.   i-2. Robert Wellington Bullis, b. 24 March 1959, Billings, MT

V9-3586.   i-3. David Arnold Bullis, b. 11 Dec 1961, Billings, MT

V9-3587.   h-2. **Robert Benjamin "Bob" Brazier,** b. 17 Dec 1938, Greer Co, OK; m. 28 April 1962, in Lodge Grass, MT, **Cheryl Telle "Terry" Miller**, b. 17 April 1943, Sheridan, Wyoming

V9-3588.   i-1. **Robert Cody Brazier,** b. 17 Feb 1963, Sheridan, Wyoming

V9-3589.   i-2. **Dona Dell Brazier,** b. 23 Nov 1965; m. 1 Sep 1984, in Lodge Grass, MT, **Gary Allen Boyd**, b. 1 Sep 1965, Sheridan, WY.

Suella Brazier and ____ Minor/ George W. Strain

f-3. **Suella Brazier**, d/o Zachary Taylor Brazier and Martha Newman, was born 9 Sep 1877, in Moore Co, TN. She first married ____ **Minor** and had one daughter; she m.2. **George W. Strain**, the widower of her younger sister. Suella died 3 Dec 1905 at the age of twenty-eight and was buried at Chico, TX, Cemetery. George W. Strain d. 18 July 1918.

Family of Suella Brazier/Minor/Strain:

V9-3590.   g-1. Marie Minor, b. 14 April 1900. Marie was only five years old when her mother died, and was raised by her step-father's brother and wife, C.B. and Willie Strain. She later lived with John W. Brazier, while attending high school in Chico, TX; Marie m. **Tom Milhollon**, b. 20 Feb 1890, a farmer in the Chico area. Tom d. 28 ?month 1969, and Marie d. 25 June 1976; they were living at the time in Henrietta, TX, and are buried in Cumby Cem, Wise Co, TX. They had two children:

V9-3591.   h-1. R. T. Milhollon, b. 8 May 1920; m. Edith Cooksey, b. 8 Dec 1923

V9-3592.   i-1. Larry Milhollon, b. 26 March 1944; m. Gwen Johnson

V9-3593.	j-1. Ricky Milhollon
V9-3594.	j-2. Randy Milhollon
V9-3595.	i-2. Sherman Travis Milhollon, b. 21 Oct 1945; m. Sherrell Witt
V9-3596.	j-1. Aryn Milhollon
V9-3597.	j-2. Cory Milhollon
V9-3598.	i-3. Donna Sue Milhollon, b. 9 Sep 1952; m. Danny Bashan
V9-3599.	j-1. Glenn Bashan
V9-3600.	j-2. Kelly Bashan
V9-3601.	i-4. Joe T. Milhollon, b. 19 Feb 1957; m. Linda Parker
V9-3602.	j-1. Jackie Milhollon
V9-3603.	j-2. Lisa Milhollon
V9-3604.	j-3. J. T. Milhollon, Jr
V9-3605.	i-5. David Milhollon, b. 19 Nov 1964; m. Lisa Stinnett
V9-3606.	h-2. Dorothy Milhollon, b. 22 Dec 1932; m. Ray Sanders, b. 13 April 1921
V9-3607.	i-1. Pamela Jean Sanders, b. 13 Aug 1951; m. Lloyd Beckworth
V9-3608.	j-1. Tammie Beckworth,
V9-3609.	i-2. James Ray Sanders, b. 5 June 1955
V9-3610.	i-3. Kendall Wayne, Sanders, b. 28 Dec 1958
V9-3611.	g-2. Joe Strain, b. 19 Sep 1904, s/o Suella Brazier/Minor and her second husband, George W. Strain; m. Ada Russell. Joe d. 1984; Ada d. 24 April 1977.
V9-3612.	h-1. Gracie Jo Strain, b. 8 Nov 1926, d. 27 Oct 1979; m. Roland Hartis
V9-3613.	i-1. Brenda Hartis, b. 13 March 1958; m. Jim Maynor
V9-3614.	h-2. Nelda Pearl Strain, b. 25 Feb 1930; m.1. Nathan Stockard, m.2. E. J. Lancaster
V9-3615.	i-1. Judy Stockard, b. 2 March 1948; m. Don Kolar
V9-3616.	j-1. Mike Kolar, b. 6 May 1965
V9-3617.	j-2. Donna Kolar, b. 11 Dec 1971
V9-3618.	j-3. Tim Kolar, b. 13 April 1973
V9-3619.	i-2. Sherry Stockard, b. 16 June 1957
V9-3620.	h-3. Mary Louise Strain, b. 29 Dec 1932; m. Sully Lanier, m.2. Hansel Jackson
V9-3621.	i-1. Randy Lanier, b. 20 July 1951; m. Karen Lynn Wilder
V9-3622.	j-1. Sheldon Lanier, b. 22 March 1972
V9-3623.	j-2. Vickie Lanier, b. 1 March 1974
V9-3624.	j-3. Sully Jo Lanier, b. 18 Feb 1979

V9-3625.   h-4. Jimmy Strain, d. in infancy
V9-3626.   h-5. Jerry Strain, b. 21 Aug 1944; m.1. Laura Lees and
             had two children; m.2. Maria Mercer and they have a
             daughter
V9-3627.   i-1. Erica Strain, b. 15 Sep 1971
V9-3628.   i-2. Brian Strain, b. 27 Oct 1973
V9-3629.   i-3. Frances Nicole Strain, b. 11 Aug 1981

Laura Oleva Brazier and George W. Strain

f-4. **Laura Oleva Brazier**, d/o Zachary Taylor Brazier and Martha
Newman, was born in Moore Co, TN, on 5 Nov 1879.   She married
George W. Strain, and had one son.   Laura died 25 March 1902 at the
age of twenty-three.   George m.2. Laura's older sister, Suella, who was
a widow with one little child.
Child of Laura Brazier and George W. Strain:
V9-3630.   g-1. George Raymond Strain, b. 28 Jan 1901; m.1. Artie
             Howard; m.2. Belle Lewis.   Raymond had no children,
             though he helped rear Belle's daughter, Lois McClellan.

James Henry Taylor Brazier and Annis Humphrey

f-5. **James Henry Taylor Brazier**, s/o Zachary Taylor Brazier and
Martha Newman, was born in Moore Co, TN, in 1881, just before the
family moved to Texas.   He married *Annie Humphrey* and had seven
children.   Henry died in 1952 and Annie in 1961; both are buried in the
Chico, Texas Cemetery.   They had seven children:
Family of James Henry and Annie (Humphrey) Brazier:
V9-3631.   g-1. **Elzie "R.D." Brazier,** b. 1906, Wise Co, TX; lived Irving,
             TX.   Lost an eye when young, while opening a sugar sack
             with scissors; m. *Marie* _____ and had six boys and two
             girls.
V9-3632.   h-1. **Dannie Marie Brazier,** m. _____ *Barrow*
V9-3633.   h-2. **Yancy Brazier**
V9-3634.   h-3. ? **Mary Brazier**
V9-3635.   h-4-7. The names of the other sons are not known,
             though they live in the Dallas area.
V9-3636.   g-2. **Stella Brazier,** b. 1908; m. *Raymond Bird*
V9-3637.   h-1. Raymond Bird, Jr.
V9-3638.   h-2. Bettie Alice Bird, m. _____ Hobbs
V9-3639.   g-3. **Daulton Brazier,** b. c1918, living Fort Worth; no children

V9-3640.   g-4. **John Henry Brazier, Jr,** living in Bridgeport, TX; m. *Marie* _____

V9-3641.   h-1. **John Henry "J.H." Brazier, III;** m. and has children

V9-3642.   h-2. **Barbara Brazier,** m. _____ *Munn* and has children

V9-3643.   h-3. **Bobby Brazier;** m. and has children

V9-3644.   h-4. **Billy Brazier;** m. and has children

V9-3645.   g-5. **Melvin Brazier,** b. 1909, d. 1982; married twice and had two children, one by each marriage:

V9-3646.   h-1. **Ammine Brazier,** m. _____ *Morris*, of Athens, TX

V9-3647.   h-2. **James M. Brazier,** of Bridgeport, TX

V9-3648.   g-6. **John Lee Brazier,** b. 1914, d. 1980; married twice and had two children by first marriage, a son who died in infancy and

V9-3649.   h-2. **Joyce Brazier**; m. _____ Harris;

V9-3650.   h-3. **Janice Brazier**; m. _____ Capshaw. a daughter by the second marriage

V9-3651.   g-7. **Zelma Brazier,** b. 1916, d. 1956; m.1. _____ Shipley; m.2. _____Queen

V9-3652.   h-1. Billy Joe Shipley

V9-3653.   h-2. _____ Queen

V9-3654.   h-3. _____ Queen

Frances Asberry Brazier and Alice Womack

e-10. **Francis Asberry "Berry" Brazier**, the tenth child of William Jean "Billy" Brazier and his wife, Perlina Hazlewood, b. 11 March 1850 in TN, d. after 1900 census, Franklin Co, TN and is buried in the Brazier cem, Moore Co, TN (per cem records), but there is no stone; m. *Alice Rebecca Womack*, b. 23 Dec 1861, Lincoln Co, TN (area now in Moore Co), d. 1 Nov 1933, d/o William R. Womack and Catherine R. Bailey.

Berry and Alice lived in Franklin Co, TN, though they are said to have separated and Berry returned to Moore Co. Alice lived for many years with her youngest son, Thomas Newton "Newt" Brazier, and is buried in the Mt. Vernon Cem in Franklin Co, TN, beside her son "Newt."

Writes Kathy B. Brannon, 300 Ollie Howard Rd, New Market, AL 35761: The Newt of both William Jean "Billy" and of Berry are both Thomas Newton. I will tell you this, I thought it was funny at the time. When I was a little girl, I went with my Dad and Papa [Aaron] Brazier to try to find the grave of Jim Brazier (father of Aaron); he wanted to put a stone on his grave, all the kids were so small when Jim died, and Florence didn't have the money for a stone. Anyway he [Aaron] put one on the grave.

Years later, I wanted to find the grave again and get his dates off the rock and make a picture of it. The area had changed so much, because they had put in Tim Ford's Dam. So we stopped at this house and asked a man in his yard if he knew of where any Brazier's were buried in the area. He said no, but he knew some Brazier's. He gave us the directions, and we went there.

I didn't know who these folks were. The wife invited us in and told me to go and talk to her husband in the living room. I walked in and nearly went into shock! This man looked just like my Daddy!!! I told him "I don't know who you are, but you look like my Dad!" He replied "Well, honey, who is your daddy?" I told him, he said he didn't know him, then he asked me who was my grandpa? I told him Aaron Brazier.

He lit up!! He said he use to stay with us and come down from up North with a peg legged man. Well, I knew this was Uncle John Mann. Then I asked him who was his Dad? he said Newt Brazier. I lit up!! I said Uncle Newt? I've heard of him all my life!

I was so overwhelmed at how much he looked like my daddy that I brought my Daddy to see him. It was like a reunion of the Braziers. When my Grandmother Brazier died, I called them and they came to the funeral home. They were Thomas & Charlene (son of Newt); I also met Wallace. I've kept in contact with them ever since. They are just part of my family.

Family of Frances Asberry "Berry" Brazier and Alice Rebecca Wommack:
V9-3655.   f-1. **William Jean "Jim" Brazier**, b. 26 June 1880, d. 20 Oct 1915, Lincoln Co, TN; m. 16 Oct 1904, *Florence Mann*, b. ?, d. 8 July 1952, Adrian, MI, d/o Joseph Richard Mann and Margaret Missouri "Mazue" Martin. After Jim died, Florence m.2. 17 Nov 1916, Dave Brooks, and they moved to Adrian, MI, where Mr. Brooks was killed when a ditch caved in on him (year unknown). Florence died in Adrian, MI, and is buried in Palmyra Cem.

V9-3656.   g-1. **Joe Berry Brazier**, b. 20 Dec 1905 (stillborn)
V9-3657.   g-2. **Mamie Frances Brazier**, b. 6 Feb 1907; m. *James Noah Baker* (lived in Michigan)
V9-3658.   g-3. **Aaron Leroy Brazier**, b. 21 Dec 1908, d. 1 June 1976; m. 27 Feb 1926, Franklin Co, TN, *Martha Eloise "Lois" Holman*, b. ?, d. 21 Aug 1994, d/o Newton Edward Holman and Malvenia Idee Fanning.

Aaron and Lois are buried in Taylor Cem, Walnut Grove, Madison Co, AL (grandparents of Kathy Brannon).

V9-3659.   h-1. **Bonnie Evelyn Mae Brazier**, b. 17 Nov 1926, Franklin Co, AL; m. *Jack Blanton*

V9-3660.   h-2. **Elton Leroy Brazier**, b. Sep 1928, Franklin Co, TN; m. *Virginia Ethlene McClure,*

V9-3661.   h-3. **James Edward Brazier**, b. 28 April 1931, Lincoln Co, TN; m. *Shirley Elenora Holland*; living in Madison Co, AL (Kathy's parents)

V9-3662.   i-x. **Kathy Brazier**; m. _____ *Brannon*

V9-3663.   h-4. **Josephine Brazier**, b. 25 May 1933, Beville, Mich; m.1. *Rufus King Gray*, d. in Birmingham, AL; m.2. *J.D. Terrell*; they live in Madison Co, AL.

V9-3664.   h-5. **Frances Marlene Brazier**, b. 23 Nov 1937; m.1. *Howard Brown* (divorced); m.2. *Frank Meli*; they live in TN.

V9-3665.   h-6. **Betty Lovern Brazier**, b. 12 Jan 1941; m. *Foster Ray Posey* (he is dec'd); she lived in Jackson Co, AL.

V9-3666.   h-7. **Aaron Leroy "Jr" Brazier, II**, b. 14 Sep 1946, Madison Co, AL; m. *Sherry Kay Hepler*; they live in Madison Co, AL.

V9-3667.   g-4. **Bonnie Alice Brazier**, b. 3 March 1910, d. 5 Aug 1983, Adrian, MI; m. *Samuel Snead*

V9-3668.   g-5. **James Henry Brazier**, b. 25 July 1911; m. *Vesma Hutto*

V9-3669.   f-2. **Lucy Brazier;** oldest daughter; no further info

V9-3670.   f-3. **Nannie Brazier;** no further info

V9-3671.   f-4. **Lillie Brazier;** m. *Jim Soloman*

V9-3672.   g-1. William Soloman; m. Marie Woodward. (ch: Jessie "Pete" Soloman, d. 1979; m. Georgia Luterall)

V9-3673.   f-5. **John Brazier;** m. *Ilah Hannah*

V9-3674.   g-1. **Bailey Brazier;** m. *Ora Walker*

V9-3675.   g-2. **Bessie Brazier;** m.1. *Jim Soloman*, m.2. *Marion Walker*

V9-3676.   g-3. **Berry Luke Brazier;** m. *Alice Brown*

V9-3677.   g-4. **J. D. Brazier;** m. *Ophelia _____.*

V9-3678.   f-6. **Mary Brazier;** m. *Herman Grant*

V9-3679.   g-1. William Grant

V9-3680.   g-2. Mary Dell Grant, d. young

V9-3681.   g-3. Gracie Grant; m. Harvell Evans
V9-3682.   g-4. Alice Grant
V9-3683.   g-5. Ray Grant
V9-3684.   g-6. Margie Grant; m. Bert Wombie
V9-3685.   g-7. Bruce Grant
V9-3686.   g-8. Frank Grant
V9-3687.   g-9. Mary Grant, d. 21 Nov 1980
V9-3688.   f-7. **Birdie Brazier,** b. 22 Jan 1894, d. 2 Sep 1985; m. *John Painter*
V9-3689.   g-1. Wilson Painter, d. 18 Oct 1969; m. Wilma Casey
V9-3690.   g-2. Alma Lee Painter, d. 10 Dec 1957; m. Clarence Waggoner
V9-3691.   g-3. Thomas Painter; m. Clara Waggoner
V9-3692.   g-4. Aubrey Painter; m. Christeen Soloman
V9-3693.   g-5. Clydeth Painter; m. Odie Marlew
V9-3694.   g-6. J.D. Painter
V9-3695.   g-7. Floy Painter, d. at age 3
V9-3696.   f-8. **Thomas Newton "Newt" Brazier,** b. 13 Jan 1898, Franklin Co, TN; m. 1920, *Birdie Hall*
V9-3697.   g-1. **Thomas Brazier,** b. 1921; m. *Charlene Jennings*
V9-3698.   g-2. **Bonnie Mae Brazier,** b. 15 Dec 1922; m. *Thomas Brown*
V9-3699.   g-3. **Leroy Brazier,** b. 3 Nov 1924; m. *Opal Hill*
V9-3700.   g-4. **Wallace Brazier,** b. 14 May 1928; m. *Ophelia Frame*
V9-3701.   g-5. **Glendon Brazier,** b. 28 Oct 1931

Perlina Brazier
and William Jacob Evans

e-13. **Perlina Susan Cordelia "Deed" Brazier,** (d/o William J. "Billy" Brazier and Perlina Hazlewood), b. 5 Oct 1856, Lincoln Co, TN, d. 1947, Moore Co, TN; m. c1879, *William Jacob "Jake" Evans* (great-grandparents of Robert Dale Sweeney <rdsweeney@vallnet.com>, who sent data), b. 27 July 1848, Lincolm Co, TN, d. 7 April 1900, TN, s/o William Stanley Evans and Elizabeth Waggoner. Both "Deed" and "Jake" are buried in Lynchburg Cem, Moore Co, TN.

"Jake" had four children by a previous marriage: Laura Bell Evans, b. 13 July 1871, m. General Beauregard Tipps ("General" is his name, not rank); John William Evans, b. 18 June 1873, m. Sallie C. _____"; Emma Elizabeth Evans, b. 21 Aug 1874, m. Will Mitchell; and Lucy Louraney Evans, b. 2 May 1878, m. William McKenzie.

Robert Dale Sweeney writes: "My great-grandmother Perlina Susan Cordelia (Brazier) Evans I remember well--a silent, fierce-looking old woman, apparently capable of unlimited malevolence--who I have always heard was half-Cherokee. It was in an attempt to prove this that I undertook, after an absence of over thirty years, once again to work on my family history. Obviously this didn't work out, and the story, however plausibly attested, is very likely, like most such stories, founded on a distortion or misunderstanding of whatever facts might lie behind them.

The story of Lucy Kelly Brazier might possibly be the source of this story, although there is a curious possibility that it may, in fact, be true. The Cherokees, whose repute is such that they have been substituted for other tribes in such stories, were, like many other tribes, matrilineal, and her mother's direct maternal line goes back to Henry Ligon's wife, the mysterious Elizabeth _____. If she was, in fact, an Indian, then great-grandmother's mother would have been an Indian, and the understanding of this would have broken down at about the time her mother would have lived.

Family of Perlina Susan Cordelia Brazier and William Jacob Evans:

V9-3702.   f-1. Cora Elizabeth Evans, b. 18 Feb 1880; m. John Tipps (brother of General Beauregard Tipps)
V9-3703.   g-1. May Tipps, m. W.B. "Bee" Garris; they had a dau: Dorothy Garris.
V9-3704.   g-2. Era Tipps, m. H.F. Coke
V9-3705.   g-3. Ernest Tipps, m. Lucille Damron
V9-3706.   g-4. Raybella Tipps, b. 15 May 1913, d. 24 Oct 1918,
V9-3707.   f-2. Ida Rosalee Evans, b. 30 Aug 1881, d. 11 Oct 1881, age 6 weeks
V9-3708.   f-3. Walter Jackson Evans, b. 13 March 1885, d. 26 Aug 1885, 5 months
V9-3709.   f-4. *Mary Myrtle Joyce Evans, b. 18 Jan 1886; m. John Wesley Limbaugh. (see below)
V9-3710.   f-5. Albert Stanley Evans, b. 30 Jan 1888, d. 23 Nov 1889, age 1½.
V9-3711.   f-6. *Robert Renegar "Bob" Evans, b. 30 Aug 1890; m.1. 21 July 1915, Della Josephine Allen, m.2. Viola (Solomon) Tipps,
V9-3712.   f-7. Felix Carl Evans, b. 21 June 1893, d. (suicide) 18 April 1940; m.1. Mary Millsap; m.2. Lizzie Mae (Copeland) Bobo. Ch: James W. Evans, 1921–1941; Thelma, b. 1924; Lyndal, b. Sept 1926; and Carl Evans Jr, b. before 1930.

V9-3713.　　f-8. Effie Vergie Evans, b. 15 Aug 1895, d. 1926, bur Lynchburg Cem; n.m.

V9-3714.　　f-9. W. Jake Evans, (apparently NOT William Jacob), b. 20 Aug 1898, d. 8 April 1967, Winchester, TN, not long after his farm in Franklin Co, TN was taken for construction of Tims Ford Dam; m. Annie Simpson, b. 11 Feb 1894, d. 8 April 1976, Tullahoma, TN

V9-3715.　　　　g-1. Joseph <u>Stanley</u> Evans, b. 16 Oct 1930, Franklin Co, TN; m. 12 July 1958, Rachel Irene Tanskersley, b. 24 Jan 1935, Moore Co, TN

V9-3716.　　　　h-1. Becky Diane Evans, b. 16 July 1959; m. 1982, in Winchester, TN, Carl Thomas Rogers. ch: Dustin and Casey Rogers

V9-3717.　　　　h-2. Mark Allen Evans, b. 16 Oct 1962, Tullahoma, TN

V9-3718.　　　　h-3. Philip Dale Evans, b. 30 Oct 1966; m. 3 Sep 1994, Franklin Co, TN, Amy Lynn Abel, from Florida. no ch.

Myrtle Joyce Evans
and John Wesley Limbaugh

f-4. Mary Myrtle <u>Joyce</u> Evans, b. 18 Jan 1886 (d/o Perlina Susan Cordelia Brazier and William Jacob Evans); m. John Wesley Limbaugh.

From Robert Dale Sweeney: Among Mother's papers I also found a letter and a sheaf of family group sheets which had been sent her by Eugene F. Limbaugh, 805 South Rose Farm Road, Woodstock, IL 60098. The letter is undated, but the envelope was postmarked 26 October 1985 at Woodstock. These sheets show the descendants of John Wesley Limbaugh and Joyce Myrtle Evans (incidentally, I do not know whether they or their children first moved to the Chicago area, or when):

Family of Myrtle Joyce Evans and John Wesley Limbaugh:

V9-3719.   g-1. Thomas Jefferson Limbaugh, b. 18 Nov 1908; m.1. 7 March 1927 to Mildred Carlson, b. 25 Aug 1905, d. 7 Oct 1963, d/o Fred Lars and Alma Augusta (_____) Carlson; m.2. Mary Brown.

Children of Thomas Jefferson Limbaugh and Mildred Carlson:

V9-3720.   h-1. Willard Wesley Limbaugh, b. 13 Sep 1927; m.1. Bette Fuller, second Mary Mellen. Children by first wife:

V9-3721.   i-1. Jeannie Limbaugh (adopted), b. 18 Jan 1946; m. ____ Rapp.

V9-3722.   i-2. Connie Limbaugh, b. 29 May 1948.

V9-3723.   i-3. Susan Limbaugh, b. ___ Feb 1951.

V9-3724.   i-4. Jonathan Limbaugh, b. 7 March 1959; m. Depta (first or last name?)

V9-3725.   i-5. Wendy Limbaugh, b. 20 May 1961.

V9-3726.   Children of second wife (he does not say whether by a previous husband or whether adopted):

V9-3727.   i-x. David Mellen.

V9-3728.   i-x. Peggy Mellen.

V9-3729.   i-x. Roger Mellen.

V9-3730.   h-2. Alma Joyce Limbaugh, b. 22 Nov 1929; m. 18 Sep 1948, Cyran Zank, b. 11 April 1927, s/o George and Anna (Goetch) Zank. (4105 Country Club Road, Ridgefield, IL).

V9-3731.   i-1. Michael Scott Zank, b. 25 July 1949; m. 14 Feb 1976, Jerry Lynn Woodson.

V9-3732.   j-1. Kate Anna Zank, b. 17 Sep 1977.

V9-3733.   j-2. Scott Michael Zank, b. 15 May 1979.

V9-3734.   i-2. Jodie Lisa Zank, b. 29 Sep 1954; m. 20 Oct 1979, Mark Lefevre, b. 4 July 1946, Michigan.

V9-3735.   j-1. Mathew Jason Lefevre, b. 13 Aug 1982.

V9-3736.   i-3. Jill Annette Zank, b. 14 July 1960; m. Thomas Freund. Child:

V9-3737.   j-1. Shauna Rosanne Freund, b. 3 Sep 1983.

V9-3738.   h-3. Gloria May Limbaugh, b. 28 Feb 1931, Freemont Street, Woodstock, IL; m.1. Arnold Harvey; m.2. Dirk H. Aissen, b. 23 Oct 1941, Sherman Hospital, Elgin, IL (3613 West Bull Valley Road, McHenry, IL). Children (by first husband):

V9-3739.	i-1. Deborah Marie Harvey, b. 12 July 1950; m.1. Theodore Jost; m.2. Kevin Werle; m.3. Steven D. Embry.
V9-3740.	j-1. Jennifer May Jost, b. 27 Aug 1970.
V9-3741.	j-2. Theodore Joseph Jost, b. 19 Sep 1970 (sic in letter).
V9-3742.	j-3. John C. Werle, b. 16 July 1977.
V9-3743.	j-4. Steven D. Embry Jr, b. 26 Sep 1984.
V9-3744.	i-2. Larry Lynn Harvey, b. 25 April 1952 (twin); m. 16 April 1971, Mary Hopp, b. 12 Oct 1954.
V9-3745.	j-1. Holly Ann Harvey, b. 9 Sep 1971.
V9-3746.	j-2. Larry Lynn Harvey, Jr., b. 22 Nov 1973.
V9-3747.	j-3. Emily Marie Harvey, b. 10 Dec 1975.
V9-3748.	j-4. Brandon Joseph Harvey, b. 8 Nov 1977.
V9-3749.	j-5. Mariah Irene Harvey, b. 31 Dec 1981.
V9-3750.	j-6. Travis Scott Harvey, b. 9 Nov 1983.
V9-3751.	i-3. Terry Lee Harvey, b. 25 April 1952 (twin); m.1. Kimberly Ort (1 ch; divorced); m.2. Tami Knabusch (2 ch)
V9-3752.	j-1. Jessica Leeann Harvey, b. 24 May 1977.
V9-3753.	j-2. Dawn Lindsay Harvey, b. 1 Jan 1982.
V9-3754.	j-3. Joseph Michael Harvey, b. 26 June 1984.
V9-3755.	i-4. Colleen Joy Harvey, b. 30 Oct 1954; m. and divorced _____ Dolby.
V9-3756.	i-5. Steven Arnold Harvey, b. 29 Nov 1955; m. Donna Navrosky, b. 8 July 1956.
V9-3757.	j-1. Trumaine Charles Harvey, b. 6 July 1983.
V9-3758.	i-6. Brian Eugene Harvey, b. 29 Nov 1960; m. Ann Ashton, b. 21 Feb 1959.
V9-3759.	j-1. William Brian Harvey (adopted), b. 7 June 1975.
V9-3760.	j-2. Nicole Marie Harvey, b. 17 May 1982.
V9-3761.	j-3. Sara Ann Harvey, b. 8 Nov 1984.
V9-3762.	h-4. Marilyn Rose Limbaugh, b. 5 Jan 1933, Ridgefield, IL; m. 18 March 1950, James Albert Amettis, b. 2 Feb 1930, s/o James and Emma (Beyer) Amettis.
V9-3763.	i-1. Thomas Amettis, b. 26 May 1954, Sycamore, IL.
V9-3764.	i-2. Randal Amettis, b. 13 June 1956, Sycamore, IL.
V9-3765.	i-3. Barry Amettis, b. 30 Jan 1958, Sycamore, IL; m. 24 Feb 1979, Lisa Houston.
V9-3766.	j-1. Kyle Joseph Amettis, b. 21 Nov 1983.

V9-3767. i-4. Anthony Amettis, b. 26 March 1961, Sycamore, IL; m. 17 July 1983, Joy McAbee.

V9-3768. i-5. Joel Amettis, b. 29 Dec 1961, Sycamore, IL.

V9-3769. i-6. Gerald Amettis, b. 13 Oct 1966, Sycamore, IL.

V9-3770. i-7. Christine Amettis, b. 4 Jan 1968, Harvard, IL.

V9-3771. g-2. Leila Evans Limbaugh; m. ____ Anderson.

V9-3772. g-3. Robert James Limbaugh, b. 14 June 1913, Franklin Co, TN; m. 26 March 1936, Willie Frances Trisler, b. 10 Sep 1913 Harrodsburg, Kentucky, d/o Irving and Willie Frances (Godfrey) Trisler, d. 29 May 1961.

V9-3773. h-1. Robert Wayne Limbaugh, b. 2 May 1937, Woodstock, IL; m. 20 Sep 1958 Nancy J. McHale, b. 19 July 1940, d/o Laurel and Marjorie (Temple) McHale.

V9-3774. i-1. Don Robert Limbaugh, b. 26 May 1959 Bellville, IL; m. 1 Aug 1981 Donna Stanger, b. 10 Aug 1961, d/o Donald Kenneth and Dorothy (Grabbert) Stanger.

V9-3775. j-1. Emily Marie Limbaugh, b. 2 Feb 1983, Woodstock, IL.

V9-3776. i-2. Kristin Laurel Limbaugh, b. 27 May 1964, Woodstock, IL.

V9-3777. h-2. Eugene Francis Limbaugh, b. 6 July 1940; m. 14 June 1958, Helen Lois Hunt, b. 22 May 1939, d/o Nelsen Stanley and Helen Dorothy (Thompson) Hunt.

V9-3778. i-1. Elaine Carol Limbaugh, b. 7 Oct 1958, Woodstock, IL.

V9-3779. i-2. Lynell Rae Limbaugh, b. 24 Aug 1964, Woodstock, IL.

V9-3780. i-3. Brad Eugene Limbaugh, b. 21 Sep 1965, Woodstock, IL.

V9-3781. h-3. Kenneth Lynn Limbaugh, b. 22 July 1945, Woodstock, IL; m. 28 April 1962 Joy Lane Hawthorne, b. 7 Sep 1945, d/o Glenn S. and Violet I. Hawthorne.

V9-3782. i-1. James Lee Limbaugh, b. 19 July 1963, Woodstock, IL.

V9-3783. i-2. Scot Alan Limbaugh, b. 24 May 1964 Harvard, IL; m. 8 Sep 1984 Greenwood, IL to Donna Jean Huff, b. 17 May 1965, Woodstock, IL, d/o Earl Hermon and Jean (Borg) Huff.

V9-3784. h-4. Clarence William Limbaugh, b. 22 May 1915 Franklin Co, TN; m. Lorraine Yanke, b. 4 Oct 1920,

	d/o Alvin and Genevieve (Goddard) Yanke, d. 18 Oct 1981, bur Greenwood Cem, McHenry Co, IL.
V9-3785.	i-1. Lavonne Rose Limbaugh, b. 4 Oct 1948, d. ____ 1948, bur Greenwood Cem.
V9-3786.	i-2. David Alvin Limbaugh, b. 28 Sep 1950; m.1. Sharon Ann Jordan; m.2. Paula Eva Zelazguez (Allen). Children by first wife:
V9-3787.	j-1. Lee Ann Michelle Limbaugh, b. 30 Jan 1969.
V9-3788.	j-2. Greta Sue Limbaugh, b. 29 Nov 1972.
V9-3789.	j-3. Rachel Grace Limbaugh, b. 19 March 1978. Child of second wife by previous marriage:
V9-3790.	j-4. Joshua Edgar Allen, b. 15 April 1972),

Robert Renegar Evans and Della Allen

f-6. Robert Renegar "Bob" Evans, b. 30 Aug 1890 (s/o Perlina Susan Cordelia Brazier and William Jacob Evans); m.1. 21 July 1915, Della Josephine Allen; m.2. Viola Solomon Tipps, b. 28 Sept 1891, TX, d. 18 March 1936, TN.

Robert Dale Sweeney writes: Robert Renegar Evans, my grandfather, was a farmer, a skilled carpenter and house builder, and famous for his prodigious memory. He had a hobby of remembering people's birthdays, and was reputed, with some exaggeration, to know the birthday of every person in Moore County.

He was born 30 Aug 1890, married 21 July 1915 Della Josephine Allen, d/o James Bascomb Allen and Althamyra (or Altha Myra) Jane Wiseman, who was born 23 Sep 1891, Comanche, TX (where her father and his brothers, according to family tradition, broke wild horses and shipped them back to Tennessee) and d. 18 March 1936 in Moore County, Tennessee of a pulmonary disease which baffled the doctors of the time, and caused their family to move for a while in the late 1920's first to Comanche, Texas, and then to Clovis, New Mexico, in both of which places she had relatives.

(He was also a first cousin of Miss Mary (Evans) Bobo (Mrs. Lacey Jackson Bobo), proprietor of the famous Miss Mary Bobo's Boarding House in Lynchburg, Tennessee, now known world-wide from the advertisements for Jack Daniel's, which now owns and runs it, and Miss Ophelia (Evans), the wife of Lem Motlow, nephew of Jack Daniel and his successor as proprietor (see a bottle) of Jack Daniel's Distillery, daughters of his father's brother Daniel Scivally Evans).

Robert Renegar Evans was later married to Viola Solomon Tipps (N.B. the spelling here and elsewhere), widow of Dan Tipps, s/o General Beauregard Tipps, who survived him.

Robert Renegar "Bob" Evans and Della Josephine Allen had 3 children:

V9-3791.   g-1. Ova Ruth Evans, my mother, b. 14 Feb 1917, Moore Co, TN, d. 16 Feb 1995 at Fayetteville, TN; married 29 July 1934, Moore Co, TN, Claude Raymond Sweeney, who was born 7 Dec 1905, Moore Co, TN, and d. 17 Oct 1978 in Huntsville, Alabama, s/o Alfred Levi Sweeney and Mietta Dora Copeland. She had 2 children:

V9-3792.   h-1. Vivian Sweeney, b. and d. 22 May 1936, Moore Co, TN,.

V9-3793.   h-2. Robert Dale Sweeney, b. 9 Jan 1939, Fayetteville, TN, B.A. S.C.L. The University of the South, Sewanee, TN, 1959; Fulbright Scholar, Georg-August University, Goettingen, Germany 1959-1960; Ph. D. (Classical Philology) Harvard University 1965,; Instructor in Greek and Latin Languages and Literatures, Wayne State University, Detroit 1965; Instructor to Assistant Professor, Dartmouth College 1965-1969; Associate Professor, Vanderbilt University 1969-1983 (resigned); Guggenheim Fellow 1974-1975; Visiting Professor, Concordia College, Moorhead, Minnesota 1985-1986; Visiting Assistant Professor, University of Cincinnati 1986-1987; coach and instructor of fencing at Vanderbilt (playing coach of the Club there), Concordia, Wright State University, Fairborn, Ohio, and now Sewanee, various part-time positions in (Ancient) History at Cincinnati and Wright State, now retired. Author of *Prolegomena to an Edition of the Scholia to Statius*, E.J. Brill, Leiden 1969, *Lactantii Placidi in Statii Thebaida Commentum...*, Vol. I (Volume II is in preparation), B.G. Teubner, Stuttgart and Leipzig 1997, as well as the usual academic small beer. Never married.

V9-3794.   g-2. Harry Clyde Evans, b. 14 Dec 1920, Moore Co, TN; m. (in Georgia) Edna Ivey, b. 20 Dec 1923, living, Moore Co, TN. He had one child:

V9-3795.   h-1. Barbara Jean Evans, b. 6 Nov 1948, Moore Co, TN; m. 22 Oct 1966, Moore Co, TN, Billy Norris Durm, b.

23 May 1948). Since 1994, she has been Register of Deeds, Moore Co, TN. She has two children:

V9-3796.   i-1. Billy Troy Durm, b. 26 Aug 1967; m. Dawn Lindeman. Two ch: i. Ashley Brianna Durm, b. 1 Oct 1992; ii. Justin Troy Durm, b. 3 Jan 1994.

V9-3797.   i-2. Gregory Allen Durm, b. 17 March 1970. Unmarried.

V9-3798.   g-3. Paul Allen Evans, b. 4 Dec 1922, Moore Co, TN; m. lastly Virginia Hamilton, d. 19 Feb 1993, Sarasota, Florida. He was married to (and presumably divorced from) Maureen _____ in the late 1940's in Detroit, Michigan. There may possibly have been other marriages and children. He and Virginia Hamilton Evans adopted 4 children:

V9-3799.   h-1. Paul Evans, Jr., b. 7 June 1950 (reputedly his legitimized son). Now married to Ardith _____ and living in Bradenton, Florida. He has been married several times before, but has never had any children.

V9-3800.   h-2. Carol Virginia Evans, b. 10 Aug 1948, Detroit, now married to Eugene Waterstraw and living in Lakeland, Florida. She is supposedly the maternal half-sister of Paul Evans, Jr. She was previously married to and divorced from Tim Porter, and has one son (by someone else): Robert Evans, who married Dawn _____.

V9-3801.   h-3. Vicki Lee Evans, b. 22 March 1963.

V9-3802.   h-4. Della Jo(sephine?) Evans, b. 25 Dec 1964.

28. Rev. ELIJAH BRAZIER, of NC & TN

c-5. **Rev. Elijah Brazier**, b. c1774 in North Carolina, s/o William Brazier of Surry Co and gs/o James Brazier of Cumberland Co, NC; m. *Nancy* _____ .

Elijah, a Methodist Minister, was ordained Elder by Bishop McKendree; settled 1818 in Lincoln Co, TN, where he died 15 Dec 1846. (ref: *Genealogical Abstracts ... from Nashville Christian Advocate*, Issue 21, Fri. March 19, 1847, p.4. col.2.).

Elijah and his brother, James, moved together and lived near each other most of their lives. Elijah, according to a descendant of James, came to Franklin Co, TN as early as 1818. Census data verifies this, as well as the brothers moving together.

Census Data

The censuses show repeatedly that Elijah's wife was older than he.

1800 Census, Greenville Co, SC:
p.265 Elijah Brasher 21100-20010-00 age 16-26, b. 1774-1784 (if census-taker came before his birthday, he would be 26 yrs old; he turned 27 in 1800); wife was older, 26-45, b. 1755-1774. If the boy 10-16 is their son, they sure got an early start; the child was born when Elijah was 16 at the oldest, 10 at the youngest. Maybe these were wife's children by a previous marriage?

boy	10-16, b. 1784-1790
boy	0-10, b. 1790-1800
girl	0-10, b. 1790-1800
girl	0-10, b. 1790-1800
boy	0-10, b. 1790-1800

These may all be the wife's children. Descendants of James knew only of Wiley, b. 1801, and Elijah Jr, b. 1806; judging from the 1830 census, there had to be at least three others.

1810 Census of Rowan County, North Carolina,
Elijah Brazier, 10100-00010. b. 1765-1784, wife is older, b. 1755-1774. Where are all those children from the 1800 census?
James Brazier, b. 1765-1784, 1 boy, 3 girls under 10.

1820 Census, Franklin Co, TN:
p.23 Elijah Brasier   121101-11001
p.23 James Brasier   110001-12100

1830 Census, Franklin Co, TN: p.100: 00012001-01100001
Elijah Brazier,   50-60, b. 1770-80
    fem,   50-60, b. 1770-80
    male,   20-30, b. 1800-1810   ?Wiley, b. c1801
    male,   20-30, b. 1800-1810   ?Elijah, Jr. b. c1806
    male,   15-20, b. 1810-1815
    fem,   10-15, b. 1815-1820   ?unknown dau, who m. John
                                                    Baker, c1830
    fem,   5-10, b. 1820-1825

1840 Census, Franklin Co, TN:
Elijah Brazier, Sr   60-70 (b.177?) wife is older
    wife   70-80 (b.176?)
Elijah Brazier, Jr.   30-40 (b.180?)
    wife   20-30 (b.181?) — [Eliza? see 1860, Franklin]
Wiley Brazier   40-50 (b.179?)
    wife   20-30 (b.181?)
    son   0-5 (b.1835-40)
    son   0-5 (b.1835-40)

1840, Franklin Co, TN, p.45: (101001-211121)
John Baker,   40-50 (b. 1795)
    wife,   30-40 (b. 1800-1810; d/o Elijah Brazier, Sr)
    dau,   20-30 (b. 1810-1820; can't be by this wife)
    dau,   20-30 (b. 1810-1820)
    dau,   15-20 (b. 1820-1825)
    son,   15-20 (b. 1820-1825)
    dau,   10-15 (b. 1825-1830)
    dau,   5-10 (b. 1830-1835)
    son,   0-5   (b. 1835-1840) ? Elijah Baker
    dau,   0-5   (b. 1835-1840) ? D.H. Baker
    dau,   0-5   (b. 1835-1840) ? Nancy C. Baker

1860 Census, Franklin County, TN:
Wiley Brasier   59 (b.1801)

1860 Census, Franklin County, TN:
Elijah Brasier   53 b.1806
    Eliza   48 b.1812
    Mary J.   14 b.1846

1860 Census, Franklin County, TN:
W.M. Brasier   21 (b. 1838-39) [prob. oldest s/o Wiley]
    Sarah J.   21 (b.1838-39)
    Mary L.   3/12 (b. 1860)

Deeds, Franklin Co, TN, 1807-1899:

- Elizabeth Brazier, 30 acres on n. side Elk River, from Wiley Brazier (Book V, p.448)
- Elizabeth Brazier, 120 acres, from Cannon Newton (Book F, p.143)
- Elizabeth Brazier, 83 1/2 acres, from Wiley Brazier Jr (Book V, p.100)
- Elizabeth Brazier Sr, 200 acres on Elk River, from W. J. & Elizabeth Brazier (Book O, p.129)
- James Brazier, 42 acres adj school land, from Jesse Bynum (Book 6, p.303)
- James Brazier, 13 acres and 448 acres between Big Hurricane Creek and Turkey Creek (Book 4, p.272)
- James Brazier, 12 acres, from William Tankusley (Book 2, p.448)
- James Brasier, 43 acres on Turkey Creek, from B. B. Brandon (Book 2, p.449)
- James Brasier, 223 acres on Shellyville Road, from John Atkins (Book O, p.429)
- James Brasier, 228 acres on both sides of Turkey Creek, from Mathew W. Watson (Book X, p.544)
- James Brazier, 12 acres, from W & M Tankusley (Book X, p.543)
- James West Brazier, 93 acres on Big Hurricane Creek, from J. J. Shasteen (Book 10, p.443)
- Mrs. Mary Brazier, a lot in Awalt on Fall Lick Creek, from J T Graham (Book 17, p.274)
- Wiley J. Brazier, 94 acres in Owl Hollow, from Elijah Brazier (Book V, p.154)
- Wiley J. Brazier, by act of Assembly, 21 Feb 1852, ? in Owl Hollow, adj Elijah Brazier (Book W, p.402)
- Wiley J. & Elizabeth Brazier, 200 acres on Daughters Creek, from Joseph Hilton, (Book O, p.15)
- ? ? on Elk Creek (Book P, p.495-6)

Rev. Elijah Brazier died 15 Dec 1846, and estate proceedings opened at once: (research by Janet Burks)
Franklin Co, TN Settlements, Adm, Exec, Guardian, Roll 47 microfilm 1811-1848: Elijah Brazier
p.212: inventory **16 Jun 1847, Meredith Pearson, Admr**
p.334: sale, p.402: sale 16 Jan 1847 some persons who bought: Willie Brazier, Robert C. Parks, Lim Brazier, Elijah Brazier, John Baker, A.G. Wiseman

Franklin Co, TN Settlement, Adm, Exec, Guardians (no index) (microfilm-research by Janet Burks), Bk Feb 1851-Mar 1854
p.7: **JOHN BAKER** guardian for his minor children: Elijah, D.H., Nancy S, Elizabeth, Saline, John, and Samuel Baker. 11 Mar 1850 received from M. Pearson Adm. of **ELIJAH BRAZIER dec'd.** the sum of $85.44 etc. down to Nov 1844 report of sd wards of John Baker /s/ John Baker 3 Feb 1851.
p242 JOHN BAKER 5 May 1852 he had received a total of $297.86 from M. Pearson Adm. of Elijah Brazier [SR]
M Pearson Adm 11 Mar 1850 $85.44 interest 11.20
M Pearson Adm 1 Oct 1849 $25.00 interest 4.20
M Pearson Adm 11 Mar 1850 $44.95 interest 8.91
M Pearson Adm 1 Nov 1849 $1.54 interest 13.92
Total: $297.86
pd Clerks for guardian bond .50, recording one report .75, making record of this settlement 1.50,
guardian for services $10.00 and $12.75 for a Total: $285.11

p.417. settlement made 5 May 1852 $285.11 with interest $17.10 total $302.21. pd clk for making this settlement 1.50, guardian services 5.00, 4.50 for total of $292.71....
2 May 1853 he has now paid ELIJAH BAKER who is now of age his full shares; to the others he is debted the sum of $246.50 to be equally distributed.

Family of Rev. Elijah Brazier

Family sheet for Rev. Elijah Brazier, of Franklin Co, TN
   Elijah Brazier, b. NC, c1774, d. Franklin Co, TN, 15 Dec 1846; m. Nancy _____. He had at least five children (1830 Census).
V9-3803.   d-1. ***William "Wiley" J. Brazier**, b. 1801, Rowan Co, NC, d. c1875, Lincoln Co, TN; m. *Elizabeth Dowthard*
V9-3804.   d-2. ***Elijah Brazier Jr,** b. c1806, per census (or 15 July 1796, per stone), Rowan Co, NC, d. 4 Dec 1888, Franklin Co, TN; m. *Elizabeth McElroy*, b. 8 Aug 1812 (48 in 1860 Census), d. 12 March 1889, both bur Harmony Cem, Franklin Co, TN.
V9-3805.   d-3. son, b. 1810-15
V9-3806.   d-4. dau, b. 1815-1820 (probably the one who m. John Baker)
V9-3807.   d-5. dau, b. 1820-1825

JOHN BAKER guardian for his minor children, received payment from estate of Rev. Elijah Brazier:

V9-3808.　e-1. Elijah Baker, b. c1831-32 (of age on 2 May 1853)
V9-3809.　e-2. D.H. Baker,
V9-3810.　e-3. Nancy S. Baker,
V9-3811.　e-4. Elizabeth Baker,
V9-3812.　e-5. Saline Baker,
V9-3813.　e-6. John Baker,
V9-3814.　e-7. Samuel Baker,

A fragment of a Franklin Co, TN, Deeds, Bk ?, p.?:
This agreement made the second day of June in the year of our Lord One Thousand Eight Hundred and Thirty Seven, (2 June 1837) by and between Elijah Brazier Sr, of the County of Franklin and State of Tennessee, of the one part and Wiley J. Brazier & Elijah Brazier Jr, his sons, of the County and State of aforesaid of the other part one certain tract or parcel of land situated, lying and being in the county of Franklin, State of Tennessee, on Daughters Creek, a South Branch of Elk River and bounded as follows, to wit Beginning on a Chain Marker I.A. Running thence north to and thru Hickory on White's south boundary line, thence east to a white oak, thence south to a stake on a bluff near Daughters Creek, thence west to the beginning containing two hundred acres of land to same , more or less, with its appertances to have and to hold the aforesaid tract or parcel of land with all and singular rights profits, and pertaining to the only and proper use and hehoof of them the said Wiley J. Brazier & Elijah Brazier their heirs and assigns forever. Witnesses are:
Wm. N. Taylor, W. W. Brazelton.

William "Wiley" J. Brazier and Elizabeth Dowthard

Family of William "Wiley" J. Brazier and Elizabeth Dowthard: all born Franklin Co, TN. H/H 104-133 in Lincoln Co, TN in 1860 Census, is James Braser, 19; Elizabeth, 40; Fountin, 17; Jerry, 14; and Newton, 15. H/H 113-113 in Lincoln Co, 1860: William Brazier, 22, the oldest son.

V9-3815.　e-1. **William M. Brazier,** b. 1838, died in a military hospital in 1862 in Georgia. He is buried in a military cemetery in Marietta, Cobb Co, GA. Susie Toal got this information from UDC, GA. The family never knew what happened to him; he just "never came home." Probably the W.M.

Brasier, age 21, in the 1860 census of Franklin Co, TN, with wife, Sarah J., age 21, and dau, Mary L., age 3/12.

V9-3816.   e-2. **James W. "Bully Jim" Brazier,** b. 1839, d. c1889; m.1. ***Lou Williamson***, m.2. 3 Nov 1868, *[Mary?] Jane Brown*. Franklin Co, TN Marriages: 3 Nov 1868: James W. Brazier to M.J. Brown, by J. Hudgins, M.G., 3 Nov 1868. (see *35,000 Tennessee Marriage Records and Bonds, 1783-1870*, by Rev. Silas Emmett Lucas, Jr. and Mrs Ella Lee Sheffield, 3 vols.)

V9-3817.   f-1. **Will Brazier,** d. unmarried at age 22

V9-3818.   f-2. **Tom Brazier,** moved to GA

V9-3819.   f-3. **Jessie Lee Brazier,** moved to Decatur, AL and d. there

V9-3820.   g-1. **Tom Brazier**

V9-3821.   g-2. **Albert Brazier**

V9-3822.   g-3. **O.V. Brazier**

V9-3823.   g-4. **Carl Brazier**

V9-3824.   g-5. **Billy Brazier**

V9-3825.   g-6. **Audrey Brazier**

V9-3826.   g-7. **Dorthary Brazier,** m. _____ Crow

V9-3827.   g-8. **Jesse O'Neill Brazier**

V9-3828.   f-4. **Carl Buford Brazier,** moved to Florida and d. there

V9-3829.   f-5. **Daisy Brazier,** m. _____ ***Richardson*** and moved to Texas

V9-3830.   f-6. **Lena Brazier,** m. _____ ***McQuary*** and lived So. Pittsburg

V9-3831.   f-7. **Leona Brazier,** d. Chattanooga, TN; m. _____ ***Houchan***

V9-3832.   e-3. **Fountaine Harris Brazier,** b. 1 May 1841, d. 6 Aug 1924, Bristol, Ellis Co, TX; m. 13 Aug 1872, Lincoln Co, TN, ***Nancy Elizabeth Ann Lee***, b. 8 July 1851, d. 27 Sep 1919, Crisp, TX, d/o R. R. Lee and Margret Barber. Both Fountaine and Nancy bur Crisp Cem, Ellis Co, TX. They moved to Texas in 1882. They had three sets of twin girls who died at birth or shortly after. (Data from Suzie Brazier Toal, Ferris, TX.)

V9-3833.   f-1. **Lillie Ann Brazier,** d. at age of 12

V9-3834.   f-2. son **(?Robert) Brazier**, b. 1873, d. at age 5 in Alabama

V9-3835.   f-3. **John William Brazier,** b. 13 Aug 1877, d. 6 June 1937, Crisp, Ellis Co, TX

V9-3836.	f-4. **James Calvin Brazier,** b. 12 March 1886, d. 11 Nov 1929 at Bristol, Ellis Co, TX; m. 13 Jan 1917, **Susan C. Pequese**
V9-3837.	f-5. **Charles Alexander Brazier,** b. 26 April 1890 in Bristol, TX, d. there, 5 May 1966; m. 23 May 1925, **Emma M. Bishop.** Emma had a daughter, Oletha Pearl, by a previous marriage, who went by the name, Oletha Pearl Brazier, b. 24 Feb 1920 (??), d. 1980, Bristol, TX; m. Earnest Autry
V9-3838.	g-1. **Charles Alexander Brazier Jr,** b. 8 Aug 1927, in Farris, Ellis Co, TX, d. 1992; m. 23 Dec 1949, **Martha C. Long**
V9-3839.	h-1. **Della Beth Brazier,** b. 6 Dec 1952, Dallas, TX; m.1. 14 May 1982, **Arthur Davis**; m.2. **Doug Anderson**
V9-3840.	h-2. **Charles Brent Brazier,** b. 8 Aug 1955, Dallas, TX; m. 10 Dec 1976, **Helen J. West**
V9-3841.	h-3. **Mark Kevin Brazier,** b. 17 April 1959; m. 14 Oct 1976, **Rhonda Jo Vaughn,**
V9-3842.	g-2. **Fountaine Harris Brazier, II,** b. 5 Oct 1928, Farris, TX; d. unmarried 17 May 1976
V9-3843.	g-3. **Kenneth Arthur Brazier,** b. 6 April 1930, Farris, TX; d. 25 Dec 1949, Bristol, TX
V9-3844.	g-4. **Cora Louise Brazier,** b. 17 June 1931, Farris, TX; m. 28 Sep 1951, **William D. Yates**
V9-3845.	g-5. **Sherman Obie Brazier,** b. 5 July 1935, Bristol, TX; m. 21 April 1966, **Mary Anderson**
V9-3846.	g-6. **Susan Elaine Brazier,** b. 27 April 1943, Bristol, TX; m. 30 Jan 1965, **Tlen Toal**
V9-3847.	e-4. **Newton A. Brazier,** b. 1843; m. 5 Oct 1885, Lincoln Co, TN ("by Jno J. Short"), **Sally Rhea** (Ray on the marriage record), and they moved to Ardmore, Giles Co, TN, which is on the state line and part of the town is in Alabama. Newt, Sally, John and Julia are all bur Elkton Cem, Ardmore, AL.
V9-3848.	f-1. **John Rhea Brazier,** b. c1887, Lincoln Co, TN, d. 28(?) Dec 1951, Giles Co, TN; m.1. 15 May 1910, Lincoln Co, TN ("by David Strang"), **Julia Newsom,** d/o Charles Newsom and Fannie Hill, of Mulberry, who are bur in Mulberry Cem, Lincoln Co, TN. John and Julia had four daughters. John ?m.2. **Nina Gilliam.**

V9-3849.	g-1. **Jesse Rhea Brazier,**
V9-3850.	g-2. **Mary Dell Brazier,**
V9-3851.	g-3. **Fanny Ruth Brazier,** (later changed her name to Virginia Ruth)
V9-3852.	g-4. **Louise Brazier,** who d. when her mother died.
V9-3853.	e-5. **Ira Brazier,** b. 1845, d. 1872 (Jerry on some census records.)

Elijah Brazier Jr and Elizabeth McElroy

Family of d-2. Elijah Brazier Jr and Elizabeth McElroy:

V9-3854.	e-x. **Mary Jane Brazier,** b. 1 Aug 1845, Franklin Co, TN; d. 17 Jan 1921, bur. Harmony Cem. Franklin Co, TN; m. 9 Dec 1868, **George W. Brazelton,**. (Franklin Co, TN Marriages: W.G. Brazelton to Mary J. Brazier, married 9 Dec 1868; see *35,000 Tennessee Marriage Records and Bonds, 1783-1870,* by Rev. Silas Emmett Lucas Jr and Mrs Ella Lee Sheffield, 3 vols.). Both bur Harmony, Franklin Co, TN.
V9-3855.	f-1. Charlie Brazelton; m. Josie Baker
V9-3856.	f-2. Nora Brazelton, b. 20 Jan 1878, Franklin Co, TN; d. 29 July 1960; m. Lee Limbaugh
V9-3857.	g-1. Gordon Limbaugh, b. 12 March 1905, d. 11 March 1970; m. Elizabeth Ikard
V9-3858.	g-2. Wilma Limbaugh, b. 19 Sep 1908; m. James Bedford

Unaccounted for:

Some of the Braziers moved to Harrison Co, Texas, c1845.

1870 Census, Harrison Co, TX:

Brazier, M. J.	60	b. SC 1810, farmer
Hannah Brazier	61	b. SC 1809
W. F.(or A.) Brazier	20	b. TX 1850
W.C. Brazier	18	b. TX 1852
Sam'l Brazier	15	b. TX 1855

1870 Census, Harrison Co, TX:

Brazier, Jas	36	b. SC 1834, farmer
Ellen Brazier	32	b. TX 1838
M. M. Brazier	11	b. TX 1859
Sara H. Brazier	4	b. TX 1866
Jas W. Brazier	2	b. TX 1868

UNSOLVED QUESTION: James E. Brazier

JAMES E. BRAZIER -- In 1832, in Franklin Co, TN, Robert and Lucinda (Brazier) Smith and James Brazier, "orphan of William Brazier," chose Robert Smith's father, the Rev. Joseph Smith, as James's guardian. Lucinda was a sister to James Brazier. See *Moore Co, TN, Genealogies Extracted from Chancery Court Loose Records*, by Judy Henley Phillips and Shirley Whitely Cato (1990), p.?]

Our best candidate for this William Brazier is the one b. 1797, s/o Elijah Brazier of Cumberland Co, NC, who was s/o James Brazier of Cumberland County; that is, a cousin of the James and Elijah who moved to Tennessee together, who were sons of Elijah of Cumberland's brother, William. If so, we could posit at least a part of a family sheet:

c-6. **William Brazier**, b. NC, 1797, d. c1832; s/o b-3. Elijah Brazier of Cumberland Co, NC, gs/o James Brazier of Cumberland Co, NC.

V9-3859.   d-1. **James E. Brazier**, b. NC, 16 Feb 1817; d. 30 Oct 1893, bur Marble Plains Cem, Franklin Co, TN (surname spelled "Brasier" on headstone); m. 3 Feb 1838, *Rachel Brandon*, b. 23 Aug 1825, d. 3 July 1863 (also on her headstone: "married to James Brasier Feb 4, 1838"), d/o Lemuel Brandon.

James E. Brazier and Rachel Brandon had four children, but the two names from 1860 Census don't agree with other records.

Note also that Rachel Brandon was only 12 when she and James Brasier married and, according to the 1840 census, had two children by the time she was 15-20.

This Rachel is not to be confused with Rachel Brandon, b. 3 Dec 1803, d/o Joseph Brandon (Josiah, on Rev.War pension papers) and Rachel Brown of Burke Co, NC. Widow Rachel Brandon received a Rev. War widow's pension (see below). Joseph (Josiah) Brandon is believed to be a brother to Lemuel Brandon.

V9-3860.   d-2. **Lucinda Brazier**, b. c1818; m. *Robert Smith*, s/o Rev. Joseph Smith. Note that Lucinda was only 14 years old in 1832, the time of the court record dealing with James's guardianship. She and Robert Smith were probably too young to become guardians; therefore they asked Robert's father. Any Smith descendants have any data on Lucinda's ancestry? or children?

1840 Census of Franklin Co TN:
James E. Brazier 20-30 (b.1810-20)
    wife   15-20 (b.1820-25)
    son   0-5 (b.1835-40)
    son   0-5 (b.1835-40)
    ? grandmother ?   70-80 (b.1760-70)

1860 Census, Franklin Co, Tn:
james Brasier   44 B.1816
    Rachel E.   37 b.1823
    Lemuel G.   17 b.1843
    James W.   9 b.1851

Rev. War Pension of Josiah Brandon, W335 West Tenn. #19088(?) $80/year issued 31 July 1833. Rachel BRANDON, widow. Tenn. #665 $80/year, issued 20 Feb. 1845.

16 Oct. 1832. Lincoln Count Tenn.

Josiah BRANDON, age 72, states he entered the service in 1776 or 1777 under Capt. Samuel DAVIDSON of Burke County N. C., of which he was a resident. He helped to build Fort Royal which is now Old Fort Royal Post Office in Burke county. He served three months as a Ranger under Capt. CUNNINGHAM and fought Indians across the Blue Ridge in the fall of 1779. In the winter of 1779 he joined Capt. BOYKIN's company of Light Horse and pursued the British under Capt. CUNNINGHAM in South Carolina until he was driven into the British garrison at 96. In March of 1780 joined Maj. McDOWELL's Corps from Burke County and served 30 days in Indian Territory. In the fall of 1780 the Indians attacked the settlement near Old Fort and "John DAVIDSON and his family were butchered in the most brutal and savage manner." BRANDON then joined Capt. WALKER and his rangers on a three month tour.

Clergyman Elijah BRAZER of Franklin County and John BAKER of Lincoln County vouched for BRANDON.

John Baker is probably the neighbor to Elijah in 1820:

In 1820 Franklin Co ,TN census (alphabetical order) on page 23:

Elijah BRAZIER 121101-11001

James Brazier 110001-12101

John Baker 2/u 10(b 1810-1820), 1/16-26 (born 1794-1804) fem-1/u 10, 1/16-26 (b. 1794-1804)

Janet Baker Burks, of Tyler, TX, (Janet Burks <mrsrose@cox-internet.com>) is trying to confirm Rev. Elijah Brazier's children (sons and daughters) and who John Baker might be, listed in the pension application with Clergyman Elijah Brazier. She's not sure if he is John Baker born 1786 in Burke Co, NC (son of Charles) or if he is another John Baker that might be Elijah's son-in-law. Where did this Elijah Brazier reside before Franklin Co, TN?

Family of James E. Brazier and Rachel Brandon

Moore Co, TN Genealogies Extracted from Chancery Court Loose Records, by Judy Henley Phillips and Shirley Whitely Cato (1990), p. 14, gives the children of James E. and Rachel (Brandon) Brazier as:

V9-3861. e-1. **Ellen Lezinka Brazier**, m. *Sam Parks* [Franklin Co, TN Marriages: 24 Aug 1859: J. M. Parks to E. Z. Brazier, by D. D. Smith, J. P.]

V9-3862. e-2. **J. W. L. Brazier**, b. 9 Jan 1850, Franklin, Co, TN, d. 13 Oct 1914; m. *America Brown* (Data from Selena Cunningham <cunningham@amvet. net>)

V9-3863. e-3. **William Brazier**,

On the same page is an entry: James J. Brazier was 45 in 1898 [that is, b. c1853]. He lived in Civil District 5 of Moore Co, TN.

Confusion: Rachel Brandon Brazier, wife of James E. Brazier, died 3 July 1863, according to her headstone. The estate of Lemuel Brandon, her father, whose will was dated 21 June 1860 and probate opened in July 1860, named only her husband. The heirs named in Lemuel Brandon's estate papers include: Samuel Parks and his wife Elener L. Parks; James Brazier Jr, citizens of Franklin Co, TN. Lazireke Brazier and Rachel Brazier, minors, are mentioned, I believe, as heirs, under care of James Brazier, Jr.

There is a case, James Brazier vs. Lazireke Brazier and Rachel Brazier, who were minors without regular guardians and resided in Bedford Co, TN. (ref: *Moore Co, TN Genealogies*, p.13.)

Elener L. Parks cannot be the same person as the minor without gaurdian, Lazireke Brazier; so the two minor girls, Lazireke and Rachel Brazier in Bedford Co, must be grandchildren. If they were daughters, James E. Brazier, who lived until 1893, would have been guardian, by right of being the father.

29. ELIJAH BRAZIER,
s/o James Brazier of Cumberland

b-3. **Elijah Brazier**, (s/o James Brazier, the Cumberland Carpenter, and Sarah, his wife), b. 15 July 1756, d. before March 1818; m.1. *Sarah* _____, d. 31 Aug 1814 (data from Eva Mae Davis Martin, g.g.gdau); m.2. *Rebekah* _____.

In 1796, Elijah bought a Bible and wrote in it: "Elijah Brazier his book May the 8th 1796. bought of Phillip Sands. Elijah Brazier was born in the year of our Lord July 15th, 1756." In 1814, he recorded the death of his wife: "Sarah Brazier departed this life the last day of August in the year of our Lord 1814." His widow was named Rebekah (Rebecca).

Elijah is on the 1777 Tax List of Cumberland Co, in the district of Capt Robert Cobb, 100 acres. He had just turned 21, and was near his father, James. On the 1779 Tax list, he had 400 acres. In 1783, he received NC State land grants of 50 and 59 acres on Parker's Creek. (Cumberland Deed Bk 15 p.300; Cumberland Deed Bk 15, p.468)

Cumberland Co, NC Deed Book 7, p.100: 4 Nov 1782, James Brazier of Cumberland Co to Elijah Brazier of Cumberland Co, "that the said James Brazier for and in consideration of the love and affection for my son Elijah Brazier" land in Cumberland County on NE side of NW branch of Cape Fear River, 100a, being the plantation where I now live near where the Earl of Granville's line crosses the River.

/s/ James Brazier

wits: John Pope, Thomas Bogs, Wm Scoggins.

On the 1790 census, Cumberland Co, NC, Elijah Brazier's household contained 2 males over 16 (one of them himself), one male under 16, five females; and three slaves. In the 1800 census (p. 390), four males were in his household, four females, and three slaves (21001-10210-03). In the 1810 census (p.587), three males were in his household, two females, and seven slaves (02001-00110-07). These figures do not altogether fit Elijah's family.

On 19 Jan 1795, he was issued entry permit #1512 for another 50 acres, adjoining his own land. He died in Cumberland County after Feb 1815, when he transferred intervivos 250 acres on Parker's Creek to his son, William, (Book 28, p.170) and 200 acres on the Cape Fear River to his son, Elijah W. (Book 28, p.936), retaining a life interest.

Cumberland Co, NC Deed Book 28, p.936: 23 May 1813, Elijah Brazier of Cumberland Co, NC, to Elijah Wesley Brazier of Cumberland for natural love and affection to my son, land in Cumberland Co, on NE side of NW branch of Cape Fear River, 200a, being the land and plantation joining the land whereon I now live.
/s/ Elijah Brazier
wits: D. Holt, John Flinton.

Cumberland Co, NC Deed Book 28, p.170: 5 Jan 1815, Elijah Brazier of Cumberland Co, NC, to William Brazier for the natural affection that I have for my son William Brazier, land on NE side of NW Branch of Cape Fear River, 250a, it being the land & plantation whereon I now live; beginning on the river bank not far from where the Earl of Granville's line crosses the Cape Fear River thence eastward to Parker's creek to Jacks Branch, Bookers corner, Elijah W. Brazier's corner.
/s/ Elijah Brazier
wits: D. Holt, Elijah W. Brazier.

Cumberland Co, NC Deed Book 28, p.33: 9 Feb 1815, Elijah Brazier of Cumberland Co, NC, to Sarah Blalock & Rebecca Smith for the natural love and affection I have for my two daughters, two Negroes & one feather bed, one cow. First of all, I give my daughter Sarah Blalock one feather bed and one cow. To daughter Rebecca Smith, one Negro boy named Jack and to my two daughters, Sarah Blalock and Rebecca Smith, one Negro boy named Jim.
/s/ Elijah Brazier
wits: Elijah W. Brazier, Daniel Holt.

Considering the flurry of these deeds, we might conjecture that Elijah may have been ill and feeling the imminence of death, and was trying to set his affairs in order. At any rate, he died before 20 March 1818:

Cumberland Co, NC, Inventory and Accounts, 20 March 1818: A list of property sold by the admr of Elijah Brazier, 20th March 1818. Names: Nathan Prince, Thomas Basham, Barnaba Thomas, James Battle, Buswell Rollings, Young Burt, David Stewart, James Burt, David Holt, Nathan Kimball, Charles Blalock [son-in-law], Jones Stephens, Benton Drake, Wiley Womack, Jesse Jones, Daniel McDaniel, Thomas Branch,

Richard Smith [son-in-law], James Booker, John Blalock, Rebeckah Brazier [widow], George Luthar, Rosy Wommack, Owen Dowd, Wiley Jones.

Richard Smith, a son-in-law, bought one lot of books and one crock and coffee(?); Looking glass and three guns; open headed cock and meal bay (?); Table, lumber and ??; scythe and cradle).

From the division of the estate (Book 28, p.133), Virginia Blalock determined these heirs:

Family of Elijah Brazier and Sarah ____:

V9-3864.   c-1. **James Brazier "Jr"**, b. c?1778, when his father was 22 years old (called "Jr" to distinguish him from his grandfather, James Brazier, the Cumberland Carpenter), living in 1789, when he got 250 acres of land from his grandfather; called James "Jr" in some deeds; d. bef. 1806, when deeds show his siblings deeding to their father, Elijah, land that had belonged to James "Jr." (See under Bathsheba Brazier, below.)

V9-3865.   c-2. ***Sarah Anne Brazier,** b. c1780, Cumberland Co, NC; d. c1844, Harrison Co, TX or Jackson Co, AL; m. c1801 **Charles Blalock**,

V9-3866.   c-3. ***Bathsheba (or Barsheba) Brazier,** b. bef. 1785, d. 1841, Lauderdale Co, AL; m. bef. 1814, **John Wesley McDougal**, moved to Lauderdale Co, AL.

V9-3867.   c-4. ***Rebecca Brazier,** b. NC, c1786, d. 1833, Selma, Dallas Co, AL, bur Farmington Bapt Ch cem, Tishomingo Co, MS; m. 17 May 1813, in Cumberland Co, NC, **Richard Smith**

V9-3868.   c-5. ***Elijah Wesley Brazier,** b. c1792, Cumberland Co, NC; m. **Anna Jordan**, b. c1802; moved to Monroe Co, GA; see below.

V9-3869.   c-6. ***William Brazier,** b. 1797, d. c1832. Probably the father of Lucinda Brazier Parks and James E. Brazier of Franklin Co, TN. See Unsolved Questions, above.

Sarah Anne Brazier
and Charles Blalock:

d-2. **Sarah Anne Brazier**, (d/o Elijah and Sarah Brazier), b. c1780, Cumberland Co, NC; d. c1844, Harrison Co, TX or Jackson Co, AL; m. c1800, *Charles Blalock*, b. 2 June 1773; d. 2 June 1856, s/o William Blalock and Lucy Womack. Data from descendant Virginia Blalock. Nine children, all but last born Cumberland Co, NC:

V9-3870. d-1. Lucy Blalock, b. 3 Dec 1802; m. Berry Johnson

V9-3871. d-2. Frances B. "Fanny" Blalock, b. 1804; m. Dr. David Hendon

V9-3872. d-3. James Stuart Blalock, b. 1806, d. 1862; m.1. Nancy Jenkins, (2 ch); m.2. Jane Price, b. 1818, d. 1874 (7 ch)

V9-3873. e-1. William Brazier Blalock, b. 1830, d. 1900; m. Elizabeth Jane Dye, b. 1837, d. 1918

V9-3874. e-2. Mary Francis Blalock, b. 1832, d. 1922; m. Vincent Gray

V9-3875. e-3. Thomas Henry Benton Blalock, b. 1837; m. Anne Albina Turner, b. 1846

V9-3876. e-4. Nancy Vitura Blalock, b. 1838

V9-3877. e-5. Charles H. Blalock, b. 1841

V9-3878. e-6. Sarah A. Blalock, b. & d. 1844

V9-3879. e-7. Emily Jane Blalock, b. 1848, d. 1858

V9-3880. e-8. James A. Blalock, b. 1850, d. 1898

V9-3881. e-9. Lucy Ann Blalock, b. 1855

V9-3882. d-4. William Blalock, b. 1809

V9-3883. d-5. Rebecca Blalock, b. 1811, m. James Sharp

V9-3884. d-6. Elijah Brazier Blalock, b. 23 Aug 1813, d. 1895; m. Susan Catherine Harrison, b. ?, d. 1898

V9-3885. e-1. Francis Blalock, b. 1845, d. 1858

V9-3886. e-2. Simmons Harrison Blalock, b. 1848, d. 1867

V9-3887. e-3. Thomas H. Blalock, b. 1849, d. 1917

V9-3888. e-4. Matilda Texana Blalock, b. 1853, d. 1945

V9-3889. e-5. Charles Richard Blalock, b. 28 July 1854, d. 1898; m. Mary Elizabeth Baker

V9-3890. f-x. Roscoe Conkling Blalock, b. 9 Sep 1881; m. Parmelia Hannah Haughton

V9-3891. g-x. Wyatt Conkling Blalock, b. 12 Feb 1909; m. Cleo Mae Beel

V9-3892. h-x. Virginia Dale Blalock, b. 30 Sep 1945; (12318 Welland Drive, Houston, TX 77031)

V9-3893.	e-6. William B. Blalock, b. 1856
V9-3894.	e-7. Elijah Brazier Blalock, b. 1862, d. 1928; m. Mittie Calloway
V9-3895.	e-8. Lizzie Blalock, b. 1863
V9-3896.	e-9. Jacob Giles Blalock, b. 1864, d. 1881
V9-3897.	d-7. Richard Womack Blalock, b. 22 Dec 1815, d. 1883; m. Emily Catherine Price
V9-3898.	e-1. Charles Stuart Blalock, b. 1840, d. 1895
V9-3899.	e-2. Nancy Blalock, b. 1843
V9-3900.	e-3. Angie Price Blalock, b. 1846, d. 1942
V9-3901.	d-8. Sarah Jane Blalock, b. 1824; m. Harden Blalock
V9-3902.	d-9. Charles Dickens Blalock, b. 12 Dec 1824, Autauga Co, AL, d. 1918; m. Vashti Russell, b. 1829, d. 1899
V9-3903.	e-1. Sarah Francis Blalock, b. 1850
V9-3904.	e-2. John Wesley Blalock, b. 1851
V9-3905.	e-3. Susan Elizabeth Blalock, b. 1853
V9-3906.	e-4. Lucy Margaret Blalock, b. 1855
V9-3907.	e-5. Richard Brazier Blalock, b. 1857
V9-3908.	e-6. Nancy Alice Blalock, b. 1860
V9-3909.	e-7. James William Blalock, b. 1862
V9-3910.	e-8. Charles Elijah Blalock, b. 1862
V9-3911.	e-9. Thomas Blalock, b. 1865
V9-3912.	e-10. Mary Ann Blalock, b. 1867
V9-3913.	e-11. Marshall Manuel Blalock, b. 1869
V9-3914.	e-12. Martha Ellen Blalock, b. 1872

Bathsheba Brazier
and John Wesley McDougal

c-3. **Bathsheba (or Barsheba) Brazier,** (d/o Elijah and Sarah Brazier), b. bef. 1785, Cumberland Co, NC; d. 1841, Lauderdale Co, AL; m. c1800, **John Wesley McDougal Jr**, b. ?, d. 1822, Lauderdale Co, AL, s/o John Wesley McDougal Sr, (1764-1800). This family moved to Lauderdale Co, AL (data from Jeff L. Bott <sandflat@aol.com>)

May 29, 1806: Bathsheba Brazier of Cumberland Co, NC, to Elijah Brazier of Cumberland Co, for $50, land that descended to me upon the death of James Brazier Jr [her brother], it being the land that was given by James Brazier Sr to his grandson in his last will and testament. (Cumberland Co, NC, Deed Book 28, p.169; wits: David Holt, Charles Blalock)

Family of Bathsheba Brazier and John Wesley McDougal:

V9-3915.   d-1. William McDougal,
V9-3916.   d-2. Lucy McDougal, b. _?_, d. 19 Oct 1945, AL; m. 19 Dec
            1829, Lauderdale Co, AL, Stephen R. Moore
V9-3917.   d-3. Joseph McDougal, b. 30 Oct 1809, NC, d. 19 Aug 1856,
            Smith Co, TX, bur McDougal Cem, Tyler, Smith Co., TX,
            age: 46 (GGG Grandfather of Jeff Bott); m. c1830,
            Lauderdale Co, AL, Amira M. McMurry, b. 4 April 1810,
            AL, d. 15 Nov 1864, Smith Co, TX, age 54, d/o James
            McMurry (1774-1858) and Rebecca ____ (1775-1851)
V9-3918.   e-1. John W. McDougal (1833-1873)
V9-3919.   e-2. Rebecca Ann McDougal (1835-1876)
V9-3920.   e-3. James Riley McDougal (1839-1905)
V9-3921.   e-4. Alexander A. McDougal (1839-1908)
V9-3922.   e-5. Henry F. McDougal (1842-1873)
V9-3923.   e-6. Joseph Monroe McDougal (1845-1916)
V9-3924.   e-7. Malinda C. McDougal (1850-1852)
V9-3925.   d-4. Sarah McDougal,
V9-3926.   d-5. Eliza McDougal,
V9-3927.   d-6. John Wesley McDougal III, b. 1812, Cumberland Co, NC,
            d. 6 Sep 1868, Tishomingo Co, MS, age 56, bur Dean
            Cem, Crow's Neck, Paden, Tishomingo Co, MS; m. 13 Nov
            1833, Lauderdale Co, AL, Nancy Vawter, b. 1817, Maury
            Co, TN, d. Feb 1896, Tishomingo Co, MS, age: 79, bur
            Dean Cem, Crow's Neck, Paden, Tishomingo Co, MS
V9-3928.   e-1. Mary Jane McDougal (1834-)
V9-3929.   e-2. Sarah "Sallie" McDougal (1836-)
V9-3930.   e-3. Martha McDougal (1837-1935)
V9-3931.   e-4. John Wesley McDougal IV (1840-1916)
V9-3932.   e-5. James Thomas McDougal (1842-1931)
V9-3933.   e-6. Amanda E. McDougal (1844-1912)
V9-3934.   e-7. Margaret E. McDougal (1851-1944)
V9-3935.   d-6. Sarah McDougal, b. c1815, Cumberland Co, NC

Rebecca Brazier
and Richard Smith

c-4. **Rebecca Brazier,** (d/o Elijah and Sarah Brazier), b. NC, c1786,
d. 1833, Selma, Dallas Co, AL, bur Farmington Bapt Ch cem, Tishomingo
Co, MS; m. 17 May 1813, in Cumberland Co, NC, **Richard Smith**, with
Richard Blalock as bondsman. Richard Smith, b. 1792, d. 1863, was s/o
David Smith and Ann Blalock.

Cumberland Co, NC Deed Book 26, p.191: 25 April 1811, Rebecah Brazier of Cumberland Co, NC, to Elijah Brazier of Cumberland Co, $50, tract of land that descended to Rebecah Brazier by the death of James Brazier (her brother), it being the land that was given by James Brazier Sr to his grandson in his Last Will and Testament. /s/ Rebecah Brazier. wits: John McDougald, Sarah Blalock, Charles Blalock.

Richard's immigrant ancestor, Ezekiel Smith, was born c1717 in Scotland. According to the family legend, he was transported to America for poaching on the king's land. He is believed to have settled in South Carolina (near Charleston?) in 1734.

His son David was born c1740 and fought in the Revolutionary War.

David's son Daniel was born c1760, and he also fought in the Revolutionary War.

Daniel's son Richard was born in North Carolina (?). He moved to Alabama where he lived between two rivers near Selma, Autauga Co, AL.

After Rebecca died, Richard moved with his family about 1834 from Selma, AL, to Farmington, MS, when his son William Richard was eleven or twelve years old. He is supposed to have started this town. He died during the Civil War and is buried at Farmington Baptist Church about three miles east of Corinth, MS. The grave is unmarked now because Union soldiers took some of the gravestones to build a baking oven.

Richard Smith m.2. Mary Hannah Walker. Nine ch: Sarah, Thomas, William Hardy, Matilda, Nancy Rebecca, Lorenzo Benson, Malissa Jane, Cinderella, and Elias Archibald Smith.

Family of Rebecca Brazier and Richard Smith:

V9-3936.   d-1. Wesley Brazier Smith, b. Cumberland Co, NC, 1813, d. after 1882, MS; m. 1839 in Tishomingo Co, MS, Mary Jane Dean (5 ch), b. Iuka, MS, d. Autauga Co, AL

V9-3937.   e-1. Virginia Ann Smith, m. 1873, J. Wiley Davis

V9-3938.   f-1. Luther Wesley Davis, b. 5 May 1888; m. Maude B. Kyser

V9-3939.   g-1. Eva Mae Davis, b. 20 July 1918; m. Ernest Martin

V9-3940.   f-2. Bettie Jan Davis, m. _____ Langston

V9-3941.   d-2. Stephen Douglas Smith, b. 1817; m. Sophie Ball, b. West Point, MS (lived at West Point, MS)

V9-3942.   d-3. William Richard Smith, b. 1823, near Selma, AL

V9-3943.   e-1. William Ira Smith, b. 13 Jan 1840, near Corinth, MS, d. 1909; m. Esther Jane Lynch. Eight ch: Lorena, Daisy, William Ira Jr, Kenneth Eugene, Houston, Charles Galloway, Esther Jane, and Velma Smith.

^{V9}-3944.   e-2. Nancy Ann Smith, b. Feb 1850; m. John W. Mincy
^{V9}-3945.   e-3. Cornelia Elizabeth Smith, b. 1855; m. Frank L.
                George (moved to Honey Grove, Tx)
^{V9}-3946.   d-4. Ann Smith, b. 1819 (lived east of Corinth, MS)
^{V9}-3947.   d-5. John D. Smith, b. 1825, near Selma, Autauga Co, AL, d.
                after 1880; m.1. Elizabeth ____; m.2. in Tishomingo, MS,
                Nancy Blakeney
^{V9}-3948.   d-6. Lucy Smith,

Elijah Wesley Brazier
and Anna Jordan

c-5. **Elijah Wesley Brazier**, (s/o Elijah and Sarah Brazier), b. Cumberland Co, NC, c1792 (58 in 1850, Monroe Co, GA), d. c1853, Stewart Co, GA; m. **Anna Jordan**, b. c1802 (48 in 1850), d. 1880, Stewart Co, GA. (See also sketch of "The Elijah Wesley Brazier Family" in *History of Stewart Co, GA,* p.670).

Cumberland Co, NC Deed Book 28, p.936: 23 May 1813, Elijah Brazier of Cumberland Co, NC, to Elijah Wesley Brazier of Cumberland Co, for natural love and affection to my son, land in Cumberland Co, on NE side of NW branch of Cape Fear River, 200a, being the land and plantation joining the land whereon I now live.
        /s/ Elijah Brazier
wits: D. Holt, John Flinton.

Cumberland Co, NC Deed Book 30, p.148:   March 1818, Elijah Brazier of Cumberland Co, NC, to James Battle of Cumberland Co, $375, land on the NE side of the NE branch of Cape Fear River near the mouth of Parkers Creek, adj William Brazier and Lucy King, 200a.
        /s/ Elijah W Brazier
wits: David Holt, Huckaby. June Term 1818

This last deed would indicate that Elijah Wesley Brazier sold his land on Parker's Creek in Cumberland County about the time his father died and immediately left the area. Most of his children seem to have been born in Georgia in the 1820s.

Family of Elijah Wesley Brazier and Anna Jordan:
^{V9}-3949.   d-1. **John C. Brazier**, b. c1820 (30 in 1850), killed in Battle
                of Ringgold, Georgia, in 1864; m.1. 12 Feb 1843, Monroe
                Co, GA, ***Martha J. Pringle***, b. c1830 (20 in 1850). (Book

A, p.210; see also *37,000 Early GA Marriages*, publ 1975, by Joseph T. Maddox); m.2. 24 Oct 1849 **Pathonio or Parthena (Indian?)**, Upson Co, GA. (*37,000 Early GA Marriages*). Some land records have John indexed erroneously as John E. Brazier, but Virginia Blalock says all the deeds read John C.

V9-3950.   d-2. **Rhoda Ann Brazier** (*Hist. Stewart Co*, has "Anna"), b. 10 March 1825, in Upson Co, GA, d. 6 Dec 1912 in Crockett, Houston Co, TX; m. 26 March 1846, Monroe Co, GA (Book B, p.13), **Leroy Washington Cooper**, b. 16 Oct 1822, Gwinnett Co, GA, d. 25 Oct 1900, Crockett, TX, s/o Lewis and Anna Cooper.

V9-3951.   e-1. Antoinette "Nettie" Cooper, b. 1847

V9-3952.   e-2. Georgia Cooper, b. 6 Dec 1848; m 1867, in Crockett, TX, Harvin Washington Moore, b. 2 May 1832, Athens, Limestone Co, AL, d. 7 Feb 1912, Crockett, Houston Co, TX

V9-3953.   e-3. J. Louis Cooper, b. 1852

V9-3954.   e-4. Leroy Nathaniel Cooper, b. 18 Noc 1855, Griffin, GA, d. Waco, TX

V9-3955.   d-3. *****Elijah Wesley Brazier Jr**, b. in Georgia, 1828 (says *Hist. Stewart Co, GA*, p.670) (23 in 1850), d. 1855; m. 26 Jan 1848, Monroe Co, GA (Book B, p.28), **Amanda Rebecca Bush**, b. 16 July 1829

V9-3956.   d-4. **Cynthia Brazier**, m. 26 Jan 1843, Monroe Co, GA, (Book A, p.209), **Edmund L. (or J. or T.) Davis**, Ch: Charles and James K. Davis.

V9-3957.   d-5. **Martha Brazier**, b. c1830 (20 in 1850, Monroe Co, GA),

V9-3958.   d-6. **William Henry H. Brazier**, b. c1839 (11 in 1850, Monroe Co, GA), was a Captain in Wheeler's Cavalry during Civil War. After the Civil War, Wm H. Brazier moved with his sisters to Union Springs, AL, southeast of Montgomery (*Hist Stew Co*, p.670)

Elijah, the dad, and Wesley, the son, are in the same household in 1850 Monroe Co, GA, census, along with some others.

1850 Census, Monroe Co, GA,

Wesley Brazier,	23, farmer, b. GA, c1727
Amanda R. Brazier,	20
James Brazier,	1
John C. Brazier,	30 [Wesley's brother]

Pertania Brazier,   20 [John C.'s wife]
E.W. Brazier,   58, b. c1792, [fa/o Wesley & s/o Elijah of Cumberland]
Ann Brazier,   48, [wife of Elijah W. Brazier]
Martha Brazier,   20 [Wesley's sister]
Wm. H. H. (Brazier?), 11 [Wesley's brother]

Elijah Wesley Brazier Jr
and Amanda Bush

d-3. **Elijah <u>Wesley</u> Brazier Jr**, (s/o Elijah Wesley Brazier and Anna Jordan), b. in Georgia, 1828 (says *Hist. Stewart Co, GA*, p.670) (23 in 1850), d. 1855; m. 26 Jan 1848, Monroe Co, GA (Book B, p.28), **Amanda Rebecca Bush**, b. 16 July 1829, Monroe Co, GA, d. 11 Feb 1896, Monroe Co, GA (1829-1898 says gravestone at Fredonia Congregational Church), d/o Jackson Bush and Lavinia Brantley.

After Elijah died young, Amanda moved back to Monroe Co, GA to be with her father. Amanda m.2. 1858, Monroe Co, GA (Book B, p.102), Wilbur H. Bankston (will of W.H. Bankston, dated 24 Feb 1888, proved 10 Dec 1888, names wife, Amanda, and adds E.W. Brazier [Elijah Wesley III] in a codicil. Amanda is buried beside Wm. H. Bankston and identified as "wife of.") Wesley and Amanda had 3 children; Amanda and Wm Bankston had 5: H.E.; J. Bush; Stanton Brantley; William Benjamin; and William Wallace. (*History of Stewart Co, GA*, p.671)

V9-3959.   e-1. **James Berrian Brazier**, b. 6 July 1849, Monroe Co, GA, d. 4 March 1935, Stewart Co, GA; James Berrian Brazier returned to Stewart Co, where on 26 June 1873, he m. **Mrs. Virginia Serena Smith**, widow of Henry Smith, who was killed in the war, d/o John Smith and Serena L. Williams. Virginia was born 22 June 1848, Stewart Co, GA, d. 10 April 1933, Stewart Co, GA.

V9-3960.   f-1. **Maggie Willie Brazier**, b. 5 April 1874; m. **W.E. Holton,**

V9-3961.   f-2. **John Wesley Brazier**, b. 4 Oct 1875, d. 11 Feb 1957

V9-3962.   f-3. **Benjamin Hinton Brazier**, b. 2 Jan 1879, lived in Charlotte, NC

V9-3963.   f-4. **Serena Amanda Brazier**, b. 26 Dec 1880; m. **C.C. Sapp**, of Newton, GA

V9-3964.   f-5. infant son **Brazier**, b. 16 Nov 1882, d. 11 Dec 1882

V9-3965.   f-6. **Jamie Evelyn Brazier**, b. 2 Feb 1884; m. **Howard Holton**, Lived Camilla GA. Jamie Brazier Holton was one of the informants for sketch in *History of Stewart Co, GA*.

V9-3966.   f-7. **Mary Virginia Brazier**, b. 22 March 1886, d. 7 March 1914; m. 16 April 1910, ***Dr. Melton Walton***,

V9-3967.   e-2. **Lucia Ann Lavincia Brazier**, b. 1 Dec 1850, d. 31 Aug 1933, in Texas; m. ***Mark McFall***, moved to Texas.

V9-3968.   e-3. **Elijah Wesley Brazier, III**, b. 12 Feb 1854, Stewart Co, GA, d. 13 June 1924, Lamar Co, GA; m.1. 23 Dec 1875, Monroe Co, GA (Book C, p.385), ***Emma Owen***, (1 son), b. 1854, d. 1924; m.2. 23 Dec 1878, Monroe Co, GA (Book D, p.307), ***Sarah "Sallie" Sappington***, b. 1855, d. 1911

V9-3969.   f-1. **Luther Brazier**, b. 22 Jan 1877, d. 5 May 1953

V9-3970.   f-2. **Stella R. Brazier**, b. 29 Sep 1879, d. March 1950

V9-3971.   f-3. **John Ellis Brazier**, b. 29 March 1882, d. 29 March 1942

V9-3972.   f-4. **Vallie Brazier**, b. 17 Aug 1885; m. ***John Stallings***,

30. ELIJAH BRAZIER,
Brother? of James Brazier,
of Cumberland Co, NC

a-2. **Elijah Brazier**, (very speculative: b. 20 April 1726, d. 1790, Cumberland Co, NC). The records just about make it necessary that we posit a brother, Elijah, for James Brazier of Cumberland Co, NC.

Elijah Brasher, b. 1726, d. 1790, would be just the right age to be a brother of James Brazier who d. Cumberland Co, NC, 1789. I've always thought that James had to have a brother named Elijah.

Will of Elijah Brazier, dated 1790, Cumberland Co, NC, names children Elijah Jr and Laban; grandchildren James and Leah Brazier. (ref: *Old N.C. Wills, 1760-1800*, research reported by Lois Breshears Cooper, of Hobbs, NM.)

Note that William Brazier, s/o James Brazier of Cumberland, also named a son Laban in his will dated 20 Sep 1813, in Surry Co, NC. And both this Elijah and James of Cumberland had grand-daughters named Leah in their wills.

This Elijah is definitely not the Elijah who was s/o James and Sarah Brazier, of Cumberland Co, NC. 1790 Heads of Household census, Cumberland Co, NC: **Elijah Braser**, 2 males 16+, 1 male 0-16, 5 fem, and 3 slaves. This man apparently has a son born before 1774, one born after 1774, a wife and four daughters. Those numbers do not exactly fit the family.

This is not **Elijah Brazier**, b. 15 July 1756, d. before March 1818 (data from Eva Mae Davis Martin, g.g.gdau); transferred land he had gotten in James's estate, intervivos to sons, William and Elijah Wesley Brazier; m.1. *Sarah* _____, d. 31 Aug 1814; m.2. *Rebekah* _____. This family is accounted for in records of Cumberland Co, NC, and Monroe and Stewart Co, GA.

Nor is he **Elijah Brazier**, s/o William Brazier, s/o James of Cumberland. That Elijah is well accounted for in Franklin Co, TN.

Elijah Brazier, b. 1726

A beginning of a family group sheet for this Elijah, based on his will and the 1790 census of Cumberland Co, NC:

Family of Elijah Brazier, b. 1726, d. 1790 (rather speculative):

V9-3973.   b-1. ***Elijah Brazier Jr**, b. c?1750; He's 70-80 in 1830 census, Blount Co, AL; 80-90 in 1840 census, Jackson Co, AL, in hh of Elijah Brazier, [III].

V9-3974.   b-2. **Laban Brazier**,

V9-3975.   b-3. **(son) Brazier**, d. bef. 1790

V9-3976.   c-1. **James Brazier**,

V9-3977.   c-2. **Leah Brazier**,

Elijah Brazier, Jr, b. c1750

b-1. **Elijah Brazier Jr**, b. c?1750; He's 70-80 in 1830 census, Blount Co, AL; 80-90 in 1840 census, Jackson Co, AL, in hh of Elijah Brazier, [III].

V9-3978.   c-1. **(son) Brazier**, b. 1774 or before (over 16 in 1790).

V9-3979.   c-2. ***Elijah Brazier, Sr [III]**, b. after 1774 (under 16 in 1790). ??could be Elijah Brazier, b. NC, 1776, who had a son, Elijah Brazier, b. SC, 1800.

V9-3980.   c-3. dau **Brazier**, (??Rebekka Brazier, m. in Madison Co, AL)

Elijah Brazier, III, b. 1776

c-2. ***Elijah Brazier, Sr, [III]**, b. NC, 1776, (under 16 in 1790), (74 in 1850, Jackson Co, AL, in hh of son, Elijah Brazier, Jr.)

V9-3981.   d-1. **John Brashers**, b. c1798, (20-30 in 1830, Blount Co, AL, with two sons in his household: 20001-00001), d. c Aug 1860, Marshall Co, AL; m. *Harriet Louiza* _____. In 1850, they were living in District22, Marshall Co, AL

    In 1870, the mother, **Harriet Louiza Brazier**, is head of household with son, William Brazier, b. 1855, AL, at home. Above her (hh #104-104) is a widow named **Julia A. Brazier**, b. 1837, AL, with children **Mary L. Brazier**, b. 1861, AL; and **Martha A. Brazier**, b. 1864, AL, probably widow of a son killed in the Civil War.

V9-3982.   e-1. **Jonathan D. Brashers/Brazier**, b. 1828, Blount Co, AL (0-5 in 1830); m. *Mourning E. Brazier*, b. 1831, AL

V9-3983.   f-1. **Parthena A. Brazier**, b. Sept 1850, Marshall Co, AL

V9-3984.	e-2. **son Brashers/Brazier**, b. 1829 (0-5 in 1830)
V9-3985.	e-3. **John G. Brazier**, b. 1832, Blount Co, AL
V9-3986.	e-4. **Utha Brazier**, b. 1834
V9-3987.	e-5. **James Brazier**, b. 1836
V9-3988.	e-6. **Thomas Brazier**, b. 1837
V9-3989.	e-7. **Narcissa C. Brazier**, b. 1839
V9-3990.	e-8. **Joseph G. Brazier**, b. 1840
V9-3991.	e-9. **Harriett L. Brazier**, b. 1842
V9-3992.	e-10. **Rebecca B. Brazier**, b. 1848
V9-3993.	e-11. **Lucinda Brazier**, b. June 1850
V9-3994.	e-12. **Van R. Brazier**, b. 1854
V9-3995.	e-13. **William Brazier**, b. 1855.
V9-3996.	d-2. ***Elijah Brashers/Brazier, Jr [IV]**, b. 1800 (20-30 in 1830, Blount Co, AL; 40-50 in 1840, Jackson Co, AL; 50 in 1850, Jackson Co, AL), d. 1868, Jackson Co, AL; m.1. _____ (probably) *Hart*, who d. c1842; m.2. *Elizabeth "Betsy" Stephens*, Elijah had 15 children; see separate chapter.
V9-3997.	d-3. ?**Thomas Brazier**, b. SC
V9-3998.	d-4. **Rebecca Brazier**, b. SC

Unaccounted for data:

Elijah William Brazier, m. 11 Jan 1815, in Cumberland Co, NC, *Macon Edwards*. They had a son:
Groves Middleton (or Madison) Brazier,

Will of Nancy Edwards (?what county?) names her daughter, Makon Brazier and grandson, Groves Middleton (or Madison) Brazier, who appears in Chatham Co, NC records up to about 1850. Groves was also associated with Orange/Chatham Co: Chatham Co, Deeds Index (Index doesn't have dates, and "to/from" notes are absent from some):

Book D, p.305: Tho. Brazor to Joshua Hudley
Book H, p.72: John Brazure to Joshua Hudley
Book S, p.393: Elijah Brazier/John Partridge "not ret'd"
Book W, p.149: Samuel Brazhire/ Jacob Brooks
Book AE, p.355: Groves M. Brazaire/ Jas. Ausley
Book AJ, p.130: G.M. Brazier & wife/ Jas. D. Pullins

William Brazier, m. 24 Dec 1815, Chatham Co, NC, *Rebeccah Wamack*
Mrs. Rebecca Brazier, m. 1827, Cumberland Co, NC, John Woodal

Ancestors of Jo Ann B. Hall

William Brazier, b. 20 Aug 1814, prob. NC, d. 14 Sep 1874, Maury Co, TN; m. 1836, Wilcox Co, AL, **Cassy Angeline Offutt**. They lived in Wilcox Co, AL, where four children were born; about 1850, they moved to Maury Co, TN, where Cassy died; William m.2. 7 Aug 1852, **Susan Elizabeth Barker**, d/o Alexander Barker and Margaret Dodson.

V9-3999.   x-1. **William Edwin Brazier**, b. 1840, Wilcox Co, AL, d. 16 July 1897, Maury Co, TN; m.1. 1866, **Laura Bane Huey**, b. 1850, Maury Co, TN, d. 1931, Denton, TX, d/o James Henry Huey, b. 1 June 1812, Maury Co, TN, d. Jan 1892, Collins Co, TX; m.2. 23 May 1841 [***error: a man wouldn't marry 2nd when 1 year old] , **Elizabeth Parsons Moore**, b. 1816, NC, d. 23 Aug 1893, Collins Co, TX.

V9-4000.   y-1. **Charles Huey Brazier**, b. 2 Nov 1883, Columbia, TN, d. 16 Dec 1964, Ft. Worth, TX; m.1. 2 Aug 1906, **Ombra Dean King**, b. 23 Oct 1883, Pilot Point, TX, d. 21 Feb 1957, Ft. Worth, TX, d/o Joseph Hawkins King, b. 14 June 1856, Madison Co, AL, d. 8 Jan 1929, Ft. Worth TX; m.2. 23 Jan 1883 [***error: a man wont marry 2nd before he's born], **Anna Jane Phipps**, b. 20 Oct 1861, Madison Co, AL, d. 30 June 1935, Ft. Worth, TX

V9-4001.   z-1. **Jo Ann Brazier**, b. 8 Oct 1923, Ft. Worth, TX; m.1. **Nathan B. Williams**, m.2. **Ralph F. Hall**, b. 17 Feb 1927, Lawrence, KS

Jo Ann B. Hall (in 1986) 123 Cooper Circle, Oak Ridge, TN 37830

from Robert E. Reed, P.O.Box 97, Garberville, CA 95440 (in 1986) to Dan Yarbrough:

James Brazier, m. 12 Jan 1820, Maury Co, TN, **Rebecca Pace**,

Corintha Brazier, m. 28 Oct 1858, Maury Co, TN, **Elisha Barker**, s/o Alexander and Margeret (Dodson) Barker

V9-4002.   "**Robert H.B. Brazier**, (b. England, d. 5 Jan 1837, Raleigh, NC), cartographer and civil engineer, was born of unknown parentage in Great Britain, where he received his professional training ... following a severe ice storm during the Christmas holidays of 1836, Brazier fell from a pair of high steps and died of the effects in Raleigh. He was survived by his wife, Rachel, and his young son, James Henderson Brazier, both of whom were members of the Episcopal Church. Brazier appears to have been an Anglican...." (See article "Robert H.B. Brazier" in *Dictionary of NC Biography*, ed. Wm. S. Powell, Vol. I, A-C,)

[V9]-4003.   1. **Charles Henry Brazier**.   The death of Charles Henry Brazier at Hillsboro, NC, on 11 Sep 1821, "infant son of Robert H. Brazier of this city" was reported in the Raleigh *Register*, 21 Sep 1821.

[V9]-4004.   2. **James Henderson Brazier**, "young son" in 1837.

31. ELIJAH BRAZIER Sr, of Jackson Co, AL

This one's dates don't match up to be son or grandson of James Brazier of Cumberland Co, NC. He's one of the reasons I think we have to posit a brother named Elijah for James Brazier of Cumberland. This branch of the family seems to like naming the first son for the father, rather than the grandfather or a favorite brother.

Background Records

c-x. **Elijah Brazier Sr**, b. NC, c1776 (age 74 in 1850 Census, Jackson Co, AL), is a generation too young to be a s/o a-2. Elijah Brazier, b. c1726; he's a better age to be a grandson and, for want of better information, I'm going to number him that way. This Elijah Sr had a son, Elijah Jr. A sketch of the life of Elijah Sr was included in the biography of his son, Elijah Jr, in a *History of North and West Texas*, p. 594:

"Elijah Brashear [Jr], was a South Carolina settler and went into Jackson county in early life, was a poor man with a large family and lived off his labor on the farm. He was born in South Carolina and died soon after our subject's birth. His [second] wife was Bettie Stephens...

"By his first marriage, Elijah Brashear, Junior, was the father of
- Bettie, who married Ezekiel Faulkner, died in Alabama;
- Sarah, died in Alabama as the wife of James Colbert and like her sister left a family;
- Nancy;
- Linda, wife of Tom Fears, who died in Alabama leaving a family;
- Martha, wife of Abe Greenlee, died in Tennessee leaving a family;
- Velina, died in Tennessee, leaving a family.

"Betsy Stephens was his second wife and her children were:
- William, who died during the war;
- Ellis, who also passed away in the Confederate service;
- Arminda, who died in Alabama;
- George W.;

- Rebecka, wife of Joe Fears, died in Illinois, leaving a family;
- Louisa C., Mrs. A.J. Messers, of Montague County;
- Elijah, our subject; and
- Solomon.

(data from Jimmie Ryan): Elijah lived on land in Jackson Co, AL, which had belonged to John B. Stephens. We know when Solomon Stephens marries Nancy Brazier, he is in the NW corner of the property. Velina Brazier has the SE and SW corner of the property, and Elisa Brazier (either widow of Elijah, b. 1800's, or Elizabeth Brazier, oldest child of Elijah, b. 1800) has the NE corner — this land will later transfer to sons: George Washington, Elijah "Lidge," and Solomon Brazier.

The property which Elijah "Lidge" Brazier, III, bought in Blount Co, AL, was from Rebecca' family, and was a wedding gift.

George Washington Brazier's land was a wedding gift from James Belton Loveless, Ida's father, and was a part of his mothers farm he received after her death.

His sister Mary had already married William Freeman of Cullman and moved to his family compound by 1880.

This land was in the northern section of the county. Gen. Sherman, in his march to the sea, went through here, burning everything and destroying crops. The family was left devastated. Those in the southern part of the county were hit less hard. The younger children of the family went, after about 1866, to live with them.

Elijah Brazier Sr is with his son or grandson, Elijah Brazier Jr, in the following censuses:

1830 census, Blount Co, AL page 35/36:
Elijah Brashers: 0000000001-000000001 (age 70-80, b. 1750s)
Elijah Brashers, Jr: 00001-12001 (age 20-30, b. 1800)
John Brashers: 20001-00001 (age 20-30)
1840 Census, Jackson Co, AL: p.28 Elijah Brazeer (01000010001-111201) old man in H/H, 80-90, b. 1750's —

1850 Census, Jackson Co, AL: p.88, #534

Elijah Brasier [Jr],	50, b. SC, c1800, farmer
Elizabeth Brazier	22, b. c1828, AL
Nancy Brazier	18, b. c1832, AL
Hart Brazier	15, b. c1835, AL, laborer
Marha [sic] Brazier, f	13, b. c1837, AL
William Brazier	7, b. c1843, AL
Jane Brazier	4, b. c1846, AL
Ellis Brazier	3, b. c1847, AL

| George W. Brazier | 1, b. c1849, AL |
| Elijah Brazier [Sr] | 74, b. c1776, North Carolina, cannot read or write |

1860 Census, Jackson Co, AL: p.331 #451

Elijah Brazier [Jr],	50 [?! should be 60], b. NC
William Brazier	17, b. c1843, AL
Jane Brazier	15, b. c1845, AL
Ellis Brazier	12, b. c1848, AL
George Brazier	10, b. c1850, AL
Lorenza Brazier, f	4, b. c1856, AL [misreading for Louisa]
Elijah Brazier [III]	2, b. c1858, AL

[one more child: Solomon Brazier, b. May 1861]

Elijah Brazier Jr died in the 1860's. "His wife, Miss Betsy Stephens, brought the children to years of maturity and passed away at the old home in December 1884" (*Hist No & West Texas*). The four youngest children are in the household of William and Elizabeth Messer in 1870; Elizabeth, the older daughter, m.2. 3 Feb 1869, (second wife of) William Messer.

William Messer, m.1. Sarah Elizabeth _____, b. 1824, AL, d. 1862-68; they had children:

▸ James Messer, 1843;
▸ John W. Messer, 1845;
▸ Mary Messer, 1847;
▸ Jesse Messer, 1848;
▸ Allen J. Messer, b. March 1850, m. 4 Jan 1871, Louisa C. Brazier, d/o Elijah Brazier Jr and Betsy Stephens;
▸ David Messer, 1859;
▸ Susanna Messer, 1855;
▸ Martha J. Messer, 1857;
▸ Sarah Messer, 1860; and
▸ Louisa Messer, 1862.

1870 Census, Jackson Co, AL: p. 116b, #686,

William Messer,	52, b. TN, Big Coon Post Office:
Elizabeth,	47, b. AL,
—[Messer children; see above]	
George Brasher	21, b. AL, c1849, laborer
Louisa C. Brasher	15, b. AL, c1855
Elijah Brasher	11, b. AL, c1858
Solomon Brasher	9, b. AL, c1861

John Stephens, b. 1666, d. 1700; m. Elizabeth _____. (4 ch)
1. John Stephens,

2. Charles Stephens,
3. Elizabeth Stephens,
4. Jeremiah Stephens, b. 1689, d. 1760; m. _____, (5 ch)
    1. *Samuel Stephens,
    2. Adam Stephens,
    3. William Stephens,
    4. Jeremiah Stephens, Jr,
    5. John Stephens,

Samuel Stephens, b. _?_, d. 30 Oct 1778. Enlisted as a private in Capt Nathaniel Fox's 6th Virginia Regiment, of the Continental Forces, on 15 Jan 1777. Late that same year, he became ill, and died on 30 Oct 1778. He and his spouse had 3 ch.

1. John Stephens, b. _?_, d. 22 Oct 1810
2. Daniel Stephens, b. _?_, d. c1833
3. *Josiah Stephens, Sr,, b. 1770, NC; d. 26 June 1848, Jackson Co, AL; m. Nancy Vann, b. 1772, d. 21 Sept 1857, Oran, Palo Pinto Co, TX, d/o Luke Vann.
    1. William Stephens, (possible parent of Betsy Stephens)
    2. Josiah Stephens, Jr, (land adjoined Elijah's in Jackson Co)
    3. Ellis Stephens,

In 1812, Josiah Sr and Nancy were living in Tennessee, where he entered the War of 1812, on 12 Dec 1812, under command of Capt George Carpenter's Company of the Tennessee and served until Feb 1813.

After the war, Josiah helped cut a road in the service of Andrew Jackson, which ran from Columbia, TN, through Muscle Shoals, AL, and then diagonally across Mississippi, to Madisonville, Louisiana. This road was called "Jackson's Military Road," and was built between 1816 and 1820.

In 1850, Nancy (Vann) Stephens, 78 (b. c1772) was living with her son, William Stephens, in Jackson Co, AL (Jackson Co, AL, census, p. 127a). William is a candidate to be parent of Miss Betsy (Stephens) Brazier.

Elijah Brazier Jr and Betsy Stephens

c-x. **Elijah Brazier [Jr]**, b. SC, c1800 (age 50 in 1850, Jackson Co, AL); d. 1860-70,(3 Feb 1869, Jackson Co, AL, p.711); m.1. _____ (probably _____ **Hart**, d/o James Hart, who lived four or five farms upfrom Elijah in 1830); m.2. c1842, **Elizabeth "Betsy" Stephens**, b. c1824; d. Dec 1884.

Elijah Bradsher counted in 1830 census of Blount Co, AL, p.17: 00001-12001.

Elijah Brazeer was counted in 1840 Census of Jackson Co, AL, p.28, 01000010001-111201. The man 80-90 is believed to be his grandfather, Elijah Brazier, b. 1750s.

Elijah Brazier was counted in 1850 Census of Jackson Co, AL, p.88, #534. His father, Elijah, b. 1776, is in his household, age 74.

Elijah Brazier was counted in 1860 Census of Jackson Co, AL, p.331, #451.

He died in Jackson Co, AL, c1868. He had 15 children, by two wives:

Family of Elijah Brazier Jr and his first wife, _____: (from Census and *History of North and West Texas*; some data collected by Dan Yarbrough).

V9-4005.   d-1. ***Elizabeth Brazier,** b. AL, c1822 (28 in 1850 Jackson), d. AL; m.1. 20 March 1847, **Ezekiel Faulkner**, "by W.H. Laurence, JP (Morgan Co, AL, Marriage Records, Bk A, p.527); m.2. 4 Aug 1864 (Jackson Co, AL, p.711), **William Messer**, b. c1823?.

V9-4006.   d-2. **Linda Brazier**, b. 1825 in Madison, AL, and died in childbirth, 5 April 1845 in Jackson Co, AL; m. **Thomas W. Fears**, c1844 in Jackson Co, AL, b. 1824 in Scottsboro, Jackson Co, AL, and died bef. 1900 in Jobe, Oregon Co, MO, son of Jacob Fears and Aisley Holt.

V9-4008.   e-1. Johnathan Elijah Fears, (twin), b. 5 Apr 1845, Jackson, AL; d. 16 May 1904, Union, Pike, IN; m. Sarah E. _____; b. 1858, IN,

V9-4009.   e-2. Elias Fears, (twin), b. 5 Apr 1845, Jackson, AL; d. 1891, Bedford, TN.

V9-4010.   d-3. ***Sarah Brazier**, b. AL, c1823; m. **James Colbert**, b. GA, c1816; d. AL.

V9-4011.   d-4. ***Nancy Brazier,** b. 3 May 1831, AL; d. 20 Jan 1909, Sunset, Montague Co, TX; m. 13 Oct 1851, (Jackson Co, AL, p.41), **Solomon S. "Dick" Stephens**, b. 25 June 1833, Jackson Co, AL; d. 23 July 1915, Sunset, TX. Solomon Stephens was a nephew of Betsy Stephens, second wife of Elijah Brazier Jr, Nancy's father. See list of children below.

V9-4012. d-5. **Velina Hart Brazier,** b. AL, c1835 (Hart = 15 in 1850 Jackson), may be the person who died in Jackson Co, AL, before 1870, of wounds suffered in the Civil War. Velina came to own "Elisa" Brazier's original land patent, Certificate #3167, which was incorporated into homestead certificates 29033 and 30019, which represent the SW¼ of NE¼, Sec 5, T3S, R5E, and SE¼ of NW¼, Sec 5, T3S, R5E, Huntsville Principal Meridian. Bordering parcels are in the names of Ellis Stephens and John F. Precise. (Thanks to Jimmie Ryan for the data.)

V9-4013. d-6. **Martha Brazier,** b. AL, c1837 (13 in 1850 Jackson), d. TN; m. *Abel "Abe" Greenlee,* (Franklin Co, TN Marriages: Abel Greenlee to Martha Brazier, by John Nugent, J.P., 3 March 1853)

V9-4014. ?d-7.? **Mary Ann Brazier**, m. 31 March 1869, *F.M. Medcalf,* (Jackson Co, AL, p.738)

Family of Elijah Brazier Jr and Bettie Stephens:

V9-4015. d-8. **William Brazier,** b. AL, 1843, first child of Bettie Stephens, Elijah's second wife; d. 27 March 1864, Rock Island Arsenal, Rock Island Prison Barracks, Rock Island, IL.

V9-4016. d-9. ***Amanda Jane Brazier,** b. AL, 1846, d. 1899, Jackson Co, AL; m. 4 Aug 1864 (Jackson Co, AL, p.288), *Andrew Worthen,*

V9-4017. d-10. **Ellis Brazier,** b. AL, 1847; d. in Civil War 16 Dec 1863, from wounds he sustained in battle; Noted in family tradition that he died as he was walking home to Alabama from prisoner of war camp after Civil War. Bur: 16 Dec 1863, Section 0 Site 83 Camp Chase Confederate Cemetery, Columbus, Franklin Co, OH. He was counted in Elijah's household in 1850 and 1860, Jackson Co, AL.

V9-4018. d-11. ***George Washington Brazier/Brashear,** b. AL, 18 Jan 1849, d. 4 Sept 1907, TX; m. 4 April 1884 (Jackson Co, AL), *Ida Lee Loveless,* living in Montague Co, TX in 1900

V9-4019. d-12. ***Rebecca Brazier,** b. June 1853, d. 28 April 1911, Saline Co, IL; m. 18 Jan 1870 (Jackson Co, AL), *Joseph Henry Fears,* b. 1853. Great-grandparents of Bill J. Fears <bjf@grnco.net>

V9-4020. d-13. ***Louise C. Brazier,** b. 12 May 1855, d. 22 June 1913; m. 4 Jan 1871 (Jackson Co, AL, p.948), *Allen J. Messer,*

b. March 1850, s/o William Messer and his first wife, Sarah Elizabeth _____. William Messer's second wife was Elizabeth Brazier, Louisa's oldest half-sister.

V9-4021.   d-14. **Elijah Brazier, [III],** b. 1 Aug 1858, d. 19 May 1915; m. 2 Dec 1877 (Jackson Co, AL, p.188), **Rebecca Cornelison,**

V9-4022.   d-15. **Solomon Brazier,** b. May 1861, Jackson Co, AL; m. 11 Jan 1885 (Jackson Co, AL, Bk ?, p.458), **Martha S. Precise,**

David R. Precise, age 18 (b. c1837, Jackson Co, AL), and Robert P. Precise, age 18 (b. c1837, Jackson Co, AL), both enrolled 6 Sep 1863 as privates in Co A, First Independent Videttes Cavalry, Jackson Co, AL. Relationship to Martha, if any, is unknown. John F. Precise held homestead 29092 in Jackson Co, AL, 1 Dec 1859, borders land of Velina Brazier, Solomon Brazier's half-brother.

ELIZABETH BRAZIER and EZEKIAL FAULKNER

d-1. ***Elizabeth Brazier,** b. AL, c1822 (28 in 1850 Jackson), d. AL; m.1. 20 March 1847, **Ezekiel Faulkner,** "by W.H. Laurence, JP (Morgan Co, AL, Marriage Records, Bk A, p.527); m.2. (at age 42) 4 Aug 1864 (Jackson Co, AL, p.711), **William Messer,** b. c1823?, s/o Jacob Messer and Sarah "Sallie" _____. William was in 1st AL Cavalry, C.S.A. with his two sons, John W. and Jesse, and his brother, Henry A.J. "Jack" Messer.

Children of Elizabeth Brazierand Ezekial Faulkner:
V9-4023.   e-1. William W. Faulkner, b. 1849, Limestone Co, AL; m. Elizabeth _____.
V9-4024.   e-2. Sarah E. Faulkner, b. 1851, Limestone Co, AL,
V9-4025.   e-3. Mary Jane Faulkner, b. 1852, Limestone Co, AL,
V9-4026.   e-4. Thomas F. Faulkner, b. 1854, Limestone Co, AL,
V9-4027.   e-5. Lucinda Faulkner, b. 1858, Limestone Co, AL,

SARAH BRAZIER and JAMES COLBERT

d-2. **Sarah Brazier,** b. Al, c1828, d/o Elijah Brazier Jr and his first wife, d. AL; m. 27 April 1843, in Orin, Madison Co, AL, **James Samuel Colbert,** b. 1828, Franklin Co, TN, d. Madison Co, AL, s/o James Colbert and Holly Burke. They are in the 1870 Census of Jackson Co, AL, #15. Their land was in T6 R5.

V9-4028.   e-1. Malissa Colbert, b. c1852; m. Jacob W. Whorton, b. c1853
V9-4029.   e-2. Velina Colbert, b. c1853
V9-4030.   e-3. Solomon M. Colbert, b. c1856; m. 27 Jan 1884, in Jefferson Co, MS, Francis Smith
V9-4031.   e-4. Martha Colbert, b. 22 April 1859, Jackson Co, AL, d. 23 March 1944, Royal Oak, MI; m. 27 Jan 1878, in Madison, AL, Hiram James White, b. 19 April 1855, Cherokee, AL, d. 13 Dec 1913, Crawford Co, AR.
V9-4032.   e-5. Susan Colbert, b. April 1860, Jackson Co, AL
V9-4033.   e-6. Caroline Colbert, b. c1863, Woodsville, Jackson Co, AL
V9-4034.   e-7. William Colbert, b. c1865, Woodsville, Jackson Co, AL
V9-4035.   e-8. John C. Colbert, b. c1866, Woodsville, Jackson Co, AL, d. 13 April 1947, Madison Co, AL; m. Fannie Jane Gurley, b. 8 March 1872, d. 1 Aug 1933

NANCY BRAZIER and SOLOMON S. STEPHENS

d-3. **Nancy Brazier**, d/o Elijah Brazier Jr and his first wife, was born 3 May 1831, AL; d. 20 Jan 1909, Sunset, Montague Co, TX, bur Denver Cem, Sunset, Montague Co, TX; m. 13 Oct 1851, **Solomon S. "Dick" Stephens**, b. 25 June 1833, Jackson Co, AL; d. 23 July 1915, Sunset, TX, s/o Ellis Stephens, who held the homestead next to Elijah Brazier's original homestead in Jackson Co, AL. Solomon was a nephew to Elizabeth "Bettie" Stephens, Elijah's second wife.

Solomon and Nancy were H/H #309, in the 1900 Census of Montague Co, Texas, p.2478, pct #8. They had been married 50 years. Both are buried Denver Cem. 7 miles northeast of Sunset, Montague Co, TX.

Family of Solomon S. "Dick" Stephens and Nancy Brazier:
V9-4036.   e-1. Henry H. Stephens, b. Oct 1853, Jackson Co, AL; raised family in Fayetteville, AR; m. Nov 1874, Jackson Co, AL, Mary F. Fowler, b. 1858, AL
V9-4037.   e-2. John Wesley Stephens, b. 10 July 1854, Jackson Co, AL, d. Sep 1930, Lawton, Comanche Co, OK; m. 9 Aug 1883, Montague Co, TX, Cassandra B. Caswell, b. 4 March 1864, Magnolia, Columbia Co, AR, d. 24 Jan 1919, Sunset, Montague Co, TX
V9-4038.   e-3. Joseph Stephens, b. 1858, Jackson Co, AL
V9-4039.   e-4. Mary Jane Stephens, b. 28 May 1860, Jackson Co, AL; d. 3 Dec 1921; m. William Caswell

^{V9}-4040.   e-5. Solomon Stephens, Jr, b. 1863, Jackson Co, AL; d. Harmon Co, OK, unmarried.

^{V9}-4041.   e-6. William B. "Billie" Stephens, b. 19 June 1866, Jackson Co, AL; d. 3 Aug 1927, Sunset, Montague Co, TX; m. 29 Dec 1889, in Jackson Co, AL, Sophia Ann Brewer

^{V9}-4042.   e-7. Andrew Jackson "Pete" Stephens, b. Feb 1869, Jackson Co, AL; d. 1964, Hale Center, TX; m. Sally Caswell

^{V9}-4043.   e-8. Lillie Elizabeth "Betty" Stephens, b. 1871, Jackson Co, AL; d. Sunset, Montague Co, TX

AMANDA JANE BRAZIER and ANDREW WORTHEN

d-9. **Amanda Jane Brazier,** (d/o Elijah Brazier Jr and Elizabeth "Betsy" Stephens, his second wife), b. AL, 1846, d. 1899, Jackson Co, AL; m. 4 Aug 1864, (Jackson Co, AL, p.288), (second wife of) *Andrew Jackson Worthen*, b. c1828, Jackson Co, AL, d. there July 1879, s/o David Benton Worthen and Levisa _____. Both Amanda and Andrew bur Sanders Mill Creek Cem, Jackson Co, AL. They are #544, p.106 in the 1870 Census, Jackson Co, AL. Andrew Worthen's children by his first marriage included: George, 1848; Eleanor, 1849; Malinda F., 1852; Malissa R., 1854; Sinia C., 1856; James M., 1858; William A., 1860; and Andrew J., 1862.

Family of Andrew Worthen and Amanda Jane Brazier:

^{V9}-4044.   e-1. Mildred Sophronia Worthen, b. c1865, Jackson Co, AL; m. Joseph M. Sanders.

^{V9}-4045.   e-2. John Spellman Worthen, b. c1867, Jackson Co, AL, d. c1923, TX; m. 16 Oct 1887 (in the home of her parents) Josephine Cox, b. 8 June 1870, Franklin Co, TN, d. 19 June 1961, Dallas, TX, bur Grove Hill Cem, Dallas, TX, d/o Alexander Cox and Polliann Thomas

^{V9}-4046.   f-1. Estill Odell Worthen, b. 28 May 1909, near Denver, Montague Co, TX, d. 18 Sep 1997, Van Zandt Co, TX, bur Grove Hill Cem, Dallas, TX; m. 10 Feb 1931, in Dallas, TX, Gladys Rosa Lobb, b. 9 Oct 1911, London, England, d/o Frederick Henry Lobb and Lucy Mary Ann Elliston. On 19 Feb 1942, Gladys was naturalized in U.S. Dist Court of North Texas.

^{V9}-4047.   f-2. William Albert Worthen,

^{V9}-4048.   f-3. Mary Jane Worthen,

^{V9}-4049.   f-4. Ettie Worthen,

V9-4050.	f-5. Murril Jose Worthen,
V9-4051.	f-6. Minne Beatrice Worthen,
V9-4052.	f-7. Bulah Lee Worthen,
V9-4053.	f-8. Myrtle Agnes Worthen,
V9-4054.	f-9. John Herbert Worthen,
V9-4055.	e-3. Thomas Benjamin Worthen, b. Aug 1869, Jackson Co, AL, d. 27 July 1947; m. 4 March 1889, Sarah Millesa Potter, b. 6 May 1869, AL. Thomas and Sarah are #9, Tupelo pct, Jackson Co, AL, p.154a, in 1900, with children:
V9-4056.	f-1. Rhoda Jane Worthen, b. Dec 1889
V9-4057.	f-2. Lucy Viola Worthen, b. May 1891
V9-4058.	f-3. Samuel Andrew Worthen, b. Feb 1894
V9-4059.	f-4. Minnie Phrenia Worthen, b. Jan 1896
V9-4060.	f-5. Martha Malinda Worthen, b. Sep 1898
V9-4061.	f-6. Fronia C. Worthen,
V9-4062.	f-7. Juanita M. Worthen,
V9-4063.	f-8. ____ Worthen,
V9-4064.	f-9. Earnest R. Worthen,
V9-4065.	f-10. Davey Thomas Worthen,
V9-4066.	f-11. Edith Worthen,
V9-4067.	e-4. Icy Phrenia "Thena" Worthen, b. 16 Nov 1871, Tupelo, Jackson Co, AL, d. 20 Oct 1965. Shawnee, Pottowatomie Co, OK, bur Tecumseh Mission Cem, Pottowotomie Co, OK; m. Joseph M.G. Sanders, b. _?_, d. 1943, Shawnee, OK. (15 ch)
V9-4068.	f-1. Wiley A. Sanders, b. March 1889, Jackson Co, AL
V9-4069.	f-2. Jane Sanders, b. 1890, Jackson Co, AL
V9-4070.	f-3. Henry J. Sanders, b. Jan 1891, AL
V9-4071.	f-4. Joseph Sanders, b. c1893, AL
V9-4072.	f-5. Eliza L. Sanders, b. Oct 1894, AL
V9-4073.	f-6. John Washington Sanders, b. 24 Sept 1896, d. 2 May 1962
V9-4074.	f-7. Sarah E. Sanders, b. Aug 1893, AL
V9-4075.	f-8. Myrtle E. Sanders, b. Feb 1900, AL
V9-4076.	f-9. Monroe Sanders, b. c1902, AL
V9-4077.	f-10. Phenie Emma Sanders, b. 8 June 1903, AL (or Eufala, OK), b. 6 May 1986, OK city, OK.
V9-4078.	f-11. Laura Sanders, b. c1905, Eufala, McIntosh Co, OK
V9-4079.	f-12. Wallace Sanders, b. c1907, Eufala, McIntosh Co, OK, d. Ok city, OK
V9-4080.	f-13. Alra Sanders, b. c1909, Eufala, McIntosh Co, OK

^{V9}-4081.   f-14. Anna Sanders, b. 2 Oct 1910, Eufala, McIntosh Co,
               OK, d. 30 Dec 1989, Shawnee, Pottowatomie Co, OK
^{V9}-4082.   f-15. Alice Sanders,

GEORGE WASHINGTON BRASHER
and IDA LOVELESS

d-11. **George Washington Brazier/Brashear**, (s/o Elijah Brazier Jr
and his second wife, Elizabeth "Betsy" Stephens), b. Maynard Cove,
Jackson Co, AL, 18 Jan 1849, d. 4 Sep 1907, Montague Co, TX, bur
Smyrna Cem, Montague Co, TX; m. 4 April 1884, in Jackson Co, AL, *Ida
Lee Loveless*, b. 23 July 1865, New Albany, IN, d. 17April 1943,
Montague Co, TX, bur Smyrna Cem, d/o James Belton Loveless
(1834–1900) and Sarah Josephine Crawford (1846–1922), gs/o Seaborn
Loveless (1807–1841) and Nancy Hail (1810–1870). George W. and Ida
Lee are great-grandparents of Jimmie Ryan <Altafae@aol.com>.

James Belton Loveless was born in SC, was a teacher in GA c1850 to
end of Civil War. After the war, he relocated briefly to IN and worked as
a manager in an iron works. Moved to AL in 1868 and settled in Jackson
Co, where he homesteaded 160 acres near Maynard Cove, about 12 miles
north of Scottsboro. The patent was granted in 1884. He was both a
farmer and a Methodist-Episcopal Circuit Rider. I don't know if he ever
taught again (data from David Wilson <davidcwilson@hotmail.com>,
great-grandson of James Seaborn Loveless and Sarah Elizabeth Davis.)

G.W. and Ida Lee Brazier homesteaded 40 acres adjoining her
parents' farm: homestead certificate #6736, for 39.85 acres, 30 June
1891. Shortly thereafter, they moved to Texas, and 200 acres of land
went to James Seborne Loveless, Ida Lee's immediately younger brother
and ancestor of David Wilson.

George Brazier/Brashear changed the spelling of the family name
from Brazier to Brashear when moving from Alabama to Texas, c1900.

Family of George W. Brazier/Brashear and Ida Lee Loveless:
^{V9}-4083.   e-1. unknown Brashear, b. & d. 1885
^{V9}-4084.   e-2. **Lula L. Brashear**, b. 2 March 1887, Jackson Co, AL, d.
               23 March 1897, Montague Co, TX, age ten, bur Smyrna
               Cem, Montague Co, TX.
^{V9}-4085.   e-3. **Albert Morgan Brashear**, b. 4 March 1890, Jackson Co,
               AL, d. Aug 1967, Fresno, CA; m. *Rhoda Cynthia
               Elizabeth Cornelison*, b. 7 Feb 1890, AL, d. July 1975,
               Fresno, CA

V9-4086.   f-1. **Mable Lottie Brashear**, b. 1910
V9-4087.   f-2. **Vera Lucille Brashear**, b. 1912
V9-4088.   f-3. **William Albert Brashear**, b. 1914
V9-4089.   f-4. **LaRue Brashear**, b. 1918
V9-4090.   f-5. **Mildred Elizabeth Brashear**, b. 1921
V9-4091.   f-6. **Melba Christine Brashear**, b. 1924, d. c1946
V9-4092.   f-7. **Janet Ruth Brashear**, b. 1929
V9-4093.   e-4. **Sarah "Sallie" Louisa Catherine Brashear**, b. 2 May 1892, Scottsboro, Jackson Co, AL, d. from cancer, 13 Nov 1966, Ontario, CA; m. *Luther William "Bill" Brown*, b. 6 Aug 1885, Hicks, TX, d. 28 Sep 1942, Chickasha, OK. Luther homesteaded 160 acres near El Reno, Caddo Co, OK (patent #47075), 23 Feb 1909. The patent was signed by Theodore Roosevelt "to secure homesteads to actual settlers on the public domain," in accordance with the Act of Congress, approved 20 May 1862. Grandparents of Jimmie Ryan, who sent data.
V9-4094.   f-1. Solomon Albert "Jack" Brown, b. 1910, d. 1995; m. Grace _____
V9-4095.   f-2. William Elman "Bud" Brown, b. 1912, d. 1989, bur Chickasha, OK; m. Tina _____
V9-4096.   f-3. Ann Brown, b. 3 Aug 1921, St Jo, TX; m. Charles Edward Brady
V9-4097.   f-4. Alta Fae Brown, b. 9 Oct 1924, St Jo, TX, d. 19 Sept 1967, Corona, CA (auto accident), bur Crestlawn Mem Park, Riverside, CA; m.1. Lewis Keith Glass; m.2. James Edward Ryan, b. 1919, New York; m.3. Oliver Wallace Scobey, b. 5 Feb 1921, Stuart, Hughes Co, OK, d. 5 Nov 1960, Brentwood, Contra Costa Co, CA, bur Union Cem, Contra Costa Co, CA, s/o Angus R. Scobey and Agnes Bell Irwin
V9-4098.   g-x. Jimmie Ryan,
V9-4099.   f-5. Viola Sue Brown, b. after 1925.
V9-4100.   e-5. **George Allen Brashear**, b. 7 Nov 1899, Jackson Co, AL, d. 22 July 1972, Montague Co, TX; m. *Ruby O. Lowrance*, b. 20 Aug 1900, d. 1 Nov 1986, both bur Sunset Cem, Montague Co, TX.
V9-4101.   f-1. **Mozelle Brashear**, b. 1922, d. 1994
V9-4102.   f-2. **Verdell Brashear**, (twin), b. 4 Oct 1925, Montague Co, TX, d. 9 Oct 1925
V9-4103.   f-3. **Maggie Nell Brashear**, (twin), b. 4 Oct 1925, Montague Co, TX, d. 8 Oct 1925

V9-4104.   f-4. **Margaret Aleene Brashear**, c. 1930; m. *Bob Callahan*

V9-4105.   f-5. **Frances Lucille Brashear**, b. 25 Dec 1932, Montague Co, TX

V9-4106.   e-6. **Charles Lewis Brashear**, b. 30 Oct 1902, d. Oct 1978, Bowie, Montague Co, TX; m. *Velma Caswell,*

V9-4107.   f-1. **Leola Brashear**, b. 1921

V9-4108.   f-2. **Myrle Brashear**, b. 1925

V9-4109.   f-3. **Doris L. Brashear**, b. 1939, d. 1940, Montague Co, TX

V9-4110.   e-7. **Ida Elva Brashear**, b. 5 Aug 1905, d. on her second birthday, 5 Aug 1907, Montague Co, TX, bur Smyrna Cem, Montague Co, TX.

1900 <u>Census, Montague Co, TX, p. 247b, pct #8</u>: #303

George W. Brasher,	b. Jan 1849 - 51 AL Ire AL
Ida L (wife)	b. July 1865 - 34 Ind SC Ga
	(Married 16 yrs. 5 children, 5 living, but only 3 listed)
Albert M. (son)	b. March 1890 - 10 AL AL Ind
Sarah A. (daughter)	b. May 1892 - 8 AL AL Ind
George A. (son)	b. Nov 1899 - 1/2 TX AL Ind

Rebecca Brazier and Joseph Henry Fears

d-12. **Rebecca Brazier,** (d/o Elijah Brazier Jr and Elizabeth "Bettie" Stephens), b. June 1853 (per 1900 census, Saline Co, IL), Jackson Co, AL, d. 28 April 1911, Saline Co, IL; m.1. 18 Jan 1870 (Jackson Co, AL, "by J.H. Garland, JP," Bk A, p.835), *Joseph Henry Fears*, b. 1853, Jackson Co, AL, d. c1892, Saline Co, IL, s/o William May Fears and Martha J. "Mattie" Sanders.

Rebecca and Joe were both 17 when they married. William and Elizabeth Messer, and William and Martha J. Fears signed the marriage license. About 1873-74, they moved to Saline Co, IL, where they are Dw #14 in Somerset Pct in the 1880 census, taken 9-10 June, with 4 children. In 1900, Rebecca is a widow, with three sons still at home: Charlie, 18, Jesse, 10, and Joseph, 8; she had borne 9 children, only six of them living.

Rebecca m.2. 26 April 1893, at Harrisburg, Saline Co, IL (bk H, p.35), *William A. Dillon*, b. IL, c1859 (41 in 1900), d. before 1900. After Rebecca died, Charlie, Jesse, and Joseph Fears all moved to Greene Co, AR, where their brothers, George W. and Benjamin Fears lived. Rebecca Brazier and Joseph Fears are great-grandparents of Bill J. Fears <bjf@grnco.net>

Family of Rebeccah Brashear and Joseph Henry Fears:

V9-4111.   e-1. George W. Fears, b. c1873, Jackson Co, AL (7 in 1880

V9-4112.   e-2. Henry A. Fears, b. c1875, Saline Co, IL (5 in 1880)

V9-4113.   e-3. Benjamin M. Fears, b. c1877, Saline Co, IL (3 in 1880)

V9-4114.   e-4. Lorenzo D. Fears, b. April 1880, Saline Co, IL (2/12 in June, 1880)

V9-4115.   e-5. Charles Fears, b. May 1882 (per 1900 census), Saline Co, IL

V9-4116.   e-6. Jesse Fears, b. Sept 1889 (per 1900 census), Saline Co, IL

V9-4117.   e-7. Joseph Fears, b. Oct 1891 (per 1900 census), Saline Co, IL

LOUISA BRAZIER and ALLEN J. MESSER

d-13. **Louisa C. Brazier**, (d/o Elijah Brazier Jr and his second wife, Elizabeth "Bettie" Stephens), b. 12 May 1855, Jackson Co, AL, d. 22 June 1913; m. 4 Jan 1871 (Jackson Co, AL, Bk A, p.948), **Allen Jackson Messer**, b. March 1850, Jackson Co, AL, d. 4 Dec 1912, Montague Co, TX, s/o William Messer and his first wife, Sarah Elizabeth _____. William Messer's second wife was Elizabeth Brazier, Louisa's oldest half-sister.

Family of Louisa C. Brazier and Allen J. Messer:

V9-4118.   e-1. Jessie M. Messer, b. 1873

V9-4119.   e-2. William Jackson "Willie" Messer, b. 12 March 1875, Scottsboro, Jackson Co, AL, d. 12 Nov 1947, Borger, TX; m. Mary Willingham, b. Oct 1879, Montague Co, TX.

V9-4120.   f-1. Sybil Messer, b. 1898, d. 1976

V9-4121.   f-2. Hallie Norvill Messer, b. 1900, d. 1971

V9-4122.   f-3. Avery Bill Messer, b. 1902, d. 1962

V9-4123.   f-4. Nora Elizabeth Messer, b. 1909

V9-4124.   e-3.

V9-4125.   e-4. George Washington Messer, b. 21 Feb 1879, Jackson Co, AL, d. 11 March 1899, Montague Co, TX, bur Smyrna Cem, Montague Co, TX

V9-4126.   f-1. Laverne Nix Messer, b. 1913

V9-4127.   e-5.

V9-4128.   e-6 Jesse G. Messer, b. June 1881, Jackson Co, AL

V9-4129.   e-7. Sarah "Sallie" Messer, b. March 1886, Socttsboro, Jackson Co, AL; m. c1905, in Montague Co, TX, Henry Willingham, b. 1884, TX

James Brazier, of Cumberland Co, NC

^{V9}-4130.   e-8. James Arthur Messer, b. Nov 1890, Jackson Co, AL, d. 1931

^{V9}-4131.   f-1. Laverne Nix Messer, b. 1913

1900 Census, Montague Co, TX: p.255a, pct #8:

Allen J. Messer	b. March 1850 - 50 AL TN AL
Louise C. (wife)	b. May 1855 - 45 AL SC AL(Marr 29 yrs, 8 ch, 4 living)
Jessey G. (son)	b. June 1881 - 18 AL AL AL
Sallie (dau)	b. March 1886 - 14 AL AL AL
Arthur (son)	b. Nov 1890 - 9 AL AL AL
Solomon Brasher	b. May 1861 - 37, AL, SC, AL (bro-in-law)

ELIJAH BRASHEAR, III
and REBECCA CORNELISON

d-14. **Elijah Brashear III**, (s/o Elijah Brazier Jr and Elizabeth "Bettie" Stephens), b. 1 Aug 1858, Jackson Co, AL, d. 19 May 1915, Montague Co, TX; m. 1 Dec 1876, Jackson Co, AL (Bk C, p.188), **Rebecca Frances Cornelison**, b. 28 Dec 1859, Jackson Co, AL, d. 15 Dec 1944, Montague Co, TX, d/o John Calvin Cornelison and Rhoda Weaver.

Elijah held homestead certificate #24919, containing 79.70 acres, in Jackson Co, AL, SW 1/4, SE 1/4, Sec 34, T17S, R15 W, Huntsville Principal Meridian, 1 Sep 1849.

From *History of North and West Texas*, p. 594: "In July 1889, Elijah Brashear, one of the prominent and successful farmers of Dry Valley, Montague Co [Texas], unloaded his family and few effects at Sunset, preparatory to becoming a permanent Settler...

Elijah and Rebecca Brashear

"He came to Texas from Jackson Co, Alabama, where his birth occurred 1 Aug 1858.... Elijah Brashear grew up without an education because the educational facilities of his home neighborhood were so poor and the domestic harassments in his childhood were such as to preclude the possibility of his attending school. He, therefore, has passed through his wonderfully successful career without the ability to read or write. He separated from his mother's home when he married and his assets on beginning life amounted to a pony, a cow, and a couple of beds. He rented land to farm for a time and then homesteaded a tract on the mountain, off of which he was enabled to eke out a little more than a living. With the proceeds of the sale of this place he came to Texas and, when he left the train at Sunset, two hundred dollars, his wife and children and a few household effects constituted his visible capital.

"He contracted for an eighty acre tract five miles northeast of Sunset, cultivated it four years, sold it and located at Thompson's Chapel, where he again bought and where he enjoyed a degree of prosperity and remained nine years. Selling there, the came into Dry Valley and purchased two hundred and sixty acres, which his and his family's labor paid for out of the products of the soil. He has extended his domains out across the valley, as his finances justified. He has cultivated the staple crops of the soil and his chief gain has come through "king cotton," the legal tender plant of the south.

"In Jackson Co, Alabama, December 1, 1876, Mr. Brashear married Rebecca F. Cornelison, a daughter of John and Rhoda (Weaver) Cornelison, whose children were: Mrs. Brashear; Sarah A.; William L.; Mary C.; John C.; and Martha J. Losing his first wife by death, Mr. Cornelison married again, his wife being Martha Carrick, who bore him five other children.

"Mr. and Mrs. Brashear's marriage has resulted in the following issue: Rhoda J.; Bettie L.; Lewis W.; Henry V.; Lillie M.; Luther C.; and Stella F." [That list leaves out first-born son: John W.]

A newspsper clipping from 1898: "Mr. & Mrs. Elijah Brashear of Denver, Texas, visited their old home in Maynard's Cove, Jackson Co, Ala." [Maynard's Cove was located in T3 R5E.]

Family of Elijah Brazier/Brashear III and Rebecca F. Cornelison:

V9-4132.   e-1. **John W. Brashear**, b. 1879, (age 1, in 1880) Jackson Co, AL

V9-4133.   e-2. **Rhoda Jane Brashear**, b. c1881, d. bef. 1900

V9-4134.   e-3. **Betty L. Brashear**, b. July 1883

V9-4135.   e-4. ***Lewis Weldon Brashear**, b. 4 March 1885, d. Nov 1941; m. in Fruitland, TX, 11 Feb 1906, ***Daisy Bell***, b. 6 Nov 1887, d. 12 Sept 1958,

V9-4136.   e-5. **Henry Virgil Brashar**, b. 9 Oct 1888, Cumberland Mountain, Jackson Co, AL, d. 11 Sept 1940, Phoenix, Maricopa Co, AZ, bur Lewis Hazelton Cem, Buckeye, AZ; m. _____

^{V9}-4137.   f-1.   **Archie Lee
"Felix" Brashar**, b. 5 Oct 1907, d. 5
Sept 1940

^{V9}-4138.   f-2. **Leander Vivian
Brashar**, b. 3 Dec 1908, Hollis
Harmon Co, OK, d. 25 Dec 1986; m.1.
Goldie _____; m.2. Luella _____,

^{V9}-4139.   f-3.   **Virgil Doward
Brashar**, b. 5 July 1915, Hollis,
Harmon Co, OK, d. 21 Sept 1941

^{V9}-4140.   f-4.   **Ivan Edward
Brashar**, b. 2 Feb
1917, Hollis,
Harmon Co, OK, d.
7 Dec 1941

^{V9}-4141.   f-5.   **Olivia May
Brashar**, b. 22
Sept 1922, Hollis,
Harmon Co, OK, d.
29 Sept 1940

Lewis W. and Daisey (Bell) Brashear, father of Marvin Brashear.

^{V9}-4142.   f-6.   **Exie Leona
Brashar**, b. 17 Nov
1923, Hollis,
Harmon Co, OK, d.
13 Feb 1989

^{V9}-4143.   f-7.   **Alice Lauerna
Brashar**, b. 22 Sept
1933, Luther, OK (or
Grove area), d. 15
May 1970

^{V9}-4144.   e-6. **Lillie M. Brashear**, b.
April 1890

^{V9}-4145.   e-7. **Luther C. Brashear**, b.
Aug 1893

^{V9}-4146.   e-8. **Stella F. Brashear**, b.
July 1896

Marvin and Bess Brashear

1880 Census, Jackson Co, AL: p.135a #59
Elijah Brazier   22, AL, TN, AL
 Rebecca Brazier 20 AL, AL, AL
 John W. Brazier 1 AL, AL, AL

1900 Census, Montague Co, TX: p.249a, pct #8
#336 Elijah Brasier b. Aug 1858 - 42 AL SC AL
 Rebecca (wife) b. Aug 1859 - 41 AL AL AL
       (married 22 yrs. 9 children, 7 living, 6 listed)
 John W. (son), b. 1879, (1 in 1880, Jackson Co, AL)
 Rhoda J.   b. c1881, d. bef. 1900
 Betty (dau) b. July 1883 - 16 AL AL AL
 Louis (son) b. March 1885 - 15 AL AL AL
 Henry (son) b. Sep 1887 - 12 AL AL AL
 Littie (dau) b. April 1890 - 7 TX AL AL
 Luther (son) b. Aug 1893 - 6 TX AL AL
 Stella (dau) b. July 1896 - 3 TX AL AL

Lewis Weldon Brashear
and Daisy Bell

e-4. **Lewis Weldon Brashear**, (s/o Elijah Brazier/Brashear III and Rebecca F. Cornelison), b. 4 March 1885, d. Nov 1941; m. in Fruitland, TX, 11 Feb 1906, *Daisy Bell*, b. 6 Nov 1887, d. 12 Sept 1958.

He bought 405 acres from his father, Elijah, and established his homestead, which he farmed for approximately three years. He took the money made from his cotton crop and invested with his half-uncle, in 50 steers. They purchased these from Charley Cross, and shipped them to Ft. Worth by train from Sunset, where they sold, losing their entire investment.

After discussing their situation, the uncle decided he and his boys would pick cotton to regain their losses, but Mr. Brashear after some thought said, "I am going to scout the country and find a few head that are too cheap." This was the beginning of a very successful career. He gathered his cattle all over the country and

Bobbie Brashear, Sr and Verna Mae
Johnson (photo: Verna Mae)

drove them by herds on horseback to Sunset and shipped to Ft. Worth by train.

Obit: Lewis W. Brashear, Friday, November 7, 1941 (from *The Sunset Signal*). He was born March 4, 1885 in Alabama. He came to Texas when he was four years old. He was united in marriage to Miss Daisey Bell of the Salona community in 1906. Three children was born to this couple: one girl and two boys. The girl died when she was quite small...."

Family of Lewis Weldon Brashear and Daisy Bell:

V9-4147.　　f-1. **Marvin W. Brashear**, b. 4 Sept 1909; m. 6 March 1932, ***Bess Williams***. d/o George Williams and Lee McDaniel

V9-4148.　　　g-1. **Bobbie Brashear**, b. 1 Nov 1934; m. ***Verna Mae Johnson***, b. 29 March 1935, of Henrietta.

V9-4149.　　　　h-1. **Bobbie Brashear, Jr**, b. 29 Dec 1955; m. ***Lisa Jackson***, of Midway

V9-4150.　　　　　i-1. **Jennifer Brashear**, b. 14 May 1974; m. ***Lyal Glover***

V9-4151.　　　　　i-2. **Brandon Brashear**, b. 27 Nov 1981; m. ***Annette _____***

V9-4152.　　　　　　j-1. **Kelsey Brashear**,

V9-4153.　　　　　　j-2. **Caleb Brashear**,

V9-4154.　　　　　i-3. **Casey Brashear**, b. 30 Dec 1982; m. ***Heather Martelle _____***

V9-4155.　　　　　i-4. **Matthew Brashear**, b. 24 Dec 1984

V9-4156.　　　　h-2. ***Jan Brashear***, b. 11 July 1958; m. ***Kevin Browning***

V9-4157.　　　　　i-1. Tiffany Browning.

Marvin and Bob Brashear in Dry Valley, near Sunset, Texas.

b. 16 Nov 1979;
m. Clay Egenbacker
V9-4158.   j - 1 .   C y
Egenbacker, b. 20 Oct 2004
V9-4159.   i - 2 . C h a n c e
Browning, b. 1 March 1984
V9-4160.   h-3. **Lance Brashear**,
(attended Midwestern State University in
Wichita Fall, TX); m. once, but has no
children.
V9-4161.   f-2. **Ona Bell Brashear**, b.
1916, d. 1920
V9-4162.   f-3. **Lewis Weldon Brashear,
Jr**, b. 5 Aug 1921, d. 3 June 1977; m.
Mildred Barlow.
V9-4163.   g-1.   **Sandy Brashear**,
m.1. *Bill Van Winkle*; m.x.   *Bob
Jenkins* in Ft. Worth
V9-4164.   h-1. Keela Van Winkle
V9-4165.   h-2. Brent Van Winkle
V9-4166.   h-3. Shane Jenkins (adopted)

L. Weldon, Jr. was the son of Lewis and Daisey Brashear. He and Mildred have one daughter, Sandy and two grandchildren.

Marvin Brashear established his home in Dry Valley. He farmed and
ranched, prior to the formation of Brashear Brothers Cattle Company, a
partnership with his brother, Weldon, which they operated until Weldon's
death. Marvin operated the business alone while Weldon served in the
United State Army from 15 Sept 1944 to 17 April 1946.

After Weldon's return, the two traveled through East Texas,
purchasing large herds, trucking them to Bowie, where they were sold to
both local and out-of-town buyers.

Bobbie joined his father and uncle in the business in 1961. This
made three successful generations of cattle buyers and was the largest
operation of its kind in North Texas.

Marvin, Bess, and Bobbie moved to Bowie in 1947, where Bobbie
completed high school in 1951. He played on the first State
Championship Basketball team his senior year. After graduation, he

attended Arlington State for two years, then transferred to Rice University in Houston. He played basketball in Arlington and Rice and was captain of his team his senior year. ...

Bobbie, Jr, followed in his father's footsteps, playing on the 1974 Bowie High School State Championship team and in college.

Mr. and Mrs. Elijah Brashear and all their descendants deceased to date are buried in the Salona Cemetery.

The Brashear Men: left to right: Caleb and Brandon Brashear; Bobbie, Jr; Casey Brashear; Lyal Glover; Chance Browning; Lance Brashear (in back); Kevin Browning; Cy and Clay Egenbacker (in back); Bobbie Brashear, Sr; Matt Brashear (Photo Verna Mae Brashear)

The Brashear women: Left to right: Tiffany (Browning) Egenbacher; Jennifer (Brashear) Glover; Heather Martelle Brashear (Casey's wife); Annette Brashear (Brandon's wife) Kelsey Brashear (Annette's dau); Verna Mae (Johnson) Brashear; and Jan (Brashear) Browning. (Photo: Verna Mae Johnson Brashear)

James Brazier, of Cumberland Co, NC   487

32. HARRIS, WILLIAM and GIDEON BRAZIER, of Iredell Co, NC

Harris Brazier

V9-4167.   a-3. **Harris Brazier**, b. ?, d. 1787, Iredell Co, NC. (This would have to be Rowan Co, NC, for Iredell was not formed until 1788.) He is another candidate to be a brother of James Brazier of Cumberland Co, NC.

Iredell County, North Carolina, is on the upper waters of the Catawba River, some 50 miles almost directly north of present-day Charlotte. It was formed in 1788 from the western part of Rowan County. The old Indian trading path from Asheboro to Winston-Salem ran through it, as does the modern Interstate 40.

Harris Brazier and William Brazier and their descendants, also, favored some of the standard Brazier names: William, James, Elijah, Thomas, Henry. But I still have no idea of how, or if, they are related to the Braziers of Cumberland County, or Orange/Chatham/ Greenville.

Will of Harris Brazier, of Rocky Creek, Iredell Co, NC, 9 Aug 1787 (Book 11, p.695): son David to receive certain land; sons James and William to get land, dividing corner. No mention of wife, nor does wife sign anything.

Family of Harris Brazier: (I'm guessing at the order of birth and adding data from land records below):

V9-4168.   b-1. **David Brazier,** d. bef. 1819; m. *Elizabeth* _____. In a record (Book J, p.?) of 1819, James Campbell lists heirs of the late David Brazier of Iredell Co, 1. Harris Brazier; 2. Elizabeth Brazier, "now McKenzie"; 3. Henry Brazier.

V9-4169.   c-1. **Harris Brazier**. [probably the oldest son], In 1801, he got 50 acres on Rocky Creek from David Brazier and wife, Elizabeth, see Book G, p.351

V9-4170.   c-2. **Elizabeth Brazier**, m. _____ *McKenzie*. In 1802, David Brazier deeded to his daughter Elizabeth, 50 acres on Rocky Creek, including house and stock, see Book J, p.341

V9-4171.   c-3. **Henry Brazier/Brasher** (Henry Brasher is in the 1820 Census of Iredell Co, NC)

V9-4172.   b-2. **James Brazier**

V9-4173.   b-3. **William Brazier**, b.?, d. c1827. **Will of William Brazier** in Nov 1827, in Iredell Co (Book 29, p.183) divides land "Sunrise" between sons James and William.

V9-4174.   c-1. **James Brazier**

V9-4175.   c-2. **William Brazier**

Mertie Brazier reports these deeds:

Rowan Co, Deed Book 11, p.695: 9 Aug 1787, NC State Grant #1508 to Richard Remington, 640 acres. (?? same book and page refs as "Will of Harris Brazier" above.???)

Iredell Co, Deed Book A, p.284, 22 March 1791 (Iredell was split off from Rowan in 1788): Richard Remington sold all or part of grant to John Huntsman.

Iredell Co, Deed Book B. p.194, 4 Aug 1794, John Huntsman sold 100 acres to David Brazier.

Iredell Co, Deed Book D, p.463, 5 Oct 1801, David Brazier and wife, Elizabeth, sold 50 acres to Harris Brazier.

Iredell Co, Deed Book Q, p.174, 21 Aug 1811, Harris Brazier (no wife mentioned) sold 60 acres to John McClellan, part of State grant to Richard Remington, who sold to John Huntsman, who sold to David Brazier, who sold to his son Harris Brazier, except 8 acres on the East side next to John Armstrong is what John Armstrong let Harris Brazier have.

William Brazier

V9-4176.   a-4. **William Brazier**, d. Iredell Co, c1795. **Will of William Brazier**, of Elk Shoal Creek, Iredell Co, NC, 30 May 1795 (Book 14, p.87), names sons Elijah, James, David, Harris. William Brazier had bought 200 acres in Iredell Co, on 3 July 1789 (Deed Book 11, p.58). This William is apparently a brother of Harris Brazier, above.

V9-4177.   b-1. **Elijah Brazier**

V9-4178.   b-2. **James Brazier**

V9-4179.   b-3. **David Brazier**

V9-4180.   b-4. **Harris Brazier**

These men must have known the SC colony. The Pendleton S.C. *Messenger*, issue of 12 July 1826, reported that there were letters in the Pendleton Post Office for Harris Brasher.

What is this: Iredell Co, NC, Book D, p. 581, David Brazier?

"The Brazier grave yard is in a clump of trees, off road near Yadkin Valley Church, in Davie Co, NC. There may not be stones for Braziers."

STRAYS

No Thomas named in any of the wills, yet 1800 Census of Iredell lists **Thomas Bashier**, 10012-21001 (two men over 45 , b. bef. 1755 [grandpa living with a mature son?] and one woman over 45, plus some young sprouts).

And the 1810 Census of Iredell lists Thomas Brashears, 01001-0201 (1 male over 45-b. bef 1765; 1 m. 10-16; 2 fem 10-16; 1 fem 26-45). Looks like the old man died. Any deaths of record in Iredell, 1800-1810? There was also a **Henry Braseur** in the 1810 Iredell Census.

Gideon Brazier/Bosher

And here's some records for someone to look up in Iredell Co (try Rowan Co for dates before 1788):

9 May 1787, ?? the court? ordered that **Gideon Brazier**, a poor child, be bound out to John Groove. Such records usually listed the late father, or something. He's the right age and this happens at the right time for him to be an orphan of Harris Brazier. Same man as these following?

Gideon Brasher (Brashur, Brashar) served from Iredell County in the War of 1812, Pvt. in Col. Alston's, 3rd Regiment, South Carolina.

Is this Gideon II?

[V9]-4181.   **Gideon Brasier**, b. Sussex Co, Delaware, 6 Sep 1804, d. Eaton, Preble Co. Ohio, 18 Sep 1886. He migrated from Delaware to Ohio in 1838, was married three times, and raised 13 children, all of whom he survived except three:

[V9]-4182.   Noah Brasier,

[V9]-4183.   _____ Brasier, m. Isaac Monosmith

[V9]-4184.   _____ Brasier, m. Henry Clark

(Reported in the Eaton (OH) *Democrat*, 23 Sep 1886.

From Heidi _____ <Geogi9486@aol.com>
My ancestor is **William Putman Brasier**-- his father is **Noah Brasier** &
his mother was ***Elisabeth Neff***. Both in Preble Co. Ohio, the town of
Eaton.

(See also chapter "Gideon Brazier" later in this book)

Some descendants who sent data:
Virginia Dale Blalock, 12318 Welland Drive, Houston, TX 77031
Mertie Brazier, Rt 2, Box 301, Chico, TX 76030
Suzie Brazier Toal, 1401 Mewton Rd, Ferris, TX 75125-9457
Wanda Irby, P.O.Box 612, Seymour, TX 76380-0612
Jeff L. Bott <sandflat@aol.com>
Robert Dale Sweeney <rdsweeney@charter.net>
Jimmie Ryan, 3315 E. 2nd St, #4, Long Beach, CA 90803;
<Altafae@aol.com>

NON-BRASHEARS FAMILIES

THE BRASHER, BRÉSER, BRASIER, BRAZIER FAMILY

OF NEW YORK CITY

33. HENRY BRÉSER/BRASHER, French Huguenot, and SUSANNAH SPICER

[1]-x. Henry Bréser, or Brézier, or Bresart, a French Huguenot who had been living for some years in Nazing, Essex County, England, came to New England in 1635, about the same time as John Eliot. He or another was in New Haven, Connecticut, in 1639. And there was a Henry or Harry Bréser in the Dutch Colony, Niew Amsterdam, in 1637. Henry Bréser came to spell his surname Brasher and founded a large and prominent family in New York City.

In Niew Amsterdam (later New York), most if not all of the family were members of the Dutch Reformed Church, which was an excellent records-keeper. They recorded births, baptism, marriages, etc in the church records, often adding some bit of family data, such as parents, sisters, etc. By the middle of the 1800s, these old records were decaying very badly; so the church embarked up a long project (a dozen years or more) of copying the records into books with fresh paper. These books were called "Manuals" and were numbered by the year they were copied: thus, the Manual of 1856, the Manual of 1864, etc. Shirley Brasher McCoy and others have sent me copies and extracts of these records. The surname appears in these records variously as Brasher, Braisjer, Bradejor, Brazier, etc, all of which are consistent with a Dutch clerk attempting to spell a French surname.

They apparently pronounce the surname BRAY-zher, not BRASH-er or Bra-SHEAR, the other two, main pronunciations of similar names. They left quite a number of records in Old New York, before and after it was taken over by the English.

In 1896, at the request of descendants in Hillsboro, Ohio, R.H. Green researched the Dutch Reformed Church records, as well as civil records, and published a longish article on this family in the *New York Genealogical and Biographical Record*, Vol XXVII (1896), pp.37-42, which I am here rearranging to make the families and descent easier for me to read.

Toward the end of the last century, Dr. Lewis B. Brasher, of Denver, (LBB; b. 7 Sept 1844, KY) did a great amount of research which he shared with Rev. John Lakin Brasher, of Alabama and which I am using, but his notes are not always clearly stated. I'm also adding information from other sources, which I'll try to identify.

Still, there are lots of gaps, lines that got lost, though they must have produced descendants. Even what I have is often incomplete: lacks birth date, or marriage, or other details. So, if anyone has any corrections, additions, deletions, emendations, revisions, anything--please send them to me with whatever documentation you have. I also like old family stories, anecdotes, descriptions of body and personality, to help these statistics come alive.

One family legend holds that the surname comes down from Phillippe Bras-de-fer, who is reported to have killed so many Saracens in one day in the First Crusade that he was given the name Bras-de-fer, "Arm of Iron." This family gained considerable prominence in the sixteenth century, but one branch became Huguenot, was driven out of France into Holland, and landed in 1620 at Nieu Amsterdamm in their own boat. There were supposed to be three brothers, who settled in and around what is today New York City. One branch eventually removed to Kentucky. In 1607, a descendant of the Catholic branch of the family was supposed to be Governor General of Canada.

[I have problems believing such family mythology: First: a surname derived from "Bras-de-Fer" is inconsistent with the French "Bréser"–you just don't change from "é" to "a" in an accented syllable; nor from "f" to "zh"; second, there was no Canada in 1607, only a few sick folk at

Jamestown, Virginia. French fishermen didn't start staying over the winter on the Québec coast until about 1614, and they certainly didn't have anything that could be called a Governor-General.

While there had been many "visits" to the New York area, especially from Henry Hudson's "discovery" of the river in 1609, there were no permanent residents until 1624 when about 30 Protestant, Walloon families were transported, only eight of whom remained at Manhattan, the rest going up-river to found Fort Orange (present-day Albany). Manhattan Island was not "purchased" until 1626, and in 1633, the population of the colony was about 200. The Walloons were from the Dutch-Belgian lowlands; they are the ones who brought the Dutch Reformed Church to Niew Amsterdam.]

HENRY BRÉSER'S LAND RECORDS

Henry Bréser/Brasher patented 33 acres on Manhattan Island in 1644, near the present Franklin Square, extending to Wolferts Valley. He resided many years in Smiths Valley--this was the C.J. Clooper estate (says R.H. Green, the family's first genealogist), between Franklin Square and Wall Street, usually called Maiden Lane, and Pearl, "worth £1,500." The patent on file in *Book of Patents*, Book GG (Dutch Language), Office of Secretary of State, Albany, New York, is dated 1645:

We, William Kieft, Director General, and council in behalf of the High and Mighty Lords the States General of the United Netherlands His Highness Prince of Orange and the Noble Lords, the Manager of the Incorporated Merchantile Company, and New Netherlands residing, by These Presents do publish and declare We on this day, the date underwritten, have given and granted unto Henry Brasher a piece of land lying at the East River betwixt the land of Cornelis Dirksen, Ferryman, South by East from the beach 132 rods, thence 45 rods East a little southerly till the maize land, further on through this maize land till to the Valley (Marsh) 109 rods, along the Valley (Marsh) N. E. by N. 20 rods, further again to the woods, next to the land of Jan Vette, W.N.W. till to the woods and through the woods next to the land of Frederick Lubbertsen to the East River, N. by West 120 rods along the strand to the place of beginning 56 rods amounting in all to 16 Morgens, 468 rods: with express condition and terms that the said Henry Brasher, or they who by virtue of these Presents, to his action may hereafter succeed, shall acknowledge the Noble Lords, the Managers aforesaid as their Lord and Patroon under the Sovereignty of the High and Mighty Lords the States General, and unto their Director and

Counsil here, shall in all things be conformed, as all good citizens are in duty bound.

Provided, also, that the said Henry Brasher or they who to his action may hereafter succeed, shall further more be subject to all such burdens and imposts as already by the Noble Lords have been enacted or such as hereafter may yet be enacted. Constituting over the same the aforesaid Henry Brasher, in our stead, in the real and actual possession of the aforesaid land: giving him by these Presents full might, authority and special license the above described parcel of land to enter, cultivate, inhabit and occupy in like manner as he may lawfully do with other his patrimonial land and effects without our, the Grantors in quality aforesaid, thereunto any longer having reserving, and saving any part, motion or control whatever. But to the behoof of aforesaid from all desisting from the time forth and Forevermore.

Promising, moreover, this Transport firmly, invicably, irrevocably to maintain, fulfill and execute and to do all that in equity we are bound to do.

Witness, these Presents, by us undersigned, and confirmed by our Seal in red wax out from below.

Done at Fort Amsterdam in New Netherlands,
this 4th day of September, A.D. 1645. *William Kieft*
By order of the Noble Lords,
the Director General   *Cornelis Van Tienhoven*, Secy.
and Council of New Netherlands.

[It's maybe a little hard for us, today, to imagine planting your maize on Wall Street or cultivating Times Square, but that's exactly the land that is involved.]

On 3 Aug 1651, Henry received a patent near Brooklyn Ferry and bought a house and lot in Gravesend in 1659. He lived on the East River side of the city in 1657, and was admitted as a small burgher, 17 April 1657.

[Where he was in 1664, when the English drove out the Dutch Colonists and took over in New York, is not mentioned.]

He lived on the south side of Wall Street between Broadway and Pearl in 1674, and in 1676 was assessed for building a new dock and other matters, 12 shillings, 6 pence, on a valuation of £100. On Long Island, he was called a magistrate. He died in 1690 and left a will (see below).

Spicer Family

In 1643, Henry settled at Gravesend, Long Island, and married, Susanna, widow of William Walters, and daughter of Thomas Spicer of Gravesend, L.I. She (or another) is sometimes called Susanna Thomas. *Marriages in the Reformed Dutch Church in New York*: 9 Oct 1644, "Henry Brasher of the Province of Essex, Eng. to Susanna Walters, widow of Wm. Walters."

Thomas Spicer was baptized 3 Feb 1592, at Barfreston, England, the son of Nicholas and Martha (Grant) Spicer. Thomas Spicer m.1. 4 Feb 1626, Ann Grant, in Sandwich, Kent Co, England, and they had two children:

Susanna Spicer, who m.1. William Walters, m.2. Henry Brazier; and Ann Spicer, who m. John Lake.

Thomas Spicer m.2. 5 Feb 1635, Michal ____, widow of John Jenkins, and they had one son, Samuel Spicer, bapt 30 July 1637 (re: *Spicer Family*, by Susan Billings Meech, and "Samuel Spicer and his Descendants," by Rev. John R. Stevenson, N.J. Hist. Coll, v.13, 2nd ser, p.41ff).

HENRY AND SUSANNAH'S WILLS

Will of Henry Brasher, Dated 23 April 1689, Proven 4 Feb 1690, City Hall, New York, Book 3, p.199, Book 144, p.147:

In the name of God, Amen. The twenty third April anno Dom. one thousand, six hundred and eighty nine. I, Henry Brasher, of ye City of New Yorke, Turner, although weak in body yett in good, perfect and sound minde, memory and understanding, praise be the Almighty God for same, therefore do make and ordaine this my last WILL and Testament in manner and forme following, that is to say. First, I commend my soule unto ye hands of ye Almighty God from whom I received it, by whom of his grace I trust to be saved and received into Eternal rest through the Death of my Savior and Redeemer Jesus Christ; my body, in hopes of a joyful Resurrection, I commit to the Earth and decent Christian Burial with such charges and in such place as my Executrix, henceafter named, shall think fitt and convenient--to whose care and management I wholly commit the same, and as touching my goods and chattels, lands, tenements and all other Real and personall estate whatsoever or wheresoever with which it hath pleased God to indow me in the World; my debts and funerall charges first being sattisfyed and paid, I dispose of the same as followeth.

Imprimis: I give and bequeath unto my sonne Henry Brasher Tenn shippings to be paid within two months after my decease. [probably "shillings"--prob a clerical error.]

Item. I give and bequeath unto my other two sonnes Isaack and Abraham Brasher five shilling each of them, to be paid within two months after my decease.

Item. I give and bequeath unto my daughters each of them, five shippings to be paid within two months after my decease.

Item. All the remainder of my Estate, both Reall and personall whatsoever or wheresoever, I give and bequeath unto my well beloved wife Susannah Brasher, to have and to hold unto the said Susannah her heirs and Assignes forever, to make sayle or dispose of as she shall see fitt; and

Lastly, I will that my loving wife, Susannah Brasher to be my sole and only Executrix of this my last WILL and Testament of the Estate herein Given, bequeathed and Divised, and likewise to have the whole and sole disposall of the same without controuls; not being lyable to give an account to any one whatsoever for concerning the premises, hereby Revoking all former WILLS or Testaments by me made any time before the date hereof.

In witness whereof, I, the said Henry Brasher, have hereto sett my hand and seale the day and yeare above written.

Henry Brasher, Senior   (seale)

Signed, sealed and D.D. in the presence of Ebenezer Willson, Adolph Pidtoy, Graft.

New York, Feb. 4, 1690. Appeared before me Adolph Pidtoy and declared before me that he was present when Henry Brasher set his hand and seal to this writing as Last WILL and his act and deed.

P.D. Cancy, Mayor

Recorded in the Book of Records of the City of New York, Feby 9, 1690, Abrah Gouverneur

Will of Susannah Bresier, 20 July 1694 (Book 5, p.85)

(Recorded for Abram Brasier)

In the name of God, Amen. The 20 day of July in ye 6 yr. of ye reign of our Sovereign Lorde and Lady William and Mary, by the Grace of God of England, Scotland, France, and Ireland King and Queen, Defenders of ye Faith, etc; and in ye year of our Lord God One thousand six hundred and ninety-four, I Susannah Brasier of ye Citty of New Yorke being sound in body and of good and perfect remembrance, Praise be to Almighty God, knowing that I am naturally born and ordained to dye and to pass from this transitory life, Minding too put in order my Estate to ye intent there should be no strife for the same after my decease, and to avoid all occasion of trouble and charges, I do make this to be my last Will and Testament in manner and form following, vis:

First, I recommend my soule to Almighty God and to his sonne Jesus Christ my Savior and Redeemer, in whose precious blood I sett ye whole and only hope of my salvation: my boddy in hope of Joyfull Resurrection I commit to the Earth to be decently buried.

Secondly: Having full power of ye Will of my deceased husband Henry Bresier, dated ye 23rd April 1689, to dispose of all of his Estate both Reall and Personall doe dispose as vis: I do give to my sonne Henry Bresier the half of ye grounds in ye Smight Valy where he hath built upon during his life and after his decease shall devolve to his daughter Susannah and by her decease to ye next survival and to his daughter Susannah two of my Biggest Platters.

Item. I doe give to my sonne Isaack Brasier ye other half of ye ground in Smiths Valy during his life time and after his decease shall devolve to his daughter Susannah and by her decease to ye next survivant and to his daughter two pewter platters, being Susannah.

Item. I doe give to my sonne Abraham Brasier my house and ground in this Citty with condition that ye same shall be appraised after my decease and what shall be found to be more worth than the grounds in Smiths Valy ye surplus shall be payd to my four daughters or their children in four equal shares: and my 2d sonne is to have and to hold ye said house and ground during his life and after his decease to his sonne Henry and by his decease to ye next surviving.

Item. My said sonne Abraham Bresier shall have all his father's tools and a negro boy paying to my daughter Sarah nine pounds one month after my decease; but ye surplus of ye house shall be payd six years after my decease in equal portions.

Item. I doe make and bequeath to my daughter Susannah all my wearing appearell and for her children one pe Serge to Clothe them which appearell shall be for her and her daughter Susanna.

Item. I doe make and bequeath to all my grandchildren each a silver spoon of tenn shillings.

Item. I doe make and bequeath to Mary Barnis (Barnes, Baring, Barnus?) daughter of Mary Bresier a bed steed, bedd Pillow, Pillow bears and coverletts with cueting and vallous and all furniture where I sleep in and also two plates, 2 platters, a bason and an Iron Pott and a Mohair petticote.

Item: I do make and bequeath to Susanna Barnes my morning gown lyeing with silk and a silk waist coat.

Item: I doe give to my Grandchild Henry Bresier sonne of Abram Brasier a silver cupp a silver dram cup and a silver spoon.

Item: I doe make to my sonne Abram Brasier one great brass Pott and a great copper Kittle, two platters, and two plates and on ye silver spoons I will and desire that shall be in each spoon my name and ye name of ye grandchild.

Item: I will that ye piece of meaddow next to Butchers at Mespatths Hill shall be disposed of for paying my burriall expenses and to pay for ye silver spoons given to my grandchildren and ye remainder to sheare alike amongst all my children and by decease to their representatives.

I doe make hereby my sonne Abram Bresier and Abram Mesier my friend to be my exectors of ye Estate which I shall leave by decease granting to them such power and authority as belongeth to them according to law in the premises.

I doe declare to be my last Will and Testament and desire it may be performed after my decease giving also to my sonne Isaak ye great pitch Pott.

In Witness whereof I have hereunto sett my hand and seal dated alt supra.

Susannah Bresier

Witnesses: P.D. Lanoy

Peter Mesier

Abraham Mesier

The foregoing Record of Susannah Brasiers Will examined and Compd. with the Original this 7 Dec 1749.

Benjamin Fletcher, Capt. General

admits above Will 27 Nov 1694.

Henry and Susannah's Family

Henry Bréser/Brasher had ten and Susannah eleven children. Ten of them were baptized in the New York Dutch Reform Church, presumably soon after they were born; "my daughter Susanna" of the will was not registered. (See *Records of the Dutch Reform Church*. The Manual of 1857, p.747-8 lists all of Henry's children's baptisms, two of Henry Jr's, two of Isaac's and some miscellaneous.) Part of the first two generations of Henry and Susannah's descendants are:

2-1. ***Susanna (née Walters) Bréser**, b. c1643/4. We are forced to add Susanna, even though her birth was not registered, because of mother Susannah's will; she was probably a daughter by Susannah's first marriage and was adopted by Henry, or at least went by the name Bréser or Brasher; m. c1672, Lt. William Churchill. See below.

²⁻2. **Mary Breser**, bap. 29 Sept 1645; prob. d. before 1694; m. 21 May 1668, Thomas Barnes (*NY Marr.* Prev. to 1784, O'Callaghan) and had children:

    ³⁻1. Mary Barnes

    ³⁻2. Susanna Barnes

²⁻3. **Willem Breser**, bap. 18 Nov 1646; probably died before either of his parents, since neither he nor his children were mentioned in the wills. Green gives a couple of possible marriages with 1671 dates, but he knew of no further descendants in this branch.

    ³⁻1. **Diryck Breser**, bap. 1 Oct 1684, s/o William and Susanna Breser; prob. d. before 1694.

    ³⁻2. **Willem Breser**, prob. d. before 1694.

²⁻4. **Rebecca Breser**, b. 22 April 1648 in New Amsterdam, (Gravesend, Kings Co, New York), bap. 26 April 1648, d. 6 Aug 1700 in Middletown, Monmouth Co, New Jersey; m. 22 April 1665 (*NY Marr.* Prev. to 1784, O'Callaghan), **Peter Tilton**, b. 16 Jan 1642, Lynn, Essex Co, MA, d. 15 Dec 1699, Middletown, Monmouth Co, NJ, s/o John Tilton and Mary Goodie Pearsall.

    ³⁻1. Rebecca Tilton, bapt. 28 Dec 1667

²⁻5. **Breser Breser**, bap. 9 Feb 1653;

²⁻6. **Machtelt Breser**, bap. 21 Nov 1655;

²⁻7. **Martan (or Martha) Breser**, bap. 20 May 1657

²⁻8. **Sara Breser**, bap. 14 Dec 1659; m. William Preay and/or m. 12 Nov 1690, John Theobold

²⁻9. **Henry Breser**, or **Brasher**, Jr, bap. 29 July 1663, d. about 1710; m. 5 Aug 1685, Maryken Van Alst, daughter of Joris Van Alst, of Mispat Kills, son of Stephen Van Alst of Bruges, West Flanders (Manual of 1862, p.565). [Joris Van Alst m. 1652, Geesje, d/o Herman Hendricksson.]

    ³⁻1. **Henry Breser**, a single man licensed 23 April 1711 to marry Sarah Andries, young woman from Bergen, N.J. (14 April 1711 says Manual of 1862, p.565). He was killed in the negro outbreak, 7 April 1712. His widow removed to Bergen, where 3 April 1713, she was licensed to marry Caspar Preyer.

    ³⁻2. **Susanna Breser**, bap. 31 March 1686; m. Isaac Bedlow

    ³⁻3. **Geesje Breser**, bap. 21 March 1690; m. 7 Jan 1708 (Manual of 1862, p.565) Daniel Lewis, but had no issue.

²⁻10. ***Isaac Braisjer**, or **Bradejor**, bap. 16 May 1666; m. 9 June 1690, Altje Colevelt (17 May 1690, says Manual of 1862, p.565). Altje, bap. in Brooklyn 6 March 1670, dau of Lawrence Colevelt; five children. Two of Isaac's sons became prominent land-owners in Manhattan

and figure in land transactions until about 1800. See "Isaac Braisjer and his sons," below.

2-11. ***Abraham Brasier**, or **Brasher**, bap. 25 Nov 1668; m. 12 Nov 1690, Lysbet Schouten (18 Oct 1690, says Manual of 1862, p.565). Abraham became a Revolutionist a century before the American rebellion and his sons and grandsons were passionate participants in the Revolution. His family emphasized military and political action. He and Lysbet had seven children and many grandchildren; see "Abraham Brasier, the Revolutionist," below.

Susannah Brasier and Lt. William Churchill

Susanna Brasier, m. 1672, Lt. Wm. Churchill, believed to have come over as an Ensign of the Merchant Marines, which in 1664 seized New Amsterdam in the name of the Duke of York, according to a descendant, Mary Sherwood Hale. If 18 in 1672, Susanna would have been born c1644, before Henry and the widow Walters were married. Mrs. Hale says "Susanna was of the family of Abraham Brashear of New York," member of the Committee of Safety and member of the council and assembly. (See HSB p.33) The altercation that Susanna's brother Abraham was involved in, the Leisler Rebellion, was in 1689, 87 years before the Committee of Safety was formed in 1776. Somebody besides me is capable of being confused and scrambling the ancestral eggs. Note also that practically every child of Henry and Susannah that had children named a girl Susanna, including "my daughter Susanna" and "her daughter Susanna," who was mentioned in grandmother Susannah's will.

Mary Sherwood Hale descended from a son of Susannah and William Churchill (ref: ltr of Mary Sherwood Hale to HSB, 23 Sept 1927; see HSB, p. 33):

2nd. gen. Robert Churchill, b. 1677, m. 1694, Sarah, d/o John and Elizabeth Cabell, step dau of Thomas Sherwood, II

3rd. gen. Eleanor Churchill, b. 1695, d. 1754; m. c1733, Thomas Sherwood, III (cf. wills of Robert Churchill and Thos. Sherwood)

4th. gen. John Sherwood, d. 1777; m. 1761, Mary Graham

5th. gen. Asa Sherwood, b. 1762, d. 1834; m. 1783, Molly Phillips

6th. gen. William Sherwood, b. 1793, d. 1875, m. 1856, Lucy A. Rice

7th. gen. Mary Sherwood, m. 1876, Charles N. Hale

33a. ANOTHER HENRY/HARRY BRESER/BRASHER?

There are so many stray names in the 1600's in New York that we almost have to insist that the original Henry Bréser, who acts rather like a Huguenot refugee, had a brother, or a cousin. Or that someone else named Brasher came to the Dutch colony in the very early days. Any ideas, anyone? I'm wondering particularly if there wasn't a second man named Henry Bresher or Brasher, an Englishman? All we'd need to confuse things completely is for him to have married a girl named Susannah (Susannah Thomas, maybe!, who is mentioned in some records as a wife of Henry or Harry Brasher). Several of the following children are approximately the same ages as Henry and Susannah (Spicer) Bréser's children:

Doc. Hist. State of NY (O'Callaghan), XI:393 refers to Bayard suit for damages for false imprisonment, includes Harry Bresher, an Englishman. (Bayard was involved in the Leisler Rebellion of 1689.)

GARRET BRASHER
and CATHERINA HARDENBROOK

Garret Hendrickson Breser/Brasher, (also called "Henry E. Brasher") took oath as native of Flatbush, 1687 (if 21 at the time, he was b. bef. 1666), may have been a brother or another son, or just a "cousin." He's at least as old as Henry Bréser, Jr.

Gerrit Brasher m. Catherina Hardenbrook, 25 May 1689 (Marriages in Dutch Reform Church, Manual of 1862, p.565). Their son, Hendrick "George" Brasher, bapt 6 Dec 1691.

Gerrit and Catherina's daughter, Anne Avory, made a will in New Jersey, in which she named her brothers and sisters:

"I, Anne Avory, late of the city of New York, but now of the city of New Brunswick, New Jersey, widow, being in tolerable health. I bequeath to my sisters, Mary Brasier and Sarah Hay, all my wearing apparel, both linen and woolen. It is my will that the land belonging to me in the County of Albany, be sold as soon as convenient and the proceeds with the rest of my personal estate be divided in five equal parts, one fifth to my brother Frances Brasier, one fifth to my sister Mary Brasier, one fifth to my sister Sarah Hay, one fifth to my sister Francis Lagrange, wife of Barnadus Lagrange, and the remaining one fifth to my nephew Meads Brasier (son of my brother George). I appoint my brother Frances Brasier and my brother-in-law Barnadus Lagrange executors." Dated June 4, 1777, Probate March 16, 1785. (Book 37, p.435)

Family of Gerrit Hendrickson Brasher and Catherina Hardenbrook (m. 25 May 1689) Order uncertain.

1. **Hendrick (also called George) Bresser**, bapt. 6 Dec 1691, lived Kingston, NY; m. Jannetje Terwilliger. Three children in records of Dutch Reform Church:
   1. **Een (?Annie) Bresser**, bap. 20 May 1733
   2. **Meads Brasier**, m. 23 Oct 1770 (*NY Marr.* Bk 16:227), Elizabeth Dash
   3. **Frances Brasier**, d. bef. 1766; m. Elizabeth Beckman, b. 30 Aug 1738, d. 9 Nov 1810, Somerset Co, NJ [will, inventory], d/o William Beckman
2. **Frances Brasier**, [? Somerset Co, NJ, Will of Francis Brasier, 1784, Book 26, p.537]
3. **Anne Brasier**, d. c1785, apparently w/o issue, since her will named only siblings and a nephew; m. John? Avory
4. **Mary Brasier**, unm. in 1785 [? Somerset Co, NJ, Will of Mary Brasier, 1786, Book 28, p. 500]
5. **Sarah Brasier**, m. _____ Hay
6. **Francis Brasher**, m. Barnadus Lagrange

Who? Phillip [sic] Brasher died intestate, 1785, Essex County, NJ (Book 27, p.376.
James Brasier did intestate 1761, inventory 1761, Salem County, NJ (Book 11, p.37)

15 Sept 1756, John Dalby and Margaret his wife deed house and lot in Montgomery Ward on Queen Street, known as lot 12 of land of late William Beckman, to Isaac Stantenburg, Elizabeth Brazier, John Montague, and Cornelia Ryckman. (Book 40, p. 272)

13 Nov 1766, Isaac Stantenburg, gunsmith, and Annaka, his wife; John Montague, baker, & Maria his wife; and Tobias Ryckman, cordwainer of N.J. and Cornelia, his wife, deed ?? (Receipt of £750) to Elisabeth Brasiers, widow (name also spelled Brasher in the deed).

William Beckman, therefore, had children:

1. Annaka Beckman, m. Isaac Stantenburg
2. Elizabeth Beckman, widow by 1766, m. Frances Brazier
3. Maria Beckman, m. John Montague
4. Cornelia Beckman, m. Tobias Ryckman

MORE STRAYS

Thomas Brazier, doorkeeper of the legislature, 1719-1722, was paid for express to Connecticut, June 1719, £11, 17sh, 5d. by Gov. Hunter. July 19, asked appointment as gunner at Fort George, NY, and Oct 22 was paid £6 for services by Gov. Burnet.

Thomas Brasier acted as witness to the will of Gertrude Van Courtlandt, in 1718.

Will of Thomas Brasier, Yeoman, of Apperfield, Ulster Co, devised £100 to his brother, Richard Brasier, and all the rest of the estate to Lydia, his own wife "for the use of herself and our children"; signed 6 Nov 1725. Probate 24 Sept 1726 (Book 10, p.257).

Lydia Brasier acted as witness to the will of John Avory in 1733. Anne Avory, widow, d. c1785, in New Jersey (see will above).

Joseph Isaac Brisser, in Col. Abraham De Peyster's Regt., 1700. (*Doc. Hist. of State of NY*, O'Callaghan, 1850, Vol. I, p.233)

Joseph Isaac (?) Brasher on 1703 Census of North Ward, NYC, with a wife, and one female child. (*Doc. Hist. State NY*, I:616). Also mentioned as head of family in New York, 1703, in Valentine's *New York City*, p.346, where he is also mentioned as Fireman (freeman?) of New York, 1683 and 1740 (which <u>could</u> be his birth and death dates).

New Eng. Hist. & Gen Reg. (Vol 16, p.35) mentions that
Capt. Brasier Brazer, d. 1759;
Jas. Brasier, m. 1759;
Simion Brazier, d. 1757;
Thomas ?Brasier [different Thomas] d. 1764, age 73 [b. c1691].

The Records of the Dutch Reform Church, Manual of 1864, p.568, lists a number of baptisms that I can't yet place. They are right under baptisms for Abraham's children and three of Isaac's children (Henry, 16 Jan 1698; Isaac, 11 Aug 1700; Aaltye, 2 Oct 1702) and there is a great deal of overlap with names of Henry, b. 1698's children, but these are just a generation too early:

   group a. **Hendricus Brasher**, 3 Oct 1708
        Daniel Brasher, 24 Oct 1711
        Wilkeson Brasher, 28 March 1714
        Elizabeth Brasher, 20 Jan 1720
   group b. **Margarietje Brasher**, 25 Nov 1716
        Sara Brasher, 25 Jan 1718
        Marjarietje Brasher, 12 Oct 1720

Mary Brazier, m. 16 Sept 1697, Philip Wilkinson (*NY Gen. Biog. Rec.* Vol 3-4, p.192). This is Not Mary, d/o Henry and Susannah, who d. before Susannah's will, 1694.

The Manual of 1862, p.565, lists these marriages, as yet unaccounted for.

12 Nov 1690, Sarah Brazier to John Theobald
24 July 1705, Susanna Brasher to Isaac Pettvies
28 April 1716, Sarah Brayser to Thos. Smit
2 Dec 1732, John Brasher to Annatye Van Gelder
30 Aug 1746, Abraham Brasher to Jane Sikkels
4 May 1756, Catharina Brasher to Albert Ryckman
21 May 1770, Mary Brasher (widow) to Jno. Tanner

Some other marriages, not yet accounted for, from *New York Marriages, Previous to 1784*, by O'Callaghan:

Abigail Brisher m. 24 July 1753, Stephen Leach (*NY Marr.* Bk I:77)
Mary Brazier m. 23 Dec 1757, Peter Ablin (*NY Marr.* Bk 1:751)
Elenor Brasher m. 2 June 1759, Alex Dunlap (*NY Marr.* Bk 2:302)
William Brasier m. 17 July 1761, Catharine Norwood (*NY Marr.* Bk 4:301)
William Brasher m. 13 May 1761, Margaret Root (*NY Marr.* Bk 4:188)
Susannah Brasher m. 24 Sept 1761, Jas. Gillihan (*NY Marr.* Bk 5:96)
Hannah Brashier m. 16 April 1783, John B. Alton (*NY Marr.* Bk 38:98)

33b. ISAAC BRAISJER AND HIS SONS

[2-]10. **Isaac Braisjer**, or **Bradejor**, (s/o Henry Bréser and Susannah Spicer), bap. 16 May 1666, d. c1779; m. 9 June 1690 (17 May 1690, says Manual of 1862, p.565), Altje (Eleanor) Colevelt, bap. in Brooklyn 6 March 1670, dau of Lawrence Colevelt. Letter of administration issued 17 June 1779 to Elinor, wife, of Isaac Brazier, wharfbuilder, who had died intestate. (*NY Hist Soc*, V.33 for year 1900)

Isaac Braisjer (Brasher) and Altje (Eleanor) Colevelt had five children: (Manuals of 1863, p. 748, and 1864, p. 775) *The Records of the Dutch Reform Church*, Manual of 1864, p.568, lists baptisms for three of Isaac's children (Henry, 16 Jan 1698; Isaac, 11 Aug 1700; Aaltye, 2 Oct 1702)

[3-]1. **Susanna Brasier**, bap. 7 July 1691 (Manual of 1857, p.747-8)

[3-]2. **Maria Brasier**, bap. 25 Dec 1695 (Manual of 1857, p.747-8)

[3-]3. ***Henricus (Henry) Brasier or Brasher**, bap. 16 Jan 1698 (Manual of 1864, p.568); m. 19 Nov 1727, Abigail Pearsall (Manual of 1862, p.565)

[3-]4. ***Isaac Brasier or Brasher**, bap. 11 Aug 1700 (Manual of 1864, p.568); m. Jannet De Voe or DeFoer. (Manual of 1862, p.565, says Jane Cox.)

[3-]5. **Aaltye Brasier**, bap. 2 Oct 1702 (Manual of 1864, p.568)

Henricus (Henry) Brasher and Abigail Pearsall

[3-]3. **Henricus (Henry) Brasher (or Breser)**, bap. 16 Jan 1698, was the son of Isaac Breser and Altje "Eleanor" Colevelt and grandson of Henry Bréser the immigrant. On 19 Nov 1727 (Manual of 1862, p.565), he married **Abigail Pearsall**; they lived in Montgomery ward. Letters of administration issued 18 Aug 1779 to Abigail, wife of Henry Brazier, pilot, who had died intestate. (*NY Hist Soc*, V.33 for year 1900). However, wife Abigail apparently died soon, for letters of administration were issued 2 June 1786 to Abigail Earle, wife of Morris Earle and daughter of Henry Brasher, of Queens Co, Yeoman, decd. Also on 2 June 1786, letters of administration were issued to Abigail Earle, daughter of Abigail Brasher, widow, of New York City. (*NY Hist Soc*, v.39 for year 1894)

Henry Brasher and Abigail Pearsall had eight children, according to R.H. Green; some of these may not be theirs:

[4-]1. **Isaac Brasher**, bap. 17 July 1728; d. c1791. On 29 June 1791, Eleanor Brasher, widow of Isaac Brasher, advertised for sale the "pleasant Island in the East River, known as The Two Brothers."

[5-]1. **Henry Brasher**, m. Gennetta _____ (see Deeds 44:368)

⁴⁻2. **Maria Brasher**, bap. 11 Feb 1730
⁴⁻3. **Aaltje Brasher**, also called 'Elinor,' bap. 9 April 1732; d. 17 Sept 1806, age 75; m. 19 March 1754 (Manual of 1862, p.565) John (or Johan) Berrien, b. 27 Sept 1720, d. 26 Dec 1773, bur. Trinity Yard.
⁴⁻4. **Willem Brasher**, bap. 6 Nov 1734; ?possibly the one who surveyed Lake Champlain in 1759 for Amherst, and the one who m. Catharine Norwood, 17 July 1761. Probably died without issue before 1771, for he is not mentioned in any of the estate deeds below.
⁴⁻5. **Abigail Brasher**, bap. 26 Jan 1737; m. Morris Earle
  ⁵⁻1. Henry Brasher Earle
⁴⁻6. **Sara Brasher**, bap. 6 April 1740, m. 14 July 1763 (*NY Marr.* Bk 7:265) Andrew Allsop
⁴⁻7. **Henry Brasher, or Braser, Jr.**, bap. 3 Nov 1742; d. bef. 1779; m. 1 Jan 1766, Cathalyntje ?Catharine Dyks
  ⁵⁻1. **Henry Brasher, III**, b. c1768, m. Frances _____
  ⁵⁻2. **Margaret Brasher**, b. c1770, m. Cooper Palmer, or Palmer Cooper, or maybe he was _____ Palmer, a Cooper by trade.
  ⁵⁻3. **Abigail Brasher**, b. c1772, m. Thomas A. Andrews
  ⁵⁻4. **Hannah Brasher**, b. c1774; m. 16 April 17<u>8</u>3, John B. Alton (*NY Marr*, Bk 38, p.98) (?Jno Dalton, surgeon, in deed below? Dates don't match. Marriage possibly 17<u>9</u>3?)
⁴⁻8. **Daniel Brasher**, bap. 25 Oct 1749

Henry Jr's Estate

Henry Brasher, Jr, son of Henry Brasher, was issued letters of administration, 31 May 1771, in the estate of Henry Brasher, of New York, who had died intestate (*NY Hist Soc*, v.31 for year 1898). However, Henry Jr seem to have died not long after, and his brother Isaac acted as a sort of executor of the estate, making several deeds of gift to his sisters and brother Henry's children, which establish family relationships:

5 Feb 1779, Isaac Brasher, blacksmith, and Elenor, his wife, gift deed to Henry Brasher and Margaret Brasher, his nephew and niece, children of Henry Brasher the younger, dec'd, a lot where of Henry Brasher, father of said Isaac died seized, in Montgomery Ward. (Book 50, p.106)

5 Feb 1779, Isaac Brasher, and Elenor his wife, gift deed to Abigail (Brasher) Earle, his sister, 1/2 of lot (whereof Henry Brasher, father of said Isaac Brasher, died seized) lying in Montgomery Ward, fronting East

on Queen 45 ft. N. 170 ft. Recorded for Henry Brasher Earle, 25 Oct 1803. (Book 65, p.414)

5 Feb 1779, Isaac Brasher, and Elenor his wife, gift deed to Elinor Berrien, née Elinor Brasher, his sister, lot (whereof Henry Brasher, father of said Isaac died siezed). (Book 109, p.450)

This last deed also alludes to Catherine Brasher occupying the lot of the late Henry Brasher. This would suggest that Isaac's brother, Henry, was married to Catharine _____. [1 Jan 1766, Henricus Brasher m. Cathalyntje Dyke (Manual of 1862, p.565).

Who? 14 Dec 1765, Cathalyntze Braser m. Thos. Thorne (Manual of 1862, p.565)]

2 Oct 1787, Henry Brasher [s/o Isaac and Eleanor] and Gennetta, his wife, deed to Dan'l Tocker (?Tooker) (Book 43, p.481). Ellinor Brasher, widow of Isaac Brasher and mother of Henry Brasher, relinquishes dower in the property last mentioned. signed Neeltie Brasher (Book 44, p.368).

14 July 1788, Henry Brasher, Gent. deeds 2 lots in Montgomery Ward to Jno. Dalton, Surgeon, consideration 1400. Elinor Brasher, mother of said Henry Brasher releases dower in said lots. (LBB of Denver did not give book and page)

5 Jan 1789, Henry Brasher, Gent, sale of lot for debt, to Garadus Hardenbrook Jr. (Book 113, p.454)

Henry Brasher Jr, nephew of Isaac Brasher, was also active:

14 Aug 1782, Henry Brasher deeds a lot on Cherry Street to Abigail (née Brasher), wife of Thos. A. Andrews, his sister. (Book 41, p.250)

20 May 1784, Henry Brasher deeds a lot on Cherry Street to Hannah Brasher, his sister, Witness: Eleanor Brasher. (Book 41, p.198)

7 April 1791, Henry Brasher and his sister, Margaret (Brasher) Palmer, deed ground for street in Montgomery Ward westerly on Fair Street and fronting Elbow Street, and in nearby Cliff Street, 24 ft. on Fair St. opposite Elbow St., extending 70 ft. (Book 269, p.12)

17 July 1794, Henry Brasher, mariner, and Frances his wife, to Palmer Cooper and his wife Margaret (Brasher) Palmer, lot lying in 5th Ward (Montgomery) same received by Henry and Margaret from Isaac Brasher and Elener, his wife. (Book 50, p. 108). Don't let their funny lack of punctuation fool you. I think the man's name was _____ Palmer and that he was a cooper by trade.

24 Nov 1794, Elinor Brasher, widow of Isaac Brasher, late of N.Y. and father of Henry Brasher,... Gen Deed (Book 50, p. 345) [Dr. LBB's notes don't say what to whom.]

Do these belong here? From gravestones in Trinity Church Yard:
Henry Brasher, Jr., s/o Henry and Geneva Brasher, d. 19 Sept 1787, age 9 mo. 25 days.
Isaac Brasher, s/o Henry and Geneva Brasher, d. 12 Oct 1760, age 29 (b. 1731)

Aaltje (or Ellen) Brasher and John Berrien

[4]-3. **Aaltje (or Ellen) Brasher**, (d/o Henry Brasher and Abigail Pearall), m. John Berrien (of French Huguenot ancestry), b. 27 Sept 1720. John Berrien became a merchant in New York, though he appears at one time to have commanded a vessel. He died 26 Dec 1773 and is buried in Trinity Churchyard. His widow died 17 Sept 1806, age 75. (ref: *The Annals of Newtown in Queens County, New York*, by James Riker Jr, c1852)

Children of John and Aaltje Elinor/Ellen (Brasher) Berrien:
[5]-1. Abigail Berrien, b. 8 Jan 1754, m. Capt. Alexander Cameron
[5]-2. John Berrien, b. 20 Dec 1756
[5]-3. Sarah Berrien, b. 31 Dec 1758; m. Jacob Hegemon
[5]-4. "Henry Brasher Herrian, s/o John and Eleanor Herrian, d. 19 Dec 1759"; bur. Trinity Church Yard.
[5]-5. Daniel Berrien, b. 20 Aug 1762, d. 1795, of yellow fever. Daniel was a shipbuilder.
[5]-6. Mary Berrian, b. 28 Oct 1765, d. 2 Aug 1770; bur Trinity Church Yard

Isaac Braisjer or Bradejor Jr and Jannet DeVor

[3]-4. Isaac Braisjer, or Brasher, bap. 11 Aug 1700, son of Isaac Breser (or Brasher) and his wife, Eleanor Aaltje Colevelt, and grandson of Henry Bréser the immigrant; married 23 Aug 1723, Jannet DuFooer, (or DeVoe, DeFour, Defoer, etc.) (Manual of 1862, p.565, says Jane Cox.); "Jennetie, wife of Isaac Brasher, d. 22 April 1788, age 93 yrs, 3 mos. 2 days" (b. 20 Feb 1695); Private in Artillery Co, 1738 (Manual of 1852, p.502); They had five children:
[4]-1. **Elizabeth Brasher**, bap. 24 May 1724
[4]-2. **Aeltje Brasher**, bap. 19 May 1726, d. young; name re-used
[4]-3. **Isaac Brasher, III**, bap. 14 Feb 1731, d. 12 Oct 1760

[4]-4. **David Brasher**, bap. 15 June 1733; m. 3 Dec 1758, Maria Anderson. "David, son of Isaac and Jane Brasher, d. 14 Dec 1758, age 25." (Manual of 1862, p.565, says Edward Brasher m. 3 Dec 1758, Maria Anderson.)

[4]-5. **Aeltje Brasher**, bap. 13 July 1737

33c. ABRAHAM BRASIER, the Revolutionist, and LYSBET SHOUTEN

In 1689, at the age of 20, [2-]11. **Abraham Brasher**, s/o Henry Bréser and Susannah (née Spicer/widow Walters), was one of the leading adherents of Gov. Jacob Leisler, who seized power in New York on the occasion of William of Orange coming to the throne in England and the expulsion of King James. An aristocratic party in New York strenuously opposed Gov. Leisler, doubtless because he had grabbed power before they could.

In 1689, Abraham Brasher assisted the soldiers in taking Colonel Bayard and was commissioned Ensign in DeBroun's company, 17 Dec 1689.

He made affidavit in June, 1690, styling himself Ensign, aged 21. He was Lieutenant in command of the fort in the city and Sheriff from Jan 8 to March.

After Jacob Leisler surrendered his authority in 1692 to Governor Sloughter, who was appointed by King William, Leisler's jealous enemies instituted the charge of high-treason against him and some of his adherents, including Abraham Brasher. They were hastily tried, convicted, and sentenced to be hanged and beheaded. Leisler and his son-in-law were executed; the others were held in prison 17 months.

Abraham was imprisoned by Governor Sloughter with nine others for treason. In 1692, he petitioned for pardon. Gov. Fletcher mentions him in Oct 1693 as under indictment for treason and the murder of Broun and others. He was finally pardoned 20 Feb 1702 by the king.

He was apparently free to go about his usual business after about 1692 and even take public office during the whole indictment. He was made a burgher 6 Sept 1698. He was listed as Ensign in Col. Abraham De Peyster's Regt. 1700 (O'Callaghan, *Doc. Hist. St. NY*, v.I, p.232). Abraham Brasier was assistant Alderman of the East ward 1699-1702 and, on 13 May 1702, petitioned against usurpations of Thomas Noell, Mayor. (See O'Callaghan, II:197-235 for several details relating to Abraham's part in the Leisler Rebellion and its aftermath.)

Abraham Brasher was on a 1703 Census of the East Ward, with a wife, one male child, and one female child. (*Doc Hist State NY*, I:611)

[2-]11. **Abraham Brasier**, or **Brasher Sr**, bap. 25 Nov 1668; m. 12 Nov 1690, *Lysbet Schouten*; seven children:

[3-]1. **John or Johann Brasier or Brasher**, bap. 25 Dec 1694 (Manual of 1857, p.747-8), died young; name re-used.

³⁻2. ***Lucas Brasier or Brasher**, bap. 20 Dec 1697; had several children, including the famous Col. Abraham Brasher, the Liberty Boy. See below.

³⁻3. **Susanna Brasier or Brasher**, bap. 28 Jan 1700 (Manual of 1864, p.568)

³⁻4. **Elizabeth Brasier or Brasher**, bap. 24 May 1701 (Manual of 1864, p.568)

³⁻5. ***John Brasier or Brasher**, bap. 15 March 1704 (Manual of 1864, p.568); was a carpenter, made freeman 19 Nov 1734; m. 18 May 1737, Susanna Baker

³⁻6. ***Abraham Brasier or Brasher, III** , bap. 30 Dec 1705 (Manual of 1864, p.568); was a baker and sea-captain. see below.

³⁻7. **Ephraim Brasier or Brasher Sr.**, bap. 2 June 1710 (Manual of 1864, p.568); m. 29 May 1740, Catharine Van Kauren (Kiunn, says Manual of 1862, p.565); Private in Artillery Co. 1738 (Manual of 1852, p.502); three children:

> ⁴⁻1. ***Ephraim Brasher Jr.**, bap. 18 April 1744 (?), d. 1810; was a silversmith and goldsmith of note and a Lt. in Col. Lasher's regiment in the Revolution, see "Lt. Ephraim Brasher and his Doubloon," below.
>
> ⁴⁻2. **Marritje "Margaret" Brasher**, bap. 19 June 1748, m. Robert Walker of Stratford, Fairfield Co, CT
>
> ⁴⁻3. **Abraham Brasher, IV**, bap. 12 Sept 1750; d. bef 1790, leaving a widow and four children (*The Numismatist*, June 1964, p.752)

The Will of Abraham Brasher, turner: 15 June 1717: I, Abraham Brasher, of New York, turner, being weak in body. I leave to my son Luke, all the working tools as belongs to my trade, and my largest gun. All the rest I leave to my wife Elizabeth, during her widowhood. But ... (if she remarries), she shall resign up all lands, tenements, and goods to my children, no division to be made until my youngest son, Ephraim, is of age. (*NY Hist Soc*, v.35 for the year 1902)

Wife, Elizabeth, was made executor, but, in the probate, widow Susannah Brasher was confirmed as executor.

Lucas "Luke" Brasher and Judith Gasherie

³⁻2. **Lucas "Luke" Brasher**, (or Bradejor, as he appears in some records), bap. 20 Dec 1697, d. 1736, was the son of Abraham Brasher and Elizabeth Schouten and grandson of Henry Bréser the immigrant; m. (Manual of 1862, p.565) 24 Nov 1723, Judith Gasherie, dau of Stephen and Engletie (Schoonmaker) Gasherie, from Marenne, France.

Judith bap. 30 May 1702. From *Memorials of the Huguenots in America--Special Reference to their Emigration into PA* (in Archives, Richmond VA): "In the Bethelem congregation was a number of members of Huguenot extraction. Judith Brasher (née Gasherie) was born at Esopus (now Kingston, NY) whither her parents had fled the revocation." [The Edict of Nantes, 13 April 1598, which granted religious and civil liberties to Huguenots, was revoked in 1685 by Louis XIV. This revocation caused a wild emigration of Huguenots from France.]

Luke Brasher and Judith Gasherie had seven children:

4-1. **Abraham Brasher**, bap. 13 Sept 1724, d. young

4-2. **Engeltie Brasher**, bap. 3 April 1726

4-3. **Elizabeth Brasher**, bap. 9 Aug 1727, d. young; name re-used

4-4. **Elizabeth Brasher**, bap. 4 March 1729

4-5. **Susanna Brasher**, bap. 31 Jan 1731; m. 16 Jan 1764, John Stiles (Manual of 1862, p.565; *NY Marr.* Bk 9:19)

4-6. **Judith Brasher**, bap. 14 May 1732

4-7. **[Col.] Abraham Brasher**, b. 2 Dec 1734, bap. 4 Dec 1734; m. Helena Kortright. Abraham became a prominent leader of "The Liberty Boys" during the Revolution.

John Brasher and Susannah Baker

3-5. **John Brasher**, (the second one by the name) son of Abraham Brasher and Elizabeth Schouten, was 13 at the time of his father's death. He was apprenticed to a carpenter, to learn the trade. "Indenture of John Brasier, son of Abraham Brasier, deceased and with the consent of his Mother Elizabeth Brasier, to John Kinder, Joyner, for seven years from Aug 6, 1719. ... And at the end of said term, shall give unto his said Apprentice One New hatt, Four New Neckcloths, Two Speckled Handkerchiefs, Six New Shirts, A New Coat, Wastcoat, and Breches, four pair of Stockings, two pair of shoes, all New. /Signed Aug 6, 1719 by John Brasier, in the Presence of Larans Garaner, Edward Pennant. Acknowledged August 6, 1719 before Philip Cortlandt, Alderman and Justice of the Peace. Registered for Mr. John Kinder the 8th day of August Anno Dom 1719. (*NY Hist Soc*, v.42)

John Brasier or Brasher, bap. 15 March 1704 (Manual of 1864, p.568); was a carpenter, made freeman 19 Nov 1734; m. 18 May 1737, Susanna Baker (Manual of 1862, p.565; *NY Marr.* Bk 1, p.6 says 16 May 1737); was Private in Artillery Co. 1738 (Manual of 1852, p.498); will dated 1 Aug 1764 (Book 24, p.46) names children (order not certain):

⁴⁻1. ***Henry Brasher**, bapt. 3 Nov 1742, d. KY, 1825. This is Lt. Henry Brasher, of Lasher's Regiment, who later moved to Kentucky, Ohio, and Indiana (Letter of Dr. Lewis B. Brasher). Note the names of descendants in KY: Jacob, John, Lawrence, etc. See below.

⁴⁻2. **Jacob Brasher**

⁴⁻3. **Lawrence Brasher**, felt-maker (1769 List of Freemen, NY City, Manual of 1856, p.480; head of household in South Ward, NYC, in 1790)

⁴⁻4. **Baker Brasher**, member of NYC militia in 1775

⁴⁻5. **Susanna Brasher**

⁴⁻6. **Elizabeth Brasher**

The Will of John Brasher: I, John Brasher, of New York, carpenter, August 1, 1764. I leave to my son Henry all my goods and personal estate. Also all that dwelling house and lot in New York, where I now live, and all other lands, messuages and tenements. In Trust, to sell all said houses and lots for the best price that can be got. From the proceeds all debts to be paid and the remainder to my sons, Henry, Jacob, Lawrence, and Baker, and my daughters Susanah, and Elizabeth. The part of my daughter Susanah is to be put at interest and the interest paid to her "during her present couverture." Proved 12 Sept 1764. (Book 24, p.46; see also *NY Hist Soc*, v. 30, for year 1897).

Baker Brasher is on a list of New York City Militia, 25 April 1775. Apparently he was issued weapons: an undated receipt: "County of New York Do hereby severally Acknowledge that we Good firelock Bayonent Car touch Box and Belt and do promise hereafter on demand ... Baker Brasher." A list of the guard for 28 April 1775 included Baker Brasher. "Ordered that a corpell and three men be opinted at Capt. Seares ... Baker Brasher ... (went of at 12 o'clock)." Undated: Centinels at the Door: Baker Brasher. "Name of the guards for Monday night": Baker Brasher. (*NY Hist Soc*, v.48)

Abraham Brasher Jr and Elizabeth Daly

³⁻6. **Abraham Brasher Jr**, was the son of Abraham Breser or Brasier and Elizabeth Schouten, and grandson of Henry Bréser the immigrant. He was bap. 30 Dec 1705; m. 10 Nov 1734 (Manual of 1862, p.565) Elizabeth Daly, dau of Philip Daly. Abraham served as alderman, 1738-40, was owner of the brigantine, Friendship, and applied for a commission for its master in May 1761. The Dutch Reformed Church

Manual of 1865, p.785, quotes the "New York Weekly Post Boy" of 9 Sept 1745: "Abraham Brasher, Captain of ship 'Four Brothers,' for London." He had ?five or six children:

4-1. **Elizabeth Brasher**, bap. 21 Sept 1735; m. 12 April 1755 (Manual of 1862, p.565), Wm. DePeyster

4-2. **Cornelia Brasher**, bap. 13 April 1738; m. 5 Oct 1788, Benj. Hoyit

4-3. **Susanna Brasher**, bap. 8 July 1739; m. 24 Sept 1761, Jas. Gillihen

4-4. **Maria Brasher**, bap. 24 Jan 1742

4-5. **Abraham Brasher, III**, bap. 19 Feb 1744; was a saddler, made freeman New York 9 Feb 1769 (1769 List of Freemen, NY City, Manual of 1856, p.480); 2nd Lt. in Col. Lasher's grenadier company, 1776; member of the Committee of One Hundred, and the New York Provincial Congress, 1775; called Colonel in 1776-7, and was a representative in the Legislature, 1777-83.

4-6? **Philip Brasher**, b. c1745-6, d. 1785. This is somewhat hypothetical; see discussion under Philip Brasher, below.

33d. COL. ABRAHAM BRASHER,
The Liberty Boy

[4-7]. **Col. Abraham Brasher**, b. 2 Dec 1734, d. 1782, son of Lucas Brasher and Judith Gasherie, was a gunsmith and "Merchant of New York." He was made freeman 3 Nov 1747; he was a member of the [Revolutionary] Committees of 51, 60, and 100 and a delegate to the first three Provisional Congresses. In July 1776, the window leads were taken (i.e. stolen) from his house [by the British, to make bullets from the lead]. On 9 June 1776, he was on a Committee to superintend the removal of British prisoners, and, on 7 Nov 1776, with Isaac Roosevelt, he reported that the muster rolls of the schooner, "General Putnam," had been examined.

Walter Barret's *Old Merchants of New York*, Vol III, p.29-32 gives a sketch of his life. It tells this story of Abraham's courtship of Helen Kortright: A Mr. C. D. had courted her for a year, then went to Europe, but did not write. Helen was "true" however, and refused to entertain any other suitors. "In fact, a young man would not pass muster in the city unless he had been refused by the beautiful Miss Kortright. All this while, there was one beau that the mother liked. The daughter did not, and avoided him whenever she possibly could. If he called, she was busy and would not come down. Still he came. Then she began to wonder at his loving patience and forebearance under her scorn. One morning, he caught her before she could escape from the reception room.

"Helen, why do you always fly from me? Why will you not give me an opportunity of declaring my attachment to you? Let this morning decide my fate."

"Very well, sir. I do not wish to keep any gentleman in a state of suspension. I cannot encourage your addresses. I esteem you, but I will tell you frankly, that I feel a preference for Mr. C.D. who is in London; and if he returns with the same sentiment for me as when he left, I shall probably marry him."

"Are you certainly engaged to him?"

"No, sir, not engaged verbally, but mentally."

"Then, my dear Miss Helen, suppose you continue to be verbally engaged to me, and mentally engaged to him."

"Would you marry any young lady under such circumstances?"

"Yes, you, with all my heart and soul."

"Would you risk your future happiness, and marry a lady who prefers another?"

"Miss Helen, I will risk anything to obtain you, and I will be amply compensated for every risk, and it shall be the study of my life to make you happy."

The ice was broken, and they talked freely upon this subject. The lover in London did not come home. The New York lover was here, and finally consent was obtained, and on the 13th of July, 1758 (new style), Abraham Brasher, son of Luke and Judith Brasher, was married to the lovely Helen Kortright, by the Rev. Doctor Barclay, of Trinity Church.

Abraham was one of the earliest patriots and was hunted by the British. On 19 Dec 1777, only a few hours after his son Abraham K. Brasher was born, the British burned his house at Parasmus. After a Major Byles had been shot dead in the yard and the house was on fire, Helen requested permission of the British soldiers to carry out her sick mother. Permission was granted, and, as they slowly carried the bed out into the yard, Col. Brasher crawled out under it, in the presence of 200 British soldiers, and escaped after they had left.

Abraham Brasher lead a Battalion in Col. Lasher's Regiment. He was active among the "Liberty Boys" and wrote many stirring songs of the revolution, the most popular being "The General's Trip to Morristown." (Cf. *Revolutionary War Manusripts, N.Y. State Lib, 50, 31*; Barrett's *Old Merchants of N. Y. City*; *New York in the Revolution*; and especially Brodhead, *Doc. & Colonial Hist of New York*, Vol 3, pp. 740, 743, 765, 811; Vol. 4, pp. 55, 83, 212, 220.)

"At the residence of Col. Brasher, John Pintard met Eliza Brasher, a daughter of the patriotic Colonel. They became engaged, and in 1785 they were married. A more splendid couple never approached the marriage altar. He was a very handsome man, and she was the very loveliest girl in the land. Her hair was black and massive, and done up on the cushions of that day, made her look magnificent--this, too, combined with the most lovely face, made her,--as she was for many years--a charming woman. He, too, looked well, with his powdered hair, blue coat, standing collar, and handsome person. If our girls in 1863, would adopt the style and mode of dressing the hair one hundred years ago, they would look a thousand times more lovely than now. Pity the girls "don't see it!" *Old Merhants*, p.222: the author got carried away with his own tastes there!

Abraham and Helena's great-great-great-grandson, Craig Colgate Jr, of Washington, D.C., published a book, *Helena Kortright Brasher, 1739-1819*, in 1987. Some excerpts: "I do not have the impression that Helena Kortright Brasher had a particularly happy life. Though she may have been content in her husband, and he in her, she lost him at a comparatively early age, in difficult circumstances. ... I have a typescript of her diary. From it, one gets a picture of increasing troubles crowding around the old lady--declining health, money (she apparently loaned a good sum to Gasherie, who somehow lost it all), and worries over her namesake, Helen, who did not marry until she was 31, a very, very old age to remain single in those days.

"She did not get along well with her son-in-law, Samuel Davies Craig, who married his wife about 3 months before the birth of their first and only child, Benjamin Davies Kortright Craig. She lived with the Craig family for a time, together with her sister, Mrs. John Wilkinson Hansom (Maria Kortright), but things were not easy as several extracts from the correspondence of John Pintard (Collections of the New York Historical Society) demonstrate:

Aug 12, 1819: "Mama had to accompany her Mother to see new lodgings, as Mr. Craig will not consent to accomdate the old ladies any longer. The weather was blustering and unfavorable and with all possible research this object is unaccomplished."

April 13, 1819: "Grandma is not yet suited with lodgings and I fear will find some difficulty. At any rate, they can stay till accommodated with Aunt Craig's. The rents of the houses and markets are so very high that board wages must bear some proportion. It is painful at the very close of life to see these good old ladies thus exposed to wander from place to place without any fixed residence to die in. I confess, my dearest daughter, that the reflection gives me the utmost pain, and I have only to be thankful that I have not been the cause of their destitution. Nor would your Aunt Helen part with a mother who lavished on her what ought to have been her support and comfort in her old days, were it not for Mr. C. who has few sympathies beyond his own personal wants and comforts."

"Helen Kortright Brasher, widow of Colonel Abraham Brasher, died in New York City on November 3, 1819, eighty years of age. She was buried in the Pintard Vault of the French Church. When this was demolished in 1831, her remains were removed to St. Clements. I believe this church has also gone. Her remains may have been then taken, along with those of John and Elizabeth Brasher Pintard, to St. Michael's Cemetery, Astoria, Long Island."

Col. Abraham Brasher, b. 2 Dec 1734, bap. 4 Dec 1734, d. 1782 in exile at Morristown, New Jersey, 1782, and was buried there in Presbyterian Cem. He m. 13 July 1758, Helena Kortright, d/o Cornelius and Hester (Cannon) Kortright. Helena was b. 1739, christened 18 April 1739, d. 3 Nov 1819.

Abraham and Helena had ten children:

⁵-1. **Judith Brasher**, b. 29 May 1759, d. 20 Oct 1811; m. Col. Fitch Hall of Boston. Five children (*Old Merchants of NY*, p.221)
    ⁶-1. Fitch Hall, Jr., b. 25 Jan 1785, d. 1807; m. _____ Mitchell
    ⁶-2. Benjamin Hall, b. 27 July 1786, d. young
    ⁶-3. William Hall, b. 1 May 1790, d. c1820
    ⁶-4. Helen Hall, m. _____ Levins, of Boston
    ⁶-5. Emily Hall, m. Nathaniel Curtis, of Boston
⁵-2. **Cornelius Brasher**, b. 28 Oct 1760, d. 29 Aug 1761; name re-used
⁵-3. **Cornelius Brasher**, b. 11 Dec 1762, d. 11 Jan 1764
⁵-4. **Elizabeth Brasher**, b. 2 Sept 1766; d. 13 Oct 1838; m. 1785, John Pintard, b. 1759, d. 1866.
    ⁶-1. Louisa H. Pintard, b. 1796, d. 1868; m. Thos. L. Sevoss, b. 1786, d. 1866
⁵-5. **Abraham Brasher**, b. 18 Feb 1769, d. 17 Dec 1769
⁵-6. **Hester Brasher**, b. 6 July 1770, d. 5 Sept 1771
⁵-7. **Mary Brasher**, b. 8 July 1771, d. 20 Aug 1771
⁵-8. **Gasherie Brasher**, b. 3 Feb 1773, d. 1803; m. Jane Abeel, d/o Gerrit Abeel. Jane left a will in 1806; Gasherie sailed from New York, 13 March 1803 and was lost at sea. He left five children, according to *Old Merchants of NYC*, 4th series, p. 29, 31. Jane's will, however, did not name any Brasher children; still, a series of deeds does suggest that Jane's Abeel heirs gave property "back" to Gasherie's children.
    ⁶-1. **John Pintard Brasher**; m. Mary _____
    ⁶-2. **Mary Brasher**; m. George Godweiss Jr
    ⁶-3. **Ellen Brasher**
    ⁶-4. **Jane Brasher**; m. Gerritt Bluker
    ⁶-5. **Julia Brasher**, m. Robt. D. Weeks
⁵-9. **Helena Kortright Brasher**, b. 19 Dec 1777 (twin); d. 5 March 1853; lic/m. 16/18 May 1808, Samuel Davies Craig, d. 2 March 1856
    ⁶-1. Benjamin Davies Kortright Craig, b. Aug 1808, d. 1879; m.1. 1839, Anne Wagstaff Thomas; m.2. 1859, Virginia Healy
⁵-10. **Abraham Kortright Brasher**, b. 19 Dec 1777 (twin); d. 1813 at Drontheim, Norway. Abraham K. Brasher was a sea captain, commanded a vessel. Will of Abraham K. Brasher, 25 Nov 1812, to mother, Helena; to sister Helen and her son, Benjamin Davis Craig; silver mug with family "court of arms" to nephew Jno. Pintard Brasher with request that as it was his grandfather's, Abraham Brasher's, he will preserve it; etc. default of which, mug to be given to nephew Benj. D. Craig; brother-in-law, Samuel Craig.

Will of Jane Brasher, 3 Nov 1806 (Book 46, p.517) names heirs: Gerrit Abul; Evart Abul; John Abul; Jose Roosevelt; George Godweiss, Jr, and Mary his wife; Gerrit B. Bluker and Jane his wife; and Peter Byvanck, default possessors of 3 lots, petitioned to be divided by partition sale.

10 Feb 1824, deed from above: John P. Brasher; Mary Brasher; Robt. D. Weeks and Julia his wife; Mary Abul, Isabella Abul Howell, Jane Abul Howell, Mary Abul Howell, by guardian C. N. Abul; G. B. Abul. (Book 173, p. 238) [LBB did not say what was being deeded, nor to whom. He did add a note, without reference, that Mary Abul, wife of Garrit Abul, was daughter of Eyert Byvanck, married 1760.]

Will of Abraham Brasher, merchant, 6 Jan 1774 (he didn't die until 1782; the twins were born after this will was made): I, Abraham Brasher, merchant, of the city of New York, being in good health. My funeral charges to be paid as soon as may be after my decease. I leave to my beloved son Gasharie, when twenty-one or married, the tract of land in Marbletown, Ulster County, commonly called Gasheries Bucht, containing 112 acres. My executors to have full power to lease or sell this land, at their discretion; the proceeds to be put at interest on good and sufficient security; the rent or interest from time to time towards the support of my beloved wife Helena and her children. The land or principal to be delivered to my son Gasherie, when 21 or married should he die in non-age or single, then the land to pass, with above limitation, to the next son I may have born before my son Gasherie's death as above; should there be no other son born, then the land is to be considered part of my estate and disposed of hereinafter mentioned. Unto my said son, or the next son I may have, my small collection of books when of sufficient age for them to be serviceable, and at my executors discretion. Unto my son Gasherie, and my daughters, Judith and Elizabeth, each, respectively when 21, or married £350; and to such child or children hereafter born of my wife Helena, the like sum at majority or marriage. Unto my wife, all her wearing apparel, my household furniture. The remainder of my estate, real and personal, to be sold or otherwise disposed of by my executors; the proceeds of sale to be put at interest for the support of my wife and children until the youngest is 21 or is married. Should all my children die in non-age, and single, the interest of the whole estate to go to my wife's support, and £1000 of the principal entirely at her disposal; the residue at her decease, unto the sons of my cousins, Phillip, Ephraim, and Henry Brasher, of the City of New York, in equal shares, payable when each son is 21. I make my wife Helena, and my brothers-in-law, Lawrence Kortright, William Rickets, Van Cortlandt, and Henry Van Vleck and Cornelius Peter Low, all of the city of New York, merchants, executors.

Dated Jan 6, 1774. Proved Feb 13, 1784. (Book 36, p.244)

Philip, Ephraim, and Henry Brasher, the cousins who served with him so early and so consistently in Col. Lasher's 1st New York Regiment, all enlisted and/or were commissioned on 14 Sept 1775, ten months before the Declaration of Independence.

O'Callaghan, *Calendar of New York Hist. Mss. Rev. Papers*:

Abraham Brasher "committee man," Lt. Col. 1st NY Battalion, Lasher's Regt.

Philip Brasher, Adjutant (in German Fusilers Co.) 1st NY Batt, commissioned 14 Sept 1775, Col. Lasher's Regt.)

Ephraim Brasher, 3rd Lt., Grenadiers Co. Col. Lasher's 1st NY Batt., commissioned 14 Sept 1775

Henry Brasher, 1st Lt, 29 Aug 1775; 3rd Lt. "Prussian Blues" Co., of 1st Regt, commissioned 14 Sept 1775; 2nd Lt. 1st Regt. "Lasher's Regt", 29 Jan 1776.

Capt ____ Brasher, in Col. Malcombs Batt. (This was Henry: O'Callaghan, p.27, says Henry was Capt. in Malcom's Batt., Col. Lasher's Regt. Henry's pension applications bear this out.)

Abraham Brasher, Jr. 2nd Lt. 8th Co. 1st NY Continental Regt, Alex McDougale, Col.

Abraham E. Brasher, 2nd Lt, 9th NY Troops, Col. Goose Van Schaick's Regt., 1775; 1st Lt, 1st NY Batt, 1776

Brodhead, *Doc. & Colonial Hist of New York*, Vol 4, p.601, lists as members of Committee of 100, 1 May 1775:

#21 - Abraham Brasher

1st Regt, Adj. - Philip Brashier

2nd Lt. Grenadier Co. - Abraham Brashier [Abraham Jr]

33e. LT./CAPT. HENRY BRASHER and LUCY CLARKE

[4-]1. **Henry Brasher**, bap 3 Nov 1742. New York City, was the son of John (Johannes) Brasher and his wife, Susanna Baker, grandson of Abraham Brasher Sr, of the Leisler Rebellion, and great-grandson of Henry Bréser the immigrant. He married 6 Feb 1764, *Lucy Clarke* (*NY Marr.* Bk 8:51). This may have been the Henry Braser who received £14/10 on 18 July 1755, for going express from Pookeepsie to Albany and Norwalk, and on 2 Sept 1755, received £7/10 for going express to the assembly at Albany; but he was young at the time (13 years).

He was Second Lieutenant in the company of Prussian Blues, Col. Lasher's regiment, N. Y. Militia, who voted to enter the service of Congress against the King in 1776; later Capt. in Col. Malcolm's command. Apparently, all his and Lucy's children were born in New York.

Children of Henry and Lucy (Clarke) Brasher: some bapt at NY Pres. Church

[5-]1. *****John Brasher**, b. 15 May 1764, d. 1840; m.1. Sarah _____; m.2. Keziah Broun of N.J.

[5-]2. **Abraham Brasher**, b. 26 July 1766, bapt. 10 Aug 1766

[5-]3. **Elizabeth Brasher**, b. 21 Jan 1769, bapt. 19 Feb 1769

[5-]4. **Lucy Brasher**, b. 18 Nov 1770, bapt. 3 Jan 1773; m.1. ____ Woolman; m.2. ____ Reed

[5-]5. *****Robert Clarke Brasher**, b. 8 Dec 1772; m. Hannah Seamon

[5-]6. **Charles Lee Brasher**, b. 31 July 1775, enumerated 1810 Census, Boone Co, KY, p.57 [1850 Census, Boone Co, KY, Dist 1, p.119: Jane Brashear]. Possibly Charles Brasher, m. Mary Black, 18 Oct 1799, BD, marr. by John Taylor, bond Elijah Horsley, Bk A-1, Boone Co, KY--

    [6-]1. **Sarah Brasher**, m. 1818 in Glasgow, Barren Co, KY, Dr. Isaac Westerfield, and started a Westerfield Family Bible; Sarah's great-granddaughter, Lida Brasher White, owns the Bible (1983).

    [6-]?. possible child: **Robert Hood Brasher**, who named a son Robert Westerfield Brasher. See "Westerfields," below.

[5-]7. *****Jacob Brasher**, m. 1 Jan 1804, (Boone Co, KY, Bk A:3, "by Alexander Mcpherson, bone Archd. H. Reid,) *Sarah Black*, d/o ?Lewis Black

[5-]8. **Susan Brasher**, unm.

5-9. **Sarah Brasher**, m. *George Black*, brother of Sarah (Black) Brasher and s/o ?Lewis Black

Henry and his family moved to Ohio, near Cincinnati in 1790. He is listed on "An Act to Establish the Town of Newport," Campbell Co, KY, in 1795 (ref: "Acts Approved by the Gen. Assembly," *KY Ancestors*, v.29, no.2, 1993-4), where he lived and was a Justice of the Peace. He was a member of the commission to organize the county and served on the first Board of Commissioners (see Campbell Co, Court Order Book A, p.103).

On 17 Dec 1793, James Taylor Sr of Caroline Co, VA and John Bartle of Mason Co, KY, sold 12 lots in Newport for 60 pounds. Witnesses: John Pennington Smith, Robert Kean, Henry Brashears, Boazdell Aleck (Mason Co, KY, Deed, Bk A, p.397). This looks like a sale to establish the city center, official building, etc. William Taylor had originally been granted huge plots of land in the Ohio Territory in 1787, presumably for Rev. War service.

Henry's son, John Brasher, was recommended in 1797 to the Executive Committee as "a proper person to be appointed a magistrate of this county" (Campbell Co Court Order Book A, p. 102). Henry's son, Charles Brasher, was appointed Under-sheriff of Campbell Co by Sheriff William Reddick, at the Sept 1797 Court (Court Order Book A, p.111).

"The Governor nominated and by and with the consent of the Senate made the following appointments: John Bush, Henry Brashier, John Hall, James Miller, Squire Grant, and John Ewing, Justices of Campbell Co." (Dept of State Archives, Campbell Co, p.2).

In the 1808 Tax List of Campbell Co, Henry Brasher is listed as "gon to boon" (Boone Co, KY, where his son, Charles lived). Several others are listed as "gone to the falls," "gon over the Ohigho," "gone to Sincinati," and "to Orleens," and the like.

Henry applied for a Revolutionary War pension from "Indiana District," later Dearborn County, Indiana.

United States of America)
Indiana District   )
Be it remembered that on the fifth day of September, Eighteen hundred and eighteen, before me the subscribing judge of the District Court of the United States in the District aforesaid [it became Dearborn County in a few years], personally appeared Henry Brasher, aged Seventy six years [b. 1742], resident of the said district, who being by me first duly sworn according to law on his oath makes the following declarations in order to obtain the provisions made by the late act of

Congress entitled "An act to provide for certain persons engaged in land and Naval service of the United States in the Revolutionary War--

"That the said Henry Brasher was appointed in the spring of 1775 an ensign in the company of Infantry commanded by Captain James ?Brown in the Regiment of Infantry commanded by Col. Malcolm in the New York line on the continental establishment in the Revolutionary War; that he remained in the said service somewhat upwards of two years in which service he rose successively to the rank of Lieutenant and Captain-- when he became so afflicted with sciatica or rheumatick pains as to be unable to continue in service where upon he resigned-- he cannot now walk without the aid of crutches-- he was in the battles of Long Island, Kings Bridges, and White Plains-- his service commissions have been lost by accident or carelessness-- and that he is in reduced circumstances and stands in need of the assistance of his country for support. ..." /s/ R. Parke

On 1 Dec 1819, John Brasher (age 55, b. 1764), made affidavit before Judge James Carnahan of Hamilton County, Ohio, corroborating his father's petition.

And on 14 April 1824, Henry Dugan, "upwards of eighty-eight years," made affidavit in Dearborn County, Indiana, that he had enlisted in a company of Infantry in 1776, commanded by Capt. Henry Brasher, and fought with him in the Battles of Long Island and Harsterns Marsh, and that he "has recently seen the man, is well acquainted with his person, and perfectly satisfied as to the identity of the said Henry Brasher."

Henry got his pension, but died before the first payment arrived. He is said to have dropped dead in 1825 when asked to be a part of the reception committee for a visit of Revolutionary War French General LaFayette to the U.S.

JOHN BRASHER, s/o Capt. Henry

[5-]1. **John Brasher**, b. New York City, 15 May 1764, d. KY, 1840, s/o Henry Brasher and Lucy Clarke, was a Private in the Revolution and moved to Springfield twp, Northwest Territory (later Ohio) c1797-8. He was with the family c1790, lived in Newport, KY, 1790s.

On 5 Sept 1796, an Indenture of Bargain and Sale from the Trustees of Newport [Campbell Co, KY] to John Brasher was acknowledged by the said Trustees and ordered to be recorded (Campbell Co, KY, Order Book A, p.59).

John lived in Hamilton Co, Ohio in 1819.

The 1850 Census of Kenton Co, KY, lists a J. Brashears, 4th Ward, Covington, p.547. (Kenton Co formed from Campbell in 1840).

John Brasher m. *Sarah* _____, b. 1764?, d. 16 April 1814, age 52 yrs, 10 mos. [She would have to be born June 1861, to be 52 yrs, 10 mos in April 1814, eh? Was she Sarah Hayms? Capt. Henry's branch of the family frequently uses family surnames as middle names.]

Dr. Lewis B. Brasher, of Denver, sent these family sheets to Dr. John Lakin Brasher, of Attalla, AL; he was apparently copying Bible records. (He names his father's brothers, but doesn't name his father!)

6-1. ***Joseph H. (Hayms?) Brasher**, b. 12 Sept 1795, Newport, KY. This is apparently Dr. L.B.B.'s "uncle Joe" who moved to Texas, whom he and Rev. J.L.B. corresponded about. See family sheet below.

6-2. _____ **Brasher**, b. KY, 1796, d. KY, 1874.

7-1. **Dr. Lewis B. (?Black) Brasher**, b. KY 7 Sept 1844

6-3. **Thomas R. Brasher**, b. 6 March 1797, Newport, KY

6-4. **Robert Clarke Brasher I**, b. 18 Oct 1798, Springfield Twp, Northwest Territory (later, state of Ohio)

6-5. **John B. Brasher**, b. 12 June 1800, N.W. Terr.

6-6. **Adm. Byrd Brasher**, b. 29 May 1803, Springfield Twp, State of Ohio; drowned in 1854.

[LBB next listed the death of his grandmother, Sarah Brasher, 16 April 1814; then listed two births, which some identify as sons. So, did John m.2. Keziah Broun/Brown, d/o ?Ephraim Brown?]

6-7. **Ephraim Brown Brasher**, b. 21 Nov 1816, Springfield

6-8. **Lawrence Lovegrove Brasher**, b. 1 July 1819.

6-1. **Joseph H. Brasher**, Lewis B. Brasher's "Uncle Joe" of Texas, b. 12 Sept 1795; d. 1 Dec 1861; m. 10 Feb 1818, *Elizabeth Glass*, b. 13 Feb 1802, d. 10 Aug 1843. Joseph and Elizabeth had bad luck with getting children to live very long, and Elizabeth died a week after the last one was born. Joseph H. Brasher, 64, is #215/231 in Fayette Co, TX, in 1860, with son Charles, 17, at home. Son Joseph, 22, b. MO, is Laborer in HH #920/1241, working for J.P. Reynolds, b. MD, c1815, farmer, $2300, $3800, and wife, Susan, b. MO, c1830, and dau, Josephine, b. TX, c1849.

7-1. **A.B. Brasher**, b. 27 Jan 1821; d. 29 July 1821, age 6 months

7-2. **Robert Clarke Brasher II**, b. 20 June 1823; d. 20 July 1823, lived 1 day; name re-used

7-3. **Sarah Brasher**, b. 24 Aug 1824; d. 10 July 1852, age 28

7-4. **Amanda Brasher**, b. April 1826; d. 9 April 1826, d. infancy

7-5. **Susan Brasher**, b. 6 July 1829

7-6. **Isabella Brasher**, b. 14 July 1832

7-7. **Mary Brasher**, b. 18 Sept 1834

7-8. **George Brasher**, b. 20 Feb 1836; d. Oct 1862, age 26

⁷-9. **Joseph Brasher**, b. 13 June 1838; d. 26 Feb 1870, age 32; born MO, per 1860 Fayette, TX,

⁷-10. **Charles M. Brasher**, b. 16 June 1841; born in Texas, per 1860 Fayette Co, TX

⁷-11. **Robert Clarke Brasher III**, b. 3 Aug 1843; d. 5 Oct 1843, age 2 months

ROBERT CLARKE BRASHER
and HANNAH SEAMON

⁵-5. **Robert Clarke Brasher I**, b. 8 Dec 1772, d. at Lebanon, OH, 26 March 1846, s/o Henry and Lucy (Clarke) Brasher; m. *Hannah Seamon*, b. 11 May 1782, d. at Livingston, IL, 27 Sept 1842, d/o William Seamon of Washington, PA (data from Robert C. Brasher's family bible, in possession (1993) of Ralph Brasher, 2427 W. Main, Belleville, IL 62223; see BFB 36:6 & 100:10). In 1816, Henry and family moved from Cincinnati, OH, to Terre Haute, IN. From the family bible, Ralph Brasher writes: "Children born to them were: Henry, Sarah, née Carsons (sic), Amy, Lucy, Mary, Amanda, Robert Clark, or William, and Ransom Hunt Brasher" and "Henry Brasher Jr was drowned in the Mississippi River near Randolph, 1 May 1853."

Family of Robert Clarke Brasher and Hannah Seamon:

⁶-1. **Henry Brasher**, b. 6 July 1800; m. 31 Aug 1826, *Susan McKee*, b. 30 Aug 1808

    ⁷-1. **Robert Brasher**, b. 1 Nov 1827; m. 20 Jan 1856, *Julia Susannah Brown*, b. 28 June 1831

        ⁸-1. **Alice Brasher**, b. 3 Dec 1853

    ⁷-2. **Ruth McKee Brasher**, m. *William Slaughter*,

    ⁷-3. **Mariann Ragan Brasher**, m. 25 Dec 1850, *William Brasher Boswell*,

⁶-2. **Sarah Brasher**, b. 26 Sept 1801; m. *Thomas Rogers*,

    ⁷-1. Lawrence Rogers, b. 7 May 1826; m. 2 March 1851, *Rachel Richardson*, b. 10 April 1832

⁶-3. **Elizabeth Brasher**, b. 24 June 1802

⁶-4. **Amy Brasher**, b. 25 Nov 1805; m. *Wells A. Hubbard*,

⁶-5. **Lucy Ann Brasher**, b. 23 Jan 1807

⁶-6. **Mary Brasher**, b. 6 April 1810

⁶-7. **Amanda Melvina Fitzellen Brasher**, b. 27 March 1814; m. *Sanders Phillips*,

⁶-8. **Robert Clarke Brasher IV**, (?twin) b. 14 April 1817

⁶-9. **William Seamon Brasher**, (?twin) b. 14 April 1817; m. *Catherine Burns*,

⁶⁻10. **Ransom Hunt Brasher**, b. 17 April 1820, Terre Haute, IN. He was the third white child born in Terre Haute. Ransom m. 29 Dec 1842, *Mary Ann Stewart*, b. 25 Feb 1821, d/o Henry Stewart of Blanford, MA, and Rhoda Nutt of London, MA

   ⁷⁻1. **Albert Laer Brasher**, b. 13 Oct 1843, d. 31 Dec 1931; m. *Samira Ann Burris*, b. 7 April 1844, d. 7 April 1935

      ⁸⁻1. **Albert Ransom Brasher**, b. 9 Feb 1868, d. 10 April 1958; m. *Eddie Launa Preston*, b. 25 May 1869, d. 18 Feb 1942

         ⁹⁻1. **Eddie Launa Brasher**, b. 1 Nov 1895

         ⁹⁻2. **Albert Ralph Brasher**, b. 26 Jan 1910

   ⁷⁻2. **Cyrus Nutt Brasher**, b. 26 Oct 1847, d. 31 March 1857

Ralph Brasher, 2427 W. Main, Belleville, IL 62223, owns the family bible of the first Robert Clarke Brasher. He writes: "It was published in 1801 by Matthew Carey of Philadelphia, the first extensive American publisher. I appears to have been the first edition published in the U.S. "Parson" Weems, the biographer of Washington, toured the country for about thirty years, selling Carey's publications. Probably sold several thousand of the bibles.

"The first entry in the bible is the following narrative: Early in the 17th century [sic; probably means early 1700s] Henry Brasher and his brother left Germany for the U.S. coming by way of Scotland. While at sea their vessel was lost. They were both rescued, but by different vessels. Henry landed in N.Y., the brother in Charleston, S.C. They both supposed the other dead for nearly 100 years; till their descendants learned this fact.

"Henry married Sarrah [we have her name as Lucy] Clark while in New York, but came to Ohio. They had children: John, Jacob, Sarrah (née Black) [??; she m. George Black], Charles, Lucy, and Robert Clark, the original owner of this bible."

As with many another family legend, some details do not square with the documents about the family! Four generations separate the immigrant Henry Bréser and Capt. Henry Brasher, who moved to Ohio.

JACOB BRASHER and SARAH BLACK

⁵⁻7. Jacob Brasher, s/o Capt. Henry Brasher and Lucy Clarke, m. *Sarah Black*, Jacob Brasher and Sarah (Black) had five children:

⁶⁻1. **Benjamin Brasher**,

⁶⁻2. **Charles Brasher**,

⁶⁻3. **Albert Brasher**,

⁶⁻4. **John Brasher**,

⁶⁻5. **Elizabeth Brasher**, m. *Madison Sebrie*,

    ⁷⁻1. Sultana Sebrie, m. Capt. John Wilson Farrell,

        ⁸⁻1. James Madison Farrell, d. young

        ⁸⁻2. Wm. Price Farrell, d. young

        ⁸⁻3. Ida Brasher Farrel, m. Albert Matthews. Ida was Regent of the DAR at Hillsboro, Ohio; in 1896, she had one child surviving: Helen Brasher Matthews.

The 1860 census index of Kenton Co, KY (formed from Campbell Co in 1840):
Andrew Brasher, age 8, b. KY, p.406, line 3, 7th Ward, Covington
Charles Brasher, age 51, b. OH, p.74, line 14, Steamboat pilot

WESTERFIELDS

Robert Hood "Ivan" Brasher, b. KY, ?possible son of Charles Lee Brasher and a wife, _____ Hood (this is pure speculation); m. *Julien Anne "Sarah" McManame*, b. June 1817, Kentucky, d. Oakland, Calif, 15 Feb 1909, widow, age 91 years, 8 months, of "Pneumonia, Asthma, Senility, and General disability," according to her death certificate (#9-003045), copy in possession in 1982 of Betty Brasher, widow of William Brasher of Taft, CA. Why the couple were called "Ivan" and "Sarah" is not known. Both "Julia Ann" and her son, "Field," lived at 1114 14th St. Oakland, CA, at the time of their deaths.

1. **Robert Westerfield "Field" Brasher**, b. 6 Feb 1842, Indiana, d. 27 May 1909, Oakland, CA (death Cert. #9-011403); m. *Kate Hibbens*, b. 1847, d. age 37, 1885, Ione, CA, d/o Willie Hibbens. Evelyn Brasher Evans referred to her as "Florence;" her listing in 1870 Census of Lawrenceburg, Dearborn Co, IN gives her name as "Kate." They had 9 children, but Evelyn and Betty mentioned only their lines.

    1. **Lewis Hood Brasher**, b. June 1867 (was in the 1900 Census of California as L. Hood Brasher)

    2. **William "Willie" Summerville Brasher**, b. 1869, Indiana, d. 1952, CA; m. 1894 in Los Angeles, CA, *Rosannah Carolina Morss*, b. 1872 in Cambria, CA, d. c1953, Taft, CA. d/o Cyrus Dudley Morss & Mary Ellen Kane of Maryland. Cyrus s/o Jacob and Terrah Morss, who crossed the prairies in a covered wagon in 1849 and settled 150 miles south of San Francisco.

        1. **Evelyn B. Brasher**, b. 16 Nov 1898, Santa Monica, CA, living in 1982 in Oakland, CA; m. *Jack B. Evans*, b. 1898, Uvalde, TX, d. c1960. They had five children.

2. **William "Bill" Waldon Brasher**, b. 21 Nov 1899, Santa
   Monica, CA, d. 23 July 1962; m. 10 July 1927, ***Betty Martha
   Eynaud***, b. 30 May 1910, Bakersfield, CA and living in 1982.
   They had five children.
2. **Cornelia Brasher**, in H/H of Robert W. "Field" Brasher in 1870,
   Dearborn Co, IN. The children referred to her as "Aunt Neal."
?. **George Brasher**, a possible brother of Robert W.

Who? 1880 Census, Lawrenceburg twp, Dearborn Co, IN, Dist 47, p.13,
No.2, 22 June 1880, ennumerator Alexander Beckman (copied by Betty
Brasher, of Taft, CA: Film #40880-377984): #128:
Thomas Brasher, 56, b. c1824, Indiana, Farmer
   Ellevina, 51, b. c1829, Indiana, wife, keeping house
   Florence, 27, b. c1853, IN, dau
   Casper, 25, b. c1855, IN, son
   Fannie, 19, b. c1861, IN, dau
   Clara, 17, b. c1863, IN, dau
   Cora, 16, b. c1864, IN, dau
   William, 14, b. c1866, IN, son
   Walter, 12, b. c1868, son

33f. LT. EPHRAIM BRASHER JR AND HIS DOUBLOON

[4-]1. **Ephraim Brasher, Jr**, bapt. 18 April 1744, son of Ephraim Brasier Sr, and his wife, Catharine Van Kauren, grandson of Abraham Brasier Sr, and great-grandson of Henry Breser the immigrant. The *Old Middle Dutch Church Records* say he was born 1734 and died 10 Nov 1810, aged 66 [should be born 17_4_4]. He enlisted at the first call to arms and was a Lt. of grenadiers in Col. Lasher's Regiment; he eventually rose to the rank of Major in the militia after the war. In 1783, he was on a Committee of Exiles to make arrangements for Evacuation Day, when the British forces withdrew from New York; and also on a Committee to conduct the Procession on that day. Previous to this, he had signed congratulatory addresses to Gen. Washington and Gov. Clinton. (cf. *New York in the Revolution*, p. 218)

He was also a noted goldsmith, who lived at 1 Cherry Street, next door to where George Washington moved when he retired from the Presidency. Ephraim had a silver and gold shop at 77 Queen Street. He minted the now-famous "Brasher Doubloon," in 1787. Seven of these coins are known to exist today. They vary in weight a little, but average about 408 grains, worth about $16, which is about the weight of the gold Spanish Doubloon of that time--hence the name. It was about the size of the pence of the time, slightly larger than our penny.

On the face of the coin is a rising sun and a landscape, under which the surname BRASHER is cast. The legend says "NOVA EBORACA [NEW YORK] * COLUMBIA * EXCELSIOR." On the obverse is a spread eagle, holding an olive branch and a sheaf of arrows. The legend reads "UNUM E PLURIBUS * 1787." All of the coins are stamped with EB in an oval, which was Ephraim Brasher's hallmark.

Ephraim Brasher:
Originator of the Famous Brasher Doubloon
by Richard A. Bagg, and Q. David Bowers
Excerpts from *The Numismatist*, Feb 1980, p.274-279:

The 1787 gold doubloon issued by Ephraim Brasher, New York goldsmith, silversmith, and jeweler, is probably the most famous American coin in the entire world. In the few instances that specimens have appeared in auction sale catalogues during the past century, great acclaim and publicity have accompanied the offerings. There has even been a motion picture entitled *The Brasher Doubloon*, [20th Century Fox, 1947; based on Raymond Chandler's novel, *High Window*, 1942], which used this coin as its theme. ...

Ephraim Brasher was born in 1744 of Dutch ancestry. The family had several branches, some of which used such spelling variations as Brasier, Brazier, Breser, Bresert, and Bradejor. We are told by his great-great-great granddaughter, Deborah, that the name is not pronounced BRASH-er; "The 'a' is long, and the 's' is pronounced like a 'z'--so the right pronunciation is BRAY-zher." The family produced several silversmiths over the years, including Ephraim's younger brother, Abraham.

[1766, the year of his marriage] saw one of the earliest appearances of work attributed to Brasher's silversmithing. A silver coffeepot bearing his hallmark, presently housed in the Abbott-Lenox Fund Collection in the New York Historical Society, has been attributed to 1766, when he was 22 years old. ...

Although there is some controversy on the subject, it is generally believed that Brasher performed the service of assaying, testing, and evaluating foreign gold coins. He would then counterstamp those pieces he deemed to be genuine and sufficient in weight with his initials EB in an oval stamp [his hallmark] as a guarantee. Several specimens of foreign gold coins marked in this way are known today, including a rose guinea of George II, a quarter guinea of George I, and a "half joe" of Joseph I (which was offered in the sale of the James Ten Eyck Collection in 1922). ...

Among his other duties, Brasher served as assayer for the United States Mint. [During the 1780's, he petitioned several times, some times with John Bailey, a goldsmith and sometime partner whose shop was at 22 Queen Street, for permission to mint coins. The Brasher

Doubloons may have been minted as specimen pieces to support his petitions--or they may have been coins intended for circulation--or they may have been souvenir pieces; one was said to be a gift to George Washington.] ...

The 1787 doubloons bearing the full surname, BRASHER, as a signature do not have a value marked on them. This was not an unusual situation during this period. When the United States Mint first produced gold coins they bore no mark to identify the denomination, probably following the tradition they were accustomed to, as British gold denominations were not identified. The same was also true of numerous foreign issues then in circulation. The value was determined by the metallic purity and weight. For this reason, the countermark, "EB," which appears on all known examples of the Brasher doubloon would have been a further indication of the coin's quality.

Brasher had obtained considerable fame and a reputation for the quality of his silver and gold products. George Washington owned various pieces crafted by Brasher. Among the items in the inventory of the Washington household were two tea trays identified with the EB in an oval. ... When planning his move to 3 Cherry Street, Washington requested Samuel Osgood, past commissioner of the Treasury, "to put the same and the furniture thereof in proper condition for the residence and use of the President of the United States." Brasher's shop [at 77] Queen Street was only a short distance north of his home on Cherry Street and it was therefore convenient for Osgood to purchase "sundry articles of plate," which totaled slightly over 283 pounds sterling.

In April 1790, following his move to Broadway, Washington paid 8 pounds, 8 shillings, and 4 pence for "4 silver skewers" to Brasher, who was also supplying his wares to other notables such as George Clinton. Brasher's esteemed reputation is attested to by the patronage of these prominent people, especially that of the President, a patronage which must have been seen as the equivalent of royal patronage by a citizenry accustomed to judging by such signs. It would have been logical for him to believe that gold coins prominently bearing his name would be accepted in the channels of commerce.

In addition to his activities in silversmithing and goldsmithing, Brasher was busy in civic affairs. In 1784 and 1785, he served as sanitary commissioner. From 1786 to 1791, according to the minutes of the Common Council, he was paid as a coroner, "for taking inquest on dead bodies." He served as an assistant justice from 1794 to 1797, and election inspector from 1796 to 1809, and as commissioner of excise between 1806 and 1810.

The records show a second marriage for Brasher on December 2, 1797. When he died in 1810, he bequeathed to his wife Mary "all my estate both real and personal." In 1811, the City Directory lists: "Brasher, widow of Ephraim" and marks the end of Brasher's contribution to our monetary system.

Brasher's doubloons first attracted the attention of coin collectors in 1838, when Adam Eckfeldt discovered a piece among some gold coins which were sent to the Mint for assaying and melting. He saved the piece and placed it in the Mint cabinet. [This is the coin that eventually came to The Smithsonian.] ... The first appearance of a 1787 Brasher doubloon [at a sale] was anticipated at the sale of the Seavey Collection, catalogued by W. H. Strobridge in 1873. However, the entire collection was purchased intact by Lorin G. Parmelee prior to the sale and the event was cancelled.

[In 1875, in Sylvester Crosby's monumental work, *The Early Coins of America*, four of the coins were known to exist.] "They are owned by Mr. Bushnell, Mr. Parmelee, Mr. Stickeney, and the United State Mint at Philadelphia; the first has the punch-mark on the breast of the eagle."

The first actual sale finally occurred in 1882 at the public auction sale of the Charles I. Bushnell specimen. ... The price was $505. ... Today, this piece remains as the only specimen of the variety with the EB punched on the eagle's breast rather than on the wing.

Today, five specimens of the 1787 doubloon, with punch-mark on the eagle's wing can be traced. ...

In 1964, the six known Brasher Doubloons were located at The Smithsonian Institution, Yale University, two at Johns Hopkins University, one in "a midwest collection," and one in the Coin and Currency Institute.

GOLD COIN RECOVERED
Miama (UPI) a $16 gold piece once owned by George Washington and now believed the world's most valuable coin has been recovered from the loot of a $1 million theft, an insurance adjuster said here today.

Richard F. Andrews, an adjustor who specializes in recovering stolen goods, said the "Brasher Doubloon," worth between $100,000 and $150,000 was recovered in south Florida during the weekend.

The coin was one of about 4,000 coins stolen from the Sterling Memorial Library at Yale University, New Haven, Conn., on May 23, 1965.

Andrews would not say how or from whom the coin was recovered.

The coin, which Andrews displayed to newsmen at a conference, was gold and obviously old. It had irregular edges, the style of coins minted by goldsmiths before the national mint was established.

Andrews said the coin was named the "Brasher Doubloon" after the goldsmith who minted it, Ephraim Brasher. Andrews said Brasher was a neighbor to George Washington in New York and gave Washington the coin in 1787.

TRAP BRINGS RECOVERY OF $100,000 DOUBLOON

Maimi (UPI) A Miami detective posing as a rare coin buyer Monday recovered the $100,000 Brasher Doubloon, part of a $1.5 million rare coin collection stolen from the home of multimillionaire Willis DuPont.

Four persons were arrested as the trap was sprung in a Miami motel room. ...

The Brasher Doubloon was among the rare coins taken when five masked men robbed the plush DuPont estate in Miami, Oct 7. DuPont, 31, his pretty wife and a servant were bound and gagged while the bandits ransacked the house, nibbling on a roast pork they had found in the refrigerator.

Some of the DuPont coins were recovered by a Miami private detective who paid $50,000 in ransom last March. The recovery of those 16 coins led to the arrest of three men in Philadelphia.

The Brasher Doubloon apparently was one of the rare coins struck by Ephraim Brasher, a goldsmith who lived in New York around 1785.

Ephraim Brasher's estate

Will of Ephraim Brasher, goldsmith: to his wife, Mary, the house he now resides in on Cherry Street; mentions sister, Margaret Walker. [LBB did not give date, nor book and page refs.]

The article in *The Numismatist*, June 1964, p.752, says he was married twice, but there were no children by either marriage, and notes that his will did not name any children, but gave "all real and personal property" to wife Mary.

Ephraim Brasher Jr. was married twice: m.1. 8 Nov 1766, Ann Gilbert (Manual of 1862, p.565); Ann was a sister of William Gilbert, a fellow goldsmith.

Ephraim m.2. 25 Nov 1797, Mary Austin (*New York Gazette and General Advocate*, Dec 4, 1797)

Apparently, Ephraim had no children.

33g. PHILIP BRASHER, the Adjutant

Philip Brasher, the Adjutant, is sort of a problem; we don't know for certain who he belongs to, but he is almost certainly a son of Abraham Brasher Jr and his wife, Elizabeth Daly, dau of Philip Daly. However, there is a tomb in St. Paul's Churchyard on lower Broadway, New York City, which is called Philip Brasher's tomb and bears the date 1758. If that's his death-date, he belongs to the generation of the sons of Abraham Brasher Sr. I think, however, there is an error carved in that stone, and that Philip Brasher died in 1785.

Col. Abraham Brasher, The "Liberty Boy," s/o Lucas Brasher and Judith Gasherie, made a bequest in his will to "sons of my cousins, Philip, Ephraim, and Henry Brasher."

Col. Abraham Brasher's grown uncles, i.e. Lucas's brothers (who would have be fathers of Philip, Ephraim and Henry), are:

3-5. **John Brasier or Brasher**, bap. 15 March 1704 (Manual of 1864, p.568); was a carpenter, made freeman 19 Nov 1734; m. 18 May 1737, Susanna Baker. Parents of Lt/Capt Henry Brasher. John's children are accounted for by his will, and there is no Philip among them.

3-6. **Abraham Brasier or Brasher Jr**, bap. 30 Dec 1705 (Manual of 1864, p.568); was a baker and sea-captain; m. Elizabeth Daly, d/o Philip Daly. Parents of Abraham Brasher III, who served with Col Abraham Brasher, The Liberty Boy, and most likely parents of Philip Brasher, the stray, who is probably the Philip who was Adjutant in Col Lasher's Regiment.

3-7. **Ephraim Brasier or Brasher Sr.**, bap. 2 June 1710 (Manual of 1864, p.568); m. 29 May 1740, Catharine Van Kauren (Kiunn, says Manual of 1862, p.565). Parents of Lt. Ephraim Brasher Jr. Ephraim Brasher Sr had a son, Abraham, but no son, Philip.

Because Abraham Brasher Jr married Elizabeth Daly, a daughter of Philip Daly, he looks like the most probable candidate to be father of Philip Brasher, Col. Abraham Brasher's cousin. The children of all the other uncles are accounted for. It would clinch it all, if someone discovered that the Daly's were Marston heirs.

The town of Brasher in Lawrence County in upstate New York was named 21 April 1825 in honor of Philip Brasher of Brooklyn, apparently a son of this Philip, who had bought portions of territory from the heirs

---

of Thomas Marston, who had acquired his title to the land in 1809. See "Philip Brasher, The Alderman," below.

[4]-6? **Philip Brasher**, merchant (1769 List of Freemen, NY City, Manual of 1856, p.480); must have been born bef. 1745; m. 11 Dec 1766, **Philander Hester Ling** (or Lyng) (*NY Marr.* Bk 10:198; bonds by Philip Brazier, of New York City, merchant, and John Burt Lyng, of New York City, goldsmith, probably her father).

This Philip was Adjutant of Col. Lasher's militia regiment during the Revolution.

Letters of administration issued 7 March 1785, to widow, Philander, of New York, in estate of Philip Brasher, shopkeeper of New York, who had died intestate. (*NY Hist Soc*, v.37, p.?) Could that tomb inscription of 1758 be a reversal of 1785? And who was the Phillip [sic] Brasher, who died intestate 1785 in Essex Co, NJ? (Book 27, p.376)

[Philip, the Adjutant, was married in 1766, therefore can't be son of Ephraim Jr, the silver/goldsmith, who was b. 1744 and had married only a month earlier in 1766.]

Philip Brasher, Alderman

Another Philip Brasher, probably Philip Jr, was admitted to practice law in New York City on 27 Nov 1788:

BY THE HONORABLE JAMES DUANE
Esquire, Mayor of the City of New York

TO ALL WHOM these presents shall come or may concern, Greetings, **KNOW YE** that Philip Brasher, Gentleman, having been duly examined and regularly admitted as an Attorney at Law by the Mayors Court of the City of New York, in and for the said City on the Twenty seventh day of November, instant, I DO HEREBY licence and authorize the said Philip Brasher to appear in the said court and there to practice as an Attorney at Law according to the rules and customs of the said Court and the Laws of the State.

GIVEN under my hand and seal at the City of New York, the twenty seventh day of November in the year of our Lord One thousand seven hundred and Eighty Eight--
Jam. Duane, E.

If Philip was 21 at the time, he was probably born c1767. The very old, very fragile parchment document (framed) is owned by descendants Milton Brasher (d. 1986) and his daughter, Melode.

Philip Brasher, the lawyer, was Asst. Alderman, 3rd Ward, 1799-1800, Alderman, 1802, and Alderman 2nd Ward, 1803-4.

According to another Philip Brasher, (Director of Personnel at Princeton University, NJ, and class of '06), a Philip Brasher was chairman of the committee in 1803 which built the New York City Hall and paid for most of it out of his own pocket. The City of New York still owes the family £567/7/6, with interest since 1803. (Letter of 31 Jan 1928 to HSB.)

Philip Brasher was a representative in the New York Legislature from New York in 1816, 1822-3, 1826-8, and from Kings Co, 1834-5.

The town of Brasher in Lawrence County in upstate New York was named 21 April 1825 in honor of Philip Brasher of Brooklyn, who had bought portions of territory from the heirs of Thomas Marston, who had acquired his title to the land in 1809. Comments from the town historian, Grace O'Brien: Both the Deer and St. Regis Rivers flow north across the town until they unite. ... Most of the revenue of the early settlers came from cutting soft wood. ... The land is better adapted to grazing than dairying. ... Navigation on the St. Regis River in Brasher was very important. ... A boat capable of Carrying ten barrels of Potash was run between Hogansburg and the Landing.

Nearby are the communities "Brasher Settlement," "Brasher Falls," a manufacturing village on St. Regis River, southwest corner of town; "Brasher Center," a hamlet on St. Regis River; and "Brasher Ironworks," on Deer River, 2.5 miles above its mouth.

[5]-1. **Phillip Brasher**, (almost certainly s/o Philip Brasher, the Adjutant) was an Alderman of the City of New York and helped in getting New York and Brooklyn joined. [Speculation: He must have married a girl named Marston! Just look at how often that name is used as a middle name among his children!]

Phillip Brasher, the Alderman, had five children:
[6]-1. **Thomas Marston Brasher**, a Captain in the Navy; no children
[6]-2. ***Phillip Marston Brasher**,
[6]-3. **William Marston Brasher**,
    [7]-1. **Louise Brasher**, married twice
       [8]-1. William Brasher Clayton (by first marriage)
       [8]-2. Jane _____ (by second marriage)
    [7]-2. **Frederick Brasher**, who was murdered

[6]-4. **Philandra Louise Brasher**, who never married. Probably named for her grandmother, Philander Ling.
[6]-5. **Cornelia Brasher**, who never married.

[6]-2. Philip Marston Brasher, m.1. _____
    [7]-1. **Archie Brasher**, m. _____
        [8]-1. **Philip Brasher**, no children
        [8]-2. **Katherine Marie Louise Brasher**, b. c1871, no children. Marie, a niece to Rex Brasher, with whom she lived, was only two years younger than he. That means her father had to be at least 20 years older than his younger half-brother.
    [7]-2. **Philip Brasher**, never married
Philip Marston Brasher, m.2. Laura Bull, who apparenly was much younger. Some 20 years seem to have passed between the children by the first marriage and these children by the second.
    [7]-3. **Reginald I. "Rex" Brasher**, b. 1869, d. 29 Feb 1960, aged 91. Became a famous ornithologist and painter of birds. Lived in Chickadee Valley, near Kent, Conn. unmarried. He devoted his life to the monumental, 12-volume *Birds and Trees of North America*, published in 1932. See TIME review-article below.
    [7]-4. ***Charles Brasher**,
    [7]-5. **Laura Brasher**, who went into a convent in Maryland.

[7]-4. Charles Brasher, m. _____ and had five children:
    [8]-1. **Madelon Brasher**, d. 1975, m. _____
        [9]-1. Joann _____; res. East Boston
        [9]-2. Michele _____; res. Long Island
        [9]-3. Martin _____; res. Long Island
    [8]-2. **Philip Brasher**, d. 1976, m.1. Mary _____; lived in Texas
        [9]-1. **Philip Brasher, Jr**,
    Philip Brasher, m.2. Rose _____
        [9]-2. **Leon Brasher**,
        [9]-3. **Rex Brasher**,
        [9]-4. **Charles Milton Brasher**,
        [9]-5. **Rose Marie Brasher**,
    [8]-3. **Milton Evans Brasher**, b. 21 April 1905, d. 11 Feb 1986; Milt was a noted animal sculptor; m. 3 Feb 1934, Marie Alvarez, b. 23 May 1907
        [9]-1. **Melode Brasher**,
        [9]-2. **Deborah E. Brasher**,
    [8]-4. **Charles Brasher**, d. 1978; m. Liana _____
        [9]-1. **Christine Brasher**, res. Forked River, NJ

⁹⁻2. **Charles Brasher**,
⁹⁻3. **Bruce Brasher**, M.D. (did internship in Birmingham; res. Philadelphia, PA)
⁸⁻5. **Robert Brasher**, living in 1983.
⁹⁻1. **Robert Brasher**, res. Old Lyme, CT
⁹⁻2. **Michele Brasher**, res. Ft Lee, NJ

(Sources: letter from Milt Brasher to Revis Brasher, of Leeds, AL, 19 April 1983; letter from Mrs. Milt Brasher to Revis Brasher, 26 Nov 1989; and notes of Revis Brasher, s/o Jasper Brasher.

Rex Brasher, Painter of Birds

(Excerpts from **TIME**, Sept 12, 1932)

Reginald I. "Rex" Brasher (pronounced BRAY-sher) has done 900 plates showing 1,200 species of North American birds. Every coloration difference due to age, sex, season, or attitude, has been shown, bringing the total of figures to 3,000. All are based on sketches drawn in the field over a period of 44 years.

The son of amateur ornithologist Philip Marston Brasher (for whom the Brasher warbler was named), Rex early heard his father's criticism of the famed Audubon bird plates, which often carry naturalism, composition, and color beyond the point of probability. In 1879, aged 10, Rex Brasher decided to paint all the birds in North America himself. After his father died, he learned taxidermy, went to St. Francis College (Brooklyn), and at 15 to work in the engraving department of Tiffany & Co. No longer prosperous was his family, whose founder, according to the family legend, had come to Manhattan in 1621 as the wealthy Frenchman Bras de Fer; one of whose members had commanded the forts in the 1690 Leisler Rebellion; another of whom is reputedly still owed £567 for paying for Manhattan's City Hall in 1803. Rex Brasher had no art training except at Tiffany's and at a Portland, Maine photo-engraver's. At 19, he set sail in a sloop down the Atlantic coast. In one spring afternoon on the deserted waste of Long Island's Far Rockaway, he saw 86 different species of birds. He sold his sloop in Key West and went back to Brooklyn to paint what he had seen. In 1900, he burned the 400 pictures he had. In 1905, he burned most of what he had done over. He figured he could do still better with more time, but he was getting a little panicky. He started the final version.

In 1928, his 900 plates were finished. Printer William Edwin Rudge told him it would cost $500,000 to reproduce them in four colors, losing most of the color exactitude. So Rex Brasher sat down to make a 500 edition of his 900 plates in twelve volumes, each plate to be reproduced

---

in black & white photogravure, then copied from the original in water-colors by himself.

When he had done 100 copies of the first volume in six months, he realized by simple arithmetic that he could not live long enough to finish. He reduced the edition to 100. ...

The 75 subscribers, leafing last week through the twelve handsome volumes, each 13 by 18 in. and 2 in. thick, inevitably measured Brasher against his predecessors. ... Critics perceive that Brasher has held faithfully to the probable background and the actual bird, rarely permitting himself a flourish. ... Rex Brasher alone has had simultaneously the time, the ability, the monumental persistence, the hard-headed fidelity to do all of the birds of North America.

from **The New York Times**, 1 March 1960:
REX BRASHER, 91, PAINTER OF BIRDS
Gaylordsville, Conn. Feb 29 (AP)--Rex Brasher, who was credited with painting every type of bird in North America, died today at his home after a brief illness. He was 91 years old.

Mr. Brasher, a bachelor, lived in Kent for thirty-five years and did most of his work there. His paintings included 1,200 species and sub-species of birds.

He hand-colored almost 1,000,000 prints of his original paintings. He worked until two years ago, when his eyesight grew dim.

Mr. Brasher announced in 1932, after forty years of painting birds, that he felt his work had been completed. During his years of artistic work, he had often found it necessary to make financial ends meet by doing laboring tasks of all kinds, particularly road building and house-painting. ...

In 1935, Mr. Brasher offered the paintings to the State of Connecticut, providing a suitable repository could be found for them. Three years later, he took the pictures back after the failure of various attempts to raise funds for a museum in which to display them.

The paintings were then sent to Washington to be exhibited as "Birds and Trees of North America" in Explorer's Hall of the National Geographic Society. ...

The State of Connecticut bought the Brasher collection for $74,000 in 1941. Twelve years later, it started to exhibit them in rotation at the Harkness Memorial State Park, overlooking Block Island, in a large manor house there, bequeathed to the state by the widow of Edward S. Harkness. ...

Today, (1991), Rex's 874 original water-colors are in the Connecticut State Musuem of Natural History, Carl W. Rettenmeyer, Director, at the

University of Connecticut, 75 North Eagleville Road, U-23, Room 312, Storrs, CT 06268. The museum sells a biography: *Rex Brasher, Painter of Birds*, by his nephew, Milton E. Brasher.

In 1960, Rex's nephew, Milton E. Brasher, wrote his daughter, Melode: "At least Rex got some of the credit due him in those widespread eulogies. ... he was indeed the world's greatest bird artist and a master of background landscapes.

"The more I think of the tremendous scope of his work--the thousands of bird subjects, the research needed to draw them and paint them with fidelity to color and feather accuracy--the research on trees and then, as if this were not enough--the beautiful backgrounds that have gone into every painting, I say--this whole achievement is unbelievable.

"And having come to this new appreciation of his work--and having read some of his autobiographical writings, I have formed a desire if not a complete resolution to write a biography that will in a measure give credit to one individual's fantastic life work. Whether I have the resolve strong enough--and the energy--is another matter."

He found the energy to go with the resolve-- and published *Rex Brasher, Painter of Birds*.

Other Non-Brashear(s) Families

34. REV. PLEASANT BRASHIER

Rev. Pleasant Brashier, b. South Carolina, c1800 (50 in 1850, Marlboro Co, SC; 80 in 1880 Census, Enterprise, Clarke Co, MS); m. **Rebecca Marie Moore**, b. c1800 (50 in 1850, Marlboro Co, SC), d/o Benjamin Moore Sr and Frances Stubbs, who were devout Quakers.

Pleasant Brashier was a Methodist Minister in Bennetsville, Marlboro Co, South Carolina, where all of his children were born. About 1855-57, he moved to Clarke Co, MS, where he was living alone in Enterprise Community, at the time of the 1880 Census. His ancestry is still a mystery to me.

From *A History of Marlboro, SC*, by Rev. Ja. W. Thomas, p.185-6, originally published 1897; reprinted 1971 by Marlboro Historical Society: "Benjamin Moore Sr, son of James and Drucilla Moore, was born in Richmond County, North Carolina in 1769. He was orphaned at an early age, and came to Marlboro in his early manhood. His wife was Frances Stubbs, the daughter of William Stubbs and Elizabeth Hubbard.

"In the year 1816, he purchased the farm upon which J. Alexander Moore lives, paying $1.94 per acre, which he thought was a high price for land. It was bought of Major Drury Robertson, who owned a territory of land reaching from Goodwin's Mill to Pipkin's Mill. The Major valued the land principally on account of the virgin timber, which was then found in unbroken profusion, and perhaps inserted a timber reservation clause in some of the deeds. The grandsons of Benjamin Moore Sr value the land because from it they produce a bale of cotton per acre and provision crops in like proportion.

"Benjamin Moore Sr died in 1846 and left a large family of sons and daughters. Rebecca Moore, his dau, m. Rev. Pleasant Brazier, and moved to Alabama before the late war." See also *Stubbs of Marlboro County*, p.33, 52, 225, 229, and *Clarke Co [MS] History*, p.17, 141, 201

The family of Benjamin Moore Sr and Frances Stubbs: (order not certain, because Rev. J.W. Thomas names all the daughters first, then all the sons)

1. Rebecca Moore, m. **Rev. Pleasant Brazier**,
2. Drucilla Moore, m. William Odom,
3. Nancy Moore, alive in 1846 (father's estate) dead in 1848 (mother's estate), m.1. Abram Odom, m.2. Younger Huckaby,
4. Catherine Moore, m. Theophilus Odom,
5. Mary Moore, m. William Easterling and settled in Mississippi
6. Permilia Moore, (Pamela in estate proceedings), m. Stephen Wallace,
7. William Moore, ("oldest son") m. Mary Adams, and settled in Adamsville,
8. James Moore, m.1. _____ Easterling, widow of _____ Jones and d/o Henry Easterling; m.2. Sarah Bethea, d/o Samuel Bethea,
9. Alfred Y. Moore, m.1. Mary A. Jones, d/o Rev. John Jones; m.2. Elizabeth Odom, d/o Philip Odom,
10. Benjamin Moore Jr, m.1. Mintie Easterling, m.2. Elizabeth Pearson,
11. Duncan W. Moore, b. 25 Nov 1819 ("youngest son") m. Martha Spears, d/o James Spears and Deborah Bethea,

These same 11 children are named in Benjamin Moore Sr's estate settlement (Estate file 27-3, Marlboro Co, SC), adm 17 Aug 1846 by Widow Fanny & sons William & Benjamin Jr, execs; Duncan Moore and William T. Ellerbe, bondsmen. See also estate settlement of Frances (Stubbs) Moore: Will signed 16 Aug 1848, probate 15 Dec 1848, (file #11-28, Marlboro Co, SC).

Family of John or William Stubbs and Rebecca Conner:

1. Lewis Stubbs,
2. James Stubbs,
3. Thomas Stubbs,
4. William Stubbs, m. Elizabeth Hubbard, they lived at "the Brazier Place on Cheraw Road," per *The History of Marlboro County*. Their daughter, Frances Stubbs, m. Benjamin Moore Sr.
5. John Stubbs,
6. Peter Stubbs,

Pleasant Brashier/Brazier is listed in the following censuses:
1830 Marlboro Co, SC Census, p.47
1840 Marlboro Co, SC Census, p.208
1850 Marlboro Co, SC Census, p.152, Fam #439
1859 Clarke Co [MS] Marriage Book A

1860 Clarke Co, MS Census, Fam #618
1870 Clarke Co, MS Census. p.8, Fam#37
1880 Clarke Co, MS Census, ED113, SH47, LN32

1850 <u>Census, Marlboro Co, SC</u>: p.152, Fam #439
Pleasant Brazier, 50, b. 1800, SC, farmer
   Rebecca, 50, b. 1800
   Mary Brazier, b. 1825
   William Brazier, b. 1829
   June or Jane Brazier, b. 1835
   James Brazier, b. 1838
   Christopher D. Brazier, b. 1839
   Robert Brazier, b. 1841
   Cornelia Brazier, b. 1848
   Also in H/H: John Brazier, 24, b. 1826, trader

On p.146, in H/H of William and Mary Moore (age 42 and 40):
Miss M. Brazier, 19, b. 1831, SC. This looks like daughter, Mary Brashier, working for a neighbor, believed to be Rebecca (Moore) Brashier's brother.

Pleasant Brashier and Rebecca Moore

V9-4185.   1-x. **Rev. Pleasant Brashier**, b. 1800, SC, d. after 1880 Census, Clarke Co, MS; m. **Rebecca Marie Moore**, b. c1801, d. bef. 1857, d/o Benjamin Moore Sr and Frances Stubbs; 13 children, all born Bennettsville, Marlboro Co, SC:

V9-4186.   2-1. ***Benjamin F. Brashier**, b. c1821, SC (39 in 1860), lived Dyer Co, TN, 1857; m. **Sarah Jane** ____, b. c1837, TN (23 in 1860); m.2. 26 Jan 1870, Dyer Co, TN, **K.J. Caliway**.

V9-4187.   2-2. **Mary Jane(?) Brashier**, b. c1825, Bennettsville, Marlboro Co, SC; ?may have m. 1854, in Wayne Co, MS, **Stephen G. Shoemake**, b. c1832 (18 in 1860, Wayne Co, MS), s/o Blakeley Shoemake and Elisa _____.   ?ch

V9-4188.   2-3. ***John Washington Brashier**, (twin) b. 5 Sept 1827, d. 25 Feb 1919; m. 9 April 1855, **Antoinette S. Arrington Lang**, b. 18 Oct 1836

V9-4189.   2-4. **Martha Brashier**, (twin) b. 5 Sept 1827, SC, d. 13 Oct 1900, bur Geneva Presbyterian Church Cemetery in Matherville, Wayne Co, MS. Stone reads "Martha Wife of Silas Eggerton"; m. 28 June 1856, Clarke Co, MS (Bk A, p.162), **Silas Eggerton**, b. 26 April 1835, d. 10 Oct 1883, bur Quitman Cem. They are in the census of Clarke Co, MS, 1870 (p.665b) and 1880 (ED 113, Sh 23, Ln 12, Beat

1) with a family. The 1900 Wayne Co, MS Census (ED 111, Sh 12A, Ln 34-36) lists Sallie Eggerton 41, head of household, born March 1859, single, merchant; Martha Eggerton, 73, mother, born Sept 1826, widow, b. SC; and John Eggerton, 23, born Sept 1876, single, mechanick.

V9-4190.   3-1. Sallie J. Eggerton, b. March 1859 (13 in 1870; 22 in 1880; 41 in 1900)

V9-4191.   3-2. George Eggerton, b. c1859 (11 in 1870; 21 in 1880); m. Emma _____, b. c1857 (per 1880 census)

V9-4192.   3-3. Caroline Eggerton, b. c1864 (6 in 1870; not in 1880)

V9-4193.   3-4. Mary A. Eggerton, b. c1866 (4 in 1870; 14 in 1880)

V9-4194.   3-5. Wilson Eggerton, b. c1868-69 (1 in 1870, 12 in 1880)

V9-4195.   3-6. John Eggerton, b. Sept 1876 (5 in 1880; 23 in 1900)

V9-4196.   2-5. **William M. Brashier**, b. Dec 1830, d. 1911, Wayne Co, MS; m.lic. 20 Jan 1866, Clarke Co, MS (Bk B), to marry **Mary Bounds** (the license was never completed, so we think they never married); m.1. 10 May 1868, Jasper Co, MS (Bk 2, p.152; transposed date, 1886 in WPA copy of *Jasper Co MS Marr*) **Sarah Jane Touchstone**; m.2. 6 Feb 1881, Wayne Co, MS, **Cynthia Coker**, b. Dec 1848, MS.

V9-4197.   2-6. **May Brashier**, b. c1831

V9-4198.   2-7. **Charles Brashier**, b. c1832, ?d. young; not in 1850 census

V9-4199.   2-8. **Green Brashier**, b. c1833, ?d. young; not in 1850 census

V9-4200.   2-9. **Jane Brashier**, b. c1835

V9-4201.   2-10. ***James T. Brashier**, b. c1837; m. c1866, **Nancy _____**, b. c1846 (She is listed in the special 1866 Census of Mississippi).

V9-4202.   2-11. ***Christopher Dudley "Kit" Brashier**, b. c1839, d. c1878; m. 1867, **Nancy Jane Sykes**.

V9-4203.   2-12. ***Robert B. Brashier**, b. 26 June 1840, d. 3 April 1902, Clarke Co, MS; Listed in 1850 census as Robert D. Brashier, but all other records as Robert B. Brashier; m. 20 Sept 1867, Clarke Co, MS, **Louise Isabell Welsen**, b. 2 Jan 1843, d. 24 July 1904, Clarke Co, MS.

V9-4204.   2-13. **Cornelia Brashier**, b. c1848, not in 1860 Census

BENJAMIN F. BRASHIER
and SARAH JANE _____ / K.J. CALIWAY

2-1. Benjamin F. Brashier, b. c1821, SC (39 in 1860), lived Dyer Co, TN, 1857; m. *Sarah Jane* ____, b. c1837, TN (23 in 1860); m.2. 26 Jan 1870, (Dyer Co, TN, Marriages, by Byron and Barbara Sisler), *K.J. Caliway.*

On 2 Nov 1857, in Dyer Co, TN, Benjamin F. Brazier and wife, Sarah Jane Brazier, give their power of attorney to William Moore "to collect, etc. from estate of our grandmother Frances Moore of Marlboro Co, SC." See Marlboro Deed Book T, p.272, 2 Jan 1858, (regarding inheritance from his grandmother).

Benjamin apparent died between 1870 and 1873, for his second wife, K.J. (Caliway) Brashier, m.2. 23 March 1873, J.D. Bradley (Dyer Co, TN, Marriages, by Byron and Barbara Sisler).

B.F. & S.J. Brazier are in the 1860 census, Dyer Co, TN, p.331, fam #85, with two ch: S.J. (fem) and J.B. (male). The 1870 Census, 12th-Civil Dist, Dyer Co, TN (printed p.162, handwritten p.2) adds more. Benjamin F. is listed at P.M. Braizier, 49 in 1870, i.e. b. 1821, (that's the right age) and wife is Amy, age 32, b. c1838. (Was K.J. Caliway called "Amy," as a nickname?)

<u>Family</u> <u>of</u> <u>Benjamin</u> <u>F.</u> <u>Brashier</u> <u>and</u> <u>Sarah</u> <u>Jane</u> _____.

V9-4205.	3-1.	**S. June Brazier**, b. c1854, TN, (6 in 1860)
V9-4206.	3-2.	**John B. Brazier**, b. c1856, TN (4 in 1860)
V9-4207.	3-3.	**Thomas Brazier**, b. c1858, TN (14 in 1870)
V9-4208.	3-4.	**Willi Brazier** (fem), b. c1860, TN (10 in 1870)
V9-4209.	3-5.	**Jesse Brazier**, b. c1861, TN (9 in 1870)
V9-4210.	3-6.	**Nina Brazier**, b. c1863, TN (7 in 1870)
V9-4211.	3-7.	**Milly Brazier**, b. c1865, TN (5 in 1870)

Stray (possible other dau) **Charity Ann Brashier**, m. 21 Jan 1878, *W.H. Nelson* (Dyer Co, TN, Marriages, by Byron and Barbara Sisler.

JOHN WASHINGTON BRASHIER and
ANTOINETTE S. ARRINGTON

2-2. John Washington Brashier, (twin, s/o Rev. Pleasant Brashier and Rebecca Marie Moore), b. 5 Sept 1826, d. 25 Feb 1919, bur DeSoto Cem, Quitman, Clarke Co, MS; m. 9 April 1855, (Clarke Co, MS Marr Bk A, p.104), *Antoinette S. Arrington Lang*, b. 18 Oct 1836, d. 12 Aug

1899, widow of _____ Lang, and d/o Dr. Anthony Arrington and Mary "Polly" Arrington (Anthony and Polly were 1st cousins).

John is in the Marlboro Co, SC 1850 census, p.152, fam #439; the 1860 census, Clarke Co, MS, p.66, fam #442; the 1880 and 1910 censuses of Clarke Co, MS.

He enlisted 1 Oct 1862 in Co. D, 5th Regt, Minute Men, Army of the State of Mississippi; discharged by reason of excessive numbers, 12 Sept 1862. Enlisted 12 April 1864, Co. B, 1st Mississippi Cavalry Reserves. His unit surrendered 4 May 1865 at Citronelle, AL, by Gen. R. Taylor.

John Washington Brashier and Antoinette S. Arrington are both bur De Soto Cem, Quitman, Clarke Co, MS; they had 11 children, all b. Clarke Co, MS:

V9-4212. 3-1. **Rebecca Brashier**, b. c1856, d. _____; m. 12 June 1878, Clarke Co, MS, ***T.F. Cherry***,

V9-4213. 3-2. ***John Calhoun Brashier***, b. 1 Jan 1857, Quitman, Clarke Co, MS; d. 11 Dec 1936; m.1. 7 Feb 1877, ***Julia Eugenia Parker***, b. 8 Sept 1858, Clarke Co, MD, d. 25 Jan 1906, Clarke Co, MS (5 ch); m.2. 20 Nov 1890, ***Martha Jane Evans Boyce***, b. 2 Nov 1869, d. 9 Nov 1908, Clarke Co, MS, bur Salem Cem, Clarke Co, MS (5 ch); m.3. 17 Nov 1909, Clarke Co, MS (Bk 2, p.32) ***Belle Hailes***, b. 1879, d. 1931, Clarke Co, MS (1 ch)

V9-4214. 3-3. ***Benjamin Franklin Brashier***, b. 24 Feb 1860, d. 5 Feb 1931; m. 1 June 1882, ***Belinda Jane McDonald***, b. 3 Oct 1866, d. 20 Jan 1938, both bur McGowan's Chapel Cem, Clarke Co, MS.

V9-4215. 3-4. **Dollye Brashier**, b. 17 Jan 1865, d. 13 Dec 1940; m. ***John Jay Parker***, b. 17 March 1849, d. 2 Feb 1939; bur together under one stone, Salem Cem, Clarke Co, MS, "In loving memory."

V9-4216. 4-1. Searcy Parker,

V9-4217. 3-5. **Selma Brashier**, b. c1865-7; m. 22 Dec 1881, Clarke Co, MS (Bk E, p.45) ***David Odom***,

V9-4218. 4-1. Idalee Odom,

V9-4219. 4-x. others

V9-4220. 3-6. **Jenny Brashier**, b. c1868; m. ***Will Jentry***,

V9-4221. 3-7. **Mourning Brashier**, b. 25 March 1868, d. 7 July 1877, age 9, bur. Quitman Cem, Clarke Co, MS

V9-4222. 3-8. **Mary "Polly" Brashier**, b. c1870; m. ***Walter Evans***,

V9-4223. 3-9. **Lucy Brashier**, b. c1873; m. 10 March 1891, ***Henry S. Wilkins***,

V9-4224.   4-1. Howell Wilkins, m. Cora Mae Riley
V9-4225.   4-2. girl Wilkins,
V9-4226.   3-10. **Elizabeth "Lizzie" Brashier**, b. c1876; m. 12 Sept
             1896, Clarke Co, MS, *J.A. Hailes,*
V9-4227.   4-1. Jeptha A. Hailes,

John Calhoun Brashier
and Julia Eugenia Parker/
Martha Jane Evans Boyce/ Belle Hailes

3-2. ***John Calhoun Brashier**, (s/o John Washington Brashier and
Antoinette S. Arrington), b. 1 Jan 1857, Quitman, Clarke Co, MS; d. 11
Dec 1936, bur Salem Cem, Quitman, Clarke Co, MS; m.1. 7 Feb 1877,
Clarke Co, MS, *Julia Eugenia Parker*, b. 8 Sept 1858, Clarke Co, MD,
d. 25 Jan 1906, Clarke Co, MS, bur Salem Cem, d/o Thomas S. Parker
and Emily Amy Gantt; John and Julia were divorced c1890 (5 ch); m.2.
20 Nov 1890, in Clarke Co, MS, *Martha Jane Evans Boyce*, b. 2 Nov
1869, d. 9 Nov 1908, Clarke Co, MS, bur Salem Cem, Clarke Co, MS (5
ch; div); m.3. 17 Nov 1909, in Clarke Co, MS (Bk 2, p.32) *Belle Hailes*,
b. 1879, d. 1931, Clarke Co, MS (1 ch).

John C. Brashier, 1857—1936 is buried in Salem Cem, Quitman,
Clarke Co, MS. Along with his is "mother" Belle Hailes Brashier,
1870—1931 "Beloved one, we love you." Belle's brother and his wife are
apparently buried nearby: "father" Jefferson A. Hailes, 13 Sept 1868—11
July 1934, and "mother" Elizabeth Hailes, 26 April 1875—7 Jan 1954.
Her mother may have been the next burial: "grandmother" Elizabeth
Hailes, 29 March 1850—10 Nov 1936 "Forever with the Lord." There is
also a William S. Hailes, 14 Sept 1874—8 Dec1960; and a Glen S. Hailes,
13 Sept 1905—2 Nov 1968.

John and his family are #442, 1860 Census, Quitman P.O, Clarke Co,
MS; ED 113, p.45. Ln36, 1880 Census, Clarke Co, MS; ED 2, p.7, Ln1,
1900 Census Clarke Co, MS, Beat 1; ED 3, p.9, Ln74, 1920 Census,
Clarke Co, MS. (data from Thomas Van Ness; see also "The Pleasant
Brashier Family" in *History of Clarke Co*, by Mary June Reese.)

Children of John Calhoun Brashier and Julia Eugenia Parker:
V9-4228.   4-1. **John Henry Brashier**, b. 1 Jan 1877, d. March 1945,
             bur Salem Cem; m. 14 March 1897, Jasper Co, MS (Bk 5,
             p.483), *Emma Neely*, b. c1878, MS
V9-4229.   5-1. **Earl Lee Brashier**, b. 1898, MS, d. 1951, bur Salem
             Cem, Clarke Co, MS, Masonic stone.

V9-4230.   5-2. **John Henry Brashier Jr**, b. 4 Jan 1899, Clarke Co, MS, d. 18 Sept 1932, Clarke Co, MS; m. 21 Sept 1922, Clarke Co, MS (Bk _, p.278) *Lola Blanche Little*, b. c1905

V9-4231.   5-3. **Roy F. Brashier**, b. c1902; m. 9 Nov 1923, Clarke Co, MS (Bk 4, p.450), *Mildred Rogers*

V9-4232.   4-2. **Cora Lee Brashier**, b, 27 July 1879, d. 7 Aug 1968; m.lic 23 Feb 1895, Clarke Co, MS, *William Joseph Evans*, b. 1875, d. 1963

V9-4233.   4-3. ***Benjamin Thomas Brashier**, b. 14 April 1884, d. 27 Aug 1970; m. 13 Sept 1903, *Margaret Clara Rigby*, b. 12 Sept 1886, Melvin, Choctaw Co, AL, d. 5 Feb 1974, Quitman, Clarke Co, MS

V9-4234.   4-4. **Lyda Julia Brashier**, b. 12 Sept 1886; m. *Dr. Percy W. Johnston*, (info from *History of Clarke Co*)

V9-4235.   5-1. Percy W. Johnston Jr; m. Mary Varnon Gibson

V9-4236.   5-2. James Burr Johnston; m. Phyllis Irene Glass, b. Maine

V9-4237.   4-5. **Earl Sayle Brashier**, b. 3 Sept 1888 (Earl was a Veterinarian; info from Danna B. Elliott and *History of Clarke Co*, via Thomas Van Ness); m. *Annie Laurie Finnin*,

Children of John Calhoun Brashier and Mattie Jane Evans Boyce:

V9-4238.   4-6. **Charles Bradford Brashier**, b. 25 Oct 1895, d. 31 Dec 1963, bur Salem Cem, Quitman, Clarke Co, MS, "A friend to all"; m. 1 Jan 1923, Wayne Co, MS, *Mattie Kathrin Rogers*, b. 13 March 1896, d. 24 April 1965, bur Salem Cem, Quitman, Clarke Co, MS, "A friend to all."

V9-4239.   5-1. **Charlie Bradford Brashier Jr**, m. *Madelon Ruth Husband*

V9-4240.   4-7. **Chester Edward Brashier**, b. 4 Aug 1893, d. 9 June 1963; m.1. *Alda H. Hamilton*, b. 15 Dec 1903, d. 26 April 1955 (7 ch), bur together, Salem Cem, Quitman, Clarke Co, MS, "Rest is thine and sweet remembrance ours"; m.2. *Kate _____*. Kate B. Brashier, b. 23 May 1899, d. 28 April 1982, is buried beside Chester and Alda.

V9-4241.   5-1. **Bea Hamilton Brashier**,

V9-4242.   5-2. _____ **Brashier**,

V9-4243.   5-3. _____ **Brashier**,

V9-4244.   5-4. _____ **Brashier**,

V9-4245.   5-5. _____ **Brashier**,

V9-4246.   5-6. _____ **Brashier**,

V9-4247.   5-7. **Edward Hamilton Brashier**

V9-4248.   4-8. **Jesse W. Brashier**, b. 2 Feb 1898, d. 11 Jan 1956, bur Salem cem, Quitman, Clarke Co, MS, "Daddy", "Beloved one, Farewall"; m. 22 Dec 1925, Smith Co, MS, **Vondelle Clisson**, b. 14 Nov 1909, d. 13 May 1995, bur Salem cem, Quitman, Clarke Co, MS, "mother", "Beloved Angel." Jesse may also have m.2. **Dee Adair**. Jesse had 8 children, according to Danna B. Elliot, but I only have two:

V9-4249.   5-1. **Pauline Brashier**,

V9-4250.   5-2. **Frances Brashier**,

V9-4251.   4-9. **Hilda France "Ann" Brashier**, b. 3 Feb 1901, d. 2 Dec 1997. Age 96; m. **Paul J. Coker**, b. 11 Sept 1901, d. 5 Sept 1991; the share a double stone in Salem Cem, Quitman, Clarke Co, MS, "At rest."

V9-4252.   5-1. Frances Coker, m. William Wallace Lowry

V9-4253.   5-2. Pauline Coker, m. Martin Harwell

V9-4254.   4-10. **Earl Lee Brashier**, b. c1898 or 1903, d. 1952; m. 29 Dec 1918, Newton Co, MS (Bk F, p.271), **Carrol Davis**

V9-4255.   Child of John Calhoun Brashier and Belle Hailes:

V9-4256.   4-11. **Joseph Tillman Brashier**, b. 17 Jan 1911, d. 15 July 1980, bur Salem Cem, Quitman, Clarke Co, MS, "Rest in Peace"; m. **Lucille Prince**, b. 21 Aug 1911, d. 20 Jan 1999, age 87, bur beside Joseph Tillman.

V9-4257.   5-1. **Alma Jo Prince Brashier**, step-dau; m. **David Kelly**

V9-4258.   5-2. **Pat Brashier**, m. **John Woody Blanchard**

Benjamin Thomas Brashier
and Margaret Clara Rigby

4-3. **Benjamin Thomas Brashier**, b. 14 April 1884, Quitman, Clarke County, MS; d. 27 Aug 1970; bur. Salem Cemetery, Quitman, Clarke County, MS; m. 13 Sept 1903, **Margaret Clara Rigby**, b. 12 Sept 1886, Melvin, Choctaw Co, AL, d. 5 Feb 1974, Clarke Co, MS. They have one gravestone, which is set backwards and says: "Memory Lane," "Book of Life," "Mother," and "Father."

Clara was d/o William Green Rigby, b. 31 May 1852, Houston Co, GA, d. 15 March 1934, Clarke Co, MS, who m. 28 Aug 1872, Margaret McInnis, b. 1 Aug 1848, AL, d. 24 April 1937, MS.

Ben and Margaret had 7 children, all born Rt 2, Shubata, Clarke Co, MS:

V9-4259.   5-1. **Leila Mae Brashier**, b. 27 Oct 1904, d. 15 Dec 1957; m. 18 June 1925, *John D. Cockrell,*

V9-4260.   6-1. Harold Merritt Cockrell, b. 26 Sept 1930; m. Lee _____,

V9-4261.   7-1. Karen Cockrell,

V9-4262.   7-2. Jane Cockrell,

V9-4263.   7-3. John Eric Cockrell,

V9-4264.   7-4. Merritt Cockrell,

V9-4265.   6-2. Mary Elizabeth Cockrell, b. 16 Aug 1935; m. William Morgan,

V9-4266.   7-1. Elizabeth Ann Morgan,

V9-4267.   7-2. William Morgan Jr,

V9-4268.   7-3. Melissa Morgan,

V9-4269.   6-3. John Arthur Cockrell, b. 3 April 1939; m. Brenda _____, b. 22 July 1946

V9-4270.   7-1. Leila Angela Cockrell, b. 1 Oct 1966

V9-4271.   6-4. Lillian Mae Cockrell,

V9-4272.   5-2. ***Clifton Leonard Brashier***, b. 10 Oct 1906, d. 11 Feb 1964, bur Salem Cem, Quitman, Clarke Co, MS, "Daddy", "We will meet again"; m. 6 June 1929, *Ellen Lesley Lyons,* b. 5 Jan 1911, Dallas Co, TX, d. there 6 April 1992

V9-4273.   5-3. **Emmett Lawrence Brashier**, b. 16 Feb 1909, d. 15 Feb 1990, bur Salem Cem, Quitman, Clarke Co, MS, "At rest"; m. *Lucille Mason,*

V9-4274.   6-1. **Robert Emmett "Bobby" Brashier**,

V9-4275.   5-4. **Clara Blanche Brashier**, b. 14 Sept 1911; m.1. 13 July 1935, *Robert Eugene Goodwin,* b. 1908, d. 1942; m.2. Jan 1951, *Reuben Watts,*

V9-4276.   6-1. Robert Eugene Goodwin Jr, b. 26 June 1936; m. Nancy _____,

V9-4277.   7-1. Ronald Goodwin,

V9-4278.   7-2. James Goodwin,

V9-4279.   6-2. Margaret Blanche Goodwin, b. 15 July 1942; m. Charles Dooley,

V9-4280.   7-1. Regina Kay Dooley, b. 29 Sept 1961

V9-4281.   7-2. Kimberly Jill Dooley, b. 6 April 1963

V9-4282.   7-3. Charles Dooley, b. 31 Dec 1964

V9-4283.   5-5. **William Calhoun Brashier**, b. 16 June 1914, d. 15 June 1915, age 1 (meningitis), bur Salem Cem, Quitman, Clarke Co, MS, "Weep not, Father and Mother, for me; for I am waiting in glory for thee."

V9-4284.   5-6. **Benjamin Thomas Brashier Jr**, b. 27 Feb 1922; m. 6 May 1951, *Jeanette Cade*,

V9-4285.   6-1. **Margaret Sue Brashier**, b. 24 April 1952

V9-4286.   6-2. **Larry Brashier**, b. 16 Sept 1954

V9-4287.   6-3. **Benny Joe Brashier**, b. 4 March 1959, d. 2 Oct 1984, bur Salem Cem, Clarke Co, MS

V9-4288.   6-4. **Brenda Joyce Brashier**, b. 19 April 1962

V9-4289.   5-7. **Margaret Julia Brashier**, b. 12 Sept 1924; m. 6 Jan 1946, *Warren E. Husband*. They moved to Jackson, MS.

V9-4290.   6-1. Warren Wayne Husband, b. 12 April 1950

V9-4291.   6-2. Paul Edward Husband, b. 19 Nov 1951

V9-4292.   6-3. Sharon Kay Husband, b, 20 April 1967

Clifton Leonard Brashier and Ellen Lesley Lyons

5-2. **Clifton Leonard Brashier**, b. 10 Oct 1906, Shubuta, Clarke Co, MS, d. 11 Feb 1964, Houston, Harris Co, TX, bur. Salem Cem, Quitman, Clarke Co, MS; m. 6 June 1929, *Ellen Lesley Lyons*, b. 5 Jan 1911, Rose Hill, Dallas Co, TX, d. 6 April 1992, d/o John Henry Lyons, b. 8 Nov 1883, Dallas Co, TX, d. there 24 Feb 1957 & (m. 14 Feb 1909) Lena Claude Lesley, b. 18 Nov 1888, Van Buren Co, AR, d. 5 Sept 1981, Dallas Co, TX

V9-4293.   6-1. **Doris Ellena Brashier**, b. 11 Aug 1930, Garland, Dallas Co, TX; m. 18 Aug 1949, *Earl Lee "Jack" McDaniel Jr*, b. 1 Jan 1930,

V9-4294.   7-1. Marilyn Lesley McDaniel, b. 31 May 1953, Dallas, TX; m. 27 Nov 1974, John Scott Freeze, no ch.

V9-4295.   7-2. Virginia Ann "Gigi" McDaniel, b. 6 May 1961, Dallas, TX; m. 7 Feb 1987, Clinton Boyd Kerns,

V9-4296.   8-1. Morgan Elizabeth Kerns, b. 25 Aug 1990

V9-4297.   8-2. Helen Irene Kerns,

V9-4298.   6-2. **Dixie Evelyn Brashier**, b. 2 June 1932, Garland, Dallas Co, TX, d. 28 Feb 1988, bur Mineola, TX; m.1. 17 June 1949, at Brunswick, GA, *Donsel W. Scoggins*, m.2. *J.D. Fitzgerald*,

V9-4299.   7-1. John Dwight Scoggins, b. 31 March 1950, Dallas, Dallas Co, TX; m.1. 30 Nov 1968 at Garland, Dallas Co, TX, Patricia Ann McKinnie, (3 ch); m.2. Darla Higgins, m.3. Judy Rae Rau, m.4. Kendra Jeane Williams, b. 20 Aug 1957

V9-4300.   8-1. John Dwight Scoggins II, b. 16 May 1969

V9-4301.   8-2. Dusti Renee Scoggins, b. 16 Nov 1970

V9-4302.   8-3. Derika Ellen Scoggins, b. 15 April 1976

V9-4303.   8-4. Justin Richard Scoggins, (twin) b. 22 May 1982

V9-4304.   8-5. Darin Donsel Scoggins, (twin) b. 22 May 1982

V9-4305.   7-2. Janet Diane Scoggins, b. 17 July 1955, Dallas, Dallas Co, TX; m.1. 10 Feb 1973, Danny Wayne Wells, (1 ch); m.2. Paul Thomas Payne, (2 ch)

V9-4306.   8-1. Matthew Wayne Wells, b. 28 Sept 1973

V9-4307.   8-2. Heather Michelle Payne, b. 15 Sept 1976

V9-4308.   8-3. Jason Paul Payne, b. 14 Aug 1978

V9-4309.   7-3. Donna Beth Scoggins, b. 25 Aug 1963; m. Mark Koonce,

V9-4310.   8-1. Amanda Koonce,

V9-4311.   8-2. Adam Koonce,

V9-4312.   6-3. **Danna Elaine Brashier**, b. 3 March 1935, Rose Hill, Dallas Co, TX; m. 30 April 1954, Dallas Co, TX, **Herbert Eugene Elliott**, b. 28 June 1929, Sulphur Springs, Hopkins Co, TX, s/o Jesse Bryan "Jack" Elliott and Edna Earl Byrd.

V9-4313.   7-1. Ellen Elaine Elliott, b. 29 Jan 1955, Commerce, Hunt Co, TX; m. 16 Aug 1975, at San Antonio, TX, Russell Floyd Bartee,

V9-4314.   8-1. Kristin Renee Bartee, b. 11 Dec 1977

V9-4315.   8-2. Jonathan Eric Bartee, b. 16 Jan 1981

V9-4316.   8-3. Erin Lesley Bartee, b. 11 Aug 1983

V9-4317.   7-2. Jane Ann Elliott, b. 2 Feb 1956, Dallas, Dallas Co, TX; m. 13 Aug 1977, at San Antonio, TX, Douglas Dwain Baucum,

V9-4318.   8-1. Wesley Elliott Baucum, b. 26 Nov 1983

V9-4319.   8-2. Charles Douglas Baucum, (twin) b. 16 June 1987

V9-4320.   8-3. Michael John Baucum, (twin) b. 16 June 1987

V9-4321.   7-3. John Herbert Elliott, b. 16 June 1957, San Antonio, Bexar Co, TX; m. 21 June 1980, Woodward, Woodward Co, OK, Janice Diana Marshall,

V9-4322.   8-1. Jesse Bryan Elliott, b. 31 May 1986

V9-4323.   8-2. Joni Patricia Elliott, b. 11 Feb 1992

V9-4324.   8-3. Jacki Diana Elliott, b. 16 Dec 1993

V9-4325.   7-4. Patti Gayle Elliott, b. 3 Feb 1963, San Antonio, Bexar Co, TX; m. 25 Feb 1989, at San Antonio, TX, Daniel Anthony DiLoreto, b. 14 Sept 1960, MD.

V9-4326.   8-1. Anthony John DiLoreto, b. 1 Nov 1996

V9-4327.   8-2. Joseph Daniel DiLoreto, b. 4 June 1998

Benjamin Franklin Brashier
and Belinda Jane McDonald

[3]3. **Benjamin Franklin "Pap" Brashier**, (s/o John Washington Brashier and Antoinette S. Arrington), b. 24 Feb 1860, d. 5 Feb 1931; m. 1 June 1882, *Belinda Jane McDonald*, b. 3 Oct 1866, d. 20 Jan 1938, both bur McGowan's Chapel Cem, Clarke Co, MS.

Family of Benjamin Franklin Brashier and Belinda Jane McDonald:

[V9]-4328. 4-1. **Nellie (or Nettie) Brashier**, b. c1883; m. 5 Nov 1899, Clarke Co, MS, *J.W. Stevens*

[V9]-4329. 5-1. Lyda Stevens,

[V9]-4330. 5-2. Forrest Stevens,

[V9]-4331. 5-3. Bertha Lee Stevens,

[V9]-4332. 4-2. **Bessie Brashier**, b. Dec 1884; m. _____ *Dedwilder or Dedwylder*

[V9]-4333. 5-1. Charles Dedwylder,

[V9]-4334. 5-2. Thomas "Luke" Dedwilder,

[V9]-4335. 4-3. **Mae Brashier**, b. March 1887, d. _____, Cuba, FLorida (suicide), bur Cem at Harmony, MS; m. _____ *Barefield*

[V9]-4336. 5-1. Vivian Barefield,

[V9]-4337. 5-2. Daniel Barefield,

[V9]-4338. 5-3. Willie Barefield,

[V9]-4339. 5-4. Grace Barefield,

[V9]-4340. 5-5. Jewel Barefield,

[V9]-4341. 4-4. *****Robert Harvey "Harry" Brashier**, b. 20 Feb 1889, d. 9 Jan 1943; m. 13 July 1912, *Estelle Smiley*, b. 27 Jan 1891, d. 23 Nov 1943

[V9]-4342. 4-5. **Benjamin A. Brashier**, b. Feb 1891, d. _____, Santa Rosa, TX; m. 6 April 1913, Clarke Co, MS (Bk 2, p.449) *Ava Daniel*, and had several children, some of whom lived in Texas.

[V9]-4343. 5-1. **Hal Brashier**,

[V9]-4344. 5-2. **Ben Brashier**,

[V9]-4345. 5-3. **Joe Brashier**,

[V9]-4346. 5-4. **Gladys Brashier**,

[V9]-4347. 5-5. **Sybil Brashier**,

[V9]-4348. 4-6. **Mollie Brashier**, Nov 1893, d. _____; m. *Noah Lee*,

[V9]-4349. 5-1. Maxine Lee, m. _____ Grayson,

[V9]-4350. 5-2. J.B. Lee,

[V9]-4351. 5-3. Bernadine Lee,

[V9]-4352. 5-4. Inez Lee,

V9-4353.   4-7. **Ruth Brashier**, b. Feb 1896, d. _____, bur Magnolia
            Cem, Meridian, MS; m.1. _____ *McGowan*, m.2. *Otis*
            Hayes,
V9-4354.   5-1. Doris McGowan, m. Lloyd B. Satterfield,
V9-4355.   5-2. Catherine McGowan, m. John L. Pogue,
V9-4356.   4-8. **John W. Brashier Sr**, b. 8 April 1900, d. 6 April 1970; m.
            8 June 1923, Clarke Co, MS (Bk 4, p.17), *Christine*
            Shannon,
V9-4357.   5-1. **John W. Brashier Jr**, b. _____ 1927, d. 12 Sept
            1972, bur Magnolia Cem, Meridian, MS; m. _____
V9-4358.   6-x. **James H. Brashier**, 10540-A Byrd Doerner Road,
            Collinsville, MS 39325; 601/737-8919
V9-4359.   4-9. **Hattie Lou Brashier**, b. 8 Dec 1903, d. _____, bur
            Magnolia Cem, Meridian, MS; m. *K.A. Britt*,
V9-4360.   5-1. Jo Marie Britt, m. _____ Crowell, lives in Forrest,
            MS
V9-4361.   5-2. Harry Louis Britt, b. _____, d. _____, bur Magnolia
            Cem, Meridian, MS;
(not quite sure where these next two belong)
V9-4362.   4-10. **Jo Marie Brashier**
V9-4363.   4-11. **Harry Lamise Brashier**

Robert Harvey "Harry" Brashier
and Estelle Smiley

⁴-4. **Robert Harvey "Harry" Brashier**, (s/o Benjamin Franklin
Brashier and Belinda Jane McDonald), b. 20 Feb 1889, d. 9 Jan 1943
(lived in 1920 in Lauderdale Co, MS; census ED 45, Sh 14b, Ln 70); m.
13 July 1912, Jasper Co, MS (Bk 1, p.358), *Estelle Smiley*, b. 27 Jan
1891, d. 23 Nov 1943

V9-4364.   5-1. **Estelle Brashier**, b. 6 Sept 1914, d. April 1993; m.
            James Christopher Hearn, b. July 1914, d. 27 Dec 90
            (1920 Census, Lauderdale Co, SM, ED 45, Sh 14b, Ln70)
V9-4365.   6-1. James Christopher Hearn Jr, b. 8 March 1947,
            Mobile, AL; m. 6 Aug 1985, Marsha Davis, b. 27 April
            1956
V9-4366.   7-1. Bryan Davis Hearn, b. 15 May 1987
V9-4367.   6-2. Memri Dell Hearn, b. 3 May 1948, Mobile, AL (born
            Memrie Dell; name changed legally); m.1. Dick
            Saunders, m.2. Glenn Lerch,
V9-4368.   7-1. Jason Saunders, b. 31 Dec 1972
V9-4369.   7-2. Andrew Saunders, b. 13 Sept 1975

V9-4370.   7-3. Patrick Saunders, b. 27 Oct 1978
V9-4371.   5-2. **Mildred Brashier**, b. 27 May 1918; m. ***David Benton Holmes III***, b. 15 Dec 1919, 6 Oct 2004
V9-4372.   6-1. Nicole Holmes, b. 20 Oct 1943; m. Baker Haskins Bush,
V9-4373.   7-1. Nicole Haskins Bush,
V9-4374.   7-2. Margaret Brashier Bush,
V9-4375.   7-3. David Holmes Bush,
V9-4376.   6-2. David Benton Holmes IV, b. 25 July 1947; m. Linda Taylor,
V9-4377.   7-1. Lisa Renee Holmes, m.1. _____ West, m.2. _____ Cooper,
V9-4378.   8-1. David Wayne West,
V9-4379.   8-2. Dylan Shawn Cooper,
V9-4380.   8-3. Savannah Drew Cooper,
V9-4381.   6-3. John Collier Holmes, b. 28 Feb 1950; m. Susan Angi Juniper,
V9-4382.   7-1. Chelsea Lorraine Holmes,

WILLIAM M. BRASHIER and
SARAH JANE TOUCHSTONE

2-5. **William M. Brashier**, (s/o Rev. Pleasant Brashier and Rebecca Marie Moore), b. Dec 1830, Bennettsville, Marlboro Co, SC, d. 1911, Wayne Co, MS; m.lic. 20 Jan 1866, Clarke Co, MS (Bk B), to marry ***Mary Bounds*** (the license was never completed, so we believe they never married); m.1. 10 May 1868, Jasper Co, MS (Bk 2, p.152; transposed date, 1886, in WPA copy of *Jasper Co MS Marr*) ***Sarah Jane Touchstone***, b. c1848, MS (22 in 1870, Jasper Co, MS) d. after 1880 census; m.2. 6 Feb 1881, Wayne Co, MS, ***Cynthia Coker***, b. Dec 1848, MS.

William and family are in the following censuses:
1850 Census, Marlboro Co, SC, Fam #439, p.152;
1860 Census, Clarke Co, MS; ED 130, p.1, Ln12, Fam #442, p.66h;
1870 Agricultural Schedule in Jasper Co., MS, for William M. Brashier on page 7 Line 15 of the Southeast Beat July 30, 1870 (printed page 583, Dw #166, Fam #166) and Christopher D. Brashier on page 5 line 14 July 29, 1870. Mary A. Bounds, widow or wife of J.C. Bounds, lives nearby (p.584, #176-176) with a family of eleven children.
1880 Census, Wayne Co, MS; ED 13, Sh 2, Ln13;
1900 Census, Wayne Co, MS; ED 135, Sh 9a, Ln16;

1910 Census, Wayne Co, MS.

About 1855-56, William assaulted John W. Graham in Marlboro Co, SC; he was tried, convicted and fined. (Marlboro Co, SC, Court Records).

On 25 Aug 1861, he enlisted in Co. F (later Co. K; A. McNeill's Co), 8th Miss Infantry; from 25 Dec 1861 to 14 Jan 1862, he was on sick-leave at home; from Jan 1862 until April 1862, he was listed as a deserter, but was probably sick at home; 31 Aug 1862, present for duty; 10 Sept 1862, AWOL; Jan 1863 to 13 May 1864, present for duty; 13 May 1864, captured near Dalton, GA; 21 May 1864, sent to prisoner of war camp at Camp Morton, IN.

Family of William M. Brashier and Sarah Jane Touchstone:

V9-4383.   3-1. **Mary Frances Brashier**, b. c1869 (age 1 in 1870, Jasper Co, MS); m. 13 Dec 1882, Wayne Co, MS (Bk 1, p.289), ***S.E. Haigler***. 1880 Census, Wayne Co, MS: ED 130, Sh 1, Ln 12 Beat 4

V9-4384.   3-2. **Greene T. Brashier**, b. June 1874, MS, d. 1946, Wayne Co, MS, bur Zion's Rest Cemetery in Northwest Wayne Co; m. 24 Dec 1894, Clarke Co, MS (Bk G, p.129), ***Addie Permilia Leggett***, b. Nov 1875 MS, d. 1941, Wayne Co, MS, bur Zion's Rest Cemetery in Northwest Wayne Co. 1880 Census, Wayne Co, MS: ED 130, Sh 1, Ln 12 Beat 4 (parents' listing); 1900 Census Wayne Co, MS: ED 13, Sh 2, Ln 15; 1920 Census Wayne Co, MS: ED 151, Sh 1, Ln 1; Additional source: Interview with James Harold Brashier by Thomas E. Van Ness.

V9-4385.   4-1. **Julius Waldo Brashier**, b. Oct 1894, d. 1958; m.1. bef 1916, ***Annie McNeil*** (1 ch); m.2. after 1917, ***Louise Weymoth***, b. 1895, d. 1964 (4 ch). 1900 Census, Wayne Co, MS: ED 13, Sh 2, Ln 17; Data: Outline Descendant Tree from Leland Beard, sent to Thomas Van Ness.

V9-4386.   5-1. **Trilby Brashier**, b. 1916; m. ***Vivian L. Lightsey***, b. 1921

V9-4387.   5-2. **Gene Brashier**,

V9-4388.   5-3. **Audrey Brashier**,

V9-4389.   5-4. **Weymoth Brashier**,

V9-4390.   5-5. **Walter Mack Brashier**, b. 1928, d. 1948, bur Zion's Rest Cemetery in Northwest Wayne Co.

V9-4391.   4-2. **Erlie Lee Brashier**, b. Dec 1896, d. 1971; m. ***Nannie Walters***. 1900 Census, Wayne Co, MS: ED 13, Sh 2,

Ln 18; 1920 Census, Wayne Co, MS: ED 151, Sh 1, Ln 3

V9-4392.   5-1. **Thomas Trasher Brashier**, m. *Cynthia Dynethea Herrington*, b. 1947

V9-4393.   5-2. **Martin Luther Brashier**,

V9-4394.   5-3. **Mary George Brashier**, b. 1927, d. 1991

V9-4395.   5-4. **Henry Sonny Brashier**, b. 1929, d. 1998

V9-4396.   4-3. **Helen Daisy Brashier**, b. Oct 1898, d. 1995; m. *William David Beard*, b. 1892, d. 1967

V9-4397.   5-1. Leland Collette Beard, b. 1922; m. Emma Jean Sanders, b. 1923

V9-4398.   5-2. Leonard Monroe Beard, b. 1923, d. 1962; m. Marshia Jean McDonald, b. 1927, d. 1986

V9-4399.   5-3. Mary Kathleen Beard, b. 1924; m. Edward Vincent Baron; m.2. Warren Cecil Stafford; m.3. Wayne Levec Ward, b. 1925

V9-4400.   5-4. Alma Louise Beard, b. 1925; m. Dale Samuel Shaffner, b. 1924

V9-4401.   5-5. Billy David Beard, b. 1930; m. Mary Johnette Carpenter, b. 1932

V9-4402.   4-4. **Nathaniel Green Brashier**, b. Feb 1900, Wayne Co, MS, d. 1958 Wayne Co, MS, bur Zion's Rest Cemetery in Northwest Wayne Co.

V9-4403.   4-5. **Janie Joyce Brashier**, b. c1904; m. *Alvie Clark*, b. 1889, d. 1976

V9-4404.   5-1. Tommy Eugene Clark; m. Delores Sue Herrington

V9-4405.   5-2. William Harold Clark, d. 1996; m. Janice Voss

V9-4406.   5-3. Dorothy Elizabeth Clark; m. James Pitts

V9-4407.   5-4. James Danville Clark; m. _____ Carman

V9-4408.   5-5. Edward Carol Clark, b. 1925; m. Debbie Brumfield

V9-4409.   5-6. Allie Joyce Clark, b. 1928, d. 1983; m.1. Hayward Sykes; m.2. Bruce Davis; m.3. Joe Cercelleo

V9-4410.   5-7. Addie Pearl Clark, b. 1930; m. Norman Marsdale Stockman, b. 1927

V9-4411.   5-8. Troy Clark; m. Ralph Vallet

V9-4412.   4-6. **Freda Maureen Brashier**; m.1. *Johnny Prater*, m.2. _____ *Maldonado*

V9-4413.   5-1. Patsy Prater; m. James McClarin

V9-4414.   5-2. Johnny Prater,

V9-4415.	5-3. Louise Prater,
V9-4416.	5-4. Judy Prater,
V9-4417.	4-7. **Gwendolyn Brashier**
V9-4418.	4-8. **Elsie Lorena Brashier**, b. 23 Oct 1921 Wayne Co, MS, d. 20 May 1992 Wayne Co, MS, bur Zion's Rest Cemetery in Northwest Wayne Co; m.1. *Noah Anderson*; m.2. *John Albers*,
V9-4419.	5-1. Frankie Anderson
V9-4420.	5-2. Carolyn Anderson
V9-4421.	5-3. Connie Anderson
V9-4422.	4-9. **Mary Frances Brashier**, b. 16 Dec 1901 Wayne Co, MS, d. 23 March 1967 Wayne Co, MS, bur Zion's Rest Cemetery in Northwest Wayne Co.
V9-4423.	4-10. **Addie Lois Brashier**, b. 1905, d. 1982; m. *John Slayton*
V9-4424.	4-11. **Henry Leland Brashier**, b. 6 Jan 1907, d. 30 June 1985, bur Zion's Rest Cemetery in Northwest Wayne Co; m. *Ruby Woodward*
V9-4425.	5-1. **Howard Kelly Brashier**,
V9-4426.	5-2. **Laura Ann Brashier**; m. *Riley Sanford Hinton*
V9-4427.	5-3. **Edward Brashier**, b. 1926; m. *Sybil White*
V9-4428.	5-4. **Bonnie Jean Brashier**, b. 1929; m. *Ralph Thornton*
V9-4429.	5-5. **James Hardy Brashier**, b. 1933; m. *Dorothy Martin*
V9-4430.	4-12. **Bill Brashier**, b. 5 July 1909 Wayne Co, MS, d. 3 Oct 1991 Wayne Co, MS, bur Zion's Rest Cemetery in Northwest Wayne Co; m. *Gurchia Mildred Herrington*, b. 1912
V9-4431.	5-1. **Barney Roland Brashier**, b. 1929; m. *Evelyn Louise Brown*, b. 1933
V9-4432.	5-2. **William Eugene Brashier Sr**, b. 1932; m. *Sarah Alice Edwards*
V9-4433.	5-3. **Sidney Laverne Brashier**, b. 1938; m. *Sarah Staples*
V9-4434.	5-4. **Glenda L. Brashier**, b. 14 Oct 1945, d. 26 Sept 1946, bur Zion's Rest Cemetery in Northwest Wayne Co.
V9-4435.	4-13. **John Harold Brashier**, b. 1911, d. 1979; m. *Ruby Pearl Simms*, b. 1918
V9-4436.	5-1. **Thomas Harold Brashier**, b. 1936; m. *Mary Stutzman*

5-2. **Julius Werner Brashier**, b. 1939; m. *Melba Jeraldine Clark*

V9-4438. 4-14. **Charles Russel Brashier**, b. 1915

V9-4439. 4-15. **Fansider Brashier**, b. 1918

JAMES T. BRASHIER and NANCY ____

2-10. **James T. Brashier**, (s/o Rev. Pleasant Brashier and Rebecca Marie Moore), b. c1837; m. c1866, **Nancy** ____, b. c1846 (she is listed in the special 1866 Census of Mississippi). They are in the 1880 Census, Clarke Co, MS: ED 114, Sh 53, Ln 40, Beat 2, Fam #416, and 1900 Census, Clarke Co, MS: ED 2, Sh 8, Ln 21.

James lived in Clarke Co, MS, in 1857: 19 March 1857, Clarke Co, MS, James T. Braisher, gives his power of attorney to Francis Goodwin "to collect for me what is still due from estate of Grandmother Frances Moore." (Marlboro Co, SC, Deeds, Bk T, p.167). Filed on 26 May 1857. *The Stubbs of Marlboro County* is in error in listing this power of attorney as originating in Tennessee.

On 4 July 1864, James appears on a list of casualties, 8th Miss Inf, in the Battle of Tishamingo Creek; wounded severely in leg. (Series 1, Vol. 39, part 1, p.230). Between 22 Aug and 17 Sept 1864, James enlisted in Co. F, 2nd Regt. Inf, Miss State Troops for 30 days. enlisted by J.W. Lankford. Left sick at Macon.

Family of James T. Brashier and Nancy ____:

V9-4440. 3-1. **Learce Brashier**, b. c1866

V9-4441. 3-2. **Belle Brashier**, b. c1868

V9-4442. 3-3. **Alonzo Brashier**, b. May 1871, d. bef. 1910; m. *Mollie* ____, b. March 1872, d. bef. 1910. They both died before 1910, when the children were living with cousins or adopted.

V9-4443. 4-1. **James Brashier,** b. Nov 1899

V9-4444. 4-2. **Matthew Brashier**, b. Feb 1900

V9-4445. 4-3. **Luther Brashier**, b. c1902

V9-4446. 3-4. **Charles L. Brashier**, b. c1875, d. bef. 1910; m. 1 July 1898, Clarke Co, MS: (Bk G, p.463), *Rosa Lee Moody*, b. 1875, AL. 1880 Census, Clarke Co, MS: ED 114, Sh 53, Ln 41 Beat 2 Fam #416. Thomas Van Ness: The groom in the marriage cited is listed as C.L. Brashier. This is the only C. Brashier I have listed that fits timewise that is not otherwise married. Thomas Van Ness's speculation: Rosa Lee Moody was married to C.L. Brashier and had custody of Grady and Albert in the 1910 Census, Jones Co, MS: ED 81, Sh 3A, Ln 42. The dates are right for the father to have been Charles Brashier, son of James T. Brashier, but I have no verification.

V9-4447.   **4-1. Grady Brashier**, b. c1900

V9-4448.   **4-2. Albert Brashier**, b. c1903

V9-4449.   **3-5. Cuning Brashier**, b. c1877

V9-4450.   **3-6. Sally Brashier**, b. Dec 1879

CHRISTOPHER DUDLEY BRASHIER and NANCY JANE SYKES

2-11. **Christopher Dudley "Kit" Brashier**, (s/o Rev. Pleasant Brashier and Rebecca Marie Moore), b. c1839, d. c1878 at 38 from an injury caused when a Civil war wound caused him to slip and injure himself while cutting wood with an ax; bur Quitman Cem, Clarke Co, MS: "Co D, 14th Miss Inf, C.S.A," no dates; m. 19 Sept 1867, Clarke Co, MS (Bk C, p.80), *Nancy Jane Sykes*, b. 27 Dec 1846, AL, d. 11 Dec 1928, Vossburg, Jasper Co, MS.

They are Fam# 840, p.582, 1870 Census, Jasper Co, MS, Southeast beat, and the survivors are in the 1880 Census, Clarke Co, MS: ED 114, Sh 63, Ln 15, and the 1900 Census, Clarke Co. MS: ED 3, Sh 1, Ln 16. They had three sons and a daughter. The three brothers all worked for the railroad and/or farmed.

Christopher Dudley Brashier served in three Confederate units. In May 1861, Christopher D. Brashier enlisted in Co. D (Quitman Invincibles), 14 Miss Inf Regt. On 16 Feb 1862, surrendered at Ft. Donelson, severely wounded arm and leg. Discharged, 19 Oct 1862, Holly Springs, MS (Confederate Service Rec. 14 Miss Inf Regt). On 30 Sept 1863, he enlisted in Hams Regt under Capt. Wm P. Curlee. In April 1864, he enlisted in Co. B, 1st Miss Cav. Reserves. On 4 May 1865, unit surrendered by Gen. R. Taylor at Citronelle, AL. On 13 May 1865, Christopher was released on parole at Meridian, MS.

Family of Christopher Dudley Brashier and Nancy Jane Sykes:

V9-4451.   **3-1. *Charles Dudley Brashier**, b. 22 July 1868, Jasper Co, MS, d. 29 Jan 1903, Clarke Co, MS; m. 1 Sept 1891, *Jennie Bell Baker*, b. 27 July 1873, Clarke Co, MS, d. 15 Dec 1948, Clarke Co, MS,

V9-4452.   3-2. **James E. Brashier**, b. June 1870, Clarke Co, MS; m. 20 Dec 1895, Clarke Co, MS (Bk G, p.233), *Lucy A. Rowell*, b. Oct 1879, MS

V9-4453.   4-1. **Frank P. Brashier**, b. Aug 1898

V9-4454.   3-3. *****Nancy Alice Brashier**, b. 30 April 1873, d. 13 Feb 1955, bur in Vossburg, Jasper Co, MS; m. 10 Feb 1889, Clarke Co, MS (Bk F, p.3), *Benjamin Forest Holland*, b. 6 April 1865, d. 26 Jan 1952

V9-4455.   3-4. *****William Robert Brashier**, b. 30 March 1876, Clarke County, MS, d. 1952 in New Orleans, LA; m. 10 Jan 1900, Jasper Co, MS, (Bk 6, p.79), *Sallie Estelle Allen*, b. Jan 1878, Vossburg, MS.

Charles Dudley Brashier and Jennie Bell Baker

3-1. **Charles Dudley Brashier**, (s/o Christopher Dudley Brashier and Nancy Jane Sykes), b. 22 July 1868, Jasper Co, MS, d. 29 Jan 1903, Clarke Co, MS, when an unscheduled express train ran into his hand cart during a thunderstorm as he pumped his way to work on the railroad; m. 1 Sept 1891, Clarke Co, MS (Bk F, p.132), *Jennie Bell Baker*, b. 27 July 1873, Clarke Co, MS, d. 15 Dec 1948, Clarke Co, MS, both bur West Pleasant Grove Cemetery Clarke Co, MS. Ancestors of Thomas E. Van Ness's wife. They are on the 1870 Census, Jasper Co, MS, Southeast beat, p.581; 1880 Census, Clarke Co, MS: ED 114, Sh 63, Ln 15.

V9-4456.   4-1. **Christopher Denton Brashier**, b. c1893; m. 19 Aug 1920, Clarke Co, MS (Bk 4, p.44), *Dollie Leggett*. They are in the 1910 Census, Jasper Co, MS:, ED 22, Sh 17, Ln 10 (Microfilm has ED's mixed up) and the 1920 Census, Clarke Co, MS: ED 3, Sh 8, Ln 70.

V9-4457.   5-1. **Edith Nebraska Brashier**, m. *George Farr*

V9-4458.   4-2. **James Arthur Brashier**, b. 28 Oct 1894, Clarke Co, MS, d. 6 July 1974, Clarke Co, MS; m. 19 March 1921, at Quitman, Clarke Co, MS, *Leila Pearl (or Lula) Elam*, b. 17 Oct 1903, Lauderdale Co, MS, d. 1 April 1998, Hinds Co, MS, bur McGowan's Chapel Cemetery, Clarke Co, MS. Census 1910 Jasper Co, MS: ED 22, Sh 17, Ln 10 (Microfilm has ED's mixed up); Census 1920 Clarke Co. ED 3, Sh 8, Ln 71. Additional source: 1997 Interview with James Harold Brashier. James Arthur Brashier was Pvt. 1st Class, in 1918, Co. E, 141st Infantry, U.S. Army (from

"Records of Discharges of Soldiers and Sailors"). Leila's sister, Allie Elam, married Artis Parker Brashier, brother of James.

V9-4459.   5-1. **James Harold Brashier**; m. *Eula Neal*

V9-4460.   5-2. **Charles Warren Brashier**, b. 19 Jan 1923, Clarke Co, MS, d. 14 Sept 1991, Clarke Co, bur McGowan's Chapel Cem. He was a Postal Clerk and served in U.S. Navy WWII; m. *Doris Hargrove*

V9-4461.   5-3. **Doris Eloise Brashier**, b. 5 Dec 1924, d. 16 Oct 1995, Jackson, Hinds Co, MS; m.1. *Artis Brandon Castle*; m.2. *Robert Jay*

V9-4462.   5-4. **Hazel Brashier**; m. *Alfred Moss*, b. 1914, d. 1969, who worked for City Bus Co.

V9-4463.   5-5. **Bobbie Jean Brashier**, b. 6 Feb 1929, Clarke Co, MS, d. 3 July 1929, Clarke Co, MS, bur McGowan's Chapel Cemetery Clarke Co.

V9-4464.   5-6. **Joe Edward Brashier**, (twin) b. 6 July 1933, Clarke Co, MS, d. 17 May 1934, Clarke Co, MS

V9-4465.   5-7. **John Elam Brashier**, (twin) b. 6 July 1933, Clarke Co, MS, d. 22 May 1934, Clarke Co, MS

V9-4466.   4-3. **Charles Ranzy Brashier**, b. c1897, d. 10 May 1979; m. *Lena Pugh*, b. 24 May 1914, d. 29 Oct 1994, buried together in New Hope United Methodist Cem, Old River Road, Wayne Co, MS. In the same cemetery are Lena's (apparent) parents: Allen P. Pugh, 14 Dec 1875—14 Feb 1948 and Betty Lee Pugh, 15 Feb 1883—15 Aug 1969. Also an apparent brother: John Mabry Pugh, 16 July 1908—13 Oct 1965.

V9-4467.   4-4. **Robert Wesley Brashier,** b. 5 Nov 1898, Clarke Co, MS, d. 15 Dec 1983, bur Zion's Rest Cemetery in Northwest Wayne Co, MS; m. 29 Aug 1920, Wayne Co, MS (Bk 6, p.23), *Kate Reynolds*, b. 08 Feb1902, d. 15 Jan 1996, bur Zion's Rest Cemetery in Northwest Wayne Co. (Info from Jewel Downey of Enterprise, MS.)

V9-4468.   5-1. **Mildred Brashier**, b. 1921

V9-4469.   5-2. **Robert Wesley Brashier, Jr**; m. *Nellie _____*

V9-4470.   4-5. **Artis Parker Brashier**, b. 11 Oct 1900, d. 1 April 1933, Harmony, Clarke Co, MS, bur Quinnelly Cem. near McGowan's Chapel; m. 20 Feb 19__, Los Angeles, CA, *Allie Elam*, b. 10 May 1907, Harmony, Clarke Co, MS. Sister to Leila Pearl Elam, who married James Arthur Brashier, brother of Artis.

V9-4471.	5-1. **Kathryn L. Brashier**, b. 6 July 1925, d. 9-12 Sept 1973, Michigan, bur Quinnelly Cem. near McGowan's chapel; m. at Meridian, Lauderdale Co, MS, **Clarence Osman**
V9-4472.	5-2. Infant Daughter **Brashier**, b. 1928
V9-4473.	5-3. **Billie Ray Brashier**, b. 1929. He was a camera man in Hollywood; m. in Hollywood, CA, _____unknown
V9-4474.	5-4. Infant Son1 **Brashier**, b. 1931
V9-4475.	5-5. Infant Son2 **Brashier**, b. 1933
V9-4476.	4-6. **Charles Bell Brashier**, b. c1903; m.1. **Alma Culpepper**, m.2. **Beatrice Smith** (info from Ethel McLeod)
V9-4477.	5-1. **Charles Bell Brashier, Jr**

Nancy Alice Brashier
and Benjamin Forest Holland

³-3. **Nancy Alice Brashier**, (d/o Christopher Dudley Brashier and Nancy Jane Sykes), b. 30 April 1873, d. 13 Feb 1955, bur in Vossburg, Jasper Co, MS; m. 10 Feb 1889, Clarke Co, MS (Bk F, p.3), **Benjamin Forest Holland**, b. 6 April 1865, d. 26 Jan 1952, bur in Vossburg, Jasper Co, MS.

V9-4478.	4-1. Forest Jefferson Holland; m. Nannie Pennington
V9-4479.	5-1. Katharine Holland
V9-4480.	5-2. Myrtle Holland
V9-4481.	5-3. Ruth Holland
V9-4482.	5-4. Jayce Holland
V9-4483.	4-2. Verda Jane Holland; m. Erman Mason
V9-4484.	4-3. Warner Edward Holland
V9-4485.	5-1. Warner Edward Holland, Jr
V9-4486.	5-2. Girl Holland
V9-4487.	5-3. Girl Holland
V9-4488.	4-4. William Benjamin Holland
V9-4489.	4-5. Virgie Elizabeth Holland; m. John Buford Baker
V9-4490.	5-1. Lois Baker; m. J. A. Broadway
V9-4491.	5-2. John Buford Baker, Jr
V9-4492.	5-3. Tommy Baker
V9-4493.	5-4. Rose Marie Baker; m. _____ Lightsey
V9-4494.	4-6. Charles Zelton Holland; m. Ann Bell Arledge
V9-4495.	5-1. Charles Holland
V9-4496.	5-2. James Holland
V9-4497.	5-3. Mary Ann Holland; m. Sam Anderson
V9-4498.	5-4. Robert Holland; m. Marsha Fleming

^{V9}-4499.   5-5. Becky Holland; m. Roger Wise
^{V9}-4500.   4-7. Ida Lucille Holland
^{V9}-4501.   4-8. James Coyt Holland
^{V9}-4502.   4-9. Alice Marie Holland
^{V9}-4503.   4-10. Earl Holland
^{V9}-4504.   4-11. Ethel Eloise Holland; m.1. _____ Roper; m.2. _____
              Lightsey; m.3. _____ McLeod
^{V9}-4505.   4-12. Mildred Tivola Holland; m. Donald _____
^{V9}-4506.   4-13. Mary Etta Holland. died in infancy

William Robert Brasher and Sallie Estelle Allen

³-4. **William Robert Brasher**, (s/o Christopher Dudley Brashier and Nancy Jane Sykes), b. 30 March 1876, Clarke County, MS, d. 2 Jan 1952 in New Orleans, LA; m. 10 Jan 1900, Jasper Co, MS, (Bk 6, p.79), **Sallie Estelle Allen**, b. 17 Jan 1878, Vossburg, Jasper Co, MS, d. 2 May 1959, New Orleans, LA, both bur Garden of Memories Cem, New Orleans. William worked for the railroad for years. Census 1880 Clarke Co, MS: Beat 2, p. 63; Census 1900 Clarke Co, MS: Beat 2; Census 1910 Lauderdale Co, MS: Meridian City, ED 44, Sh 3 (Additional source: Email 12 Oct 1998 from Bill Norwood to Thomas E Van Ness, containing Descendancy tree.)

^{V9}-4507.   4-1. **Lloyd Brasher**, b. 14 Nov 1900, Vossburg, Jasper Co, MS, d. June 1958 at sea; m. **Ruth Marmouget**, b. 5 March 1904, New Orleans, LA, d. Sept 1984, New Orleans, LA.
^{V9}-4508.   5-1. **Diane Brasher**; m. _____ **Russell**
^{V9}-4509.   4-2. **Anna Pearl Brasher**, b. 5 Aug 1906, Vossburg, Jasper Co, MS, d. 12 March 1996, New Orleans, LA; m. **Gustave Edwin Carlson, II**, b. 21 Nov 1897, TX, d. Feb 1973, New Orleans, LA
^{V9}-4510.   5-1. Gustave Edwin Carlson, III, b. 27 Sept 1934, d. May 1970, New Orleans, LA; m.1. Flo Nelson; m.2. Helen _____; m.3. _____
^{V9}-4511.   6-1. Charissa E. Carlson,
^{V9}-4512.   6-2. Lauren A. Carlson, m. _____ Crawford
^{V9}-4513.   7-1. Jennifer Leigh Crawford
^{V9}-4514.   4-3. **Louise Edna Brasher**, b. 7 Sept 1912, d. 21 March 1990, Dallas, TX; m. 10 Sept 1935, in New Orleans, LA, **Louis Phillip Paquet**, b. 9 April 1892, New Orleans, LA, d. 19 Oct 1944, New Orleans, LA; m.2. 15 Aug 1950, in St Francis Xavier Catholic Church, Metairie, LA, **Alexandre**

	Francis LeDoux, b. 12 Sept 1909, New Orleans, LA, d. 3 Jan 1969, New Orleans, LA.
V9-4515.	5-1. Gwendolyn Paquet, b. 8 Jan 1937, New Orleans, LA; m. 7 Jan 1961, Fred Rankin Grote, b. 20 Sept 1931, TX
V9-4516.	6-1. Gwendolyn Louise Grote, b. 28 May 1962; m. 7 Nov 1992, Cory Paul Farrugia
V9-4517.	7-1. Molly Elizabeth Farrugia, b. 17 Feb 1995
V9-4518.	6-2. Fred Rankin Grote Jr, b. 17 July 1963; m.1. 30 June 1984, Mary Clair Echoles (1 ch); m.2. 14 Aug 1993, in Dallas, TX, Nancy Elizabeth Holbrook
V9-4519.	7-1. Ashley Clair Grote, b. 24 Jan 1989
V9-4520.	7-2. Fred Rankin Grote III, b. 18 May 1994
V9-4521.	7-3. Nancy Ann Grote, b. 17 Feb 1998
V9-4522.	5-2. Alexander Francis LeDoux, Jr. b. 3 Dec 1953, New Orleans, LA; m. 8 July 1978, in New Orleans, LA, Elma Leonce Ireland, b. 14 Feb 1954, New Orleans, LA
V9-4523.	6-1. Kathleen Louise LeDoux, b. 9 April 1984, New Orleans, LA
V9-4524.	6-2. Patricia Ann LeDoux, b. 7 Dec 1987, New Orleans, LA
V9-4525.	6-3. Colleen Elizabeth LeDoux, b. 9 April 1990, New Orleans, LA
V9-4526.	4-4. **Margaret Brasher**, b. 8 Nov 1914, New Orleans, LA; m.1. 18 Aug 1935, St. Bernard Parish, LA, **Joseph Robert Norwood**, b. 16 Nov 1896, Collins, Covington Co, MS, d. 16 Feb 1943, in VA Hospital, Hines, IL; m.2. c1952, in New Orleans, **John Thomas Olmstead**, b. c1904, Boston, MA, d. 11 Nov 1968, Grand Prairie, TX
V9-4527.	5-1. Joseph Robert Norwood Jr, b. 2 Aug 1936, New Orleans, LA, d. 18 Nov 1996, New Orleans, LA
V9-4528.	5-2. William Bowers Norwood, b. 15 Dec 1939, New Orleans, LA; m. 31 March 1962, in New Orleans, LA, Joan Marion Bayhi, b. 1 Sept 1943 New Orleans, LA
V9-4529.	6-1. James William Norwood, b. 30 March 1963, Ellsworth AFB, South Dakota; m. 6 July 1985, in Wimbledon, North Dakota, Shelene Marie Samek, b. 28 July 1963, Jamestown, North Dakota
V9-4530.	7-1. Kaitlin Rose Norwood, b. 27 March 1991, St Gabriel Hosp, Little Falls, Minnesota

V9-4531.	7-2. Brennan James Norwood, b. 24 Feb 1995, St Gabriel Hosp, Little Falls, Minnesota
V9-4532.	7-3. Ian David Norwood, b. 11 Aug 1996, St Gabriel Hosp, Little Falls, Minnesota
V9-4533.	6-2. Michael Wayne Norwood, b. 3 Feb 1966, Ellsworth AFB, South Dakota; m. 29 Aug 1994, Fargo, North Dakota, Nancy Jane Wilson, b. 26 May 1968, Bismarck, North Dakota
V9-4534.	6-3. Donald James Norwood, b. 13 March 1970, March AFB, Riverside, CA
V9-4535.	6-4. Susan Elaine Norwood, b. 15 Dec 1971, Ellsworth AFB, South Dakota; m. 26 May 1998, in London, Ontario, Canada, Nicholas John Cowan, b. 7 Dec 1965, Canada

ROBERT B. BRASHIER
and LOUISE ISABELL WELSEN

[2]-12. **Robert B. Brashier**, (s/o Rev. Pleasant Brashier and Rebecca Marie Moore), b. 26 June 1840, Marlboro Co, SC, d. 3 April 1902, Clarke Co, MS, bur Desoto Cem, Clarke Co, MS, south of Quitman according to Cemetery survey found in Quitman Public Library, Quitman, MS ; m. 20 Sept 1867, Clarke Co, MS, *Louise Isabell Welsen*, b. 2 Jan 1843, 24 July 1904, Clarke Co, MS. (probably her second marriage, for marriage license lists her as Mrs. Bille (?Belle) Welsen and she seems to have had a daughter by a first marriage).
Census 1850 Marlboro Co, SC, p.152, fam# 439;
Census 1860 Clarke Co, MS, p.665B, fam#618;
Census 1880 Clarke Co, MS: ED 114, Sh 64, Ln 47 Fam # 592;
Census 1900 Clarke Co, MS: ED 3, Sh 17, Ln 84.

On 8 May 1861, Robert enlisted in Co. D, 14th Miss Inf; surrendered 16 Feb 1862 at Ft. Donelson; Sept 1862, exchanged at Vicksburg; about Feb 1863, became a teamster by order of Gen. Loring and Regt. Colonel; captured May 1863 and sent to prison Camp, marked as deserter on roll; released 14 May 1865 on his oath of Allegiance to US.

V9-4536.	3-1. Arewina Welsen, b. c1864

Salem Cem, Quitman, Clarke Co, MS

Mary Rebecca, wife of A. BRASHIER   16 Mar 1871   16 Jun 1904
  "She was a kind and affectionate wife,
   a fond mother, and a friend to all."

"Bill" Harold BRASHIER   6 Jul 1929   27 Oct 1973
(CS) Earl Lee BRASHIER   1898   1951   (Masonic)
Benny Joe BRASHIER   4 Mar 1959   2 Oct 1984

Row 5 (L-R):
(GS) Joe Tillman BRASHIER   17 Jan 1911   15 Jul 1980
    "Rest in peace"
(FHM) Lucille PRINCE BRASHIER   Born 21 Aug 1911   Died 20 Jan
1999   Age 87
GS on concrete base) John H. BRASHIER 4 Oct 1899 18 Sep 1932
(CS) William Calhoun, son of B. T. & Clara BRASHIER
    16 Jun 1914   15 Jun 1916
  "Weep not Father and Mother for me,
    for I am waiting in glory for thee."

BRASHIER (DM - one stone, both names - stone backwards)   "Memory
lane"
  "Book of Life" Clara RIGBY   12 Sep 1886   5 Feb 1974   (footstone):
Mother
  Ben T.   14 Apr 1884   27 Aug 1970   "Book of Life"   (footstone):
Father

Daddy Leonard BRASHIER   10 Oct 1906   11 Feb 1964
    "We will meet again."
Emmett L. BRASHIER   16 Feb 1909   15 Feb 1990
    "At rest"
(DBS) (GS) Paul J. COKER   11 Sep 1901   5 Sep 1991
    "At rest"
    (GS) Hilda Ann COKER   3 Feb 1901   2 Dec 1997
    "At rest"
      (FHM) Hilda Ann BRASHIER COKER   Born 3 Feb 1901   Died 2
Dec 1997   Age 96
(GB) Charles B. BRASHIER, Sr.   25 Oct 1895   31 Dec 1963
    "A friend to all"
(GB) Mattie R. BRASHIER   13 Mar 1896   24 Apr 1965
    "A friend to all"
BRASHIER (DM)
  Ralph Calhoun   1 Oct 1924   5 Jan 1992
  Alice Dean   12 Nov 1931   (one date)
(CS) Mother Elizabeth Hailes   26 Apr 1875   17 Jan 1954
    "A tender mother and a faithful friend"
(CS) Father Jefferson A. Hailes   13 Sep 1868   11 Jul 1934

"Tho' lost to sight, to memory dear"
(CS) Grandmother Elizabeth E. Hailes   29 Mar 1850   10 Nov 1936
"Forever with the Lord"
(CS) Mother Belle Hailes Brashier   1879   1931
   "Beloved one, we love you."
   (footmarker): B. H. B.
(CS) Father John C. BRASHIER   1857   1936
Glen S. HAILES   13 Sep 1905   2 Nov 1968
(CS) HAILES (headstone)
   (footstone): William S. HAILES   14 Sep 1874   8 Dec 1960
Row 7 (L-R):
(DBS) (GS) Mother Vondelle GLISSON BRASHIER   14 Nov 1909   13
May 1995   "Beloved angel"
      (GS) Daddy Jesse W. BRASHIER, Sr.   2 Feb 1898   11 Jan 1956
"Beloved one farewell"
Kate B. BRASHIER   23 May 1899   28 Apr 1982
(GS) Father Chester E. BRASHIER   4 Aug 1893   9 Jun 1963
   "Rest is thine and sweet remembrance ours."
   (footmarker): C. E. B.
(GS) Mother Alda H. BRASHIER   15 Dec 1903   26 Apr 1955
   "Rest is thine and sweet remembrance ours."
PARKER (DM - one stone, both names)
   (CS) Father John Jay   17 Mar 1849   2 Feb 1939   "In loving
memory"   (Masonic)
      (footmarker): J. J. P.
   (CS) Mother Dollie BRASHER   17 Jan 1865   13 Dec 1940   "In
loving memory"
      (footmarker): D. B. P.

New Hope United Methodist Cemetery
Old River Road, Wayne County, Mississippi
Compiled by Jerry D. Mason, 11 October, 2003

BRASHIER
Charles R. Brashier; died May 10, 1979 "In Loving Memory"
Lena Pugh Brashier; May 24, 1914 - Oct. 29, 1994

PUGH (Lena's parents)
Allen P.; Dec. 14, 1875 - Feb. 14, 1948
Betty Lee; Feb. 15, 1883 - Aug. 15, 1969

BROTHER: John Mabry Pugh; July 16, 1908 - Oct. 13, 1965

Stray data:

(from Thomas E. VanNess <tevanness@juno.com>)
In the Dyer Co. TN Marriages book by Byron and Barbara Sistler in the Birmingham Public Library Tutwiler Collection:
    B.F. Brazier m. 26 Jan 1870, K.J. Caliway (?? second marriage?)
    J.C. Brashears m. 3 Sept 1867, Rebecca J. Hawkins

In the 1870 Census, I found Samuel Braser, Pg 57 printed or 25 handwritten in Civil Dist 4, Fam #173.

In the 1880 Census, I found:
Tha? Brazier, ED 5 p.32(handwritten) 286(printed) LN 46
Elleck Boshears ED 12 p.21(HW) 44A(printed) Ln 19, Fam #151, 8th Civil Dist.

Thomas E. Van Ness <tevanness@juno.com>
1900 Census Clarke Co. MS ED 3 SH 4 LN 21

Brasher, William B. Head, b. Oct 1840, 59, m. 32		AL AL AL
Mary E. Brasher, b. Aug 1845, age 54, m. 32 ch:8- 5		MS MS MS
George W. Brasher, b. Aug 1877 22 S		MS AL MS
James B. Brasher, b. July 1882 17 S		MS AL MS
Ella M. Brasher, b. June 1888 11 S		MS AL MS

[V9]-4537.   **William B. Brasher**, b. Oct 1832, AL, (parents b. AL); m. c1868 (m. 32 yrs in 1900), **Mary E.** ____, b. Aug 1845, MS (54 in 1900), ch: 8-5

[V9]-4538.   1.
[V9]-4539.   2.
[V9]-4540.   3.
[V9]-4541.   4.
[V9]-4542.   5.
[V9]-4543.   6. **George W. Brasher**, b. Aug 1877, MS (22 in 1900)
[V9]-4544.   7. **James B. Brasher**, b. July 1882, MS (17 in 1900)
[V9]-4545.   8. **Ella M. Brasher**, b. June 1888, MS (11 in 1900)

(Sources:
Thomas E. Van Ness, <tevanness@juno.com> 3117 Paradise Acres, Hoover, AL 35244
Doris Brashier McDaniel, 9959 Waterfront Dr, Rockwall, TX 75087
Danna Brashier Elliott, P.O.Box 7, Sulphur Springs, TX 75483-0007; 903/945-2897 (Danna is Pres of Hopkins Co (TX) Gen Soc.)
Patti Elliott DiLoreto, 914 Springvale Dr, San Antonio, TX 78227; 210/674-1528
James C. Hearn, 1965 Edenbridge Way, Nashville, TN 37215. 615/309-5562
Mildred Holmes, Meridian, MS; now deceased.
James H. Brashier, 10540-A Byrd Doerner Road, Collinsville, MS 39325; 601/737-8919
Bill Norwood, <joanbill@gfherald.infi.net> 2650 26th Ave So, #307, Grand Forks, ND 58201

35. ZACHARIAH BRAZIER/BRASHER

Considerable confusion surrounds **Zachariah Brazier,** b. 1715, s/o Robert Brazier of Kent Co, England. Many Brashear researchers have suggested him as a son for Robert Brasseur/Brashear, the Huguenot immigrant to VA c1635. In addition, many try to make Zachariah's second wife, Elizabeth Fowke, into the wife of Robert Brasseur, the Huguenot immigrant. The documents (and dates!) do not support these ideas. In most references, this man is referred to as *Zachariah Brazier*. He left a number of records in South Carolina, before moving to Virginia.

from *The Huguenots of Colonial South Carolina,* by Hirsh, 1928, p.97: "In 1725, when extant records of St. Philips Church begin, we find French Protestants active in its life. The record of July 13, 1725, shows that Francis LeBrasseur, recently dec'd, was a church warden. There is evidence of very few pews owned or rented in St. Philips by Huguenots after 1725. In 1743, Zachariah Brazier applied for a pew in the choir loft (MS Vestry Bk, 1732-56, March 19, 1743, Charleston, Berkeley Co, SC)."

from *South Carolina Jury Lists, 1718-1783,* by Mary Bondurant Warren:
1720 Co not entered   Jury 2 Braiseur, Francis
1744 St. Philips Co Jury 2 Brazier, Zachariah
1744 St. Philips Co Jury 3 Brazier, Zachariah

From these records, we might be tempted to think that Zachariah Brazier was a son of Francis LeBrasseur, but he wasn't. He was s/o Robert Brazier, of Kent Co, ENGLAND.

Francis LeBrasseur, of Charlestown, SC

[V9]-4546.   Francis LeBrasseur came into South Carolina from Barbados about 1690, and his surname appears in the records variously as DeBrassieur, Le Brassieur, and Brasseur. On 29 Aug 1717, he made affidavit (according to Leonardo Andrea) that he was 40 years old, or

---

thereabouts— that is, born c1677. He died prior to 13 Jul 1725 and left a will.

The LeBrasseur family, from Barbados, settled in Charleston and were long active in that city's history and prominent in one of the few Huguenot Churches to flourish in America. He was at one time a guardian of Christopher Arthur, a minor. He was a church warden at St. Philip's Church and a wealthy merchant of Charlestown. On 7 Oct 1719, Mrs. Catherine LeBrasseur, wife of Francis LeBrasseur, made affidavit that her husband was at the time in Barbados, presumably on some commercial venture.

Francis LeBrassieur and his wife, Catherine, had at least one child:

V9-4547.   **Francis LeBrassieur**, *the younger*, m. 29 Jan 1730, at Charles Town, Anne Mellish, widow of Richard Splatt (Misc. Recds, BB, p.174). Francis the younger d. 1736, and left a will.

The Will of Francis LeBrasseur, Merchant of Charles Town, SC, dated 27 Nov 1736, probate 13 Jan 1736/7:

- debts and expenses;
- to white servant boy, Jacob Marky, 15 lbs;
- to my negro man, Philander, yearly a set of clothes;
- to my negro woman, Sahina, yearly a set of clothes;
- to Rev. Alexander Gorden and Capt. Thomas Gadsden, 10 lbs ea;
- to Benjamin Whitaker and James Green, 50 lbs ea;
- to my daughters, Anne and Charlotte, 2800 acres on Pedee River;
- to my daughters, Anne and Charlotte, all household furniture, plate, wearing apparel, goods and chattel, and all residue;

Exectrs: My beloved wife, Anne Le Brasseur, and my good friends, Ralph Izard of Goose Creek, Esq, and Jacob Motte of Charles Town, Merchant;

Witnesses: Thomas Gadsden, James Greene, Susanna Harrison;

Proved 13 Jan 1736/7 by Thomas Gadsden and Susanna Harrison.

Thomas Gadsden renounced the 10 lbs legacy to him.

Index to SC deeds, 171⁹⁻ 1785- 1800- Charleston: (Call # 975.7 R2c)

Le Brasseur, Francis & Arthur Dominick,   Feomnt, Bk V, p.138
      ditto   to Elizabeth Gadsden,   Sale,   Bk I, p.176
Le Brasseur, Ann, Lessor, to Peter Calvett, Lessee,   Lease and Release, Bk V, p.221
Le Brasseur, Ann, Lessor, to John Watson, Lessee,   Lease and Release, Bk V, p. 142.

Captain Zachariah Brazier's first marriage

South Carolina Marriages, 1688-1799, comp. Brent H. Holcomb, 1983: **Zacheriah Brazier** & **Mary Ann Fairfax**, 7 Apr 1740, P. License, St. Phillip's.

Ships Registers in the SC Archives, 1734-1780, all Charleston, SC:
29 May 1745, Zechariah Brazier, Master of Schooner "Friendship"
30 Oct 1746, Zechariah Brasier, Owner of Schooner "Molley"
18 May 1748, Zachariah Braisier, Master of Schooner "Banjo"
25 May 1749, Zachariah Brazier, Master of Brigantine "Dolphin"

The Papers of Henry Laurens, v.1, p.43: "For some days past, a Small Privateer has infested our coast, drove one of the Winyaw Pettiaugas aground & then plunder'd her, but the People escaped to shore & afterward got her off again."

This is apparently the same incident reported in the *Gazette*, of Aug 24, 1747, per footnote in Laurens Papers: "Capt **Brazier** sailed from hence to Winyaw, and was chased soon after he got over this bar by a Spanish Privateer; but, being well acquainted with the Coast, he ran his vessel ashore, and retired with his crew unseen by the Enemy; Saw the privateer's boat come on board his Schooner, and (upon a hard Gale of Wind coming on) go off again, upon which he immediately re-took possession, got her off and sailed her into Bull's-Head inlet, off which place he was again chased."

Captain Zachariah Brazier
and Elizabeth Fowke

Several genealogies, including John Bennett Boddie's, *Historical Southern Families,* show that

Robert Offley, of London, England, m. Anne Osborne, d/o Sir Edward Osborne, Lord Mayor of London, and had (at least) daughters Ann and Sarah.
a-1. Ann Offley, m. Robert Hays, b. c1601, came to Lower Norfolk, VA, 1637
    b-1. Alexander Hays,
    b-2. Nathaniel Hays, moved to Prince George Co, VA
    b-3. Adam Hays, m. Susan Ivy, moved to Prince George Co, VA
    NOTE: a John Hays was first owner of a mill located on Hays Creek in Augusta Co, VA, 1742

a-2. Sarah Offley; m. Capt. Adam Thoroughgood,
 b-1. Elizabeth Thoroughgood, m. Capt. John Michael,
 b-2. Ann Thoroughgood, b. c1632; m.1. Job Chandler, m.2. c1661 (2nd wife of) Col. Gerard Fowke, sixth son of Roger and Mary Fowke of Gunston Hall, Staffordshire, England; Gentleman of the Bed Chamber to Charles I and Col. in Royal Army; he escaped to VA in 1651 after the battle of Worcester. He was a Burgess of Westmoreland Co, VA in 1663, merchant and planter; owned "Geneston," "Cedar Hill," "Hill Top," in VA and "Port Tobacco" in Charles Co, MD; d. 1669, MD.
   Children of Col. Gerard Fowke and Ann Thoroughgood, per "M.H.M. XVI—No.1, March, 1921," cited in a note in *Across the Years in Prince George's County*, p.136:
  c-1. Adam Fowke, d. young
  c-2. Elizabeth Fowke, m. William Dent,
  c-3. Gerard Fowke Jr, m. 1686, Sarah Burdett, of Charles Co, MD
   Children of Gerard Fowke and Sarah Burdett, per *Across the Years*:
   d-1. Gerard Fowke, died single
   d-2. *Capt. Chandler Fowke, m. Mary Tassaker, of VA
   d-3. Roger Fowke, m. Ann Stone,
   d-4. Anne Fowke, m. Roger Alexander, founder of Alexandria, VA
   d-5. Frances Fowke, m. Dr. Gustavus Brown, of Charles Co, MD
    e-5. Anne Brown, m. Rev. Samuel Claggett, father (by his first wife, Elizabeth Gantt) of Rev. Thomas John Claggett, first Bishop of the Protestant Episcopal Church in America, consecrated 1792.
   d-6. Catherine Fowke, m. Ellsworth Bayne,
   d-7. *Elizabeth Fowke, m. Col. William Philips.
  c-4. Mary Fowke, m. her cousin, George Mason, s/o Col. George Mason, progenitor of "Gunston Hall," VA, and author of the Virginia Bill of Rights (per *Dinwiddie Papers*, p.xiii; also listed in *Across the Years*).

I've put another generation in here (over what Boddie has), based on Philips and Fowke family records, which are corroborated by Brown and Claggett family records and the record in *Across the Years*. A son born between 1661 when Col. Gerard Fowke married Mrs. Ann (Thoroughgood) Chandler, and 1669, when he died, would be 47-54 years old when Capt. Chandler Fowke married Mary Tassaker in 1716. Considering that Chandler and Mary had 12 children, that's getting started awfully late. We need a Gerard Fowke Jr, s/o Col. Gerard Fowke and Ann Thoroughgood, to be parents of the Gerard Fowke, who m. Sarah Burdett and was father of the Capt. Chandler Fowke who m. Ann Tassaker and the Elizabeth Fowke, who m. Col. William Philips.

This portion of an old [1857] genealogy confuses the first Gerard Fowke in this country with the Gerard Fowke, Esq, of King George Co, VA, who m. Sarah Burdett and/or Elizabeth Dinwiddie.

"Col. Gerard Fowke was the first of his name who came to this country. He was Colonel in the British Army, and Gentleman of the Privy Chamber to Charles I. He came to Virginia about the time that his unfortunate monarch was beheaded. One of his sons settled in Maryland. His son, Chandler Fowke, Esq, settled in King George Co, VA. He had three sons--Chander, Gerard, and Richard. Chandler married a Miss Harrison, Gerard married a Miss Dinwiddie, and Richard married a Miss Bumbary. Their sister, Elizabeth Fowke, married a Mr. Z. Brazier, (son of Robert Brazier, of Isle of Thanet, Kent Co, Eng).

[Overwharton Parish records in Brown Family records, see below, say Gerard, 1718; Elizabeth, 1727; Chandler, 1732, and Richard, 1741, were children Capt. Chandler Fowke and Mary Tassaker, who m. 1716 in Stafford Co, VA. There has to be another generation in here! The Philips family records also require another generation.]

Chandler, the eldest of the children [he wasn't eldest], had three sons-- William, John, and Thomas. William married his first cousin, Jenny Fowke, of Maryland, and John went south with his sister, Jenny.

"Mr. Gerard Fowke (the second brother) had issue also--Chandler and Roger, who went south; Gerard; William (m. a Miss Bronaugh); Robert Dinwiddie (m. a Miss Peachy); Elizabeth (m. Col William Philips of Stafford; error: he's a generation off); and another dau (who m. Mr. Johnston and resided in KY).

"Richard Fowke, Esq, died in the Army. He also left a family." (ref: *Old Churches, Ministers, and Families of VA*, by Bishop Wm. Meade, Gen. Publ Co, orig: 1857, reprint: 1978, pp.482-3).

Chandler Fowke and Mary Tassaker

d-2. Capt. Chandler Fowke, of Virginia, son of Gerard Fowke Jr, Esq, and Sarah Burdett, m. c1716, Mary Tassaker, eldest d/o Col. Richard Tassaker, Stafford Co, VA, who settled in King George Co, VA, having inherited "Pasipatanzy," later removed to "Gunston Hall," Stafford Co, where he died. Capt. Chandler Fowke, of Gunston Hall, in Stafford Co, d. 10 Feb 1745 (ref. Parish Registers of St. Paul, King George Co, and Aquia and Overwharton Parishes, Stafford Co, as given in *VA Genealogies*, "Brown Family," p.157; FHL fiche #6046678). Chandler and Mary (Tassaker) Fowke had 12 children, of whom Gerard, Chandler, Richard, and Elizabeth had children, which may be why Bishop Meade thought they only had three sons and a daughter:

e-1. Chandler Fowke Jr, b. 7 Nov 1717; d. young? name re-used

e-2. Gerard Fowke, b. c1718, d. 1781; m. Elizabeth Dinwiddie, d/o Lawrence Dinwiddie, Provost of Glasgow, Scotland, and niece of Robert Dinwiddie, Gov. of VA.

    f-1. Chandler Fowke, went south

    f-2. Roger Fowke, went south

    f-3. William Fowke, m. Miss Bronaugh

    f-4. Robert Dinwiddie Fowke, m. Miss Peachy

    f-5. Elizabeth Fowke,

        f-6. __dau__ Fowke, m. Mr. Johnson, res. in KY

e-3. William Chandler Fowke, b. Sept 1723, d. young? name re-used.

e-4. John Fowke, b. 17 Jan 1724/5, d. 16 Apr 1740

e-5. ***Elizabeth Fowke***, b. 27 Apr 1727 (Overwharton Parish Records); m.1. Richard Buckner; m.2. 12 Nov 1759 (St. Paul Parish Records; see also pre-nuptial agreement below), **Capt. Zachariah Brazier**, 1715-1797 (Stafford & Prince Co, VA), son of Robert Brazier of Isle of Thanet, Kent Co, England... one child.

    f-1. **Sarah Harrison Brazier**, m. Jonathan Cannon, s/o Luke Cannon of Ireland and had children:

        g-1. Grandison Cannon, d. bef. 1857

        g-2. Elizabeth Cannon, d. bef. 1857

        g-3. John Cannon,

        g-4. Sarah Edith Cannon, d. bef. 1857; m. 14 May1817, her cousin, Col. William Fowke Phillips Sr, b. 1795, s/o her aunt d7. Elizabeth (Fowke) Philips. See below.

e-6. Ann Fowke, b. 6 Feb 1729, d. 8 Dec 1732; name re-used

e-7. Chandler Fowke, "youngest son of Chandler and Mary Fowkes," b. 3 May 1732, d. 18 Feb 1810; m. Mary Harrison

    f-1. William Fowke, m. his first cousin, Jenny Fowke, of MD

    f-2. John Fowke, went south with his sister, Jenny

    f-3. Thomas Fowke,

    f-4. Jenny Fowke,

e-8. Sarah Fowke, b. 10 Aug 1734, d. 14 Oct 1739

e-9. Ann Fowke, "youngest daughter of Chandler and Mary Fowke," b. 4 Apr 1737; m. ?Hooe

e-10. Susanna Fowke, b. 27 Oct 1739; m. 15 Mar 17__, Henry Payton
e-11. Richard Fowke, b. 11 Dec 1741; m. 16 Mar 1760, Anne Bunbury; Richard died in the Army, but left a family also.
e-12. William Fowke, b. 31 May 1743, d. 2 Dec 1743

Elizabeth Fowke and Col. William Philips

d-7. Elizabeth Fowke, d/o Gerard Fowke Jr and Sarah Burdett, m. Col. William Philips, b. c1746, Stafford Co, VA, s/o James Philips of South Wales and a Miss Griffin of Stafford Co. William Philips was High-Sheriff of Stafford, and died about 1797.

Col. William Philips and Elizabeth Fowke had twelve children, "six of whom are now living [Bishop Meade, 1857]", including:
e-1. __dau__ Philips, b. c1774 (83 in 1857), "the eldest," m. _____ Jones
e-12. Col. William Fowke Philips Sr, b. c1795 (62 in 1857, "the youngest"; m. his cousin Sarah Edith Cannon (gd/o Zachariah Brazier), of Prince William County, VA, by whom he had seven children:
f-1. Laura Philips,
f-2. Mary Caroline Philips,
f-3. William Fowke Philips Jr,
f-4. Laura E.S. Philips, m. Wm. B. Carr of London Co, VA,
f-5. Dinwiddie Brazier Philips, m. Miss Nannie F. Walden, d/o William Walden of Rapp Co, VA,
f-6. Virginia Edith Philips,
f-7. Roberta Gustavia Philips.

Much the same data on Zachariah is given in *The Dinwiddie Papers*, v.1. p.xxiii, where he is referred to as Zachariah Brazier.

Their Pre-Nuptial Arrangements

Capt. Zachariah Brazier and Mrs. Elizabeth (Fowke) Buckner, widow, married when he was 44 and she was 32, which seems to have been of some concern to the parties:

Stafford Co, VA, Deed Bk P, p.241-3: This indenture tripartite made 5th November 1759, between Capt ZACHARIAS BRAZIER of the one part, and Mrs. ELIZABETH BUCKNER, of County of Stafford, Widow, of second part, and GERARD FOOKE & CHANDLER FOWKE, of sd County, Gent, and JAMES BOWIE, of Town of Port Royal, Merchant, of third part,

Whereas a Marriage by God is shortly to be had between the sd Zacharia & Elizabeth, and Elizabeth is now possessed in her own right of a number of Negroe slaves, among them the following (6 named, but not in the copy I have)...

Now, this indenture witnesseth that Elizabeth in consideration of the Intended Marriage and with consent of said Zacharias that a suitable and comfortable provision may be made for her in case she survives him, doth grant to said Gerard Fooke, Chandler Fooke, and James Bowie, the said Negroes upon the Trusts and to purposes mentioned, That is to say, that ...[Zacharias] will permitt the said Elizabeth and her assigns to hold said Negroes and take the rent and profits thereof to her own proper use untell the said Marriage shall take effect and after solumnized ... [Elizabeth] will permit said Zacharias and his assigns to enjoy the same and take the rent and profits during his natural life [and?] after death of Zacharias will permit Elizabeth and her assigns to possess so long as she shall live and upon [death] Trustees ... shall devide among all and every the Sons and Daughters of sd Zacharias and Elizabeth — if they leave any such issue, provided if Elizabeth should happen to survive Zacharias without leaving any issue of this Marriage, that then the Negroes with their increase remain to said Elizabeth and her heirs, as if sd Marriage had never taken effect.

/s/ Zachr. Brazier
/s/ Elizabeth Buckner

Presence Wm. Stuart, Zachr. Taliaferro,
Mary Taliaferro, Susanne Fooke

At Court held for Stafford County, 13th November 1759, Deed of Contract admitted to record.

Zachariah's and Elizabeth's dates look exactly a century too late to be part of the Brasseur/Brashear family: Zachariah and Elizabeth (Fowke) Brazier would need to be born c1627, not 1715 and/or 1727, to be related to our Robert Brasseur of Isle of Thanet.

Brazier Family of Kent Co, England

Now, second think: there *was*, since ancient times, a <u>Brazier</u> family in Kent. "The southern side of Leavesgreen (the remainder of which is in Keston) is within this parish [Cowdham], where there is an old mansion called *"Old Court"* or *"Old House"*, which was for many generations, and till lately, the residence of the Braziers; it is now [1797] called Leavesgreen farm, and belongs to the widow of George Butler, esq. There is much coppice wood dispersed over several parts of it."

(Vol.2, p.60 of *History and Topographical Survey of the County of Kent*, by Edward Hasted, 12 Vols, publ Canterbury, 1797-1801; repr. E.P.Publ, Ltd, 1972).

"Cowdham is within the ecclesiastical jurisdiction of the diocese of Rochester, and deanry of Dartford. The Church is dedicated to St. Peter and St. Paul ... In this church ... are ... monuments and inscriptions ... for the family of Brazier, of "Old House," in this parish ... (same ref. Vol.2, p.74-5).

Zachariah seems to me to be from an altogether different family.

36. TWO (Or More) WILLIAM BRASIERS,

DR. WILLIAM BRASIER, of Edgefield Co, SC

"Dr. William Brasier, though a native of England, died in Aiken, then a part of Edgefield, in July 1843, and may be claimed as an Edgefield practioner, though much of his life was spent elsewhere. Dr. Maximilian Laborde has left us, in an Obituary notice, all we know of this rather remarkable character. Born in London about A.D. 1740, (being something like one hundred years old when he died) of highly respectable parentage, one of his cousins, Captain Lambert, of the British Navy, fell at the capture of the Java by the Constitution; another, General Lambert, was in command of the British reserve at the Battle of New Orleans; he obtained favor of the British Government and secured a collectorship at the port of St. Christopher, in the West Indies. Here he turned missionary to the negroes, preaching the doctrine of John Wesley.

"About 1791, he was invited to Charleston by a Society of Primitive Wesleyan Methodists, to take charge of their Congregation. Here he determined upon the study of medicine and repaired to Philadelphia for that purpose, a year or two after. Receiving an invitation from Dr. Rush, who discovered rare talent in the student, to go into his office, he prosecuted his studies among the inmates of the Philadelphia Almshouse, for six months of the year 1795. He then returned South and practiced medicine at and near Augusta, Ga, and in Edgefield until 1803, when he was again called to Charleston to take charge of the church, by which he had been invited in 1791. Nine months after, he abandoned the pulpit and removed to Columbia, where he practiced medicine a short time; thence he returned to the neighborhood of Edgefield Court House, where he practiced his profession until about 1827. Five or six years were then spent in the Valley of the Mississippi." (from History of Edgefield County, South Carolina, from the Earliest Settlements to 1897, by John A. Chapman, p.344)

1820 Census, Edgefield Co, SC:
p.098 William Brazier   001101-0011045+, w/1 m 16-18

On 10 Mar 1826, William Brashier Sr of Edgefield District, SC, purchased a 300-acres tract of land in Greenville District, commonly known as Paris's Mountain, from Waddy Thompson Jr. (Greenville Deeds, Book P, p.192)

On 26 Jul 1842, William Brasier of SC, for love and affection unto dau Charlotte (Brasier) Randolph, wife of James H. Randolph, in trust to Geo. Towns, for the use of my dau & my grandchildren, the children of my dec'd dau, the former wife of the said James H. and the children of the said Charlotte, the plantation conveyed to me by Gen. Waddy Thompson lying on Paris Mt. in Greenville Dist. (Greenville Deeds, Book U, p.90)

from The Greenville Mountaineer, 1825-1863 (see *SC Mag of Ancestral Research*, v.5 (1977):

"It is with great diffidence that this writer attempts this notice of the death of Dr. Wm. Brazier, who departed from this life in Aiken, SC, in July last from which place it was his intention to start for Greenville to his family. His diffidence arises from the utter impossibility he feels of doing even partical [sic] justice to the character of that excellent man, whose useful life would furnish matter for the ablest biographer: but it would seem meek to notice it now, tho feebly set forth, from the consideration set forth below, to wit: the death of his venerable consort ... He was a zealous minister of the Gospel, holding forth the views of the pious Mr. Wesley during his early life in the West Indies but long since had ceased; he declined preaching for the practice of medicine, in both of which spheres ... he was eminently useful.

"... Departed this life on the 22 ult.... at the residence of her son-in-law, J.H. Randolph, near Greenville, SC: Mrs. Ann Brazier, consort of Dr. Wm. Brasier, aged the rise of 80 years, who embraced religion at a very young period of life and attached herself to the Methodist Church."

Charlotte Brazier, m. 22 Dec 1841 (Edgefield Dist, SC), James H. Randolph, of Greenville Dist (*Edgefield SC Marriage Records*, by McClendon).

DR. WILLIAM BRAZIER, Surgeon, of VA

There is a **William Brazier** in early Virginia that needs accounting for: **Charles City County,** Court Orders, 1664-1665 (Charles City County is on the north bank of the James River estuary, upstream from Williamsburg but below Henrico Co).

In Sept, 1664, "Capt. John Eppes hath proved rights by testimony to 400 acres of land for the Charge of importacon of John Lewis, **Willm' Bras'ier** (?Brashier), Peter Seaman, Richd Wright, Sarah Smith, Sarah Croshaw, Sarah Richds, John Mawe." (*Va. Col. Abstracts*, by Beverly Fleet, v.3, p.499). The date makes it pretty impossible that this was the William Brazier who was transported in 1676, age 19, (therefore b. c1657) as an indentured servant from London to Maryland on the ship, *Elizabeth.* So we have yet another man who is unaccounted for.

William Brazier, Chirogeon, in list of "Surgeons and Doctors" in old manuscript of 168[9-]90, in *Old Rappahomock Virginia.*

Will of Henry Willson, of Farnham Parish, Rappahannock Co, VA, dated 14 Mar 1686, proved 10 Mar 1688: paragraph 8: "Item: I give and bequeath unto **Will Brasier** all Chirurgion my weights and scales and with other instruments belonging to a Chirurgion to be delivered to him on demand after my decease." (*Wills of Rappahannock Co, VA, 1656-1692*, p.140)

Will of John Overton, planter, of Farnham Parish, Rappahannock Co, VA, dated 14 Sep 1688, proved 1 Jul 1691, signed, sealed, declared in presence of: Richard White, Charles Dickson, **William Braseer.** (*Wills of Rappahannock Co, VA, 1656-1692*, p.148.)

However, 4 Mar 1686: Attachment granted to Alexandr: Swan against the estate of Doctr William Brash(blot) returned to this court (*Summary of the Minutes of Old Rappahannock Court, 1685-1687*, p.80). We believe, without very strong documentation, that Dr. William Brazier and/or his sons moved to the Eastern Shores of Maryland.

WILLIAM BRAZIERS
of the Eastern Shore of Maryland

Somerset, an original county, was created in 1666 on the Maryland peninsula below Delaware, and stretched from Chesapeake Bay to the Atlantic. In 1742, Worcester was formed from the eastern part of Somerset, i.e. the Atlantic shore, and in 1867, Wicomico was formed from northern parts of Somerset and Worcester.

William, William, and James Mumford Brazier

Patented 1 Sep 1688 by **William Brazier** in Pocomoke, 100 acres, a resurvey from Lloyd's Grove, for 250 acres. ?Called "Bradshaw's Purchase"?

1718, March -- **William Brazier** sold land called "Bradshaw's Purchase" in Worcester Co, MD, to John Broughton. (*Land Records of Worcester Co, 1666-1810*, by Ruth Dryden [975.221 D799]

1723 -- **William Brazer** listed as taxable in Somerset Co. MD. (*Citizens of the Eastern Shores of Maryland, 165⁹·1750*, by F. Wright, p.3. [975.21 W945])

1723 -- Richard Wharton willed plantation, unnamed, to wife, Anne Wharton, to go at her decease to her grandchild, **James Mumford Brazier**. (*Land Records of Worcester Co, 1666-1810*, by Ruth Dryden, p.134.) This reference is in a discussion of a plantation called "Convenience." Anne would have been married, first, to a Brasher/ Brazier. Her son, William Brasher/Brazier, was apparently Richard Wharton's executor: MDHR Accounts (Somerset Co), Bk 7, p.428, 6 Jul 1726: The account of Will Brasher, exec of the last will and testament of Richard Wharton, late of Somerset Co. Dec'd ... charges himself with inventory worth £38/7/0 "and prayeth for no salary."

1731, Apr 6 -- William Wharton sold 200 acres to **William Brazier**, land that Wm. Stevens willed to Richard Wharton and that became right of his son, Richard who died without issue. William Wharton is heir to Richard. This also was in the discussion of "Convenience." This William Brazier would have been the father of James Mumford Brazier.

That particular **William Brazier**, s/o Anne (__?__) Brasher-Wharton, apparently died about 1733: MDHR Inventories (Somerset Co) Bk 17, p.426, 22 Aug 1733: Came <u>Anne</u> <u>Brasier</u>, <u>adm</u>^x of <u>William</u> <u>Brasier</u> and made oath on the Holy Evangelist of Almighty God that the within is a just and perfect inv^{'t} to the best of her knowledge, of all and singular the goods and chattels of the dec'^d that has yet come to her hands and that what shall hereafter come to her hands or possession she will further Acct for and that she knows of no concealment of any part or parcel thereof by any person whatsoever and that if she dothe discover any concealment or suspect any to be, she will acquaint Comm^r Genl for the time being or his deputy with such discovery or cause of suspicion thatit may be enquired into & that she will well & truely give an Acct of all and every part of the dec'^{d'}s personal estate that shall hereafter come to her hands or possession or knowledge. Sworn before me .... Nehemiah King, D [Deputy?] Com^r of Samerset C^{ty}.

1734, Dec 15 -- **James Mumford Brazier** sold 200 acres, now called "Good Success." Patented 1759, for 140 acres. (*Land Records of Worcester Co, 1666-1810*, by Ruth Dryden, p.134. (In discussion of "Hickman's Neglect")

1736, April 10 -- **James Mumford Brazier** sold 100 acres (?part of "Bradshaw's Purchase") to William Conner. (*Land Records of Worcester Co, 1666-1810*, by Ruth Dryden [975.221 D799]

Other William Braziers

1748, -- **William Brazier** patented 62 acres, called "Brazier's Adventure," in Colburn's District, #6, Map 32, Worcester Co. NE part.

1754, Nov 9 -- **William Brazier** sold 62 acres (?"Brazier's Adventure") to Jno Godfrey. (*Land Records of Worcester Co, 1666-1810*, by Ruth Dryden, p.73. [975.221 D799]

1753, Oct 5 -- Plantation "Connecticut" patented to James Tubbs, Selby Hickman, and Jesse Hickman, for 71 acres.

1756, Sep 10 -- "Connecticut" re-surveyed for **William Brazier**, 46 acres sold to him by Tubbs, Hickman, and Hickman, to 140 acres. (*Land Records of Worcester Co, 1666-1810*, by Ruth Dryden, p.131.

Another William Brazier, d. c1754:

MdHR Testamentary Proceedings (Worcester Co) Bk 36, p.23, March Court 1754: Citation against James Baker and John Morrill, sureties on the Estate of **William Brazier**, late of Worcester Co. to show cause why they do not pass a final acct (at the instance and request of William Brazier, apparently his son.)

Bk 36, p.39, May Court 1754: Sheriff's certificate: he had "the body of John Merrile" but James Baker was not to be found in his bailiwick. Case continued to next session of court.

Bk 36, p.58, July Court 1754: Daniel Delany, Esqr, represented John Merrile, but the case was continued to the second Tuesday of July.

Bk 36, p.72: Case continued again to next court. Jas Baker "non est."

Bk 36, p.109, Jan Court 1755: Continued again, Citation unchanged.

Bk 36, p, 127, March Court 1755: New Citation issued for James Baker. Continued.

Bk 36, p.149, May Court 1755. Whole process reviewed and renewed.

Bk 36, p.176, July Court 1755: More of the same. Sheriff had not returned the issue and was held in contempt.

Bk 36, p.200, Sep Court 1755: Attachment issued per order to the Coronor of Worcester Co. against Ephraim Waggaman, Sheriff ... for neglecting ... Coronor makes no return. Case renewed.

Bk 36, p.254, Jan Court 1756: Still, Coronor makes no return.

Bk 36, p.271, March Court 1756: Ordered that the case be renewed.

Bk 36, p.292, May Court 1756: Renewed again.

But we've still got William Brazier's aplenty:

1759 -- **William Brazier** and Jacob Rodgers patent 60 acres, called "Brazier's Discovery." Resurveyed to the partnership, 7 Mar 1761. (*Land Records of Worcester Co, 1666-1810*, by Ruth Dryden, p.73

1759 -- "Hickman's Neglect" patented, 140 acres by **William Brazier**.

1760, Jul 26 -- **William Brazier** sold 140 acres to Abner Lamb. (*Land Records of Worcester Co, 1666-1810*, by Ruth Dryden, p.294.

1761, Jul 3 -- "Brazier's Discovery," 453 acres, a re-survey patented to **William Brazier**.

1 Sep 1761, Vestry of St. Martin's Parish, Worcester Co, met and pews in the new church were assigned: **William Brasher** assigned #15, along with John Mumford, Armwell Showell, Benjamin Hackwood, Walter Evans, and Rebeckar Harrison (Minutes of St. Martin's Parish, Worster Co, MD, p.76; FHL film #0924759).

1 May 1764, Vestry of St. Martin's Parish made choice of **William Brazher** for Church Warding [sic] at Prince George's Chappel. The following vestrymen were present - and there appeared Kendall Collier and Henry Hudson to qualifie as vestrymen and William Brazher as Warding (Minutes of St. Martin's Parish, Worster Co, MD, p.85; FHL film #0924759).

1770, Dec 13 -- **William Brazier** sold 269 acres to David Mifflin of Accomack Co. VA. 17 Jun 1771, William Brazier and Wife Sarah

Brazier, confirmation of previous sale to Daniel Mifflin. (*Land Records of Worcester Co, 1666-1810*, by Ruth Dryden, p.458.

1794 — One of our William Braziers (Brassier, in one of the records) died in 1794, Worcester County, MD, and named a son Belitha Brassier. Bond 21 Sept 1794, Jerard(?) Townsend and Samuel Johnson, (unreadable). (Thanks to Kathy Ballew, <kaballew@comcast.net> for this information, 23 Mar 2005. She is interested in grandson, Levin Brazier and his wife, Nancy Hitchens.) Belitha Brazier had a son, Levin Brazier, b. 15 March 1782; m. in Worcester Co, MD, 1810, Nancy Hitchens.

At the February Court 1797, Levin Brazier, orphan of Belitha, aged 15 on next 15th March, was apprenticed to Asher Burrough, (unreadable). Securities: George Bell, Annanias Deal. Levin became a shoemaker. (Worcester County Orphans Court, 1792/1797, p. 414, February Court, 1797.)

In 1811, David Taylor was apprenticed to Levin Brazier, shoemaker.

1809, May 17 -- **Jno & Eliz Brazier** sold 100 acres, called "Hog Quarter," to Edward Hammond, land that William Cropper had granted to his daughter, Elizabeth Slattery, now wife of John Brazier. (*Land Records of Worcester Co, 1666-1810*, by Ruth Dryden, p.302.

1810 -- Census of Worcester Co. MD: Godfrey Brazier
1830 -- Census of Worcester Co. MD: James Brazier; William Washington Brazier
1850 -- Census of Worcester Co. MD: Jacob Brazier; William Washington Brazier
1860 -- Census of Worcester Co. MD: William Washington Brazier

Georgene says:
Children of William and Ann Bradshaw (Parish Records of _____, p.15, 17, 21; film 0006302):
1. Mary Bradshaw, b. 7 Jan 1670
2. Ann Bradshaw, b. 18 Apr 1673
3. Katherine Bradshaw, b. 18 Mar 1764
4. William Bradshaw, b. 27 Mar 1675
5. Ursula Bradshaw, b. 14 May 1683
Child of William and Rebecca Bradshaw (same source)
6. William Bradshaw, b. 8 Nov 1689

37. EDWARD BRASIER,
of Charlestown, Mass.

What I know of Edward Brasier and his descendants is primarily based on *The New England Historical and Genealogical Register* and the *Genealogical Dictionary of the First Settlers of New England*, comp by James Savage, reprint 1986. Some information has been added from John Bennett Boddie's *Southside Virginia Families*, (Baltimore: Genealogical Publishing Co, 1966), Vol 2, p.117-19, and *Calendar of Historical Manuscripts in the Office of the Secretary of State of New York*, O'Callaghan, 1865.

Edward Brasier was born c1603 (age 80 in 1683, per court files) and died 3 May 1689. He was living in Cambridge in 1647 (*New Eng Hist Gen Reg*, v.7, p.175). He paid his taxes in Charlestown in 1653; bought 1.5 acres of land and a house from R. Temple, one part bought of R. Kettell, other of W. Bridges; owned 4 acres on northwest line of Cambridge; in 1654, he bought a hay lot of Mr. Hurst, bounded on the west by Palgrave, on the east by Davison.

Edward Brazier was living in Charlestown, 1658, where his children were born after he was 57 years old: 1660-1667. Edward d. 3 May 1689. (ref: *Genealogical Dictionary of the First Settlers of New England*, Vol. I, comp. by James Savage, rpt 1986)

[same ref: <u>Austen</u> <u>Bratcher</u>, of Charlestown, died in 1630 at the hand of Walter Palmer. A jury was charged to inquire of it, and Palmer was discharged. This might be a source of other families?]

[V9-]4548.   a-x.   Edward Brasier made his will 11 May 1683. It entered probate 1 Oct 1689. Devised to wife half of house, etc; to son, the other half, to have the whole after wife's death; to son, 3 acre lot in Cambridge. Wife and son exrs. The inventory included: house and orchard, one acre; 2 acre hay lot; 3.5 acres by Cambridge line (3 acres "by the line," and half in Cambridge); two lots on Mystic side.

Edward Brasier m. ***Magdelen*** _____, who was admitted to the church in 1656. But, later, "Maudeline Brasier, Irish woman, lately of

New London; at Mungo Crawford's, Dec. 28, 1681; not accepted as inhabitant of Boston (per selectmen's records)." *SVF*, p.117.

Family of Edward and Madeline Brasier:
V9-4549.   b-1. ***Thomas Brasier**, bapt. 29 Feb 1660; m. ***Elizabeth*** _____, bapt 8 Oct 1699, d. prior to 1725 (per deed)
V9-4550.   b-2. **Elizabeth Brasier**, b. 10 Jun 1663, d. 7 Jul 1663
V9-4551.   b-3. **Abigail Brasier**, Dec. (2) 1660
V9-4552.   b-4. **Rebecca Brasier**, b. 13 Nov 1667, d. 8 Nov 1672
V9-4553.   b-5. **Sarah Brasier**, d. 18 Oct 1678 of small pox

Thomas Brasier, s/o Edward Brasier

b-1. **Thomas Brasier**, (only son of Edward Brasier), bapt. 29 Feb 1660; m. ***Elizabeth*** _____, bapt 8 Oct 1699, d. prior to 1725 (per deed)
V9-4554.   c-1. ***Thomas Brasier Jr**, b. 2 Aug 1691; d. 1764
V9-4555.   c-2. ***Edward Brashier**, b. 15 Jan 1693
V9-4556.   c-3. **Elizabeth Brasier**, b. 13 Dec 1695; m. 18 Aug 1725, ***Jonas Allen***,
V9-4557.   c-4. **Benjamin Brasier**, b. 30 Jan 1697/8
V9-4558.   c-5. **Mary Brasier**, b. 16 Oct (or 5 Nov) 1699, d. 4 May 1721

All of the above, except Abigail and Mary, were baptized at once, 15 Oct 1699.

Thomas Brasier, Jr, and Hannah Webb

V9-3904. c-1. **Thomas Brasier Jr**, s/o Thomas Brasier and g-s/o Edward Brasier, was born 2 Aug 1691; he was a housewright (i.e. a carpenter), who was admitted to the church 2 Feb 1717/8. On 6 Nov 1713, he married **Hannah Webb**, who was admitted to the church 18 Aug 1717.

His taxes were abated in 1721-2, but he paid from 1727-1763. With his brothers, Edward and Benjamin, he deeded 4 acres, in 1729, to D. Russell, bounded on north by the Cambridge Road, southwest by the Cambridge line, east by Elkanah Welch. Also in 1729, the three brothers deeded 3 acres on the Charlestown line to A. Bordman, Jr.

In 1736, he hired (rented) the house of Thomas Hender.

In 1751, the three brothers [?bought] 2 acres and a shed, bounded on the northeast by Joseph Lynde, on southeast by a ditch next to Jos. Lynde, on northwest by a ditch next to Minot, southwest by a cove; they had right of a private way through Jos. Lynde. Recorded, 1764. In

1760, they [?bought] an additional 1.25 acres called Brasier's Orchard, bounded on N & S by Joseph Lynde and the lane through Miller's farm; on the E by said land. This was also recorded, 1764.

Thomas Brasier [sic] died 1764, age 73, in ?New York. (Cal Hist Mss ... NY, v.16, p.35)

Children of Thomas Brasier Jr and Hannah Webb:

V9-4559. d-1. ***Thomas Brasier, III**, b. and bapt. 25 Jul 1714; m. ***Hannah Ivory,***

V9-4560. d-2. **Hannah Brasier**, b. 17 (or 20) Jan 1716/7; m. 1739, ***Zachariah Davis Jr,***

V9-4561. d-3. ***Christopher Brasier**, bapt. 7 Dec 1718; m. ***Mary Knapp,***

V9-4562. d-4. **Mary Brasier**, bapt. 19 Feb 1720/1; m. 1743, ***James Ridgway,***

V9-4563. d-5. ***Simeon Brasier**, b. 18 (or 19) May 1723; d. 1757 ?in NY; m. ***Mary Pool,***

V9-4564. d-6. **Samuel Brasier**, b. 28 (or 30) Jun 1728, d. 20 Sep 1729; age 14 mos.

V9-4565. d-7. ***Samuel Brasier**, b. 28 April (or 3 May) 1730

Thomas Brazier, III and Hannah Ivory

V9-3909. d-1. **Thomas Brasier, III**, b. 25 Jul 1714, was also a housewright; he died in 1754. His will was dated 27 Jul 1754, entered probate 30 Dec 1754, and devised to wife improvement of pasture in Eastfield, and all property. On 12 Nov 1741, he married ***Hannah Ivory***, b. c1714, d. 2 Sep 1758 (her gravestone says in her 44th year). They apparently had no children, for Hannah's will dated 22 Aug 1758, probated 9 Sep 1758, devised 1/3 of estate to sister Mary, wife of Samuel Preston; 1/3 to John Ivory, etc.; ?remainder to Sarah, wife of J.I.; to John I, Jr; to Mary and Catharine, daughters of Joseph Frothingham.

V9-3911. d-3. **Christopher Brasier**, bapt 1718, s/o Thomas Brasier Jr, was a mason in Boston. On 10 Apr 1744, he married in Boston, ***Mary Knapp***, b. c1718, d. 29 Oct 1799 (age 81, says her gravestone in Mall burying ground, Boston). In 1784, Christopher, with his sister, Mary Ridgway, sold the northeast half of lot (house burnt) lately occupied by Thomas Brasier, to William Newhall, bounded on north by road, southwest by river, northwest by Kendall, excepting a small house and yard and a horse-house 3 x 18 ft, with private way to street. Recorded

1788. Also in 1788, Christopher, along with Polly and Hannah Ridgway, all of Boston, sold the house and land to William Newhall, all bounded by Newhall.

V9-3913. d-5. **Simeon Brasier**, b. 18 May 1723, s/o Thomas Brasier Jr, m. 5 May 1748, *Ann Pool*. They were taxed in 1744, 1748, 1756. Simion Brazier [sic] d. 1757 (Cal. Mss. ... NY, Vol. 16, p.35)

V9-3916. d-7. **Samuel Brasier**, b. 28 Apr 1730, s/o Thomas Brasier Jr. In 1760, he bought of Elizabeth Hender, 1/2 of the house occupied by Thomas Brazier, his father, bound on southeast by road, southeast the other half, northwest by Kendall, southwest by river; recorded 1767. Submitted claim for loss, 1775.

Edward Brasier
and Mary ____/ Esther Frothingham

V9-3905. c-2. **Edward Brasier**, b. 15 Jan 1693, s/o Thomas Brasier, and g-s/o Edward Brasier, was a bricklayer of Boston, who was admitted to the church 16 Aug 1719. He had bad luck with getting wives and children who would survive: m.1. *Mary* ____, d. 27 Aug 1719 (age 18 yrs, 7 mos, says her gravestone in Charleston); m.2. 29 Nov 1722, *Esther Frothingham*, by whom he had one child: **Ester Brasier**, bapt. 22 Mar 1723/4 (there were two more baptisms in North-Boston, 1726 and 1729; possibly more); m.3. *Mary Baker*, d. 7 Apr 1750 (age 38 says her gravestone in Granary); m.4. 10 Jan 1750/1, *Ann Negus*.

In 1720, he bought a lot that adjoined Burying Hill, from B. Lawrence, recorded 1755. Edward Brasier and wife, Ann, sold part of the same lot with a house to Thomas Wood, in 1755, bounded on south by way up to burying ground 100, north road 50, north Jonathan Rand 50. In 1729, he and his brothers, Thomas and Benjamin, sold to Bordman (see above). In 1730, Edward Brazier and wife, with Abigail Frothingham [?wife's sister or mother], sold a 4 1/4 acre pasture to E. Hartshorn, bounded east H. Phillips' heirs 17 poles; west, range 17; north, T. Call 40; and on Bridgen and E. Hartshorn 40. In 1732, Edward Brazier and wife, with Abigail Frothingham, sold 1/2 of a wood lot laid out to M. Price, entry #70, and 5 commons making 14 acres, to T. Oakes and J. Waters, bounded north & south, ranges; west, John Johnson; east, Isaac Cole; recorded 1735.

Benjamin Brasier

^{v9-}3907. c-4. **Benjamin Brasier**, b. 30 Jan 1697/81, s/o Thomas Brasier, and g-s/o Edward Brasier, was a yeoman. He was taxed from 1727-58. In 1725, he quit claim deeded to his sister, Elizabeth, all his interest in the estates of his father, Thomas, and his grandfather, Edward; recorded 1728. He was a party, with his brothers, Thomas and Edward, in the deed to Bordman in 1729, already noted. In 1734, he sold 6 acres to Benjamin Tufts, bounded south by Medford line, north by range, west by B.T., east by J. Foye; rec. 1752.

Capt. Ben Brazer/Brazier, d. 1759 (Cal. Hist Mss ... New York, v.16, p.35) His son, Benjamin Jr, also a soldier, was still living in the 1770's; so this must be Benjamin the elder.

On ?? Mar 1726, Benjamin Brasier married **Abigail Osborne**, who was at Stoneham, age 80, in 1779 (per archives).

Children of Benjamin Brasier and Abigail Osborne:
^{v9-}4566. d-1. ***Benjamin Brasier Jr**, b. 6 Jan 1726/7
^{v9-}4567. d-2. **John Brasier**, b. 20 Apr 1729
^{v9-}4568. d-3. **James Brasier**, b. 20 Oct 1732; ? James Brazier, m. 1759 (Cal Hist Mss ... New York, v.16, p.35) Did he remove to New York, and disappear from Massachusetts records? Looks like it.
^{v9-}4569. d-4. ***Thomas Brasier IV**, b. 10 Jul 1731

Benjamin Brasier, Jr, and Alice Phillips

^{v9-}3916. d-1. **Benjamin Brasier Jr**, b. 6 Jan 1726/7, s/o Benjamin Brasier, Sr, g-s/o Thomas Brasier, and g-g-s/o Edward Brasier; m. 9 Oct 1749, **Alice Phillips**, who d. in Boston, 30 Mar 1804, age 79. Benjamin Brasier, Jr, was one of the six soldiers sent from Charlestown to Cape Breton. He was in the army, as servant to Richard Devens, 1752; enlisted 1757 and was allowed pay "what the town allows and bounty"; was in jail 18 Oct to 8 Nov 1776 (?because of Revolution). He was taxed in 1748, 1756, 1758, 1765, 1766, 1770; abatement of taxes considered 17 Oct 1770 and granted 1772, 1774. In 1756, he and the heirs of H. Phillips deeded house etc, formerly of H. Phillips, to W. Wyer. "Mr. Brazier d. May 12, 1789" (Devens). Benjamin and Alice had 9 children:
^{v9-}4570. e-1. **Abigail Brasier**, bapt. 18 Aug 1751 (died young)
^{v9-}4571. e-2. **Benjamin Brasier III**, bapt. 18 Aug 1751
^{v9-}4572. e-3. ***John Brasier**, bapt 8 Apr 1753; m. **Mary Grubb**,
^{v9-}4573. e-4. **Samuel Brasier**, bapt. 3 Mar 1755
^{v9-}4574. e-5. **Alice Brasier**, bapt. 3 Jul 1757

^{V9-}4575.   e-6. **James Brasier**, bapt. 23 Nov 1760
^{V9-}4576.   e-7. **Timothy Brasier**, bapt. 26 Jun 1763
^{V9-}4577.   e-8. **Abigail Brasier**, bapt. 9 Feb 1766 (second use of name)
^{V9-}4578.   e-9. **Ann Brasier**, bapt. 20 May 1770

^{V9-}3922. e-3. **John Brasier**, b. c1753, s/o Benjamin Brasier Jr, g-s/o Benjamin Brasier Sr, g-g-s/o Thomas Brasier, and g-g-g-s/o Edward Brasier, was a ships-carpenter; m. *Mary Grubb*, bans publ. 1774; lived in Cambridge after 1775. In 1779, he bought a house from W. Stimpson, bounded southwest by street 15; southeast by Barber's Lane 50; northeast by T. Harding 22; northwest by Sarah Capen 34. He sold the same house in 1791 to Thomas Hooper. In 1789, he bought a plot from the Thomas and James Capen estate, bounded on northeast by Stephen Brown; rec. 1792. He sold the same to T. Hooper, in 1791. He submitted a claim for loss in 1775 (?Revolution damage?)

Thomas Brasier, IV, and Esther Howard

^{V9-}3919. d-4. **Thomas Brasier IV**, b. 10 Jul 1731, s/o Benjamin Brasier Sr, g-s/o Thomas Brasier, and g-g-s/o Edward Brasier; m.1. 17 Apr 1755, in Gloucester, *Esther Howard*, m.2. (bans publ. 25 Sep 1775), *Hannah Cooper*, who died a widow (consumption) 19 Dec 1797 (funeral 22 Dec), age 53. Thomas Brasier, IV, was at Fort Cumberland in 1759 (family at home); was in census of 1789 with wife and children Thomas and Hannah; died of consumption, 20 May 1791. He had 8 children by his two wives, the last three, apparently by Hannah, were baptized in Waltham.

^{V9-}4579.   e-1. **John Brasier**, bapt. 27 Mar 1757 (d. young; name re-used)
^{V9-}4580.   e-2. **Abigail Brasier**, bapt. 17 Jan 1762
^{V9-}4581.   e-3. **John Brasier**, bapt. 18 Dec 1763
^{V9-}4582.   e-4. **Benjamin Brasier**, bapt. 4 Sep 1768
^{V9-}4583.   e-5. **Esther Brasier**, bapt. 27 Mar 1770
^{V9-}4584.   e-6. **Joseph Brasier**, bapt. 1776
^{V9-}4585.   e-7. **William Brasier**, bapt. 1781
^{V9-}4586.   e-8. **Hannah Brasier**, bapt. 1783

Unidentified Brasiers

^{V9-}4587.   Unidentified: **James Brasier**, a glazier and wharfinger, b. 1720-22 (age 60 in 1782, per archives; age 64 and lame in old folks home in 1784); m.1. 14 Aug 1757, *Elizabeth Souther*, who died 19 Jul

1767, age 35 says her gravestone; m.2. 10 Dec 1767, **Abigail Phipps**, who was admitted to the church, 18 Dec 1768. He was taxed 1756-1773. In 1761, he bought a house on 39 ft. of Bow St. from W. Barber, which he sold in 1779 to Eben Breed. On 21 Nov 1761, he bought 1/2 of a house from Isaac Rand, along with 1/2 of a well and a way to it, bounded south Bow st. 12; north by A. Snow 16; west by Isaac Rand; east by heirs of Edmund Rand. The same day, he bought the other half from Edmund Rand's administrators. For it, he executed a mortgage to Isaac Rand in 1761, and discharged it in 1787. In 1787, he sold the southwest corner of his property to O. Holden, beginning on Bow St. running east on S. Conant's line 105; north on Isaac Snow's 31; west on James Brasier's 104; south on Bow St 26. In 1789, he sold to W. Goodwin a right to a pump and well; rec. 1804.

His will was dated 14 May 1788. "Mr. Brazier died, May 12, 1789" (Devens). Will entered probate, 10 Nov 1797, and devised all to wife; at her decease, 1/2 to James Brasier and 1/2 to Abigail Brasier. No inventory.

His widow, Abigail, was in the census of 1789. In 1816, she sold the estate on Bow St. to S. Knowles, who sold to Eben Baker, 1826.

V9-4588. 1. **James Brasier**, b. 20 (bapt. 25) Jun 1758 (d. young; name re-used)

V9-4589. 2. **Elizabeth Brasier**, bapt. 6 Jun 1762

V9-4590. 3. **James Brasier**, bapt. 25 May 1766; lived Harwich; sold 1795 a house to Matthew Bridge, beg. northwest corner on N. Holden, running southwest along Bow St. 26; south on line of D. Austin 95; east on M. Bridge, S. Moore; north on N. Holden 95. In 1775, a James Brasier of Charlestown and a James Brasier of Cambridge claimed for loss. Him?

V9-4591. 4. **Abigail Brasier**, bapt. 14 Aug 1768 (d. young; name re-used)

V9-4592. 5. **Abigail Brasier**, bapt. 3 Mar 1771

V9-4593. 6. **Mary Brasier**, bapt. 2 May 1773

V9-4594. **Thomas Brasier**, b. c1770; m. 9 Jan 1794, **Elizabeth Reid**, in census of 1789, lived near Thomas, s/o Benjamin, Sr.; d. 23 Aug 1815, age 45 says his gravestone, ergo born c1770. Four children:

V9-4595. 1. **James Brasier**, b. 23 Jul 1795

V9-4596. 2. **Joseph Brasier**, b. 26 Apr 1799

V9-4597. 3. **Margaret Brasier**, b. 20 Apr 1801

V9-4598. 4. **Esther-Ann Brasier**, b. Feb 1810, d. 19 Sep 1810, age 7 mos (gravestone)

^{V9}-4599.   **John Brazer**, merchant, of Boston.

In 1802, sold a lot on Wapping St. to Thomas Rand; mortgaged it back, which was discharged in 1804. Same as to Thomas Barnes.

^{V9}-4600.   **Zachariah Brasher** and his wife, *Bathsheba*, had a child:

^{V9}-4601.   1. **S. (or Z. for Zachariah) Harrison Brasher**, b. 12 Mar 1734, Falmouth (Portsmouth) Maine. (*New Eng Hist & Gen Reg. v.14*, p.144). Zachariah H. Brazier m. 3 Dec 1759 to *Sarah Gustini*, (same ref. v.14, p.224). Harrison Brasier m. (2nd?) *Betsey Turner* (data from Tina Brazier Plummer, a descendant <dplummer@ime.net>). They were parents of

^{V9}-4602.   x. **James Brazier/Brasier**, b. abt 1805, in Cushing, Lincoln Co, Maine, d. 26 Apr 1864; m. 25 Feb 1858, Windsor, Maine, *Hannah Elizabeth Jackson*, b. 14 Jul 1830, Windsor, Maine, d. 13 Oct 1901, Cushing, ME, bur Cushing, ME. They had 7 children - one of whom was

^{V9}-4603.   y. **Daniel Brasier**, b. 08 Mar 1862, Cushing, Knox Co, ME, d. 04 Jul 1903, Thomaston, Knox Co, ME; m. 17 Jan 1891,Thomaston, ME, *Ida Ellen Vose*, b. 04 Feb 1862, Cushing, Knox Co, Maine, d. 09 Mar 1944. They had 5 children- one of whom was

^{V9}-4604.   z. **Maurice James Brazier**, b. 08 Dec 1894, d. 1978; m. *Jennie Robinson*. They had 1 child

^{V9}-4605.   a-x. **Maurice Arthur Brazier** (Tina's grandfather), b. 02 Jun 1920, d. 19 Jan 1988; m. *Arlene Louise Stanley*. They had 4 children - one of whom was Tina's father

^{V9}-4606.   b-x. **Kenneth Robinson Brazier**, b. 05 May 1943, Thomaston, Knox Co, ME; he had three daughters one of whom is

^{V9}-4607.   c-x. **Tina Brazier**; m. *Dave Plummer*.

^{V9}-4608.   **James Brasier**, soap-boiler, of Roxbury and Charlestown; m. 12 Apr 1818, *Elizabeth-Hicks Hunt*, d/o John Hunt of Watertown, sister of Mrs. D. Goodwin.

The following line of Nancy Williams must belong to this family somehow, but how? I'd bet research on James Brasier and Elizabeth Hicks-Hunt would be a good Hunt.

V9-4609. a. **Franklin J. Brazier**, b. 8 Feb 1830, Boston, MA, d. 14 Aug 1872?; m. ***Abbie Chaney***, Among their children:

V9-4610. b. **Charles Goodwin Brazier**, b. 10 Oct 1867, Cambridge, MA, d. 10 Apr 1947, St. Pete (?), FL; m. ***Oliva Maria Merrill***, Among their children:

V9-4611. c. **Charles Goodwin Brazier Jr**, b. 5 Feb 1902, Boston, MA, d. 12 Jan 1984, Laguna Hills, CA; m. ***Ellen Gertrude Scott***,

V9-4612. d. ? _____ Brazier; m. _____ Williams

V9-4613. e. Nancy Williams, 606 Linden Ct, O'Fallon, IL 62269

38. GIDEON BRAZIER/BRASHIER

Gideon Brashier and Jerusha Thacker

Gideon Brashier, m. 3 Dec 1807, *Jerusha Thacker*

V9-4614.   b-x. **Mary Sapphira Brashier**, b. 3 May 1820, Wythe Co, VA, d. 30 Dec 1873, Wise Co, VA, bur Duncan Gap, Harricane, VA; m. c1840, Lockhard A. Hamilton, b. 4 July 1821, Grayson Co, VA, d. c1905, Dickenson Co, VA. Data from Ginger ____ <eaglewmn@bellsouth.net>. Barry O'Neill, Box 64, Belspring, VA 24058 <kmoneil@i-plus.net> says they had 11 children. Another contact: Shane Hicks <shanehicks@hotmail.com>. Among the children:

V9-4615.   c-x. Hester Ann Hamilton, b. c1860, Bland Co, VA, d. 8 July 1883, Dickenson Co, VA; m. 7 Nov 1873, in Wise Co, VA, James Henderson Mullins, b. 6 Nov 1855, Wise Co, VA, d. 27 May 1939. Among the children:

V9-4616.   d-x. William Lockhardt Mullins, b. 26 Aug 1882, d. 16 Feb 1898, Washington Co, VA; m. Amanda "Mandy" Perry, b. 25 March 1879, VA. Among the children:

V9-4617.   e-x. Andy Ernest Mullins, b. 28 Sep 1910, d. 24 Dec 1991; m. 11 Sep 1931, Nettie Bentley. Among the children:

V9-4618.   f-x. Thelma Marie Mullins. Among the children:

V9-4619.   g-x. Ginger _____ <eaglewmn@bellsouth.net>

A different Gideon Bosher: s/o John Bosher

John Bosher, m. Ona Unity Wheeler, d/o Charles Wheeler Jr and Nancy Stewart (http://www.familytreemaker.com/users/w/h/e/Roy-W-Wheeler/GENE0001-0006.html)

V9-4620.   1. *Leonard Bosher, b. c1814, Cumberland Co, VA, d. c1878, Kanawha County, WV; m. 5 Jun 1856, Chesterfield Co,

VA, a second cousin, Rebecca Wheeler, d/o Samuel
Wheeler Jr and Nancy Allen.

V9-4621. 2. *Gideon Bosher, b. c1814, Cumberland Co, VA, d. 31 May
1887, Richmond, VA, bur Maury Cem; m. 5 May 1845,
(per *Cumberland Co, VA, Marriages, 1840-1846*), Rebecca
B. Chenault, d/o Henry Chenault and Ann Wheeler.

V9-4622. 3. *Nancy Bosher, b. Oct 1819, Cumberland Co, VA, d. 17
Mar 1902, Manchester, Chesterfield Co, VA; m. 12 Apr
1841, Cumberland Co, VA, Shirley Dowdy, (per
Cumberland Co, VA, Marriages, 1840-1846; Unity Bosher,
mother of the bride, gave her consent.)

V9-4623. 4. Artemesia Bosher, b. ?; m. 19 Oct 1840, Horace Dowdy,
(per *Cumberland Co, VA, Marriages, 1840-1846*; Bondsmen
were Thomas J. Smith and Gideon Bosher. John Bosher,
Father of the bride, gave his consent.)

V9-4624. 5. Thomas Bosher; m. 27 Jan 1846, (per *Cumberland Co, VA,
Marriages, 1840-1846*), Sarah Ann Lowry.

Cumberland Co, VA, Deeds, Book 24, p.106 (12 Sep 1840): This
indenture made and entered into the twelfth day of September One
Thousand eight hundred and forty between Leonard Bosher and Gideon
Bosher of the county of Cumberland of the one part and William S.
McAshan of the Town of Caira and the said county of Cumberland of the
other part, Witnesseth that the said Leonard and Gideon Bosher, for and
in consideration of the sum of three hundred and twelve dollars and
twenty five cents, to them in hand paid by the said William S. McAshan,
the receipt whereof is hereby acknowledged, have granted bargained and
sold and by the presents do grant bargain and sell to the said William S.
McAshan the entire interest of John and Ona Bosher in the Estate of the
late Charles Wheeler, dec'd, now in possession of Nancy Wheeler, widow
and relict of the said Charles Wheeler, held by her as dower of the said
estate, consisting of land, negroes, and other property, the land lying and
being in the county of Buckingham, adjoining the lands of Col. Valentine
Parish and Alexander Trent Jr, containing by estimation seventy five
acres be the same more or less; also the interest of the said John and
Ona Bosher in the slaves belonging to the said Estate, numbering at
present ten, together with the future incres of the female slaves. To have
and to hold the aforesaid property; to him the said William S. McAshan
his heirs and assigns forever, and the said Leonard and Gideon Bosher
for themselves and their heirs, hereby warrant and defend and will
forever warrant and defend the said William S. McAshan and his heirs in
good and lawful title in fee simple, in and

to the above conveyed land and premises and other property, free of the claim or claims of all persons whatever. In witness whereof the said Leonard and Gideon Bosher have hereunto set their hand and affixed their seals the day and year first above written.

/s/ Leonard Bosher

Gideon [X] Bosher

Children of Leonard Bosher and Rebecca Wheeler:

V9-4625.   1. Samuel Wheeler Bosher, b. 8 Apr 1854, Cumberland Co, VA, d. 1932, Kanawha Co, WV
V9-4626.   2. William Bosher, b. 6 Mar 1859, Cambell's Creek, Kanawha Co, WV, d. 4 Feb 1925, Winifrede, Kanawha Co, WV
V9-4627.   3. Artimisia Bosher, b. c1860, Kanawha Co, WV, d. WV
V9-4628.   4. James Bosher, b. c1861, Elk River, Kanawha Co, WV, d. 1871, Kanawha Co, WV
V9-4629.   5. John Bosher, b. Feb 1865, Elk River, Kanawha Co, WV, d. 20 Jul 1955, Kanawha Co, WV
V9-4630.   6. Nancy Bosher, b. c1866, Kanawha Co, WV (listed in 1910 census with brother, Samuel, and mother, Rebecca)
V9-4631.   7. Mary E. Bosher, b. c1868, Kanawha Co, WV; m. William Clendenin
V9-4632.   8. Charles H. Bosher, b. c1875, Kanawha Co, WV, d. 1948, WV
V9-4633.   9. Edward Bosher, b. c1879

Children of Gideon Bosher and Rebecca Chenault: (first six b. Cumberland Co, VA; 1860 census, Manchester P.O., Chesterfield Co, VA)

V9-4634.   1. Sophia Bosher, b. c1846,
V9-4635.   2. Martha Bosher, b. c1848; m. 1 Jul 1885, Chesterfield Co, VA, James W. Newby
V9-4636.   3. Ann I. Bosher, b. c1849,
V9-4637.   4. Rebecca Bosher, b. 11 Nov 1853,
V9-4638.   5. William Robert Bosher, b. Mar 1854, d. 18 Mar 1927, Prince Georges Co, VA
V9-4639.   6. Gideon Bosher Jr, b. 18 Jun 1855, d. Chesterfield Co, VA
V9-4640.   7. Judith H. Bosher, b. ?, Chesterfield Co, VA, d. 11 Jun 1856, Chesterfield Co, VA

Children of Nancy Bosher and Shirley Dowdy (all b. Cumberland Co, VA; 1870 census, Madison twp, Cumberland Co, VA)

V9-4641. 1. John T. Dowdy, b. c1842; m. 4 Jul 1872, Manchester, Chesterfield Co, VA, Emma J. King

V9-4642. 2. Shirley P. Dowdy, b. 15 Mar 1845, d. 1 Jan 1893, Richmond, VA; m. 1 Mar 1870, Manchester, Chesterfield Co, VA, E. A. Blunt

V9-4643. 3. Lucy Ann Dowdy, b. c1848; m. 21 Dec 1869, Manchester, Chesterfield Co, VA, J.B. Donley

V9-4644. 4. Albert Dowdy, b. 15 Jul 1857, d. 15 Feb 1912, Richmond, VA.

INDEX

Note: I have made an effort to index names as they appear in documents. Where the surname is spelled in more than one way, e.g. both Brashear and Brashears in the same document, you will find that person indexed both ways. Also, check under variant spellings for the object of your search: Breshear(s), Boshears, Beshears, Brasher, Brashers, Brashier(s), etc.

Abbott
Ashley Renee 327
Brian Willis 328
Clifford Allen 328
Daniel Sterling 327
David Michael 327
Dwayne Allen 328
Elizabeth Anne 328
Gardner B. 327
James Gardner 327
Jamie Lee 327
Jennifer Lynn 327
Jessica Lynn 327
John W. 327
John William 327
Lisa 327
Nathan Lee 327
Paul Allen 328
Sarah Lorraine 328
Susanne Noelle 328

Abeel
Gerrit 519
Jane 519

Abel
Amy Lynn 432

Abell
Martha Virginia 122

Abercrombie
Mary 249

Ablin
Peter 505

Abul
C. N. 520
G. B. 520
Garrit 520
Mary 520

Abul (Abeel)

Evart 520
Gerrit 520
John 520

Ace
Iva 331

Adair
Dee 550

Adams
Mary 19, 543
Queen T. "Tiny" 292
Rebecca Smith 246

Adcock
Angie 261
Tom 410

Aissen
Dirk H. 433

Akehurst
Daniel 243
Filia Christi 243

Akers
Jean Tabb 288

Albers
John 559

Aldrich
Velma 36

Alexander
Joseph Henry 76
Julia Roene 322
Laura Mae 142
Roger 575
Walter "Pat" 160

Alford
Alice Audna 79
Alma 137

Allen
Beth 169

Brenda 52
Corrine Bellzora 49
Della Josephine . 431, 436
Henry 21
Ida 392
James Bascomb 436
Jonas 589
Joshua Edgar 436
Mary Jane Evans 389
Nancy 598
Sallie Estelle ... 562, 565
Sterling Washington . 405

Allgood
Donald H. 228
Donna K. 228
Donnie H 228
Douglas S. 228

Allison
Elsey 89, 90
James Monroe 89
Lottie Ann Patterson .. 89
Maggie Adams 89
Mary Ann 88, 90
Nancy 353

Allsop
Andrew 507

Alton
John B. 505, 507

Alvarez
Marie 538

Amettis
Anthony 435
Barry 434
Christine 435
Gerald 435
James 434
James Albert 434

Joel 435
Kyle Joseph 434
Randal 434
Thomas 434

Andereck
Eliza Jane "Jennie" . . . 37

Anderson
Bertha 352
Carolyn 559
Connie 559
Dotty 56
Doug 445
Eleanor 65
Frankie 559
George 362, 366
Georgia 109
Helen 123
John 366
Maria 510
Mary 445
Noah 559
Sam 564
William, Sr 366

Andrew
Aaron 41
Leann 41

Andrews
Thomas A. 507
Thos. A. 508

Andries
Sarah 500

Archibeque
Ashlee Mechelle 404
Dwayne Cruz 404
Paul 404
Tiara Cruz 404

Arendt
Julia Delia 90
Peter 90

Arers
Murle 38

Argo
Frank 19

Arledge
Ann Bell 564

Armstrong
Annie 410
Ben 410
Frank 410
George 410
Gladys 410
Henry B. 410
J. B. 410

Mary 410
Maude 410

Arrington
Anthony 547
Antoinette S. 546
Mary "Polly" 547

Arter
Joseph 312

Arthur
Anne Marie 292
Edna Earle 310

Artre
Helen Ann 391

Asberry
Tabitha 158, 159

Asbury
J-- 75
James 121
Lindsey 75

Ash
Alexander Hoyt 393
Lydia 191
Samuel Barnett 393
Susan Rebecca 191

Ashley
Florence 350
Job and James 350
Larry Joe 49

Ashton
Ann 434

Atchley
Allie Mae 143

Atkins
John 441
Wade 349

Atkinson
Phillip 378

Atteberry
Charlie Washington . . 136

Atterberry
Alice 136
John Valentine 136

Atterbury
Joe G 123

Austin
Benjamin Green 181
John 181
Laura 181
Louisa 164, 171
Mary 534
Robert Lewis 181
Wesley 164, 176, 181

Autry
Earnest 445

Avory
Anne 504
Anne (Brasher) 502
John 503, 504

Awtrey
John 244
Sarah 244

Ayers
Olive "Olley" 374

Bach
Margaret 287

Bacon
Dorothy Ann "Dolly . . . 167
Mary Olevia 398

Badger
Connie 40

Bailey
Catherine R. 427
Chris H. 264
Cora 230
John 531
Nancy 257
Rebecca Elizabeth . . . 331
Sarah 257

Bain
John 47
Margarita "Maggie" . . . 26

Baker
Albert 419
Anna Bell 101
Bobby 419
Buford 419
D.H. 442, 443
Debbie 419
Elijah 442, 443
Elizabeth . . 419, 442, 443
Ella Carlet 18
James 585, 586
James Noah 428
Jennie Bell 561, 562
Jimmie 419
Joanna 283
John 441-443, 448
John Buford 564
John Buford, Jr 564
Josie 446
Lois 564
Mary 591
Mary Elizabeth 453
Mary J. 388, 405
Mary L. 405

602

Nancy S. 443
Rose Marie 564
Saline 442, 443
Samuel 442, 443
Selah Jane 347
Shannon Leigh 128
Susanna . . 513, 522, 535
Tommy 564
Wallace 419

Baldridge
Margaret Annett 36

Baldwin
Absalom 156
Annie 157
Cordella 158
Hester M 156
Martha 157
Nancy 157
Samantha 156
Sarah F 156
Sylvester Lilburn 156
Thomas . . . 154, 156, 157
William 157, 158

Bales
Karen Leora 202

Baley
James Frank 116

Ball
Bennett 257
Moses, Jr 257
Nancy 257
Sallie M 127
Wesley 257

Ballinger
Mary Ruth 61
Robert 61

Baltimore
Virginia 413

Baltzell
Daniel Rufus 269

Bandy
Wilma 41

Bankston
H.E. 459
J. Bush 459
Stanton Brantley 459
Wilbur H. 459
William Benjamin 459
William Wallace 459

Barbee
Dawn 310

Barber
Anita 336

Emma 24
Frank Othello 336
Margret 444

Barbour
Dana Barbour 198
David Denton 198
Farron 198
Sidney 198

Barefield
Daniel 554
Grace 554
Jewel 554
Vivian 554
Willie 554

Barger
Lois 332

Barker
Alexander 464
Carl 382
Clyde J. 382
Delbert 381
Donald Lee 381
Dorothy May 381
Edna 382
Elijah Claude 382
Elisha 464
Ellis Thomas 381
Elmer Lloyd 380
Eva Estella 380
Fannie Anise 381
Gladys Blanche 382
Grace 382
Guy Cary 381
Henry Dean 382
Horace Harrison 381
Howard Taft 381
Irma 381
James Dewey 381
Julia Flora 382
Laverne Ruth 63
Lyle Frank 381
Mabel 381
Martha Ann 380
Mildred 381
Nancy Jane 380
Reuben Lloyd 380
Ronald Lee 381
Ruth Juliette 381
Ruth Pauline 381
Sarah Anise 381
Susan Elizabeth 464
Thomas Frank 381
Thomas Otis 380
Virginia 381

Wanda 381
Wilbur Eugene 381
William Ellis 381

Barkl(e)y
John 383

Barkley
Adam Jay 422
Harry 422

Barlow
Mildred 485

Barnes
Mary 500
Mary Elizabeth "Lizzie"
. . . . 244
Susanna 500
Thomas 500

Baron
Edward Vincent 558

Barr
Phyliss 61

Barriage
Kenneth 47

Barrow
Dannie Marie Brazier . 426

Bartee
Erin Lesley 553
Jonathan Eric 553
Kristin Renee 553
Russell Floyd 553

Bartel
Gary Dean 136

Bartholow
Darlene Etta 143
Donald 142
Glenda Ola 143
Norman Ralph 143
Sherman Ralph . 142, 143
Thelma Lorene 143

Barton
Gary Kenneth 201
Robert Keith 201
Roger Maris 286
Sandra K. 201

Basham
Elizabeth 222

Bashan
Danny 425
Glenn 425
Kelly 425

Bashier
Thomas 490

Bateman

603

Crystal 132
Battenfield
Walsie Ellen 77
Baucum
Charles Douglas 553
Douglas Dwain 553
Michael John 553
Wesley Elliott 553
Bauguss
Mary 347
Baur
Heidi 320
Baxter
Banner 290
Bayhi
Joan Marion 566
Bayless
Cynthia Ann 20
Dennis Ray 20
James 20
James Earl 20
Quincy Jameson 20
Bayne
Ellsworth 575
Beaden
Patsy 248
Beal
Catherine 249
Martha 249
Mary 249
Bean
Emily Ann 18, 24
Jewel 412
Beanblossom
Grant Marshall 42
William Dane 42
William Kurt 42
Beard
Alma Louise 558
Billy David 558
Leland 557
Leland Collette 558
Leonard Monroe 558
Mary Kathleen 558
William David 558
Beasley
Edna J. 87
Jessie L. 87
John V. 87
Minnie B. 87
Owen S. 87
Robert 87
Thomas Alvie 87

Beatty
William W 97
Beckman
Annaka 503
Cornelia 503
Elizabeth 503
Maria 503
William 503
Beckworth
Lloyd 425
Tammie 425
Bedford
James 446
Bedlow
Isaac 500
Beel
Cleo Mae 453
Beeler
Ann E. 378
Harriet 378
Jennie V. 378
Joseph 378
Lilly Fremont 378
Lydia A. 378
Mary Alice 378
Nancy W. 378
Nettie F. 378
Olive 379
William H. 378
Beevers
Jechariah Dean 404
Tone Dane 404
Bejar
Fobert 160
Belander
Olivette 136
Belding
Richard 297
Bell
Betty 114
Buddy 114
Daisy 481, 483
Danny Joe xiv
Doris 114
Hamilton 336
Henry 113
Jimmy 114
Johnny 114
Karen Lynn xiv
Nancy 114
Patty 114
Phillip Drew xiv
Rhonda Gale 52

Stanley Farris xiv
Bellah
Dwight Davidson . . . 396,
403
Florence Josephine . . 396
Mary Sue 396
Ronnie Bruce 403
Samuel Irvin 403
Samuel Walter 396
Scott 403
Belt
Catherine 304
Florence "Flossie" . . . 321
Harrison Benjamin . . . 321
Harrison Benjamin "Red", Jr
. . . . 321
Mildred Geraldine . . . 321
Willa Bea 321
Benjamin
Bradley Dean 42
Don 42
Mikaela Brooke 42
Benner
Daniel 252
Elizabeth "Maggie" . . 253
Elizabeth A. 252
Bennett
Benton 282
Harry H. 24
Margaret Angelina . 34, 36
Theresa Joe Bentley . 400
Bentley
Amber Michelle 401
Bradley Jack 401
Bryan Adam 400
Clyde Samuel 400
Dakota Keith 400
Elizabeth 343
Heather Louise 401
James Alvin 394, 400
James R. 273
James Ray 400
Miranda Ellen 400
Nettie 597
Patrick Shawn 401
Phillip James 400
Robert 273
Shawn Lee 400
Summer D'Anne 400
Theresa Joe 400
Tiffany Ann 400
Benton
Gladys 354
Berchak

Henry Lee 321
Judith Katherine "Katie" 321

Bergant
Mariann 381

Berrien
Abigail 509
Daniel 509
Elinor 508
Henry Brasher 509
John 507, 509
Mary 509
Sarah 509

Berry
Frankie Jean 169

Bersheres
B.E 157
Mary M 157
Rebecca 157

Beshear
Alma 81
Alta 81
Arie 80
Arney M. 80
Artie 82
Aubry 80
Audra 80
Benny Harrison 82
Elmer, Jr 81
Etta 81
Gaytha 82
George 82
Ira B. 81
James H. "Jim" 81
Leon 82
Millie Francis 81
Richard "Dick" 81
Roy 81
Roy Leo 81
Ruby 82
Troy 81
Troy Cleo 81

Beshears
A.C. "Pete" 326
Aaron 344
Aaron Essley ... 345, 349
Aaron Hegman 350
Aaron Lee 346
Aaron Wayne 113
Absolim 154
Adam 20
Addie 326
Addison Clyde 112
Adlaide 345

Agnes 90
Agnes Teresa 105
Albert Gaither 345
Albert Wayne 124
Aley Lidy Elizabeth .. 350
Alfred 351
Alfred Thomas 322
Alfred Thomas, Jr ... 322
Alice 81, 97, 175, 351
Alice (Mrs.) 78
Allen 326
Alva M. 115
Alvis Leo 19
Aly Adina 348
Amanda 322
Amanda Jane "MJ" .. 326
Ambrose 159
Ambrose B 123
Amy 324
Annie C. 18
Annie E 112
April 94
Araminta 118
Arthur "Doc" Leon 81
Arthur C 114
Arthur K. 108
Arthur Roy 115
Asa 352
Austin Butler 124
Austin Butler Jr 124
Ava Aldreen 25, 30
Averil Wayne 113
Averil Wayne Jr 113
Basil Lorenzo ... 108, 112
Bazy (Bazil?) 114
Beatrice 325, 350
Belva Alice 348
Benjamin "Dick" "Benny
    Dick" 80
Bernice 325
Bernice J. 351
Bertha L. 93
Bertha Rachel 160
Bessie 120
Beth Michelle 113
Beulah May 25, 30
Billie Joe, Jr 94
Billie Ray 94
Billy 26, 326
Billy Joe 94
Birdie 98
Bitty Idamae 19, 20
Blanche H. 165
Braden 158
Braden (?Brandon) .. 159

Brandon 159
Brenda Joyce 354
Brenda Lee 23
Brendon Boyd 113
Brian Edward 29
Calvin 326
Carl Ray 20
Caroline 88
Carrie Virginia "Sister"
.... 351
Cassie Marie 20
Catherine L. 173
Chandra 20
Charles Daniel 101
Charles Daniel, II 102
Charles G. 172
Charles Gabriel "Gabe"
.... 174
Charles H. 346
Charles McCune 113
Charlotte A 108
Chester W. 165
Clare 105
Clarence 18
Clarence Joseph 165
Clarissa Catherine .. 344,
                346
Cleo Abner 19, 21
Cleo Edward 23
Clyde Marion ... 101, 102
Columbus 165
Cora Ella 345
Cordelia 19, 120
Cordelia "Goldie" Keturah
.... 108
Cornelius Clingman .. 345
Cyrus 18
Cyrus Edward 25, 29
Daniel Fowle, Sr 345
Daniel Ray 114
Danielle Allyssa 353
David 20, 94
David Andrew 353
David Andrew, Jr 353
David R. 354
Deanna 114
Dell 26
Della A. 123
Delphia 326
Devin Roy 115
Don O. 121
Donald 79
Dora 165, 324
Dora B. 348
Dora Lee 90, 92

Doris Mozelle 354
Doris Virginia 353
Dorothy Faye 353
Dulcemia 90
Earl A 115
Edith 326
Edith E. 119
Edmond 25
Edna 79
Edna Beatrice 111
Elberta Ann 105
Elias 117
Elijah 84, 88
Eliza 322
Elizabeth . . . 88, 126, 345
Elizabeth Ann "Beth" . 105
Elizabeth C. 72, 74
Elizabeth Lee 348
Ella 352
Ella Gray 101
Elmer 81, 326
Elmer (Robert/Randall?)
. . . . 325
Elmer Jackson 124
Elva 325, 326
Elva Lucille 326
Elvin 79
Elzie Densmore 350
Emily Dulcinia 322
Emma Lucretia . 122, 125
Emma P 108
Erma 79
Ernest 79
Ernest, Jr 79
Esther 79
Eugene 97, 105
Eula Mercedes 124
Eura May 98
Eva 79, 114, 325
Eva Lena 115
Evaline Ruth 119
Evelyn Elizabeth 26
Ezra M 115
Fay Everette 119
Floyd William 111
Francis Earl 123
Francis Earl Jr 123
Francis Joseph 105
Fred L. 173
Freddie Joe 19
Garret Patrick 24
Gene Abner 23
Gene Elliott 24
George 79
George R. 94

George Washington . . 325
Gerald Wayne 124
Gertie 348
Gilbert Guy 325
Ginnie 105
Glen Bert 326
Glenn Newton 122
Goldie 160
Grover Cleveland "Cleve"
. . . . 351
Gwendolyn Lenore . . . 352
Harley 159
Harvey S. 78
Hazel Bernice 22
Hazil 94
Heg Hamilton 345
Helen R. 165
Henry 165
Henry Arthur "Art" . 18, 25
Henry Lee 348, 350
Herman Dee 20
Herman Donald 20
Hiram E 119
Homer Anderson 115
Homer B 112
Howard 350
Hubert Oscar 326
Ida Catherine 113
Ida Mae 326
Ida Mary 345
Ida Virginia 348
Idona 123
Irvin Cecil 79
Irwin Scott 353
Isaac L. 322
Jack R. 122
Jack "Archie" 326
Jackson "John" . . 85, 118
James 90
James Anderson . . 72, 78
James Arvell 325
James C 97, 98
James Dickson 350
James E 113
James Franklin 326
James Freeman 173
James Garland 325
James J. 98
James Monroe 322
James N. 88
James R. 165
James Robert 108
James W 84, 97
James Walter 350
James William 112

Janet 29
Janice Gay 123
Jay Bazzel 114
Jeremiah, Jr 73
Jerry 79
Jesse 159, 165
Jesse Bazel 113
Jessie 326
Jodica 108
Joe 18
Joe Brandon 24
Joe L. 173
Joel Marion, a.k.a. Joseph
Marion 98
Johanna F. 88
John 344, 345, 347
John B. 164
John E. 173
John Lee 121
John Leonard 351
John Leonard "Jack", Jr
. . . . 352
John Leonard, Sr 352
John Leonard,III 352
John Leonard,IV 353
John Napoleon 108
John R. 322
John Sherman . 345, 348,
349
John W 97
Joseph 106
Joseph Clyde 103
Joseph Francis 104
Joseph Franklin 349
Joseph Marion 98
Josephine 350
Judith Ann 123
Julia A 98
Julia A. 349
Julia Ubania (or Ann?)
. . . . 324
Julius Martin 350
Katherine 90
Katherine Florence . . 121
Kathleen 354
Kathy 26
Katie D. 94
Keith Anthony 106
Kenneth 115
Kevin 105
Kiter Virginia 350
Konnie 27
L.G. 26
L.T. 326
Lacy 350

Laura 105, 352, 353
Leanne 81
Lee Iris 79
Lela 354
Lena 115
Leni I 112
Leonard Lee 20
Leroy 90
Lester Lee 121
Lillian "Lillie" 159
Lillie 19, 165
Lillie Alberta . . . 345, 348,
349
Lillie Faye 81
Lisa Mechele 29
Lois 348
Lois Ellen 23
Lola 19, 326
Lonnie Joe 19
Loucinda 90
Louise 326
Loy Oscar 326
Lucille E. 94
Lucinda Jane . . 118, 125,
126
Lucretia Elizabeth "Lizzie"
. . . . 116
Lucy J 117
Luke 26
Lula Dee 92
Luster Clarence "Buster"
. . . . 79
Luther Andrew 25, 26
MaeFern 326
Maggie D. 91
Malinda "Lin" 344
Manfield "Max" 351
Manie 351
Marceille 326
Margaret 326
Margaret Jane 322
Marita M. 94
Marjorie Ruth 114
Marshall Clinton 346
Marta Gayle 20
Martha 79, 91, 344
Martha A 119
Martha C. 89, 165
Martha E 97
Martha E. "Mattie" 98
Martha "Patsie" 344
Marvin Wheeler 112
Mary 26
Mary A. 89
Mary Ann 322

Mary Blanche 111
Mary E 98, 115
Mary Elizabeth . . 108, 348
Mary Margaret 115
Mary Rebecca 350
Mary "Polly" 344
Mattie 91
Maureen Frances . . . 105
Max Edward 29
Melba Joyce 24
Melissa "Sis" 120
Mertie May 108
Mildred 92
Minnie F. 172
Minnie Lorene 19
Miranda 322
Mirtie 165
Missoura Pearlina 18
Mollie 90
Myrtle 93
Nancy 88, 89
Nancy J. 172
Nannette Sarah 105
Nettie M. 345
Nina A. 173
Noah 326
Noah Call 350
Nora Perditta 91, 94
Obie 325, 326
Odell 352, 353
Odis 326
Ola 326
Ollie 326
Ollie Eugene 112
Ollie Mae 18
Ona 326
Oneta Fern 113
Onie Nell Dell 25, 28
Orpha 353
Orville Anderson 117
Parker 348
Patricia Ann 105
Patty 75
Paul 105, 348
Paul Garland "Bruce" . 325
Paul W. 119
Paulina 84, 85
Paulina A 108
Pearl J. 173
Percie Orah 109
Perlie Logene 109
Philip 154
Preston 25
Preston Pebble 25
Preston Pebble "Presley"

. . . . 18, 24
Ray Alfred 354
Ray Thomas 114
Ray Vaughan "Dock" . 345
Raylene Sue 114
Raymond C., Jr 91
Raymond C., Sr 91
Reid W 97
Reta Louise 113
Retha Lou 326
Rettie Victoria 345
Reuben Alfred 90, 92
Rexie Coulter 91
Rhonda 27
Richard Clyde 105
Ricky 106
Robert 83, 154
Robert Anderson . 72, 85,
114
Robert Archie 94
Robert Arendt 91
Robert Glenn 348
Robert Hurley 121
Robert L. 121
Robert T. 88, 90
Robert "Bob" 351
Robin 94
Roland Freeman 111
Rose Ethel 112
Roy E 113
Ruby 91
Ruby V 119
Russell Caldwell 122
Ruth Cleveland 114
Sallie (or Sarah) Ellen
. . . . 110
Samantha 353
Samuel T 159
Samuel T. 159
Sanford L., Jr 79
Sanford L., Sr 79
Sarah 19, 90
Sarah C. 348
Sarah Evelyn 345
Sean Michael 416
Selay Lebeth 350
Shane Elliott 24
Sharon 79
Sheila Kay 30
Sherry Lynn 23
Sid 159
Susan G. 88
Susie 327
Thelma Jo 326
Thelma Sue 113

Theresa M. 105
Thomas 73, 416
Thomas Aaron 348
Thomas J 108
Thomas Jackson 17
Thomas Lee 20
Thomas Scott 353
Thomas Wesley 19
Thurman 18
Thursday (or Tuesday)
. . . . 81
Traci Jean 23
Vada Blanche 354
Velma Gladys 111
Velma May 124
Vernie Lee 108
Virgie 18
Walter Carl 119
Walter R. 119
Wanda Lou 27
Wanda Beatrice 124
Wanda Sue 25, 124
Webb 350
Wesley Aaron 24
Wesley V. 173
Wilburn Lee 29
Willard Wayne 124
William 101, 116
William Abner 17, 18
William B 114
William Bazil 72, 111
William Bazwell (?Basil)
. . . . 84, 106, 108
William C. 322
William Cleveland . . 159,
160
William Cowles 346
William David "Bill" . . . 324
William E. 172
William Elze 90
William Franklin 344, 348,
349
William H . . . 97, 98, 108,
110
William M.R. 348
William Moody 350
William R. 159
William Ray 20
William Robert 119
William "Bill" Riley 78
Willie Mae 326
Willie Thomas 345
Wilson 72
Winfield Scott . . 345, 351-
353

Zebulon Vance "Zeb" . 348
Zepha S 110
Zerelda Hazeltine . . . 120
Zola 18
Zora Adina 345
Besherse
Alvin Lewis 70
Doug 70
Douglas R. 69
Solomon 70
Bethea
Deborah 543
Samuel 543
Sarah 543
Bettisworth
Maurice 109
Beyer
Emma 434
Bias
Hiram 339
Biddlecombe
James 244
Mary 244
Bierman
Shirley 42
Biggs
Ella Mae 18, 24
Lloyd William 416
Taylor Aaron 416
William Jamie 416
Billions
William Jean 413
Bingham
Darrell 42
Deena Renee 42
Bird
Bettie Alice 426
Raymond 426
Raymond, Jr 426
Birkette
Melissa 354
Nathan 354
Steve 354
Bishears
Catharine "Catie" 342
Martha 343
Mary 342
Sarah "Sallie" 342
Bishop
Emma M. 445
Heidi Lynn 52
Tennie Johnson 417
Bittle

James Westley 390
John David 390
Mary Priscilla 390
Naomi Ruth 390
Nathan Aaron 390
Paul David 390
Rebecca Ann 390
W. A. 390
Bivins
Elias 339
Willie Reeves Hardin . 336
Black
Donald 354
George 523
Lewis 522, 523
Mary 522
Sarah 522, 527
Blackburn
Edmund 345
Edna 247
Martha Ellen 346
Mary Alice 349
Sarah Camilla . 344, 348,
349
Blackman
Elaine 244
Blackmon
Isaac Marshall 184
Lester 184
Blackwell
Carol 354
Elizabeth . . 264-268, 270-
272
Blades
Ransom 222
Sarah Jane 222
Blair
Amber Renee 396
Bobby Don "Donnie" . 396
Bobby Lee 396
Brandon Lee 396
Breon 396
Dwight Lee 396
Justin Don 396
Kristi Dawn 396
Shawn 396
Vicki 396
Blake
Joseph 368
Mary 367
William 367
Blakely
Mary 216

608

Blakeney
Nancy 457
Blalock
Angie Price 454
Ann 455
Charles . . . 452, 453, 456
Charles Dickens 454
Charles Elijah 454
Charles H. 453
Charles Richard 453
Charles Stuart 454
Elijah Brazier . . . 453, 454
Emily Jane 453
Frances B. "Fanny" . . 453
Francis 453
Harden 454
Jacob Giles 454
James A. 453
James Stuart 453
James William 454
John Wesley 454
Lizzie 454
Lucy 453
Lucy Ann 453
Lucy Margaret 454
Marshall Manuel 454
Martha Ellen 454
Mary Ann 454
Mary Francis 453
Nancy 454
Nancy Alice 454
Nancy Vitura 453
Rebecca 453
Richard 455
Richard Brazier 454
Richard Womack 454
Roscoe Conkling 453
Sarah 451, 456
Sarah A. 453
Sarah Francis 454
Sarah Jane 454
Simmons Harrison . . . 453
Susan Elizabeth 454
Thomas 454
Thomas H. 453
Thomas Henry Benton
. . . . 453
Virginia 458
Virginia Dale 453
William 453
William B. 454
William Brazier 453
Wyatt Conkling 453
Blanchard

John Woody 550
Bland
Christine Louise 58
Elmo 121
LaVerne 58
Leland B. 121
Mary Jo 114
Orville L. Jr, ... 121
Orville L., Sr 121
Patricia Denise 58
Pauline 121
Vernon Virgil 58
Blanks
Mary Jane Daniel 66
Blanton
Brian Keith 128
Grady 128
Jack 429
Mikalya Dawn 128
Blasbo
Barbara Jo 419
Blevins
Laura Jean 128
Blichington
Sarah Beth 50
Blocker
Amanda Lucindy 216
Catherine 217
Delitha Ellen 217
Drinda Malinda 217
Elijah C. 216
Elizabeth E. 216
Emilie Arminda 217
George R. 217
George W. 216
Hiram Abraham 217
J. Calvin 217
James Wesley 216
John 217
Joseph 217
Lyle 217
Mary 217
Michael M. 216
Michael Mitchell 217
Samantha Elizabeth . 217
Sarah 217
Susan F. 216
William Jasper 216
Blockson
Nora 233
Bluker
Gerrit B. 520
Gerritt 519

Blumenstock
Amy Lynn 41
Blunt
E. A. 600
Blythe
Lucy Adeline 66, 68
Ora 66
William 68
Boatman
Elizabeth 199
Boatright
Judy 55
Bobo
Lizzie Mae (Copeland)
. . . . 431
Maxie Pearl Brashears
. . . . 312
Bodine
James 35
Margaret 35
Bohrer
David 210
Rachel 210
Robert 210
Bolden
Monroe 414
Boldwyn
Robin 38
Bolinger
Christian Dawson . . . 212
Jason Dawson 212
Ryan Dawson 212
Ward 212
Bolling
Nancy 182
Bollinger
Devoe 79
Lydia Geraldine 79
Susan Catherine 78
Bond
Sandra Sue 129
Bonham
M. 88
William B. 88
William T 88
Booker
Franklin 156
Boone
Daniel 247
Rebecca 247
Bopp
Gary 62

609

Gary, Jr, ... 62
Gerald 62
Harry 62
Michelle 62
Robert 62

Borg
Jean 435

Boshears
Cornelius "Neil S." Brown
. . . . 261
Jeremiah 193
Jeremiah Nathan 261
Neil S. Brown 261

Bosher
Ann I. 599
Artemesia 598
Charles H. 599
Edward 599
Gideon 597-599
Gideon, Jr 599
James 599
John 597-599
Judith H. 599
Leonard 597, 599
Martha 599
Mary E. 599
Nancy 598-600
Rebecca 599
Samuel Wheeler 599
Sophia 599
Thomas 598
William 599
William Robert 599

Boshers
Carl 309, 312

Boss
Emmit Robert 27

Boswell
William Brasher 526

Bott
Jeff L. 454

Bounds
Mary 545, 556

Bowels
Durleene 20

Bowman
Jim 419

Boxx
Bill 273

Boyce
Martha Jane Evans . 547,
548

Boyd

Ada A. (?Anna) 187
Celia Frances 115
Daisy Edith 113
Gary Allen 424
John Wasson 113
Kay 285
R.I 115
Wanda 196

Bozarth
Helen 329

Bracey
Tommy 136

Brackin
James 223
Jerry Anne 224
Vernon Everett 224

Braddy
Lisa 42

Bradejor
Isaac 500, 506

Braden
Elsie 224, 236

Bradford
David Lee 30
Frank Edward 30
George 90
Glover Franklin . . . 25, 30
Herbert Franklin 30
Virginia May 30

Bradley
Charity 274
Emma 178
J.D. 546
James "Jim" 290
Minerva 187

Bradshaw
Ann 587
Hazel Ramona 28
Katherine 587
Kelly Lynn 234
Mary 587
Ursula 587
William 587

Brady
Charles Edward 477

Braezar
James 362, 363

Braisher
James 367
John 367
William 367

Braisjer
Isaac 500, 506, 509

Braizar
James 366

Braizier
John 362

Branch
James O. 58

Brandon
B. B. 441
Joseph 447
Josiah 447, 448
Lemuel 447
Rachel 447, 449

Brannon
Kathy 429
Kathy B. 427
Kathy Brazier 429

Brans
Maude 416

Bransford
Mary 246

Brantley
Lavinia 459
Mary 246

Braser
Cathalyntze 508
Samuel 570

Braseur
Henry 490

Brashar
Alice Lauerna 482
Archie Lee "Felix" . . . 482
Exie Leona 482
Gideon 490
Ivan Edward 482
Leander Vivian 482
Olivia May 482
Virgil Doward 482

Brashars
Corrinda 156

Brashear
Absalom 135, 154
Ada A. 256
Adda 289
Agnes 290
Ailsey 185
Albert 317
Albert Morgan 476
Alice 318
Alonzo D. . . 193, 194, 204
Alvan V. 255
Amanda 254
Amy 236
Andrew P 187

Ann Marie 191
Anna Holland 335
Anna Mae 336
Anne Elizabeth "Betty"
.... 239
Annexa 259
Annie 334
Arminda 466
Arnetta Virginia 281
Artie 195
Asa 193
Asa D. 193-195, 197, 204
Barbara 321
Barton 85
Benedict 249, 250
Benjamin 304
Benjamin H. 291
Benjamin, Sr ... 247, 303
Benjamin, V 191
Bertha 334
Bertie D. 197
Betsy 466
Bettie 224, 229
Betty L. 481
Bevie Glee 198
Bobbie 484
Bobbie, Jr 484
Bobby 254
Brandon 484
Caitlyn Marian 256
Caleb 484
Carl 278
Carol Evelyn 256
Carroll 186
Casey 484
Catherine 321, 335
Charles 324, 334
Charles E. 317
Charles Lewis 478
Cherrie Peart 281
Christina 285
Clara 289, 335
Clarence 289
Clega Lois 226
Cosma 285
Daisy 289
Danny 356
Dave 254
David 334
Donald Everett 281
Donald J. 278
Donnie 254
Doris L. 478
Dowell 254
Earl "Shack" 289

Earl Shacklette "Shack"
.... 289
Eden, Jr 187
Edgar Maurice 281
Edgar Thorne 281
Edith 189
Edith May 189
Edward 188, 317
Eleanor 191, 279
Eleanor L. (or C.) 184
Elias 317
Elijah 467
Elijah, III 480
Elijah, Jr 466
Eliza 317
Elizabeth . 247, 248, 260,
303, 304, 317
Elizabeth Betty Jane . 289
Elizabeth T. "Dixie" ... 85
Ella Louise 223, 227
Ella Mae 225
Ellis 466
Ellis M. 193-195
Elsie 279
Emily 192
Emma 290
Emma Bell 199
Enoch 296
Erve "Seven" 254
Estella Minnie 281
Eva 254
Everett R. 288
F. N. 289
Fay A. 280
Frances Lucille 478
Francis 191, 335
Francis "Frank" 279
Frank 279, 313
Frank jr 279
Frank Wesley 314
Frank, Jr 279
Franklin 335
Fred Loren 236
Geniene 320
George 334
George Allen 477
George W. 335, 466
George Washington . 471,
476
George Woodford ... 187
Georgia Ann 198
Gerald Edwin 186
Gilberte 185
Gilly Ann 224
Goebel 254

Grace 288
Grover Elroy 290
Grover Elroy, Jr 290
Guy Hiram 184
Guy Winford 237
Harold Earl 256
Harvey Smith ... 223, 224
Hazel 320
Henry 259
Henry Alonzo 254
Henry Virgil 481
Henry "Six" 254
Hobert 278
Huie 195
I. 317
Ida Elva 478
Ida Virginia 292
Ignatius "Nacy" 190
Ignatius, Jr 291, 303
Ignatius, Sr 303
Irma 279
Irvin 190
Isaac Wright 257
Isabelle 299
James 317
James Asa 195
James Barton 85
James Basham 222
James Clark 287, 288
James E. 280
James E., Jr 280
James Harrison 185
James R. 225
James W 187
James W. 187
Jan 484
Jane 192, 193, 522
Janet Ruth 477
Jay 292
Jay M. 292
Jay Michael 292
Jennifer 484
Jenny Clyde 201
Jeremiah 248
Jesse 32, 289
Jewell Blake 199
Jim Gordon 237
Jimmye 195
Joanne 254
Joel 292
John . 250, 258, 259, 274,
332, 334
John A. 184
John Alfred 279
John C. 292

611

John F. 335
John Leslie 197
John Richard 187
John Richard "J.R." . . 187, 188
John T. 308
John W. 481
John Wesley 314
John William 256
Jolie Ann 292
Jonathan Marshall . . . 292
Joseph 248, 279
Joseph E. 280
Joseph Erick 278
Joshua Derrick 278
Juanita 254
Julia 193
Julia (Smith) 279
Julius Guthrie 291
Julius Guthrie, Jr 291
Karen Leah 313
Katie Lee 287, 288
Kelsey 484
Lance 485
Larry 320
LaRue 477
Laura 334
Laura I. 280
Laura Jane 241
Lawrence 289
Lawrence "Jake" 289
Lemuel 193
Lenzy 291
Leola 478
Leslie 321
Letitia (or Lutitia) 187
Lewis Weldon . . 481, 483
Lewis Weldon, Jr 485
Lillie 202
Lillie M. 482
Linda 466
Linda Jean 313
Lois 320
Lola Beatrice 204
Lonnie Van 254
Lorelle G. 226
Lou Bell 194, 196
Louisa 318
Louisa C. 467
Lula L. 476
Luther C. 482
Mabel 334
Mable Lottie 477
Maggie 335
Maggie Nell 477

Marcus William 184
Margaret Aleene 478
Margaret P 187
Margaret P. 187
Margaret R. 280
Margery 248
Marie 186
Marion 321
Marion Eleanor 256
Mark Lewis 224
Martha 154, 304, 466
Martha A. 317
Martha E. 318
Martha Lynn 289
Martha "Patsy" 185
Marvin K. 195
Marvin W. 484
Mary . 244, 254, 256, 299, 317, 334
Mary "Tom" 187
Mary A. 184
Mary Ardella 223
Mary Cook 239
Mary Jane 191
Mary Jean 281
Mary Wilmult 236
Mary "Polly" 157
Mary "Tom" 187
Matthew 484
Meade E. . . 193, 194, 197
Medora 191
Melba Christine 477
Micajah Samuel 185
Micajah Samuel "Cage" 185
Mildred Elizabeth 477
Mildred Leona 237
Milton C. 255
Minnie 290
Mozelle 477
Myrl C. 197
Myrle 478
Myrtle 223
Nancy 254, 466
Napoleon Reginald . . 280
Neil 320
Nicholas Ray 183
Nola Jane 225
Ona Bell 485
Ora 290
Orville (AKA Dick) . . . 313
Orvillle 313
Otho 190, 280, 282
Otho R. 280
Otto 289

Patricia 320
Patricia Anne 281
Phebe 317
Philip, Sr 154
Phoebe 318
R. A. 256
R.U. 289
Rachel 250
Raymond 254
Rebecca 257
Rebecka 467
Reginald 280
Reuben D. 223
Rhoda Jane 481
Richard Gassaway . . . 254
Robert . . . 154, 290, 303, 304, 321
Robert A. 191
Robert Ayres 256
Robert D.L. 280
Robert E. 255
Robert E.L. 280
Robert Edward, "Jr" . . 255
Robert Eugene 254
Robert H. 255, 291
Robert Horace 256
Robert Horace, jR . . . 256
Robert J. the elder . . . 255
Robert J., the younger 255
Robert N. 335
Robert S. "Old Bob" . . 285
Robert Terrel 272
Robert "Sug" 254
Roy "Monk" 254
Ruby 289
Ruby Bell 194, 196
Russell Clifford 289
Ruth 285
Ruth Carolina 304
Ruth Caroline 303
Rutha 337, 338
Ruthie 254
Sallie 259
Sammye 195
Samuel . . 135, 250, 285, 316-318
Samuel Eden . . . 187, 189
Samuel Marion 320
Samuel Ray 285
Samuel Thomas 187
Samuel, III 250
Samuel, Jr . 248, 303, 304
Samuel, Sr . 247, 303, 304
Sandy 485

Sarah 184, 317, 466
Sarah A 188
Sarah A. 187, 188
Sarah Alice 254
Sarah E. 289
Sarah Rhea Hankins . 276
Sarah "Sallie" Louisa
   Catherine 477
Snoden Trullinger ... 320
Solomon 467
Stella 285
Stella F. 482
Sue 254
Terence 280
Terry 321
Thomas ... 183, 191, 335
Thomas Benton 285
Thomas C. 190
Thomas Cook 238
Tobias 304
Valerie 321
Van Swangdon 254
Velina 466
Vera Lucille 477
Verdell 477
Vicki 321
Virgil 187
W.L. 334
Washington 280
Wayne 308
William ... 183, 224, 236,
   248, 281, 334, 335, 466
William Albert 477
William C. "Bill" 285
William Harrison 185
William Henry .. 191, 336
William Henry, Jr 336
William Irwin 189
William James Leftwich
   69
William S. 335
William Silas (W.S.) "Red
   Will" 285
William Thomas 335
Winford Richard 237
Brashear/Brassers
   Richard 361
Brashears
   Absalom 17, 73, 83
   Absalom J. 295
   Acie 283
   Ada J. 253
   Adaline 296
   Aggie 308
   Albert 300, 305

Alexander Martin 182
Alfred (or Albert) 296
Alice 168
Alphons 293
Alva 185
Amanda A. (or R.) ... 298
Amanda Lucy 135
Amanda M. 296
Amber Mercedes 278
Amelia Frances 252
Andrew 159
Anissa Nicole 286
Ann 31
Anna 155
Anna Pearl 67
Annie Elizabeth 293
Ardella 168
Arnold 68
Arnold Lee 263
Arnold Lee, II 264
Artina 164, 176, 181
Artis Bell (Stewart) 68
Augustus 306
Basil 220, 221
Bat 305
Battieste 305
Benjamin .. 162, 163, 306
Benton 285
Bernice Gertrude 67
Berry 308
Berry Franklin 310
Bertha 292
Bertrand 67
Bessie 307
Beulah 66
Beverly Ann 328
Bill 305
Bostyn Logan 286
Brashears 305
Britannia E 157
Britannia E. 157
Britysh 286
Buster 305
Carol Lynn 328
Carolyn A. 340
Carrie 306
Catharine "Catie" 343
Cecil 263
Charles Henry .. 310, 311
Charles Loren 275
Charles V. 253
Charles W 67
Charles W. 67
Charles "Chuck" Henry, Jr
   310

Charley 305, 306
Cheryl Ann 310
Clara 66, 158, 159
Clara E. 252
Cora A. 308
Cora E. 252
Coralee Helen 328
Dennis 68
Diane Lenel 237
Dollie 293
Donna Carol 310
Dorcas G. 249
Doris 310
Dorothy Marie 296
Douglas V. 290, 291
E. Morton 66
Earl 263, 290, 291
Ed 306
Edward 305
Edward Pierson 180
Effie B. 293
Eliza 296
Elizabeth H. 274
Elizabeth L. 67
Elizabeth "Eliza" 323
Ernest Napoleon 66
Ethel 321
Eugene 306
Evangeline 67
Ezekiel 283
Fannie Ray 285
Filip N. 288
Flossie 306
Floyd 263
Floyd E 168
Frances 252
Frank 168
Furmon 67
Gabe 173
Gabriella Susan 168
Gayland B. 291
George 305
George Alfred Caldwell
   182
George Ridgely . 252, 253
George W. 297, 305
George William . 253, 297
George William, Jr ... 253
Gerald Benton 286
Gerald Craig 286
Geraldine 310
Gilbert 33
Gladys 263
Grace May 185
Grafton Finley 253

613

Gregg Thomas 68
Grover Cleveland 67
Guyann 237
Heather Renee 286
Helen Kathleen "Kathie"
. . . . 310
Henrietta 306
Henry 69
Henry C. 306
Henry G 68
Henry G. 68
Henry William 340
Henry, Jr 340
Herbert 293
Humphrey Godman . . 250
Ida 306
Ida L 308
Iona Elizabeth 168
Ira 155, 296
Isa May 306
Isaac 221
Isaac/Isaiah 73
Isabelle 297
Ithra, Sr 316
Iva 253, 291
Ivey 305
J R 308
J.C. 570
J.W 84
James . . . 165, 173, 182,
295
James Edom 311
James F. 253
James L 33
James L. 33
James W. "Jim" 66
James "Jim" 66, 340
Jane 298
Jeanne Bradley 329
Jemima 164, 166
Jemima Martha 178
Jeremey 286
Jeremiah, Jr 73
Jeremy Benton 286
Jesse . . . 31, 73, 164, 257
Jimmy 310, 311
Job Wesley 172
John . . 33, 156, 167, 168,
306, 323
John B. 165
John Clayton 249
John H 158
John H. J. 156
John James Lafayette
. . . . 262, 263

John Robert 275
John W. 275, 308
John Wesley 182
John Wesley Bolling . 17,
182
John William . . 33, 65, 66
John William "Willie" Jr
. . . . 66, 68
John William "Willie", Jr
. . . . 66, 68
John Willis 327
Johnie Tobias 306
Joseph Henry 262
Joshua 253, 286
Joshua, jR 252
Julia Ann 252
Julia F. 306
Julia H. 308
Julia M. 252
Kansas (or Arkansas) . 71
Katherine 253
Keith Richard 237
Kenneth Leo 253
Kirby 283
Lafayette M. 283
Lee Roy 168
Leonard 185
Lewis 164, 175
Lewis Greene 172
Lewis Hayden 67
Lida B. 306
Lightfoot Veol 310
Lillie C. 291
Linda Kay 237
Linnea Marie 286
Lois Cora 327
Lois Cornelia 66
Lonzo 290
Louisa 156, 173
Louise M. 309
Lovel Sumner . . 297, 307
Lovinia J 156
Lucy Elizabeth Cross . 250
Luella 66
Lula V. 291
Luna Jewel 310
Luva E. 253
Machell 264
Manerva C 156
Margaret 312
Margarette Ellen 168
Marie 66
Marina 164, 181
Marion 263
Marion Columbus . . . 165

Mark David 264
Marsham 292
Martha 156, 342
Martha A. 322
Martha H. 307
Martha H. (Grissom) . 300
Martha J 167
Martha "Patsy" 157
Martin 164, 171
Martin A. 182
Martin S.J. 172
Marvin 263
Marvin Melvery 31
Mary . 167, 172, 214, 216,
275, 297, 308, 342
Mary "Polly" 214
Mary Ann 33, 179
Mary Ann "Polly" 33
Mary C. 252
Mary Claudia 180
Mary Estella 306
Mary Frances 311
Mary J. 307
Mary L 308
Mary L. 309
Mary M 157
Mary M. 157
Mary Prince 307
Mary Prudence 253
Mary Samantha 253
Mary "Polly" 158
Maxie 68
Maxie L. 68
Maxie Pearl 312
May 185, 290, 291
Maybelle 68
Melinda C. 291
Minnie 307, 308
Minnie Elizabeth 179
Monicha 264
Myrtle 66
Nan L. 253
Nancy 83, 275, 307
Nancy Artemie "Nanny"
. . . . 172
Nancy C 33
Nancy C. 33
Nancy Ella 66
Nancy J 156, 158
Napolean P 308
Nellie 69
Nina L. 253
Nina Lillian 180
Ollie Gertrude 291
Ona Christine 185

Ora 291
Orenia 292
Orland Yates 67
Oscar E 67
Oscar E. 67
Parthena "Thena" . . . 134
Pauline 178
Pearl Carman 185
Pearl Vestina 264
Percy 283
Philip 31, 73, 154
Philip Boyer 292
Philip Jr 83
Philip Sr 83, 162
Philip, Jr 17, 31, 73
Philip, Sr 17, 31, 73
Phillip 134, 300
Phillip, Sr 134
Phoebe 213, 220
Polly 305
Preston 25
Queen A. 292
Richard 305, 307
Richard Gassaway . . . 252
Robert . . . 17, 73, 83, 84,
134, 162
Robert B. 276
Robert Lee 180
Robert Leroy . . . 308, 309
Robert Lewis . . . 178, 180
Robert Samuel . . 213, 220
Robert W. 275
Robert William 328
Ronnie 310
Roy 291
Roy English 309
Rube 307
Rutha 336
Sadie L. 309
Safrona 156
Samuel . . 156, 159, 164,
166, 167, 275, 300
Samuel R 156
Samuel T 159
Samuel T. 159
Sarah 157, 168
Sarah "Sally" 221
Sarah Ann 250
Sarah Burton 296
Sarah J 168
Sarah M 308
Sarah White 300, 301
Sarah "Sallie" . . . 342, 343
Sheila 275
Shirley 311

Sinna 164
Stamp 321
Steven Leonard 237
Susan M 308
Susie 293, 307
Synda (or Sydney) 70
Thelma Mae 67
Thomas 68, 73, 163, 253,
490
Thomas H. 253
Thomas Hammond . 252,
253
Thomas Walter 253
Thurmon 67
Tobias 307
Tola 306
Turner 307
Tyler Wayne 310
Urey Hubert 67
Valdon A 33
Valdon A. 31, 33
Van Stiffler 253
Vera 65
Vickey Denice 237
Victoria 291
Viola 307
W. J. 290
W.J. 291
Walford 66
Walter 308
Walter Scott 66
Walter "Watt" 222
Wardell 66
Wilbur 66
Will Tom 311
William . . . 156, 172, 252,
253, 308, 322
William B 84
William Bazwell 84
William Bradley 310
William Brannon 286
William Brent 286
William C. 249
William Clayton 249
William Colonel Runnels
. . . . 182
William D. 262
William Edom 311
William Edwin . . 310, 311
William Emmett 180
William F. 252
William Guy 68
William Henry . . 283, 312
William Hjalmar 286
William J. 307

William James Leftwich
. . . . 31, 69
William Joey 286
William Joshua 178
William Marquess . 65, 68
William R. 159
William Riley 277
William Silas "Bill", Jr . 285
Willie 305
Wilson 73
Zadock 300
Zaza 73
Brashears (Beshears)
Jesse 164
Brasher
A.B. 525
Aaltje "Elinor" 507
Aaltje (or Ellen) 509
Abigail 506-508
Abraham . 501, 505, 511,
513, 519, 522, 535
Abraham (Col) . . 517, 518
Abraham E. 521
Abraham K. 517
Abraham Kortright . . . 519
Abraham, III 512, 515
Abraham, IV 512
Abraham, Jr . . . 514, 521,
535
Abraham, Sr 511
Abraham, Will of . . . 512,
520
Abrahamm Jr 535
Adm. Byrd 525
Aeltje 509, 510
Albert Laer 527
Albert Ralph 527
Albert Ransom 527
Alice 526
Alyssa 212
Amanda 525
Amanda Melvina Fitzellen
. . . . 526
Amy 526
Andrew 528
Anna Pearl 565
Archie 538
Asa D 194
Asa Davis 209
Asis S. (?Asa) 208
Avon E. 209
Baker 514
Benjamin 527
Bert Valentine 210
Bert Valentine, III 210

615

Bert Valentine, Jr 210
Bert Valentine, Sr ... 210
Bert Vessie 208, 210
Betty 528
Bruce 539
Capt Asa 257
Casper 529
Catharina 505
Catherine 508
Catherine Marie 210
Charles .. 527, 528, 538,
                       539
Charles H 208
Charles Lee 522, 528
Charles M. 526
Charles Milton 538
Charles Riddle 272
Christine 538
Clara 529
Cora 529
Cornelia ... 515, 529, 538
Cornelius 519
Cyrus Nutt 527
Daniel 504, 507
David 510
Deborah E. 538
Derrick 212
Diane 565
Dorothy 210
Eddie Launa 527
Edward 510
Eleanor 508
Elenor 505
Elinor 508
Eliza 517
Elizabeth . 504, 509, 512-
      515, 522, 526, 528
Ella M. 570
Ellen 519
Ellevina 529
Engeltie 513
Ephraim 521, 535
Ephraim Brown 525
Ephraim, Jr ... 512, 530,
                534, 535
Ephraim, Sr 512, 535
Eva Louise 273
Evelyn 528
Evelyn B. 528
Fannie 529
Florence 529
Francis 503
Frederick 537
Garret Hendrickson .. 502
Gasherie 519

George 525, 529
George W. 570
Gideon 490
Hannah 507, 508
Harriette Ellen 274
Helen Keating 209
Helen Kortright 518
Helen Marie 212
Helena Kortright 519
Hen, Jry 508
Hendrick "George" ... 502
Hendricus 504
Henricus 508
Henricus (Henry) 506
Henry 489, 492, 494, 496,
  502, 506, 507, 509, 514,
      521-523, 526, 535
Henry, III 507
Henry, Jr 500, 507
Hester 519
Isaac 506, 507, 509
Isaac, III 509
Isabella 525
Jacob 514, 522, 527
James B. 570
Jane 519
Jasper 539
John . 505, 512, 513, 522,
          524, 527, 535
John (Johannes) 522
John B. 525
John Lakin 493, 525
John or Johann 511
John Pintard 519
John, "Jr" 247
Joseph 526
Joseph H. 525
Joseph H. (Hayms?) . 525
Joseph Isaac 504
Judith 513, 519
Julia 519
Katherine Marie Louise
                   538
Laura 538
Lawrence 514
Lawrence Lovegrove . 525
Leon 538
Lewis B. 493, 525
Lewis B. (?Black) 525
Lewis Hood 528
Lloyd 565
Lomax 208
Louise 537
Louise Edna 565
Lucas 512

Lucas "Luke" 512
Lucy 522
Lucy Ann 526
Madelon 538
Margaret 507, 566
Margarietje 504
Marguerite Marie 273
Maria 507, 515
Mariann Ragan 526
Marifrancis 209
Marjarietje 504
Marritje "Margaret" ... 512
Martha 274
Mary . 247, 505, 519, 525,
                     526
Mary Eleanor 210
Mary Ida 274
Melode 538, 541
Michael Lawrence ... 212
Michele 539
Milton E. 541
Milton Evans 538
Mithilda Ann "Tillie" .. 274
Neeltie 508
Patricia Ann 211
Philandra Louise 538
Philip . 515, 521, 535-538
Philip Marston .. 538, 539
Philip, Jr 538
Phillip 503
Phillip Marston 537
Rachel A. 208
Ralph 526
Ralph Gustave 274
Ransom Hunt 527
Reginald I. "Rex" ... 538,
                     539
Revis 539
Rex 538
Robert 526, 539
Robert Allen, Jr 274
Robert Allen, Sr 273
Robert Christopher .. 210
Robert Clarke 522
Robert Clarke, I . 525, 526
Robert Clarke, II 525
Robert Clarke, III 526
Robert Clarke, IV 526
Robert H. 277
Robert Hood 522
Robert Hood "Ivan" .. 528
Robert Terrel 272
Robert Westerfield ... 522
Robert Westerfield "Field"
          528

616

Rose Marie 538
Ruth McKee 526
S. (or Z. for Zachariah)
   Harrison 595
Sara 504, 507
Sarah . 522, 523, 525, 526
Sarah Jane 208
Seaborn 208
Susan 522, 525
Susanna .. 505, 512-515
Susannah 505, 512
Tabitha L. 209
Talitha C. 209
Thomas 529
Thomas Frederick ... 210
Thomas Marston 537
Thomas R. 525
Walter 529
Wilkeson 504
Willem 507
William ... 505, 528, 529,
               586
William B. 570
William Henry 208
William Marston 537
William Robert 565
William Seamon 526
William Thaddeus ... 210
William "Bill" Waldon . 529
William "Willie" Summerville
              528
Zachariah 595
Zaza, Sr 208

Brashers
Angela 276
Bessie 307
Betsy 308
Carolyn 275
Deborah 276
Deborah K. 276
Doulis W. "Woody", Sr
              276
Doulis W., Jr 276
Eveline 275
Freddie 236
Gail Delores 236
Gary 276
Janis 236
John 357, 365
John R. 275
Margaret 275
Mary W. 307
Nathan 275
Obadiah Memery 275
Robert Eugene 276

Robert Henry 275
Thomas C. 277
Tiffany 276
William Riley 277
Brashier
Blanche 551
Addie Lois 559
Albert 561
Alma Jo Prince 550
Alonzo 560
Artis Parker 563
Audrey 557
Barney Roland 559
Bea Hamilton 549
Belle 560
Ben 554
Benjamin A. 554
Benjamin F. 544, 546
Benjamin Franklin ... 547
Benjamin Franklin "Pap"
             554
Benjamin Thomas .. 549,
             550
Benjamin Thomas, Jr . 552
Benny Joe 552
Bessie 554
Bill 559
Billie Ray 564
Bobbie Jean 563
Bonnie Jean 559
Brenda Joyce 552
Charity Ann 546
Charles 545
Charles Bell 564
Charles Bell, Jr 564
Charles Bradford ... 549
Charles Dudley . 561, 562
Charles Ranzy 563
Charles Russel 560
Charles Warren 563
Charlie Bradford, Jr .. 549
Chester Edward 549
Christopher Denton .. 562
Christopher Dudley "Kit"
          545, 561
Clifton Leonard . 551, 552
Cora Lee 549
Cornelia 545
Cuning 561
Danna B. 549
Danna Elaine 553
Dixie Evelyn 552
Dollye 547
Doris Ellena 552
Doris Eloise 563

Earl Lee 548, 550
Earl Sayle 549
Edith Nebraska 562
Edward 559
Edward Hamilton 550
Elizabeth "Lizzie" 548
Elsie Lorena 559
Emmett Lawrence ... 551
Erlie Lee 557
Estelle 555
Fansider 560
Frances 550
Frank P. 562
Freda Maureen 558
Gene 557
Gideon 597
Gladys 554
Glenda L. 559
Grady 561
Green 545
Greene T 557
Gwendolyn 559
Hal 554
Hannah 505
Harry Lamise 555
Hattie Lou 555
Hazel 563
Helen Daisy 558
Henry Leland 559
Henry Sonny 558
Hilda France "Ann" .. 550
Howard Kelly 559
James 560
James Arthur ... 562, 563
James E. 562
James H. 555
James Hardy 559
James Harold 563
James T. 545, 560
Jane 545
Janie Joyce 558
Jenny 547
Jesse W. 550
Jo Marie 555
Joe 554
Joe Edward 563
John Calhoun .. 547, 548
John Elam 563
John Harold 559
John Henry 548
John Henry, Jr 549
John W., Jr 555
John W., Sr 555
John Washington ... 544,
             546

617

Joseph Tillman 550
Julius Waldo 557
Julius Werner 560
Kathryn L. 564
Larry 552
Laura Ann 559
Learce 560
Leila Mae 551
Lucy 547
Luther 560
Lyda Julia 549
Mae 554
Margaret Julia 552
Margaret Sue 552
Martha 544
Martin Luther 558
Mary Frances . . . 557, 559
Mary George 558
Mary Jane 544
Mary Sapphira 597
Mary "Polly" 547
Matthew 560
May 545
Mildred 556, 563
Mollie 554
Mourning 547
Nancy Alice 562, 564
Nathaniel Green 558
Nellie (or Nettie) 554
Pat 550
Pauline 550
Pleasant 542, 544
Rebecca 547
Robert B. 545, 567
Robert Emmett "Bobby"
. . . . 551
Robert Harvey "Harry"
. . . . 554, 555
Robert Wesley 563
Robert Wesley, Jr . . . 563
Roy F. 549
Ruth 555
Sally 561
Selma 547
Sidney Laverne 559
Sybil 554
Thomas Harold 559
Thomas Trasher 558
Trilby 557
Walter Mack 557
Weymoth 557
William Calhoun 551
William Eugene 559
William M. 545, 556
William Robert 562

Brashur
Gideon 490
Brasier
Aaltye 506
Abigail 589, 592-594
Abraham 501
Abraham, Sr 511
Alice 592
Alice Dora 331
Ann 593
Anne 503, 585
Benjamin . . 589, 592, 593
Benjamin, Jr 592
Benjamin,III 592
Blanche 329
Charlotte 582
Christopher 590
Daniel 595
Donald McCosh 331
Donna Jo 329, 331
Edward . . . 588, 589, 591
Elizabeth 589, 594
Ester 591
Esther 593
Esther-Ann 594
Frances 503
George Washington . 330,
331
Gideon 330, 490
Hannah 590, 593
Hattie Effie 331
Henricus (Henry) 506
Hiram 329
Ida Melissa 332
Isaac 329, 506
James 503, 592-595
James Dallas 331
Jas 504
John . . 360, 362, 592, 593
John F. 330
John M., III 361
Jonathan 330
Joseph 593, 594
Julie Ann 331
Lucinda 330
Lydia 504
Margaret 594
Maria 506
Mary . . 503, 589, 590, 594
Maude Ora 331
Meads 503
Noah 490
Paulina 330
Raymond 329
Rebecca 589

Reuben 364
Richard 504
Samuel 590-592
Samuel Alonzo 331
Sarah 503, 589
Simeon 590, 591
Susanna . . 330, 501, 506
Thomas . . . 504, 589, 594
Thomas, Jr 589
Thomas,III 590
Thomas,IV 592, 593
Timothy 593
Westley 330
William 505, 581, 593
William Elmer 331
William Putman 491
Brasil
Edna Earle 79
Brasseur
Benois/Benjamin 357
John 356, 357, 361
John III 357
John, III 362
John, Jr 356-358
Martha 245
Mary 357, 359
Richard 358
Robert 245, 357
Brasseur/Brashear
Robert 572
Brasseur/Brazer
John, Jr 359
Brasseur/Brazier
John, IV 362
Brassier
Belitha 587
Richard 363
Brassiers
Richard 362
Brassieur
Mary 244
Brassure
Elizabeth 361
Robert 361
Bratcher
Austen 588
Brayser
Sarah 505
Brazelton
Charlie 446
George W. 446
Nora 446
Brazer

618

Brasier 504
Elizabeth 360
John 360, 595
John (John Brasseur, Jr)
. . . . 359
Richard 360
William 584

Brazher
William 586

Brazier
Aaron Leroy 428
Aaron Leroy "Jr", II . . . 429
Adam Keith 412
Albert 444
Alton 417
Alverene 419
Amanda Jane . . 471, 474
Ammine 427
Andrea Lynn 412
Angela Robin 416
Anne 410
Annette 416
Arthur James 413
Arthur James, Jr 414
Audrey 444
Bailey 429
Barbara 427
Barbara Ann 413
Bathsheba (or Barsheba)
. . . . 452, 454
Benjamin Hinton 459
Bernice 415
Berry Luke 429
Bessie 429
Betsy 466
Betty Jean 415
Betty Lovern 429
Betty Lucille 415
Beulah 423
Beverly Ann 422
Billy 427, 444
Billy Glenn 416
Birdie 430
Bobby 415, 427
Bobby Gene 413
Bonnie Alice 429
Bonnie Evelyn Mae . . 429
Bonnie Mae 430
Bruce Wayne 412
C. M. 368
Carl 444
Carl Buford 444
Carrie 382
Charles Alan 414
Charles Alexander . . . 445

Charles Alexander, Jr
. . . . 445
Charles Brent 445
Charles Goodwin 596
Charles Goodwin, Jr . 596
Charles Henry 465
Charles Huey 464
Charles William 411
Charles William "Bill" . 411
Charlie Osborn 414
Charlotte 582
Christiana 369, 371
Christopher Randall . . 412
Cleon Freeman 412
Clifford 410
Cora Louise 445
Corey Thomas 412
Corintha 464
Cretia 372, 374
Cynthia 405, 458
Cynthia Rae 416
Daisy 444
Dannie Marie 426
Darrell Brazier 413
Daulton 426
David 488, 489
David Edward "Duck" . 415
David Leroy 419
Debbie 414
Della Beth 445
Delores 414
Denise 414
Diane 413
Dona 414
Dona Dell 424
Donald 414, 415
Dorthary 444
Dovie Mae Della 411
E.Z. 418
Earlene 418
Earnest Price 415
Earnest Rayman 416
Edna 383
Edna L. 417
Edward 417
Elijah   368, 369, 371, 372,
374, 375, 377, 382, 386,
389, 439, 441, 447, 448,
450, 457, 461, 489
Elijah W. 451
Elijah Wesley . . 356, 451,
452, 457
Elijah Wesley, jR . . . 458,
459
Elijah William 463

Elijah, III 472
Elijah, Jr . . 443, 446, 462,
466, 468, 470
Elijah, Jr [IV] 463
Elijah, Sr 443, 466
Elijah, Sr [III] 462
Elizabeth . 376, 387, 441,
472, 479, 488, 503
Elizabeth "Betsy" . . . 470,
472
Ellen 410
Ellen Lezinka 449
Ellis 471
Elmira 382
Elton Leroy 429
Elzie "R.D." 426
Ethel Emma 410
Evon 419
Fanny Ruth 446
Fountaine Harris 444
Fountaine Harris, II . . 445
Frances 503
Frances Asberry 411
Frances Marlene 429
Francis Asberry "Berry"
. . . . 410, 427
Franklin J. 596
Fred 383
Gaston W. "Dock" . . . 410
Geneva 413
George Andrew 416
George W. 405, 476
George Washington . . 471
George William 421
Gideon 490
Gladys 422
Glendon 430
Glenn 416
Godfrey 587
Groves   Middleton   (or
Madison) 463
Hamer 382
Hannah 376, 377
Harmon D. 418
Harriet Louiza 462
Harriett L. 463
Harris 488, 489
Harry 383
Henry 384, 489, 496
Henry Carey 413
Herbert Moody 414
Holland 417
Ira 446
J. D. 429
J. W. L. 449

J.B. 415
J.W. 409
Jackie 419
Jacob 587
James . . . 356, 362, 363,
    366-369, 371, 372, 374,
    376, 382, 386, 387, 389,
    394, 413, 439, 441, 447,
    448, 462-464, 489, 587
James A. 405
James Berrian 459
James Byington 422
James Calvin 445
James E. 447, 449
James Edward . . 415, 429
James Henderson . . 464,
    465
James Henry 429
James Henry Taylor . 420,
    426
James M. . . 409, 417, 427
James Madison 383
James Mumford . 584, 585
James Oscar 417
James W. 418
James W. "Bully Jim" . 444
James Walter "Jim" . . 419
James, "Jr" . . 372, 452
Jamie Evelyn 459
Janice 427
Janice Ann 415
Janie Lavone 415
Jesse 546
Jesse O'Neill 444
Jesse Rhea 446
Jessie Lee 444
Jimmy Dole 414
Jno & Eliz 587
Jo Ann 464
Joanna Leigh 414
Joe Berry 428
John . 368, 369, 372, 374,
    375, 382, 384, 429, 462,
    587
John Asberry 417
John B. 546
John C. 457
John Ellis 460
John G. 463
John Henry "J.H.", III . 427
John Henry, Jr 427
John Lee 427
John Rhea 445
John W. 408, 424
John Wesley 459

John William 444
John William "J.W." . 420,
    421
John, IV 363
Jonathan D. 462
Joseph G. 463
Josephine 429
Joyce 414, 427
Joyce Ann 419
Juanida 413
Julia A. 462
Julia Louise 422
Kathy 429
Kenneth Arthur 445
Kenneth Robinson . . . 595
Laban 368, 372, 374, 384,
    462
Lamar 419
Landon 419
Larry 419
Larry Joe 414
Laura Oleva 420, 426
Lavone Brazier 416
Leah 368, 462
Lee R. B. "Bud" 415
Lee Roy 417
Lee "R.B." 415
Lemuel 405
Lena 444
Lena Mae 416
Leona 444
Leroy 430
Levin 587
Lewis 383, 384
Lillie 429
Lillie Ann 444
Lilly Faye 416
Lim 441
Linda 470
Lou Anna 417
Louisa C. 468, 479
Louise 446
Louise C. 471
Lucia Ann Lavincia . . 460
Lucinda 447, 463
Lucrecia 382
Lucy 429
Lucy Kelly 431
Lula Caroline 412
Luther 460
Lydia 405
Lydia Ann 376
Mabel 383
Mable 419
Maggie Willie 459

Mamie Frances 428
Margaret Edith 413
Marilda C. "Rilda" 409
Marilyn Sue 422
Mark Kevin 445
Martha 458, 471
Martha A. 462
Martha Elizabeth 405
Martha M. 410
Marvin 419
Mary 382, 429, 505
Mary A. Elizabeth "Polly"
    408
Mary Ann 471
Mary Caroline "Callie" 405
Mary D. 375
Mary Dell 446
Mary Esther 421
Mary H. "Polly" 388
Mary Jane 446
Mary L. 444, 462
Mary Virginia 460
Mary "Polly" 374
Mattie Jane 415
Mattie Margaret 422
Mattie Pearl 420
Maudine 412
Maurice Arthur 595
Maurice James 595
Maymie Catherine . . . 419
Melissa Jo 414
Melville 382
Melville Christy 383
Melvin 427
Melvin C. 382
Mertie 388, 422, 489
Mildred 415
Milly 546
Mitchell Keith 412
Mourning E. 462
Myra Dale 412
Nancy 374, 375, 378, 414,
    470, 473
Nancy C. "Nan" 410
Nancy Ellen 388, 392
Nancy Ellen 394
Nancy R. 405
Nannie 429
Narcissa C. 463
Nathan Elonzo "Lon" . 417
Nellie Ann 418
Nellie P. 417
Newton A. 445
Nina 546
Nora Eloise 423

620

O.V. 444
Obediah 417
Oletha Pearl 445
Oliver 385
Otho Benjamin C. . . . 420, 423
Otho Benjamin, Jr . . . 423
Ovena 419
Parthena A. 462
Pathonio or Parthena (Indian?) 458
Patricia Ann 424
Perlina Susan Cordelia "Deed" 410, 430
Phoebe (Febe) Ann . . 409
Pleasant 543
Polly 372
R.L. 418
Rachel 405
Randall Warren 412
Rebecca . 452, 455, 463, 471, 478
Rebecca B. 463
Rebekka 462
Rhoda Ann 458
Robert . . . 444, 572, 576, 577
Robert Benjamin "Bob" 424
Robert Cody 424
Robert H.B. 464
Robert Walter . . 417, 418
Roland Dawson 412
Ronald Loyd 415
Rosa M. 419
Roy Clayborn 412
Roy David 412
Ruben 364
Ruby 416
Ruthie Lee 418
S. June 546
Sally M. 387, 389
Sarah 385, 405, 470, 472, 505
Sarah Anne 452, 453
Sarah Harrison 577
Sarah J. 444
Serena Amanda 459
Shadrach 376
Sherman Obie 445
Simion 504
Sion S. 388, 405
Solomon 472
Stella 426
Stella R. 460

Suella 420, 424
Susan Elaine 445
Thelma Louise 413
Thomas . . 385, 386, 413, 430, 463, 504, 546
Thomas Newton "Newt" . . . 409, 410, 427, 430
Thomas Riley . . 409, 411, 416
Thomas William 412
Tina 595
Tom 444
Utha 463
Vallie 460
Van R. 463
Velina Hart 471
Virginia Ruth 446
Wallace 430
Walter 423
Wanda Pauline 414
Wesley Johnson 422
Wilber 382
Wiley 372, 374, 441
Wiley J. 443
Wiley, Jr 441
Willi 546
William . . . 368, 369, 372, 374, 382, 384-387, 389, 394, 447, 449, 451, 452, 457, 463, 464, 471, 488, 489, 583-587
William (Surgeon) . . . 583
William E. 405
William Edwin 464
William Henry H. 458
William J. 409
William Jean "Billy" . 386, 388, 407
William Jean "Jim" . . . 428
William Loyd 414
William M. 443
William Washington . . 587
William "Wiley" J. 443
Willie 441
Willie (or Wiley) A.E. "Sue" 410
Willie Suella 417
Yancy 426
Zachariah . . 572, 576-578
Zachary Taylor . 409, 411, 420
Zacheriah 574
Zelma 427

Brazier/Brasher
John, V, ... 364

Brazier/Brasier
James 595
Brazier/Brassier
John M, III 360
Braziers
Belitha 587
Levin 587
William 587
Brazzer
Thomas T. 364
Breakiron
Gartright 249
Breckenridge
Emma R. 274
Breder
Christine 40
Breeden
Malinda Ellen 320
Brengle
Doris 122
Harold G. 122
Helen 122
Jacob Bruce 122
Mildred 122
Bresart
Henry 492
Breser
Breser 500
Diryck 500
Garret Hendrickson . . 502
Geesje 500
Henry 500
Henry, Jr 500
Machtelt 500
Martan (or Martha) . . . 500
Mary 500
Rebecca 500
Sara 500
Susanna 500
Willem 500
Bréser
Henry 492, 494
Susanna (née Walters) 499
Breshears
Aline 341
Atsy 312
Barbara Lynn 314
Christine Lori 315
Clora Elizabeth "Liz" . 341
Daisy 109
Doyle Neil 315
Earna R. 340, 341

Florence 109
Gertrude Ellen 109
Hardin 312
Helen 314
Ivan 314
James Robert 109
John 341
John Francis "Little Frank"
. . . . 313
John Wayne 314
John William 314
Juanita Mae 314
Julia Florence 109
Leonard Thomas 314
Lloyd Thomas 314
Lowell 315
Madison Golman 313
Margaret 110
Marion Lloyd 314
Perry Westerfield . . . 314
Ralph 315
Ralph Lee 341
William Arthur 312
William Lewis 109
Zephalinda 109

Bresher
Henry 502
Bresier
Susannah 497
Bresler
Stella Joan 140
Bresnehen
Morris 185
Bresser
Een (?Annie) 503
Hendrick "George" . . . 503
Meads 503
Brewer
Irene 412
Mike 411
Rita 412
Sophia Anna 474
Brézier
Henry 492
Briant
Emily Henry Josephine
. . . . 396
Brice
Bessie 121
Cutie Inez 121
Delcie 121
Elizabeth 121
James Roy 121

James Samuel 120
Lena 121
Zelma 121
Bridges
John W 68
John W. 68
John W. Jr 68
John W., Jr 68
Leonard Lisha 68
Lucy Adeline (Blythe) . 66,
68
Bridgewater
Nancy 125
William Leon 130
Briscoe
David 92
Jerry 92
John 117
Raymond 92
Thad A 117
Brisher
Abigail 505
Brisser
Joseph Isaac 504
Bristow
Emily 322
Samuel Houston 322
Britt
Harry Louis 555
Jo Marie 555
K.A. 555
Broadway
J. A. 564
Broak
Donna Jean 131
Brockell
Margaret 116
Brocus
Martha 304
Brook
Nell M. 139
Brooker
Bennett 321
Judy Lenora 321
Brooks
Charles 382
Donald Dean 315
Lowell 319
Martha "Patsy" 389
Brooksheare
Thomas Baker 129
Broom

Banner 290
Ora 290
Victoria 290, 291
Broughton
John 584
Broun
Keziah 522
Browder
Pearl 37
Sarah Emeline 331
Brown
Alice 429
Alta Fae 477
Amanda 415
America 449
Ann 477
Anna F 156
Anne 575
Barbara Louise 112
Bridgett Gail 416
Carl 79
Cathy Lanett 416
Celesta Jean 198
Chadley 415
Charles William 112
Cheryl Lucille 415
Clarence Lloyd 112
Clarinda 84, 97, 98
Corey 415
Debra Jo 416
Durand Levoyd 415
Elizabeth 272, 280
Elmer 63
Ephraim 525
Etta Lou 79
Evelyn Louise 559
Gary Dale 415
Gustavus 575
Harold 200
Homer Ben 112
Howard 429
Jeffery Glenn 416
Jerry Lee 59
Joe 119
Joseph 272
Julia Susannah 526
Keith Lee 59
Kenneth Harold 416
Keziah 525
Larry Duane 237
Louis 293
Luther William "Bill" . . 477
M.J. 418
Marie 67

622

Marshall 237
Mary 433
Mary Lillian 112
Matthew 415
Nancy 190
Norma Lee 200
Orien Ray 112
Raymond Rose 112
Rhonda Denise 416
Richard Alan "Rich" . . 234
Ruth 280
Solomon Albert "Jack"
. . . . 477
Tamara Lynn 237
Thomas 430
Vernie L. 415
Vernie L., Jr. 415
Vicki Jean 59
Viola Sue 477
William 97
William Elman "Bud" . 477
[Mary?] Jane 444

Browning
Chance 485
Kevin 484
Tiffany 484

Brukett
Charlie David 331

Brumfield
Debbie 558

Bryan
William 114

Bryant
Charlie 409
Daisy 42, 55
Fred Carter 235
Graem Kiernan 235
Jan Jacob 235
Kaela Leanne 235
Sheryl Lynn 60

Buckner
Brittania 158
Edward 158
Elizabeth (Fowke) . . . 578
Ellen 158
Emma 157
Francis 158
Hettie 158
James 158
James G 157
James G. 157
Louisa 158
Mary A. 158
Moses 157

Rachel 158
Rebecca 157
Retanna 157
Richard 157, 577
Richard I 157
Stephen 158
William 158

Bull
Laura 538

Bullis
Charles Alvin 424
Charles Lowell 424
David Arnold 424
Robert Wellington . . . 424

Bullock
Claudia Melissa 179
John Harrison 179
Lu Willie 179
Rebecca Ann 179
Robert Lewis 179
Valerie Chloe 179
William J. 179

Bumgarner
Henry 343

Bunbury
Anne 578

Burd
Margaret 281

Burdett
Sarah 575, 576, 578

Burge
Alyssa 41
Barbara Lua 40
Chad Ernie 39
Christopher Edwin . . . 41
Connor 41
David Kieth 39
Donald 39
Jerry Lee 41
John Paul 41
John Scott 41
Khristy Dawn 39
Michael Paul 39
Nonda Fay 40
Paul Dwight 39
Paul Steven 39
Tiffy 41
Tina Marie 39
Tyler Paul 39

Burgess
Charles R. 67
Garner 67

Burke

Holly 472
Burkett
Elizabeth 85, 118
Burks
Elijah, Jr 442
Janet 442
Janet Baker 448
William "Wiley" J. 442
Burleson
Henry 76
Burleyson
Rebecca "Becky" 40
Burning
Albert 63
Brad 63
Brenda 63
Sandra 63
Burns
Catherine 526
Nichodemus 220
Burris
Annette 203
Samira Ann 527
Burrough
Asher 587
Burroughs
Claudie 124
Sara Beth 124
Scott Alan 124
Shawn Christopher . . 124
Sheila Renee 124
Burrow
Minnie Lee 411
Burrows
John 164
Burrus
Isaac 168
Bush
Amanda Rebecca . . 458, 459
Baker Haskins 556
David Holmes 556
Jackson 459
Lena Marie Inez 142
Margaret Brashier . . . 556
Nicole Haskins 556
Butler
Elizabeth 35
Francis M 123
George 579
Martha 246
Myra V 123
Susan 168

623

Button

Minnie Elizabeth 314
Roy Horace 315
Walter Joseph 314
William Ralph 314

Byas

J.L. 391
Jack Lynn 391
Jana Lynn 391
Jason Lee 391
Shelly Nan 391
Steven Dale 391

Bybee

Leta May Button 314

Bynum

Bonita 169
Catherine Lee 169
Charlotte A 170
Daniel Cade 170
Debra Janet 170
Elizabeth 170
Elizabeth Rose 169
Elmer Graves 169
Eugene Warren 169
Glenna Faye 169
Gregg Richardson ... 169
Isham Richardson ... 168
Isham Richardson Jr . 169
Isham Richardson, Jr . 169
Janet Marleta 170
Jason 170
Jennine Marie 170
Jesse 441
John W 169
Joseph Payne 170
Karl Joseph 170
Kellianne 170
Kevin 170
Kurtis A 170
LaRita Fern 169
Linda 170
Mickey Charles 169
Paul J 170
Phillip Melvin 169
Ralph Edward 170
Randall J 170
Rocky Carl 169
Rose Ellen 169
Tammy Lee 170
Terry Lane 170
Tina Marie 169
Toi Lane 169
Trent Christopher 170
Vickie Jo 170

Byrd

Edna Earl 553
George Washington . . 267
Hugh Roberts 267
Joseph 267
Sophronia 266

Byrum

John E. 334

Byvanck

Eyert 520
Peter 520

Cabell

John 501
Sarah 501

Cade

Jeanette 552

Cadman

Diana Lynn 202

Cager

Dorothy xiv

Cagle

Aretha Lorraine 71
James Alexander 71
John J 71
Thomas Jefferson ... 71

Cain

James T. 301
Martha Francis 301
Stephanie Denise ... 210

Caldwell

Matilda Tea 121
Samuel R 98

Calhoun

Lucy A........... 39

Caliway

K.J. 544, 546

Callahan

Bob 478

Callan

Lloyd Jerome 179
Savannah Faith 180

Calloway

Benny 354
Elaine 354
Florence 350
James Blaine "J.B." . . 354
Jim 350
Karen 354
Michael 354
Mittie 454

Cameron

Alexander 509

Camp

Annie Naomi 244
Hosea 244
John 244
Margaret "Peggy" 244
Mary 244
Nathaniel 244

Campbell

Ada Mae 71
Daisey 91
Dylan Alexander 278
John 418
Johnathan Scott 278
Paula 38
Peggy Kathryn 29
Smith Alexander 71
Valta Lou 50

Cannon

Elizabeth 577
Grandison 577
Hester 519
John 577
Jonathan 577
Luke 577
Sarah Edith 577, 578

Canter

Ellen 348, 349

Cantrell

Franklin D. 226
Gary D. 226
Johnnie 419
Lisa D. 226
Sarah 419
T. Douglas 226

Capshaw

Janice 427

Carder

Blanche 140
Rachel 53

Cardwell

J. Osco 348

Carl

Kathryn 237

Carlile

Dan 30
Danielle 30
David 30

Carlson

Charissa E. 565
Dale 96
Fred Lars 433
Gustave Edwin, II ... 565
Gustave Edwin, III ... 565

624

Lauren A. 565
Mildred 433
Ray E. 242

Carlyle
Archie Logan 63
Bob Loren 63
Charles Edwin 63
Flossie Lillian 63
James 62
Myrtle Anna 63
Pleasant Garfield 62
William Loren 63
Zelma Irene 62

Carmack
Horace 273

Carman
Alma Ellen 185, 186
Annie Elizabeth 186
Elizabeth Eleanor . . . 186
Ella Louise 186
Emiley Alice 186
Isaac Newton 186
James Edward 186
James H. B. 185
Marcus Linus 186
Margaret Lee 186
Mary Jane 186

Carnell
Delores Faye 50
Jesse Warren, Jr 50

Carney
Betty 327

Carnline
Monette Lacy 23

Carpenter
Kenneth 64
Mary Johnette 558
N.F. 159
Ralph/Kenneth 64
William 159

Carr
Rita 21
Wm. B. 578

Carrel
Caroline 170

Carsteen
Betty Jo 237

Carter
Barbara Jean 49
Charles Earl 56
Cornelius 140
Earline 57
Orville 140

Ruth 344
Silas Adam 140
Will 57

Cartwright
Verna 179

Cary
Mattie May 380

Casaus
Casey Tye 404
Ernest J., Sr 404
Ernie J. 404
Montana Rose 404

Casey
Talitha 208
Wilma 430

Cash
Walter 223

Castellari
Alfred 45
Alice Marie 45
Shirley Ann 46

Castle
Artis Brandon 563

Caswell
Cassandra B. 473
Oma W 187
Oma W. 187
Sally 474
Velma 478
William 473

Cathey
Dorothy H. 293
Mary Ann Martin 292
Mary Lucinda 294
Mary Lucinda "Synda"
. . . . 292
Samuel Newton . 292, 294

Catryl
Frances Permelia . . 190,
303

Caughron
William 154

Cavin
Victoria 44

Cawthon
Nancy Annette 286

Cercelleo
Joe 558

Cerio
Frank Edwain 328
Krista Lauren 328

Chaffin

Ellie 45

Chalfant
Chilnissae J. 282

Chambers
Chester M. 55
Fredrick Leroy 55
Robert Chester 55
William Edward 55

Chandler
Anna 319
Job 575
Peter 266
Raymond 531

Chaney
Abbie 596

Chapman
Amy Brashear 236
Jessie 236
Mary Jane 167

Chappell
James 347
John 63

Cheeves
Bertha 415

Chenault
Henry 598
Rebecca 599
Rebecca B. 598

Cherry
T.F. 547

Chester
Brianna Renee 133
David 133

Childers
Lloyd 25

Childres
Lloyd 28

Childress
Helen 199

Christian
Sylvia 414

Chunn
Annie Elizabeth 272
John 272

Church
Alexander,IV 343
Alma 354
Aly Queen Esther . . . 347
Amelia 343
Annie Dora 346
Arthur 410
Bynum Lufate 346

Calvin Horace Greely 347
Caroline 343
Catherine 343
Christopher 354
Clyde Mathus 347
Coila Mae 346
Daniel Welborn Jones
. . . . 347
David 343
Edmund Call 346
Esther Maybelle 347
Fannie Ellen 346
Florence Deona 346
Gabriel 342, 343
Grover Cleveland 346
Harrison Henry 347
Harrison Loranso Dow
. . . . 347
Henry Harrison . . 344, 346
Ina 347
James Monroe 348
Joel M. 343
Jordon 343
Laura 347
Lena Mary 347
Levi Harrison 346
Lillian 347
Mae 347
Mary 354
Mary Idella 346
Michael 354
Nancy Elizabeth 347
Nettie 346
Ninnie 348
Rebecca Lou Ellen . . 347
Richard Hackette . . . 346
Robert 354
Robert Page 347
Ronald Lee 354
Sallie Clarissa Virginia
. . . . 347
Scott 354
Selena V. . . 344, 345, 347
Thomas Aaron 346
Thomas Mack 346
Walter Grady 346
Willard Vann 346
William John Wesley . 346
Willie 346
Winfield Scott Jr 347
Winfield Scott, Sr . . . 347
Winnie Mae 347
Winston 343
Zeb 347
Zora Camilla 347

Churchill
Eleanor 501
Robert 501
William 499, 501
Cisneros
Jody Lynn 401
Claggett
Samuel 575
Thomas John 575
Clark
Addie Pearl 558
Allie Joyce 558
Alvie 558
Barbara 420
Dorothy Elizabeth . . . 558
Dorothy Lea 228
Edward Carol 558
Elizabeth M. 76
Henry 490
Howard Dudley 380
J.D. 404
James Danville 558
James M. 418
Jenise Renee 22
John E. 76
Lynda Joy 420
Marcella 197
Melba Jeraldine 560
Mirtie 118
Napolian 76
Nattie 159
Nettie 159
Noah Gerald 65
Peggy Sue 228
Pharis C. 228
Pricilla Lynn 404
Rebecca F. 76
S. G. 159
Thomas 86
Tommy Eugene 558
Troy 558
Wallace 420
William Harold 558
William "Will" T 115
Clarke
Lucy 522
Clasper
Austin 40
MacKenzie 40
Tyron 40
Claus
Albert 280
Claxton
Freda Sue 144

Judith Ann 144
Noah 143
Otto Wilson 143
Clay
Henry 39
Clayton
Clara G 108
George W 112
Katherine "Kate" 108, 112
Stephanie 189
William Brasher 537
Cleghorn
Marriett 269
Clemens
Kristine Louise 234
Clements
Elizabeth Cornelia . . . 127
Clemons
Bessie 293
Clary 293
David 293
Florence 293
Harvey 293
James "Jimmie" 293
Katie 293
Margie 293
Mary 293
Nellie R. 293
Rachel "Dollie" 293
Samuel 293
William Penn 293
Clendenin
William 599
Cleveland
Artus J. 338
Clines
Pearl 236
Clinkenbeard
George 237
Clisson
Vondelle 550
Clossen
Gordon Vaughn 52
John Adams 52
Lisa Michele 52
Michael Vaughn 52
Michael Vaughn, Jr . . . 52
Nancy Jane 52
Sallie Ann 52
Clowe
Irene 67
Cluster

Mary Jane 119

Cobb
Robert 450
Ruth (Beshears) 352

Cobble
Jane 388
Terresa 388
William 386, 388

Cochrum
Jim 35

Cocke
Brazure 359
Elizabeth 359
Henry 359
James Powell 359
Mary 359
Thomas 357, 359
Thomas, Jr 359
William 357

Cockrell
Harold Merritt 551
Jane 551
John Arthur 551
John D. 551
John Eric 551
Karen 551
Leila Angela 551
Lillian Mae 551
Mary Elizabeth 551
Merritt 551

Cody
Cooleen 45

Coggins
William C. 412

Coke
H.F. 431

Coker
Cynthia 545, 556
Frances 550
Paul J. 550
Pauline 550

Colbert
Bradley Dewite 416
Caroline 473
Charles 416
James 466, 470, 472
James Samuel 472
John C. 473
Malissa 473
Martha 473
Solomon M. 473
Susan 473
Velina 473

William 473

Coldren
Jesse 282

Cole.
Walter 273

Coleman
Carrie Mae 94
Ethel Maudine 412
Hunt 97

Colevelt
Altje 500
Altje (Eleanor) 506
Eleanor Aaltje 509
Lawrence 500, 506

Colgate
Craig, Jr 517

Collier
Clara C. 229
Joseph 229
Kendall 586

Collins
George 167

Colton
Shiela 41

Combs
Alfred Washington . . . 312
Andrew Jackson 312
Charlie 136
Edward D. 312
Flora 287
James Alvery 287
Judy 136
Lindsey 286, 287
Malinda 287
Nancy 136
Norman 312
Watson W. 287

Compton
Ima Jean 310

Conn
Marc Glaspy 410

Conner
Bridget 365
Debbie 195
Judy S. 314
Rebecca 543
Sarah 59
William 585

Connoy
James 168

Conway
Nettie J. 331

Cook

Jesse Aaron 406
Pearl Elizabeth 66
Sanford D. 66

Cooksey
Edith 424

Cooledge
Nancy E. 339

Cooley
Annis 398

Coon
Michael 201
Nathan Tyler 201
Zachary Michael 201

Cooper
Antoinette "Nettie" . . . 458
Dylan Shawn 556
Eura Dell 403
Georgia 458
Hannah 593
Hollis 31
J. Louis 458
James 31
Leroy Nathaniel 458
Leroy Washington . . . 458
Lewis 458
Palmer 507, 508
Savannah Drew 556

Cooperrider
Sarah Catherine . . 35, 64
William 64

Copeland
Aaron Thomas 233
Deborah Renee 233
Gary Wayne 233
John Thomas 246
Matthew Allen 233
Melissa Ann 43
Mietta Dora 437
Mildred 246
Paul 43
Peggy 20
Peter Lee 233
Richard Allen 233
Rubecca Sue 233
Sarah Mary 246
Suzanna Michelle . . . 233
Wayne Carroll 233

Copelin
Alma 79
James Larkin 79

Copenhagen
Ronald Gene 230

Copley

Eula 417

Coranante
Theresa M. Beshears
. . . . 105

Cormick
Irene 49

Cornelison
John Calvin 480
Rebecca 472
Rebecca Frances . . . 480
Rhoda Cynthia Elizabeth
. . . . 476

Cornelius
Frances Pauline 414
William 415

Cornett
Bertha Rosalie 350
Bertie Leota 348

Cortlandt
Van 521

Cotner
Forest 335

Cotrell
Pat 208

Cottrell
Arthur Albert 211
Dawn Marie 211
Denise Mary 211
Eric Martin 211
Gail Louise 211
Pat 208
Timothy Scott 211

Couch
Mary Alice 392

Courtney
Bertha Irene 271

Cover
Clara 380

Cowan
Nicholas John 567

Cowden
Cordelia 116

Cowser
Ovena 418

Cox
Alexander 474
Byron 319
David Earl 132
Deborah Lynn 132
George Earl 132
Jane 506, 509
Josephine 474

Kenneth 319
Margaret Fanny 262
Mary Beth 234
Stanley William 234
Terrie Ann 132
W. 234
Whitney 132
William 319

Cox/Maybee
Mary Beth 234

Craft
Jane 224

Craig
Benjamin Davies Kortright
. . . . 518, 519
Samuel Davies . 518, 519

Crandall
C.J. 26
Clifton Wesley 26
Kyle 26
Lynnette 26
Russell 26
Teresa 26

Crane
Ada Mae 61
Elizabeth 343

Cravens
Owen 92

Crawford
Amanda E 115
Elizabeth 331
Ella Katherine 285
George 283, 285
Jennifer Leigh 565
John 421
Margaret 283
Sarah Josephine 476

Crayens
Edward Allen 53
James Edward 53
James Edward, Jr 53
Staci Lynn 53
Tammy Lynn 53

Craytor
Amanda Gail 23
Cody Wayne 24
Kyle James 24
Tracy Dean 23

Crear
Mary Louise 109
William 109

Creech
William 257

Creed
Dwight 57
Garry Earl 57
Garry Earl, Jr 57

Creek
Jeremy Shane 200
Jerry Wayne 200
Joshua Cameron 200

Crick
Sarah 33

Crippen
Debbie 41

Cronquist
Catherine Elizabeth . . 230
John 230

Crook
John Seldon 331
Josephine Maude . . . 331

Croom
Marta Beshears 17
Marta Gayle Beshears . 20

Cropper
William 587

Crosby
Jo Lynn 422
Sue Ann 422
William Robert 422

Crosnon
Anna (Brahears) 155
Elizabeth E 155
George T 155
George T. 155
L.C 155
Reuben L 155

Cross
Mary 248

Crosser
Karen Irene 44

Crow
Dorthary Brazier 444
Samuel Houston 265

Cruger
Emma 62

Crump
Frances Jeanette 390

Cruteson
Ricky 419

Cryer
Alice 322

Culmore
Albert 105
Albert, Jr 105

Geralynn 105
Lisa 105

Culpepper
Alma 564

Cummings
Peter S. 37

Cunningham
Cassandra Lynn 129
Selena 449
Tawni Leann 129
Wesley 201
Wesley Cole 201
William Elmer 129

Curry
Sarah "Sally" 329

Curtis
Francis 139
Ira M. 46
Nathaniel 519

Cutburth
Betty 91
Sandri Kay 398

Dailey
Barry David 24
James David 24
Vincent Eugene 24
Zoleta 92

Dake
Gertie Lula Alice 138

Dalby
John 503

Dalton
Debra Lyn 45
Jno 508

Daly
Abraham, III 535
Elizabeth 514, 535
Philip 514, 535

Damiano
Jeffrey Alan 232
Robin Marie 232
Ryan 232

Damron
Lucille 431

Daniel
Ava 554
Emeline 76
Febe 409
John J. 409
Mary Louise 401
Tom 409

Darnell

Edna Florence 110
Edwin Lawrence 110
Ernest 110
Fount L 110
Gracie 408
James W. 408
Jim 408
John 408
Laura L. 408
Martha 409
Mary 409
Sam 408
Sarah A. 409
Susan P. 408
W. L. "Billy", Jr 408
W.L. "Will" "Billy" 408

Darrington
Lawrence 269

Dash
Elizabeth 503

Daugette
Ann 413

Daugherty
Emily Elizabeth 201
Jordan Michael 201
Timothy 201
William 266

Davidson
Ada 283
Amos W. 283
Anna 282
Elizabeth 280, 282
Haddie 282
Jacob 282
Jacob and Mary 280
John H. 281, 282
Kate 282
Lou 282
Mary 282

Davis
Aaron Mitchell 133
Anne 83
Arthur 445
Bettie Jan 456
Bruce 558
Carrol 550
Christi Lynn 61
Darren Paul 61
Darri Clifton 61
Debra Nell 61
Donald Ray 61
Donya Dee 61
Douglas Arthur 61
Edmund L. (or J. or T.)

. . . . 458
Elizabeth 239
Eva Mae 456
J. Wiley 456
John T. 348
John Thomas 155
Karis Nicole 133
Lewis 362
Linda Jean 49
Louisiana 208
Luther Wesley 456
Marsha 555
Natalie 26
Paul Ray 60
Ray 60
Robert 360, 361
Thomas 246
Zachariah 590

Dawson
Emma 285
Fyrn 315

Day
Elizabeth 64
Ellia 55
Sarah Frances 35, 53
William T. 53

De Voe
Jannet 506

Deadmond
Belle 57
Brenton Keith 60
Brian Wayne 61
Briana Kay 60
Calila Mae 61
Charles 65
Clifford 59
Dalene 57
Darrell Leroy 60
Darrus Eugene 60
David Allen 61
Dean 65
Delores Fern 59
Donna Ellen 61
Dwight 65
Edna Ruth 54
Everett E. 64
Floyd 65
Gail Dee 59
Garry Dean 59
Hershel Dean 59
Ira 64
Irwin Dale 65
Isabelle 64
Ivan Lynn 59

Jefferson 55
John 64, 65
Joseph 64
Joseph E. 64
Joseph Oscar 59
Karen Rae 60
Kevin Wayne 60
Larkin 65
Lillian Dell 65
Linnie R. 57
Lovell Lynora 59
Marnell Elaine 61
Matthew Dirk 61
Michael Lawrence 60
Mitchell Allen 61
Myrtle F. 55
Phyllis Maxine 60
Rebecca Lynn 60
Richard Lee 60
Richard Lee, Jr 60
Roger Keith 61
Samuel Allen 57
Steve 58
Steven 60
Tammy Lea 60
Wilson 64

Dean
Dana 283
Elnora 270
James 63
Mary Jane 456
Michelle 283
Patience Anna (Marshall)
. . . . 269
Thomas B. 269

Deatch
Bradley 93
Dawn 92
Mike 92

DeBoer
William Ray 47

DeBusk
Bessie Inez 25, 29

Dedwylder
Charles 554
Thomas "Luke" 554

DeFoer
Jannet 506

Deike
Helen Ruth 160

Delany
Daniel 586

DeLarue

Ella Dora 255

Deming
Tammie Wood 247

Dempsey
Allison Faith 197
Amanda Hope 197
Betty 194, 205
Chloe Marie 197
Donald 196
Karen Elizabeth 197
Timothy Dunn 196

Dennis
Lowell Wallace 226
Lowell Wallace, Jr . . . 226
Sandra Denise 226

Denniston
Ann 119
Jane 119

Dent
William 575

Denton
Barbara 198
Dawn 198
Dona 198
Frieda 198
Gene Edward 198
James 198
Lorene 198
Ruby 198
Simon, Jr 198
Simon, Sr 198
Steve 198
Summer 198

Denty
Sebrina Kay 412

DePeyster
William 515

DeVoe
Jannet 509

Dial
Deborah 374
Robert 375
Shadrach 375

Dickson/Dixon
Edward R. 394

Dieckhoff
Colby 341
Jordan 341
Shanna 341
Tim 341

Diehl
Elisabeth Regina Anna
. . . . 130

Diggs
Alfred H. 271

Dike
Martha E. 172

Dillon
William A. 478

DiLoreto
Anthony John 553
Daniel Anthony . . . 553
Joseph Daniel . . . 553

Dinwiddie
Elizabeth 576, 577
Lawrence 577
Robert 577

Dishman
Dale Hullett 226
Ella Mae 226
Florence Earlene . . . 226
Harvey Lee 226
Harvey Neil 226
Hubert 226
Hubert Mack 226
Hulett 225
Hulett, Jr 226
Huronica Katherine . 226
Jimmy Ray 226
Leroy 225
Linda Ann 226
Mary Alice 226
Patsy 226
Russell L 226

Dix
James Hobert 42
Joshua Leon 42
Sydney Jean 42

Dodson
Catherine Annette . . . 402
Chad Kynor 397
Margaret 464

Domer
Daisy Ellen 253
John 253

Donley
J.B. 600

Donoho
Brad Andrew 59
Brett Alan 59
Ethel 60
Janice Leight 59
Tulley Andrew 59

Dooley
Charles 551
Gertie 137

Kimberly Jill 551
Regina Kay 551
Dooly
Etha Pearl 340, 341
Dorland
Edith 179
Dorsey
Frank 239
Henrietta 239
Kate Winder 239
Lucy Sprigg 239
William Roderick 239
William Roderick Jr . . 239
William Roderick, III . . 239
Dotson
Cody 93
Jerry 93
Mary Ellen 93
Pauline 395
Sandra J. 413
Shanna 93
Doucette
Mona Jean 170
Reno 170
Douglas
Jane 383
Dow
Heather Michelle 212
Ian Matthew 212
Matthew Daryl 212
Mel 212
Dowdy
Albert 600
Horace 598
John T. 600
Lucy Ann 600
Shirley 598, 600
Shirley P. 600
Dowell
Mary 247
Dowler
Harold G. 274
Downey
Hazel 320
Dowthard
Elizabeth 442, 443
Doyd
Reba 62
Doyle
Agnes 103
Alan Lynn 404
Carline 324
Jennifer JaNeal 405

Ronald Melvin 404
Shawna Renee 405
Stacy Leann 404
Draper
Tom 201
DuBose
Julius 160
DuFooer
Jannet 509
Dugan
Henry 524
Dugger
Clara Ann 310
Duggins
Micajah "Cage" 339
Duncan
Dale Calvin 23
Kaitlynn 23
Kim Ellen 23
Kristen 23
Richard 23
Dunford
Anna Elizabeth . 108, 109
Dunlap
Alex 505
Dunn
Betty Jane 196
Grecia 196
Harold Wayne 196
John Albridge 196
Sherri 196
Thomas Jackson 196
Durm
Ashley Brianna 438
Billy Norris 437
Billy Troy 438
Gregory Allen 438
Justin Troy 438
Durrell
David C. 380
Dutton
Jo Ann 129
Duvall
Alexander 248
Dvorak
Pauline Utterback . . . 257
Dyer
John William 185
Dyke
Cathalyntje 508
Dyks
Cathalyntje ?Catharine

. . . . 507
Dyson
Nancy 188
Eades
Paulina 110
Eakright
Alexander Blake 96
Jeff 96
Logan Steven 96
Victoria Nicole 96
Earl
Patricia Ann Beshears
. . . . 105
Earle
Abigail 506
Abigail (Brasher) 507
Henry Brasher . . 507, 508
Morris 506, 507
Easten
Evelyn Martha 47
Easterling
Henry 543
Mintie 543
William 543
Easterwood
Wanda Annette 412
Eastman
Carolyn 62
Eathridge
Mary Sue 194, 197
Eberhard
Ester 48
Echoles
Mary Clair 566
Eddington
George 159
Edwards
Clarence 292
Cynthia Dian 401
Douglas 96
Gary Dean 401
Gladys 325
Macon 463
Mary 63
Mattie (Hamilton) . . . 326
Nancy 463
Sarah Alice 559
Steven Andrew 401
Egenbacker
Clay 485
Cy 485
Eggerton

Caroline 545
George 545
John 545
Mary A. 545
Sallie J. 545
Silas 544
Wilson 545

Eilbeck
Ann 214

Eish
Barbara 45

Eisnmann
Bernard 48
Ronnie 48

Elam
Allie 563
Leila Pearl 563
Leila Pearl (or Lula) .. 562

Elder
Katherine Beshears ... 90

Eliot
John 492

Elkins
Louise 416

Elledge
Betty 93
George L. 93
George, Jr 94
Jackie 93
John 93
Millie 93
Sandra 93

Eller
Finley A. 345

Elliott
Ellen Elaine 553
George 92
Herbert Eugene 553
Jacki Diana 553
Jane Ann 553
Jesse Bryan 553
Jesse Bryan "Jack" .. 553
John Herbert 553
Joni Patricia 553
Patti Gayle 553

Ellis
Elmer 91
Elmer S. 91
Greg 91
Samuel 194
Sarah Jane   193-195, 197,
204
Susan 91

Elliston
Lucy Mary Ann 474

Elmore
Janice Paulette 226
Paul 226

Ely
Alice 118

Elzea
Alta M. 120
Jesse 120

Embry
Steven D. 434
Steven D., Jr 434

Emerson
Calvin Ray 132
James Mark 132

Endris
Deborah Kathryn 22

Engessler
Pete 331

England
Esther 226
Leonard 139
Sue 139

Eoff
Ada Mae 319
Delores June 319
Donna Jean 319
Dorothy Lois 319
Ida E. J. "Myrtle" 319
Robert Nelson 319
William Ellsworth 319
William Sanford "Jake"
.... 318, 319
William "Sandford" ... 318
William "Sanford" ... 317,
319

Epling
Amber McKay 200
Caleb Patrick 200
Patrick 200

Epperson
Anthony 91, 92
Bert 91
Eugene 91
Franklin 91
Garnett Lee 92
James 91
Joe W. 90, 92
Martha Beshears 91
Richard Lee 91
Robert 91
Roy 91

William 91
William Edward Huck .. 92

Ernst
Ivyline Ann 43

Estes
Ed Hill 310
Otis 198

Etchison
Carolyn Brashers 275

Etheridge
Mildred 412

Ethridge
Anna 312

Eubanks
Chaste C. 244
Chester Lafayette ... 244
Drewry Alvin 244
Drewry Lyman 244
John D. 135
Nancy 135
Nina Agnes 179

Evans
Albert Stanley 431
Alma Louise 406
Barbara Jean 437
Becky Diane 432
Bertha C. 406
Bessie Edith 111
Beulah Ethel 111
Carl, Jr 431
Carol Virginia 438
Clarence I. 406
Cora Elizabeth 431
Cora I. 406
Della Jo(sephine?) ... 438
Donna Almeda 406
Effie Vergie 432
Elizabeth Mariah 119
Emma Elizabeth 430
Fannie 115
Felix Carl 431
Fern Almeta 123
Francis Marion 111
Harry Clyde 437
Harvell 430
Ida Rosalee 431
Isaac C. 405
Jack B. 528
James Carroll 405
James W. 431
John C. 409
John William 430
Joseph Stanley 432
Josie Lou 417

632

Laura Bell 430
Lola Z 114
Lucy Josephine 406
Lucy Louraney 430
Lyndal 431
M. Roy 417
M.C. 78
Mark Allen 432
Mary Charlotte "Lottie"
. . . . 389, 406
Mary Myrtle Joyce . . 431,
432
Ova Ruth 437
Paul Allen 438
Paul Benn 111
Paul, Jr 438
Pauline 417
Philip Dale 432
Robert Renegar "Bob"
. . . . 431, 436
Susan 57
Thelma 431
Verna 320
Vicki Lee 438
W. Jake 432
Walter 547, 586
Walter Jackson 431
William Arthur 406
William Henry 110
William Jacob "Jake" 410,
430
William Joseph 549
William Stanley 430

Everett
Rani Deanne (Clayton)
. . . . 277
Sarah A. 267

Everidge
Mary 285

Evilsizer
Jeanetta 44

Eynaud
Betty Martha 529

Fairchilds
Alice Lorine 347
Emma Parlee 391

Fairfax
Mary Ann 574

Fanning
Malvenia Idee 428

Fant
Bobbie 42

Farley

Margaret Mary 210
Farmer
Carol Ann 51
Clara 269
Dana 392
Diane 392
Kimberly Lynne 51
Lee 51
Mark Douglas 51
Melissia 392
Michael Roy 51
Nathan Douglas 392
Raymond 392
Sharon Lee 51
William James 51

Farr
George 562

Farrar
John 249
Katherine Watson . . . 249
Mary Watson 249
William Watson 249

Farrell
Ida Brasher 528
James Madison 528
John Wilson 528
William Price 528

Farrow
Alvah Howard 249
Howard Watson 250
Marion Stratton 250

Farrugia
Cory Paul 566
Molly Elizabeth 566

Farthing
Oscar 62

Faulconer
Nan (Carlisle) 296

Faulk
Janet 304

Faulkner
Ezekiel 466, 470, 472
Joe E. 273
Joe T. 273
Judith Ann 273
Kaye Don 273
Lucinda 472
Mary Jane 472
Sarah E. 472
Thomas F. 472
William W. 472

Fauntleroy
Sally Conrad 242

Fears
Benjamin M. 479
Bill J. 471
Charles 479
Elias 470
George W. 479
Henry A. 479
Jesse 479
Joe 467
Johnathan Elijah 470
Joseph 479
Joseph Henry . . 471, 478
Lorenzo D. 479
Thomas W. 470
Tom 466
William May 478

Featherstone
Walker 124

Fechtler
Patricia Marie 54

Feeback
Jeri 327

Feihel
Barbara 353

Felgenhauser
Stephen Joseph 39
Steven Michael 39

Felkins
Letha Gladys 79

Feltner
Baxter J. 287
Cleda Mae 287
Fred Lonadean 287
Marcus W. 287
Robert Alvin 286
Robert Alvin, Jr 287
Roy Allen 287
Royal Francis 287

Felty
Brett E. 38
Danielle 38

Fenn
Doyle 182

Ferriel
Esther Carrol 139
Joyce Dorene 139
Loman 139
Wilda 139

Ferry
Frank Marshall 232
Kimberley Ann 232
Kristopher M. 232

Fickbohm

Alexander Save 233

Fields
Maude Armstrong . . . 410

Fike
Esther L. 120
Leonard Hamilton . . . 120
Thomas F. "Tom" 120

Finckbone
Devin Clay 56
Mindy 56

Finger
Vicki 144

Finnie
Andrew John 230
John Irwin 230
Scott Charles 230
Sean McIlwain 230

Finnin
Annie Laurie 549

Fisher
Dana Louise 380
Edward C. 380
Richard Wayne 380
Vicki Lee 42

Fishler
Connie 24

Fisk
Carole 139

Flanders
Elizabeth 289

Flatt
James 220

Fleming
Marsha 564

Fletcher
Harry 290
Jim 75
Leslie 289

Floweree
Ella N 119

Flowers
Clara Roberson 127

Floyd
John 331

Flynn
Gordon 111
Judy Elizabeth 396

Folt
Wilbur 62

Foltz
Donna Mae 63
Robert 63

Wanda Faye 63

Fonden
Arthur Olaf 232
Maxwell Arthur 232

Ford
Adella B 86
Andrew Jackson "Jack"
. . . . 394
Belle 87
Benjamin Eagleton . . . 87
Benjamin Thomas 85
Brian Lee 404
Burt 86
Carol Ann 404
Claudius C 86
Curtis James 403
Dalton Clay 404
Daniel Boone 87
Dean Allen 404
Dustin Lee 404
Ella R. 87
Emily J. 87
Emma Netta 87
Ida May 87
James Leroy 403
Jimmy Noble 405
John D 87
John or Jonathan . . 86, 87
John Steele 87
Karen Beth 405
Katherine 87
Kimberly Lynn 404
Laura 87
Levi 403
Mary 87
Matthew Ryan 405
Patricia 26
Purlina Margaret 87
Renore "Nora" 86
Roy 87
Stephen F 86
Thomas Ray 88
Timothy 85-87
Travis Shane 404
William "Willie" A. 87

Forrester
Philip 310

Foster
Ambrose 300, 301
Janet 200
Marcus D. LaFayette . 301

Fouts
Kathryn Marie 22

Foutz

Elizabeth 327

Fowke
Adam 575
Ann 577
Anne 575
Catherine 575
Chandler 575-577
Chandler, Jr 577
Elizabeth 574-578
Frances 575
Gerard 575-577
Gerard, Jr . 575, 576, 578
Jenny 576, 577
John 576, 577
Mary 575
Richard 576, 578
Robert Dinwiddie . . . 576,
577
Roger 575-577
Sarah 577
Susanna 578
Thomas 576, 577
William 576-578
William Chandler 577

Fowler
Arthur James 180
Effie J. 173, 174
John Albert 180
Margaret Evelyn 180
Mary 336
Mary F. 473
Robert Alex 180
Ron 178, 180
Thomas W. 35

Fox
Joseph Oscar 132

Frame
Ophelia 430

Francis
Henry 358
Ileene 29
Sheryle Ann 329

Frank
Clara 46
Madgalena 209, 210
William H. 268

Franklin
Melissa 414

Frazier
Carol Simone 413
Emma 323

Freeman
Alice 181

Benjamin 181
Ella 181
Gabriel 181
Gabriel M . . 163, 164, 181
Jemima 181
L.J 163
Marina 181
Myrtle 181
Samuel 181
Sterling 181
Freeze
John Scott 552
Freund
Shauna Rosanne 433
Thomas 433
Frey
Frederick 209, 210
Mary Louise 209, 210
Friel
Shirley Phillips 349
Friend
Elizabeth 338
Frimel
Carmen E. 61
Christie 58
Danty Eugene 61
Denesise Ellen 61
Kenton Ellis 61
Frost
Joseph 386
Frothingham
Esther 591
Fry
Albert Burl 312
Marjorie Glee 139
Maymie Glee 139
William Adam 139
Fugason
Paul Elmer 230
Susan Joann 230
Fugate
Mayoma 286
Fulcher
Mary Sargent 204
Fuller
Bette 433
Eva Della 245
Hattie Pearl 66
Fullerton
W.A. 323
Fulton
Richard S 136

Richard S. 136
Fultz
Lola Jane 137
Gaines
Elizabeth 194
Gallion
Martha 166
Galloway
Everett 120
Gant
Marcina 38
Gantt
Elizabeth 575
Emily Amy 548
Garber
Betty 228
Garberg
Paul J 111
Gardner
George M. 394
Garfield
Waymon 413
Garland
Patricia 105
Garmon
Cheryl Lynn 200
Eugene 200
Marsha 200
Garner
Eugene 142
Faye 229
Lyle 142
Morgan 387
Walter 142
Zelma 142
Garoutte
Frances 222
Garren
Fern 56
Garret
Sarilda Jane 268
Garris
Dorothy 431
W.B. "Bee" 431
Garrison
Aliene Marjory 226
Bobby Lee 226
Carolyn Sue 227
David Hough 227
Della Maxine 226
Dickey Ray 400
Ed 226

Joshua 226
Kelly 226
Larry Neil 227
Mural 200
Norma Jean 227
Pamela Sue 227
Ruth Ann 227
T.J. 159
Terry Lorane 226
Torri Jean 227
Gary
Zora Addie 78
Gasherie
Judith 512
Stephen 512
Gee
Creda Joy 390
D.L. 390
Darmond Legue 390
Leva Maxene 390
Lloyd Wade 390
Mark Anthony 390
Marvin Leon 390
Shelby Larry 390
Shelby Leon 390
Terron Douglass 390
Gehl
Natalie Farrow 250
Geis
Marilyn Sue 23
Geissmann
Noel 300
Gelder
Annatye Van 505
Gelvin
Diane 391
Donald 391
Mike 391
Geneau
Liza Jane 335
Gentle
John 374
Gentry
Emily Tennessee Bivens
. . . . 283
George
Billie 136
E.W. 419
Francis J 136
Frank L. 457
George Rea 136
Joe 324
John 46

Matty 136
Mimi 136
Olivette M 136
Robert Lee 136
Ted 46

Gibbons
Virginia Gail 139

Gibbs
Vivian 58

Gibson
Cordelia (Ashford) . . . 326
Mary Ann 280
Mary Varnon 549
Susan Ann 292, 294

Gilbert
Ann 534
Margaret Jane 80
Mary Alice "Allie" 80
Moses 80
William 534

Giles
Alva G. 379
Georg 361
John 361

Gilliam
Nina 445

Gillihan
Jas 505

Gillihen
Jas 515

Gilliland
Robert 214

Ginger
Deana 212

Githers
Carolyn 51

Glass
Elizabeth 525
Lewis Keith 477
Phyllis Irene 549

Glenn
Hattie 53

Glover
Eddie 92
Lyal 484

Goddard
Genevieve 436
Judy 203

Godfrey
Willie Frances 435

Godman
Sarah 250

Godweiss
George 519
George, Jr 520

Goe
Mary 247
Phillip 247
William, II 247

Goeke
Karen Sue 39

Goetch
Anna 433

Goetz
Angelea Christine 27
Brandel Lee 27
Donnie 27
Dorothy 328
Jason Lee 27

Goins
Jeanne Lucille 403

Gold
Martha 170

Golden
Lenore 256
Martha Julia "Pink" . . . 71

Gomez
Paulie 404

Gonser
Amanda Lynn 52
Brenda 52
Cinthia Alien 52
David 51
Frank Arthur 52
Gloria Jean 51
Larry Junior 51
Patricia Louise 52
Roy 51
Sandy June 51

Goodnight
Susanna J. 76

Goodrich
Mary Ann 404
Thomas 64

Goodwin
Francis 560
James 551
Margaret Blanche . . . 551
Robert Eugene 551
Robert Eugene, Jr . . . 551
Ronald 551

Gordon
Everett L. 92
Jane 92
JoAnn 92

Johnny 92
William Everett 92

Gore
Eric Wayne 113
Fannie 115
Judy 392
Lee 113
Lisa Ellen 113
Melaney Lee 113

Gorton
Brian 105
Frances 105
Kathleen 105
Matthew 105
Michael 105
Roland 105
Ronald 105
Stephan 105
Timothy 105

Goss
Dorothy 183

Grabbert
Dorothy 435

Grable
James F. 282

Graham
J T 441
John W. 557
Mary 501
Shirley 185, 187
Tabitha "Betha" 339

Grammer
Annie Lee 408
Gracie 408

Grant
Alice 430
Ann 496
Bruce 430
Ethan Nicholas 233
Frank 430
Gracie 430
Herman 429
Margie 430
Martha 496
Mary 430
Mary Dell 429
Ray 430
William 429

Grantham
Maude 165

Graven
Christi Lynn 196
James Ellis 196

Jennifer Elaine 195
William 195
William Robert, II 195
Graves
   Anne Marie 232
   Banner 388
   Danielle Nicole 232
   Fred Austin 232
   George W. 388
   Joseph 387
   Joseph F. 388
   Karen Elaine 232
   Martha C. 388
   Martha Jane 388
   Randall Keith 232
   Sandra Kay 232
   Sarah Odessa 232
   Thompson Wesley . . . 388
   William Dean 232
   William Joe 393
Gray
   Catherine Elizabeth . . 409
   Elizabeth Givens 98
   Elsie 338
   J.N. "Ike" 409
   James Cullen "Jim" . . 409
   John Shelby 409
   Lucy 409
   Mary Frances 409
   Mattie 409
   Michael Neal 235
   Rufus King 429
   Sally 243
   Samuel Riley 98
   Sarah 252
   Virginia "Jennie" . 409, 416
Graybeal
   Eve Adel 50
   Rachel Corrine 50
   Ronnie Lester 50
   Samuel Earl 50
   Sarah Elizabeth 50
Green
   Bama Whitney 310
   Cynthia 77
   Emma Jane 38
   Karen Sue 133
   Laura 350
   Laura Ann 348
   Margaret 61
   Martha 347
   Mary Francis 72, 78
   Nancy 283, 285
   R.H. 493

William A. 79
Greene
   Andrew William 233
   Charles A. 296
   Richard Lynn 233
Greenlee
   Abe 466
   Abel "Abe" 471
Greenway
   Evelyn Marie 256
Greer
   Benjamin 344
   Elizabeth 344
   Zackery 348
Gregory
   Fern 118
   Halley 90
   Halley M. 90
   James P 114
   Marvin 293
   Mary Jane 114
Gresham
   Mary 228
Gribble
   Bill 418
Griffey
   Eliza 66
Griffin
   Eliah 364
   Evelyn 226
   John 363
   Larkin 344
Griggs
   Anna Pauline 123
   Arthur Bryan 122
   Carson "Carsie" 122
   Charles M. 123
   Charles Vaughn 122
   Claude Vincil 122
   Joseph Hurley 122
   Joseph Newton 122
   Lucy Bell 123
   Mollie Pearl 122
   N.J 115
   Newton 122
   Rex 124
   Roxie May 122
   Ruth 115
Grill
   Ann 358, 359
   Jonathan 359
Grimes
   Fannie 416

Minnie 143
Grissom
   Martha H. 300
   Martha Helen 296
   William 296, 300
Groff
   Ruth Amanda 41
Groove
   John 490
Grote
   Ashley Clair 566
   Fred Rankin 566
   Fred Rankin, Jr 566
   Fred Rankin,III 566
   Gwendolyn Louise . . . 566
   Nancy Ann 566
Grubb
   Mary 593
Grubbs
   Sallie 340
   Terra 226
Guffey
   Danza Raye 397
Guinn
   Mattie 272
Gunn
   Thelma 418
Gurley
   Fannie Jane 473
Gustini
   Sarah 595
Guthrey
   G.P. 323
Guthrie
   Mary E. 291
Guy
   Emily Caroline 330
Gwaltney
   Harriet Durham 378
   Rebecca A. 379
Hacker
   Mary Elizabeth 265
Hackett
   Charles 347
Hackwood
   Benjamin 586
Hackworth
   Neil 391
   Nell 391
Hadden/Madden
   Elizabeth 300
Hadlen

Charles 232
Dorothy Theresa 232

Hadley
Jon Scott 422
Kristen Leigh 422
Lesley 422
Robin Gayle 422

Hafley
Gwen Ann 48
Kyle 48
Marilyn Kay 48
Michael 48
Richard 48

Hagwood
William 246

Hahesy
John 173

Haig
William 362

Haight
Dodie 181

Haigler
S.E. 557

Hail
Nancy 476

Haile
Eliza Maude 46

Hailes
Belle 547, 548
Elizabeth 548
J.A. 548
Jefferson A. 548
Jeptha A. 548
William S. 548

Hair
Earl 196
Ethan Michael 196

Hale
Charles N. 501
Donald Eugene 396
Mary Sherwood 501
Tracey LaDon 396

Haley
Betty 30
Colton David 30
Dallas Lee Ann 30
Robert Lee 30
Ryan Haley 30
Sean Lee 30
Virgil Ray 25, 30
Virgil Ray, Jr 30

Hall

Benjamin 519
Birdie 430
Carlton 227
Emily 519
Fitch 519
Fitch, Jr 519
Helen 519
Jeffrey David 227
Jo Ann B. 464
Lee Curmon 416
Ralph F. 464
Stephanie Lynn 416
Thomas 416
William 519

Hambleton
Edward 262
Elizabeth 262
Margaret 262
Sarah 262
William 262

Hamblin
JoAnn 247

Hamby
Cheryl 354
Rufus 349

Hamilton
Alda H. 549
Hester Ann 597
Lockhard A. 597
Virginia 438

Hammer
Laura 185

Hammond
Edward 587

Hammonds
John, Jr 141

Hancock
Donnie 41
Elizabeth Clare 379
Michael Allen 41

Handleman
Shelly 136

Hanley
Ester Jewel 58

Hannah
Ilah 429

Harbin
Elizabeth 319

Hardenbrook
Catherina 502
Garadus, Jr 508

Hardin

Mary Ann "Molly" 257

Harding
Peter 109

Hardy
John 362
Madaline 55

Hargett
Mable Maxine 43

Hargis
Leona 403
Tresa Marie 404

Hargrove
Doris 563

Harley
Debora Kay 52
Jason Lee 52
Linda Diane 52
Randal Todd 52
Raymond Edward 52
Raymond Edward, Jr . . 52
Stephen Craig 52
Susan Rae 52

Harmacek
Danica Louise 30

Harmon
Cora Elizabeth "Corky"
. . . . 297
Deanna Carole 297
Julia Mae 60
Larry Ronald 297
Virgil Kenneth 296

Harper
Phyllis Jean 58

Harrell
Ashlie Layne 329
Richard Todd 328
Thomas 328
Travis 201

Harris
Carie Irene 236
Clyde Colman "Cole" . 400
Dora 254
Earlene 82
Eunice Rozanna 298
Geraldene 82
Jack L. 201
Joyce 427
Juanita 62
Lee Ann 201
Lena 57
Mike Alan 404
Tracy Linn 201
William Estell 400

638

William Taylor "Tye" . . 400

Harrison
Mary 577
Rebeckar 586
Susan Catherine 453

Hart
Amy C. 212
Elizabeth 242
Ellis 110
James 470
Wayne 242
William 265

Hartis
Brenda 425
Roland 425

Hartley
Gertrude Maresca . . . 210

Hartzog
Fannie Pearl 354

Harvey
Arnold 433
Brandon Joseph 434
Brian Eugene 434
Clara Catherine 249
Colleen Joy 434
Dawn Lindsay 434
Deborah Marie 434
Elizabeth 250
Emily Marie 434
Holly Ann 434
Jessica Leeann 434
Joseph Michael 434
Larry Lynn 434
Larry Lynn, Jr 434
Mariah Irene 434
Nicole Marie 434
Rosanna 24
Sara Ann 434
Steven Arnold 434
Terry Lee 434
Thomas 249
Travis Scott 434
Trumaine Charles . . . 434
William Brian 434

Harwell
Martin 550
William H. 270

Hastings
Margaret 118

Haughton
Parmelia Hannah 453

Hawk
Nora 139

Hawkins
Hannah 245
John 245
Rebecca J. 570

Hawley
Jeanine 39

Hawthorne
Glenn S. 435
Joy Lane 435

Hayden
Bryan 86
Byrd 121
Carol 413
Claude 86
Elladee 121
Emily V. 86
Etta Elizabeth 86
Garnet 86
Garrett 86
George E. 86
Gilbert 121
Gloyd 87
Ida May 86
James 121
Joseph Leo 86
Lucinda Ann 266
Maggie Belle 86
Mamie 86
Marshall 87
Mattie Lena 86
Mattie Lucy 87
Ruby 121
Ruby Davis 86
Sarah Ada 86
Sarah Gertrude 86
Tuie 86
Virgil 86
William Green 86
William J. 86
Woodson 86
Zoron (or Zora) P. . . . 86

Hayes
Benjamin David 235
Billy Michael 234
Billy Michael, Jr 235
Bonnie Adele 235
Carolyn 419
Danny 199
Otis 555
Sherry 199

Hayms
Sarah 525

Hays
Adam 574

Alexander 574
James Woodsen 328
John 574
Julie Ann 328
Martha 117
Nathaniel 574
Robert 574
Steven James 328
Terry Gay 328
Tracey Helen 328

Hayzlip
Bertha Rachel 160
Dorotha 160
Edith A. 160
Goldie 160
Juanita 160
Minnie Rosette 160

Hazard
Edward Judkins 292
Olivia Kensington 292

Hazelwood
Martha 388
Nancy 123
Perlina A.E. (?Elizabeth)
. . . . 407

Hazlewood
Perlina A. E. 388

Healy
Virginia 519

Hearn
Bryan Davis 555
James Christopher . . 555
James Christopher, Jr
. . . . 555
Memri Dell 555

Hegemon
Jacob 509

Heinig
Ciera Elizabeth Abbot
. . . . 328
Gerald Thoman 328

Henderson
Homer Durl 315
John H. 274
Winnie Doris 131

Hendon
David 453

Hendricks
Toni 203

Hendricksson
Geesje 500
Herman 500

Hendrix

Alice Margaret 118
Frank Conn 118
Hiram J. "Jack" 118
Leona Bell 118
Lloyd Trammell 118
Mary 118
Noah Trammell 118
Ruth Hendrix 118

Henry
Gerald 79

Hensley
Lens W. 138
Michael 56
Peggy 56
Walter Rexall 56

Henson
Cathy Elaine 415
Virginia 412

Hentzi
Bill 314

Hepler
Sherry Kay 429

Hepner
Aubrey Jane 199
David James 199

Herrean
Mort 339
Pinky 339
Simon 339

Herrin
Sarah "Sallie" 69
Sarah "Sally" 31, 69

Herrington
Cynthia Dynethea . . . 558
Delores Sue 558
Gurchia Mildred 559

Herzing
Mike 38

Hester
Anna 265
Churchwell 270
Elizabeth 265
Louisa 270
Margaret 271
William 265

Hiatt
Laura 185

Hibbens
Kate 528
Willie 528

Hickman
Charlotte 209
Franklin 209

Helen 209
James 267
Jesse 585
Selby 585
Timothy 267

Hicks
James G 87
Raymond Earl 296
Terry Lee 23
Timothy Lee 23

Hickson
Sarah J. 267

Higdon
Carolyn 340
Carolyn A. 340
Malcolm 340

Higgenbotham
Tracy Lynn 50
Ydona 50

Higgins
Darla 552

Highfill
Melvina 136

Hill
Benjamin 48
Clayton 112
Elizabeth 244
Fannie 445
James M. 112
John 244
Lance Travis 235
Mary Kathryn 48
Opal 430
Sandra Kay 48
Sarah Jane "Sadie" . . 280
Sibert 112
Trever Maxwell 41

Hilleary
Eleanor 239, 241
Nettie 241
William 241

Hilton
Joseph 441

Hines
Rilla 326

Hinkle
Cheryle A. 256

Hinsley
Eliza 295

Hinton
Mattie J. 194, 195
Riley Sanford 559

Hitchens

Nancy 587

Hite
Clifford 381
Lester Condrad 230
Melissa Mare 230
Stefanie Nicole 230

Hoagland
Lawrence 120
Marie 120
Preston 120

Hodge
Charles 412
Mary Ann 55
Mildred Joyce 412

Hodges
Gerald 313
Lenny 390
Lewis C. 313
Sarah H. 313
Sarah M. 313

Hoffart
Judith Ann 48
Ralph 48

Hoffman
Dena 232

Hogan
Genevieve Elizabeth . 117
Jeannie R. 30

Hogg
Mary Ann 285

Hogue
Asa Albert 139

Holbrook
Nancy Elizabeth 566

Holder
Civilla Lois 403
Floyd L. 403
Marvin 180

Holland
Alice Marie 565
Amanda 26
Becky 565
Benjamin Forest   562, 564
Charles 564
Charles Zelton 564
Dusty 26
Earl 565
Ethel Eloise 565
Forest Jefferson 564
Ida Lucille 565
James 564
James Coyt 565
Jayce 564

Katharine 564
Luke 26
Mary Ann 564
Mary Etta 565
Mildred Tivola 565
Myrtle 564
Robert 564
Ruth 564
Shirley Elenora 429
Verda Jane 564
Virgie Elizabeth 564
Warner Edward 564
Warner Edward, Jr . . . 564
William Benjamin 564

Holliday
Leona 77

Holloway
Bob 136
Donald 419
Jimmie 419

Holman
Louise Virginia 86
Martha Eloise "Lois" . . 428
Newton Edward 428
Sharon Alice 412

Holmes
Chelsea Lorraine 556
David Benton,III 556
David Benton,IV 556
John Collier 556
Lisa Renee 556
Nicole 556

Holsapple
Diane 57
Robert 57

Holsonbake
Derrick 246

Holstead
Doris 180

Holt
Elizabeth 360, 361
Richard 361
Sarah Jane 35, 37

Holton
Howard 459
W.E. 459

Homer
James 299
Laura 299
Laura (or Louisa) 297

Homma
James Homer 297

Hon

Wallace 254

Hood
Francis E. 226
Henry 252
William 252

Hooper
Blanche 143
Roxie Mae 390

Hope
May 393

Hopkins
Henry "Bunk" 141
James 247
Julie 170
Mary Emily 141
Thomas 247

Hopp
Mary 434

Hoppis
Lola Isabell 77

Hopson
Georgia Lucretia 405

Horne
Sarah 369, 372, 394

Hoskinson
Barbara J. 389

Hostetter
Clarinda Pritchett 98
Emily Pritchett 98
Fannie Ellen 87
Harry 88
James E. 88
William 88

Hostler
Clarence Norvin 328
Joshua Paul 328

Houchan
Leona Brazier 444

House
Homer Leon 81
Joyce 81
Mahlon (or Mathen) . . 318
Myrtle 395

Houston
Lisa 434

Howard
Barbara 315
Elizabeth 361
Ellen Jane 330
Esther 593
G.T 108
Sherry Elaine 400

Ted 319

Howell
Charlotte Cathy 54
Isabella Abul 520
Jane Abul 520
Mary Abul 520
Patricia Sue 58

Howser
Charles W . 118, 125, 126
Chauncey Loren 130
Connie Lois 132
Elijah 125
Hattie Jane 130
Heather Marie 131
James Micah 131
Jimmie Leon 131
Julia Dianne 131
Kali Jo 131
Larry Dean 130
Lenora Ella 126
Lloyd Gary 131
Marcus Joseph 131
Mattie Jane 130
Melanie Ruth 131
Michael Christopher . . 131
Otis Roy 130
Otto Lloyd 131
Ronnie Gene 131
Shalanna D'Ann 131
Sommer Michelle 131
Susan Armanthia 130
William Leon 130

Hoy
Michael 235

Hoyit
Benj 515

Hubbard
Elizabeth 542, 543
Wells A. 526

Hubble
Pamela 415

Huber
Eric Philip 210
Sarah Noel 211
Victoria Marie 211

Huckaby
Younger 543

Huckabye
Meredith 413

Huckenberry
Maggy 63

Hudson
Henry 586

641

John 360
Lucy 411
William 360
Huey
Alvia Josephine 169
James Henry 464
Laura Bane 464
Huff
Donna Jean 435
Earl Hermon 435
Huffer
Jean 418
Huffman
Christi Dawn 397
Emma Jean 397
Frances 122
Glenda Kaye 397
Hoyt Leon 396
Jeffery Paul 397
John Henry 396
Johnnie Ray 397
Kenneth Joe 397
Robert E. 396
Hughes
Adaline 330
Amanda 329
Hughs
Caswell Jackson (Magor)
. . . . 78
Charles E. 78
Ina A. 78
Peter E. 78
William O. 78
Hukle
Madeline Jane 381
Huland
Amanda 297, 299
Mack 299
Mattie 297, 299
Hull
Michael James "Mike"
. . . . 235
Hulland
Mack 297
Hulse
Joe 25
Humbert
Albert 256
Humphrey
Annie 420, 426
Humphreys
Georgene 31
Sarah 312

Hundt
Mathilda 273
Hunt
Bessie 417
Elizabeth-Hicks 595
Helen Lois 435
Nelsen Stanley 435
Wiley 410
Hunter
John 375
Reuben 375
Hurley
Beverly Ann 131
Husband
Madelon Ruth 549
Paul Edward 552
Sharon Kay 552
Warren E. 552
Warren Wayne 552
Hutchinson
Margaret E. (Rogers) . 84,
106
Hutchison
Elizabeth Mariah (Evans)
. . . . 119
Hutto
Vesma 429
Hutton
Mary Pearce 255
Ikard
Elizabeth 446
Ingram
Jolene 398
Martin 165
Inman
Benjamin F. 331
Irby
James Thomas . 394, 400
Wanda Fay 401
Ireland
Elma Leonce 566
Irwin
Agnes Bell 477
Ishmael
John G. 275
Isman
Ben 123
Isturis
Dereck Micheal 27
Vince Gomez, III 27
Vincent Gomez, IV 27
Ivey

Edna 437
Ivory
Hannah 590
Ivy
Susan 574
Jackson
Ada May 87
Adrian Clark 56
Andrew 87
Clyde 36
Earl J. 36
Earnest Todd 36
Eleanor 56
Elisha 36
Elizabeth A. 301
Elmer 56
Elva Eileen 111
Everet 56
G.W. 414
George 300, 301
Gerald Wayne 414
Hannah Elizabeth . . . 595
Hansel 425
Horace Green 87
Irl Raymond 87
James, Sr 300
Janice Paulette 414
Leonard Charles 414
Lisa 484
Lola Belle 87
Marguerita E. 36
Mary 301
Mary Jane 217
Nancy 36
Rick 63
Terry Martin 414
William Joseph 36
Jacques
Pauline 170
James
Amos 350
Angie 322
Jemima 85
John 191
Vera 68
Jansons
Deb 71
Jay
Robert 563
Jeffers
Terry Joy 244, 245
Terry Lee 245
Jeffords

Felicia 58

Jeffries
  Lydia Jewell 314

Jenkins
  Ann 249
  Bob 485
  Caroll (Brashear) 186
  Cora Belle 187
  Hannah 249
  James 249
  James A 187
  James A. 187
  John 248, 249, 496
  Joseph 248
  Joseph Nelson 249
  Levi 249
  Margaret 249
  Mary 249
  Michal 496
  Nancy 453
  Osborn 249
  Shane 485

Jennings
  Charlene 430
  Don 336, 339

Jent
  Billy 286
  Callie 286, 287
  David Wendall 48
  Glenda Kay 48
  James Wendell 48
  Lesa Anne 48
  Mark Alan 48
  R.J. 48

Jentry
  Will 547

Jeter
  Elizer 246

Jewell
  Claud V 119
  Elizabeth 119
  Ella 119
  Felix 119
  Lem 119
  Leta 119
  Minnie 119
  Moses E 119

Jirik
  Ann Marie 236
  Anthony Albert 236
  Dale Robert 236
  Frank Albert 236

Johns

Authur 390
Johnnie Evelyn 219
Perry 406

Johnson
  Anna 321
  Annie Elizabeth 242
  Benjamin 233
  Benjamin Barnett "Barney"
  233
  Berry 453
  Bruce L. 27
  Charlie D. 18
  Clo Ann 170
  D. 18
  Delmer 321
  E.R. 241
  Elisha "Lish" 36
  Elizabeth Ann 111
  Fred 18
  George 317
  George W. 319
  Gordon 321
  Gwen 424
  Hebert 321
  Helen 321
  Henrietta 241
  Henry A 120
  Ida Belle 319
  Jewel 422
  Jimmie 26
  Jimmie Austin 27
  Jimmie Brent 27
  Jimmie Greg 27
  Joan 170
  Joseph 239, 241, 368
  Joseph Alexander . . . 241
  Karen Marie 235
  Laura J 243
  Leah Michelle 27
  Liesel Dristin 27
  Lilly 322
  Mary Eleanor . . . 240, 241
  Mary Louisa 243
  Oma 321
  Otis Ray 18
  Ozea 322
  Robin 212
  Selma 321
  Stacy Marie 128
  Thomas Brashear . . . 242
  Thomas Roger 239
  Tonya Michelle 27
  Verna Mae 484
  William Channing 242
  William Hilleary . 239, 241

William?) Allan 321
"Bud" 321

Johnston
  Bernice 354
  Brad 65
  Brenda 65
  Brian 65
  Bruce 65
  Edwin Clive 354
  Floyd Nelson 65
  Gail Gale 65
  Gerald 65
  James Burr 549
  Jenna 28
  Percy W. 549
  Percy W., Jr 549
  Roma 65

Jones
  Alma Marie 95, 96
  Angie Nicole 39
  Ann 247, 303, 304
  Brittany 200
  Chris 200
  Emma 395
  Gary 200
  Isaac 195
  James 259
  James W. 259
  Jerry Daniel 133
  Jessie M. 48
  John 270, 543
  Kathy 39
  Katie 200
  Kerri Lee 200
  Ma 303
  Mary 247
  Mary A. 543
  Mary Elizabeth 292
  Micah 133
  Robert William 268
  Sarah 330
  Sarah Elizabeth 277
  Sarah Emeline (Browder)
  331
  Tanner 133
  William 247

Jordan
  Anna 452, 457
  Caroly Winona 351
  David Anthony 351
  Della Irene 254
  Eliza Jane 101
  Elizabeth 244
  James 364

643

Joseph 243
Lloyd James 351
Lloyd James, Jr 351
Mary Melissa 351
Sharon Ann 436
Sharon Joann 351
Sheila Faye 351
Tina Maire 351
Zachariah 364

Joseph
Joseph 248

Jost
Jennifer May 434
Theodore 434
Theodore Joseph 434

Jourdan
Adam Leroy 60
George 59
Patti Jean 60
Ronnie Lee 59
Ronnie Lee, Jr 59
Stanley David 60
Thomas 59
Tomona Fern 59
Willford Wayne 60
Wilma Jean 59

Joyce
Alice Mae 38

Julian
Martha Lynn Brashear
. . . . 288

Juniper
Susan Angi 556

Kamrowski
Anthony 93
Breanna 93
Donold 93
Jacob 93
Johnathon 93
Kimberly 93
Madison 93
Michael 93
Michael David 93
Myrtle 93
Robert 93
Roman 93
Tyler 93

Kane
Mary Ellen 528

Karstetter
Clara 130

Kasten
Debbie 43

Eric 43
Tiffany 43

Katzmark
Jared Scott 234
Julian David 234
Teresa 234

Kauren
Catharine Van . . 512, 535

Keating
Dorothy 210
Dorothy Ester . . . 209, 210

Keeler
Margaret 68

Keeley
Ken 26

Keeling
Paul 143

Keen
Eliza 374
Frank 239
Mary 239
Samson 374

Kees
Cicero Calvin 347
Isaac A. 347
Lonnie Levi Sr 347
Sarah "Sally" 343
Turner Harrison 347

Keesee
Paton 339
Payton 338

Keith
Anna Maxine 28

Keithley
Charles W. 88
Delila 85
Eli 85
Elizabeth 85, 118
Emily Jane 85
Irena 85
Jacob 85
John 88
Joseph 84
Joseph Jr 85
Joseph Sr 85, 118
Levicy 85
Lucy W 87
Margaret Paulina 88
Martha A 86
Mary H 87
Matilda 85
Pettis 85
Sarah L. 88

Sarah "Sally" 85
Silas 85
William 85
William E. "Eddie" 85

Kell
Jessie Lee 185

Keller
Doyle 236
Hugh 236
Martin 236
Renee 236
Ronald S 236

Kelley
Lucy Caroline 409
Winifred 209

Kelly
Charles 411
Colleen A. 319
David 550
Edith 130
Katie May 50
Lucy Caroline . . . 409, 410
Patricia 59

Kelsey
Susie K. 195

Kelso
Pearl 296

Kemp
Abijah Gotlieb "Bija" . . 394
Barnett 392
Benjamin Franklin . . . 395
Coryell Clementine "Cora-
Lee" 393
Daisy Mae 394
Dora Alice "Allie" 393
Fanny Florence . 394, 395
Hattie Louisa . . . 395, 403
James Barnett 392
Lewis Cass 393
Marion Abijah 395
Mary Louisa "Lou" . . . 394
Minnie 394
Minnie Maud 395
Minnie Rose 393
Nancy Caroline "Callie"
. . . . 394
Nancy Ellen 395
Nancy Lilly 394
Robert 394
Samuel Barnett . 393, 395
Sarah Ann 394
Sophronia Ann 393
Thomas Jesse 395
Thomas Lafayette . . . 394

644

Thomas Lafayette "Tom"
.... 394
Viola Tennessee 392
William Barnet 392
William Barnett 388, 392,
394
William Josiah 395
Wilson Rudolph "Willie"
.... 394

Kennamore
Lucy Elizabeth 275
Kennard
Jennifer Jean 49
Timothy Carter 49
Timothy Michael 49
Kennedy
Joseph 390
Pat 257
Tom 75
Kennemer
David 414
Gabriel "Gabe" Martin
.... 167
James 167
James David 167
John 167
Lee 167
Lela Lucille 414
Margaret 167
Mary 167
Nancy 167
Nora 167
Samuel Elijah W. 167
Sarah 167
Susan 167
Thomas 167
William 167
Kent
Donald L. 226
Jay Leroy 226
Kepac
Janice Lynn 233
Kepley
Debbie L. 131
Kerns
Clinton Boyd 552
Helen Irene 552
Morgan Elizabeth 552
Kerr
Polly 372
Kersey
Ann 358
John 358

Kikis
Corey Austin 232
Kelley Renee 232
Kristen Nicole 232
Peter Howard 232
Robin Elaine 232
Kilman
Minnie (Renske) 53
Kim
Jim Su 401
Kimbell
Ivy New 18, 24
Kimmous
Evelyn 390
Kincheloe
Nell 320
Kinder
John 513
King
Annie E 108
Emma J. 600
Joseph Hawkins 464
Lucy 278, 457
Noble 314
Ombra Dean 464
Rebecca Adeline 322
Sarah 70
Kingsbury
Richard 357
Kinney
Elizabeth 267
Kirch
Isabelle 239
Kirk
Lena R. 406
Kirkpatrick
Ellen Lee 394, 398
John 398
Kitchens
Allen 391
Alvin James 390
Anna May 392
Arthur Lee 390
Ashley 391
Beverly May 390
Bill 390
Cecil C. 392
Charles 391, 392
Clifford Dee 390, 391
Corda Mae 391
Curtis Edward 391
Dane 391
Donald 390

Elizabeth 389
Emmaline 391
Ethel Viola 390
Floyd Norman 390
Fred 392
George David 390
George Steven 390
George Washington . 389,
390
Grady Otho 391
Green Berry 387, 389
Hazel 392
Iliot Duard 390
Ina Elizabeth 389
Iva Mae 390
J.T. Asberry 390
James Henry 392
James Melton 389
James Morrison 392
Jess Robert 391
Jewell 391
Joel Wayne 390
John 391
John Joseph 390
John Timothy 390
Josie F. 392
Laguatta Joy 390
Larry Dean 392
Linda Mae 390
Lora 389
Louis Thomas 389
Lovell Gene 391
Madison Danielle 391
Margaret 392
Martha A. 392
Martha L. 389
Marvin Keith 390
Marvin Lee 390
Mary Adeline 390
Mary L. 389, 392
Milburn Lafayette 390
Minnie May 391
Nancy 389
Nancy J. 391
Nancy Jane 392
Naomi Gertrude 390
Nettie Janita 390
Norma Lee 391
Onie Lee 392
Otis Roy 390
Paul Curtis 391
Paul Ray 390
Paul Stewart 390
Pearl Elizabeth 390
Randall 391

Richard Edward 391
Robert Dale 390
Roberta Evelyn 391
Samuel 389
Samuel Asberry 389
Samuel Westley 389
Sarah S. 391
Sedonia Lora 389
Shirley Maxine 390
Taylor Leigh 391
Velma Sedonia 390
Wade 392
William Andrew 392
William Floyd 391
William Green "Billy" . 391
William L. 389
William Newton 389
William Seth 392
William Zachariah . . . 391
Winnie 389
Zachary 391

Klapp
Andrew 202
Daniel 202
Sean 202

Klein
Emily 101, 102

Klepac
Janice 210

Knabusch
Tami 434

Knapp
Mary 590

Knight
Martha 128

Knollie
Mary 127

Knowles
Andrew 199
Rachel Faith 199
Richard Gregory 199

Knudsen
Bill 139

Knutti
Brad 203
Tara 203
Timothy Stone 203

Koenig
Edward L. 249
Emil L. 249
Robert Farrar 249

Koeppe
Mary C. 54

Koester
Joyce Ann 47

Kolar
Don 425
Donna 425
Mike 425
Tim 425

Koller
Lynn 26

Kolstad
Bruce Howard 232
Markus Joel 232
Michael Bruce 232

Koonce
Adam 553
Amanda 553
Mark 553

Kortright
Cornelius 518
Helen 516
Helena 513, 518
Lawrence 521
Maria 518

Kraft
Nannie Boyd 113

Krezman
Kimberly Ann 30

Krick
David 203
Marilyn 203
Nila Ardene 204

Kriglein
Mary (Jordan) 350
Mary Melissa (Jordan)
. . . . 351

Krueger
Ida 379

Kruger
Mary 48

Krum
Lois 30

Kurlich
Rich 248

Kyser
Maude B. 456

Lackey
Mary Julia 410

Lacy
Donald R. 274
Hopkins 277
Theophilus 277

Ladd
Hester 270

Laffew
Christine 62

Lagrange
Barnadus 503

Lahey
Jane Yohe 279
Joseph B. 279

Laird
Rosa 111

Lake
John 496

Lamb
Barbara 194
Barbara Louise 200
James Haskell 200
Lauren Elizabeth 200
Millie Jane 18
Molly Kathryn 200
Stacy Walker 200

Lammers
Sharon Kay 117

Lancaster
E. J. 425
Vickie 199

Land
Lowell L. 131
Taran Elaine 131

Landis
Laura 185

Landreth
Ada Mae 319
Lena Ann 319

Landrum
Eltin 215

Laney
Mary 227

Lang
Antoinette S. Arrington
. . . . 544, 546
Charles 340
Rosa Ann 340

Lange
Dennis 389
Samuel Zachary 389

Lanier
Randy 425
Sheldon 425
Sully 425
Sully Jo 425
Vickie 425

Lankford

Mary 122

Larkin
William 290

Larson
Anderson Eugene . . . 116
Charles Alfred 117
Charlie 116
Cloletus A.R. 117
Glenn Harold 117
Grace Elizabeth 116
Otis Ray 117

Latta
Jane Alice 41

Lauchsteadt
Gustave 273
Ida Hilda Ada 273

Laws
Sterling 88

Lay
Ben 179

Leach
Bettie 261
Sandra Jo 131
Stephen 505

Leaf
Lulu 239

Leather
J.W 163

LeBrasseur
Francis 572

LeBrassieur
Francis, the Younger . 573

Leckie
Daisey Sarilly 423

Ledbetter
Cindy 338
Katie 339
Levi W. 339
Rachel 171
Truett 170

Ledford
Jesse 416
Pearl 263

LeDoux
Alexander Francis, Jr . 566
Alexandre Francis . . . 565
Colleen Elizabeth 566
Kathleen Louise 566
Patricia Ann 566

Lee
Alfred 80
Bernadine 554

BokHu 401
Brandy Lynn 41
Broadus 347
Bruce Wayne 41
David S. 347
Delorse Ann 46
Edgar 293
Harold 40
Inez 554
J.B. 554
Jang Uk 401
Mamie 347
Maude 347
Maxine 554
Nancy Elizabeth . 345, 349
Nancy Elizabeth Ann . 444
Noah 554
Pansy 347
R. R. 444
Robert 347
Shannon Sue 40
Steve Wayne 40
Venie Mae 80
Wade 347
William 349

Lees
Laura 426

Lefevre
Mark 433
Mathew Jason 433

Lefler
Millie 159

Leggett
Addie Permilia 557
Dollie 562

Leicher
Elizabeth 304

Leininger
Brent 40

Leisler
Jacob 511

Leonard
"Dolly" 279

Lerch
Glenn 555

Lesley
Lena Claude 552

Lethure
Winney 246

Letterman
Cloval 144

Levitt
Emma 396

Lewis
Belle 426
Daniel 500
George 417
James 417
Lem A. 417
Leonard 417
Yvette Marie 96

Light
Jessica 93

Lightsey
Vivian L. 557

Ligon
Henry 431

Lile
Mary 227

Lillard
Luanne 254

Limbaugh
Alma Joyce 433
Brad Eugene 435
Clarence William 435
Clyde 418
Connie 433
Daisy 417
David Alvin 436
Don Robert 435
Elaine Carol 435
Emily Marie 435
Eugene F. 432
Eugene Francis 435
Gloria May 433
Gordon 446
Greta Sue 436
Hazel Leola 418
James Lee 435
Jeannie 433
Joel 418
John Wesley . . . 431, 432
Jonathan 433
Kenneth Lynn 435
Kristin Laurel 435
Lavonne Rose 436
Lee 446
Lee Ann Michelle 436
Leila Evans 435
Letha Zone 418
Lynell Rae 435
Marilyn Rose 434
R.J. (or R.T.) 418
Rachel Grace 436
Robert James 435
Robert Wayne 435
Ruthie Brazier 387

Scot Alan 435
Susan 433
Thomas Jefferson . . . 433
Walter Clyde, Jr 418
Wendy 433
Willard Wesley 433
William Benjamin 418
William Marshall 418
Wilma 446

Lindeman
Dawn 438

Linderman
Judith Ann 353
Sarah 353
Thomas 353

Lindsay
Bonita 303
Felix Hubert 303
Peggy Irene 303
William 304
William Brashear . . . 303, 304
William Brashear, III . 303
William Brashear, Jr . 303

Lindsey
John 198

Ling
John Burt 536
Philander 538
Philander Hester 536

Link
Agnes Mae 186

Lipprado
Lug Palino 59

Little
Lola Blanche 549

Littlejohn
Rachel Ann 413

Livesay
Terri Gayle 54

Llewellen
Elvira J 97
Grace 87
Zephalinda 108

Llewellyn
Zephalinda 84, 106

Lloyd
Aquilla Durham 379
Azula 379
Catherine 378
Charles R. 379
Clara R. 379
Deborah 378

Eben 379
Elijah 379
Ella 379
Emmet 379
Henry I. 379
Herbert "Bert" 379
Hulder 378
Jackson 379
Jackson T. 379
John 378
John Meyer 379
Julia Ann 380
Labon Brazier 378
Lucie B. 379
Mary "Mollie" 379
Nancy 379
Nancy Catherine 379
Reuben 375, 378
Reuben L. 379
Sarah Alice 379
Timothy 379

Lobb
Frederick Henry 474
Gladys Rosa 474

Locke
Anna 293

Logan
Bobbie Orville 229
Carolyn Louise 229
Emmett 229
George W. 223, 227
Gilla Adaline "Addie" . 227
Henry Eldon 229
James 227
James Orville 229
L.P. 79
Lillie Smith 228
Reuben Monroe 229
Virgil Edward 229

Lomax
Elizabeth 208

Long
Martha C. 445
Sarah 84, 88

Loughrey
Daniel 203
Katherine 203
William 202
William Joseph 203

Love
Andrew 267
Bobby 23

Loveless
Ida Lee . . . . . . c. 471, 476

James Belton 476
James Seborne 476
Seaborn 476

Loven
Florence 18, 24

Low
Cornelius Peter 521

Lowe
Edwin 354
Gregory 355
Ray 354
Sharon 354
Sybil 234
Valerie 354

Lowrance
Ruby O. 477

Lowry
Sarah Ann 598
William Wallace 550

Lozano
Robert 26

Lucas
Lucy 183
Silas Emmett 444

Lucckesi
Dwayne Lawrance . . . 28
Nickolas Giovanni . . . 28
Stephanie Marie 28

Lundgren
Charles Emerson 232
Lisa Joan 232
Nancy Lynn 232

Lupkins
Mary Lydia 391

Lusch
Connie 63
Robert 63

Lusk
Marion James "Bunk" 395
Sarah Florence 394

Luster
Golf 185

Luterall
Georgia 429

Luttrell
Aaron Lee 43
Arlin Leroy 43
Carissa Lynn 43
Charles Frederick 55
Charles Fredrick 42
Cheryl Lynn 43
Crystal 43

Garrett Raymond 43
Garrison Robert 43
Gary Lee 43
Kelly Marie 43
Kevin Patrick 43
Marie 55
Ramonda May 43
Raymond Chesley 42
Raymond Leroy 42

Lyle
Margaret Ann 266

Lynch
Esther Jane 456

Lynn
Jody 60

Lyons
Angela Ruth 54
Anissa Mickela "Mickie"
. . . . 54
Charles Franklin 54
Charles Fredrick 54
Charles Monroe "Jim" . 54
Dale Rodney 54
Daren Michael "Darry Mike"
. . . . 54
Ellen Lesley 551, 552
James Monroe 54
Jerome Christopher . . . 54
John Henry 552
Marie Annette 54
Melanie Leann 54
Mitchell Lane 54
Patrick William 54
Reginald Ferinand 54

Magee
Catherine Jenny "Katie"
. . . . 379

Magner
Anita Louise 252

Maiden
Jessie P. 119

Majek
Cora 178

Major
Nora 61

Malady
Peter 267

Malick/Mallett
Will 339

Malicote
Sarah "Sally" 261

Malla
Edward 227

Michele Denise 227
Malone
Ted 79
Malrey
Rachel 35
Mann
Carolyn June 233
Chad Steen 233
Florence 428
Jeffrey Dean 233
Joseph Richard 428
Ryan Scott 233
Terressa Lynn 233
William Norman 233
Manning
Jim 409
Mansker
Ada Mae 139
Agnes 141
B.F. 141
Barbara Jean 142
Benjamin Franklin . . . 140
Berchia Ethyl 139
Beulah Pearl 143
Beverly 141
Beverly Ann 139
Brenda 143
Clella 139
Curtis Layne 139
Daniel Elijah 142
Darren Keith 141
Delores May 142
Delsa Leather 139
Dennis 141
Dixie 143
Donald Louis 142
Donna June 142
Earnest Earl 142
Earnest, Jr 142
Ella Mae 138
Frances Evelyn 142
Fred 143
Frieda Joan 141
Gail 140
Gail Gibbons 144
Gail Jeanne 140
Gary Lee 142
Geneva Irene 141
Gertrude 141
Icy Ola 140
James 140
Jeanetta 143
John Henry 141
John Leslie 142

Johnny 142
Karen 143
Kenneth James 140
Kermit Braden 139
Larry Dale 141
Laura 141
Laura Bell 138
Laura May 143
Lela Jane 140
Lisa Marie 141
Margaret 141
Margaret Eva "Maggie"
. . . . 140
Marilyn 143
Mary Ellen 141
May 142
Michael Hayden 140
Michael W. 137, 144
Minnie 142
Nancy Lee 142
Nellie Dora 140
Ollie 143
Ollie Rayborn 138
Patrick Alan 140
Paul 140
Ralph Douglas 141
Rosa Adeline 142
Rosa Lee 142
Russell 139
Sharon Kay 141
Sheila Faye 141
Shirley Lavon 142
Stella Mae 139
Stephen Dale 140
Thurman "Bill" Hayden
. . . . 139, 144
Virginia 141
Wiley 141
Wiley, Jr 141
Willard Gene 142
William Harry . . . 139, 144
William Henry . 135, 137,
146
William L. 140
Wilma 142
Maples
Clyde 419
Mar
Eleanor 352
Marano
Melissa 105
Michael 105
Mike 105
Marbury

Elizabeth 300

March
Horace 256

Marcus
Martha E. 77

Marker
Clarice 213

Markham
Goldie K. 390
Harold Feldon 51
Larry Wayne Feldon . . 51

Marklein
Linda Ann 117

Marko
David 202
Kayla 202
Larry 202
Lori 202

Marlew
Odie 430

Marmouget
Ruth 565

Marquess
Helen Louise 68

Marsell
Rita 38

Marsh
Dean Anita 235
Kimberly Dell 397
Louis Dale 397
Sherman Wade 397

Marshall
Alma F. 291
Alma Florence 291
Annie 417
Anthony Ray 42
Christine Ann 42
Hayden 417
Jane 269
Janice Diana 553
Lizzie 418
Patience Anna 269
Rosa 159
Willard Ray 42

Marshel
Earl 47
Johnny Ray 47
Melinda K. 47
Michael Ray 47

Marston
Thomas 536

Martin

Angel Michell 416
Danny Ross 235
Dorothy 559
Elizabeth 265
Ernest 456
Holy Gail 416
Ila Monehta 244
Margaret Missouri "Mazue"
. . . . 428
Mary Louisa 215
Muriel Ann 113
R. C. 270
Sam 416
Sam Perry 113

Masini
Martha Louise 27

Mason
Alexander 214-216
Allen D. 38
Charles Edgar 38
Daniel . . . 213, 214, 216
Diana 38
Donald O. 38
Elizabeth . 215, 218, 316,
318
Erman 564
George 214, 575
Henry P. 215
James 215
James Phillip 38
Jesse Green, Sr 215
Jesse H. 215
Jesse H., Jr 215
John Calloway 215
John W. 215
Julie Ann 38
Linda Jane 38
Lucille 551
Margaret 215, 216
Margaret Lucinda 215
Martha E. 215
Mary 214
Mary Jane 215
Nancy Adeline 215
Nancy Jane 215
Nancy M. 38
Nathaniel 213, 221
Orville H. 38
Phebe Haney 215
Phillip 277
Phillip J. 214
Raymond Neal 38
Robert 213
Robert Doyle 38
Sarah 245

Sharlene Kay 38
Susan Alana 38
Trent James 38
Trey William 38
Warren 213
William L. 215

Massey
Ada 228
Lewis 405

Masterson
Thomas 220

Matlock
Moore 220

Matson
William R. 86

Mattei
Lee 249

Matthews
Albert 528
Eva 122
Helen Brasher 528

Mauney
Julia 381

May
Carl 44
Jeff 235
Jim 25
Joyce 20
Matilda C 85

Maybee
Emily Rose 235
Erik Nilson 235
Harold 234
Jessica Lynn 235
Mark Orrin 235
Melody Ann "Dee Dee"
. . . . 235
Mikelyn Gay "Miki" . . . 235
Mona Rosa 222
Monica Jean "Mickey"
. . . . 234
Morgan Sheamarie . . 235
Orrin Smith 234

Maybee/Bryant
Erik Nilson 235

Mayhew
Hallie Cuba 197

Mayhill
Albert W. 45

Maynard
D.M. 335
Frank 128
Morton Armand 191

650

Maynor
Jim 425
Mays
Norene 412
McCabe
Darrell 143
Emmaglee 143
Nadine 143
Patsy Lou 143
Willard Cecil 142
McCain
Bradley Dean 180
Cyndia Jeneane 179
Fred Brashears 179
Freddy Dean 179
Ila Lucile 179
Ina Jean 180
Joyce 175
Minnie Euleta 179
Regina Ruth 180
Richard Powers 180
Ruby Joyce 179
Thomas Jackson 179
Thomas Jackson, Jr . 179
Thomas Lewis 179
Winnie Kathleen 179
McCarthy
Frances Teresa 103
Owen 103
McClain
Blaine L. 89
Chester 89
Delbert 89
Dennis Harvey 119
Ernest 89
Helen 89
Jesse 89
Linda Lee 119
Mildred 89
Raygene 89
Raymond 89
Teresa Ann 119
William H 119
McClanahan
Pearly 143
McClarin
James 558
McClellan
Lois 426
McClelland
Mary Frances 57
McClure
Nona Faye 170

Virginia Ethlene 429
McClusky
Patricia 416
McCormack
Mary 264
McCosh
Alva Lindly 331
Lois Effa 331
McCoun
George 89
Robert 89
McCoy
Patricia 180
Shannon Lynn 52
Shirley Brasher 493
Tom 52
McCravey
James 264
McCrory
John Knox 111
John Knox Jr 111
Nancy Sue 111
Nelda Evans Rohr . . . 111
Sally Kay 111
McDaniel
Earl Lee "Jack", Jr . . . 552
Ivan Anthony 58
Ivan Eugene 58
Ivan Wayne 58
Jeffery Keith 58
Kathy Marlain 58
Larry Edward 58
Lee 484
Lillie 229
Lola Jean 58
Lynn 58
Margina 58
Marilyn Lesley 552
Virginia Ann "Gigi" . . . 552
McDannold
Dranis A. 88
McDavies
Mary 139
McDonald
Belinda Jane . . . 547, 554
Lucille 422
Marshia Jean 558
Pat 257
McDougal
Alexander A. 455
Amanda E. 455
Eliza 455
Henry F. 455

Virginia Ethlene 429
James Riley 455
James Thomas 455
John W. 455
John Wesley 452
John Wesley, III 455
John Wesley, Jr 454
John Wesley,Sr 454
Joseph 455
Joseph Monroe 455
Lucy 455
Malinda C. 455
Margaret E. 455
Martha 455
Mary Jane 455
Rebecca Ann 455
Sarah 455
Sarah "Sallie" 455
William 455
McDougald
John 456
McElroy
Elizabeth 442, 446
McEntire
Merinda 335
McFall
Mark 460
McFerron
George E. 280
McFerrons
Richard 280
McGaughey
Brandon 210
Cameron 210
Dan V. 210
Jordan Thaddeus 210
McGee
Betsy 419
Fines Ewing 268
Sissy 408
McGeeHee
Tom 410
McGeHee
Lottie 409
Tom 409
McGinnis
Harrison P. 330
Mary H. 330, 331
McGowan
Catherine 555
Doris 555
McGraw
Mary Ann 253
McGrew

Alma 120
Elizabeth 120
Iola 120
Jesse 116
Leonard Smith 120
Susan Melissa 120
Vicy 120
William E. 117
McGuire
Floy 293
McHale
Laurel 435
Nancy J. 435
McHatton
Alcestes 90
McInnis
Margaret 550
Mcintire
James 220
W.P. 334
McIntosh
Robert T 88
McKay
Dewey Lee 401
Lois Ellen 401
McKee
Mary 392
Susan 526
McKelvey
Samuel 418
McKendree
Bishop 439
McKenzie
Elizabeth Brazier 488
William 430
Wilma Nadine 315
McKinney
Charles Elbert 47
Edward Allen 47
Eleanor Sue 47
Ella 66
Glen Travis 47
Linda Irene 47
Loren Allen 47
Loren Allen, III 47
Loren Allen, Jr 47
Loretta Jean 47
Tammy Lee 47
Terri Jean 47
Trina Lynn 47
William David 47
McKinnie
Patricia Ann 552

McKnab
Norma 382
McKnight
Leanne Beshears 81
Matthew Thomas 131
McKnoun
Eva 59
Mclerkin
A. Harvey 273
Carolyn Louise 273
McManame
Julien Anne "Sarah" . . 528
McMarty
Edna 62
McMasters
Donna 391
E.G. 391
Jennifer 391
Tommy Grant 391
McMichael
Cayla 30
Christa 30
Cody 30
Steve 29
McMillen
Janice Kay 124
McMorris
James 365
McMurry
Amira M. 455
James 455
Lealan 205
McNally
Helen Theresa 104
McNatt
Ada 233
McNecky
Velma "Wilma" 65
McNeeley
Rebecca 17
McNeil
Annie 557
McNeley
Martha Miranda 71
McNight
Alexander 338
McNutt
John 220
Mcpherson
Alexander 522
McPherterson

Alter 415
McQuary
Lena Brazier 444
McQuery
Georgann 68
McVey
Samuel 379
Meador
Ada Leota 62
Charles Lee 62
Lee Joshua 62
Meadows
Cecil 43
Leslie 43
Medcalf
F.M. 471
Meech
Susan Billings 496
Meeks
Samuel Seedal . . . 25, 30
Meilock
Anne Marie 292
Meli
Frank 429
Mellen
David 433
Mary 433
Peggy 433
Roger 433
Mellish
Anne 573
Melton
Julie Ann Ball 286
Mercado
Christina 192
Daniel 192
John 192
Shannon Orr 192
Mercer
Margaret 260
Maria 426
Meredith
Leonard 237
Margie 237
Ray 36
Merreill
Ernest Ray 381
Horace M. 381
Merrile
John 586
Merrill
Oliva Maria 596

652

Mervin
Mary E. 17
Messer
Allen J. 468, 471
Allen Jackson 479
Avery Bill 479
David 468
George Washington . . 479
Hallie Norvill 479
Henry A.J. "Jack" 472
Jacob 472
James 468
James Arthur 480
Jesse 468, 472
Jesse G. 479
Jessie M. 479
John W. 468, 472
Laverne Nix 479, 480
Louisa 468
Martha J. 468
Mary 468
Nora Elizabeth 479
Sarah 468
Sarah "Sallie" 479
Susanna 468
Sybil 479
William . . . 468, 470, 472, 479
William Jackson "Willie"
. . . . 479
Messers
A.J. 467
Metcalf
Alexandra Elizabeth . . 211
Brenda Marie 211
Daniel Grady 211
Jessica Brooke 211
Monica Rose 211
Nicholas Edward 211
Parney 325
Rebecca Francis 211
Timothy Edward 211
Zachary Joseph 211
Metzken
Gladys 180
Meyers
Clora Elizabeth "Liz" . 340
Donald W. "Hamburger"
. . . . 340, 341
Dwayne 341
Ernie 341
Karen 341
Kyle 341
Maxine 45

Rayne 341
Michaud
Georgia Marie 95
Philip 95
Mickoelson
Betty Joann 227
Middleton
Hannah Elizabeth . . . 316
Mielock
Ed 291
Mifflin
Daniel 587
David 586
Mikeal
Asa Burton 347
Belle Boyd 347
Betty Nell 347
Cicero 349
Coy M. 347
Eliza 349
Enoch Reeves, Sr . . . 347
Fanny Pearl 347
John Wilburn 347
Lee Edward 347
Loy Martha Catherine 347
Max H. 347
Ruth Marie 347
Scott Tillman 347
Mikel
Henry M. 191
Henry M., Jr 191
Otho Brashear 191
Milhollon
Aryn 425
Cory 425
David 425
Donna Sue 425
Dorothy 425
J. T., Jr 425
Jackie 425
Joe T. 425
Larry 424
Lisa 425
R. T. 424
Randy 425
Ricky 425
Sherman Travis 425
Tom 424
Miller
Brandon D. 93
Bryan J. 93
Charles Floyd 193
Charley 259

Cheryl Telle "Terry" . . 424
Flemon 113
George E. 193
James 93
James Eldon 193
Jennifer 93
Kathy 113
Larry Earl 54
Laura L. 93
Lenora "Nora" Ethel . . 353
Marvin 113
Mary 281
Maude 409
May Nioka 179
Nancy 113
Nora 352
Owen "Booney" 93
Paige D. 93
Pittman 113
Richard 113
Virgina 193
William 193
William D. 93
William Henry 193
William R. 93
Mills
Albert N. 78
Anderson Prentis 77
Benjamin Franklin 77
Bertha 77
Byrd Francis 77
Caswell 72, 74
Charles 76
Charles H. 78
Elizabeth C. Beshears 72, 74
Frederic 77
George B. 77
George W. 77
Harvey Anglish "Harve"
. . . . 77
Henry Wilson "Dick" . . . 77
Hulds L. 76
Ida M. B. 76
James William 76
Jesse 76
Joel Jackson "Jack" . . . 78
John 76
John Thomas 76
Johney Jacob "Jake" . . 77
Leonidas L. 77
Lucy Iona 78
Madison H. 77
Mary Ann 76
Mary E. 76

Matilda L. 77
Millie Frances 76
Nancy C. 77
Terry 76
Vicie E. 77
William R. C. 77
William Robert 77

Millsap
Mary 431

Millspaugh
David 203
Greg 204
Lee 203
Roger 203

Mincy
John W. 457

Minor
Marie 424
Suella Brazier . . 420, 424

Minton
Carylin 160
Jack 160
Marylin 160
Nannie 287

Mitchell
Amelia 193
Annette 398
Beverlie Custer 398
Brenda 398
David 354
Delma Lou "Doodle" . 398
Doris Ray 398
Gordon 201
Harlis Leo 398
James 354
James "Jimmy", Jr . . . 354
Kenneth Joe 398
Kenneth Raymond . . . 398
Lorraine 354
Louise 354
Richard Franklin 398
Robert "Bobby" 353
Shelley Ann 354
Terrell Wade "T.W." . . 398
Will 430
William F. 353
William F. "Billy" , jr . . 353

Mitchem
Alexander 166
Artina 166
Benjamin Lewis 166
Charles 166
Edwin 166
James Alfred . . . 164, 166

James E. 166
John/Johnie 166
Marina Gabriella 166
Samuel B. 166

Mitras
Pete 111

Modlin
Clyde 59
Glenda Jean 59

Moffett
Benjamin 242
Carrie 242
Eleanor J. 242
Laura Pritchard 242
Robert 242

Monosmith
Isaac 490

Monroe
Bruno Perriera 235
John Dennis 235
Jon Christopher 235

Montague
John 503

Moody
Rosa Lee 560
Sharon Louise 396

Moore
Alfred Y. 543
Amanda J. 196
Amanda Jane . . 194, 195
Amy Karis 133
Anna Michelle 132
Benjamin 542
Benjamin, Jr 543
Benjamin, Sr . . 543, 544
Betty Jean 133
Carol Denise 132
Catherine 543
Daniel 413
Della 69
Donna Marie 391
Drucilla 543
Duncan W. 543
Elizabeth Parsons . . . 464
Ethan William 133
Eugene Albert 139
Harvey 63
Harvin Washington . . 458
Idella 69
J. Alexander 542
James 543
James and Drucilla . . 542
James Shaw 26
Jessa Dene 133

Jessie 62
Jimmie Ellis 133
John Eric 133
John G 108
L.O 133
Larry 51
Lawrence 58
Lewis Wayne 133
Lisa Elaine 133
Lois 331
Louisa 296
Luclihoma 296
Martha Ann 132
Mary 543
Mary Magdaline . . . 18, 24
Maxine 139
Morgan LeAnn 132
Nancy 543
Natalie Sue 133
Nellie 24, 381
Nellie Edith 25, 26
Noel Dean 139
Nora "Mae" 63
Permilia 543
Rebecca 543
Rebecca Marie . 542, 544
Sandra Kay 58
Stephen R. 455
Theodore 139
Timothy William 132
Tina Marie 51
Verna Ruth 139
Victoria Renee 133
Virgil Marvin Edgar Lee
. . . . 139
William 543, 546
William E 132
William Royce 132

Morehead
J.R. 29
Myrtle 415
Nita Kay 29

Moreland
Lewis Edward 129
William Riley 129

Morgan
Blanche 254
Cora Lee 314
Elizabeth Ann 551
Hazel 254
Ira Dawson 381
James 47
Melissa 551
Michael 48

Pamela Gail 204
Ruth Barker 380
William 551
William, Jr 551

Morisano
Anthony John 105
Anthony Nicholas 105
Maureen Frances Beshears
. . . . 105
Sarah Marie 105

Morlock
Jack 202
Janet 202
Kelly 202
Kevin 202
Tammy 202
Terry 202
Timmy 202

Mornewer
Leah Marie 48

Morrill
John 585

Morris
Ammine Brazier 427
Tilda "Tillie" 224

Morrison
Derek Craig 57
Diana 57
Jess 57
Jess E. 57
Michael 57
Stanley 57

Morss
Cyrus Dudley 528
Jacob 528
Rosannah Carolina . . 528

Morton
Ruth 314

Moseley
Ann 246
Anna 246
Anne 245
Benjamin 245, 246
Clement P. 246
Daniel 246
Edward 245, 246
Elisha 246
Elizabeth 245, 246
Gracey 246
Henry 245
Jack 118
Jesse 246
John 245, 246

Lydia 246
Martha 245, 246
Mary 246
Penelope 246
Rachel 246
Robert 245, 246
Robert D. 245
Robert T. (S.) 246
Sarah 246
Sarah\Selah 245
Susanna 246
Thomas 246
Thomas T. 246
William 245
William Brantley 246
William, Jr 245
William,III 245
William,IV 245

Moser
Harley 354
Shirley Ann 354

Mosley
Bessie Mae 293
Kelly 412
Velor 293

Moss
Alfred 563
James 389

Mosteller
Gary 20

Mott
Dorothy F. 283

Moutardier
Andrew 197

Mouton
Marie Martha 303

Muldoon
Lucille 65

Mullins
Andy Ernest 597
Denise 131
James Henderson . . . 597
Thelma Marie 597
William Lockhardt . . . 597

Mulvaney
Patrica Louise 43

Mumford
John 586

Munn
Barbara Brazier 427

Murphy
Julia Ann 31, 33
Louisa M. 338

Murr
Betty Jo 21
Bonnie Mae 21

Murray
Donnie Dale 315
Eliza 260
Thomas 260
William H. (Alfalfa Bill)
. . . . 260
Zella Lou 314

Musich
Susan 183

Myers
Cora Elizabeth "Corky"
. . . . 297
Edward Eugene 57
Effie 34
Frankie Lee 57
George 34, 35
Hattie 34
Herbert Edward 57
Hershall 63
Isaac Benjamin 34
James Edward 57
John 34, 35
Marsha 65
Mattie 34
Mischelle Jean 57
Robert William 57
Rosie 34
Sandra Jeremy 51
Stephen Wayne 51
Stephen Wayne, Jr . . . 51
Stephenie Diana 51
Thresia Lynn 57
Tylaine Gayle 57
Virgil Lee 57
Willie 34

Nagel
Bill 383
Gary 39

Nail
Joseph 277

Napper
Cynthia 416

Nart
John Van 290

Nations
Libby 298

Navrosky
Donna 434

Neal
Eula 563

Nearmyer
Kenneth 115
Neely
Emma 548
Joyce Wilma 263
Neff
Elisabeth 491
Negus
Ann 591
Nehring
Ruth 352
Neilson
Jewel Rayborn . . 136, 140
Nelson
Amy Elizabeth 232
Cole 297, 299
Emma 351
Flo 565
Gabriel 297, 299
Gary Brian 232
Isabel 247
Jemima 193
Jennifer Anne 232
W.H. 546
Will 299
Wilson 299
Neuson
John 18
Newald
Alfred 63
Newberry
Kenneth Allen 45
Newby
James W. 599
Newell
Ethel 34
Tina 234
Newman
Dee 228
Cynthia Ann 228
Douglas Shawn 314
Ernest Harold 228
Ethel 289
G. Louise 228, 229
Gabriel Douglas 314
James Ernest 228
Martha E. 409, 420
Mary Jane 35, 37
Ray 229
Samuel 35, 37
Tammy Jo 228
Tone Dee 228
Newsom

Charles 445
Julia 445
Newson
Edith Hadley . . . 209, 210
Newton
Cannon 441
Peggy 311
Shirley 311
Tavie 311
Tom 311
Nichols
Shadrack 191
William W. 191
Nicks
Phoebe 213
Quinton 213
Nixon
Bob Claude 405
Doris Williams 405
No
In Hwo 328
Noble
Clay 403
Cleve 403
Clint 403
Curt Henry 395, 403
Curt Henry, Jr 403
Florence 403
Luther 282
Ned 403
Ruby Violet 403
Wilsie Louise "Midge"
. . . . 405
Nokes
Nancy 31, 69
Noldt
Marion Farrow 249
Noller
August 61
Kevin 61
Randy 61
Roy W., Jr 61
Roy W., Sr 61
Valeri 61
Norem
Clarence Herbert 52
Norvell
Owen 406
Norwood
Brennan James 567
Catharine 505, 507
Donald James 567
Ian David 567

James William 566
Joseph Robert 566
Joseph Robert, Jr . . . 566
Kaitlin Rose 566
Michael Wayne 567
Susan Elaine 567
William Bowers 566
Notsinger
Hubert 350
Nott
Anne 245
Nunn
Josephine 379
Nutt
Rhoda 527
Nutter
Heather Lynn 234
James Douglas 234
Joshua 234
O'Keefe
Clarence 45
Gerald Edgar 45
Norma Jean 45
Odom
Abram 543
David 547
Elizabeth 543
Idalee 547
Philip . . . . : 543
Theophilus 543
William 543
Offley
Ann 574
Robert 574
Sarah 575
Offutt
Cassy Angeline 464
Oland
Brad 118
Olazabel
Rachael 197
Vic 197
Victor 197
Olebeare
Ruby Mae 124
Oliver
Robert 195
Olmstead
John Thomas 566
Olson
Donald Edward 230
Traci Diane 230

Olson/Pelegrin
Traci Diane 230
Orme
Mary 303
Orr
Elizabeth Jane 101
James McGee 101
Marion Campbell 101
William Campbell 101
Orrill
Edgar P. 332
Ort
Kimberly 434
Osborne
Abigail 592
Anne 574
Sir Edward 574
Osman
Clarence 564
Ostickenberg
Oscar 228
Randy H. 228
Sandra K. 228
Otsberg
Laurel 286
Ott
Pamela Sue 117
Outlaw
Inez L. 121
John W. 121
Lewis 121
Raymond B. 121
Overbeck
Ada Angeline 55
August 54
Elizabeth Lucille 55
Fredrick H. 54
Lillie May "Lil" 54
Mary Kathryn "Bunny" . 54
Overton
John 583
Overturf
Jack 56
Jonathan 157
Levi 155
Mary 155
Mary Ann 134
Richard 56
Owen
Emma 460
Flora 68
John 110

Mina Moody 204
Owens
Alia "Alley" 344
Amos 156
Andrew 345
Barnard 344
Frank 171
Hattie Lee 168
John Quincey 171
Larkin 344
Mary 345
Nancy J. (Norman) ... 156
Olivia 41
Sarah Jane 345
Troy 40
William C 168
William Columbus ... 168
Owensby
Carrie 136
O'Mara
Keith 297
Pace
Rebecca 464
Page
Robert Gordon 55
Paige
Kristie 129
Painter
Alma Ellen (Carman) . 185
Alma Lee 430
Aubrey 430
Clydeth 430
Floy 430
George H. 185
J.D. 430
Jacob 163
John 430
Thomas 430
Wilson 430
Pak
Chong Um 328
Palmer
Adrienne "Addie" Christine
.... 23
Alan Lee 23
Benjamin Cole 23
Cooper 507
Curtis Duane 22
Floyd Duane 22
Floyd Wayne 22
Grant Joseph 23
Hazel (Beshears) 17
Jacob Daniel 22

Joseph Errett 113
Kelly Ann 22
Kyle Alan 23
Madge 113
Margaret (Brasher) .. 508
Robert Joseph 113
Scott Michael 22
Thomas G 113
Victoria May 22
Walter 588
Paquet
Gwendolyn 566
Louis Phillip 565
Parastar
Donald 185
Gilberte Brashear ... 185
Jimmy 185
Pardue
Gladys 195
Parker
Art J. 25, 28
Benjamin Franklin 50
Cecil Raymond 29
Clara Mae 51
Debra Elaine 29
Debra Ellen 53
Donald 53
Doris Jean 53
Edward Arthur "Tuffy" . 29
Edward Guy 29
Effie M 115
Emily Lou 29
Evelyn 51
Fern Adeline 50
Frank 50
Jacob Raymond 29
James Allen 53
James Allen, Jr 53
Jennifer Melissa 29
John Jay 547
Julia Eugenia ... 547, 548
Laura Katherine 128
Linda 425
Lois Faye 52
Lori Denise 53
Mary Elizabeth 52
Patricia Ann 28
Riley Dennis 28
Ruth Ann 53
Searcy 547
Thomas 128
Thomas S. 548
William Dwain 52
Parkman

David Lee 96
Ian Geoffrey 96

Parks
J.M. 418
Robert C. 441
Sam 449

Parr
Alice J. 378
Andrew 378
Andrew Jackson 378
Mattie Nancy 378

Parsley
Ruby 391

Parsons
Annie Mae 346
Hannah Caroline 348
Martha Lee 20

Partridge
Delbert 378

Pate
Royce Lee 260

Patterson
Caroline Frances "Cari"
. . . . 204
Connor James 204
Dean Alan 204
Dillon Scott 204
Elmer 390
Frank Lee 204
Jake Aaron 204
Jennifer Nicole 204
June 201
Katherine 281
Kyle Anthony "Tony" . 204
Lee Crosswhite 204
Lisa Fredrica 29
Michael Frank 204
Michael Frederick . . . 204
Nancy 187
Nicholas Lee 204
Nicky Lee 204
Penny Lynn 204
Robby Frank 204
Scott Alan 204
William 154

Paul
Josephine 95

Paulson
Elberta "Bert" 103
Olaf John 103

Paxton
Lovanna Mae 115

Payne

Geni Lynn 412
Gregory S. 412
Heather Michelle 553
Jason Paul 553
Jessica 196
Mary Ann 286
Melinda 343
Paul Thomas 553
Rhoda Catherine 343

Payton
Henry 578
Sarah "Sally" Ellen . . . 289
William R. 289

Pearce
Essie 414
Richard Miles 208

Pearsall
Abigail 506
Mary Goodie 500

Pearson
Elizabeth 543
Meredith 441

Pearth
Rachel Ann 280

Peckat
Gloria 160

Peirce
Aaron Scott 117
Charles Lee 116
Christopher Sean 117
Edgar Lee 116
Lorrie Ellen 117
Lynne Marie 116
Rachel Lee 117
Raymond Earl 116
Ronnie Ray 117
Stacy Lynn 117

Pelfrey
Donna Rae 278

Pell
Danny 353
David 353
Melissa 353

Pelton
Charles 51
John 51

Pender
Corrina 202
Molly 202
Wesley 202

Pendergraft
Herman Charles 325
James A. "Jim" "Doc" . 324

Larry 324
Rosette 326
Rosie 325
William David 325

Pennington
Nannie 564

Pequese
Susan C 445

Perez
Robert 234
Steven 21

Perkins
Calva 143
Geraldine 143
Imogene 143
Joe Weaver 412
Sherrie 234
Worth 143

Perriera
Rejanne SantAna . . . 235

Perrin
Donald O. 27

Perry
Addie "Nancy" 67
Amanda "Mandy" 597
Anna Belle 199
Barbara 247
Elizabeth 247
Isaac 71
Isaac Floid 71
James 247
John Henry 247
Kathryn 247
Levi 198
Lulu 63
Sadie Mae 198

Perryman
Cynathia "Cindy" Darlene
. . . . 310
Gary Don 130
Tony Shea 130

Peterman
George L. 253
Sarah Louise 253

Peterson
Floyd Douglas 325
Floyd Montgomery . . . 324
Lee Roy 325
Lynn Ann Atkins 44
Mark 325
Matilda Elizabeth "Tilly"
. . . . 325
Oscar Tait "Pete" 325

Pettitt
Marvin Clifford 402
Pettvies
Isaac 505
Petty
Ida E. 392
Mary Ann 164, 175
Pearl B. 392
William H. 392
Pettyjohn
Ella N. 140
Everett C. 140
Howard 140
James W. 140
Pearl 140
William T. 140
Pfieffer
J.F. 180
Pheasant
David 143
Jerry 142
Robert 143
Phelps
Andrea Ann 131
Philips
Dinwiddie Brazier 578
James 578
Laura 578
Laura E.S. 578
Mary Caroline 578
Roberta Gustavia 578
Virginia Edith 578
William 575, 576, 578
William Fowke, Jr . . . 578
William Fowke, Sr . . . 578
Phillips
Alice 592
Anna Snowbell 349
Calvin F. 218
Carol 49
Champ 89
Chanie 348
Clara Estora 347
Clyde Iredell "Pat" . . . 349
Connie Janine 200
Darcus Belle 323
Delmar 349
Edith Jane 383
Eli 349
Elijah Day 383
Elizabeth (Fowke) . . . 577
Ennis 347
Ethel Mae 319

Freddy 49
Greely Curtis 347
Horace Harrison 347
How Columbus 347
Isabella Ellen 218
James Blaine 347
James Henry 218
James M. 217
John 218
Johnson Alonzo 349
Joseph A. 218
Lou Eva Mae 347
Margaret Ann 219
Martha Ann "Polly" 17
Martin Philo 345
Mary 62, 345
Mary Etta 218
Mildred Leota 349
Millard Monroe 347
Molly 501
Nancy Jane 218
Nathan 348, 349
Robert Franklin 349
Samuel Paul 49
Sanders 526
Sarah Frances 218
Sarah Pauline "Polly" . 347
Vertie Reeves 349
Wade Harold 347
William Fowke, Sr . . . 577
William Joseph Sr . . . 347
William Thomas 218
William "Henry" 319
Zacharia 218
Zachariah 218
Phipps
Abigail 594
Anna Jane 464
Pickering
Nancy E. 66
Pickle
Emaline 317
Lydia 317
Pierce
Ermil 46
Georgia 142
Nell 271
Pierson
Claudia Ann 179, 180
Pigg
Bradley Morgan 416
Donna Faye 416
Eva 56
Keith 416

Pilkenton
James M. 345
Pillegrini
Henry 230
Timothy Paul 230
Pintard
John 517, 519
Louisa H. 519
Pitchford
Michael 270
Pitt
Mary 357
Pitts
Ann Maria 238
Charles H. 239
James 558
Jimmie Ruth 415
Lucy Marie 314
Pitzer
Jane 89
Plumlee
Beulah Mae 228
Dee 228
George Dee 228
Larry Dee 229
Lyndall Ada 228
Tolbert Fanning 228
Vickie Kay 229
Plummer
Dave 595
Pocernish
Jerri Lynn 44
Norma Jean 44
Poe
Lucinda 89, 90
Pogue
Floyd 413
John L. 555
Poindexter
Perry 67
Pointer
Garret Daniel 199
Larry 199
Pokojski
Kathryn Sue 60
Pollard
Daniel H 116
Fanny Mae 67
Samuel 67
Pontious
Tanna Rae 40
Pool

659

Ann 591
Mary 590

Poor
Lisa 391

Porter
Eleanor 43
Wanda 354

Posey
Barbara 42
Foster Ray 429

Post
Alfred B 112

Potter
Ralph 235
Sarah Millesa 475

Potts
Christine 203
Craig 203
Enoch 338
Fred 338
Jeff 203
Lee 203
Lindsey 203
Raymond 203

Powell
Atha 201
Edward Garnett 201
Fannie 325
Janice Ann 201
John Madison 345
Lucylle 201
Mayme Lee 201
Sarah E. 201
William Archie 205

Prater
Johnny 558
Judy 559
Louise 559
Patsy 558

Precise
David R. 472
John F. 471
Martha S. 472
Robert P. 472

Pressnell
Carlos Eugene 415
Joseph 415

Preston
Eddie Launa 527

Preyer
Caspar 500

Price
Emily Catherine 454

Jane 453
Maude Emily 383
William 364

Prince
Alma Jo 550
Lucille 550

Prine
James Eddie 315

Pringle
Martha J. 457

Pritchett
Ada 98
Clarinda 98
Claude 91
Edward 98
Emily 98
Harvey 98
Jessie 98
Mattie 98
Olie 91
Sidney 98
William 98

Proctor
Luther 179

Pryer
Carrie Lynn 234
Kevin Lee 234
Korey Lee 234
Roger Lee 233

Pryor
Francis 308
Kimberly Sue 54

Pugh
Allen P. 563
Betty Lee 563
John Mabry 563
Lena 563

Purdy
Viola "Belle" Maybelle 296

Pursifull
Grace 94

Pursley
Sarah 164
William, III 166

Purtle
Delilah 78

Purvis
Hazil Beshears 94

P'Pool
Frances 67
Laymon 67

Quarles

Bruce 293

Quick
David Gerald 39

Quinlan
Margaret Marie 103

Quinton
Rachell 262
Walter 262

Rae
Newton 157

Rager
Christopher 23

Raines
Alfred Lee 20
Alice 24
Alice Mae 19
Benjamin 24
Benjamin Franklin . 19, 20
Bert Edward 24
Beulah Hazel 19, 21
Bonnie Elaine 21
Carolyn Sue 21
Dale Willey 21
Evelyn Kay 21
Forest Mathew 21
Geraldine 21
Henry Edward 20
James Alfred 24
Jeremiah Oscar 24
Jerry Ben 21
Jerry William 21
Judith Ann 21
Larry Wayne 21
Leah Darlene 21
Leamon Oscar 21
Mark Stevan 21
Melvin Ray 21
Oleta Faye 21
Othal Viola 20
Rose Marie 21
Ruby Mae 21
Wanda Laverne 21

Rains
Bryan Keith 132
Caleb Zachary 132
Cayden Matthew 132
Colton Daniel 132
George 24

Ramsburg
Helen 242

Randolph
Isaac McAlpin 267
James H. 582

Ranger
Eliza Jane 379
Rappeli
Danny Raymai 49
Gus 49
Joy Lynn 49
Rau
Judy Rae 552
Rawlings
John 358
Ray
Anne 183
J.W. 18
Jack W. 414
James 141
James Marlon 157
Johnie Lee 418
Louisa 141
Thomas 247
Zelpha Adeline 141
Ray/Rae
Newton 157
Rayborn
George Washington . . 138
Jesse Winett 138
Jewel Juanita 138
Marjorie Leone 138
William Howard 138
Wilma Ione 138
Raymer
Elizabeth 289
Raymond
Louisa 98
Rea
Abraham S. 137
Adeline 134
Adeline Elizabeth . . . 135,
137
Benjamin F. 136
Bob 136
Burl 136
Carthena 135
Chloe Dora 136
Clifford 136
Daniel Robert 134
Dearl 136
Emma D. 136
Ferby 135
Franklin 157
Hallie 137
Harry 136, 137
Hazel 137
Irene 137

J. Harvey 136
James 136, 137
James Henry 135
James Thomas 135
Madeline 137
Maurice Van 137
Oleta 136
Paul 137
Rosie E. 136
Thomas Edison 136
Thomas H. B. 134
Thomas Henry 134
Ward 137
Wayne 136
William J.P. 134
Reach
Edwin 391
Read
Robbie Taylor 69
Reaves
Albert 138
Elmer 138
Gladys 138
Ila 138
James W. 138
Nellie 138
Ollie 138
Rhoda 138
Stella 138
Redding
Betty 352
Charles 352
Essie 352
Eugene 352
John L. 352
Josephine "Josie" . . . 352
Miles 352
Patsy 352
Redman
Neva 40
Redmon
Susie Ann 69
Reed
Danny Gayle 50
Danny Gayle, Jr 50
David Warren 51
Dennis Jason 51
Diana Dawn 51
Effie 326
Joyce Jean 51
Mary Arizona 322
Pearl 50
Robert Bruce 51
Robert E. 464

Tammy Michele 51
Reese
Chester 175
Richard 172, 175
Reeves
Austin John 398
Brian Lynn 397
Jared Brian 398
Martha 245
Reid
Elizabeth 594
Reiff
Frances Marie 204
Reimer
Jonathan Paul 117
Kimberly Ann 117
Paul Gerhardt 117
Stefanie Lynne 117
Reinert
Mary Ellen 116
Reinke
Fred 352
Remer
Pearl Lorrain 404
Renfro
Norma Ann 21
Renner
Catherine 252
Rentz
Foah O. 111
Roland 111
Roland, Jr 111
Rettig
Diana 38
Revara
Winnona Marguerita . 228
Rexroat
Marsha 402
Rey
Peter 357
Reyault
Christopher 356
Reynolds
Kate 563
Rhea
Esther 277
John 276, 277
John, Sr 277
Margaret 277
Nancy 277
Sally 445
Sally L. 277

William 277

Rhodes
Robyn Ann 286

Rice
Al 25
Ambrose L. 297, 299
Andrew 117
G.W. 297, 299
Hattie 346
John 220, 282
John B. 221
John Tandy 270
Lucy A. 501
Rebecca 220
Rhoda 117
Stephen 213, 220

Rich
Lawrence 404
Linda Kay 404

Richards
Elize A. 379
Richard 35

Richardson
Anita Gwenn 401
Billy Jack 402
Clarence Ray 402
Daisy Brazier 444
Darla Kay 402
Elinore Nadine 400
Gary Ray 402
Gordon Clarence 402
Ina Gertrude 402
Jermey Scott 402
Jerry Lee 402
Joe 354
Justin Ray 402
Karl Ray 402
Kristopher James 402
Larry Wayne 402
Lena Lucille 403
Loyd Ray 401
Minnie Leora 396
Necia Leigh 402
Nettie May 396
Norma 392
Rachel 526
Randi Michelle 402
Ray Cecil 403
Rebecca Lynn 402
Rufus Clay 394, 395
Virginia Pearl 398
Walter Calvin . . . 394, 398
Walter Dale 401
Wanda Fay 394, 400

Rickbohm
Todd G. 233

Rickert
Fred 283
Freddie 283
Nancy Ann 283

Rickets
William 521

Ricketts
Dwayne Steven 416
James Steven 416
John Edward 416
Justin Daniel 416
Luther 416
Steven James 416

Riddle
Betty Louise 232
Buster 391
Debra Kay 391
Elizabeth Arlene 230
Eula Maxine 230
James 230
Marilyn Roseanne . . . 230
Marsh Lea 230
Robert Ellis 230
William Ernest 230

Ridgway
Alzoma 123
James 590

Rife
Daniel Bryand 397
George Philip 397
Lynda Denise 397
Philip Ben 397
Tammy Kaye 397

Rigby
Margaret Clara . . 549, 550
William Green 550

Riser
Barbara Yvonne 130
Deryl Calcote 130

Risley
Ken 336
Noah 338
Susan Jane 338

Roam
Harley Preston . . 394, 400
Harley Preston, Sr . . . 400
Harley Robin 401
Jennifer Lee 401
Roy Robin 401

Roark
Deborah Lynn 402

Robbins
Janet (Stevens 192

Roberts
Alfred Marion 266
Amanda 265, 266
Amanda J. 266
Andrew 94
Asa Ellis 264, 268
Bazzel 271
Calvin 269
Caroline M 122
Charles Melvin 95
Charles Wilson 269
Daniel Jerod 96
David 232, 265
Elias 257
Elias R. "Robbie" 264
Elijah 265
Elizabeth 264
Elizabeth Canses 270
Elizabeth Jane 266
Emilee Cheyenne 96
Florence Elizabeth . . . 269
Francis Marion "Jack"
. . . . 266
Frank Andrew 95
Frank Aubrey 95
George W. 269
George Washington . . 265
Georgia Ruth 95
Hugh 267
Hugh Ellis 269
Hugh F. 265
India A. 267
James E. 78
James Mitchell 271
John 271
John C. 264
John Calvin 264-268, 270-
272
John Francis 266
Joseph A. 270
Julia Ann 267
Julie Lynette 96
Linda Margaret 95
Lucinda Francis 268
Manda Isibel 270
Margaret 269, 272
Margaret A. 265
Martha Mandring 268
Mary A. 264
Mary L. 265
Mary Lee 267
Mary Savannah 270
Millie Frances 72, 78

Monroe 269
Nancy Ruth 95
Nellie Marie 96
Nora Lee 95
Rebecca 271
Rebecca Elizabeth . . . 272
Rebecca J. 264
Richard 95
Richard Lee 96
Richard Lee, Jr 96
Robert Samuel 270
Rosa Della 269
Samuel H. 270
Samuel Henry 266
Sarah Angeline 269
Sarah E. 265
Sarah Jane 268
Scotland L. C. 271
Snyder E. 214
Susan Elizabeth 267
Vina Tennessee 270
Walter 271
William 269
William Charles 95
William H. 265
William L. 272
William Louis . . . 264, 270
William Lyle 266
William Melvin 94

Robertson
Holt 416
Xerxes 312

Robinson
Effie 224, 236
Jennie 595
Marie 37
Ollie Blanton 116
Ollie Blanton Jr 116

Rodden
Audie Faye Elizabeth . . 80

Rodgers
Alexandra Megan 22
Jacob 586
Jordan Dale 22
K. Curtis Dale 22

Rodono
Angela Marie 211
Anthony James 211
Dominic Joseph 211
Paul Arthur 211
Richard Lawrence . . . 211

Rodriguez
Sylvia Navarro 127

Rogers

Brigette 353
Carl Thoms 432
Casey 432
Dustin 432
Edith 419
Lawrence 526
Leonard 311
Margaret E . . 84, 106, 108
Mattie Kathrin 549
Mildred 549
Peggy 311
Thomas 526

Rohr
Cary Eugene 111
Chester Arthur 111
Eugene Mitchel 111
Kerwin Dean 111
Nelda Evans 111
Wyman Mitchell 111

Roland
Barbara 85

Roles
William 322

Ronstance
Aaron Joseph 41
Jeffery Allen 41
Noah Scott 41
Scott Joseph 41
Stacy Jo 41

Roosevelt
Jose 520

Root
Margaret 505

Rose
Albert 224, 229
Beulah Helen 232
Burl Efton 232
Edward 139
Eula Odessa 229
Joan Darlene 232
John 383
Laurena 383
Mona Marie 234
Nancy Jean 232
Sarah J. 308
Walter 120

Ross
Anna Agnes 393
Bernard B. 55
Bob 56
Grace R. 36
Isaac 55
Isaac John 36
Jack 56

John 422
Willia 179

Rostance
Bertram Joseph 40
Joseph L. 40
Rebecca Sue 40

Roten
Margaret 346
Martisha Cordelia . . . 346
Mattie 346

Rouley
Mary Viola 47

Rowe
David Allen 234
Gerald Lawrence 234
Gerald Lawrence, Jr . 234
Gerald Lawrence,III . . 234
J.T. Lewis 234
Jeffrey Allen 234
John Edward 234
Karley Alys 234
Marcellus 199
Vearl 138

Rowell
Lucy A. 562

Royall
Richard 170

Rucker
Elizabeth A. "Bettie" . . 323

Rudloff
Velma Oleta 390

Rudy
Carol Sue 53
Kenneth Allen 53
Leroy Allen 53
Leroy Willford 53
Mellissa Jean 53

Rumble
Henry 249

Runnels
Ben 389
Henderson 389
Leonard 389
Lula 389
Mary Elizabeth 389
Willie 389

Rupp
Howard 280
Melody 203

Russell
Ada 425
Edy 336
James 40

Maude C. "Maudie" .. 226
Nicholas 41
Ron 170
Vashti 454

Russler
Catherine 64

Ruth
Mary "Polly" 215

Rutherford
Amy Louise 169

Ryan
James Edward 477
Jimmie 471, 476, 477

Ryckman
Albert 505
Cornelia 503
Tobias 503

Sadler
Richard Ray 60
William Lester 228

Sailor
Jean Carol 47

Samek
Shelene Marie 566

Sample
Alexix 43

Sampo
Gina 327

Sampsell
Artelia 271

Sanchez
Rosie 404

Sanders
Alice 476
Alra 475
Anna 476
Caledonia "Callie" ... 159
Eliza L. 475
Emma Jean 558
Henry J. 475
James 168
James Ray 425
Jane 475
Jess 179
John Washington 475
Joseph 475
Joseph M. 474
Joseph M.G. 475
Kendall Wayne 425
Laura 475
Martha J. "Mattie" ... 478
Monroe 475
Myrtle E. 475

Nannie 168
Pamela Jean 425
Phenie Emma 475
Ray 425
Sarah E. 475
Wallace 475
Wiley A. 475

Sands
Earl Raymond 65
Eugene Rollin 65
Glen 65
Rollins 65
Wayne 65

Sandy
Adriah 63
William 330

Sanford
Charles Thomas 310
Ronald 310
Samanatha "Sammie" Karon
.... 310

Sangster
Lawrence 239

Sapp
C.C. 459

Sappington
Sarah "Sallie" 460

Sargent
Barbara Snyder 158
Bradley Jonathan 161
Christopher Ray 161
Crystal Faith 161
Jody Ray 161
Robert Duane 161
Robert Duane, III 161
Robert Duane, Jr 161
Steve Raymond 161
Tyler Lee 161

Sartin/Sartain
Kelly 343

Sasser
Liaze 242

Satterfield
Elizabeth 220
James 220
Lloyd B. 555

Saunders
Andrew 555
Dick 555
Jason 555
Patrick 556

Sayre
Annie Lee 123

Elizabeth 123
Francis Alvin 123
Hazel 123
John Henry "Hank" ... 123

Scaggs
Valerie Ann 39

Scarbough
Sandy Moore 60

Scarbrough
Darla 60
Darla Kay 58
Glen Albert 58
Glen Earl 58
Kay LaVonne 58
Levi 58
Rocky Lee 58
Ronnie Gene 58

Schaefer
Esther 381

Schaffer
Christine Marie 46
Robert Michael 46
Samuel 46
Sandra Sue 46

Schaubert
Clarence 62
Hazel Marie 62
Maxine 62
Robert Clarence 62

Schleuter
Barbarba Ruth 62
Eugene 62
William 62
William A. 62

Schmidt
John Scott 116
Judianne Marie 117
Robert 116

Schmitt
Kathlene Marie 43

Schoonmaker
Engletie 512

Schoonover
Al 57
Jill 57
John 57
Kevin Scott 57
Timmy 57

Schouten
Lysbet 501, 511

Schulse
Elizabeth "Eliza" C. .. 183
Mark 183

Schumbach
Arch 123
Schwamb
Louis 272
Scobey
Angus R. 477
Oliver Wallace 477
Scoggins
Darin Donsel 553
Derika Ellen 553
Donna Beth 553
Donsel W. 552
Dusti Renee 552
Janet Diane 553
John Dwight 552
John Dwight, II 552
Justin Richard 553
Scott
Clora Dell 269
Ellen Gertrude 596
Francis Perry 269
Harriett W. 338
Homer 86
Louise 86
Michael Ray 114
Mitchel Eugene 114
Ronnie 114
Scribneron
Glenda Sue 227
Scrivner
John 156
Seamon
Hannah 522, 526
William 526
Sears
Lauron Lemens 406
Seaton
Sarah Ann 256
Seay
David 187, 189
Sebrie
Madison 528
Sultana 528
Seddelmeyer
Claude 202
Seely
Arron Patrick 233
Cooper 233
Seevers
Charles Newton 95
Charles Thomas 96
Jaden Thomas 96

Joylynn Rose 96
Tanner Ryan 96
Sells
William Ernest 95
William Ernest, Jr 95
Sessions
William 245
Settle
Joy 198
Severn
Rebecca 249
Severt
Clementine Brown . . . 346
Sevoss
Thos. L. 519
Sewald
Carol Marie 230
Peter "Pete" 230
Shackleford
Cora 108
Ione E. Kirtly 108
Mollie 108
Willis Green 108
Shaffer
Frederick, Jr 301
Shaffner
Dale Samuel 558
Shain
Dinah 96
Shanafelt
Emma 55
Shanefelt
Emma M. 36
Shankel
Elisha 26
Peter 26
Shannon
Christine 555
John Dudley 205
William Frances 205
Sharp
Jane 24
Shasteen
J. J. 441
Luisa Jane 388
Shaver
Jessie, Jr 419
Shaw
Barbara 327
Danny Ray 46
George 56
Hettie Mae 314

Ralph 46
Robin 56
Susan Darlene 46
Shea
Cora Dorothy 327
Shearer
Elizabeth (Brazier) . . . 376
Sheets
Amanda R. 379
Sheffield
Mrs Ella Lee 444
Shell
Elizabeth "Betsy" 31
Shelton
Louisa 408
Shepherd
Nelia 344, 347
Thomas 348
Sherrell
Myrtle 266
Sherroll
Henrietta 269
Sherwood
Asa 501
John 501
Mary 501
Thomas, II 501
Thomas, III 501
William 501
Shields
Ada Marie Cuthbirth . . 141
Karley Elizabeth 200
Lewis 19
Randy 200
Sidney 382
Shipley
Billy Joe 427
Shipman
Bonnie 275
Shlegle
William R. 192
Shlinder
Glen Ray 20
Linda Joyce 20
Millie 20
Minnie Lou 20
Odus B. 19
Thomas 20
Shoat
Maude 290
Shoemake
Blakeley 544

665

Stephen G. 544
Shoemaker
Stacey 60
Shonhart
Noel 94
Shopteaw
Eddie 63
Shores
Holly Gayle 199
Sue Lynn 199
Vernie Clifton 199
Willis Murl 199
Short
Ruby 81
Shoults
Mary Ann 185
Show
Ida 253
Showell
Armwell 586
Shutt
Bethany 61
Brad 61
Cassandre 62
Dusty 61
Holly 61
Terry 61
Travis 61
Sielert
David 331
Donna Jo Brasier 329
Sikkels
Jane 505
Siler
Sharaon 29
Sills
Carolyn 338
Cursey 338
J. H. 338
Joshua Henry 338
Silvey
Bryant 88, 89
James H. 89
Loudustie 89
Margaret A. 89
Mary May 267
Samuel Louis 89
Sarah E. 89
Susan E. 89
William E. 89
Simmons
Clinton Alan 402

Elizabeth 363
George 363, 364
Kayla Lynnette 402
Martha 183
Susan 363
William 363
Simms
Ruby Pearl 559
Simpkins
Margaret 312
Simpson
Annie 432
Bill 292
Elmer 38
Jamie 38
Jane 38
Jim O. 38
Robert 292
Sims
Abner Austin 128
Arthur Paul 129
Billie Don 127
Charles Edward 129
Charles Edward Jr . . . 129
Chelsea Renee 129
Christopher Ryan 129
Fonda 128
Gray 220
James Carlisle 127
Janiece Aline 128
Jo Dene 127
John Anthony 129
John Robert 128
Johnnie Raymon 127
Johnny Maurice 127
Judith Ann 128
Larry 127
Leslie Ann 128
Lisa Ann 128
Lulu 55
Margaret Ann 129
Mark 128
Michael 128
Mildred Pauline 128
Milton Carlisle 127
Nancy Kaye 130
Robert 127
Robert Brown 127
Robert Brown Jr 127
Robert Milton 127
Sandra Sue 129
Steven Ray 129
Wanda Fae 128
Wesley Ralph 129

William Horace 127
Sinclair
Ananias 35
Singleton
Pamela Sue 402
Sinklear
Polly 91, 92
Sinks
Andrew 37
Sitz
Brian 200
Briana Taylor 200
Cynthia Lauren 200
Skaggs
Ali Elizabeth 196
Chris 196
Josephine 289
Kalee Dunn 196
Sarah 137
Skillman
Josiah 39
Mary 39
Slabaugh
Marian 111
Slane
Maggie Belle 381
Slater
Mary Louise 48
Slattery
Elizabeth 587
Slaughter
Georgia 94
James Allen 245
James Sydney 245
Mattie Lou 245
William 526
Slayton
John 559
Sligar
Diana Lynn 61
Smallwood
Jean 187
Smart
John S.C. 191
Smedley
Nancy 246
Smiley
Estelle 554, 555
Gary 170
Jerry Dean 171
Richard Lee 171
Smit

Thos 505

Smith
Addie 234
Algie Kipling 199
Algie Ray 199
Andy 390
Anise 226
Ann 457
Beatrice 564
Bobby Sue 419
Chad Andrew 26
Charles Galloway 456
Cornelia Elizabeth . . . 457
Daisy 456
Dallas 236
Daniel 456
David 390, 455, 456
Edwin G. 226
Esther 180
Esther Jane 456
Eunice "Lora" 116
Everett F 116
Ezekiel 456
Francis 473
Fred 199
George Andrew Jackson
. . . . 18, 24
George Andrew Jackson
"Jack" 24
Gwynn 412
Harry 94
Hazel Lorraine 95
Henry 459
Houston 456
Ida Andrew . . . 18, 24, 25
Ida Joan 404
Isabelle "Lucy" 25
James 363
Jennifer Suellen 390
Jess 25
John 218, 264, 459
John D. 457
John M. 25, 394
Joseph 447
Karol Lee 199
Kathy 26
Kellie Adelle 403
Kenneth Eugene 456
Lemmie 417
Lequetta 419
Linda Fay 26
Linda Kay 226
Lisa Fay 236
Lonnie Charles 26
Lorena 456

Lucille E. Beshears . . . 94
Lucinda (Brazier) 447
Lucy 457
Luther R 116
Macy Ofield 26
Mary 113, 387
Mary J. 25
Mary JoAnn 204
Mary Lois 390
Mary Susan (Toney) . 264
Mary "Polly" 394
Milly 323
Nancy Ann 457
Noland 413
Ollie Edwin 116
Ollie Edwin Jr 116
Rebecca 451
Rebecca "Becky" . . . 25
Richard 455, 456
Rita Kay 116
Robert 447
Roberta Gail 226
Rosetta 390
Rowena 18, 25
Roy C. 227
Samantha May 116
Sandra K. 390
Sarita 263
Stephen Douglas 456
Susannah 363
Theodore Printis 393
Thomas J. 598
Velma 456
Verna Taulbee 288
Virginia Ann 456
Virginia Serena 459
Wayne 47
Weneton 390
Wesley Brazier 456
William Ira 456
William Ira Jr 456
William Richard 456
William Thomas 390

Smothers
Nancy 135

Snead
Samuel 429

Snider
Doris Ann 189
James Langford 189

Snow
Robert L. 41
Sherry 41

Snyder

Barbara Ann 161
Carl Lee 160
Deborah 161
Diana Lynn 161
Edward 353
Edward, Jr 353
Evelyn 161
Harold 63
James 161
Janet 160
LaDonna 161
Laura 353
Mark 160
Martin V. 318
Michael 161
Raymond Lee 160
Reba 63
William 160

Solley
Alonzo Edwin 327
Cecil James 327
Marvest Preston 327
Michael C. 327
Michael Dale 327
Pauline 327
Ruth Lois 327
William 327
Wilma Doyce 327

Soloman
Christeen 430
Jessie "Pete" 429
Jim 429
Mattie 417
William 429

South
Thomas 345

Southard
Charles 79
Jobe 79

Souther
Elizabeth 593

Sparks
Brenda Ann 397
Bryan Wade 398
Lee 195
Misty Marie 398
Roland Wade 397
Terry Wade 398

Speake
Lee B 130

Spearman
Brian Allen 327

Spears

667

James 543
Lewis Anderson 350
Martha 543
Winnie Alice 350

Speer
Cornelius C. 216
Emley Elizabeth 217
George H., II 216
George Hopkins . 215, 216
George Hopkins, Jr . . 217
John 215
John, Jr 215
John, Sr 216
Mary Elmina 216
Mary Jane 217
Nathaniel Mason 215
Phoebe Brashears . . . 215
Samantha (Mason) . . 216
Thomas Jefferson . . . 216
William 216

Speers
Amanda C. 218
Anna Louise Tennessee
. . . . 219
Elizabeth 219
Elmer 220
Franklin Monroe 218
George 219
George Newton 219
James William 219
John Lindsey 219
John T. 219
John, Jr 218
Lizzie 219
Maggie 219
Marion Monroe 219
Martha Jane 219
Mary 219
Minnie 219
Nathaniel H. 219
Nathaniel Mason 219
Phoebe Brashears . . . 218
Rosetta 219
Samuel Jefferson 219
Steve 220
Virgil 219
William Thomas D. . . 218

Speigel
Helen 254

Spence
Gordon Arthur 297

Spencer
Luther 408
Martha L. 407

Reece 350
Rick 39
Ryan Matthew 40
Sara Michelle 40

Spicer
Ann 496
Nicholas 496
Samuel 496
Susanna 496
Thomas 496

Spivey
Steve 310

Splatt
Richard 573

Splinter
Kimberly Ann 28

Sponberg
Ester 286

Spotts
Samuel 191

Sprague
Jane 116

Sproull
Lawrence W. 58
Lenora Fern 59
Nellie Louise 59
Raymond Franklin . . . 59
William R. 59

Sprouse
Carl M. 204
James 204
John Wesley 204
Martha "Mattie" . 194, 204

Stacy
Corzillia York Brashear
. . . . 288

Stafford
Van Rachel 314
Warren Cecil 558

Stailfy
Jerry 129

Stallings
John 460
Malachi 246

Stamp
Laura R.C. 393

Stanert
Homer Lee 226

Stanford
George S. 201
Larry G. 201
Norma Jean 201

William Clyde 201
Stanger
Donald Kenneth 435
Donna 435

Stanley
Arlene Louise 595
Eliza A. 36
Linda 414

Stantenburg
Isaac 503

Stanton
Warren 124

Staples
Sarah 559

Starns
Alfred Carter "Alf" 323
Edgar H. 323
Elizabeth Ann 323
Elliott Franklin 323
F.F. 322
George W. 322, 323
George W. "Gus" 323
Harry C. "Dock" 323
James L. "Jim" 323
Jason 323
Lewis N. 323
Martha 323
Mary E. "Mollie" 323
Maude 323
Nancy 323
Nancy C. 323
Nicholas 323
Sallie I. 323
Samantha R. 323
Susan C. 323
Walter 323
William Nicholas 323

Steelman
Annie 19
Beulah 19
Claud 293
J. E. 19
Joseph Ellis 19
L. C. 19
Lonnie 19

Steen
Randall Jan 233
Tiffany Renee 233

Stephans
JoEllen 204

Stephens
Adam 469
Amanda 267

Andrew Jackson "Pete"
.... 474
Bettie 466, 468
Charles 469
Daniel 469
Elizabeth 469
Elizabeth "Betsy" ... 463,
470
Elizabeth "Bettie" 473
Ellis 469, 471, 473
Henry H. 473
Jeremiah 469
Jeremiah, Jr 469
John 468, 469
John Wesley 473
Joseph 473
Josiah 469
Josiah, Jr 469
Lillie Elizabeth "Betty" 474
Mary Jane 473
Samuel 469
Solomon S. "Dick" .. 470,
473
Solomon, Jr 474
William 469
William B. "Billie" 474

Stepp
Ethel B. 136

Steppe
Carrie Leigh 96

Stevens
Bertha Lee 554
Forrest 554
J.W. 554
Janet 192
Lee Ann 192
LeeAnn 192
Lyda 554

Stevenson
John R. 496

Stewart
Artis Bell 68
Douglas James 233
Henry 527
Howard 237
Howard Eugene 236
Mary Ann 527
Nancy 597
Randy 237
Vanessa 41
William John 68

Stidum
Grand 87

Stiffler

John 252
Mary 252
Stinnett
Linda Jean 415
Lisa 425
Stockard
Jim 425
Judy 425
Sherry 425
Stockman
Norman Marsdale ... 558
Stolz
Jerry Edward 415
Stone
Amanda 202
Angela 203
Ann 575
Chloe 202
Donna 203
Elaine 203
Eliza 296
Elizabeth "Lizzie" 340
Ervin 202
Garland 202
Gary G. 203
Jeremy 203
Jill 203
John 202
Lance 203
Lottie 203
Louie Dale 202
Maureen 202
Melissa 202
Michael 202
Nathan 202
Renee 203
Rex 203
Robert 202
Ryan 203
Traci 203
Tracy 202
Tyler 203
Vernon 203
Stovall
Hagar 336
Martha "Patsy" 291
Stover
Robert 36
Strain
Alma Esther 420, 421
Brian 426
C.B. 424
Erica 426
Frances Nicole 426

George Raymond ... 426
George W. . 420, 424, 426
Gracie Jo 425
Jerry 426
Jimmy 426
Joe 425
Mary Louise 425
Nelda Pearl 425
Willie 424
Straisner
Dallas Belzora 260
Elizabeth LeAndrea .. 260
Healeder Elizabeth Drucilla
.... 260
Henrietta W. 260
James 260
Jefferson 260
Jefferson F. 260
Julia Frances 260
Lula Missouri 260
Mary Margaret 260
Michael 260
Nancy C. 260
Rhoda Charlotty 260
Rose Zinna Rebecca Jane
.... 260
Sarah P. 260
William Jasper 260
Strandridge
Martha 419
Strandtman
Mary Jane 422
Strandtmann
Donna Theresa 422
Phil 422
Streater
Edw 357
Strickland
Rosa 173
Stromberg
Hjalmar 286
Rowena Deborah Elizabeth
.... 285
Stuart
Elizabeth 343
Stubbs
Frances 542-544
James 543
John 543
John or William 543
Lewis 543
Peter 543
Thomas 543

William 542, 543

Stull
Darlene 94

Stutzman
Mary 559

Styles
Bessie 351
Flora Direne 351
James "Big Jim" 351
John Murphy 350
John Murphy, Jr 351
Johnsie 351
Margaret 351
Robert 351
Shirley Jean 351

Suddeth
Clarence 64

Suey
Sarah 141

Sullivan
Jessica Layne 328
Mable 180
Robert 328
Scott Alexander 328

Sullivant
Arminta Elizabeth . . . 141

Summer
Josh 131

Summerville
Annetta 36
Jack 36
John Alva 36
Robert 36

Sumner
Leona 209

Sumners
Geraldine 236
W. 236

Sunser
Nancy 121

Sward
David 422

Sweeney
Alfred Levi 437
Claude Raymond 437
Robert Dale . . . 430, 432,
                436, 437
Vivian 437

Swickard
Oneida Lee 170

Swift
Richard Moss 204

Tennessee 204

Sykes
Hayward 558
Nancy Jane 545, 561

Tabb
Jean 288
Roy Eldred 287, 288
Roy Everett 287, 288

Taber
Gloria 336
James 336
John 336
William 336

Tabor
Averil 338
Bennett 338
Ede (Edy?) 339
Edy 336
Eliza 339
Fanny 339
George McKinley 338
Gloria 338
Henry 336-338
Henry William 339
Hiram 339
Isaac 336, 339
Jacob 339
James 336, 339
John Franklin 339
John M. 338
John William 338
Manerva 338
Mary 339
Minerva 339
Nancy Jane 339
Phoebe 339
Ray 338
Robert 339
Russell 336
Rutha Eda (Edy?) . . . 339
Sally 339
Sarah 339
Susan 339
Tabitha 338
William 336
William J. 338

Tallent
Jane 267
John 266
Jonathan 266
Lucy A. 266
Margaret 266
William A. 266, 272

Talley

Aletta Key 237
Dennis 237
Edna Mae 236
James 79
Norman 237
Verl 236

Tankersley
Vance 310

Tankusley
W & M 441
William 441

Tanner
Frank 109
Franklin D 122
Henry 109
Jno 505
Raymond 109

Tanskersley
Rachel Irene 432

Tarpley
James 244
James, Jr 244
Mary 244
Winifred 244

Tassaker
Mary 575, 576
Richard 576

Tate
Delbert 143
Edith 141
Eloise Sue 60
Gary 56
John 56
Warren 413

Tatum
Bailey Suzanne 310
Clifton Eugene 310
Clifton Eugene, III . . . 310
Clifton Eugene, Jr . . . 310
Philip Scott 310
Preston Scott 310
Tiffany 310
Xanthia Nicole 310

Taulbee
Archie 288
Dwight David 288
Granvel P. 288

Taylor
David 587
Delie 70
Gregory 315
John 414
John A. (or H.) 70

John Thomas 419
Lemuel Eugene 70
Lillie 199
Linda 556
Martha Ellen 77
Nancy 70
Octavia "Octie" 70
Richard 69
Richard, Jr 69
Rosemary 414
Sarah Leweller 70
V. (Church) 342

Teague
Eugenia Diana 350
George 87

Tefertillar
Henry 134

Temple
Marjorie 435

Tenney
Margie Raye 397

Terrell
J.D. 429

Terwilliger
Jannetje 503

Teters
Thelma Lovina 314

Thacker
Jerusha 597

Thayer
Vera May 95

Theobald
John 505

Theobold
John 500

Therman
Jill 51
Richard 51

Thingvold
Glenda 287

Thomas
Anne Wagstaff 519
Bill 285
Brian John 23
Clinton Andrew 23
Cory David 23
James Harlan 390
Joe H. 285
Jonathan Brian 23
Norma 353
Polliann 474
Richard 418
Robin Beshears 94

Sheri 62
Susanna 496
Susannah 502
Sylvia Mae 390
Terry Joe 132
Tommie 23
Velma Faye 130
Willie 390

Thompson
America 332, 334
Annette Elizabeth . . . 228
Carrie E. 334
Elizabeth 245
Erick 228
Helen Dorothy 435
Herman 416
James Timothy 416
Jeannie 324
John 381
Nathaniel 332, 334
Nora 415
Robert Hanley 228
Tommy 44
Tommy Joseph 44
Tyler John 44
William 245

Thornberry
Hazel Ruth 419
Jim Wiley 419
Jo Ann 419
Lamar 419

Thorne
Thos 508

Thornton
Cindy Lynell 24
Ralph 559

Thoroughgood
Adam 575
Ann 575
Elizabeth 575

Thursk
Grace 381

Tibbs
Richard J. 55

Tidwell
Everett 237
Lavonna M. 237
Margaret 261

Tijerina
David Ricardo 52
Maria Susan 52
Ramiro 52

Tilghman

Sarah 250

Tilton
John 500
Peter 500
Rebecca 500

Timmerman
Jack 56
Tim Hugh 56

Timson
Judith 402

Tine
Felitha Cumile 339

Tinnon
Cynthia Ann "Cindy" . . . 79

Tipps
Era 431
Ernest 431
General Beauregard   430, 431
John 431
Leona Laura 127
May 431
Raybella 431
Viola (Solomon) 431
Viola Solomon 436

Tipton
Rebecca Ann 161

Toal
Susan Elaine Brazier . 445
Suzie Brazier 444
Tlen 445

Tocker
Dan'l 508

Tolman
Oba 423
Oba Rho 423
Otha Ernest 423
Tom 423
Vaughn 423

Tomilson
Margaret 118

Tomlinson
Ella T. 349
Levi 349
Maggie 349

Toney
"Elizabeth" M. 268
Cynthia Minerva 268
Mary Susan 264

Tooles
Robt 357

Torley

671

Edward 87
Touchstone
Sarah Jane 545, 556
Toups
Lena Clotile 303
Tower
Benton 195
Christian Benjamin .. 196
Matthew Ryan 196
Townsend
Beulah 391
Cordia Anne 420, 423
John 367
Myrtle 391
Trammell
Lilly M. 77
Rosa Lea 77
William Perry 77
Tredway
Mary Eliza 108, 110
William F 110
Trent
James 156
Trice
Kennie 419
Trisler
Irving 435
Willie Frances 435
Tritch
Lucille 274
Trott
Sarah 259
True
Elizabeth 39
Truhitte
Bobby Lee 27
Carolyn Annette 28
Jacklyn Lavern 28
Jeffery Michael 28
Robert Leonard 27
Ronnie Lee 27
Tubbs
James 585
Tucker
Bob 419
Hetty Jo 169
Kathy Smith 133
Linda 412
Turbaugh
Debbie Ann 235
Turley
Ed 110

Turnbough
Vanessa 93
Turner
Anne Albina 453
Betsey 595
Carrie Ann 286
Dorcas 247
Dorothy 122
Earl 123
Edwin J. 201
Eldon T. 21
Floyd 179
George A. 323
John 247
Lillie 419
May 418
Scott 179
Sylvester 123
Virginia L. 123
Zella R. 123
Turpin
Sarah 246
Twyman
James 189
Ubanks
Lori 40
Uhls
Nellie 65
Underwood
Nimrod 265
Toni Reneau 204
Unseld
Mary E. 291
Unsell
Lucretia A 85, 114
Upton
Arlosa 188
Bessie 413
Charles Thomas 412
Ernest Leonard 412
George A 188
George A. 188
George Washington .. 289
Georgeanne 188
Georgianne 187
Herbert Clifton 413
James Donald 413
Leona 287, 288
Mary Helen 412
Millie 188
Nadean 413
Paralee 289
Paralee Brite 288

Samuel E 188
Samuel E. 187, 188
Sarah Catherine 413
Virginia 413
William Eli 412
Wilma May 412
Utsinger
Nancy Brashears 275
Utterback
Bill 295
Iola 108
Vallet
Ralph 558
Van Alst
Joris 500
Maryken 500
Stephen 500
Van Dyck
Carolyn (Sills) 338
van Leesburgh
Vera 47
Van Ness
Charles L. 560
Georgia Ann 128
Thomas ... 549, 557, 560
Van Winkle
Bill 485
Brent 485
Vandenburg
Helen 70
Vandevort
Paul 249
William 249
VanHooser
Candy Sue 233
Vann
Edmond Edward 246
Luke 469
Margaret 245
Nancy 469
Vaughan
Shirley 38
Vaughn
Earl 63
Rhonda Jo 445
Vawter
Nancy 455
Vernon
Maggie 283
Vibbert
Eric 198
Vincent

Johnny 199
Megan 199
Victor 198
Vineyard
David 229
Wilma 229
Vinger
Gulbran 247
Vleck
Henry Van 521
Vogel
Grace Etta (Fair) 383
Marjorie 383, 384
Vose
Ida Ellen 595
Voss
Charles 63
Charles, Jr 63
Christina 63
Cindy 63
Harry 63
Janice 558
Lisa 63
Theresa 63
Troy Richard 63
Walter 63
Vowell
Clayton 59
Waddle
Ada Lee 233
Agaytha Ann 233
Donna Jean 234
Henry 233
Henry Lee Daniel 233
Rose Carol 233
Wade
Alisha Ruth 201
David Meade 201
Deborah Ann 201
Jason Daniel 201
Kyle Dean 201
Lucien Shirley 201
Waggoner
Clara 430
Clarence 430
Elizabeth 430
George 386
Lee 410
Wagner
Carl 45
Emily May 45
Frank Earl 45
Shirley 94

Walden
Nannie F. 578
William 578
Waldmeier
Loren 114
Thomas Frank 114
Walker
Alsie 140
Earl 381
Elizabeth 58
James Harmon 199
James Winthrop 230
Jeff 401
Jerry 344
Lena Lovell 200
Linda Arlene 230
Marion 429
Mary Hannah 456
Ora 429
Robert 512
Ruth Ellen 230
Sheldon 58
Thelma Gray 200
Willa Dean 201
William 344
Winthrop Charles "Win"
. . . . 230
Walkley
Patricia 93
Wall
Rachele Michelle 27
Wallace
Alpha O. 115
Eugene P. 115
Frank 115
Gaytha (Beshear) 82
Lorraine 130
Stephen 543
Waller
Beulah 291
Nancy Jane 415
Wallis
Teackle 239
Walraven
Susan Lorraine 328
Walsh
Selona 352, 353
Selona "Lon" Josephine
. . . . 345, 351
Walters
Mary Christine 230
Nannie 557
Polly 329

Richard C. 330
William 496
Walthall
Deomae 422
Walton
Melton 460
Wamack
Rebeccah 463
Wampler
Bryon Lee 227
Debra Lynn 227
Derrill Jean 227
Ronda Elaine 227
William Blain 227
Ward
Beverly J. 40
Linda 196
Trina Jo 132
Wayne Levec 558
Warden
Mary Catherine 268
Sarilda Jane (Garret) . 268
William 268
Warfield
Henry McTier 239
Warren
Cindy 40
John, Jr 377
Louise 63
Olive "Olley" 374
Phillip 46
Victor D. 46
Washam
Carl 227
Carl Delmer 228
Ella Geraldine 228
Florine Elizabeth 227
John 227
Washington
George 214, 530, 532
Wasson
Susan Morton 111
Waterman
Edith 124
Waters
Joseph "Pete" 344
Waterstraw
Eugene 438
Watkins
Alice May 45
Andrew John 45
Arlene Fay 46

Benjamin 45
Dorthy May 45
Edward Eli March 45
Eli 45
Ellen Faye 45
Eva 45
Floyd Raymond "Bill" .. 45
Frank 45
Frank (Brown) Eli 45
Glen Raymond 45
Helen Faye 45
Irma L. (Bonnie) 45
J.D. 46
John D. 46
John Floyd 45
Joyce Colleen 45
Kara Colleen 45
Kevin 46
Leah 46
Leroy Joseph 45
Mary Louise 45
Newton Edwin "Tony" . 45
Rebecca Lyn 45
Ruby 45
Shirley Ann 45
Silvia May 46
Thomas Franklin 45
Wendy 45

Watson
Barbara 247
Laura 249
Lucille Marie 127
Martha Addie 223
Mathew W. 441
Robert 247

Watts
Reuben 551

Weatherford
Stanley 123

Weaver
Fairy Ellen 314
Harry E. 331
J. W. 406
Nell Elizabeth 380
Rhoda 480
William C. 380

Webb
Ann Lynn 52
Hannah 589
Jaunita Luginia 52
Jaunita Luginia, Jr 52
Martha Ann 391
Mary Susan 165
Peggy Sue 52

Ruby Lucille 319

Weber
August F. 394
Susan 88

Webster
Louise 254

Weeks
Robt. D. 519

Weimholt
Jessica Marie 96

Weldon
Grover 290

Wells
Danny Wayne 553
Matthew Wayne 553

Welsen
Arewina 567
Louise Isabell ... 545, 567

Wempe
Sylvester 53

Weninger
James Charles 329
Virginia Lois 329

Werle
John C. 434
Kevin 434

Wesley
Barbara 63

Wessling
Bernajean 283
Bernie 283

West
Bertha 416
Camden G. 209
David C. 209
David Wayne 556
Doris J. 57
F.A. 209
Frank D. 209
Helen J. 445
Jason 354
John L. 209
Kristi 354
Kristie Paige 129
Nora Zilpha 380
Samuel L. 209
Stephanie 354
Terry 354

Westberry
Gary 171

Wester
Margaret 271

Westfall
Bertha 319
Charles 317, 318
George 317
Hallie 319
Martha E. 317
Robert 318, 319

Wetzler
George 34
Georgie 34
John 34
William 34

Weymoth
Louise 557

Whalen
Susan 63

Whan
Christopher 202
David 202
Jeremy 202
Kara 202

Wharton
Richard 584
William 584

Wheat
Betty Lou 199
Halqua 197
James Michael 199
Jim 257
Joseph Lee 199
Joseph Lee, Jr 199
Katherine 199
Keith Taylor 199
Leslie Dawn 199
Natasha Belle 199
Oral Lee 199
Othan 197
Virginia Rose 199

Wheeler
Ann 598
Charles 597
Darrell 93
Donna 92
Ellie May 93
Gene 92
Johnny 93
Ona Unity 597
Patricia 93
Rebecca 598, 599
Samuel 598
Vernon 93
Zella 112

Whitaker

Alice 357
Lydia 375, 382

White
Danny L 128
Faye 380
Gladys Opel 401
Helen Julia 380
Herbert O. 380
Hiram James 473
Laura 380
Lida Brasher 522
Mary 300
Park R. 379
Perry Samuel 380
Rodney Lee 128
Sarah Ann 17
Sybil 559
Walter George 380
Zachary Lee 129

Whitehead
Christopher 59
Christopher Casey 59
Tammy Lee 59

Whitfield
Lindsay Elizabeth . . . 304
Rhonda 304
Ross Elliot 303
Ross Stuart 303

Whitford
Clayborn 389
Frances Marion 389
Isaac 389
Lewis 389
Winnie 389

Whitney
Christine Francetta . . . 46
Debora Marie 45
Elenor Louise 46
John Ira 46
Julie Gaye 46
Robert Allen, III 45
Robert Allen, Jr 45
Steven Anthony 46

Whitten
Thomas Jr 83
Thomas Sr 83
William 83

Whitton
Elizabeth 83, 84
George 83
Jeremiah 83
Mary 83
Robert 83
Thomas 83

William 83

Whitworth
Sarah 311

Whorton
Alexander Wilbur "Dick"
. . . . 81
Alford 81
Austin 81
Beulah 81
Clifford 81
Della 81
Fay 81
Jacob W. 473
Jay 81
Lula 81
Miranda Clinton 78
Orville 81
Oscar 81
Ruby 81
Sylvester 81

Wier
Laurie 71

Wilburn
Blanche 297

Wilcox
Jennifer 29

Wilder
Karen Lynn 425

Wiley
Joyce 418

Wilkerson
Mary 164
Mary "Polly" 164

Wilkes
Kathleen 60
Wilma D. 59

Wilkins
Henry S. 547
Howell 548

Wilkinson
Jessie 402
Judy A. 167
Julius King 379
Melville Cox 379
Philip 505

Wilkison
Elizabeth 279

Wilks
Helen 329

Williams
Ada Lucille 57
Addeline Ada 58
Adrian M. 208

Allie Alice Eliza 36
Amanda Joyce 324
Amber 44
Ann 49
Anthony Wayne 40
Arthur Franklin 37
Arthur Newton 48
Atsy Geneva 312
B.W. 412
Barbara 56
Bertha 64, 65
Berthold 50
Bess 484
Bessie May 37
Bessie Mildred 57
Betty 65
Bobbie 55
Bradley Paul 38
Brian Robert 39
Brian Scott 44
Bryan Jeffrey 310
Bryce Michael 48
Cary Robert 55
Charles Carter 49
Charles E. 48
Charles Newton 49
Charles Wayne 47
Charles Wayne, III . . . 48
Charles Wayne, Jr . . . 48
Clara Alice 64
Clarence Edward 37
Claude Wellington 63
Clay 66
Cleo I. 55
Clyde 64
Cora Ann 37
Curtis 40
Damos 196
Dan 65
Delbert Melvin 48
Delbert Melvin, Jr 48
Denny Lee 40
Diana Lee 47
Dicy (or Lucy) 34
Dicy C. 35
Dicy Daisey 49
Donald Lee 40
Dorothy May 42
Dorthy Jane 49
Doug 40, 56
Earl Dale 49
Earnie Lawrence 64
Edgar Allen 37
Edward Lee 46
Elaine 65

675

Eleanor Maude 47
Elizabeth 34
Elizabeth Ann 44
Ella Marie 62
Elsie Viola 37
Emma May 62
Enoch 35, 64
Ernest Clyde 37
Essie Jeannetta 128
Esta May 65
Ester Bernice 46
Evelyn Gertrude 50
Everett Lawrence 56
Everett Samuel 49
Everett, Jr 56
Fannie Mae 56
Ferrold 65
Gay 49
George 55, 484
George Newton 55
Gerald Dean 44
Gertrude Ellen "Alice" . 65
Glen Allen 38
Glenda Joyce 38
Grace 65
Gregory Allen 40
Guy 119
Harold 65
Harry Eugene 44
Harry Thomas 62
Hazel Dell 38
Hazel Fern 64
Helen Glendabell 48
Ida Miranda 400
Ira Thomas 61
James Bunt 35
James E. 245
James Henry 37
James Lawrence 56
James Leslie 56
James Luther 37
James Matthew 40
James N. 34, 35
Jefferson William Lawson
. . . . 36
Jessica Nichole 44
Jessie M. 49
Jim Pete 35
John 35, 66
John Harry 43
John Harvey 39
John J. 33, 34
John Joseph 34, 35
John Michael 44
John Paul 38

Johnnie 36
Joseph 312
Judy Arlene 42
Julia Lee 49
K. Dwaine 33
Katherine 290, 291
Kathy 47
Kathy Lynn 42
Keith Byran 38
Keith Douglas 38
Kelly Ann 40
Kendra Jeane 552
Kenneth 55
Kenneth Dwaine 41
Kenneth Dwight 41
Kerry 56
Kim 55
Kip Lea 38
Larry Edward 46
Lashley Dunn 196
Laura Lynn 196
Lavenia 66
Leslie Allen 55
Lillie Belle 53
Linda Kay 131
Lisa Jean 49
Lloyd Enoch 65
Lola Idene 58
Lonnie Ray 42
Lorene Rose 64
Luke 246
Lulu Monita 63
Mary 35
Mary (May) 44
Mary Alice 46
Mary Ann 56
Mary Ellen 49
Mary Frances . . . 310, 311
Mary Jane 116
Mary Lucille 39
Mary Margaret 47
Mary Virginia 47
Mattie Attala 245
Maude 66
Maude Louise 62
Maybelle 66
Merle Edgar 38
Michael 38
Michael Alan 44
Mildred Lucille 56
Minnie Amilia 35
Minnie Lucille 37
Myrlle 66
Myrtie 64
Nancy 596

Nancy Ellen 39
Nancy Minerva "Minnie"
. . . . 50
Naomi Ruth 64
Nathan B. 464
Nelda Fay 56
Nellie May 62
Nena Kay 42
Newton Anderson 46
Newton Charles . . . 35, 37
Neysa Catherine 42
Nora Frances 61
Olive Zoelle 58
Oliver David 50
Opal "Azalie" 56
Ora Florence . . . 223, 224
Otis 115
Otto 35
Pansey Alice 64
Peggy 391
Peggy Ann 119
Peter 234
Philip Allen 35
Phillip Allen 53
Phillip Logan 62
Pinkney David 34, 36
Randy Kieth 42
Raymond 65
Rebecca Katelyn 310
Reggie 65
Renee Arlette 46
Richard Anthony 46
Rick 50
Robert 48, 66
Robert Douglas 55
Robert Floyd 44
Roger 50, 55
Ronald "Ronnie" Wayne
. . . . 38
Rosa Ellen 36
Ruby Diamond 65
Russell Dean 44
Sadie Pearl 37
Samuel Casey 49
Sarah 35
Sarah Margaret 35
Serena L. 459
Silas 36
Silas Earl 37
Stephanie Marie 40
Stephen Edgar 38
Susan Diane 44
Teri Lynn 44
Thelma Mae 64
Timothy Michael 48

Tobbie Lynn 38
Tom J. 35
Tommy 66
Ursula Gertrude 37
Valdon 35
Velma Dene 58
Victor Blake 40
Victoria Jean 44
Viola Irene 63
Virgil Newton 46
Virginia 65
Virginia Lee 64
Vivian Fern 62
Walter Enoch 37
Walter Harrington 37
Wanda 48
Wilburn Haile 47
Willard 35, 64
William 34, 64
William Jeffrey 310
Willie W. 49
Zola Louise 49
Zola M. 48

Williamson
Eloise 416
Lou 444

Willingham
Henry 479
Mary 479
Mildred 412

Willis
Jack Thurmond 401
Melissa Louise 401
William 274

Willman
Mary Lou 403

Wills
Mary 191

Willson
Henry 583

Wilson
Brian 304
Aaron Jr 73
Aaron Sr 73
Aaron, Jr 73
Aaron, Sr 73
Alan Porter 43
Ann . 17, 31, 73, 83, 134,
154, 162
Anna 134
Ashley Rae 304
Bob 336
Coy 118
Daniel 73

David 476
David Alan 43
Doris 118
Elisha 34
Ezekiel 34
Frank Emmett 303
Frank Emmett, iii 304
Fred Allen 415
Gabriel 73
George 34
George Edward 118
Gertrude 379
Gwynn 118
Jack Clinton 131
James 73
James Franklyn 43
Jesse Linton 131
Jessica Diane 131
John 73
John Emmett 304
Lloyd 119
Mark Joseph 304
Martha 137
Mary 34
Mary Arminta 119
Maxwell Brian 304
Mayme Jane 139
Melinda 84, 97
Moses 73
Nancy Jane 567
Patsy . . 73, 134, 154, 162
Phillip 34
Ray 119
Rhonda Anita 303
Sam 43
Samuel William 304
Thomas 73, 139
Thomas J. 378
Thomas Jr 73
Thomas Sr 73
Thomas, Jr 73
Thomas, Sr 73
Tracy Dawn 415
William 34

Wineinger
Cassandra Loraine . . 20
Wesley 20

Winn
Genubuth 244
Permelia Foster 245

Winner
Leon 123
Lisa 123
Sam 123

Winslow
Deanne Marie 232

Winters
Barbara Ann 323
John M. 324

Wise
Roger 565

Wiseman
A.G. 441
AlthaMyra Jane 436

Witt
Sherrell 425

Wohlgeman
Benjamin Arthur 228

Wolf
Ada Beth 200
Brad 200
Dawson Bradley 200
Harriet 279
Ruth M. 279

Wolford
Vicki Sue 233

Wollf
Elizabeth Cora 329
Kristopher Francis . . . 329
Melissa Francis 329
Robert Alfred 329
Robert Alfred, Jr 329

Wolper
Ronald Mark 132

Wolski
John 56
Michael 56

Wolterman
Al 283
Billy 283

Womack
Alice 410
Alice Rebecca 427
Lucy 453
William R. 427

Wombie
Bert 430

Wood
Agnes 139
Arthur 298
Cecil Earl 140
Eugenia 267
Florence 298
George Henry 298
Ina 298
Ivey 298

Jesse 138
Jesse Hayden 140
Jewell Gladys 138
John William 298
Mary Ruth 131
Naomi 298
Nettie Arlie 138
Nora Velma 139
Opal 138
Robert Dewey 298
Rosie 298
Ruth 140, 298
Thomas L. " Tommy" . 298
William 298
William and Nannie . . 298
William Edgar 298

Woodal
John 463

Woodcock
Patricia 329

Woodhall
James 111

Woodie
Naamon 343, 344

Woodley
Helen Christine 26

Woodruff
Lydia Ann 377
Lydia Ann (Brazier) . . 376

Woods
Mary 197

Woodson
Allen 120
George 120
Jerry Lynn 433
Leonard 120
Lestie May 120
Lloyd 120
Mabel 120
Mary Belle 120
Mayo 120

Woodward
Dudley 189
Eliza Sophronia [Ann?]
. . . . 392
F. L. 189
John 405
Josiah Grandon 392
Marie 429
Minnie Brown 189
Nancy Amanda 395
Nancy R. Brazier 405
Ruby 559

Woody
Jonathan 344
Jonathan P. 344

Wooley
Daisy 381

Woolsey
Linda Faye 132
Michelle Jean 129

Wooters
Guy 42
Patti Jo 42

Worsham
Gilbert Bruce 271

Worster
Nora Ellamus 336
Thomas M. 336

Worthem
Andrew 471
Andrew J. 474
Andrew Jackson 474
Bulah Lee 475
Davey Thomas 475
David Benton 474
Earnest R. 475
Edith 475
Eleanor 474
Estill Odell 474
Ettie 474
Fronia C. 475
George 474
Icy Phrenia "Thena" . . 475
James M. 474
John Herbert 475
John Spellman 474
Juanita M. 475
Lucy Viola 475
Malinda F. 474
Malissa R. 474
Martha Malinda 475
Mary Jane 474
Mildred Sophronia . . . 474
Minne Beatrice 475
Minnie Phrenia 475
Murril Jose 475
Myrtle Agnes 475
Rhoda Jane 475
Samuel Andrew 475
Sinia C. 474
Thomas Benjamin . . . 475
William A. 474
William Albert 474

Worthley
Allen Talcott 180

Wright

Berdette 403
Bettie 261
Bill 19
Corliss E. 157
Edgar Lee 19
Edna Mae 19
Hettie Noble 314
Mattie Lee 412
Rachel 208
Vessie Buel 314
Virgene "Kay" 287
William 264

Wyatt
Caroline 275
John 274
John Harmon 274
Lelia Sheets 346
Margaret Catherine . . 272
Martha A. 274
Mary Jane 274
Nancy M. 274
Sarah E. 274
Sarah M. 274
Tennessee C. 274
Virginia C. 274
William 274

Wynn
Michael 226
William 226

Yager
Christi Jean 28

Yancey
Frances Hammons . . 315

Yanke
Lorraine 435

Yarbrough
Dan 464, 470
Emily 171

Yardley
Caroline 50

Yates
Annie Flavil 346
Ethel May 54
Eva Francis 55
Evelyn Mae 53
Franklin 53
Orville Roy 53
Robert Leslie 53
William 336
William D. 445

Yaw
Charles Martin "Marty" . 44
Gregg 44

Lauren Christine 44
Yeater
Ulyssus Grant 268
Yocum
Felitha Cumile (Tine) . 339
Lora Lee 23
Yohe
John S. 279
York
Corzillia 288
Younce
Cynthia Ellen ... 345, 349
Young
A.C. 199
Barry Allen 50
Clifford Lee 50
Diane Elizabeth 50
Douglas 327
Francis Jane 208
Gobel 200

Kathleen 311
Kirstyn 327
Klyil Mara 327
Laura Elizabeth 200
Leah Jewell 201
Martha 286
Norman J 50
Rena Odell 415
Rickie Wilson 200
William Jackson 50
William Jackson, Jr ... 50
Youngblood
Francis Marion 80
Zahourek
Bart Mitchel 28
Carley June 29
Christol Joy 29
Jeffrey Wayne 28
Jeri Ann 29
Macy Lynne 28

Michael Shawn 28
Stak Conard 28
Zank
Cyran 433
George 433
Jill Annette 433
Jodie Lisa 433
Kate Anna 433
Michael Scott 433
Scott Michael 433
Zelazguez
Paula Eva 436
Zeleneck
Robert 418
Zenor
Kathy 203
Zimmerman
David 202

679

www.ingramcontent.com/pod-product-compliance
Lightning Source LLC
Chambersburg PA
CBHW021153160426
42812CB00080B/2706